Alexander Graham Bell, Edward Miner Gallaudet

Education of Deaf Children

Evidence of Edward Miner Gallaudet and Alexander Graham Bell

Alexander Graham Bell, Edward Miner Gallaudet

Education of Deaf Children
Evidence of Edward Miner Gallaudet and Alexander Graham Bell

ISBN/EAN: 9783337136222

Printed in Europe, USA, Canada, Australia, Japan

Cover: Foto ©Paul-Georg Meister /pixelio.de

More available books at **www.hansebooks.com**

OF

DEAF CHILDREN:

EVIDENCE

OF

EDWARD MINER GALLAUDET AND ALEXANDER GRAHAM BELL,

PRESENTED TO THE

ROYAL COMMISSION OF THE UNITED KINGDOM ON THE CONDITION OF THE BLIND, THE DEAF AND DUMB, ETC.

WITH

ACCOMPANYING PAPERS, POSTSCRIPTS, AND AN INDEX.

EDITED BY

JOSEPH C. GORDON,

Professor of Mathematics, etc., in the National College for the Deaf, Washington, U. S. A.

INTRODUCTORY.

This book has been printed, through the liberality of the Volta Bureau, to signalize an educational movement of international interest.

The object of the movement referred to is, to secure provision for the elementary education of every deaf child in the United Kingdom, and incidentally to promote the greatest efficiency practicable in the instruction afforded.

In furtherance of this end, a Commission created by the Crown in 1885, with special reference to the blind, was instructed, January 20, 1886, to enlarge the scope of inquiry, and was empowered "to investigate and report upon the condition and education of the deaf and dumb."

This Commission endeavored to examine the whole field of deaf-mute instruction with characteristic British thoroughness and energy. Schools upon the Continent were visited, and in London the Commissioners held one hundred and sixteen sittings, calling before them for examination forty-three persons as experts specially interested in the welfare of the deaf, and deemed capable of giving information of great value upon the subjects of inquiry.

The complete report of the Commission forms a great work of 1574 large octavo pages in four volumes, which was presented to Parliament in 1889, upon the conclusion of the labors of the Commission.

The direct evidence in this volume has been extracted from the third volume of the Report of the Royal Commission. It includes the testimony of President EDWARD MINER GALLAUDET, Ph. D., LL.D., and of Mr. ALEXANDER GRAHAM BELL, Ph. D., M. D., etc. Dr. GALLAUDET, President of the National Deaf-Mute College, and Chairman of the Standing Executive Committee of Conventions of American Instructors of the Deaf, appeared before the Commission in November, 1886, upon the invitation of the British Government communicated through the Secretary of State. President GALLAUDET appeared as the accredited representative of the profession in America. His evidence, with the accompanying exhibits, is found in Part I. of this volume Eighteen months later, in June. 1888. Dr. BELL appeared, on the invitation of the Royal Commission, and testified, incorporating in his evidence replies obtained by him from seventy-five *per cent.* of the heads of schools in America to special points upon which information was sought by the Commission. Dr. BELL's evidence, etc., appears in Part II. of this work.

The Table of Contents and the Index to this volume indicate in some measure the magnitude of the labor of love undertaken by President GALLAUDET and Dr. BELL. The variety and importance of the subjects discussed by these eminent men make it inexpedient to attempt to give an epitome of their evidence, or a critical estimate of the value of the matter presented by them. It is sufficient to say that every intelligent friend of deaf children who reads this book will not only be the wiser for the reading, but will be stimulated to greater efforts for the welfare of the deaf.

To readers unfamiliar with the deaf, and with the history of deaf-mute instruction, who may note antagonistic and divergent views in these pages, the writer would say that the art of instructing and educating the deaf is still in its youth. Though philosophers had demonstrated "the practicability of this extraordinary art" and a hundred instances, or more, of instructed deaf-mutes had flashed their feeble rays of light along the ages, the learned JOHN BULWER, contemporary of MILTON, and BUTLER, and BACON, met with no encouragement whatever in the earliest effort on record to found a school for those "originally deafe and dumb." Referring to his project, BULWER says: "I soon perceived by falling into discourse with some rationall men about such a designe that the attempt seemed so paradoxicall, prodigious, and Hyperbolicall, that it did rather amuse than satisfie their understandings." Indeed, more than a century followed, in which DALGARNO, and WALLIS, and HOLDER, of Oxford, and DEUSING, and VAN HELMONT, and AMMAN, on the continent, wrote apparently upon the sand before the first enduring schools were established by BRAIDWOOD, DE L'ÉPÉE, and HEINICKE, who groped their way in darkness along an unbeaten path. Living octogenarians may have known persons who were the first pupils in the schools of these pioneers.

The problems which have confronted all laborers in this field are many and difficult; and though able and well-equipped minds have been devoted to the solution of them, few, if any, fundamental principles have been established, and definite methods of procedure have not found general acceptance. The education of the deaf has not passed yet beyond the experimental stage. Though methods and systems may be sharply differentiated, I am persuaded from personal observation, from conversation with instructors, and from a study of the literature of the subject, that the instruction of the deaf is in a state of transition and of progress which renders the shibboleths of the past, vague, and of doubtful utility aside from the historical interest which may attach to them.

The teaching of language, as the key to knowledge, rightly holds the foremost place in the instruction of the deaf. In this branch, radical reforms are steadily making progress which have not been subjected as yet to statistical inquiry. Subordinate to language-teaching, though holding a more prominent place in current thought and discussion, is the teaching of speech. Figures are at hand to illustrate the progress of this phase of improvement in the education of the deaf in the United States. In 1887, the total number of deaf children under instruction was 7,978, of whom 2,556, or 32 per cent., were taught articulation; in 1891, four years later, 9,232 deaf children were under instruction, of whom 4,245, or 46 per cent., received instruction in articulation. In the former year, out of 577 teachers, 171, or 29.6 per cent., were engaged in teaching speech; in the latter, out of 686 teachers, 258, or 37.6 per cent., were teachers of speech. The reader is referred to page 259 in Part III. for interesting tables which more fully illustrate the growth of speech-teaching in the United States.

The returns of pupils *taught by speech* are incomplete. The number reported for 1891 is 963, or 10.4 per cent. of the entire number of deaf pupils attending school. 365 of these were in the New England States where they formed 64.7 per cent. of the whole number of pupils, and 72.1 per cent. of the pupils receiving instruction in speech.

The following table, presenting the statistics of speech-teaching in the United States by geographical groups, has been compiled from the returns tabulated by Dr. E. A. FAY in the *American Annals* for January, 1892:

STATISTICS OF SPEECH-TEACHING IN SCHOOLS FOR THE DEAF IN THE UNITED STATES FOR 1891, ARRANGED IN FOUR TERRITORIAL GROUPS.

Territorial Groups.	Number of Schools.	Pupils.			Teachers.		
		Whole number.	Number taught Articulation.	Per cent. taught Articulation.	Whole number.	Articulation teachers.	Per cent. of Articulation teachers.
New England States	8	564	506	89.9	62	49	79.
Middle States, Maryland and District of Columbia	16	2,648	1,793	68.6	215	115	53.5
Central and Western States and Territories	32	3,830	1,307	34.1	262	70	26.7
Southern States	19	2,190	649	29.6	147	24	16.3
Total	75	9,232	4,255	46	686	258	37.6

Much of the progress indicated above may be of a superficial character, but the schools of the future will realize substantial benefits from the intelligence, independence, and zeal which characterize the workers in many of our schools who have already broadened and deepened the education of the deaf along various lines to an extent unattempted and undreamed of in other lands.

American readers will be interested in knowing that the evidence presented by President GALLAUDET and Dr. BELL exerted a marked influence in England. A copy of the official summary of the recommendations of the Commission may be found in Part III. of this volume. A bill founded largely upon these recommendations, but applying to Scotland only, was introduced into the House of Lords by the Marquis of LOTHIAN, President of the Scotch Educational Department, on the 22d of May, 1890. This bill passed both Houses of Parliament, received the Royal assent, and has become a law.

A bill drawn up by the government to make better provision for the elementary education of the blind and of the deaf in England and Wales was introduced by Viscount CRANBROOK, the Lord President of the Council, into the House of Lords, and it was ordered to be printed July 1st, 1890. This bill, subsequently amended, passed the House of Lords but did not reach the Commons. A copy of this bill will be found in Postscripts, Part III. Taking advantage of the public discussion and criticism of the original bill a new bill was introduced into the House of Lords the succeeding winter and passed, but was not presented to the House of Commons.

Assurances have been given that the government will for the third time bring this measure before Parliament at the coming session and that a vigorous effort will be made to render operative by legislation the following recommendations: Substantial subsidies to existing institutions of approved standing, the founding of new institutions and day-schools if necessary, capitation grants with provision for maintenance in necessitous cases, compulsory attendance, governmental inspection with reports upon "the knowledge of written language, speech, and the general efficiency of the schools under whatever system,' non-interference with methods of instruction so long as the result in written or spoken language is satisfactory, and saving clauses respecting the rights and obligations of parents in regard to choice of school, religious training, and contributing to the support of children according to ability.

Notwithstanding threatened opposition from several associations in no way connected with the education of the deaf, there is reason to believe that the perfected measure will command the support of well-informed friends of the deaf and of philanthropists without regard to party affiliations. Partisan opposition is apprehended from party men having at best a superficial acquaintance with the subject of deaf-mute instruction. The main grounds upon which opposition is anticipated are the fear of sectarianism and the fear of exclusiveness in the management of institutions. Outside of the few schools organized and maintained expressly in the interest of some particular creed or cult, sectarianism is practically unknown in schools for the deaf either in Great Britain or in the United States.

The fear of exclusiveness in the management of schools may not be altogether groundless. In America examples of fossilized corporations are not unknown. But there is need of caution in the application of a remedy, and too great care cannot be exercised in devising safeguards against the introduction of party politics under the cloak of "popular control." The efficiency of a few schools in America has been seriously impaired by the operation of vicious laws. These laws made it possible for "practical politicians" to secure the control and management of certain State schools as a reward for partisan services. The baneful effects have been fully realized in widespread demoralization in but few cases. But even in cases where partisanship has been held in abeyance, trustees have been selected whose highest conception of duty has found expression in a balance-sheet more creditable to an almshouse or a prison than to a highly specialized educational establishment.

The spectre of sectarianism need occasion our British friends no alarm, but vigilance must be exercised to shut out partisanship and incompetency from all possibility of controlling schools for the deaf.

It is to be hoped most earnestly that Parliament will be aroused from its lethargy, and, in response to the appeals of an enlightened and ever-growing public sentiment, that it may be led with wisdom to legislate for the welfare of deaf children for whom no provision is assured by law, and thus to remove a reproach which rests upon the British government alone among the great powers of the world.

It may be noted that POSTSCRIPTS, Part III., contains matter not submitted to the Commission nor heretofore printed. Here, in connection with a series of charts of Visible Speech, may be found, for the first time in print, an exposition of Visible Speech, with special reference to the application of the system to the teaching of deaf children. The latest available statistics of schools for the deaf in the United Kingdom, Germany, and in the United States, are also given in this part in the pages preceding the index.

The editor's acknowledgments are due to Harper & Brothers, A. S. Barnes & Co., Wm. Wood & Co., and to the publishers of the "American Supplement to the Encyclopedia Britannica," for courteous permission to use copyrighted matter appearing in the Exhibits. Acknowledgment is due also to the authors of papers which have been taken from the AMERICAN ANNALS OF THE DEAF.

In the preparation of these pages for the press I have been kindly assisted by A. W. MCCURDY, Esq., by the Hon. JOHN HITZ, and by others who, though unnamed, have rendered services none the less appreciated.

J. C. GORDON.

NATIONAL COLLEGE FOR THE DEAF,
KENDALL GREEN,
WASHINGTON, D. C., *January 1st*, 1892.

TABLE OF CONTENTS.

PAGE.

INTRODUCTION, *Professor Gordon* iii

PART I.

PRESIDENT GALLAUDET'S EVIDENCE 1–39

EXHIBITS BY PRESIDENT GALLAUDET:

Census Returns for 1830, 1840, 1850, *Dr. H. P. Peet* 43

Census Returns for 1850, 1860, 1870, *Dr. E. A. Fay* 49

Census Returns for 1880, *Dr. E. A. Fay* 51

Report of Committee on Forms for Registration of Statistics 52

History of the Education of the Deaf in the United States, *President Gallaudet* 54

Deaf-Mutes, *Dr. E. A. Fay* 60

Statistics of Schools for the Deaf for 1885 72

The True Combined System, *Mr. A. L. E. Crouter* 76

Comprehensive Education in its Philosophy and Practice, *Dr. G. O. Fay* 79

Oral and Aural Training, Report of Address by *President Gallaudet* 81

A System of Education adapted to all Deaf-Mutes not excluding the Feebler-minded, *Dr. Job Williams* 82

Poetry of the Deaf, *President Gallaudet* 83

The "American" Manual Alphabet, *Professor Gordon* 94

The Manual Alphabet as a part of the Public-School Course. *Mr. James Denison* 98

How Shall the Deaf be Educated? *President Gallaudet* 100

Milan Convention, *President Gallaudet* 104

Exhibits of Proceedings, ANNALS, and School-Reports 110

PART II.

DR. BELL'S EVIDENCE 1–66

EXHIBITS BY DR. BELL:

Census Returns of New England for 1880 67

An Open Letter concerning the bill relating to the instruction of deaf-mutes in incorporated cities and villages 69

Extracts from the Laws of Wisconsin 73

Facts and Opinions Relating to the Deaf, from America:

Circular Letter to Superintendents and Principals 74

I. Visible Speech 75

II. Auricular Instruction 78

III. Intermarriages of the Deaf 88

IV. Instruction of the Deaf 106

V. Statistics of Articulation-Teaching 124

VI. Miscellaneous Material 126

Articulation-Teaching in 1883 130

The Semi-Deaf 131

Exhibits of Photograph, School-Reports, Memoir, Genealogical Charts 132

Is there a Correlation between Defects of the Senses? 134

The Brown Family; the Allen Family 136

What Kind of Trades Shall be Taught? *Rev. Edward Everett Hale, D. D.* 137

Auricular Instruction 139

Exhibits of *Deaf-Mutes' Journal*, Catalogue of Deaf Children of Deaf Parents, Charts of Visible Speech 143

EXHIBITS BY DR. BELL—*Continued:*

Visible Speech as a Means of Communicating Articulation to Deaf-Mutes 144
Upon a Method of Teaching Language to a Very Young Congenitally Deaf Child 150
Fallacies Concerning the Deaf 155
Discussion: *President Gallaudet. Hon. G. G. Hubbard. Dr. Bell* 161
Deaf Classes in the Public Schools 168
Discussion: *Dr. Gillett* and others 170
Notions of the Deaf and Dumb before Instruction. *Harvey P. Peet, LL.D.* 173
Singular Observation of Dr. Itard 185
Deaf-Mutes of Chilmark 186
The Lovejoy Family, *with chart* 187
Visible Speech at the Belleville Convention 189
Miss Worcester's Method 192
The Deaf in the Eleventh Census 197
Report of Census Committee 201
Final Form of Schedule 203

PART III.

POSTSCRIPTS:

Comments on Dr. Bell's Evidence. *President Gallaudet* 207
The Census of 1880; Reply to President Gallaudet's Comments, *Rev. F. H. Wines* 212
Deaf Children of Deaf Parents: Revised Tables 214
The Massachusetts Census of 1885: TABLES 228
Graphical Charts, etc 241
Visible-Speech and Line-Writing 248
Summary of Recommendations of the Royal Commission 254
Governmental Bill for England and Wales 255
Methods of Instruction in American Schools, with Statistics, *Dr. Fay* 257
Comparative Statistics of American Schools for a number of years, *Dr. Bell* 259
Statistics of Schools in the United Kingdom, *Professor Gordon* 260
Statistics of Schools in Germany, etc 261
INDEX .... i–xxvi

PART I.

Evidence of President Gallaudet, with accompanying Exhibits.

Royal Commission on the Blind, the Deaf and Dumb, &c.

32 Abingdon Street, Westminster.

Tuesday, 9th November, 1886.

Present:

The Right Hon. the LORD EGERTON OF TATTON in the Chair.

Admiral Sir E. Sotheby, K.C.B.
William Woodall, Esq., M.P.
F. J. Campbell, Esq., LL.D.
W. Tindal Robertson, Esq., M.D.
T. R. Armitage, Esq., M.D.
The Rev. W. Blomefield Sleight, M.A.

The Rev. Charles Mansfield Owen, M.A.
E. C. Johnson, Esq.
W. Auchincloss Arrol, Esq.
B. St. John Ackers, Esq.
Charles Few, Esq.
Charles E. D. Black, Esq., *Secretary*.

Dr. E. M. Gallaudet, examined.

Dr. E. M. Gallaudet.

9 Nov. 1886.

13,101. (*Chairman.*) You are president of the National Deaf-Mute College at Washington?—That is my office. I am president of the corporation of that institution, as well as of the Faculty of Instruction, the corporation being the governing body.

13,102. You were recently at a convention in California of instructors of deaf-mutes in America?—Yes; I have here a minute from the proceedings of that convention, which I beg leave to present as a credential from that convention, giving its views with reference to my coming to give evidence before this Commission, which will show the Commission what constituency I represent relating to institutions for the education of the deaf in America; and before I read this minute, I should like to say that at this convention there were actual instructors and principals from 43 of the 67 schools in our country. This convention met in California in July, and it may be taken as having been the largest and most representative convention that has ever been held in America, consisting, as it did, of members from schools of all the different methods in our country. The minute is as follows: "Minute unanimously adopted by the Eleventh Convention of American Instructors of the Deaf, at Berkeley, Cal., July 21, 1886. The American Instructors of the Deaf, assembled in Convention at Berkeley, Cal., desire to congratulate their professional brethren in Great Britain and Ireland upon the appointment of the Royal Commission to inquire into the Education of the Blind and of the Deaf, and beg leave to express the hope that the labors of the Commission will result in the recognition by the British Government of the just claim of blind and deaf children to education by the State. We learn with pleasure that the Royal Commission has invited Dr. E. M. Gallaudet, President of the National Deaf-Mute College, and Chairman of the executive committee of this Convention, to appear before them; and we take this occasion to commend President Gallaudet to the Commission as one who possesses in the highest degree our confidence and esteem." I hold the office of chairman of the standing executive committee of that convention, which is held quadrennially, and my office as chairman of the standing executive committee places me at the head of the organization in the interim between its meetings.

13,103. You have had previous meetings?—Quite a number.

13,104. How long have these quadrennial meetings been held?—Since 1851.

13,105. Can you furnish us with any statistics of the number of deaf-mutes in the United States; has there been any accurate census made of them?—I am prepared to furnish such statistics. I have a brief statement before me giving some comparative results of figures with references to extended statements, which I am prepared to leave with the Commission, in the form of documents. I may say that during the last 50 years the statistics of the deaf and dumb have been increasingly full in our country, and an interesting question with us has been the proportion of deaf to the general population, and whether or not that proportion was increasing or diminishing. In 1830, out of a white population of 10,532,060, there were 5,363 deaf-mutes, giving a ratio of one in 1,964. Ten years later, in a population of 14,189,218 white people, there were 6,682 deaf-mutes, giving a ratio of one in 2,123. In 1850, with a population of 19,630,738 white people, there were 9,469 deaf-mutes, giving a ratio of one in 2,079. I have given the white population for the reason that it appeared, on an examination of these results, that the enumeration of blacks was very erroneous, so much so that to take the few millions of blacks in our country in those three decades and mass them with the whites, would give an entirely erroneous impression as to the proper proportion, so I leave them out up to 1850. In 1850 much more care was taken, and the total population being in that year 23,191,876, there were 9,803 deaf-mutes, making the proportion one in 2,365, rather diminishing the ratio. In 1860 the proportion remained almost exactly the same, one in 2,452, the total population being 31,443,321, and the number of deaf-mutes being 12,821. In 1870 the proportion remained still almost exactly the same, one in 2,379, the total population being 38,558,371, and the number of deaf-mutes being 16,205. I would refer the Commissioners to our *Annals*, Vol. V, p. 9; Vol. XIX, p. 107; and Vol. XXVIII, p. 206, where very suggestive and valuable articles are to be found with regard to these statistics, and where conclusions are drawn which may be taken as quite authoritative. In 1880, our last census, the proportion increases to one in 1,480 (the population being 50,155,783, and the number of deaf-mutes 33,878) which is quite a remarkable change, and the cause of this apparent great increase in the number of deaf-mutes has been a subject of very considerable discussion among specialists in our country. There are those who have said that it has grown out of the intermarriage of deaf-mutes; it is seriously doubted by others whether that has had an important influence on the result, for an examination of the actual reports made in the taking of this 1880 census shows that the officers in charge of this special branch of the census, in their great zeal to have a very full and perfect census of deaf-mutes, erred on the other side, and in many cases enumerated the same person twice, and even three times. It is extremely difficult to arrive at an absolutely certain result with regard to the proportion of deaf-mutes at the last census, but a suf-

Dr. E. M. Gallaudet.

9 Nov. 1886.

ficient number of errors of the character I have mentioned have been found in examining the reports to make it practically certain that the ratio of the deaf to the whole population has not materially increased over the figures of the previous censuses. It may be taken that the ratio before 1880 was too small, and it may be presumed that one in 1,800 would represent accurately the proportion; and this figure of one in 1,480, if it were corrected for error, would come to very nearly the same proportion of one in 1,800, and that may be taken as undoubtedly very nearly the proportion of our deaf-mutes in our population in America to-day.

13,106. After all, the figures are not absolutely accurate?—In the volumes of the *Annals* to which I make reference, articles will be found written by specialists, who have very carefully considered these figures, drawing certain conclusions from them.

13,107. But after all they are only specialists?—Yes, the figures cannot be taken as absolutely accurate. We have not been able to arrive at a result which we could say was absolutely accurate.

13,108. You say that according to the last census, the number of deaf and dumb in the United States was 33,878?—In one paper that I was looking at, giving a report of the proceedings at one of the conventions, the number is stated to be not less than 35,000. This figure is less than 34,000. The 35,000 may have been given as round numbers. This was six years ago. We have had no census since 1880.

13,109. Probably 35,000 would be the number at the present time?—It is quite possible. In connection with the statistics of the deaf and dumb, I may mention that there are to be found in the Report of the Special Committee of the Fifth Conference of Principals (which is set out in the *Annals*, Vol. XXX, p. 52), suggestions of forms for collecting and preserving statistics of the deaf admitted to schools. Those suggested forms were prepared by a special committee appointed by a conference of principals held in Minnesota two years ago. I draw attention to them for the reason that an earnest effort has been made in America to induce all the schools to adopt these forms, which are very full and clear, for collecting and preserving statistics relative to deaf-mutes, and which forms might probably be found useful as suggesting something which might be adopted in England.

13,110. I observe in one of the reports, allusion is made to boards of charity, and boards of education; will you explain the respective functions of those two boards?—Boards of charity are organized and authorized by the legislatures of our States. There is a board of charity in the State of Massachusetts, for instance, and another in the State of Illinois, and they are in the nature of commissions; a certain number of men are appointed by the legislatures, or authority is given by the legislatures to the Governor to appoint a certain number of men to supervise all the charitable institutions, and sometimes institutions for correction are included in those commissions, and they make reports to the legislatures. They have in varying degrees authority conferred upon them to interfere even with the management of those institutions.

13,111. Are the organization and government of schools for the deaf under the general boards of education, or under the boards of charity?—The practice varies. When I come to my next head I will give some particulars with regard to the relation of the State to the schools. In connection with my first head (Statistics of the Deaf in America), I may refer the Commissioners to an historical sketch of the schools for the deaf, in America, in an article in the *Annals*, Vol. XXXI, p. 130, reprinted from the American Supplement to the Encyclopedia Britannica, and also to an exceedingly valuable article by Professor Fay, of the College at Washington, in Buck's Reference Handbook of the Medical Sciences, published recently in New York, which article contains very valuable information with reference to statistics, and various other points. A copy of Professor Fay's article is submitted.

13,112. Will you now go to your second head, the exterior organization of schools for the deaf in America?—In speaking of the exterior organization of schools for the deaf, it may be said that we have three different forms in America. First, we have the corporate form, where a certain number of persons are erected by law into a body corporate and politic, who exercise control over the institutions which they are authorized to create and sustain. That form of government exists in New England, in New York State, in Pennsylvania, and at Washington, the institutition at which place is sustained by the Federal Government. There is then another form, called the State Institution, where the legislature of the State creates a committee or board of directors, or trustees as they may be termed, into whose hands it places the care and government of the institution, and the property belonging to such institutions under this State organization belongs absolutely to the State; the lands and buildings are vested in the State (in the other case the property is vested in the corporation, who hold it as corporations usually hold property). The State organization exists in the South and West generally. We have then a third organization in some of our cities of day schools for deaf-mutes, which are organized and governed by school boards, and sustained out of the taxes paid in the cities for the support of public schools, so that we have this variety of organization in our country, and variety also of method of support; the Washington institution being supported out of the general Treasury of the United States, and so is a burden on the whole country, the State institutions being sustained by taxes raised in the States, while in the cities the school organization is sustained out of the city taxes.

13,113. Is there any education rate?—We have in most of our States a general education rate.

13,114. In other cases the schools are supported by the general taxes of the cities?—Yes.

13,115. In how many cities are there these day schools?—There are day schools in about six or seven. I should be glad to be allowed to say, in connection with these various organizations, that the corporate organization in our country seems to have been the one under which the very best results have been reached, for reasons which I conceive to be very well worthy of the consideration of the Commission.

13,116. Have they any endowments?—Some of them have endowments, two or three.

13,117. Do you think that important?—I think it is quite desirable, where they have endowments, that they should be allowed to use the income of them; not to have them interfered with by the State. But I was going to say, that in the cases of the State organizations, those which are under the legislatures of the States, where we have changes of political parties from time to time, very disastrous results have occurred from the interference of the State authorities in the management of these institutions, purely for the sake of party patronage, valued and experienced instructors, and even principals, being replaced by persons very little competent to manage such institutions, solely for the purpose of giving places to persons of the dominant political party for the time being.

13,118. Is that difficulty avoided in the case of the corporate institutions?—I think I am justified in saying that, in the case of the corporate institutions, that difficulty is absolutely avoided.

13,119. I see that the President of the United States is the head of the college of which you are the President?—Yes.

13,120. Is he the head of the college *ex officio*?—Yes; the President in his office as patron has the duty of attaching his signature to the diplomas which attest the degrees which are conferred by our college at Washington, and it is usual for the President to be present and preside at the anniversaries of the college. Our present President takes an active interest in the college, and his predecessors in office have befriended the college since its organization.

13,121. The President is not the head of all these corporate bodies?—No; he is, by law of Congress, the head of this institution.

13,122. Because it is situated in Washington?—Because it is situated in Washington and because it is very largely sustained by appropriations by the General Government. I ought to say, with reference to these corporations, in several instances they have on them officers of the States which contribute to the support of those corporate institutions, that is to say, to the education and support of the pupils in them. In New England the institutions have several of the State officers of the different States of New England on their boards, and in the corporation of the institution at Washington, there are at present two Senators and two Members of the House of Representatives, who take part in the government of the institution. The institution may, in fact, be termed a mixed corporation.

13,123. Are those Senators and Members of the House of Representatives elected from time to time, or are they members of the corporation for life?—The members of the Senate and House are appointed at the beginning of each Congress. I should correct myself and say that one Senator is appointed by the President of the Senate; the other Senator happens to be a member of our board. Then as regards the two Members of the House of Representatives appointed by the Speaker, their term of office is for two years; they may be reappointed at the end of that term. All the other members of the corporation of our institution in Washington and these other corporate institutions are permanent. I ought to speak of the organization of one institution in America, in the State of Maryland, which is quite peculiar, and in which some of the difficulties which attend the organization of the other State schools seem to be done away with. The appointment of the board of visitors is vested in the Governor of the State, and he is authorized to make appointments which are permanent, that is to say, for life, or till resignation; so that the board is appointed under the authority of the State. It is a board that cannot be changed by the action of a political party. That has always seemed to me a very wise arrangement, assuming that the Governor selects men well fitted to govern the affairs of the institution. I ought also to add, to show the relations of these corporate institutions to the State, that the support of the pupils is in most cases provided for by an allowance from the State for each pupil. That allowance is paid on a statement given of the number of pupils in the institution. Pennsylvania pays the institution at Philadelphia 275 dollars per annum for each child received and cared for in that institution.

13,124. Are those institutions so receiving grants from the State subject to inspection, and are the grants subject to approval by Government inspectors?—The institutions so receiving grants are subject to inspection. The inspection is usually managed by a committee appointed by the legislature to visit, inspect, and report, and of course any irregularity would immediately affect the action of the State in reference to this *per capita* allowance.

13,125. How many institutions for the deaf and dumb are there in the United States?—That brings me to the third head in the programme of topics that I have taken the liberty of submitting to the Commission, viz., the interior organization of the schools in the United States, their number, the cost of buildings and so forth. There are at present 67 schools for the deaf in the United States. Of those, 14 are corporate, but practically supported by the State in the manner I have mentioned, with the exception that two or three of them have rather large endowments, and therefore the contribution of the State is not for their entire support, but only for their partial support; it supplements the income from those endowments. While for the Philadelphia Institution the State of Pennsylvania pays 275 dollars per annum for each child, the States of New England pay about 175 dollars per annum, the other 100 dollars being provided out of the endowments of the institution. The endowment of the Hartford Institution grew out of a very large appropriation of public lands by Congress in the very early history of the institution. The lands were sold, and the funds invested in interest-paying securities. 34 of the 67 are State institutions. There are eight day-schools, and 11 schools of a private and denominational character, which cannot be said to be public schools at all, making 67 as the entire number. Of those 67 schools, 38 are now carried on on the combined system of instruction, 14 on the manual method, 12 on the oral method, one is reported as experimental, and in two the methods pursued are not known. The number of pupils in those institutions last year was 7,801, the number of teachers was 540: 228 of them being male and 312 female; the proportion of teachers to children being as 1 to 14. The number of pupils taught speech and lip-reading amounted to 3,032. To give an idea of the amount expended upon these institutions in what we call the plant, I may say that the buildings and grounds have cost in sterling money 1,700,000*l.*, and for their annual support there is expended 280,000*l.* The plant per pupil, including the expense of building, grounds, and everything that is permanent, is estimated at 212*l.* 10*s.* *per capita*, and the average annual *per capita* cost of educating those pupils is 38*l.*; that is, excluding the interest on plant. If that was taken into account, that amount would be a little increased; but that is more fully given in detail in the *Annals*, volume XXXI, p. 82.

13,126. To whom is the executive management of these institutions committed?—With reference to the interior organization of these schools, I should mention that the institutions are usually governed by a principal or superintendent, who is the chief executive officer, and a committee, or board of directors as they are usually termed, or trustees, to act as the legislative body. In most instances they take no part in the interior government of the institution. They digest the regulations for its government, and draw out its general line of policy, the executive management being committed to the superintendent or principal who is subject to and responsible to the board. There are a few institutions where a condition of things exist which we call the double-headed system, where there are two executive officers, neither of whom is responsible to the other, but both of whom are responsible to the board of direction, and by those who may perhaps be said to be best competent to judge as to the efficiency of such an arrangement, it is an arrangement very greatly to be deprecated.

13,127. Is one of those officers the head of the educational department, while the other is at the head of the housekeeping?—Yes; where it is attempted to govern an institution in that way, a certain amount of friction is found to exist, and the results reached have not been found satisfactory at all; so that it is laid down as a principle that the best thing to be got in the interior organization of such institutions is a man who is an experienced teacher, and who is capable of assuming the executive control of the entire institution. The reason

Dr. E. M. Gallaudet.

9 Nov. 1886.

for this may be briefly stated thus: that though the domestic department may be thought, on casual reflection, to be separate from the educational department, yet the same individuals, the pupils, are under these two kinds of management, and very often there is friction if two heads are governing; and there are only a few institutions in our country where this arrangement exists. I should like to add, on this matter of the interior organization of our schools, that, as a rule, the principal or superintendent who has charge of the institution is not required to teach; he is understood, with very few exceptions, to have been an experienced instructor, but is not required to devote hours each day to the teaching of a class; that is felt in the organization of our institutions to be of very great importance, for the reason that it gives the head of the institution time to be present more or less in all the classes, and to superintend the work of those doing the actual work of teaching. In the case of two or three State institutions, there have been men appointed to take charge of them who have been absolutely ignorant of the method of teaching the deaf, and they have gone on with a principal teacher under them, that principal teacher conducting the operations of the school. Such an arrangement is thought to be a very unfortunate one. It places a man at the head of the institution who cannot in any way direct the work for the carrying out of which the institution has been established; but that has been the result of political interference.

We have also in the interior organization of our institutions one arrangement that I conceive to be of very great importance, viz., that the classes are taught in separate rooms. I have found in my visits to schools in England that a number of them have several classes in a large school room, the classes being in various parts of the room. We think that an unfortunate arrangement, and great pains are taken in our institutions to avoid it. I do not know one where that arrangement exists. It is thought that separate class-rooms should be made use of for separate classes, so that the teacher of one class should not be interfered with by the operations of other classes. Under this head of interior organization I may say a word with regard to religious instruction.

There are a few institutions (I think limited to the State of New York) which are of a denominational character, which receive aid from the State. That is not the usual rule in the United States. The general rule is that religious instruction of a very simple and undenominational character shall be given, the pupils being taught the general principles of religion, and religious services—prayers and other services—being conducted by instructors who may be members of different denominations. So that it is the policy of American institutions to give religious instruction, but to give it in a careful, guarded, undenominational manner, allowing, of course, free access to the institution to religious teachers who may be desired by the parents of the pupils to be present and give instruction from time to time to the pupils.

13,128. Is religious instruction given in all the ordinary schools?—It is the rule to give religious instruction to a very slight extent, hardly more than the reading of the Bible and a prayer, and in some schools not even that is given. It depends on the action of the local school boards.

13,129. Do the day-schools come under the same category?—I think most of them have a brief religious service; they would come under the same rule as an ordinary day-school.

13,130. Can you tell us what the private schools are, whether they are on the combined system, the oral system, or the manual system?—Of the private schools, 11 in number, five are oral schools, three are combined, one is experimental, and in two the method is not given. The number of pupils in those schools is, altogether, only 165.

13,131. For all practical purposes the private schools are not worth considering?—Hardly.

13,132. Now, will you tell us something with regard to the methods of instruction, the duration of pupilage, and the courses of study?—A very brief reference is probably necessary to the early work of the schools for deaf-mutes in America. The method introduced 70 years ago in our first schools was the manual method. The decision to adopt the manual method grew out of two considerations; one was that the founder of deaf-mute education in America received his instruction as to teaching from the Abbé Sicard, in Paris, who at that time, in the year 1816, was practising mainly the manual method; he taught articulation, but not to any large number of pupils or to any great extent. Then it was thought by those who established the first institutions in America that, in view of the fact that the public purse, aided by private benevolence, would provide, perhaps, only for a term of instruction of four years, or at the utmost five years, the manual method would probably produce results of greater value to the pupils than if the other method, the oral method, were pursued, and for those two reasons the manual method was made use of in the institutions of America at the beginning, and for many years. In 1860, however, the question of teaching deaf-mutes to speak was brought forward quite prominently in America in several directions, and not very long after, about 1867, oral schools were established on a small scale in New York and Northampton.

13,133. Was the oral method introduced from Germany?—The suggestion that it should be introduced originated, I think, mainly in a report made by Horace Mann, who visited the German schools some years before that, and reported very favorably with reference to the oral method. The accepted term of pupilage by that time had increased, and it was possible to secure the assistance of the State, and to make use of funds from private sources, so as to continue the term of pupilage to seven and eight, and sometimes even nine or 10 years, and it was felt that it was desirable to teach speech to deaf-mutes: in fact, there were those who urged that that method should take precedence of the other. The older institutions, at least one of them, the one in Washington, in 1867 sent a representative to Europe to make an examination of the schools for deaf-mutes in the various countries of Europe, and to ascertain the results of the different methods. The result of this examination was a report which recommended very strongly the introduction of the teaching of articulation in all schools for the deaf. These distinctive oral schools, which were established in the first instance at New York, and Northampton in Massachusetts, about the same time, 1867, went forward in their work in a manner that won the approval of the teachers of the older schools, and in 1868 a conference of principals was held at Washington, representing quite a large number of old schools for the deaf in America, at which conference a decided approval was expressed of the recommendations of the report made at the instance of the institution at Washington in 1867, that the teaching of articulation should be introduced into all the schools for deaf-mutes in America. The introduction of that method was gradual; it was not possible to secure immediately the action of boards of direction favorable to that change, but from year to year more of the old schools have adopted the method of teaching to speak, and so now the method of teaching speech may be said to prevail in all the prominent institutions of America.

13,134. Are you speaking of the combined system or of the purely oral system?—I am speaking of teaching speech. I do not mean to say that these schools have become what may be termed pure oral schools, for we conceive that the term "pure oral" really does not convey a correct impression. To say that a school is a pure oral school is to say what is almost an impossibility.

13,135. You mean signs will be used?—Signs will be used. It is not practicable to banish them any further than from actual use in the school room, which may be done with difficulty, but signs will be made use of at certain stages of the instruction, more or less, to assist in reaching the end desired. The number of schools where speech is taught is now 50 out of the 67. Only 14 remain on the purely manual method; of those some are known to be making arrangements to introduce the teaching of speech, and will probably do so within a short time.

13,136. You have told us that there are 34 State schools?—Yes; and then there are the 14 corporate schools.

13,137. Making together 48?—The 48 would be called public schools, not counting the day-schools.

13,138. Will all those have either the combined system or the purely oral system?—Out of those 48 schools the oral method is more or less practised in 36 schools.

13,139. The majority of the leading schools adopt the pure oral system, or the combined system?—A very large majority are carrying on the combined system. That means that in a large majority of the public schools speech is taught to as great a number of pupils as it is found possible to teach with success; that is the policy in these combined-system schools. That would lead me to ask permission to read the resolutions passed at the Convention in California this last summer, which I conceive to be of very great importance, and they will be seen to cover very broad ground with reference to this conflict of methods, as it is frequently termed, which has existed for many years, but which now may be said to have come practically to an end. A report of this Convention is published in the "International Record of Charities and Correction," a periodical not devoted specially to the interests of the deaf and dumb, but covering many subjects of an allied character. Before I read the resolution I will read what a writer in that periodical says in speaking of the Convention: "The "proceedings were marked by an unusual degree "of harmony. The conflict of theories and methods "which has occupied so much of the time and at"tention of previous conventions was almost wholly "absent. It was unanimously agreed that, like "other people, the deaf differ widely in their men"tal and physical conditions, and, therefore, meth"ods of instruction differing as widely are necessary "for the highest development of the class. * * * "The war between the two prominent systems of "instruction—the 'manual' and the 'oral'—which "has been carried on so vigorously for many years, "may be said to be practically ended, not through "the victory of one side or the other, but through "the better understanding of each other's methods "and results. Discussions between men actuated "only by philanthropic purposes, and upon matters "in which selfish interest does not enter, lead to "cordial recognition of whatever strength there "may exist in each other's position, and the yield"ing of untenable points, until they find themselves "occupying common ground. Such has been the "outcome of the long controversy upon the oral "*versus* the manual method. The method of the "future is the 'combined' or 'American' method, "in which the best features of both systems are in"corporated. This method is outlined in papers "read at the Berkeley Convention by Dr. G. O. Fay, "of Hartford, and Professor A. L. E. Crouter, of "Philadelphia, and covered by resolutions intro"duced by Dr. E. M. Gallaudet, of Washington, "and adopted without a dissenting voice."

13,140. You endorse all that is said there?—Yes. I commend the resolutions which I am about to read to this Commission as a representation of the ablest and most recent thought on the subject; the resolutions being the outcome of papers read by gentlemen who are both highly educated men; one of them, Dr. Fay, who was at the head of the Ohio Institution for many years, and who is now at Hartford, and the other, Professor Crouter, who is at the head of the Philadelphia Institution. In Philadelphia the oral school exists quite separate from the manual portion of the institution. The action of the Convention is stated as follows, and I will remind the Commission that representatives from the so-called oral schools, or, as they are termed in England, pure oral schools, of Northampton, New York, Pennsylvania, and Portland, Maine, were present at this Convention, and gave their votes for this action. I speak of that as a matter of very great importance, because it was really a burying of the hatchet.

13,141. The resolutions were passed by a unanimous vote?—By a unanimous vote; I introduced the resolutions, and they were seconded by the most prominent professor in the Institution for the Improved Instruction of the Deaf at New York, which is our pure oral school *par excellence*. The resolutions which were unanimously adopted were as follows: "Whereas the experience of many years "in the instruction of the deaf has plainly shown "that among the members of this class of persons "great differences exist in mental and physical con"dition, and in capacity for improvement, making "results easily possible in certain cases which are "practically and sometimes actually unattainable in "others, these differences suggesting very widely "different treatment with different individuals; it "is, therefore, resolved, that the system of instruc"tion existing at present in America commends it"self to the world, for the reason that its tendency "is to include all known methods and expedients "which have been found to be of value in the edu"cation of the deaf, while it allows diversity and in"dependence of action, working at the same time "harmoniously, and aiming at the attainment of an "object common to all. Resolved, That earnest "and persistent endeavors should be made in every "school for the deaf to teach every pupil to speak "and read from the lips, and that such effort should "only be abandoned when it is plainly evident that "the measure of success attainable is so small as not "to justify the necessary amount of labor." I think it will be evident to the Commission that these resolutions approve an effort in the direction of oral teaching which may be said to be absolutely going to the extreme; that is to say, that if practice proves that all can be taught to speak, then manualists would be very glad to have that result reached. I call attention to the fact that those who had schools in which the manual method alone was used voted for this resolution, that in all schools all the children ought to be taught to speak who can be taught to speak; and it is with a very great degree of satisfaction that I present this result to the Commission, for we conceive that we have arrived in America at a conclusion with regard to this long vexed question of methods, a conclusion which approves of every effort being made in the direction of the oral method, the importance of which we admit. When I say "we" I speak as representing perhaps those who favor the combined system, and I would draw a distinction between the words "method" and "system." In America we apply the term "method" to the oral mode of instruction of the deaf, to the manual mode, and to another method of which I have not yet spoken, but to which I shall allude presently. We call those "methods" of instructing the deaf, and the "system" of which we speak in America as the "combined system" is one which allows of the bringing together of all "methods" under varying conditions.

Dr. E. M. Gallaudet.

9 Nov. 1886.

For example, the Philadelphia Institution has a separate oral branch in which pupils who are found to succeed well in speech are taught on what would be termed here in England the pure oral method. This which was started as a manual school is now conducted under what is called the combined system. The same institution has in its larger establishment classes which are taught entirely without the use of signs or the manual alphabet; and, again, there are classes which are taught by means of the use of the manual alphabet and signs, finding that there are a certain number of pupils who will not succeed with speech. And on that point I may, perhaps, be allowed to say a word with a good deal of earnestness. Those of us who started in our work in America as manual teachers do claim, and we ask that the claim be recognized, that it is possible for us to take a disinterested view of the oral method and judge of its results with unprejudiced minds. We have watched the progress of the oral mode of teaching the deaf, both in our own country and in foreign countries, and we do not hesitate to say that where the attempt is made on the part of a certain locality, a province or State, to carry on a school for the instruction of the deaf, there will be a very large number of pupils who under the most favorable circumstances will not attain to a degree of success in speech and lip-reading which would warrant the time and labor and money that is necessary to carry on a school on what is termed the pure oral method. I was in Paris a few days ago, and I was told that the expense *per capita* of the pupils in the institution there is, without counting the cost of plant, 1,500 francs, equal to 300 dollars, or 60*l*., which is very much larger than the average cost of educating the deaf and dumb in our country. The number of teachers they employ is very much greater, and the expense is very much larger; and we who have had long experience in this matter of the education of the deaf have come to the conclusion that there is too large a proportion of the whole number of pupils that do not succeed in speech to make it right to continue that method for all.

13,142. As you have mentioned Paris, do you know at what age the oral system is begun to be taught in the schools in France?—I think at about eight years of age.

13,143. I think not till 10?—I was not aware of that.

13,144. Is it your experience in America, that in order to teach language well you ought to begin to teach it at the age of six or seven?—Our experience is, that if we are to teach language well we should begin at about the age of seven. My own opinion is, that we should not begin to teach deaf and dumb children language at a younger age than seven. Some advocate beginning at four or five.

13,145. You would treat deaf and dumb children the same as you would other children, as far as possible?—Yes.

13,146. Has it ever struck you that if you delay the teaching of the oral system beyond a certain age the vocal chords will get stiff, and that there will be a want of flexibility about them which will prevent a proper development of the voice?—I should say that to defer it beyond the age of 12, 13, or 14, in boys especially, would be very unfortunate.

13,147. Many of their pupils in Paris are older?—Yes. A third method which we are now practising in America with some exceedingly interesting results may be spoken of as the aural or auricular method. A very considerable percentage of those who are classed in the community as deaf-mutes have a degree of hearing which makes it entirely possible that they may be educated through the ear. The percentage is put variously at from 12 to 25 per cent., which even at the lowest figure is a large percentage of the whole number. The first movement in reference to the aural teaching of the deaf was made in Nebraska four years ago, and it was found in that institution that the percentage was quite large of those who were capable of being taught by the ear. I saw in that institution a little more than two years ago a class which was being taught entirely upon this method, and the process of teaching was an exceedingly interesting one. The class consisted, perhaps, of 11 or 12 pupils. There had been a careful examination of the amount of hearing possessed by each of these pupils, and that pupil who heard the least was placed at the teacher's right hand, the one who had a little more hearing was placed next, and the one who had a little more further on, while the one who had the greatest amount of hearing was furthest removed from the teacher. The teacher then in a voice elevated above the ordinary tone was able to dictate to those pupils, and they had all of them been actually taught to use that hearing which they possessed, which prior to the instruction was not supposed to have been sufficient to be made available at all as a means of instruction. In other words, those pupils were gradually ceasing to be deaf-mutes; they were speaking very well, and they were hearing as well as persons whom we call hard-of-hearing persons. The result would be that, having come to the school under the legal appellation of "deaf-mutes," they would go out of the school not deaf-mutes at all.

13,148. How is that result attained?—The process I can describe a little more fully by reference to the result of a very interesting experiment which we tried in the primary school connected with our college at Washington. In that primary school we try a good many experiments, and we do what we can to develop various methods. The children come in at the age of seven, and they continue in the school for eight or nine years. We had a boy who entered before we began to teach articulation. He was accredited to us as a deaf-mute from one year of age. He lost his hearing in infancy before he learnt to speak; he was absolutely dumb, and the degree of hearing that he possessed was not supposed to be of any account at all. He was registered as hearing slightly very loud noises. Not long after he entered we began teaching him speech, and he was taught to articulate. His progress was only moderate; his success was so imperfect that after a year's effort it was almost decided to give up attempting to teach him any further, but his teacher discovered, purely accidentally, that in uttering a word when the boy's face was turned away from him the boy reproduced the sound. With the use of the hearing tube it was presently discovered that the boy could repeat the vowel sounds and many of the consonant sounds without difficulty; he could repeat words the meaning of which he did not in the least degree understand. The teacher then at once began to educate his hearing. This degree of hearing which the boy possessed had never been enough for him to hold any conversation with members of his family or with any person at an ordinary distance from him.

13,149. Was the speaking tube that was used an ordinary speaking tube?—Yes, a flexible speaking tube. Within two years after that time I exhibited this boy before the National Academy of Sciences at Washington, and talked with him through the tube without difficulty, and to-day he has advanced far enough to be a student in our college: he is a young man full of promise, and he hears well enough to be able to sit by the side of either of you gentlemen and carry on a conversation with you through the tube.

13,150. The fact is that his power of hearing had been overlooked?—Just so.

13,151. There was no extra mechanism in the tube?—No. The result in that case shows that a very small amount of hearing, untrained to be useful, has existed in hundreds of deaf persons who have gone on through life dumb and hard of hearing, and classed as deaf, whereas they might, under this aural or auricular method of instruction, have been taken entirely out of the category of deaf-mutes.

13,152. Is there any medical inspection of these children before they enter school, and is any attempt made by the doctors to improve the hearing if the passages have become clogged by cold or disease?—Yes, in all our better schools there is a careful medical inspection of the children as they enter; it is usually the case that all means have been exhausted to benefit the hearing by the parents and friends of the children before they are brought to the institution. An examination by the medical man exhibits that fact. There are a few instances where the hearing by medical treatment has been improved, but they are very few. I commend this auricular method to all who are interested in the education of the deaf as one deserving of very great attention, because, if we take the number of the deaf who are capable of being taught aurally as amounting to 10 per cent. only, it is conferring upon them a great boon to teach them aurally; it is a greater boon even than giving them the power of imperfect speech.

13,153. With regard to the facility of giving and receiving instruction in such a case as that to which you have just referred, can the boy take his place with the others in the class, or does he require the teacher's individual attention?—In the class at Nebraska, of which I have just been speaking, I think the boys hear when the teacher's voice is raised to a certain *timbre*. When the teacher elevates his voice to a certain pitch they have no difficulty in hearing him.

13,154. Would the teacher use the tube?—Yes, at times, but she was able to make the pupils in her class hear without the use of the speaking tube; they were so arranged that the one that heard the least was placed nearest to her, and the one who had a little more hearing was placed next, and so on.

13,155. No mechanical contrivance is made use of for increasing the volume of sound?—Mr. Edison, who is himself very deaf, told me a few years ago that he was working very hard to bring out some appliance by which the volume of sound might be so increased that a deaf person might hear with great ease.

13,156. Has Professor Bell taken that question up?—To a certain extent, I think.

13,157. Is Professor Bell an advocate of the aural method?—Yes, as well as the oral method. Every one who has heard of the results of the aural method is in favor of it wherever subjects are found that are adapted for it.

13,158. I see it stated that in some of these schools where the sign-system prevailed, or used to prevail principally, there was a great lack of knowledge of the English language; was that so, or is it so still?—It is a fact that in many schools for the deaf certain pupils even after a number of years' teaching, are lacking in the ability to use language idiomatically; the number of such pupils is not found to be greater in manual schools than in oral schools. It goes without saying that there are manual schools and manual schools, and that there are oral schools and oral schools; there will come into the management of schools of any class carelessness in the appointment of teachers, or there may be incompetent teachers appointed through the absence of sufficient funds to secure competent teachers; and so, undoubtedly, in manual schools there may be found pupils who will not succeed well in the idiomatic use of language who might have succeeded better if they had had better teaching. But it is also true that, under the best teaching, in the oral method as well as in the manual method, there will be found a certain number of deaf-mutes who seem to lack the ability to attain to an absolutely idiomatic use of language. That, I think, is a fact that cannot be disputed, that under the best auspices and the best teaching, with the full period of instruction, there will be found pupils whose mental capacity seems to be lacking in some respects, and who will never be able to attain an idiomatic use of their vernacular.

13,159. Would not the use of the manual system, that is to say, finger-language, as against the sign-system, tend to a more accurate knowledge of language?—I do not know what you call the sign-system.

13,160. In some of the schools in our country we have seen children taught entirely by signs, without any finger-language?—I know of no school in America where any sign-system is exclusively used.

13,161. But are signs used as an assistance to teaching?—Yes, as an assistance to manual spelling and writing. The use of signs is resorted to for the purpose of explanation, but in none of our schools are the children exclusively taught by any such system.

13,162. The use of the sign and manual system does not lead to an accurate knowledge of language, does it?—I can answer that question very readily by making this statement: that it is admitted, without question, that an injudicious and incompetent teacher may make such an improper and inordinate use of gestures in the work of teaching in the class-room as to militate very strongly against the best success on the part of the pupils in the attainment of idiomatic language. That, I might say, goes without saying, and that in some of the manual schools such teachers have been found is too true. It may be said, on the other hand, that in manual schools where thoroughly competent and judicious teachers are employed the use of signs is not only found to be no impediment in the acquisition of the power of using language idiomatically, but is found to be a great help in reaching that end; so that the whole question would turn on whether the use of gestures was one that was subject to criticism on general grounds, as being injudicious and undesirable, or whether a proper use was made of gestures by the teacher.

13,163. Do you think that under the oral system there is the same difficulty as to a limited vocabulary as in the manual system?—I do. I think there is the same difficulty.

13,164. Deaf-mutes under both systems are able to make use of only a limited vocabulary?—Naturally. Very little reflection will show us that a hearing person is compelled, whether he will or no, to hear an amount of verbal language on all occasions, that is simply out of all proportion to anything that can possibly be conveyed to one who is deaf, even under the most favorable circumstances; so that the vocabulary of a hearing person is necessarily much larger than that of a deaf person. The vocabulary of a deaf person could not possibly be equal to that of a hearing person until after a very long period of education.

13,165. I have before me a report of the proceedings of a meeting held in July, 1884, in the Senate Chamber, Madison, Wisconsin, in which you say:— "I urge most earnestly that those persons that reject the manual alphabet, and who reject signs for the deaf, while they are giving them speech and lip-reading, are doing them a cruel wrong, in this: that they are dooming them to a greater social isolation than they are compelled to submit to who have no speech, but who still use the manual alphabet and signs"?—In my memorandum of the topics upon which, perhaps, you might desire me to give evidence, I have made a note of that very point, the comparative social isolation of persons who are taught on the oral method, and who

Dr. E. M. Gallaudet.

9 Nov. 1886.

are taught to reject the use of signs and the manual alphabet, comparing persons so taught with others who have the use of signs and the manual alphabet; and from a considerably extended experience of persons who have been taught in both ways, I do not hesitate to express the opinion, that one who has been taught orally, and who does not use the manual alphabet in his family or among his circle of friends, is far more isolated in society than one who has not the power of speech, but who uses freely the manual alphabet and the language of signs. I speak from an experience that extends over the period of my whole conscious life, beginning in my infancy with my mother (who was a mute, who never heard and who never spoke, with whom I communicated freely by signs from the earliest days of my infancy, and with whom I learnt to communicate before I learnt the use of my voice), and extending over all the years of my life, mingling as I have in my earlier years with deaf people who had not the power of speech, and in later years with people who had the power of speech which they had gained from having been instructed in oral schools, or under private tutelage, where a single person has had the advantage of the instruction of many teachers; and I could mention the names of many persons (which I forbear to do) whose intelligence and education were of the highest order, but who have persistently rejected the use of the manual alphabet and signs and only used speech, who could make themselves understood to their friends pretty freely, and to strangers with greater or less freedom and facility, but whose social isolation I am certain has been greater than that of others, whom I could also name, who have not had the power of speech, but who have had the use of the finger-alphabet, and who could use signs in holding communication with those who understand signs; and the emphasis of the opinion which I want to express lies just in this: speech made use of by a person who is totally deaf, and who depends on lip-reading for his answers from others, is at the best a means of communication which is often unsatisfactory, involving many repetitions, involving much guessing, involving frequent misunderstanding, involving a feeling of dislike on the part of the person conversing with the deaf-mute to repeat so many times what he wants to convey to the deaf-mute, and a doubt in his mind whether he has been understood, this leading to an embarrassment in communication which frequently results, in a greater or less degree, in the social isolation of the person so depending on speech and lip-reading for communication with the outer world. I could give the names of persons whom I know in the highest society in America, who are more or less socially isolated on account of the acknowledged and admitted difficulty on many occasions, and under many circumstances, of making the means of communication of speech and lip-reading available exactly and quickly, and without very much repetition. I know many persons in America who are acquainted with these educated deaf persons, and who say to me, "I dread to meet so-and-so, for I am expected to speak, and that person is expected to understand my lip-movements. It is not always that my lip-movements are understood, and it is not always that I can understand his speech." That is the feeling which many people have who meet such a person in society, and, therefore, the deaf person is let alone and but little conversation is attempted because it is carried on with such difficulty. I myself have sometimes at dinner parties sat by the side of a highly educated deaf person who has been educated on the oral system and who rejects the use of the finger-alphabet and signs, and I have spoken with him more or less on a limited range of topics and carried on a conversation that was agreeable so far as it went, but I have found it impossible to branch off on a totally different subject as with an ordinary person. I have felt that I would give anything if I could speak with my fingers with that person for five minutes. On the other hand, a person who depends on the finger-alphabet entirely, and who has not the power of oral speech or the power to read lip movements, if he has the power of forming friendships, will have a circle of friends who will acquire, for his sake, the finger-alphabet, and with the use of the finger-alphabet conversation can be sustained as fluently, as readily, and as perfectly as if he had speech. In other words, a deaf person, who has the finger-alphabet as a means of communication, will have in his own family those who will learn to use it freely and fluently for his sake, and he has a circle of friends who will also acquire the finger-alphabet so as to be able to carry on a conversation with him easily, and his social isolation will be less absolute than the social isolation of a person who depends entirely upon speech and lip-reading, and rejects the use of the manual alphabet. I speak from experience of a very great number of both classes of persons.

13,166. At the meeting at Madison, I see Dr. Bell quotes you as having said this: "I see, running "through it all" (that is to say, the paper which had been read), "the fact, which I am very glad to "have acknowledged here so plainly in this Con- "vention, and which we have all to look in the face, "that the deaf and dumb in our institutions, as a "class, do not master the English language." Then Dr. Bell again quotes you as saying: "If we want "the children of our institutions for the deaf and "dumb to master the English language, what have "we to do with the sign-language? I answer, "As little as possible." As I understand, you say an over-use of the sign-system is a dangerous thing?—Yes.

13,167. Is it the tendency in schools on the combined system in America, and in schools where the manual alphabet is taught, to depend more on the manual alphabet than on signs in order to get a more accurate knowledge of the English language? —Yes, the tendency in the American schools is to a diminishing use of the language of signs. At Indianapolis, where I made that statement which was quoted by Dr. Bell, at Madison, the subject of the use of signs in class-rooms was under discussion. At that time, 16 years ago, there were in many of our schools in America teachers who were very careless, reckless, and unjustifiable in their use of gestures, and the result was a very unsatisfactory development of the power of idiomatic expression; so at the discussion at Indianapolis I said that I felt that there was such a thing as a very pernicious and dangerous use of the sign-language in the instruction of the deaf.

13,168. When you speak of the sign-language, you mean gestures—conventional signs?—Yes.

13,169. Those signs vary in different countries and in different schools?—Yes; in different countries, and, to a certain extent, in different schools. I raised my voice at Indianapolis to warn teachers against making too great a use of sign-language, and insisted that in the instruction of the deaf the language of signs should be used as little as possible.

13,170. You say that that meeting at Indianapolis was 16 years ago?—Yes.

13,171. Therefore, what you said then does not accurately represent the danger to which schools are liable now?—No; we were fighting against certain evils then existing in schools. With regard to the comparative social isolation which results from oral teaching, I may refer to an incident which occurred this last summer. One of the professors of our college at Washington was spending some time in New England, and he himself being a great bicyclist attended a meeting of bicyclists at a town called

Dr. E. M. Gallaudet.

9 Nov. 1886.

Brattleboro'. He noticed at that meeting a young man of very prepossessing appearance with a bicycle, who had come to attend the meeting, and he observed that he spoke on his fingers to some one near him. This professor speaks very well, and has always spoken, but he lost his hearing at ten years of age. He noticed this young man speaking on his fingers, and he naturally sought to make his acquaintance, he himself being a deaf man. He found that the young man was well educated, that he used his fingers very freely, and that he used even the language of signs; and he found to his surprise that he had been wholly educated at a pure oral school. He was the son of wealthy parents, and had been a long time at school, and completed his education there, and he spoke very well and read from the lips very well; but he told this professor of our college at Washington that, while among his intimate friends, he always spoke and read from the lips, and did so very well in a certain limited range of subjects, yet he found that in general society he got on more satisfactorily and pleasantly by using the manual alphabet; and therefore he adopted the use of it, and his friends learnt it for his sake. He being a person who had never been in a manual school or a sign-school, still found it was necessary for him to learn to converse with his fingers, in order to avoid a certain degree of social isolation to which he would have been subjected if he had confined himself to the oral method. Then I will refer to the case of a Wisconsin lady who became deaf at the age of 16, and who became an exceedingly good lip-reader. She called at my house with a lady friend of my wife's, and we were made acquainted and entered into conversation. She read my lips very readily, and we talked together for a little time, and I marvelled at her success in carrying on the conversation. Presently she said, "I "did not understand that last sentence; will you "spell it on your fingers?"; so I spelt it on my fingers. I said, "How is it that you resort to "speaking by your fingers?" She replied, "Do "you think I would be so foolish as to reject a "means of communication which is absolutely certain and reliable for one which I often find myself "blundering in? Whenever my speech and lip-"reading fails I like to resort to my fingers; that "is sure and certain while the other is doubtful." Then, again, I have the acquaintance of a gentleman in Philadelphia who became deaf after he had grown up, who is a very good lithographer, and he told me not a great while ago that, while he could speak, and read lip-movements, and often passed as a person who heard, yet invariably, when he entered into any business contract, he resorted to writing; he did not dare to depend on the power of lip-reading, because in carrying on conversation by that means there was a liability to mistakes. I refer to those cases simply to show that while people advocate this teaching of speech and lip-reading, we know (to use a commercial phrase) there is a discount to be allowed upon it.

13,172. You said that the age at which children should be sent to school was seven years; should they be taught writing before they go to school?—Most of our institutions in their circulars recommend to the parents and friends of deaf children where they are able to do so to teach them writing at home; to teach them the use of simple words. I do not think the majority come to the institutions having been so taught; that is urged, but I think the majority of them do not come to the institutions with any knowledge at all. I should here like to refer the Commission to a very careful comparison of results of teaching by the oral method and the combined system, which was made in the oldest school in America, Hartford, by its principal in the case of more than 30 pupils who came to that institution from the oral schools in New England after having been in those schools a longer or shorter time. The paper to which I refer in which that comparison was made was presented at the conference of principals held in Minnesota two years ago, and is found in the record of the proceedings of that conference, pages 182–196, 197, which I will leave with the Commission. The paper gives the results arrived at from a careful examination of those pupils, running over a period of eight or nine years. The results are tabulated, and a comparison of the results due to oral teaching and manual teaching, or teaching by the combined system, is given which is not found, I think, elsewhere.

13,173. Will you now favor the Commission with any observations that you have to make with reference to the duration of pupilage and the courses of study?—With reference to the duration of pupilage and courses of study, in our institutions in America we endeavor to have a course of study practically the same as that which is pursued in the schools for the hearing. We take up the elementary study of geography, arithmetic, and history, and some little study of physics, perhaps, and occasionally some study of physiology, which we deem of importance even in the case of those who go through a limited course of teaching; and in nearly all, I may say all, the larger institutions in America, quite an important feature is made of instruction in art. We develop as far as possible the power of drawing, and instruction is given in the branches of art of painting and sculpture. Wood carving has come into great prominence in the last few years, and many institutions are establishing departments for instruction in the art, carrying it forward to a very high degree of development. I may speak particularly of the institution at Illinois, which is the largest in America, where they have a department of art with a teacher at the head, and four or five assistants, who devote themselves entirely to the instruction of the pupils of the institution in art.

13,174. Do they turn out many artists?—A large number, and an increasingly large number. They turn out artists of various degrees of talent, but an artist who is able to work in decorative art, designing, and things of that kind may be very successful, though he may not be able to paint landscapes or portraits.

13,175. Do you know Mr. Moore?—Yes, I know him very well. He is one who was never taught to speak. He has not been orally taught. He was taught under the manual method.

13,176. Are you aware that he is able to get several hundred pounds for his pictures?—Yes; he set a very good example by patient and long study for a number of years before he began to sell any pictures.

13,177. (*Mr. Woodall.*) Is what is aimed at to make picture-makers?—No, it is general instruction in art that is given. We do not encourage the pupils to be portrait painters or landscape painters. In many cases in our large cities in which these deaf persons who have been instructed in art come into competition with others they have done extremely well.

13,178. (*Chairman.*) The instruction they receive in art enables some of them to become draughtsmen for engineers and architects, and so on?—Yes. In making drawings for woodcuts for illustrated papers many of the pupils have succeeded extremely well.

13,179. (*Mr. Woodall.*) Is anything done in the way of kindergarten teaching with a view to leading up to their industrial art teaching. In your primary school which you spoke of at Washington have you any kindergarten teaching?—We have not in the primary school at Washington, but in several of the schools there are departments for kindergarten work, and at our convention in California

Dr. E. M. Gallaudet.

9 Nov. 1886.

considerable prominence was given to the matter of kindergarten instruction for the deaf, and I know one or two, perhaps three, institutions in America in which there are seperate departments for kindergarten instruction, where the children who are put under the instruction which is given in that department are very young, and are kept quite separate from the older ones.

13,180. Do you recognize any useful relationship between the kindergarten teaching and the subsequent teaching in art?—I should say the one would naturally be a good preparation for the other.

13,181. (*Chairman.*) With regard to industrial training, have the boys any industrial training given them while at school, or does it begin after the education pure and simple is finished?—There are some schools in America into whose curriculum industrial training does not enter; they depend entirely upon the apprenticeship of their pupils after they leave the school to mechanics with whom they may learn trades, and so be prepared to become mechanics; but that is the practice of a small number of schools comparatively; by far the greater number have a larger or smaller number of shops in which trades are taught. In the whole number of our schools in the United States only 14 have no industrial department, and eight of these 14 are day schools, so that there are only six of those institutions which would be called public institutions in America which have no industrial departments; those that have an industrial department and those that have not are named in the table in the *Annals* to which I have referred. The feeling is decided among the managers of our institutions in favor of teaching trades while the pupils are in school. As to the amount of time that is given to industrial training, in some of the institutions, there is a division of the day between the forenoon and the afternoon, the boys being in the shops during one-half of the day and in school the other half; and in other institutions the school hours are prolonged during a part of the afternoon for two or three hours, as the case may be, and industrial work given at a later time in the day; but as to the result of this training I can certainly say that a vast number of very competent mechanics have been turned out of these industrial departments of our institutions.

13,182. At what age are they turned out?—Varying from 16 to 20.

13,183. Do they keep them as long as that?—If they enter at 10 years of age they may remain 10 years in some of our schools.

13,184. You spoke of seven years as being the age at which they commence school?—When they commence school at the age of 10 they would be retained to the age of 16 or 17; the time of their being discharged would vary from the age of 14 or 15 to 20, but if the children were discharged at the age of 13 or 14 they would hardly be old enough to learn a trade while in school.

13,185. What is the age at which you begin to give them industrial training; how long after they have been at school?—It would depend on the age at which they entered.

13,186. Would you begin their industrial training at 12, 13, or 14, according to the age at which they entered?—It would again depend on the physical condition of the boys; some at 12 years of age would be quite as capable of beginning to learn a trade as others at 14.

13,187. What is the industrial work that is taught?—I have here a list of the trades taught; baking, basket making, bookbinding, broom making, cabinet making, carpentry, chair making, cooking, clay modelling, coopery, dressmaking, farming, gardening, glazing, knitting, mattress-making, painting, printing, sewing, shoemaking, tailoring, wood carving, wood engraving, and wood turning.

13,188. Those are taught at different schools?—Yes, not all at the same school; here is one school, the New York Institution, where, besides art, baking, cabinet-making, carpentering, clay modelling, and dressmaking are taught; then in another, the Pennsylvania School, cooking, dressmaking, knitting, printing, shoemaking, and tailoring are taught. In Kentucky five trades are taught, in Ohio four, in Virginia six, in Indiana three, in Tennessee two, in North Carolina ten, in Illinois ten, in Georgia only one, and in South Carolina three; the number of trades taught varies.

13,189. Do the pupils assist in the ordinary house work of the institution?—To a very considerable extent. I may say that one of the reasons that induces us in America to be very earnest in teaching these boys trades, while they are in the school, is that the difficulty of apprenticing them after they leave school is very great, owing to the existence of very close trades unions in our country, under whose regulations the number of apprentices is limited.

13,190. Do they keep out the deaf and dumb from any prejudice against them?—They keep them out as they would any one they did not wish to admit. They are not excluded simply because they are deaf, but still there would be those who would rather turn the cold shoulder to them because they were. We conceive it to be of great importance to give them this manual training even though they may not follow, after leaving the institution, the trade that they have been taught. We conceive it to be an important point, because dexterity in one trade, the training of the hand and the eye in the use of tools, prepares the boy for success in, perhaps, several different directions, and in point of fact, we find that there is that success. The institution for the improved instruction of the deaf and dumb in New York city favors very much the limitation of industries taught to the deaf and dumb to those of a higher character; that is, those in which the element of art may come to a greater or less extent. The authorities of that institution believe that it is well to endeavor to get the deaf to take up wood carving and lithography, and industries of that sort, rather than to relegate the deaf to carpentry, and shoemaking, and such trades; but that feeling does not prevail throughout the country. It is felt in a large number of institutions throughout the country that ordinary industries are as valuable to the deaf and dumb as those that may be said to be more refined. They succeed extremely well as gardeners. I could mention one colored boy who seemed to possess very little intellectual power; we thought him at one time almost an imbecile, but he developed afterwards considerably, and lately he has become a competent gardener.

13,191. Are colored boys taught in the same classes with the others?—In our primary school in which we have 60 pupils, eight or nine are blacks.

13,192. Are they taught in a class by themselves?—No, they are mixed with the others in the classes; in the sleeping apartments and at the table they are separated in deference to the caste prejudice, which still continues in our country to a certain extent, but in the classes they come together; the day-schools have no shops. I ought to say that in America we do not consider day-schools as capable of finishing the entire education necessary for the deaf, and we consider them rather as an expedient, better than nothing, as being schools into which the younger children can come, and where they can remain, perhaps, one, or two, or three years, but from which they ought to go to the boarding schools to reach the best results. The sentiment in America is against the extension of day-schools, and in favor very much of bringing the deaf together in boarding schools.

13,193. You said that some of these day-schools are conducted on the oral method?—Yes.

13,194. Would there not be more difficulty in teaching by oral method in a day-school than in an institution, looking to the probability that if a child goes back to its parents and friends it would necessarily make use of signs before it could make itself understood?—My own opinion is that the child in going home to its parents would, perhaps, get a practice in speech which would be a benefit to it.

13,195. Do you think that generally in America parents endeavor to assist the instruction of their children in the oral system?—Where they are in day-schools, and they go home to their parents, I think they do, and when they go home from boarding schools, I think the parents and friends in the vast majority of cases take pains to keep up the speech of their children. We find often when they return from their holidays that their speech is improved.

13,196. It depends on the parents taking an intelligent interest in their children?—Very much.

13,197. Are any objections felt in America to collecting together the deaf and dumb in institutions in view of the probability that friendships will be formed resulting in intermarriage in after-life?—There may possibly be such objections, but we believe they are so far counterbalanced by the advantages to be gained in having the deaf in schools where they may be taught as such and receive the benefit of special training, that we think that the best way of treating those possible objections is to make the pupils, as they advance in intelligence, feel the importance of avoiding such marriages. Later on, I will go into that rather more fully.

13,198. Is there any separation of the sexes at school after the age of 13 or 14, or are they kept together?—They are separated altogether, excepting in the class-room; they come together in the class-room; in many institutions, where there are a sufficient number to classify the boys and girls separately, they have separate classes, but there are institutions where, as a matter of preference, in the dining-room, the boys and the girls are seated together at tables; and it is claimed by those who keep up that practice, that the effect is good—that the boys are improved in manner by association with the girls, and that the girls are in no way injured by being thus associated with the boys in a sort of little family; but universally, in all matters of domestic arrangement, the dormitories, the sitting-rooms, and the play-grounds, the girls and boys are carefully separated.

13,199. Do the deaf and dumb find any difficulty in getting employment as soon as they leave school?—They do not find any great difficulty in securing employment; they secure employment with considerable facility, and the number of unemployed deaf in America would be found to be very small.

13,200. There is no prejudice against the employment of the deaf and dumb?—No general prejudice. There may be found individual masters who would not like to employ deaf persons, but generally speaking, there is no prejudice against them.

13,201. Will you give us the substance of what you wish to say about the sign-system, as distinguished from the manual, as bearing upon the answer which you gave to me on the quotation which I made from a former speech of yours, made 16 years ago, at Indianapolis?—In answer to the question, I beg leave to present two quotations. The first is from a paper of Dr. Fay, presented at the Convention in California this last summer, on the general subject of the education and care of the deaf. He speaks here with reference to the two methods often spoken of as the French and the German, or the manual and the oral, and makes some important comparisons, which I will read, as they bear very much on one or two of the answers given under that head. Dr. Fay says: "Errors of "proportion have divided the educators of the deaf "into schools of opinion, not exactly hostile, but "certainly separate and narrow. The schools of "France, for a century, and subsequently the schools "of the United States, while theoretically favorable "to the teaching of articulation, have demonstrated, "only and mainly, through long practice, the importance and possibilities of pantomime and the "uses of the manual alphabet, supplemented by "written speech. They have applied these instruments with great skill and energy, and have produced a remarkable body of silent scholars easily "superior in scholarship to anything that oralists "have been able to produce. French and American "schools, true to their traditions, have been backward, however, in taking up and applying, with "equal skill and energy, the teaching of oral speech. "Might not a fraction of their silent, written scholarship have been well exchanged for a degree of oral "skill? Such seems to be their own present conviction. We are now witnessing the introduction of "the systematic teaching of articulation into all the "prominent institutions of Europe and America. "And the pursuance of this policy has exhibited the "fact that the development of the faculties and the "acquisition of verbal speech by pantomime, by finger-spelling, and by books, are an excellent preliminary training, the full peer of all rival expedients, for teaching associated and subsequent "oral speech itself. The pupil has something to "say, and can be more easily taught to say it. The "present need of our historic schools is to expand "their scope still more widely, so as to include and "attach to themselves all that is valuable in oral "schools. If a longer school period shall be found "necessary for the best results, it should not, will "not, be withheld. Another school of opinion, "represented by the schools of Germany for a century, and by a few recently opened in the United "States, ignores the pantomime of the deaf and uses "none. It omits the finger-alphabet and proposes "to teach the deaf at the start, and with no intermediate step, oral speech itself, and by it all "branches of desirable knowledge. Though opposed to the use of extempore sign-pictures, it "uses all printed pictures freely. It omits evidently "and rejects such illustrations as the pupil is likely "to imitate and to incorporate into signs of his own. "It is communicating instruction with great and increasing skill, and to a proportion of pupils steadily enlarging. The partially deaf, and those who "have heard in early years, succeed from the start. "An additional number, some of them totally deaf "from birth, succeed to a certain extent, practically "useful. A large number do not acquire it sufficiently "to be able to rely upon it, singularly evanescent, "in after-life. At school they habitually invent and "illicitly use a gesture-language for social relief, "and feel more confidence in their pencil than in "their voice. The time spent in oral teaching has "crowded out some topics taught in the sign-schools. "The range of written scholarship, including English composition and the ability to read newspapers, is considerably lower. This deficiency is justified by those who are responsible for it by the "compensating value of the oral speech acquired "or attempted. These schools have yet to learn "that, in omitting the use of pantomime and finger-spelling, they ignore the uneducated mute's best "friend. They take away a ladder, the only ladder "known, by which all the deaf can easily rise. They "require the mute, scorning all climbing steps and "gradual approaches, to clear at one bound the "chasm that separates the deaf from the hearing. "They force the recruit at once upon frowning "breastworks. They apply a method derived from "the functions of the hearing mind, and not at all "from the essential, the universal functions of the "mind of the deaf. Attempting the best thing for "all the deaf by a method heroic, they succeed with "a smaller number, less than half, and, holding no

Dr. E. M. Gallaudet.

9 Nov. 1886.

"middle ground substantially, culpably fail with a "considerable number. The brilliancy of the operation is clouded by its frequently fatal issue. "These schools, excellent, ambitious, and ably officered, need, in behalf of many of their pupils, to "incorporate into the early years of their course all "that is valuable in the sign-schools. The removal "of intervening barriers will make the two jarring "methods friends—astonished to remember that "they ever differed. Pantomime and finger-spelling, as jealously excluded now from oral schools "as the 'long keels of the northmen,' will prove a "boon, a help, and not a hindrance, to all their pupils. They will all easily rise, and rapidly, to the "plane of written speech; and those capable of taking the higher step, the last, the crowning oral "one, will not be the less able for having a broader "elementary base." I present that as the expression of what I conceive to be the best thought of the present day in America relative to what is spoken of as the combined system. It gives everything to the oral teaching that it can accomplish, and it still holds on to much that belongs to what may now be termed the old manual method, which exists no longer as the only method of teaching the deaf, but which still, the writer conceives (and there are a large majority who sustain his view), should not be given up.

13,202. Might I ask what was the view taken with regard to the aural system at that California convention; how far was it considered to be practicable in a sufficient number of cases?—It would vary in different localities, from 10 to 20 per cent. of the whole number of deaf-mutes. Coming now to the other citation pertinent to the matter, to what extent signs are valuable in the instruction of the deaf, and in the life of the deaf, I would read this short paragraph from an article published in a handbook of medical science, on the general subject of gesture language, which I was asked to prepare with a view of giving information to medical men with regard to the treatment of the deaf: "At this point the question will naturally arise in many minds: 'Does the "'sign-language give the deaf in these respects *all* "'that speech affords to the hearing?' The experience and observation of the writer leads him to "answer the question with a decided affirmative. "On many occasions it has been his privilege to interpret, through signs to the deaf, addresses given "in speech; he has addressed assemblages of deaf "persons many times, using signs for the original "expression of thought; he has seen hundreds of "lectures and public debates given originally in "signs; he has seen conventions of deaf-mutes, in "which no word was spoken, and yet all the forms "of parliamentary proceeding were observed, and "the most excited and earnest discussions carried "on; he has seen the ordinances of religion administered, and the full services of the church carried "on in signs; and all this with the assurance growing out of his own complete understanding of the "language, a knowledge of which dates back to his "earliest childhood, that for all the purposes above "enumerated, gestural expression is in no respect "inferior, and is in many respects superior, to articulate speech as a means of communicating ideas. "But the greatest value of the sign-language to the "deaf, when the whole period of their lives is taken "into account, is to be found in the facility it affords "for free and unconstrained social intercourse. And "in this, as in the matter of public addresses, nothing has been discovered that can fully take its "place. It may even be asserted, that so long as "the deaf remain without hearing, nothing else can "give them what speech affords their more favored "brethren. They may have much pleasant intercourse with others by the employment of writing "tablets; they may even enjoy conversation under "many limitations with single individuals through "articulation and lip-reading; with the aid of the "manual alphabet they may have a still wider and "more enjoyable range for the interchange of "thought; but it is only by employing signs that "they can gain the pleasure and profit that comes "from conversation in the social circle, that they "can enjoy such freedom of intercommunication as "shall make it possible for them to forget they are "deaf."

13,203. Does not the language of signs convey sometimes a slightly different idea to different people; for instance, take it in this way: Supposing a sermon was preached in signs, would every member of the congregation write the sermon down in exactly the same language?—No, not at all.

13,204. Then, clearly, there is room for a great latitude and variety of language?—That the ideas would be expressed clearly and distinctly is as probable even as that the ideas would be so expressed in a case where a congregation heard a sermon preached orally.

13,205. I do not see how that is reconciled with what you said 16 years ago; that the effect of signs tends to make the language inaccurate or obscure?—I was speaking then distinctly of the use of signs in teaching, which I deprecate in the class-room; but for purposes of lecturing, for purposes of public addresses, for purposes of social intercommunication, I insist that the language of signs is of such value, and the source of so much enjoyment and pleasure in the intercourse of the deaf, that it is cruel to take it away from them.

13,206. But I thought that from the passage you read out, you proved more than that; that you proved that everybody who has speech should use signs, because it is the more expressive of the two, as the Italian does?—I think there are circumstances where the language of signs is more expressive than that of speech. I often find myself better able to express certain ideas through the means of the gestural language than through the means of speech.

13,207. (*Mr. Johnson.*) You wrote that passage for the guidance of the medical profession, I understand?—Yes, this is one article in their handbook, intended to guide them in the treatment of these children.

13,208. (*Chairman.*) Going on to the higher education of the deaf, would you in the higher education of the deaf give all the lectures by signs rather than by the manual alphabet?—My preference would be to use the language of signs in most lectures; there might be some very much of a technical character, and in which scientific terms would be largely used, where the manual alphabet would be preferable.

13,209. You would not give lectures in Mathematics or Logic by signs, would you?—To a considerable extent; but in the use of the gesture language the interjection of words spelt upon the fingers is very common.

13,210. The mixture of the two would be necessary?—Quite necessary.

13,211. In order to give precision in certain cases?—Yes. You ask me, with regard to the higher education of the deaf, to speak somewhat to that point; and I will, therefore, with your permission, make a statement as to the establishment of the college at Washington in which the higher education of the deaf is provided for; and I have brought with me a few copies of a map which represents the grounds and buildings of the institution, which the Commission might be interested to look at, so as to get an idea of the extent and the arrangement of the grounds and buildings, that is, of the institution, including both the primary school and the college; they are quite distinct in their organization. This map shows the grounds and the arrangement of the buildings. I am sure it would be of a little interest in connection with the higher education of the deaf, to know how it came about that the Government of the United States became committed to the support of such a work; for it is probably well known, even in this country, that, constitutionally, the Government of the United States would not be at liberty to appropriate the money of the country at large for the support of an ordinary educational institution; in fact, that point in the progress of the relations of the college with the Congress at Washington has been often raised. The institution at Washington was begun in 1857 as a primary school. One of the clauses in the Act of Incorporation gave no limit, in providing for the period during which children should be received and educated, as to the time which they could be retained in the institution. They were simply to be received and retained there while they were of teachable age. That simple omission to place any limit on the course of instruction, suggested to those who had charge of the institution in its early years, that the course of instruction might be extended so as to cover the secondary or collegiate course. So in 1864, after the primary school had existed for seven years, it was suggested to the Board of Directors by the then superintendent of the institution, that the course of instruction should be extended to include collegiate training. The Board of Directors accepted the suggestion. Congress was asked to pass an additional act authorizing the institution to confer collegiate degrees. This act was passed before the Collegiate Department was organized, and in 1864 the simple pressing forward of a few of the more capable pupils of the school into collegiate study formed the nucleus of what became later the National College. Congress made an appropriation for enlarging the grounds at that time, and later for additions to buildings, but no appropriation whatever for the maintenance of students in the college who were unable to pay their expenses. Private charity was appealed to successfully to secure annual contributions for support of young men in the college who were unable to pay their own expenses. At a certain point, a little later, I think it was in 1866, I (if I may be allowed to speak in the first person, for I was then President of the college) received a letter from the Honorable Thaddeus Stevens, who was then the leader of the House of Representatives, in that position on account of his being at the head of the Committee on Appropriations, saying that in his district there was a young man who wished to come to the college at Washington, who was deaf, had never been in a school for the deaf, but had become deaf, who was poor but very intelligent, and asking me if he could be admitted without charge. I replied that he could not, and I called upon Mr. Stevens to explain the reasons why he could not. He grew very much excited (he had previously been a friend of the institution, and the means of securing appropriations for it) and asked why his constituent could not be received without charge. I replied, that there was no law for it; and in very emphatic language, which I need not repeat, he declared that there should be a law for it; and in a very few weeks he succeeded in passing through Congress a law for the admission of a certain number of young men from the States and Territories on a free basis; and that formed the beginning of our authority from Congress to receive young men into the college from the States and Territories, giving them board and tuition without charge when their circumstances were such as to make it impossible for them or their friends to meet the expense of paying.

13,212. And did the State vote the sum of money requisite for the purpose?—Not the State. The Federal Government gave those annual appropriations, increasing from year to year, and sufficient to cover the increased expenses owing to the reception of these young men, the majority of whom are in circumstances which make it impossible for them to pay.

13,213. But do not the State Governments also pay?—They contribute nothing.

13,214. But with regard to those in the primary school, do not the State Governments pay so much?—In the primary school at Washington the majority of the pupils are from the District of Columbia, and so they are paid for by the United-States Government, as we have no local government in Washington.

13,215. Are you quoting this college as a model for the rest of the United States, or is that the only one?—It is the only one, and the only one that is at present needed; that is to say, it is able to furnish the secondary or collegiate education for all the deaf that are fit to take that course of study; so that we can say no other is needed at present in our country. We quote that as something very desirable to have, if possible, in other countries.

13,216. As I understand it, all the education of the deaf and dumb is practically free in cases where the poverty of the parent requires it?—It is so.

13,217. Free; being borne either by the State or by the Federal Government?—Yes; so that even through the college the education of the deaf is practically free.

13,218. All education is free in America?—All primary education, but not all collegiate education. The deaf have an advantage there over the hearing.

13,219. (*Mr. Woodall.*) These pupils in Washington are received from all parts of the country?—Yes.

13,220. (*Chairman.*) Are they maintained there free?—It would not include, for instance, their clothing.

13,221. And in the holidays they go home at their own expense?—Yes.

13,222. They have their college-training free?—Yes.

13,223. And their board and lodging free?—Yes.

13,224. (*Mr. Woodall.*) There is no system like what prevails in France?—No. We had what are called scholarships given by private individuals. These private individuals paid for certain students at the college an annual sum which was equivalent to the charge which we made to ordinary students for board and tuition; but those terminated and have not been renewed, and now the entire help of students needing help comes from the general fund appropriated by the Congress of the United States.

13,225. (*Mr. Johnson.*) There are certain people who do pay?—Yes.

13,226. It is only those who are unable to pay who claim a free education from the State?—Yes, those who are able to pay are expected to do so.

13,227. (*Chairman.*) Practically, what proportions pay?—Only about 5 per cent. pay their expenses; and it ought to be said in connection with that, that the distances in our country from Washington are so great to all the outlying States, that even though the circumstances of a deaf young man may be tolerably comfortable he has to pay in coming and going such a large cost for transportation, besides going home during the holidays and expenses in connection with that, that we assist young men who are not in a condition that we should call one of absolute poverty, but whose means are straitened and are not sufficient to enable them to pay their expenses; but they all provide their travelling expenses, their clothing and books, and what may be called their incidental expenses.

13,228. (*Mr. Woodall.*) What assistance do you give them?—We make them no charge for board or tuition. In no case do we assume the actual support in an eleemosynary sense of any of these young men who are following their higher education. I

Dr. E. M. Gallaudet.

9 Nov. 1886.

may say that we have been asked to do so by the managers of institutions in different parts of the country, and I have steadily refused, and have been sustained by the directors in refusing to adopt any course which seemed to make the collegiate education of the deaf an absolute eleemosynary act. I claim that the deaf young man who is not able by his own energies or by the assistance of friends to clothe himself and pay his way to Washington and back had better not have the higher education.

13,229. (*Chairman.*) Is this institution full, and what number does it contain?—In the primary school it contains 65 at present, and in the college 50. We have room for probably 25 or 30 more in our buildings.

13,230. What proportion of those in the primary school go up to the higher education?—A very small proportion, hardly one a year from our primary school. Before leaving the subject of the Governmental support of the institution, I would say that at present the annual appropriation for the support of the institution in all its branches by Congress is a little over 10,000*l.*, which makes, it will be seen at once, a very large *per capita* for the number of pupils and students, say 120, that would be taught during any given year. This large expense grows out of the necessity of paying large salaries to the professors in our college. One of the professors in our college, the one who is most highly paid, receives a salary of 3,000 dollars, or 600*l.*, and a house; and two others receive a salary of 2,400 dollars, or 480*l.*, and a house. The others receive rather smaller salaries, but these large salaries which it is necessary to pay men of sufficient ability to teach in the college carry the *per capita* cost up to the high point that it is.

13,231. What is that point?—It is quite 100*l.* a year.

13,232. That does not take into calculation the interest on the capital sum that has been spent on buildings and on land?—No.

13,233. (*Dr. Campbell.*) What is about the proportion in the primary department, and what in the collegiate?—The primary department is quite a different thing.

13,234. (*Chairman.*) Do you separate the expenses?—I have not done so in my calculation. This sum of 10,000*l.* covers the entire institution in both departments.

13,235. But of course there must be very much greater expense in educating the higher department than in educating the primary department?—Yes.

13,236. It means therefore practically that the expense of the higher classes is not only 100*l.* per head, but a great deal more; because in that calculation of 100*l.* you are giving them credit for the lower sum per head that the primary school costs?—Yes. But to compare the cost of the college with, for instance, the Government Schools at Annapolis and West Point for naval and military training, the expenses there run up to 1,000 and 1,500 dollars *per capita* per annum, and the expenses of young men securing a collegiate education in our colleges in America run up to a much higher sum than it costs in our college. I should pass on to give an idea of the course of study pursued in the college at Washington, and then to speak of some of the practical results of the higher education of the deaf, what they can do in after-life, how they succeed, and what they accomplish. I may state that the form of admission is given in the appendix to the report of the institution. The course of study taken up at the college supplements that carried forward in the best and most advanced of our State schools, our primary schools. The applicant for admission to the college is supposed to have completed arithmetic, and to have completed primary studies of course, and comes in then to what is termed on page 27 of our report an introductory course of one year in a course of five years; and in this first year of the five of the course, which is termed our collegiate course, algebra, the study of English grammar and history, and original compositions, and Latin are pursued. Latin is begun at the beginning of this year, the lowest year of the five in the collegiate course. Then in the freshman year we continue in mathematics, algebra, and take up geometry; in English, original compositions; in Latin, the study of Sallust and Cicero is carried on; Greek is an optional study; and the course of history is continued. Then in the next year, the sophomore year, mathematics go on to trigonometry, mensuration, and surveying; zoölogy is taken up, and botany and chemistry; Latin is continued with Virgil's Æneid; Greek is an optional study, and there is quite a course in English. The next year, the junior year, mathematics are continued to the calculus and mechanics; physics are taken up; in chemistry, laboratory practice and qualitative analysis; and physiology. French is then taken up and continued during the year; and history and English and logic are studied. In the next year, the senior year, in English literature quite an extended course is pursued; German is taken up and continued for the year; natural science is taken up, and the elements of mental science; moral science is taken up, æsthetics, political philosophy, and international law. That affords an idea of the course of study pursued in the college which is necessary to secure a degree, and examinations in those studies are made at the end of each three months, each semestre, and then a record is made of the marks obtained in the recitations and the examinations, and it is required that a certain standard should be reached (a standard of 6½ on a scale of 10) in order to enable the student to pass. And I may say that we have had whole classes that have reached the end of the college course, the average of which has been above 9 on a scale of 10 in recitations and marks for the entire course.

13,237. (*Dr. Campbell.*) In connection with the study of languages, it is always written, I suppose, never oral in any case; take, for instance, French or German?—We do use speech in a good many cases, and speech is used as a means of communication in a great many cases where it is practicable. Of course we do receive students who have not power of speech, and with them the method of communication is mainly the manual alphabet. I may say that in the recitations and in the class-room the sign-language is very little employed, the students being taught by writing and the manual alphabet.

13,238. But do the deaf people learn to speak French or German?—Not to any very great extent. Now, with regard to the admission of young men who may come to us for the purpose of pursuing special courses, although our full course is five years we may have young men who come to us and study for two or three years, and leave us with certificates of honorable dismission, showing what studies they have pursued. These of course take no regular diploma, and go out with no degree, but a good many young men take in our college what is tantamount to a high-school course of study, such a course as will be beneficial to them in after-life, the particular course depending upon what pursuit they intend to take up.

13,239. (*Chairman.*) I see that free admission is given also to those whose fathers are in the military or naval service?—Yes: that is the law of Congress. We rarely have a case of that sort; we have not had one for several years, but it is open to such, if such a case should occur. With regard to the admission of young men into this higher school at Washington, I am able to say that the whole country has been represented with the single exception of the Pacific States. The distance by which we are separated from the Pacific involving a very large cost of transportation, has prevented the representation of any of

Dr. E. M. Gallaudet.

9 Nov. 1886.

the Pacific States in our college; but the South and the Middle States, and the West and the East, have been represented in a proportion almost exactly comparing with the proportion of the population of those different sections; and in this publication, which was printed three years ago, the number of students received, and even their names, and the States from which they came are given. So that running it over, it will be found that nearly every State, with the exception of the Pacific States, has been represented in proportion to its population. And that has been an interesting fact to us, and one that has commended the college to the liberality of Congress, for it sees at once that since our system of general education is so extended it is possible for deaf boys to be found in all parts of the country sufficiently advanced in their primary instruction to enable them to come into the higher school. I may mention that we have had two very estimable young men from the United Kingdom; in fact, three. One young man came to us after a short residence in America in one of the primary schools, who was from Scotland. His father was a professor in one of the higher schools there, and this young man came to us and graduated, and is now a teacher in one of the western schools. Two other young men have come from Ireland. One after staying with us for three years developed Bright's disease, and died after returning home. He was a bright, intelligent young man. The other is with us now, and I will mention his name, Francis Maginn. His father is a clergyman of the Church of England, in Ireland, near Cork; his uncle was the distinguished "doctor" of Frazer's Magazine, William Maginn, and his family is one that is well known in Ireland. He has been with us for two years, and is a very promising young man, sure I think to make his mark somewhere when he gets through his course of study. He is enthusiastic in his appreciation of his opportunities with us, and was extremely anxious that I should make it appear before the Commission that the higher education of the deaf was a practicable thing, and an important thing. He said he was feeling it in his own case, and that he expected to come back to Great Britain after two years more, and do something that would show that it was worth while for him to have had this higher education.

13,240. Do any of these students go out into the liberal professions, law, medicine, or the Church?—I will answer that by reading a brief paragraph. This was written three years ago: "Forty who "have gone out from the college have been engaged "in teaching; three have become editors and pub- "lishers of newspapers; three others have taken "positions connected with journalism; 10 have en- "tered the civil service of the Government. One "of these, who had risen rapidly to a high and re- "sponsible position, lately resigned to enter upon "the practice of law in patent cases in Cincinnati; "one, while filling a position as instructor in a "Western institution, has rendered important ser- "vice to the Coast Survey as a microscopist; one "has become an accomplished draughtsman in the "office of a New York architect; one has for several "years filled the position of recorder's clerk in a "large Western city; two have taken places in the "faculty of their *alma mater*, and are rendering "valuable returns as instructors where they were "students but a short time since; some have gone "into mercantile and other offices; some have un- "dertaken business on their own account; while "not a few have chosen agricultural and mechani- "cal pursuits, in which the advantages of thorough "mental training will give them a superiority over "those not so well educated. Of those alluded to "as having engaged in teaching, one has been the "principal of a flourishing institution in Pennsyl- "vania; another of a day-school in Cincinnati, and "later of the Colorado Institution; a third has "had charge of the Oregon Institution and a fourth "is at the head of a day-school in St. Louis." And I would be glad to add to this enumeration a very interesting case which has come up since this publication was issued of a young man, who came to us, who was entirely deaf from birth, and had never learnt to speak. He devoted himself to chemistry especially, while he was in college, though he pursued the full scientific course, and received a degree in science. He became after his graduation an assayer in a prominent smelting establishment in Chicago, and soon rose to take the chief position there. He has had submitted to him on many occasions disputes between other practical chemists in Chicago, his judgment being relied on as very good; he has contributed to scientific publications several articles, some of which have been translated into German scientific publications; and now quite recently he has been called to St. Louis, where he has been appointed chief practical chemist to an immense sugar refinery. And when I say that this young man graduated from our college only four years ago, and is now only 28 years of age, I think you will agree with me that the deaf, with the higher training, may find their way into positions of practical use, and be able to stand side by side with those who have all their faculties. I should add that this young man has not the advantage of speech; he communicates entirely by writing or by the fingers. I merely speak of that to show that this practice of the oral method with the deaf is not essential to the highest success in the various pursuits which they take up. I may say that one or two of our young men have studied for the ministry, but none of our own graduates have been ordained. There have been three deaf men ordained to the ministry in America, and they are serving their own people very well in different parts of the country.

13,241. Do any of your students become doctors?—Doctors they do not try to be, because from their deafness they cannot make the necessary examinations of patients. I ought to speak in this connection of a young man whose case interested me very much in the past summer. He is a farmer in Vermont. He spent two years with us. He was a young fellow of great intelligence, but not of the highest scholarship, but while he was with us he knew that he was to be a farmer, his father having a farm which he was to inherit, and so he pursued his studies with the view to making himself an intelligent and scientific farmer. I was at his house in Vermont last summer, and I heard from his neighbors that he was absolutely the best farmer in the whole district; that he made more money out of his farm than any other farmer; that it was in better condition than any other; that he knew more than any farmer in the whole neighborhood; that he was able to read intelligently the best scientific papers that have a bearing upon farming; and that his farm was a model of excellence. That would show that the higher instruction has its uses even with the deaf young men who go into farming. This young man also is one who has no power of speech. Of course instances could be added, but it goes without saying that our graduates have little difficulty in finding their way into positions which they would be utterly unable to take had they not had the higher training that is given in the college. I think that I ought to ask to be permitted to give a little specimen of the excellence of the literary work of the graduates of the college. Some of our graduates have even aspired to be poets, which might be a surprise. Here are a dozen lines which, if your Lordship would allow me, I should like to read, because they give a very interesting insight into the mental condition of one who has become deaf in childhood. These lines take the form of a

Dr. E. M. Gallaudet.

9 Nov. 1886.

sonnet, which describes the condition of those who have become absolutely deaf, after having heard, perhaps, for a few years during childhood:

"They are like one who shuts his eyes to dream
  Of some bright vista in his fading past;
  And suddenly the faces that were lost
In long forgetfulness before him seem.
Th' uplifted brow, the love-lit eye whose beam
  Could ever o'er his soul a radiance cast,
  Numberless charms that long ago have ask't
The homage of his fresh young life's esteem:
  For sometimes, from the silence that they bear,
Well up the tones that erst formed half their joys
  A strain of music floats to the dull ear,
Or low, melodious murmur of a voice,
  Till all the chords of harmony vibrant are
With consciousness of deeply slumb'ring pow'rs."

I quote from an article on the poetry of the deaf which I contributed to the "*Annals*" three years ago, Vol. XXIX, p. 204.

13,242. (*Rev. W. B. Sleight.*) How was he educated?—Upon the manual system. He received his college education with us. He was at the Hartford School previously. He was not a mute from birth, but became technically a deaf-mute, though retaining the power of speech, not having heard after his childhood, and all his education was carried on in schools for the deaf.

13,243. (*Mr. Johnson.*) At what age did he become deaf?—At the age of 10.

13,244. (*Chairman.*) Do the degrees which you give at your college bear comparison with those given in the universities of the country?—They bear comparison with the other colleges of the country. An university degree is in advance of what we give, but the degree of Bachelor of Arts compares with the degrees given in the ordinary colleges of our country. With us the term college means an institution which is not quite up to the standard of what you would term your full university course. We have universities in America which give this full course quite equal to the universities here.

13,245. I was rather asking the question with regard to the universities?—There is just that distinction which I have mentioned.

13,246. I will ask you now about the condition of the deaf after they have left the ordinary schools of the country. You have told us, to a certain extent, with regard to their industrial training and the occupations which are pursued?—Yes, but I have not spoken as to how successful they are in after-life in any detail, or how they bear themselves in society in general. The 70th Report of the oldest institution in the United States, that of Hartford, issued this same year, 1886, gives a very valuable account, which I will not attempt to read at all in detail, of a very large number of their graduates about whom they have taken pains to collect information; and a glance at a list like this would show you the number of occupations pursued by the graduates of this school. There are 50 or 60 different occupations, and there are observations with reference to the wages which they earn.

13,247. Is it not a question with the deaf in the same way as it is with the blind?—It is not so serious with the deaf.

13,248. You do not find any difficulty, probably, any more than we do, in their getting employment?—No, no serious difficulty. This report might come in as an appendix to show the comparison of the wages they earn and what they do; and the general statement can be made that the deaf, as a class, with education, are self-supporting. And I think it well, in connection with the statement, to call attention to this point which I have had occasion in one or two instances before Congressional Committees to lay some emphasis upon, and which is not generally appreciated; that is to say, when the condition of the uneducated deaf, their dependent condition, the small amounts that they earn, the limited intelligence that they show in employments, and the cost of carrying them through the ordinary course of an average life, are taken on the one hand, and on the other the expense of educating the deaf in boarding schools at the public expense, paying for their sustenance as well as their education, then taking the period necessary to carry out this education, whether it be seven or eight years, when this calculation is entered into, it is found that the saving to the State in actual pounds, shillings, and pence, by educating them, is simply enormous. I will not stop to give figures. I have made the calculation, and I have presented it to the Congressional Committees; and, as a general observation, I may say that while it is perfectly conceded that it is an additional expense to educate the deaf in boarding schools, it is not generally understood that, even taking this addition into account, the saving to the State is enormous over what they would lose through the helpless and dependent condition in which the uneducated deaf are found during nearly the whole period of their lives. The question is often raised by those who have the levying of rates and assessing taxes. They say that it costs so much more to board these children, and that it should be considered a matter of pure charity. But we do not so look at it in America.

13,249. It is a matter of interest you would say?—It is a matter of pure selfish interest that we take these deaf people out of the condition of ignorant dependence, and, by the expenditure of an amount of money easily calculated, we turn them over into the other side, the producers and self-supporters, and gainers of wealth to the community; and the gain to the State is simply enormous by the change effected by education. And there is one other consideration in connection with that, which has had some prominence given to it in our own country. It has been urged, on the one hand, that the deaf could be educated in day-schools, and the expense of their education much diminished. On the other hand, it has been also urged that the parents of the deaf in the community have the right to their having the best education, and, if the best education can only be obtained in boarding schools, then it is right that they should have that education in boarding schools, and that no parents, or few parents, would consider that the absence of a child from home in a boarding school was to be weighed as over and against the expense of supporting that child at home. Any parent would rather have the child at home than send him away for the sake of merely gaining the cost of his sustenance. So, all over our States, the doors of these schools have been opened to the children of the well-to-do, and even rich, as well as to those who are poor, and in some States it is considered absolutely a portion of the system of public education, and no statement of poverty or inability to pay is required, and that has become the tendency and practice in all parts of the country.

13,250. That is associated with the general free education that prevails in America?—Yes.

13,251. One cannot understand that there should be any reason why the deaf and dumb should be excluded from that?—Yes. The disposition to associate together in a clannish manner of the deaf after leaving school has been made the subject of considerable discussion in our country, and it has been urged that schools should be so organized, if possible, as to prevent this clannish association of the deaf in after-life, with a view to prevent too much intermarriage of the deaf, from the fear that intermarriage of the deaf might increase the amount of deafness in the community, that their children might be more apt to be deaf than other children.

13,252. Have you any statistics to give us showing the effect of the intermarriage of the deaf?—The statistics are far from being complete. Mr. Alexander Graham Bell, who, I believe, has been

Dr. E. M. Gallaudet.

9 Nov. 1886.

invited to give evidence before this Commission, has made, during the last two or three years, quite a study of the matter of the intermarriage of the deaf, and has presented to some of our scientific associations papers in relation to the possibility of the formation by intermarriage of a deaf variety of the human race. If Mr. Bell should appear before you, undoubtedly he would give you a great deal of information on that point. His studies, he admits, up to this time, are incomplete; the data he has had at his command have not been sufficiently numerous to enable him to make a complete statement: but it is a subject which engages the attention of all teachers of the deaf, and they feel it to be important that deaf pupils going out of the institutions should be perfectly aware as to wherein lie the dangers of intermarriage. And, in connection with this, it may be interesting to say that while we have not facts and figures to make a complete statement, we have enough data to show very clearly that the mere fact of one who is totally deaf marrying another who is totally deaf, does not at all suggest that their children are likely to be deaf; for the reason that if the parties have both of them acquired deafness by accident, there is no greater likelihood that their children will be deaf than the children of other persons.

13,253. You are not competent, perhaps, to speak on the question of deafness running in families?—I can say that in America there is quite a body of statistics at hand with reference to certain families in which deafness seems to have run, and to have visited, in a considerable number, the members of these families, and it is certain that, wherever there is found, by the presence of more than one deaf person in a family, any evidence of a tendency to deafness, if a person belonging to that family, whether deaf or not, marries a person whether deaf or not belonging to another family in which deafness has run, you find that the children are, in a large proportion of cases, liable to be deaf. It is not the fact of the deafness of the contracting parties; but, if you find a family where there is evidence of a disposition to deafness, and members of that family marry into another family with a similar disposition to deafness, they are very apt to have deaf children; so, these institutions for the deaf, which stand in *loco parentis* to the pupils, many of them, take great pains to advise the pupils to be very careful, and to exercise a caution which people often do not exercise in regard to marriage, and where they know there is a disposition to deafness in a family to avoid marrying any one belonging to that family.

13,254. Are you aware whether the marriage of first cousins produces deafness?—It is a subject that has received a great deal of attention.

13,255. Perhaps you would refer us to any statistics that are reliable on the subject, if there are any?—I can refer rather to papers and discussions based upon the rather limited area of facts which bear upon the subject.

13,256. We do not desire to go into the details now, but if there are statistics, perhaps you would kindly hand them in in your evidence?—Yes. *See* Topical Index of the *American Annals of the Deaf*.

13,257. The next point is, what education does the State require in the teachers of the deaf and dumb, and what are the qualifications for the teachers required by the State?—I am sorry to say that we have not in America any normal school, or any examining board with reference to the qualifications of teachers before whom applicants for the position should go and prove their capacity. In each institution it is a matter for the governing body of the institution itself to determine the qualifications of the teachers. The course pursued is usually this: To take into the institution a young person, male or female, who has a sufficient amount of education and ability to make it probable that he or she will succeed as a teacher of the deaf; and then for the principal of the institution, with the assistance of the teachers who are already experienced, to train this young teacher in the art of teaching the deaf. And in this way a body of very capable and experienced teachers has been raised up in America in the different schools. In some institutions there has been pressure to bring them down to small salaries, and that keeps out teachers of the greatest efficiency from these institutions.

13,258. Does that system insure an uniformity of teaching in the schools, or would it not rather tend to produce uniformity of teaching in each particular school rather than throughout the whole of the schools?—I think that would be the tendency, although I think that in a country so large as ours, considering our political organization, and that local matters are quite independent of the Federal Government, it would be impossible to establish through the Federal Government any general system of examination. There has been a serious thought of establishing in connection with our college at Washington a training school for teachers, and the establishment of such a school would no doubt be attended with good results; but that is still in the future.

13,259. You have only the judgment and discretion of the governing body to ensure that the teachers are good ones?—Yes, and yet it can be said that the practice has been in America to require that the applicants for positions as teachers should be men and women of very high order of education. A very large proportion of our men teachers of the deaf are, what would be called in England, university men; that is to say, graduates of colleges, men with high attainments; and running back for a series of years, we can point to many men who have gone out from institutions in which they have been teachers of the deaf, and taken positions of the highest eminence in literary and scientific pursuits. I could cite the names of several presidents of colleges who were teachers in institutions for the deaf; and it is an interesting fact that both the candidates in the recent canvass for the highest position in our country, that of the President, Mr. Cleveland, and Mr. Blaine, began life as teachers of the blind. I mention this to show that men of a sort who might be expected to rise to high positions, are often found among the ranks of our teachers.

13,260. Is not that the case in America generally; there is no separate profession, a man begins his life as one thing, and ends it as another?—Yes. It ought to be said in connection with the employment of our teachers, a great object in the organization of our institutions is to secure permanency, and we pay salaries, for example, on which they can marry, and settle, and feel that the work of teaching the deaf is to be their life-work. That has an effect not only in the actual efficiency of the single and given institution, but also it has the tendency to establish, as it were, a profession in which it is possible to have an *esprit de corps*, and the opportunity for promotion. Teachers, for instance, look forward to the time when they may be principals, and they feel even if they are not, that they are to be well paid and enabled to live comfortably, and have their families about them; and so they consider that they are entering on a work which is to be their life-work; and experience of course is very valuable from year to year.

13,261. I think you stated that the principals in the ordinary State institutions were appointed by the President?—By the directing body that has been named by the Legislature.

13,262. Not by the President?—No. You understand that we have in our State constitutions a Governor and the members of the Legislature, and

Dr. E. M. Gallaudet.
—
9 Nov. 1886.

those officers are supreme in their own State. The President has nothing to do with what may be termed State patronage, only with what may be termed Federal patronage. So that in these State institutions the principals and teachers would be appointed by a Board of Directors or Trustees who are constituted by the Act of the Legislature; and when the complexion of the Legislature changes, for instance, from Republican to Democratic, or from Democratic to Republican, it often happens that the Board of Directors or Trustees changes also.

13,263. The principals of these institutions are liable to being changed by these bodies for political reasons?—Yes; and it has happened that when the existing law of the State was such that the removal could not be made of the principal of the institution, the entire existing law has been repealed, and a new law enacted, to enable him to be removed. To such a pass are we come, I am sorry to say. I do not speak of it with anything but mortification. It is a most pernicious system, and the results have been painful. I have seen men put into the office of teacher who had absolutely no knowledge whatever of teaching. The only qualification of one man put at the head of a large institution was that he was a very good dentist.

13,264. What you have said about the teachers is subject therefore to these contingencies which may or may not be prejudicial to the education of the deaf and dumb?—Yes. So that it is true that in many of these institutions governed by the State, the teachers are persons whose claim to be teachers is not a good claim; but in the corporate schools, those whose management is in the hands of a permanent board, the teachers are taken with great care.

13,265. Are the teachers who are chosen with great care often sent out of other schools for the deaf, or do they often follow a career in the body in which they have been first brought up?—They frequently change their place. If they are paid a certain salary in one school, and have the offer of a much better one in another, and if it is for their advantage to make the change they make it. I have a single note under this head of teachers and their relations to the institutions, to say that we have no arrangements in America in our schools for the deaf for paying our teachers by results. In the education of the deaf it would, in my judgment, be almost impossible to judge of the teacher's efficiency by any scale which could be marked by results, for often a class of deaf children of secondary mental power may have been labored with by the teacher of the utmost devotion and earnestness, and yet the result in marks on any scale that might be applied to all deaf pupils would show comparatively but little progress. That very teacher might be the one who had worked harder than any other in the whole school. So that we have never made any attempt in America to pay our teachers by results, but simply to have that supervision over them by the principal in charge, which would make him satisfied that they are doing the best that can be done.

13,266. I think you have told us, with reference to the conferences, that they have now been in practice for some years, and take place every four years?—We have two bodies of instructors of the deaf meeting in America, one termed the conference of principals, which meets every four years, and the other the convention of instructors, including principals, which also meets every four years. These meetings alternate with each other, so that we have a meeting every two years, one year the conference of principals and the other the convention of instructors; and those meetings have been continued since 1851, with an interregnum during the time of our civil war, when, for a few years, they were suspended. I have brought with me, and I shall leave at the disposition of the Commission, a number of copies of the proceedings of different conventions and conferences that have been held, in which there is a great amount of material of great value bearing upon the work of instructing the deaf in America. And I cannot speak too favorably of these conferences and of the importance with which they are regarded in our work in America. They bring teachers together. For instance, at this last convention in California, half of the time of the convention was taken up in normal sections; teachers of known capacity and experience were selected to take charge of certain subjects of instruction and to hold meetings of such teachers as were interested in those particular branches of instruction. They interchanged methods and means of instructing from one teacher to another, and so a normal school was carried on for a certain period that was productive of great benefit. And to these conventions the principals of the institutions are generally sent by the governing boards of the institutions and their travelling expenses paid; and in some instances teachers are sent, and their travelling expenses paid. The conventions themselves and the conferences are usually held in some institution during the vacation, and the institution which invites them entertains the members of the convention during its period. For example, the California institution, by a vote of the Legislature, expended about 3,000 dollars in entertaining this convention that was held last July, continuing a little over a week.

13,267. It comes out of the funds of the State, then?—Yes, or of the institution; but the travelling expenses of the members may be paid for each one by the institution which sends them; but the institution which entertains the convention meets the expense of boarding it, and of publishing the proceedings. It is considered by the managers of our institutions that the presence of such a meeting, such a body of teachers of the deaf, is of value to the State where it is held in influencing public opinion, in increasing interest in the work of teaching the deaf, and in disseminating knowledge as to what it is; and so institutions are found every two years that are quite willing to bear the expense of entertaining these conferences and conventions.

13,268. Then it is rather through conferences such as these that you would get uniformity of teaching in America than in any other way?—The tendency is very strongly not towards absolute uniformity but harmony of action, which we feel is better than absolute uniformity. Different teachers have very different opinions as to the methods that come out in these conventions, and they find that those with whom they differ have a good many things that they are glad to learn; and so there comes about a harmony of action and a good feeling among the different teachers in the deaf schools all over the country, that we think is very much better than absolute uniformity.

13,269. Do these conferences generally end in the passing of certain resolutions?—Very rarely. It is not sought to pass resolutions which should bind the sentiments or practice of the members of the convention.

13,270. Papers are read?—And discussions had, and methods brought forward and their importance heard; but the resolutions which I presented here were almost the only resolutions of that character. Of course there are complimentary resolutions passed, but the practice of our conventions is not to attempt to bind the members to any particular course or particular method. The convention, as I mentioned a little while ago, has a standing executive committee, and under that committee is published a publication known as the *American Annals*, a quarterly publication which has been published for many years. I have a set of the *Annals* here. I have brought it over for purposes of reference, and I have a good many citations noted in my notes from the *Annals* which would be of value perhaps to the Commission. That concludes the ninth point upon which you are asking questions. If you were prepared to pass on to the tenth point I should have something further to say with regard to these publications.

13,271. Are the periodicals which are published in the interest of the deaf and dumb under the control and under the guidance of these conventions, or are there any other independent ones?—There are other independent periodicals published in the interest of the deaf themselves and for their instruction and general entertainment; that is to say, there are newspapers published for them; but the only publication which is in the interest of the education of the deaf is this of the *Annals*, which has run now through a period of 31 years. I have here an index to those *Annals*, the whole set of volumes, which has been prepared at considerable expense and with great care, so that any one looking over this index can refer to this series of publications in a very easy manner. Any topic upon which it is desired to get information and on which information exists in the *Annals*, can be found by reference to this index. And I should like to say, that this publication is sustained in a manner somewhat peculiar. It is not a publication which merely depends upon the subscription of those who may desire to have it and read it, but from a very early point in the history of its publication this method has been pursued and found to be successful. The institutions were asked by the standing executive committee to contribute in proportion to the number of pupils in their respective schools to the support of this periodical, and an assessment has been made by the committee of certain sums upon the different institutions, which in general has been accepted. Of course these assessments were not at all compulsory, merely voluntary, but they have been so generally accepted that it has been possible to publish the *Annals* on a liberal scale, to pay an editor to take charge of it, and to pay contributors for articles contributed, which has stimulated teachers and others to write for the *Annals* in a way which has made it a periodical of increasing value. The assessments have been paid out of the general funds of the various schools of the country by vote of their respective boards of direction, and the money has been disbursed under the direction of the standing committee, and accounted for to the conventions as they have met from time to time. I am very pleased to be able, through the assistance and courtesy of the New York Institution for the Deaf, and by the co-operation of Dr. Isaac Lewis Peet, who is at the head of it, and who succeeded his father, who was for many years at the head of the institution, to present in the name of the New York Institution, and of the Institution of Washington to the Commission this complete set of the *Annals* which I have brought with me as a matter of reference. It consists of 31 volumes, and with this index it is now a little difficult to get in a complete form; and if the Commission will accept it from these two institutions in America, it will give the managers of the institutions great pleasure, I am sure. It may serve as a library for the Commission to delve in for themselves and to get information from, which may perhaps be helpful as the work of the Commission goes on; for these *Annals* speak of the education of the deaf not only in America but all over the world, and this may be said to be a mine of information which can serve many purposes.

13,272. I am sure the Royal Commission are most sensible of the kindness which has prompted the giving of so handsome a present to the Commission, and it will be most valuable for our labors. The Secretary will write officially and thank the institutions which have so kindly furnished the volumes; and we thank you for the way in which you have presented them to the Royal Commission?—I also present a couple of volumes relating to the work of the Columbia Institution at Washington. That is the corporate name of the institution which includes both the college and the primary school. They are the official reports to Congress of the institution during a period of 25 years. Under the matter of periodicals published in the interest of the education of the deaf, I ought, perhaps, to say a word with reference to papers published by different institutions. Where printing offices are in existence, it is quite the custom for the institutions to publish each of them a little paper, larger or smaller according to circumstances, in which there is much of interest in reference to the teaching of their pupils, and which serves to interest parents and the people generally of the State where the institution exists.

13,273. You mean a sort of school magazine?—Yes, a sort of school magazine; and then there are one or two other papers that are published in the interest of the deaf quite independently of any institution. I have brought with me two or three copies that might be looked over at the convenience of members of the Commission. Perhaps the particular interest in these copies would be that they contain accounts of two or three conventions of the deaf themselves that were held this last summer,—associations which were organized by the *alumni* of the respective State schools. They meet from time to time. They have benevolent contributions sometimes, and they raise money for certain purposes of a charitable nature; and in the proceedings of these meetings will be found papers presented by the deaf themselves, addresses made which have been reported, which would be interesting as showing the point of intelligence which they reach after they leave the various schools of the country and the college. I have also copies of the American Manual Alphabet, which is not of much use in England, but which has been prepared to assist parents of the deaf by Professor Gordon, of the college at Washington.

13,274. Is the one-handed alphabet considered advantageous?—We prefer it in America very much; but that is a question, of course, whether it is better than the two-handed or not; we think it is. And, in connection with the alphabet, I have cited in my notes a paper presented to the convention at California by an instructor of the deaf, urging the teaching of the manual alphabet in all schools, so that all the children in the country may know the manual alphabet, and be able to converse that way with deaf mutes when other means fail, and when the lips are not perfect enough for oral communication to fall back upon that; and this paper was well received. (*Annals*, Vol. XXXI, p. 233.) It happens that when I was in Geneva lately, the American consul told me that three or four years ago he was extremely ill with an attack of hemorrhage of the lungs; his physician absolutely forbade him to speak or even to exert himself to write; but having learnt the manual alphabet, and it being known by members of his family, he communicated with them with ease, without making any exertion which might bring on any possible return of the hemorrhage; and he was quite ready to advocate the teaching of the manual alphabet.

13,275. I see in one of the books mention of a Milwaukee, Wisconsin, Phonological Institute; is that different from any other institution?—It is an oral school; it is only another name for it, that is all. I did not call attention just now, when speaking of the college at Washington, to the fact that we have 100 acres, which land lies within two miles of the National Capitol building itself. Though we hold it now, we may not think it necessary to hold it for all time, the whole of it; but if the time should come when the city should extend out around it, a part of it might be sold and a very ample portion

Dr. E. M. Gallaudet.

9 Nov. 1886

still remain, and, from the proceeds of the portion sold, might be formed an endowment for the institution. We carry on a farm here (*pointing to a picture*), and an orchard, and have our own dairy, and raise quite enough to feed a large number of dairy cows.

13,276. Can you tell us anything with regard to any of the Canadian institutions of the deaf and dumb; have you any special knowledge of them?—The list of Canadian institutions is included in the *Annals* of last January, but beyond that I am not able to give any very definite information, excepting that I may say this, that I know that they are mainly upon the combined system—institutions which accept instruction in speech and give it to as large a number of their pupils as possible.

13,277. You do not think that there is any substantial difference in the teaching in the Canadian institutions?—No; but in the management there is. For instance, the management of the Ontario Institution is in the hands of an inspector or a government official who controls quite a number of public institutions; there is no board of directors; it is under the control of an inspector who, with the approval of a body representing the Government, appoints the principal and subordinate officers The Mackay Institution at Montreal, I believe, is a corporation.

13,278. (*Dr. Campbell.*) Is the inspector of that institution at Ontario a superintendent of general education?—I do not think he is.

13,279. (*Chairman.*) Do you think that if a paper of questions was sent round by this Commission to the different institutions for the deaf and dumb in the United States, the managers of those institutions would be willing to furnish any replies to those questions for the use of the Commission? I only ask the question in case we should wish to supplement the information which you have already given us?—I have no doubt the majority of them would be quite willing to go through a great deal of trouble and pains to answer such questions. We are in the habit of answering such questions in our own country; for instance, to our department of education which exists at Washington. That sends round circulars which ask a good many questions which we grumble over a little, but always answer.

13,280. Is the inspection in each State carried out by an inspector-general of the educational institutions, or is there a special inspector for the deaf and dumb?—The practice differs very widely in that respect. There are some of the States in which there have been appointed these commissioners of public charities in general, and they inspect and visit and report upon the schools for the deaf as well as a number of other benevolent establishments; but the practice is not uniform throughout the country at all. I think, in general, the management of the institution is left very much to the local organization which governs it, and then it is subject to the determination which may be made from time to time by a legislative committee, or in some of the States the governor takes pains to visit (in some he is required to visit) and report upon the condition of schools for the deaf.

13,281. Have you any deaf and dumb and blind in any of your institutions?—We have quite a number in America scattered through the country.

13,282. Do the deaf and dumb and blind generally go to the blind institutions or to the deaf and dumb institutions?—I think generally to the deaf and dumb institutions.

13,283. I ask that question because Mr. Hall says "We have three deaf and dumb and blind in my institution"?—That would indicate that certainly some are found in blind schools. I think for purposes of education; on reflection I remember a blind deaf-mute who is in the blind institution in Maryland. There must be some of that class of persons in the blind schools. Of course, I am not able to answer with regard to that. I know that there are a number in the deaf-mute schools. There are one or two in New York and in some of the other schools.

13,284. Do you think it is advantageous at all that the deaf and dumb and blind should be associated together in any industrial works; for instance, we have had occasion sometimes to see a deaf and dumb person employed in the institutions for the blind; that is to say, to give sighted superintendence where sighted superintendence is necessary; have you any experience of that?—I have no experience of that sort of employment or mingling of the two classes. I can see no reason why in certain circumstances it might not be of some help, but not I think for the benefit of the deaf, but perhaps for the assistance of the blind.

13,285. In your opinion the deaf and dumb are able to earn their livelihood without being included in any blind institutions?—Yes; I do not think it is necessary to establish special places where the deaf and dumb may be helped to earn their living. I think they can earn their living side by side with the hearing.

13,286. Do any of the deaf and dumb institutions give any grants for the apprenticing out of young men, or is that generally done by the parents and friends?—It is generally done by the parents and friends. I cannot say with certainty that there are any that make a practice of doing that. I think there have been some that have had funds at their disposal perhaps for a short time, which have enabled them to help a certain number in that way, but the practice being so general in the schools in America of teaching industrial work while the pupil is in school, it would not be natural that they should make arrangements for having these grants to apprentice their pupils to masters when they go out.

13,287. In fact, they are generally turned out of school with sufficient knowledge of some trade which they can practice in after-life?—That is the rule.

The witness withdrew.

Adjourned to to-morrow at eleven o'clock.

32 ABINGDON STREET, WESTMINSTER.

WEDNESDAY, 10TH NOVEMBER, 1886.

PRESENT:

THE RIGHT HON. THE LORD EGERTON OF TATTON IN THE CHAIR.

Admiral SIR E. SOTHEBY, K.C.B.
W. TINDAL ROBERTSON, Esq., M.D.
B. ST. JOHN ACKERS, Esq.
T. R. ARMITAGE, Esq., M.D.
W. AUCHINCLOSS ARROL, Esq.
F. J. CAMPBELL, Esq., LL.D.
E. C. JOHNSON, Esq.
CHARLES FEW, Esq.
WILLIAM WOODALL, Esq., M.P.
The Rev. W. BLOMEFIELD SLEIGHT, M.A.
The Rev. CHARLES MANSFIELD OWEN, M.A.
CHARLES E. D. BLACK, Esq., *Secretary*.

Dr. E. M. GALLAUDET further examined.

Dr. E. M. Gallaudet. 10 Nov. 1886.

13,288. (*Mr. Johnson.*) I suppose you consider that the statistics with which you have been kind enough to furnish the Commission, are on the whole fairly correct?—I think they are quite as reliable as any statistics that could be found. Taking them in connection with the articles in the *Annals* to which I make reference, which explain them and give elucidations of the results which are given in the figures, I think one might arrive at a very approximately accurate idea with reference to what those statistics profess to show.

13,289. Did I rightly understand you to say that there were in America only twelve schools where the pure oral system was taught?—Yes.

13,290. In those oral schools is there no other system whatever taught but the oral?—I think if you will allow me in answering the question to make use of the word "method" instead of the word "system," I would prefer to use that word. I said yesterday that we apply the word "system" to that which may include two or three methods. I am quite certain that in those schools the oral method alone is used.

13,291. Is any pure and simple oral teaching carried on in the other 38 combined system schools, or the 14 manual method schools?—In the 14 manual method schools there would be no oral teaching whatever; in the 38 combined system schools I am certain that there are many distinctively oral classes in which all the instruction is given orally, and not only that, but in more than one of those institutions that are classified as maintaining the combined system there are branches—separate schools—under one board of direction, in which the oral method is exclusively practised, so that the figure of 12 as applied to oral schools would simply mean those which were exclusively oral schools, while in the others which are put down as practising the combined system, there are distinctively oral classes: and then there are separate oral schools, branches of the larger institutions.

13,292. Wherever the pure oral method is taught in those combined system schools, are the children who are instructed in the oral mode separated from those instructed in the sign and manual mode?—Naturally where there are these separate schools—these branches—they are quite isolated from those children who are taught more or less by the use of signs and the manual alphabet. In the larger institutions, where there are these separate oral classes, I do not think that any effort is made to isolate the children taught upon the oral method out of school; to isolate them out of school from the others who may be taught more or less by the use of signs.

13,293. Is it the custom in America where some of the children are being taught on the oral mode, to put those children into a separate room or buildings, and are those children who are learning on the oral mode allowed to associate out of school with those who are being taught by the sign and manual mode?—The custom is, in general, with very rare exceptions, I should say, not more than one or two, to allow the free association of the pupils after school hours who are taught on the different methods. I can hardly think of any other case than that of Pennsylvania, which has its oral branch: I think there is one other institution, but I am not able at this moment to name it, that has a similar arrangement of an oral branch, and in those two there would be a complete separation.

13,294. (*Chairman.*) In those cases where you speak of an oral branch, you refer to an absolutely separate building?—Yes.

13,295. It is not like the case at Manchester, one building divided in the middle?—No.

13,296. (*Mr. Johnson.*) Is it desirable, in your opinion, to separate those who are taught orally from those who are taught by the sign and manual method?—My opinion is that nothing is gained by it. In fact, I may go further, and express my opinion that a great deal is lost by it: for in my judgment the association of children who are taught orally with those who are taught by signs, and the permission to use the sign-language with a considerable amount of freedom out of school, greatly assists in the mental development of those children who are taught on the oral method.

13,297. When you speak of the oral method, do you mean the oral method, as we understand it here, pure and simple?—I do. Perhaps I ought to add, that it may be that I have not an exactly clear apprehension of what is meant in England by the term "pure oral method."

13,298. The pure oral method, I should say, would be the method advocated by the Congress at Milan?—Even at Milan there was quite a difference of opinion as to what should be meant by the term "*La méthode orale pure.*" There were those who maintained that that should mean the absolute exclusion of signs from all instruction. There were others who claimed that it should mean that at the earlier stages natural signs, not conventional signs, might be made use of by the teacher in assisting to the end desired; so that, if I may be allowed to say so, there is quite a difference of opinion as to what the term should be understood to mean. If I may state in as few words as possible my understanding of this term the "pure oral method," I may say that I understand it to mean that method by which speech is made not only the great end to be attained in instructing the deaf, but to the largest possible extent the means of communication between teacher and pupil, from the earliest stage of education. If that is the understanding in England of the term "pure oral method" (though in America we do not use the word "pure"—we simply say "the oral method"), then the term "oral method," where I have used it in speaking of our schools, means in practice the same as the term "pure oral method" in England.

13,299. It would be a difficulty to define it from your point of view, because, as I understand, in your combined system schools they teach lip-reading and a certain amount of speech. As I understand, in America, speech is required to be a part of your education in the combined system, but your

Dr. E. M. Gallaudet.

10 Nov. 1886.

pure oral system does not find so many advocates as it does, perhaps, in other countries?—In America, in the schools which are maintained on the combined system, the practice differs in different schools. There are schools in which these oral classes, to which I referred a moment ago, exist, and in those the teaching cannot be differentiated in any essential particular from that teaching which would be given in the pure oral schools of England. We have schools carried on on the combined system, as it were—the oral method within the other. I will explain another method: Classes are organized in which the general instruction is given by means of writing, the manual alphabet, and some use of signs in explanation, and the pupils go for half an hour or an hour every day to a teacher who teaches them speech and lip-reading; that is quite another method, and results are reached by that method which some teachers find to be equally satisfactory with the results reached where speech is the main means of communication in giving instruction; but those two different manners—if I may use the term—of carrying on instruction in speech may be found in schools which are conducted on the combined system. So it must not be understood that in those schools there is no pure oral teaching; on the contrary, the whole policy in those schools to-day (and I am sure that I do not misrepresent the management of those schools on the combined system) is to give oral instruction, as far as possible to as many as possible, and by those means which in practice may be found best to conduce to that end.

13,300. There is another system which you mentioned, the aural system: I understood you to say that from 12 to 25 per cent. of those who are classed as deaf could be improved through the ear. That, of course, applies to persons who have not been born deaf?—On the contrary, a number of very interesting cases have come under the notice of careful observers in the different schools in America of children who were congenitally hard of hearing, if I may use that expression. They were so hard of hearing from birth that their hearing was never educated by the ordinary means, so that they have reached in several instances school age without having made any use of their hearing whatever, so far as the acquisition of the power of speech is concerned, or so far as learning to understand what is spoken by others is concerned; so that though they are not congenitally deaf they are congenitally so hard of hearing that they stand on arriving at school age in the category of deaf-mutes, and not a small number of such persons have been found among the general class of deaf-mutes.

13,301. Is the amelioration of their condition dependent on the training of the school, or is it dependent on medical treatment?—It is dependent on the training of the school. The condition of the ear will be found to be such that medical treatment will not improve it.

13,302. I suppose there is a medical examination in the case of every child that comes to a school for instruction?—In all our best establishments.

13,303. That is only on admission, I understood you to say?—In many of our well-managed schools those examinations are made from time to time.

13,304. Is any effort made to improve the defective organ by medical treatment as a general rule?—No effort is made as a general rule, simply because the examination has shown that such efforts have been made previously and failed.

13,305. We have heard a great deal in this country of the Milan International Congress; were you present at that Congress?—Yes.

13,306. I see that a number of resolutions were arrived at by that Congress, and I think the Commission would be very glad to know if you could give us some idea of the opinion of those in America best calculated to express an opinion upon the results arrived at at that Congress?—The feeling in America was that the resolutions adopted by that Convention, giving a formal approval to the pure oral method, were not entitled to very great weight. The Convention was far from being a representative body. I mean to say that there was no basis of representation, so that a particular institution or a particular country should be considered as being represented by a certain number of delegates. My own opinion at the time was, and nothing has since occurred to change it, that the decision of the Convention at Milan as regards the pure oral system, as expressed in these resolutions, was not to be taken as of very great weight in determining questions of method, and that opinion was entertained by a very large majority of the teachers of the deaf in America, including many who taught then and teach now on the oral method. In justice to the few who hold to a different opinion I should say there were some teachers in America who accepted the decision of the Milan Convention as expressing their views. I am not aware that the opinion or the practice of any teacher in America, or of any school in America, has been changed by this action of the Milan Convention.

13,307. May I take it that from your own experience the combined system, with as much vocalization as can be added, is the method that you would recommend?—I should say oral teaching should be included.

13,308. Is that the method which is recommended in America?—That is the method which is recommended by the resolutions which I had the honor to read to the Commission yesterday, as coming from the largest Convention that has ever been held in America, and at which all methods were represented. My views are in accordance with the recommendations in those resolutions, and I have held those views during now a period of 19 years. I may say frankly, that my experience prior to that time was such as to lead me to depreciate and undervalue the oral teaching of the deaf, and I wrote and spoke and worked as a manual teacher purely up to 1867; but when I then visited Europe and examined the oral schools, especially in Germany, I became satisfied that I had failed to grasp the situation theretofore, and I accepted at once the addition of the oral method as a necessity in any system that aimed to reach the highest good of the deaf. In a convention at Indianapolis, some quotations from speeches at which were alluded to yesterday, I was assailed by one of the old and very respected manualists as the degenerate son of a worthy sire, because I had fallen from the grace of the manual method. I survived the accusation. I do not know that I am less respected now than I was then.

13,309. (*Rev. C. Mansfield Owen.*) Do you consider it essential if State aid is to be given, that the State should enforce the adoption of any one method of instruction?—I should conceive it to be extremely deplorable if such State aid were coupled with such a restriction.

13,310. From your experience do you think that articulation can be successfully taught to those who have been born deaf, or who have lost their hearing in early infancy?—My experience leads me to say that in a very considerable number of cases success, and entire success, may be attained with deaf children who were born deaf or lost their hearing very early in life.

13,311. Have you ever known instances of deaf children who have been transferred from the oral method to the manual method because they failed under the oral method?—I have known many such instances.

13,312. Have the children in those cases succeeded under the manual method?—Yes.

13,313. Though they had previously failed under the oral method?—Yes.

13,314. When you said yesterday that the language

of signs is diminishing, do I rightly understand you to wish the manual alphabet to be used more and signs less?—I recommend a restricted use of signs in the class-rooms; I would have the use of signs restricted as far as possible in the class-rooms, and the manual alphabet used rather more freely than I know it has been used in many of the manual and even the combined schools.

13,315. Do I rightly understand that you decidedly deprecate the adoption of the oral method to the absolute exclusion of the other methods?—I go even so far as to say that that oral method will conduce to the best results which does not disdain to make some use of signs and a considerable use of the manual alphabet; in other words, that the pure oral method, which attempts to exclude signs and which excludes the manual alphabet, I do not conceive can reach the best results under any circumstances.

13,316. Speaking from your experience, what proportion of pupils educated on the oral method are, in your opinion, enabled to rely solely upon articulation and lip-reading as a means of communication with hearing persons in after-life?—The question is a difficult one to answer. It is a question which I asked myself many times when I was visiting schools for the deaf in Europe in 1867. I received answers to that question from a number of very prominent oral teachers of the deaf who were then actively engaged in some of the foremost schools of Europe; if it be desired I can give a reference to their answers, which are contained in my report on my visit to those schools in 1867. Speaking for myself, I should find it extremely difficult to give an intelligent answer to that question, for my experience with deaf children taught orally is not wide enough. I mean to say that it is mainly confined to a single institution, but I have the opinions on that question of Mr. Hill of Weisenfels, Mr. Hirsch of Rotterdam, and M. Vaisse of Paris, and one or two others, which were expressed at that time and which might be laid before the Commission.

13,317. Do you find that orally-taught pupils when they are not under supervision converse with each other manually or *viva voce*?—They converse with each other manually, almost wholly, even in the pure oral schools.

13,318. (*Chairman.*) You are speaking of America?—I should say it is the same in every country.

13,319. (*Rev. C. Mansfield Owen.*) Do orally-taught pupils after leaving school keep up their speech and lip-reading, or does your experience lead you to believe that they prefer to talk with their fingers, and that their speech and lip-reading falls into disuse?—I think it depends very much upon the energy and mental capacity of the deaf person. I am sure that very many of the deaf who have been orally taught not only keep up their use of speech and lip-reading but improve it after leaving school, it is quite possible that they may do so, but because some do so, others who do not should not be perhaps seriously blamed, because their failure to do so proceeds from their very different mental constitution, a less persistence in the will, and a variety of causes. It is equally true that a large number of deaf persons orally taught, on leaving school, do allow their use of speech and lip-reading to fall into considerable desuetude, they resort to the use of signs and the manual alphabet, and they associate with deaf persons with whom they may speak freely by those means.

13,320. In America, I understand, you do not make any special effort to follow up the pupils in after-life, to know what system they keep to?—On the contrary, the managers of the various schools do take pains to inquire what their graduates are doing, and to urge and encourage those who have been orally taught to keep up the practice of that very valuable acquisition of speech and lip-reading. There are reports existing of some of the schools in America where very careful inquiries have been made to see whether the use of speech has been continued, whether it has improved, or whether it has grown less perfect; those reports are easily attainable.

13,321. In America, have you missionaries who assist you in that way, keeping the pupils in touch with the institutions?—Yes.

13,322. And they are able to report upon the method of communication which the pupils have adopted after leaving the institution?—Yes.

13,323. I presume you would consider the evidence of those missionaries very important?—I should, decidedly.

13,324. It has been stated in evidence that the pupil's "power of gathering from the lips of others "is within very narrow limits during the school "period"; if that be so, do you consider it a proof of the inefficiency of the method of instruction?—I should say that that is undoubtedly true, but I do not consider that it is an evidence of the inefficiency of that method of instruction: it is simply evidence that the instruction has not yet been carried on to a successful point.

13,325. Do you consider that orally-taught pupils can go out into the world and converse freely with all with whom they come in contact?—Quite the contrary. I have known very few of whom that statement could be made with truth. I have known a few, but the number is so small that it would be represented by not more than one or two or three per cent. of the whole number of orally taught.

13,326. Have you ever known instances of orally-taught pupils dispensing in after-life entirely with the sign and finger-alphabet and the use of pen and pencil in their communication with the world?—I have known those of whom I have been told that they did dispense with even the pen and pencil and paper; certainly they did with the use of signs and the finger-alphabet.

13,327. Have you known of such cases yourself?—Yes, I have known of such cases.

13,328. Have you known of many?—Not many.

13,329. You think such cases would be the exception, and not the rule?—Decidedly the exception and not the rule.

13,330. Have you known of any taught on the pure oral method who could understand sermons or lectures if they could see clearly the utterances of those who were speaking or preaching, as the case might be?—The most important word in that question is the shortest—the word "if"; so much depends upon that "if"—*if* they can see clearly. I should answer the question as you have given it, yes, but I should immediately say that the usual environment of a deaf person who is present on any occasion where public speaking is going on, is sure to be that which would render it impossible for him to see clearly the lips and vocal organs of the one who is speaking.

13,331. To take another example: Supposing there are one or two persons sitting round a table talking, have you ever seen an orally-taught person appear to understand or take part in the general conversation?—You limit it to one or two.

13,332. I mean in a room, in ordinary society?—I have never seen one who could take part with any freedom in the general conversation of a number of persons sitting round a table, for instance. Instead of "take part" I ought to say "take very much part." Taking part in the conversation round a table might mean that this deaf person orally taught would speak to one person across the table and do pretty well; he might be said to be taking part in the conversation at the table, but, properly speaking, taking part in a conversation would be when a

Dr. E. M. Gallaudet.

10 Nov. 1886.

number of people were talking, for this orally-taught person to glance from one to another and catch up the threads of conversation and join in them, and have his word to say upon them, that is what I understand to be meant by "taking part in "the general conversation," and my answer remains as before, with that explanation.

13,333. How long had the oral system been in vogue in America before you produced some good pupils who in after-life could converse?—In the institution at Washington several years. Much to my regret the institution at Washington, the primary school, did not adopt the oral method immediately after the recommendation which I had the honor to make to our Board of Direction in 1867; the reason for this was owing to the fact that the whole energy of the management of the institution at Washington was then being directed to securing Governmental aid for the college, and to promoting the development of the college. As our primary school was small, the directors thought it was not essential that oral teaching should be immediately introduced, and it was therefore deferred for a few years.

13,334. Speaking from your knowledge, do you think that in fifteen or twenty years after the system was adopted, good results ought to be produced?—I should think so.

13,335. You think that would be plenty of time?—Ample time.

13,336. I believe that in America no pains or expense have been spared to attain full information on this oral system?—That is so.

13,337. Were deputations sent from America to Germany to examine into the subject?—There were as early as before 1850. I think it was 1848, but I am not quite able to speak to the exact date.

13,338. What were the reports on the system adopted in Germany?—The reports given at that time were unfavorable to the oral method; upon the whole they gave approval to a certain amount of instruction in articulation to such deaf and dumb as had some power of speech or had some little power of hearing, but they did not recommend its general adoption.

13,339. Then as I understand, the fact that the oral system is not adopted universally in America cannot be attributed to want of knowledge of the subject?—Certainly not. We have had abundant knowledge of what has been done in any country in the world.

13,340. If the oral system is adopted to the exclusion of any other system, you consider it detrimental to the best interest of the children?—I should consider it extremely so.

13,341. It has been stated in evidence by an oral teacher that a boy educated on the oral system could, after three years' instruction, write an ordinary letter; have you known such cases in America?—Yes, I have; and I have also known cases where they have been taught upon the manual method where they could write quite as well and quite as accurately.

13,342. Taking an equal length of time, do you consider that a manual pupil or an oral pupil is the better instructed?—I should without question give the preference to the pupil manually instructed so for as the development of his mind is concerned and the aggregate amount of knowledge gained.

13,343. By which system do you consider that pupils attain a greater grasp of language?—When either method is carried on as it should be, and good teachers are employed, as between the oral method and the manual method, I have not been able to ascertain that any superiority is to be accorded to one over the other as to accuracy in the use of idiomatic language.

13,344. With regard to the cost per head, what is the cost per head in America as compared with that in Paris; I think you said it was 60*l*., roughly speaking, in Paris?—38*l*. is the average cost per head in America as compared with 60*l*. in Paris.

13,345. Do you take into consideration the interest on plant?—Not in either case.

13,346. What compulsion can the State put upon parents, or the representatives of the parents, to send deaf and dumb children to school?—I think in two or three only of the States of our Union in America are there laws which authorize any public officer to compel the attendance of deaf and dumb children in the schools.

13,347. Then when the State gives aid to an institution, is it the rule to insist upon inspection?—Yes; it depends on the will of the State Government to what extent that inspection should be carried. In New England it is an inspection made by the Governor and his council, or by the Governor and a committee of the legislature. In some other States it is made by a Board of Charities constituted for such purpose, and again in other States it is made, as I said yesterday, by the actual governing body which controls the institution absolutely and reports to the State Government.

13,348. There are no school inspectors, as such, like we have in England?—No.

13,349. Will you tell us a little more of the oral branch of the Pennsylvania Institution?—The oral branch of the institution at Pennsylvania is one that I briefly alluded to yesterday, and it exists with a method of organization which in the report which I made in 1867 on the European schools for the deaf, I commended as perhaps the ideal method of organization. I found it then existing in Copenhagen, where there were two schools under Government inspection under the same general management, and there was a carefully arranged process of selection and discrimination among the pupils received and provided for by the management of those two schools, which formed practically a single institution, so that a very wise selection was made of pupils who should be taught upon the oral method or upon the manual method. That is the arrangement at Philadelphia, this oral branch occupying buildings which are under the charge of a matron, and quite separated by two or three miles, I think, from the buildings of the main institution. Those children who are found to be specially ready in speech and in lip-reading, and who do not need perhaps—I say perhaps, in order to be consistent with what I said a little while ago as to the value of signs and the manual alphabet in all teaching of the deaf—who do not need, perhaps, the assistance of those means of instruction, are separated from those who use signs and the manual alphabet, and are taught on as pure an oral method as can be found anywhere in the world. Mr. Crouter, the very able and esteemed principal of this Pennsylvania institution, presented to the California Convention a paper on "The True Combined System" of instruction, and I venture to give it some words of commendation, even more decided than I gave it in referring to it yesterday; and he gives opinions and results of the practice. This method is carried on in this, one of the oldest of the manual schools in America, which now takes its place, in my opinion, in the van of oral teaching.

13,350. With regard to religious instruction; what do you think is the best method of conducting religious instruction for the deaf and dumb?—There are in existence organizations in many parts of our country for the religious instruction of the deaf after they leave school. There are missions for their assistance, the headquarters of one of which is in New York, my brother, Dr. Thomas Gallaudet,

Dr. E. M. Gallaudet.

10 Nov. 1886.

D. D., being at the head of that organization; he has several assistants, two of whom are deaf and who are in holy orders, and he has services with the aid of those assistants in very many of the cities of the Union, in the West, and in the South, and in the East. Those services have been found to be a great help to the deaf in their moral and religious life, and more than that, that organization has been the means of giving them assistance and comfort in a great variety of ways, helping them in their efforts to gain a livelihood, and to live decently and respectably. The work is regarded in America as a matter of very great importance, and those missions to the deaf are sustained very liberally. It is known to be absolutely impossible to carry them on excepting by the employment of a means of communication which shall be manual; it is impossible to conduct a service for the deaf orally which would be intelligible to any considerable number of those attending it.

13,351. Do pure orally-taught persons, after they leave the institutions, attend those services?—Yes.

13,352. Do they acquire the sign and manual language after they leave the institution?—Very readily.

13,353. In order to participate in those services?—Yes, and to enjoy social intercourse with those similarly afflicted.

13,354. All the services are conducted in the sign and manual language?—Yes.

13,355. You said that the Federal Government takes great interest in the amelioration of the condition of the deaf and dumb, and you said that the President of the United States is *ex-officio* patron of your college; does he take a personal interest in the present movement for the advancement of deaf and dumb education?—He does take a very warm interest in it. He began his life as a teacher of the blind, and he has never ceased to take an interest in institutions for the benefit of the blind and deaf, and he is patron of our institution at Washington for the deaf. The President has on several occasions manifested his interest by attending the anniversaries, and in other ways. On the morning that I left Washington to answer the invitation to give evidence before this Commission, I called upon the President to take my leave, and to inform him of the purpose for which I was to be absent from the country by the permission of the Government, and he expressed very great interest, not only in our work in America, but in the work proposed to be done by this Commission, which I explained to him at some length as far as I was aware of it; and before the day was over he sent me this note, which it may be of interest to the Commission to know is entirely written and directed by his own hand, expressive of his great interest in the object of my visit to England, and in the work of the Commission:

"EXECUTIVE MANSION,
"WASHINGTON, October 6th, 1886.

"Professor E. M. GALLAUDET.

"MY DEAR SIR: I am very glad to learn that you have been invited to give information before a Commission organized under the auspices of the British Government to inquire concerning the subjects of the education of the blind, the deaf, and the dumb. A country that contributes so largely from its public funds for these purposes, and with such gratifying results, ought to be able to furnish much that is interesting and profitable in such an investigation; and no person, I believe, can better represent our achievements in this field of inquiry than yourself. I hope that the trip you are to make in answer to this invitation will be pleasant, and in furtherance of the objects which you have so earnestly at heart.

"Yours sincerely,

"GROVER CLEVELAND."

13,356. (*Mr. Arrol.*) You stated yesterday that one in 1,800 of the population in America is deaf; can you give the Commission any information as to how that proportion compares with the proportion in the continent of Europe?—The proportion on the continent of Europe, as well as I remember, varies more or less. In the mountainous countries, where physical disabilities, such as goitre and cretinism, and other evidences of physical deterioration exist, the number is much larger; but I think (I speak quite from memory, and not from any recent examination of the figures), that the proportion in the countries of Europe in which ordinary physical vigor and development exist, does not differ very much from that in America.

13,357. Can you inform the Commission what the proportion may be of persons who are born deaf?—Rather less than one-half. A reference to the tables which I have submitted as an appendix to my evidence, would give that; there are two or three tables where that would be stated quite definitely, and the causes of deafness are there rehearsed.

13,358. Yesterday you mentioned, that of the 7,800 under tuition, you excluded 186 taught at pure oral schools?—Those were private schools.

13,359. You have mentioned that there are rather over 3,000 being taught articulation; what may be the reason why such a large proportion as the remainder are not being taught articulation?—Partly because there are still 14 manual schools in America where no speech is taught, and then further, because in some of the larger institutions which are carried on on the combined system, the oral method has been recently introduced, and means are not available for the employment of teachers enough to teach as many of the pupils as might be taught orally, and further, because a large number of the pupils in our schools have been found to be not likely to succeed well in oral attainments, and so their instruction in that branch has been given up.

13,360. What may that large number represent in proportion?—I give only my own opinion, but it is that the proportion of the deaf who will not be likely to succeed in speech, to an extent to justify the expense and labor of teaching them orally, would certainly rise to 40 per cent.

13,361. In connection with most of your schools, apparently, you have industrial departments?—Yes.

13,362. Fourteen only have no industrial branch connected with them; are those the private and the public board schools that have no manufacturing departments connected with them?—Eight of those 14 are day schools, and of the other six my impression is that at least three would be those private schools of which we spoke, so that only three of the public institutions of America can be said to be absolutely without an industrial department.

13,363. It is considered necessary to have an industrial department?—It is considered quite essential to the proper preparation of a young deaf and dumb person to go out and make his way in the world.

13,364. Did I rightly understand you to express the opinion that it is to the benefit of the deaf and dumb adults that they should be connected with the parent school or institution through missionaries?—I did not say that it was desirable, in my opinion, that they should be connected with the parent institution through the intervention of missionaries connected with the institution; those missionaries are not sustained by the institutions, but by organizations in which funds are contributed by persons disposed to carry on this missionary work among the deaf; they are not directly connected with the institutions.

13,365. How many missionaries have you trained and sent out from your college at Washington?—I think that three or four of the graduates of the college have gone out to become missionaries among that class. I am not able to speak with definiteness of the number, but I know several have. It may be

Dr. E. M. Gallaudet.

10 Nov. 1886.

five. I may repeat what I said a little while ago. I think it very important that these missions should be carried on for the benefit of the adult deaf.

13,366. Is it found that State aid in America conflicts with charitable benevolence?—It is found that so far as what might be termed annual subscriptions to aid in the ordinary support of schools for the deaf go, the general giving of State aid in America does away almost absolutely with such annual subscriptions, but it by no means stands in the way of bequests and legacies which in some instances have been quite large in amount; for example, in 1865 or 1866, a Mr. Clark, in Massachusetts, left a very handsome fortune for the establishment of an oral school for the deaf, which was established at Northampton. I think the endowment of that institution—I am speaking without any recent reference to the figures —is 50,000*l.* or 60,000*l.*, and that endowment was made, of course, long after State aid had been freely given in all that region of country. The Pennsylvania institution has large endowments which yield an income, which is devoted to certain purposes, and I am under the impression that in the case of that institution there are certain sums paid to those who leave to assist them in making their way with master mechanics as a sort of apprenticeship money. So that in the matter of legacies and charitable gifts to institutions the giving of State aid has not stood in the way of their continuance.

13,367. In America you consider it absolutely necessary for the Government to subsidize all these charitable institutions for the deaf and dumb?—It would be difficult to accomplish the end in any other way. It is looked on as a thing which it is right the State should provide for.

13,368. Do you or not consider that it is necessary, after a deaf and dumb person has been thoroughly educated, that he should in any way receive a subsidy or grant to assist him in industrial pursuits or in earning a living in some other way?—That would depend a great deal upon the amount of industrial training that he had received while he was in school, and upon the age at which he left school, which would, of course, come in to affect the matter of the amount of industrial training which he might have received. Of course, if he was an accomplished mechanic, he would be able to go out and make his way without assistance; if he were not an accomplished workman, either from the fact of the short time that he had been under instruction, or from having been in a school where a sufficient number of industries were not taught, or from the fact that his education began at so early an age and closed at so early an age as to make it quite out of the question to teach him a trade while in school, I think it would be a very advisable thing that there should be funds existing, from the income of which there might be a sum of money paid to assist him in making a start.

13,369. The inspection of your institutions, I apprehend, is conducted by a board connected with the State, or connected with the institution; would it not be more thorough and more satisfactory to have Federal State inspection?—That would be quite inconsistent with the whole spirit of our Government; it would not be tolerated in the States at all; in fact, it would be inconsistent with the constitution of the several States for Federal inspection to attempt to extend itself into schools sustained either as corporate schools or State schools by the State Governments.

13,370. Do not you think that that system of inspection would be more thorough?—My own opinion is that the inspection of a local board of men having a local interest, and, therefore, a personal interest, in the success of the school, would be likely to lead to better results than an examination which was made by an inspector or a board of inspectors appointed to go over a very large amount of territory and examine institutions all over the country. I think I said yesterday that in America the ideal exterior organization of an institution was felt to be a corporate institution with the assistance of the State, and without much interference, either in the way of inspection or otherwise, by the State, but depending for its successful development on the earnestness and activity of the men constituting the local board of management, and on a desire to show results comparing favorably with those of other institutions.

13,371. Perhaps you may have formed an opinion upon the reasons why the pure oral system, after being tried so thoroughly in this country towards the end of the last century and the beginning of this, should have been in a measure abandoned till recently?—My opinion is that it was for the reasons which operate to make my own opinion unfavorable to the attempt to force all the deaf into education on the oral method. It is undoubtedly the fact that when that is insisted on the result is that a very large number of deaf who are perfectly capable of being educated on the manual method are likely to be set aside as almost imbecile because they cannot succeed on the oral method. That, in point of fact, has been the case. In many countries where the attempt to teach all on the oral method is persisted in the results in a large number of cases are sure to be so unsatisfactory that it is not at all strange that the tide of public opinion should set back and sweep the oral method off and revert to the manual method. In my opinion, the only way, perhaps I should not say the only way but the best way, to preserve the oral method in its best uses is to acknowledge that it is not possible to apply it to all, but that it is applicable to a certain number, and that other methods should be adopted for those who did not succeed with the oral method.

13,372. You made a tour of inspection in 1867, and visited some 36 schools; would you favor the Commission with your views in respect to what you found on your recent visit as to the increased amount of teaching under the oral system?—I know, as a matter of fact, that in France and Italy and in England the oral method is now employed in a much greater proportion than it was at that time.

13,373. Can you say to what extent?—I am not able to say to what extent; I know that quite a large number of the prominent schools in France have adopted it.

13,374. (*Chairman.*) It is not a question of adoption, it is now the law of the country that the oral method shall be taught in all schools?—I was not aware of that.

13,375. And, as I am told, the reason why the age of admission is at present fixed so high is because it is a survival of the old manual system, and they are gradually lowering it in France?—I was not aware of that.

13,376. (*Dr. Tindal Robertson.*) Is the physical condition of the deaf and dumb who have come under your superintendence equal to that of ordinary children?—I find that it is probably, and I think almost certainly, a little lower, not very much lower, but a little lower, for the reason that the deafness supervenes, in very many cases, in consequence of severe attacks of disease; those attacks of disease leave the system not only with the auditory organ destroyed, but with other conditions of feebleness, so that those cases where that physical deterioration has occurred would come in to lower the average a little, but not very much. I should say that, generally speaking, the physical condition of the deaf and dumb might be stated to be good.

13,377. Except in those cases where deafness occurs as a *sequela* to other diseases?—Yes.

13,378. Are there medical men attached to your institutions?—Yes.

13,379. Are examinations always made in the case of children who come into the school?—Yes.

13,380. (*Chairman.*) And periodically too?—Yes.

13,381. (*Dr. Tindal Robertson.*) In the case of death are there any post-mortem examinations?—There have been in some cases, but usually where the death happens from some well understood cause no post-mortem examination is made.

13,382. In cases where post-mortem examinations are made, is there any record of any abnormal appearances kept?—No; among some of our instructors the wish has been expressed that such examinations should be made more frequently.

13,383. Do you think that such a thing might be advisable, and might lead to information upon the subject which would be very useful?—I should be inclined to say so.

13,384. (*Dr. Armitage.*) You grant diplomas at your college; how are they granted?—The directors of our institution at Washington, which includes the college and the primary school as well, are named in our annual report; they consist of one Senator appointed by the President of the Senate, two Members of the House appointed by the Speaker of the House, and six directors, who hold a permanent position. The vote of that Board, of which I am the President, and before which recommendations come from the faculty of the college, is necessary in the conferring of degrees, the degrees being conferred upon the recommendation of the faculty.

13,385. In point of fact, you are self-contained; the professors, as I understand you, and the president examine the pupils as to their fitness to obtain the diploma?—Yes.

13,386. Do the ordinary primary State schools throughout the country grant diplomas to the pupils when they leave school?—I understand you to mean by diplomas, degrees; in no instance do they give such diplomas; they may give a certificate; the pupils receive a certificate of honorable dismissal or graduation from these schools.

13,387. You spoke of graduates from these State schools; did you mean by that simply those who had passed through the course of the school?—I think, if I remember rightly, when I used the term "graduates," I referred to those who had gone regularly through these primary State schools as pupils; they would be classed generally as graduates of those schools.

13,388. By the word "graduates" you simply meant former pupils?—No, but those only who have completed the prescribed full course of study.

13,389. To continue Dr. Robertson's questions as to physical training, are gymnastics and free exercises and out-door games carried on in considerable extent in your American schools?—To a considerable extent; I regret to say not to as great an extent as would be deemed desirable. Six years ago at Washington we completed and opened a very well equipped gymnasium, in which physical training is carried on under the direction of a well educated and competent drill master and instructor. Since that time quite a number of State institutions have followed the example set at Washington, and have erected and equipped gymnasiums more or less perfect in their appliances for physical training. It is admitted on all hands that that is extremely desirable, and I think those appliances for physical training will soon be introduced in our institutions generally; physical training by such means is of even greater importance to the deaf, if that were possible, than to those who are not deaf.

13,390. As to another question which was touched upon yesterday, are intermarriages among the deaf frequent in America?—They may be said to be quite frequent.

13,391. Taking the whole of the marriages of the deaf, can you give us an idea what the percentage of those who have intermarried is to the whole number of marriages?—I am sorry to say I am not able to answer that question in figures. I can say, in general, that the number of intermarriages of deaf persons would considerably exceed the number of marriages where only one of the contracting parties was deaf.

13,392. Do you think that the intermarriage of the deaf and dumb leads to bad results?—I think the whole subject depends on a matter of which I spoke yesterday. As a matter of fact, there are a considerable number of families now existing in America, the parents in which are both deaf, and in which there are to be found a large, not to say a lamentable, proportion of deaf children. My opinion is, that those marriages, on examination, would be found to be between parties who belong to families in which there was an indubitable tendency to deafness, proved by the existence in those families of a considerable number of deaf persons. It is also true that there are a large number of families in America where both parents are deaf in which no deaf children are to be found. The general opinion is that a deaf person in a family with a tendency to deafness should not marry a person of another family with a similar tendency. Where that is avoided the danger of deaf offspring is diminished to a very small figure. Marriages of the deaf are encouraged in America rather than otherwise by the officers of institutions; it is found unquestionably that the happiness of the deaf is immensely increased by happy marriages; of course they may make unhappy marriages as well as hearing people?—I have myself taken occasion in several articles that I have published to caution the deaf in the matter of marriage, and to urge that where it is practicable they should make choice of a partner who hears, for unquestionably it is more to the advantage of the offspring to have only one parent deaf than to have two parents deaf.

13,393. Do you believe that when the deaf contract marriages that question is considered frequently?—I think it is more and more considered.

13,394. You think that they would endeavor to avoid marrying into a family where there was a hereditary tendency to deafness?—I think it is more and more considered; the officers of the institutions take more and more pains to guard against such marriages.

13,395. Is the evil that we are referring to fully appreciated by the missionaries?—I am not able to say that.

13,396. Your brother, Dr. Gallaudet, is at the head of one of the missionary organizations?—My brother is at the head of one of the largest missionary organizations in America; he appreciates the danger of which we are speaking fully, and would certainly exercise his influence to prevent unsuitable marriages.

13,397. You think it desirable that the missionaries should throw their whole influence into the scale to prevent marriages where there is a tendency to deafness in both families?—Most undoubtedly I do.

13,398. Can you suggest any other way in which such intermarriages can be prevented or discountenanced?—I have given the subject from first to last a great deal of thought, and I can see no other way. I think legislation upon the subject would be inconsistent with public sentiment. I think there is no better way of dealing with the matter than for the teachers, and those who have any interest in the deaf after they leave school, to give them the best advice they can upon the subject, and endeavor to

Dr. E. M. Gallaudet.

10 Nov. 1886.

lead them to do that which is best in the matter of marriage.

13,399. Is the matter one which is much insisted on in literature which is published specially for the deaf?—I do not think it has been very much insisted on.

13,400. (*Admiral Sotheby.*) Taking into consideration the great difficulty and the time required in teaching the deaf and dumb, do you consider that industrial training during the period of school life militates against the best development of education?—Not if the period of school life can be prolonged to at least seven years; if it is cut short of that it might be a question whether, in giving too much time to industrial training, you might not be lessening the value of the other department of instruction.

13,401. Would not you say that a little industrial training while they were under education might be beneficial to their health and be a relaxation?—Yes, I should say that industrial training rightly carried on might be beneficial to health.

13,402. You have stated that you were present at the Convention at Milan?—Yes.

13,403. Are you aware that the French went there strongly prejudiced against the oral system?—I have heard it said that a number of teachers went from France who were previously manual teachers. I have no positive knowledge that they went there with any strong prejudice against the oral method.

13,404. Are you aware that the French Commissioner and the teachers who went from France to that Convention came away converts to the oral system?—That is a fact quite well known.

13,405. And then a law was passed in Paris that the oral system should be adopted as the State system?—So I understand.

13,406. I think you said that for church and platform purposes the sign and manual system is certainly the best?—Certainly the best, and the only method, so far as I am aware, by which one can succeed in imparting information to a considerable audience of deaf persons.

13,407. Who makes out the syllabus for the religious instruction in the schools in America?—Whatever body controls the course of instruction in the school.

13,408. The syllabus is not drawn up by the superintendent himself?—If the board of directors authorize the superintendent so to do it may be done by the superintendent himself; it may be done by a committee; it may be done in any manner that the board of direction direct.

13,409. There is a regular syllabus made out?—Yes, for a certain amount of religious instruction.

13,410. Do you consider that the deaf and dumb will fairly compare with hearing people as to morality?—I consider that they will.

13,411. You say that deaf-mutes lose much social intercourse if their conversation is confined to the lip system; do you find in America many people who understand the sign and manual system or the manual system only so as to be able to converse with them?—I find in America that a very large number of people understand the manual alphabet, through the means of which they converse readily with deaf persons who have never been taught orally.

13,412. And they prefer doing that?—They prefer it in many instances; they find it a means of communication more direct and more agreeable, less coupled with the necessity for repetition, and less liable to misunderstanding than the oral method of communication.

13,413. Do you consider that the deaf and dumb are able to take their part with hearing people in all manly sports?—So far as hunting and shooting are concerned, for my own part I advise the deaf to let them alone, for so much depends on what may come to one through the ears if one goes hunting or shooting that it is dangerous for them to engage in those sports. But we find that the deaf are quite capable of taking part in such games as cricket, or base-ball, or foot-ball, and we encourage them to do so.

13,414. You would probably add swimming to the list of manly exercises in which they might safely take part?—Yes; we have a swimming school in connection with our gymnasium at Washington.

13,415. I understood you to say that between certain times 40 had left the college at Washington, and are now occupying very lucrative positions; what would that period be?—My statement was that 40 who had gone out from the college had been engaged in teaching. I enumerated a large number of others who were engaged in various pursuits, but the 40 had become teachers of the deaf, and the period during which they left the college and entered upon those various pursuits would extend over about 20 years.

13,416. (*Rev. W. Blomefield Sleight.*) At what age do you consider that the education should begin under the oral method, and at what age under the manual method?—My own judgment is in favor of beginning the instruction of deaf-mutes in school at the age of seven years as a rule. In certain cases where the physical development is very decided, and the home associations are such as to make it desirable that the child should be placed in school at a younger age, it might be placed there satisfactorily at the age of six, or even a little younger. That would apply to either method. I should say, further, that wherever it is practicable for the child to receive instruction at an earlier age at home, or even in a kindergarten with other children, not depriving the child of that opportunity for play and free run which a child needs till it is seven years of age, the instruction should begin at an earlier age than the age I have mentioned as that at which it is proper for a child to be placed in school.

13,417. You will admit that the degrees of the affliction of deaf-mutism vary very considerably; under what heads would you classify deaf-mutes?—The class should always be spoken of as the deaf; the term "deaf-mute" should only be applied to such as are totally deaf and completely dumb. Besides this sub-class we should then have the speaking deaf, the semi-speaking deaf, the speaking semi-deaf, the mute semi-deaf, the hearing mute, and the hearing semi-mute; those last two classes being usually persons of feeble mental powers. I ventured to lay down that classification a few years ago in an article published in the *International Review* on the question, "How should the deaf "be educated?" which had previously been submitted to a meeting of the American Social Science Association, and I think the classification has been accepted as one of some importance in discovering just how to deal with the differently constituted units of the great class usually spoken of as the deaf and dumb; and by assigning the various members of the great class of the deaf to those various sub-classes very important results are obtained in the way of classifying them for different modes of instruction. If you will allow me I will explain a little the meaning of those sub-classes: "The speak-"ing deaf" would include a child who has learnt to speak and lost his hearing after he was five or six or seven years old. Of course he is perfectly deaf, but he speaks fairly well; still in the eye of the law he is classed as a deaf-mute, for he cannot go to an ordinary school. Then the "semi speaking deaf" person is one who lost his hearing—we might say at perhaps two or three years of age—who retains the power of uttering disconnected words, but has not the power of expressing himself in connected language. He would have one advantage over the absolute deaf-mute in starting on his course of instruction, and it would probably be considered advisable that having this limited power of speech he should in his course of instruction come under the oral method. Then we come to the "speaking semi-deaf," comprising cases where from disease a child might lose his hearing partially and still have the power of speech, who was so deaf as not to be able to enter an ordinary school, but who could hear enough to be taught on the aural method. Then as an example of the cases that would come under the sub-class of "mute semi-deaf," I may refer to the case I spoke of yesterday: the boy who came into our institution deaf, as we supposed, from the first year of his infancy, but who had, as we discovered, an amount of hearing sufficient to be able to be taught on the aural method. Then the next sub-class, the "hearing mute," would comprise such children as hear perfectly well but who do not speak; such are almost invariably idiots. When we find a child who hears perfectly well but who does not speak, and numbers of such are brought to me as deaf-mutes, I almost without exception have to send them to schools for feeble-minded children.

Hearing mutes and hearing semi-mutes, when found to be dumb *only* because of feeble-mindedness should not, speaking with precision, be regarded as belonging among the deaf and dumb. I have included them only because of misconceptions which seem to be deeply rooted in the uninstructed public mind.

13,418. As I understand you, there are exceptions?—There are exceptions where through some malformation of the vocal organs there is an inability to speak; one such case I can recall recently in the Washington Institution, where we were able to overcome the defect in the vocal organs and to teach the boy to speak very well after some little practice.

13,419. (*Dr. Armitage.*) Was that defect overcome by a surgical operation?—No; there had been a partial paralysis of the vocal organs, a feebleness of muscular power and a disinclination on the part of the boy to make an effort to speak. We encouraged him to speak, and after some time he attained a reasonable degree of success in speech.

13,420. (*Chairman.*) It was a case of restoration of the voice which had been lost through partial paralysis?—Yes; the restoration of the voice being effected not by surgical or medical treatment but simply by patient instruction on the part of the teacher.

13,421. (*Dr. Armitage.*) By encouraging the child to make use of the organ which had been long disused?—Yes.

13,422. (*Dr. Tindal Robertson.*) Was the child before he came into the institution badly fed, and did his physical condition improve *pari passu* with the recovery of his speech?—Yes; he was a child of an inebriate father, and he had grown up under very poor surroundings.

13,423. (*Rev. W. Blomefield Sleight.*) In schools where the manual system was taught, should not every endeavor be made to develop the power of speech of those who manifested any such power?—That is what I have now for 19 years urged very earnestly, and what has come to be the accepted practice in our American schools. Manual schools which adopted that method would be no longer manual schools, they would then be combined schools.

13,424. (*Chairman.*) In the manual schools all those who were not absolutely deaf would be forced to continue on the sign and manual system, whereas they ought to be treated on the oral system?—Yes, and if such pupils were allowed to remain in manual schools they would have a great wrong done them. I should deprecate very strongly their remaining any longer in manual schools.

13,425. (*Rev. W. Blomefield Sleight.*) What, in your opinion, is the greatest alleviation that can be given to the deaf and dumb?—If I rightly understand the purport of the question, the greatest alleviation which could be given to the deaf would be that their minds should be developed, and that they should be given the power of expressing themselves in verbal language by their fingers or by writing, and given the power of reading books. Then, when they have the vernacular of their country, they come in easy association and contact with those who can read and write, and are able to communicate by writing. The giving of speech to the deaf, while it is admitted by everyone to be a very valuable thing, occupies a secondary position by the side of the mental development which may be brought about by a course of training which will open up to a deaf person all the stores of literature. Of course oral training is not an essential thing in the education of the deaf—it is an important thing, but by no means a thing of such transcendent importance as some pure oralists would have the world believe.

13,426. By what method can a knowledge of written language be best imparted to the mass of the deaf?—To the mass of the deaf I should not hesitate to say that a knowledge of the use of written language can be best imparted by the use of the manual alphabet, by signs, and by writing.

13,427. On referring to the *American Annals of the Deaf and Dumb* (January, 1881), I see you stated at the Milan Conference: "In my opinion it is by "the practice of the combined system that the great-"est advantage to the greatest number may be se-"cured." Is that still your opinion?—I have seen nothing to induce me to change or modify that opinion in the least.

13,428. Can you give us the number of children that are being taught under the oral method, the number who are being taught under the manual method, and who are being taught under the combined system in your American schools?—In oral schools, 583; in manual schools, 430; in combined schools, 6,788.

13,429. Did you before the oral system came into prominence teach speaking to semi-mutes in your institution, at Washington?—I am sorry to say we did not; we ought to have done so.

13,430. Was any such teaching given in other schools?—In a few of the manual schools in America teaching speech to the semi-deaf and the semi-mute was practised before the matter of oral instruction attained much prominence as it began to do 20 years ago.

13,431. (*Chairman.*) You said that there were only two schools at first?—Yes, both started in 1867.

13,432. (*Rev. W. Blomefield Sleight.*) Could all deaf-mutes be taught to talk and read from the lips with success?—In my opinion, decidedly not.

13,433. In pure oral schools would you prohibit the use of signs altogether?—I should not, for the reason that I am very slow to attempt the impossible.

13,434. Can you give us the proportion of children in the oral schools who were born deaf?—I am not able to give the proportion of such children.

13,435. Is it your opinion that it is easier to instruct a child who was born deaf in the oral method than one who has become deaf?—I should say that there are to be found children who were born deaf who learn to speak much more easily than other children who might be placed by their sides who were not born deaf; but if you take the two sub-classes of those born deaf and those not born deaf then the sub-class of those not born deaf would

Dr. E. M. Gallaudet.

10 Nov. 1886.

learn to speak much more readily than the sub-class of those born deaf.

13,436. Taking them as a whole?—Taking them as a whole.

13,437. What length of time is needed to educate a child under the manual method, and what length of time is necessary to educate a child under the oral method. I am speaking of ordinary school education?—In my opinion, with a child of average intelligence, not less than seven years if the manual method were entirely used, and if the oral method were used I should add at least a year or two to reach the same results so far as the intellectual development of the pupil is concerned.

13,438. Are the oral schools ready to admit all children or do they practically make a selection?—I am credibly informed that they practically make selections. I know as a matter of fact that in a number of instances where application has been made for the admission of pupils into oral schools the application has been refused, that is to say, pupils have been refused admission into oral schools because, in the judgment of the teachers of such schools, they were not likely to succeed in speech I have had under my charge in Washington pupils who would prove that fact.

13,439. How do children taught under the oral method communicate with those taught under the manual method?—Naturally by signs and the manual alphabet.

13,440. Principally by signs, or principally by the manual alphabet?—Rather more by signs, I should say.

13,441. By what system do deaf-mutes make themselves best understood with the outside world?—It goes without saying that a deaf person who may be taken as a shining success under the oral method may communicate with the outside world more readily and with less loss of time than one who is reduced to the necessity of writing; but taking the whole number of deaf who have been orally educated as compared with the whole number of deaf who have been only manually educated, in my opinion the deaf educated under the manual method would have the precedence over those educated under the oral method, taking them *en masse;* that is to say, if those educated under the oral method undertook to make their communications through the means of speech, there would be so many of them that would speak imperfectly and read from the lips imperfectly that the average of those that would be able to communicate with any degree of success with the outside world would be less than the average of those educated under the manual method.

13,442. Do you find that children who have been educated on the oral method, when they leave school are inclined to congregate together, and that those educated under the manual method are inclined to cling together?—The tendency, in the great majority of cases, is for the two classes to mingle as one class after leaving school, those educated in oral schools mingling freely with those educated in manual schools.

13,443. Then how do those who are orally taught converse with those who have been taught by the manual method?—Almost entirely by signs, supplemented by the manual alphabet.

13,444. By which method do you consider the brightness and general happiness of a deaf child's life may be best promoted?—I have said on a former occasion in America, that if, by a process which of course is impossible, I could be projected back to a period of existence which antedated my mother's life, and could choose for her, it being a necessity that she should be born deaf, whether, on the one hand, she should be educated upon the oral method, and should be denied through her life the use of signs and the manual alphabet, even allowing that she might be educated under the oral method with very great success, or whether, on the other hand, she should be well educated, so far as mental development was concerned, but should have no speech, and should be allowed the free use of signs, and the manual alphabet, considering her happiness, I should choose the latter unquestionably; that is to say, that she should remain mute during her whole life, without the power of speech or lip-reading, but be allowed to have the use of signs and the manual alphabet. My mother, as is known, was a deaf-mute, and of course I observed her life, so far as I was able, after I arrived at a sufficient age to be observant, and I have no hesitation in saying that in my judgment the happiness of a deaf person is greater who may be educated without speech, but still who uses the manual alphabet and signs, than one (and I hope I shall not be misunderstood) who has the power of speech and lip-reading but refuses to use signs and the manual alphabet. I know of such persons, and I am certain that their lives are more isolated, and they have a less degree of happiness in society and among their friends than those who without speech still use freely signs and the manual alphabet. I would not be understood, in giving this answer, to undervalue the usefulness of speech to the deaf, but understanding the question as put to me to have reference to the general happiness of the person, I should not hesitate to say that one taught under the manual method would have a great superiority over one taught on the pure oral method, with all that that implies.

13,445. Do you think that the heart, the imagination, the soul, and the affections of a deaf mute, can ever be so deeply stirred by speech and lip-reading, as by the manual method?—I do not think they can ever be so deeply stirred or strongly moved as by the use of gestures.

13,446. Were you present at the conference of principals of American institutions in 1884?—I was.

13,447. Did Mr. Williams produce specimens of the composition of oral and manual pupils?—He did. I have made reference to that paper of Mr. Williams', which is published in the proceedings of that conference (which I have left with the Commission for them to refer to if they should wish to do so), in which that comparison is presented with very great clearness.

13,448. At what age do you admit students to the Washington College?—We have no absolute limit of age; we require an entrance examination; we have admitted students as young as between 15 and 16 into the college; we prefer that boys of so young an age should not generally be received; we prefer that they should not enter under 16, and for the reason that the discipline of a college is naturally not so rigid as that of a primary school; and we think that the age of 16 should be reached before boys should be allowed that latitude that is given to the students in a college.

13,449. What percentage of your students take their degree?—I think about 25 per cent. of those who enter the college graduate in the full course; the others pursue the courses I spoke of yesterday; they select special courses, cutting short their period of connection with the college to two or three years.

13,450. You have at present 50 students?—About 50.

13,451. Can you tell the Commission how many of those have been educated under the oral method, and how many under the manual method?—I think five or six of those have been educated in oral schools; they came to us from oral schools; the remainder having mainly come from schools where the combined system is maintained.

13,452. By what method do you interpret the lectures to them?—By the use of gestures entirely.

Dr. E. M. Gallaudet.

10 Nov. 1886.

13,453. Do you or your professors ever deliver lectures to them *viva voce?*—We never do; we know it would be useless to attempt it even to those who read well from the lips.

13,454. (*Chairman.*) You consider it would be a waste of time?—We should not be understood at all; some few sentences might be understood, but no continuous lecture could be given to a dozen deaf-mutes orally, in my judgment, with any success.

13,455. (*Rev. W. B. Sleight.*) Do not you consider that teaching by the lips is, after all, a gesture method?—I have always called it a gesture method; it is a method in which signs are used; the signs are very small, and they are made by the vocal organs, but they are gestures for all that. The method of teaching by lip-reading is a sign method. Certain movements of the vocal organs are taught, in a perfectly arbitrary manner, to mean certain things; these signs are perfectly arbitrary, which the gestures and manual movements of those who have been taught by the sign and manual method are not; they are pantomimic and ideographic, which the signs made by vocal organs never can be.

13,456. Where did Mr. Magin receive his primary education, and by what method?—My impression is that he was at a school at Belfast. He was a teacher in a London school before he came to Washington, but I think he was at Belfast.

13,457. Where the sign and manual system was taught?—Yes. He has no power of speech.

13,458. You mentioned that 40 who have gone out from your college are engaged as teachers; are any of those 40 engaged as teachers in oral schools?—It is quite impossible that they should be, unless in oral schools they resort to some instruction in the sign and manual alphabet. It is impracticable for deaf persons to be teachers in oral schools.

13,459. Does not the industrial training which you give your pupils somewhat interfere with their education?—In my opinion, not unless it is made to occupy too large a proportion of the time from day to day; it could be made, of course, to occupy an amount of time which would seriously militate against the proper advancement of the pupil in the intellectual department; but, ordinarily speaking, the amount of time that would be given to industrial work in our schools would not interfere with very good progress being made in the school.

13,460. Of what real value do you consider speech and speech-reading to be to deaf-mutes in the prosecution of their callings in after-life?—I think that, in the frequently arising circumstances in which they may be placed, the power to speak and read from the lips of others gives them a decided advantage over those not able to speak or read from the lips; it would be very difficult to state to what extent that would be an advantage. It goes without saying, that a deaf person who has the power of expressing himself so that strangers, or even those who are not strangers, can understand him pretty readily and reading from the lips, has a great advantage over one who cannot do that. At the same time it is only right to say that there are a vast number of deaf-mutes living now who have been educated without speech who have got on in the world with entire success; who have maintained themselves and their families, and have even amassed wealth; they have, in fact, practically succeeded in all the essential elements of success in life without speech. I think, however, that any such deaf-mutes who had had the power of speech added to their other attainments would have had an advantage in their contest with the world.

13,461. You mentioned three cases of young men doing very successfully in after-life who had been trained by the sign method; could you give cases that have been taught on the oral system doing so successfully?—I know cases of young men who have been taught in the oral method who are now succeeding very well and doing admirable work, maintaining themselves in a very creditable manner.

13,462. How do you consider the condition of the educated deaf compares with that of others of a similar station in the matters of, say, thrift, industry, perseverance, and honesty?—I think it compares very favorably with that of other persons of their station; possibly on the whole they get on better than the mass of persons do of their station in life, for the reason that their training in special schools has been of a character to develop in them those peculiarities of character and constitution that tend to success; in other words, one may say, that the training in the special schools for the deaf tends to raise the general standard of capability.

13,463. I believe I am right in stating that, with regard to most of the deaf and dumb institutions in our country, no industrial workshops are attached to them: from your experience in America, do you think that it is of use to the deaf and dumb to have these industrial workshops?—In America I think so. I am not perhaps sufficiently well acquainted with the conditions of labor in this country, and the difficulties which attend the entering into various trades by young people who would be apprenticed, to be able to express an opinion as to what would be the desirable thing in this country. In general, however, the opinion is very decided in America that it is well to give instruction in industrial pursuits while the pupils are at school.

13,464. Would it be possible for a debate or a discussion to be carried on among deaf-mutes by articulation?—I have never heard of such a discussion or debate, and I doubt whether it is practicable. I have heard of conventions of deaf-mutes meeting in Germany where the oral method alone is practised, and that they invariably carry on their discussions by gestures.

13,465. I was going to ask you some questions on the religious question, but I think Mr. Owen has touched pretty fully upon that subject; but I will just put this question: Do you think that the hearts of your audience, of your congregation, could ever be as deeply touched by the oral system as they can by the manual; in a sermon I am speaking of now?—I feel very certain that they could not; in fact I have never yet known the case where any body of deaf persons sufficiently large to be called an audience could be spoken with at any great length orally at all. I do not think it can be done. I know that in some of the oral schools there are religious exercises conducted orally for a certain number of the pupils, and they usually consist of reading passages of scripture, the offering of prayers, which are more or less familiar, and perhaps a simple exposition which is understandable in part only, even by those who are the best lip-readers.

13,466. In your opinion could higher and larger results be obtained by the combined system than by any single method?—That is my opinion very decidedly. I have maintained that on all occasions for a number of years.

13,467. One question occurred to me to-day: are any aural cases found among those who have become deaf?—Yes, quite a number; for in the instances where deafness is caused by disease, it not infrequently happens that the organ of hearing is not entirely destroyed, but the hearing is only partially destroyed, so that in quite a number of cases where the aural or auricular education of the deaf is possible, it is true that deafness has supervened as the result of accident or disease.

13,468. The progress of disease may have stopped the ears?—Yes. As, for example, with scarlet fever; the tympanum may have been perforated, and the organs of the ear may have been disturbed, but not so far destroyed as to render hearing impossible.

Dr. E. M. Gallaudet. 10 Nov. 1886.

13,469. Do you approve of deaf and dumb persons being employed as teachers in institutions?—I do give my approval to the employment, in a reasonable proportion, of deaf persons as teachers of the deaf, and I think that when this proportion is not too great, this policy is to be decidedly preferred over that of employing hearing persons for the entire corps of instruction, and for the reason that the deaf, having had themselves a personal experience of the difficulties that surround the education of the deaf, are, in many respects, better able to teach persons of their own class than others who may be equally intelligent and equally capable who are without the experimental knowledge. I favor decidedly the employment of a certain proportion of deaf teachers in schools for the deaf.

13,470. I will put one more question. I will quote from the same article as before in the *American Annals* for 1881. You say: "I do not fear to "predict that the system of the future, that on "which all opposing elements will unite, and in the "upholding of which all hostility and animosity "will be transformed into generous emulation, is "the combined system;" is that your opinion still?—That is my opinion very decidedly, and I have had some recent reasons for strengthening that opinion, and for the entertaining of that hope as concerns other countries than my own. And I may add that I consider that the element of harmonious action which is found in the teaching of the deaf in America seems to have added a greater strength to the cause; that when teachers of the deaf in various methods are fighting among themselves, the public has less interest in sustaining the work than when they are acting in harmony.

13,471. (*Dr. Campbell.*) In the first instance, I would like to put a question which I have been requested to put, and I will do so before forgetting it, and that is, whether you have ever known a deaf and dumb person to speak so perfectly that you would be unable to distinguish him from an ordinary speaking person?—I have known a very few such persons. I was very much impressed when in Rotterdam, a number of years ago, with a pupil of Mr. Hirsch, who is a very eminent teacher of the oral method, of the name of Polano, who was born deaf, and who spoke in a manner that was simply marvellous. I had a long conversation with him. I walked with him arm in arm through the streets in rather a hurried manner to catch a train for which I was a little belated, and to get to which I was unable to find a carriage when I wanted it, and, to my great surprise, we were able to carry on the conversation with our faces very slightly turned towards one another, at least, with my face very slightly turned towards his. He caught the expression of my speech from a side view of my mouth, and I was able to understand him with perfect ease; and I can say of him that his speech seemed to me like the speech of a person who had always heard.

13,472. (*Chairman.*) Did he speak in English?—He spoke in German.

13,473. And do you know whether he was deaf from early life?—He was born deaf, and had a sister born deaf. That is a marked exception. I have also the acquaintance of a lady in America who has been taught to speak. I think she is a congenitally deaf person, and she was largely taught to speak by her own mother, who was very earnest and patient with her. She speaks in a voice that suggests her being a foreigner. Her voice is not quite natural; her pronunciation is a little peculiar; but she speaks with great fluency, and reads from the lips with great readiness, and altogether might converse with you for half an hour, and you would never dream she was deaf. She would stand in my own country as, I think, the most accomplished speaker and lip-reader among deaf persons I have ever known; and she had a private education, not in a school at all. But such instances are really very rare among the orally-taught deaf.

13,474. With regard to the blind, I hold that the blind themselves in using methods and so forth, are really the best judges in regard to the best apparatus, and specially as to things that apply to the touch and so forth. I should like to inquire, taking the deaf themselves, where they have been well taught both by the oral system and by the manual method, what the opinion is among that class in regard to the best method of teaching their class; is it that the combined is the best, or do they generally take either one side or the other?—I have met many deaf young men who have come to our college from the oral schools, and I have yet to remember to have learnt from any one of them that he held the opinion that the oral method was the only method that should be used in the education of the deaf. I think, without an exception, I may say I am sure without an exception, among those young men who have come to our college from the oral schools (and naturally before they get to our college course they are adults, and their judgment is worthy of considerable weight), their opinion would be in favor of a combined system which would include oral schools, even some pure oral schools, for those who might unquestionably succeed well on the oral method, at the same time it would require manual schools and manual teaching for a considerable proportion who would not be able to succeed on the oral method; and the same view would be held by those who have come to us from manual or from combined schools. In short, I think I may speak for the educated deaf in America, and say that the weight of their opinion is in favor of the combined system of educating the deaf.

13,475. In regard to the subject of marriage between deaf-mutes, you remarked that where both parties had an hereditary tendency to deafness you would discourage it; would you not go further and say that if either of the parties had an hereditary tendency, I mean from their parents, and it was known that it was in the family you would discourage their marrying even with an ordinary person?—It would depend very much on circumstances. I should say that taking a person whose family had the tendency to deafness, perhaps not very strongly pronounced, suppose that person had the opportunity of marrying another of a family where there was not the slightest tendency to deafness and where there was health and strength and vigor, there would be a considerable presumption that such a marriage might tend to eliminate the tendency to deafness; in other words, the man being the one that belonged to the family where deafness existed, the woman being of a strong and vigorous constitution, the probability would be strong that their children would not be deaf. So that it would depend on the circumstances of the individual case. It might be perhaps said in general that such persons might be advised not to marry at all, but I can easily conceive of a case arising where that would seem a very cold-hearted piece of advice to give them.

13,476. I quite admit that, but the great point is that where there is this tendency unless the circumstances are very favorable and such as you state them, there the tendency would be to hand down the calamity. I should like in the next place to know whether among the educators of the deaf and dumb in America the same thing prevails as among the blind in this respect, that so far as possible we should increase the public feeling against terming the schools for the deaf-mutes and the blind, and so forth, charity schools? The idea I want to convey is this, that it is detrimental to the class; for instance, it would be advantageous to the blind if their education was regarded in the ordinary sense, not as a charity, but as a part of the great system of the education of the country, as it is in some of the States I know, and that is growing. Is that so with the education of the deaf and dumb?—The instructors of the deaf seem very strongly disposed to ask that legislators and the public shall look upon the education of the deaf as a matter not at all of charity, but as a pure matter of right when it is admitted in any State or Nation that general public education is the right of the people; and they feel it so much that they have in several instances sharply criticized the census officers for having the particulars relating to the deaf classified with those relating to the insane and even the criminal, which is often done. That answers your question as to the opinion and feeling of the teachers of the deaf in America on that subject. They look upon it as a matter purely of educational interest, and one that should be so regarded at all points.

13,477. And for that reason the whole idea of asylums, and the consideration of charity, is as far as possible being obliterated?—That is the fact, that the word asylum is very offensive to the vast majority of teachers and officers of institutions for the deaf in America, and to the deaf themselves, conveying an idea which is wholly inconsistent with what is actually done in the institutions for the teaching of the deaf. There are but two institutions now that retain the name of asylum, the old parent school at Hartford, which, I am very sorry to say, holds on to the name, and one in Texas. I hope the day is not far distant when the oldest and most dignified of the institutions, and I will not say the least dignified, but one of the younger, will remove that word from the corporate name of their institutions.

13,478. Would there not have to be Government action to effect that at Hartford, they having originally received a large grant from the Federal Government, they would have to get the consent of the Federal Government to the change of name; is not that the reason?—That may be so in part. A mere petition to Congress, I believe, would be all that would be needed to authorize the asylum at Hartford to change its name. And I think the State Legislature of Connecticut could do it. The institution is incorporated solely under the laws of Connecticut, and when the Government of the United States gave a large tract of land, this donation was given to a corporation existing under the laws of the State of Connecticut only.

13,479. Was that donation of land in the case of Hartford given on the condition that the deaf and dumb from other States should be taken at 100 dollars per annum to be educated in the school?—I do not think any such condition was attached. As a matter of fact for many years the institution at Hartford did receive pupils from Connecticut and from the other States, and, in fact, from any, on the payment of 100 dollars per head, because from the invested fund they had money enough to make up the difference; but I do not think any law was passed. They changed the requisition in later years; they require now more than 100 dollars.

13,480. I should like to know whether there is any tendency among deaf-mutes more than ordinary persons to secret vices, whether your attention has ever been called to that?—I would answer that, so far as I am able to speak, I think not. That there is that tendency, of course, goes without saying, and in an establishment where many children and youths are brought together there must be much watchfulness to reduce the practice of such vices to the lowest possible point. Human nature is human nature, and I do not know that there is any more of it in the deaf than there is in other people.

13,481. (*Chairman.*) I should like to ask you some further questions. You told us that you have visited most of the institutions for the deaf and dumb, both in England and on the Continent, and you have visited specially the oral schools, where the German system is adopted?—Quite a number of them.

13,482. Do you think that the oral schools in Germany are more advanced in the success of their teaching than in England and in America, as far as your knowledge goes?—I am really not able to speak from a recent examination of those schools.

13,483. How long ago was it that you visited them?—It runs back now to my visit of 1867, so that I am not able to speak of recent advances in Germany.

13,484. I think that you have visited later than that date the schools at Milan?—Yes, at the time of the convention, six years ago.

13,485. Did you find the oral system there carried out to a very full degree?—I found it in a very high state of perfection.

13,486. From your visits both to Germany and Italy, do you think that the German or the Italian language lends itself more readily to the oral system than English does?—Speaking in a rising way of the facility and adaptedness of language for the purposes of oral instruction, I think that the German language is probably best fitted for success in speech of the deaf; the Italian would follow, the French would follow that, and the English would be found the most difficult of the four. That is my experience, and I think that that view is generally held. German is the easiest, in fact, there every letter is pronounced. Then follows the Italian; that has a great advantage in its liquid sounds, and its open expression of the mouth, especially in lip-reading. Then again the French is less difficult than English. I believe that view would be sustained generally, and may be taken as one reason why in schools of English-speaking countries it should not be absolutely insisted upon that all the deaf should be educated under the oral system. It is an absolutely practical question.

13,487. Then I understand you generally from your evidence to say, that, although the combined system is the one that is gaining most ground in America, yet it is in consequence of the older schools having adopted the oral system more or less, that you have formed that opinion?—Quite so. It is true that the effort made 20 years ago by the promoters of the oral teaching, which was at first ridiculed and resisted by very many of the old teachers in schools where the manual method was used, has resulted most beneficially to the welfare of the whole mass of the deaf, and that the managers of the old manual schools have been compelled in many instances, often at first against their will, to recognize the value of oral teaching to at least a large portion of the deaf, and so they have come at length to accept it very heartily.

13,488. Are the schools in the United States for the deaf and dumb all conducted and built on as large and as liberal a scale as those at Washington?—Very many of them are. I have visited within two or three years the schools of the South, (that is a portion of the country which you are aware, suffered very much from the war 20 years ago), and I was extremely gratified to notice that the Legislatures even in those States had been ready to make handsome provision for the education of the deaf, in putting up commodious buildings, providing large grounds, introducing the oral teaching, and generally reaching results that would compare favorably with the results of any part of our country. In the richer States in the west, and the north, and the east, there are many other establishments that are provided for as to grounds and buildings on a scale quite as commodious and extensive as the institution at Washington.

13, 489. In all those cases is the ground itself and the grant for the building provided at the expense

Dr. E. M. Gallaudet.

10 Nov. 1886.

of the State, or is it in any case, or generally by private munificence?—The practice differs in different parts of the country. In the State of New York, the recent policy has been for the State to decline to appropriate money for the purchase of ground, or very much for the erection of buildings. They have been provided by the donations of residents of the locality in which it was proposed to establish these institutions; and after they are established and provided for as to the grounds and buildings, then the State under a general law, gives a *per capita* allowance to all the schools in the State for the deaf.

13,490. We had evidence from Mr. Hall, that New York gives a subsidy of 20,000 dollars a year to the education of the blind; do you know at all whether the same system of large grants of that kind applies to the education of the deaf and dumb?—No, it does not, and for this reason: the institution of which Mr. Hall speaks, in New York, is a State institution, pure and simple. There are no such institutions for the deaf in New York.

13,491. Is there not one at New York for the deaf on the oral system?—Yes, but it is a corporate institution. This one for the blind stands rather by itself as a State institution, under the control of the State Legislature. Purely State institutions are those which the State absolutely controls: corporate institutions are those which the State may assist to the extent I have described.

13,492. My question was whether there is any similar grant by New York to the deaf and dumb, to that which is made to the blind?—I am quite sure there is not.

13,493. (*Dr. Campbell.*) In these corporate institutions where the State pays for the education of the blind, in most of them, not in all, the State has the power of appointing a certain number of the governing body, has it not?—That is the fact. The entity of the corporation exists, the autonomy, but there comes into it as there does at the institution in Washington, this element of State supervision by the presence of directors on the part of the State.

13,494. (*Mr. Johnson.*) I suppose as a general principle the State goes hand in hand with benevolence?—Yes.

13,495. (*Chairman.*) But what I wanted to know is this: With regard to New York. I think you told us that there is only a pure oral school at New York?—Do you mean the city or the State?

13,496. I have got in my notes that the leading school in New York was a pure oral one; I have not a note as to whether that applied to the State or to the city?—That is not the case in the city. The leading school in the city is one that is sustained on the combined system. There is a very flourishing oral school in the city which has 200 pupils, but the other has as many as 400.

13,497. I wanted to elicit by my question, whether side by side in a large city like New York there were the means of education on the two systems?—Quite so.

13,498. Therefore, of course, nobody would be forced to go either to the one system or to the other, but he would have the option of both?—Yes; and in the whole of New England there is a legislative provision which makes it possible for the parent of any deaf child to elect whether that child shall go to Northampton, where there is a pure oral school, or to Hartford, where there is a combined-system school: they may choose; and it has very often been the case that parents having had their children in the oral school for a year or two, and not finding their progress satisfactory, have placed them in the other. They change from one to the other.

13,499. They have that power?—They have that power.

13,500. Do you think that it should be attempted to teach all the children the oral system, and that in the case of those who are failures, after a certain time it should be given up and they should be taught the manual system; so that all should have the opportunity of being tested as to their capabilities of learning the oral system: do you think that that is desirable?—My opinion is very earnest on that point. I do urge it strongly, and I am glad to be able to say that opinion is gaining ground very much in my own country: and I think the time is very near when persistent efforts will be made to give to every child the opportunity of learning to speak, and that those efforts will only be intermitted or given up altogether when it seems to be certain that the child will not be able to succeed in speech.

13,501. Assuming that it is desirable that the oral system should be taught if it can be taught it would be quite possible to teach every child, say for one or two years, on the oral system, and yet not lose any material portion of the time available for instruction. If the child was found to be unfitted for the oral system it might then go on at the age of nine to the manual system, and not be in a worse position than children were before under the old system with the advantage that in that way every child would have its capacity for speech tested?—I can only give my assent in this qualified manner, that I should hardly lay down a limit of two or three years as the period for which it is necessary that the oral system should be taught; because sometimes in six months it might be very plainly shown that the child was making no progress at all; in other cases it could not be settled in six months, or there would be a certain measure of success that would suggest that the effort should be continued. And then the same thing may happen with the deaf as we find happens in our education of the blacks in America. We find in many instances that when the blacks begin their course of instruction their minds develop very rapidly, and after two or three years they reach a certain point and seem incapable of going on further. That is the case with the black race. So in the case of the deaf, it might be that for a year or two the deaf child might do very well in speech, and then it would seem to be impossible for him to go any further. With that qualification I would assent to the views suggested in your question.

13,502. Would you carry out that in the combined system by a system simply of separate classes, or of separate instruction in a separate building, and draft them off from the one building to the other as their education required?—My impression would be that the result could be reached in either way. The separate building and the separate school, for instance, such as I have spoken of in Philadelphia, would seem to be suggested only in cases which from the very start might be counted as quite hopeful cases. Let them be placed at once in a school of that sort; but in the matter of determining whether others are going to succeed or not, I think that experiment could be made and results ascertained either by instruction in a class or in some other way. In a variety of ways the test might be made. I do not think it is necessary to lay down one rigid method of making that test, if only the test is faithfully and fully made.

13,503. I gathered from what you said that you would not forbid the use of signs in connection with the early teaching of the oral system?—So far from it, I should say that the test can be certainly in my judgment better made by placing the teacher in possession of any means of communication that is free and full between the child and the teacher. So that in my opinion the use of signs during these experimental years is far from being detrimental, it even assists the teacher: and I have seen oral teachers carry a pupil right over a difficulty in speech by the judicious use of gesture: so that I have no question, but that in oral teaching the use of signs is often of great assistance.

13,504. (*Mr. Johnson.*) Can the pure oral system according to your American view be carried on side by side with that of manual signs or the alphabet; you are aware that it is on the pure oral method that so much controversy has arisen in England?—I certainly say that classes in which the oral method (if I may use that form of expression instead of "the pure oral method") is rigidly adhered to, may exist side by side in institutions or schools with classes where signs are used and more or less interchange of the use of signs goes on, and at the same time extremely satisfactory results in speech be attained. There is evidence of that in many of our best schools.

13,505. (*Chairman.*) I should be glad if you could give us the daily routine of teaching and the play-hours and meals in your primary school and also in your college at Washington; could you hand that in, or is it stated in any report?—With regard to the college I can give it to you now. In the college, recitations begin in the morning at a quarter past eight, and they are continued in lengths of three-quarters of an hour each.

13,506. What time do the students rise in the morning?—They breakfast at seven. The first recitation is at a quarter past eight, the recitations continuing after that for three-quarters of an hour duration, with 15 minutes interval between one recitation and the next, until mid-day, when at half past 12 their principal meal is served. Occasionally a recitation is had in the afternoon from two to three, when it is necessary. That is not always done. When the arrangement of classes makes it possible to have all the actual recitations during the forenoon a study time is prescribed from half past one until half past three in the afternoon, when the students are expected to be in their rooms.

13,507. Have they no recreation until after dinner?—The recitations end at 12. They go into the dining-room at half past 12, and usually spend half an hour in the dining-room and have half an hour for recreation, until they go into their rooms to study at half past one. Then from half past three till six o'clock they are quite at liberty, with the exception of an hour taken on four days of the week for physical training at the gymnasium, which of course is exercise for them. At six o'clock their supper is served, and from half past seven to ten they are supposed to be at study. There is a little latitude allowed with reference to that; they may be engaged in writing letters part of the time, or sometimes they have permission to be absent in order to pay social visits; but those are the prescribed hours.

13,508. Will you explain to us exactly what "recitations" are?—"Recitations" means in the college the meeting of the instructor with the class for the purpose of examination in a portion which has been prescribed in some text-book, and the time is spent in examining the class to see whether they have acquired an understanding of that portion of the text-book. These examinations go on from day to day.

13,509. In fact, it is question and answer on the part of the teacher and students?—Yes. These differ from the exercises of the class-room, as they would be understood in an ordinary school, where the scholars are expected to be in the class-room with their teacher and do their study there, and have explanations from the teacher there, and so forth. The studying of the students in the college is all done in their private rooms, and they come to the class-room for this purpose of recitation and meeting their instructor, and showing that they have properly mastered the portions assigned for study in the text-book.

13,510. What proportion of those instructions are given by the finger-language, and what by signs? Of course there are some things that cannot be expressed by signs?—Very little is done in the recitations of the college by signs. The greater part of the communication between the pupils and the teacher is by the manual alphabet. Some portions of it, where the pupil is a good lip-reader and speaker, are given orally, but it is found to be difficult under that method to have the attention of the entire class to everything that is said by pupil and instructor as well; so that the manual alphabet and writing on large slate tablets, or writing theses on paper, may be said to be the means used mainly for giving the question and answer in recitation.

13,511. Do you make use of looking-glasses in your class-rooms to assist the view of the teachers?—In oral teaching we do.

13,512. And in all cases they are in separate rooms for oral teaching?—Yes, we have no two classes in one room.

13,513. What proportion of the teachers are of the first class or second class; that is to say, what proportion of the teachers in your college are upper teachers, and what proportion lower teachers?—In our college we have an active faculty of six professors, including myself. My own professorship is that of moral and political science. Then there are three regular—we term them— professors and two assistant professors. That is the only division of rank in the college. Those two assistant professors are graduates of the college, deaf men who speak very well, and they will probably in a year or two be promoted to be professors.

13,514. Are they deaf men who have had speech and then become deaf?—Yes.

13,515. Can you tell us the remuneration of the professors generally in the college?—In our college the professor who ranks next myself, and now acts as president in my absence, receives 3,000 dollars and a house. Two other professors receive 2,400 dollars each and a house. Of the assistant professors, one receives 1,500 dollars and a house, who is a man with a family; and the other, who is a bachelor, receives 1,500 dollars and a suite of rooms, and is boarded in the family of the institution.

13,516. There are no totally congenitally deaf professors?—Not in the college.

13,517. But in the primary school are there?—In the primary school we have one.

13,518. Is your primary school, in connection with this institution at Washington, a fair sample of the other deaf and dumb schools in America in its methods of teaching; I mean is it a pattern that is followed?—I may say this, that the general method and arrangement of classes and giving instruction is quite the same as prevails in the State institutions, the primary schools, throughout the country.

13,519. Could you give us in the same way the daily routine of a combined school?—In the tables which I have referred to on one or two occasions, contained in the January number of the *Annals* of this year, that is stated very fully with reference to each school.

13,520. When I was speaking of your visit to the Continent, there was one question which I omitted to ask you. You have before referred to the Convention at Milan. I should like to know whether, having been present there, you can inform us what the constitution of the Convention was. You have, perhaps, already given a description of it elsewhere which you might read to us?—I referred to it, and said in general that it was not looked upon as a representative body, but I am able to say, quoting from an article which I published after the meeting at Milan (which took place in 1880) that "out of "the 164 active members of the Convention, 87, or "a clear majority of 10, were from Italy; that 56 "were from France, making, with the Italian members, a majority of seven-eighths; that of the "eight English delegates, six were ardent articulationists, and only two at all favorable to any other

Dr. E. M. Gallaudet.

10 Nov. 1886.

"method; a proportion, which entirely misrepresents the present" (in 1880) "sentiment of English teachers of the deaf; that the only truly representative delegation present was that from the United States, consisting of five members duly accredited to the Milan meeting by a conference of principals of American Institutions for the Deaf and Dumb held at Northampton last May, in which the supporters of the several methods of instruction now made use of in this country (including all that are known in the world) were assembled in friendly council; that the American delegates represented 51 schools, containing over 6,000 pupils, a greater number than was represented by all the other 159 delegates taken together; that the Convention allowed the American delegates to be out-voted in the proportion of nearly 10 to one by the representatives of the two schools of Milan, they being accorded 46 seats in the Convention." I think that would be sufficient to make it evident that the Convention at Milan was in no sense a representative body; it was an assemblage in which it happened that those who were in favor of the oral method were largely in the ascendant at the beginning. There were two very large oral schools at Milan which had produced remarkably good results, and those two schools were accorded 46 seats in the Convention; and that had this result, that on a vote, if any vote was taken affecting the pure oral system, the remonstrance of any of us from America who felt that the pure oral method was not the best for all the deaf, was of no avail.

13,521. Are you aware at all of the steps that were taken by the permanent committee for endeavoring to obtain a convention of a representative character on that occasion?—I am well aware that the invitation of the committee which went out before this meeting at Milan was extended to all teachers of the deaf of institutions of every sort and every method in all countries.

13,522. (*Mr. St. John Ackers.*) So that everybody had an opportunity of coming?—Most certainly everybody had an opportunity of coming, but when we from America, five in number, had come (and we could not bring a hundred from America owing to the shortness even of an American purse) and we were in a position actually to represent the whole body of institutions in America, as I have said in my article there, representing some 6,000 pupils and over 50 schools, we were allowed five votes and no more in making up the conclusion which was reached by this Milan Convention. The invitation was broad enough to every one, but when it was found that from America there were five only who represented this large constituency, there was no motion made to limit the representation from Italy or from France, or even from the schools in Milan, where 46 persons were allowed each to cast his ballot, and determine the results, as against five votes which we had when we had a backing of 6,000 pupils, as compared with 300 of theirs. I think it is evident that, while the invitation was broad enough to the Convention, when it came to be constituted and it was found who were there, and what they represented, no notice whatever was taken of the fact that the five American delegates, or the eight English delegates, represented a far larger and stronger constituency than these Italians and French delegates who outvoted all the rest.

13,523. (*Chairman.*) I think you have furnished us in this report of your college with various facts with regard to gymnastic training; I understand that you have, not very long ago, fitted out a complete gymnasium?—You will find a drawing of it in that number.

13,524. And you have also a large swimming school and two bowling alleys?—Yes.

13,525. Do you find that the health of the inmates of the college has been improved since those have been added to the institution?—We find that there has been a remarkable improvement, both physically and morally. A moment's reflection may show you that when a lot of youths like that have the opportunity of working off their physical strength and vigor and steam in gymnastic exercises, they are much more amenable to discipline; and so we find the effect to be wonderfully helpful both from a physical and moral point of view; and I may, by relating a little incident, show how marked that result has been. At an anniversary which occurred two years ago when the first class of our college which had gone completely through the college course of gymnastic training, appeared before the public, Mr. Bayard, now our Secretary of State in America, and then a director of the institution, was on the platform, and after the exercises were over he said to me: "I want to ask you a question. I was very much struck with the fact that every young man who came up on to this platform to deliver his address at graduation and to receive his degree, came up with a firm, manly, vigorous step. Now, I have noticed in ordinary colleges that a certain number will be men who look feeble and delicate." I said: "You remember this is the first class that has been entirely through its course in gymnastic training." The fact was that there were two young men among that number who entered the college apparently soon to die. One with a hollow, flat chest and no muscles at all seemed to be a candidate for an early grave from consumption. He came out as well-rounded and vigorous as any of the others. And I cannot speak in too strong terms of the importance of gymnastic training for the deaf.

13,526. I think you have kept some statistics with regard to the muscular improvement and measurement round the chest, also, of some of your pupils?—Yes, we have done so: and they will be found in the twenty-fifth of the annual reports bound up in the volumes I have left with you.

13,527. Will you kindly refer us to the passage?—There is a paragraph in our report made in June, 1882, with reference to some of the results of physical training. The paragraph is as follows: "The results growing out of the work done in our new gymnasium have been most gratifying, whether they are regarded from a moral or a physical point of view. The morale of the institution was never as high as during the past year. The instances where discipline became necessary have been very few as compared with former years, and the reactive effects of an improved physique on the mental and moral faculties has been markedly favorable in many instances. During the six months from November 1 to May 1, all the students of the college and the older boys from the primary school were required to spend four hours a week in active gymnastic exercises, viz., an hour on Monday, Tuesday, Thursday, and Friday of each week. These exercises consisted of dumb-bell practice, in concert, intended to open the lungs, stir the blood, and set in motion the whole body, and in the development of special muscles by the use of a number of ingeniously prepared machines, designed and furnished by Dr. D. A. Sargent, the director of the gymnasium of Harvard University. The dumb-bell exercise was acquired with great readiness, and given with precision, the idea of rhythm and time in marching being conveyed by the assistance of drum beats. The great benefit arising from the use of the special apparatus has been clearly shown in the uniform increase of chest girths, arm girths, &c.; in the erect carriage and springy step of the students, and above all in the desire for *regular* exercise, as shown in their work on days when the "exercise was not compulsory. The physique of "each student was carefully recorded in a series of "42 measurements taken at the beginning and "again at the end of the season. The average "chest girth of about 50 young men showed the "following gains:—

	November.	May.
"Inflated - -	·897	·918
"Repose - -	·853	·864

"The measurements given are decimals of a "meter.

"The greatest gain in chest girth was:—

	November.	May.
"Inflated -	·890	·972
"Repose -	·855	·910

"Some interesting cases occurred of the develop-"ment of limbs into symmetrical proportions where "marked discrepancies existed when the first meas-"urements were taken. A single illustration will "be sufficient:—

	November.	May.
"Right calf - -	·377	·388
"Left calf - -	·373	·388
"Upper right arm -	·297	·305
"Upper left arm -	·300	·305"

We were able to produce symmetry in that young man whose left side at one time had probably been slightly paralyzed.

13,528. (*Mr. Johnson.*) With regard to what you have said about the Milan Conference, I should like to put a question to you. Have you any idea what are the opinions of the teachers of the deaf and dumb in America as to the adoption by the London School Board of the oral system of teaching; has it been made a subject of any comment or consideration amongst the teachers of the deaf and dumb in America?—I can say that it has not been in any formal manner in convention, but it has been commented upon, and decided regret has been expressed that where so many children were to be taken care of as in these schools in London, that rigid rule has been laid down, and it has been felt that the best results would not be obtained.

13,529. Were those gentlemen whom you consulted, or with whom you talked, aware how it was that the London School Board came to that conclusion; might they have been guided, do you think, by the results of the Milan International Convention?—It has been a subject of complaint in America among teachers there, that the action of the Milan Convention seemed to have had an effect in England far greater than we could bring ourselves to recognize in America as proper; but that has always been spoken of as a matter of some little surprise.

13,530. (*Rev. C. M. Owen.*) Because it was not of a sufficiently representative character?—Precisely so.

13,531. (*Admiral Sir E. Sotheby.*) What are the hours that the professors are supposed to be present in the college; how many hours?—The professors of the college are on an average engaged in three recitations each day, of from three-quarters of an hour to an hour each. That, however, does not represent by any means the entire amount of time that they give to the work of their professionships, for essays are submitted to them, preparations are made for lectures, and much work is done outside those three hours. They are required to give lectures, and to perform duties, and attend faculty meetings, and to do other things in connection with the work of their professionships that would very much extend the hours that were given to their duties. So that in speaking of the hours given to duty by college professors, it would be extremely difficult and unjust to make any comparison between them, and the hours that might be expected to be required of teachers in a primary school, who would go into the school-room and remain in it five hours.

13,532. How many hours do you think the professors give altogether, from the time they go into the college, until they come out of it?—They are supposed to give all their strength.

13,533. But then they are professors elsewhere, are they not?—No, they are not.

13,534. They hold no other office?—No.

13,535. They cannot?—They would not be expected to.

The witness withdrew.

Adjourned to Friday, December 3, at twelve o'clock.

EXHIBITS.

The following Exhibits were made by Pres. E. M. Gallaudet during the course of his evidence before the Royal Commission.

CENSUS RETURNS FOR 1830, 1840, 1850.

[This Exhibit consisted of the following article by Harvey P. Peet, LL. D., entitled "Statistics of the Deaf and Dumb," published in the *American Annals of the Deaf* for October, 1852, Vol. V, pp. 1-21.]

My attention has been, by various circumstances, recently drawn to the subject set forth in the heading of this paper; and I have taken pains to procure from the Census Office such Tables as could be furnished, from the returns of the last Census, respecting the deaf and dumb. Some of these Tables, so far as I know, have not yet been made public, and though by no means as full and complete as we could wish, yet by comparison with the results of European enumerations, and with the returns of the Census of 1830 and 1840, some conclusions can be formed, not without interest and value, to those interested in the deaf and dumb.

It is greatly to be regretted that Congress has not yet authorized the printing of the list of all the Deaf and Dumb in the Union, as asked for by the memorial presented in pursuance of a resolution of the Convention of 1850, and there is some reason to fear (judging from the report of the committee on printing the Census) that the printing of this most interesting and valuable document may finally be refused. There is reason to hope, however, that if it be not printed, a manuscript copy may be obtained from the Census Office; in which case, at least the results of a careful examination of it will be made public in due time.

In the meanwhile, I have been obliged to content myself with the tables obligingly furnished me from the Census Office, which exhibit no smaller subdivisions than States, and in the classification of the deaf and dumb, though better adapted to the purposes of comparison than that adopted in the two former enumerations, is far from being as minute as could be desired. One of these Tables, which has been published in the National Intelligencer, and thus has become generally accessible, gives the number in each State, of the deaf and dumb, blind, insane, and idiotic, distinguished according to sex, and whether white, free colored, or slaves. The other Table, which has not, as I am aware, yet been published, includes the deaf and dumb only, in two separate statements, first, classed as white, and free colored, and each again distinguished as male and female, and as under ten; ten and under thirty; thirty and under seventy, and seventy and upward. Columns had been set apart for those unable to read and write, but no figures are found in them. In the second part of this Table, all the free (white and colored included together and the sexes not distinguished) are classed as born in the State, born in the United States, born in foreign countries, and place of birth unknown. Respecting the slaves deaf and dumb, a statement is given of their ages only.

The whole number returned, as "*born in the State*," is 6,937; "*born in the United States*," 1,959; "*born in foreign countries*," 567; place of birth unknown, 151, of whom 112 were returned from Illinois, probably nearly all by the neglect of a single assistant marshal. Of the 1,959, about 210 or 220 are known to have been attending school out of their own State, to which nearly all of them will return, leaving only about 1,740 who really resided in a State not their native State; or less than one emigrant to four who remained at home. The classification of the general population in respect to place of nativity has not yet been completed. When it is made public, we shall be able to say positively what proportion of deaf-mutes are found among emigrants. That their proportion is probably smaller than among those who remain at home, I shall presently show from other considerations. I will here only remark that the number of deaf-mutes of foreign birth is only about one-seventeenth of the whole (slaves not included), and as there have been more than a million and a half of emigrants landed in the country within the last ten years, and more than three-quarters of a million within the preceding ten, it may safely be estimated that the population of foreign birth is much more than one-seventeenth part of the whole free population.

Neither has the classification of the general population according to age yet been completed. In order to compare the numbers of the deaf and dumb of the several ages embraced in the official table with the whole population of the same age and color, I have been obliged to estimate the numbers of the present population of the different ages as in the same proportion that they were in the same States in 1840: which, though not strictly accurate, will, it is believed, be found very nearly so. With these preliminary remarks, I pass to the proposed brief examination of the statistics of the deaf and dumb.

It is only since the instruction of the deaf and dumb began to attract general attention, and to receive the aid of governments, a period comparatively very recent, that any enumerations of this class of population have been made. Consequently the statistics of the deaf and dumb are yet very imperfect. Something, however, has been done, both by order of governments and by the conductors of institutions who have kept records respecting their pupils, within the last thirty years, and the materials thus collected already present a respectable bulk, and give promise of permanent value.

One result of the different enumerations made is that, as far back as they extend (only twenty-five or thirty years at most) the number of deaf-mutes in a given country is not found to vary greatly from a certain proportion to the population of the country. Whatever the causes of deafness may be, they are found so far constant that, in any populous and long-settled district, the proportion of deaf-mutes seldom varies greatly from one period to another. And though different countries, or differently circumstanced districts of the same country, may vary very considerably in their proportions of deaf-mutes, yet even this variation has its limits. A few extreme cases excepted, there is, I believe, no country inhabited by Europeans or their descendants, in which, in a population of a million, there are less than three hundred and fifty deaf-mutes, or more than about eight hundred.

Of the extreme cases that have been referred to, the most remarkable are presented by certain districts of Switzerland, and the adjoining Duchy of Baden in Germany. The Canton of Berne contained, in 1836, 1,954 deaf-mutes in a population of 401,000, nearly one deaf-mute in every two hundred souls. In that country, deaf-dumbness seems often connected with, or complicated by the greater infirmity of *cretinism*, so prevalent in many parts of Switzerland.

Throughout Germany, with the exception of Baden, where the proportion of deaf-mutes is said to be as high as one in five hundred souls; the proportion, in any considerable district, only varies from one in 1,240 souls in Wurtemburg, to one in 2,180 in Saxony. And I believe there are no countries in which deaf-mutes have yet been enumerated, Switzerland and Baden excepted, in which the proportions much transcend these limits, whether on the one side or on the other.

Prussia seems to represent nearly the mean proportion, both of Germany and of Europe, having about one deaf-mute in every 1,550 souls. And this proportion being found nearly the average of all the countries in which enumerations of the deaf-mute population have yet been made, has been assumed to represent the general proportion in the whole human family, thus enabling us to estimate that, at a very moderate computation of the population of the world, there must be at least half a million of our fellow-beings bereft of the faculties of hearing and speech. It must be remembered, however, that, with the single exception of the colored population of the United States, enumerations of deaf-mutes have only been made among nations of European races. Among the Asiatic, African, and aboriginal American races the results may prove quite different. A few years since, the Rev. Samuel R. Brown, formerly a teacher of the deaf and dumb in the New York Institution, and then a missionary in China, made particular inquiry in that country for deaf-mutes, but never met one, and could only hear of one case. Blindness, however, was very common in the celestial empire. I shall by and by show that in our own country deaf-dumbness is less prevalent among the African race than among the whites, while with blindness the cases are reversed. It would not be surprising if the same peculiarity—greater liability to deafness, and less to blindness—should hereafter be found to characterize the white races, when data shall have been obtained for comparing them in this respect with the other great divisions of the human family.

I may here add that from the returns of the late Census, insanity is more prevalent than idiocy among the whites, and idiocy more prevalent than insanity among the blacks, another marked characteristic of the races, which I leave to the consideration of those who have made physiology a study.

Speaking of the greater liability of one race than another to certain infirmities, it may be observed that it would not be surprising if different families of the European stock should be found liable in different degrees to the loss of hearing, the Teutonic races, for instance, more than the Celtic: but this is a point which must be left to the result of future investigations, no data now existing for forming a satisfactory judgment on it. But as the first enumeration of the deaf and dumb of Ireland has just been made at the instance of Dr. Wilde, of Dublin, who will spare no pains to make the returns accurate and comprehensive, when the results are made public, they may, perhaps, by comparison with enumerations made in this and other countries where Teutonic races prevail, enable us to form satisfactory conclusions on this as well as on many other points of interest.

That a liability to deafness should run through a whole race need not surprise us, for deafness certainly *runs in families*. And though perhaps only one in fifty of deaf-mute heads of families may have deaf-mute children, yet they are more liable to have such children, other causes being equal, than heads of families who have no family predisposition. Cases are recorded, though rare, in which deafness has appeared in certain families through three generations.*

The inquiry respecting the liability of different races to deaf-dumbness is quite a novel one, but greater attention has been paid to the question of the influence of climate and of modes of living on the prevalence of this infirmity. Switzerland, where the proportion of deaf-mutes is excessively great, is a cold, mountainous, and humid region. Saxony and Belgium, where this proportion is small, are comparatively level, dry, and fertile. Warm countries, as Tuscany, appear to contain, on the whole, a smaller proportion of deaf-mutes than cold countries, as Denmark and Scotland, but the difference is not great nor very uniform. Still it is very probable climate has an important influence on the prevalence of deafness, though among the many causes that may influence the proportion of deaf-mutes in a given district it is difficult to judge how much of the result is due to each.

Hence it is that no satisfactory conclusions can be formed from the proportions in districts of small population. It is only by collecting together a number of districts similar in climate, elevation, or other circumstances, so that the operation of other causes may nearly balance each other, and the influence we wish to investigate run through the whole, or be manifestly deficient in the whole, that we can confidently pronounce on the effect of such influences. Such a laborious comparison of Census returns to any extent has never yet been made, but it is in contemplation to attempt it in part when we are in possession of the list of the deaf and dumb in the United States. Meantime, from the general statement we have some conclusions may be formed not wholly uninteresting or uninstructive.

The value of the enumerations of the deaf and dumb made in this country, before the last made in 1850, has been greatly impaired, both by the scantiness of the particulars noted, and by the carelessness of the returning officers. The most remarkable instance of this carelessness is in the fact that many white deaf-mutes must, in 1830 and 1840, have been placed in the column appropriated to colored deaf-mutes (we have noted colored deaf-mutes returned from certain towns from which no colored population was returned); the effect of which was to propagate widely what now proves to be a very erroneous idea, that deaf mutes were far more numerous, proportionally, among the colored population of the Northern States than among the whites. The last census (in taking which a line was given to every individual noting the color, sex, age, etc., of each opposite his or her name) has set this right, and shown that in fact the proportion of deaf-mutes, as I have already remarked, is much smaller among the free colored people than among the whites, the case with the blind being just the reverse. Among the slaves the proportion of deaf-mutes is still much smaller. There may be here some reason to distrust the accuracy of the census, as we can hardly imagine the master or overseer of a large number of slaves as ready and accurate in giving a description of each, as the head of an ordinary family in giving a description of each member of the family, and the smallest proportion of deaf-mutes returned among the slaves is in those States where they are owned in the largest numbers by few masters. Still it would be quite consistent with the theory of the greater liability of the white race to deafness to find the free colored, who have in general, a larger admixture of white blood, more liable to that infirmity than the slaves. The difference between these two classes may be owing in part to this, and in part to the greater inaccuracy of the enumeration of the slaves.

Besides the influence of climate and of race, it has been held that a want of physical comforts and of enlightened care in infancy, tends to increase the prevalence of deafness as of other infirmities. It has been believed that deafness is more common, in proportion to numbers, among the poor who inhabit uncomfortable and unwholesome dwellings, and take comparatively little care of the wants of their children, than among the more intelligent and better provided classes. On this point, however, we have as yet little definite statistical information.

The great apparent proportion of deaf-mutes among the free people of color used to be cited in confirmation of this theory, as this class of population are generally among the poorest and worst lodged: but, as we have seen, this proves to be a mere error in the returns. And the fact that the smallest proportion of deaf-mutes is returned from great cities where poverty is found in the most miserable extremes, is certainly unfavorable to the theory under consideration. It may be, indeed, that the returns from cities are more inaccurate

* Twenty-eighth Report of the American Asylum, p. 41.

than from country districts, but we may also suppose that in the great mortality among children in cities and in unhealthy localities, deaf and dumb children, or those liable to become so, being probably below the average in soundness of constitution and tenacity of life, perish more readily than others.

In examining the returns of the census, I will not go into the details of each State. The population of some of the States is too small to make the proportion of deaf-mutes of much statistical value, and moreover, in the several New England States, this proportion is greatly affected by the fact that a large proportion of their deaf-mutes were absent from the families to which they belong, being collected into one school at Hartford. A like circumstance affects the proportion in the Middle States, though to a less degree. I shall therefore class the States in sections, so arranged as to place together those most alike in certain circumstances.

For the purpose of comparing the last census with the former ones, I shall, for the convenience of availing myself of calculations previously made, class the States as 1, New England; 2, The four Middle States, New York, New Jersey, Pennsylvania, and Delaware; 3, The Northwestern States, from Ohio to Iowa; 4, The Southern Atlantic States from Maryland to Georgia; 5, The Southwestern and extreme Southern from Florida to Missouri; 6, The extreme Western which appear for the first time in the last census in two divisions, first, Texas and New Mexico, second, California and the Territories. For the purpose of comparing different sections of the Union together, I shall presently make a different division of the States.

The annexed Table exhibits the numbers and proportion to the whole population of the same color of the white deaf and dumb at each census in each of the six or seven great sections of the Union just defined.

There seem to be certain periods when deafness becomes in a small degree epidemic in a certain district. Hence we find an increase in the proportion of deaf-mute children, not as I shall hereafter explain, at the census taken while those children are in early infancy and the deaf-mutism of many of them yet unrecognized, but at the next succeeding census. At the third census the proportion generally decreases; and if the epidemic period be not repeated, it settles down to the average or below it. Thus, in New Jersey there was in 1830, one deaf-mute to 1,352 souls; in 1,840, one to 1,953, and in 1850, only one to 2,220.* The decrease in the Northwestern States, between 1830 and 1840, may be owing, besides the supposed inaccuracy of the census, to the great emigration into that region, there always being a smaller proportion of deaf-mutes in a population composed of recent immigrants than in a stationary population; and the increase of the last census can only be ascribed to one of these epidemic periods, probably occurring between 1830 and 1840, though not affecting the census till 1850.

Among the causes that make deafness more prevalent at certain periods than at others, are various diseases, as scarlet fever, small-pox and measles, in the case of accidental deafness; and in cases of congenital deafness, maternal anxiety, to which many cases are ascribed, with what degree of truth it would be presumptuous now to judge, may sometimes become epidemic. At least there are certain years in which the nervous system of females is rendered more than usually excitable, and shocks that may have a deleterious influence on the offspring are more common. This is particularly the case in a country that is the seat of war. Many mothers in France have ascribed the infirmity of their congenitally deaf children to alarms sustained during the invasion of France by the Allies in 1814 and 1815, and its subsequent occupation. When we are able

TABLE I.

STATES.	1830 White Population.	1830 Whole D. & D.	Ratio.	1840 White Population.	1840 Whole D. & D.	Ratio.	1850 White Population.	1850 Whole D. & D.	Ratio.
New England	1,933,338	1,074	1·1800	2,212,165	1,194	1·1854	2,705,772	1,504	1·1799
Four Middle States	3,541,430	1,842	1·1923	4,465,154	2,029	1·2201	5,845,449	2,750	1·2125
Six N. W. States	1,454,135	648	1·2244	2,938,307	1,057	1·2780	4,671,381	2,163	1·2160
Total Northern States	6,928,903	3,564	1·1944	9,615,626	4,280	1·2247	13,222,602	6,417	1·2060
Five S. States and D. C.	2,040,483	1,115	1·1830	2,240,901	1,252	1·1790	2,701,277	1,483	1·1821
Eight S. W. States	1,562,674	684	1·2284	2,332,601	1,150	1·2028	3,297,574	1,486	1·2220
Total Southern States	3,603,157	1,799	1·2003	4,573,502	2,402	1·1904	5,998,851	2,969	1·2020
Texas and New Mexico	......	......	......	......	......	......	215,630	77	1·2800
California, Utah, Oregon, and Minnesota.	......	......	......	......	......	......	193,655	6	1·52,276
Total of the U. S.	10,532,060	5,363	1·1964	14,189,218	6,682	1·2123	19,630,738	9,469	1·2070
Total Atlantic States	7,515,251	4,031	1·1864	8,918,310	4,475	1·1993	11,252,498	5,737	1·1961
Total Western States and Territories.	3,016,809	1,332	1·2250	5,270,908	2,207	1·2388	8,378,240	3,732	1,2245

From this Table it will be seen that the proportion of deaf-mutes, in each great section of the Union, has remained tolerably uniform. In New England, it has, within the twenty years, varied only between 1.1799 and 1.1854; in the Southern Atlantic States, only between 1.1790 and 1.1830; in the Middle States, between 1.1923 and 1.2201; in the Southwestern States, between 1.2028 and 1.2220. The greatest disturbance of the ratio has been in the Northwestern States, where it was 1.2244 in 1830, 1.2780 in 1840, and 1.2160 in 1850. This fluctuation of the proportion of deaf-mutes in the Northwestern States I am hardly prepared to account for. It may be owing, in part, to an unusual inaccuracy in taking the census of 1840 in these States; and in part, to unknown causes by which deafness may have been rendered more prevalent in that region since about the year 1835 than between 1825 and 1835. This is a point that demands some examination.

to make out a more minute statement of the ages of our deaf-mute population than we yet possess, we shall examine whether a proportion larger than the average seems to have been born in time of war. It should be added, that some of the diseases that destroy the sense of hearing may operate before birth, and it is possible these diseases may have certain periods of prevalence.

Another cause which has been assigned for the birth of deaf-mute children in many cases—viz., the intermarriage of near relatives, can only be verified by an extensive inquiry into individual cases; and not from the usual returns of a census. The data we now possess are not sufficient to enable us to form any satisfactory conclusions on that point.

Before examining whether the returns throw any light on the influence of climate on the proportion

* The numbers in each case corrected by allowing for deaf-mutes then attending schools out of the State.

of deaf-mutes, it is necessary to attend to the influence of emigration. I have already remarked that a population composed chiefly of recent immigrants generally presents a small proportion of deaf-mutes. This is strikingly exemplified in California, and the recently settled Territories, which only present six deaf-mutes in a population of 193,000, and the Table already given shows that, while the Atlantic States taken together have one deaf-mute in 1,961 souls, the Western and Southwestern have only one in 2,245. But to show more clearly the influence both of emigration and of climate, we will arrange the States, leaving out the extreme west, in a somewhat different order. The six New England States may remain together; but the Middle States we will extend to the Potomac by adding Maryland and the District; annex Missouri to the northwestern section; form a new section under the name of Central States, to comprise Virginia, Kentucky, North Carolina, South Carolina and Tennessee, and class together the remaining Southern and South-western States, including Texas, as extreme Southern States.

TABLE II.

Census of 1850.

SECTIONS.	White Population.	WHITE D. AND D.		WHITE BLIND.		WHITE INSANE.		WHITE IDIOTS.	
		No.	Ratio.	No.	Ratio.	No.	Ratio.	No.	Ratio.
6 New England....	2,705,772	1,504	1·1799	1,201	1·2253	3,796	1·716	2,368	1·1142
5 Middle States....	6,302,066	2,961	1·2128	2,439	1·2584	5,308	1·1137	3,870	1·1630
11 S. N. E. Poto...	9,007,838	4,465	1·2018	3,640	1·2475	9,104	1·190	6,238	1·1444
7 N. W. States......	5,263,158	2,407	1·2186	1,645	1·3200	2,441	1·2153	3,314	1·1588
5 Central States....	3,241,803	1,881	1·1729	1,881	1·1729	2,517	1·1288	3,329	1·974
7 Extra S. States..	1,862,454	682	1·2731	731	1·2548	873	1·2110	1,301	1·1431

By comparing the New England with the northwestern, and the central with the extreme southern, we see the influence of emigration, which it will be observed, is even greater in the case of the blind than of the deaf and dumb. In other words, a smaller population of adult deaf mutes, and of families containing deaf-mute children are tempted to emigrate than of the general population, and of the blind a still smaller proportion.

And by comparing the States northeast of the Potomac and northwest of the Ohio with the extreme Southern States, we see the influence of climate. In the former the deaf and dumb are more numerous; in the latter, lying much more under the sun, the blind are more numerous. In the Central States, the relative influence of climate on the proportion of the deaf and dumb and of the blind appears to be balanced, for in those States the numbers of those two classes are equal.

And though it is aside from the purpose of this paper, it may not be without interest to add in passing, that insanity is proportionably more prevalent at the north and particularly at the east, and idiocy at the south and west.

In the following table we have placed in contrast the white and colored races:

TABLE III.

POPULATION.		DEAF AND DUMB.		BLIND.		INSANE.		IDIOTS.	
		No.	Ratio.	No.	Ratio.	No.	Ratio.	No.	Ratio.
Whites,	19,630,738	9,469	1·2073	7,997	1·2455	15,156	1·1295	14,230	1·1384
Free colored,	428,661	145	1·2956	491	1·867	321	1·1335	436	1·983
Slaves,	3,204,089	489	1·6552	1,211	1·2646	291	1·11011	1,040	1·3081
Total colored, 3,632,750		634	1·5730	1,705	1·2131	612	1·5936	1,476	1·2461

I have already remarked on the probable greater inaccuracy of the returns with respect to the slaves than with respect to either of the other classes. In South Carolina, where the slaves far outnumber the whites, there are returned upon a slave population of nearly 385,000, only fifteen deaf-mutes, fifty-two blind, nine insane, and fifty idiots. On the other hand in the adjoining State of North Carolina, with a slave population of only 288,412, there are returned slaves deaf and dumb fifty-two, blind 117, insane twenty-four, idiots 138, in each case from twice to thrice the number, and from two and a half times to five times the proportion. It is not easy to imagine any other cause for this excessive difference between the two adjoining States, than the greater inaccuracy of the census, when it relates to slaves collected in large bodies on a few plantations.

Allowing for this inaccuracy, we shall find blindness and idiocy, as I have already remarked, more prevalent among the colored races than among the whites, and deafness and insanity less so. Why this should be so, and why the proportion of insane among the slaves should be so small as after making every allowance it must be, are questions which I am not now prepared to discuss, but would suggest them to physiologists as interesting topics of inquiry.

The proportion between the sexes of each class under consideration is a subject of some interest. Among the population at large, the males exceed the females in the ratio of about twenty-five to twenty-four, but among the deaf and dumb, the males are to the females nearly as five to four. Similar results have been presented by European enumerations. Among the blind and the idiotic, the disproportion of males is still greater, being as four to three; but among the insane, the sexes are nearly equal. I may add that even in countries where the total female population exceeds the male, the male deaf-mutes have been found far to outnumber the females.

I will detain the reader upon but one other topic connected with the census returns, the ages of the deaf-mutes returned. This is a point of considerable importance, going to show that probably one-half or more of the deaf-mutes, under ten years of age, were unrecognized or overlooked. I have already remarked that not having yet obtained a statement of the ages of the general population according to the last census, I have considered it to be sufficiently accurate for my purpose to assume that the proportion of the different ages does not differ materially from the proportion of the same ages in 1840.

In the table which has been obligingly furnished me from the Census Office, there must be a serious error in the number returned as over seventy, for one-half of the whole number over that age are returned from two States, Massachusetts and Pennsylvania; and I know of no causes to collect aged deaf-mutes in those two States. The effect is, to make the number of deaf-mutes in Massachusetts, over seventy years of age, more than one-tenth of the whole, and in Pennsylvania, more than one-eighteenth. Such proportions, being four times as great as the proportion of persons of seventy and upward in the general population, are utterly incredible. I can only account for this result by supposing that some of the assistant marshals, in each of the two States, have erroneously returned as deaf and dumb a number of old people who had merely become deaf by age. The proportions of deaf-mute septungenarians in the other twenty-nine States do not but little exceed the proportion of persons of the same age among the whole population; but as the error just considered may have had some influence in the other returns too, we must accept very cautiously the favorable view of the comparative longevity of the deaf and dumb which is presented on the face of the returns.

I will, therefore, include in one sum deaf-mutes between thirty and seventy, and those over seventy. Computing the whole population of the same color, sex, and age, as being in like proportion to the total population of that color as it was in 1840, we have:

TABLE IV.—WHITES.

1. *Males.*

	Population.	Deaf and Dumb.	Ratio.
Under ten...........	3,174,500	888	1·3570
Of ten to thirty....	4,092,100	2,634	1·1550
Above thirty........	2,702,000	1,638	1·1700
	2. *Females.*		
Under ten...........	3,029,800	720	1·4200
Of ten to thirty....	3,987,600	2,082	1·1930
Above thirty........	2,584,000	1,400	1·1750

[N. B. Seventy-one males and thirty-six females were returned from Illinois, whose ages were not given.]

From this Table it appears that the proportion of deaf-mutes returned as under ten is with each sex considerably less than half as large as the proportion between ten and thirty. This result is nearly uniform in every district of considerable population, wherever enumerations of deaf-mutes have been made, whether in America or Europe.* To put the point in a clearer light, we will compare the present number of deaf-mutes over ten years of age with the whole number returned ten years ago:

White deaf and dumb, present number over ten.......	7,754
White deaf and dumb, whole number returned in 1840.	6,682
Increase..	1,072

If the ages of 107 from Illinois just mentioned were known, this difference would be found still greater, at least 1,150.

The present white population over ten is estimated at..	13,426,200
Whole white population in 1840..........................	14,189,200
Decrease in ten years..................................	763,000

It is impossible to ascribe the increase in the number of the deaf and dumb above shown to emigration from abroad, for in 1850 the whole number of deaf-mutes returned as of foreign birth including those under ten, and those who were in the country before 1840, was only 567, hardly half the increase; and we have just seen that the emigration of persons born before 1840 has fallen short by three-quarters of a million at least, to balance the loss by death to the whole white population who were living in the United States in 1840.

We have already shown that the gain to the deaf-mute population by immigration is probably less in proportion than to the general population. It may then be safely assumed that the number who were living in 1840 should have decreased in 1850 by the excess of deaths over immigration at least one-eighteenth part. And as we find in 1850, about 7,832 over ten, allowing for those in Illinois, we find by this rule the number in 1840 should have been 8,292, instead of the returned number, 6,682, a difference of 1,610, or 24 per cent., which, as the general proportion of deaf-mutes to the whole population has but slightly varied, can only be ascribed to the imperfectness of the returns where young children are in question. Allowing a proportional deficiency in the returns for 1850, we shall have—

Number of white deaf-mutes returned..................	9,669
Add 24 per cent..	2,272
Approximation to the real number........................	11,941

This estimate may possibly prove rather too high, for if we add the whole 2,272 to the number now returned as under ten it will make the proportion of deaf-mutes under that age 1·1600, whereas the average proportion between the ages of ten and thirty is only 1·1740. To keep on the safe side, therefore, we will only suppose the number under ten ought to be as large in proportion to the population of the same age as the number between ten and thirty, which would give 3,566 white deaf mutes under ten, instead of 1,608, and make the total of white deaf and dumb 11,377. To this should be added an increase of at least six per cent. for the two years since June, 1850, making the probable present number 12,060.

Applying the same correction to the number returned from my own State, New York, we shall have:

White deaf mutes returned under ten.	181	propor.	1·4865
Making this proportion equal to the next, we have..............................	499	"	1·1770
Deaf mutes returned between ten and thirty....................................	726	"	1·1770
Deaf mutes returned over thirty......	390	"	1·2290
Whole number returned................	1,297	"	1·2351
Number corrected as above............	1,615	"	1·1888

Only ten colored deaf-mutes were returned in a colored population of 47,397. Colored deaf-mutes, I need hardly say, are in this and other Northern States as much entitled as the whites to the means of education, and several are, or have been in the New York Institution, and I believe in other Northern institutions.

Applying the same test to New York that has just been applied to the returns from the whole Union, we find that, in 1840, the number of white deaf-mutes returned was 1,039. In 1850 there were

* See Eighteenth Report of the N. Y. Institution, page 59, and Twenty-third Report, page 19 and sequel.

returned 1,117 above ten years of age, an increase of one-thirteenth part. The whole white population, in 1840, was 2,378,890; the estimated number above ten in 1850, is 2,176,400, a decrease of more than one-twelfth part. If there has been a similar decrease, by excess of deaths and emigration over immigration among the deaf and dumb, in order that there may be 1,117 deaf-mutes over ten now, there should have been 1,220 deaf-mutes in 1840, instead of the returned number, 1,039; and making a proportional correction in the whole number returned for 1850, we shall have 1,521 white deaf-mutes in the State—a smaller number than was just obtained by estimating the proportion under ten to be as great as the proportion between ten and thirty. I am inclined to believe from the number of applicants for admission into the New York Institution, the last estimated number 1,521, is, to say the least, not too high.

The causes of the great deficiency in the number returned as under ten years of age are, the difficulty of determining in the first year or two, whether the child hears or not (in fact the conviction that the child is deaf is often only forced on the parents when, at the usual age, it proves unable to learn to speak), and in the case of children who have become accidentally deaf, yet retaining the ability to utter a few words, the unwillinguess of the parents to class them with the deaf and dumb.

It is easy to show that the same causes operate in every State. Taking the six New England States together we find, in 1840, white deaf-mutes 1,194. In 1850, the number over ten was 1,337, an *increase* of 143, or one-seventh. The whole white population, in 1840, was 2,212,165; the white population over ten in 1850 was not far from 2,009,700, a *decrease* of 202,400, or nearly one-tenth.

In Ohio, the proportion of deaf-mutes in the population under ten is only 1·4200; in the population of ten and under thirty, it is at least 1·1500, nearly thrice as great.

The following table will give these proportions for the few States for which I have found leisure to calculate them:

TABLE V.

Showing proportions of white deaf-mutes to the white population of the same age in 1850.

STATES.	Under 10.	10 to 30.	Over 30.	Total.
New England	1·4180	1·1740	1·1290	1·1709
New York	1·4825	1·1770	1·2290	1·2351
Pennsylvania	1·3060	1·1680	1·1560	1·1871
Virginia	1·3080	1·1250	1·1230	1·1541
Tennessee	1·3650	1·2150	1·1960	1·2259
Alabama	1·4320	1·2160	1·2350	1·2777
Ohio	1·4200	1·1490	1·2030	1·2083
The Union, Males	1·3570	1·1550	1·1700	1·1920
The Union, Females	1·4200	1·1930	1·1750	1·2265
Do. both sexes	1·3880	1·1740	1·1725	1·2073*

Whatever may be the numbers of deaf-mute children, or of those destined to become such, under the age of ten, the returns of the number between ten and thirty may be assumed to be tolerably correct. And, judging from the ages of the general population, we estimate as one-sixteenth of those between ten and thirty the number between twelve and thirteen (which is the best age of admission into an institution, and the age prescribed in the New York Institution and some others). According to this estimate, we have calculated for each section of the Union, and for several of the States, the number which, if we propose to educate the whole, should be admitted annually; and the number which, allowing an average continuance of six years (and less should not be prescribed for deaf-mutes of fair capacity), should now be in school; adding the number actually in school at the date of my last advices.

* It is to be noted that the seventy one males and thirty-six females in Illinois whose ages are unknown are included in the total.

TABLE VI.

STATES.	Whole D. and D. ten to thirty.	Should be annually admitted.	Should be in School.	Actually in School.	Deficiency.
New England	626	39	234	194	1-6
New York	726	45	273	217	1-5
Pennsylvania	555	35	210	101	1-2
All the five Middle States	1,485	93	558	307	1 3
Virginia	320	20	120	60	1-2
All the five Central States	982	612	369	214	5-12
Seven extreme Southern	335	21	126	40	2-3
Seven Northwestern	1,326*	83	498	365	1-4
Ohio	542	34	204	130	1-3
The whole Union, including California and Territories.	4,770	298	1,788	1,180	1-3

In New England and the Middle States the number in school has been corrected by allowing for pupils from other sections of the Union and from the Canadas. In the Northwestern and Central sections of the Union it is estimated the number from those sections in Eastern institutions is equal to the number in their schools from the extreme South. The last-named section has as yet but one young and small, but prospering, institution, that of Cave Spring, Georgia; but sends several pupils to institutions farther north.

From this Table it appears that the most ample provision for the education of the deaf and dumb is made in New England and New York; that the extreme Southern States are those in which there is the greatest deficiency, and next to them, I regret to say, stands Pennsylvania. The Table is probably too favorable to the Northwestern States, as those States have increased since 1850 more in proportion than the Eastern and Southern States. If we allow for the increase since June, 1850, the deficiency will be still greater, especially in Pennsylvania, and in the Northwestern and extreme Southern States.

Of the apparent deficiency, however, a part is owing to pupils continuing in school less than six years, in a few cases, because a longer term is not allowed by the State, but in much the greater number, through the selfishness or mistaken kinduess of their friends. If we were to calculate by the number of admissions annually, comparing it with the number given above who *ought* to be admitted annually, we should come nearer to the actual number who do receive more or less instruction. In the New York Institution, for instance, the admissions, not including the readmissions, for three years past have averaged forty-four; and allowing five of these to be from beyond the State, there will remain thirty-nine admissions from our own State annually, a deficiency of only about one-seventh. And as the New York Institution, for some years past, has never refused any proper applicants, it may safely be affirmed that means of education are provided for all the deaf and dumb in that great State, who are not kept from school either by physical or mental disease, or by the apathy, ignorance or mistaken fondness of their own natural guardians.

After making every allowance, however, the deficiency in Pennsylvania and in the States farther south and west will still continue deplorably large. I am persuaded that the friends of the deaf-mute in these sections of the Union will not rest content to fall so far short of the good end at which we all aim, the restoration to usefulness and happiness and Christianity of all the deaf and dumb. In the Southern and Western States the cause has made most encouraging advances within a few years, and we may well hope the period is not remote when the means of education will be provided for every child in our broad and favored land, whether able to hear and speak, or, by a dispensation of Providence, deaf and dumb.

* Of the 107 returned from Illinois, whose ages are not given, half are supposed to be between ten and thirty.

CENSUS RETURNS FOR 1850, 1860, 1870.

[This Exhibit consisted of the following editorial from the *American Annals of the Deaf* for April, 1874, Vol. XIX, pp. 104–109, reviewing the Ninth Annual Report of the Board of State Charities of Massachusetts.]

Ninth Annual Report of the Board of State Charities of Massachusetts. Boston: Wright & Potter, State Printers. 1873. 8vo, p. 602.

Under the ungracious and distasteful heading, "The Defectives," this report gives some valuable statistics and makes some interesting comments upon the census of 1870, with regard to the deaf-mute, blind, idiotic, and insane classes. We extract from it a portion of the remarks relating to the deaf and dumb:

"The United States Census Office, in its reports, admits the peculiar liability to error in all statistics concerning defectives, particularly the deaf and dumb. Assistant marshals, whatever instructions may be given to them, oftentimes return the deaf only as deaf and dumb, even where the infirmity arises solely from age. But there are difficulties which even care and discrimination cannot avoid. There are partial states of deafness and dumbness which it is not easy to classify. Besides, the several classes pass into each other by imperceptible gradations.

"In the returns for the early census reports, idiots were often classed as deaf and dumb; but the distinction is now too well understood to make the error common in those of 1860 and 1870.

"Deaf and dumb children under ten years of age are to a great extent omitted by the census-takers, even to the proportion of one-half. The defect is not ascertained for some months after birth, and when ascertained is not readily admitted by parents.

"Even the names of grown persons are sometimes intentionally withheld by the member of the household who makes the answers to the assistant marshal, and who may or may not have an excuse for the omission other than a reluctance to admit the disability in the household. The marshal, when familiar with the community, is able not infrequently to verify the answers by personal knowledge; but where his district is large or the population dense and changing, the error passes uncorrected into the record. Assistant marshals have stated such cases to the secretary. One also has come within his own observation, where there are two deaf-mutes in a family, and one only appeared as such on the census returns. The other was a young man who became a mute at the age of five years. Since that time he has been a pupil of the American Asylum for the Deaf and Dumb, at Hartford, and was reported as a deaf-mute in the State census of 1865. One of his parents, however, reported only one deaf-mute, omitting the one referred to. It should be added, however, that while with the general public he communicates only by the sign-language,* and is also entirely destitute of the faculty of hearing, he articulates at home a few words remembered from his early childhood, before the disability commenced; and this fact was the reason for omitting to report him as a deaf-mute.

"By far the larger proportion of the deaf-mutes returned are between the ages of ten and twenty. This is not because the proportion is greater between those ages, but because the deaf-mutes at this period of life being to a considerable extent collected in institutions are not likely to escape attention. Such deaf-mutes are often returned twice—once for the place in which they live, and once for that in which they are at school. Such duplications the Census Office endeavors to eliminate, but not always with success.

"Deaf-mutes of all ages, even where the disability is well known and understood by the family and neighborhood, are often omitted, by reason of the haste or carelessness of the assistant marshals. This is more true of cities than of rural districts, as in the former the officer has much less, if indeed he has any, acquaintance with the people whom he is numbering and describing. Accordingly deaf-dumbness appears in the census to prevail in cities less than in country towns; while as a fact it exists more in the former than in the latter.

"A smaller proportion of deaf-mutes is reported among the foreign than among the native population. This is due in part to the greater difficulty of conducting the inquiries with immigrants, and in part to the circumstance that this class is not so likely to emigrate.

"In several ways indicated, and perhaps in others, errors arise in the enumeration of the deaf mutes: but it is found that duplications are not very frequent, while omissions are not uncommon. As a general result, therefore, the numbers as reported by the United States, or even by the State census, are far below their actual numbers. A noteworthy instance of this occurred in the census of 1860, which reported the number of deaf-mutes in Massachusetts as 427, and in the State census of 1865, which reported the number as 561; but the former secretary of this board, Mr. Sanborn, in his fourth report (pp. 139–141) comes to the conclusion that, including children under five years of age, there were 950, and perhaps 1,000."*

It should be stated here that Gen. Walker, late Commissioner of the Census, accounts in part for this difference by saying that Mr. Sanborn included in his estimate the deaf-mutes of Massachusetts who were in school at Hartford; while in the census these pupils were reported among the deaf-mutes in Connecticut. The report continues:

"The Census Office, in its report for 1860, estimated—although the proportion was much less by the returns—that there was in this country one deaf-mute to 1,500 inhabitants—a proportion but little smaller than that of Europe. The report for 1870, as will be seen, gives, however, a proportion of only one in 2,380. In fact the proportion would be considerably larger if a true enumeration were to be made. The number reported by the census of 1870 is 16,205; but if the proportion estimated by the census report of 1860 held good for 1870, the actual number of deaf-mutes in the United States at the latter date must have exceeded 25,000.

"By the census of 1850 there was one deaf-mute in every 2,365.8 inhabitants; by that of 1860, one in 2,452.5; and by that of 1870, one in 2,379.4.

"The New England States contain, according to the census of 1870, deaf-mutes in the proportion of one in every 2,058.9 of their whole population; the Middle States, *i. e.*, New York, New Jersey, Pennsylvania, and Delaware, one in 2,547.2; the Southern States, including under that designation all the territory embraced by the old slave States, except Delaware and that part of Virginia now constituting West Virginia, one in 2,366.6; the Western States and Territories, one in 2,312.5; the Pacific section of the country, one in 4,295.6.

"These figures and proportions cannot be regarded as expressing the absolute, but only the relative, numbers of the defective classes in the different

* Why not by writing? The author of the report evidently supposes that the sign-language, and nothing else, is taught the pupils of our institutions. See also p. 108.—ED. *Annals.*

* By a recent revision of his list, as we learn from the last report of the Clarke Institution (p. 9), Mr Sanborn has recorded the names of about 1,100 Massachusetts deaf-mutes. The list is still imperfect. "The whole number cannot be less than 1,200, and may exceed 1,600."—ED. *Annals.*

sections. According to them the deaf-mutes are most numerous in proportion to the population in the New England States, and fewest in the Pacific section.

"The following table shows the enumeration of deaf-mutes by the United States census in the years 1850, 1860, and 1870:

STATES AND TERRITORIES.	Census of 1850.	Census of 1860.	Census of 1870.
STATES.			
Maine	266	297	299
New Hampshire	162	163	170
Vermont	148	144	148
Massachusetts	358	127	538
Rhode Island	65	56	64
Connecticut	404	395	475
New York	1,263	1,579	1,783
New Jersey	189	212	231
Pennsylvania	1,145	1,357	1,433
Delaware	54	56	61
Maryland	261	237	384
Virginia	642	816	534
West Virginia	....	....	218
North Carolina	471	468	619
South Carolina	165	203	212
Georgia	266	388	326
Florida	24	24	48
Alabama	210	275	401
Mississippi	107	208	245
Louisiana	117	239	197
Texas	59	181	232
Arkansas	84	131	265
Tennessee	377	436	570
Kentucky	563	652	723
Missouri	282	498	790
Illinois	356	743	833
Indiana	537	600	872
Ohio	915	959	1,339
Michigan	125	277	455
Wisconsin	69	313	459
Iowa	59	252	549
California	7	57	141
Minnesota	....	33	166
Oregon	....	15	23
Kansas	....	27	121
Nebraska	....	11	55
Nevada	....	....	4
TERRITORIES.			
District of Columbia	19	47	134
New Mexico	34	35	48
Utah	....	7	18
Dakota	....	....	4
Washington	....	3	6
Arizona	....	....	....
Colorado	....	....	4
Idaho	....	....	1
Montana	....	....	5
Wyoming	....	....	2
Totals	9,803	12,821	16,205

"It is not proposed here, in anticipation of the forthcoming comments of the Census Office upon the returns, to discuss the causes of the relative distribution of the defective classes among the different sections of the country. One, however, may be referred to: that of foreign immigration, which is a prominent element in the population of all the Northern States, but the least promising part of which is most likely to settle on or near the Atlantic seaboard.

"The apparent frequency of these disabilities in the New England States, as compared with other sections of the country, as shown by the census, may be accounted for in part by a more complete enumeration in those States, which is itself due to the fact that the defectives are more generally known and provided for than in newer communities."

The report also contains a statistical table of the deaf-mutes in Massachusetts, prepared from the census returns on file at the State-house, which differs somewhat from the tables given in the census report. It divides the deaf-mutes into three classes: the deaf and dumb, the deaf only, and the dumb only. The census report gives the number of deaf-mutes in Massachusetts as 538; this table gives 507 deaf and dumb, 74 deaf, and 49 dumb. Doubtless some of the last named would be more properly included among the deaf and dumb or the idiotic.

With regard to the tendency to aggregation among deaf-mutes, and its results, the report says:

"One class of defectives, the deaf-mutes, are quite often found to be collected in certain localities. To an extent not equalled by blindness, the absence of speech and hearing isolates those who experience it from the general community. The artificial language, which, for the most part, has been the only one taught them (!!), though sufficing in general for mutual intercourse, only aggravates the difficulty of communication with the world at large, and intensifies the sympathy and tendency to associate with others similarly afflicted. Thus little communities of deaf-mutes are formed, and through intermarriage the defect is perpetuated. Whoever examines the detailed tables given hereafter will notice some marked instances of aggregation of deaf-mutes. Thus the small town of Chilmark has 16 cases of deaf-mutes; West Roxbury, 5; Pittsfield, 4; Boxford, 4; Deerfield, 8; Leverett, 4; Chicopee, 4; Randolph, 4; Medway, 4; Blackstone, 5.

"The hereditary character of the defect is apparent in many instances. The 16 cases in Chilmark include but four family names, and deaf-mutes of the same name are observed in other localities. A family of three deaf-mutes in West Roxbury has kindred of the same name and defect elsewhere in Norfolk county. Very many families have two or more deaf-mute members."

CENSUS RETURNS FOR 1880.

[This Exhibit consisted of the following notice concerning the compendium of the Tenth Census, published in the *American Annals of the Deaf* for July, 1883, Vol. XXVIII, pp. 205-206.]

The Tenth Census.—The volume of the Tenth Census Report (1880), containing the deaf-mute returns, is not yet published, but the "Compendium" recently issued gives some of its statistics. They certainly show much greater completeness than those of any previous census, and there seems to be every reason to believe that the great pains taken to insure accuracy and eliminate errors have been very successful. The following extract from the tables of Mr. Wines' preliminary report, published in the Compendium shows the considerable apparent increase in the number of deaf-mutes in the United States during the last thirty years as compared with the whole population—an increase only apparent, doubtless, and due to the greater accuracy of the Tenth Census:

	1880.	1870.	1860.	1850.
Total population	50,155,783	38,558,371	31,443,321	23,191,876
Deaf-mutes	33,878	16,205	12,821	9,803
No. in each million of population	675	420	408	423

The following table gives the number of deaf-mutes in the several States and Territories in 1880, indicating also sex, nativity, and race:

States and Territories.	Total.	Male.	Female.	Native.	Foreign.	White.	Colored.
Alabama	693	383	310	684	9	405	288
Arizona	7	6	1	6	1	7	
Arkansas	489	249	240	483	6	417	72
California	382	232	150	306	76	365	17
Colorado	85	44	41	74	11	84	1
Connecticut	565	318	247	505	60	559	6
Dakota	63	37	26	32	31	62	1
Delaware	84	39	45	80	4	72	12
District of Columbia	169	121	48	162	7	133	36
Florida	118	69	49	111	7	55	63
Georgia	819	420	399	812	7	499	320
Idaho	7	3	4	5	2	7	
Illinois	2,202	1,239	963	1,876	326	2,179	23
Indiana	1,764	967	797	1,669	95	1,739	25
Iowa	1,052	582	470	893	159	1,046	6
Kansas	651	372	279	583	68	629	22
Kentucky	1,275	669	606	1,248	27	1,107	168
Louisiana	524	296	228	505	19	388	136
Maine	455	258	197	428	27	454	1
Maryland	671	366	305	629	42	515	156
Massachusetts	978	524	454	806	172	969	9
Michigan	1,166	637	529	929	237	1,152	14
Minnesota	500	297	203	327	173	500	
Mississippi	606	320	286	604	2	317	289
Missouri	1,598	872	726	1,501	97	1,523	75
Montana	9	8	1	9	......	7	2
Nebraska	287	159	128	228	59	284	3
Nevada	10	8	2	9	1	9	1
New Hampshire	221	125	96	201	20	219	2
New Jersey	527	265	262	456	71	520	7
New Mexico	70	40	30	66	4	58	12
New York	3,762	1,998	1,764	3,168	594	3,736	26
North Carolina	1,032	578	454	1,027	5	724	308
Ohio	2,301	1,227	1,074	2,082	219	2,255	46
Oregon	102	56	46	87	15	97	5
Pennsylvania	3,079	1,697	1,382	2,820	259	3,047	32
Rhode Island	150	85	65	114	36	145	5
South Carolina	564	297	267	559	5	301	263
Tennessee	1,108	599	509	1,098	10	868	240
Texas	771	447	324	718	53	614	157
Utah	118	60	58	69	49	118	
Vermont	212	114	98	194	18	212	
Virginia	998	544	454	992	6	705	293
Washington	24	15	9	22	2	24	
West Virginia	520	295	225	510	10	510	10
Wisconsin	1,079	622	457	810	269	1,074	5
Wyoming	11	8	3	10	1	11	
The United States	33,878	18,567	15,311	30,507	3,371	30,661	*3,217

*Among the "Colored" are included 3 Chinese and 37 Indians. Of the Chinese, 2 are in California and 1 in Oregon. Of the Indians, 6 are in California, 1 in Dakota, 7 in Michigan, 2 in Montana, 1 in Nevada, 11 in New Mexico, 1 in Ohio, 4 in Oregon, 1 in Virginia, and 3 in Wyoming.

REPORT OF THE COMMITTEE ON STATISTICS.

[This Exhibit consisted of the following report, published in the *American Annals of the Deaf* for January, 1885, Vol. XXX, pp. 52-58.]

The Committee appointed by the Fifth Conference of Principals, at Faribault, Minn., "to prepare a blank form for the collection of statistics concerning the deaf and dumb," have performed, to the best of their ability, the duty assigned them, and beg leave to report, as directed, through the *Annals*.

The Committee met at Faribault on the evening of the 13th of July, and after a general discussion of the subject assigned to them requested Dr. E. M. Gallaudet, Dr. A. G. Bell, and Mr. A. L. E. Crouter to act as a Sub-Committee.

In accordance with a call issued by the Chairman, a meeting of the Sub-Committee was held at the National Deaf-Mute College, Washington, Nov. 22, 1884, at half-past ten A. M. Dr. Gallaudet, Dr. Bell, and Mr. Crouter were present.

It was voted that Dr. E. A. Fay be requested to sit with the Sub-Committee and to act as its Secretary.

It was agreed to take the form of statistics used by the Pennsylvania Institution as the basis upon which, with such amendments as might be adopted, a blank form for the collection of statistics should be prepared for publication in the *Annals*.

The Sub-Committees proceeded to consider the proposed form, and after making some progress in the work adjourned at one P. M., to meet on the following day at eleven o'clock.

The Sub-Committee met, pursuant to adjournment, Nov. 23, 1884, at 11 o'clock. Messrs. Gallaudet, Bell, Crouter, and Fay were present.

The consideration of a blank form for statistics was resumed, and a form was agreed upon, subject to the approval of the absent members of the full Committee. Forms of questions for inquiry were also adopted, subject to the same conditions. The Chairman and Secretary were authorized to put the forms adopted into shape, communicate with the absent members, and prepare a report for the next number of the *Annals*.

The Chairman was authorized to present the following communication to the Standing Executive Committee of the Convention of American Instrutors of the Deaf and Dumb:

GENTLEMEN: We beg leave to call your attention to certain forms for the collection and preservation of statistics concerning the deaf which we have prepared and are about to publish in the *American Annals*, in pursuance of the instructions of the Fifth Conference of Principals of American Institutions for the Deaf and Dumb. We would respectfully suggest that great good might be accomplished if you, in your capacity as representatives of the Convention, would cause blank forms to be printed, as proposed in what we have prepared, which might be furnished to the various institutions and schools at cost, and so facilitate the collection of uniform and full statistics.

Dr. Bell was authorized to request a Committee of the American Otological Society to designate the probably real causes of deafness as related to the cause usually assigned by parents and friends.

The Committee then adjourned.

The members of the Committee attach much importance to the request they make of the Standing Executive Committee of the Convention, and entertain the hope that the Committee or the Convention may find it practicable to arrange for the codification from time to time of such information as may be gathered concerning the deaf in the manner proposed by this Committee—perhaps by the establishment at some central point of a permanent bureau of statistics, with which all the schools may be induced to place themselves in regular communication.

The following heading of a blank form for the registration of statistics, questions to be asked on the admission of pupils, and questions to be asked of former pupils and of their employers, are recommended by the Committee:

*Heading of Blank Form for the Registration of Statistics.**

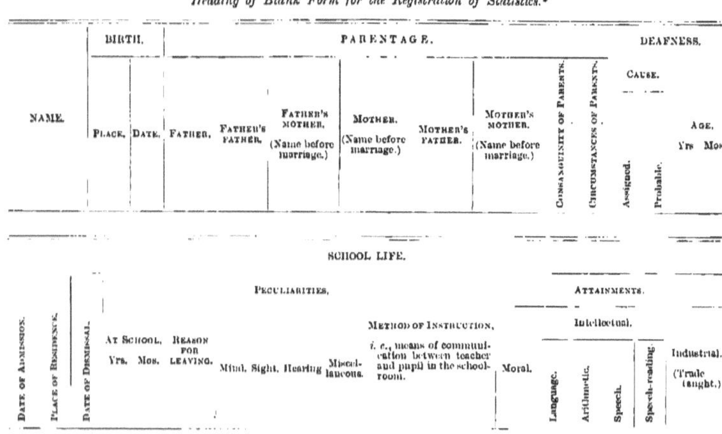

NAME.	BIRTH.		PARENTAGE.								DEAFNESS.			
											CAUSE.		AGE.	
	PLACE.	DATE.	FATHER.	FATHER'S FATHER.	FATHER'S MOTHER. (Name before marriage.)	MOTHER. (Name before marriage.)	MOTHER'S FATHER.	MOTHER'S MOTHER. (Name before marriage.)	CONSANGUINITY OF PARENTS.	CIRCUMSTANCES OF PARENTS.	Assigned.	Probable.	Yrs	Mos.

SCHOOL LIFE.

DATE OF ADMISSION.	PLACE OF RESIDENCE.	DATE OF DISMISSAL.	AT SCHOOL.		REASON FOR LEAVING.	PECULIARITIES.				METHOD OF INSTRUCTION, i. e., means of communication between teacher and pupil in the school-room.	ATTAINMENTS.					
												Intellectual.				
			Yrs.	Mos.		Mind.	Sight.	Hearing.	Miscellaneous.		Moral.	Language.	Arithmetic.	Speech.	Speech-reading.	Industrial. (Trade taught.)

* This heading is here divided into three sections, to accommodate the size of the pages of the *Annals*. For actual use it is proposed to print it in one unbroken block at the head of a sheet of paper 4 x 1½ feet in size, affording space on each page for the registration of twenty names. The questions to be asked of parents, of former pupils, and of employers, are to be printed on large sheets with spaces for the answers to be written on the same sheets.

Heading of Blank Form for the Registration of Statistics—Continued.

	OCCUPATION AFTER LEAVING.		INTERCOURSE WITH HEARING PERSONS.				FAMILY RELATIONS. (Mention names.)								CONDUCT AND CHARACTER.	RESIDENCE.		DEATH.		CORRESPONDENCE.		GENERAL REMARKS.
					POWERS OF SPEECH.			HUSBAND OR WIFE.					CHILDREN.									
DATE OF INFORMATION.	TRADE.	SELF-SUPPORTING.	HOW CONDUCTED.	IMPROVEMENT IN LANGUAGE SINCE LEAVING.	Speech.	Speech-reading.	DEAF RELATIVES.	Hearing.	Congenitally deaf.	Adventitiously deaf.	Related before marriage.	DEAF RELATIVES OF HUSBAND OR WIFE.	Hearing.	Deaf.		COUNTRY, VILLAGE, OR TOWN.	P. O. ADDRESS.	CAUSE.	DATE.	FILE.	No.	

Questions to be asked on the Admission of Pupils.

1. What is the child's full name?
2. When born? (Give year, month, and day.)
3. Where born?
4. Was the child born deaf?
5. If not born deaf, at what age was hearing lost?
6. From what cause?
7. Is the child totally, or partially deaf?
8. What noise can the child hear?
9. To what extent can the child hear the sound of the voice?
10. Have efforts been made to cure the deafness; and if any, in what way and with what results?
11. Can the child understand anything by reading from the lips of the person speaking?
12. Is the child totally dumb?
13. Can the child utter any intelligible words?
14. Does the child communicate by signs intelligible to those with whom it has constant intercourse?
15. What have been the general moral conduct and disposition of the child?
16. What is the state of the child's health in general?
17. What is the condition of the child's eyesight?
18. Is the child free from fits, from scrofulous ulcerations, and from every symptom of acute, chronic, or cutaneous disease?
19. Has the child had the small-pox?
20. Has the child been vaccinated?
21. Has the child had scarlet fever, measles, mumps, whooping-cough, or any other disease? (State which.)
22. Has the child been under instruction at any time; if so, where and for how long?
23. Can the child read or write?
24. Has the child learned to peform any manual labor, or ever been usefully employed; if so, in what?
25. Does the child live with its parents? If not, state with whom it lives, and where, and how it is maintained?
26. Give the father's full name.
27. Give full names of father's parents before their marriage.
28. Give the mother's full name before marriage.
29. Give full names of mother's parents before their marriage.
30. Where do the child's parents reside? (Give county, township, and nearest P. O.)
31. Where was the father born?
32. Where was the mother born?
33. Is the father deaf?
34. If the father is deaf, was he born so, or at what age and from what cause did he become deaf?
35. Is the mother deaf?
36. If the mother is deaf, was she born so, or at what age and from what cause did she become deaf?
37. Were the father and mother cousins, or related in any degree before marriage?
38. What are the parents' occupations?
39. Has the father any, and, if any, what deaf relatives? (Give their names.)
40. Has the mother any, and, if any, what deaf relatives? (Give their names.)
41. How many children have the parents had? (Give their full names, with dates of birth and death, if any have died.)
42. Name those born deaf.
43. Name those who have become deaf, and give cause of deafness and age at which deafness occurred.
44. Give post-office address of parent or guadian.

Questions to be Asked of Former Pupils.

1. Were you taught a trade while at school? If so, what trade?
2. What has been your occupation since leaving school?
3. Have you been able to support yourself by it?
4. Give the name and post-office address of your present employer.
5. Was it difficult for you to learn your present trade?
6. Have you had any great difficulty in obtaining your employment?
7. Did the instruction which you received in the shops or sewing-room when at school aid you in learning your present occupation?
8. Have you any difficulty in communicating with hearing and speaking persons?
9. How do you usually communicate with them?
10. Has your knowledge of language improved since you left school?
11. Do you think a longer term of instruction would have been profitable to you?
12. Were you taught articulation and lip-reading at school?
13. If so, have you continued to practise them, or either of them?
14. Can you understand persons when they speak to you?
15. Can other persons understand you when you speak to them?
16. Are your associates mostly deaf or hearing persons?
17. Are you connected with any church? If so, name the church and pastor.
18. Who were your teachers while at school?
19. Are you married? Give full name of husband, or of wife before marriage.
20. Did you marry a deaf or a hearing person? If deaf, where educated?
21. Was your wife (or husband) born deaf?
22. Are you and your wife (or husband) cousins, or were you related in any degree before marriage?
23. Have you or your wife (or husband) any deaf relatives? If so, name them.
24. Have you any children, and how many? Give names and dates of birth and death, if any have died.
25. Were any of your children born deaf? If so, name them.
26. Name any who have become deaf since birth, and give causes of deafness, and age at which deafness occurred.
27. Do you know of any deaf-mute children who have not been at school?
28. If so, will you please send the names and addresses of their parents or guardians?
29. Do you live in the country, in a town, or in a village?
30. Give your name and post-office address.
31. Add anything further concerning yourself that you think would be of interest.

Questions to be Asked of Employers.

1. Is —— ——, a deaf person in your employment?
2. What is trade?
3. Had he greater difficulty in learning the trade than hearing persons usually have?
4. How does he communicate with you and others?
5. Can he articulate so as to be understood; and, if at all, how much?
6. Can he understand the speech of others by reading from their lips; if so, how much,
7. Is he self-supporting?
8. What are general character and conduct?
9. In what estimate is he held in the community?
10. Does he apparently lead a happyand contented life?
11. Give any further particulars of interest.

The foregoing forms and questions are submitted to the institutions and schools for the deaf in America in the hope that they will meet with general approval, and in the belief that, through their adoption and use, information of very great value concerning the deaf in this country may be obtained and made available for reference.

Respectfully submitted.

EDWARD M. GALLAUDET,
ALEXANDER GRAHAM BELL,
PHILIP G. GILLETT,
A. L. E. CROUTER,
JOB WILLIAMS,
Committee.

WASHINGTON, D. C., *December* 12, 1884.

HISTORY OF THE EDUCATION OF THE DEAF IN THE UNITED STATES.

[This Exhibit consisted of the following article by President Gallaudet, published in 1883 in the American Supplement to the Encyclopædia Britannica, and reprinted by permission in the *American Annals of the Deaf*, April, 1886, Vol. XXXI, pp. 130-147.]

The first attempt, of which any record now appears, to teach the deaf in America, was made by the Rev. John Stanford, about the year 1810. He was then acting as chaplain to the almshouse of the city of New York, and found in that establishment several deaf-mute children, whom he undertook to teach by causing them to write the names of familiar objects on slates. Finding the work of imparting a knowledge of language to deaf-mutes more difficult than he had expected, demanding more time than he could afford, he was compelled to relinquish his undertaking. His interest, however, in the education of the deaf continued, and he was a few years later one of the founders of the New York institution for the Instruction of the Deaf and Dumb.

The first effort to teach deaf-mutes in the United States in any systematic manner was made in Goochland county, Va., in 1812, in the family of Col. William Bolling, who had three deaf children, and whose brother and sister had been taught some years before in Edinburgh, in the school established by Thomas Braidwood, and carried on there by the Braidwood family. John Braidwood, a grandson of Thomas, came to America in 1812, with the design of establishing an institution for the instruction of the deaf on a large scale. Col. Bolling invited young Braidwood to take charge of the training of his three children, and later advanced funds to aid in the organization of a permanent school in Baltimore. But Braidwood, though possessed of skill and ability as a teacher, squandered the funds intrusted to him in an irregular manner of life. He was twice assisted by Col. Bolling in efforts to set up a private school in Virginia; he made a feeble attempt at carrying on a school in New York city, and finally died a victim to intemperance.

The establishment of the first actual school for the deaf in America grew out of the interest manifested by the late Rev. Thos. H. Gallaudet, LL. D., of Hartford, Conn., in a deaf-mute daughter of Dr. Mason F. Cogswell, of that city, in 1814. Dr. Gallaudet had just graduated from the Andover Theological Seminary, and was expecting to enter the Congregational ministry. Having some months of leisure during the winter of 1814-'15, he devoted considerable time to the instruction of the child, Alice Cogswell, and succeeded in imparting to her a knowledge of many simple words and sentences. This success led her father, Dr. M. F. Cogswell, to entertain the idea of the establishment of a school for the deaf in his own town, where his child, with others similarly afflicted, might be educated. A number of gentlemen met at Dr. Cogswell's house, March 13, 1815, to consider the suggestion, and these gentlemen appointed Dr. Cogswell and Mr. Ward Woodbridge, a committee to raise funds to defray the expense of sending a suitable person to Europe for the purpose of acquiring the art of teaching deaf-mutes. Mr. Woodbridge heading the list with a liberal subscription, secured the pledge of a sufficient sum in a single day. Dr. Gallaudet was urged to undertake the labor of establishing the proposed institution, and after some hesitation consented to do so. He sailed for Europe on the 25th of April, 1815, was unsuccessful in his efforts to obtain the necessary training in Great Britain, but was cordially received by the Abbe Sicard, the Director of the Institution for Deaf-Mutes in Paris. After acquainting himself with the method pursued by that eminent teacher, Dr. Gallaudet returned to Hartford in August, 1816.

He devoted his time during the following autumn and winter to the collection of funds for the new institution, and the school was opened April 15, 1817, in Hartford, with about twenty pupils. The first grant of public funds in behalf of the education of the deaf in this country was an appropriation made in October, 1816, by the legislature of Connecticut, of $5,000 in aid of the new institution. During the winter of 1818-'19 the Congress of the United States made a grant of a township of land (more than 23,000 acres) to the institution. This was sold to good advantage, yielding a fund of more than $300,000, the income from which has accrued to the benefit, mainly, of the New England States, by diminishing the *per capita* cost of educating the deaf in that section of the country. The institution thus established remained under the management of Dr. Gallaudet fourteen years. It has been sustained in a course of unbroken prosperity, and holds a place at the present time of highest rank among the local schools of the country. More than 2,000 children have been educated to lives of usefulness within its walls, many of its teachers have been called upon to organize and take charge of schools in various parts of the country, many persons have come to it to fit themselves to become teachers of the deaf, and this now venerable institution is justly looked up to and honored as the *mother school* of sixty-four in which the education of the deaf is provided for in the United States at the present time.

The second school for the education of the deaf in America was opened in New York city, in May, 1818. The suggestion for its establishment came from the unsuccessful effort of John Braidwood, already referred to, in which the interest of Dr. Samuel Akerly was excited. With the co-operation of Dr. Samuel L. Mitchell, a society was organized with the distinguished De Witt Clinton at its head, which was incorporated by the legislature of New York, April 15, 1817, under the name of the New York Institution for the Instruction of the Deaf and Dumb.

The means for the support of the Institution were, at first, subscriptions and donations, with payments from such parents of pupils as had means. The city of New York soon provided for ten day-scholars, and the legislature of the State promptly followed, first with donations of money, but soon (in 1821) with a permanent and specific provision for thirty-two State pupils. The liberality of the legislature has continued without interruption, increasing from year to year, and now embraces seven institutions located within the limits of the State, in which 1,300 children are receiving education.

The New York Institution was for several years after its opening under the charge of Dr. Akerly. In 1821 Mr. Horace Loofborrow became the principal teacher and occupied that position for ten years.

The work of the Institution had many difficulties and drawbacks, arising in part from the lack of well-qualified and competent teachers, and from the irregular attendance of pupils, a large proportion of whom were day-scholars. But in 1831 the Institution made a new departure by securing the services of the late Harvey P. Peet, LL. D, as principal, in which office were united the duties previously delegated to the superintendent and the principal teacher.

Dr. Peet had been for several years connected with the Institution at Hartford, in the capacity of steward, and possessed qualifications, both natural acquired, which well fitted him to assume the direction of such an establishment. As an assistant of Dr. Gallaudet, at Hartford, he had come to understand that the task of teaching the deaf demanded for its successful performance persons of exceptional ability and zeal. And the excellent results that followed his administration were owing in a large degree to his selection of his assistants. Among them were a number of young men of great talent, several of whom, after devoting years to teaching the deaf, left the profession to become distinguished in science, literature, and the work of general education.

The Institution remained under the able and energetic control of Dr. Peet for nearly thirty-six years, and at the time of his resignation, in 1867, the Institution had educated nearly 2,000 children. Under the management of Dr. Isaac Lewis Peet, who succeeded his father in the office of principal, the New York Institution has held its place in public esteem, and for many years enjoyed the distinction of being the largest school for the deaf in the world. Within a short time, however, the numbers of the Illinois and Pennsylvania Institutions have exceeded those of the New York.

Massachusetts was the next State to provide for the education of the deaf at public expense, making an appropriation in 1819, for the support of twenty beneficiaries in the school at Hartford. Pennsylvania followed the example of her eastern sisters in 1820. The Board of Directors of the Pennsylvania Institution for the Deaf and Dumb was organized April 20, 1820, under the presidency of the Right Rev. Wm. White, D. D. Some months previously Mr. David G. Seixas had opened a private day-school for the deaf in his own house in Philadelphia. Among his first pupils was John Carlin, who has attained distinction as an artist, and as the only congenital deaf-mute who has ever succeeded in composing poetry. This school was adopted by the organization just alluded to. Mr. Seixas was appointed principal, funds were freely advanced by benevolent persons in Philadelphia, and the infant institution well provided for during the summer, fall, and winter of 1820–'21. In February, 1821, the legislature of Pennsylvania passed an act incorporating the Institution, and authorized the education of fifty children at the expense of the State.

Mr. Seixas, after filling the office of principal for eighteen months, was succeeded temporarily by Mr. Laurent Clerc, the distinguished deaf-mute pupil of Sicard, who accompanied Dr. Gallaudet on his return from France, and rendered valuable services for many years as a teacher in the Institution at Hartford. Mr. Clerc, after remaining seven months in Philadelphia, systematizing the work and methods of the school, returned to his labors at Hartford, and was succeeded by Mr. Lewis Weld, who had acquired the art of teaching the deaf as an assistant of Dr. Gallaudet at Hartford. Under the management of Mr. Weld, which continued until 1830, when he was called to succeed Dr. Gallaudet as principal of the Hartford school, the Institution became well established. Its usefulness has increased during the years of its existence, and it now has more than 400 pupils.

The State of New Hampshire made provision in 1821 for the education of ten deaf-mutes in the Hartford Institution; and in the same year the legislature of New Jersey passed an act making an annual appropriation for the education of the deaf and dumb of the State "in some suitable and convenient institution." Under the provisions of this law the deaf of New Jersey were educated at New York and Philadelphia until 1883.

In Kentucky the fourth school was established in 1823. The legislature passed an act, Dec. 7, 1822, establishing a school for deaf-mutes, and providing for its support. The passage of this act was mainly due to the efforts of Gen. Elias Barbee. The school was opened for pupils at Danville, April 27, 1823, and placed in charge of Rev. John R. Kerr, a gentleman of good education, but without experience in teaching the deaf. Two deaf-mutes, young men, were successively employed as teachers, but were found to be incompetent. The board of directors, finding it impossible to secure the services of an experienced instructor of deaf-mutes, engaged John A. Jacobs, a young man of unusual ability, who was then pursuing his studies at Centre College, Danville, Ky. Mr. Jacobs went to Hartford to seek the aid of Dr. Gallaudet and his assistants in acquiring the art of teaching the deaf. He remained an inmate of the Hartford Institution for eighteen months, and then, before he had completed his twentieth year, returned to Kentucky to assume the direction of the school at Danville. He conducted the affairs of the Kentucky Institution with marked ability and success for a period of forty-four years.

In this connection we take occasion to condemn the mistake of placing at the head of institutions for the deaf men without previous knowledge of the art of teaching that class of persons. No censure can be too severe on such action, at once seriously injurious to the interests of pupils, and insulting to the body of teachers employed in various institutions, among whom may be found men fitted by experience and natural ability to assume the direction of an institution. If, indeed, it prove a matter of difficulty to secure the services of such a man, then let the wise example of the directors of the Kentucky Institution be followed, and the crime avoided of appointing, for political or personal considerations, inexperienced men to positions which can only be properly filled by specialists.

Maine and Vermont were the next States to provide for the education of the deaf, each making appropriations in 1825 to maintain beneficiaries at the Hartford Institution. During the same year a school for the deaf was opened in Canajoharie, N. Y., the establishment of which was authorized by an act of the legislature, passed in 1822. Mr. Wm. Reid, a graduate of Union College, spent some time at the New York Institution, in 1825, preparing himself to be principal of this school, and assumed the direction of it at its opening. This Institution was kept up until the year 1836, when it was discontinued, and its pupils, together with Mr. Oran W. Morris, were transferred to the New York Institution, Mr. Morris becoming an instructor therein. Mr. Levi S. Backus, one of the earliest pupils of the Hartford Institution, was an instructor in this school, and when it closed Mr. Backus became the editor of *The Radii*, a weekly newspaper published at Fort Plain, N. Y., and for many years was the only deaf-mute editor in the world.

In December, 1825, an act was passed by the legislature of New Jersey to "incorporate and endow the New Jersey Institution for the Deaf and Dumb," but the Institution was not organized at that time, the provision by the State, previously made for maintaining beneficiaries in the New York and Philadelphia schools, being deemed adequate to the wants of the deaf in New Jersey. In 1883 a school was opened at Chambersburg, near Trenton, where the deaf children of New Jersey are now successfully educated.

In May, 1827, a school for the deaf was opened at Tallmadge, Summit county, Ohio, where in the family of Mr. Justus Bradley were three deaf-mute girls. These, with eight other deaf-mutes, were placed under the instruction of Mr. C. Smith, a deaf-mute, who had been for six years a pupil in the Hartford Institution. The school was sustained by private charity, with the exception of $100 granted by the legislature of Ohio in 1828. An unsuccessful effort had been made in Ohio to provide for the education of the deaf by the citizens of Cincinnati in 1821, who went so far as to send the Rev.

James Chute to Hartford to acquire the art of teaching from Dr. Gallaudet.

This enterprise was opposed in the legislature mainly on account of the proposed location of the school, which was not a central one. In January, 1827, the legislature of Ohio passed an act providing for the establishment of an institution for the deaf. The organization of the board of directors was effected in July following, with the Rev. James Hoge, D. D., as president. In March, 1828, Mr. Horatio N. Hubbell, who had been chosen principal, went to Hartford to secure a knowledge of the art of teaching the deaf, remaining there about a year and a half. In January, 1829, the legislature located the Institution at Columbus, and it was opened for pupils in October of that year. This school has continued in successful operation, and now stands fourth in the country in point of numbers. Mr. Hubbell, the first principal, presided over the Institution with honor and success for twenty-four years, when he voluntarily retired.

In 1835, the States of South Carolina and Georgia made provision for the maintenance of beneficiaries at the Hartford Institution, continuing to send pupils thither until schools were organized within their own limits; the latter State establishing an institution in 1846, and the former in 1849.

In 1839, an institution for the education, under the same roof, of the two classes, the deaf and the blind, was opened at Staunton, Va., receiving the bounty of the State from the outset. The department for deaf-mutes was placed under the charge of Rev. Joseph D. Tyler, who had been for seven years an instructor in the Hartford Institution. Mr. Tyler's able management, which continued until his death, in 1851, did much to settle the Institution on firm foundations. During the civil war its operations were restricted by lack of funds, and by the diversion of its buildings to the uses of a military hospital.

In the year 1842, a deaf-mute young man, who had been a pupil in the school at New York, collected a half-dozen deaf-mutes in Park county, Indiana, and began teaching them. Not being well fitted for the work, his school was continued only a year. Attention was, however, directed by his undertaking to the importance of deaf-mute education in Indiana, and the legislature voted him $200 as a compensation for his services.

In 1843, a law was enacted with great unanimity, as a preliminary measure, by which a tax was levied of two mills on each $100, for the purpose of supporting an institution for the education of the deaf. In May of that year Mr. William Willard, a well-educated deaf-mute, who had been an instructor for twelve years in the school at Columbus, visited Indianapolis and interested himself in the organization of the new institution. With the indorsement of prominent citizens of the State, Mr. Willard spent the summer in travelling over the State in search of pupils, and in October a school was opened under his direction with 16 pupils. An act incorporating the new Institution was passed Jan. 15, 1844, and a board of directors was organized. Mr. Willard's school was adopted by the board, and he remained in charge a second year, when Mr. James S. Brown, who had been for four years an instructor in the Ohio Institution, was placed at the head of the Institution. Mr. Willard continued to teach for many years. Under Mr. Brown's management the Institution enjoyed a healthy and rapid development. Liberal appropriations were judiciously expended under his direction, and by the end of 1851 commodious buildings, capable of accommodating 200 pupils, were completed.

In 1845, Rhode Island made provision for the education of her deaf-mutes in the Hartford Institution. Since 1877 there has been a School for the Deaf in Providence.

The Tennessee School for the Deaf and Dumb was incorporated in the winter of 1843-'44. Rev. R. B McMullen was the first president of the board of trustees. The organization of the institution was due to the strong rivalry then existing between Middle and East Tennessee. A bill was proposed to the legislature by a member from Middle Tennessee for the establishment of an institution for the blind at Nashville, when Gen. Cocke, a prominent member from East Tennessee, immediately arose and proposed an amendment providing for a school for the deaf to be located at Knoxville. Rev. Thomas MacIntire, Ph. D., for four years previously an instructor in the Ohio Institution, was appointed principal, Jan. 1, 1845, and the school was opened at Knoxville April 14, but no pupil applied for admission. This was partly owing to the fact that payment for board and tuition was expected, but mainly to an indisposition on the part of parents to allow their deaf children to leave home. After waiting a month, without obtaining pupils, the board determined to issue new circulars offering free board and tuition to a limited number. This brought six pupils, whose instruction was commenced early in June. The number of pupils increased to ten, and the school was closed in February, 1846, for lack of funds. In the absence of funds from the State, private benevolence was successfully appealed to, and during the summer of 1846 suitable grounds and buildings were secured, and the school was reopened with thirteen pupils. Circumstances led Dr. MacIntire, since become well known as the successful superintendent for many years of the Indiana Institution, and later of the Michigan and Western Pennsylvania Institutions, to resign in August, 1850, after having done much to build up the school in Tennessee. This Institution has passed through many vicissitudes, being suspended and much injured during the civil war; but it was reopened after the war, and has since received liberal aid from the State. It is now in a flourishing condition.

During the summer of 1843 Mr. William D. Cooke, then connected with the school at Staunton, Va., made a tour in North Carolina, accompanied by a young deaf-mute, for the purpose of exciting an interest in the education of the deaf. He gave exhibitions of the manner of teaching, and urged in a number of public meetings the importance of providing for the instruction of the deaf. As a result of his efforts the legislature passed an act in January, 1845, establishing an institution and providing for its support. Mr. Cooke was appointed principal, and the school was opened May 1, 1845, with seven pupils, which number increased to seventeen before the close of the session. In April, 1848, the cornerstone of a permanent building was laid by the Masonic fraternity, and Dr. Peet, the principal of the New York Institution, delivered an address. This Institution was continued without interruption during the civil war, and is now in a flourishing condition.

The legislature of Illinois passed an act establishing an institution for the deaf Feb. 23, 1839, and appropriating one quarter per cent. of the interest upon the school, college, and seminary fund to the Institution. The board of directors was organized under the presidency of Joseph Duncan, Esq., June 29, 1839, but owing to a variety of causes, especially the disturbance in the value of bank currency, which was wide-spread at that period, the completion of the buildings of the Institution was delayed until the autumn of 1845. The school was located at Jacksonville, and was opened for pupils Dec. 1, 1845. Mr. Thomas Officer, for five years previous an instructor in the Ohio Institution, was appointed principal. In the first year the number of pupils was 9, and in the following year 14. Mr. Officer proved an eminently capable principal, and during the ten years he continued in charge of the Institution its growth was rapid and healthy. At the time of his resignation, in 1855, permanent buildings for the Institution were completed, and the number of pupils had risen beyond 150. Philip G. Gillett, LL. D., was appointed principal of the Institution in 1856, and is still in office. Dr. Gillett had been for four years an instructor in the Indiana Institution. Under his very energetic and able management the Illinois Institution has had a growth unparalleled in the history of schools for the deaf. Liberal appropriations from the State have provided for the improvement and enlargement of the buildings; the moneys granted have been so well expended that the school at Jacksonville is to-day probably superior in the convenience of its arrangements and appointments to any other establishment for the education of the deaf; and in the number of its pupils it leads the world, 504 being reported in December, 1885.

Of the institutions, the story of whose origin has now been briefly sketched, ten are in full operation, and these ten were established within thirty years from the time when Dr. Thomas H. Gallaudet began his pioneer work at Hartford.

During the thirty-five years which have followed the opening of the Illinois Institution more than fifty schools for the deaf have been established in our country, and fifty-four of them are now in operation.

Of these fifty-four schools, three are deserving of particular notice, for the reason that in connection with their development new and important features in deaf-mute education have been perfected.

In 1856, an adventurer from the city of New York brought with him to Washington, D. C., five little deaf-mute children whom he had gathered from the almshouses and streets of the metropolis. With the aid of a number of benevolent citizens he succeeded in setting up a school, and in collecting half a score of deaf and blind children belonging to the District of Columbia. Most prominent among the friends of the school was the Hon. Amos Kendall, who soon discovered that the would-be founder of the new institution was a man wholly unworthy of confidence. A little investigation showed that he had been maltreating the children under his care, and misusing the funds intrusted to his hands. Mr. Kendall preferred charges against him in the criminal court of the District, and was constituted by the court the legal guardian of the children brought from New York. The others having been removed from the school by their parents, Mr. Kendall took measures for the organization of an institution in due and proper form. An act of Congress was approved Feb. 16, 1857, incorporating the Columbia Institution for the Instruction of the Deaf and Dumb and the Blind, naming a provisional board of directors, with Mr. Kendall as its president. In May of the same year the board appointed Edward M. Gallaudet and Mrs. Sophia Gallaudet, the youngest son and the widow of Dr. Gallaudet, of Hartford, as superintendent and matron of the new Institution. Mr. Gallaudet had been for eighteen months an instructor in the Hartford school. On the 13th of June, in temporary buildings provided by the liberality of Mr. Kendall, the school was opened with five pupils. In the spring of 1859 Mr. Kendall added to his former benefactions by erecting a substantial brick structure, and deeding this, together with two acres of ground, to the Institution. The total value of his gifts to the Institution amounted to about $13,000. In 1862 Congress appropriated $9,000 for the enlargement of buildings, and by this act enabled the Institution to provide fully for the education of the deaf and blind of the District.

In their report for 1862 the directors laid before Congress a proposal for the enlargement of the scope of the Institution by the establishment of a collegiate department, which might afford the deaf of the country an opportunity to engage in the higher courses of study open to other youth in colleges. The desirableness of providing a college for the deaf had been urged for several years by prominent instructors, foremost among whom was the Rev. Wm. W. Turner, for many years an instructor in the Hartford Institution, and for ten years its principal. Congress acted favorably on the suggestion of the directors of the Columbia Institution, and in 1864 passed an act authorizing the board to confer collegiate degrees. An addition of $3,100 was made to the annual grant of Congress for the support of the Institution, and the sum of $26,000 was appropriated to enlarge the grounds and buildings.

The collegiate department, under the name of the *National Deaf-Mute College*, was publicly inaugurated June 28, 1864—the honorary degree of Master of Arts being conferred on John Carlin, to whom reference has been made. Mr. Carlin delivered an oration on this occasion, as did also the venerable and distinguished deaf-mute, Laurent Clerc, M. A., who had assisted the elder Dr. Gallaudet in organizing the Hartford school. At the same time Edward M. Gallaudet, who had filled the office of superintendent of the Institution from its opening in 1857, was installed as president of the corporation and of the board of directors.

The development of the College for the Deaf, still the only one in the world, has been most gratifying. Opening with 7 students in September, 1864, it had during the last year reported 48, representing 26 States and the Federal District. More than 300 young men have availed themselves of its advantages, leaving its walls to enter upon lives of usefulness as teachers, editors, lawyers, farmers, business men, specialists in science, and officials in government departments. Private benevolence in the cities of Washington, Philadelphia, Boston, and Hartford, Conn., responded liberally to appeals in behalf of the College in its early days, upwards of $15,000 having been contributed in these cities by individuals. Congress has supplemented these private benefactions by liberal appropriations for buildings and grounds, besides granting an annual sum for the payment of the salaries of the professors and for the assistance of students unable to meet their own expenses. An able faculty of seven professors affords the students an opportunity of pursuing study in the several courses usually open in colleges. The primary department of the Columbia Institution, which in 1885 received the name of the Kendall School, has flourished, although its numbers are naturally small.

The department for the blind, organized when the institution was opened in 1857, and never containing more than ten pupils, was discontinued in 1865, Congress making provision for the education of the blind of the District in the Maryland Institution at Baltimore.

During the first half century of deaf-mute education the method pursued was, with very inconsiderable exceptions, that derived by the elder Dr. Gallaudet from the Abbe Sicard in Paris. This was the manual, which is well described by Professor E. A. Fay as "The course of instruction which employs the sign-language, the manual alphabet, and writing as the chief means in the education of the deaf, and has facility in the comprehension and use of written language as the principal object. The degree of relative importance given to these three means varies in different schools, but it is a difference only of degree, and the end aimed at is the same in all. If the pupils have some power of speech before coming to school, or if they possess a considerable degree of hearing, their teachers usually try to improve their utterance by practice; but no special teachers are employed for this purpose, and comparatively little attention is given to articulation."

Prior to the year 1867 the importance and feasibility of teaching deaf-mutes to speak orally had been urged by several American writers, notably by

Horace Mann, who made a tour of Europe in 1843, when he visited some of the German schools for the deaf, in which articulation was the prominent feature. Mr. Mann urged the superiority of the German method over that pursued in America. His report excited so much interest that the Hartford and New York schools sent gentlemen abroad, who visited many schools where the oral method was practised. They reported that the manual method produced better results than the oral. Some little effort was, however, made to teach articulation to semi-mute and semi-deaf pupils: but this was not long continued. Although the suggestions of Horace Mann led to no immediate practical result, they were not forgotten. Dr. Samuel G. Howe, the distinguished teacher of the blind (still better known as the instructor of the blind deaf-mutes, Laura Bridgman and Oliver Caswell), was Mann's travelling companion in Europe in 1843, and shared his views as to the importance of oral teaching for the deaf. In 1864, seconded by Mr. Gardiner Greene Hubbard, of Cambridge, one of whose children was deaf; by Frank B. Sanborn and others, Dr. Howe made an effort to secure the incorporation of an oral school for the deaf in Massachusetts. This was successfully opposed by the friends of the Hartford school, in which the beneficiaries of Massachusetts were then educated, on the ground that for the mass of deaf-mutes, if one method were to be chosen to the exclusion of the other, which was what the oralists urged, the manual method would accomplish the most beneficial results. The controversy between these two parties was brought to an end, as many a similar struggle has been, by the discovery that each was demanding too much, and that a *juste milieu* of practicability could be found. In the autumn of 1864 Miss Harriet B. Rogers, a sister of the lady who, under Dr. Howe's direction, taught Laura Bridgman and Oliver Caswell, undertook to teach a deaf-mute child to speak. Meeting with encouraging success, she advertised in November, 1865, for other pupils, limiting the number to seven. In June, 1866, she opened her school at Chelmsford, Mass., with five scholars. In 1866 and 1867 the board of State charities, of which Dr. Howe was chairman, and F. B. Sanborn, secretary, continued to press the importance of oral teaching for the deaf upon the attention of the legislature of Massachusetts. At this juncture John Clarke, Esq., of Northampton, Mass., proposed to contribute towards the endowment of a school for deaf-mutes in Massachusetts. His generous offer was communicated to the legislature by Governor Bullock in January, 1867. In June following the Clarke Institution for the Instruction of Deaf-Mutes, at Northampton, was incorporated, and organized on the 15th of July with G. G. Hubbard as president. Miss Rogers, of Chelmsford, accepted an invitation to take charge of the new institution, and, having transferred her pupils to Northampton, the Clarke Institution was formally opened Oct. 1, and at the date of the first annual report—Jan. 21, 1868—had 20 pupils. The purpose, as to method and scope, as to the kind of pupils desired, of the Institution, was made clear in the first report: "The Clarke Institution differs from all other American institutions (for the deaf) in this, that it receives pupils at as early an age as they are admitted in our common schools, and in teaching by articulation and lip-reading only." "This Institution is especially adapted for the education of the semi-deaf and semi-mute pupils, but others may be admitted."

The success of the Clarke Institution has been marked in every particular. Never having claimed to be able to teach *all* deaf-mutes to speak and read from the lips, it has developed the speech of the semi-deaf and the semi-mute, besides imparting the power of speech to many congenital deaf-mutes in a very satisfactory manner. The endowment of the school by Mr. Clarke was munificent, and in 1877 the value of its real and personal estate was reported to be over $350,000. The number of its pupils in December, 1885, was 89.

In the city of New York during the year 1866 Mr. Bernhard Engelsmann, who had had several year's experience as an instructor in the Hebrew (oral) School for the Deaf in Vienna, undertook to instruct a few deaf-mute children by the German or oral method. The parents of these children, together with a number of prominent Hebrew gentlemen of the city, met on Feb. 27, 1867, at the residence of Mr. Isaac Rosenfeld with the purpose of extending the advantages of Mr. Engelsmann's school to the children of parents who might be unable to pay the necessary expenses. So promptly were measures taken for the raising of funds that Mr. Engelsmann's school, under a formal organization, was opened with ten pupils on March 1, 1867, at No. 134 West Twenty-seventh street, antedating the opening of the Clarke Institution by exactly seven months. The school, which was sustained wholly by private subscriptions and the payment of tuition by parents until 1870, was not incorporated, however, until Jan. 11, 1869. In 1870 the legislature of New York provided for the education of beneficiaries in the Institution on the same terms and conditions as those prescribed for the old New York Institution, making also a special appropriation to enable the Institution to prepare for the reception of State and county pupils. In 1871 another special appropriation, this time of $25,000, was made by the legislature. Mr. Engelsmann was succeeded in 1869 by Mr. F. A. Rising, and he in 1873 by Mr. D. Greenberger, who, like Mr. Engelsmann, had been a teacher in the Hebrew School for the Deaf at Vienna.

The growth of the Institution has been rapid and healthy. The number of pupils reported as present in December, 1885, was 161. The permanent buildings of the Institution, erected at a cost of $134,904.53, on Lexington Avenue between Sixty-seventh and Sixty-eighth streets, were formally dedicated Nov. 29, 1881.

Still a third event, which gave an added and most influential impetus to the movement in favor of oral teaching, occurred during the year 1867. The directors of the Columbia Institution at Washington, having their attention called to the movements on foot in Massachusetts, in behalf of the oral method, and the persistent assertions there made that the oral method was to be preferred to the manual, which claims were stoutly disputed by the authorities of the Hartford Institution, decided to send their president, Edward M. Gallaudet, LL. D., to Europe, for the purpose of making a thorough examination of all the methods pursued in that part of the world. President Gallaudet spent six months abroad, and visited about forty institutions, including in his tour all the countries of Europe except Spain, Portugal, Greece, and Turkey.

In his report to the board of directors, Oct. 23, 1867, President Gallaudet took very different ground with reference to the oral method from that maintained by the gentlemen who had been sent out by the New York and Hartford schools some twenty years before. Giving the preference, as his father did, to the manual method, if the whole body of the deaf are to be restricted to one kind of instruction, he admitted the practicability of teaching a large proportion of the deaf to speak and to read from the lips, and advocated the introduction of articulation as a branch of instruction in all the schools of this country. Influenced by the recommendations of President Gallaudet, the directors of the Washington Institution authorized the calling together of a conference of the principals of all the American schools for the deaf, to be held at Washington in the spring of 1868. In response to this invitation the principals of fifteen institutions out of the twenty-five then existing in the country, together with one vice-principal and two ex-principals (Drs.

Poet and Turner), met on May 12, 1868, and remained in session five days. Many subjects of interest and importance to the cause of deaf-mute education were considered by the Conference, that of articulation occupying a prominent place. After full discussion the following was unanimously adopted:

Resolved, That in the opinion of this Conference it is the duty of all institutions for the education of the deaf and dumb to provide adequate means for imparting instruction in articulation and in lip-reading, to such of their pupils as may be able to engage with profit in exercises of this nature.

The action of this conference, taken in connection with the establishment at about the same time of the oral schools at Northampton and New York, gave a great impulse to the cause of the oral teaching of the deaf of America.

In nearly all the large schools, and in many of the smaller ones, classes in articulation were soon formed. So rapidly has this branch of instruction found favor in this country, that to-day, among the sixty-four schools, only ten are to be found where speech is not taught. And these ten schools contain only 430 pupils out of the 7,801 that were under instruction during the year 1885. The strictly oral schools are eleven in number, and had in that year 583 pupils. It will be seen, therefore, that at the present time a majority of the schools in this country sustain the combined system, and that this latter class of schools includes more than six-sevenths of the whole number of pupils under instruction during 1885.

The distinctive features of the "manual method" have already been given. For a brief and clear explanation of the other two, we quote again from Professor Fay in the *American Annals of the Deaf and Dumb* (January, 1882):

By the *oral method* is meant that in which signs are used as little as possible; the manual alphabet is generally discarded altogether: and articulation and lip-reading, together with writing, are made the chief means as well as the end of instruction. Here, too, there is a difference in different schools in the extent to which the use of signs is allowed in the early part of the course; but it is a difference only of degree, and the end aimed at is the same in all.

The *combined method* is not so easy to define, as the term is applied to several distinct methods, such as (1) the free use of both signs and articulation, with the same pupils and by the same teachers, throughout the course of instruction; (2) the general instruction of all the pupils by means of the manual method, with the special training of a part of them in articulation and lip-reading as an accomplishment; (3) the instruction of some pupils by the manual method and others by the oral method in the same institution; (4)—though this is rather a combined *system*—the employment of the manual method and the oral method in separate schools under the same general management, pupils being sent to one establishment or the other, as seems best with regard to each individual case.

In conclusion, it may be stated that in no country of the world is the education of the deaf so well provided for as in the United States, and in no country have public appropriations in aid of this object been as liberal as in our own.

EDWARD M. GALLAUDET, PH. D., LL. D.,
President of the National College,
Washington, D. C.

DEAF-MUTES.

[This Exhibit consisted of the following article by Prof. E. A. Fay, reprinted in the *American Annals of the Deaf*, 1888, July and October numbers, Vol. XXXIII, pp. 109-216, 241-259. It is reprinted here by permission of William Wood and Company, owners of the copyright.]

[The following article is extracted, by kind permission of the publishers, from Buck's "Reference Handbook of the Medical Sciences" (William Wood and Company, New York, 1886). The aim of the article was not only to present facts of interest to scientific men, but to place physicians in a position to answer such questions as are likely to be asked by the parents of deaf children, and to enable them to give suitable instruction and advice. It was understood that the writer was not to discuss the comparative value of the various methods of instruction, but that this branch of the subject was to be committed to two prominent advocates of the combined method and of the oral method respectively. Extracts from one of these articles by Professor Gallaudet were published in the *Annals* last year (vol. xxxii, pp. 141-147); the other, which was to have been written by Miss Caroline A. Yale, Principal of the Clarke Institution, has not yet appeared in the Handbook. The following article is admitted to the *Annals* at the request of several members of the profession. Much of its matter may be found in the completed volumes of the *Annals*, but it is here presented in a more compact form.—E. A. F.]

DEFINITION AND CLASSIFICATION.

The word "deaf-mutes" signifies, strictly speaking, persons who, having been born deaf, or having lost their hearing in early life, have not acquired the power of speech. There is usually no defect in the vocal organs, except such imperfection of development as may be the result of lack of exercise; muteness is simply the consequence of deafness. Ordinary children learn to speak by hearing and imitating the sounds made by others; the deaf child does not hear such sounds, therefore does not imitate them, therefore remains mute.

The term "deaf-mutes" seems to have originated in the United States within the last fifty years. The synonymous term generally employed in England, and still frequently used in this country, is "deaf and dumb." Of these two designations "deaf-mute" is the preferable one; for (1) the words "deaf and dumb" tend to perpetuate the popular error that deafness and dumbness are two distinct physical defects, instead of standing, as above explained, in the relation to each other of cause and effect; and (2) the word "dumb" is open to the further objection that it carries with it an implication of stupidity and brutishness, being associated in the minds of many people with disparaging allusions to the lower animals, as in the scriptural expression "dumb dogs," and in Longfellow's reference to "dumb-driven cattle" (Dudley: *Annals*, 1880).

There are many persons usually spoken of as "deaf-mutes," or "deaf and dumb," and educated in institutions established for the instruction of this class, who are not properly described by either of these terms Some of them, having lost their hearing by accident or disease after they had learned articulate language, still retain their speech notwithstanding their deafness; others, formerly mute, have acquired the art of speech through the instruction of skilful teachers of articulation. Such persons are not really "dumb" or "mute," and their improper classification as such—especially in the case of those who have learned to speak before losing their hearing—gives rise to serious errors in the mind of the public concerning the nature of deaf-mute education and its results. The strictly correct designation for the whole class of persons under consideration in this article is "the deaf," a term which is coming more and more into use, and which will probably ere long supersede "deaf and dumb" altogether, leaving the word "deaf-mute" to be applied to persons deaf from birth or infancy, who have not acquired the use of articulate speech. The progress that has already been made in this direction is indicated by the corporate titles of our schools for the education of the deaf. Those first established were called "asylums for the deaf and dumb;" then, as soon as the nature of the work began to be understood, came "institutions for the education of the deaf and dumb;" later, when the objections above mentioned to the word "dumb" were felt, "institutions for the education of deaf-mutes" were founded; while those most recently established are entitled simply "schools for the deaf."

Some of the deaf are either born deaf, or, losing their hearing in early infancy from unobserved causes, are supposed to have been so born; others become deaf from various diseases or from accidents. The deaf are thus divided into two great classes: the "congenitally" and the "adventitously" deaf, or, as they are often called, "congenital deaf-mutes" and "adventitious deaf-mutes." Except where hearing is known to have existed, it is impossible to say positively to which of these classes a deaf person belongs (see Proportion of Congenital and Adventitious Cases, *infra*); the distinction nevertheless is an important one.

Among the adventitiously deaf, a large proportion lose their hearing in early childhood, before they have learned articulate language; in other cases, where some progress in speaking has been made, the length and severity of the disease that causes deafness, often temporarily affecting the brain at the same time, seems to efface the language previously acquired; and in others the neglect of parents and friends to aid and encourage the deaf child in the extraordinary efforts necessary for the retention of speech after hearing is lost, produces the same result. Speech as well as hearing is gone, and the child as truly belongs to the class of "deaf-mutes" as if he had never heard. No doubt there is a difference in his mental condition—greater or less according to the age at which deafness occurred—from that of the congenital deaf-mute. (See Mental Condition and Characteristics, *infra*.) But inasmuch as, before receiving special instruction, there is no apparent difference in any respect between persons of this class and congenital deaf-mutes, while the real difference is much less than that which separates them from the class to be described in the next paragraph, they may be designated for educational purposes as "quasi-congenital deaf-mutes" (Storrs: *Annals*, 1883).

Many persons have lost their hearing by accident or disease, after having acquired the use of articulate speech, and retain this speech more or less perfectly notwithstanding their deafness. If the loss of hearing occurs in adult life, they usually escape the improper classification with deaf-mutes above referred to; but if it happens in childhood, so that they cannot be educated in the usual manner of hearing children, but must be sent to special schools for instruction, they are erroneously included among deaf-mutes. Many of the processes of deaf-mute instruction are, it is true, equally applicable to persons of this class, and they may therefore properly be associated with deaf-mutes for the purpose of education; but they differ from deaf-mutes essentially, not only in having the ability to express themselves orally, but still more in their natural mode of thought, which is in words and not in gestures. (See Mental Condition and Characteristics, *infra*.) This difference is fully recognized by all teachers of the deaf, who in this country distinguish the members of this class by the useful and convenient, though not accurately descriptive, title of "semi-mutes."

The deaf may be further classified according to the degree of their deafness. Deafness varies all the way from a slight difficulty in hearing to the inability to perceive the loudest sounds. Persons in whom the defect is so slight as to allow of their education through the ear in ordinary schools are never regarded as deaf-mutes, and do not come within the scope of the present article; they may be designated as simply "hard of hearing." The whole class of the deaf, aside from the hard of hearing, are divided into "the totally deaf" and "the semi-deaf." The totally deaf may belong either to the congenital or adventitious classes, and the same is true of the semi-deaf. The semi-deaf are often semi-mute also, having acquired language before their hearing was lost, or possessing sufficient hearing to distinguish and learn words and sentences spoken in a loud voice or through a hearing-tube. In other cases of the semi-deaf, where no use whatever has been made at home of their slight degree of hearing—its very existence often being unknown to parents and friends—experience has shown, as will be explained more fully under the sub-title "Auricular Instruction," that this slight degree of hearing may often be educated, and, apparently, by education developed, so that a considerable number of pupils who enter the institution as deaf-mutes may be graduated as merely hard of hearing.

The term "mute" is often used as synonymous with deaf-mute, but it should be avoided as less exact, since it may also refer to persons who hear, but are not able to speak on account of feeble mental power or of some defect in the vocal organs. It is open to the further objection that it suggests to many minds an undertaker's assistant at a funeral. Persons "mute" or "semi-mute," but not deaf, are, of course, not to be included among deaf-mutes, and are not suitable candidates for admission to schools for the deaf. If, as is usually the case, their muteness is due to defective mental power, they may properly be sent to a school for the feeble-minded, where the skilful efforts of devoted teachers often succeed in awakening the dormant intellect, imparting speech, and restoring the child to society.

We have, then, as terms of definition and classification essential to a discussion of the subject, (1) the whole class of "the deaf," sometimes called "the deaf and dumb," "deaf-mutes," and "mutes;" (2) the division of this class into, (*a*) "the congenitally deaf" and "the adventitiously deaf;" (*b*) "deaf-mutes" and "semi-mutes;" (*c*) "the totally deaf," "the semi-deaf," and "the hard of hearing." Some combinations of these terms often convenient, and other terms so self-explaining as not to need definition, are "congenital deaf-mutes" and "quasi-congenital deaf-mutes;" "the congenitally semi-deaf" and "the adventitiously semi-deaf;" "the speaking deaf" and "the semi-speaking deaf" (including semi-mutes and such deaf-mutes as have been taught articulation); "the speaking semi-deaf" and "the mute semi-deaf;" "the hearing mute" and "the hearing semi-mute;" the last two classes being usually persons of feeble mental power and not belonging to the general class of the deaf (E. M. Gallaudet, *International Review*, 1881).

EXTENT OF DEAF-MUTISM.

For a large part of the world we have, of course, no statistics of deaf-mutism; but during several decades most of the countries of Europe and North America have included such statistics in their census returns. The returns from different countries, and from different parts of the same country, show remarkable differences in the extent of deaf-mutism. These differences are doubtless due in part to the greater accuracy with which the census is taken in some places than in others; but it is probable that climate, race, and modes of living have considerable influence. Mountainous regions give a larger proportion of deaf-mutes than low, level countries; the Caucasian than the African race; Jews than Christians; the poor and ignorant than the intelligent and well-to-do classes. Compare, for instance, in the following table the statistics of Switzerland with those of Belgium and the Netherlands; the white with the colored population of the United States; the Jews in Bavaria and Prussia with the Catholic and Protestant inhabitants of those countries. The table is compiled from Mayr ("*Beiträge zur Statistik*," etc., 1877), Hartmann ("*Taubstummenheit*," etc., 1880), and the Tenth Census of the United States, 1880. Of the United States Census returns it may be remarked that extraordinary pains were taken by Mr. F. H. Wines, the expert and special agent in charge of the statistics of the "defective" classes for this census, to secure accuracy and eliminate errors. In consequence, probably, of their greater correctness, they show a larger proportion of deaf-mutes than any previous census of the United States.

	Date of census.	Total population.	Number of deaf-mutes.	Number of deaf-mutes in each million of population.
Austria	1869	20,394,980	19,701	966
Belgium	1858	4,529,560	1,989	439
France	1872	36,102,921	22,610	626
Germany	1871	39,862,133	38,489	966
Great Britain and Ireland	1871	31,845,379	19,237	604
Hungary	1870	15,417,327	20,699	1,343
Netherlands	1869	3,575,080	1,199	335
Norway	1865	1,701,756	1,569	922
Spain	1860	15,658,531	10,905	696
Sweden	1870	4,168,525	4,266	1,023
Switzerland	1870	2,669,147	6,544	2,452
United States	1880	50,155,783	33,878	675
United States: White	1880	43,402,970	30,661	706
United States: Colored	1880	6,580,793	3,177	483
Jews in Bavaria and Prussia	1871	....	....	1,632
Christians in Bavaria and Prussia	1871	....	....	949

The statistics of the twelve countries above named show an average of 920 deaf-mutes in every million of population. If we suppose the proportion to be the same for the entire population of the globe, the total number of deaf-mutes in the world is nearly 1,500,000.

PROPORTION OF CONGENITAL AND ADVENTITIOUS CASES.

The deaf are divided into two principal classes—those who are supposed to have been born without hearing (the congenitally deaf), and those who could hear at birth and have become deaf afterwards from disease or accident (the adventitiously deaf). The following are some of the fullest statistics that have been obtained on this subject:

	Total number of cases.	Number of congenital cases.	Number of adventitious cases.	Congenital cases in 1,000.	Adventitious cases in 1,000.
Fifteen European countries	5,171	3,465	1,706	670	330
United States Census, 1880	22,473	12,155	10,318	541	459
Twenty European schools	1,455	630	825	433	567
Seventeen American schools	6,018	2,578	3,440	428	572

The results given in this table for European countries and those of the United States Census show an excess of congenital over adventitious cases: while those compiled from the reports of European and American schools give an excess of adventitious over congenital cases. The statistics of European countries are compiled from Schmalz ("*Ueber die Taubstummen*," etc., 1848), and Hartmann ("*Taubstummenheit*," etc., 1880), who do not indicate the sources from which they are derived: those of European and American schools are compiled from the official reports of the principals of those schools, and are unquestionably more trustworthy than the census reports, inasmuch as the inquiries made by principals on the admission of pupils are generally more intelligent and careful than those of the census-takers. We may conclude then that, so far at least as the result can be determined by the testimony of parents and friends under the questioning of competent investigators, adventitious cases of deafness are more numerous than congenital cases.

It may be remarked that the earlier reports of schools for the deaf give a much larger proportion of congenital cases than the later ones. Thus seven American schools, about the year 1850, report a total of 3,381 cases of pupils admitted up to that time, of whom 1,812, or 536 in a thousand, were congenital, and 1,569, or 464 in a thousand, were adventitious; while of 272 pupils admitted into six schools in the year 1873, only 88 are recorded as congenital, the remaining 184 being adventitious. The statistics of the Western New York Institution, established at Rochester, N. Y., in 1876, contrast still more strongly with those of the older schools. Of the 241 pupils admitted since that time only 20 have been recorded as congenital, the remaining 221 being adventitious. In Europe similar decrease in the proportion of congenital deaf-mutes, though in a less degree, is shown by comparing the cases reported by Hartmann in 1880 with those given by Schmalz in 1848. Of the 3,982 cases compiled by Schmalz, 2,810, or 705 in a thousand, were congenital, and 1,172, or 295 in a thousand, were adventitious; of the 2,644 given by Hartmann (including the twenty European schools cited above and the districts of Nassau, Cologne, and Magdeburg), 1,285, or 486 in a thousand, were congenital, and 1,359, or 514 in a thousand, were adventitious. This change is, perhaps, to be attributed to the increased prevalence during recent years, both in Europe and America, of some of the diseases often resulting in deafness, especially cerebro-spinal meningitis; perhaps, also, to the greater skill of physicians in these later days in the treatment of scarlet, typhoid, and other fevers, enabling them to save the lives of their patients in more cases than formerly. The life is saved; but, often from the neglect of proper precautions against exposure after the physician's attendance has been discontinued, the hearing is lost (Ackers: "Deaf not Dumb," 1876).

Although the statistics of congenital and adventitious deafness reported by the principals of schools for the deaf are more reliable than those of the census-takers, they are probably far from correct. Their only sources are the statements of parents and friends when they bring their deaf children to school; and, however willing parents and friends may be to state the facts correctly, in many cases it is not in their power to do so. Deafness is not usually discovered until the child arrives at the age when children generally begin to talk; at that time it is impossible to say whether the deafness has existed from birth; or hearing has been lost at some time since birth. If the child has suffered from some unmistakable disease that is known to be a frequent cause of deafness, the case is recorded as adventitious; it may possibly, however, have been congenital. If, on the other hand, no such disease is remembered, the case is recorded as congenital; but it is, perhaps, quite as likely that hearing has been lost in consequence of some unnoticed inflammation of the mucous membrane of the tympanic cavity of the air-passages immediately after birth, or at some subsequent period before the deafness was observed. Deafness truly congenital is probably of much rarer occurrence than is indicated by the most trustworthy statistics.

CAUSES OF DEAF-MUTISM.

The immediate cause of mutism, in the great majority of persons who do not speak, is simply deafness. (See Definition and Classification, *supra*.) Where this is not the case, as occasionally occurs in children improperly brought to schools for the deaf, there is usually some mental defect which has prevented the development of speech. Such mutism "is the result of the absence either of ideas, or of reflex action in the motor organs of speech. In the former case, imbeciles have nothing to say; in the latter, they feel no desire to speak" (Griesinger: "Mental Pathology," etc., 1867). Very rarely, indeed, it happens that mutism is due to some defect or paralysis of the vocal organs that interferes with articulation. But as neither of these groups of "hearing mutes" belongs to the class of deaf-mutes, they do not come within the scope of the present topic. Since deafness is the immediate cause of mutism in all deaf-mutes, in order to ascertain the causes of deaf-mutism we must inquire into the causes of deafness.

The causes of deafness may be divided into direct and indirect causes. The direct causes are the defects in the organ of hearing, whether congenital or adventitious, which prevent the perception of sound. The indirect causes are the circumstances of environment, disease or accident, either ante-natal or post-natal, or both, accompanying or preceding deafness in so large a number of cases as to give us reason to suppose that they have an important influence in producing those defects. The first class of causes, the manner in which they are produced, and the manner in which they produce deafness, I do not venture to discuss; they are treated elsewhere in this "Handbook" by competent otologists. The indirect causes of which I shall speak are those that have been observed by teachers of the deaf, or gathered by them from the statements of the parents and friends of the children brought to them for instruction.

In discussing this subject it has until recently been usual, setting out with the classification of the deaf into congenital and adventitious cases, to ascribe all the former to ante-natal, and all the latter to post-natal, causes. This distinction cannot be maintained. There are probably both congenital and adventitious cases (though a much smaller number of the former than is generally supposed), and there are, doubtless, both ante-natal and post-natal causes; but (see Proportion of Congenital and Adventitious Cases, *supra*) it is impossible in any case of supposed congenital deaf-mutism to say certainly that it is not adventitious, while, as will appear below, there is reason to believe that ante-natal causes often combine with post-natal to produce adventitious deafness. Every case should be considered by itself; just as careful inquiry should be made, on the one hand, concerning all possible ante-natal causes in cases known to be adventitious as in those supposed to be congenital, and, on the other, concerning all possible post-natal causes in cases supposed to be congenital as in those known to be adventitious. This has not usually been done; when it is, we may expect to arrive at a much clearer understanding of the causes of deafness than has yet been reached.

Heredity.—The first, and probably the most effective, indirect cause of deaf-mutism is heredity. This is sometimes questioned, for the reason that deaf parents do not, as a rule, have deaf children; but, aside from the fact that the exceptions to this rule are of themselves numerous enough to establish the principle of heredity, its existence is clearly proved by the large number of deaf persons who are related to one another by blood. Out of 5,823 pupils admitted into six American schools up to the year 1877, 1,719, or 295 in a thousand, had one or more deaf relatives (Bell: "Memoir upon the Formation of a Deaf Variety of the Human Race," 1884). Of 2,106 pupils admitted into the Hartford school up to the same year (included in the 5,823 cases just mentioned), 593 had one or more deaf brothers and sisters; 271 had two or more; 116, three or more; 51, four or more; 15, five or more; 11, six or more. Of these same 2,106 pupils, 693, or 329 in a thousand, had one or more deaf relatives; 374 had two or more; 224, three or more; 120, four or more; 65, five or more; 35, six or more; 15, seven or more; 9, eight or more; 4, ten or more; 3, fifteen or more. Probably many of these cases are counted more than once in the statistics, making the groups of related deaf persons much fewer than the total number of related deaf persons reported; but they none the less forcibly illustrate the tendency of deafness to prevail in certain families—a tendency which can be explained only by the principle of heredity. There are some families in the United States that have become famous in the annals of deaf-mutism for the large number of deaf-mutes they contain Among these may be mentioned the Brown family, of New Hampshire, having deaf-mutes in four consecutive generations, and numbering at least thirty-four such cases; the Hoagland family, of Kentucky, containing 21 deaf-mutes in three consecutive generations; and a group of ten families residing in neighboring villages in Maine. not known certainly to be connected, but containing in all 105 deaf-mutes (Bell: "Memoir," etc.)

Of the 5,823 cases above mentioned, 2,262 were recorded as congenital, and of these 1,234, or 545 in a thousand, had deaf relatives; 2,864 were adventitious, and of these 396, or 138 in a thousand, had deaf relatives. The large proportion of cases supposed to be congenital, among those having deaf relatives, indicates that the hereditary tendency to deafness, where it exists, is generally so strong as to produce the result—whether independently or in conjunction with some other indirect cause that is not observed—either before or soon after birth; while the considerable number of known adventitious cases having deaf relatives shows that the inherited tendency not infrequently awaits the concurrence of some disease not hereditary in its character, or of accident, before manifesting itself. Striking instances of the combination of hereditary tendency with adventitious causes to produce deafness are offered in the cases of the Surber and Huston families of Iowa, reported by Talbot in the *Annals*, 1870. The father of the Surber family is a deaf-mute, supposed to be congenital, and has several deaf-mute relatives. Of twelve children in this family, only one is supposed to have been born deaf, but four others lost their hearing, in whole or in part, from apparently adventitious causes. The father of the Huston family, and all of his brothers, became deaf, or at least hard of hearing, early in life; of the ten children, three are recorded as having been born deaf, and two as having lost their hearing by disease.

While the principle of heredity is thus clearly established as an indirect cause of deafness, it is a curious fact that, in a great majority of cases, the defect is not transmitted by deaf parents to their children. Such transmission is so rare that many writers, especially those who first investigated the subject, have denied that it ever occurs; and so late as the year 1881, the Commissioners of the Irish Census, in their Report of the Census of that year, say that, "as the result of the investigations of the censuses of 1851, 1861, and 1871, it appears evident that the question of deafness and dumbness in the parents has no influence in propagating the defect." The inquiries of the Irish Census of 1871 were conducted under the immediate direction and supervision of the late Sir William Wilde, an eminent aural surgeon and statistician. He reported that there were in Ireland 115 instances of marriages in which one or both of the partners in marriage were congenitally deaf. In 81 instances one only of the partners were congenitally deaf: from 67 such marriages 264 children were born, none of whom were deaf; in the remaining 14 instances there was no issue. There were 4 instances of the marriage of a congenitally with an adventitiously deaf person, from 3 of which 7 children resulted, one of whom was a deaf-mute. There were 13 instances of the marriage of partners, both congenitally deaf, and from 12 of these marriages 44 children resulted, of whom one was a deaf-mute, and one was deaf only. In 4 instances where one parent was congenitally deaf, the condition of the other parent and of the offspring could not be ascertained. Of the 315 children resulting from all the above-mentioned marriages, only two were deaf-mutes, and one was deaf only. Much similar testimony as to the rarity of deaf-mute children resulting from the marriage of deaf-mutes might be brought from other countries. In almost every instance, however, in which a large number of cases have been collated—as indeed in Ireland, notwithstanding the assertion of the Census Commissioners—the proportion of deaf children has been found to be greater than in the community generally.

The marriage of deaf-mutes, both with one another and with hearing persons, is far more common in the United States than in Europe. This country, therefore, affords the best field for investigating the results of such marriages, and a considerable body of statistics, though still very incomplete, has been collected by the principals of American schools for the deaf. They show, as do the Irish statistics above quoted, that many married deaf-mutes have no deaf-mute children, and that, with deaf parents as with hearing parents, hearing children are the rule, deaf children the exception; but they also show, especially when a large number of such cases are brought together, that the proportion of those exceptions with deaf-mute parents is far greater than with hearing parents. Thus, in 110 families in which one or both parents were deaf, formed by graduates of the Hartford school, there were 275 children, of whom 38 were deaf—a proportion of deaf to hearing children many times greater than in the community at large (Turner: "Proceedings of the First Conference of Principals," 1868); and of 16,719 deaf-mute pupils admitted into thirty-three American schools up to the year 1883, 207, or 12.4 in a thousand, had one or both parents deaf (Bell: "Memoir," etc.) While considerable allowance must be made in these last statistics for the fact that the deaf-mute children of deaf-mute parents are more likely to be sent to school than those of hearing parents, the proportion of such children to the whole number of deaf-mutes still remains many times greater than the proportion of deaf-mutes to the whole population.

Another curious fact shown by the statistics of deaf-mute marriages is that the proportion of deaf-mute children is greater when one of the parents is deaf and one is a hearing person, than when both parents are deaf. In 57 families formed by graduates of the Hartford school, in which one parent was deaf and the other a hearing person, there were 14 deaf children, or 24.6 deaf children for every 100 families; while in 239 families, in which both parents were deaf, there were 34 deaf children, being only 14.2 deaf children for every 100 families ("Report of the American Asylum," 1877). Dr. Bell's suggestion ("Memoir," etc.), that in many cases the hearing parent probably belonged to a family containing deaf-mutes, is doubtless the correct explanation of this phenomenon; since other statistics collated by him prove that an hereditary tendency to deafness, as indicated by the possession of deaf relatives, is a far more important element in determining the production of deaf offspring than deafness in one or both of the parents. Of 162 deaf-mutes married to hearing persons, 55 who had deaf-mute relatives had 15 deaf children; while of the remaining 107, who had not deaf relatives, only one had a deaf child. One exception to the statement at the beginning of this paragraph should be noted; where both parents are recorded as *congenitally* deaf, the proportion of deaf offspring is greater than where one of the parents is a hearing person: the strong hereditary tendency which produced deafness in both parents, before or soon after birth, being transmitted with intensified force to the children. Of the 110 families above-mentioned as reported by Turner, 24 which had both parents congenitally deaf numbered 17 deaf to 40 hearing children, being at the rate of 70.9 deaf children to every 100 families.

While the statistics of heredity are still too limited and incomplete to enable us to form positive conclusions, the following seem probable:

1. Persons who have deaf-mute relatives, whether themselves deaf-mute or hearing, marrying persons who have deaf-mute relatives, whether themselves deaf-mute or hearing, are likely to have deaf-mute children.

2. Persons deaf from birth or from early infancy, marrying each other, especially if either partner has deaf-mute relatives, are likely to have deaf-mute children.

3. Persons adventitiously deaf and not having deaf-mute relatives, marrying each other, are not likely to have deaf-mute children.

4. Deaf persons, whether congenitally or adventitiously deaf, not having deaf-mute relatives, and marrying hearing persons who have not deaf-mute relatives, are not likely to have deaf-mute children.

Consanguinity of Parents.—The consanguinity of parents is often assigned as a cause of deafness. The attention of teachers of the deaf was early called to the fact that a considerable number of their pupils were the children of parents related by blood, and for many years they have gathered statistics on this subject. The following table, compiled from the reports of four American schools, gives the statistics of the pupils admitted up to the year 1877:

	No. of families.	No. of deaf-mutes.	No. of families in 1,000.	No. of deaf-mutes in 1,000.
Parents first-cousins	45	63	48	40
Parents second-cousins...	10	19	10	15
Parents third-cousins.....	7	11	7	8
Parents fourth-cousins...	2	3	2	2
Parents uncle and niece.	1	1	1	1
Parents not related.......	880	1,181	932	925
Whole number of cases	945	1,278	1,000	1,000

While these statistics are less appalling than those presented by Boudin ("*Dangers des Unions Consanguines*," etc., 1862) with respect to some French cities (the correctness of which, however, has been denied), they are certainly striking, and seem at first glance to justify the assertion often made, that the consanguinity of parents is one of the most frequent causes of deaf-mutism, as well as of idiocy, insanity, blindness, and other calamities. But they cannot be regarded as conclusive on this point until we discover the extent to which relatives marry each other. If the proportion of the deaf-mute children of consanguineous marriages to all deaf-mutes is greater than the proportion of consanguineous marriages to all marriages, such unions are doubtless a cause of deaf-mutism; but, unfortunately, the proportion of consanguineous marriages to all marriages has not yet been ascertained.

The official statistics of marriages in Prussia, from 1875 to 1878, indicate a smaller proportion of consanguineous marriages (viz., 0.8 per cent.) than the proportion of the deaf-mute offspring of such marriages usually is, but we have no statistics on the latter point for Prussia; on the other hand, Mr. George H. Darwin's estimate of 2.2 per cent. for England, which was based on careful and ingenious calculations, though within narrow limits, shows the two proportions to be about the same for that country.

The larger proportion of deaf-mutes among Israelites than among Christians, and among mountaineers than dwellers in lowlands (see Extent of Deaf-Mutism, *supra*), is sometimes attributed to the greater frequency of consanguineous marriages among Israelites and mountaineers; but other plausible explanations of the prevalence of deafness among these classes are offered, and numerous instances are cited of communities in various parts of the world, where consanguineous marriages prevail to a great extent, and yet the children are more than ordinarily free from deaf-mutism and other defects.

My own opinion is, that consanguineous marriage is not in itself a true cause of deafness, but that the numerous instances in which deafness follows such marriages are to be considered as cases of heredity. If two persons marry, both of whom belong to a family in which an hereditary tendency to deafness exists, the tendency is transmitted to their offspring with increased intensity, and deafness in the offspring is the result; just as is the case in the marriage of two persons belonging to different families in which such a tendency exists. As a general rule, investigators seeking the causes of deafness have accepted the kinship of the parents as a sufficient cause without pursuing the subject further; whereas further inquiry would probably have revealed other adequate causes in many instances, and an analysis of all the cases in connection with the possession of deaf-mute relatives would have demonstrated the existence of an hereditary tendency to deafness on the part of many parents. Yet I should not advise relatives to marry, even where no hereditary tendency to deafness or other defect is known to exist; for as Mr. Darwin forcibly suggests, no man knows with certainty, until toward the end of life, what ills may lie hidden in his edition of the family constitution.

Maternal Impressions.—Fright or some other influence acting on the mind of the mother during pregnancy is frequently assigned by parents or friends as a cause of deafness, and striking narratives, especially with respect to gesticulating deaf persons seen by the mother for the first time during that period, are related in support of the theory. Inasmuch, however, as further inquiry usually brings to light other causes which seem to be adequate, we need not accept this as a true cause.

Scrofula.—So many deaf persons—from thirty to seventy-five per cent. in different schools—show traces of scrofula, that we are probably justified in supposing some connection to exist between this disease and deafness. "Scrofula, as a predisposing cause of deafness, acts almost always as a predisposing cause of inflammation in general, which inflammation, being excited in the ear, produces changes resulting in deafness" (Dudley Peet: *Annals*, 1856). "The organ of hearing takes a prominent place among those organs of the body that are affected by the diseases caused by scrofula; and not only do independent diseases of the ear occur more frequently in scrofulous individuals, but affections of this organ caused by other diseases, as scarlet fever, measles, etc., take a more unfavorable course in such individuals" (Hartmann: "*Taubstummenheit*," etc.) The scrofulous diathesis manifests itself quite as frequently in cases of adventitious as of supposed congenital deafness, confirming Hartmann's statement that its presence increases the likelihood that other diseases of an entirely different nature will result in deafness.

Social Circumstances.—Unfavorable social circumstances, poverty, and ignorance may probably be classed among the indirect causes of deafness, since the proportion of deaf persons among these classes seems to be greater than in the whole community. This is a matter of common observation rather than of statistical record up to the present time, but it is confirmed by some statistics recently published by the Pennsylvania Institution concerning its former pupils ("Report of Special Committee to Collect Information," etc., 1884). Of the 344 families which sent to that school 364 children, concerning whom information was obtained, 283, or almost eighty-two per cent. of the parents, were simple day-laborers or mechanics, the largest number of them, in proportion to the whole population of the State, being miners of the Lehigh, Schuylkill, and Wyoming regions. It is certainly reasonable to suppose that negligence, damp and ill-ventilated dwellings, insufficient nourishment, the lack of proper medical treatment, and other evils springing from poverty and ignorance, may combine with more direct causes to produce deafness.

Mountainous Regions.—The large percentage of deaf persons in Switzerland, as compared with all other countries of which we have statistics (see Extent of Deaf-Mutism, *supra*), and of the more mountainous regions of Switzerland, Austria, France, Spain, and Germany, as compared with the lower and more level districts (45 in 10,000 in Berne, Lucerne, and Wallis, to 24.5 in the whole of Switzerland; 30.6 in Salzburg, Steiermark, and Carinthia, to 9.7 in all Austria; 24.5 in the Alpine departments of France, to 6.26 in the whole country; 10.4 in South Germany, to 6.05 in North Germany) shows that there must be some influence in mountainous countries which, in some manner, tends to cause deafness. The opponents of consanguineous marriages charge the result to the kinship of the parents, who are said to be more likely to be related to each other than in the lowlands, on account of the scanty means of communication between different districts; others, who attach much importance to social conditions, ascribe it to the poverty of mountainous regions, and the close, unhealthy houses in which the people live in winter; others to the dampness and coldness of the climate. We must await a fuller knowledge of all the causes of deafness, and of all the circumstances of mountaineers, before we can explain this phenomenon satisfactorily.

Diseases and Accidents.—Turning to the causes which more unmistakably produce deafness after hearing is known to have existed, statistics show that it so often follows certain diseases and accidents as to leave no room for doubt that these diseases and accidents may be counted as true causes. The fullest statistics that we have on this subject are those of the United States Census of 1880; and though they were not collected by experts, yet as they correspond generally in their proportions with those recorded of the pupils in our schools, and as the returns were carefully reviewed and analyzed by competent authorities, we may consider them tolerably correct. The cause of deafness was assigned, with more or less definiteness and probability, in 9,209 cases, out of which 366 were referred to diseases of the ear, 8,250 to other diseases, and 593 to accidents; 850 cases of disease and 128 of accidents were rejected in the compilation of the returns as too vague or improbable to be counted and classified. The list of causes accepted is as follows (Wines: *Annals*, 1884):

Meningitis	2,856	Hydrocephalus	63
Scarlet fever	2,095	Teething	54
Malarial and typhoid fevers	571	Mumps	51
Measles	448	Small-pox and variola	47
Fevers, non-malarial	381	Erysipelas	36
Catarrh and catarrhal fevers	321	Fright	32
Other inflammations of the air passages	142	Water in the ear	25
Falls	323	Sunstroke	21
Abscesses	281	Noises and concussions	21
Whooping-cough	195	Tumors	11
Nervous affections	170	Chicken-pox	10
Scrofula	131	Struck by lightning	10
Quinine	78	Foreign bodies in the ear	9
Blows and contusions	74	Salt rheum	3
Inflammations of the ear	72	Malformation of the ear	2
Diphtheria	70	Syphilis	2
		Consumption	1
		Total	9,209

It will be noticed that meningitis, which in the census returns includes cerebro-spinal meningitis, pachymeningitis, convulsions, fits, etc., stands at the head of the list. The proportion of cases from this cause would probably be still further increased in a census of the deaf in the United States under thirty years of age, since epidemic cerebro-spinal meningitis has been the most frequent occasion of deafness in the pupils admitted into many of our schools during the past twenty years. The same is true of some parts of Europe, especially the northeastern provinces of Germany. Scarlet fever is second on the United States Census list, and either first or second on most of our school lists; until the prevalence of cerebro-spinal meningitis it almost always ranked first in this country. In Europe typhoid fever seems to come next after cerebral affections and before scarlet fever (Hartmann: "*Taubstummenheit*," etc.).

MENTAL CONDITION AND CHARACTERISTICS.

With respect to mental condition and characteristics, the division of the deaf into several distinct classes, mentioned at the beginning of this article, is of the greatest importance. Semi-mutes, who have acquired an idiomatic use of spoken language before hearing was lost, retain to a greater or less degree the modes of thought and mental characteristics of hearing persons. They think in words and express themselves easily and naturally in the language of their childhood. In the course of time, especially if they are not encouraged to use the voice in conversing with others, they may lose their memory of sound and may cease to pronounce words mentally; but even then, if they have learned to read and write, words in their written or printed form will serve them as natural and convenient instruments of thought.

Since semi-mutes, on account of their deafness, cannot, as a rule, be educated in common schools, and their number in any community is usually too small to justify the establishment of special schools for them, they are educated with deaf-mutes, many of the processes of instruction beyond the elementary stage being equally applicable to both classes; but the semi-mute always has a great advantage over his deaf-mute classmate in his command of language. This distinction, though it is often explained by candid teachers, is not always understood by visitors to the school-room; and the public are thus sometimes misled as to the actual attainments of deaf-mutes. In mental vigor, and in the acquisition of general knowledge, the true deaf-mute, notwithstanding he is heavily handicapped in respect to language, will not infrequently surpass the semi-mute; but most of the cases of remarkable facility in composition and of great success in articulation that astonish the undiscriminating public at exhibitions belong to the class of semi-mutes, as do also nearly all the deaf persons who have distinguished themselves in later life as authors and poets.

Between the semi-mute and the congenital deaf-mute, but more closely allied with the latter than the former, stands the "quasi-congenital" deaf-mute. He retains no conscious memory of words; he must acquire written language or vocal speech by the same laborious processes as if he had never heard; in his attempts at composition he makes the same curious mistakes as the congenital deaf-mute; and yet it is a fact often observed by teachers that children of this class do learn language more easily and successfully, and adapt themselves more readily to the modes of thought of hearing persons, than those who are born deaf or lose their hearing soon after birth. When we remember how vivid are the impressions of childhood, how full a vocabulary, and how much fuller a comprehension of language as spoken by others, a bright child obtains during the first two or three years of his life, it is not strange if the mental condition of one who loses hearing when he has reached this age is essentially different from that of one who has never heard. The wonder is rather that, of the immense mental and linguistic acquisitions he has made through the sense of hearing, so little appears to remain.

The uneducated deaf-mute who has never heard, or whose hearing has been lost in early infancy, has no knowledge whatever of the language of words. This lack of language is the key to his mental condition and characteristics. He has an intelligent mind; he observes, reasons, and forms conclusions; but his train of thought, being carried on by means of mental pictures and rude gestures, is imperfect and incomplete, while his reasoning, being based upon his own limited range of observation uncorrected by the superior wisdom and wider experience of others, is apt to lead him to erroneous conclusions (E. M. Gallaudet: *International Review*, 1875). Careful inquiries made of educated deaf-mutes with respect to their ideas before instruction have elicited the fact that, although—like young children in general—they usually accept the phenomena of nature as a matter of course, and do not trouble themselves concerning their origin, yet they do sometimes reflect on these subjects, and frame for themselves various fanciful explanations of the means by which the most striking natural phenomena are produced: as, for instance, that the wind is blown from a great bellows, and that the rain is poured down through small holes in the sky, that snow is ground out like flour from a celestial mill, that thunder and lightning are the discharges of cannon, that the stars are candles or lamps lighted every evening, that death is caused by the medicine administered to the sick person, etc., etc. None seem to have arrived at the idea of the existence of the soul, nor of a god, nor of immortality; and there are only two instances on record in which they have reflected at all upon the origin of the world and its inhabitants. One girl, who had reached the age of fifteen before coming to school, said that she "had tried to think about it, but could not;" she "thought the people came from the South;" and one very intelligent boy, at the age of nine years, having gained from his own observation an idea of the descent from parent to child, the propagation of animals, and the production of plants from seed, struggled long and earnestly with the question, whence came the first man, the first animal, and the first plant; but like many wiser men, without reaching any satisfactory conclusion.

The deaf-mute very early invents a language of signs sufficient for the expression of the common wants of his every-day life, and if he has intelligent friends who are ready to aid his attempts at the exchange of ideas in this way, or if he associates with other deaf-mutes, this language will be extended and elaborated to a high degree. It becomes his usual mode of thought; and while he may, after long years of effort by his teachers and himself, learn to think more or less in spoken or written words, the language of signs always remains his easiest and most natural method not only of expression but of thought. The language of words written or spoken is for him something strange, foreign, artificial; he may master it as the hearing student masters a foreign tongue, so that he will think in it to some extent, use it with considerable freedom, and read it understandingly and profitably; but except in very rare cases of peculiar education and environment, the language of gesture is, and always remains, the vernacular of the deaf-mute.

The language of words being a foreign language to the deaf-mute, he is liable, even after years of instruction, to make mistakes in its use. Such mistakes, of course, become less frequent as his education advances; but the deaf-mute who has never heard, or has lost his hearing in early infancy, rarely, if ever, acquires such a mastery of language as to employ it in speech or writing with the same readiness and freedom as persons who learn to speak in childhood through the hearing. The peculiarities in his phraseology are sometimes called the "deaf-mutisms," and their origin has been ascribed by some writers to the inversions of the sign-language; but their main cause, like that of the blunders of foreigners, is merely an incomplete knowledge of the language of words. The "deaf-mutisms" most frequently observed in the school-room (Pettengill: *Annals*, 1878) are the transposition of letters, as "kinfe," "tryant;" the inversion of words in compounds, as "general-major," "a looking-good man;" the coining of new words in analogy with those already learned, as "longly" (from "shortly"), "youthhood;" the doubling of negatives, as "Nobody cannot gaze at the sun;" the substitution of synonyms, as "a secret tutor;" the use of possessive pronominal adjectives agreeing in gender with the noun following instead of the antecedent, as "My mother wrote a letter to his husband;" the employment of unidiomatic though not ungrammatical phrases, as "He gave up his ghost," "Some martyrs were burned at the stakes;" and the inappropriate use of expressions in themselves correct, as "Abraham showed his piety by almost killing his son Isaac;" "Men and women forget things, but God has an uncommonly good memory."

The characteristics of an uneducated deaf-mute, especially when in unfavorable social circumstances his natural language of signs has not been developed beyond its most rudimentary stage, are what might be expected. Cut off from communication with his kind, misinterpreting alike the order of nature and the actions of his fellow-men, he is apt to become melancholy, suspicious, treacherous, and cruel. The neglect on the part of parents and friends which, from any motive whatever, allows the deaf-mute child to grow up in this condition, when, as in the United States, the benefits of education are freely offered to all, is simply criminal.

A wisely conducted education, giving the deaf-mute writing or speech as a means of communication, and imparting just views of his relations to God and his fellow-men, tends to correct the defects above-mentioned, and enables him to take his proper place in the world as an active and useful member of society. Almost the only peculiarity that distinguishes the educated deaf-mute in general from hearing persons, aside from the physical fact of deafness, and more or less constraint in the idiomatic use of language, is the manifestation of a decided preference for the society of others like himself rather than of those who hear and speak. There are deaf-mutes of whom this is not true, but they must be regarded as exceptions to the general rule. This tendency is deplored by many of their best friends, since it leads them to regard themselves as a separate class, to weaken the ties binding them to the rest of the community, which ought rather to be strengthened, and to result in their marriage with one another (E. M. Gallaudet: *Annals*, 1873). Some writers even condemn the present method of instructing the deaf, on the ground that they foster this tendency (Bell: "Memoir," etc., 1884); but no one has yet proved that there is any practicable method of instruction yielding satisfactory results that will prevent its development. It should be added that the results of the disposition of the deaf to associate together are not wholly evil; see "Religious Work for Adults," *infra*.

MORBIDITY.

Since the scrofulous diathesis frequently exists in deaf-mutes, and since the maladies that cause deafness are in some cases the result of an imperfect physical constitution, and in others leave a previously sound constitution debilitated and impaired, we should expect to find the percentage of morbidity in persons of this class higher than among hearing persons. We have few records on this point except those of our schools, and the latter not in a statistical form; but it is the general testimony of the heads of schools that their pupils, as a rule, enjoy excellent health—quite as good as the average health of hearing children. This is probably due to the regular habits, wholesome food, well-ventilated rooms, and out-of-door exercise afforded by institution life, which counteract any unfavorable constitutional tendencies that may exist.

Thirty years ago consumption was regarded as a disease to which the deaf were peculiarly liable, since statistics collected by Porter and Peet in this country, Wilde in Ireland, and Müller in Germany, showed that a large proportion of deaths among them were due to this cause (H. P. Peet: *Annals*, 1834); but within recent years consumption has not been observed to be specially prevalent among the deaf.

It is sometimes asserted that the lungs of the deaf-mutes are ill-developed on account of their lack of exercise in speech. But, aside from the fact that deaf children do generally use their voices considerably, making a great variety of sounds, the expansion of the lungs in respiration really suffices for their proper development (Hartmann: "*Taubstummenheit*"). A careful examination of the lungs of the students of the National Deaf-Mute College at Washington, with a view to cautioning them against violent gymnastic exercises in case of pulmonary weakness, showed only one out of fifty with any tendency in that direction.

The Census of the United States for 1880 gives a surprisingly large number of deaf persons who are afflicted in other respects, 245 being blind, 268 insane, 2,122 idiotic, 30 blind and insane, and 217 blind and idiotic, making a total of 2,882 who are doubly or trebly afflicted (Wines: *Annals*, 1884). These returns seem to indicate that there exists some co-relation between the several defects of the senses, since persons having one of these defects appear to be more liable to the others than persons normally constituted, and persons having two defects appear to be more liable to be otherwise afflicted than persons having a single defect (Bell: *Science*, 1885). It is not safe to comment on these statistics in advance of the publication of Mr. Wines' special Report on the Census, which will doubtless give details throwing important light upon them. I will only venture to suggest that probably a considerable number of those reported as deaf and blind have lost their sight and hearing from the same disease, and possibly some of them are deaf-mutes who have lost their sight in old age; that many of those reported as deaf-mute and idiotic are not deaf, but are mute from mental incapacity; and that a majority of those reported as deaf-mute and insane are uneducated deaf-mutes, the social condition and environment of whom are often such as would naturally result in insanity.

MORTALITY.

The reasons given above for expecting a higher rate of morbidity in deaf-mutes than in hearing persons, together with their greater liability to fatal accidents in the street, on the railway, etc., on account of their inability to hear warnings of danger, indicate the probability of a higher rate of mortality also; but there are at present no comparative tables on a scale sufficiently extended to enable us to form a definite conclusion. An inquiry made thirty years ago into the number of deaths of 650 pupils in four American schools during ten years showed a rate thirty-seven per cent. higher than in the general population (H. P. Peet: *Annals*, 1834); but two of these schools were in large cities, and their mortality was considerably greater than in schools more favorably situated, while the total numbers and the limits of age were too small for generalization. Hartmann ("*Taubstummenheit*") compares 4,247 deaf-mutes of Prussia and Bavaria with all the inhabitants of thirteen German states in quinquennial groups of ages from five to fifty years of age, and concludes that there is a somewhat greater mortality among the deaf-mutes than among the total population, but that the difference is so slight that no conclusion can be drawn from it.

It is to be hoped that the necessary statistics for determining this important question may soon be afforded, since at present some insurance companies refuse to accept risks on the lives of deaf persons on any terms, in the belief that their expectation of life is considerably less than that of hearing persons.

MARRIAGE.

Since the education of the deaf has become general, marriage among them has ceased to be rare. In Germany, according to the Census of 1871, 6.3 per cent. of the male deaf-mutes and 3 per cent. of the female deaf-mutes were married (Mayr: "*Beiträge zur Statistik*," 1877). For other countries I have no complete statistics, but the records of the graduates of American schools for the deaf indicate a much larger proportion of marriages than those given for Germany. Of 5,738 pupils admitted into five American schools up to the year 1882, 1,089, or nineteen per cent. have been married. As the total number of pupils here given includes the children in school at the date of the report, and some others not yet arrived at a marriageable age, the true percentage is considerably higher. Of 1,259 of those pupils who were born before 1840, 571, or 45.4 per cent., were married (Bell: "Memoir," etc.), and this rate is probably an approximation to the true percentage of married deaf-mutes in the United States. The larger proportion of marriages in the United States than in Germany is probably to be explained by the more prosperous circumstances of American deaf-mutes.

Of the 1,089 former pupils above recorded as married, 856, or 78.6 per cent., married deaf persons. The objection to marriages of this kind is the probability that under some circumstances the defect will be transmitted to the offspring. On the other hand it is said to be in favor of such marriages, that, as a rule, they are more likely to be harmonious and congenial than when deaf-mutes are unequally yoked together with hearing persons. As the statistics already gathered show that under certain circumstances the deaf may, and under others they cannot, marry one another without danger of transmitting the defect, we may reasonably hope that the time is not distant when the conditions under which deafness is transmitted will be so well understood that, in many cases, the deaf may be advised to follow the choice of their own hearts in this respect without any fear whatever of evil consequences: while in other cases, where they ought not to marry persons similarly afflicted, or, possibly not to marry at all, they may be warned more effectively than at present of the danger incurred. (See Heredity, *supra*.)

OCCUPATIONS.

Uneducated deaf-mutes can and do perform unskilled labor, but the competition here is so great, and they are at so much disadvantage in various ways as compared with hearing persons, that, though they are sometimes self-supporting, they are often more or less a burden upon their friends or upon the community.

With educated deaf-mutes the case is very different. In most of our American schools the importance of industrial instruction is fully recognized and several hours of each day are devoted to this purpose. The occupations taught are, for the boys, baking, basket-making, bookbinding, broom-making, cabinet-making, carpentry, chair-making, coopery, farming, gardening, glazing, mattress-making, painting, printing, shoemaking, tailoring, and wood-turning; for the girls, cooking, domestic, and ornamental sewing, both with and without the machine, dress-making, shirt-making, tailoring, and the folding and stitching of sheets for the bookbinder. Instruction in clay modelling, drawing, decorating, etc., enables some of both sexes to engage in various pursuits of industrial art and in pure art. In some instances the pupils are made thorough masters of their trades while at school, so that they immediately command remunerative positions upon graduating; and even in the greater number of cases where they merely acquire the principles of a trade, familiarity with the use of tools, dexterity, and habits of industry, they find it much easier to master the business afterward, or to learn some new trade, than would be possible if no attention had been paid to industrial education.

The list of occupations pursued by educated deaf persons includes not only the industries above mentioned as taught at school, but almost every pursuit that does not require the actual use of hearing and speech. The great majority are engaged in various branches of skilled industry; some are artists, or workers in industrial art; while among the more intelligent and highly educated, especially those who have enjoyed the advantages of the College at Washington, are many government clerks, many teachers of the deaf, several clergymen preaching to the deaf, and several editors, publishers, merchants, inventors, chemists, and lawyers.

LEGAL RIGHTS AND RESPONSIBILITIES.

Under the Justinian Code, deaf-mutes who could not read and write were classed with the insane and idiotic, and had therefore no legal rights nor responsibilities. A better comprehension of their mental condition has led to considerable modification of their legal status, so far at least as their rights are concerned. It has been decided repeatedly, both in England and America, that an uneducated deaf-mute who possesses sufficient intelligence to express his ideas, wishes, and intentions by signs can make contracts, execute deeds, dispose of property by gift or by testament, and give evidence in court. The degree of intelligence and facility of communication can usually be determined by the testimony of acquaintances or of experienced teachers of the deaf (H. P. Peet: "Legal Rights and Responsibilities of the Deaf and Dumb," 1856).

The uneducated but not unintelligent deaf-mute who commits crime against property—usually theft—is generally and properly held responsible for the act; but in the case of serious crime against the person—as, for instance, homicide under the provocation of cruelty—his moral and legal responsibility is not so easy to determine. In such cases, which have been unhappily frequent in proportion to the number of this class of persons, judges and juries, especially in view of the death penalty, have naturally shrunk from the decision that the deaf-mute without any education was morally and legally responsible, and he has either through an appeal by his counsel to the old law classing deaf-mutes with the insane and idiotic escaped trial altogether, or through the sympathy or disagreement of the jury been acquitted (I. L. Peet: "Psychical Status and Criminal Responsibility of the Totally Uneducated Deaf and Dumb," 1872).

Educated deaf-mutes who can communicate with others orally or by writing occupy the same position before the law as hearing persons.

It is creditable to the character of the present generation of deaf-mutes in the United States, as peaceable and law-abiding citizens, that of the 33,806 returned by the enumerators of the Census of 1880, only four were found in jails or other prisons (Wines: *Annals*, 1884).

ORIGIN AND GROWTH OF SCHOOLS AND METHODS.

It was not until the latter half of the eighteenth century that the first schools for the deaf were established. Before that period there were isolated cases of the education of individual deaf-mutes, beginning with the conferring of speech upon a deaf boy (supposed at the time to be miraculous) by St. John of Beverly, Archbishop of York, in the year 685, and becoming more and more numerous during the sixteenth and seventeenth centuries. Several teachers of private pupils in the seventeenth century, especially Bonet in Spain, Wallis in England, and Amman in Holland, published descriptions of their methods which were afterward found valuable in the more general instruction of the deaf.

The first instruction of deaf-mutes in schools began about the year 1760, when, nearly at the same time, three schools were established independently of one another—in Paris by the Abbe de l'Épée, in Dresden by Samuel Heinicke, and in Edinburgh by Thomas Braidwood. Heinicke's school a few years later was removed to Leipsic. Of these three teachers, De l'Épée is justly the most renowned, on account of the benevolence and disinterestedness of his character. While Heinicke and Braidwood received only the children of rich parents and kept their processes of instruction as secret as possible, De l'Épée devoted his life and his fortune to the education of the poor, and published his methods widely, in the hope that they might be made useful to deaf-mutes elsewhere.

As the successful results of the instruction given in these schools became known, others were established in other cities and countries. The first school in America was founded in Hartford, Conn., in the year 1817, by the Rev. Thomas Hopkins Gallaudet, LL. D., a young man of high education and culture, deeply religious spirit, and lively sympathy with the class to whose welfare he devoted his life. As it was supposed at that time that one school would suffice for the needs of the whole country, it received the name of the American Asylum. There are at present (1886) sixty-one such schools in the United States.

The Abbe de l'Épée, though he gave some attention to articulation teaching, depended chiefly upon an ingenious sign-language devised by himself as his means of instruction, and is thus regarded as the founder of the "manual," sometimes called the "French," method of teaching. Under his successor, the Abbe Sicard, articulation teaching was abandoned, and the manual method was pursued exclusively in the Paris and other French schools. As new schools were established in other countries, the manual method was adopted almost everywhere, except in Germany.

Heinicke and Braidwood, while not neglecting other branches of education, devoted themselves chiefly to teaching their pupils to speak and read the speech of others, and so were the founders of the "oral" or "German" method. In Great Britain the brilliant results achieved in France by De l'Épée and Sicard, which were regarded as superior to Braidwood's, led to the adoption of the manual method, or of a combination of the manual and oral methods, in the schools afterwards established. Even in Germany the ideas of De l'Épée and Sicard had considerable influence, leading to the development of a sign-language and the introduction of French methods to some extent. Within recent years, however, the tendency in Germany has been to return to the pure oral method, and this method has made great progress in other countries also, even in France supplanting the manual method to a considerable degree. At an International Convention of instructors held at Milan, Italy, in 1880, nearly all the teachers present, except those from the United States, voted in its favor, and since that date a majority of the European schools have adopted it in practice. In others a combination of the manual and oral methods is preferred.

When the first school in the United States was opened at Hartford, Dr. T. H. Gallaudet introduced the manual method, which he learned from Sicard in Paris. This method, developed and improved by able teachers in America, prevailed almost exclusively in this country until the year 1867, when two oral schools were established—one in New York and one in Massachusetts. In the same year Dr. E. M. Gallaudet, President of the National Deaf-Mute College at Washington, D. C., a son of the founder of deaf-mute instruction in America, spent six months in visiting European schools, and on his return presented a report in which, while he maintained the soundness of the principles upon which the system of instruction pursued in America was based, he strongly urged the importance and value of speech and speech-reading to the deaf and recommended that all the pupils should be afforded opportunities of acquiring these accomplishments until it plainly appeared that success was unlikely to crown their efforts: while with those who evinced facility in oral exercises the instruction should be continued during their entire school life. At a conference of Principals of American Schools, held in Washington in 1868, after a full and free discussion, President Gallaudet's views were almost unanimously adopted. Since that time most of our schools, while still using the sign-language and the manual alphabet, have made speech and speech-reading in various ways a part of the course of instruction for a part at least of their pupils, thus seeking to combine the advantages of both the oral and manual methods. The pure oral method is followed in a few schools and the pure manual in a few others; but the combined method in some form prevails in a large majority of the schools in the United States.*

On the Continent of Europe schools for the deaf are chiefly suported by tuition fees and the voluntary contributions of the benevolent, often in connection with religious societies, aided to a large extent by state, provincial, and city governments. In Great Britain they are almost wholly dependent upon tuition fees and voluntary contributions, with some assistance from Boards of Guardians of the Poor. In the United States they are generally supported by the State governments, and education in them is free to all children who are too deaf to receive instruction in the common schools.

SCHOOL AGE.

There is a difference of opinion among experienced teachers as to the best age for sending deaf children to school. On the one hand, such children have so much to learn as compared with hearing children that their education ought to be begun as early as possible: on the other, there are obvious objections to taking them away from their homes—as in the great majority of cases is necessary in order that they may receive proper instruction—while they are still very young. The decision must depend largely upon the circumstances of the individual, and the facilities offered by the State in which he resides. Where the term of instruction afforded by the State is limited to six or seven years, and where children are surrounded by favorable influences at home, probably ten or twelve is the best age for them to be sent to school, since experience has shown that the six or seven years following that age are those in which the most can be accomplished for the physical, mental, and moral development of the deaf-mute; but where, as is the case in some States, there is no limit to the term of instruction, where proper provision is made for the care and teaching of the little children by kindergarten methods apart from the older pupils, and especially where the home influences are bad, it is desirable to send them as young as six years of age. From six to ten they will make less progress at school than from ten to fourteen; but if, in addition to those four years under ten, they remain six or seven years longer, they will be able to acquire a much fuller mastery of the language of their fellow-men, and to reach a far more advanced stage of education in all respects than if their education had not been begun until the years of early childhood were passed.

BOARDING-SCHOOLS AND DAY-SCHOOLS.

The experience of more than a century has shown that the education of deaf-mutes can be most efficiently and successfully carried on in special boarding-schools. Except in large cities, the number of deaf children in the community is too small to render the organization of day-schools practicable, and in cities the evil influences that surround many of them at home, the temptations of the street out of school-hours, the danger of accidents in going to and from school, the interruptions to progress from tardiness and absence, and the lack of facilities for industrial instruction, make the results much less satisfactory than in the well-organized boarding-school, where the influences of the workshop, the play-ground, and the evening study-hour all combine with those of the school-room to promote the proper development and education of the child. Excellent work, however, is done in some of our day-schools; for children who are surrounded by good influences at home, with parents, brothers, and sisters who will take pains to guard them from harm, and to advance their education out of school, the day-school is to be recommended in some cases, especially during the earlier years of school-life, in preference to sending them away from home to the boarding-school. But for the great majority of deaf-mutes the advantage of the boarding-school over the day-school is shown in the fact that in the former the physical, intellectual, and moral welfare, of all the pupils is cared for in every way all the time, while in the latter the good gained during the five hours, more or less, that they are in the school-room five or six days of each week, is counteracted in many cases by the pernicious influences that surround them during the much larger portion of time that they are out of school.

The idea of having deaf-mutes taught in the public schools, wholly or in part with hearing children, has commended itself to many distinguished educators, and in several countries of Europe the experiment has been faithfully and zealously tried with the sanction and aid of the government. It has, however, on account of the essential difference in the methods of instruction required for deaf and hearing children, invariably resulted in failure, and all systematic and organized efforts in this direction have now been abandoned in Europe (Gordon: *Annals*, 1885). A plan for the establishment of deaf-mute schools in connection with public schools, the instruction given to be partly special and partly in common with hearing children, has recently been proposed in the United States by Dr. Alexander Graham Bell; but experienced teachers do not share his expectation that it will effect a revolution in the methods of deaf-mute instruction, nor believe that under the most favorable circumstances it will produce any other good results than those which have followed similar experiments in Europe, viz., the awakening of more interest in the subject of deaf-mute education, the growth of special schools in some places where they are needed, and in others the preparation of deaf children in common schools for their future education in special schools by teaching them habits of neatness, order, and obedience, the use of the pencil and pen, counting, and some elementary knowledge of words (Walther: "*Geschichte des Taubstummen-Bildungswesens*," 1882).

PRIVATE INSTRUCTION AT HOME.

It has been said by a high authority that "the best deaf-mute school is a school of one pupil," but the statement is not to be received without some qualification. In order to attain a mastery of spoken or written language the more individual attention the deaf child receives the better, and in this respect private instruction at home has a decided advantage over class instruction at school. On the other hand, the

* For a fuller definition and explanation of the various methods of instruction see the *Annals*, vol. xxvii, page 32.

child taught alone at home, and thus lacking the stimulus of association with others placed on an equal footing with himself, is apt to become listless in study and melancholy in disposition. The best advice, therefore, to be given to parents whose means enable them to provide a private teacher is this: Obtain a competent tutor or governess for your child at three or four years of age. Let the efforts of this teacher for seven or eight years be devoted almost wholly to giving the child language, articulation, and speech-reading by the natural or intuitive method, which imitates as closely as the nature of the case allows the manner in which hearing children learn to speak, and let the teacher's efforts be heartily seconded by all the other members of the family. When the child is ten or twelve years old send him to school to pursue other branches of study and complete his education. The command of idiomatic language acquired by the home training is something that could not be imparted at school, while the moral and intellectual development received at school could not be attained at home.

Intelligent parents and friends, whose pecuniary circumstances do not allow them to employ a private teacher, can themselves do a great deal in the way of preparing their deaf children for school-life by forming in them habits of order and obedience, and by teaching them the use of the pencil and pen, counting, and common words in their written forms. If the child already possesses speech gained before hearing was lost, great efforts should be made to retain the speech and to cultivate the habit of reading the speech of others. If any hearing exists, it should be utilized in practice, the aid of the hearing tube, trumpet, and audiphone should be tried, and whichever instrument proves most effective should be employed. In all cases the deaf child should be governed with the same firmness as his hearing brothers and sisters. While due allowance should be made for his inability to understand, and he should be protected as far as possible from the teasing of playmates, he can and should be taught strict obedience to parents, and due respect for the rights of others.

AURICULAR INSTRUCTION.

A very large proportion of persons so deaf as usually to be classed as deaf-mutes possess more or less hearing. Sixty years ago Dr. Itard estimated the proportion of the semi-deaf among deaf-mutes at eighty per cent., and a commission of the French Academy of Medicine in 1828 recommended the establishment in the Royal Institution for Deaf-Mutes at Paris of a special class for the semi-deaf, with a view to the education of the aural sense. Nothing, however, was actually accomplished in this direction until the year 1882, when Mr. J. A. Gillespie, Principal of the Nebraska Institute, having arrived, independently, at conclusions similar to Itard's, organized in his school a class of semi-deaf children. About fifteen per cent. of the pupils were found capable of instruction through the ear, directly, or with the aid of acoustic instruments. Mr. Gillespie's success led to the further investigation of the subject by a committee appointed for the purpose by the Convention of Articulation Teachers held in New York in 1884, who have tested the hearing of the pupils in various schools by means of the audiometer, the audiphone, ear-tubes, ear-trumpets, tuning-forks, bells, musical instruments, the voice, etc. While definite conclusions are not yet reached, it is evident that the hearing power that often exists unnoticed in the deaf can in many cases be educated by careful and skilful training, and that a considerable number of the pupils of our schools "can and ought," as Mr. Gillespie claims, "to be graduated as hard-of-hearing speaking people, instead of deaf-mutes, as heretofore."

MANUAL ALPHABETS.

The manual alphabets employed by educated deaf-mutes afford a means of communication more rapid and convenient than writing, and more exact than articulation and speech-reading. They are easily acquired by the friends of the deaf, and practice gives great facility in their use.

The single-hand alphabet is used in the schools of the United States following the combined and manual methods of instruction, and to some extent in those of Great Britain and her colonies. It is also employed in France, and with some variations in the other countries of Europe. It has the advantage over the two-hand alphabet of leaving one hand free for other uses, as driving, or carrying an umbrella, at the same time that one is spelling.

The two-hand alphabet is used in most of the English schools following the combined and manual methods of instruction, and educated deaf-mutes in all English-speaking countries, even where the single-hand alphabet is preferred, are generally familiar with it. It is said to admit of even greater rapidity than the single-hand alphabet.

The Dalgarno, or glove alphabet, is preferred in some schools where prominence is given to oral teaching, since it can be used by the sense of touch while the eyes of the pupil are fixed upon the teacher's lips, and, not being generally understood, it affords a less frequent means of escape from practice in speech and speech-reading. By a modification of this alphabet, employed by Dr. Alexander Graham Bell, the letters are indicated by touching various parts of the pupil's shoulder instead of the hand. All the letters of a short word or of a syllable can be made simultaneously, and the force of accent and rhythm can be given.

VISIBLE SPEECH AND LINE-WRITING.

In the year 1872, Dr. Alexander Graham Bell applied the system of "Visible Speech," invented by his father, Professor Alexander Melville Bell, to the instruction of deaf-mutes in articulation. Visible Speech is a species of phonetic writing, and, as it is based not upon sounds but upon the action of the vocal organs in producing them, its principles are as easily comprehended by the deaf as by hearing persons. Each letter of the Visible Speech Alphabet, to a person familiar with the system, is a picture of the vocal organs placed in the proper position for producing the sound indicated, so that the writing of any word in this alphabet shows its correct pronunciation. Visible Speech has been introduced into several schools in the United States, and is regarded by some teachers as a useful aid in their work. Others, including some of the most experienced oral teachers, look upon it as more of a hindrance than a help to young children, for whom, it is said, its symbols are no less arbitrary than the letters of the English alphabet. All are agreed, however, that the principles of physiological speech taught in Professor Melville Bell's works are very valuable to teachers of articulation.

Dr. Graham Bell has recently (1885) introduced a modification of one of his father's alphabets called Line-Writing, which has the advantage of being much more rapidly written than the symbols of Visible Speech heretofore used in the instruction of the deaf.

HIGHER EDUCATION.

The standard of education in schools for deaf-mutes at the present day corresponds in general to that of the common schools—an education fitting the pupil for intelligent citizenship. But there are some among the deaf who are capable of advancing beyond this standard and preparing themselves for scientific and literary pursuits. The United States makes provisions for the wants of this class in the National Deaf-Mute College established by Congress at Washington, D. C., in the year 1864, through the efforts of Edward M. Gallaudet, Ph. D., LL. D., who has been its president from the beginning. This college affords a course of training corresponding to that of American colleges in general, with such modifications as seem desirable in view of the peculiar needs of the deaf, and confers upon its graduates the usual academic degrees. Of the students who have been connected with the college a large number are now engaged in teaching, several are editors and publishers, others are in the civil service of the government, one is a lawyer practising in the Supreme Court of the United States, one is at the head of large assaying works in Chicago, one is a missionary to the deaf in Pennsylvania, and nearly all are occupying positions of a higher grade than would have been possible without the educational advantages conferred by the college course.

RELIGIOUS WORK FOR ADULTS.

The moral and religious instruction given in most of the American schools for the deaf is of an unsectarian character, the pupils being advised by their teachers to connect themselves during their vacations, or after leaving the schools, with the churches to which their parents belong. Adult deaf-mutes, however, can derive much more pleasure and profit from special services in the sign-language than from ordinary religious exercises, and in places where their numbers are sufficiently large to form a congregation the holding of such services is entirely practicable. The Rev. Thomas Gallaudet, D. D., of New York, established a church for deaf-mutes in that city in 1852, and, through his efforts and those of other friends of the deaf, arrangements are now made by which religious services in the sign-language are held weekly in several cities of the United States, and at less frequent intervals in many other places. The Episcopal Church, with which Dr. Gallaudet is connected, has been by far the most active in providing for the religious welfare of adult deaf-mutes, but other churches have also had a part in the work. There are now (1886) five ordained clergymen in the United States who are themselves deaf—three of them Episcopalians, and two Congregationalists—and there are a large number of deaf laymen who assist in missionary work. Similar work for the benefit of adult deaf-mutes is carried on in Great Britain and Ireland. In connection with the religious organizations there usually exist benevolent and relief societies, and in some cases literary and social unions. While this association of the deaf with one another, rather than with hearing persons, is to be regretted on some accounts (see Mental Condition and Characteristics, *supra*), it is also productive of good in the mutual aid and support it leads them to render, the comfort and enjoyment they derive from the free interchange of thought and sentiment, and the opportunities it affords for their intellectual, moral, and religious instruction.

STATISTICS OF SCHOOLS FOR THE DEAF 1885.

[This Exhibit consisted of the following tables from the *American Annals for the Deaf*, January, 1886, Vol. XXXI, pp. 82–91.]

SCHOOLS FOR THE EDUCATION OF THE DEAF IN THE UNITED STATES, 1885.

A.—Public Schools.

	Name.	Location.	Date of opening.	Chief Executive Officer.
1	American Asylum for the Education of the Deaf and Dumb	Hartford, Conn.	1817	Job Williams, M. A., Principal.
2	New York Institution for the Instruction of the Deaf and Dumb	Wash. Heights, New York, N. Y.	1818	Isaac Lewis Peet, LL. D., Principal; Chauncey N. Brainerd, Superintend't.
3	Pennsylvania Institution for the Deaf and Dumb	Philadelphia, (m) Pa	1820	A. L. E. Crouter, M. A., Principal.
4	Kentucky Institution for the Instruction of the Deaf and Dumb	Danville, Ky	1823	W. K. Argo, B. A., Superintendent.
5	Ohio Institution for the Education of the Deaf and Dumb	Columbus, Ohio	1829	Amasa Pratt, M. A., do.
6	Virginia Institution for the Education of the Deaf and Dumb and the Blind.	Staunton, Va	1839	Thomas S. Doyle, Principal.
7	Indiana Institution for the Education of the Deaf and Dumb	Indianapolis, Ind	1844	Eli P. Baker, Superintendent.
8	Tennessee School for the Deaf and Dumb	Knoxville, Tenn	1845	Thomas L. Moses, Principal.
9	North Carolina Institution for the Deaf and Dumb and the Blind	Raleigh, N. C	1845	W. J. Young, M. A., do.
10	Illinois Institution for the Education of the Deaf and Dumb	Jacksonville, Ill	1846	Philip G. Gillett, LL. D., Superintend't.
11	Georgia Institution for the Education of the Deaf and Dumb	Cave Spring, Ga	1846	W. O. Connor, Principal.
12	South Carolina Institution for Education of the Deaf and Dumb and the Blind.	Cedar Spring, S. C	1849	Newton F. Walker, Superintendent.
13	Missouri Institution for the Education of the Deaf and Dumb	Fulton, Mo	1851	Wm. D. Kerr, M. A., do.
14	Louisiana Institution for the Deaf and Dumb	Baton Rouge, La.	1852	John Jastremski, M. D., do.
15	Wisconsin School for the Deaf	Delavan, Wis	1852	John W. Swiler, M. A., do.
16	Michigan Institution for Educating the Deaf and Dumb	Flint, Mich	1854	M. T. Gass, M. A., do.
17	Iowa Institution for the Education of the Deaf and Dumb	Council Bluffs, Iowa	1855	Henry C. Hammond, M. A., do.
18	Mississippi Institution for the Education of the Deaf and Dumb	Jackson, Miss	1856	J. R. Dobyns, do.
19	Texas Deaf and Dumb Asylum	Austin, Texas	1856	Rev. Wm. Shapard, do.
20	Columbia Institution for the Deaf and Dumb	Kendall Green, near Wash., D. C.	1857	E. M. Gallaudet, Ph. D., LL. D., Pres't.
	A. Kendall School for the Deaf	do	1857	James Denison, M. A., Principal.
	B. National Deaf-Mute College	do	1864	E. M. Gallaudet, Ph. D., LL. D., Pres't.
21	Alabama Institution for the Deaf and Dumb and the Blind	Talladega, Ala	1860	Joseph H. Johnson, M. D., Principal.
22	California Institution for the Deaf and Dumb and the Blind	Berkeley, Cal	1860	Warring Wilkinson, M. A., do.
23	Kansas Institution for the Education of the Deaf and Dumb	Olathe, Kansas	1861	S. T. Walker, Superintendent.
24	Le Couteulx St. Mary's Institution for Deaf and Dumb	Buffalo, (l) N. Y	1862	Sister Mary Anne Burke, Principal.
25	Minnesota School for the Deaf	Faribault, Minn	1863	Jonathan L. Noyes, M. A., Sup't.
26	Institution for the Improved Instruction of Deaf-Mutes	New York, (a) N. Y.	1867	D. Greenberger, Principal.
27	Clarke Institution for Deaf-Mutes	Northampton, Mass	1867	Miss Harriet B. Rogers, Principal.
28	Arkansas Deaf-Mute Institute	Little Rock, Ark	1867	Francis D. Clarke, M. A., do.
29	Maryland School for the Deaf and Dumb	Frederick City, Md.	1868	Chas. W. Ely, M. A., do.
30	Nebraska Institute for the Deaf and Dumb	Omaha, Neb.	1869	John A. Gillespie, M. A., do.
31	Horace Mann School for the Deaf	Boston, (b) Mass	1869	Miss Sarah Fuller, do.
32	St. Joseph's Institution for the Improved Instruction of Deaf-Mutes (f).	Fordham, N. Y.	1869	Ernestine Nardin, President.
33	West Virginia Institution for the Deaf and Dumb and Blind	Romney, W. Va	1870	John C. Covell, M. A., Principal.
34	Oregon School for Deaf-Mutes	Salem, Oregon	1870	Rev. P. S. Knight, Superintendent.
35	Maryland School for Colored Blind and Deaf-Mutes	Baltimore, (c) Md	1872	F. D. Morrison, M. A., do.
36	Colorado Institute for Mute and Blind	Colorado Springs, Colo.	1874	D. C. Dudley, M. A., do.
37	Chicago Deaf-Mute Day Schools (h)	Chicago, Ill.	1875	P. A. Emery, M. A. Principal.
38	Central New York Institution for Deaf-Mutes	Rome, N. Y	1875	Edward B. Nelson, B. A., Principal.
39	Cincinnati Day-School for Deaf-Mutes	Cincinnati, (e) Ohio	1875	A. F. Wood, Principal.
40	Western Pennsylvania Institution for the Deaf and Dumb	Edgewood, near Wilkinsburg, Pa	1876	Rev. J. G. Brown, D. D., Principal.
41	Western New York Institution for Deaf-Mutes	Rochester, N. Y.	1876	Z. F. Westervelt, Principal and Sup't.
42	Portland School for the Deaf	Portland, Me	1876	Miss Ellen L. Barton, Principal.
43	Rhode Island School for the Deaf	Providence, (d) R. I.	1877	Miss Anna M. Black, do.
44	St. Louis Day-School for Deaf-Mutes	St. Louis, (g) Mo.	1878	D. A. Simpson, B. A., do.
45	New England Industrial School for Deaf-Mutes	Beverly, Mass	1880	Miss Nellie H. Swett, do.
46	Dakota School for Deaf-Mutes	Sioux Falls, D. T	1880	James Simpson, Superintendent.
47	Milwaukee Day-School for the Deaf	Milwaukee, (i) Wis	1883	Paul Binner, Principal.
48	Pennsylvania Oral School for Deaf-Mutes	Scranton, Pa	1883	Miss Emma Garrett, Principal.
49	New Jersey School for Deaf-Mutes	Chambersburg, n'r Trenton, N.J.	1883	Weston Jenkins, M. A., Superintendent.
50	Deseret School for Deaf-Mutes	Salt Lake City, Utah	1884	Henry C. White, B. A., Principal.
51	Northern New York Institution for Deaf-Mutes	Malone, N. Y	1884	Henry C. Rider, Superintendent.
52	Florida Blind and Deaf-Mute Institute	St. Augustine, Fla	1885	Park Terrell, Principal.
53	Public Schools, including the National College.			
11	Denominational and Private Schools. (k)			
64	Schools in the United States.			

(a) Lexington Ave., bet. 67th and 68th streets. (b) No. 63 Warrenton street. (c) No. 258 Saratoga street. (d) Cor. Fountain and Beverly streets. (e) Ninth street, bet. Walnut and Main. (f) This Institution has three branches; one situated at Fordham, another at Brooklyn (510 Henry street), and another at Throgg's Neck, Westchester Co., N. Y. (g) Cor. 9th and Wash. streets. (h) There are five schools in different parts of the city. Mr. Emery's address is 43 So. May street. (i) Corner 7th and Prairie streets. (k) See [B, p. 74]. (l) No. 125 Edward street. (m) Broad and Pine, and Eleventh and Clinton streets.

SCHOOLS FOR THE EDUCATION OF THE DEAF IN THE UNITED STATES, 1885—Continued.

PUBLIC SCHOOLS—Continued.

	Name.	Method of instruction.	School-hours.	Trades.†	No. of pupils. During the year.* Total.	Male.	Female.	No. taught articulation.	Present Dec. 1, 1885.	Total have rec'd instruction.	No. of instructors.† Whole No.	Male.	Female.	Deaf-mute.‡	Semi-mute.
1	American Asylum	Combined	9 to 12 and 2 to 4	Cab., Sb., Ta.	204	121	83	48	160	2,384	16	7	9	1	2
2	New York Institution	...do...	8 to 12 and 1 to 5 (b)	Art., Bak., Cab., Car., Cl., Dr., Ga., Gl., Pa., Pr., Sh., Ta.	414	262	152	(a)	388	3,074	16	8	8	3	3
3	Pennsylvania ...do...	Oral and comb'd.	8 to 12½	Ck., Dr., Kn., Pr., Sh., Ta.	466	258	208	143	426	2,159	34	10	24	2	3
4	Kentucky ...do...	Combined	8 to 1	Bo., Car., Ga., Pr., Se.	161	92	69	16	146	850	12	7	5	3	2
5	Ohio ...do...	...do...	8½ to 10¼, 10½ to 12½, 2 to 4½ (e).	Bo., Car., Pr., Sh.	458	243	215	80	377	2,093	26	15	11	6	6
6	Virginia ...do...	Oral and manual.	8½ to 1½	Bo., Cab., Car., Pr., Sh., Ta.	98	52	46	36	82	577	11	6	5	2	2
7	Indiana ...do...	Combined	8 to 1	Cab., Ch., Sh.	374	204	170	60	308	1,507	18	8	10	4	6
8	Tennessee School	...do...	8½ to 11½ and 1 to 3	Pr., Sh.	148	91	57	13	122	......	8	5	3	2	0
9	North Carolina Institution	Oral&man	8 to 2	Sh.	125	60	56	23	125	......	8	5	3	4	0
10	Illinois ...do...	Combined	8 to 11 and 12, 1 to 3 and 4½	Bak., Cab., Cl., Dr., Ga., Gl., Pa., Pr., Sh., Wc.	584	339	245	150	584	1,810	31	8	23	5	2
11	Georgia ...do...	Manual	8 to 1	Sh.	90	58	32	7	80	377	7	6	1	1	3
12	South Carolina ...do...	Combined	8 to 1	Pr., Se., Sh.	67	36	31	13	57	100	4	3	1	2	0
13	Missouri School	...do...	8 to 1	Cab., Pr., Sh.	261	160	101	60	195	903	13	6	7	2	1
14	Louisiana ...do...	......	......	......	......	......	......	......	......	......	......	......	......	......	......
15	Wisconsin ...do...	...do...	8 to 12 and 1 to 3	Ba., Car., Dr., Pr., Se., Sb.	231	140	91	61	197	722	14	6	8	3	1
16	Michigan ...do...	...do...	8 to 11 and 12½ to 3½ (b)	Ba., Cab., Car., Pr., Se., Sh.	321	176	145	85	297	1,083	18	6	12	2	3
17	Iowa ...do...	...do...	8 to 12½ and 1½ to 4½	Car., Fa., Pr., Sh.	285	160	125	70	260	657	15	8	7	2	2
18	Mississippi ...do...	...do...	8 to 1	Cab., Pr.	100	60	40	30	70	......	6	4	2	2	1
19	Texas Asylum	...do...	8½ to 1½	Bo., Car., Pr., Sh.	146	90	56	33	119	200	9	4	5	1	1
20	Columbia Institution	......	......	......	121	103	18	48	106	824	15	13	2	2	3
	A. Kendall School	...do...	8¼ to 12¼ and 2 to 3	Cab	73	55	18	48	62	545	6	4	2	2	1
	B. National College	Manual	8 to 12½ and 1½ to 3½	None	48	48	0	0	44	279	9	9	0	0	2
21	Alabama Institution	...do...	8 to 1	......	65	35	30	13	50	210	6	3	3	2	0
22	California ...do...	Combined	8 to 1	Cl., Gar., Pr., Wood-w'k'g.	138	84	54	38	122	201	9	5	4	3	0
23	Kansas ...do...	...do...	8 to 10¼, 10½ to 12¼, 1¼ to 4	Cab., Pr., Se., Sh.	225	127	98	50	189	444	14	6	8	2	2
24	Le Couteulx St. Mary's Inst.	Oral and combined	8 to 12 and 1½ to 4 (b)	Dr., Pr., Sh., Ta.	150	80	70	100	136	370	11	0	11	1	0
25	Minnesota School	Combined	8 to 12½	Co., Dr., Pr., Sh., Ta.	164	93	71	40	130	386	11	6	5	2	3
26	Institution for Imp'd Inst'n	Oral	9 to 12 and 1½ to 3½	None	182	105	77	182	161	350	15	5	10	0	0
27	Clarke Institution	...do...	9 to 12 and 2 to 4	Cab., Se.	106	55	51	106	89	250	13	0	13	0	0
28	Arkansas Institute	Combined	8 to 12½	Art., Pr., Dr., Ga., Sh.	91	46	45	64	72	239	6	2	4	1	2
29	Maryland School	...do... (and aural	7½ to 9¾, 9¾ to 12½, 2 to 4½ (e).	Cab., Pr., Sh.	110	57	53	70	98	302	10	4	6	3	1
30	Nebraska Institute	Combined	8½ to 12 and 1½ to 3	Car., Pr., Se., Wc.	123	74	49	30	106	233	9	4	5	1	1
31	Horace Mann School	Oral	9 to 2	None	91	45	46	91	78	236	9	0	9	0	0
32	St. Joseph's Institution	Combined and oral.	9 to 3½	Ba., Dr., Ga., Sh., Car., Ta.	271	114	157	271	256	452	19	1	18	2	1
33	West Virginia Institution	Combined	8½ to 1½	Cab., Pr., Sh., Ta.	76	42	34	22	64	219	6	4	2	1	2
34	Oregon School	Manual	8 to 12½	None	29	13	16	0	24	77	3	2	1	1	0
35	Md. Institution for Colored.	...do...	8 to 1	Br., Ch.	19	13	6	......	19	55	2	1	1	1	0
36	Colorado Institute	...do...	8 to 1	Car., Ck., Pr., Se.	45	24	21	9	38	82	4	3	1	0	2
37	Chicago Day-Schools	Manual	9 to 12 and 1 to 2½	None	45	22	23	10	43	130	6	2	4	1	2
38	Central N. Y. Institution	Combined	9 to 12 and 1½ to 3½	Cab., Dr., Gl., Pr., Sh.	164	102	62	15	156	270	12	8	4	3	4
39	Cincinnati Day-School	Manual	9 to 12 and 1½ to 4	None	36	22	14	0	24	80	2	1	1	2	0
40	Western Penna. Institution	Combined	8¾ to 12 and 1½ to 3½	Cab., Car., Sh.	145	98	47	29	127	230	9	4	5	0	3
41	Western New York Instit'n	...do...	8½ to 12½ and 2 to 4	Car., Ck., Gl., Dr., Ga., Pa., Pr.	179	95	84	179	165	256	14	1	13	1	1
42	Portland Day-School	Oral	9 to 12 and 2 to 4	None	46	26	20	46	45	56	5	0	5	0	0
43	Rhode Island School	...do...	9 to 1	None	32	16	16	30	26	54	4	0	4	0	0
44	St. Louis Day-School	Manual	8¾ to 12 and 1½ to 3½	None	45	31	14	......	40	80	3	1	2	1	2
45	N. E. Industrial School	Combined	9 to 12 and 2 to 4	Fa.	21	10	11	13	21	55	2	0	2	1	0
46	Dakota School	Manual	9 to 12 and 2 to 4	Fa., Gar.	36	28	8	0	30	41	2	1	1	1	1
47	Milwaukee Day-School	Oral	9 to 12 and 12½ to 2½	None	25	13	12	25	25	25	3	1	2	0	0
48	Pennsylvania Oral School	...do...	9 to 2	None	18	13	5	18	13	28	1	0	1	0	0
49	New Jersey Institution	Combined	9 to 12 and 1½ to 3½	Dr., Sh.	119	67	52	22	98	134	7	1	6	0	0
50	Deseret School	Manual	9 to 1	None	20	12	8	0	16	20	1	1	0	...	...
51	Northern New York Inst'n	Combined	9 to 12 and 1½ to 3½	None	37	30	7	7	37	37	4	4	0	0	2
52	Florida Institute	...do...	8 to 11 and 1 to 4	None	8	7	1	5	8	8	2	1	1	0	0
53	Public Schools	......	......	......	7636	4417	3219	g2511	6660	26,095	520	220	300	81	75
11	Denom'l and Pri. Sch's (d)	......	......	......	165	99	66	107	120	421	20	8	12	0	0
64	Sch'ls in the United States	......	......	......	7801	4516	3285	g2618	6780	26,516	540	228	312	81	75

*Including those who have left school during the year. †Including the principal. ‡Not including the semi-mute. (a) All the pupils are taught lip-reading for one hour daily. (b) One session for school and one for shops, by a system of rotation. (c) Two sessions for school and one for shops, by a system of rotation. (d) See page 88. (e) For the year 1884. (g) Not including the pupils of the New York Institution.

§ Bak. = Baking. Bas. = Basket-making. Bo. = Book-binding. Br. = Broom-making. Cab. = Cabinet-making. Car. = Carpentry. Ch. = Chair-making. Ck. = Cooking. Cl. = Clay modelling. Co. = Coopery. Dr. = Dress-making. Fa. = Farming. Ga. = Gardening. Gl. = Glazing. Kn. = Knitting. Ma. = Mattress-making. Pa. = Painting. Pr. = Printing. Se. = Sewing. Sh. = Shoemaking. Ta. = Tailoring. Wc. = Wood-carving. We. = Wood-engraving. Wt. = Wood-turning.

SCHOOLS FOR THE EDUCATION OF THE DEAF IN THE UNITED STATES, 1885—Continued.

PUBLIC SCHOOLS—Continued.

Name.	Vacation.	How supported.	Value of build'gs and grounds.	Expenditure last fiscal year. For support.	Expenditure last fiscal year. For build'gs and gro'ds.	No. vols. in library.
1 American Asylum	Last Wed. in June to 2d Wed. in Sept	Endowment and N. E. States.	$250,000	$47,400	....	2,000
2 New York Institution	4th Wed. in June to 1st Wed. in Sept	State, co'ties, and pay pupils.	560,500	99,949	$7,705	3,348
3 Pennsylvania ....do	Last Wed. in June to first Wed. in Sept	State and endowment	565,000	90,074	16,608	5,500
4 Kentucky ....do	Last Thurs. in June to about 1st Sept	State	142,000	31,268	6,000	1,600
5 Ohio ....do	Third Wed. in June to second Wed. in Sept	...do	700,000	77,083	8,000	2,000
6 Virginia ....do*	Wed. before 2d Thurs. in June to first Wed. in Sept	...do	175,000	34,640	....	500
7 Indiana ....do	Second Wed. in June to second Wed. in Sept	...do	459,000	52,836	2,966	3,500
8 Tennessee School	June 10 to Sept. 15	...do	125,000	24,000	12,000	600
9 North Carolina Institution.*	Second Wed. in June to second Wed. in Sept	...do	100,000	36,000	....	1,321
10 Illinois ....do	Second Wed. in June to third Wed. in Sept	...do	356,000	90,000	6,000	7,254
11 Georgia ....do	Third Wed. in June to second Wed. in Sept	...do	40,000	15,815	....	1,000
12 South Carolina ...do*	Last Wed. in June to 1st Wed. in Oct	State and pay pupils	55,000	10,843	7,850	....
13 Missouri ....do	Second Wed. in June to second Wed. in Sept	State	175,000	46,326	....	1,017
14 Louisiana ....do	....	...do	....	....	....	....
15 Wisconsin ....do	June to first Wed. in Sept	...do	97,000	40,000	11,000	700
16 Michigan ....do	June 17th to Sept. 9th	...do	475,000	45,000	....	2,306
17 Iowa ....do	Middle of June to middle of Sept	...do	350,000	38,000	24,000	....
18 Mississippi ....do	Third Wed. in June to Oct. 1st	...do	75,000	16,175	300	300
19 Texas Asylum	1st Wed. in June to 1st Wed. in Sept	State	100,000	31,580	10,508	700
20 Columbia Institution	Wed. before last Wed. in June to Thurs. before last Thurs. in Sept.	United States and pay pupils	675,000	61,332	3,000	3,000
21 Alabama ....do	June 15th to Sept. 15th	State	75,000	16,000	2,000	600
22 California ....do*	Second Wed. in June to 4th Wed. in August	...do	350,000	45,640	5,000	1,200
23 Kansas ....do	Second Wed. in June to second Wed. in Sept	...do	125,000	32,000	25,000	200
24 Le Couteulx St. Mary's Inst.	July 1st to Sept. 1st	State, co'ties, and pay pupils	120,000	30,000	5,000	200
25 Minnesota School	June 9th to second Wed. in Sept	State	200,000	32,000	10,000	1,100
26 N. Y. Inst. for Imp. Instr'n	Third Wed. in June to first Wed. in Sept	State, co'ties, and pay pupils	320,000	80,336	4,101	....
27 Clarke Institution	Forty weeks after third Wed. in Sept. to third Wed. in Sept.	Endowm't, State, and pay p'ls.	90,000	27,334	846	1,100
28 Arkansas Institute	4th Wed. in June to first Wed. in Oct	State	60,000	16,315	8,827	....
29 Maryland School	Third Wed. in June to second Wed. in Sept	...do	250,000	26,000	....	2,150
30 Nebraska Institute	Middle of June to middle of Sept	...do	80,000	23,000	12,000	825
31 Horace Mann School	Last Tues. in June to first Mon. in Sept	State and city	....	....	....	300
32 St. Joseph's Institution	Last Fri. in June to first Mon. in Sept	State, co'ties, and pay pupils	106,175	20,243	12,640	450
33 West Virginia Institution*	Forty weeks after first Mon. in Sept. to first Mon. in Sept.	State	80,000	24,957	....	710
34 Oregon School	May 1st to Sept. 1st	State and voluntary cont'ions.	5,000	5,000	1,000	....
35 Md. Institution for Colored*	June 20th to Sept. 10th	State	25,000	....	....	....
36 Colorado Institute*	First Wed. in June to first Wed. in Sept	...do	45,000	21,000	2,000	....
37 Chicago Day-Schools	Last Fri. in June to first Mon. in Sept	...do	....	....	....	....
38 Central N. Y. Institution	Second Wed. in June to third Wed. in Sept	...do	65,000	39,234	....	210
39 Cincinnati Day-School	June 21st to Sept. 6th	City	....	....	....	....
40 Western Penna. Institution	Last Wed. in June to first Wed in Sept	State and pay pupils	150,000	32,282	44,810	125
41 Western New York Inst'n	Third Mon. in June to first Mon. in Sept	State, co'ties, and pay pupils	60,000	38,311	2,560	550
42 Portland Day-School	Last Fri. before July 4th to second Mon. in Sept	State and city	....	....	....	....
43 Rhode Island School	June 26th to Sept. 1st	State	....	....	....	300
44 St. Louis Day-School	Second Thurs. in June to first Mon. in Sept	City	....	....	....	....
45 N. E. Industrial School	Middle of June to second Wed. in Sept	Voluntary contributions	....	2,772	....	375
46 Dakota School	Second Wed. in June to second Wed. in Sept	Territory	29,000	....	16,000	30
47 Milwaukee Day-School	July 3d to first Mon. in Sept	State aid	....	2,000	....	....
48 Penna. Oral School	Third week in June to Sept. 1	City and voluntary cont'ions.	....	....	....	....
49 New Jersey Institution	Last Thurs. in June to second Wed. in Sept	State	100,000	....	....	....
50 Deseret School	May 28th to August 16th	Territory	....	4,000	....	....
51 Northern N. Y. Institution	Second Wed. in June to second Wed. in Sept	State and counties	....	6,120	....	....
52 Florida Institute*	Second Mon. in June to 1st Mon. in Oct	State	16,000	....	....	....
53 Public Schools.						
11 Denominational and Private Schools.						
64 Schools in the United States.						

* Contains a department for the blind also, the expenses of which are included in the statement of expenditures.

B.—DENOMINATIONAL AND PRIVATE SCHOOLS.

Name.	Location.	Date of opening.	Chief Executive Officer.
1 Whipple's Home School for Deaf-Mutes	Mystic River, Conn.	1869	N. F. Whipple, Principal.
2 German Evangelical Lutheran Institution for the Deaf and Dumb	Norris, Mich	1875	D. H. Uhlig, Director.
3 St. John's Catholic Deaf-Mute Institute	St. Francis, Wis	1876	Rev. Chas. Fessler, President.
4 Mr. Knapp's Institute	Baltimore, Md	1877	F. Knapp, Principal.
5 St. Joseph's Deaf-Mute Institute	Hannibal, Mo	1881	Sisters of St. Joseph.
6 Mr. Bell's Private School for Deaf Children	Washington, D. C. (a)	1883	A. Graham Bell, Ph. D., Superintendent.
7 Chicago Voice and Hearing School for the Deaf	Englewood, Ill	1883	Miss Mary McCowen, Principal.
8 Private School for Teaching Deaf Children to Speak	Philadelphia, Pa. (b)	1883	Miss Mary S. Garrett, Principal.
9 Washington School for Defective Youth	Tacoma, W. T	1885	Rev. W. D. McFarland, Director.
10 Convent of Maria Consilia Deaf-Mute Institute	St. Louis, Mo. (d)	1885	Sisters of St. Joseph.
11 New Mexico School for the Deaf and Dumb	Santa Fé, N. M	1885	Lars M. Larson, B. A., Principal.

(a) No. 1234 Sixteenth Street. (b) No. 7 Merrick Street. (d) 1849 Cass Avenue.

SCHOOLS FOR THE EDUCATION OF THE DEAF IN THE UNITED STATES, 1885—Continued.

B.—DENOMINATIONAL AND PRIVATE SCHOOLS—Continued.

	Name.	No. of pupils. During the Year.* Total.	Male.	Female.	No. taught articulation.	Present Dec. 1, 1885.	No. of instructors.† Whole No.	Male.	Female.	Deaf-mute.‡	Semi-mute.	Method of Instruction.	School-hours.	Trades.
1	Whipple's Home School (c)	12	9	3	12	8	2	1	1	0	0	Oral	9 to 12 and 1 to 4½	Gardening.
2	Germ. Ev. Lutheran Institution	40	24	16	40	40	3	3	0	0	0	..do	5½ hours	None.
3	St. John's Catholic Institute	45	28	17	9	24	3	2	1	0	0	Combined	Eight hours	Farming, Printing, Sewing, Shoe-[making.
4	Mr. Knapp's Institute	...	...	...	...	...	...	...	...	...	...	Oral	9 to 2	None.
5	St. Joseph's Institute	22	8	14	9	5	1	0	1	0	0	Combined	9 to 11½ and 1 to 3½	None.
6	Mr. Bell's School	6	4	2	6	5	3	1	2	0	0	Experimental	9 to 2	None.
7	Voice and Hearing School	23	14	9	23	21	5	0	5	0	0	Oral and aural	9 to 4	None.
8	Philadelphia School	8	8	0	8	8	1	0	1	0	0	Oral	9 to 2	None.
9	Washington School	9	4	5	0	9	2	1	1	0	0	Combined	8 to 1	None.
10	Maria Consilia Institute	...	...	...	...	...	...	...	...	...	...	...	...	...
11	New Mexico School	...	...	...	...	...	...	...	...	...	...	...	...	...
11	Denom. and Private Schools	165	99	66	107	120	20	8	12	0	0			

	Name.	Vacation.	How Supported.	No. pupils have rec'd instr'n.
1	Whipple's Home School	Last Wed. in June to first Wed. in Sept	Tuition fees and State	63
2	Germ. Ev. Lutheran Inst'n	July 15th to September 1st	Tuition fees and Lutheran Congregations	119
3	St. John's Cath. Institute	End of June to first week in Sept	Voluntary contributions and tuition fees	161
4	Mr. Knapp's Institute	...	...	...
5	St. Joseph's Institute	Last week of June to first Monday in Sept	Voluntary contributions and pay pupils	22
6	Mr. Bell's School	Middle of June to October 1st	Tuition fees and Mrs. Bell	6
7	Voice and Hearing School	July 1st to Sept	Tuition fees	33
8	Philadelphia School	June 15th to Sept. 15th	Tuition fees and subscriptions	8
9	Washington School	Last Thursday in May to last Wednesday in August	Private funds of Director	9
10	Maria Consilia Institute	...	...	...
11	New Mexico School	...	...	...
11	...	...	...	421

* Including the pupils who have left during the year. † Including the principal. ‡ Not including the semi-mute teachers. (c) For the year 1884.

SCHOOLS FOR THE EDUCATION OF THE DEAF IN CANADA, 1885.

	Name.	Location.	Date of opening.	Chief Executive Officer.
1	Catholic Male Deaf and Dumb Institution for the Province of Quebec	Mile-End, n'r Mon., Can.	1848	Rev. J. B. Manseau, P. S. V., Principal.
2	Institution for the Female Deaf and Dumb of the Province of Quebec	Montreal, Can. (a)	1851	Sister Philippe, Superior.
3	Halifax Institution for the Deaf and Dumb	Halifax, N. S.	1857	J. Scott Hutton, M. A., Principal.
4	Ontario Institution for the Deaf and Dumb	Belleville, Ontario	1870	R. Mathison, Superintendent.
5	Mackay Institution for Protestant Deaf and Dumb and the Blind	Montreal, Can	1870	Miss Harriet E. McGann, Superintend't.
6	New Brunswick Deaf and Dumb Institution	Portland, N. B.	1873	A. H. Abell, Principal.
7	Fredericton Institution for the Education of the Deaf and Dumb	Fredericton, N. B.	1882	Albert F. Woodbridge, Principal.
7	Schools in Canada.			

	Name.	No. of pupils. During the Year.* Total.	Male.	Female.	No. taught articulation.	Present Dec. 1, 1885.	No. of instructors.† Whole No.	Male.	Female.	Deaf-mute.‡	Semi-mute.	Method of Instruction.	School-hours.	Trades.**
1	Catholic Institution (Male)	117	117	0	30	74	§27	27	0	3	0	Manual and oral.	Five hours	Bo., Cab., Car., Fa., Ga., Pa., Pr., Sh., Ta., Wt.
2	Catholic Institution (Female)	185	0	185	60	139	§35	0	35	0	0	......do	8½ to 11½ and 1 to 3½	Se.
3	Halifax Institution	74	39	35	10	68	5	3	2	1	0	Combined	9 to 11, 11¼ to 12¾ and 2 to 4.	Car., Ga., Sh.
4	Ontario Institution	284	168	116	33	243	15	7	8	2	2	..... do	9 to 12 and 1½ to 3	Car., Dr., Sh., Ta.
5	Mackay Institution	45	25	20	12	36	4	1	3	0	1	..... do	9 to 12 and 1½ to 3½	Cab., Car., Dr., Pr.
6	New Brunswick Institution (b)	32	23	9	0	23	2	2	0	2	0	Manual	9 to 12 and 2 to 4	Car., Fa., Pa., Se., Sh., Ta.
7	Fredericton Institution (b)	20	11	9	2	16	2	2	0	0	0	Combined	............do	None.
7	...	757	383	374	147	601	90	42	48	8	3			

	Name.	Vacation.	How Supported.	Value of build'gs and grounds.	Expenditure Last Fiscal Year: For support.	For buildings and grounds.	No. volumes in library.	Total No. pupils have received instruction.
1	Catholic Inst'n (Male)	Last Wed. in June to first Wed. in Sept	State, pupils, and vol. contributions	$80,000	...	...	600	477
2	Catholic Inst'n (Female)	July 1st to first Tues. in Sept	State and voluntary contributions	200,000	...	...	800	...
3	Halifax Institution	Second Wed. in July to first Wed. in Sept	State and voluntary contributions	...	$9,776	$2,178	...	301
4	Ontario Institution	Third Wed. in June to second Wed. in Sept.	State	202,718	38,749	1,500	1,500	707
5	Mackay Institution	Third Wed. in June to second Wed. in Sept.	State, pupils, and vol. contributions	50,000	7,700	1,848	250	103
6	New Brunswick Inst'n	May 17 to Aug. 6	Pupils and voluntary contributions	...	...	...	...	99
7	Fredericton Institution	July 1st to Sept. 1st	State and voluntary contributions	...	...	...	...	31
7	...	...	...	...	...	...	...	2,018

* Including those who have left school during the year. † Including the principal. ‡ Not including the semi-mute teachers. § Comprising industrial instructors. ** Bo.=Book-binding. Cab.=Cabinet-making. Car.=Carpentry. Dr.=Dress-making. Fa.=Farming. Ga.=Gardening. Pa.=Painting. Pr.=Printing. Se.=Sewing. Sh.=Shoemaking. Ta.=Tailoring. Wt.=Wood-turning. (a) No. 401 St. Denis street. (b) For the year 1884.

THE TRUE COMBINED SYSTEM.

[This Exhibit consisted of the following paper by Mr. A. L. E. Crouter, published in the proceedings of the Eleventh Convention of American Instructors of the Deaf, 1886, pp. 146–152.]

The relative merits of the oral, manual, and combined methods of instruction, as pursued in American institutions for the deaf, have been so frequently and fully discussed that their further consideration may possibly appear to many superfluous; but, in view of the fact that these discussions have, as yet, led to no conclusions that have been accepted by the adherents of the different methods, I trust that a brief exposition of the defects of certain of them, and of the advantages of a system which I am led by experience to believe possesses the merits of all of them, with the smallest possible proportion of the defects of any, may be of interest to the members of this convention.

In the *American Annals of the Deaf and Dumb*, of January, 1882, Professor Fay, of the National Deaf-Mute College, says, after briefly describing the oral method of instruction: "The combined method is not so easy to define, as the term is applied to several distinct methods, such as: (1) the free use of signs and articulation with the same pupils and by the same instructors, throughout the course of instruction; (2) the general instruction of all the pupils by means of the manual method, with the special training of part of them in articulation and lip-reading, as an accomplishment; (3) the instruction of some pupils by the manual method and others by the oral method, in the same institution; (4) although this is rather a combined system, the employment of the manual method and oral method in separate schools and under the same general management, pupils being placed in one establishment or the other, as seems best in each individual case."

In this concise yet comprehensive statement, Professor Fay sets forth very clearly the salient features of the four distinct methods of instructing the deaf that are severally and collectively included in the term, "The American or Combined Method."

Beyond pointing out their advantages and commending them to the serious attention of the members of the convention, and especially of those who are at the head of large schools, where a system of classification according to the natural powers of deaf children can be most fully and profitably carried out, I shall have but little to say concerning the last two of the methods enumerated; but the first and second are so fraught with what, after a somewhat lengthy personal experience, I have come to believe is hurtful to the best interests of the deaf, that I propose to state, as briefly as the nature of the subject will allow, my objections to them, and to urge their discontinuance as a part of the American system of instruction.

The first of these methods seeks, by the free use of both signs and articulation, by the same teachers, in the same classes, to instruct all deaf children in spoken and written language and other branches of study. It is to this and to the succeeding method that reference is most commonly made when the term "combined method" is used. A more appropriate name for it would be, in my opinion, the mixed method, for there can certainly be no combination between two elements for a system of instruction which not only do not work together for a common object, but positively antagonize each other. A teacher working under this method not only tries to teach, by the aid of signs, the ordinary branches of a common-school education, which, with deaf children, is a sufficiently difficult task when performed under the most favorable circumstances, but, also, attempts to impart, as a separate branch of study, a knowledge of articulation and lip-reading. Here we have two entirely distinct and independent objects to be attained, each of which ordinarily demands the whole time and attention of an earnest instructor for its accomplishment. He then must be twice a man who, unaided, can bring about their satisfactory fulfilment. Mark that the purpose is not to give instruction orally in the ordinary branches of study (this is done by manual means), but to teach articulation and lip-reading in addition to them. Time thus devoted to articulation and speech-reading, as an accomplishment, is time taken from the other branches; it is insufficient for the attainment of the object in view, and, as a result, the child usually leaves school with imperfect powers of articulation which he soon loses from a disinclination to use them (which disinclination arises principally from his own knowledge of his imperfections), and, frequently, an inadequate knowledge of other and more essential branches of study.

Oral and manual instruction cannot be successfully imparted in the same class. The methods are diametrically opposed to each other, and when pursued thus closely together they expend their powers in counteracting the influence for good that each possesses. Under this form, the semi-mute, to whom the oral method is obviously best adapted, falls gradually into the habits of manual communication, with resulting detriment to his speech and speech-reading, while, to the congenital mute, the time thus devoted to articulation is ordinarily time wasted. Another defect of this method lies in the fact that it brings together in the school-room two greatly dissimilar classes of pupils. Very often there is a greater dissimilarity between the semi-mute and the congenital mute than between the semi-mute and the hearing child. A well-known English writer has said that a child learns more in the first seven years of its existence than in all the rest of its life. While this assertion may be somewhat extravagant, it is certainly true that the development of a child's mind is proportionately much more rapid during the first four or five years of its life than afterwards, and the child who, during these years, has been in full possession of all his normal faculties, will have a better developed mind and possess greater mental powers than one who has been deaf from birth. This being true, different methods of instruction are required for different classes of pupils, if each is to make the fullest possible progress. For congenital mutes, minute explanations and constant repetitions are necessary which to semi-mutes are generally superfluous and irksome; the former are slow of comprehension, and have constantly to retrace their steps; the latter are quick, and anxious and able to press forward rapidly. Thus it happens, when the two are brought together in the same school-room to receive the same instruction, the semi-mute cannot make as rapid progress as he would if unimpeded by those who cannot keep step with him, while the true mute, in struggling to keep up with his more favored classmate, suffers not only from the disadvantage of unequal mental development, but the added one of imperfect training, the result of a defective system of classification and improper methods of instruction. The semi-mute chafes at the delay, and gradually loses interest in his studies, while the congenital mute becomes discouraged, and finally sinks into a state of indifference, from which he is with difficulty aroused.

As for the teacher, he is but human, and cannot serve two masters in the school-room any more effectually than he can out of it. His desire to make a good record as an instructor tempts him to devote his time to the most progressive portion of his class, to the neglect of those most worthy of his best efforts. The mischief that results is not the fault of the teacher, but that of the system under which he is compelled to labor; and we think we but state the truth when we assert that, to the conscientious teacher, this method is the source of constant harassment and painful misgiving concerning the best welfare of his pupils. Professor Storrs, in an able article in the *American Annals*, says: "As a teacher, then, having regard only for the best work of my class and to the maximum of advantage to the most needy, and I may add, the most interesting portion, I confess I am always unfeignedly sorry to see any semi-mute, however bright, claiming any portion of my time and effort. I know that such a pupil does not need, in any special degree, that peculiar instruction which it is my privilege to attempt to give to such as do need it." There are, I believe, few teachers who do not echo these sentiments of Professor Storrs. They appreciate more fully than any one the unequal contest the two classes are waging, and yet, though their sympathies may go out to their struggling deaf-mutes, they find themselves compelled, by the necessities of their position, to neglect the weaker for the stronger, the striplings in knowledge for their more robust competitors.

The second form of the combined method, as defined by Professor Fay, is that wherein the general instruction of all the pupils is carried on by means of the manual method, with the special training in separate classes, of a part of them, usually the semi-mutes only, in articulation and lip-reading as an accomplishment. This appears to be the most popular method of instruction in America to-day. It is also, in my opinion, the most mischievous, for it is open to all the objections urged against the previous method, and several additional ones peculiar to itself. Under it the special accomplishment of articulation and speech-reading is gained, if gained at all, at the expense of attainments far more important and practical to the pupils to whom it is generally confined, and the general progress of the rest of the class is very seriously interrupted. The training semi-mutes receive in this way very often fails to give them even a moderate dexterity in speech and speech-reading. A comparison of the attainments of pupils in schools where their whole training has been oral with those of similar standing whose training has been of the intermittent character of the so-called combined method, conclusively demonstrates to me the superiority of the former in articulation and speech-reading. This statement may seem extravagant and unwarranted by facts, but, after a careful and somewhat extended examination of the results accomplished under pure oral training, and combined training, I am bound to admit that, with some exceptions, pupils trained under the former method excel in these two respects.

And this, in the nature of things, cannot be otherwise. Instructors in oral schools are just as earnest, enthusiastic, painstaking, and capable as are the teachers of articulation in sign schools; their pupils are naturally just as bright and receptive, and why should they not accomplish more in this direction, working four or more hours a day, than we, under the combined method, working a half, or perhaps one hour a day. To expect any other result appears to me absurd. Besides, the constant means of communication in the former case being by the voice, the child comes to look upon it as the natural and only right means of communication: while in the combined school, the pupils being constantly surrounded by those who use signs, and receiving a great part of their own instruction through the medium of the same language, they soon acquire a dislike for oral instruction, and practise their powers of oral communication to a very limited degree only. They look upon it as an imposition, an irksome task from which their schoolmates are excused, and very often are found in no happy frame of mind when the hour for articulation work arrives. This, of course, makes the work of the teacher all the more severe; he has to work against the grain, which is no pleasant addition to the other difficulties of his position. Indeed, considering all the disadvantages under which they labor, it is surprising that teachers of articulation working under this method accomplish as much as they do.

While this oral work is going on in the articulation room, the teacher from whose class the pupils have been taken is indulging in thoughts not in the highest degree complimentary to an arrangement that daily breaks up his work, and is often perplexed beyond measure how best to fill in the time with so many of his pupils absent. He cannot go on with his regular course of instruction, and, consequently, a large portion of his class is obliged to suffer for the doubtful advantage afforded to a few of its members.

In short, it may be said of this form of instruction that the pupils dislike it; the teachers dislike it; it fails very largely to accomplish what it attempts; and it is a decided hindrance to the general progress of both manual and oral work.

If the experience of others confirms the truth of this picture, it is certainly time that some remedy were provided.

To me, the remedy is a very simple and effective one, and, I am glad to say, is embodied in the last two forms noted in Professor Fay's definition of the combined method.

Under the first of these two forms, oral instruction and manual instruction are given in the same institution, but in separate classes, the pupils being taught by one means or the other, as in the judgment of the Principal may appear best—manual instruction being given to those who should be manually taught, and oral instruction to those who may most profitably be taught in that way. Under this arrangement, the evils attendant upon the two first mentioned forms largely, if not wholly, disappear, and each child enjoys that form of instruction best suited to his condition.

In the institution which I have the honor to represent before this convention, this form of separate oral instruction has been pursued in two of the classes in the main school, for three years, with gratifying success. In one of them, the youngest, the pupils may be regarded as being congenitally deaf; for, if they were not born deaf, they lost their hearing so early in life that no trace of speech remained when they entered the school: the other consists mostly of semi-mutes and two bright congenitals. Although no attempt has been made to restrict these children in the use of signs out of the class-room, their progress in articulation, speech-reading, language, and arithmetic has been highly satisfactory. Indeed, I am inclined to the opinion (the future, however, may prove that in this I am wrong) that the use of signs on the grounds, in the play-rooms, and in the chapel has been an advantage to them in the way of mental development. The progress of *these pupils* is to me a matter of deep interest: if it continues uninterruptedly to the end of the course, it seems to me the possibility of prosecuting successful oral work in a manual school will be proven beyond a doubt.

There is an objection (I am willing to concede a serious, though by no means a fatal, objection) to this form of instruction, arising from the fact that the pupils who are thus being instructed orally are constantly subjected to the seductive influences of signs. To many who favor the pure oral method, this would appear an insurmountable objection, but with the experience I have had upon the subject, I do not so regard it, and maintain that, if not equal to the last, it is at least vastly superior to the first two mentioned forms. Under it, the congenital mute is not subjected to the discouragements that arise from constant competition with those who possess superior natural advantages, and the semi-mute is not retarded by those who are less quick of comprehension than himself; the teacher is not tempted to favor one pupil at the expense of the other, and is not subjected to daily interruptions of his work; and the progress of the semi-mute in articulation and lip-reading is much more rapid and permanent.

But the last form mentioned by Professor Fay affords, in my opinion, the best possible system for the instruction of the deaf. It provides instruction in separate schools, under the same general management, for both classes; those who can best be instructed manually being so instructed, and those who can best be instructed orally receiving oral instruction. The advantages of a school so organized are worthy of serious consideration. The question whether the child should be instructed orally or manually presents no disturbing difficulties since, being left to the impartial and unprejudiced judgment of the head of the school, it is solved solely with a view to the best interests of the pupil, and without any reference whatever to the discordant claims of rival methods.

It cannot be denied that, organized as most of our schools are at present, many children are compelled, owing to the selfish interests of the advocates of the methods under which they are being instructed, to undergo a course of training wholly unsuited to their condition. On the one hand are the adherents of the pure oral method, who say: Teach all orally—any deaf child that can be taught at all, can be taught to speak. And on the other hand are those equally extreme in their views who maintain that all should be instructed by the manual method, with articulation and lip-reading thrown in as an accomplishment: that to attempt more is a waste of time, and must result in great loss to the pupil in the way of mental development. And in attempting to prove the correctness of their theories, both classes of instructors do great injustice to a large proportion of the children confided to their care.

Surely the time has come when all may yield somewhat in their extreme views, and unite upon a surer, truer, and more practical system of instruction than the one they now advocate; one which, while giving the greatest freedom as to method, will secure that kind of instruction best suited to each child. This system, which at the head of this paper has been called the True Combined System of Instruction, includes, under one management, manual instruction, pure and unadulterated, for all who may most profitably be so taught, and oral instruction, pure and unadulterated, for all who can most effectually be educated by that method. It discards all attempts to provide accomplishments of any kind, and confines itself to what appears wisest, best, and most practicable for each individual case.

For all practical purposes, and in order to secure immunity from error in the choice of methods, I would divide the deaf into three classes, the congenitally deaf, the semi-deaf, and the semi-mute. With the first I would include those born deaf, and those who lose their hearing from accidental causes very early in life, say within the age of three or four years. These, for the most part, I would instruct manually. The semi-mute and the semi-deaf, and such of the congenitally deaf as appear particularly bright and quick to learn, I would instruct orally. A few months' or a year's trial will enable the Principal or Superintendent to decide whether a mistake has been made in any individual case, and if so, a change should be quickly effected. But having definitely decided on the method best adapted to each pupil, let that form be adhered to. If the child is to learn to speak, let speech be its means of communication, and not signs or writing or spelling; if, on the other hand, speech is believed to be impracticable, dismiss all attempts to teach orally, and resort fully and heartily to manual methods.

After a trial for several years of the second method of instruction as defined by Professor Fay, the managers of the Pennsylvania institution, deeming the results obtained by it unsatisfactory as regards articulation and speech-reading, determined to make a trial of the pure oral method, under the same management but in a building separate from the main institution. Accordingly, an oral school was organized at a convenient distance from the parent school, and placed in charge of a principal teacher and several assistants. The school passed through the usual vicissitudes of all such experiments. It had its friends and its foes. The former stoutly maintained that all deaf children could be taught orally, while the latter contended that very few true mutes could be benefited by that method, and that results would never warrant the outlay of time and money necessary to attain them. Happily, neither side was able to carry out its extreme views, and with the lapse of time more moderate and conservative counsels began to prevail; for, while the results were not such as its most ardent friends had expected, still, enough had been done to fully warrant the continuance of the school. It was, therefore, reorganized and brought more into harmony with the parent institution, thereby securing, as is believed, the greater efficiency of both. It is believed that a large percentage of our pupils, namely, the semi-mutes and the semi-deaf, and such of the congenitally deaf (few in number, probably) as are capable of receiving oral instruction, can and should be orally taught, and that all others, forming, to be sure, the majority of the pupils, should be taught by manual methods.

The objection so often urged against separate oral instruction, that of the increased expense, has not proven with us at all formidable. It has been found, by actual experiment, that the capita cost of maintaining a separate oral school under the same management is but slightly greater than that of the parent school. But, however this may be, when the importance of speech to a deaf person is considered, the slightly increased outlay incurred in providing it should have but little weight. When a deaf child is able to make itself understood by its voice, even though unable to read the lips, its affliction is very greatly diminished, and no one will deny that it is our duty to lighten the misfortune of deafness in every possible way.

We consider our departure no longer within the domain of experiment; it has become an accomplished fact. The two systems are working harmoniously, side by side, each contributing not a little to the success of the other, and separate oral and manual instruction will, in future, be a prominent feature of the system pursued in the Pennsylvania Institution for the Deaf and Dumb.

COMPREHENSIVE EDUCATION IN ITS PHILOSOPHY AND PRACTICE.

[This Exhibit consisted of the following paper by Mr. Gilbert O. Fay, published in the proceedings of the Eleventh Convention of American Instructors of the Deaf, 1886, pp. 159-163.]

In hearing education, teachers discuss topics before their pupils or require them to read up the same in text-books, and later to reproduce the remembered substance in language, written or oral, generally the latter. Facility of speech, an extensive diction, exists at the outset. A deaf child is not best taught by the same verbal process, destitute as he is, or nearly so, of both words and thoughts. Such a task is the Egyptian one of making bricks without straw. The wiser teacher, with true philosophy, will become for the time a gesticulating mute himself. The mute's pantomime he does not shun or seek to extirpate. He is thankful for its existence, and patiently learns to use it, that thereby he may lead the pupil up to the added understanding and use of words in their visible form—the dactylic, or finger spelled. He becomes a child himself, even a mute, that thereby he may lead his pupils up to and into their kingdom of heaven—written and oral speech. The pupil, encouraged by the fellowship of his teacher, will work along this new line of language patiently, happily, hopefully, successfully Not a single pupil will despair or fail. The script of the school-room and the type of the book will follow in close alliance. The fingers, in decimal system, will count and calculate; and their equivalents, numerical and verbal, will be committed to memory. Within a year, the pupil will write many a story with his stock of words, already amounting to five or six hundred. The same process, kept up, will conduct him subsequently through the various uses of the vocabulary of common life and the usual list of studies constituting the course. Printed language or script, previously written, will be the preferred medium of communication to the pupil in the school-room. Extempore pictures, pantomime, differing in no philosophic sense from the pictures of books, will be freely furnished in explanation of the verbal text. When neither print nor prepared script is accessible, dactylic language will be employed. But out of the school-room, in the tide of daily life, in its flood of events, great and small, in its business, its amusements, its necessities, its exigencies, verbal speech will yield precedence to the more rapid and more expressive language of signs. Spontaneous feeling will maintain itself against all precepts of teachers and their severest repressive discipline, be it sweeping or petty.

The child's first learning of language will be a process of simple imitation. Later, when ideas have increased and the reasoning faculties have measurably awakened, sentence analysis and rules of composition will be profitably introduced. No teacher, however, should forget that a wide vocabulary, scant enough at the best, with simple syntax, very simple, is preferable to longer sentences of misused words. Much should be, may be, understandingly read that should not be at any time imitated. The wide understanding and flowing facility of teachers, and the analogy of composition by hearing pupils, often mislead the teacher of the deaf into a pace and range of work entirely beyond the assimilating capacity of his pupils. The right use of qualifiers and idioms is slowly, very slowly, acquired. Verbal language is incessantly lapsing. Haste will break up a growing style, really correct, into a chaos of shreds and patches.

For deaf children at this stage there is no adequate literature existing for the occupation of their leisure hours. So called children's books, though beautifully illustrated, are decidedly too difficult verbally for deaf-mutes. To some exceptional pupils, already referred to, the editorials of the daily press and the fictions of Dickens are acceptable. But the ordinary deaf-mute needs at first books and papers upon the commonest topics, written wholly in simple sentences of eight or ten words. Such a literature is indispensable as a substitute and equivalent for the colloquial speech of the hearing. The want of it is the occasion of many idle, or worse than idle, hours among the deaf.

Following the acquisition of verbal language in its simpler and clearly visible forms of finger spelling, writing, and print, the comprehensive teacher will also undertake, along the years, as a part of the general course, and with daily drill, to give to his pupils a mastery of the vocal equivalents of the words which they already understand and freely use. The task is beset with extraordinary difficulties, and should not be pushed at one time to the weariness or disgust of the pupil. Not hearing his own voice or the voice of others, and only conscious of certain muscular action approved by his teacher, his difficulties are prodigious. Gains trifling to the hearing should be thankfully recognized and encouraged. Every deaf child can learn a few words. Many can learn to pronounce sentences fluently. With advancing education, pupils judiciously handled will have a growing ambition to add oral speech to written. Poor articulation, broken speech, is better than none. The ability to utter single words, to go no farther, adds substantial value to life. To make room for oral speech, the range of study in general knowledge and written language, already limited, need not, should not, be narrowed. Vocal training should be introduced into, or rather added to, the course of existing education in fair proportion; and it should occupy a part of the daily school time, presumably, of every pupil. A degree of proficiency in oral speech should be made a condition of graduation in the State institutions and in the National College. To secure this result, extension of time, if demanded, should be granted.

The deaf, out of school hours, should be encouraged to use dactylic and oral speech, not passing beyond the point of weariness. If they are likely to become proficient in oral speech, steady encouragement and its superior convenience will secure its permanent use. After they have acquired the correct use of dactylic speech, they should not be held permanently to its use. If unlikely to rise to the easy use of oral speech, they should not be checked in their inclination to think in pantomime. Its celerity, parallel in degree to oral speech, affords them, in thinking at least, a great relief from the tardy pace of finger spelling, be it ever so rapid and correct.

Errors of proportion have divided the educators of the deaf into schools of opinion, not exactly hostile, but certainly separate and narrow. The schools of France, for a century, and subsequently the schools of the United States, while theoretically favorable to the teaching of articulation, have demonstrated only and mainly, through long practice, the importance and possibilities of pantomime and the uses of the manual alphabet, supplemented by written speech. They have applied these instruments with great skill and energy, and have produced a remarkable body of silent scholars, easily superior in scholarship to anything that oralists have been able to produce. French and American schools, true to their traditions, have been backward, however, in taking up and applying, with equal skill and energy, the teaching of oral speech. Might not a fraction of their silent written scholarships have been well exchanged for a degree of oral skill? Such seems to be their own present conviction. We are now witnessing the introduction of the systematic teaching of articulation into all the prominent institutions of Europe and America. And the pursuance of this policy has exhibited the fact that the development of the faculties and the acquisition of verbal speech by pantomime, by finger spelling, and by books, are an excellent preliminary training, the full peer of all rival expedients, for teaching associated and subsequent oral speech itself. The pupil has something to say, and can be more easily taught to say it. The present need of our historic schools is to expand their scope still more widely, so as to include and attach to themselves all that is valuable in oral schools. If a longer school period shall be found necessary for the best results, it should not, will not, be withheld.

Another school of opinion, represented by the schools of Germany, for a century, and by a few recently opened in the United States, ignores the pantomime of the deaf, and uses none. It omits the finger alphabet, and proposes to teach the deaf at the start, and with no intermediate step, oral speech itself, and by it all branches of desirable knowledge. Though opposed to the use of extempore sign pictures, it uses all printed pictures freely. It omits evidently and rejects such illustrations as the pupil is likely to imitate and to incorporate into signs of his own. It is communicating instruction with great and increasing skill, and to a proportion of pupils steadily enlarging. The partially deaf and those who have heard in early years succeed from the start. An additional number, some of them totally deaf from birth, succeed to a limited extent, practically useful. A large number do not acquire it sufficiently to be able to rely upon it, singularly evanescent, in after-life. At school they habitually invent and illicitly use a gesture-language for social relief, and feel more confidence in their pencil than in their voice. The time spent in oral teaching has crowded out some topics taught in the sign schools. The range of written scholarship, including English composition and the ability to read newspapers, is considerably lower. The deficiency is justified by those who are responsible for it by the compensating value of the oral speech, acquired or attempted.

These schools have yet to learn that, in omitting the use of pantomime and finger spelling, they ignore the uneducated mute's best friend. They take away a ladder, the only ladder known, by which all the deaf can easily rise. They require the mute, scorning all climbing steps and gradual approaches, to clear at one bound the chasm that separates the deaf from the hearing. They force the recruit at once upon frowning breastworks. They apply a method derived from the functions of the hearing mind, and not at all from the essential, the universal functions of the mind of the deaf. Attempting the best things for all the deaf by a method heroic, they succeed with a small number, less than half, and, holding no middle ground, substantially, culpably fail with a considerable number. The brilliancy of the operation is clouded by its frequently fatal issue.

These schools, excellent, ambitious, and ably officered, need, in behalf of many of their pupils, to incorporate into the early years of their course all that is valuable in the sign schools. The removal of intervening barriers will make the two jarring methods friends—astonished to remember that they ever differed. Pantomime and finger spelling, as jealously excluded now from oral schools as the "long keels of the Northmen," will prove a boon, a help, and not a hindrance to all their pupils. They will all easily rise, and rapidly, to the plane of written speech; and those capable of taking the higher step, the last, the crowning oral one, will not be the less able for having a broader elementary base.

To secure the best results in existing institutions, sign and oral, a degree of reorganization will be necessary, gradual or summary. It will involve in sign schools the adding of the teaching of articulation to the daily round of the duties of existing teachers, or the employment of additional articulation teachers. In oral schools it will involve the added use of pantomime and the manual alphabet by existing teachers, or the employment of additional teachers who can use them. New institutions need not be embarrassed by servile imitation of institutions time-honored simply. The line of progress is not necessarily a royal line, a dynasty. Errors may be transmitted, congenitally so. New institutions should have the enterprise and courage to select and to combine wisely, with at least one eye to the future. A great desideratum in the equipment of a school so enlarged is a collection of books, a library of them, composed in shortest words and in syntax extremely simple, with the syllabification and all silent letters clearly indicated.

It remains for our country, reverential and fearless, inventive and aspiring, and abounding in resources of money and of brain, to organize, to perfect, and to sustain, an eclectic, a combined, an American system of deaf-mute education—a system that shall be true to the nature of the deaf, and that, using all arts, shall conduct them gently, hopefully, happily, and within a reasonable time, up to the plane of oral speech. Some will talk in halting tones. Some will pause midway at written speech, and that in syntax poorly ordered. But all will, by graduated process, achieve results proportionate directly to their school time and to their receptive power.

ORAL AND AURAL TRAINING.

[This Exhibit consisted of the following report of an address by President Gallaudet before the National Academy of Sciences upon "Some Recent Results of the Oral and Aural Teaching of the Deaf under the Combined System," published in the *American Annals of the Deaf*, July, 1884, Vol. XXIX, pp. 232-233.]

The National Academy of Sciences—the most learned and distinguished body of scientific men in America—has recently manifested an unusual interest in deaf-mutes and their education. A report of their discussion at the New Haven meeting in November last of Professor Bell's fears of "the Formation of a Deaf Variety of the Human Race" was published in the January *Annals*; and at their meeting in Washington last April President E. M. Gallaudet was invited to address the Academy on "Some Recent Results of the Oral and Aural Teaching of the Deaf under the Combined System." The following report of Dr. Gallaudet's address is taken from the Washington *Post:*

Dr. Gallaudet began by referring to the fact that the instruction of the deaf, even at its inception, about the year 1760, in France, Germany, and Great Britain, was carried on under methods which differed greatly from each other. De l'Epée, in France, advocated and practised the manual method, which makes great use of the language of gestures and discards speech; while Heinicke in Germany and Braidwood in Scotland upheld the oral method, discarding signs, and giving speech the place of prominence.

From those early days to the present time there has continued a controversy between the oralists and the manualists as to the merits of the respective methods.

In America, when the first school was established in 1817, the manual method was adopted, and held its place in the schools of this country to the exclusion of the oral method for half a century. In 1867 oral schools were established in Massachusetts and in New York. Early in that year the Directors of the Institution for Deaf-mutes in Washington sent Dr. Gallaudet to Europe for the purpose of examining the methods pursued in the schools in that part of the world. After a careful study of some forty schools, during a period of six months, Dr. Gallaudet became convinced that a combined system which he found existing in a number of places conferred greater benefits on deaf-mutes than either the oral or the manual method used alone.

On his return from Europe, Dr. Gallaudet strongly recommended the introduction of oral teaching into the existing deaf-mute schools, and he had the satisfaction of knowing that this suggestion had been acted on favorably in all parts of the country, with very gratifying results.

Dr. Gallaudet stated that those who advocated the pure oral method were urging very earnestly the abandonment of signs in the education of the deaf, and were claiming that under the combined method the oral instruction of the deaf could not be carried forward successfully. He said that he would presently introduce to the Academy one of the pupils of his Institution in which the combined system was followed, that the members might judge for themselves whether the claims of the pure oralists were well founded or not. But before making this exhibition the Doctor informed the Academy that quite a new feature in the instruction of the deaf had lately been developed in the Nebraska Institution at Omaha, which was under the charge of Prof. J. A. Gillespie. It had been found that some fifteen per cent of the children in this Institution possessed more or less hearing. By means of the audiphone and other appliances, Prof. Gillespie had succeeded in developing the hearing power of these pupils in a most gratifying manner, and he urged teachers of the deaf in all parts of the world to labor in this direction, with the assurance that under this aural method a large percentage of the so-called "deaf and dumb" might be taken entirely out of that class, and become in no respect different from persons whose hearing had been impaired.

Dr. Gallaudet then called to the platform one of his pupils, a resident of Washington, John O'Rourke by name, a boy seventeen years of age, who was now in the sixth year of oral instruction. This boy, the speaker said, was entirely dumb when his oral teaching began, in the autumn of 1878. Dr. Gallaudet did not use a sign in communicating with his pupil, and resorted but once to the manual alphabet to correct a mispronunciation on the part of the boy. Many questions were asked and answered, the pupil reading from Dr. Gallaudet's lips with ease, and making his replies with a distinctness that caused them to be understood by all present. Young O'Rourke read three stanzas from Longfellow's "Psalm of Life" in a manner that elicited hearty applause.

At this point Dr. Gallaudet stated that Master O'Rourke might be taken as an illustration of the aural method, as well as of the oral, for within the past eighteen months it had been discovered that he possessed hearing in a sufficient degree to admit of cultivation. This limited power was being developed by his faithful teacher, Miss Mary Gordon, who was entitled to the credit of his progress in speech.

The audience manifested the most lively satisfaction with all that Dr. Gallaudet had presented to the Academy, and one lady present, Mrs. Caroline H. Dall, of Georgetown, who had visited many oral schools, declared that Master O'Rourke's pronunciation was superior to any she had hitherto heard from one who had once been dumb.

A SYSTEM OF EDUCATION ADAPTED TO ALL DEAF-MUTES, NOT EXCLUDING THE FEEBLER-MINDED.

[This Exhibit consisted of the following paper by Mr. Job Williams, published in the proceedings of the Fifth National Conference of Principals and Superintendents of Institutions for Deaf-Mutes, 1884, pp. 182–194.]

Throughout the United States of America, schools for the deaf, whatever may be the system of instruction employed, are maintained wholly or in large part at the public expense, and are for the benefit of *all* who are too deaf to be taught in the public schools, but whose mental capacity would entitle them to an education therein, were they possessed of hearing. The brilliant minds among this unfortunate class may be successfully taught by either the oral or the manual method, or by the combined method. Where quick perception is added to rare mental endowment, the oral system may be better, especially in the case of semi-mutes, the advantages outweighing the disadvantages. Where quick perception is wanting, though there may be rare mental capacity, there is little doubt that the combined system will produce a far higher average of results than would the oral system in the same case. In that large percentage of the deaf (perhaps a little larger among the deaf than among the hearing) who possess neither superior minds nor unusually quick perception, nearly all are willing to admit that the manual method is the only one by which satisfactory results may be attained. Unfortunately these distinctions in the condition of our pupils are not given sufficient consideration in all cases, and as a consequence, many a child is allowed to suffer in his mental development, and to an extent unknown and undreamed of in our public schools, and that would not be tolerated there; pupils are shut out from school and condemned to grow up in ignorance, a burden to themselves, to their friends and to the community, on the ground that they are too weak in mind to receive instruction, when, in fact, the fault is not in the child's mental capacity, but in the system employed by his teachers, as applied to him.

Within a few months one who occupies a high position as an educator of the deaf and who is an enthusiastic oralist, in comparing the pupils of the manual schools with those of the oral schools, has said that the manual schools (I quote directly) "are apt to gather up all that they can find, regardless of age or mental capacity." * * * "Their desire to have a large number of pupils is too great." "This desire often leads to the admission of pupils who are so deficient in mental ability that they more properly belong to an asylum for feeble-minded children." "Some of them are too old to make much progress in education." "Nowhere else are there so many unfit scholars to be found in schools for the deaf as here." "If you compare the appearance of the generality of articulating scholars with the dull, sullen, and uncouth looks of the pupils of sign schools, you will find the difference to be as great as it is between the members of a congregation of a Fifth Avenue Church and the inmates of a penitentiary." These things were said not in heated oral discussion where there was little time to weigh the force of words, but in cold type with ample time for deliberation.

The writer of this article once asked the author of the above quotations if he received all deaf-mutes who applied for admission to the school over which he presided. "Oh, no," said he, "we do not want idiots. We send them to the Institution," naming a manual school near by. Further conversation developed the fact that the term idiot, as used by him, included a large proportion of those possessing less than average ability.

Another repudiator of the use of signs as ordinarily used by the manual schools in the instruction of deaf mutes, speaking of the working of his system among the pupils of the school over which he presided, said, in substance, not long since, if a pupil is not able to make good improvement without the aid of signs, as used under the combined method, I say to him, the progress you are making is not sufficient to compensate for the money which the State is spending for your education. You must go home. So the child is left to grow up in ignorance.

Now, I wish to submit to this company of educators of deaf-mutes, whether such treatment of deaf-mutes as is indicated by the foregoing quotation, is just to them. Is it Christian? Is it even humane? Do not those children, possessing degrees of mental ability between idiocy and mediocrity, have as strong a claim upon our sympathy and our aid, as do those of higher mental endowments? Is not their need even greater than that of their more gifted brethren? Are we not placed in our positions to labor for the education of *all* deaf-mutes, rather than to secure brilliant results and gain credit for our methods, while aiding only the better part of that class?

How would it work in our common schools to teach only those children having good mental endowment, and leave the slow and the dull to get on as best they could without the assistance of school instruction?

The above quoted charges, intended as a reproach to the manual schools, we receive as a high compliment to the philanthropy and Christian spirit of the managers of these schools. Such schools receive *all* whose mental capacity would entitle them to admission to our common schools, if they possessed hearing. They exist for the elevation of deaf-mutes as a class, not solely for the specially gifted among them. Such they gladly receive, and they claim to do as good work in and for them as is done anywhere. But if a child's mental condition does not give promise of brilliant success in his education, they labor with and for it just as faithfully, as earnestly, as they do with those possessing a higher order of mind, and oftentimes with results which, though less in amount, are equally marked. A dull class requires from its instructor as much skill, as much tact, as much versatility, more patience, more perseverance, more cheerful courage, than a bright one, and the teacher who can make even moderate progress with such a class, certainly deserves no less praise than the instructor who makes long strides in progress with a class possessing superior mental endowments. The actual improvement in the mental and moral condition of the child is often greater in the former case than in the latter. That this class of pupils do not call forth the applause of the unthinking part of the public we are aware, but to gain that is not the chief aim of our schools. It is the glory of the schools employing the combined method of instruction, that they are able to reach all grades of mental ability, and to give to each child as much instruction as his mental capacity will enable him to hold. They do not profess to furnish brain power, but the sign-language enables them to gauge unerringly the mental capacity of a child, and to cultivate and use all the mind that it has, be it much or little.

Let me cite a few facts. Some years ago a bright boy, who lost his hearing at four months of age, was found in the streets by an enthusiastic advocate of the oral system, who took him in charge and endeavored to teach him articulation and lip-reading. After a protracted effort in that direction with no apparent success, it was decided that the cause of the failure must be mental weakness, and the boy was accordingly sent to a school for feeble-minded children. After two years of experiment there it was discovered that the boy was not an idiot, but was simply deaf, and accordingly he was sent to a manual school for instruction. He had learned to write a few words and found his mental level in a class of three or four weeks' standing. He proved to be a boy of more than average ability, a fair language scholar, and in arithmetic one of the quickest and most accurate in his class. In all his studies he did well, and, after six years of instruction, left school that he might go to work. For ten years he has had steady employment; from his earnings has provided a neat and comfortable home for his wife and little ones, and, as the fruit of his industry and economy, has quite a sum of money credited to his account in the savings bank. He is able to make his way anywhere and to do business with any intelligent person. He is an honest, industrious, thrifty, and respected citizen.

Let me state another fact. A son of a Massachusetts farmer lost his hearing at the age of five and a half years. Being a semi-mute, as was natural and right, his parents desired to have him keep up his articulation. They went a step further and determined that all his instruction should be received through articulation. Accordingly the boy was placed in an oral school from which signs were rigidly excluded. He did not prove a promising subject for instruction in that way. His failure was attributed to mental incapacity, and his father was urged to place him in the school for feeble-minded children at South Boston. Not satisfied as to the correctness of the teacher's conclusion, his father took him to a manual school to see what could be done for him by the combined method of instruction. He proved to be a bright boy, remained nine years, and graduated with credit from the first class. He is an intelligent man, honest and industrious, with steady work and good wages.

As an example of a different class of cases, let me instance the following: A bright boy lost his hearing through sickness at the age of five and a half years. He was sent to school and taught by the oral method for seven years. His progress in articulation and lip-reading was excellent. His parents decided to send him to a manual school, where it was found that his mental progress had been such only as to qualify him to enter a class of four years' standing, and in no respect was he in advance of the average of the class. He continued with the class three years till their graduation and then entered the Deaf-Mute College at Washington.

A bright girl, deaf in infancy, at the age of eighteen entered a manual school after having received instruction for eleven years by the oral method. Her lip-reading was remarkably good, and her articulation such that she could generally be understood by strangers, after they had become a little accustomed to her voice. Her mental attainments were only such as to qualify her for admission to a class of six years' standing, and her scholarship was not above the average of the class.

Though both of the last two pupils mentioned were considered by their oral teachers very successful in acquiring articulation and lip-reading, yet it cannot be claimed for either of them, as is sometimes done in such instances, that the progress, even in these branches, through the oral method was so much greater than it would have been through the combined method, as to compensate for the loss of time in mental development, for in neither case was the articulation or lip-reading much superior to that of pupils of equal native ability who had been instructed under the combined method, in those special branches, much less time than they had been under instruction by the oral method.

Let us apply another test to these two systems. Several years ago a boy, who became deaf at the age of two and a half years, and who had been under instruction by the oral method for ten years, entered a manual school at the age of eighteen. He had been accustomed to describe pictures and to write imaginative stories suggested by them. To test his ability to express his ideas in the English language, a picture was placed before him and he was told to write the thoughts which were suggested to his mind by it. Next, the same picture was placed before a toto-congenital mute, who had been two years under instruction by the manual method, and the same directions were given to him as to the first boy. Then the same picture and the same directions were given to a toto-congenital mute, who had been under instruction by the manual method only four years. No suggestions whatever, except such as the child received from the picture itself, were given to any one of the pupils. All three of them were bright and, as far as we could judge, of about equal native ability.

The three following compositions were the result of the experiment. They are given *verbatim et literatim* and in the order of their mention.

The picture, entitled "Temptation," may be found in the Junior Chatterbox for 1879.

[By a pupil who had been under instruction ten years by the oral method.]

A woman is poor, and a man gave Barrel apple to her, and she have no money. She was think and Will sell the apples. She sat in the street, and some people want eat apples & we gave money to her about it. Two Boys asked her How much cost a apple. She said 5 cents. He don't pay it, and we walked all around in the street and Woman stay is too long time because she is very tired and two boys saw her and he walked no noise thief and ran off. He are very Bad boy because we thief apples to poor woman. Two boy are not pretty He are Bad & thief—A apple on the table in side walk. Why we was thief apples. I think because we was *very very* hungry. Will he are very bad boy made hungry. I think A woman is cold day—Basket on the table or ground. Cloth & Box & umbrella on the Basket. I saw picture about Two Boy & woman & apples & Basket—*Brick* Look *like is* Bad Boy.

[By a toto-congenital mute who had been taught two years by the manual method.]

Last summer a woman sold many apples near a house. She sat on a chair. Soon she slept. Two bad boys walked. They saw the woman sleep. One of them walked quietly. He took one apple out of a box. Many apples rolled and fell on the ground. The noise awoke the woman. The woman stood up. She saw two bad boys. She took an umbrella out of a basket. She struck the boys with the umbrella. The umbrella broke. The boys were frightened and ran. The woman put the apples into the box. She kept the apples in the box. She did not sell the apples. She went home.

[By a toto-congenital mute taught four years by the manual method.]

An old lady had many apples. She looked poor and she wished to earn. She thought she would like to sell many apples. She carried some apples in a large basket. Then she put the apples on the table. There was the basket, an old umbrella and a bushel under the table. One day, while she was sleeping near the table, two boys saw the apples on the table. They saw the old lady sleeping near the table. One of the boys stole one of the apples. When the boys ran away, the old lady awoke and saw the boy eating the apple. She screamed and called them. The boys refused to come to her. The old lady told them that she would call the policeman if they would not come to her, but they refused to go. The old lady saw the policeman walking in the street. She called him and then the policeman came to her and said to her, "What is the matter." Then the old lady told him that while she was sleeping, the boy stole one of her apples and ran away. The policeman was very angry with the boys. He looked for the boys who stole the apple from the lady. At last he found the boys near the tree. He caught them and led them to the lady. One of the boys, who did not steal the apple, told the policeman that the other boy stole the apple. The policeman caught the boy who stole the apple and put him in prison in a few days. In a few days the boy was very sorry. He told the policeman that he promised not to steal anything again. He led the boy to the lady. Then the boy told her about the things and asked her to forgive him. She was very kind and forgave him. The boy went to his home. He never stole anything again. He was happy.

I have tried to state the above cases fairly and I believe that I have succeeded in doing so. Yet I am aware that there is some ground for the criticism that it is impossible to tell what varying conditions there may be in minds of apparently equal strength and force. Where the variation is all in one direction, however, the presumption is very strong that it arises from the same cause. In these cases we should attribute it without fear of successful contradiction to the method of instruction.

But to avoid even the slightest suspicion of injustice, let us take the same pupil under the two systems and see what results we find.

A boy much above the average in strength and sharpness of mind was placed in an oral school where he remained for one and a half years. At the end of that time he was transferred to a manual school by his parents. When he entered the latter school what articulation he had acquired was well-nigh unintelligible. He had learned quite a vocabulary. What practical use he could make of it, the following letter, which is an exact copy of one written by him a few days after his arrival there, will show:

HARTFORD, *Oct.* 12, 1882.

DEAR MOTHER AND A.—I am going the go. The wants are apples on box of school. Louis boy good all the time read. Mother her good in the a little to come for Mother dollars $2.00 wants to come Louis or call Fred and Jennie to be love sorry. The come little for The boots wants on come Miss W. on school the teacher that see you very Louis. He playing all the time good school likes. Mr. P. W. the keeps. Sleeps night eight morn on the hats wants home box come school reads all the time very White Good eats many fats Louis very good Boys house playing rain on the Wet Louis boots wants come on the cold snow Louis help Mr. S. the boys calls all the time Louis talks teachers Miss R. Boys cries all the time reproves Miss W.

The following is the unaided production of the same boy after he had been under instruction by the combined method just six months.

[A few days before it was written two travelling showmen with a bear visited the asylum yard and performed for the entertainment of the pupils.]

HARTFORD, *April* 2, 1883.

MY DEAR MOTHER: I send the letter to mother. Tuesday me see a bear. Two men and bear come. Mr. W. leads two men and yellow bear. The boy walks and runs. The man throws a stick at the bear. The bear takes a stick. He climbs a tree. We stand near the bear. The bear is funny. We laugh at the bear. The bear is not cross. He is kind. The man shakes the bear. The bear kisses the man. Some boys stroke yellow bear. The bear scratches almost one boy, many girls looks at a bear. An other man holds a hat in the hand. Mr. W. and Mr. W. give some money into the hat. The man thanks them. Two men and bear go. We wave our hats. Many boys run to school. The boys fall on the floor. Mr. W. laughs. I am well. What does mother do? I think of my mother. I do not expect to letter from mother. Are you well? What does James do? I love mother. I write the long letter. What does Harry make in the shop? I am proud. I study my lessons all the time. I try to become a good boy. I make round tables all the time. I am not tired. We play ball. I am happy. I said mother shows the letter to A. I said Harry writes the letter. He sends the letter to me. I do not expect Harry's letters. How many horses has Harry? I see Harry's horses. What does Mr. P. do? C. is sick. He stays at home. He is better. C. comes. I see C. Miss K.'s mother is very sick. She does not come to school. Mr. F. teaches Miss K.'s class.

Take another similar illustration. The two letters following were written by the same pupil—one who had been under instruction by the oral method, for more than five years, before entering a manual school. The first was written a few days after her admission to the latter school, and the second after she had been under instruction by the combined method for six months. Both are unaided productions and are copied *verbatim et literatim.*

HARTFORD, *Nov.* 3, 1879.

MY DEAR MOTHER: I like sews somethings cloths. I have went to store. I like see the store. Hughs gives to me and reads paper. I will to thank you and the reads paper. I am glad to letter. A—. L—. gives to me and nuts. I like to A—. L—. My teachers names is Miss W. Please give to me write letter the Marys. I like to school. You have to very well. Last Sunday I reads the books. I am very tired. Place give to me and stamps sister Marys. Do you like to school. You have the works. You sews the somethings cloths. You are well. I read the books. I like to school. I see the store. I have to beautiful. I walked see the tree.

HARTFORD, *June* 1, 1880.

MY DEAR MOTHER: I hope you are well and happy. I like to wash the dishes and work. I am well. Last Saturday I did not go to the city. I went in the yard. They sat on the seat and were quiet. In three weeks all the pupils shall go home and will be happy. Last Friday Miss W—. gave the dates and lemonade to the pupils in her class. The pupils ate date and drank lemonade and liked them. The pupils thanked Miss W—. She was kind. Sometime I shall go in Boston.

Your loving daughter.

Other cases where the improvement has been as marked as in those just quoted have come under my observation, but these are sufficient to illustrate my point. For the sake of brevity I have condensed into the following table facts which might easily be expanded into many pages. Not a case is given of which I have not personal knowledge, and so far as I know the table embraces every pupil who has entered the school, with which it is my fortune to be connected, after having been previously instructed by the oral method, excepting two—the one of whom died soon after entering school, and the other of whom had so much hearing and has attended the public school so much as to make it difficult to tell just where the credit of his attainments belonged.

[Because of the difficulty of characterizing the mental development in any concise way, I have adopted the plan in column four of the following table of gauging that development by the standing of the class which the pupil's attainments qualified him to enter; *e. g.*, the mark 2 in that column indicates that the pupil against whose name it stands was able to go into a class of two years' standing and work fairly with the class. The mark 0 in the same column indicates that the pupil was qualified only to enter the youngest class in school.]

	Age when deafness occurred.	Time under instruction by the oral method.	Age when admitted to the American Asylum.	Mental development when admitted to American asylum.	Attainments in articulation at admission.	Attainments in lip reading at admission.	Mental capacity as indicated by progress und'r the combined method.	Progress in articulation under the combined method.	Progress in lip reading und'r the combined method.
	1	2	3	4	5	6	7	8	9
1	½ year.	2 yrs. at scl. for idiots.	13 years.	0	Poor.	0	Good.	0	0
2	5¼ years.	6 weeks.	9 years.	0	0	0	Good.	0	0
3	5½ years.	7 years.	15 years.	4 years.	Good.	Good.	Very Good.	Good.	Good.
4	4 years.	9 years.	15 years.	5 years.	Poor.	Good.	Very Good.	Fair.	Good.
5	1 year.	4 years.	15 years.	2 years.	Very poor.	Poor.	Fair.	Poor.	Poor.
6	Congen.	4 years.	13 years.	0	0	0	Fair.	0	0
7	3¾ years.	6 years.	12 years.	1 year.	Poor.	Poor.	Poor.	Very poor.	Very Poor.
8	2 years.	6½ years.	15 years.	2½ years.	0	0	Good.	0	0
9	2 years.	5½ years.	15 years.	1 year.	Very poor.	Poor.	Fair.	0	Good.
10	2½ years.	10 years.	17 years.	4 years.	Fair.	Fair.	Good.	Good.	Good.
11	Congen.	2 years.	10 years.	0	0	0	Fair.	0	0
12	1½ years.	11 years.	18 years.	7 years.	Fair.	Very good.	Very Good.	Good.	Good.
13	Congen.	3 years.	10 years.	1½ years.	0	0	Very Good.	0	0
14	Congen.	3½ years.	11 years.	0	0	0	Poor.	0	0
15	5-6 years.	½ year.	10 years.	0	0	0	Poor.	0	0
16	Congen.	....	8 years.	0	0	0	Poor.	0	0
17	Congen.	1 year.	9 years.	0	0	0	Poor.	0	0
18	1½ years.	5 years.	12 years.	1 year.	0	0	Fair.	0	0
19	Congen.	1½ years.	15 years.	1 year.	Poor.	Poor.	Very good.	Good.	Good.
20	½ year.	....	8 years.	0	0	0	Fair.	0	0
21	2 years.	5 years.	18 years.	2 years.	Poor.	Fair.	Good.	Good.	Good.
22	2½ years.	7 years.	13 years.	1 year.	0	0	Fair.	0	0
23	3 years.	4 years.	13 years.	0	Poor.	0	Good.	Good.	....
24	6 years.	5 years.	16 years.	1 year.	Good.	Good.	Very good.	Good.	Good.
25	Congen.	1 year.	10 years.	0	Poor.	Fair.	Very good.	Good.	Good.
26	6½ years.	4 years.	15 years.	4 years.	Good.	Good.	Very good.	Good.	Good.
27	Congen.	2 years.	16 years.	0	0	0	0	0	0
28	3½ years.	3 years.	10 years.	1 year.	0	0	Fair.	0	0
29	4-5-6 yrs.	1 year.	8 years.	0	0	0	Very Poor.	0	0
30	3 years.	4½ years.	11 years.	1 year.	....	....	Good.	....	....
31	Congen.	1 year.	8 years.	0	0	0	Very good.	0	0
32	3 years.	2 years.	9 years.	0	Poor.	Poor.	Very good.	Fair.	Fair.

It will be seen by a glance at the foregoing table that eight of those on the list are marked *very good* in mental capacity, as shown by their progress here. Of these eight, three entered the Deaf-Mute College at Washington after graduating at the American Asylum; two graduated with credit; two were obliged to leave school to go to work, and one is still in school, maintaining a very high standing in scholarship.

Of the eight marked as *fair* in capacity, I do not think there is one who will not be able to earn a comfortable support, and to communicate with comparative ease with those about him.

That even those marked *poor* in capacity are far from being idiots, the following specimens of their unaided productions will show.

[The following translation from signs was written by the pupil marked No. 17, in the foregoing table, after nine years of instruction under the combined system.]

"One day a boy was playing near a barn yard. A calf was standing on the ground near a fence. He saw it. He pulled some grass and then gave it them to eat. The boy wanted to ride on the calf's back. He coaxed it to the fence. He jumped over the fence, and jumped on the calf's back. The calf was frightened. Many stones lay on the ground. The calf threw the boy away. The large stone struck his head. The blood ran over his face. He began to cry and scream. The lady heard him. She came to the fence. His mother heard the boy. She came to the fence. The lady and his mother carried him into the house. The boy was very weak and sick. They lay him on his bed. His mother washed his face. She was very kind to him. She gave him nice milk to drink. The boy was sorry that he ever had been to ride on the calf's back."

[The following is a translation from signs written by the pupil marked No. 29, in the foregoing table, after eight years of instruction under the combined system.]

"Some years ago A merchant lived in England, he owned a dog A gentleman called him, the dog opened his mouth. The gentleman gave one penny, he ran to Baker. The merchant gave cake to him, he run to the gentleman, he put his hand into his pocket, he took it out of her pocket, he ran to the Bakery, the merchant looked at the bad penny, his head shook, he ran to the gentleman's house, he scratched the door, the gentleman heard the dog a noise, he called the servant, he opened the door, he showed the bad penny to him, the dog put the penny on the doorsteps, he ran away, he ran to the Bakery, the gentleman found it, he went to the Bakery, he put it into the drawer, he saw the dog, the merchant and the gentleman laughed at him, he went to the Bakery, he bought two candy, he thought that he ate two candy."

We do not claim success in all cases equal to that shown in the foregoing quotations and letters. It would be folly for us to do so, since the secret of supplying mental capacity, where nature has left a deficiency, has not yet been revealed to us. We *do* claim, however, that these cases, together with the facts given in the table following them, show very plainly three things, viz: First, That the mental development even of pupils who succeed in acquiring fair articulation and lip-reading is much more rapid in many, yes, nearly all, cases under the combined method than under the oral method. Secondly, That many, who utterly fail of progress under the oral method, may reach a fair degree of mental development through the manual method. Thirdly, It is very conclusively shown by the above quoted productions of pupils who have been tried under both systems of instruction, that the sign-language is not responsible for the inaccuracies in the language of deaf-mutes and the peculiarities of language, commonly styled deaf-mutisms. They are to be attributed only to a want of familiarity with the proper forms of written language. Moreover, we assert (would there was some process by which we could give samples of articulation on paper!) that the pupils who have come from oral schools to us, even the cases of marked success in articulation and lip-reading, show no better results in those branches than articulating pupils who have received all their instruction by the combined method *for the same length of time*. Not for a moment would we argue that there should be no schools of pure oralism. That is an excellent method for some of the semi-deaf and of the semi-mute. The success in *some* such cases is sufficient to more than compensate for any loss there may be in general mental development. In some such cases I have urged parents to send their children to a school using the pure oral method.

But we believe that many pupils who plod along in the oral schools with very indifferent success to the end of the course, dwarfed in mind and disheartened, by a different method might have their mental power stimulated and strengthened, and might as a consequence gain better results than they now do, even in the special branches of articulation and lip-reading. We believe that a majority of the pupils taught by the pure oral method would be better fitted to go forth to the duties of life, would come much nearer than they now do to being "restored to society," had they been taught by the combined method. Surely the difficulties in the path of every deaf-mute are very great, and any degree of success, even when every possible advantage is afforded him, deserves praise, but to take away his most natural, most efficient aid and then attribute to the stupidity of the child the failure which fairly may be laid at the door of the method employed in his instruction, is certainly very unjust, and seems to those who understand his mental difficulties and peculiarities heartless, if not inhuman. Idiots there are among the deaf as well as among the hearing, but we have yet to learn that the proportion is any greater in the one case than in the other.

Not all with perfect hearing can learn music. Not all good language scholars can become proficient in mathematics. Not all can succeed as mechanics. Genius does not always run to art. Why should it be thought strange that not all the deaf can succeed in acquiring articulation and lip-reading?

Let the work be prosecuted with a large-hearted, Christian philanthropy, remembering that the sole motive in it should be the advancement of our pupils—advancement both mental and moral—the advancement of the weak not less than that of the strong. The teacher's ease, or pride in brilliant results, or impatience at the plodding pace of the very dull, should never shut out from school a single deaf-mute, who can there be helped to a higher plane of life. Let us be broad enough to own that our method of instruction may not be the best method for all the deaf, and when it becomes apparent that any pupil will probably receive more development by another method, let us be generous enough to give it the advantage of that method.

POETRY OF THE DEAF.

[From *Harper's Magazine*, copyright 1884, by Harper and Brothers. Reprinted by permission.]

[This Exhibit consisted of the following article by Pres. Gallaudet, published in *Harper's Magazine* for March, 1884, reprinted in the *American Annals of the Deaf* for July, 1884, Vol. XXIX, pp. 200-222.]

Edgar Allan Poe, in his essay on *The Poetic Principle*, defines the "poetry of words" as "the rhythmical creation of beauty."

"Contenting myself," he says, "with the certainty that music, in its various modes of metre, rhythm, and rhyme, is of so vast a moment in poetry as never to be wisely rejected—is so vitally important an adjunct that he is simply silly who declines its assistance—I will not now pause to maintain its absolute essentiality."

If this *dictum* of so great a master of the music of verse is accepted, the declaration that poetry may be fully appreciated, and even produced, by those bereft of the sense through which alone music can be enjoyed, presents an apparent absurdity.

It is no easy matter, if indeed it be at all possible, for us who possess the sense of hearing to place ourselves in the position of those who dwell for a lifetime in a world of silence. The constitution of their minds lacks absolutely an element that forms a part of ours, from the baby days when the mother's lullaby soothes to sleep, to the hour when (whether the creation of the imagination, or something more real, who can tell ?) the song of angels thrills the soul of the dying saint.

It is not likely that the interesting questions in mental science as to what is the difference between the normal mind and that in which the sense of hearing has not existed will ever be fully answered. But it is evidently impossible that the congenitally deaf should have any proper idea of sound, and hence of music.

Hardly more likely does it seem that those whose hearing was destroyed in early childhood can retain the memory of sound to a degree sufficient to enable them to become musical composers, even in the poetic sense. And yet the interesting fact appears that the deaf, in no inconsiderable numbers, have essayed to mount on the wing of poetic expression; to what extent and with what success it is the purpose of this paper to show.

In the first number of the *American Annals of the Deaf and Dumb*, the editor introduces a poem by a deaf-mute, with the following note:

How shall he who has not now and never has had the sense of hearing, who is totally without what the musicians call an "ear," succeed in preserving all the niceties of accent, measure and rhythm? We should almost as soon expect a man born blind to become a landscape painter as one born deaf to produce poetry of even tolerable merit. Accordingly such cases are very rare. Indeed, among the thousands of educated deaf and dumb persons in this country and in Europe, we know of but one example of the kind. We refer to John Carlin, a former pupil of the Pennsylvania Institution for the Deaf and Dumb, and now a miniature painter of decided merit in New York city. At our request Mr. Carlin has communicated the following article for publication in our *Annals*. It is published precisely as it came from his own hand. We have not felt ourselves at liberty to add, subtract, or change the position of a single word.*

Mr. Carlin is still living in New York, enjoying a vigorous old age, and recently, in compliance with a request from the writer for information as to the manner in which he came to write verses, furnished the following statement:

I was born deaf, and have since been so. I was graduated from the Pennsylvania Institution in 1825, at the tender age of twelve years, after four years' schooling. I was never taught articulation. I am still profoundly dumb; and, being totally deaf, I have no idea of vocal sounds.

During my youth and early manhood I took delight in reading Shakespeare, Milton, and Pope. While studying art under Delaroche, at Paris, I illustrated in outlines "Paradise Lost," and also Bunyan's *Pilgrim's Progress*, a poem in prose. Notwithstanding my ignorance of the rules of versification, I scribbled verses. Ever desirous to be a good poet, I made strenuous endeavors to discover where and how to master the art of poetry, and in every endeavor I failed. My pen danced on, the poetic flow of my imagination having found an outlet in discordant verses, which demonstrated that I was still ignorant of the secret of poesy.

All hearing persons to whom I showed my attempts at poetry were unable to explain fully where the difficulty lay, and, by reason of my congenital deafness, and the subsequent inability of my ear to catch and con long and short syllables intonated in strictly poetic feet, either iambic or trochaic, dactylic or anapæstic, I was convinced that I could never be what I so ardently desired—a correct writer of verses. But when I made a professional sojourn at Springfield, Massachusetts, in the winter of 1842, I had the good fortune to become acquainted with the Rev. Dr. W. B. O. Peabody, and took the first opportunity to lay my case before him, with one of my efforts for his critical perusal. He soon saw my deficiency in the knowledge of regular rhythm, and, after careful reflection, he definitely opened my eyes to the right way to my goal, by directing me to study Walker's *Pronouncing Dictionary*, and also his *Rhyming Dictionary*, a book which contains all the fundamental principles of poetry. Besides he gave me hints about poetizing correctly.

JOHN CARLIN.

Long and patiently I plodded in the way pointed out to me by that good man, treasuring in my sensorium as many accented syllables as I could, that they might be easily called to mind at any time without my having to consult the dictionaries. The advice which Bryant, the poet, personally gave me—"Read the best English poets"—has proved a valuable guide in poetical composition.

During the last thirty years Mr. Carlin has produced a considerable number of short poems, many of which have been copied widely in the newspapers. One, entitled "A Scene on Long Island," in blank verse, is to be found in *The American Reader*, published by A. Dekalb Farr, and is remarkable for a certain majesty of movement, which shows how fully Mr. Carlin has overcome the most serious difficulties growing out of his deafness.

The following, as a specimen of our author's composition in rhyme, is, however, all we have room for in this article:

TO THE FIRE-FLIES.

Awake, ye sparklers, bright and gay,
  Still nestling in your lair!
The twilight glories fade away,
  And gloom pervades the air.
Come, then, ye merry elves of light,
Illuminate the tranquil night,
While low and high ye blithely fly,
Flitting meteors 'neath the sky.

*As the poem referred to, "The Mute's Lament," was published in full in the *Annals*, vol. i, p. 15, it is omitted here.—*Ed. Annals.*

The twinkling stars appear anon,
Shine feebly from on high;
The humble glow-worms hasten on
To bear them company.
O come, ye lustrous sylphs of night,
Display with them your fairy light,
While low and high ye blithely fly,
Flitting meteors 'neath the sky.

The trees are hushed, the streamlet's still
The frogs their vigils keep;
The nodding grain on yonder hill
And flowers together sleep.
O rise, ye sprightly flies of fire,
This slumbering scene with life inspire,
While low and high ye blithely fly,
Flitting meteors 'neath the sky.

The old folks doze, the maidens fair
Their wooing swains delight;
Then rise ye from your wat'ry lair
To cheer the solemn night.
O sparklers, in the hour of dreams
Fling merrily your witching gleams,
While low and high ye blithely fly,
Flitting meteors 'neath the sky.

In recognition of his high attainments as a writer, and of his earnest devotion to letters, Mr. Carlin was invited to deliver an address at the public inauguration of the National Deaf-Mute College at Washington, D. C., in June, 1864, and was on that occasion made a Master of Arts, this being the first instance of the conferring of a degree by the new College; and he still enjoys the distinction of being the only *deaf-mute* poet the world has ever known.

Of all other deaf poets—that is to say, those who lost their hearing in childhood, and hence have retained some memory of sound—the wonder is only less in degree, as compared with the congenitally deaf, that they can, after long years of complete silence, give utterance to their thoughts and feelings in strict accord oftentimes with the rules of "metre, rhyme, and rhythm." And the marvel is the greater when it is known, as is the case with several persons presently to be alluded to, that hearing was lost long before the mind had received any appreciable poetic influence from without.

The peculiar mental condition of those to whom sound is only a memory is well expressed in verse by two of their own number.

The following is from the pen of Professor Amos G. Draper, of the Faculty of the College at Washington, who became totally deaf at the age of ten years:

They are like one who shuts his eyes to dream
Of some bright vista in his fading past;
And suddenly the faces that were lost
In long forgetfulness before him seem—
Th' uplifted brow, the love-lit eyes whose beam
Could ever o'er his soul a radiance cast,
Numberless charms that long ago have askt
The homage of his fresh young life's esteem;
For sometimes, from the silence that they bear,
Well up the tones that erst formed half their joys—
A strain of music floats to the dull ear,
Or low, melodious murmur of a voice,
Till all the chords of harmony vibrant are
With consciousness of deeply slumb'ring pow'rs.

Miss Angie A. Fuller,* who lost hearing at the age of thirteen, and was educated in part at the Illinois Institution for the Deaf and Dumb, has written a number of very creditable short poems, from one of which, "The Semi-mute's Soliloquy," the following extract will be of interest in connection with Mr. Draper's sonnet:

No sound! no sound! an alien though at home,
An exile even in my native land;
A prisoner too, for though at will I roam,
Yet chained and manacled I oft must stand
Unmoved, though sounds vibrate on every hand.

No sound! no sound! yet often I have heard,
Echoing through dear memory's sacred hall,
The buzz of bees, the rare song of a bird,
The melody of rain-drops as they fall,
The wind's wild notes, or Sabbath bells' sweet call.

No outward sound! yet often I perceive
Kind angel voices speaking to my soul
Sweetly consoling charges to believe
That this life is a part, and not the whole
Of being—its beginning, not its goal.

No sound! except the echoes of the past,
Seeming at times, in tones now loud, now low,
The voices of a congregation vast
Praising the God from whom all blessings flow,
Until my heart with rapture is aglow.

In our own country several are found besides those already referred to who may justly claim to be recognized as deaf poets. Most prominent among these is James Nack, who died in New York, September, 1879, at the age of seventy-one.

JAMES NACK.

Mr. Nack lost his hearing in his ninth year, entered the New York Institution for the Deaf and Dumb as a pupil within a few months after this event, and remained there four years. His first publication was a volume of poems, written between his fourteenth and seventeenth years, entitled *The Legend of the Rocks, and Other Poems.*

One of the leading reviews of that day speaks of the volume in terms of most enthusiastic praise, calling the author an intellectual wonder, and ranking his writings above the productions of Chatterton, and those of Byron in his earlier years.

In 1839 Mr. Nack published a volume entitled *Earl Rupert, and Other Poems;* in 1850, *The Immortal, a Dramatic Romance;* and in 1859, *The Romance of the Ring, The Spirit of Vengeance, and Other Poems.*

The following may be taken as a specimen of his style in his miscellaneous pieces:

THE RINGLET.

Though to thee this little tress
Brings no thought of loveliness,
Nothing that my eye can meet
For that eye hath charm as sweet;
Nor such witchery is spread
By the locks on beauty's head,
Whether their dishevelled dance
Floats in wild luxuriance,
Or their gently waving rings
Fall in sunny glisterings,
Or in their ambrosial wreath
Violets and roses breathe,
Or, in regal band controlled,
They entwine with gems and gold—
Whether their light clusters through
Peeps the laughing eye of blue,
Or the shade of raven wing
O'er the eye of night they fling.
Know, if thou wouldst have me tell
Whence it hath derived a spell
Far all other charms above—
'Twas her first fond gift of love.

* Miss Fuller, who resides in Savanna, Illinois, is now nearly blind; but, in spite of her disabilities, she has recently published a volume of poems, entitled *The Venture.*

By a singular coincidence, during the year that brought deafness to James Nack, the same affliction befell another boy of equal age, who was destined to attain prominence as a writer and as a poet.

John R. Burnet, born in northern New Jersey in 1808, made totally deaf by disease in 1817, published in 1835, *Tales of the Deaf and Dumb, with Miscellaneous Poems*. This book attracted great attention, and was successful both as a pecuniary venture and in a literary point of view. During the thirty years following its publication Mr. Burnet was a frequent contributor to the periodical press of the country, articles from his pen appearing in the *Biblical Repository*, the *North American Review*, the *American Annals of the Deaf and Dumb*, and other journals.

In 1871 Mr. Burnet received the degree of Master of Arts from the Deaf-Mute College at Washington, which, in the language of one of the reports of the New York Institution for the Deaf and Dumb, "honored itself in honoring this the most eminent of the semi-mute scholars in this country."

We have room in this paper for only a few lines of Mr. Burnet's, which we take from a piece entitled

THE BATTLE OF TRENTON.

December 26, 1776.

Great Washington rides through the silent ranks,
Speaks cheering words, then turns to hide a tear;
That so much hope is left he renders thanks,
And breathes for victory a silent prayer.

He gives the word—*Embark!* A few frail boats
Are freighted with the last hope of the free;
And with these fragile vessels sinks or floats
Thy cause forever, weeping Liberty!

Row on! brave sons of Freedom! prove your might;
Push through the crashing and dashing surge!
A mighty stake lies on your strength this night;
With oar and pole and axe your course still urge!

Though chill the sleet your limbs—oh, do not quail!
Though last your toil for hours—oh, do not tire!
A holy cause rests on you, if you fail,
The world's last hope of Freedom must expire.

Howard Glyndon is a name not infrequently appearing in our current magazines and literary newspapers as the author of pieces in prose and verse. Probably few persons are aware that this writer is a lady who has been totally deaf from early childhood. Her primary education was conducted in the Missouri Institution for the Deaf and Dumb, from which she graduated in 1857. She took leave of her teachers and classmates in a poetical address of considerable literary merit, which was published in the *American Annals of the Deaf and Dumb*, together with an article in prose under her real name, Laura C. Redden. Her ambition was to succeed in literary pursuits, and many who were in Washington twenty years ago will remember her as an attractive lady with a voice hardly rising above a whisper; fragile and very youthful in appearance, as she was then in years, but exhibiting an earnestness and independence which gave promise of the success that has since crowned her labors.

Miss Redden (now Mrs. Edward W. Searing) was an acceptable correspondent of many daily and weekly journals while she remained in Washington, and in 1865 she published, under the patronage of some of our most distinguished public men, a volume of poems entitled *Idyls of Battle*, which added to her growing reputation. In 1873 she published another volume, *Sounds from Secret Chambers*, in which may be found much that is beautiful in thought and expression. From this volume we take the following, entitled:

WHICH IS BEST?

What if I saved from trampling feet
The drooping plumes of a wounded bird,
And tended its hurt with a gentle hand
Till its new life stirred?

What if it nestled against my cheek,
And tamed its shyness upon my breast,
Until I believed that it loved me more
Than its old-time nest?

And if some day, when I prize it most,
It should leave my hand with a sudden spring,
And cleave the blue of the summer sky
With a freshened wing,

And never pause at my pleading call,
Never come back to my desolate breast,
And forget I had saved its life, and forget
I had loved it best—

Should I never open my arms again
To any helpless or suffering thing?
Never bind up the bruised heart,
Nor the broken wing?

Better a thousand times to bear
A blow in place of an earned caress,
Than to turn aside into selfish ways,
Or to pity less.

Better the long-abiding pain
Of a wronged love in its sufferance meek
Than the hardened heart and the bitter tongue
And the sullen cheek.

Mrs. Mary Toles Peet is the author of a considerable number of short pieces in verse, all of which are graceful and finished in style and full of poetic feeling. Mrs. Peet lost her hearing at the age of thirteen, and was for two years a pupil in the New York Institution for the Deaf and Dumb, of him whose wife she afterward became, Dr. Isaac Lewis Peet, the well-known principal of that Institution.

"HOWARD GLYNDON."

MRS. MARY TOLES PEET.

In the year 1853, not long after the death of the founder of deaf-mute education in America, Rev. Dr. Thomas H. Gallaudet, LL.D., the deaf and dumb of the whole country contributed of their means for the erection of a monument to their great benefactor on the grounds of the parent school, at Hartford, Connecticut.

The occasion of the unveiling of this monument was commemorated by Mrs. Peet in lines the following quotation from which will illustrate her modes of thought and expression:

THE GALLAUDET MONUMENT.

No flaunting banners wave,
No pomp surrounds his grave,
No arch triumphal blazons forth his name;
More fitting pile we raise
For one whose brightest days
Were given to deeds worth a far nobler fame.

Plain monumental stone,
Whereon the summer's sun
And autumn moonbeams silently will die,
O'er thee soft gales of spring
May float with unseen wing,
And mingle here with the mute pilgrim's sigh.

And while we linger round
This consecrated ground,
Perchance, as starbeams mirrored in the wave,
His spirit, lingering near,
May be reflected here
In silent hearts, inspiring works of love.

Among the students of the College for Deaf-Mutes at Washington, compositions in verse are not uncommon, and there are those of their number who will no doubt be hereafter known as poets.

Besides Professor Draper, already alluded to, one other graduate of the College deserves mention as a writer of verse. William L. Bird, of Connecticut, graduated from the College in 1870. He served for a short time as a clerk in the Census Office, taught for a year the most advanced class in the Virginia Institution for the Deaf and Dumb, at Staunton, whence he removed to Hartford, Connecticut, to take a position as instructor in the school where his early education was conducted.

WILLIAM L. BIRD.

Mr. Bird lost his hearing in the seventh year of his age, after having attended school as a hearing child for a single session. In his tenth year he became a pupil of the Institution at Hartford, where he remained until he entered College in 1866.

Giving the brightest promise of a successful and useful life as a teacher and as a writer, he was suddenly stricken with a mortal disease, and died in 1879 at his post in Hartford.

Mr. Bird published no verses during his lifetime, but among his papers ample evidence was found that he was a true poet, and he undoubtedly would have been known as such had his life been spared. In proof of which the following lines will, we believe, be accepted:

THE OCEAN.

I stand alone
On wave-washed stone
To fathom thine immensity.
With merry glance
Thy wide expanse
Smiles, oh! so brightly upon me.
Art thou my friend, blue, sparkling sea?

With your cool breeze
My brow you ease,
And brush the pain and care away.
Your waves, the while,
With sunny smile,
Around my feet in snowy spray
Of fleecy lightness dance and play.

So light of heart,
So void of art,
Your waves' low laugh is mocking me.
I hear their voice—
"Come play, rejoice;
Come, be as happy as are we:
Why should you not thus happy be?"

Alas! I know
That, deep below,
And tangled up in sea-weeds, lies,
Where light dares not
Disturb the spot,
He who alone can cheer my eyes.
O sea! why wear this sparkling guise?

Last, but not least, we may include in our catalogue one who is not only deaf, but dumb and blind. For it is a fact that Laura Bridgman, the mere mention of whose name touches a chord of sympathy in every heart, has lately, in the evening of her days, given expression to her reflections in a form that is highly poetic, even though her lines do not follow the modern models of versification.

LAURA BRIDGMAN.

Several incidents of recent occurrence in the life of this remarkable woman, most influential among which, no doubt, was the death, six years ago, of her benefactor and devoted friend, Dr. Howe, have seemed to give a poetic turn to the current of her thought and feeling. And the following can hardly be read without emotion when one remembers the deep shadows under which the writer has walked and dwelt all the days of her earthly pilgrimage:

HOLY HOME.

Heaven is holy home.
Holy home is from everlasting to everlasting.
Holy home is summerly.
I pass this dark home toward a light home.
Earthly home shall perish,
But holy home shall endure forever.
Earthly home is wintery.
Hard it is for us to appreciate the radiance of holy home because
of the blindness of our minds.
How glorious holy home is, and still more than a beam of sun!
By the finger of God my eyes and my ears shall be opened;
The string of my tongue shall be loosed.
With sweeter joys in heaven I shall hear and speak and see.

What glorious rapture in holy home for me to hear the angels sing and perform upon instruments!
Also that I can behold the beauty of heavenly home.
Jesus Christ has gone to prepare a place for those who love and believe Him.
My zealous hope is that sinners might turn themselves from the power of darkness unto light divine.
When I die, God will make me happy.
In heaven music is sweeter than honey, and finer than a diamond.

The earliest specimen of poetry by the deaf is to be found in a rare and interesting work entitled *Vox Oculis Subjecta*, by Francis Green, of Boston, published anonymously in London in 1783. The lines are given as the composition of a pupil of Braidwood, the first teacher of deaf-mutes in Great Britain, and appeared in 1768. They are as follows:

ON SEEING GARRICK ACT.

When Britain's *Roscius* on the stage appears,
Who charms all eyes, and (*I am told*) all *ears*,
With ease the various passions I can trace,
Clearly reflected from that wondrous face,
Whilst true conception with just action joined
Strongly impress each image on my mind.
What need of sounds, when plainly I descry
Th' expressive features and the speaking eye?—
That eye whose bright and penetrating ray
Doth Shakespeare's meaning to my soul convey.
Best commentator on great Shakespeare's text!
When *Garrick* acts *no* passage seems perplext.

The most voluminous writer of poetry among the deaf is Mrs. Tonna, better known under her assumed name of Charlotte Elizabeth. She became totally deaf at nine years of age, no sound of any kind ever reaching her afterward. She was, however, acutely sensitive to vibrations, whether conveyed through the air or through a solid medium. In this way the vibrations from an organ or from the sounding-board of a piano gave her great pleasure, and from her recollection of Handel's music she took great delight in it.

On one occasion, when she had reached the age of twenty-three, a new country-dance was played. The tune was called the "Recovery," the rhythm of which is very peculiar. She was as usual at her station, with her hands on the sounding-board, when some friends expressed a doubt as to the possibility of her forming any idea of the tune. She sat down at once, and wrote a song which followed the tune in all its changes with absolute precision.

There is a piece of Mrs. Tonna's beginning

"No generous toil declining,"

which is quite difficult to read as poetry until the reader is made familiar with an old song entitled "A rose-tree in full bearing," to which it is perfectly adapted.

Besides many short poems and her numerous well-known prose works, Mrs. Tonna published four separate volumes of poetry—*The Convent Bell; Izram, a Mexican Tale; Osric, a Missionary Tale;* and *The Garden, with Other Poems.**

Among the prose writers of the world who became deaf in childhood, the place of highest rank will without question be accorded to John Kitto, the famous Bible commentator.

His published poetical compositions cover only some three hundred lines, in his interesting work on the *Lost Senses*. By way of apology for their introduction, Kitto earnestly disclaims any desire to be recognized as a poet, but his specimens plainly indicate that he might have gained distinction as a writer of verse had he devoted himself to poetry with half the interest he showed in his prose works.

The reasons for his indisposition to attempt the writing of poetry appear in the conviction he expresses that deafness is an insuperable obstacle to rhythmical composition.

"For want of oral guidance in hearing others speak," he says, "it is next to impossible that the deaf man should have that knowledge of quantity and rhythm which is so essential to harmonious voice. He would also be unsafe in his rhymes, for rhyme lies in assonances which can often only be determined by the ear, and verse will require words which one who became deaf in early life will never have heard. It is therefore not wonderful that the deaf-mutes and those who have become deaf in childhood never do attempt to contend with difficulties which seem absolutely insuperable. I am utterly ignorant of any verse--for I will not venture to call my own such—written by any any persons under such circumstances. With those who become deaf after adult age has been attained the case may be different, although I am not aware of any poetry which even such persons have given to the world."

Kitto follows this expression of what seems rather a surprising ignorance by an interesting description of the way in which he learned to read poetry, and how he was led at length in early life to attempt to express his thoughts in rhyme and metre. All along insisting on the impossibility of his being able to compose in correct verse, he concludes by saying: "And as there is no other way of settling the question which has been mooted, I will venture to introduce a few specimens. If the reader can discover the formal errors, the bad rhymes, the halting, hopping, stumping feet, which I am unable to detect, then my proposition is demonstrated; but if he can make no such discoveries, it must be admitted with some qualification. But I must earnestly stipulate that the reader shall bear in mind the single experimental purpose for which these lines are introduced."

That Kitto's poetry is better than his reasoning will be proved by the following:

ALTERNATIVES.

Were all the beams that ever shone
From all the stars of day and night
Collected in one single cone,
Unutterably bright,
I'd give them for one glance of heaven
Which might but hint of sin forgiven.

Could all the voices and glad sounds
Which have not fallen on my sense
Be rendered up in one hour's bounds,
A gift immense,
I'd for one whisper to my heart
Give all the joy this might impart.

If the sweet scents of every flower—
Each one of which cheers more than wine—
One plant could from its petals pour,
And that were mine,
I would give up that glorious prize
For one faint breath from paradise.

A volume of poems, entitled *Day-Dreams of the Deaf*, was published in London in 1858, from the pen of William Henry Simpson, who had been some years previously a teacher in the school for deaf-mutes on the Old Kent Road, London. Simpson lost his hearing in boyhood, after having learned to read, and continued the education in the school where he was afterwards an instructor. In an introductory note to his poems he quotes Kitto's reference to the "insuperable difficulties" that stand in the way of the writing of poetry by the deaf, "at the risk," as he adds, "of laying himself open to the charge of vanity, for the purpose of introducing some of my own compositions to public notice, being unwilling that the statement (proceeding as it does from one whose dictum, right or wrong, must of necessity carry weight with it, from the similarity of his own case to that on which he writes) should pass unnoticed, while I had it in my power to correct an erroneous impression."

Some of Simpson's verses are little more than "machine poetry," while others show skill in rhythmical writing as well as feeling.

The following song is perhaps a fair specimen of his most pleasing efforts:

*The incidents relating to Mrs. Tonna are taken from a sketch of her life by her husband, in the *North British Review*.

Old Time is a good old man,
  What though his step be not gay,
He trudges along as well as he can,
He trudges along still with equal span,
    With his scythe in his hand,
    And his time-piece of sand,
  And his single lock glossy and gray.

Full many the joys he bears,
  Full many the griefs he brings,
Yet thinketh he naught of the load of cares
Contained in his wallet, nor wots who shares,
    But indifferent smiles
    On the world and its wiles,
  On beggar's lot or the fate of kings.

The years in their flight he measures,
  As round his dial they climb:
But we, alas! scarce value his treasures,
We thinking now of the season's pleasures,
    When our cares we lay by,
    When we banish each sigh
  For the song and the dance at Christmas time.

Hail, then, December, though old and hoary!
  Fresh fagots pile on the bright fire,
And listen awhile to the comical story.
The year's departure, let's crown with glory.
    By the embers' bright glow,
    We'll defy frost and snow,
  While the whistling wind joins in the choir.

One piece of Simpson's, which was widely quoted in the newspapers at the time of its publication, will be of interest to Americans even at this day. It is entitled "Lines on Reading the Narrative of Frederick Douglass, an Escaped American Slave." We will not occupy space for the entire poem, but will transcribe a few stanzas that will serve as a specimen of the whole:

He told his wrongs in simple strain,
  Unmix'd with aught of guile:
Of sad days spent in toil and pain,
  Uncheer'd by kindly smile;
How long he bore the galling chain,
  The badge of bondage vile.

And all for what? His skin was dark,
  His soul was therefore base!
By nature, feature, born the slave
  Of all the white man's race.
Thus argued pious heads and grave,
  With eloquence and grace. . . .

Back to thy native land and tell
  How England loves the slave,
How million hearts responsive swell
  Against each servile knave
Who still his follow-man would sell,
  Yet heavenly favors crave.

Lift up, lift up thy voice and win
  Many to freedom's cause;
Rest not till all thy kith and kin
  Live under equal laws;
Blot from thy land one cursed sin,
  And win the world's applause!

Passing from England to the continent of Europe, we find several deaf poets, most prominent among whom is Pélissier, totally deaf from early childhood, and for many years a teacher of deaf-mutes in the famous Institution founded by the Abbé de l'Épée in Paris more than a century ago. Mr. Pélissier published a volume of poems in 1844, which gained high praises from the critics.

Edouard Morel, the editor of the *Annales de l'Education des Sourds-muets et des Aveugles*, reviews the book at length, and pronounces Pélissier a true poet, commending most warmly the marvellous skill with which he expresses his thoughts in accordance with the rules of rhyme, rhythm, and metre. Morel quotes a specimen of Pélissier's verse with the following warm introduction:

"Lisez cette strophe de Pélissier dans son invocation à sa muse, et dites moi si l'on pourrait croire que c'est la lyre d'un poëte privé de l'ouïe et de la parôle, qui a produit ce chant mélodieux."

Viens égayer ma vie,
Muse, je t'y convie.
Couronne moi de fleurs!
Pour comble de faveurs,
Ah! daigne me sourire.
Soit qu'en proie au délire
Je chante dans mes vers
Le roi de l'univers,
Soit qu'ivre d'harmonie,
Aux hauteurs du genie,
Faible et novice, encor
J'ose prendre l'essor.

In 1855 a small volume of poems was published at Toulouse, written by a former pupil of the school for deaf-mutes in that city, by the name of S. B. Châtelain. Professor Léon Vaïsse, for many years director of the Institution for Deaf-Mutes at Paris, pronounces Châtelain's work "very good verse," of equal value, probably, with Pélissier's.

Châtelain was the son of a captain in the French army; he suffered from delicate health all his life, and became entirely blind before his death, which occurred a few years since.

Urbain Borie, born at Sarlat, France, in 1846, and who lost his hearing at five years of age, has written some twenty poems, a number of which have been published. Borie was for eight years a teacher in the Paris Institution for Deaf-Mutes, and now fills a position as clerk in a lawyer's office.

The following piece, published in 1878, received honorable mention at a meeting of poets presided over by Victor Hugo:

LA RÉPUBLIQUE.

Un enfant gisait sur la terre,
  Presque nu, sans abri, sans pain;
Le malheureux cherchait sa mère;
  Sa voix l'appelait, mais en vain.
Dans le pays de sa naissance,
  Nul n'eut pitié de sa douleur.
Le pauvre enfant venait en France
  Pour mettre fin à son malheur.

"Qui m'aidera dans ma misère?"
  Disait-il: "je me sens mourir."
Une voix répond: "Moi, ta mère;
  Mon bonheur est de secourir;
Viens donc au foyer domestique;
  En vrai fils tu seras traité;
Enfant, je suis la République,
  Je suis la paix, la liberté.

"Enfant, écoute-moi: mon chaume,
  Je l'ouvre à tous les malheureux,
Des pauvres je suis le royaume,
  Le travail seul y fait les preux;
Et sans l'orgueil du diadème
  Mon droit toujours est respecté;
Car partout on recherche, on aime
  La bienfaisante liberté.

"Enfant, aux lieux qui t'ont vu naître
  Tu diras en parlant de moi:
'J'ai vu régner l'ordre sans maître,
  Le peuple respecter le loi;
Au travail sans cesse il s'applique;
  Sa devise est fraternité;
J'ai vu la sainte République,
  Le bonheur par la liberté!'"

The only deaf writer of verse in Europe remaining to be noticed is Frithiof Carlbom, born in Eskilstuna, Sweden, in 1835.

Carlbom lost his hearing at about five years of age; was received as a pupil by the Royal Institution for the Deaf and Dumb at Stockholm in 1844, remaining there four years. After four years of private instruction at home he entered the Royal Academy of Fine Arts in 1852, where he remained until 1863. Here he received six silver medals, and in the competition for the royal prize medal in 1863 he gained the *accessit*. The same year he was made principal of the "Silent School"—a day school for deaf-mutes in Stockholm, of which he still has charge.

Mr. C. Kierkegaard-Ekbohrn, the principal of the Royal Institution for Deaf-Mutes at Bollnas, to whom we are indebted for the facts concerning Carlbom, says of him: "He has not written more than a small collection of lyrical poems, and some songs and verses for different occasions. His versification is fine, and he is here, especially by the deaf and by us teachers, regarded as a genius. As an instructor of our deaf brethren he is admirable; one of the most skilful teachers in our country."

For the benefit of students of Scandinavian literature we will insert a specimen of Carlbom's verse:

UPPÅL.

Bort jordiska minnen,
Bort sorger och smärta!
Jag afkastar bogan, som trycker min sjül.

Bort töcken, försvinnen!
Kom lugn till mitt hjerta!
Kom engel, befria materiens träl.

Låt fri ifrån gruset
Min tanke sig svinga,
Som förr till den Allgodes saliga verld!

Åck låt mig åt ljuset,
At kärleken bringa
Min flämtande lampa förr'n veken är tärd.

Åt hvem blef väl gifvet
Sitt öde ransaka?
En lag blott vi vete: "Till jord åter blif!"

Din skänk utaf lifvet
Tag gerna tillbaka!
Blott döden mig för till söllare lif.

A young Swede, who became deaf in his twelfth year, was graduated from the Minnesota School for Deaf-Mutes, and is now a student in the College at Washington, has made the following literal translation of Carlbom's verses:

HEAVENWARD.

Away all earthly thoughts,
Away sorrows and pain!
I throw off the fetters that depress my soul.

Away shadows, vanish!
Come quiet to my heart!
Come, angel, liberate the slave of matter.

Let, free from earth, my thought,
Itself heavenward swing,
To the blest world of the ever-kind Father.

Oh! let me toward light,
Let me toward love bring
My flickering lamp, ere the wick is consumed.

Indeed, to whom was granted
His own fate to descry?
But one law we know: "Return again to dust!"

Thy gift of life to me!
Fain take back unto thee!
Death alone can bring me to a happier land.

—*Translated by Olof Hanson.*

It would be foreign to the purpose of this article to attempt to criticise from a literary point of view the verses we have quoted, or to give any estimate of their value respectively as literary productions. We leave this to the reader, contenting ourselves with having made what we believe to be a unique collection of writings by representatives of a peculiar and most interesting class of persons—a class hitherto commanding little attention in the world of letters, but destined, we feel assured, with the increasing advantages afforded it, to contribute in the future its due share to the aggregate of intellectual production.

NOTE BY THE AUTHOR.

Since the publication of the foregoing article in *Harper's Magazine* my attention has been called to the writings of several deaf authors, which I should have deemed worthy of notice had I known of them before reading the final proof of the article.

Miss Alice C. Jennings, of Boston, Mass., who became totally deaf in childhood, has published a volume of poems entitled, "Heart Echoes." Her verse shows no little skill in its construction, and often gives evidence of true poetic feeling. A specimen of Miss Jennings' poetry may be found on page 248 of vol. xxvi of the *Annals*.

Miss Rachel J. Philbrick, of Savannah, Georgia, who lost her hearing at the age of twelve, and who has struggled under the burden of invalidism for, now, thirty years, has written several very creditable romances in prose, and has occasionally expressed herself in verse. Lines on the death of Garfield were printed in Cambridge, Mass., in September, 1881, and in *Desire Wentworth, a Romance of Provincial Times*, a song occurs, which, though somewhat faulty in metre, gives expression to poetic ideas.

Morrison Heady, of Louisville, Ky., has published volumes of prose and poetry under conditions peculiarly trying. He has been for many years not only deaf, but blind. He writes with a machine which punctures his paper with sharp points, making characters which he can read with the ends of his fingers, and from which a copyist prepares his manuscript for the press.

Mrs. M. A. M. Cramer, of Milwaukee, Wis., who lost her hearing at five years of age, has written a number of short poems. She has been a contributor to the Chicago *Tribune* over the signature "Morna," to the New York *Citizen* as "Barbara O'Brien," and to *Good Cheer*, the *Galaxy*, and other periodicals in her own name.

A number of fugitive pieces by deaf persons have recently come under my notice, the writing of which would hardly entitle their authors to be named as deaf poets. Some of them, however, are of such merit as to suggest that the roll of honor in this department of literature will be added to in the near future.

An interesting incident in the experience of Pélissier, the French deaf-mute poet, has been brought to light by Professor Gordon, of the College Faculty, which is related in *l'Impartial* for July, 1858. Pélissier wrote a poem of great merit entitled, *Ma Mère! Mon Dieu!* which was read with effect by Mlle. Favart, the actress, at an entainment given in Paris in aid of *la Société Centrale d'éducation et d'assistance pour les sourds-muets en France.* Some months later a speaking man, Decombes by name, published at Lyons a poem under the same name as that by Pélissier, and so similar in its form and expression, that a suit was brought against Decombes' publisher for plagiarism. The suit was successful and the plagiarist punished in accordance with the provisions of the penal code.

[This Exhibit consisted of the following illustrated paper by Professor Gordon, printed in diminutive quarto, pp. 40, abridged from the historical sketch of Manual Spelling in his "Practical Hints to Parents of Young Deaf Children Concerning Preliminary Home-Training," pp. 32-40:]

THE "AMERICAN" MANUAL ALPHABET.

"I'll speak to thee in silence."—*Cymb., Act V, Sc. 4.*

KENDALL GREEN, *March* 9, 1886.

The author's thanks are hereby expressed to Dr. Alexander Graham Bell, Dr. Edward Allen Fay, Mr. J. A. Boland, and to all the kind friends who have "lent a helping hand" in the preparation of this little work.

J. C. GORDON.

To promote the convenient and useful art of finger-spelling is the object of this little monograph.

The origin of this ancient art is not known, but evidences of its existence have been traced, from the Assyrian antiquities down to the fifteenth century, upon monuments of art. The venerable Bede, "the wise Saxon," described finger-spelling more than a thousand years ago, and three manual alphabets are figured in an edition of his works printed in 1532. These are based upon the finger-signs for numbers which were used by the ancient Egyptians, Greeks, and Romans.

Monks, under rigid vows of silence, and other scholars who had special reasons to prize secret and silent modes of communication, beyond doubt invented and used many forms of manual alphabets as well as systems of signs or gestures. Rossellius, a Florentine monk, figured no less than three one-hand alphabets in 1579. Two-hand alphabets, or mixed alphabets of various forms, were in use among school-boys in Spain, France, and England centuries ago, and in some form such alphabets probably survive with the "child-lore" and the games inherited in turn by successive generations of children throughout Christendom.

The Spanish one-hand alphabet, which contains certain forms found in the Florentine's plates of 1579, was the first finger-alphabet adopted in teaching spoken and written language to the deaf. The happy thought of this adaptation is attributed to the pious and learned monk, Pedro Ponce de Leon (1520-1584). This alphabet, beautifully engraved, appears in the famous work of Juan Pablo Bonet, secretary to the Constable of Castile, which was published a century after the birth of Ponce or in 1620. This work, borrowed largely from Ponce no doubt, is the oldest practical treatise extant upon the art of teaching the deaf-born to speak and to use the common language of life.

The Spanish alphabet, somewhat modified, was introduced into France by the brilliant Pereire and his gifted deaf pupil, Saboureux de Fontenay, where it speedily supplanted the clumsy alphabets employed in teaching the deaf by the Abbe de l'Épée and the Abbe Deschamps. The same alphabet, with a few slight changes, was adopted by Dr. T. H. Gallaudet, in the school for deaf children opened at Hartford, in 1817, and it is now known in almost every hamlet in the land.

Finger-spelling is to the deaf a borrowed art. It was originated neither by them nor by their teachers, nor is it essential to their education, yet its value can hardly be over-estimated. To the deaf-born the mastery of common language is an extremely difficult task. Intelligible speech in certain cases is wellnigh impossible. Writing is slow, wearisome, lifeless, and often impracticable. Finger-spelling, which may have the rapidity of deliberate speech, and three times that of writing, permits dramatic action, emphasis, accuracy, and easy repetition, thus keeping the senses alert and vividly impressing the forms of words and sentences upon the mind. It compels practice in our language and encourages and stimulates the child in his efforts to master it. "Pupils who consent to spell out their thoughts soon leave behind them those who will be persuaded to do nothing but gesticulate." [*Ed. Am. Annals*, 1853.]

It was a favorite idea of Dr. T. H. Gallaudet that finger-spelling might be advantageously used in teaching hearing children to spell well, a theory which has been fully confirmed by experience.

It is, however, chiefly with a view to promoting the welfare of thousands of more or less educated deaf persons, who depend largely upon finger-spelled English in their social and business relations, that this little hand-book has been prepared, and this simple art commended, gentle reader, to you. Taken up as a pastime, often, it has proved useful in business and in the home. It is of special value in the sick-room, and it has been used by many, after the voice was gone, to convey messages of importance and last words of love, trust, and peace.

This alphabet can be learned in an hour. It has been learned by close application in ten minutes. The plates represent, for the first time, typical positions of the fingers, hand and forearm, from an absolutely uniform point of view, in front of the person spelling, or as seen in a large mirror by the user himself. They were engraved by the "Joyce process" from drawings by Mr. Harry Cunningham, based upon photographs subjected to competent criticism. The forms were determined from a study of scores of mediæval and modern plates as well as current usage. The arm should be held in an easy position near the body. It is not necessary to move it, but a slight leverage at the elbow is permissible, provided the hand delivers the letters steadily within an imaginary immovable ring of, say, ten inches in diameter. The fingers need not be so closely held nor firmly flexed as shown, but all sprawling should be avoided. Certain letters as *c, d, i, j, k, l, m, n, o, q, u, v, w*, and *z*, resemble written or printed forms. *J* is simply traced in the air with the little finger, and *z* in like manner with the index finger. *H, u*, and *n* differ only in the position of the hand, and *t* is formed as in "taking off baby's nose." These ten words contain all the letters: "adz, fan, map, cow, box, jar, sky, hat, quill, glove." Practise upon each of these for five minutes. It will do you no harm to have a verse of Scripture or some favorite quotation "at your fingers' ends" every morning of your life.

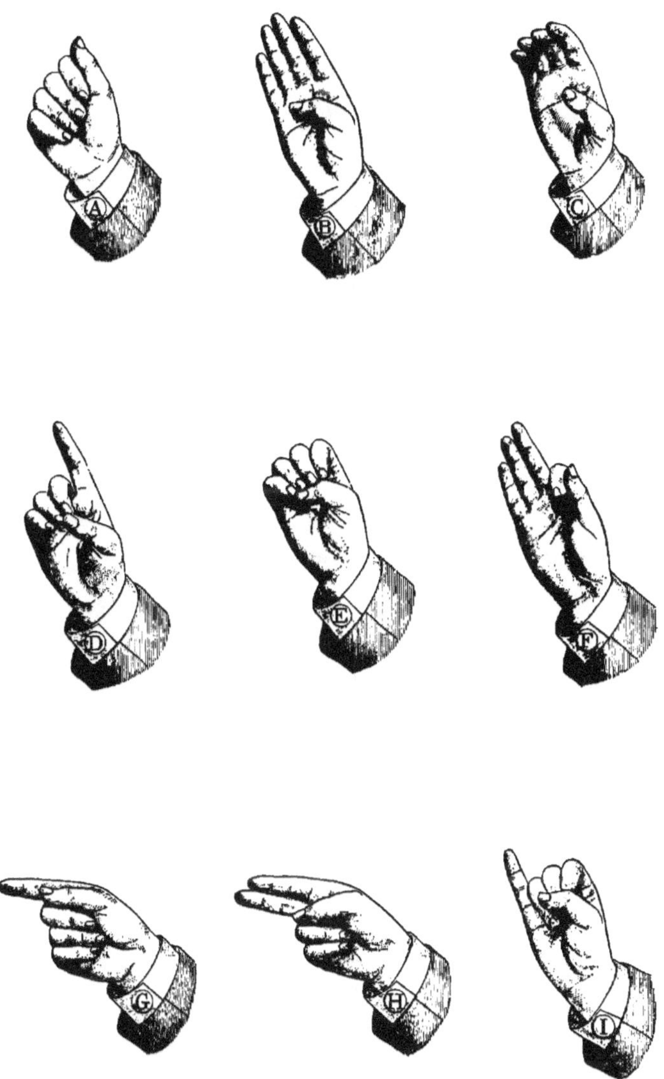

[THE "AMERICAN" MANUAL ALPHABET.]

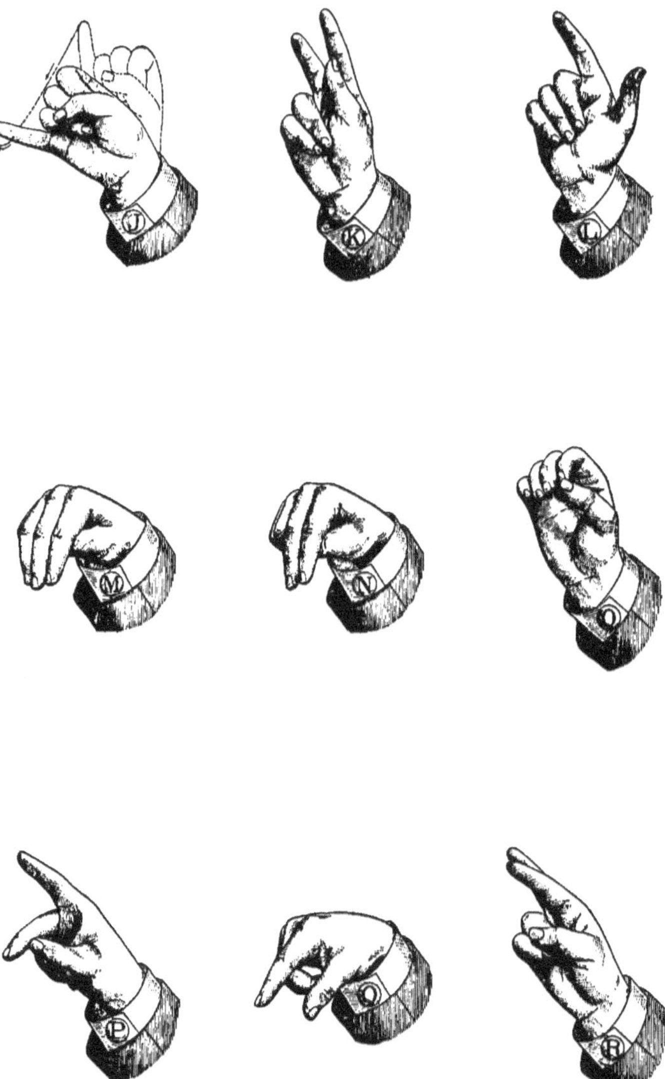

[THE "AMERICAN" MANUAL ALPHABET.]

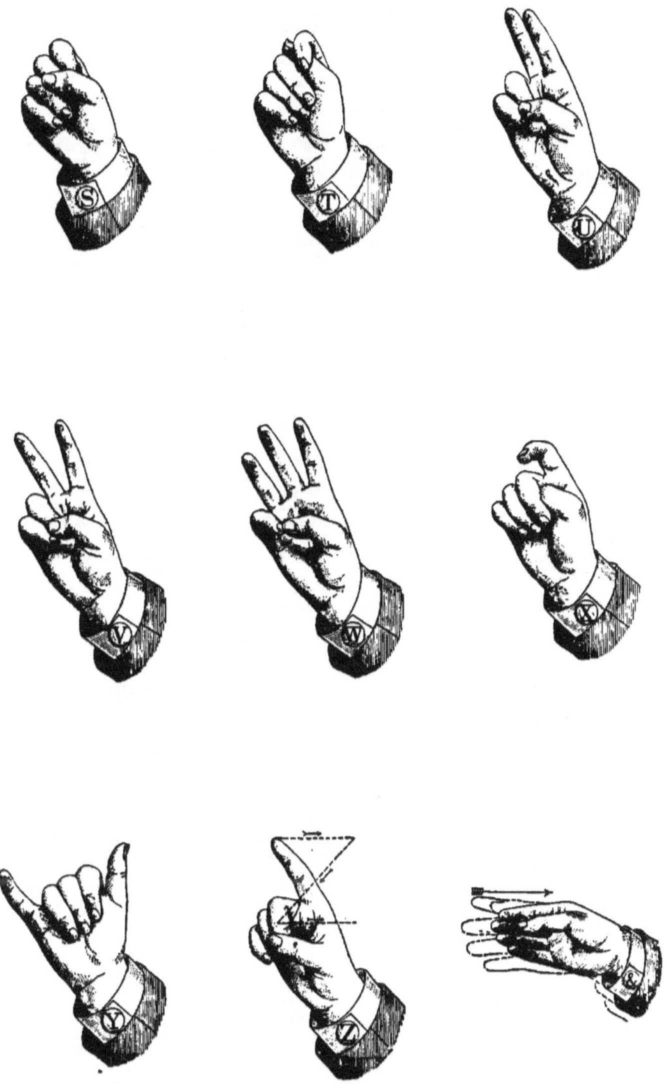

[THE "AMERICAN" MANUAL ALPHABET.]

THE MANUAL ALPHABET AS A PART OF THE PUBLIC-SCHOOL COURSE.

[This Exhibit consisted of the following paper by James Denison, M.A., Principal of the Kendall School for the Deaf, Washington, D. C., from the *American Annals of the Deaf*, October, 1886, Vol. XXXI, pp 233-239:]

In some English magazine I remember reading a few years ago a story to the following effect:

A burglar, intent upon robbery, had obtained entrance to a bed-room, where the lady of the house, awakened from sleep by the noise of his movements, was intimidated from giving an alarm by his fierce threats of violence. Hearing footsteps approaching, the robber concealed himself behind the bed, first cautioning the occupant that the least whisper of his presence would be at the risk of her life. The husband entered, unsuspicious of the fact that, from his place of concealment, the robber, with levelled pistol and finger on trigger, was breathlessly watching and listening.

The situation was full of peril—more easily imagined than described. The least allusion to the truth might have been instant death to the beloved husband, and probably to the wife also.

Now it happened that in their younger days they had learned the manual alphabet of the deaf, and had frequently since, as occasion suggested, communicated with each other by it. Unseen by the robber, the lady gave her husband on her fingers an inkling of the state of matters. He took in the situation at a glance—literally at a glance—and making a misleading remark about something he had forgotten to bring, he was out of the room and in a moment back again with fire-arms and assistance, and the burglar was captured, and robbery and possible murder prevented: and this by the manual alphabet, an accomplishment easily and carelessly learned years before, with no thought of its future employment in such an emergency.

This case, extreme as it may seem, only illustrates the general rule that in daily life circumstances are constantly arising in which there is an imperative necessity of saying something directly to the person most interested in a way not to attract too greatly the undesired attention of others, and of saying it quickly, perspicaciously, felicitously, without using the voice.

Writing is a medium of communication that answers these purposes at certain moments, and on certain occasions. It is undoubtedly an indispensable medium where distance, exactitude of statement, future reference, extent of matter, are to be considered. There is no need of enlarging upon this phase of its usefulness; it is universally acknowledged.

There are indisputably times and places in which the finger alphabet fulfils, as writing cannot do it, the conditions of expression where vocal utterance is either not desirable or not possible; where to use pen or pencil would be either an inconvenience, a waste of time, or a sheer impossibility.

How often at social gatherings—I am not alluding to the deaf in this connection—do we not see individuals, separated from each other by the crowd or the length of the room, vainly striving, by bewildering contortions of the countenance or noddings of the head, to convey a piece of information upon which may hinge the ease and pleasure of the evening. Repeatedly it must have occurred to the looker-on, as he noticed the mortification or blank disappointment depicted upon their faces at the futility of their attempts to reach a common understanding, that the finger-alphabet would have furnished them with a means of perfectly accomplishing that object without attracting undesirable attention by uncouth gestures, or obliging them to make themselves conspicuous by raising the voice beyond the proper pitch.

Probably no one has ever left a promiscuous gathering of any kind without recalling an unfortunate moment, made so by a lapse of memory, or some misinformation as to the name, identity, or profession of a person interviewed, where the use of the finger-alphabet on the part of a kindly-disposed third person would have saved him from an awkward blunder.

In concerts, where music has charms to still every other sound; in the church, where any other voice than that from pulpit or choir would shock the congregation from centre to circumference; in the theatre, where the owner of a voice in orchestra or gallery finds himself the focus of a hundred lorgnettes; and again, amid the noise and rattle of the machine shop, factory, or railroad, how often arises an imperious necessity of making a communication to another. How handy—old Saxon word this, but pat to the purpose, is it not?—How handy at such times and places would come the manual alphabet, achieving the end sought for completely, and without the least friction or disturbance!

Outside of the confessedly deaf, how many persons there are who, resenting with warmth the imputation of not being the possessors of a perfect auditory apparatus, are yet hardly ever addressed except in tones more or less raised above the conversational pitch. Often in certain situations the recollection of the fact that the voice must be thus heightened is an effectual preventive of anything being said at all. Thus timely, pleasurable, or valuable information has been withheld when the finger-alphabet could and would have put it where it would have done the most good.

To the invalid and to the sick room the manual alphabet comes, as it were, with healing on its wings. Has not every home its sick room dedicated to the goddess of perfect quiet, every family its invalid, a sort of living original of the marble statue of silence with finger forever on lip? How the sound of the human voice, be it ever so modulated and repressed, racks the ear of the nervous sick one! How the whisper of the nurse or the subdued tones of the physician startle him from the repose upon which his recovery depends, and turns his thoughts into channels that lead to apprehension and despondency! How perfectly, how beautifully, the manual alphabet performs its functions here; every weary nerve in the sufferer's body cries out, "God bless it!" And again, on the other hand, when the invalid is incapacitated by disease or exhaustion from using his voice, what a solace to him and his attendants it is if he can still express his wants by the silent, unlaborious motion of his fingers.

In this connection it is not out of place to refer to a more solemn subject—that of the death-bed. Some of you who have stood by the dying ere the soul has taken its flight may recall—and with what feelings I will not say—that last appealing look and those vain endeavors of the departing one to express some final desire. It is a well-known fact that the vocal chords give way long before the muscles of the hand; the dying man is "speechless," while his fingers move at will. How many last messages to be treasured thenceforth as a most precious heritage have been lost to the loving ones remaining behind—lost because the finger-alphabet was not known.

Members of the family of Dr. Thomas Hopkins Gallaudet have told me that in his last moments such precious and ever to be remembered messages continued to come from his fingers after his tongue was paralyzed in death. The same may be said of the Rev. B. M. Fay, father of Professor Fay of Kendall Green, who passed away last year; of Grace Aguilar, known to us through her "Days of Bruce," "Home Influence," and other writings, of whom the *Annals** says: "In her final illness, when the power of speech was gone, she conversed with her friends in the manual alphabet, and her last words thus expressed were, 'Though he slay me, yet will I trust in him.'" Dr. Harvey P. Peet, in an obituary notice of Martha Dudley in the same periodical,† states the same fact as regards her last hours, and mentions at the same time how "Mrs. Peet, after she became wholly speechless, spelled with her fingers distinctly the word 'Mother,' which incident is commemorated in a touching little poem of Mrs. Sigourney, 'The last word of the dying.'"

Thus far I have mentioned only a tithe of the circumstances in which a knowledge of the manual alphabet would be an advantage—I may say, an immeasurable advantage—to hearing people. A moment's thought will suggest to any one so many further illustrations to the same effect that there would not be space or time to give them all.

I must, however, mention one more. The finger-alphabet possesses acknowledged and, in the opinion of those familiar with its use, an unequalled excellence as a means of education in orthography. The care and deliberation with which the letters are formed, and the concentration of mind that the process involves, insure precision beyond any other method.

At Kendall Green, and possibly at other places similarly situated in regard to schools for the deaf, where the hearing children of the locality are formed into little schools for private instruction, the finger-alphabet has been practically and successfully tested in this respect. The teachers like it. "It makes the pupil so particular," they say. I have in mind now children of deaf parents, early used to this alphabet, who, on entering public schools, easily led their classes in spelling, to the wonderment of their teachers until the reason was explained.

Once more I have recourse to the *Annals*:‡

"It was a favorite idea of the late Rev. T. H. Gallaudet, the lamented illustrious pioneer of deaf-mute education in this country, that the practice of spelling words with the manual alphabet, even by hearing and speaking children, might be made very serviceable to them, by familiarizing them with the correct orthography of words aside from the use of the ear. The principle upon which the idea is based we think to be this: The more varied the form under which language is presented to the mind through the different senses, the more perfect will be the knowledge of it acquired, and the more permanently will it be retained."

In view of the incontestably great usefulness of the manual alphabet to the hearing, and considering the comparatively little labor and time needed to acquire it, has not the day arrived when some determined effort should be made to adopt it into the public-school system of the country? Should not this matter be urged upon the attention of teachers and boards of trustees of the public schools? Could not they be persuaded to hang charts of the manual alphabet on the walls of their school-rooms, with cuts large enough to be seen without effort from the farthest corner? Could not they be led to try the experiment of using this alphabet as a means of drill in spelling instead of the present method of writing out long lists of words? The same course, by the way, might be found useful in recitations in geography.

Would not the school-room work move on in smoother grooves, with less jar to nerve and temper, if a pupil, instead of speaking aloud and thus distracting the attention of others from their studies, simply spelled out on his hand a request or a question to the teacher? Would not the teacher himself feel more satisfaction in making a remark to a pupil in this way, having once caught his eye, than in interrupting the work of a whole class to do it?

The objection may be made that the result would be a demoralization of discipline; that pupils will have still another means of talking in school regardless of rules. To this it might be answered that there will always be more or less of this unauthorized interchange of ideas in every school-room; and that if it should be carried on through the finger alphabet there would be less disturbance than if any other medium were employed. But in truth the teacher possesses a check on the abuse of the manual alphabet in the fact that he is himself skilled in its use, and can tell what his pupils may be saying. A teacher in the High School at Washington informs me that all unlawful attempts of this sort ceased at once when his pupils found that their remarks were no riddle to him.

In keeping this matter within legitimate bounds, everything, of course, depends upon whether the teacher has tact, influence, character. Lacking these qualities, he has no right to be where and what he is. With them, he is sure of commanding the respect and obedience of his pupils for whatever regulations his judgment may lead him to make. Where the manual alphabet is employed, as it is in schools for the deaf, its use is under proper control. Why need the case be different elsewhere?

If, thus far, I have failed to expatiate upon the benefit—great beyond conception—that the introduction of the manual alphabet into the schools of the hearing would confer upon the deaf-mute himself, it is because this is something that needs only to be suggested to be recognized in all its force and extent. When we think how the general use of the manual alphabet would throw wide open the doors of communication between the deaf-mute and the hearing—doors that now open with difficulty and close again almost as soon as opened; when with the mind's eye we see the deaf child's intellect and heart unfolding from tender years in the sunlight of knowledge under conditions more analogous to those of his hearing playmate; when we behold the deaf adult, wherever he finds himself, whether in places of business, in political meetings, in religious assemblies, in social gatherings, placed in perfect unison with his neighbors and surroundings; when we realize that he moves among his peers with no feeling of isolation; when we know that there may be more instances than heretofore in which "the charm of waving hands," but without the evil taint of the charm that Vivien wiled away from Merlin, shall knit together for life the heart of the deaf and that of the hearing, how can we, as members of our noble profession, hesitate to give our vote, individually and collectively, for the general diffusion of the manual alphabet through the public-school system of the country? No; let us not hesitate; let us not even doubt:

> Our doubts are traitors,
> And make us lose the good we oft might win,
> By fearing to attempt.

* Vol. xvii, page 132.
† Vol. v, page 81.
‡ David E. Bartlett, *Annals*, vol. v, page 33.

HOW SHALL THE DEAF BE EDUCATED?

[This Exhibit consisted of the following article by Pres. Gallaudet, entitled "How Shall the Deaf be Educated?" published in the *International Review*, December, 1881, and reprinted here by permission of A. S. Barnes & Co., owners of the copyright. An abstract of this paper was given in the *American Annals of the Deaf* for January, 1882, Vol. XXVII, pp. 57, 58:]

The heated controversies which have been sustained for many years as to the merits of rival methods of instructing the deaf have, in part, grown out of a mistaken idea of classification, and partly out of an imperfect understanding of the capabilities of the persons to be taught. The synonymous terms *deaf-mute* and *deaf and dumb* have been applied to individuals supposed to form a class in the community.

Schemes for the amelioration of the condition of these persons have been urged in the several civilized countries, based on the presumption that what would be suited to one would be equally helpful to all. A certain method of instruction has been successfully made use of in certain instances, and the advocates of this method have insisted that none other should be used with any deaf-mutes. Enthusiastic teachers have been blind to the fact that the "class" for which they labor must be properly divided and subdivided; that the mental and physical peculiarities of each subdivision must be carefully differentiated; that the capabilities of each individual, even, must be understood before it can be determined what means of improvement may be resorted to with the greatest likelihood of success. It is believed that no attempt has ever been made to effect a definite division of the class "deaf and dumb" into its proper sub-classes, orders, etc., and it is not proposed to undertake this at the present time, but only to suggest a few terms which might be employed in such a classification.

First of all, the *class* should always be spoken of as *the deaf*. The term *deaf-mute* should only be applied to such as are totally deaf and completely dumb. Besides this sub-class, we should then have the *speaking-deaf*, the *semi-speaking-deaf*, the *speaking-semi-deaf*, the *mute-semi-deaf*, the *hearing-mute*, the *hearing-semi-mute*—these last two sub-classes being usually persons of feeble mental power. In all these sub-classes there would be found those of normal mental capacity, those of a capacity a little less than normal, others of still weaker mental power, and so on until the condition of imbecility is reached. The imitative faculty would be also found to exist in varying degrees; there would be differences in the power of visual perception, of tactile perception, as well as diversities of temperament, all of which would call for separate classification. It will not be claimed that for each *order* thus indicated a special method of instruction is required; but it is urged that with a *class*, involving such essential differences among its sub-classes and orders, no single method can be expected to be successful.

The question, then, which demands consideration is not, What is the best *method* of instructing the deaf? but rather, *How* shall the deaf be educated? And it should be understood that by *education* is implied such a course of instruction and training as shall enable its subjects to communicate intelligibly with others; to acquire information from books and to write; to engage in some avocation that may yield the means of support; and to comprehend their duties to their fellow-men, to their country, and to their God. For the education of any person, the prime requisite is the possession of a means of communicating ideas to the pupil, either from the living teacher or from books. This the normal child possesses in that language which is acquired during the years of infancy by imitation and without special effort. It is also true that a considerable number of the deaf gain speech before losing their hearing, many of them retaining their facility of language in spite of total deafness. But a large proportion of the deaf are without language until they come under the care of special instructors. The first labor in the education of these, therefore, is to supply their lack of the means of communicating with others. In the attempt to do this, we are compelled to ascertain what forms of language they can acquire, and then to determine which they shall be encouraged to use.

It is beyond all question that the form of communication natural to the deaf is that of signs and gestures. In this they seek to express their thoughts and feelings while yet untaught by others. And instances are numerous where children born deaf have so far developed this means of communication in their families as to have created what may, not improperly, be termed a *language*—limited in its scope it is true, and yet as full in its vocabulary as the languages of the most intelligent Indian tribes or even of some half-civilized nations.* When this gesture language is still further developed, as it has has been in the United States, and in several of the countries of Europe by intelligent teachers of the deaf, it can be made to serve as a vehicle of thought for the conveyance of the most elevated and abstruse ideas. But the language of signs is not, as some suppose, the only means of communication possible to the deaf. It may be remarked, in passing, that many visitors to the College for Deaf-Mutes at Washington have said that they supposed the students gained *all* their instruction through signs, being unable to use books or written language. The very early as well as the later history of the education of the deaf has proved that to persons born totally deaf the power of vocal utterance has been imparted, together with an ability to comprehend the speech of others, from the movement of the lips, which has practically placed them in possession of oral language.

The means of communication possible to the deaf are, then, three in number: 1. The language of signs; 2. Oral language; 3. Written language. Either of these may be taught independently of the other. The feasibility of teaching the deaf to express themselves in writing, and to understand printed and written language, except in cases where the mind is feeble, is universally admitted; and the importance of this feature of their education, whatever method be employed, is nowhere disputed. It is with reference to the use of signs and speech that wide differences have existed in the past and still exist; which it is the purpose of this article to reconcile, and, if possible, set forever at rest.

First of all, it may be said that for all the deaf who have acquired speech before losing hearing—these including the *speaking-deaf*, the *semi-speaking-deaf*, and the *speaking-semi-deaf*—it is most desirable that speech should be employed in their instruction to the greatest possible extent. They should be taught to read from the lips as early as possible, and their imperfections in utterance should be corrected. If it were true that all *deaf-mutes* (the word is used in the limited sense explained above) were able to master oral language, there would be no question as to the desirableness of attempting to bring them into possession of this means of communication. And just at this point in the shaded

* It will be understood that such words as *language*, *vocabulary*, and the like, are made use of in speaking of a voiceless and tongueless means of communication, only because of the lack of English words whose etymology would be consistent with the ideas to be expressed.

pathway of experiment and conjecture, through the twilight of which one must pass before entering the clear light of demonstration and the certain road of accomplished fact, appears the will-o'-the-wisp which has encouraged much effort only to crown it with disappointment.

As has already been stated, instances are numerous where congenitally deaf persons have been taught to speak well. This has been done in nearly every country of Christendom, and in every generation from the days when Pedro Ponce de Leon, three centuries ago in Spain, taught children "deaf from birth to speak, to read, write, and keep accounts, to repeat prayers, to serve the mass, to know the doctrines of the Christian religion, and to confess themselves *viva voce*." Schools have existed in Germany for more than a century where the attempt has been made, and is continued to the present day, to teach all deaf-mutes to speak. And a method, not pursued to any extent in this country until within the last fifteen years, which is frequently spoken of as *new*, is in fact the oldest of all methods of educating persons deprived of hearing and speech. In tracing the history of this interesting feature of the training of the deaf, it is not difficult to determine what has led so many teachers and others to believe that their general education might be conducted by the oral method. And this cannot be better made clear than by the relation of an incident which occurred in the experience of the writer some years since. Having spent a very interesting day in company with one of the most eminent and successful teachers of speech to the deaf now living in Europe, the writer raised the question whether it were true that a good many of his pupils did not *succeed* in speech. "Oh, yes!" he replied, "that is true; but it is all owing to the laziness or stupidity of my assistants." Now this good man had, a quarter of a century before, been wonderfully successful with a son and daughter of a prominent physician of Rotterdam. Out of this success had grown up a school liberally endowed by the benevolent in that city; and because of this success with his early highly gifted pupils, this teacher had persistently, in the face of all discouragements, held to the oral method with all who came to him. He had never attempted to divide the deaf into classes: he had not taken proper account of their widely differing capabilities. What had answered in two cases, or a few, *must* succeed with all; and so when his logic and his results disagreed, he ungenerously laid the blame on those who had, no doubt, labored with zeal and intelligence hardly inferior to his own. Other teachers meeting with pupils who could not master speech have accounted for their failures in various ways, many most unjustly assuming that all who failed to acquire the power of vocal utterance were deficient in intellect; and from not a few schools such children have been cruelly dismissed as incapable of receiving any instruction, when in point of fact their minds were normal, and they might have been well educated under a method dependent on signs and writing as means of communication.

Without taking further space to prove what will, it is believed, be very generally admitted even by promoters of the oral method of teaching the deaf—viz., that many *deaf-mutes* are found whose acquisitions in speech, even under the most favorable circumstances, will be very imperfect—the writer believes he is justified in assuming that with certain *deaf-mutes* it is not desirable to encourage the use of oral language. For these, signs and verbal language in the form of books, writing, and the manual alphabet should be cultivated as means of communication between teacher and pupil, for self-development and for social intercourse. It is with satisfaction that a quotation in support of this view is made from the writings of an English instructor of the deaf, who though young in his work has achieved excellent results in oral teaching, and who has taken a very advanced position in favor of the oral method. Mr. Arthur A. Kinsey, Principal of the Training College for Teachers of the Deaf on the German Method, Ealing, near London, in a paper presented to the International Convention of Instructors of the Deaf, held at Milan in September, 1880, says:

> "I propose to classify those for whom we are laboring according to their physical and mental condition. I shall ask your consent to placing the simply deaf on the one side, and those deaf and otherwise afflicted on the other; in this latter class I include those suffering from defective brain power, imperfect vision, extreme constitutional weakness, or serious malformation of the vocal and articulating organs. The first division it is proposed to instruct on the German system; the second, on the French."

"Defective brain power," referred to by Mr. Kinsey, must not be understood to mean only imbecility, for the term is applicable to imperfect or weak memory, lack of the imitative faculty, slowness of apprehension, nervousness, and other conditions familiar to those who have had to do with the deaf. "Imperfect vision" includes near-sightedness, far-sightedness, and other abnormal states of the visual organs, as common among the deaf as with others, all of which stand in the way of success in artificial speech, for this depends on the eye no less than on the vocal organs. Taking Mr. Kinsey's classification, we have a large percentage of the deaf with whom any effort to teach oral language is to be discouraged. The oral method, therefore, is not to be accepted, as many of its promoters insist, as the universal and only means of educating the deaf, but is to be made use of with a certain proportion only.

The question will now be raised and answered, whether those deaf persons who cannot learn to speak are to be regarded as inferior to those who can, and are, consequently, more to be pitied. This is frequently a matter of great concern to parents who have deaf children about to enter upon a course of instruction; and it is true that not a few teachers and supporters of the oral method would have the world believe that those taught under it have a far more valuable education than others. At the Milan Convention already alluded to, where the oral method was most ardently advocated, the suggestion made by a pupil on exhibition that a deaf person without speech was no better than a monkey was received with undisguised marks of approbation. A most emphatic protest is here entered against the acceptance of any such idea, or anything approaching to it; and it will be shown that, while the acquisition of speech by the deaf is a thing to be desired and valued, inability to gain it does not stand in the way of securing an education, in the fullest sense of that term; and it will be shown, further, that educated *deaf-mutes* (the word is used in its limited sense) possess certain advantages over those who mutism has been removed by education. The history of the instruction of the deaf in the world reveals the fact that in the United States and in all the countries of middle and northern Europe, except Germany, deaf children have been educated in large numbers without an attempt having been made to give them speech. With this education they have been able, with very few exceptions, to provide for their support by their own intelligent labor; a large proportion of them have married and reared families, often marrying hearing persons; they have mingled freely in society; they have proved themselves good citizens, and have, as a rule, lived lives of piety, enjoying the comfort of an intelligent religious faith.

Since the preparation of this paper was begun, a letter was shown the writer by the senior professor in the College for Deaf-Mutes at Washington, which gives an interesting, though of course imperfect, picture of the course in life of one who was a pupil of the professor while he was an instructor in the institution for the deaf and dumb at Hartford.

This letter so well illustrates several points relating to the condition of a person deaf from infancy, educated without speech, that no apology is made for inserting it entire. It is given, of course, precisely as composed by the writer.

AT HOME, *May* 6, 1881.

MY DEAR TEACHER AND FRIEND: I was indeed delighted to hear from you, and that little Minerva was not entirely forgotten. Many thanks for the letter and your photo. You have changed somewhat since I saw you. You did not have any beard or mustache when I saw you last. That changed your look very much. You say you are *gray!* How I wish I could see you, to have a chat such as we used to have at Hartford. I remember the pleasant good times. Let us go back to the year 1860—that was in the fall when we talked about my domestic affairs, while that little daughter of mine was lying asleep on the sofa in the parlor. She is a young lady now, as nice and lovely as can be. Well, you thought you saw my husband then. Yes, but he died the following summer from the effects of a severe fall. He left me two dear little children, Minnie, now aged 24, and Dannie, aged 22, a very nice young man, and are still living with us. I was again married, in 1868, to Mr. F——, a councilman, and have three children by him, Edith, aged 10, Bertha 7, and Lewis 6. All can hear and talk, and are attending school—can use the sign-language fluently.

Mr. F——is a very agreeable companion and an indulgent father to his children, even to Minnie and Dannie, and has done everything to make us happy. He was an only child and an old BACHELOR too, when he married me. Oh, is it not sweet to be called an old man's DARLING? He is a hearing man and handsome. We live on a nice farm lying at the foot south of "Woonsocket Hill"—a very pleasant location. I like living in the country the best.

Do you remember my brother Charles and my sister Desire? They were at school at the same time you was there. They live a little way from here, and of course we see each other almost every day. Charles was married a year ago at the ripe of age of 52 to a young deaf-mute lady aged 20, late of New York. They seem to be very happy together. Sister Desire is living with them, having been divorced from her husband for his neglect and misconduct. She has a son aged 22, and am sorry to say that he is like his father and is away somewhere.

My dear mother died a year ago aged 86 years.—Oh, I must tell you that she and President Garfield's mother were *cousins*. We descended from Maturin Ballou: I have plenty of proofs. Are you acquainted with General Garfield? I am going to write a letter to Grandma Eliza Garfield soon. Mother often spoke of her. Mother's maiden name was Freelove Ballou.

I think I have changed some since I saw you. Have grown fleshy. Not gray yet, and am almost 46 years. My teeth are as good as when I left school. I am well embalmed I guess, —ha! ha! I am still lively, gay, fun-loving as ever, and as happy as fat clams in high-tide! Among my pleasures and blessings I do not forget my dear Heavenly Father, and always am thankful. I shall send you my photo taken two weeks ago. Does it look like little Minerva—what do you think of it? Have I aged a great deal? I can almost see you smile. Whenever you come East please drop into Little Rhody and give us a visit. We shall all be happy to see you. I have so often spoke of you that they are almost acquainted with you. Will you please favor me with a lock of your hair—do I ask too much? I am making a wreath out of hairs of my choicest friends. The whitest lock I have is my old teacher Mr. Turner.

I have written all I think would interest you, and quite a lengthy letter—I fear a tiresome one too. Will now close with hopes to hear from you soon. God bless you! I am

Affectionately yours,

MRS. F——.

It will be noticed that very few errors of language appear in Mrs. F.'s composition; that as a *deaf-mute* widow with two children she was able to make an advantageous match with a hearing man (and it may be remarked that her first husband was also a hearing man); in short, that, in spite of her total deafness and unrelieved dumbness, she has lived a happy and useful life in free intercourse with hearing people, apparently at no great disadvantage on account of her physical disabilities.

Now it is not designed, in showing that *deaf-mutes* who have not learned to speak may nevertheless live happy and useful lives, to underrate the importance of adding speech to their other acquirements whenever it is possible to do so; nor yet to shield from a certain measure of criticism those teachers of the deaf in our own and other countries who have neglected or rejected the teaching of oral language in the education of the deaf. But it is the wish of the writer to emphasize the fact that teaching the deaf to speak and to read from the lips of others is not educating them, that it is not the thing of paramount importance, that it is not even an element of the *greatest* consequence. It is urged, therefore, without hesitation, that in cases where the process of imparting speech is found to be attended with great difficulties, and the degree of success in the early stages is small, it is better to discontinue the effort, relying on signs, writing, and the manual alphabet for the prosecution of the great work of education which is still entirely practicable.

It has been intimated that educated *deaf-mutes* possess certain advantages over those to whom the power of speech has been imparted, and the writer is well aware that many promoters of articulation will smile at this proposition—which he wishes, however, seriously to discuss, with no purpose of undervaluing speech, but with a view of encouraging and comforting those who may fail in their endeavor to overcome dumbness. In the first place the *deaf-mute* in the manual alphabet—facility in the use of which may be readily acquired by his friends and acquaintances—has a means of communication at his command for all the social and business relations of life *far more certain, comprehensive, and satisfactory than speech and lip-reading.* For it must be understood by the unprofessional that the ability to speak and read from the lips, enjoyed by many totally deaf persons, is by no means the same thing as normal speech and hearing, though some teachers of articulation would have the world believe that it is. There is a degree of uncertainty varying with circumstances, demanding repetition, explanation, and at times a resort to writing, which often makes oral communication with deaf persons far from satisfactory and comfortable. With many such persons conversation is limited to commonplaces. With most of them the free interchange of the "social circle" is impossible, communication being restricted to two persons, and these so placed with reference to each other that the vocal organs of each shall be in full view of the other. Now when conversation is carried on between two persons, or in the social circle, through the manual alphabet, all these difficulties disappear. Thought is transmitted from the fingers through the eyes to the brain with as great readiness and exactitude as from the tongue through the ear; both these processes are natural; neither of them puts a strain upon Nature. But when the eye is compelled to recognize the differences, often slight, which appear in the external aspect of the organs of speech when vocal sounds are uttered, a demand is made upon Nature to which she is not always able to respond. There is consequently a necessity for such close attention in order to lose as little as possible of what is being said, that the mind is not free to attend to the *subject* of conversation, but is occupied rather with the effort to understand. This serious drawback is entirely absent from communications by means of the manual alphabet.

The writer trusts he may be pardoned for saying that in respect to this matter of the relative comfort, fulness, and exactitude of the two means of conversing with deaf persons, just described, he has had opportunities for extended personal experiment. With the finger alphabet he has been familiar from his childhood, and its use is as easy to him as speech. Within the past ten or twelve years he has met many well educated deaf persons who declined to use the manual alphabet, and depended wholly on speech and lip-reading in their communications with others. With these he has found himself laboring under restrictions, such as have been referred to, which detracted not a little from the freedom and consequently from the pleasure of conversation; and he does not remember a single instance of such intercourse when he was not led to reflect on the great advantage attaching to the use of the finger alphabet by the deaf. At this point the question naturally arises, "What hinders deaf persons who have the power of speech and the ability to read from the lips of others from using the manual alphabet at will?" to which it may be replied, "Nothing whatever." And when the question follows, "Why then do they not avail themselves of its benefits?" the answer is, "Because they have been unwisely advised by their teachers to abstain from its use, as well as from the use of the sign-language, in the hope of attaining thereby to greater perfection in speech and lip-reading than they would be likely to do if they allowed themselves other means of communication." And moreover, they have in many instances been inspired by their teachers with a false shame of being taken for *deaf-mutes*, and their vanity has been inflamed by being assured that through the acquisition of speech they would be removed from the class in which their natural disability had placed them, and so "restored to society," whatever that phrase, so often used by promoters of the oral method, may mean.

The limits of this paper will not allow an exhaustive discussion of these points; but the attention of the reader may be directed to the fact that speech and the manual alphabet do not constitute two languages, rendering it important that only one should be cultivated at a time—they are merely two forms of expressing the same language, and hence may be used interchangeably without fear of evil results. And those whose greatest interest in the education of the deaf centres on perfecting them in speech and lip-reading should remember that with all their skill and zeal they cannot give the slightest hint of *actual hearing* to their pupils, and that failing in this they must remain *a class* in the community; also, that it is a mistaken kindness to cause their pupils to look down on such deaf persons as may fail to acquire speech. Besides having the important advantage of the use of the manual alphabet, *deaf-mutes* are more favorably situated than the *speaking-deaf* in this, that their lack of speech gives them an additional hold on the sympathies of others. They are felt to be more in need of a helping hand than those who undertake to communicate as the world does. The graceful movements by which they convey their ideas are attractive and interesting; while the speech of the deaf, never perfect and often painfully defective, is repellent and sometimes even distressing. Not a few parents of young deaf-mutes, having heard the speech of those who had been taught to articulate, have insisted that their children should *not* be instructed in speech, so disagreeable to them was the utterance of a totally deaf person. Still another advantage do well-educated *deaf-mutes* enjoy over the *speaking-deaf*—and this is the *free enjoyment and use* of the language of signs. The terms "free enjoyment and use" are emphasized because it is true that the *speaking-deaf* do make a certain use of signs, in spite of the prohibition that is sought to be enforced in the oral schools. Assuming to reject them, both teachers and pupils resort to them, the latter often surreptitiously, for the simple reason that among the deaf they serve a purpose of which, in many instances, nothing can take the place. And this is a proof, though not the only one, of what has been already claimed—that the language of signs is natural to the deaf.

There is at present connected with the college at Washington a young man of rather more than average intelligence, whose first training was received in an oral school where signs were very little used. After some years he was placed in an institution where the sign-language in its full development was freely employed. This young man has assured the writer that the acquisition and use of the language of signs seemed to open a new world to him. Thought was stimulated; a freedom of intercourse with others, unknown before, was developed; the enjoyment of public speaking (through signs) was added; and the general pleasure of life doubled. What is true in the case of this young man has been true of others, and would be of many more were they similarly favored by circumstances. Without any attempt to discuss this point exhaustively, it may be said that totally deaf persons can directly enjoy public speaking—such as lectures, preaching, addresses, and discussions—only through the medium of the sign-language. A friend may give them the substance of spoken discourses with the manual alphabet; but the claim, made by some, that when they have mastered lip-reading they can understand public speaking, is not well founded. To be *en rapport* with them, one who would address them directly must employ that language which alone is natural to them. The writer has seen so much of the pleasure and profit derived by the deaf from addresses made to them in *their own language*, that he can think only with pity of the loss sustained by those who, from mistaken notions of their own advantage, decline to make use of the means of communication which benignant Nature has especially designed for them. Strange as it seems to these who know in their own experience what the resources and value of the sign-language are in the education of the deaf, there are some who reject it and place it under a ban. That its use may be carried to injurious excess by injudicious persons is admitted; but the same is true of many things which man cannot spare from the social economy.

In urging the use of the language of signs, to a greater or less degree, in all schools for the deaf, no stronger arguments can be presented than are given by one of the most distinguished and successful teachers of *articulation* in Germany, the late Moritz Hill of Weissenfels, whose experience as an instructor of the deaf in speech extended over a period of more than forty years. In his comprehensive work, "Der gegenwärtige Zustand des Taubstummen-Bildungswesens in Deutschland," Mr. Hill alludes to the fact that some persons have charged upon the "German method" the proscription of every species of pantomimic language, and says: "Such an idea must be attributed to malevolence or to unpardonable levity. This practice is contrary to nature and repugnant to the rules of sound educational science." And then, after condemning even more sharply those who would attempt to educate the deaf without signs, he gives the following comprehensive estimate of the value of the sign-language:

"I acknowledge in this language of natural signs—

"1. One of the two universally intelligible innate forms of expression granted by God to mankind—a form which is in reality more or less employed by every human being.

"2. The only form of expression which by the deaf and dumb child can be fashioned without the aid of extraordinary practice, just as his mother tongue suffices to the hearing child, eventually arranging itself into forms of thought, and unfolding itself into spoken language.

"3. The reflex of actual experiences.

"4. The element in which the mental life of the deaf-mute begins to germinate and grow; the only means whereby on his admission to the school he may express his thoughts, feelings, and wishes.

"5. A very imperfect natural production, because it remains for the most part abandoned to a limited sphere of hap-hazard culture.

"6. A valuable mirror for the teacher, in which the intellectual stand-point of his pupil is exhibited to him.

"7. At first the only, and consequently indispensable, means of comprehension between teacher and pupil, but not a language which we merely need to translate into ours in order to induct him into the latter tongue.

"8. An instrument of mental development and substantial instruction made use of in the intercourse of the pupils with each other; for example, the well-known beneficial influences which result from the association of the new pupils with the more advanced.

"9. A means, but not the only one, whereby to supply a lack of clearness in other methods of communication, and leading back, in extraordinary cases, to the real object, or to its representation in drawing or model.

"10. The most convenient, quick, and certain means in many cases of making one's self understood by deaf-mutes, whether during tuition or out of school hours, and therefore also employed, perhaps, very often without need, even without volition.

"11. A very welcome means of revisal and correction when articulation brings into use, for example, an ambiguous word.

"12. A most efficacious means of assisting even pupils in the higher degrees of school training, giving light, warmth, animation to spoken language, which for some time after its introduction continues dull and insipid.

"13. A practical means of communication with others beyond the walls of the deaf and dumb institution, whether it be used by itself or in connection with articulation."

Then, after extending somewhat the train of thought suggested by these clearly stated points, the author thus concludes what he has to say in this part of his book on the use of signs:

"But it is particularly in the teaching of religion that the language of pantomime plays an important part, especially when it is not only necessary to instruct but to operate on sentiment and will, either because here this language is indispensable to express the moral state of man, his thoughts and his actions, or that the word alone *makes too little impression on the eye of the mute* to produce, without the aid of pantomime, the desired effect in a manner sure and sufficient."

Who will take the responsibility of proscribing the use of the language of signs in the general education of the deaf in the face of such testimony from such a source, after such an experience?

The importance of the sign-language to the deaf might be still further discussed; but the limits of this paper will allow nothing more than the remark that the fifth point quoted from Hill shows that with all his appreciation of the value of signs he had never developed them, as the French and American instructors have done, for certainly they have not been left to "a limited sphere of hap-hazard culture" in France or in the United States.

It now remains to answer, in a practical manner, the question chosen as the title to this paper. That no one method is to displace all others has, it is believed, been made evident. There must then be a system that shall include every method which can be shown to be of real service to any sub-class or order of the deaf. The writer has made use, in several publications, of the term "Combined System" in advocating the cause of the deaf. This term is thought to be an expressive one, and is certainly broad enough to include everything that is valuable to the deaf. That there may be no misapprehension of its meaning an attempt will be made to show how it is susceptible of somewhat different applications under conditions not identical. In a small State or section, where for economical reasons it would be impracticable to have more than one institution for the education of the deaf, the Combined System would suggest divisions and classes in which oral instruction would be emphasized and made prominent, while in other divisions and classes no attention would be paid to this branch. In such States as New York, Ohio, Pennsylvania, Indiana, and Illinois, the Combined System would call for the establishment of separate schools in which the several methods might be pursued, care being taken that the capabilities of the pupil and the peculiarity of the method should be in harmony. And as it is true that, in the country generally, articulation ought to have a more prominent place in the education of the deaf than is at present accorded to it, it is to be hoped that the example set by New England and New York of maintaining schools in which only those pupils shall be retained who are found capable of success in speech, may be speedily followed by Pennsylvania, Ohio, Indiana, and Illinois, in all which States there is urgent need of increased provision for this branch of public instruction.*

Having secured, under the Combined System, either in separate schools or in well divided classes, the application of the different methods accepted as valuable to the diverse capabilities of the deaf, the use of the manual alphabet and the language of signs in all schools is to be urged—these means of communication being employed, of course, to a much greater extent in silent schools than in those following the oral method. But in the latter it is earnestly recommended that advanced pupils, such as have practically mastered speech, be afforded the great advantage of receiving moral and religious instruction through signs, as well as the benefit of lectures and addresses of a secular character. It would thus become necessary that all teachers of the deaf should be familiar with the manual alphabet, and that in every oral school there should be one or more of the instructors well versed in the language of signs. In the silent schools care should be taken in the employment of signs, lest their excessive use interfere with the progress of the pupil in mastering verbal language; and in such schools the use of the manual alphabet should be encouraged even with very young pupils, as a means of conversation among themselves and with their teachers. The importance of employing in all schools only well-trained teachers, and such as possess a natural fitness for the work of instruction, cannot be overestimated; for no method, however valuable in itself, can be successful, except when practised by able and skilful hands. And if to secure the services of such it be necessary to pay what may seem to be large salaries, it is to be hoped that the spirit of benevolence, which leads legislatures to provide for so humane a work as the education of the deaf, will not fail of providing that the work may be done in the best possible manner.

Economy in public expenditure, as in private, is no doubt a virtue; but its over-cultivation produces the vice of parsimony as readily in the one case as in the other. And it is a fact greatly to be deplored, that, in schools for the deaf as in others, the welfare of pupils has suffered because of a disposition to make use of inferior services in order that appropriations and taxation may be slightly diminished. An evil largely due to such mistaken ideas of economy must not be overlooked in this connection; namely, the enlargement of single institutions until the number of pupils under one management is counted by many hundreds. It is argued that one school of four or five hundred pupils can be conducted at much less than double the expense of two schools, each of half the number. Granting this, it will be admitted on the other hand by all candid persons, that the congregation of large numbers of children away from their homes for purposes of education involves many evils, which may be in a great degree avoided by allowing the numbers in a single establishment to be no more than is necessary to a suitable arrangement of grades and classes.

At the beginning of this article an allusion was made to "heated controversies" which have been maintained with more or less bitterness as to the merits of rival methods of instructing the deaf.

Perhaps this effort to answer the question *How shall the deaf be educated?* can be closed in no more satisfactory manner than by recording the gratifying fact, that while in Europe these "controversies" are continued in a spirit which is not always magnanimous, or even fair, in our own country harmony prevails among those whose views as to the relative advantages of the different methods are not yet in perfect accord. Cordial interchange of sentiments takes place in conventions to which all teachers, of whatever shade of opinion, are invited. Success under any method is recognized and applauded. And a tendency is plainly discernible towards a general approval of such a Combined System as has been described, in the successful operation of which, throughout our whole country, the best possible results are to be anticipated.

* By the benevolent bequests of a lady recently deceased in Philadelphia, the authorities of the Pennsylvania Institution for the Deaf and Dumb have come into the possession of funds, with which they have determined to establish two separate schools for small children in Philadelphia—one following the oral method, the other the sign method.

EXHIBIT TO QUERY 13,427.

MILAN CONVENTION.

[This Exhibit consisted of the following Report upon the Milan Convention by Pres. Gallaudet, published in the *Annals* for January, 1881, Vol. XXVI, pp. 1-16:]

The readers of the *Annals* will remember that in the summer of 1878, during the progress of the French Universal Exhibition, a meeting of instructors of the deaf and dumb was hastily convened, to which the commanding name of International Convention (*Congrès Universel*) was given. Twenty-seven teachers attended this gathering, out of which number twenty-three were from France; Sweden, Austria, Switzerland, and Belgium each furnishing a single delegate. The character of the assemblage, therefore, did not correspond with its title, and as an attempted representation of the work and various methods of deaf-mute instruction in the world, as well as of the opinions held by instructors, the Convention of Paris was a failure. Moreover, it is well known that the management of the Convention was in the hands of the promoters of articulation, and more especially under the control of representatives of the Pereire Society (*la Société Pereire*), an association established some years since in Paris for the purpose of securing the recognition of Pereire as the first teacher of deaf-mutes in France, and to bring about the general adoption of the oral method, which was practised by Pereire. It is probably not so generally known that several great-grandsons of Pereire are now living in Paris; that they are united in a very wealthy banking firm, and that they have been contributing large sums of money during the past few years for the support of the Pereire Society, and the Pereire School for deaf-mutes, of which Mr. Magnat is the principal.

The Paris Convention appointed a committee of twelve of its own members to make arrangements for a second international meeting. Of those composing this committee, eleven were from France, and a very large majority were ardent promoters of the method of articulation. Milan was selected as the place in which the Convention of 1880 should be held, in which city are to be found two institutions formerly conducted on the method of the Abbe de l'Épée, but which for the past ten years have been giving the greatest possible prominence to articulation.

When the Convention came to be organized, the head of one of the Milan schools, the Abbe Tarra, was made President, and the leading instructor in the other school, Professor Fornari, was made Secretary. Of the four Vice-Presidents and four Vice-Secretaries, seven were pronounced supporters of articulation.

Two days before the opening of the Convention were devoted to public examinations of the Milan schools, at which the delegates were earnestly urged to be present; and during one-half of each day that the Convention was in session no sittings were held, in order to leave the members free to visit the Milan schools.

All these facts are mentioned in order to show—which certainly cannot be disputed—that in arranging for the Convention the promoters of articulation secured every possible advantage to themselves, imparting a partisan character to the whole affair from the very outset. And the sequel will prove that the Convention at Milan was no more international or representative in its composition than that of Paris; that its formal utterances are no more to be taken as representing the sentiments of teachers of the deaf and dumb throughout the world than are the resolutions of a party nominating convention to be regarded as a fair expression of the opinions of the whole community.

And yet a journal of no less prominence and influence than the London *Times* gravely announces, in a labored editorial published a few days after the adjournment of the Milan Convention, that "no more representative body could have been collected than that which at Milan has declared for oral teaching for the deaf, and for nothing but oral teaching," and speaks of the action of the Convention as expressing a "virtual unanimity of preference for oral teaching which might seem to overbear all possibility of opposition."

With such stupidity, if it be nothing worse, on the part of the conductors of one of the leading journals of the world, it is not easy to be patient.

If the editors of the *Times* had taken the slightest pains to inquire, they would have learned that out of the one hundred and sixty-four active members of the Convention *eighty-seven*, or a clear majority of ten, were from Italy; that *fifty-six* were from France, making, with the Italian members, a majority of *seven-eighths;* that, of the eight English delegates, six were ardent articulationists, and only two at all favorable to any other method—a proportion which entirely misrepresents the present sentiment of English teachers of the deaf; that the only truly representative delegation present was that from the United States, consisting of five members, duly accredited to the Milan meeting by a Conference of Principals of American Institutions for the Deaf and Dumb held at Northampton last May, in which the supporters of the several methods of instruction now made use of in this country (including all that are known in the world) were assembled in friendly council; that the American delegates represented fifty-one schools, containing over six thousand pupils—a greater number than was represented by all the other one hundred and fifty-nine delegates taken together; that the Convention allowed the American delegates to be out-voted in the proportion of nearly *ten* to *one* by the representatives of the two schools of Milan, they being accorded *forty-six* seats in the Convention.

Possibly, if all these facts had come to the knowledge of the editors of the *Times* before the publication of the article quoted from above, less might have been said as to the "representative" character of the Milan meeting.

But we are not yet done with the "Thunderer" of Great Britain, for it is unfortunate in the correspondents it employs as well as in its editorial staff.

In an account of the public examinations, so called, of the Milan schools, given on the two days preceding the assembling of the Convention, the *Times* reporter says:

"Let it be noted that the medium of examination —the sole medium of communication, in fact, between pupil and examiner, whether teacher or visitor—was speech—speech alone. Every word of the examination was uttered audibly; every word of the answer was spoken in like manner, audibly and loudly. There was not even in this country, where gesture and action so commonly accompany speech, the least resort to signs or finger language. * * * Deaf children were addressed just as if they were not deaf, in spoken language, and they one and all answered in spoken language, though in our country we call them dumb."

Now, while this was all true, the English letter-writer failed to report that the examinations followed very closely the printed programmes; that the answers were in many instances begun before the examiner had completed his question; that no real examination was made by outside persons; that many pupils were asked very few questions, while certain other pupils were examined at great length; that these discriminations were made by the teachers in every instance; that no information was given as to the history of any pupil—that is to say, as to whether deafness was congenital or acquired, and whether speech had been developed before hearing was lost or not; that the impression was thus sought to be conveyed to the audiences that all the speech possessed by all the pupils had been imparted to them by their teachers, which was certainly not the case. In view of all which we do not hesitate to characterize these so-called examinations as mere exhibitions, deserving to have very little influence with the professional observer.

The labors of the Convention began at noon on Monday, Sept. 6, and all the time of that day's session was consumed in complimentary speeches and the election of officers.

The subjects presented for discussion by the Committee on Organization were grouped in four classes, as follows: (1) Those relating to buildings, and all material arrangements for the accommodation of inmates of institutions; (2) everything concerning the details of instruction; (3) the various methods of teaching; (4) special questions.

After what has been said as to the organization and complexion of the Convention, it will surprise no one that, among the many topics suggested in the programme, that of methods of instruction should have engrossed the time of the Convention to the exclusion of almost everything else.

Discussion was begun on the second day by the presentation of a printed volume of one hundred and sixteen pages, prepared by Mr. Magnat, principal of the Pereire school for deaf-mutes in Paris. In this brochure all the topics included in the first three groups were treated *in extenso*. A small portion only of this volume was read to the Convention. As an evidence of the *entente cordiale* existing between the head of the Pereire family and those who are working under its patronage, the dedication of this volume is interesting:

"*A Monsieur Eugène Pereire, Président du Comité d'organisation du Congrès international de Milan. Hommage de parfait attachment.*

"MAGNAT."

Mrs. B. St. John Ackers, well known to the readers of the *Annals* as an accomplished English lady who has been for some years superintending the education of a deaf daughter, read a paper on the "Mental development of the deaf under the German system."

Mrs. Ackers was followed by Miss Susanna E. Hull, of London, the mistress of a private school for deaf-mutes, in a paper entitled "My experience of various methods of educating the deaf-born."

Both these ladies urged in eloquent language the superiority of the German or oral method over the French or sign method, but neither recognized the objection which may be raised against the oral method for *all* deaf-mutes: that, in point of fact, a large proportion of the deaf are incapable of attaining any real success in speech and lip-reading.

The writer of this article opposed the use of either the German or the French method to the exclusion of the other, and advocated a combined system, in which all available means should be employed, these being wisely adapted to the diverse conditions of those who are to be taught.

He admitted the propriety of maintaining schools in which the oral method should prevail, but insisted that at the same time other schools should be provided for the benefit of those who are incapable of success in speech.

These views, however, found little favor in the Convention, and after a debate, absorbing three entire days, in which the presiding officer, the Abbe Tarra, was the most prominent speaker, he occupying more than two hours on two successive days, the following resolutions were adopted, the only negative voices being those of the American delegates and one English delegate, Mr. Richard Elliott, headmaster of the old London Institution:

1. "The Convention, considering the incontestable superiority of speech over signs, (1) for restoring deaf-mutes to social life, (2) for giving them greater facility of language, declares that the method of articulation should have the preference over that of signs in the instruction and education of the deaf and dumb."

2. "Considering that the simultaneous use of signs and speech has the disadvantage of injuring speech and lip-reading and precision of ideas, the Convention declares that the pure oral method ought to be preferred."

On the fifth day of the meeting the writer of this article was invited by the President to read a paper he had prepared on the higher or collegiate education of the deaf and dumb, suggested by the second of the special questions proposed in the programme:

"Where and how can those whom deafness has prevented from pursuing classical studies receive an education equivalent to that of the higher schools open to hearing and speaking students? Should it be in a higher department of the institutions for the deaf and dumb, or in a special institution? With special or with ordinary instructors?"

The writer argued in favor of the establishment of colleges for the deaf in the several countries of Europe, and maintained that, even with the highest possible facility in speech and lip-reading, the number of deaf students that could pass successfully through an ordinary college would be very small. The effort to give the higher education in each institution to the mere handful that would be capable of receiving it was objected to as expensive and impracticable. The writer demonstrated the practicability of his ideas by giving a history of the successful progress, during the last sixteen years, of the National Deaf-Mute College at Washington.

The suggestion of the founding of colleges for the deaf in Europe was warmly endorsed by Mr. Hugentobler, of Lyons, Padre Marchiò, of Siena, and the Abbe Balestra, of Paris. The President expressed the thanks of the Convention for the paper on Collegiate Education, and desired a copy for publication.

The suggestion was made that the Convention give a formal expression of its approval of the idea of establishing colleges for the deaf in Europe, but Herr Treibel, of Berlin, followed by others, urged that the higher education should not be undertaken in Europe while so many deaf-mutes were unable to secure even the primary education.

The discussion on the subject was closed by the adoption of the following: "Considering that a great number of deaf-mutes do not receive the benefit of instruction, and that this is due to the poverty of their families and the want of suitable institutions, the Convention resolves that Governments ought to take the necessary steps so that all the deaf and dumb shall receive instruction."

The writer had the pleasure of stating to the Convention that the provision urged by the resolution was already made, with very rare exceptions, throughout the States of the American Union. The remainder of the session of Friday was occupied in the discussion of a few details in the work of teaching, more especially concerning instruction in grammar.

On Saturday, the closing day of the meeting, resolutions were adopted urging the preparation of special text-books to be used in teaching deaf-mutes by the oral method; advising the entrance of pupils into school between the ages of eight and ten years, and their continuance under instruction for at least seven years; advising that no more than ten pupils be assigned to one instructor, and counselling a gradual and progressive substitution of the oral method in institutions in which it is not now employed.

It was decided that the next International Convention should be held at Basle, in August, 1883, and after the usual complimentary speeches and resolutions, the Convention adjourned.

The following papers prepared for the Convention were not read, but will be published in the proceedings: "Advantages to the Deaf of the 'German' system in after-life," by B. St. John Ackers; "On the Education of the Deaf," by Arthur A. Kinsey, Principal of the Training College for Teachers of the Deaf on the German method, Ealing, near London; "Speech and lip-reading for the Deaf; a teacher's testimony to the German system," by David Buxton, Ph. D., Secretary of the Society for training teachers of the Deaf and Diffusion of the "German" system in the United Kingdom; and "The Combined System," by the venerable and eminent Monseigneur De Haerne, of Brussels, whose labors and writings in behalf of deaf-mute education are so well known and so highly appreciated in America.

That the business committee did not arrange for the reading of this last paper is an additional proof of the partisan character of the management of the Convention, for in the discussion of the matter of methods fully nine-tenths of the time was occupied by the advocates of the pure oral method. It is, however, not difficult to understand that, in a convention largely made up of ecclesiastics of the Roman Church, the promoters of the pure oral method should have preferred that so high an authority as Monseigneur De Haerne should not be heard in opposition to their views. Had he been present at the Convention, it is probable that the majority in favor of the pure oral method would have been considerably less than it was. And in this connection we are constrained to mention a fact that is not without a certain significance in estimating the value to be placed on the conclusions of the Convention.

A majority of the French delegates were members of an ecclesiastical order called the Brotherhood of St. Gabriel. Many of these brothers expressed the opinion freely in private conversation that signs could not be dispensed with in the instruction of deaf-mutes, and also that not all deaf-mutes could succeed under the oral method. They took no part, however, in the debate until towards the close, when Frère Hubert, inspector of the schools under the direction of the Brothers, rose and announced his conversion to the "pure oral method," closing his little speech by giving thanks to M. Eugène Pereire, through whose liberality the members of his brotherhood had been enabled to visit Milan and attend the Convention. And not a brother of St. Gabriel voted against the method of Pereire.

Having now given a brief outline of the proceedings of the Convention, and having demonstrated, as we believe, that it was wholly partisan in its management and not at all representative in its composition or manner of voting, we will attempt to show that the declarations of the Convention (as to methods) are in some respects inconsistent with the expressed views of their prominent supporters, and that these conclusions are based on unsound premises; in fine, that they are deserving of no weight whatever with broad-minded, candid, and progressive friends of deaf-mutes.

If the reader will turn back to resolutions one and two, and will consider them together, it will be perceived that not only is the method of articulation given the preference over that of signs, but that signs are not to be used simultaneously with speech; in other words, all use of signs is to be prohibited in the instruction of deaf-mutes. That such was the requirement of the "pure oral method" its supporters maintained most earnestly at certain points in the debate, and yet at certain other stages of the discussion it was admitted that signs *are* used under the "pure oral method," and Professor Fornari offered a resolution in which he endeavored to state in terms to what extent signs were to be employed. This resolution was supported by Mr. Hugentobler and several of the more conservative supporters of articulation. But the radicals felt that the admissions of Fornari's resolution would be inconsistent with the term "pure oral," with which they had resolved to christen their method, and of course did not sustain the motion.

Unfortunate pure oralists! Either horn of the dilemma was found to be an uneasy and painful resting place. If they admitted that signs were employed, the world would smile at the use of the words "*pure oral.*" If they told the world they had banished signs, the records of the Convention would testify against them, for it was distinctly acknowledged that "natural signs," "those which are used and understood by hearing persons," "might be employed in the earlier stages of instruction."

The writer recalls an incident which occurred during his boyhood, when a young Frenchman, just arrived in this country and quite ignorant of English, visited his father's house. This young man had never before seen a deaf-mute, but on meeting the mother of the family, who was a mute, he at once began talking with her by signs, and continued conversation for more than an hour on a great variety of subjects, making, of course, only such signs as are "used and understood by hearing persons."

It is well known that the signs in use among the Indians of North America, who are certainly "hearing persons," cover a wide range of ideas.

But it is unnecessary to pursue the subject further to show that the so-called "pure oral method," exists only in name. We are not done, however, with the inconsistencies of some of its prominent supporters.

None of the delegates at Milan were more earnest advocates of the "pure oral method" than Mr. Arthur A. Kinsey, who was kind enough to present the writer with a copy of the paper he had prepared for the Milan Convention,* from which we quote the following:

"Before proceeding further, I should propose to classify those for whom we are laboring according to their physical and mental condition. I shall ask your consent to placing the simply deaf on the one side, and those deaf and otherwise afflicted on the other: in this latter class I include those suffering from defective brain power, imperfect vision, extreme constitutional weakness, or serious malformation of the vocal and articulating organs.

"The first division it is proposed to instruct on the 'German' system; *the second on the 'French.'* [The italics are ours.]

"At the present time the special schools in Germany do not reject those suffering other serious ailments in addition to deafness. All the deaf are admitted to the advantages of instruction, regardless of other defect being unhappily present.

"But the question which I desire to present to you is—Should this continue?

"Where time, money, and teaching power are limited, where pupils are in excess of school accommodation at the special institutions, would it not be wiser to teach those merely deaf upon the 'German' system,—those who would really profit by such instruction and put it to real practical and valuable use in after-life,—than to keep back such pupils for

* See preceding column.

the sake of doubly afflicted ones, who, despite all effort and skill, would only be advanced to a *certain attainment in spoken language of trifling and most uncertain value.* [Again the italics are ours.] * *

"The children that this method [the German] is incompetent to deal with should be cared for by other means not requiring so much capability on the part of the afflicted."

If we may be pardoned for the use of a little slang, we will venture the opinion that few instances are to be met with of a more complete "give-away" of one's self than the foregoing. Consistent pure oralist! in the Convention he votes and shouts for "*la méthode orale pure*," and then submits a paper in which it is proposed to establish and maintain schools on the "French" or "sign" method, in which it is acknowledged that there are certain deaf-mutes with whom the "German" method is "incompetent to deal," and who, under it, "despite all effort and skill, would only be advanced to a certain attainment in spoken language of trifling and most uncertain value." We beg to call the attention of the London *Times* to this record, and to suggest that if Mr. Kinsey is to be taken as a specimen "pure oralist," there may be something unreliable in the declarations of that "representative body" "which at Milan has declared for oral teaching for the deaf, and for nothing but oral teaching." But we forgive Mr. Kinsey his inconsistencies, and gladly take him on his record, and extend to him the right hand of fellowship. Far from being a "pure oralist," he is plainly in favor of a "combined system" —a system which welcomes every practicable means of advancing and perfecting the education of *all* the deaf and dumb; a system which approves of the establishment of schools in which the oral method may be employed, provided that at the same time other schools can be maintained for the benefit of those who are incapable of success in speech; a system which is in operation to-day in New England, with its oral schools at Northampton, Boston, Portland, Providence, and Mystic; with the large and well-known institution at Hartford, where the sign method is still employed with excellent results.

Lest some of Mr. Kinsey's friends should think we are too fast in placing him where we do, we will consider for a moment, before passing to other matters, just how much is involved in his division of deaf-mutes into two classes, as quoted above.

In this he displays more far-sightedness than we had given him credit for, and we cannot but admire the discretion with which he leaves an open door, and by no means a narrow one, for the convenient exit of those with whom the "German" method is found to be "incompetent to deal."

"Defective brain power;" most happily chosen expression! For it is applicable to imperfect or weak memory, lack of the imitative faculty, slowness of apprehension, nervousness, and a score of other conditions familiar to those who have had to do with deaf-mutes. "Imperfect vision," including "near-sightedness," "far-sightedness," and other abnormal states of the visual organs (common among deaf mutes), which would stand in the way of success in artificial speech, for this is an achievement of the eye no less than of the vocal organs. "Constitutional weakness" would furnish a very considerable percentage of the whole number to be educated, and we drop the word "extreme," for surely a predisposition to colds, sore-throat, and catarrhal affections operates seriously against the attainment of speech by deaf-mutes. And when we add those suffering from "serious malformation of the vocal or articulating organs," we have an aggregate sufficiently large to call for not a few of the "French method" schools Mr. Kinsey so wisely recommends.

But enough has been said to show that the expressed views of prominent "pure oralists" in the Milan Convention are inconsistent with the "declarations" for which they voted. We will now endeavor to make it apparent that these declarations are based on unsound premises.

Taking into account the whole body of deaf-mutes, and the time and money that is available for their education, it is not true that the method based on speech has an "incontestable superiority" over that based on signs.

And first of all, for that class with which, on the authority of Mr. Kinsey, the "German method is incompetent to deal," the boot is quite on the other leg. As to the proportion indicated by this class opinions differ, but in the judgment of some of the ablest instructors of articulation in Europe it outnumbers the other with whom success in speech is practicable.

As to the "incontestable superiority" of speech even for these, all depends on the environment. Given ample funds, implying a large proportion of teachers, and ample time, implying a long term of school training, the superiority of "speech" is admitted. On the other hand, with a period of teaching restricted to four or five years, and funds so limited that but one teacher to twenty or more pupils can be allowed, then we do not hesitate to claim that results of greater practical value to the deaf-mute have been reached and will hereafter be attained under the method of de l'Épée than under that of Heinicke.

A short time since the writer met for the first time a deaf-mute of about forty years of age, a resident of Natick, Mass. He communicated with us by signs, through the use of the manual alphabet, and by writing. He had never learned to speak.

What followed may be taken as a fair sample of this deaf-mute's ability to use his vernacular, while the facts brought out will give some idea as to his success and pleasure in mingling with those who hear and speak. In presenting the following questions and receiving the answers writing was the sole medium of communication:

"Were you born deaf?"

"Yes, sir; I was born deaf and dumb. I can hear loud whistle of an engine plainly."

"How many years were you at the Hartford Institution, and in what year did you leave school?"

"Six years. I was nine years old when I went to school; 1847; left there in 1853; before I went to school my mother learned me the finger-alphabet and many words, and also learned to write. Mrs. Vice-President Henry Wilson was my school-mate."

"How have you been employed since you left school?"

"When I left school, farming with my brother seven years; left it on account of hard work. I went into a shoe manufactory, where I have been employed eighteen years, and am still at work."

"Have you had any difficulty in earning enough to support yourself?"

"No, sir; I have not had any difficulty in earning enough to support myself since I left school. Now I am in very comfortable circumstances, and will be able to support myself as long as I live. My wages in the shop are good."

"Have you made many friends among hearing and speaking people?"

"Yes, sir; a great many. I enjoy associating with them very much. They are very good and kind to me."

"How have you conversed with these friends?"

"By writing, and one and two-hand alphabet."

"How many persons have learned the finger alphabet, so as to be able to talk with you?"

"A good many. I cannot count them. They enjoy talking with me very much. Very often they tell me what they are speaking with the others and what the others say."

"When a train of thought passes through your mind, do your ideas take shape in signs or in words?"

"In words always, since that is the way in which my ideas are expressed."

That among the graduates of the deaf-mute schools of this country large numbers may be found who have been equally successful in making their way in the world, equally happy in their relations with hearing people, and equally correct in their use of language with the person just alluded to, is too well known to be successfully disputed.

Now, if the person above described could have had his term of study extended fifty per cent., and could have acquired speech and lip-reading, in addition to what he secured at Hartford, he would, of course, have been the gainer. But with his school-term limited to six years, with, perhaps, only a second or third rate ability to acquire speech, necessitating the devotion of the greater part of his time to speech alone, we do not hesitate to claim the "incontestable superiority," in his case, for the method based on signs. And what is true in this instance will apply in many others.

We now desire to direct attention to a few glaring misstatements to be found in papers presented to the Convention by some of the English delegates, giving evidence of a degree of ignorance or carelessness on their part which, if it is to be taken as an index of their general method of investigation, will readily account for this greatest of all blunders in ascribing an incontestable superiority to the method of speech over that based on signs in the general education of the deaf.

Towards the close of Miss Hull's paper we find the following:

"When we look at the home life, the social life, and, above all, the religious life of the deaf, at how much greater advantage are those who can freely converse with others by speech and lip-reading, compared with the disciples of the sign-language, who must necessarily confine their intercourse within a circle—the limited circle—of those who have learned the same mode of converse with themselves."

The reader of this paragraph is plainly left to infer that a deaf-mute, educated without speech, has no means of holding intercourse with his fellow-men save through the use of the language of signs. We beg to inform Miss Hull that deaf-mutes taught on the "sign method" learn to read and write; that they often carry on extended conversations with hearing people in writing; moreover, that they have in the manual alphabet a means of communication easily and very frequently acquired by their hearing friends, which is in many particulars, and under many circumstances, a much more satisfactory medium of conversation than speech and lip-reading.

In the paper presented by Mr. Ackers the following will be found on page 8:

"The contrast was most marked between those taught under the 'German' system, with whom we conversed by word of mouth, and those who had been taught under the 'French' system, unable to converse with us who were unacquainted with signs and the manual alphabet, and whose attempts at writing were most difficult, and in many cases impossible to understand owing to the language of their country being to them a foreign language. That the language of their country will be ever thus, even to the most highly educated, will be admitted by even the staunchest supporters of those systems. Dr. E. M. Gallaudet acknowledged this to me, and said that I might mention that even one so highly gifted by nature and education as his own mother never, even in later years, could be said to have lost in her writings all 'deaf-mutisms.'"

To those who are at all familiar with educated deaf-mutes in this country it will not be necessary to say anything in reply to the misstatements contained in the above paragraph. But for the benefit of the general reader we will state that we know of no even moderately staunch supporter of the 'French' method who admits that the language of their country ever remains as a foreign language to the most highly educated of the deaf and dumb taught under that method; that thousands of deaf-mutes in this country have a fair mastery of verbal language, though they remain dumb: that the writer's mother, far from being "highly gifted by education," had the misfortune to have reached adult years before the first school for mutes in this country was opened, and enjoyed only three years of instruction; that she, in spite of these disadvantages, gained so good a command of the language of her country as to be able to sustain a voluminous correspondence with members of her family and others, even into extreme old age, never experiencing any difficulty in expressing her ideas in verbal language, which, if not always correct, was usually so, and was certainly more free from errors than that of many hearing persons who have enjoyed far greater educational advantages than were hers.

We venture to promise our friend Mr. Ackers, whose disinterested and generous labors in the cause of deaf-mute instruction command our warmest admiration, that on the occasion of his next visit to America we will place him in communication with educated deaf-mutes whose attainments in verbal language will greatly modify his present views as to the possible results of the "French" method of instruction.

In Mr. Kinsey's paper we find the following on page 22:

"These remarks are addressed, not at my 'German system' brothers, but at those engaged on other methods in my mind far less satisfactory, and I think are not uncalled for, when I remember the words addressed by the head of a National College for the Deaf and Dumb, viz., that he 'had felt diffident about conferring a degree on a young man upon his graduating who was not competent to construct a grammatically correct sentence in his own native language.'"

We will not say that the above is an intentional misrepresentation, but we will say that it is entirely an unwarrantable statement. What we did "address" to Mr. Kinsey on the occasion alluded to was, that in a certain instance we hesitated to confer a degree on a young man who, while he had sustained all the examinations required for his degree, was not always able to use his vernacular correctly. And Mr. Kinsey does not need to be informed that among the hearing and speaking graduates of colleges, both in England and America, there are to be found those who are not always faultless in their use of their "own native language."

Perhaps the most glaring evidence of a lack of knowledge of the subject with which one was attempting to deal is found in an utterance of the President of the Convention, the Abbe Tarra, whose professional reputation is that of a *master* of the sign method, which he once taught, as well as of the oral, of which he was the high-priest and apostle at Milan.

He closed his oration in favor of the pure oral method as follows:

"Speech is addressed to the intellect, while gestures speak coarsely to the senses. I used signs for many years in my religious teaching, but decided definitely to give them up and adopt the pure oral system, because I am convinced that my pupils, instead of understanding the abstract ideas I intended to convey to them, were only placed in possession of grossly material images."

Nothing more than this is needed to stamp the Abbe Tarra, in the minds of accomplished instructors of the deaf under the sign method in this country, as a mere tyro in the use of the language of signs. For every *master* of that language knows how completely it may be made to convey and clearly express the highest religious and moral truths and sentiments.

The limits we have assigned ourselves in this article will not allow the insertion of a number of points we have in mind quite pertinent to the general line of thought suggested by the proceedings of the Convention, and we can only express the hope, in closing, that, in spite of the little value to be attached to the so-called *conclusions*, good results may flow from the meeting, in an increased interest towards deaf-mutes throughout Europe. And we believe that the sober second thought of many, even, who were carried away by the enthusiasm of the hour at Milan, and so were led to vote for impracticable and even impossible things, will deter them from attempting manifest absurdities.

In addition to the foregoing exhibits, the books and pamplets named in the three following exhibits were presented by President Gallaudet to the Royal Commission:

PROCEEDINGS.

EXHIBIT TO QUERY 13,266.

[This Exhibit consisted of copies of the proceedings of the following Conventions and Conferences:]

First Convention of American Instructors of the Deaf, New York, 1850.
Second Convention of American Instructors of the Deaf, Hartford, Conn., 1851.
Third Convention of American Instructors of the Deaf, Columbus, Ohio, 1853.
Fourth Convention of American Instructors of the Deaf, Staunton, Va., 1856.
Fifth Convention of American Instructors of the Deaf, Jacksonville, Ill., 1858.
Sixth Convention of American Instructors of the Deaf. [See First Conference of Principals.]
Seventh Convention of American Instructors of the Deaf, Indianapolis, Ind., 1870.
Eighth Convention of American Instructors of the Deaf, Belleville, Ont., 1874.
Ninth Convention of American Instructors of the Deaf, Columbus, O., 1878.
Tenth Convention of American Instructors of the Deaf, Jacksonville, Ill., 1882.
First Conference of Principals (counted also as the Sixth Convention), Washington, D. C., 1868.
Second Conference of Principals, Flint, Mich., 1872.
Third Conference of Principals, Philadelphia, Pa., 1876.
Fourth Conference of Principals, Northampton, Mass., 1880.
Fifth Conference of Principals, Faribault, Minn., 1884.

EXHIBIT TO QUERY 13,271.

ANNALS.

[This Exhibit consisted of thirty-one volumes of the *American Annals of the Deaf*, constituting a complete set up to the end of 1866. These volumes were presented to the Royal Commission on behalf of the New York Institution and the Institution at Washington.]

EXHIBIT TO QUERY 13,272.

SCHOOL REPORTS.

[This Exhibit consisted of the following reports of American Schools for the Deaf:]

The Institutions at Hartford, New York, Columbus, Philadelphia, Indianapolis, and Washington, with catalogues of the College at Washington.

PART II.

Evidence of Dr. Alexander Graham Bell, with accompanying Exhibits.

ROYAL COMMISSION ON CONDITION OF THE BLIND, &c.

6, Old Palace Yard, S.W., London.

Thursday, 14th June, 1888.

PRESENT:

THE RIGHT HON. THE LORD EGERTON OF TATTON IN THE CHAIR.

SIR TINDAL ROBERTSON, M.P.
B. ST. JOHN ACKERS, ESQ
T. R. ARMITAGE, ESQ., M.D.
F. J. CAMPBELL, ESQ., LL.D.
EDMUND C. JOHNSON, ESQ.

ROBERT McDONNELL, ESQ., M.D., F.R.S.
WILLIAM WOODALL, ESQ., M.P.
THE REV. W. BLOMEFIELD SLEIGHT, M.A.
THE REV. CHARLES MANSFIELD OWEN, M.A.
L. VAN OVEN, ESQ.

CHARLES E. D. BLACK, ESQ., *Secretary.*

Mr. A. GRAHAM BELL (Washington) examined.

Mr. A. G. Bell. — 14 June 1888.

21,355. (*Chairman.*) You are well known to have taken a great interest in the education and general condition of the deaf. I think you have before you President Gallaudet's evidence before this Commission with regard to the education of the deaf and dumb in the United States. Is there anything in what he says with regard to the education of the deaf and dumb in America that you would like to supplement or to make any remark on?—There are a few points which I should like to enlarge upon a little, in which I think Dr. Gallaudet has been misled, in relation to the statistics of the deaf and dumb as given in the census of 1880: which is the best census we have had taken in the United States. It was well known to Dr. Gallaudet, and to the other superintendents and principals of American institutions, that many deaf mutes were reported twice, once from the institution where they were receiving instruction, and once from their homes. Then there were numerous cases of persons who were reported as deaf mutes who became deaf at 80 years of age and 40 years of age, and so a good many of the principals and superintendents may have formed an idea that the census of 1880 is unreliable, and that the numbers of deaf mutes are as much overstated in that census as they were understated in the former census; they have a right to have that belief, but I am in a position to show that they are wrong and that the census of 1880 is very reliable.

21,356. You are now referring to Dr. Gallaudet's answer to question 13,105, in which he says: "It "may be taken that the ratio before 1880 was too "small, and it may be presumed that one in 1,800 "would represent accurately the proportion?"—Yes.

21,357. You wish to make some remarks with reference to that statement?—Yes; of course it is not improbable that there may be duplicates in the returns obtained in 1880, but to my personal knowledge very great efforts were made by the census commission to eliminate all those duplicates, and to eliminate all cases where the persons reported had become deaf in adult life; certainly there could be no such error as would change the proportion of the deaf and dumb from one in 1,480 of the population to one in 1,800. According to Dr. Gallaudet's assumption the number of deaf mutes in the country on the 1st of June, 1880, would be 27,864, that is one in 1,800 of the population, instead of 33,878, as given in the last census, the difference being 6,014 duplicates—that is to say, between one-fifth and one-sixth of the whole number. The actual number given in the census is 33,878, that is one deaf mute in 1,480 of the population. Dr. Gallaudet assumes that there is one deaf mute in 1,800 of the population, and if you make the calculation on the whole population of the country, which is 50,155,783, you will find that that yields a resultant of 27,864, which is a difference of 6,014 cases that are attributed to duplicates. That is a very serious charge against our census, and on seeing this statement I immediately telegraphed to the Rev. Frederick Wines, who has charge of this department of the census, telling him that the accuracy of the United States census had been attacked before the Commission on account of duplicates, and asking from him a reply to present to the Commission. I received the reply just before starting, and it is as follows:—"Springfield, May 28th, 1888. My dear Sir,—I "thank you most sincerely for your kindness in informing me by telegraph that the accuracy of the "last census relating to deaf mutes has been attacked "before the Royal Commission. It is the first that "I have heard of it, and it is rather difficult to know "how to answer an attack which one has not seen. "No census that has been taken, in any country "since the world began, can claim to be free from "inaccuracy; and no one knows this so well as the "census taker. But every census before that of "1880 has erred in the matter of the enumeration "of the deaf, on the side of omissions rather than "duplication of names. There are two ways in "which duplications may occur. First, a deaf mute "may be enumerated in the institution of which he "is a pupil and an inmate, and he may also be enumerated at the place where his family resides. Second, it is possible that some physician, in reporting "to me the names of lunatics and idiots within the "sphere of his personal and professional knowledge, may have reported a deaf mute also. But "the greatest possible pains were taken to purge "the list of all duplicates; and, if any have remained "undetected, it has probably been owing to the misspelling of names in cases where two different "spellings were possible. But the number of such duplications can in no event have been considerable. "A liberal estimate would not, I think, place it "above 100 in all, which, as you know, is scarcely "worthy of notice in an investigation of such magnitude. And the duplications, granting that they "exist (which I do not admit without proof, of which "none has been laid before me), are much more than "counterbalanced by the known omissions. If you "will look at the enumeration by age, you will perceive that the number of deaf mutes returned "under the age of five years is much less than it "must actually have been, as is especially evident "when attention is directed to the number of congenital deaf mutes. I have no doubt that, whatever "may have been said to the Royal Commission by "some person unknown to me, the number of deaf "mutes in the United States exceeds rather than "falls below the number reported in the census. "If there is any subject which I should like to urge, "had I the opportunity to do so, before the Commission, it would be the necessity of more liberal "provision for the training of the idiotic and feeble-minded, who are less likely to be fully represented "before it, than either the deaf or the blind." I am in a position to support Mr. Wines in a remarkable manner. It so happens that I have had access to the original schedules of the census returns, and

Mr. A. G. Bell.

14 June 1888.

I have noticed the pains and the care with which deaf mutes have been hunted up, hundreds and thousands of letters have been written to ascertain the accuracy of the returns: and for purposes of my own I have made a card catalogue of the deaf mutes in the United States: the undertaking was enormous, and is not completed yet; but for some months I have had in my possession, arranged in alphabetical order, the names of 23,969 deaf mutes from the census—that is nearly 24,000—these have been copied on cards from the census returns, and then I have had them arranged in alphabetical order, so as to bring all the surnames together, and so as to examine cases where a large number of deaf mutes would appear of the same surname, so that if any considerable duplication existed—if between one-fifth and one-sixth of the total number were duplicates—I must have observed it. But there is a method of testing the figures by which you may judge for yourself. I happen to have in my possession an official copy of the Returns of the deaf mutes of the six New England States, numbering 2,581. Now, if you come to look over those you will find, if Dr. Gallaudet is right, no less than 461 duplications of names. I should be happy to place this before the Commission for their examination (*handing it in*). It will, perhaps, be interesting also to you to examine the kind of material that has been collected; but I must say that my study of the census returns has given me great confidence in the accuracy of the 1880 census, and has led me to the conclusion that a great deal of pains has been taken to eliminate dupicates and ascertain the truth. Mr. Wines, as you see in his letter, is of opinion that instead of the numbers of the deaf and dumb being over estimated in the 1880 census they were under estimated.

21,358. That would generally be likely to be the case?—Yes. He estimated that there were, in 1880, probably 35,000 deaf mutes in the United States instead of the actual number shown. Of course that is a matter of opinion.

21,359. Have you any remarks to make on any other statement of Dr. Gallaudet?—Of course there are many points on which I differ from Dr. Gallaudet, but those are chiefly differences of opinion. I should like to supplement Dr. Gallaudet's historical sketch of the schools and the organisation of schools, given in answer to questions 13,111 and 13,112. I think his statements are very accurate, but I should like to say a few words on the policy of the States in dealing with their deaf and dumb, from the time when the instruction of that class began to be taken up by the Government. In 1815, when the first school was established, the number of deaf and dumb was not known; they were supposed to be few in number and widely scattered through an enormous extent of country, and a policy was adopted, which I shall term a policy of centralisation—a policy to reach the deaf and dumb by taking them away from their homes and bringing them together into some central institution. The Federal Government made a grant of land to the American Asylum in order that this school might be a school for all the deaf and dumb of the United States, and there were many who seriously doubted whether there would be enough pupils to support a school. The plan of centralisation soon failed. The National School at Hartford could not accommodate a fraction of the number of the pupils who made their appearance. The State Governments then took action, and the plan that was then first adopted was the plan of centralisation in each State, and the attempt was made to bring into one school the deaf mutes of the State. But, as statistics regarding the deaf became more accurate, these State institutions were found to be insufficient to accommodate the deaf mutes, and a gradual splitting up of the large institutions has taken place. The central institution in New York has been split up into seven or eight distinct institutions, scattered in different parts of the State. We have now over 50 State institutions.

21,360. We were told that there are 67?—I cannot tell you the exact number without consulting my notes. I am speaking of the centralised institutions, but it was found that they were not enough to accommodate the deaf children who required instruction, and another move toward decentralisation took place in the establishment of day schools in the large cities. We have now 69 institutions, including day schools and private schools. The Census returns of the United States of 1880 show that there were 15,059 deaf children of school age (that is to say, "from five years old to twenty"), and 5,393 in all the institutions put together. I find on examining the census that the day schools are not taken into account, but the total number in the day schools is comparatively small. At all events, whatever the actual number of deaf children growing up without instruction may be, it is evident that whatever allowance we may make, certainly we have as many deaf children of school age growing up without instruction as there are in all the schools and institutions in the United States put together. This, I think, has arisen largely from the policy adopted by the States, the policy of centralisation. Mothers will not part with their children except upon compulsion. In a country like ours the value of physical labour is so great as to prevent many children from being sent to school, especially in country districts. The whole plan of centralisation has failed to bring under instruction one-half of the deaf children of school age. When I came to examine the statistics of each State, I found a similar condition of affairs in every State, showing that the fault is in the system, and is not remediable by any increase in the number of institutions. A certain per-centage of pupils will escape instruction. I have therefore urged the adoption of the policy of decentralisation to bring schools as near to the homes of the children as possible; to extend the day school plan, to supplement our institution plan by an enlarged development of day schools, acting upon the principle that the nearer the school can be brought to the home of the pupil, the less likelihood is there that he will escape instruction. Other reasons also urged me some years ago to advocate the policy of decentralisation, and I would supplement Dr. Gallaudet's testimony by pointing out to you how far that policy has been adopted in one particular State. It may be within the knowledge of the members of this Commission that a conference of teachers of the deaf met in the Senate Chamber at Madison, Wisconsin, to confer with the teachers of the hearing, at a meeting of the National Educational Association. At that meeting I advocated the policy of decentralisation. Great interest was excited in Wisconsin, as a bill had been brought forward before the Wisconsin Legislature advocating the same thing. It was the first attempt to embody in a law the policy of decentralisation; whether it will be successful or not I do not know. I am not a law maker, but I can see very clearly the principle involved, and when the Committee of the Legislature invited me to visit Wisconsin and speak upon the subject of this Bill I did so, and embodied the substance of my remarks in an open letter, which was addressed to the members of the Legislature and Senate of Wisconsin, a copy of which I beg leave to present to the Commission, which will show you my views upon that subject (*handing it in*).

21,361. (*Mr. St. John Ackers.*) What was the date of that meeting at Wisconsin? — The meeting in Madison was July 16th, 1884; the date of the letter is February, 1885; the Bill passed on April 15th, 1885, and it was amended on March 12th, 1887. I have printed copies of this Bill which I will hand in; the printer, however, has placed the amendments before the Bill itself.

21,362. (*Chairman.*) Is there any attendance officer in the United States to see that every child goes to school?—Yes, in some cities.

21,363. Not in the rural districts? — I cannot

Mr. A. G. Bell.

14 June 1888.

speak with authority; in Boston there are what are called truant officers. I have urged that there should be no law of compulsion, unless you can offer a choice between a day school and an institution. I recognise the right of the community to see that deaf children are educated, for uneducated they may be a danger to the community in which they live; but I do not recognise the right of the community to take a child away from his own parents without their consent; unless it can be clearly shown that his education necessitates removal from home; but if the State could offer to the parent of a deaf child either an institution or a day school, then I could advocate compulsory education. In this Bill, to which I have directed your attention, the object has been to facilitate the giving of State aid to day schools. Hitherto the State has recognised only the central institution, and if parents want their children educated at home, or if they start a school and provide a teacher they do it out of their own pockets, and get no State aid. This Bill is to encourage the growth of these little schools, so that if there should be one parent of one deaf and dumb child he can have State aid to get a teacher; such teacher being approved by the State superintendent of public instruction. He will get 100 dollars from the State Treasury through the machinery that has been provided. If he applies to the nearest school board and asks for a school for his deaf child the teacher will say yours is the only child, or there are only two or three, well the parent will say, if you can get this State aid of 300 dollars for these three children, I and the other parents will meet the balance required to pay the salary of a teacher. That is the idea. It is only an experiment; it is a new departure, but I think it is an important departure. Immediately on the passing of the Bill a worthy private school that had been struggling along without recognition by the State, the Phonological Institute at Milwaukee, at once received State aid, and became a public school under the public school system of Milwaukee. Two years ago another little school with six pupils started at Lacrosse in Wisconsin, under the provisions of this Bill, and I hope by degrees, as parents find the advantages that may be derived from these little schools, that the whole of the State of Wisconsin may be dotted over with little day schools around the central institution which will then be enough to accommodate all the children who cannot attend a day school.

21,364. Are these schools conducted on the oral or the combined system?—The oral system.

21,365. Those established in that State?—Those established in that State under the provisions of the Bill. The Central Institution is on the combined plan. The teachers in those new schools much prefer the teaching of articulation, but in the Bill there are no provisions with regard to the method of instruction. I do not advocate any restriction in regard to methods of instruction, nor did the promoters of the Bill. We are very much inclined to believe in America, with my friend Dr. Gallaudet, that diversity in methods is favourable to progress, but what we want is some superior power over the institutions and schools to collect statistics and test the results of instruction; we have no such machinery. In Wisconsin we have a general superintendent, but generally throughout the State there is no general system of State inspection.

21,366. That you advocate?—Yes. I would not impose my own ideas upon any school. I would not have one method of instruction if I could. I think that honest men differ, and that the proper way to test methods is by results, and there are no statistics extant by which we can test results. I go to the conventions of teachers of the deaf in America and listen to the discussions between the sign and manual and the oral teachers, and then I study historically what happened a hundred years ago. The same arguments and the same things are reproduced. The same arguments have been brought forward for a hundred years, and the questions raised have not been settled. The reason is we have no mechanism for testing methods of instruction by results. I would urge upon this Commission the importance of devising and bringing into operation some practical method of testing by results, and getting statistics relating to adult deaf and dumb to show the influence of methods of education on their after life. I would not have you put any restriction on methods, diversity is favourable, but I would have you avoid centralisation. We have found another evil to spring from centralisation in America, a centralised institution in a great State becomes oppressive; an established method of instruction, like an established religion, becomes intolerant, it crushes out the little schools that appear round about it. And, by-the-bye, in that connexion I would like to direct your attention to what Dr. Gallaudet says in answer to question 13,131. He says "For all practical purposes the private schools are hardly worth considering." I say they are. There is a great lesson to be learnt from private schools. The existence of private schools in a country like ours, where the States are munificent in their benefactions to the deaf and dumb, is an anomaly. Why do these private schools exist? They express the existence of grave dissatisfaction with the institutions—that is their significance—and when you come to examine the statistics of those private schools you will find that they are of two classes, one purely religious and the other purely oral.

21,367. You mean the dissatisfaction is partly on religious grounds and partly with regard to not teaching speech?—Yes, and the day schools also are expressive of dissatisfaction with the life in the institution. As you examine the statistics of these private schools another thing becomes significant, they keep changing. A little school starts up and then it will go out of the list of private schools and become a State institution. It struggles along for a short period in adversity, because it cannot get the recognition of the State; it cannot at first get State aid, and then when it gets State aid it goes out of the list of private schools, so they always seem to be small in number. There are several States in which day schools have been established in the large centres of population, supported partly by the State and partly by the cities in which they are established; but the effect of this Bill that was passed in the Wisconsin Legislature will be to push the day school system into the rural districts, and into the smaller districts of the country, where only a few children can be brought together. The expense of the education of a deaf child at an institution is so great as to render it a matter of economy to the State to send a teacher wherever you can have four or five deaf children brought together rather than take them to an institution.

21,368. (*Mr. Woodall.*) There is nothing to prevent any municipality under the public school system establishing a day school for the deaf and dumb?—Nothing except the expense, and that does prevent the establishment of such schools except in the large cities.

21,369. (*Chairman.*) In answer to question 13,115, Dr. Gallaudet says, "There are day schools in about "six or seven cities, and the next question is have "they any endowments?" To which his answer is, "Some of them have endowments, two or three." Therefore, it is a very small number which have endowments. Practically, with the exception of Wisconsin and these two or three day schools, they are not generally recognised or subsidised by the State?—I do not know; these private schools, as I say, are significant; the policy of centralisation has rendered it necessary for the institutions to give religious instruction to their pupils. It is true this is done in a very guarded and a very proper way, but still that has led to the dissatisfaction and the establishment of denominational schools, chiefly Roman Catholic, these are chiefly, I think, upon the sign system.

Mr. A. G. Bell.

14 June 1888.

21,370. In answer to question 13.128, Dr. Gallaudet says: "It is the rule to give religious instruction to a very slight extent, hardly more than the reading of the Bible and a prayer, and in some schools not even that is given." Does that apply generally to schools in which the deaf and dumb are taught?—I think that it does. There are some parents that object to that, and others say it is not enough.

21,371. Some parents object to any religious instruction being given at all?—Some object to any religious instruction being given at all, and others wish it to be given according to their own creed or denomination, and so we have a number of denominational schools that appear among the private schools, for those are generally not recognised by the State, excepting in the State of New York. The private schools (other than denominational) are exclusively oral, and the meaning of that is that there are certain parents and persons dissatisfied with the instruction given in the institutions, and they would rather pay for the instruction of their children by the oral method than send them free of charge where their speech is not attended to—that is the significance of it. So I do not agree with Dr. Gallaudet in thinking that these schools are hardly worth considering. In fact these private schools have effected a great reformation in the United States. They represent a germ of life, a very little hing in itself, but it keeps pushing and growing. Every now and then one of the little schools will become an institution. The teachers in these oral schools, who are nearly all ladies, who hardly ever venture to express an opinion in public, have worked quietly and silently and the establishment of those schools has effected a great reformation. They have forced the institutions to give attention to speech.

21,372. From Dr. Gallaudet's evidence generally I think we should form the impression that combined schools are in the majority in America—your evidence rather tends to show that there is a wish for more instruction in speech such as is given in the pure oral schools?—Yes, that is my reasoning on the subject. I may be wrong.

21,373. There is a dissatisfaction with the State schools and that shows itself by the formation of these private schools?—Yes.

21,374. Dr. Gallaudet says that the present feeling is in favour of adding the oral system to the sign system, which means the combined system. You say that the establishment of these private oral schools shows that there is an inclination to go still further, and to give more instruction in speech than is given in the combined schools?—Yes; and as these private oral schools increase in size and show successful results, the institutions become alarmed and immediately commence to teach speech to a portion of their pupils, so I look upon these private oral schools as a lever which is enforcing greater and greater attention to the teaching of speech and speech reading in our institutions, but I cannot follow Dr. Gallaudet in his classification of methods. I do not recognise any combined method or system, and I notice that the very institution that he brings forward as a typical combined institution—the Pennsylvania Institution—discards the idea; this shows the vagueness with which the term is used. In answer to question 13,141, speaking of the Pennsylvania Institution, which is undoubtedly one of the finest of our institutions, and is doing real good honest work in all branches of education, oral and otherwise, he says:—"The system of which we speak in America as the 'combined system,' is one which allows of the bringing together of all methods under varying conditions. For example, the Philadelphia Institution has a separate oral branch in which pupils who are found to succeed well in speech are taught on what would be termed here in England the pure oral method. This, which was started as a manual school, is now conducted under what is called the combined system." In a note which the principal of this institution has sent to me occurs this statement: "The combined system has no place in our school at present." I have no doubt it is a combined system in the mind of Dr. Gallaudet, but it shows the vagueness with which the term is used, that the principal of that very institution uses that language. I think it is very important that we should consider the proper classification not only of the methods of instruction, but of the deaf. I agree with Dr. Gallaudet that the Philadelphia Institution is a model institution: there is no dispute as to what is done, but one terms it an institution on the combined system and the other does not. I may as well say here that before I left America I was anxious to present before the Royal Commission a picture of the condition of the education of the deaf and dumb in America, and to give to you the views of the principals and superintendents themselves upon the questions in which you are interested. I therefore directed a circular letter to the principals and superintendents of all the institutions and day schools and private schools in America, including Canada, and I have received replies from 58, and the mass of material collected is very valuable. I was in hopes to have been able to present to you this testimony in printed form at least a day before my own examination. On account of the shortness of time I have been unable to do so, but by the kindness of Messrs. Spottiswoode I have been able to get the greater portion of it in print in the shape of proof. Messrs. Spottiswoode have set their whole establishment to work upon it, and I am able to hand to you the answers to some of the questions (*handing in the same*). This is what Principal Crouter says of his own institution: "The combined system has no place in our school at present. Our pupils are taught either orally or manually." And then, in answer to another question, he says: "I believe in oral instruction (separate oral) for all deaf children who can be successfully instructed by that method, and in sign instruction for those who cannot." There is one other point of fact in Dr. Gallaudet's testimony to which I should like to refer. In answer to question 13,139 he states:—"A very large majority of the leading schools are carrying on the combined system. That means that in a large majority of the public schools speech is taught to as great a number of pupils as it is found possible to teach with success; that is the policy in these combined system schools." I know that this is not done, whatever the policy may be.

21,375. (*Dr. Campbell.*) When he says "public schools," does he refer to ordinary public schools?—I think that he is referring to all the institutions and schools that are supported by the State or the city.

21,376. Probably when Dr. Gallaudet was speaking of the combined system being taught at the Philadelphia Institution he meant that the pupils there were taught by either system, not that each pupil was taught both orally and by the sign system, that may be so?—Yes, it is either one or the other that is taught at that institution, but not both combined. I have here a tabular statement showing the amount of teaching of articulation in the United States in May 1883. Out of 6,232 pupils in the United States, 1,991, or 31·9 per cent., were taught articulation, and 4,241, or 68·1 per cent., had no instruction whatever in speech.

21,377. Upon that I would ask you this: Do you think that 68 per cent. of the deaf and dumb in America could not be taught articulation?—Undoubtedly not; they could all be taught articulation. I do not think they could all be taught to read from the mouth.

21,378. Are those 6,232 under instruction at the present time?—No, this refers to May 1883.

21,379. There was an increase between 1880 and 1883 from 5,393 to 6,232?—Yes; those were not all; this information was obtained through a circular let-

Mr.
A. G. Bell.
14 June 1888.

ter of inquiry directed to the principals of the institutions by the principal of the Clarke Institution at Northampton. Here are the full results of that inquiry (*handing in the table*). In looking at the totals you will find that 6,232 was the total number and 1,991 was the number taught articulation. Then discriminating those who were taught orally from those who used articulation simply as an accomplishment, who had instruction for an hour or half an hour a day, we find that the number orally taught was 886, or 14 per cent.; 1,105, or 18 per cent., were taught speech as an accomplishment, making no use of it in the schoolroom; and 4,241, or 68 per cent., received no instruction whatever in articulation; that is in 1883. The total number of pupils under instruction in 1883 was 7,169, and of these 6,232 were reported to the Clarke Institution.

21,380. Since that time have you reason to believe that the number of pupils receiving oral instruction had increased?—In 1884 out of 6,228 pupils, 2,041 or 32·8 per cent. were taught articulation, which is an increase, and 4,187 or 67·2 per cent. were not. In 1885 out of 6,780 pupils, 2,618 or 38·6 per cent. were taught articulation; that is an increase again; and 4,162 or 61·4 per cent were not. In 1886 out of 6,596 pupils, 2,484 or 35·7 per cent. were taught articulation, that is a decrease, and 4,472 or 64·3 per cent. were not. In 1887, this is the year that Dr. Gallaudet speaks to, out of 6,862 pupils, 2,556 or 37·2 per cent. were taught articulation, and 4,306 or 62·8 per cent. were not taught speech at all.*

NATURAL CLASSIFICATION OF THE DEAF.

Age at which deafness occurred.	Amount of Hearing Power.										
	0	10	20	30	40	50	60	70	80	90	100
0											
1											
2											
3											
4											
5											
6											
7											
8											
9											
10											
11											
12											
13											
14											
15											
16											
17											
18											
19											
20											

*For amended reply *see* queries 21,496 and 21,497.

CLASSIFICATION INTO EIGHT GROUPS.

Period of Life when Deafness occurred.	The Deaf.	
	Totally Deaf.	Semi-Deaf.
From birth or infancy (*i. e.*, less than 2 years of age).	1	2
From early childhood (*i. e.*, 2 years and less than 5).	3	4
From late childhood (*i. e.*, 5 years and less than 14).	5	6
From youth (*i. e.*, 14 years and less than 21).	7	8

21,381. (*Dr. Campbell.*) In regard to that year when there was a falling off, do you know what the cause of it was?—I do not know the cause. We might analyse the statistics and discover the cause, but I have not gone sufficiently into them to do so.

21,382. (*Chairman.*) Your opinion is, that all those that could be taught to speak at all could be taught to speak orally, even if they could not be taught to lip read?—Undoubtedly. I am too familiar with the mechanical nature of speech to doubt it for a moment.

21,383. With regard to the classification of the deaf, have you any suggestions to make?—I am very much dissatisfied with all the classifications I have seen. They seem to me to be based upon an inconstant quality, the character of the speech (which can be modified by instruction). We classify the deaf according to the amount of muteness, and that amount of muteness can be remedied by instruction. It leads to a false classification, as false as if we were to classify them by the amount of ignorance, which is also remediable. I would suggest a natural classification of the deaf. It is now universally recognised that those whom we term deaf mutes are simply persons who are deaf from childhood; that the natural defect is a single defect and not a double one, and muteness or dumbness is the result of the natural defect and not a defect in itself. I would classify pupils by the natural defect alone, and there are only two elements to be determined which would completely define, as it were by means of lines of latitude and longitude, the position of a deaf child in the whole mass of the deaf. These two elements to be determined are (1) the age or period of life at which the deafness occurred, and (2) the amount of the defect. If we say that a child became totally deaf at five it is understood what that means. We do not require to say that he is a semi-mute—that is the resultant—and if we say a child was born deaf we know that the mental condition must be entirely different. In America we measure the amount of hearing power of a child, so that we can say that a child has a hearing power of 10, 20, 30, 40, 50, or 60. Let us represent that by vertical lines, the lines of longitude of our map, and represent the age at which the deafness occurred by horizontal lines or lines of latitude upon the map, then we completely define on that map the position of any deaf person. If you do not measure precisely the amount of hearing power you may measure it roughly. You may divide the deaf into two great classes, which you may term the totally deaf and the semi-deaf—those who have not a sufficient amount of hearing to perceive the difference of vocal sounds and those who have. Then, again, if you did not know the precise age at which a child became deaf you could classify roughly by periods. For instance, you might put in one class

Mr. A. G. Bell.

14 June 1888.

all those who had been deaf from birth or infancy, *i. e.*, those who had become deaf under the age of two years. Then those who had become deaf between two and five might constitute the "deaf from early childhood," and those who became deaf from five to the age of puberty the "deaf from late childhood," and above that the "deaf from youth," and if you followed that classification you would divide the deaf into eight groups, each group having marked characteristics of its own. I would recommend to the serious attention of the Commissioners some natural classification of the deaf under those two heads, the amount of the defect and the age or period at which the deafness occurred Another point is important, how is it that we fail to discover so many of the little deaf children we desire to bring under instruction? Their parents will not call them deaf mutes. For instance, a child becomes deaf from scarlet fever, at the age of 4½. The census taker comes along and says, "Are there any deaf "mutes in this house?" The parent says "No." But suppose the census taker asked if there were any persons in the house who were deaf or hard of hearing, the answer would be "Yes, my child can-"not hear since he had the scarlet fever." Then if the census taker said "At what age did the deafness "occur?" The answer would be "4½ years." I would recommend that such questions as those should be asked by your census takers when they take the next census. I am now urging upon the census authorities in the United States the advisability of asking the questions, "Are there any deaf "or hard of hearing persons in this house, and if so "at what age did the deafness occur?" and if you cannot get at the age, at what period of life did it occur. The census takers might get at that as nearly as they could; then after that the census taker could ask about deaf mutes; if you get these particulars you can completely determine the case: we can get at those who belong to the class called "deaf and dumb" without hurting the feelings of the parents of those children, and it is those little children we want to reach.

21,384. (*Sir Tindal Robertson.*) Would you recommend that the census takers should inquire into the cause of the deafness?—Certainly, all the information which could be got should be got in the census return, but the recording of the fact of the deafness and the age at which it occurred would enable us to find out the deaf children of school age in time to bring them under instruction.

21,385. (*Chairman.*) With regard to classification of methods of instruction have you any remarks to make?—It seems to me that we want to think very carefully over the methods of instruction, and find some suitable and natural classification of them. I cannot say that I have hit upon such a classification, but I have some ideas upon the subject to offer you which perhaps you may think worthy of consideration. In this classification I cannot see any place for the combined system, it is neither one thing nor the other. When we come to consider that the possibility of instructing a deaf child is based upon the possibility of teaching a language of communication whereby ideas may be imparted and the mind cultivated, I think in that language of communication we have a basis of classification. You cannot very well have a combination. It is difficult for a person to think in two languages. There is some one language in which a child thinks: the question is, what is that? Whatever your method of instruction may be the child thinks in some form of expression. When we think we think in words—or rather *with words*, for I presume no one really does think in words, although we have a consciousness of what we mean by "thinking in a language." We think in the English language, and when we come to learn French or German we are still English, and we translate. What is the language a deaf child thinks in? It is the language which is habitually used by the people around to impart ideas to the child. That is the basis of classification to my mind, and you may divide that broadly into two classes, one the ordinary language of the people and the other a special language. I do not care whether it is sign language, or German or French. It is a language special to the child if it is not the language of the people. You have those cases in which the language of communication is the ordinary language of the people, and you have those cases in which the language of communication and thought is a special language different from the language of the people.

CLASSIFICATION OF METHODS OF INSTRUCTION.

Basis of Classification.	Class to which the Method belongs.	Sub-group.	Specific Methods of Instruction.
The language employed to impart ideas.	Ordinary Language Methods.	(1.) Manual Methods.	(a.) The Manual Alphabet Method.
		(2.) Oral Methods.	(b.) The Speech-reading Method.
			(c.) The Auricular Method.
	Special Language Methods.	(3.) Sign Methods.	(d.) The Sign-language Method.

21,386. Before a deaf and dumb child has had any instruction at all his mind is the same as that of a speaking child or a hearing child; why should there be a special language for a deaf and dumb child differing from that for a speaking child?—We all start in life without a language, and we all acquire a language by instruction.

21,387. By imitation?—By imitating the language spoken by those round about us; any language that a deaf and dumb child can imitate, that is clearly perceived by his senses, that is used by the people round about him, he will learn by imitation. If people round about him do not use any language that he can acquire by imitation he goes to work to invent one, and the moment a child commences to invent a language of his own he has got to the age when he should be taught a language. He wants to express ideas. It seems to me that the classification of methods of instruction should be based upon whether the language of the people is used as the language of communication, or a special language not the language of the people. Now we may divide the "ordinary language of the people" into two sub-classifications, viz.: (1) Its written (or "manual") form, and (2) its spoken (or "oral") form; and among the sub-divisions of "special language" would come (3) a language in the form of gestures (or "signs").

"Manual," "oral," and "sign" methods may be still further sub-divided according to the mode in which the language is presented to the pupil so as to designate specific methods of instruction.

1. Under "manual methods" would come (*a*) "*the manual alphabet method*," which rejects the sign-language and relies upon writing and a finger alphabet.

2. Under "oral methods" would come (*b*) "*the* "*speech-reading method*" (pure oral), and (*c*) "*the* "*auricular method*," the spoken language of the people being presented in the one case to the eye, and in the other to the ear; and

3. Under "sign methods" would come (*d*) "*the* "*sign-language method*," used in America where the "combined system" is employed.

There we get a distinct basis on which to build, broad enough to include other possible methods.

21,388. Is not the old classification more simple, namely, (1) language, and (2) signs; the one appealing to the eye and the other to the ear?—I only submit this, without very much confidence, to the Commission as a basis upon which we might perhaps arrive at some reasonable classification of methods.

21,389. (*Mr. Johnson.*) What you call a special language would be sign language?—The language

Mr. A. G. Bell.

14 June 1888.

of signs is a special language; it is immaterial whether it is a sign language, or French, or German, or Hottentot; it is not the ordinary language of the people, and when a deaf and dumb child is taught in sign language he thinks in that sign language, and he has to go through the mental process of translation when he comes to use English, and it is that difficulty which separates the deaf who are so taught from the hearing world in adult life, and leads the deaf to keep together and not mix with hearing people, and to intermarry and have deaf children.

21,390. That is on the hypothesis that he is taught signs?—On the hypothesis that he is taught a language that is not the language of the people.

21,391. What is your definition of special language?—I mean by the term any language that is special to the deaf and not used by the people among whom they live.

21,392. (*Chairman.*) Do you think much can be done in the way of improving the hearing of the deaf?—When we realise the truth of the fact that there is no other defect in those that we term deaf mutes than the simple defect of deafness, we may also realise that there may be degrees in the amount of that deafness, and we have been startled in America by the discovery that large numbers of those who are congenitally deaf are only very slightly hard of hearing; they suffer from such a slight disability of hearing that, had the defect occurred after they had learned to speak, they never would have appeared in an institution for the deaf and dumb. Now, the difficulty is to ascertain the amount of hearing possessed by an apparently deaf child. Experiments have been made with hearing tubes and various appliances for a great number of years past. The first case on record in which an attempt was made to ascertain to what extent a deaf person could be made to hear occurred before 1867, when Mr. Whipple in Connecticut, who had a deaf mute son, tried to teach him to speak. Mr. Whipple, who was a man of little culture and education, was dissatisfied with the instruction given in the institution at Hartford, and he set his son up in front of him and shouted at him, and mouthed at him, and the boy learned to speak. Mr Whipple thereupon formed the erroneous idea that all deaf children could be taught to speak in that way. He produced his son to the Principal of the American Asylum in Hartford, and the principal of that institution went behind the boy, about a foot behind his ear, and spoke to him, and the boy answered him. The principal unfortunately came to the conclusion that it was a case of fraud or self-delusion, and that the boy was not a deaf mute at all. He failed to see in this case the beginning of a great discovery, that the hearing power could be educated and utilised.*

21,393. We have had evidence of the fact that instruction in speech does develop a certain amount of hearing?—Then I will not trouble you by going into the history of the development of that mode of treatment of the deaf, but I will proceed to give the per-centage of those that are capable of receiving auricular instruction.

21,394. When a child first comes into school are any means taken to ascertain the amount of hearing that the child possesses and how far any of these auricular appliances would be a benefit to him?—It is very difficult to ascertain the amount of hearing a child possesses. In the first instance in the case of young children, they almost always appear to hear.

21,395. You mean they always say they hear?—Yes; it is well known that in our institutions for the deaf the pupils are summoned in from the school ground by ringing a dinner bell, that indicates that a good number of them can hear, and I suggested the experiment of counting the number of pupils who could hear the ringing of a bell, and so determine the per-centage, but Dr. Gillett of the Illinois Institution replies, "I find all my children can hear "the ringing of the dinner bell, but only five per "cent. can hear the school bell." Mr. S. T. Walker, the Superintendent of the Kansas Institution, says, that out of 161 pupils tested "88 said they could "hear, but 48 of these also said they heard when "the bell was not rung." Still, some very interesting statistics have resulted from the experiments that have been made within the last month in America upon that question, and I have been able to get a per-centage of cases where there is partial hearing. I find that out of 1,475 pupils tested 304, or 20·6 per cent., can hear the ringing of a bell.

21,396. How was that tested?—Mr. Walker (Superintendent of the Kansas Institution) describes the method as follows:—"I had them turn their backs "to me each trial, and at a signal face me and tell "who heard. These trials were repeated several "times and one or two of them were false trials, "when the bell was not touched. Notwithstanding "48 of the 161 tried answered that they heard the "bell *every time*, even when it was not touched. "Knowing that to make statistics of real effect (or "rather the conclusions drawn from them) they "should be as nearly correct as possible, I was care-"ful to have these tests correct."

21,397. (*Dr. Campbell.*) It would make a great difference whether the children stood on a wooden floor or a stone floor; have you any information as to what sort of floor they stood on?—No. In the proof I handed to you you will find some remarkable testimony regarding auricular instruction. Those are reports from the institutions which have pursued auricular instruction as a distinct method, giving details of the instruction, and the method of instruction, and giving full statistics.

21,398. (*Chairman.*) Would the system of auricular instruction, if it were systematically and constantly pursued, tend to develop the general hearing?—The apparent hearing power is enormously developed by it.

21,399. (*Mr. Van Oven.*) In such a case as you referred to just now, do you think the continuous shouting in a boy's ear would tend to develop the power of hearing?—Yes. It is extremely doubtful whether it produces any real improvement in the hearing proper, but there is a marvellous improvement in the power of discriminating sounds, but that comes, I think (and it seems to be the prevailing impression in America), from an increased knowledge of language and increased attention, but certainly it is the case that pupils who at first exhibit very little power of imitation when you speak into a hearing tube, after being taught orally and auricularly for a few months, come to understand through that hearing tube, and to discriminate sounds, which they could not discriminate before, and it is a great problem whether there is any improvement in the hearing or not. I am inclined to think there may be some slight improvement, due to that cause, because when we perform the act of listening we use a muscle, in the action of listening there is a contraction of a muscle adjusting the tension of the membrane, and why should not that muscle grow by use, like other muscles of the body. I must say, however, that this opinion is contrary to the opinion of all the aurists to whom I have spoken. Take a congenitally deaf child, he has no language, that lack of language is an element in making his deafness appear greater than it is really is. Suppose a Chinaman were to test your hearing by asking you to imitate some

* Mr. Whipple attempted to put his ideas into operation by opening a private school, "The Whipple Home School," at Mystic, Conn. He succeeded in teaching all his pupils to speak though not to hear. After his death the school was carried on by one of his sons ("Zeno," I think), who proved to be a successful and ingenious teacher, and who invented a very interesting form of alphabet (known as "Whipple's Natural Alphabet"), for the purpose of teaching articulation. The characters were pictorial of the positions of the vocal organs in uttering sounds, thus having the same basal idea as my father's system of "visible speech," but it was devised, I believe, quite independently of my father. Mr. Zeno Whipple (the inventor of the alphabet) died a few years ago, but the school still exists among the private schools.

Mr. A. G. Bell.

14 June 1888.

Chinese word or phrase, it would be rather hard on you if he attributed your inability to repeat that word or phrase to lack of hearing. A deaf child has to contend against the difficulty of the want of familiarity with the language. The English language is Chinese to that child, and as he advances in knowledge of language he also advances in power of perception. I may refer to a remarkable instance of what can be done in the way of auricular instruction: there is a young man, a teacher in the New York Institution, Mr. Jones, who was a congenital deaf mute, or became deaf very early in life. He passed through the whole curriculum of that institution as a deaf mute, he graduated from that institution and went through the course in the National College at Washington as a deaf mute; he then married a hearing lady and became a teacher in the New York Institution. Just about this time experiments, which attracted a great deal of attention in America, were being made in the Nebraska Institution, where it was shown that 16 per cent. of the pupils could be taught auricularly, and that of those the majority could be turned out of school as simply "hard of hearing speaking persons," and not as deaf mutes. The wife of this gentleman knowing he had some hearing, thought she would like to try some experiments with him, and she sat to work to teach him to speak; and he has learnt to speak and learnt to hear. When I was at the New York Institution, I placed him at the end of the schoolroom, and I talked with him, and he answered me, then I went out of the room backwards into the passage a considerable distance away, and I could carry on a conversation with him by shouting to him.

21,400. Is any special instrument other than the ear trumpet used?—The tendency seems to be to discard instrumental aids, but the majority of teachers prefer to use, temporarily at least, what is known as the Currier "Conico-cylindrical conversation tubes, with duplex ear-piece. This *(producing it)* is a photograph of a class at the New York Institution for the Deaf and Dumb which will show the nature of the apparatus. Each child has a duplex tube (two speaking tubes connected to a single ear-piece). The teacher speaks into one of the speaking tubes, and the child itself into the other, the idea being that he may hear his own voice and compare the intonation of his voice with that which proceeds from the teacher. In class instruction the teacher takes a whole bunch of these speaking tubes in his hand at once, and speaks into them all at the same time. This operation is shown in the photograph. I may say that this auricular instruction is carried on as a separate method of instruction in four schools in America. The endeavour was first to test the hearing of all the pupils, and then to form an auricular class.

21,401. Are those schools oral exclusively?—No. Three of them are what Dr. Gallaudet would call combined schools. The other is a private oral school.

21,402. Are they leading schools in America?—Three of them are State institutions. Each one is a leading school in its own State, and I presume no principal would like me to discriminate between one institution and another. I have statistics from Nebraska if you would care to have them. At Nebraska they started a class to test whether the audiphone was of any value, each child placed one against the teeth, and all the children who seemed to perceive any sound were placed in a class by themselves, and attempts were made to get them to imitate the sounds uttered by the teacher; it was found that a certain portion did so, and then it was found that the audiphone was of no use, and that they could do just as well without it. That was the origin of this auricular class, and Mr. Gillespie, the Principal, states that his belief is that 16 per cent. of all the pupils in our institutions are capable of auricular instruction. In New York experiments were made by myself in conjunction with Mr. Currier and Mr. Clarke, and in Washington by Professor Gordon. We had been appointed a committee to investigate this subject of hearing power, and we devised an apparatus which we have called an audiometer, for measuring the power of hearing, and I have brought one of these instruments with me which I shall have great pleasure in presenting to the Commission. The hearing power of several hundred deaf mutes has been tested by an apparatus like this. It consists essentially of two coils of wire and a magneto generator, which generates an intermittent current of electricity in one of the coils, the other coil being connected with a telephone, and currents are induced in the secondary coil by the action of the first, but the intensity of the induced current depends on the distance between the the two coils, so that if you get the two coils in close proximity you get a tremendous noise; but as you draw one coil away from the other the sound becomes less and less till at a certain distance no sound can be perceived. Then the distance between the two coils we take as the measure of the hearing power.

21,403. *(Rev. Mr. Owen.)* Is that audiometer your invention?—Partly my invention and partly Mr. Clarke's. We got it up among us, and it has served a very useful purpose. We do not know how far it may be of value; it is of value in giving numerical estimates of hearing, but it takes a great length of time to test hearing. We tested the hearing of the pupils in the New York Institution by that instrument, and also by the ringing of a bell and also by shouting, and I came to the conclusion that if a child can hear the ringing of a bell there is some hope for him by auricular instruction. A curious point in connexion with this auricular instruction was this, that some of those who would not be termed semi-deaf developed into hard of hearing persons by instruction in the institution. I think 16 or 17 per cent. of the whole number of pupils in our schools will prove fit subjects for auricular instruction. In Nebraska the principal has stated it to be 16 per cent. and in Arkansas the principal has also stated it to be 16 per cent., and in the New York Institution the auricular teacher has stated it to be 17 per cent. In the private school, "The Voice and Hearing School," the per-centage is greater. The per-centage of those known to be semi-deaf by the principals of institutions I find to be this. Of 5,060 pupils, 462, or 9·1 per cent., are known to be semi-deaf, that is the minimum per-centage, and we know now from the experiments which have been made in auricular instruction that a large number who are not known to be semi-deaf turn out to be semi-deaf. From the bell experiments the per-centage was 20·6, which I take to be the maximum per-centage, so that probably 16 or 17 per cent. would turn out to be the true average per-centage. It will be unnecessary for me to speak about methods of instruction or apparatus used, for those are fully entered into in the reports which I have placed in your hands from those who have had most experience in that class of work. I may say here that in experiments with this audiometer I tested the hearing power of over 700 children in the public schools in Washington in order to arrive at an idea of what the normal hearing was, and I found that there are children in our public schools who hear worse than the best cases of deaf mutes in our institutions, and if we could classify the deafness of the whole population we would find a complete gradation from perfect hearing down to no hearing at all.

21,404. *(Rev. Mr. Sleight.)* Has any one perfect hearing?—Probably not, for there is generally a difference between the hearing power of the two ears. There is one other apparatus I have brought here (which is an improvement, perhaps, upon that which I have just shown you) which has not been tested yet; but it tests hearing with more facility than the other instrument.

EXHIBIT TO QUERY 21.400.

DIAGRAM No. 2.

COMPARISON OF THE CONGENITALLY AND NON-CONGENITALLY DEAF ADMITTED TO THE AMERICAN ASYLUM AND ILLINOIS INSTITUTION.

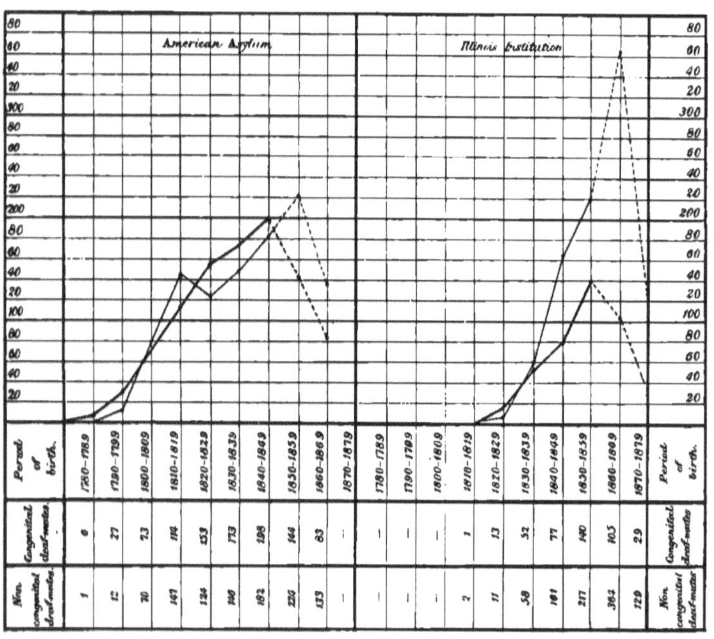

Period of birth	American Asylum: Congenital deaf-mutes	American Asylum: Non congenital deaf-mutes	Illinois Institution: Congenital deaf-mutes	Illinois Institution: Non congenital deaf-mutes
1780–1789	6	1	–	–
1790–1799	27	12	–	–
1800–1809	73	70	–	–
1810–1819	114	141	1	2
1820–1829	153	124	13	11
1830–1839	173	146	52	58
1840–1849	198	182	77	181
1850–1859	144	224	140	217
1860–1869	83	133	105	364
1870–1879	–	–	29	129

The dark lines indicate those pupils who were born deaf, and the light lines those who became deaf from disease or accident.
The pupils are arranged according to period of birth.

DIAGRAM Nº I.

ANALYSIS OF 22472 CASES OF DEAF MUTES LIVING ON 1ST JUNE 1880.

FROM THE CENSUS RETURNS FOR THE UNITED STATES.

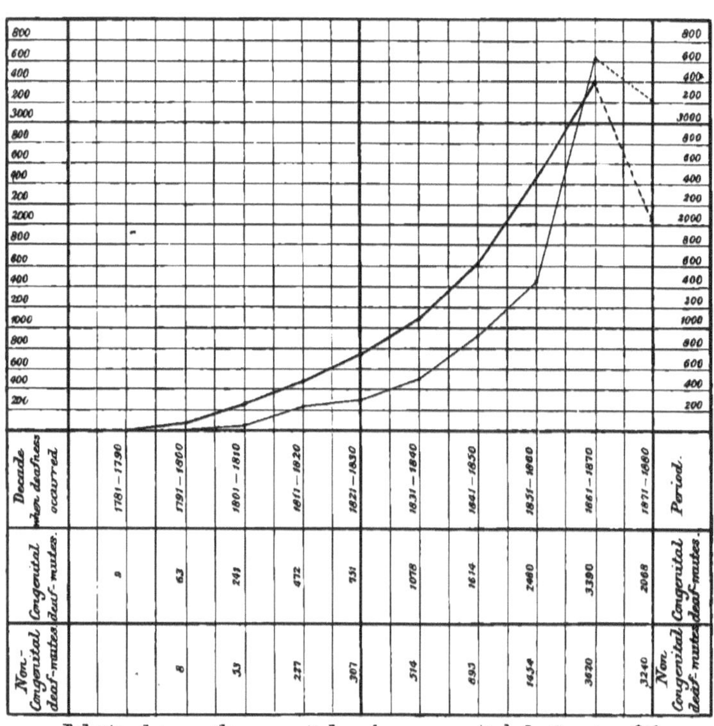

Relation between the congenital and non-congenital deaf-mutes of the country, according to the Rev. Fred. H. Wines.
The congenital deaf-mutes are indicated by the dark line; the non-congenital, by the light line. These deaf-mutes are arranged according to the period when deafness occurred.

21,405. (*Chairman.*) Must you have electricity for that too?—Yes; this takes advantage of the principle of the induction balance. There are two coils here, if they are kept in this position no human ear can perceive any sound, but if this is moved a hair's breadth the normal ear will perceive a sound, so that you can at once select those who have got normal hearing from those who have not.

21,406. (*Mr. Van Oven.*) Is this your invention?—Yes.

21,407. (*Chairman.*) Would you now give us your opinion as to the causes of deafness; you have gone into the matter very fully, I believe?—I do not know that I am capable or competent to give much detailed information on the causes of deafness. I can allude to some of the principal causes in the United States.

21,408. Are there any statistics for that purpose?—Every institution report records the causes of deafness of the pupils admitted. I may say here that I have brought over a large collection of institution reports in case the members of the Commission would like to look over them. In each of these reports you will find the causes of deafness of the pupils admitted. I would, perhaps, rather speak of the causes of deafness of the whole deaf mute population.

21,409. Can you present it to us in a classified form?—Yes. I can present some light on the causes of deafness. The full returns of the census with regard to the causes of deafness has not yet been published; it is the very last thing to be published; but I have, in my "Memoir upon the formation of a deaf variety of the human race," a copy of which I would like you to consult, given on page 35 (*See* Diagram No. 1) the results of an investigation of 22,472 cases of deaf mutes reported in the census, dividing these into two classes: those who are reported deaf from birth, and those who are reported deaf from disease or accident. You will observe that the curves are very remarkable. I may say further on the point, that these cases are also classified according to the period when deafness occurred. The vertical height of the curve indicates the number of deaf mutes who became deaf at a certain period, which is indicated by the horizontal distance.

21,410. What does the dark line at the top indicate, where it gets to 3,400?—That indicates that there were about 3,400 congenital deaf mutes who became deaf in the period from 1861 to 1870, in that decade. (The actual number was 3,390.) If you refer down you will see that. The vertical height indicates the number of cases that became deaf, and the horizontal extension indicates the decade in which that deafness occurred. In the case of the congenital deaf mutes it indicates the period of birth also. In the case of non-congenital deaf mutes it does not indicate the period of birth.

21,411. Then the dotted line seems to go back to 2,000 in the decade from 1871 to 1880?—Yes; but it is to be observed that these are the younger deaf mutes, of whom probably many were not enumerated. You will find on page 36 these words, "Mr. Wines says that in proportion to the degree "of their youth, the younger deaf mutes are not "enumerated. Fewer deaf mutes who are babes in "arms are enumerated than at the age of three "years, and fewer at three years than at seven. "The apparent maximum at seven is not the actual "maximum; the actual maximum is at some "younger age not yet ascertained." In fact you can see from Diagram No. 1 that the census of 1880 shows a proportionately less number of deaf-mutes who lost hearing in the decade of 1871-80 than in the previous decade. Owing to this apparent deficiency the line for that decade has been dotted to call attention to it. It appears as though the younger deaf mutes were not fully returned. That led Mr. Wines to suppose that the total number of deaf mutes in the United States, if it could be ascertained, would amount to 35,000 instead of 33,878.

21,412. What is the next line below that?—The light line is a graphical representation on the same plan of the deaf mutes who become deaf from disease.

21,413. This table begins at eight years old?—Yes, at any age; but the period there refers not to the period of birth, but to the period when deafness occurred. Now you will observe one general result that you may obtain by a glance at the tables, viz., that there has been an enormous increase in the last few years in the numbers of the non-congenitally deaf, so great as to reverse the whole relation between the two classes. You see the curves cross one another. In the case of the younger deaf mutes, the majority are non-congenitally deaf; in the case of the older deaf mutes, the majority were born deaf. It will also be seen that this result is not due to a diminution in the number of the congenitally deaf. The curve formed by the congenitally deaf is a perfectly symmetrical curve; there is a regular increase at a regular rate, and a mathematician could project it where it is deficient.

21,414. I do not quite know why one of these lines begins at the third line, and the other begins at the fifth line apparently; has it anything to do with the ages?—If you take the extreme left corner of the diagram at the lower point as your starting point, that is the origin for the axes of co-ordinates; that is the lower left-hand corner, where the vertical and horizontal lines cross one another. That point is on the vertical line indicating the decade 1771 to 1780, but no deaf mutes were living in 1880 who were born in that decade, so that neither of the curves extend as far as that. Now, if you go two lines to your right, where the actual curve commences, that indicates the period from 1781 to 1790. It is the dark line that commences there. This shows that some of the congenital deaf mutes who were living in 1880 were born in that decade. By reference to the figures you will find that nine were born in that period.

21,415. (*Mr. Woodall.*) I thought you expected us, in this diagram, to see the average ages of the children at which certain results were obtained? No, except in the case of the congenitally deaf, because there the period of birth coincides with the period when deafness occurred. This enormous rise of the light line indicates a period when there was an enormous increase in the number of persons who became deaf from disease.

21,416. (*Chairman.*) Will you call attention to the general results, apart from the diagram?—The general result is this, that the numbers of the non-congenitally deaf are subject to great and sudden fluctuations on account of epidemic diseases which cause deafness; whereas the numbers of the congenitally deaf are not subject to these sudden changes. In the second diagram you will observe a comparison of the congenitally and non-congenitally deaf admitted to the American Asylum and the Illinois Institution. In the American Asylum you will see that there were two periods when there was an abnormal increase in the number of persons who became deaf from disease. In the Illinois Institution the increase in the number of persons who became deaf from disease has been so great within the last few years that I call special attention to it. I will read from my paper what I say: "In regard "to the Illinois pupils (Diagram No. 2) it will be "observed that the increase in the numbers of the "non-congenitally deaf is so enormous that, of the "pupils who were born in the decade 1860–69, "there were more than three times as many non-con-"genitally deaf as there were congenitally deaf, and "of those born in 1870–79 more than four times, "whereas the census returns show that more than "half of all the deaf mutes living in this country "(1880) were born deaf." There is, therefore, evidence that, taking the deaf mutes as a whole, there has been of recent years a great epidemic; and on examining the statistics of the various institutions I find that it is due to an epidemic of cerebro-spinal

Mr. A. G. Bell.

14 June 1888.

meningitis, which now takes the first rank as the deafness-producing disease of America.

21,417. (*Chairman.*) Is that consequent upon some particular condition of life?—I am not able to say.

21,418. (*Dr. McDonnell.*) "Spotted fever," I see in the note, is another name for it?—Yes, so it is stated. These cases often become deaf suddenly, in half an hour.

21,419. (*Chairman.*) Is that an inherited disease, or is it caused by some affection of the patient concerned?—I am not competent to decide that; I think it is not inherited. There are evidences of two great epidemics of cerebro-spinal meningitis in America which caused deafness, one occurring in the decade from 1810 to 1819, and that is the cause, by-the-bye, of that sudden sharp curve about the period in the American Asylum diagram (Diagram 2), and also probably the cause of the irregularity in the non-congenital curve for the deaf-mutes of the country (Diagram 1), occurring at that same period (1811-1820). If this is so, it indicates that the earlier epidemic extended over the whole country sufficiently to affect the relation between the congenital and non-congenital classes. That died away, and about 1840 scarlet fever assumed the first rank as the deafness-producing disease. Since the period of the Civil War scarlet fever has gradually taken second rank, and the cerebro-spinal meningitis is now the prevailing cause. Few, if any, deaf-mutes have appeared in our institutions who became deaf from cerebro-spinal meningitis in the period from 1820 to 1860.

21,420. (*Mr. Woodall.*) Perhaps you will explain whether the epidemic was more felt in Illinois than in the other States?—I do not know; but there is evidence that it has been felt all over the country; all the institution reports show it, and it affects, as you see, the relation of the non-congenital to the congenital cases in the whole country; it has reversed the whole relation.

21,421. (*Rev. Mr. Sleight.*) Why is the line in diagram 2 (Illinois Institution) dotted from 1860 to 1869?—Because there we know the curves are incomplete; they are inaccurate because all the pupils who became deaf in that decade, who would ultimately be sent to that school, had not been admitted into the institution at the period when the report was made, from which these diagrams were made.

21,422. (*Sir Tindal Robertson.*) What is the average age at which deafness occurs?—I have no idea of that.

21,423. With regard to this particular epidemic that would be a most interesting point?—You will see these reports, and if the question is one of importance to the Commission I shall be glad to examine the point and see what we can determine. We cannot determine it from the census returns, because the ages and causes of deafness have not been fully published.

21,424. Could it be ascertained whether at the same time there was any corresponding disease with the same results with regards to adults?—Not from the institution reports.

21,425. From any other sources?—Yes; we have sources of information from which much information could be obtained. We could certainly obtain statistics relating to deaths, but I do not know whether the fact of deafness in adults could be obtained. Dr. Billings, of the Army and Navy Medical Library (Washington, D. C.), could give you information upon this point.

21,426. (*Mr. Woodall.*) You have probably explained just now what can be said with regard to the extraordinary increase of congenital deafness over the period traversed by your diagram?—I have not touched the question of the congenitally deaf yet; we are now on the non-congenitally deaf.

21,427. But I observe that the increase in non-congenital deafness shown in the diagram of Illinois is corroborated by the general increase over the States generally?—Yes.

21,428. But the relative n
ness in the two institution
does not exactly correspon
Congenital deafness over th
appears to have reached a l
in the period of 1870, than
rate institution?—That is
The report from which the A
was made was issued in 1
able, say, for two decades b
are rarely admitted till the
and some do not appear u
is not reliable for the dec
reports from the American
was a decrease, not that the
there for that period, but s
who were born in that de
would ultimately be sent
peared in the institution at
was made (1877). The I
again is a later report, 1882
1846; whereas the Americ
from 1815. That explain
Put the two diagrams tog
American Asylum for the
Illinois Institution for the
approximates more closel
census returns.

21,429. But looking at
might almost have been
neither congenital nor non-
preceding the period of
not know that. And in th
few, because they were n
census returns are only f
alive in 1880.

21,430. That I take it
mind, that you have been
making stricter scrutiny in
causes whose existence was

21,431. (*Rev. Mr. Sleigh*
more accurate returns you
Yes. There is one import
between the institution re
turns. The institution ret
were admitted, their dates
of whether they were alive
were made. The census
deaf who were living on 1s
direct your attention to a
may be wrong in my dedu
an important point that we
curves as these, and thro
growth of the deaf-mute
erence to the earlier defect
attempted to do so on the
ing page 40 in my Memoir
think it is very importa
should form an opinion as
reasoning is correct or not
upon the earlier censuses.
we compare the relative n
mutes and hearing person
should give us the relation
genital deaf population an
at the period when they w
tion that the death rates a
down equally; that is the
go. If we assume that th
now exists between conge
ing persons *of the same*
resents the proportion of
the whole population born
were born, we have the n
growth of the congenitall
that of the population at la
that the congenital deaf m
increasing at a greater rat
large; that is evident from

21,432. (*Mr. Woodall.*)
these are gross figures, ar
relative figures to the pop

To face question No 21431.

DIAGRAM No 3.

Comparison of the congenitally deaf population with population at large, in the United States.

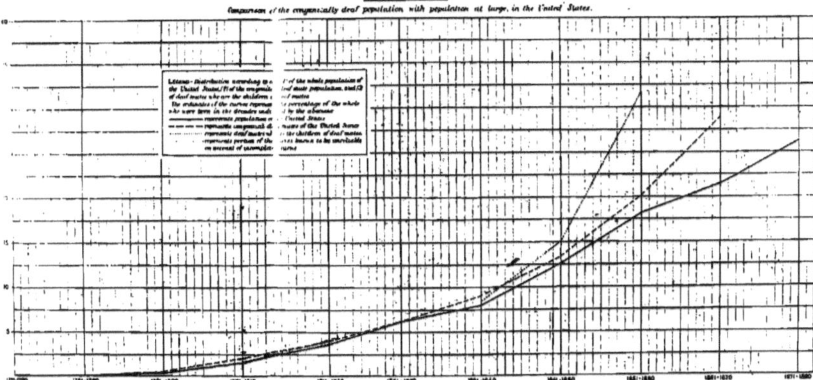

Mr. A. G. Bell.

14 June 1888.

21,433. In the diagram which you have presented, showing the relative proportion of congenital and non-congenital cases of deaf mutism in the United States, the ascending scale indicates the actual gross numbers and not the per-centage to the general population at all?—Yes, that is true for the first diagram presented.

21,434. Would not a table showing the general population of the United States during that period, and its wonderful increase, have something like the same appearance as this diagram presents?—I have shown that.

21,435. For the entire population?—Yes, for the entire population of the United States; it is shown on the diagram No. 3. But it would be difficult to represent on the same scale, the absolute number of the whole population and the absolute number of the deaf population; and I have therefore taken per-centages so as to give them on the same scale; the lower dark line indicates the distribution according to age of the whole population of 50,155,783. Then the second line indicates the distribution according to age of the congenitally deaf population: and if you look in the Appendix to my Memoir, you will find the table and all the figures given from which the table is made. I would like very much that the Commission should realise that this demonstration (because it seems to my mind to be a demonstration) that the congenitally deaf mute population is increasing at a greater rate than the population at large, is independent of the errors of the earlier census reports. All the material is taken from the 1880 census alone. The table to which I refer is Table U in the Appendix, on page 77. It is as follows:—

Deaf-mute population of the United States compared with the population at large.

Period of Birth.	Population of the United States (1880), classified according to period of birth, and the number of persons born in each period reduced to a percentage of the whole.		12,164 congenital deaf-mutes living June 1, 1880, classified according to period of birth, and the number of deaf-mutes born in each period reduced to a percentage of the whole.		Deaf-mutes both of whose parents were deaf-mutes, classified according to period of birth, and the number of deaf-mutes born in each period reduced to a percentage of the whole.	
	Number of persons.	Percentage.	Congenital deaf-mutes.	Percentage.	Deaf-mutes both of whose parents were deaf and dumb.	Percentage.
1871-1880 - - -	13,394,176	26·7051	2,068	17·015	19	14·3
1861-1870 - - -	10,726,601	21·3866	3,398	27·958	41	30·8
1851-1860 - - -	9,168,393	18·2798	2,460	20·240	42	31·6
1841-1850 - - -	6,369,362	12·6992	1,614	13·280	20	15·0
1831-1840 - - -	4,558,256	9·0882	1,078	8·870	11	8·3
1821-1830 - - -	3,111,317	6·2033	751	6·179	—	—
1811-1820 - - -	1,830,095	3·6488	472	3·883	—	—
1801-1810 - - -	776,507	1·5482	241	1·983	—	—
1791-1800 - - -	196,197	0·3912	63	0·518	—	—
1781-1790 - - -	20,863	0·0416	9	0·074	—	—
—— 1780 - - -	4,016	0·0080	—	—	—	—
Total - -	50,155,783	100·0000	12,154	100·000	133	100·0

21,436. In effect there has been a very remarkable growth of the general population of the United States, a still greater growth of the congenitally deaf, and in a much greater ratio—especially from 1840 to 1860—of deaf mutes born of deaf mutes?—Yes.

21,437. (*Mr. Van Oven.*) But there is an immense falling off from 1871 to 1880?—These are the deaf children of deaf mutes. The apparent falling off does not necessarily mean a real falling off. These deaf children were returned to me as having been at some time pupils of institutions. Few pupils make their appearance at school before they are 10 or 12 years of age, so that many of the younger deaf children had not appeared in school at the time the returns were made to me. But there is another point. The line forming the line for deaf mute children born of deaf mutes commences suddenly. There are none at all before the decade 1831–1840.

21,438. (*Chairman.*) Is that an absolute fact, or is it only unrecorded?—I think it is an absolute fact, but that is simply my opinion. When I come to enter upon that subject (which I would rather not do just now) I will deal more fully with it. There are cases of deaf mutes who have one parent deaf, who were born earlier. But even with the fuller information now in my possession, the only case I have found of a deaf child with both parents deaf before that decade was a female born in 1829, but this case requires verification. Then there was no other case until 1833 that I have found; there may be others, of course. But the important point is that the line starts suddenly. It does not extend back to the beginning of the century like the others.

21,439. I think you said that you would give us a classified return of the causes of deafness, so far as you can?—If the Commission would like it, I should be glad if they would put any definite questions, and I shall be glad to see what I can do in the way of solving them between now and the next meeting.

21.440. The classification of these causes of deafness in the United States we have not got in a tabular form?—I shall be happy to do what I can to arrive at that.*

21,441. Are there any other causes of deafness to which you wish to draw particular attention on which you have made any particular remarks; you have told us of scarlet fever and cerebro-spinal meningitis?—The causes of congenital deafness are very obscure. There is a very prevalent impression among the parents of congenital deaf mutes that mental impressions upon the mother during the period of pregnancy have an influence on the child. I must say that I am not inclined to believe that; but I must say that in my examination and inquiries among parents I found that belief very prevalent. It is evident that one of the chief causes of congenital deafness is a hereditary pre-disposition. That is manifested by the fact that of the 2,262 congenital deaf mutes, mentioned on page 13 of my memoir, more than one half, or 54·5 per cent., had other members of their family deaf and dumb.

21,442. Is arrested development the cause of deafness? Sir William Dalby says that in the first class of causes he would place deafness as due to arrested development before birth, which is quite unpreventable?—I am very much inclined to think that there is a great deal in that.

21,443. (*Sir Tindal Robertson.*) Can you tell us

* *See* reply to Query 21,487.

Mr. A. G. Bell.

14 June 1888.

whether that idea of mental impressions is shared by experienced medical men, specialists, in America, or is only a sort of popular idea?—It is a sort of popular idea.

21,444. Have you any particular book upon the question written by a recognised medical authority which throws any light upon this particular question of causes of deafness?—I believe not. I am now engaged in a very elaborate investigation by which I hope to arrive at some light. It is based on this fact: that 54·5 per cent. have deaf mute relatives. From that fact I deduce this consequence that heredity plays a part in the production of congenital deafness. If there is no deafness in the ancestry, it is something else in the family which is not specially indicated. If it is not deafness, how are we going to find it out? I have formulated a plan of research, from which I expect to obtain important results. It is to examine the ancestry of families containing three or more deaf children. If one child in a family is born deaf, it may be accidental; if two children in a family are born deaf, it is a little less likely to be accidental; but if there are three or more children born deaf, I think we may confidently assume that there is something to be discovered in the ancestry. Therefore I have started a genealogical inquiry which has now assumed enormous proportions. I felt that one man could hope to do very little, and that it would be better to take a limited area of country and examine all the cases in that area in which three or more children had been born deaf. I have taken as the base of my operations the New England States, and I have experts, genealogists, at work who have been engaged for nearly four years in tracing the ancestry of all the families that I have any record of in the New England States, that have three or four deaf children. My plan is this: I trace the ancestry up in every branch. I do not know what it is we are going to look for except that it is probably something abnormal. Therefore we search for any peculiarities or abnormalities among the ancestors, or the brothers and sisters of the ancestors. My idea is that, where we have got a good number of cases of distinct families having no deafness in the ancestry, but where three or more deaf children have appeared, we should take and put together these genealogies, make a sort of composite photograph, and see what sort of abnormalities appear in common in the ancestry; and that will have something to do with the deafness.

21,445. (*Sir Tindal Robertson.*) Taking into consideration blood relationships?—Yes.

21,446. (*Chairman.*) We have had evidence before us that consanguinity has a very important bearing?—Without taking up the time of the Commission, I should like them to look at these papers. Those will give you an idea of the mass of material which I am collecting. This is the index to the genealogical material I am collecting with regard to the ancestry of deaf mutes in the New England States.

21,447. With us in 35 institutions, there have been 56 cases resulting from the marriages of first cousins, 11 of second cousins, of other relatives, two; and 28 cases which were children of deaf and dumb parents. Therefore the deaf and dumb marriages of first cousins appear to be double the number of those of children of deaf and dumb parents. And that is not quite a disposing cause, because a great many more first cousins have married of course than are the parents of deaf and dumb children?—I presume that the Commission is familiar with the researches of Dr. George Darwin, of Cambridge, who has investigated that very point of consanguineous marriages. If I remember rightly he examined the institutions for the deaf and dumb in this country, and found the per-centage of deaf mutes who are the children of first cousins; so, too, he took the blind and the idiotic, and so forth, but he did not stop there as others have done, he took the per-centage of children with no defects at all in the schools, and found the per-centage the same. And so far as my researches have gone, I have given considerable attention to this subject, and I can see no proof; at least we have no statistics that undeniably prove that a consanguineous marriage is a cause of deafness; but I do see abundant proof that a consanguineous marriage occurring in a family in which there is already deafness increases the deafness in the offspring; it is simply a case of selection; the family peculiarities, whatever they are, are increased. However, I must refer you to one source of information which seems to me to give the most plausible proof that consanguineous marriages may be a cause of deafness, that is the report of the Halifax Institution for 1877; it is out of print. The principal of that institution has only one copy. He had two, and he presented me with one. If the Commission have not got it at hand I have it here; and I think the statistics that are in that report are very striking with regard to consanguineous marriages. But again with regard to this subject, if the Commission desire me to search the reports of the American institutions, and make tabular statements, I shall only be too glad to do so.

21,448. (*Mr. Woodall.*) In stating Dr. Darwin's view, I understand you to concur in it?—Yes, so far as my researches go. In regard to the question of arrested development in the nervous system, I may direct the attention of the Commission to a very curious phenomenon. White cats that have blue eyes are always deaf; it is a very curious thing. Darwin (the father) explains this peculiarity upon the hypothesis of arrested development of the nervous system. He says that all kittens when they are born are deaf. Not only are their eyes closed, but their ears are closed also, and if you avoid making a current of air, and simply make a loud noise by clanging together a poker and shovel, you cannot awake kittens if they are asleep. Now when the eyes are first opened they are always blue; they change afterwards, and Darwin says that supposing an arrest of development to occur in the nervous system at the period of closed eyelids, the eyes will be permanently blue, and the kitten permanently deaf. In proof of that I may say that there was a French doctor, whose name I forget for the moment, who observed a white kitten with blue eyes, and tested its hearing as well as he could, and studied it, and when this cat grew to be about one year of age, he found that the eyes began to change colour, and then the cat began to hear. In the case of deaf mutes, I have sought to see whether we have anything similar in the blue eyes. I counted the blue eyes in one institution, and I found a very abnormal proportion of blue eyes in the New York institution, but I do not hold that as conclusive at all, because in New York State the Roman Catholic children go to a separate school, and they belong largely to the dark eyed races. I wish, however, to direct the attention of the Commission to one very curious thing. I cannot assert it as a fact, but I think it is of importance. I have found a few cases of deaf mutes who have eyes and hair that do not match, and every one of those was partially blind.

21,449. (*Chairman.*) More or less albinos?—No, light blue eyes and black hair. And on examining a school for the idiotic in Elwin, Pennsylvania, my attention was immediately struck with the fact that about 50 per cent. of the children in the primary school there had eyes and hair that did not match. Some had very light blue eyes and black hair, and others had very dark eyes and light flaxen hair. It is a subject that should be kept in mind. Now with regard to correlation there is an undoubted correlation between blindness and deafness and idiocy. I will not take up the time of the Commission by going into details, but will refer you to an article upon that subject I published in "Science" of February the 13th, 1885, in a paper entitled "Is "there a Correlation between Defects of the "Senses?" I will just refer to a few of the general

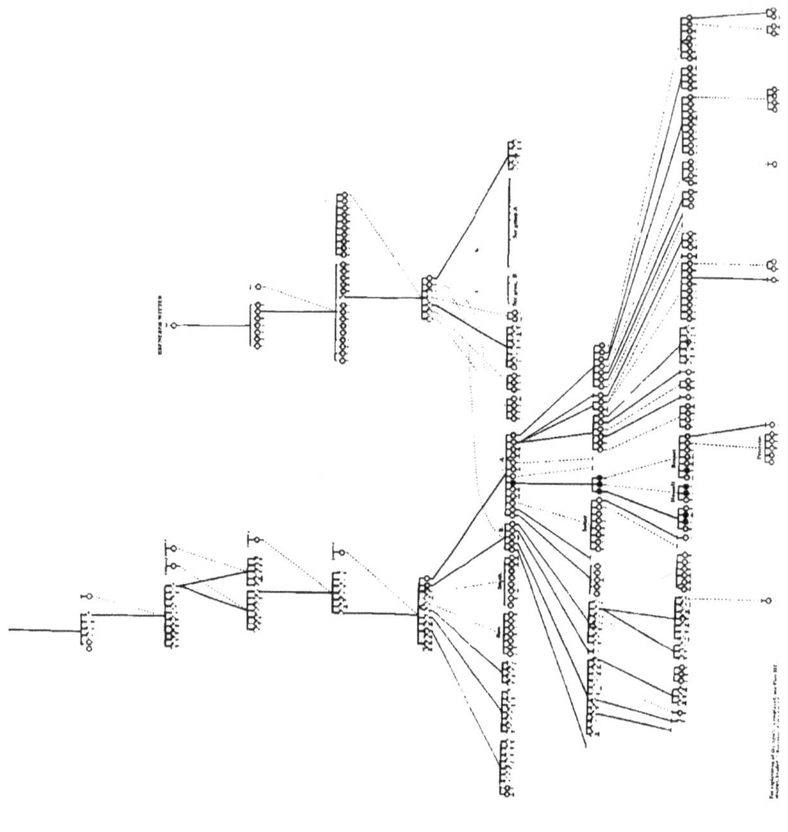

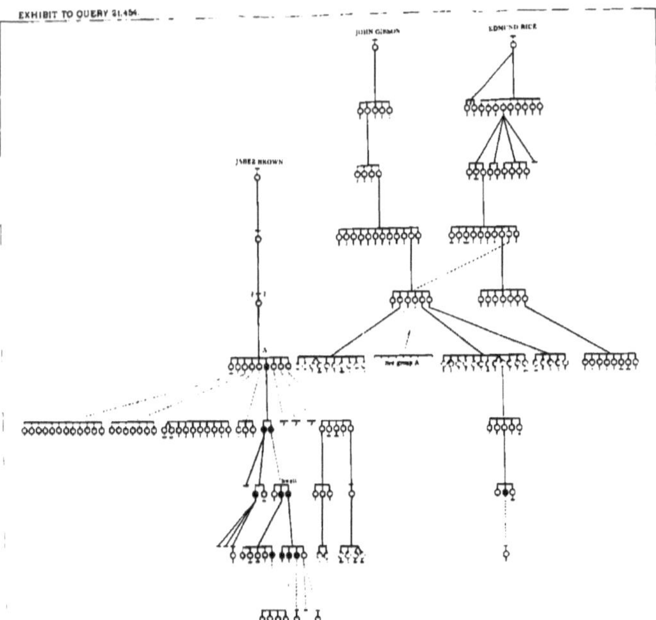
EXHIBIT TO QUERY 31,454.
JOHN GIBSON
EDMUND RICE
JABEZ BROWN
A
See group A

remarks. There are 14½ times as many blind persons among the deaf and dumb in proportion to the population as there are in the community at large, and 46 times as many idiotic; there are 14 times as many deaf mutes among the blind as there are in the population at large, and 19 times as many idiots.

21,450. Then you think that there would be a peculiar fitness in this Royal Commission inquiring into the education of the idiotic, so far as they can be educated together, with the education of the blind and the deaf and dumb?—No;* I bring this forward as bearing on the causes of deafness. I say that these three things probably have some common cause. I would say that there does not seem to be any great correlation between deafness and insanity, so far as the census returns show. My genealogical researches, on the other hand, indicate that while comparatively few deaf mutes are insane, insanity has appeared not infrequently among the brothers and sisters of ancestors of deaf-mutes. I would recommend this paper to the Commission. I present them with a copy of "Science" containing it. I suggest there that it may be possible, in a certain proportion of cases of blindness, deafness, and idiocy, that they may spring from a common cause, probably from arrested development of the nervous system. I find that it is not uncommon for deaf mutes, especially where they belong to a family having a number of deaf mutes, to have cousins, not brothers and sisters, who are idiots; as if the defect had struck down in one branch as deafness, and in the other as idiocy. In concluding this subject of the causes of congenital deafness, I think we must undoubtedly assume that in the majority of cases some ancestral cause operates, whatever it may be; and I am very much inclined to the belief that there is an arrest in the development of the nervous system. I find all around the points, where deaf mutes appear in large numbers, evidences of other disturbances in the nervous system, paralysis, chorea (St. Vitus's Dance), and epilepsy; and it is probable that in regard to congenital deafness in families, there is some cause in the nervous system that is inherited—it may not be deafness—but heredity plays a part. There is one other point associated with congenital deafness, and that is, variability. You will find abnormalities all round the points where you find numerous deaf mutes. I am specially struck with one point that may turn out to be nothing more than a coincidence when I come to take the per-centage, I allude to the presence of twins and sometimes triplets in the families of the ancestors of large families of deaf mutes. I do not know what the association is, but it occurs so frequently in the families that I have been investigating as to have attracted the special attention of my correspondent, Mrs. Pratt, who first pointed it out to me. In that connexion, I may say that one of the Siamese Twins had deaf and dumb children. The Siamese Twins, in America, married two sisters, and one had deaf and dumb children. And in Martha's Vineyard, in Chilmark, where one person in every 25 of the population is a deaf mute, you have evidence of variability—various sex peculiarities which cannot very well be spoken of in the Commission; and you have dwarfs, and you have six-fingered persons.

21,451. (*Dr. Campbell.*) Can you form any idea of how soon you will be able to publish the results of this investigation?—I cannot say. I have no idea. I have been at work upon it four years. I expect to publish one part of it this autumn. That is the part which refers to the deaf mutes in Martha's Vineyard. That has proved to be an interesting field, being an island where consanguineous marriages have occurred, and I have been able to trace the ancestry. As you will observe by my reports, the ancestry is traced in every branch. That has been very difficult work, but I have got the ancestry traced up through 10 or 12 generations. The rest of the work may take years.

21,452. (*Mr. Woodall.*) Where is Martha's Vineyard?—In the southern part of Massachusetts; it is one of our largest islands, between 50 and 60 miles from Boston.

21,453. (*Chairman.*) What is the population, about?—The population of this little hamlet (Chilmark), where deafness occurs is only 500, and there are 20 deaf mutes. I have a list of 72 deaf mutes born in that place, or whose ancestors came from there. But on the 1st of June, 1880, there were 20 deaf mutes there to a population of 500, which is one in 25 of the population.

21,454. (*Mr. Woodall.*) Without pursuing in anything like detail, what you refer to with regard to the peculiarities of sex, were they monstrosities?—Yes, what are called hermaphrodites. And then there are other curious sex peculiarities. I will tell you one. In the Brown family of Henniker, New Hampshire, in which deafness has gone down through four generations, there is a very remarkable sex peculiarity. The first deaf mute in this family is one of nine children, and they are all girls except the deaf mute, and he is a boy. In his mother's family they are all boys except one girl, and in her mother's family they are all girls except one boy. And in all these three cases the families are large. I will show you another case with regard to twins and triplets. That is the Allen family. That is a very curious case. In this case the deafness has gone down through three generations, and the third generation is very young. In the family containing the first deaf mute there were twelve brothers and sisters, including a case of twins.

21,455. (*Sir Tindal Robertson.*) Was the deaf mute a twin?—No. Go up to the father of the family and you have among his brothers and sisters a pair of twins and a case of triplets. I am constantly struck with the appearance of twins. Whether they have any significance or not I do not know; one is apt to be misled. It may be that twins and triplets are as common in the community at large; but it is a point which is attracting my attention. In this same family you have correlation with idiocy. The first deaf mute has a brother who is insane; then he has another brother who has one child insane and one child who is all right. That child has a child who is feeble-minded. Go up on the mother's side here. The mother had a brother and one of his children was feeble-minded. You find here is insanity again. All round the point where the deafness occurs you find evidences of something generally affecting the nervous system in connexion with the brain. In such families you sometimes find consanguineous marriage taking place. There is a case I have in which seven children are deaf mutes. There was no deafness in the ancestors that was known, and no consanguineous marriage.

21,456. That does not stop pro-creation?—I do not think so. But in this case one of these seven deaf mutes married his first cousin and had a number of children who could all hear and speak, but three of them were feeble-minded. There again is something to indicate that the thing intensified might be in the brain and not in the ears at all.

21,457. (*Chairman.*) With regard to the education of the deaf and dumb in America, are there any special points on which you wish to dwell; what are the main points that influence you in regard to your being in favor of the day school system rather than the special institution system of education; what are the dangers to which you think the institution system open?—There are a number of distinct lines of reasoning that all point as a conclusion to the advisability of increasing the number of day schools

* I do not wish my reply to this query to go upon record in the negative. Reflection convinces me that the education of the feeble-minded should be inquired into by the British Government. I know from what I have seen in America that much can be done for the idiotic, and many that would otherwise be a burden upon the public can be taught to be self-supporting. The causes of idiocy are so inter-related to the causes of deafness and blindness that I think there would be a peculiar fitness in this Royal Commission inquiring into the condition of the idiotic.

Mr. A. G. Bell.

14 June 1888.

and making them as small as possible.* In theory the best school for a deaf child is a school with only one in it; but of course it is impracticable: it is too expensive. I believe the best way to arrive at the solution of such a problem as the character of the best school is to formulate your ideal school, recognising that it is impracticable, but coming up as near to it as you can. In my "Memoir upon the "formation of a deaf variety of the human race," I have formulated one of the principal reasons for the advisability in my opinion of extending the day school system on page 45. I say "I think all will "agree that the evidence shows a tendency to the "formation of a deaf variety of the human race in "America. What remedial measures can be taken "to lessen or check this tendency? We shall consider the subject under two heads: (1) repressive: "(2) preventive measures." Repressive measures I abandon. On page 46 I take up the question of preventive measures, and I would request the very close attention of the Commission to this point, for it really forms the central point of my idea of the day schools with regard to preventive measures (that is in regard to preventing the inter-marriages of the deaf and dumb). I say:—"The most promising method of lessening the evil appears to lie "in the adoption of preventive measures. In our "search for such measures we should be guided by "the following principle: (1) Determine the causes "that promote inter-marriages among the deaf and "dumb; and (2) remove them. The immediate "cause is undoubtedly the preference that adult "deaf mutes exhibit for the companionship of deaf "mutes rather than that of hearing persons. "Among the causes that contribute to bring about "this preference we may note: (1) segregation for "the purposes of education; and (2) the use, as a "means of communication, of a language which is "different from that of the people. These, then, "are two of the points that should be avoided in "the adoption of preventive measures. Nearly all "the other causes I have investigated are ultimately "referable to these. Segregation really lies at the "root of the whole matter; for from this the other "causes have themselves been evolved by the operation of the natural law of adaptation to the environment. We commence our efforts on behalf "of the deaf mute by changing his social environment. The tendency is, then, towards accommodation to the new conditions. In process of time "the adaptation becomes complete; and when, at "last, we restore him to the world as an adult, he "finds that the social conditions to which he has "become accustomed do not exist outside of his "school-life. His efforts are then directed to the "restoration of these conditions, with the result of "inter-marriage and a tendency to the formation of "a deaf-mute community."

21,458. (*Mr. Woodall.*) Is that so?—Yes. "The "grand central principle that should guide us then "in our search for preventive measure should be *the "retention of the normal environment during the period of education.* The natural tendency towards "adaptation would then co-operate with instruction to produce accommodation to *the permanent "conditions of life.* The direction of change should, "therefore, be towards the establishment of small "schools and the extension of the day school plan. "The practicability of any great development of day "schools will depend upon the possibility of conducting very small schools of this kind economically "to the State: for the scattered condition of the "deaf and dumb in the community precludes the "idea of large day schools, excepting in the great "centres of population. The principle referred to "above indicates that such schools should be of the "minimum size possible; for the school that would "most perfectly fulfil the condition required would "contain only one deaf child. It also points to the "advisability of co-education with hearing children; "but this is not practicable to any great extent. No "instruction can be given through the ear, and complete co-education would only therefore be possible "by a change in the methods of teaching hearing "children. It is useless to expect that such a change "would be made for the benefit of the deaf and "dumb on account of their limited number. Partial "co-education is, however, possible, for some studies "are pursued in the common schools in which information is gained through the eye. For "instance, deaf mutes could profitably enter the "same classes with hearing children for practice in "writing, drawing, map-drawing, arithmetic on the "black-board, sewing, &c. For other subjects "special methods of instruction would be necessary, "and these demand the employment of special "teachers. They do not, however, necessitate "special schools or buildings, and a small room in "a public school building would accommodate as "many deaf children as one teacher could successfully instruct. Considerations of economy render "advisable the appropriation of a room of this kind, "as the appliances of a large school might thus be "obtained without special outlay. The average *per "capita* cost of the education of a deaf child in an "American institution is \$223·28 c. per annum. "Very small day schools could be maintained at no "greater cost."

21,459. Is that over the whole of the States?—That is the average arrived at from the average of 34 institutions; they are not my figures; I quote them from the principal of the Illinois Institution in 1882. Perhaps Dr. Gallaudet's testimony will be more reliable.

21,460. 250 and 260 dollars I find was paid by the States generally *per capita*?—You will find the table from which the *per capita* is calculated in the Appendix, Table X.

21,461. (*Chairman.*) I wanted to ask you this question. In Germany they have a large number of institutions, and they have a certain number of every day schools; but where the oral system is taught there is no inter-marriage practically by the deaf and dumb; and therefore while you are advocating, in order to prevent the inter-marriage of the deaf and dumb, day schools instead of institutions, would it not be far more simple to follow the example of Germany, and would you not consider that if you give them speech, you take away the great inducement to inter-marriage. Or is it practicable to do that. If it is not impracticable it is more simple, but is it practicable?—We do not find the facts in America the same as you state. The pupils of our oral schools do marry deaf mutes.

21,462. But do they do so exclusively, or do they not also after they leave school mix with those on the sign system?—A larger per-centage of the pupils on the oral system marry hearing persons than of those of the sign system.

21,463. I assume that you wish to prevent this calamity happening of the formation of a deaf variety of the human race; the question is whether you can arrive at that in the best way by your system, that is to say, by doing away with institutions, and having day schools, so as to prevent the possibility of the deaf and dumb being thrown together so much when young. Would you not attain your object better by assisting their learning speech as far as possible?—I do not advocate the abolishment of institutions. I am only on the line of researches. I propose to keep our institutions.

21,464. It is a very serious question you raised of doing away with the institutions altogether?—We could not do that; that is a step backwards. It may be done by the process of natural selection. I do not propose to do that; I propose to supplement the institutions by a large development of small day schools, and leave in each state at least one institution which shall accommodate the children who cannot attend day schools; and, where it is practicable in any State, let the day schools be affiliated with the public schools so that the children shall be in the public school buildings, in a special room under a special teacher, but thrown in contact with

* See replies to Queries 21,457; 21,464; 21,468; 21,469.

Mr. A. G. Bell.

11 June 1888.

the hearing children in every possible way. One of the lines of argument that lead to the same result is my desire that all deaf children should be taught to use their vocal organs, and to speak. The conditions in an institution are unfavourable to this, because there are few people there who can hear them speak; so that if they are placed in an institution the English language is of little use to them: and if you want a child to make a rapid advance in the English language you must make the language of use.

21,465. Do you think it would be an advantage to the deaf and dumb children to be brought in contact with speaking children in play hours?—Undoubtedly; I am very strongly of that opinion.

21,466. In London, besides our institutions, we have a certain number of school board schools, in which the deaf and dumb children are in many cases in a part of the same building where the ordinary hearing children are taught, and to a certain extent they mix with them. If that were to be carried out as it could be carried out in large towns, and is being carried out in England in large towns, it would obviate your suggestion for the deaf and dumb being kept together in a separate class?—Yes.

21,467. Do you see any objection to that system?—No; I do not believe you can carry on co-education with hearing children. I do not think that that is a practicable thing for a large number: there are individual cases where it may be done. But I think that partial co-education is not only possible but practicable; and it would be an advantage to the deaf to have a special teacher in a special room in the same building with a large number of ordinary children.

21,468. Do you think it advisable, after deaf and dumb have had a sufficient education (I am assuming that they are being educated in speech) to enable them to go out into the world, after they had had eight or ten years in a private school or with separate education, which you admit they must have, that they should if possible go to some technical school where they can be taught in common with other children the rudiments of practical mechanics and drawing, and other elements of industrial trades, say from 14 to 16 or 16 to 18. Do you think that that is a step in the right direction?—I think it is. In the day schools in Boston no industrial training is provided by the city, and the principal, through a private fund, has sent a number of her boys to the Institute of Technology, where the Russian workshop system is introduced, where the pupils are not taught a specific trade, but are taught the elements, the use of tools and the elements of a trade; and these boys have found no difficulty in getting good employment. There are two other points that occur to me with regard to day schools. A boy who is brought up in close association with a large number of hearing children will derive a great advantage in adult life from his knowledge of these hearing children, even though he never communicates with them. They will be the men and women among whom his lot in life is cast, and they will help him in getting on in life; they will remember that he was a schoolfellow and will help him.

21,469. That must be on the oral system, otherwise there would be no means of communication between them?—Let there be any means of communication that they can get, or if they do not communicate at all it will still be an advantage. Boys are not always rough. When these children grow up to be men and women they will remember the deaf children, even if they never spoke a word to them; and these deaf children will have friends in the hearing community who will help them to business and places: whereas, if they kept away from hearing persons and go out into the world without knowing any, they find it much harder to get employment. The other point is still more important: it is this, that the institution plan does not bring half the deaf children under instruction. You can get the children into day school at a younger age, and make the institutions places of higher learning. You can reach the children at an age when they cannot go from home; you can carry the school to the door of the home. The institution system of America has not brought under instruction one-half the deaf children, and teachers tell me the same elsewhere. The reason is the same; that the parents will not part with their children. I should propose to supplement the institution plan therefore by these little feeders which will reach those pupils at a younger age. They will occupy a field that the institutions cannot touch and will prove of advantage to the institutions by bringing the pupils into the institutions at a much further state of advancement than if they had had no previous instruction at all.

21,470. I see that in your American schools the industrial department is introduced into most of them. I see from the evidence that out of the whole number only about 14 have no industrial departments; eight of these are day schools, so that only six have no industrial departments in connexion with them: I suppose that is so?—I believe so.

21,471. How late do the majority of your pupils remain in the institutions: how long do you keep them?—I do not think that I am competent to give an opinion as to that. But I may say in regard to the pursuits of the deaf and dumb in adult life, that it is very obvious that they do not follow the trades which they are taught in institutions. And yet, as a class, they are self-supporting. How did they acquire the trades by which they earn their livelihood and which were not taught them in school? In ordinary shops, by simple observation and experience. That is a very important point as to how far it is advantageous to teach specific trades in institutions: because the institution is necessarily limited to the choice of very few trades. A boy, whatever his abilities may be, is obliged to become a boot maker or a cabinet maker; whereas he might prefer something else. And all these deaf children go into competition with one another where they are not wanted. I think that the tendency should be to scatter the deaf and dumb in different employments rather than to bring them all into two or three trades; and that it would be better to teach the elements of trades in institutions rather than specific trades. I would commend to the attention of the Commission on that subject a paper by the Rev. Edward Everett Hale, of Boston, as to what occupations and trades should be taught to the orphans in our orphan asylums. It should have a practical bearing on the education of the deaf. It is reprinted in the American Annals of the Deaf. I can say, in one word, that Mr. Hale advocates giving the highest training.

21,472. Secondary training?—Yes, to orphans or public charities, because they will come into less competition with the outside world than if they are taught lower occupations, and the same thing applies to the deaf and dumb. Art training is of great importance with regard to them. I would recommend the Commission to look at that article, and I will furnish the reference to it. [See Annals for January 1887, Vol. XXXII., pp. 16 to 20. "What kind of Trades shall be taught?" By the Rev. Edward Everett Hale, D.D., of Boston, Mass.]

The witness withdrew.

Adjourned to Thursday next at 12 o'clock.

6, Old Palace Yard, S.W.

Thursday, 21st June, 1888.

PRESENT:

THE RIGHT HON. THE LORD EGERTON OF TATTON IN THE CHAIR.

ADMIRAL SIR E. SOTHEBY, K. C. B.
SIR TINDAL ROBERTSON, M.P.
B. ST. JOHN ACKERS, ESQ.
T. R. ARMITAGE, ESQ., M.D.
F. J. CAMPBELL, ESQ., LL.D.
WILLIAM WOODALL, ESQ., M.P.
THE REV. W. BLOMEFIELD SLEIGHT, M.A.
THE REV. CHARLES MANSFIELD OWEN, M.A.
L. VAN OVEN, ESQ.

CHARLES E. D. BLACK, ESQ., *Secretary.*

Mr. A. GRAHAM BELL recalled and further examined.

Mr. A. G. Bell.
21 June 1888.

21,473. (*Chairman.*) I believe you desire to amplify some of the answers which you gave in the course of your examination before the Commission last week?—Referring first of all to my answer to question 21,383 in regard to the classification of the deaf, where I propose to classify the deaf by two elements only, the age at which the deafness occured, and the degree of the defect, that classification is sufficient for all purposes of education, but it is insufficient for investigation relating to inheritance: and I would propose that you should again divide the deaf into two broad classes according as they have deaf relatives or not. That is for the purpose of studying the inheritance of deafness, and guiding our deaf pupils in their choice of partners in life. No one desires to bring misfortune upon his offspring, and if the deaf were so classified as to distinguish those who would be likely to transmit their defect, from those who would not, many of the more intelligent of our pupils might avoid forming unions that would increase the chances of their having deaf children. (*See* foot-note.)

CLASSIFICATION of the DEAF into FOUR GROUPS as a GUIDE to MARRIAGE.

Period of Life when the Deafness Occurred.	Character of the Deafness.	
	Sporadic Deafness.	Family Deafness.*
Before birth (congenital) -	2	4
After birth (non-congenital)	1	3

* For want of a better term I characterise non-sporadic deafness as "Family Deafness"—that is deafness that seems to run in families—deafness that affects more than one member of the family. The hereditary tendency is most marked in persons who belong to families containing more than one deaf-mute. The greater the number of deaf relatives a child has, the greater is the danger of his handing down his defect to his offspring.

Persons belonging to Class 1 do not manifest a tendency to transmit the defect to their children.

Persons belonging to Class 2 do manifest such a tendency, but not so strongly as persons belonging to Classes 3 and 4.

Persons belonging to Classes 3 and 4 (especially Class 4) manifest a very decided tendency to propagate the defect.

Persons belonging to Classes 2, 3, and 4 (and their hearing brothers and sisters) increase their liability to produce deaf offspring by marrying persons belonging to Classes 2, 3, and 4 (or their hearing brothers and sisters); and diminish it by marrying persons belonging to Class 1 (or their hearing brothers and sisters), or by marrying hearing persons who have no deaf relatives. Persons belonging to Classes 2, 3, and 4 increase their liability to produce deaf offspring by marrying blood relations—especially if these relatives are on the deaf side of the family.

21,474. That of course is merely a special view of it for a special purpose?—Yes. The other classification is sufficient for educational purposes.

21,475. Would you have any objection to our putting a copy of your diagram into our report?—I shall be only too delighted for the Committee to make any use they may desire of my material. Proceeding with what I was saying I would propose to divide the deaf into two great classes, the sporadic and the non-sporadic. That is better than the distinction of congenital and non-congenital. We cannot decide who were and who were not born deaf; it is very indefinite.

21,476. Not absolutely definitely?—No, it is not possible.

21,477. Do you mean to say that a surgeon cannot tell that?—I cannot presume to say that.

21,478. I want to know from what point of view it is impossible: do you mean that it is impossible to do so with any degree of certainty, or that it is impossible from a medical point of view, by a medical man?—Medical men would be better able to answer that question than I am. But the difficulty here is that we cannot test the hearing of an infant; we cannot ascertain that a child is deaf for a long time after its birth, therefore in studying the inheritance of deafness, the proper classification would be that of sporadic and non-sporadic. As a general rule sporadic cases do not tend to have the deafness inherited; that is to say, cases in which a single member of the family is deaf, whether reported congenitally deaf or not, have a much less tendency to transmit the defect than cases where three or four members of a family are deaf and dumb, even where the latter were not born deaf.

21,479. There is another question bearing upon that point which I should like to ask you, and which is alluded to in your paper in "Science," that is to say with regard to a large number of deaf mutes who have been classed as idiots; and you say that that fact rather disturbs some of the returns; does the fact of their being classified as idiots, instead of being classified as deaf mutes, to any extent disturb the classification?—I think not to any great extent; but that subject has been very fully investigated by the officers of the census. At the same time I think that a large number of deaf mutes are returned as idiotic who are not idiotic. On the other hand, it is probable that many idiots are reported as deaf who are not deaf. The number of doubly afflicted persons may therefore be decidedly less than it appears in the census. We cannot safely assume that the returns of any isolated fact are complete.

21,480. That leads me to ask the question whether there are not many children who are simply deaf sent to idiot schools?—No doubt.

21,481. Are there not more than several?—I am inclined to think so.

21,482. And then again, on the other hand, idiotic children are sometimes sent to deaf and dumb institutions?—Yes, but they are generally rejected. The difficulty of ascertaining the correctness of the returns relating to the idiotic deaf and dumb is the difficulty of ascertaining whether the observers are competent or not to decide upon the mental condition of a deaf and dumb child. There is very considerable doubt as to the number; but the number is so enormous, as compared with the whole of the deaf and dumb population, as to show that the feeble-minded must be very much more common among the deaf and dumb than among the hearing.

21,483. You spoke of the correlation between the deaf mutes, the blind, and the idiotic; and you think that those defects may possibly all arise from a common cause?—That is my feeling. I feel that by a study of the causes of these forms of defects we shall find some common cause involving the production of congenital deafness. Then there is one further point which I wish to refer to in my answer to question 21,402, which is a question I rather avoided answering. It has reference to the schools where auricular instruction is practised as a separate department. I am asked whether they are leading schools in America, and I say that I do not like to discriminate between one institution and another.

21,484. That was not my object in asking the question; I merely wanted to know whether they were schools of great calibre, size, and so forth?—I had a feeling that this answer of mine rather cast reflections upon these schools by implication, and as I think the members of this Commission are entitled to have my honest views upon all questions, I should like to speak for one moment of those four schools which adopt auricular instruction. (1.) The Nebraska Institution is one of our leading institutions, and that is where auricular instruction was first introduced as a distinct method.

21,485. That is the view I meant to convey in speaking of the leading schools, in the sense in which you are using the term now, that is to say, one of the principal schools?—The principal of that school is a man whose opinions are always treated with respect by all members of the profession. He is a man who states his views in moderate terms, and he is very careful and guarded in his utterances, so that whatever he says regarding auricular instruction you may believe.

21,486. Has he said anything in his pamphlet bearing upon this point?—Yes, all these four schools have made reports which are printed here. (2.) Miss McCowen, who was one of the teachers in the first auricular class in the Nebraska Institution, became dissatisfied with the results of the auricular system in a combined institution, and thought that the system would be more successful in an oral school. She therefore started in Chicago a voice and hearing school, a private school. She makes a report also upon auricular teaching. In regard to Miss McCowen, I may say that she is an enthusiast. Her heart is full to overflowing with her work, and this should be borne in mind in weighing accurately whatever she may have to say. Her report seems to be very carefully worded, and I am sure it may be thoroughly relied upon.

21,487. What is the name of the principal of the Nebraska Institution?—Mr. Gillespie. I may state that a committee was appointed by the last conference of articulation teachers to investigate the whole of the grounds of this method of teaching.* I was chairman of that committee, and upon it were also Professor Gordon, of the National College for Deaf-Mutes, and Mr. Clarke, of the New York Institution. (3.) Experiments were made in the New York Institution by Mr. Clarke and Mr. Currier, the special teacher of articulation in that institution, and those experiments resulted in the formation of an auricular department in the New York Institution. Mr. Currier sends a report. I do not know much about Mr. Currier: he seems to be a good teacher of articulation. I do not know anything about his public writings, but I think from personal conversation with him, that his statements may be fully relied upon. (4.) Then Mr. Clarke, who was on the committee, and who was one of the teachers of the New York Institution, has recently become the principal of the Arkansas Institution, and an auricular department has been conducted in that school, and Mr. Clarke sends us a report. Before Mr. Clarke went to the Arkansas Institution it was in an unsatisfactory condition. It has yet a reputation to make. Mr. Clarke has made an honourable record as a teacher, and from my personal knowledge of him I can fully commend his report to the Commission. Referring now to what appears at question 21,439, I am happy to be able to present the Commission with a very full classification of the causes of deafness. In fact I have here a short analysis of the chief points relating to the deaf and dumb, which, if the Commission desire it, I will incorporate in my evidence. This is an analysis of the tenth census of the United States relating to the deaf and dumb results, compiled from published statements of Rev. Fred. H. Wines, expert and special agent of the tenth census for the defective, dependent, and delinquent classes:—

DEAF and DUMB of the UNITED STATES (1880).

Where found.

At home or in private families	27,867
In schools (excluding day schools)	5,393
In almshouses	511
In benevolent institutions	79
In hospitals or asylums for the insane	24
In prisons	4
	33,878

Sexes.

Males	18,567
Females	15,311
	33,878

Ages.

Under 6 years of age	1,437
6 to 16 years of age	10,046
Over 16 and under 21	5,013
21 years of age and over	17,382
Total	33,878

Age when deafness occurred:—	
Born deaf	12,155
Under 5 years of age	7,289
5 to 9 years of age	2,235
10 to 14 years of age	694
15 years of age	100
Unknown	11,405
Total	33,878

*For Report of this Committee, written by Professor Gordon, see Annals, Vol. xxx, p. 59.

Mr. A. G. Bell.

21 June 1888.

Causes of deafness :—

Congenital - - - -	12,155
Adventitious - - - -	10,318
Not stated - - - -	11,405
Total -	33,878

Causes of adventitious deafness :—

Causes assigned, accepted and tabulated - - - - -	9,209
Causes assigned, rejected as too vague or improbable to be counted or classified - - - -	978
No cause assigned - - - -	131
Total	- 10,318

Causes of adventitious deafness assigned with more or less definitiveness and probability in the following cases :—

Accident - - - - -	593
Diseases of ear - - - - -	366
Other diseases - - - - -	8,250
Total -	9,209

21,488. What would be the other diseases that would generally be reckoned as causes?—I have here an analysis of all the causes of adventitious deafness that have been accepted in the United States, which have been accepted and tallied by the officers of the 1880 census. They are as follows :—

Meningitis - - - -	- 2,856
Scarlet fever - - - -	- 2,695
Malaria and typhoid fevers -	571
Measles - - - - -	418
Fevers (non-malarial) - -	381
Catarrh and catarrhal fevers -	324
Other inflammations of air-passages -	142
Falls - - - - -	323
Abscesses - - - - -	281
Whooping-cough - - - -	195
Nervous affections - - - -	170
Scrofula - - - - -	131
Quinine - - - - -	78
Blows and contusions - - - -	74
Inflammations of the ear - - - -	72
Diphtheria - - - - -	70
Hydrocephalus - - - - -	63
Teething - - - - -	54
Mumps - - - - -	51
Small-pox and variola - - - -	47
Erysipelas - - - - -	36
Fright - - - - -	32
Water in the ear - - - - -	25
Sunstroke - - - - -	21
Noises and concussions - - - -	21
Tumors - - - - -	11
Chicken-pox - - - - -	10
Struck by lightning - - - -	10
Foreign bodies in the ear - - -	9
Salt rheum - - - - -	3
Malformation of the ear - - - -	2
Syphilis - - - - -	2
Consumption - - - - -	1
Total	- 9,209

21,489. You spoke of making one of your divisions as between those who are deaf at certain ages as giving you a clue to those who would be able to use speech to begin with. As I gather all those after five would be those who have remains of speech to begin with?—Yes.

21,490. It is important to know the number of those who have remains of speech left, in order to know the number of those who would be suitable for oral schools; I suppose you may say that all those above three years of age would be suitable?—In my opinion those who become deaf in early childhood (two and less than five years) constitute a doubtful class. They have all spoken, but the habit of speech has not been fully formed, so that they readily forget how to articulate unless constantly encouraged to speak at home. Many of them easily regain the power of speech by instruction in school. Whether or not, however, they retain remnants of speech when admitted to school, their minds are in a much more mature condition than those who became deaf in infancy (under two years) and they should not therefore be classed with them. Those who become deaf in late childhood (five or more years of age) certainly retain some recollection of speech, even though they may have been neglected at home. Their speech is very readily preserved and improved, and they speedily acquire the power of speech-reading by eye.

21,491. What you have given us now will be sufficiently near for our purposes; you have got those at five years old?—Yes.

21,492. You have already told us that it is difficult to say whether they are actually congenitally deaf, or whether they have become deaf before they speak?—You have simply to accept the returns. It may be that a large number of those who became deaf in infancy were congenitally deaf; but we can not ascertain it certainly. I think that members of the Commission may rely upon this analysis of causes of adventitious deafness, these causes having been analysed by experts. As a general rule the causes assigned cannot be relied upon in all our institution reports. The causes are very vague and improbable in a large proportion of cases, and as you see even in the census returns, there are a very large number, nearly a thousand, rejected as improbable. The others were submitted to competent medical inspection and classified in this way. I have here another table which I have prepared, and which I think the Commission might like to have. It is a table of comparison showing the growth of American schools for the deaf from 1857 to 1887—statistics compiled from the American Annals of the Deaf, and it is as follows :—

Date.	Total Number of Schools.	Total number of Pupils.	Number of Pupils taught Articulation.	Total Number of Teachers.	Number of Deaf Teachers.	Number of Articulation Teachers.
1857	20	1,721	—	95	—	—
1863	22	2,012	—	—	—	—
1866	24	2,469	—	119	—	—
1867	24	2,576	—	120	—	—
1868	27	2,898	—	170	71	—
1869	30	3,246	—	187	77	—
1870	34	3,784	—	222	94	—
1871	38	4,068	—	260	110	—
1872	36	4,253	—	271	107	—
1873	38	4,252	—	274	104	—
1874	44	4,892	—	290	98	—
1875	48	5,309	—	321	111	—
1876	49	5,010	—	304	104	—
1877	49	5,711	—	356	111	—
1878	49	6,166	—	375	126	—
1879	51	6,431	—	388	113	—
1880	55	6,798	—	425	132	—
1881	55	7,019	—	444	147	—
1882	55	7,155	—	481	154	—
1883	58	7,169	—	497	151	—
1884	61	7,485	2,041	508	155	—
1885	64	7,801	2,618	540	156	—
1886	66	8,050	2,484	566	158	134
1887	69	7,978	2,556	577	155	171

21,493. Are you at all aware how far the tables in the American Annals of the Deaf and Dumb in deaf and dumb institutions throughout the world are accurate; have you ever made it your business to test in any way the accuracy of those tables?—Yes, they are considered by the profession to be thoroughly reliable for America. The American Annals of the Deaf is the official organ of communication, and is supported by the institutions. Its information is collected every year by a circular letter of inquiry addressed to the institutions, and the institutions recognise the importance of correct statements; and I think that these statistics may be considered as being thoroughly reliable for America.

21,494. I see that the number of articulation teachers increase in a much larger ratio than the number of sign teachers; do you draw any deductions from that; is there any proportionate increase in the number of articulation pupils, or has it been found necessary to have a larger number of teachers so as to have smaller classes?—I have not analysed these returns, but I think it is undoubtedly the case that articulation teachers have a smaller number of pupils.

21,495. There is a proportionately larger increase in the number of articulation teachers as compared with the number of articulation pupils. I want to know whether it was for the causes that I asked you about you do not draw any deduction from that?—No; I do not draw any deduction, because the number of articulation teachers has only been noted in the Annals for two years past. Of course, articulation teachers were employed before, but we do not know their number. We cannot safely generalise from only two observations. The institutions have devoted a great deal more attention to speech recently, but where you find one articulation teacher for 60 or more pupils, the articulation cannot be very perfect. In such cases the pupils come to the articulation teacher for only a short period of time every day.

21,496. (*Dr. Campbell.*) As a rule, how many do they have at once?—In the oral schools I think the number ten is supposed to be about the limit that can be satisfactorily handled. I should like here to refer to my answer 21,380 in regard to the growth of articulation teaching in the United States. I find that the totals from which I calculated the percentages are the total number of pupils who were present on the 1st of December in the year, instead of the total number present during the year, which is a larger number and affects the percentage. The number taught articulation is correct, but the effect of the error is to increase the percentage of those who are taught articulation, and to reduce the percentage of those who are not taught articulation.

21,497. (*Chairman.*) Have you any table to put in with regard to this point?—I have a table showing the growth of articulation teaching in the United States, which is as follows:—

Year.	Total.	Taught Articulation.	Not taught Articulation.	Percentage taught Articulation.	Percentage not taught.
1883*.	6,232	1,991	4,241	31·9	68·1
1884	7,482	2,041	5,441	27·3	72·7
1885	7,801	2,618	5,183	33·5	66·5
1886	8,050	2,484	5,566	30·8	69·2
1887	7,978	2,556	5,422	32·0	68·0
1888*	4,944	2,213	2,731	44·8	55·2

* The totals for 1883 and 1888 are not complete, but the number of cases is so large as probably to yield a correct percentage. It may be possible, however, that the institutions which failed to make returns were those which paid least attention to articulation, in which case the percentage taught articulation may be excessive.

I have corrected the totals. I give you now the total for 1888 from my returns. You will find the full returns for articulation teaching in the pamphlet that I have handed to you commencing on page 176, and going on to page 177; but as many of the returns were imperfect, it was impossible to arrive at a sum total. I have therefore added together only those that made returns from which we could have the total number of pupils, and the total number taught articulation. The total number of pupils that I have included in my table is 4,944, and of these 2,213 were taught speech. I have here the percentage; it is over 44.

21,498. (*Dr. Campbell.*) They are taught speech; but not the pure oral system?—It includes all who are represented as having been taught articulation. I have not been able, on account of the labour involved in analysing the returns, to find out any further detail than that it is 44·8 per cent. The percentages returned for 1883 and 1888 are very much larger than they are in the intervening period. These two periods were ascertained by circular letters of inquiry from private parties. The 1883 percentage was deduced from the replies to a circular letter from the principal of the Clarke Institution. My 1888 percentage was deduced from the answers to my circular letter of inquiry, the intervening numbers come from the totals shown in the Annals.

21,499. (*Mr. St. John Ackers.*) Does not that show that the returns in the Annals are under the mark?—Or that the others are over the mark.

Mr. A. G. Bell.

21 June 1888.

21,500. Which is it, in your opinion?—I am inclined to think that if any are incorrect the others are over the mark.

21,501. (*Mr. Woodall.*) Can you express an opinion as to whether at any time there has been a sudden growth in the matter of oral teaching, and at another time a diminution; have there been anything like waves of popularity up and down?—It may be possible. My opinion is that the increase in oral teaching in our sign institutions (the combined institutions) has been due very largely to outward pressure, to the pressure of public opinion applied from without, and there have been periods when there has been a greater amount of popular attention directed to the subject of oral teaching than at others; and it may possibly be that the number has fluctuated in the way shown.

21,502. (*Chairman.*) With regard to the results of intermarriage with the deaf, I gather from these returns which you have handed to us, that there is a considerable variety of opinion as to the results of such marriages, and in the case of some of the scientific witnesses while admitting the perfect possibility of such a result, do they not contend that it would be only after a succession of marriages of that character through a great number of generations, and under circumstances which would hardly be likely to recur in every generation?—I want you to say with regard to those points how far you agree and how far you disagree with the views expressed in some of these answers not as to the possibility, but as to the practical probability of such a thing occurring; because that is what as practical men we have to see, whether it is practically likely to happen, not so much whether it is theoretically possible. I am with you on that point, but I want rather to test your view as to the practical probability of it?—Upon this question of the intermarriages of the deaf, and the production of deaf offspring, I would like to deal with facts and not with opinions. I have in this little pamphlet presented to the attention of the Commission the evidence of scientific experts on the subject of heredity for you to ascertain the conditions that will certainly result in the production of a deaf race if they are carried out; and then I want to direct your attention to the facts to ascertain whether they are carried out or not. There are certain conditions which all these scientific experts unite in declaring will certainly establish a deaf race,—it being only a question of time.

21,503. But time is an important element?—Yes, time is an important element. It requires a number of generations. The conditions are these: that large numbers of the congenitally deaf shall marry one another, and that their congenitally deaf children, if they have any, shall again marry congenitally deaf; and that their congenitally deaf children, if they have any, shall again marry congenitally deaf and so on: that that alone will result in an increasing proportion of deaf offspring in each succeeding generation, and ultimately after a certain length of time, which we cannot calculate at the present time, a true breed or race will be formed. It is a very important question to find out whether that condition is being fulfilled and it is being fulfilled.

21,504. But does not that suppose that in each generation in order to come to an absolute variety of the human race the deaf mutes must intermarry?—Yes, or marry hearing persons belonging to families in which deafness is hereditary.

21,505. Because directly the line is broken you start afresh again, and the chances are by so much more diminished of the eventual creation of a deaf variety of the human race; you admit that I suppose?—Yes, no doubt the chances are diminished, but you do not have to start entirely afresh again. You have simply diminished the hereditary tendency which may still exist in a much stronger degree than in normal families.

Mr. A. G. Bell.

21 June 1888.

21,506. Is not that a disturbing element in the calculation. The chances are of their marrying a person who is not deaf and dumb?—Yes, if that element entered largely into the calculation. But I would like to call your attention to the facts.

21,507. What we want to know is what has happened: to what extent that constant intermarriage from one generation to another of the deaf and dumb has occurred and how far the results have issued from those marriages?—The percentage of the deaf and dumb who marry hearing persons is entirely insignificant now; they nearly all marry deaf mutes.

21,508. Is that so?—It is so. I deal with facts and not with theory. I have taken a great deal of trouble to investigate the subject, and if you will allow me I will bring forward my facts. That is the point. The deaf children of deaf mutes are not marrying hearing persons, they are marrying deaf mutes.

21,509. Shall we be able to understand this part of your evidence without tables?—Entirely, and it will not take up much of your time.

21,510. We want the conclusions founded upon facts?—I want to give you facts exclusively, and nothing else. In my memoir on page 16 I gave an analysis in Table XX. of 1,089 deaf mutes who have married. These deaf mutes are taken from the New England States, from New York State, from Ohio State, from Indiana State, and from Illinois State. Of these 1,089 deaf mutes, 856, or 78·6 per cent., were recorded to have married deaf mutes, and 233, or 21·4 per cent., married hearing persons. Then in Table XXI. I range them according to the period of birth. Of those who were born before 1810, 129 are recorded to have married. Of these 72 married deaf mutes, that is 55·8 per cent. Of those born between 1810 and 1839, 80·7 per cent. married deaf mutes. Of those born between 1840 and 1859, 84·1 per cent. married deaf mutes. Of those born after 1860 (and that does not bring it down to very recent times), 91·7 per cent. married deaf mutes. In my memoir I queried that percentage because it was based upon only 12 cases. But now let us examine the volume of evidence from America of the Illinois Institution, which gives us a larger number of cases of intermarriages of the deaf. The paragraph that I refer to is on page 57, and it is in these words: "Of the deaf mutes who have been connected with "the institution as pupils and have left it, 272 have "married deaf mutes, and 21 have married hearing "persons." That is about 93 per cent. married deaf mutes.

21,511. (*Chairman.*) Further down I see it says: "It is interesting to know that among all these only "16 have deaf mute children"?—I should like you to calculate the percentage. The absolute number is not so important as the relative number. Supposing that you take an equal number of marriages of hearing persons, how many deaf children should there be? There should not be one.

21,512. (*Dr. Campbell.*) Does the percentage which you have just given, 93 per cent. or whatever it is, mean so many persons, or many marriages; is it man and wife inclusive?—It is the percentage of the pupils who have married, that is to say, of all the pupils who have married, about 93 per cent. married deaf mutes. If they married pupils in the same institution it would reduce the number of families; and if they married deaf mutes in other institutions the number of persons coincides with the number of families.

21,513. If they married each other there would only be about 136 marriages?—Yes; I cannot ascertain that there.

21,514. (*Mr. Van Oven.*) It is an important point, is it not?—Perhaps so. For, as I understand the report, there are 16 families in which there are deaf mute children. Now, if there are only 136 families, instead of 272, the proportionate number of deaf children will be still larger than at first sight appears.

21,515. (*Chairman.*) How many are married in the institution he does not say?—No.

21,516. (*Mr. Van Oven.*) One thing is very certain, that if 272 married deaf mutes, a large number must remain in the institution, because the institution is in the State; and they would not have married from other States?—They chiefly marry in the same institution.

21,517. Therefore that would be 136, and the 21 would be those who married outside entirely?—Yes; I have for more than a year past been gathering statistics relating to this subject; it is very difficult to obtain them; I have found one means of doing so which I should very much like to bring to your attention. The deaf mutes of America have newspapers of their own, gossipy papers, speaking of their marriages, their families, and their children. I have succeeded in making complete files of some of the earlier of these deaf-mute journals for preservation; I then took these deaf-mute journals and had copied out on cards, which I submit for the inspection of the Commission, all the records of marriages, giving the names of both parties who were married. Generally the journals did not state whether the deaf mutes were born deaf or not, but I have taken these cards and as far as I have been able I have hunted up the deaf mutes that have been married in the institution reports; and now I have a collection of marriages from which we can deduce a percentage.

21,518. (*Mr. Woodall.*) When you speak of the deaf mute journals, are they published for general circulation, or are they merely printed in the institutions?—Most of them are printed in the institutions with the object of giving the pupils practice in the art of printing; they are also circulated by the institution among the former pupils. I have brought with me, in order that you may see the nature of them, a journal published in the New York Institution, and this is a volume of it (*producing the same*); and I would direct your attention very specially to one feature which is a very important element in promoting clanship in the deaf and dumb; there is a column entitled The Itemizer. I will read the heading of this column and you will see its importance and significance. "Facts relating to deaf "mutes from all parts of the world, news from every "State in the Union. The idea is to gather into "this column items that relate to deaf mutes personally or to associations of deaf mutes or to institutions for the benefit of deaf mutes. We hope "our friends and readers will keep us supplied with "items for this column. Mark items to be sent "'The Itemizer.'" You can imagine the fascination which such papers as that have for deaf mutes; they can hunt up and find the movements of their deaf friends recorded; if a deaf mute cuts his finger it is here. These papers are very valuable from a genealogical point of view, and I have been making great efforts to preserve complete files.

21,519. There is a similar paper published at Philadelphia, is there not, called "The Silent World"?—Yes, there are quite a number of such papers.

21,520. (*Chairman.*) You think these papers are objectionable because they tend to bring the deaf and dumb more together and tend to their intermarriages?—Undoubtedly. The institutions should not publish papers of that kind. Of course you cannot prevent the deaf and dumb publishing independent papers.

21,521. (*Mr. Woodall.*) But would you not say that they served certain other very useful purposes? —Yes.

21,522. (*Chairman.*) There may be other reasons why the deaf and dumb should have their own journals?—Perhaps so. The object is a very worthy one, namely, the teaching of the art of printing, but I do not think the public money should be expended in promoting clanship among the deaf and dumb. Papers of that character should, I think, if printed at all, be printed at the expense of the adult deaf mutes themselves. The institutions should encourage their pupils to read ordinary newspapers, and if printing is taught by the publication of a periodical the aim should be, in my opinion, to give the pupils of the institution (not the adults) information, in simple language, of what is going on in the great world outside, the items of news that interest hearing persons. I have somewhere in my book a table giving the results of the examination of 757 marriages reported in deaf-mute newspapers, which I have been able to use for the purposes of statistics, and the percentage of those who marry deaf mutes which comes out of this examination is 95 per cent.: that is to say, 95 per cent. of those who have married have married deaf mutes,* so that it is absolutely certain—it is no question for argument or opinion—that of the deaf who have married there has been a constantly increasing number who marry deaf mutes, until now they nearly all marry deaf mutes, and of those who marry hearing persons, in the majority of cases the hearing persons are the brothers and sister of deaf mute friends. I beg to present the Commission with the facts referred to in Queries 21,510 to 21,522 arranged in tabular form.† (*See* "Statistics of Intermarriage.")

21,523. (*Mr. Woodall.*) May we not take it that the perfecting of education has made them far more independent of a hearing and speaking mate than was the case before. I take it that formerly where they were taught the means of communication by signs only it was a great advantage to a man or woman to have a hearing and speaking husband or wife to be a medium of communication with the outer world; but as we have perfected a system by which they can themselves directly communicate with the ordinary population, there is less necessity for them to have an interpreter associated with them. Is that at all likely do you think to be one of the influences at work that tend to their intermarrying?—It may be one of the influences at work; and it certainly is a curious fact that there are no intermarriages of deaf mutes on record in the United States before the establishment of institutions. There are very few cases of marriage of deaf mutes at all before the establishment of institutions and those were exclusively with hearing persons: I have examined a few of these early cases and there are indications that even in these cases there were difficulties in the way of permission being granted to marry. For instance, I find a delay of two years between the record of an intention to marry and the actual marriage (which seems to have been solemnised to legitimatize a birth).

Mr. A. G. Bell.

21 June 1888.

21,524. (*Chairman.*) Were there any State prohibitions or restrictions as to marriage?—No, not that I know of, and you will find in the appendix at the end of the small pamphlet a letter from the librarian of the Law Library of Congress which fully investigates the subject of the marriage laws in relation to the deaf and dumb from which it seems that there could not have been any restriction.

21,525. (*Mr. Woodall.*) Does it not follow that when these young people of both sexes are taught together in the same institution, as they commonly are, that in itself would naturally lead to amorous relationships, and ultimately to marriage?—Undoubtedly that is the prime cause of the whole thing, namely, segregation. Sign language is undoubtedly a most powerful element operating in adult life, but that again has been evolved from segregation.

21,526. (*Chairman.*) I do not quite see how the fact of institutions in themselves can be said to produce intermarriage of the deaf and dumb, if it is not so in Germany where they have a larger number of the deaf brought up in institutions, I believe, as far as we gather by the enquiries that we have made, certainly in large towns, and where they are all taught on the oral system. As the result of the enquiries which we have made in Germany, we have satisfied ourselves that there was no great intermarriage of the deaf and dumb?—The oral schools in America have been too recently established to enable us to get reliable and accurate returns; but still we find that the pupils of these schools do to a large extent marry deaf mutes, but the proportion who marry hearing persons seems to be much greater than in the case of sign-pupils. For instance, in the Clarke Institution there are 17 pupils married, of whom 12 have married deaf mutes educated in other schools, and five have married hearing persons. Then there is a very curious point which is worthy of investigation. When you look at the 12 who have married deaf mutes, 10 of them are girls; it is the sought that are married more than the seekers. I see also that in the Horace Mann School, which is an oral school (only it is a day school, and the teachers have no control over the pupils after the school hours), there are three cases of intermarriage of pupils.

21,527. But supposing that these institutions were day institutions, the pupils would be thrown together just as much as if they lived in the same house, or very nearly so, would they not?—Yes, while they were in school.

21,528. Would your objection be equally strong to large day institutions?—Equally, if the pupils were brought exclusively together. We want to mingle the deaf with hearing children in every possible way. We want to have the deaf mutes brought together in as small numbers as possible, and we want them to be in close proximity with hearing children in as large numbers as possible. I wish now to speak of the deaf offspring, that is to say, of the results of intermarriage, because that is a most important point; and I want you to examine this question not from the point of view which interests me so much, which is the scientific point of view, namely, the formation of a deaf variety of the human race, that is not the practical point for you; the practical point for you to

* For analysis, *see* answer to Query 21,408.

† STATISTICS OF INTERMARRIAGE.

1. Analysis of 1,089 cases of marriage of deaf-mutes from the following States:—Maine, New Hampshire, Vermont, Massachusetts, Rhode Island, Connecticut, New York, Ohio, Indiana, and Illinois. For sources of information *see* Memoir "Upon the Formation of a deaf variety of the Human Race," foot-note to Table XII. *See also* Tables XX. and XXI. In the following Table the married deaf-mutes are classified according to period of birth.

Period of Birth.	Total recorded to have Married.	Total recorded to have married Deaf-Mutes.	Per-centage.
Before 1810 -	129	72	55·8
1810 to 1839 -	715	577	80·7
1840 to 1859 -	233	196	84·1
1860 and after -	12	11	91·7

2. Analysis of 293 cases of marriage of pupils of the Illinois Institution. *See* "Facts and Opinions," page 57.

Total recorded to have married before 1888.	Total recorded to have married Deaf-Mutes.	Per-centage.
293	272	92·8

3. Analysis of 1,443 cases of marriage of deaf-mutes from all parts of the United States—collated from records in deaf-mute newspapers. 71 of these married hearing persons, and the remainder married among themselves, the whole constituting 757 families. For full analysis, *see* reply to Query 21,848.

Total Deaf-Mutes reported to have married.	Total recorded to have married Deaf-Mutes.	Per-centage.
1,443	1,372	95·08

Mr. A. G. Bell.

21 June 1888.

consider is how far you are increasing the burden on the people by the education of the deaf offspring of deaf people; and looking at it from a merely money point of view (which I hold to be a lower point of view than the scientific one which interests me) it is a very serious and important question. The most accurate statistics on the question are those that are given by the Rev. W. W. Turner, and published on page 20 of my memoir. The general result is simply this, that with one parent who is a congenital deaf mute one-tenth of the children are deaf, and with both parents congenital deaf mutes, about one-third are born deaf.

21,529. Out of a smaller number of families?—Yes, about one-third of the children are born deaf. Now, the only principal who has given me complete statistics of the marriages from his institution is the principal of the Georgia Institution; and I would recommend your attention specially to his table on pages 60 and 61 of the pamphlet, in which he finds that 16 marriages of congenital deaf mutes produced 59 children, 19 of whom, or 32½ per cent., were deaf mutes; that is nearly a third. While that percentage is important from a scientific point of view, you are more interested, of course, in the absolute numbers. I refer you to my memoir, pages 78, 79, 80, and 81, which contains a list of deaf mutes introduced to our institutions who have one or both parents deaf. These names were returned to me by the principals and superintendents of our institutions in reply to a circular letter of enquiry. There are 207 of them. It is only an imperfect list. If you turn to pages 28 and 29 and onwards of my memoir, where I allude to families of deaf mutes, you will see a number of large families of deaf mutes, and I find that these are not included in the table at the end. In my researches I have incidentally come across altogether 124 cases, which are not included in the table at the end.

21,530. Are you speaking of the table of the Brown family?—Yes; look at the Hoagland family on page 30 where there is a Hoagland with seven deaf and dumb children. On page 32 you have another case of Sayles Works, who married a female deaf mute who had six brothers and sisters deaf and dumb, and they have six children deaf and dumb. There again these children are not included in the table at the end. Adding all these we obtain a list of 331 deaf mutes who are children of deaf mutes, but that still is very incomplete. My conclusions have been criticised by the principals and superintendents, as you will observe, on account of the incompleteness of the returns. But will you consider for one moment what that incompleteness means? It means that the results are worse than those that I have given—that there are more deaf children of deaf-mutes than those I have specified. One month before I left America, a new method of ascertaining the number of deaf children occurred to me independent of the principals. I thought I would see what could be done by reference to the census returns. Suppose, for instance, we find a number of deaf-mutes of the same surname living in the same house. Now look at their ages: May you not then be able to find out whether they are the children of deaf mutes? I will show you the sort of information I get from the census return. Here is a case. Here is a family all of the surname of Runck, all living in the same house, here is Daniel, aged 40; Annie, aged 38; Elias, aged 17; Eddy, aged 12; and Mary, aged 3, all deaf mutes living in the same house with the same surname. Here is another case: a family of the name of Holman. There is Richard, aged 40; Ruth, aged 30; George, aged 4; and Levy, aged 2. Now in such cases it is surely reasonable to assume that we have deaf mute parents with deaf mute children. I have gone over the United States Return of the Deaf and Dumb, and picked out all such cases as that. I am astonished, I am alarmed at the number that I found. These are capable of complete verification, because in the population returns the relationships are given to the head of the family, so that all we have to do is to take the numbers and hunt them up in the population returns, and find out exactly the relationship of those deaf mutes to one another. Unfortunately I have not been able to verify the list here for the Commission, for this reason, that the manuscript returns of the population are now in the hands of the binder, and are not accessible; it would take some time to bind them, but in the autumn I hope to verify every one of these cases. I have put into the shape of a card catalogue all the cases which appear to me conclusively to be children of deaf mute parents. The indications are that we have at least 607 deaf mute children of deaf mutes in the United States living before 1880.

21,531. (*Mr. Woodall.*) One or both parents being deaf mutes?—Yes. As I say these are all capable of verification, and I shall make it my duty to verify them the moment I can get at the population returns. In the meantime in order that you may examine them and see whether my judgment is reliable or not, I have had a duplicate made of my card catalogue, which I present to the Commission (*handing in the same*). It contains the names of 607 deaf mutes who are believed to be the children of deaf mutes. In every case the authority is given. Where the authority is given as A. G. B.'s memoir, the result is reliable, because I have ascertained it directly from the superintendents and principals. Where the authority is given as the census it is a matter of judgment, and your judgment is of course as good as mine. I desire to say here that quite independently of the scientific aspect of the case I should like you to take and calculate upon the basis of the average *per capita* cost what it must cost the United States to educate those children, and then I would like you to see my analyses of these children according to their ages; and to see the rate at which they are increasing; it is something tremendous. If you will allow me I will just read the figures according to the ages of birth, so that you can see quite independently of the formation of a deaf variety of the human race that we are paying in dollars and cents an increasing and increasing amount for the education of such children. That alone makes it a very serious question for statesmen to examine. Here is the analysis by ages. I have four tables which I will submit to the Commission: but I will read these by ages as it shows the increase. Of these 607 cases, 3 were born in the decade 1800 to 1809 (I take each decade). In the next decade 3 were born; in the next decade 13; in the next decade 36; in the next decade 57; in the next decade 102; in the next decade 128; in the next decade 178; that is all that I have ascertained, making a total of 520. Of those not ascertained there were 87. Dividing these according to whether the deafness was congenital or not, the following are the figures. There are 239 with regard to whom we cannot determine whether the deafness was congenital or not. That leaves 368 cases which we can divide into congenital and adventitious. Of these 368 cases, 328, or 89·1 per cent., were born deaf, and only 40, or 10·9 per cent., were not born deaf; from which we may deduce that 89 per cent. of these 607 cases are congenital deaf mutes; and if you examine whether they constitute any considerable percentage of the whole congenitally deaf mute population, you will be startled by the result. If these figures are to be relied upon (and I ask the judgment of the Commission upon that point), *one deaf mute in every 34 among the congenital deaf mutes is the child of deaf mute persons.*

21,532. (*Mr. Woodall.*) Is that a larger proportion than you would have expected to find?—Yes. My figures have hitherto been based upon 207 cases, and all the scientific testimony that I have read from my book is based on only 207 cases. I knew that my returns were imperfect, but I had no conception of that number, which shows that the matter is one of very much greater immediate importance than I had any idea of, and I do not know what scientific gentlemen would say as to the length of time which would be required to form a deaf race with so many. The number materially alters the question.

Mr. A. G. Bell.

21 June 1888.

21,533. (*Chairman.*) I presume from some of the answers to the questions which you have received, that it does not always follow that the marriage of deaf mutes produces deaf mute children in the first generation; but it often skips a generation?—That is the popular idea; I do not know of any cases to justify it; I mean that I do not know of any considerable number of cases. It is a very common idea, but I have not found any proof of it.

21,534. Certainly some of the answers to the questions distinctly state the opposite view?—Yes, but if you examine the institution reports that contain deaf relatives, you will find that a remarkably small proportion of the children have grandparents who are deaf, or great uncles or aunts who are deaf, which would be the case if the peculiarity skipped a generation.

21,535. In the Halifax Institution, out of 30 marriages 20 have been to deaf mutes and 10 to hearing persons, and the principal says:—"So far there are "probably between 30 and 40 children in these "families, and only in one case do the offspring of "these unions share the infirmity of the parent: but "that case is sadly noteworthy, all the children, five "in number, being deaf mutes. In this instance, "however, the children were, so to speak, doubly "stamped, there being several deaf mutes in the "family on both sides, as well as deafness in one of "them three generations back." There is a case, certainly, in which all the children were deaf mutes in consequence of that double stamp; but on the other hand there were a greater number who were not so affected?—The majority of children of deaf mutes can hear, but the proportion of deaf offspring of deaf mutes is enormously greater than the proportion of deaf offspring in the community at large, and that is the point. Now these deaf children are going to have a larger proportion of deaf offspring than their parents had if they marry deaf mutes, and 95 per cent. of all those who marry are going to marry deaf mutes. That is again the point; it is the continuous selection from generation to generation.

21,536. Is it the fact that deaf mutes in the United States have less instruction than the ordinary children. It is stated, I see, in the pamphlet that the common law undertakes the education of all children from 6 to 21, but in the mute State schools the pupils formerly only got five years' education; is that so?—It is the case that they get a very much less number of years instruction than the hearing children; the reason I suppose is the expense that the State is put to to board them.

21,537. They are in boarding schools are they?—Yes; I believe it would be better for the State and more economical for the State, as well as better for the children, to let their parents board them wherever it is possible, and to lengthen their time of instruction.

21,538. (*Dr. Campbell.*) Is not that state of things partly brought about because they are often drafted off to practical employment; is it not the theory that as soon as they are prepared so that they can enter into ordinary society, it is better for them to do so. A great many people have a theory, have they not, that if these children are going into practical life in some employment, they ought not to remain in one of these boarding schools too long. Many of them have eight years have they not?—Yes; but hearing children have from the age of 6 to 21.

21,539. I know that, and I agree with you that it would be better if these children were partially prepared before they went there, so that they would not begin so early; but I think that most educators of the deaf and dumb would themselves hold that they should not stay too many years in a boarding school for the deaf and dumb, but that it is better for them to get out into the world; I should like to get your opinion upon this point; I think that previously to the time of education the religious opinion of the community had something to do with the prevention of marriages between the deaf and dumb in the same way which it had amongst the blind. But what I want to ask you is this; do you not believe that the great preponderance of this evil might be removed if the State would have entirely separate institutions for girls and boys; and that if one State could not afford to have more than one institution, different States should combine, so as to have separate institutions for boys and girls; that is my theory with respect to the blind, and I want to know whether you share the same opinion with respect to the deaf and dumb?—I do not think that that would make much difference, so long as the language that is used by deaf mutes is different from the language of the community.

21,540. Do you not think that where girls and boys are seeing each other every day, and come into contact through meeting in class and society, they form the very feeling which leads to after marriage with a great majority of them?—Undoubtedly the collection of the two sexes into one institution does of itself promote intimacies and affections among the pupils. But quite independently of that, the fact of the possession of a language different from that of the community would bring the deaf together in large cities, just as the English-speaking people come together in the cities of Europe, because they have a common language. So far as I can find historically (and I have examined the subject) the first case of intermarriage of deaf mutes seems to have been the marriage (in 1819) of Laurent Clerc, the teacher whom the elder Gallaudet brought from France to America; and as I look through the literature of the subject, I see evidences that the results of that marriage were watched with very great interest and eagerness by the deaf mutes of the country. There undoubtedly was a feeling before that time that it was wrong for a deaf mute to marry a deaf mute.

21,541. (*Chairman.*) They had a feeling that it aggravated the evil?—Yes, and some of the earlier teachers of the deaf and dumb had an idea that intermarriage would lead to a deaf mute race. I was not the first to start that idea. Dr. Turner, of Hartford, was the first who produced that theory: and it was founded upon facts within his knowledge. I have simply amplified his facts.

21,542. You stated that the results of that marriage was looked upon with great interest by all the deaf and dumb at the time: what was the result?—The children all heard.

21,543. If they had not heard, the old system would have prevailed?—That is my opinion.

21,544. (*Mr. Van Oven.*) Is there any record as to whether the husband and wife,—this lady who was imported from France, and the person whom she married,—were congenital deaf mutes or became deaf in after life?—In regard to the husband we do not know. He came from France and was supposed to be congenitally deaf, but we do not know it for certain. There is one thing which may indicate that he was not. It seems that his sign-name in Paris, translated, meant the false deaf mute; so it may be that he was not born deaf. His wife, who was one of the early pupils of the American Asylum, was not born deaf, but Laurent Clerc himself was thought to be congenitally deaf, and that was what gave special interest to the case.

21,545. (*Admiral Sir E. Sotheby.*) Do you know what is the result of their children marrying?—All their children were hearing and speaking children, and all the descendants can hear.

21,546. (*Mr. Van Oven.*) But there is no proof that either of them were congenitally deaf?—No. After that time the deaf and dumb commenced to intermarry.

21,547. (*Chairman.*) Assuming then that you have proved the case (which certainly is a very strong case from the statistics) that the present system is leading to a serious increase of deaf mutes in America which should be prevented, what is your remedy for it in the way of suggesting other methods of instruc-

Mr. A. G. Bell.

21 June 1888.

tion; would you formulate any distinct plan for avoiding that which would be applicable to this country as well as America. I want you to sum up generally what you said before into any plans which you have had before your mind?—I think that I can give the Commission some general principles which will be valuable in forming a conclusion. My plan for preventing the intermarriages of deaf mutes is to examine carefully the artificial causes, whatever they may be, which have led to intermarriage and to eliminate them from our methods. If I may sum it up in my own way I would say this: I want you carefully to formulate from the scientific testimony in this little pamphlet, the breeder's way to produce a deaf variety, and then to look at the methods which have been adopted by philanthropists, and to see whether you agree with me in the conclusion that these are the ways in which the breeder would go to work. How would the breeder go to work, supposing that he wanted to make a deaf race? The first thing that he would do would be to collect all the deaf mute children at as young an age as possible, take them away from their homes and hearing people, bring them all together and make them live together from early childhood up to adult life. Is not that just what we do?

21,548. (*Admiral Sir E. Sotheby.*) How long would you keep them there?—As long as possible if you want to make a deaf race. That makes them more likely to marry one another than to marry hearing people. That is just what philanthropists have done. But that is not enough. You have certainly promoted acquaintances among the deaf; you have certainly prevented them from making acquaintances among the hearing. But still you send them out into the world, equipped, it is supposed, to mingle with the world and to take their place in society; and inasmuch as there is only one deaf mute for 1,480 of the population, it would seem rather difficult to formulate a plan that would make a deaf mute in adult life go and marry only a deaf mute. But supposing that we were to get a very ingenious breeder, supposing that we were to find a man who could formulate a plan which should compel the deaf to marry the deaf, to choose the one out of the 1,480, what plan would he adopt? Now I conceive that about the only practicable plan, but it would be efficacious, would be this: *do not let your deaf mutes think in English language;* make them think in a different language from the language of the people, and then you have got the conditions. Now then, send them out into the world, and they not only know one another and do not know hearing persons, but they think in a language of their own distinct from the language of the people. That will compel them to keep together. And is not that what we do in America? These are the two chief elements that produce deaf children in America. First, segregation which itself evolved the sign language; and secondly, the sign language which prevents the acquisition of English as the vernacular which brings the deaf children together in adult life, and forces them to marry one another. The hopeful feature about the whole case is that these are artificial conditions. You want to eliminate these conditions. The first error made by philanthropists was to take the deaf from their homes and from hearing children. We want to reverse the whole policy of centralisation. We want to adopt the policy of decentralisation to the greatest possible practicable extent. We want to bring the deaf together in as small numbers as possible, and we want to separate the deaf from hearing children as little as possible. We want them to be among their friends and in their own homes; we want to strengthen, not to weaken, the ties that unite them to home. Institution life severs the home ties of the children.

21,549. (*Chairman.*) Do you think that the principals of these institutions, knowing these facts which you have brought before us, make any attempt to discourage or prevent the marriage of deaf and dumb; because given those facts a great deal might be done if they were brought together under those circumstances; is anything done by those who have control of them when young to instil into their minds the dangers and disadvantages which they are entailing upon their offspring and those to succeed them by intermarriage?—My best answer to that is to quote the words of the principal of the Illinois Institution, who is a representative man among our teachers. At page 53 of the pamphlet, Dr. P. G. Gillett says: "I do not discourage the in-"termarriage of the deaf as they are usually more "happily mated thus than where one of the parties "only is deaf. The deaf need the companionship of "married life more than those who hear, and it is a "gross wrong to discourage it."

21,550. It is not surprising when a man of so much influence as that in America advocates their intermarriage that his advice is followed by other teachers?—Certainly not.

21,551. (*Dr. Campbell.*) Is it not quite evident also that the majority of the principals of the deaf and dumb institutions throughout the States hold the same opinions?—I think so.

21,552. (*Chairman.*) Supposing that you had another system of teaching the deaf and dumb, as long as you have got a language which separates them from the rest of the world, even if they are brought up in their own homes, will not those who have been brought up under the separate system gravitate together when they are grown up, and again just at the time when marriage would take place be brought into contact with each other after they left their own homes?—Yes, if there is a separate language that result must follow.

21,553. So that it is not enough to do away with institutions?—No, but it is not practicable to do away with institutions.

21,554. But even if you could do away with institutions, that of itself would not be enough?—No; in fact the chief cause of the intermarriage I hold to be that special language, but then that language was evolved from segregation which was the first cause; it never would have been evolved but for that.

21,555. (*Mr. Woodall.*) Among the deaf mutes themselves is there not a preference for those who are similarly circumstanced, rather than for marriage with a hearing and speaking person?—That is the immediate cause of the marriages; but then they do not know other people; they have been brought up together and have had no chance of forming acquaintances among other people.

21,556. Do you think that there is any general prejudice on the part of those who possess their faculties to the disadvantage of those who are deprived of the one or the other?—When they have not the opportunity of seeing deaf children, there is a prejudice; but when they have the opportunity there is no prejudice at all.

21,557. You have had so happy an experience as we know that I hardly know in what way to put my question; but do you think that marriages generally between those who are so similarly circumstanced, and those who are differently placed in this respect, are happier in the one case than in the other?—The opinions of the principals seem to be that they are happier when both are deaf mutes. But I know of no data myself from which we can form conclusions.

21,558. (*Mr. St. John Ackers.*) Is it not a fact that a very fair number of hearing teachers in institutions in America have married deaf and dumb ex-pupils?—I am not prepared to generalise; but I know a good many who have done so.

21,559. (*Chairman.*) Following your remarks upon the questions which affect the increase of the deaf and dumb, will you now tell us what your views are with regard to the methods of instruction, first of all in relation to what we call the special language which we have been in the habit of calling the sign language, and next with regard to the teaching of language which is known in this country as the oral system; will you give us your views as to how far the education of the deaf and dumb is affected and govcerned by those two systems?—In trying to educate the deaf child the first thing that we have to decide is through the medium of what language shall we educate him? Now I think the important principle that should guide us should be that we must teach our child to think in the language of the people among whom he lives; that is to say, that whatever method of instruction we adopt in this country, English in some form should be the language of communication and thought. The moment you use a special language that is not the language of the people, it comes between the deaf child's mind and the English language which he then acquires as a foreign language, and then certainly in adult life he will seek those who use that special language. The whole question of the education of the deaf is the question of language reading.

21,560. How far is that special language necessary, or is it necessary at all?—That special language is not necessary at all; it is in the way because it interferes with the acquisition of the vernacular. For that purpose I should like to give you my views of the special language that we use in America, and which is known as the sign language. The same results I hold would follow if we used German or any language which is not the language of the people. I think that half the misunderstandings that arise between the teachers of the various systems of instruction arise from mutual misunderstandings of the meaning of the word "signs." There are signs and signs; and I think that it would be a matter of great importance to this Commission to classify the signs in order to have a proper and suitable classification by which we might see what class of signs are harmful and what class of signs are not. I would divide signs into four broad classes: (1) Signs of the emotions, facial expressions, and so forth; (2) Dramatic signs, signs used by orators and others to emphasize the meaning of their words; (3) Imitative signs, natural pantomime by which people imitate; and (4) Symbolic signs or conventional signs; these are generally imitative in their nature but are symbolical of something else.* As an illustration of what I mean by a conventional sign, if you attach the idea of "good" to holding up the thumb, that is conventional. Or again, suppose you adopt the sign for a cap string, drawing the thumb down the cheek, for a woman: that is a conventional sign. In America the sign for the cap string now means "female." It would be applied to an animal as well as to a human being. Or if you use a shirt front with the meaning, not of a shirt front, but "white," that is a symbolical sign. The first three classes constitute natural signs. That is—signs that are naturally used and naturally understood by all mankind. The use of a symbolical or conventional sign constitutes the basis of a real sign language. I may say in regard to that sign language that when I first became interested in the subject of the education of the deaf, I came to the conclusion that it was the duty of any man who desired to benefit the deaf to study all the methods of communication that were known. I, therefore, in 1872 or 1873 began to make a study of the sign language and took lessons in it for one year. I mingled with the adult deaf mutes of Boston to get familiarity with the language and I know the language as you know French or German, or Russian, or some language that you do not think in but translate. I may not care to use it, but I know enough about it to admire it and be fascinated by it as a scientific study, and as a philological study. To see the way in which this language has arisen by a process of evolution from natural pantomime has fascinated me; and in 1878 I brought forward the subject before the Philological Society of England in London, when I advocated the study of this language by men of science. I say this in order that you may know that I do not approach this language with the bias of an oral teacher. I admire it as much as any teacher of signs can do; I think it worthy of study, and worthy of preservation; and yet I think it a mistake to use it in the education of the deaf. Now, in order that you may get clearly the distinction between the third and fourth classification, natural pantomime and sign language (that is symbolical signs), I would draw your attention to an exactly similar parallel between pictures (which correspond to pantomime) and a picture language like the Egyptian hieroglyphics (which corresponds to the sign language). In the one case you have natural signs and symbolical signs just as in the other case you have natural pictures and symbolical pictures. I think the whole difficulty with our teachers, and probably with yours, in knowing what to do with signs arises from not clearly formulating the radical differences between these kinds of signs. There is no teacher who does not use signs of the nature of Class 1 and 2; they all use expressions of face and they all use dramatic gestures. There is no teacher that objects to Class 3 in moderation being used as pictures are used; there is no teacher that would not allow his children to illustrate the meaning of a sentence or story by acting it out. Natural pantomime is a great thing to interest a child in language, but it should be used as pictures are used, as mere illustrations. *The proper use of signs is to illustrate language, not to take its place.* It is the conventional language corresponding to hieroglyphics to which objection is made. It is an arbitrary language, a conventional language, a symbolical language, exactly analogous to the Egyptian hieroglyphics, and it takes the place in the mind of the deaf child that the English language should take. I think it important we should teach our children to think in the language of the people. Now how does that language appear? It appears under two forms, the spoken and the written form. Where the spoken and written forms coincide, as in Germany and Italy, there is really one language to be learnt, and I would advocate there as in all countries similarly circumstanced the pure oral method alone. But I do not think that that plan is quite suitable for all deaf children in our country because the spoken and written languages are different.

21,561. Why are the spoken and written languages different in England, and not in Germany and Italy?—I suppose we are more conservative, I do not know; but since the introduction of printing, the written form of the language has remained comparatively fixed, whereas the spoken form of the language has shifted, so that now the pronunciation and spelling do not coincide.

21,562. That renders it more difficult of course than Italian or German?—Yes, that renders the introduction of the oral system more difficult.

21,563. I did not know to what you were alluding, I quite understand it?—We want to teach our children the English language. Now how are we going to teach any children a language? I think there is only one royal road to the learning of a language, and that is to use it for the communication of thought without translating it into any other language. The moment you teach one language through another the pupil thinks in the one language and translates into the other. You must use the language without translation, and I hold that any language that is used in the presence of deaf children will be acquired by them by imitation if the language is clearly presented to their senses. And in regard to teaching language, if you have not had the evidence of one man, a fellow countryman of your own, I recommend you to bring him before this Commission; a Scotchman (a good old Scotchman) a Scotch tutor in Oxford, who wrote upon the education of the deaf and dumb an admirable treatise, and who died and was buried and was forgotten. A hundred and fifty years afterwards his remains were discovered by Dugald Stewart on the

* CLASSIFICATION OF SIGNS.

Signs:
- Natural signs
  - 1. Emotional signs.
  - 2. Dramatic signs.
  - 3. Imitative signs.
- Conventional signs
  - 4. Symbolic signs.

Mr. A. G. Bell.

21 June 1888.

dusty shelves of an old library, and the works of George Dalgarno were reprinted by the Maitland Club of Glasgow; and if this Commission has not looked at that little work of Dalgarno's entitled "Didascalocophus" you will find that is a work containing many of the ideas of the nineteenth century. This was a man of gigantic intellect in his day, and when you consider that this was written about the year 1680 before the deaf were educated at all, you will be surprised at the clear ideas that he has. If I have any ideas of value about language teaching I give the credit to Dalgarno. You will find a reprint of his work in the Annals for January 1857, Vol. IX, pp. 14–64.

21,564. At that time they were taught language and not signs, I suppose?—They were taught nothing; the deaf were not taught at all; there was nothing in the year 1680 for the education of the deaf. His ruling principle in the way of teaching a language is, use it, and use it, and use it; he says that it is the frequency with which words come that impresses them upon the memory so that the more frequently you can present words to the eyes of the deaf child the better; all that you have to do is to present words to the eyes of the deaf child as we present words to the ears of the hearing child.

21,565. Written words?—Yes; then the child will come to understand them, and afterwards will come to use them.

21,566. But then as you have to present it only to the eyes in the first instance, how do you first begin to teach language; would your system be to write down a word and then speak it orally?—My plan would be simply to write or spell to a deaf child what I would say to a hearing child. After a time he would come to understand it—then he would imitate it and use it.

21,567. In each case you would write down a word and then speak it orally or *vice versa*; which would you begin with?—It depends entirely upon the class of the deaf that I am dealing with. Take those who are born deaf, those who have no knowledge of language; I hold that the basis of their education should be written language, the written language of the people. The spoken language presented by word of mouth, what we term speech reading in America, reading from the mouth, every child who has a knowledge of language can acquire; but I think that with the congenitally deaf to commence their education by speech reading, to commence to have the child read words from the mouth, *before he knows the language*, interferes with his mental development, retards progress in the acquisition of language, and thus defeats its own end, and retards the acquisition of speech-reading itself. I will illustrate in a moment what I mean. When you come to look at the mouth of a person so as to read from the mouth, you find that the elementary signs or positions are not clearly differentiated to the eye.

21,568. In English it is so, certainly?—Yes. For instance, take the difference between P and B and M. Here the lips are closed and accordingly the differences must be interior. All those three letters involve the closing of the lips, and the differences, whatever they may be, are interior. Whatever differences of adjustment differentiate to the ear the three sounds P, B, and M, there is nothing that can be seen by the eye, because the lips are shut, so that to a deaf child the letters P, B, and M are alike. So with T, D, and N; so with K, G, and NG; so with F and V, and so on with S and Z. In fact when you come to consider the visibility of the elementary sounds of the language they are very ambiguous. Take the case of P, B, and M again. A child cannot tell whether you say P, B, or M, but what he can tell is this—that the sound you utter is one of those three letters; he can differentiate groups, but not individual letters. He can know that whenever he sees the lips shut, it must be one of those three letters, for there are no other elements in the English language that involve the closing of the lips. So again if he sees the under lip against the upper teeth he knows that it must be either F or V, but he cannot tell which; so that so far as the elementary positions are concerned all that a deaf child can do is to determine groups of sounds. It follows from that ambiguity to the eye when you deal with words that there are many words that have the same appearance to the eye. Take such a word as "man;" there are no less than 13 words that look just alike to the eye of a deaf child; so that if you were to say the word "man" to a deaf child, he could not tell from sight alone which one of those 13 words is the word you intend. They are all homophenous with one another. Let me take the case of the words which look like the word "man;" there are for instance, pat, bat, mat, pad, bad, mad, pan, ban, man, pant, panned, band, and manned; those are all alike to the eye of the deaf child. If you say the words singly he cannot tell one from the other. But supposing you put them into a sentence; supposing that the child knows that the word is one of the group that I have given and I say "I met a (?) in the street" it could not be pat or mat and it could not be bad or mad; it is *man*. Then, again, supposing that I say "I wiped my feet upon the (?);" it must be one of those words, and it can only be *mat*. *Context differentiates the ambiguous words one from the other.* It follows from this that those who have a sufficient knowledge of the English language to be able to judge by context become good speech readers, but those who have not do not, and speech reading alone will not give them the knowledge. Those who could speak before they became deaf have that knowledge naturally. The congenitally deaf must first be given it artificially. If you were to take a pair of scissors and cut a line of writing right in half, so that you could only see the upper half or the lower half, it is evident if you show it to a man who knows the language perfectly he can read. It is ambiguous, but the context tells the meaning. But if he does *not* know the language will such a presentation of it teach it to him? I think not. So I think that if we present the English language in its spoken form to the eyes of those deaf children who know the language, we get good speech reading; but if we present it to those who do not it will not teach the language, and we only retard mental development by presenting a language to them prematurely in an ambiguous form. In order to teach the language it should be presented in a clear and unambiguous form. Writing and a manual alphabet will do that. I do not think that there is any difference of opinion among practical teachers, either here or elsewhere, that in the case of children who have natural speech, and who therefore know the language, the pure oral system should certainly be adopted with them. But in regard to the congenitally deaf where they do not know language, there diversity of opinion occurs. I am inclined to think that those children should be taught the English language in a written form before being required to rely upon the mouth alone.

21,569. With signs?—All the natural signs you like.

21,570. Would you use the finger language then; where would that come in; that maintains the language, does it not?—That maintains the English language, and I see no objection to it from a mental point of view. The objection is that it interferes with speech reading; that is the true objection. But its use in the school-room, in the oral department, is a matter entirely within the control of the teacher. Do not mix the manual alphabet and speech reading together, for then one will interfere with the other. Writing also interferes with speech-reading, if it is used to explain ambiguities of speech. Would you therefore deny a child a knowledge of written language? Certainly not. But how does a manual alphabet differ from writing? It is simply another form of alphabet—it is not a language by itself, only another kind of character or letter that can be made when writing materials are not at hand—and that has the advantage of writing in being more expeditious. But when we come to consider the deaf, I think we have more to look at than speech reading. Take the case of a congenitally deaf child; there are three misfortunes that result from his deafness; it is quite a different case altogether from a child who speaks naturally. In the first place he knows no words, so that his thoughts are carried on without words; there is a mental condition that is extraordinary, an ignorance that we cannot realise. Secondly, resulting from that, he knows no speech; he does not know spoken words, because they are addressed to his ear. And thirdly, although he has perfect eyesight and the printed page appeals to him as it does to us, he derives no ideas from written language. So we have these three necessities which are very obvious in the case of congenitally deaf children: lack of speech, lack of knowledge of written language, and lack of mental development which comes from intercourse with other minds. Now the three broad varieties of methods of instruction, the oral, the manual, and the sign methods, aim for one of those three things, *but not for them all*. A sign language teacher says it is the mental development that is most important and we will reach the mind any way, no matter about language; so he develops the mind through that language which it is easiest for the deaf child to learn, irrespective of written language and irrespective of speech. The oral teacher says the child does not speak: let us remedy that; and it is speech that is made the one object, and written language is secondary, mental development is secondary, and everything must go through speech. The manual teacher, on the other hand, thinks that written language is the only thing of value and neglects speech. So that each method aims at one of these three defects instead of all of them. I think that undoubtedly there is a great deal of truth in all the points that are made by all the teachers of all the schools. I think that if we have the mental condition of the child alone in view without reference to language, no language will reach the mind like the language of signs; it is the quickest method of reaching the mind of a deaf child. If you want a child to learn written language there is no method like using written language and spelling it and writing it on the board and on paper, and spelling it with the fingers. Use the written language all the time. Then in the case of speech, there is nothing that will develop speech like using the mouth. But if you try to send a billiard ball in three different directions at the same time, the billiard ball takes a resultant path, and I believe that the broad-minded man who looks at the whole condition of the deaf will not aim at one of these things: he will not adopt that method which is best calculated to attain one of these results at the expense of the others; *he will take the resultant path*. My own ideas upon that subject as regards the congenitally deaf are these: that those signs which are natural are really, or should be really, common to all the languages that you teach a deaf child, whether speech or otherwise. It is only the fourth class of signs that is objectionable. While I admit that the use of a sign language might *start* the mind of a deaf child more quickly than the other methods—the mental improvement is not continued but retarded as time goes on; for the printed literature, through which alone much advancement can be gained, is in another language (the English language), and he cannot profit fully by this until he has *unlearned the language he first acquired*, so as to be able to think in English. The sign language is in the way of his learning the English language, so that though his initial velocity may be very great, he soon runs against an obstacle which checks his further advance. I believe that for the congenitally deaf written language should form the basis, because it is clearly differential to the eyes; it is perfectly distinct and perfectly clear, and I think that it should be supplemented by the use of the manual alphabet, for we want that method, whatever it is, that will give us the readiest and quickest means of bringing English words to the eyes of the deaf, and I know of no more expeditious means than a manual alphabet. Then I think that every deaf child should be taught to use his vocal organs. For those little deaf children who are taught by writing and the manual alphabet, I should advocate also the teaching of speech.

Mr. A. G. Bell.

21 June 1888.

21,571. Simultaneously, not as an accomplishment?—Not as an accomplishment, but simultaneously. I would have a deaf child speak in the schoolroom all the time, and have the teacher write or spell to him. Of course I speak still of the congenital deaf. Their difficulty is a one-sided difficulty; deafness interferes with their comprehension of language *addressed to them*. There is no defect of the vocal organs to prevent them from using speech in addressing their teacher.

21,572. What would you have the teacher do, write or use speech?—I would have him write or spell so as to present the language in a clear form, and when the child has arrived at familiarity with the English language then is the time when he may profit by speech reading. Then is the time, and not till then, that he is thoroughly competent to decide upon the ambiguities of speech. I think that the oral teachers retard the acquisition of speech reading by their congenitally deaf pupils by not relying more on written language. I advise that they should be taught both written language and speech, and that while the pupil should be encouraged to use speech all the time, the teacher should rely upon written language in the earlier stages, and that as they grow up in their knowledge of language speech reading should be substituted for writing and spelling.

21,573. That is, I suppose, what is meant by the combined system in some cases. You have told us that it is very difficult to know what the combined system is, that it may be one thing or it may be another. Is that the view that is taken in America with many who say that their schools are on the combined system?—I do not know. The greatest diversity of opinion prevails about the word "combined."

21,574. What are the institutions in the United States which adopt your method: are they institutions which describe themselves as combined schools?—There are not any. The teachers in America are all extremists; they are either pure oralists, or they are sign teachers, or manual teachers. The best results I have seen in the teaching of English to little children on a large scale have been in the Western New York Institution, where sign language is abolished, and all communication is carried on by the manual alphabet, but they neglect speech. In all the schools with which I am acquainted "speech" and "speech reading" go together. It is not fully recognised that they are two distinct arts, and that a pupil may succeed in one and fail in the other.

21,575. (*Mr Woodall.*) When you speak of the Western New York Institution, do you mean the one at Western, New York?—No, I mean the one at Rochester, New York. I think it important to make a very great distinction between articulation and speech reading. All the difficulties in the way of the application of the oral method, which all men must admit is the best if it is practicable, lie in speech reading.

21,576. You think then that everybody can learn to speak?—Everybody can learn to speak, and everybody who knows the English language can learn to understand it from the mouth. If we are to teach our children to speak we have, practically, in English-speaking countries to teach them *two languages*, or rather two dialects of the same language, for the spelling and the pronunciation are very different from one another. They must learn the written form. Then keep it separate by itself, like a distinct language. During one portion of the day have all communication by writing and a manual alphabet;

Mr. A. G. Bell.

21 June 1888.

at another portion have it all by speech and speech-reading (and if writing must be used to explain ambiguities let it be phonetical writing). In the earlier stages I would use writing and a manual alphabet almost exclusively; simply teaching articulation and speech-reading for an hour or so a day. The pupils will be able to pronounce words long before speech-reading can be relied upon as the means of communication. I would then in this stage have them use their speech (instead of writing and spelling) when they communicate with their teacher *all the time*, but have the teacher continue during the greater portion of the day to address them by means of writing and a manual alphabet, but for an hour or so a day let him use speech without the manual alphabet. As the pupils become familiar with English phrases many will be found whose education could be carried on in an oral department, exclusively by oral methods. Others will not be able to understand speech from the mouth readily and easily, while they may be able themselves to speak intelligibly. In such cases they should remain under manual instruction, but speak themselves in the school-room, oral instruction being given for a limited period each day.

21,577. Then you look upon lip-reading as a subsequent part of the instruction which ought not to be begun at first?—It should be begun from the very earliest stage, but should not be relied upon as the means of communication.

21,578. I suppose you admit that unless speech is taught when young, the results of speech to the deaf are never satisfactory?—Yes, but I do not wish to assert this too positively.

21,579. That is the evidence which we have had, and we have observed ourselves that a great deal of the voice depends upon practising speech early; is that your opinion?—Undoubtedly, but I must say one word as to the method of measuring the results of speech in oral schools. I think that the method which is adopted of ascertaining the relative value of speech and signs is entirely wrong. Let us now see of all the accomplishments, and all means of communication, that are taught to a deaf child, what are those means that are of use to the child in communicating with the hearing world. (1.) First of all look at a sign institution. They use the sign language. That language is not known by the hearing world; it is of no use to them in communication there. They use the manual alphabet; that is not known to the hearing world; that is of no use in communication. There is only one thing which they have that is of use in communicating, and that is writing. That is the only bond of union between a deaf child taught by the sign method and the hearing world. (2.) So if you look at the manual method in which the sign language is excluded, and writing and the manual alphabet is used, again we find only one means of communication, viz., writing. (3.) Now you come to the oral school, and here is the point which we do not realise as a general rule,—that they have writing too. The children are taught to read and write, and they have that means of communication with the hearing world, so that whatever articulation they have, let it be of the most abominable character possible, it is something in addition to that which they have by all the other methods. We are generally apt to gauge the value of the oral method by the perfection of the speech. That has nothing to do with it at all. Whatever speech a child has is something in addition to what a child has who has no speech; and the way in which you should compare the oral schools, the manual schools, and the sign schools is to take what they have in common and compare the results then; compare their knowledge of written language, and their use of it in oral schools, manual schools, and sign-language schools; and supposing that they simply are all equal, then the oral system is better. If they are not equal, then the defect should be remedied. The claim has been made, and I am inclined to think with some justice, that in some cases they are not equal. I am inclined to think that in some cases in oral schools the knowledge of language of the congenitally deaf is not equal to that of those who are taught in manual schools, certainly not in Mr. Westervelt's schools, but that can be remedied; there is no reason in the world why written language should not be used more freely. The manual system relies on writing and neglects speech. The oral schools rely upon speech and neglect writing. But there is the means of comparing them. If you are to value speech, how are you to value it? Not by its perfection, but by its intelligibility.

21,580. As a means of communication?—Yes, that is the value of speech. But if you value the oral *method* you have to base your value on the knowledge of written language possessed by the children. If their knowledge of written language is the same as the knowledge of written language possessed by those taught on other systems, then they have something in addition in whatever power of speech they have.

21,581. Do you think that that knowledge of speech, which is very often found to a limited degree in the deaf and dumb, is valued by them as a means of intercourse as much as it ought to be valued?—It is valued in the place where it should be valued; it is valued in the homes of the children. The teachers of the deaf do not value it; they think that because speech is imperfect or perhaps painful to the ear, it is of no use. There never was a greater mistake. All those who have had anything to do with the deaf, and who may have had deaf persons in their own family, know that an imperfect articulation may be very sweet to those who love the child; and the point of value is the intelligibility of the speech. If it is intelligible that is its value. Of course the greater perfection we can get the better. But do not discard articulation because it is difficult to get it in perfection.

21,582. But where articulation is only taught as an accomplishment, as it is in some schools, there appears to be, from what we have seen and heard, a great shyness on the part of children who are deaf and dumb in an institution to exercise that speech; there does not seem any great willingness on their part to exercise speech; that is so, is it not?—Undoubtedly; the conditions in institutions are unfavourable to the practice of speech. Indeed I have known speaking children who became deaf at 12 years of age, who have gone to a sign institution, and been placed under a deaf teacher, and have come out deaf mutes—those were children who had been in our ordinary public schools. That is to say, they were deaf mutes in this sense, that they did not use their speech, that they were shy in using it; they had the ability of course, but they come out deaf mutes, and were mingling with deaf mutes in adult life.

21,583. Therefore you think it very important that everybody should have an opportunity of being taught speech?—I think it is a crime not to try to teach the deaf to speak. In our institutions, as you will find from the statistics which I have presented to you, the majority of the children have no opportunity of acquiring the art of speech; they are not dropped from articulation classes. If you look at the statistics that are collected at the end of this little volume, "Facts and Opinions relating to the Deaf," you will find that the majority of the pupils have not been dropped from articulation classes; they have not had a course of training for a year or so in speech, and then been dropped on account of their inability to acquire it; they have never had the opportunity of learning, and I hope the moral sentiment of society in future will be such that it will be considered a crime to deprive a human being of the power of articulate speech by neglecting to instruct him in the use of his vocal organs. Therefore I have urged that in all the institutions of the country, whatever method of instruction is employed, articulation should be raised at least to the level of geography and history. It should be a study that should be taught as a matter of course to every deaf child, not only on account of the benefit that it is to his health and his lungs, but as a matter of duty and conscientiousness.

Mr. A. G. Bell.

21 June 1886.

21,584. In an institution where you have some who are congenitally deaf, and others who have the remains of speech, in the one case you say that the congenitally deaf must be taught by the finger alphabet in the first instance, and that those who have some remains of speech must be taught orally. Have you any strong views as to the necessity of keeping those two classes absolutely distinct in such an institution, and not allowed to communicate with one another?—I have no strong views as to the separation of those two classes out of school hours. I think that their knowledge of written English will be increased by communication with one another by the manual alphabet. I would not, however, have the manual alphabet used in the school-room in the oral department.

21,585. Passing them up from that department to the oral school, and making the oral school an upper school?—Yes, putting all those who have a knowledge of speech in the oral school to start with; and in the case of those who have no knowledge of speech, I would give it them; but speech reading should not be used as the sole means of communication until they are familiar with the English language. Just as fast as they become familiar with the idiomatic phrases of the language, then they have the faculty of reading from the mouth, and they can be graduated into the oral classes. One point with regard to speech reading is very important. When you come to realise that context is the key to speech reading, you can see a very curious result that ordinary speech at its ordinary rate of utterance is more clearly intelligible than slow and laboured articulation. I have studied this matter very closely, and have been informed by a lady, who relies exclusively upon speech-reading, that she understands strangers more readily when they do not know that she is deaf, because they speak naturally and at the ordinary rate; but the moment they are told that she cannot hear, they commence to mouthe and make exaggerated motions, and then she finds more difficulty in understanding them. You can easily see that if context is the key to speech reading, if you speak single words to a deaf child, word by word, he does not get enough to make the context. You want to present the whole sentence to a child. But you cannot do that with a congenitally deaf child, although you can with one who knows the language. So that I hold that relying upon speech reading in the earlier stages of the congenitally deaf defeats its own end. We do not get such good speech reading as we would if the children were taught familiarity with the English language first. As already stated the conditions in an institution are not favourable to articulation and speech reading. There are few people who can hear him talk, for his companions are all deaf, and if he is put under a deaf teacher his speech is of no use. I believe that in day schools, especially in little schools where children have frequent intercourse and association with hearing children, you will get one thing that is wanting in institution life, viz., a stimulus to the acquisition of speech. There are people all round the child who can hear, the people at home and at school, the people who go to the same building can hear, so that every word that a deaf child learns to speak is a bond of union between him and his hearing companions; every word that he learns to understand from the mouth is a bond of union between them and him; and as his education advances and he becomes more able to communicate by word of mouth or by writing with those who can hear, those bonds of union will become more and more numerous until ultimately he will be absorbed into the population; whereas, if we keep him away from hearing persons speech is of no use, the English language itself is of no use. Segregation and sign language tend to separate the deaf from the hearing world. They are not restored to society. You must have small day schools and plentiful instruction in articulation and speech reading, for that alone is the means by which children can come into communication when they are too young to communicate by writing. There is one point with regard to the general matter of instruction which I should like to mention here. It is very important that in examining methods of instruction you should ask the age at which the child became deaf. The cases that are shown in America as cases in which great results have been obtained with deaf mutes have very often been cases of children who became deaf after they had learned to speak. I have thought of one method by which we can gauge the general success of our American institutions. It is rather a curious method, and Dr. Gallaudet has promised me his assistance in applying it. We have in America a national college for the higher education of the deaf, which is open to all the deaf graduates of our institutions. These persons who apply for admittance are examined: there is a matriculation examination, when certain of them are thrown out and others continue in the college; and finally, they go through the whole curriculum of the institution and some graduate. Now we know what is the proportion of the congenitally deaf to the whole deaf mute population. It is more than one-half, but of the graduates of the National College only 10 per cent. were born deaf. That to my mind indicates that as regards the congenitally deaf who form the majority of our pupils the methods of education have not been so successful as to place them on a level intellectually and mentally with those who started with speech.

21,586. I want to know with regard to this college of Dr. E. M. Gallaudet what proportion of the students come from oral schools, because he stated to us that those who had been in the oral schools mixed freely with the others, and he thought there was no objection to that: but I do not think he told us what the proportion was; can you do so?—I am unable to say what is the proportion; but Dr. E. M. Gallaudet promised to give me every facility to examine it; and I think the statistics of the National College can be used to gauge the general success of the education all over the United States.

21,587. You say in your memoir that at Dr. E. M. Gallaudet's school and college, that is, the primary school and college, there is not one single pupil using articulation as a means of instruction?—No, not one. But you will observe in the evidence from the Kendall School, which you will find in this little volume, that speech is used as a means of instruction in that school, but not as the sole means of instruction.

21,588. (*Mr. Van Oven.*) Do you not think it is possible that the reason why the percentage of congenitally deaf mutes is comparatively speaking so small in their college for the higher education of the deaf may arise from the fact that their intelligence is not so good to begin with: that the same cause which made them be born deaf in all probability may have produced less brain power; do you think that you should put it entirely upon the training?—I do not know what the cause is; but it is simply suggestive to my mind as a means of testing the methods of education.

21,589. Let me suggest that to you, because your opinion is so valuable that I should like you to say whether it is a hard and fast opinion or not?—It is not a hard and fast opinion at all. I may say, however, that so far as my observation has gone, there are many bright and intelligent minds among the congenitally deaf, and some of the brightest of our pupils have themselves been children of deaf mutes.

21,590. (*Mr. St. John Ackers*) You are, I understand, here not specially deputed by any one school of any one system in America?—I come as the representative of no system; I express merely my own opinions and my own ideas. I have invited the principals and superintendents to express their ideas for themselves in the pamphlet that I have handed to the Commission ("Facts and Opinions relating to the Deaf").

21,591. Referring to Dr. E. M. Gallaudet's evidence before this Commission in answer to question 13,140, he there mentions a convention which was held, I think, in California; do you know of that?—Yes.

Mr. A. G. Bell.

21 June 1888.

21,592. He says there, in effect at any rate, that there was an entire concensus of opinion as to the best way of teaching in America, and he says, "I "speak of that as a matter of very great importance, "because it was really a burying of the hatchet." Are we to understand that in your opinion there is a general agreement in America between teachers as to the best method to be pursued, or do you consider there is still great diversity as to what should be the system?—I know that there is the very greatest diversity of opinion among teachers; but there is a burying of the hatchet. Our teachers meet together in friendly conventions, and we discuss all these disputed questions in a friendly spirit, each having respect for the opinions of others; so that in that sense there is a burying of the hatchet. We have in our country representatives of all the methods of instruction that are used elsewhere, but instead of their being the animosities that prevent progress there is free discussion in such conventions, as the convention which was held in California. I was not present at that convention and therefore I cannot speak as to its results.

21,593. Then when these words are used in the report of that convention: "The war between the "two prominent systems of instruction, the 'manual' and the 'oral,' which has been carried on so "vigourously for many years may said to be practically ended." That does not mean that persons have come to one mind in the matter?—By no means.

21,594. But simply that each is inclined to follow his own line?—I think it means that the acrimonious war is ended. There were very bitter feuds between the upholders of the different systems; those are dead. In that respect I think that Dr. Gallaudet is right in saying that the war is ended, though the diversities remain.

21,595. The diversities are in fact as strongly marked as ever?—Yes.

21,596. Now referring to the articulation tables at the end of your memoir, to which I have already partially referred, the statistics go there, do they not, to prove conclusively that a very large proportion of the non-congenitally deaf are still debarred from articulation?—Undoubtedly the majority of them.

21,597. It is not therefore confined to the congenitally deaf; but the majority even of the others are debarred from articulation under the present prevailing system in America?—I believe that is true.

21,598. You spoke on the last occasion when you were under examination of the proper classification in the census returns; do you not consider that it would be of very great importance if a similar classification could be obtained in the census returns of all States?—Undoubtedly.

21,599. And would you not consider further that there should be uniform statistics in each school and institution?—Undoubtedly so, and in that connexion I would refer the Commission to the action of the recent conference of principals that was held in Jackson, Mississippi, very shortly before I came from America, in which the forms for the collection of statistics that Dr. Gallaudet referred to were formally accepted by the principals of all the institutions so as to produce uniformity in the collection of statistics. You will find a description of these forms in the Annals for 1885, Vol. XXX., pp. 52-58.

21,600. Would it not enormously help to a right conclusion as to the causes of deafness, and therefore to a great extent as to their prevention, if these statistics were kept in an uniform way in each institution; not only in each country but in all countries?—Undoubtedly.

21,601. And those who like yourself have spent so very large an amount of time in research in this matter would welcome such a change as being extremely beneficial?—Undoubtedly.

21,602. Then, as I understand you, it is desirable to classify so as to thoroughly understand the causes of deafness and other particulars in the census return in each individual institution, and also to classify what is meant by the different terms used in deaf mute education?—I think it is necessary.

21,603. I want to go back to what seems to me, if I may say so, the most important part of your extremely important evidence; that is, with regard to deaf children being the offspring of deaf parents. Is it not a common error even amongst those who have most to do with the deaf and dumb that congenitally deaf persons marrying are not more or not much more likely to have deaf children than other persons?—That is a very common error.

21,604. And is not this on account of the number of such persons having hearing children?—Yes.

21,605. They conclude because a very much larger number of these children are hearing children than are deaf that really there is not a very much larger proportion?—That is the reason undoubtedly. Nearly all of the objections that have come to my theories are based upon the fact that the majority of the children of congenitally deaf mutes can hear.

21,606. If the average of the children of the congenitally deaf were taken, the total number of their children, hearing and deaf, and then the number of their deaf children, and compared with those born of hearing parents, the difference would be seen at once, would it not?—Undoubtedly.

21,607. Let us now turn for a moment to page 20 of your memoir, and I am now going for the sake of convenience to deal with round figures rather than in the actual figures which appear here; for instance instead of saying one in every 1,480 I should say one in every 1,500. I would ask you in the first instance how many children you reckon should be taken as the average number of every family; do you reckon three or five or what number?—I cannot venture to say.

21,608. It does not signify much; I will take three. For the sake of argument, allowing three children to every family and allowing (this is all for the sake of argument, please to understand) half the total number of deaf to have been born so, and also allowing for the sake of argument that as many deaf are born to hearing as to deaf and dumb parents (which of course you do not agree to), would you not expect to find one child who is deaf and dumb born to every 3,000 of the population?—Undoubtedly, speaking in round numbers.

21,609. Allowing one in every 1,500 to be deaf and dumb, and allowing one-half of those to be congenitally deaf and dumb, you must double the number of the population to get one congenital case, therefore it would be one in every 3,000?—Yes.

21,610. Now can you tell us what is the minimum number that you find as the average in your researches where one or both parents are deaf, taking 50 or 60 cases?—I cannot answer the question in that form.

21,611. Will you put it in your own way?—I can answer that by taking totals. Taking the whole deaf mute population at 34,000 in round numbers, if congenital deafness was no more common among their offspring than among the offspring of hearing persons, we should expect that one in 3,000 of the deaf mute population would himself be a congenitally deaf child of deaf mute parents. We can calculate that. Upon that basis we should, by dividing 34,000 by 3,000, arrive at the total number of congenitally deaf children in the country who should themselves be the children of deaf mute parents, say 12. There should not be more than 12 congenitally deaf mute children of deaf mute parents in the country, if the children of deaf mute parents were no more liable to congenital deafness than those of others. But we have here a list of 607 deaf mute children of deaf mutes, and of these 89 per cent., that is about 540, were born deaf. So that while I cannot answer the question in detail with families, we can form some general idea looking at the whole deaf population.

21,612. Is it not a common thing for those who hold (as I see that some of the heads and other teachers of institutions in America still hold) that there is not a greater number of deaf children the offspring of deaf parents to produce statistics to show that such is the case; and when those statistics are analysed, taking their own figures, you find that a very much larger proportion are really the children of congenitally deaf parents, or where one parent is congenitally deaf, than when that is not the case?—Yes; the very figures that are brought to prove the converse of the fact show that.

21,613. You have spoken of the cases of the deaf marrying together, and you have stated, I think, that the chief causes are, in the first place, the language not being the language of the country; and secondly, their being brought together in large numbers in institutions. You have stated that, when they go out from those institutions, they cannot mix with the ordinary world, and are therefore brought together again. May I ask whether there are not in America and elsewhere adult societies, philanthropic societies, missionary societies, and social societies which very much increase the congregating of large numbers together?—Undoubtedly so; not only do we have such societies in nearly all of our large cities, but the Church missionary system extends over the whole country, and there are itinerant missionaries who travel from city to city, and bring the deaf together.

21,614. Have you had much opportunity of talking with those missionaries, and with other officials of the adult deaf and dumb societies, as to what value they place upon articulation?—I have not had much opportunity of talking upon that subject with missionaries.

21,615. You cannot therefore tell us, from your own knowledge, what line they take with regard to this subject?—No.

21,616. Is it within your knowledge that they very frequently try, and succeed, to join with the totally deaf and dumb those who have been orally taught?—It is within my knowledge that efforts are made to bring into the societies the pupils of oral schools.

21,617. I will take, for instance, the case which I personally know of Boston, where you have a large day school and where there is every effort made to prevent the pupils being together except in schools, and where they are living in their own families. Is it not the case that when they leave school, and even sometimes in the evenings before they have left school, there is a great effort made, and a successful effort, to get them to join the deaf and dumb adult society?—Yes.

21,618. And that in your opinion conduces very considerably to an extra number of marriages of the congenitally deaf and dumb?—Yes.

21,619. And therefore they increase?—Yes.

21,620. At the majority of your institutions are the pupils of the different sexes mixed?—I think in the majority of them, so far as my observation goes, they have the different sexes in the same schools.

21,621. With regard to the adult deaf and dumb societies are the majority of their meetings, whether for social or religious purposes, confined as a rule to one sex at a time or do they mingle together in these evening meetings?—Both sexes mingle together.

21,622. As a rule they are both together at the same time?—Yes.

21,623. I see that the view you take that the intermarriage of these congenitally deaf mute persons dates very much from the system of sign teaching and institution life is not held, at any rate, by certain of the professors and teachers in America. I see that there is one person mentioned in this pamphlet, page 83 from the Cathedral School in Cincinnati, who argues in this way (and I do not know that I should take much notice of this if it had not been that unfortunately we get the same argument from other places): "The world is six thousand years old, "and during all these years deaf mutes have been "born; they have intermarried and died, leaving "children after children, yet nowhere on the face of "the earth is a hereditary race of deaf mutes found." I take it that you would at once say that this is incorrect as to their having intermarried, in the sense in which you now speak of intermarriage, with regard to deaf mutes in America; inasmuch as we know perfectly well that the institution life and system did not exist, say, 150 years ago from the present time?—Yes.

21,624. May I ask you whether in your large experience in America of these different gatherings, and outside, you do not find ideas very similar practically to this which is here stated. Perhaps this is an extreme case; but is it not the case that there is a very large amount of ignorance upon this matter which, if once dispelled, and the real facts thoroughly grasped, would, in your belief, lead to a very different state of things with regard to the way in which the present institution life and sign system is regarded in America?—Undoubtedly so. Light and information are what is wanted.

21,625. You have referred to the scientific evidence which is given in your pamphlet from persons with apparently a very large knowledge on the subject: and I see that on page 95 Mr. Brewer says:—"It is conceded that the same biological laws apply "to man and brute alike. I am not aware that any "eminent biologist, naturalist, or breeder denies "this." I think we shall all agree to that. Then he goes on to say that a different race, if we may say so, is generally considered to have been thoroughly produced after four or five generations; he says: "Five generations of sires and four of dams is the "common rule." I would ask you whether, in examining these matters with regard to the intermarriages of the congenitally deaf, you would not be of opinion that in all probability it would require considerably longer than is here stated, for this reason, from my own experience at any rate, and I have had considerable experience in these matters of breeding, as our chairman knows, of certain classes of animals, it is only usual to attempt to classify them as this gentleman speaks of herd-books after several generations of similar breeding have taken place; and that when he speaks of four or five generations going back, those four or five generations really mean recorded cases after long years of similar conditions existing, not perhaps so strict; and therefore perhaps it might take a considerably longer time than the four or five generations before you could get what you might call a complete variety of the human race; do you follow me?—I do not know. I would rather in such questions trust to the scientific man; and here Prof. Brewer says in answer to that very point. He says: "Five generations of sires and four of "dams is the common rule," and here is the answer to your question: "And I imagine that the chances "of a child being born with hearing would be small "if all its ancestors for a like number of generations "had been congenitally deaf."

21,626. You think that even with four or five generations the chances would be small?—I think so.

21,627. (*Chairman.*) It is not absolutely so; but the chances would be small?—Yes. Of course I know nothing of that question myself. I have to rely upon the statements of such men as Professor Brewer.

21,628. I pass from that, which seems to me the most important of all the subjects which you have brought forward, and touch very shortly upon one or two others. I do not think that this examination would be complete without one word as to one of your family discoveries, if I may use such an expression—that of visible speech. It is a fact, is it not, that you and your father and grandfather have all worked out one after another and perfected that universal alphabet, or whatever you may prefer to call it, which is generally known by the name of visible speech?—My grandfather, my father, and myself have devoted our attention almost exclusively to the study of the mechanism of speech, articulation; and to my father is due the invention of the system of symbols known as visible speech.

21,629. That system has been in use, has it not, in the oral institutions, or some of them, in America for some years?—Yes.

21,630. Have you a chart of that system just to show to the Commission?—I have (*producing the same*).

Mr. A. G. Bell.

21 June 1888.

21,631. By that system you are able, are you not, to give to a person who understands it, although perfectly deaf, a means by which he can reproduce certain sounds which he has never heard before?—Yes.

21,632. It is a fact, is it not, that amongst other instances of this a very remarkable one took place (I remember one that took place when I was in America, but there are, of course, hundreds of others) whereby you are able to get a deaf mute to pronounce a particular word of the Hottentot language (the Hottentot click, or whatever it may be termed) which the hearing persons in the room were not able at the first attempt to produce as well?—Yes.

21,633. I should like to ask you this as a practical point, now how far, in your opinion (and it is a most valuable one), this system should have a place in the education of the deaf?—I have the feeling that the adoption of some such system as this is essential and necessary in the instruction of the congenitally deaf in obtaining perfect speech. The result will necessarily, I think, be imperfect without some such system as this.

21,634. May I ask whether in working out this system of visible speech, and in working also for the mechanism of speech, you have not been led to other important discoveries?—Undoubtedly so.

21,635. Was it not through these investigations that you were led to the great and world-wide discovery of the telephone?—Undoubtedly so; that originated from investigations relating to the teaching of articulation to the deaf.

21,636. With regard to the American institutions, do they take all the deaf that are offered to them, or is there any selection?—I have never known of there being selection. The charge has been made that certain pupils are selected, but I have not known personally of any such cases.

21,637. I judge from the evidence which you have already given that no institution in America will take weak-minded pupils, that is to say, below a certain point, never mind whether on the sign or speech system?—I referred there simply to children who were simply weak-minded and not deaf. As a matter of fact, some of our institutions do receive deaf mutes who are weak-minded. As a general rule the institutions decline to receive pupils who are weak-minded.

21,638. And that would apply to all the institutions upon whatever system?—Yes.

21,639. (*Dr. Campbell.*) Are all State institutions either for the deaf and dumb or for the blind compelled to receive all pupils unless they can be proved to be feeble-minded within certain limits, provided that their characters are satisfactory?—I do not know exactly what the legislation is upon that point.

The witness withdrew.

Adjourned to to-morrow at 11 o'clock.

SIXTY-SEVENTH DAY.

6, Old Palace Yard, S.W.

Friday, 22d June, 1888.

PRESENT:

THE RIGHT HON. THE LORD EGERTON OF TATTON IN THE CHAIR.

SIR TINDAL ROBERTSON, M.P.
B. ST. JOHN ACKERS, ESQ.
EDMUND C. JOHNSON, ESQ.
WILLIAM WOODALL, ESQ., M.P.
THE REV. W. BLOMEFIELD SLEIGHT, M.A.
THE REV. CHARLES MANSFIELD OWEN, M.A.
L. VAN OVEN, ESQ.

CHARLES E. D. BLACK, ESQ.,
Secretary.

Mr. ALEXANDER GRAHAM BELL recalled and further examined.

21,640. (*Mr. Van Oven.*) From the evidence which you have already given us it seems to be your opinion that frequent intermarriage between the deaf, especially between those who are congenitally deaf, or those who are deaf from inheritance, is likely to produce in time a race of deaf people?—That is my opinion.

21,641. You consider, therefore, that it is exceedingly important that, so far as possible, the deaf should be induced to mix with the hearing world?—Decidedly.

21,642. So as to prevent the constant association one with another?—Yes.

21,643. Therefore, without going any further into that question, you consider that on that point, however desirable they may be upon other points, all these societies which exist for the benefit of the adult deaf are to a certain extent harmful, because they collect the adult deaf together and cause them to associate with each other, and consequently in all probability would lead to intermarriage?—To a certain extent, certainly, just as I consider institutions harmful, but I do not think that we can do away with these adult associations entirely, for there will always remain a certain number of pupils who are not fitted to mingle with the world, and I do not know how else we are going to reach them and benefit them without some such association, so that, while theoretically I do consider them harmful, I think that in certain respects they are necessary, but we want to give great thought and great care to the subject of the association of the adult deaf.

21,644. I do not propose for a moment to consider or to ask you or anybody to consider the idea of suppressing such societies altogether, but I want to elicit from you your opinion, which I gather to be this, that so far as possible we should place the deaf in such a position as to render the great portion of them independent of such societies, and to a great extent not desirous of joining such societies; I conclude that that can only be done by their general admixture in the world, and that for that purpose the use of speech and lip-reading is of very great importance beyond the importance which of course attaches to the fact of the deaf-mute being able to mix with all people who are not familiar with any special mode of communication?—I agree with you entirely in your statement there.

21,645. In following this up it follows as a corollary that you consider it highly important that all the deaf should be taught to articulate with fair distinctness, and should, if possible, be able to read from the lips of others, therefore the system which is called here the oral system of instruction is in your opinion highly desirable?—Very much so.

21,646. Then again, I take it from the evidence you have given us that you think, even in school life, it is exceedingly desirable that, if possible, the sexes should be kept separate, so that school boy and girl friendships should not be encouraged, which may lead in after life to the continuation of that friendship and ultimately to marriage?—I do not wish to express too decided an opinion upon that point.

21,647. You have no decided opinion as to whether the sexes should be kept separate in school or not?—I have no decided opinion.

21,648. And even when boys and girls have got beyond childhood, and are 14 or 15 years old, do you think that they should be kept at separate schools and taught in separate establishments, or should they be taught together and play together?—I cannot say that I have formed any decided opinion upon the subject; I have devoted my attention more to the condition of the very young, where the question of the separation of the sexes does not assume importance. In regard to older pupils, I recognise that there are evils that result from the co-education of the sexes; but I also recognise that evils result from keeping persons of one sex together without opportunities for forming acquaintances with suitable persons of the opposite sex. I would therefore rather not express myself positively upon that subject.

21,649. Now, as regards the question as between day schools and residential schools, I gathered from your remarks that you consider the day school decidedly preferable if circumstances will admit of that system being carried out?—Undoubtedly so.

21,650. And I believe your reason for so holding is that you think in day schools the children are mixing in home life and in the world generally, whereas in residential schools they are only mixing among the deaf or among those so accustomed to the deaf that they become as it were a special class of the community?—Yes; and I recognise distinct classes of day schools. The day school that forms a school for the deaf apart and distinct by itself I do not think so advantageous as the day school that is in a public school where hearing children are, so that opportunities might occur for mixing the deaf children in with the hearing children in the same classes for subjects where they might profitably go together, the principle being to mingle the deaf in every way possible with the hearing.

21,651. You have just answered the question I was coming to. Consequently I may take it you are of opinion that this mixing with their hearing school-fellows in play hours, or in drill, or in other exercises, such as writing, or things of that sort, where the deaf can be taught with hearing children, is exceedingly desirable?—Exceedingly desirable and important.

21,652. Therefore, if other circumstances admit of it, you think that the plan, or rather a modification of the plan, which is at present being adopted by the London School Board, of having deaf-mute classes in the ordinary schools, is a desirable plan?—I am not familiar with the details of your London School Board plan. The principle of it is undoubtedly sound.

21,653. I am not talking of the details, but of the principle?—The principle is undoubtedly sound if those deaf classes are taught by special teachers. I do not believe that complete co-education with hearing children is a practicable thing; but if those deaf classes in your London board schools have special scholars and special teachers I consider it an admirable plan.

21,654. That is exactly the point I want your opinion upon. Now in America the system of instruction generally followed is what is called the combined system, I believe?—Yes; in my opinion that is the sign language system in disguise.

21,655. Now, as to this combined system, is it the same in all schools, or does a combined school mean a school where they do not confine themselves to one special form of instruction, but combine various forms of instruction together. For instance, a school which endeavours to teach by means of the ear as well as the mouth would be to a certain extent a combined school, although no finger language were used; would that be called a combined school in America?—I do not know. The idea underlying the term "combined" is undoubtedly a good one. The idea is to adopt an eclectic system, but the definition attached to "combined" is vague and indefinite, and you have schools that are actually classified in the Annals as "manual, oral, and combined." If "combined" includes the manual and oral, I do not see the necessity for the distinction.

21,656. Taking, for instance, the Deaf and Dumb Institution at Margate under Dr. Elliott, which is one of the largest in this country, and almost the oldest (indeed I think it is the oldest), there is a large building and a certain number of pupils are taught by the sign language and the manual alphabet, and a certain number, a great many of whom are in a separate building, are taught on what is called the pure oral system; but all the children mix together for the purposes of recreation, for dining, for drill, and for other purposes, on which occasions all the children oral or not oral are communicated with by means of the sign-and-finger language. Do you think the people of America generally would call that a "combined school?"—I think that is what is meant by a "combined school" generally in America if the sign language is employed as well as a manual alphabet.

21,657. That is to say, that they have different departments where they are using different systems, but the children who are taught orally mix with the children who use the sign-and-finger alphabet, and from time to time are educated by that means themselves?—It is my impression that that is what is usually spoken of as the "combined system" in America. But Dr. Gallaudet does not seem to define it in that way. What you have just said with regard to this English school exactly defines what appears to me to be the usual meaning of the word in America, that is, if the sign language is used as well as the manual alphabet; but you must form your own judgment upon that question, for as I say, I am not an authority upon the "combined system," and I do not believe that the term is correct. I do not think that a system using the finger alphabet—but excluding the sign-language—would be called a combined system in America.

21,658. I dwell rather at length upon this point, because it is desirable that when we talk of a certain system we should know what we are talking about; and if you talk of a school as a combined school in America, we should know what a combined school means?—Yes, as a matter of fact, in very many of the schools which are stated to be under the "combined system," that plan is adopted, in fact in most of them; that is to say, that all the children who are taught speech mingle freely with those who are not taught speech out of school hours, and use the sign language for purposes of inter-communication.

21,659. (*Mr. Woodall.*) The directors of the Pennsylvania Institution have a detached school in which the pupils are taught upon the pure oral method?—Yes.

21,660. But in the general institution a certain proportion of the pupils are taught the oral method. Am I to understand from you that those children are allowed or are not allowed to mingle with the other pupils in the ordinary exercises of the playground and in the industrial classes, for instance?—The principal of the Pennsylvania Institution attempted by an experiment to decide which plan was best for the oral pupils, exclusion from the sign pupils or mingling with the sign pupils after their school

Mr. A. G. Bell.

22 June 1888.

instruction was over; therefore for a number of years they have had two oral systems in use in the Pennsylvania Institution, one a separate and distinct school, known as the oral branch of the Pennsylvania Institution, in which all children taught orally were separated entirely from the other pupils and had no admixture; and secondly, in the main body of the Pennsylvania Institution they had an oral class, or oral classes, in which the pupils mingled afterwards in play hours with the others. They have had the two systems in that same institution, and as a general result Mr. Crouter expressed his opinion as it is quoted at the bottom of page 107 of the pamphlet "Facts and Opinions relating to the Deaf."

21,661. (*Chairman.*) After this experiment has been carried out he gives that as his deliberate opinion?—Yes, as his deliberate verdict. He says: "I "believe in oral instruction (separate oral) for all "deaf children who can be successfully instructed "by that method," and so forth.

21,662. That is that there is separate instruction, although Dr. Gallaudet calls it a combined school?—Yes.

21,663. Dr. Gallaudet may have had the other branch of the school in his mind at the time?—Yes.

21,664. (*Mr. Van Oven.*) I gather Mr. Crouter's opinion, as expressed in what you have read, to be this: that in order successfully to carry out the system of oral instruction it is necessary to restrain as far as possible the chances, or at any rate to put no encouragement in the way of the pupils so taught, for using any other mode of communication; is that what you understand Mr. Crouter's opinion to be?—That is the impression that I draw from what Mr. Crouter says, but of course the Commission can decide for themselves.

21,665. Do you share in that opinion; it is your opinion which I wish to elicit?—My opinion is that any other mode of communication than that by word of mouth and by speech-reading interferes with the art of speech-reading: but it is my opinion also that in spite of that it is advisable for other reasons—mental reasons—with the congenitally deaf to use the English language in the written form very constantly.

21,666. Consequently the system as carried out at Margate, which appears to me to be very much the system carried out in many of the combined schools in America—that is to say, a separate class-room and a separate building for the children taught on the pure oral system, those children being allowed at meal times to mix with the other children, who use the sign-and-finger alphabet, and being instructed by means of the sign-and-finger alphabet at drill and in other portions of their curriculum, is to a great extent detrimental to the full development of the oral system. I take it from what you have said that your opinion is that if these children were not only kept in a separate class but kept entirely to themselves as they are in many continental schools, the oral system would have a far better chance of producing excellent results?—As I have tried to express to this Committee, I look upon institutions or separate schools as evils, and of course, if institutions are necessary, we have got to make the best of an evil. I do not believe in separating deaf children from hearing children, but if you have got to do it then I think that the admixture of pupils who are taught speech and the admixture of pupils who are taught the sign-language out of the schoolroom is harmful to the articulation and the speech-reading of the pupils. That is the main point. Then you included in your question the manual alphabet. I would not express the same view for a school where the manual alphabet was used to the exclusion of the sign language, because then the intercourse of the pupils with one another, though to a certain extent it would interfere with the speech-reading, yet would be a constant practice in the use of the English language in one of the forms in which people have it ordinarily. It would be the same as the practice of written language. My point is that speech-reading is not all that we have to consider in the education of the deaf; the mind has to be considered as well, and my objection to the mingling of the two together where the sign language is used is that the practice outside is in the special language. If that communication outside were in the English language, I should hold that while it might not be good for speech-reading it might be good for the child on the whole.

21,667. Then I would ask why the finger alphabet is considered by you desirable in a large school in preference to the children writing down anything that they may not be able to communicate by word of mouth?—Because of the speed with which it can be used. The speed of writing, even if one scribbles, is only about 30 words a minute, whereas the speed of a manual alphabet may be as much as 100 words a minute; and we want to have the most ready and quick means of communicating English words to the pupil that we can get. Speech-reading is better still, because the speed of that comes up to 150 words or more a minute, but this speed is only practicable where the pupil has already familiarity with the language.

21,668. But admitting, as you admit, that the power of speech-reading and the power of articulation are greatly interfered with by the use of any other method of communication, do you not think that giving the finger alphabet a mode of communication which is so easy and ready and speedy will greatly retard the acquisition of the power of lip-reading and the clearness and precision of articulation; have you considered whether that loss is not, perhaps, greater than the loss of time involved by prohibiting the use of the finger alphabet, and forcing the communication to take place either by speech or writing, remembering, of course, that writing exercises give even a greater amount of instruction in language than spelling on the fingers?—If you have followed my ideas so far you will see that speech-reading is only easy to those who are vernacularly acquainted with the language. Therefore, in the case of those who know the language in either its written or spoken form, I would not have the remotest hesitation in saying that we should not use the finger alphabet, but should rely exclusively, as far as possible, on speech and speech-reading: but in the case of those who do not know the language speech-reading does not by itself teach it. A knowledge of language will teach speech-reading, but speech-reading will not teach a knowledge of language, so that, I think, that every means we can employ to make the English language familiar to the pupil should be adopted before we cause him to rely exclusively upon the mouth. In separate institutions the manual alphabet will retard speech-reading, undoubtedly, if used when the pupil has arrived at an age when he might rely upon the mouth, but the use of the manual alphabet in the schoolroom is entirely within the control of the teacher, and outside, it is important that inter-communication among pupils should be in the English language. The pupils will communicate with one another in that mode that is easiest to them. If speech-reading is easy to them they will prefer it; if it is not they will use signs, unless a manual alphabet is permitted. In schools where the deaf children have plenty of communication with hearing children, I do not see any disadvantage in having the manual alphabet in such schools. It is only in separate schools where the manual alphabet would be likely to take the place of communication by word of mouth that it is disadvantageous. If the child has opportunities of frequent admixture with hearing children, we may trust to the laziness of human nature that they will use the means of communication which is to them most easy, and it is more easy for a hearing child to talk with his deaf companion, if the deaf companion can understand him, than it is for him to spell upon his fingers, and if he cannot understand his speech, it is better that the manual alphabet should be used than that communication should be stopped. I would not put any restrictions upon the methods of communication between deaf and hearing children. Let us use every means to give a knowledge of the English language, and when that is got, reliance may be had upon speech-reading. Those who know the language first may rely upon speech-reading at once.

21,669. I have followed what you say, and I know very clearly the truth of your remark; but I must confess that I am a little dubious as to how you would advise the education to be carried on, having in view the fact that the education under the oral system must of necessity be interfered with if a finger alphabet is taught or allowed. However much I may appreciate your idea as regards a separate class being taught in a central school where the general admixture in the playground, and otherwise, is with hearing children, I cannot see that it has the same force as regards a separate school for the deaf, and I apprehend that our school board classes as they exist now, and as I feel confident they always must exist, will be to a great extent separate schools; consequently, if the finger alphabet be there taught the finger alphabet will be the general mode of communication between one pupil and another, and will be generally used by them, however much they may know of the language, and be able to read from the lips?—Of course, the views I have been expressing on the manual alphabet are simply my own individual views. The principle that underlies my ideas in the case of the manual alphabet is the absolute necessity of using with the congenitally deaf in the earlier stages of education the written forms of the language. So long as you use writing in place of the manual alphabet that meets the same end. My only advocacy of the use of manual alphabet is based upon its rapidity, and instead of it interfering with oral methods, it is necessary that the pupil should be largely taught by the written form in the earlier stages. I mean that with the congenitally deaf reliance should be had upon writing as the means of communication in the earlier stages until the pupil has become familiar with the language. In respect to speech itself I do not hold that view. I think that all children should have instruction in articulation from the very first, and that they should be caused to use their vocal organs in the schoolroom on all occasions. As I look upon it the defect in the deaf children is a one-sided defect. It interferes with the communication of other people with the child, and not the communication of the child with other people. The vocal organs are perfect, and I would have the child taught to speak and speak all the time in the schoolroom. Hence I should not put him under a deaf teacher; you must have a hearing teacher. My only point of difference with my oral friends is as to the mode in which the communication is carried on with the child. In many of our oral schools the principle is adopted that no word shall be presented in writing until after the child can read it from the mouth. That is what is meant by the pure oral in our country.

21,670. That is not the case in Germany, is it?—I cannot say; that plan I do not advocate. The plan that I would advocate is where the written word is always presented in the earlier stages with speech. Of course, with those who have a knowledge of the language, that is, those who are usually termed semi-mutes, there is no difference of opinion. We do not want the manual alphabet, we want reliance upon speech and speech-reading alone.

21,671. I take it that your idea of the mode of instructing the deaf child should be commencing by teaching articulation and by teaching language from writing?—That is it exactly.

21,672. That if it be found a child's appreciation is not sufficient to enable that child to read words easily from the lips, or that the child being a congenitally deaf mute, and never having had any language at all, the teaching of that child is greatly retarded for want of a quicker method, then that child might be placed in a separate class, and be given, in addition to the other modes of communication, the use of the finger alphabet?—Yes.

21,673. I do not understand it to be your opinion that in a school for the deaf generally, the finger alphabet should be used for all alike, whether congenitally deaf or not congenitally deaf,—whether quick of apprehension or slow of apprehension?—I may say that, to the best of my judgment, the knowledge of a manual alphabet is of no harm to any deaf child, because it is practise in the English language. I admit that if it is used in conjunction with speech to explain words that are ambiguous to the child when he does not understand them from the mouth, it interferes with the acquisition of the art of speech-reading: but that is a matter in the control of the teacher. I would not have the manual alphabet used in the schoolroom, where in your oral department explanations must be by the mouth itself or a pupil will come to rely upon the hand instead of the mouth. In communications with hearing children I do not think that the use of the manual alphabet interferes with speech-reading, because it is so much easier for a hearing child to speak to a deaf child, if he can understand, that he will always prefer it to the manual alphabet. In schools where the deaf children have the power of mingling with hearing children, I would not restrict their methods of inter-communication with the hearing children; I would let them have the manual alphabet, I would let them have signs, or any way in which you can bring them into communication with the hearing children in the full confidence that the hearing children will adopt speech as the means of communication wherever it is possible, because it is easier to the hearing child to speak than to use the other methods. Therefore I would not exclude the manual alphabet or any crude signs that the pupils could invent which would bring the deaf children into communication with the hearing children.

21,674. (*Chairman.*) You mean to say that you have no objection that the hearing children should learn signs, or the finger alphabet, because there is no temptation to them to make that the principal means of communication?—Exactly.

21,675. But, of course, where the contrary system exists you would not say the same?—In the institution life it is different, because they are all deaf, and the sign language that would grow up there would take the place of the English language, and they would never learn it. I would like my idea to be perfectly clear in regard to the matter of articulation. I come here not to advocate any system or any method; I come to express only my own views as to what is good, not for the oral method, but what is good for the child; and, in regard to articulation, I would have articulation used in all schools for the deaf. I would have the pupil use his mouth, for that is perfectly practicable; every child can be taught to speak, and the only difficulty is the mode of communicating with him on account of his deafness. I agree thoroughly with all that my oral friends would advise, that speech shall be used, and that the pupil shall speak under whatever system of instruction he is taught; that he shall communicate with his teacher by speech however defective it may be, whether you use the oral or any other method. The only difference between me and my oral friends is as to the means by which we should communicate with the deaf child. With all those who have a knowledge of the language sufficient to enable them to judge by context of the ambiguities of speech-reading, speech-reading should be used. With all those who have not that knowledge the language in its written form, or some clear form, should be used, and I see no harm there but only good in the use of the manual alphabet. After the language has been acquired I would drop the manual alphabet in the school. Let the children use it outside as much as they like, but let them communicate in the schoolroom by speech-reading. If you can have the deaf child brought into constant communication with the hearing child the manual alphabet will do him no harm.

21,676. (*Mr. Van Oren.*) I understand you to say that in America something over 44 per cent., I think you said it was 44.8 per cent., were taught articulation in one way or another; is not that a very small

Mr. A. G. Bell.

22 June 1888.

proportion?—It is according to the returns sent to me in answer to my circular letter of inquiry.

21,677. Can you suggest any reason why so few are taught articulation in America?—One reason is obvious; we cannot get teachers who are familiar with the mechanism of speech. Hearing persons grow up from early childhood to adult life and never study the mechanism of speech. You may take hundreds and thousands of our best teachers in the public schools and hardly find one who can give an intelligible description of the movements of his vocal organs in uttering the simplest sentence. Quite independently, therefore, of the difficulty of introducing speech into an institution the difficulty exists of getting teachers who know anything of the mechanism of speech. I must say on behalf of our American institutions that the principals and superintendents of all our American institutions express, so far as words can express, the desire to give every child an opportunity of acquiring speech, and only dropping a child from the articulation class when it is shown that he cannot profitably acquire it. They all express that desire, and in our last convention of teachers in California it was specially recommended that they should do it. The fact is, however, that they do not do it, and that the majority of the pupils in America do not have the opportunity of trying whether they can be taught speech or not. My researches show that 44.8 per cent. are taught speech, leaving 55.2 per cent. who are not taught speech. Now I have asked the principals to distinguish, as regards that 55.2 per cent., between those who have been dropped from articulation classes and those who have never received any instruction in articulation. Looking down this table of statistics, it is obvious that the vast majority have never had an opportunity of learning. I must, however, give the principals credit for the expressed desire to do more than they do, and I think that there is really a difficulty in the way of getting competent teachers.

21,678. (*Chairman.*) You have no system of Government inspection of schools in America, and therefore, I presume, that has never been brought prominently before the States?—That is the great difficulty.

21,679. If you had a Government inspection of schools, would not that want have been prominently brought before the States?—Yes; the great want in the whole subject of the education of the deaf is the want of competent teachers. It is not fine buildings and schools that we want, but it is teachers who first have a knowledge of the art of teaching, who have been trained to be teachers of ordinary children and who have superposed upon that any special knowledge that is required in regard to the deaf. We are fortunate in America, in giving salaries liberal enough, to bring into our schools men and women of education. We have that advantage, but there are very few of them who have been trained as teachers. I would urge upon the British Government the advisability of providing that one of the requisites for State or Government aid should be a teacher who has been trained as a teacher, who has as the basis of knowledge the knowledge how to teach ordinary children. This question of teachers is the most important point I think you can consider. The methods of instruction and the character of the schools and buildings are all secondary to the matter of teachers. One of the first things to consider is the competency of the teachers. The next thing is to see that you pay them such salaries as shall induce well-educated men and women to enter upon the work. I would recommend to your special attention in this matter the recommendations of the principal of the Halifax Institution, and who understands more of your British needs than those at the American institutions do. His recommendations are quoted at page 168 of this pamphlet: "Facts and Opinions relating to the Deaf."

21,680. (*Mr. Van Oren.*) Have you ever visited any of the German institutions?—No.

21,681. Are you acquainted with the mode at the Schleswig Institution, which is very much that which you point to, namely, that the best teachers from the public elementary schools are selected to become the teachers of the deaf, and are paid higher salaries in order to induce them to so enter themselves. Do you think that the proper plan for us to pursue here?—I think that is a very excellent plan; I think your articulation teachers should all have studied the mechanism of speech.

21,682. In special training schools for the training of teachers for the deaf?—Not necessarily in special training schools for the deaf. The knowledge of the mechanism of speech is the essential thing, and not the place where they acquire it.

21,683. Therefore your idea, if I gather it rightly, is that the teachers for the deaf should be selected from the general teachers of the country; that as good a one as possible should be selected, and should then be specially trained for the teaching of the deaf, and for that purpose should, of course, receive a higher salary?—Yes.

21,684. Now we were speaking the other day about the aural method of teaching by means of hearing; you say that you consider that 16 per cent. could be orally taught?—That seems to be about the percentage—16 to 17.

21,685. You do not mean 16 per cent. of the congenitally deaf?—No, of the whole mass of the deaf.

21,686. How would you proceed to investigate those cases which you would treat aurally?—I would proceed first to make experiments to ascertain those pupils who seemed to have any perception of sound. One of the simplest means of doing that is to take a large dinner bell, and ring this bell behind the pupil's head, and see whether he can hear it. Another method is to shout behind the pupil's back when he is not expecting it, and see whether he turns round. I fully expect from the statistics gathered that you will find that about 20·6 per cent. of the pupils will manifest a sufficient amount of hearing to hear the ringing of a dinner bell or to turn round at a shout. All those pupils I would put in a separate class for separate auricular instruction to ascertain those who might profit by such instruction. I would give all those pupils the opportunity of improving their hearing. The statistics seem to indicate that a number of those cases will have to be dropped from the auricular class, and that the true percentage will be somewhere about 16 or 17 per cent. of the whole.

21,687. When you say auricularly taught, do you mean that the whole instruction should be given by means of the ear, or should any signs be given; should they be taught at all on the oral method, or should the instruction be entirely by means of the ear trumpet?—In the Nebraska Institution, which is at present our model, the pupils are taught on the oral system, with the addition that the voice of the teacher is raised sufficiently to reach their organs of hearing. The distance of the pupil from the teacher is arranged with regard to the amount of hearing. Their general education is carried on by speech and speech-reading, with what hearing they can gain from the teacher's shouting: and then they are specially exercised in the use of their ears without their eyes by conversation carried on behind their backs. I am not sure at the present moment whether those pupils are allowed to mix with the sign pupils of the institution in which they are taught or not, and whether they are not also taught by signs. My impression is that they are kept distinct: but Mr. Gillespie has given some details; I have not yet had time to investigate the details myself.

21,688. By the exercise of the hearing faculty, is the hearing much improved, as a rule?—The apparent hearing is enormously improved; whether there is any real improvement in the hearing proper is another question; that is to say, the pupils who can not imitate sounds through the hearing tube come to understand speech—come to be merely what you may call hard of hearing: that is all we know; that is the fact. When you start their education they seem to perceive only noises. If you try to get them to imitate words you fail. Those pupils by education come to be only hard-of-hearing people, and you can carry on a conversation with them behind their

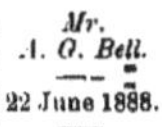

heads, so that the apparent amount of hearing is entirely changed. Of course it is a very great problem what the change is. There is no doubt at all about the fact. Whether it is due to the improvement in the hearing apparatus itself by use, or whether it is simply due to the increased knowledge of language and familiarity with the sounds that are represented, we do not know absolutely, but the opinion of teachers generally is that it is due to the greater familiarity with the language and greater attention, and not to the improvement in the hearing power. I would not reject the other hypothesis entirely; I think it is possible that there may be some improvement in the hearing power, too, although the aurists do not agree with me.

21,689. Consequently, in your opinion, all pupils in a school for the deaf should, if possible, be taught auricularly?—Undoubtedly all who are capable of it. There is one point in auricular instruction that I have not touched upon. There are some cases where the pupils appear to be totally deaf by every test that you make, with the hearing tube or by the bell being rung or by shouting, and yet who can hear and imitate sound by the audiphone. Such cases are very rare, but there are some cases. In those cases the conducting mechanism has been destroyed, and yet the internal ear exists and vibrations communicated through the bony structure of the head through the teeth are perfectly perceived. I shall never forget my surprise in the discovery of one case of that sort in New York, for, as a general rule, the audiphone is utterly worthless, and pupils who can hear with the hearing tube do not seem to hear well with the audiphone. We made a series of tests in the New York Institution. We first used the audiometer which you have here, then the hearing tube, and then the bell, and then we tried to see if they could imitate vowel sounds, and then at last we took the audiphone and tried that. I can mention one case in which they tried the audiometer without any sensation of hearing; then they tried the hearing tube, but the person did not seem to hear. Then they tried shouting but without the person hearing, nor was he able to imitate the vowel sounds. Then we came to the audiphone test, and at first we thought "it is hardly worth while to try that." However, in order to make our test complete, we tried it, and the boy could imitate speech with the audiphone. It was the greatest surprise I ever experienced. That example teaches us that though the audiphone is useless in the vast majority of cases, we should not discard it entirely. I know a few cases in adult life where it has answered. I know a lady in Washington who derives a great deal of benefit from the audiphone in society, and I presume there must be cases (I do not know how to reach them) in our institutions in which the middle ear has been destroyed, and the internal ear remains perfect, and might be reached by the audiphone; experiment should be made with it, and it should not be discarded entirely. The audiphone is a fan-shaped instrument, and any ordinary card-board fan answers the same purpose, and does just as well.

21,690. (*Rev. C. M. Owen.*) I believe you had formerly a private school at Washington for the deaf?—I had for about two years a private school.

21,691. How many pupils had you?—I limited it to four pupils.

21,692. And you only had it two years, I think?—I think that was the time.

21,693. So that you really had not time to complete the education of your pupils?—I had not.

21,694. What practical experience have you had in the teaching of the deaf and dumb?—I was for some years before the telephone took my attention from the subject, a teacher of articulation, or rather a teacher of teachers of articulation. I taught in the Horace Mann School for the Deaf in Boston; I instructed the teachers in the Clarke Institution at Northampton; I instructed the teachers at the American Asylum in Hartford in the use of my father's symbols for visible speech, and then I opened in Boston a normal training class for articulation teachers of the deaf. I had about 60 teachers under instruction altogether. In our experiments in teaching articulation we were met with the difficulty of providing pupils to give the teachers training in the art of teaching. To remedy that difficulty we opened a free class for adult deaf mutes in Boston, and quite a number of adult deaf mutes came forward and formed the experimental subjects for the teachers to work upon. At that time I was simply engaged in articulation work; I did not enter into the general subject of the education of the deaf, in fact I kept clear of it. In my introductory article on the use of visible speech which is published in the American Annals for January, 1872, you will see the position that I took then, which I have consistently kept throughout since. What I said was this: "Visible "speech takes no part in the contest between articu-"lation on the one hand and signs and manual "alphabets on the other. In presenting his system "for adoption all that the inventor means to say is "this: here is a means by which you can obtain "perfect articulation from deaf mutes; make what "use of it you choose. He places the tool in the "hands of teachers with general directions how to "use it." That has been my position from that day to this. I have advocated teaching articulation to all the deaf, but not necessarily teaching *by* articulation. You see that there is a very great distinction there; so that while I have appeared as a consistent advocate for oral training I have not always appeared as a consistent advocate of what is known as the oral method of instruction. Now as to my experience of the modes of teaching, I could not enter into this work without being interested in the more general questions of education. I did not obtrude my views upon my teachers, and my teachers went into sign institutions or into articulation schools, and all over the country to institutions of all kinds. I longed to have some little pupil upon whom I could test ideas of my own and such a case presented itself. The father and mother of a deaf child, a little boy five years of age, thought that I had good ideas upon the subject, and came to me and said, "Take "our deaf child and do what you like with him—"we trust you." I said, "I do not propose to fol-"low any method that is in use anywhere else." But they said, "We will trust you; we believe in your ideas." Accordingly they sent the child to me when he was five years of age with a nurse to look after him. I employed a lady to look after him and to relieve me of a good deal of the work of instruction, and I carried on that boy's instruction till the telephone took my attention away from the subject. That boy is now a young man: he appeared in Washington desirous of entering the National College, and I had a note from the Principal of the Kendall School saying, There is a young man at our school who has an unusual knowledge of the English language for a congenital deaf mute; he does not articulate particularly well, but his general familiarity with the English language is something remarkable, and we have cross-questioned him to find out how he was taught, and he says that you taught him, and we would like to know how you did it. I therefore wrote an account of the method of educating this child, which was published in the Annals, a copy of which I beg to present to the members of this Commission (*handing in the same*). The article will be found in the Annals for April, 1883, Vol. XXVIII., pp. 124–139, under the title, "A method of teaching "language to a very young congenitally deaf child." Now the ideas here are derived from George Dalgarno, as you will see from reading the paper. I will not go into it now at any length, but there is one point to which I would wish to direct your attention and that is how I got over the difficulty which our teachers experience with regard to the use of the manual alphabet and how I was able to use a manual alphabet that would not interfere with speech-reading. I came to the conclusion that you could use an alphabet read by the sense of touch instead of by the sense of sight (of course there was

Mr. A. G. Bell.

22 June 1888.

no difficulty in doing that where you had only a single pupil to deal with). I made a slight modification of George Dalgarno's manual alphabet, which is shown on page 10 of the pamphlet which I have just handed in; that also formed a means of communication with hearing persons. Dalgarno's plan is that the pupil should wear a white glove and that the letters of the alphabet should be written upon the fingers of the glove. Of course when this boy was with me he did not require to wear a glove because I knew the position of the letters and would touch the place on his hand, but when he was with his friends in society and they wanted to talk to him they would see the letters on the glove and touch them when they could not use the ordinary manual alphabet. But to deal with the question of communicating with the boy, my belief is that the whole difficulty in teaching language is how we are to communicate with the deaf person. My mode of education was to make school life as life-like as possible; and this boy had no regular instruction in the sense in which we use the term in general, but I would take him to the window and talk to him on his hand about what he could see going on outside. I have somewhat modified my ideas and I would certainly advocate that the parent should speak to the deaf child at the same time that he touches his hand and let the child look at his mouth so that he would get the definite communication through the hand accompanied by the movement of the mouth, when the parent is close to the child and when he is a little way off he would have the mouth alone; so that you have an education for speech-reading through the use of a manual alphabet of this kind. However, I do not desire to enlarge upon that point. The members of the Commission will be able to read this pamphlet if they wish, and I would simply say now that it is of great importance that we should consider the methods of teaching very young congenitally deaf children at home before they are old enough to go to school. This child could write a letter, and was writing letters to his friends all day long, before he was six years old. Indeed, the floor of his nursery was littered with scraps of paper on which he had been writing. I made the experiment fairly which George Dalgarno spoke of. He suggested, as I say, on page 3 of this pamphlet, "that a deaf person should "be taught to read and write in as nearly as possible "the same way that young ones are taught to "speak and understand their mother tongue. His idea was that we should talk to the deaf child just as we do to the hearing child, with the exception that our words are to be addressed to his eye instead of to his ear. Indeed, George Dalgarno carried his theory so far as to assert that the deaf infant would as soon come to understand written language as a hearing child does speech, "had the mother or nurse "but as nimble a hand as commonly they have a "tongue." That idea has been ridiculed by teachers, and I accordingly wanted to test it. To test it I determined to carry the thing out fully in the education of this child. The first education of that child commenced by my writing on the board before the child whole sentences. I did not commence with letters, or even with words, but I wrote whole sentences on the board just as I would speak to a hearing child. Whatever words came into my mind that I would want to say to the little fellow if he could hear I wrote down on the board. Persons who came and saw the boy said, "How wonderful! Does that child understand what you have written there?" I said, "Oh, no." They said, "Then why "do you write it?" I said, "He can never come to "understand it until he has first seen it. If you "speak to a baby by word of mouth does the baby "understand what you say? Of course not; he has "to hear it and hear it and hear it again before he "can understand the words which you speak." I commenced, as I say, with sentences, and then I wrote down on separate pieces of card the names of the toys, or of the things that he had to eat, and, indeed, of everything that he wanted, and I taught him to go and ask for them by picking out the card that corresponded to the thing he wanted, and I made a game of it so as to make it as easy as possible for him. My idea was to make him use written words as much as possible in place of his own little baby signs. I studied his signs for my own purpose, but I never used them; I tried to give him words in place of his signs. The moment he could recognise a written word I pretended not to understand his sign, and then he would run to the board and pick out the card for the word corresponding to the thing he wanted; he could do that before he knew a letter of the alphabet, or could use Dalgarno's alphabet. He could write whole sentences by imitation before he knew a letter.

21,695. Just in the same way, I suppose, as a child can speak before he can write?—Exactly. That was the experiment which I tried, and it was successful; and it is, I believe, the only case that has been tried according to George Dalgarno's method. It contains perfectly true methods of teaching the language. I believe from the experience I have had it is a true principle—that there is a time to teach a child a thing, and that you may teach a child a thing prematurely. Now the indication of what is the right time to teach a child a thing is when the child indicates the want or need of it. When a child begins to invent a sign for everything he wants that is a proof that he wants words. I began by expressing all ideas to him in writing; that was my sole means at first of communicating, and I kept on writing and writing things that the child did not understand. Now you may ask me how he expressed his desire to write. It was in this way: He went to the blackboard, and he wanted to be the teacher, and to make me his pupil, and took the chalk in his hand and scribbled all over the board and then made signs to me to act, because I used to make him act in his play what I had written. That was an indication that he wanted to write, but he did not know the letters. I tried to find out what he wanted me to do, and I discovered that it was to give his doll a drink of water. Thereupon I wrote upon the blackboard, "Please give dolly a "drink of water;" and then I erased the sentence so as just to leave the slightest possible trace of it on the board, and then I gave the chalk to the child, and he traced it over and pointed to me to do what he had written.

21,696. (*Mr. Woodall.*) How old was he when that occurred?—He came to me when he was about 5, and all that happened within a month or two.

21,697. Doubtless you have seen remarkable instances of a child as young as 6 being able to write with great proficiency what is pointed out to him?—Yes, you will see letters in that pamphlet written by this child without any assistance before he was 6 years of age, in which expressions occur so remarkable as to show that he thought in English, and I can give you an illustration of that.

21,698. (*Rev. W. B. Sleight.*) Was the child born deaf?—Yes, he was born deaf.

21,699. Was he a particularly intelligent child?—He has not turned out to be particularly intelligent, though he was thought to be rather a prodigy in those days.

21,700. You had good material to work upon in that case?—Yes, I had good material to work upon.

21,701. (*Mr. Woodall.*) You do not cite that particular case as the case of an abnormal child?—Not by any means.

21,702. (*Mr. Johnson.*) But it was an exceptional case, was it not? You have no more like it; you have only tried this one case I believe?—Yes; the telephone took my attention away from the subject. Now just let me read to you from this pamphlet some remarkable expressions which he has used, and which he never saw used before. He came to me on October 1st, 1872, and on page 14 of this pamphlet you will find a letter written on November 14, 1873, which is a little over a year after his first coming to me; he was then six years old, and this is a conversation which actually took place. I may say that I used writing as much as possible, and when he had not writing materials at hand he used Dalgarno's touch alphabet. The following conversation was all written on two scraps of paper:—"*Mr. Bell.* "I think you are tired and *hot* now, so we will be "*quiet* and *rest* now. What does 'rest' mean? "*George.* Rest means stop. *Mr. Bell.* Yes, dear; "it means 'stop' or 'still.' *George.* Or wait? "*Mr. Bell.* Yes. *George.* Please may I put a "your handkerchief, and be like an old woman." Note in my record book. After playing for a while he remembered that his grandmamma had made fun of him for pretending to be a woman, so he wrote: "I am not put on my towel on my head and be like an old woman, and grandma said not now, grandma will be so very sorry now." That you will remember is the case of a six-year old child. Now I will just refer you to a few remarkable expressions that show that he thought in English words. In a letter here you will find: "I matched the lamp on fire." That is perfectly expressive though he had never seen such an expression. Then he says, "The rain is not "well but rain is sick but the snow is well." However, I will not take up your time any further with these illustrations, you will be able to read the pamphlet if you wish to do so. I will only say that, in George Dalgarno's opinion, the only point of art in teaching language to a deaf child is to use no art at all—but diligence. "Let the same words be seen "and written as often by the deaf man," he says, "as they have been heard and spoken by the blind; if "their faculties of memory and understanding be "equal, the measure of knowledge also will be equal." In the teaching of language, he says, that only diligence and patience are needed on the part of the teacher, and not great abilities. "An acute man "will be impatient, and not able to stoop so much "as the other. And to clear this further," he says, "I think it will be readily assented to, that a prat-"tling nurse is a better tutrix to a foster child than "the most profoundly learned doctor of the univer-"sity.

21,703. (*Rev. Mr. Owen.*) I think that answers the question I was putting to you?—I have not completely answered your question yet. The telephone took away my attention from the practical work of teaching, but my interest has always been in the general work of the education of the deaf; and having obtained new ideas relating to the education of very young deaf children I at last determined to start the private school limited to four children in Washington, to which reference has been made, in connexion with a kindergarten school for hearing children. I will not take up your time by going into the matter any further, but will simply state that I found difficulty in getting teachers. My first teacher remained with me for a year and then married and left me. My second teacher remained with me for a year, and then her mother died and she had to go home and keep house, and then the difficulty of getting teachers seemed to me to render it advisable not to carry on the school again (it was an experimental school) until I could get either a married lady, or a man who could devote his whole attention to the work, for I could not do more than spend a very little time in the school myself. The great questions connected with the telephone law-suit so occupied my thoughts at that time that I was unable to attend properly to the school, and I have therefore given it up, but I hope only temporarily, and the children are now being educated on the same methods by their parents, who went through the parents' class in connexion with the school.

21,704. Then, as a matter of fact, you have had no practical personal experience in the American institutions, the greater number of which are carried on under what is called the "combined system"?—I have no personal experience except by observation. It is my custom to visit the institutions, and I go among the little pupils, and sit down and write to them, and try to find out what knowledge of written English they possess. I have visited quite a large number of institutions in that way as a sort of outside impartial critic; so that while I have no practical experience I have a general knowledge of some of the institutions.

21,705. You have told us that you are a warm advocate of the pure oral method, and you have quoted Principal Crouter's opinion; are you aware that Principal Crouter in a paper read before the Convention of American Instructors of the Deaf said this, and I will ask you whether you agree with it: "It is believed that a large per-centage of our pupils, "namely, semi-mutes and semi-deaf, and such of the "congenitally deaf (few in number probably) as are "capable of receiving oral instruction, can and "should be orally taught, and that all others (form-"ing to be sure the majority of the pupils) should "be taught by manual methods." Do you agree with that?—I think I have fully expressed my ideas upon that subject. There is a great deal of confusion as to what is meant by oral method. I think it means generally the "speech-reading method." I believe that all children should be taught by articulation, and taught to use articulation; but I do not think all children should be taught by articulation, that is to say, speech-reading. All who can be successfully and readily taught by speech-reading should be so taught, and those who cannot should be taught manually—by which I mean that written language should be used by the teacher. In all cases, however, the mouth should be used by the pupil as *his* means of communication. In this sense I would use an oral system for all. "Speech" for all; "speech-reading" for as many as can readily profit by it. That is my opinion.

21,706. Do you find that orally-taught pupils really use speech and lip reading in after life?—Undoubtedly, those who read with facility, and I speak from personal experience; my own wife has been orally taught, and for every word of communication she relies upon communication by word of mouth. In fact, it is my knowledge of the fact that it is perfectly practicable for a person without hearing to rely for every word of information upon the mouth of others that has led me to come forward as I have done prominently in America. I desire that all deaf children should be placed in the condition that my wife is.

21,707. You told us your wife became deaf at the age of five, I think?—Four and a half.

21,708. Undoubtedly the oral system has answered in her case?—Yes, admirably in her case.

21,709. Do you think it would have been equally successful, if she had been congenitally deaf?—I think if she had acquired a knowledge of the English language before being allowed to depend upon the mouth for information, the result would have been the same. So far as my observation has gone, if a pupil is taught to rely upon the mouth for communication before the language is acquired, it interferes with the acquisition of language; but if he is taught the language before he relies upon the mouth, then that knowledge of the language enables him to acquire the art of speech-reading.

21,710. Then you have no objection to the manual alphabet being used for the purpose of giving the child its knowledge?—I have none whatever personally.

21,711. You do not consider that the use of the manual alphabet in the earlier stages of education is a hindrance to articulation?—I do not. I think it is a great advantage to the pupil.

21,712. You were present, I believe, at the Conference of American Principals and Superintendents in America at Fairbault?—Yes.

21,713. You are reported as having said at that meeting, "I would advocate the use of a manual "alphabet," and then later on you said, "If oral "schools would only adopt the manual alphabet." Are you still of that opinion?—Undoubtedly.

21,714. Is not that what we call the "combined system"?—That is for you to define. I do not think that is what is meant by the term in America. In all the combined schools the "sign-language" is

Mr. A. G. Bell.

22 June 1888.

used, and I do not think that any method would be spoken of as "combined" which rejected the sign-language.

21,715. What I think most of us Commissioners understand by the "combined method" is that both systems, the manual system and the speech system, are used as channels and means of education to the same identical child?—Yes, but it is a very indefinite term, and in America always, I think, includes more. Sign-language as well as manual and oral instruction.

21,716. You told us that you did not object to the manual alphabet being used as a subsidiary means of education in oral schools?—I do not, undoubtedly.

21,717. That is not the pure oral system, is it?—It is not.

21,718. From your knowledge of the institutions in America do you agree with what Dr. Gallaudet says, "that they adopt the combined or American "method, that is to say, the method in which the "best features of both systems are incorporated"?—As I have said, I do not believe there is any "combined system" in America. What is known as the "combined system" is simply the sign language system in disguise. The sign language is the language of communication; I would divide the methods according to the language of communication that is used. There are two radical varieties. Special language (which in our country is the sign language) and the ordinary language of the people. Now, I discard entirely a special language as being nothing but harmful, and I would advocate the ordinary language of the people which appears in two forms—written language and spoken language. Spoken language I would have used by the pupil from the commencement of his education to the end of it, but spoken language I would not have used as a means of communication with the pupils in the earlier stages of the education of the congenitally deaf, because it is not clear to the eye, and requires a knowledge of the language to unravel the ambiguities. In that case I would have the teacher use written language, and I do not think that the manual alphabet differs from written language, excepting in this, that it is better and more expeditious.

21,719. Are you aware that the advocates of the pure oral method in England are totally opposed to the use of the manual alphabet?—I am; and so they are in America.

21,720. Then you do not agree with them on that point?—Certainly not. I would permit the pupils in every school to know and use a manual alphabet. I would not permit the use of the sign language.

21,721. You have said you scarcely approve of missions amongst the adult deaf and dumb as bringing the deaf and dumb together?—They have bad features and they have good features, and I do not wish to express a decided opinion on the subject. I can recognize that there must be many in our schools who grow up to adult life without the ability to communicate with hearing persons; they are isolated from the community and the question is, what are you to do for them. I do not mean to express any decided opinion as to that. You have got to reach them some way or other. It would be better to reach them in some other way than by bringing them together, but I do not know how to do it. It might, perhaps, be possible to bring together adults of only one sex at a time.

21,722. Do you not believe that the association of the deaf and dumb among themselves is a very great element in their happiness?—Not necessarily so. I think that the association with persons with whom they can talk and converse is an element in their happiness. If they cannot talk or converse with hearing persons then, of course, association amongst themselves is an element in their happiness, and you cannot keep them apart. We want to make every effort to help them to make friends among hearing persons of their own age.

21,723. Have you given the matter consideration as to how far religious missions to the deaf and dumb are to be carried on: would you exclude them all and, if so, how would you reach the spiritual needs of the deaf and dumb?—That is a matter that I have not given much thought to, and it is a very important matter. My thoughts have been chiefly directed to the young and to the means of reaching them and educating them and preventing this association in adult life that we have. I have not given much thought to the means of reaching the adults and benefiting them. I am not competent therefore to give an opinion upon that.

21,724. Now, as regards the day schools and institution system, I want to ask you one or two questions; do you not think that in many cases the teaching is much checked by the children going home to illiterate parents under the day school system?—It depends entirely upon the character of the home; I think in the majority of cases that the teaching is helped. But there is more than that to consider. Many parents desire to benefit and assist their children at home, but do not know what to do. In the day schools they come into personal relations with the teachers, and an exchange of ideas occurs. The teacher tells the mother what to do at home, and she does it. In an institution pupils are taken away so far from their parents; the parents never communicate with the teacher, or very rarely; and when the children go home in the holidays they do not know how to communicate with them. The children get tired of home and long for the school playground and the deaf children with whom they can communicate so freely; the ties of blood relationship are weakened and the institution becomes their home. The day school strengthens those ties of relationship. The communication between the teacher and the parent enables the parent to help the child at home; and I have seen in the Horace Mann School many instances of wonderful results achieved quite as much, I think, by the parent as by the teacher, by the co-operation of the two.

21,725. You told us that institutions do not seem to get the children at sufficiently early age; do you not get them quite early enough for their minds to be capable of receiving instruction?—Yes, but they are too old to start easily the study of language and speech, especially speech. It is in very early childhood that a language is most readily acquired. I believe with Dalgarno that it should be acquired in infancy or very early childhood. When the child comes to be 10 years of age you have to adopt methodical and grammatical ways of teaching, whereas the language should be acquired naturally in very earliest childhood by imitation if the language is constantly used by those around the child in a clearly visible form.

21,726. Do you not think that in institutions the children get the advantage of discipline, training, and moral tone which they could not get in any day schools?—I doubt whether it is an advantage to a very young child to be placed under that discipline. Kindergarten methods are more suitable. In regard to morality, I should say certainly, no. There is no person who can look after the morals of a young child like its own mother.

21,727. It seems to be generally admitted that physical training is most important for the deaf and dumb; is not that a great feature in institution life that could not be obtained in a day school?—I do not see why it could not be obtained in day schools. I think everything that can develop the lungs is of importance. Speech is of importance in that light, and I think the experience that Dr. Gallaudet enunciated in his testimony shows the enormous development in that respect in the case of his pupils at the National College by physical gymnastics; but I do not see why that means of development should be confined to institutions. In the Horace Mann School, which is a day school, there is a gymnasium, and the pupils have daily exercise with dumb-bells to develop the chest.

21,728. Have you visited the Stainer Home for teaching deaf children in connexion with the board

Mr. A. G. Bell.

22 June 1888.

schools in London?—Not yet; but I hope to do so very soon.

21,729. Then you are not prepared to answer any question with regard to that system, because you have not been there?—No.

21,730. (*Mr. Woodall.*) I want to ask you a few questions bearing upon the general system of public aid to schools in America; I suppose that each State in the Union has its own method of dealing with the deaf mutes much as it determines its own process with regard to the education of all other classes?—Yes.

21,731. And consequently there is nothing like uniformity in the general policy of the States, although there may be substantial agreement, perhaps?—There is substantial agreement in adopting the policy of the central institution for all the deaf mutes of the State, but each State has its own laws in reference to the education of the deaf.

21,732. Does every State charge itself with the responsibility of providing the means of education for the deaf mutes?—I think it does. You see in America it is very generally recognised that the safety of the Republic depends upon the education of the masses. Hence, education is a matter of State concern, and in some of our States (as in the State of Wisconsin, as you will see if you will refer to my open letter), there is actually a provision in the constitution of the State that every child should have the opportunity of education at the public expense from a certain age to a certain age.

21,733. That also appears in the constitution of some of the New England States, does it not?—I am not prepared to answer that question; but I may say that you will find, as a general rule, in each institution report the laws of the State where the institution is found relating to the deaf and dumb.

21,734. In effect may we take it that the institutions have been established on private foundations and arranged by independent boards?—I am not competent to speak upon these questions. I observe that Dr. Gallaudet has already given testimony in the matter, and he is much more competent than I am to say what the actual organization of the schools may be.

21,735. The States recognise the obligation of contributing to the institutions an amount which they regard as sufficient to bear the whole cost of the education and maintenance of the pupils sent by the State?—I think they all recognise the obligation of the State to educate the deaf and dumb.

21,736. Then, perhaps, you will state the amount usually contributed to those institutions?—I cannot do so with accuracy.

21,737. May we take it that it is as much as 250 dollars, equal to 50*l.* of our money, a year for each child?—Dr. Gillett stated the average *per capita* cost at 223 dollars 28 cents per annum. I wrote a letter to the editor of the "American Annals of the Deaf," asking him what the average *per capita* cost at the present time is. If you like I would read the letter in response, if that is the information which you desire.

21,738. May we take it that 223 dollars is the average arrived at by including States where the cost of living is much cheaper than it is in New York, for example?—Undoubtedly, and I do not think that that average *per capita* cost truly expresses the average *per capita* cost. I have not calculated it myself because I cannot trust myself upon such a matter, but I will read the letter of the editor of the "Annals" giving me the information how to calculate truly the average *per capita* cost in America, and that information will guide you just as well as it will guide me. This is his letter: "Dear Professor Bell, I do not know that any calculation of the "*per capita* expense has been made since Dr. Gillett's, with which you are familiar. The materials "for one may be found in the last January number "of the 'Annals' in the tabular statement of the "schools of the United States, which gives the "number of pupils and expenditure for support "during the year 1887 for most of the schools. "Schools having a department for the blind should "be omitted, as the number of deaf mute pupils "only is given, while the expenses of both the deaf "and the blind departments are included in the "statement of expenditures. Such schools are "marked (on the page giving expenditure) with an "asterisk. Perhaps it would be fair also to omit "the Columbia Institution as the collegiate department is included in the table of expenditures, and "the expenses of this department in proportion to "the number of students is much greater than in "any of the schools. I do not think (but I am not "sure) Dr. Gillett made either of those eliminations. Very sincerely yours, E. A. Fay."*

21,739. Are you aware of the fact that in addition to the amounts contributed by the State for maintenance and education a sum which is sometimes 30 dollars a year is given by the county for the supply of clothing to those who need that assistance?—I am not aware of the details.

21,740. I only ask these questions because I am anxious to know whether, in your opinion, this comparatively generous aid given from the public purse has had the effect of checking or diverting private benevolence from the institutions?—There is no doubt at all in my mind that private benevolence has been diverted by the very generous State aid, but we must remember that the attitude of the American mind toward questions of education is peculiar. Education at public expense is claimed as a right pertaining to American citizenship, and is not looked upon as a matter of charity. Parents often complain bitterly at the injustice of considering the education of their deaf children as a matter of "charity," when no one would dream of viewing the education of their hearing children from such a standpoint, though the hearing, as well as the deaf, are educated at public expense. It is chiefly, I think, the schools that have opposed the institutions that have received private aid—the articulation schools, for example, the Clarke Institution; that is my belief; but I may be wrong; I am not an authority upon these subjects, and, perhaps, I should not express an opinion at all.

21,741. But surely all the institutions you have named, particularly those in New York and Philadelphia, founded by private benevolence, and managed by voluntary boards under charters, are substantially kept going by the capitation grant given on the pupils sent by the State, are they not?—I should say in that whole department of the subject I am not a competent authority to speak. I have crude ideas, but I may be wrong or I may be right.

21,742. But you have said you attached a great deal of importance to the necessity of effective government inspection; can you tell the Commission what kind of investigation is now made by the State authorities in the cases where they have given money aid?—So far as I am able to judge a formal inspection of the institution is made; but, as a rule, I do not think that the persons who inspect the institutions are competent to judge of the results of the education of the deaf. For example, the members of the legislatures sometimes inspect the State institutions in a body. An exhibition of the school is given. But members of the legislature would, as a rule, accept a child who became deaf at five years of age as a fair specimen of the average "deaf-mute," and attribute his mental condition to the instruction he received in school.

21,743. But each State maintains a Superintendent of Public Instruction, does it not?—It does.

* In connexion with this subject, Rev. Fred. Wines says: "The *per capita* expense cannot be accurately calculated, "because (1) the reports do not state the *average* number "of pupils, and (2) the average number, in institutions "which are closed for a part of the year, may be either the "average for 365 days, a full year, or for the number of "days included in the actual school term. I have little "faith in any of the statements made by the officers of institutions for the deaf on this subject. They do not use "words in the same sense. The *per capita* cost could only "be approximated from the table in the Annals."

Mr. A. G. Bell.

22 June 1888.

21,744. Is it not the duty of that superintendent periodically to visit institutions that are aided by public money?—I do not know, because in many cases the institutions for the deaf and dumb occupy an anomalous position among the schools. They are very often placed under the boards of State charities instead of the boards of education. They may be, and sometimes are, under both. It may be possibly that in all cases the superintendent of public instruction inspects them, but that I do not know. It should be done.

21,745. But you are aware that the reports generally are addressed to the Senate and House of Representatives of the particular State in which the institutions are placed?—Yes.

21,746. And that the institutions have to make a return to the Government controller of the finances of the institutions?—Yes.

21,747. But all this is something quite different, I presume, from what you contemplate when you suggest that there should be an efficient and skilful system of Government inspection?—Undoubtedly; and I should say in connexion with that point that the difficulty of inspection in a State lies in the fact that as a general rule there is only one school in the State. I think that the true way to promote improvements in our methods of instruction is to have very numerous small schools. I would direct your attention to the letter of Professor Fay, the editor of the "Annals," which is the last letter on the subject of instruction of the deaf at page 175 of the pamphlet "Facts and Opinions relating to the Deaf," which I have handed in. Professor Fay says, "I will only express the hope that you will urge the "British Government to afford liberal support to "existing schools of all kinds, and to establish new "ones, without hampering them by close restrictions "of any kind as to the methods to be pursued, trusting rather to 'the survival of the fittest,' which will "be the inevitable result of the free discussion which "has been going on for some time, and is not yet "ended." There is just one point there upon which I differ from Professor Fay. I do not think that "the survival of the fittest" will operate unless there is "a struggle for existence." The different methods of instruction have been in existence for a hundred years, and the "survival of the fittest" has not brought one of them out in place of the others yet. The reason is that we have not any means of testing the results. In order to have the survival of the fittest there must be the struggle for existence. If you have got a State institution, without any competition or opposition, there is no tendency to improve.

21,748. The unfittest in that case may survive as steadily as the fittest? Yes; what you want is this: numerous small schools *dependent for life upon the results obtained.* And in testing these results I would have the British Government keep one point in view as the primary thing to test by, and it is this: to compare the results in those schools as regards their acquisition of written English; their familiarity with the written language of the people, for that is the one point in which all the methods agree; that is one of their objects: they are all trying to teach the written language of the people. I should eliminate everything else in the first test. Then supposing that all succeed equally well upon that test, the one that in addition to that teaches speech is worthy of encouragement. Next, supposing you have a number of schools under different methods that do equally well as regards the knowledge of written language and their power to articulate; then comes the still higher point, namely, the ability to read from the mouth. The thing that is common to all is the written language; therefore I say test that first, do not throw out the articulation school because the articulation is bad or painful or disagreeable, provided that the knowledge of written language acquired by those pupils is equal to the knowledge of written language acquired in some other school where speech is not taught, because that bad speech is something in addition that the pupil has got. However bad it may be it is something more than a pupil has who has no speech. Do not compare speech with a knowledge of the sign language, because the sign language is of no use in the hearing world, whereas the speech, even if imperfect, is of use if it can be understood.

21,749. You are aware that we have in this country a system in our primary schools of Government inspection and payment by results which is unique, and you are probably also aware that that has often been charged with the evil of having stereotyped the methods of instruction?—The whole subject is new to me, and I should like very much to investigate the matter, because it is a problem with me how to evolve some method applicable to America, by which we could have a supervision over our institutions as you have in this country and test by results.

21,750. While you are in this country you will give attention to that matter, I presume?—Yes.

21,751. I gather from answers that you have already given that it would be possible for the State in the most eclectic spirit to institute a system of inspection and payment to the several schools on the results attained in achieving the end which you have thus indicated while leaving each institution to pursue its own methods?—Yes, that is just the point I would keep in view, I would leave these schools free to pursue any method they like, but I would have the British Government give their aid by results.

21,752. But in order to get those results in teaching you insist that great efforts should be made to ensure the competency of the teachers employed?—It is very necessary. The great mistake in America has been to recognise what I may term as bricks and mortar as the thing to which State aid should be given. The competency of the teachers is not an element. I do not mean to say by this that we do not have good teachers, for we have. Indeed, I believe that the average of intelligence and culture among our teachers is at least equal, if not superior, to that of those employed in Europe. I would have you to recognise the importance of competent teachers, who should receive payment for each pupil in accordance with the pupil's attainments, wherever the teacher may be, whether in one particular school or another, and not confine your aid to some centralised institution.

21,753. In England in our primary schools Government grants are only given when certified teachers are employed; do you think that a good plan?—Undoubtedly.

21,754. Now with regard to the training of teachers for particular work of instructing the deaf and dumb: do I gather rightly that you think those teachers might be best obtained from the ordinary normal schools of the country rather than that they should be specially trained from the first for teaching the deaf and dumb?—That is my impression; but I do not think we want to be very strict about that, because there may be admirable teachers of the deaf who have not obtained a normal school education. But I should insist that every teacher of the deaf should have a competent knowledge of the general art and science of teaching. If they are not trained in a normal college they should be tested and examined on that point before they are allowed to teach the deaf.

21,755. Is it not the fact that the great bulk of the most competent teachers employed in the institutions at present have been trained for the ordinary public schools of the country?—I have no statistics to determine that. My own personal experience, from my knowledge of a number of teachers, is that the bulk have not been trained, but only a very small percentage have been trained, but they are as a rule persons of good general education; but very few of them, I think, have been specially trained as teachers or have passed through the normal course.

21,756. I gather that you do not advocate the establishment of a special training institution for teachers of the deaf and dumb?—I would not advocate the establishment, by the Government, of a special training school for teachers of the deaf, for this reason, that it will tend to the perpetuation of some one method of instruction. I believe that diversity in methods of instruction will be advantageous to progress, if there is competent supervision and examination of results and payment by results; and that it would be better to draw our teachers from all the normal schools of the country, and let them acquire their special training in schools and institutions for the deaf. It would be a very proper thing for special training schools to be established by private enterprise—to propagate some special method—and such teachers might be accepted and recognised by the Government, if their general qualifications come up to the Government standard.

21,757. You are familiar with the methods of training in some of the normal schools, are you not?—I am not sufficiently familiar with them for you to be able to rely upon my testimony.

21,758. May I take it that it is a rule throughout the United States that no teacher is allowed to be employed in a public school until he has completed his apprenticeship in the normal schools?—I believe that a certificate is required as a rule from the teachers of the hearing, but not from the teachers of the deaf.

21,759. I believe you have nothing in the public schools of America analogous to our pupil-teacher system, by which apprentices are employed in the actual work of teaching in the primary schools?—I am not competent to say.

21,760. Given that you have secured a properly trained teacher, you prefer day schools to institutions for the reasons you have stated?—Undoubtedly. I recognise that you cannot do away with the institutions, but I prefer the day schools wherever they can be adopted.

21,761. I think you told us that very little more than one-third of the children of school age who are known to be deaf are at present under public education?—I did not mean to convey that idea. What I meant to state was that on the 1st of June, 1880, there were 5,393 pupils in all the State institutions, excluding the day schools, whereas there were 15,059 children of school age in the country. The number in the institutions upon that particular day was, therefore, about one-third of the total I have given; but of that total, many had already received partial education in the institutions. I think, however, upon the evidence that exists we may be able to say (though this is only a matter of opinion) that there are probably as many deaf children of school age growing up without instruction in America as there are in all our institutions and schools put together. That is, as I say, matter of opinion and not proved as fact.

21,762. Whatever the proportion may be, is it not a little surprising in view of a very generous aid given from the public funds towards the maintenance as well as the education of the deaf in America?—It is very surprising, and indicates to my mind a defect in the methods of reaching the deaf and dumb. It indicates to me that the policy of centralisation, however generously supported (and it is generously supported in the United States), fails to reach a large number of the deaf and dumb; because their parents will not send them away from home. No increase in the number of institutions will remedy that evil. I would say, do not increase the number of institutions to accommodate those children who have not come in, but push out little day schools as near the homes of the children as you can, that is to say, supplement the institution system by the day school system.

21,763. I gather that you do not look to any system of compulsory attendance as the remedy?—No, I think not.

21,764. At all events, you would not advocate compulsion where the only available means of instruction is at a distant institution?—I would not advocate it.

21,765. But do you think if there were provided within a certain walking distance from the home such day schools as those you have indicated, compulsion might then be properly applied?—I think the community would then have the right to apply compulsion.

21,766. To the same extent as it is applied to the ordinary hearing child?—Yes; on one condition, that the wishes of the parents are consulted in regard to the methods of instruction.

21,767. You cited the action of the State of Wisconsin in having specially legislated for the establishment of day schools upon the models which you approve; and you told us that the State had agreed to make a grant of 100 dollars a year for each child so taught. I am not quite sure whether you told us by what particular county authority these day schools would be managed; would they be part of the Public School system?—They would be part of the Public School system under the Local School Boards in the places where the schools are established. They would be supervised by those Local School Boards, and would also come under the supervision of the State Superintendent of Public Instruction, and State aid would only be given to those local schools on the condition of their having a teacher whose competency is certified to by the State Superintendent of Public Instruction.

21,768. Supposing the actual cost of instruction of each child to be more than 100 dollars a year, would you say from what other funds the balance would come?—From the local school funds and from the parents and friends of the pupils; but I would not advise that day schools should be discriminated against by the State; that is, I would not advise that the pupils in day schools should have less aid from the State than the institutions receive.

21,769. But, presumably, the cost of giving instruction in a day school where the children go home to their parents would be very much less than in an institution?—Undoubtedly. Hence the State might afford to give a longer term of instruction at the day school.

21,770. Supposing it be not possible to establish these day schools within walking distance of the child's home, do you contemplate the establishment of local homes to which children might be sent, say from Sunday to Sunday?—I do not contemplate the establishment of local homes, excepting as an alternative to the greater evil of institutions. They are better than an institution, but not so good as a school where the children return to their own parents after the school hours are over. The cost to the State where the parents assume the cost of board is, of course, very much less than where the State assumes the cost of maintenance and board as well as education; and I would advocate in cases where the parents bear the cost of board, the State should not discriminate against the day school by making a less total appropriation for the education of a day scholar than it gives to an institution scholar. I should, therefore, advocate that the terms of instruction at the State expense in the day school should be increased, so that the same amount of money that is expended on the child at the State institution may be expended on the education of the child at the day school in the form of giving him a longer period of instruction. Now, hearing children have at the public expense an education from the age of 4 to 20 years in Wisconsin, whereas the deaf who need education so much more than the hearing are limited to a very few years in the institution on account of the expense. I hold, therefore, that if the State can be saved any expense by sending the deaf child to a day school, the term of his instruction should be lengthened until it approximates to or equals that afforded to the hearing child. In regard to homes for deaf children, I look upon the homes as an intermediate step between the day school proper, which I advocate, and the institution which is very objectionable. The objectionable feature in a system of day schools supplemented by homes is the bringing of children together into those homes for so many days exclusively without the supervision of

Mr. A. G. Bell.

22 June 1888.

their parents; but still it is a step in advance of the institution plan in my view: it is better than to take them from their parents for several months in the year.

21,771. Under the English law of compulsory attendance a limit is fixed within which there must be a suitable school available; is there anything of that kind in the laws or byelaws of the American system?—There is no relation to the hearing children.

21,772. Do you imagine that the same regulation as to distance would apply to the deaf and dumb as to the hearing children; or in their case materially different?—I think that the distance might be increased in the case of deaf children, because parents very often recognise the very great necessity of the children going to school, and would prefer to send their children, as they do in America, 18 miles by railway to attend a day school rather than send them to an institution. So I therefore think the limit of distance could be very considerably enlarged.

21,773. I have been asking you these questions because I was anxious to know whether this grant of 100 dollars per annum for each child (equal to 20*l.* a year with us) contemplates the cost of maintenance as well as the cost of education to any extent at all?—It does not contemplate maintenance at all.

21,774. Are there any facilities afforded in America in the nature of free passes by railway or tramway systems for pupils under any circumstances?—Very generally some arrangement has been made. There has recently been a law passed interfering with the granting of passes for any purpose. I do not know how far that has affected the day schools; but I know that in Boston, in the Horace Mann School, private parties very often leave money for the purpose of horse-car fares and things of that sort for the pupils; so that there is no necessity for any parent paying for the transportation of the child, if he is not able to afford it. I may say also that in my opinion day schools promote charitable enterprises much more than institutions do. In day schools at Boston, for instance, people come forward and leave money in the hands of the principal of the school for the boot and shoe fund, so that if a child comes from a home where it cannot be properly dressed she has her school dress provided. If you were to go into the school you would see nothing in the nature of a ragged school. All the children are well dressed, with clean faces and good boots and shoes. These day schools promote enterprises of that description more than the institutions do. I forgot to allude to a very important movement just established in Boston which has touched me very much, namely, the establishment of the first infant school for the deaf in America, which has just been opened this last month. I have given the whole history of it, so far as I know it, at page 165 of my pamphlet, "Facts and Opinions relating to the "Deaf." *See* "The Sarah Fuller Home for little "Children who cannot hear." It takes little children at three or four years of age.

21,775. We may assume that in such infant schools, even to a greater extent than is common in ordinary schools, great attention would be given to the kindergarten?—Undoubtedly; that would be essential.

21,776. I do not want to go into details as to the methods of instruction; but, putting the question broadly, would you regard the general kindergarten principle as applicable to every stage of the instruction of the deaf and dumb?—In the earlier stages, I think, it is essential for the very young.

21,777. That leads me up to a concluding question I would like to ask, as to the extent and character of the industrial instruction for which you would provide in conjunction with the ordinary literary work of the school?—I have a feeling that we want to interfere as little as possible with the literary work, and that the industrial education during the period of school life should be as much as possible confined to the elements of trades and the use of tools, rather than extended to the teaching of special trades or special pursuits, and that after the pupil has finished his education there should be some aid from the Government to apprentice the child to the trade or pursuit for which he evinces the best aptitude. I think they should be scattered as much as possible in different pursuits, whereas the teaching of special trades at school brings them all into one or two trades, in which they cannot all obtain employment. As regards most trades and businesses which deaf persons enter into, the deaf are able to acquire, without instruction through language, by simple observation and imitation the details of the trade, and they have no difficulty I am sure in acquiring them where they start with a competent knowledge of the use of tools and the elements of the trades. I should therefore recommend that in schools for the deaf only those elements should be taught that are common to a number of special trades, and that after the school life is finished some aid should be given by the Government to apprentice the children in different pursuits and different specific trades, scattering them as much as possible through the community.

21,778. Do you look upon the industrial training given on those principles as likely to be useful to the physical development of the pupil?—I see no reason why it should be unfavourable.

21,779. It might be directed to that as its special aim?—It might be so directed.

21,780. And you have told us already that you see no reason why physical exercises should not be as thoroughly well given in a day school as in an institution?—I see no reason. In the Horace Mann School in Boston they have regular gymnastic exercises. They have a little gymnasium in the first place where the pupils can exercise at their own desire, and, furthermore, they have regular class instruction with the dumb-bells; all the children in the school are drilled like a set of soldiers; they all make the same motions with the dumb-bells for a certain length of time each day.

21,781. Very much the same exercises, I suppose, as those that are given in the best public schools of America?—The aim is to make them the same. By-the-by, there is one feature in the Horace Mann School in Boston which I have not mentioned, which is unique. It has arisen from an accident, but as it is so very important I will direct your attention to it. The school became too small to accommodate the children, and pending the erection of a special school building, the principal sent two of her classes, the most advanced classes, into an ordinary public school building; she picked out the two classes where the progress in speech and speech-reading was most advanced, the children of which could talk well. That acts, I think, as a stimulus to the articulation of the younger children, because they want to go into the public school. It also brings the best class of pupils into contact with the public. The teachers and children of the public school converse with these selected deaf children and do not see the worst cases. It acts as a stimulus, as I say, because the children know that if they make sufficient advancement in speech-reading and articulation they will be drafted into the public school, and go into what is looked upon as a sort of upper class in the school. I think it very important that we bring the pupils of our schools—especially the older pupils—into contact with hearing persons in a greater degree as their education advances, as a preparation to entering the world. The object of their education is to fit them to live in a world of hearing people, and as their education advances they become better able to communicate with hearing persons, and should have opportunities of becoming accustomed to the conditions in which they will live in the future, instead of being left to plunge in at the conclusion of their school course, without any experience of the difficulties with which they will have to contend. The Institution plan of preparing them to enter the world reminds me of the remark of the ancient monarch who was nearly drowned, and who vowed he would never again go into the water *until he had learned to swim!* The Institutions try to teach them to swim without putting them into the water.

21,782. In American schools for the hearing and speaking children I believe a very large portion of the teachers are females; do you think that women are as well adapted for the teaching of the deaf and dumb?—I think that they are better adapted; they are more patient and understand the condition of little children a great deal better than a man does. They are able to bring themselves down to the level of the children very much better.

21,783. (*Sir Tindal Robertson.*) I know that your evidence relates more to the deaf and dumb than to the blind; but I put this question to you because you have exceptional acquaintance with telephone work and work of that kind. I would ask you whether you think that blind people, especially blind girls and blind women, might be advantageously employed in telephone work considering that they would not be required to write?—I think that a very important suggestion; it never occurred to my mind before it was suggested to me here; but there is no reason at all why the blind should not be employed in our central offices where hearing alone is required, and the telephone business certainly opens up a great avenue for the employment of the blind.

21,784. Then with regard to the question of heredity amongst the deaf and dumb, I understand you to say that you would avoid, as much as possible, the congregation together of the deaf and dumb either for educational purposes or for social intercourse in order to avoid the possibility of intermarriage?—I should adopt the principle of decentralisation in education and separate the deaf from one another as much as possible and strive to encourage bonds of union between the deaf population and the hearing population. No doubt we cannot avoid bringing the deaf together to a certain extent, but we should do it as little as possible, and we should recognise that it is an evil to be avoided if possible.

21,785. Considering that we must, as you say, bring them together to a certain extent, would you advise that in all institutions for the deaf and dumb there should be a separate school for each sex?—I must say I have not formed any decisive judgment upon the question of separating the sexes in schools; it is an unnatural thing to separate them. I have not formed any decided opinion upon that subject. What we want to do is to avoid the association of the two sexes in adult life.

21,786. Is not that much more likely to happen when they have been associated in their school life?—I think it depends a good deal upon the method of instruction and upon the character of the school. Institution life certainly tends to association in adult life, but if you have a very small day school for the deaf in the same building with a large school for the hearing, and if those deaf children associate freely with the hearing children and their own parents and friends, I think the deaf boys will see and know many more hearing girls than deaf girls. I am very undecided as to the propriety of separating the sexes, especially during the earlier period of education.

21,787. In the question I just put to you I was referring to an institution which was for the education of deaf and dumb children exclusively, would it be advisable in your opinion that in such an institution there should be separate schools for the sexes in order to avoid the great evil which your theory manifestly suggests?—I would rather not express too decided an opinion upon that. In Montreal we had a school for males and a school for females, at the first blush it seems a good thing, but I can see many objections to a separation of the sexes, especially in the case of very young children, and I would rather not express too decided an opinion upon the question. It is a matter upon which we should think carefully and come to a careful decision. I would rather not announce my views upon that subject in too rigid terms at the present time. I may say that I am inclined to think that separate schools for the two sexes, especially for the older pupils, might be advantageous, but I do not wish that to go on record as my firm conviction.

21,788. (*Mr. Johnson.*) I understand you to say that you have not a very decided opinion as to the desirability of separating the sexes in institutions for the deaf and dumb; but I assume you would not see any objection to their being brought together in an ordinary public day school?—No, I would not separate them there.

21,789. In an institution you think it might probably be desirable to separate them?—I am inclined to think it might be desirable in the case of older pupils, in the case of young pupils I do not think it so desirable.

21,790. Your experience has not been so much with old pupils as with the young?—My experience has been more with the younger pupils.

21,791. With regard to masters and mistresses for the deaf and dumb, where do you get your masters and mistresses from now?—That is a mystery; but I must say this for American institutions, that we do get men and women of ability, both as principals and teachers, but not, so far as my observation goes, specially trained as teachers.

21,792. Have you anything corresponding with our pupil-teachers system?—No. I cannot speak with authority upon this question, but my impression is that a teacher is selected by the principal, and the principal is the judge of the competency of that teacher. When a teacher once goes into the work, and has been in the work for two or three years, he or she is likely to continue, and it is very much the custom of institutions when they want new teachers to take their teachers from other institutions. This is specially the case in sign-institutions, for teachers who know the sign-language have practically a monopoly of the work; it takes so long a time for a raw teacher to acquire the language.

21,793. In some instances they take persons who know very little as regards the treatment of the deaf and dumb, and they train them in the institutions?—That is so.

21,794. But there is no training college in the States for teachers for the deaf and dumb?—No.

21,795. Do not you think it would be a desirable thing to establish such a college?—No. I think it would be advantageous perhaps to have a training school on each method, which could send out advocates of its own system, but I would not have a training college supported by the State. I think the Government should take from the training colleges for hearing persons those who would be likely to make good teachers of the deaf and send them to schools for the deaf and let them gain experience in those schools for the deaf. Special training colleges might very properly be established by private enterprise, but I do not think it would be well for the Government to do so. Government action would be apt to interfere with healthy competition between methods of instruction, by encouraging some one system at the expense of the others. I would have the Government take no part in the contest between systems of instruction otherwise than as an impartial judge of the results.

21,796. With regard to homes I do not know whether I understood you rightly that there are no such things as homes for the deaf and dumb in America in connexion with day schools?—There are such homes.

21,797. Are they very numerous or not?—I think not, but there is a day school in the city of Portland in the State of Maine, to which there were so many applications for admission that the principal was obliged to find homes for the children among private families in the city. Then some one family became a sort of head centre and received 10 or a dozen children, while there were a number of scattered homes in the city receiving in each case a

Mr. A. G. Bell.

22 June 1888.

smaller number. A very small percentage of the children who attend that school come from Portland itself; they come from other parts of the State. I am afraid that the result will be the establishment of an institution; that is to say, that the day school will become an institution. If an institution is established in that State, what I would recommend would be that it should not be in the city of Portland, but somewhere else, and that the day school should be kept in the city for the children of the city and surrounding district.

21,798. You would prefer the separate boarding-out system to the associated system?—Yes. I should prefer that, but the plan that I would prefer to all others would be that the children should be at their own homes; next to that, if that is impossible, I should prefer to have them boarded separately in families, with people who would look after them; next to that, if that is impossible, I would have a home the inmates of which should be as few as possible; after that, if that was impracticable or expensive, I should have a boarding school; but in every case I would keep my number as small as possible, and the boarding school should be constructed and operated on the cottage plan, rather than upon the dormitory system.

21,799. In those day schools where deaf and dumb children are admitted, is there any medical supervision or examination at all to determine the causes of deafness, or to ascertain whether any steps might be taken to ameliorate their condition medically and surgically?—I am not competent to speak upon that. I am acquainted with what is done in the Boston School, but not with what is done in other schools. I think in that school the teachers simply advise the parents of anything they ascertain themselves, and in some cases an examination of the children is made by a competent aurist, who, as a general rule, charges nothing for the examination; but I do not think that sort of examination by an aurist a general feature of a day school. Generally in institutions there are medical men whose names at all events appear upon the reports as doctors to the institutions, who look generally to the health of the pupils, and you will find in the reports of the institutions a report upon the health of the inmates from the medical superintendents. In some cases those are outside physicians who attend at the institutions as they go to a hospital, in other cases they are associated intimately and closely with the institution.

21,800. Do not you think, supposing there was anything like compulsory education of the deaf and dumb, that it would be a desirable thing to have a special medical supervision of the schools into which deaf and dumb children were admitted, with a view to ameliorating the deafness from which the children were suffering, where practicable?—I think it would be a very good plan.

21,801. I ask you the question because in some of the institutions we have visited in England we have found that deafness depends very much upon an enlargement of the throat and an enlargement of the glands of the ear, a condition which might be very much modified by medical treatment?—I think it is very important that the British Government should collect correct statistics relating to causes of deafness. The teachers, the principals, and the parents of the children are incompetent to decide as to the causes of deafness. The most ridiculous causes are sometimes assigned. The true causes of the deafness in particular cases in my opinion can only be arrived at by some competent system of medical supervision. Some competent medical authorities should examine the children and give a report upon the causes of deafness from a medical point of view. The results of medical treatment of diseases of the ear in America do not seem to be very encouraging.

21,802. Have you arrived at anything like a conclusion as to what is the most frequent cause of deafness among children?—The most frequent cause of congenital deafness is hereditary predisposition, as is shown by the fact that more than 54 per cent. of those who are returned as congenitally deaf have other members of their families deaf and dumb. That is the most frequent cause amongst the congenitally deaf.

21,803. What has caused the deafness in the parents of those congenitally deaf and dumb? Is syphilis a cause?—I do not find syphilis to be a cause in any large number of cases. I have examined very carefully the history of a family in which deafness has gone down through five successive generations. I had competent medical assistants to assist me in the examination. I made a special study of that family, and I specially inquired as to syphilis, because members of the family in the lower generations had fallen very much in social status, and it might be supposed that syphilitic symptoms might have had something to do with it, but I found from the doctors who had attended upon those deaf and dumb persons that in some cases an amputation had been performed—an amputation of a finger, for instance—and the person recovered perfectly from the operation; the wound healed in a way it would not have done had there been syphilis in the family. Then I have not observed Hutchinson's notched teeth in the family. I do not think syphilis is the cause of congenital deafness to any very great extent; it does cause it in some cases, undoubtedly.

21,804. In those cases it would be in the secondary or tertiary form?—I do not know. This chart shows the pedigree of the family I have referred to —the Lovejoy family, of Maine. The black dots indicate those who are deaf mutes. In the Sydney branch of the family deaf mutes have appeared for five successive generations, and this chart gives a complete account of all the descendants, deaf and hearing, so far as known, of the first deaf mute.

21,805. To go to another subject, has there been any great trial in America of the pure oral system; that is to say, a system in which signs and the manual alphabet are rigidly excluded?—That system was introduced into America about the year 1867. The schools on that system are increasing in number. I am sorry that the Commission have not had testimony before them from some one who is a pure oralist. As I have explained to the Commission, I cannot undertake to present the views of the advocates of any particular system.

21,806. Taking the education of the deaf and dumb as 100, have you any idea what would be the percentage of the purely orally taught children as far as you know, would it be a third, or a fourth, or a fifth? —In the pamphlet "Facts and Opinions relating to the Deaf" (Part V., pages 176–181) you have the materials from which you can determine that for yourselves. I have not added up the figures because the records are imperfect; some of the institutions have not made full returns. You will see that in those statistics of articulation teaching I have discriminated between those pupils to whom articulation was taught as a means of instruction and those to whom articulation was taught but not used as a means of instruction. In 1883 a similar letter of inquiry was addressed to the principals of American institutions by Miss Rogers, who was the principal of the Clarke Institution, and the result showed that at that time out of 6,232 cases 886, or 14 per cent., were under oral instruction, while 1,105, or 18 per cent., were taught articulation as an accomplishment, and 4,241, or 68 per cent., received no instruction whatever in speech. From the tables presented to you you can get the same facts for 1888. Then there is this fact in addition. Among those who are not taught articulation are a number of cases who have been dropped from articulation classes as not being suitable subjects for such instruction. I have attempted to separate those from the others, and you can get at the result for yourselves.

21,807. (*Rev. Mr. Sleight.*) Upon the question of statistics upon which you dwelt a great deal, at what period did the American census begin to take any

Mr. A. G. Bell.

22 June 1888.

note of deaf mutes?—I think the census of 1830 was the first that took note of them.

21,808. Then the earlier records of the congenitally deaf are not reliable?—Not at all reliable. I do not think any census is reliable except the 1880 census.

21,809. You said that a number of idiots were deaf mutes, what means have you of ascertaining that absolute idiots are deaf mutes?—You can find out whether an idiot can hear or not by his taking notice of sound. If an idiot is deaf he is, of course, set down as a deaf mute idiot, the deafness carrying the muteness with it; but I hope and believe that the census relating to idiotic deaf mutes is incorrect, because an ordinary observer, I think, could hardly be competent to decide upon the mental condition of deaf mutes. I know of some deaf mutes who were thought to be idiots, but who turned out to be perfectly bright and intelligent. While, of course, we have to accept the figures of the census, and while we must admit that the proportion of idiots among deaf mutes is abnormally large, yet I hardly think we can trust to the judgment of the census-taker and assume that all that are reported as idiots are idiots. In any British census I would recommend that the British Government should take care to formulate some system by which the statements of the census-takers should be checked and verified by competent observers. A great deal has been done in the United States census to eliminate errors in that respect by correspondence with physicians in the neighbourhood and by getting opinions from them.

21,810. At what age is a child capable of receiving auricular instruction?—We do not know yet at what age, the whole subject is too new and there are very great difficulties in the way of ascertaining how far a very little child can hear and so many of them pretend to hear who do not.

21,811. Sound having once reached a child's mind do you not consider that that child is more capable of being orally taught than a congenitally deaf mute?—Certainly. If the voice can reach the child through the ear I think we have got something instinctive to work on; we have the instinctive feeling in the child to help us. A child whose ancestors for generations back have made use of the vocal organs in expressing thought must have acquired some hereditary aptitude for that means of expression, a child whose ancestors for generations have received ideas through the medium of the ear must in my opinion if it has any hearing, however slight, have some hereditary aptitude for receiving language through that means. Of course I may be entirely wrong in that idea, but it is one that I give to the Commission for what it is worth.

21,812. Are not there many who consider the sign language the mother tongue of the congenitally deaf?—There are very many who do so consider it, mistakenly as I conceive. I have discussed that question very fully in public with my friend Dr. Edward Gallaudet. We always seem to be opposed to one another upon that particular question and when I give a lecture upon that subject I invite him to come and oppose me, and I publish the results of the discussion on both sides, and I have great pleasure in presenting the Commission with the result of our last friendly contest on the matter, which is contained in this pamphlet (*handing it in*). This discussion with Dr. Gallaudet is printed in the Annals for January, 1884, Vol. XXIX., pp. 32–69, under the title "Fallacies Concerning the Deaf." In the same volume, pp. 312 to 325, will be found my discussion with Dr. Philip G. Gillett, in Chicago, concerning "Deaf Classes in the Public Schools."

21,813. Language is what we want to give to deaf mutes, but given that a child can only be five years at school (the average is not five years in our own schools) by which system could you best impart a knowledge of language to a congenitally deaf mute?—By the system, whichever it is, by which you could bring the greatest repetition of English words to the senses of the child; and in that connexion I may allude to what I consider to be an important suggestion that I brought before the recent Convention of Principals held in Jackson, Mississippi, just before I came away from America, which was very favourably received by the principals, upon that very point. The method I would advocate for teaching a congenitally deaf mute would be that method by which you could produce the greatest number of repetitions of words to the eye, distinctly and clearly, in a given time. The difficulty in presenting English words to the eye of a deaf child is the difficulty in the speed of writing, or in the speed of spelling with the hand; you cannot write more than about 30 words a minute; with the manual alphabet it is possible to approximate to 100 words, but very few teachers can do it. 80 words would be the outside with an average expert teacher. Now I suggest that you should have recourse to a method by which you can get a greater speed. Before speaking of this method let me call your attention to the rate at which words are presented to the ears of hearing children. The average rate of speech to a child, using the simple words which children employ, would be about 200 a minute. A stenographer would say 150 words a minute was a very good rate of speech, but that is for language in which long words are of frequent occurrence. Nurses and mothers gabble at a tremendous rate to little children, and from experiments I have made in reading children's books aloud and counting the number of words I found that 200 words a minute is not a fast rate at which we present words to the ear of a hearing child. Now make a calculation and see what would be the number of words presented to the ear of a hearing child before he acquires our language. Suppose that all the talking that goes on in the presence of hearing children in the course of the day were to be concentrated into one long continuous gabble, and suppose we put that at three hours, the number of words that that child would have presented to his ears in the course of those three hours at 200 words a minute would be 36,000 (and as the whole vocabulary that we use with a child hardly exceeds 300 words, this means a very great repetition). We do that 365 days in the year; we do not stop on Sundays; and we do it continually for two years before the child turns round and speaks to us. Now, what we want to get at is, how can we present English words as rapidly and clearly to the eyes of a deaf child as we do to the ears of a hearing child. If we can do it with the same rate of rapidity we know perfectly well that he will learn the English language as easily as the hearing child; the difficulty is how to do it. I suggested at the recent conference a mode by which I think that result can be arrived at. I have been testing the rate at which we can take in words by the eye, though the rate at which we write is only 30 words a minute at the outside the rate at which we read words once they are written is over 350 a minute. The first time that the importance of this fact struck me was when I noticed the enormous amount of reading that is done by what are termed semi-mute pupils, and the little amount of reading that goes on among the congenitally deaf. I thought I would test the speed of that reading. I gave a deaf friend an interesting novel (she did not know the object I had), a novel which I knew would fascinate her. I made note of the time when she commenced to read. She read it through at one sitting, and when she finished it I noted the time; then I took the book and estimated the number of words in the book and found that, on an average, she had read nearly 400 words a minute; *she had read more words in an hour and a half than a hearing child hears in the course of a day*. I say there is great hope for the deaf in giving them a knowledge of language by putting books before them and accustoming them to form the habit of reading. There is a great attempt made in our institutions to adopt what is termed the natural method of teaching, but they fail in one particular, they do not realise this, that in the natural process of learning a language comprehension of the language precedes expression of

Mr. A. G. Bell.

22 June 1888.

ideas in that language. A child understands a language before he uses it, whereas the attempt is made in our schools for the deaf to make a child use the language before he understands it: for instance, in the sign institutions the process would generally be to tell a story in signs and make the pupils express the ideas in the English language before they know the English language. Very rarely do you find the converse; where they give the story in English words and get the pupils to express the meaning in signs. I would advocate as a very important thing the cultivation of the habit of reading. I would make it a regular part of our school exercise that interesting stories should be put before the children, and that they should read them whether they understand them or not. Teachers say, Why put books before deaf children and require them to read that which they do not understand? But a deaf child never can learn language till he has seen it any more than a hearing child can learn it till he has heard it, he must hear it without understanding it at first; he comes to understand it by hearing it, and a deaf child will come to understand it by seeing it. I may say that I made an experiment upon myself which has a very important bearing upon this whole subject. I obtained a Spanish book on the education of deaf mutes. I did not know anything of the Spanish language, and I determined to try how far I could understand this book by forcing myself to read it. I read about 20 or 30 pages of it, and I found I could make very little of it; the Latin roots helped me a little, and I understood a few technical terms, but that was all. I refused a dictionary altogether; a dictionary stops the current of thought; I read about 30 pages of it, and then I stopped. Now a number of words had occurred so often that they impressed themselves upon my memory; a number of other words had occurred pretty frequently, but not often enough to impress themselves on my memory; those which had occurred so frequently as to make me remember them without explaining themselves by the context I hunted up in the dictionary. Then I read a few more pages, and I found that those words, the meaning of which I had obtained from the dictionary, formed the key for the next 30 pages, and the meaning of many sentences, which otherwise would have been obscure, became apparent. Now words explained themselves by the context, and after I had turned over 30 or 40 more pages I turned to the dictionary again and found the meaning of some more words that I could remember. Having done so, I turned back and read the book a second time, and a very great portion of the meaning of that book revealed itself to me, and I felt convinced that if I wanted to learn the Spanish language I had nothing to do but to read and to read and I would learn it. The application to deaf mutes at once flashed across me. It is a most unfortunate thing that our deaf mutes do not read books; that is to say, our congenitally deaf mutes,—our semi-mutes do read,—and I think that half the credit that teachers get for the knowledge of language possessed by those who are termed semi-mutes is not due to the teaching at all, but is due to the books they read. I am strengthened in that view by what I have observed in the case of deaf friends. There are many expressions they use that are never used by persons with whom they come in contact; exceptional forms of speech common in society novels, but not usually employed in conversation. I have come to the conclusion that novels and plays that are usually banished from the libraries of our deaf and dumb institutions might prove a great means of giving language to the deaf and dumb, especially those society novels in which you have conversations in questions and answers. Ordinary books like books of history, Stanley's Travels, and so on, do not give the language of the people, it is book language; but novels and plays are the books that will facilitate the acquisition of language and stimulate the pupil to read. If you make a deaf child perforce every day, as a regular school exercise, read over not a few paragraphs of a book, but hundreds of pages, he will gradually learn language; he gets the repetition of words to the eye that the hearing child gets to the ear. I strongly recommend this plan of introducing reading as a part of the school exercise, the reading of interesting stories that hearing children love to read, introducing it as a school exercise without any explanation of the meaning, getting them to read, whether they understand what they read or not. I would recommend that some reward should be given to a child for this process of reading a book that he does not understand; that is to say, after reading an interesting story I would recommend acting it out. I would act it out in natural pantomime with him, or I would show him a picture—pictures are as tangible as signs. I would not show him the picture till after he had read in the book what was represented by the picture. Then let us trace what goes on in his mind. He obtains the idea that this language which he is reading expresses a pantomime or expresses a picture, and all the time he is reading his mind is being exercised and he is wondering what sort of pantomime it is going to be, or what sort of picture it is going to be. That is the sort of mental exercise that the child needs. If his idea was incorrect the pantomime or the picture would correct it, and if, on the other hand, the pantomime or the picture corresponded with the imaginary picture he formed in his mind, he would be doubly delighted. That, I think, is a process which should be followed in all schools for the deaf. It is the reverse of the process usually adopted. For example, in our sign schools a story will be told in signs, and pupils who know little or nothing of the English language are asked to go through the drudgery of writing it out in words. This makes of the English language a school task. Even in schools which do not use the sign language, "action writing" is resorted to before the pupils are able to read. For example, a teacher may take a book from a boy, open it, place a slip of paper in it as a mark, close it, and lay the book upon her desk. She then asks her class to express in writing what she has done. This kind of exercise is known as "action writing," and it is used in nearly every school. It is an admirable exercise in composition for older pupils, but out of place with pupils who cannot understandingly read an ordinary book. It reverses the process of nature, which demands that a child shall understand a language before he uses it. A hearing child has constant repetition of words to his ear for two years before you expect him to express himself in words. A deaf child should have constant repetition of words to his eye before you call upon him for any very great exercises in English composition. I would, therefore, have a child read books in order to learn the language, instead of studying the language in order to read books.

21,814. I know that in sign schools the children are generally taught columns and columns of nouns and adjectives to commit to memory?—That is just as useless as if you got them to learn the whole of Webster's Unabridged Dictionary. It is not words that a deaf and dumb child wants, it is how to use them. Phrases and varied forms of sentences are what he needs. Sentence forms that remain constant through the constituent words may be infinitely varied. Mere names are of little value until he has occasion to use them. The vocabulary that serves the varied wants of a hearing child rarely exceeds 300 words. Why, then, burden the memory of the deaf child with multitudinous words for which he has no need?

21,815. (*Mr. Johnson.*) You say you would give the child an interesting story to read; before you did that would you give the child any preliminary teaching of any sort?—What I did recently in the case of a little child four years of age whose father I was visiting was this: The child did not know a thing. I took up a book containing the story of the "Three Bears," and I made the child put the forefinger of her right hand on the line of words and travel along the line of words with that hand, while I took her left hand in mine and spelt the words upon that left hand (using Dalgarno's Touch-alphabet) as the child put her finger upon each printed word. My object was to be sure that the little girl had her eye fixed upon the proper word. I spelt it upon her hand, and I put emphasis and expression to it, then after a little while I took the child down and we had a little pantomime. I was the bear and the child had the idea that that was expressed some how or other by those printed words. Every time I went to the house that child brought a book and wanted me to read to her. She had obtained the idea that the words in the book expressed a pantomime. She would, by herself, take up the book from which I had read, and, looking at the words, recall the pantomime she had seen. She would point to the words, and try to explain to her deaf brother the pantomime that had been employed.

21,816. (*Rev. Mr. Sleight.*) The first word the child learnt was the word "bear"?—I do not think she learnt that either. I did not attempt any methodical instruction with the child, it was only to show the parents how I would deal with the child. The child is under methodical instruction now. I only say that is the way I would have commenced the education of the child, and carried it on if it had been in my power to do it. What I did in that case was simply to test whether a child who had not any knowledge of language or letters would get the idea that the pantomime was expressed in the book by the printed letters, and that child had that idea. Telephone matters have occupied my attention very much during the last year especially, so that I have not been able to devote much time to following up my experiments in that direction.

21,817. Did that child express her first ideas in natural signs?—In natural pantomime, helped out by crude conventional signs it had devised for itself. A congenitally deaf child always at first uses signs to express ideas for which it lacks words.

21,818. With regard to the children admitted into the infant school of which you have spoken, do the teachers begin by teaching those children articulation, or do they use signs?—I know from the lady who is the general superintendent that they will commence on the pure oral system, believing that the vocal organs of a deaf child should be exercised when very young, and believing that the power of imitation in a deaf child is very much greater in infancy than when advanced in life. The idea is that if you commence at as young an age as practicable with a deaf child on the pure oral method he will learn to read from the mouth and to speak better than if you commence later. That is the idea on which that school is carried on.

21,819. Do you think it a good system to debar these infants from the use of signs?—They do not debar them from the use of signs, they debar them from the use of conventional signs or sign language; they do not debar them from natural pantomime. Sign teachers quibble a great deal about the word "signs." There is no objection in any method of instruction to the use of natural signs so long as they do not supersede language. Oral teachers object to the use of "sign language;" then the sign teachers turn round and say that the oral teachers object to the use of "signs;" they do not, they use natural signs in every school. It is impossible to reach the mind of a child without the use of natural signs. Hearing children use natural signs in the same way—the only objection is to this conventional *language* of signs. The advocates of sign language muddle the minds of people who have not studied the question by confusing the subject of sign language with the more general subject of signs. I have read a little of what the German teachers have said on the subject of signs. They do not object to natural signs, and there is no such thing as a school in existence where natural signs are not employed, natural signs being understood to mean the signs that ordinary people employ.

21,820. (*Mr. Johnson.*) They give up natural signs when the pupils are sufficiently advanced in oral teaching?—I do not think so. I do not think anyone ever gives up natural signs; but they do not use natural signs in place of words. They are used simply to illustrate and render more interesting the word as you might smile pleasantly when saying something pleasant to a child, or as you might point to the door when you told him to go to the door. Sign teachers have ridiculed the oral method very unjustly, and they have said when an oral teacher says to a child go to the door, he at the same time points to the door, and they say that is a sign. Of course that is a sign; but that is not sign language. That is a thing done to illustrate the meaning of the English expression that the teacher had used to the child, just as is done in the case of a hearing child. We are always using natural signs. Life would be uninteresting without them. Some sign teachers seem to have the idea that a proper teacher of the oral system is a person who will tie his hands behind his back rather than use a gesture of any sort.

21,821. (*Rev. Mr. Sleight.*) Is not it a rule in oral schools that there must be no signing?—They use the word in the sense of conventional signs; they do not mean to prohibit the use of natural signs. I would recommend this Commission to endeavour to get at what is meant by some of the words used by the advocates of different methods. Half the controversy between teachers would be gone if we had distinct definitions.

21,822. Could you explain to me what is the difference in these American schools between a combined, a manual, and an oral school?—I would have to refer you to the principals of those schools. I see No. 24, Le Couteulx St. Mary's Institution, in Buffalo, is "manual, oral, and combined."

21,823. What does that mean?—It simply means that the sign language is used; that is what is meant by the word "combined," and it is a very hopeful sign that the sign teachers seem a little disinclined to state definitely that they use the sign language; they come before the public as using an eclectic system, but they do not follow it, so I translate this "manual, oral, and combined" as meaning that it is manual, oral, and sign language.

21,824. (*Mr. Van Oven.*) How do you read No. 30, the Nebraska Institute, "combined and aural?"—That is sign language and auricular; they have a special auricular department there.

21,825. How do you read No. 32, St. Joseph's Institute at Fordham, "combined and oral?"—I look upon that as sign language and oral; they have an oral department there. Of course you may combine other languages in your curriculum of studies just as you may teach French and German to your English-speaking children. Though you teach hearing children French or German they are English all the time: they think in English, and the other language is a subject of study. Now in schools where they claim to have the combined method, as a general rule they have sign language as the language of communication with the mind, and the pupils study written language and spoken language, as our hearing children study French and German in the public schools, and with similar results; the sign language is their language when they come out of school, and the other is a foreign tongue. It is very difficult to combine in the mind of a child two languages, so that he shall think equally well in both; as a general rule he thinks only in one, and the other will be a foreign language to him. In these combined schools the pupils think in the sign language, and the English language both in its written and in its spoken form is a foreign tongue to them. In the manual schools it is the written language that is the language of thought, thought being probably accompanied by motions of the fingers, and they dream on their fingers when they are asleep.

21,825*a*. (*Rev. Mr. Sleight.*) And if they are wandering in time of sickness they will wander on the hand?—Yes. Now the pupils taught on the oral method think in motions of the mouth, and there is a very important metaphysical question involved as

Mr. A. G. Bell.

22 June 1888.

to what goes on in the mind of a child when it is denied articulation, even of a crude kind. I think in the majority of our institutions children are wilfully deprived of the power of articulation by neglecting to give them the chance to learn speech.

21,826. Not wilfully deprived in the sense of doing them a wrong?—They are wilfully deprived in the sense of not giving them a chance to learn. There is an unfortunate opposition between advocates of the oral method and the advocates of the sign method, and articulation in those schools which are not pure oral schools is not put on the level of geography, or history, or arithmetic, and the pupils are not taught how to use their vocal organs, because of the prejudice against the oral system. I am not a pure oralist, but I advocate that every deaf child should be taught articulation, whatever may be the method of instruction employed. It is my opinion that in the lower stages of instruction of the congenital deaf it would be better to adopt the plan I have spoken of; but in the higher stages I would have the speech-reading method, for all that would succeed with it. If there were any that did not succeed I would continue the manual alphabet plan, not the sign language plan, for the way by which a person acquires language is by the repetition of words, so that the duller a child is the more necessary is that repetition, and the more harmful is the sign language. A dull child needs to have a greater repetition of words than a brighter child. If a child has no speech, it is a curious problem what goes on in his mind. I do not mean to settle it, but he does not think exactly as we do. I remember in the case of that little child that I experimented with before the telephone took my attention from the subject. I came down stairs one day and found him sitting at the bottom of the stairs, and his fingers were moving; he was thinking to himself upon his hands, and I read his thoughts. He was sitting with one boot on and the other off, and he was spelling to himself, "Grandmamma says I must not go out to the stable."

21,827. (*Mr. Johnson.*) Has any evidence been obtained in the case of any educated deaf and dumb person to show what was the previous condition of mind of that person before he was educated?—The late Dr. H. L. Peet attempted to solve that question, and there is printed in one of the earlier numbers of the Annals (Vol. VIII., p. 1) a very interesting paper by him upon "The Notions of the Deaf and Dumb before Instruction." Bebian's theory (Annals, Vol. VIII., p. 105) is, "that the deaf and dumb do not " think either in signs or words, but only in images " and ideas." My feeling is that they must think in pictures. A succession of pictures probably passes before the mind. I am not sure that we do not all think in pictures, but our pictures come labelled with language attached to them.

21,828. But often in ordinary dreaming a conversation goes on; there can be no conversation in the dreams of the deaf and dumb when they have no knowledge of language?—Excepting pantomimic conversations.

21,829. (*Rev. Mr. Sleight.*) Referring to this school for infants which you have spoken of, is not that beginning the institution system much earlier in the child's life than the institutions at present do?—Yes.

21,830. One of your strong points is that you object to children being taken from their mothers; but in that school for infants they are doing so?—I do not say that I advocate that system. I was simply directing attention to the fact that it is the first infant school in America; I consider it a great misfortune to take children away from a good home; but in cases where children have not good homes, and in cases where no attempts are made to instruct them at home, it is a problem what is best to be done. I do not think such a school as that is the best kind of infant school. I would rather have a kindergarten where the children could live at home. I was only directing attention to the matter in which this school came into existence without intending to express any opinion, favourable or otherwise, to the plan itself. But I certainly think that a child should be brought under instruction in language in infancy.

21,831. You would approve of institutions for children whose homes are not what homes should be?—I do not approve of institutions at all, except so far as they are absolutely necessary. I consider them as evils to be avoided as much as possible. I do not approve of taking a child out of the condition in which nature has placed him. I would not take a child away from its home unless it was absolutely necessary. It would be better to find another home for a child in a hearing family than to place it in an institution.

21,832. Have you ever tested the amount of knowledge of written language possessed by pupils in the American institutions on the combined system?—I have.

21,833. What have you found?—Of course, the experience of any one man cannot be taken as a gauge of the whole of the pupils under instruction in all the schools, but I have found as a general rule with little pupils who have been under instruction less than two years that it is difficult to carry on any sort of conversation in writing without the use of signs or some pantomime. I am alluding only to little pupils. I do not examine the older pupils much when I make visits to any of these institutions. I try to get hold of the congenitally deaf. I do not care much about the semi-mutes; their method of education is settled, namely, pure oral. Those that I am more interested in are those who are congenitally deaf, and those who were deaf before the age when speech was acquired, so that when I go into a school I ask for those children who are congenitally deaf, or who have not had any knowledge of language, and who have been there less than two years. A child should learn a language in two years, and, as a general rule, in the combined schools I have visited I find that I cannot carry on a conversation in writing with children who have been under instruction less than two years. In the Rochester school I was able to do this.

21,834. You would never put a deaf mute on the same footing as a hearing child, a hearing child would always have the advantage?—A deaf child has an advantage over a hearing child in this respect, that he is shut up with books, and he ought to be ahead of a hearing child in mental attainments, it is only the difficulty of teaching them the language. The semi-mutes, that is, those who are deaf from late childhood, are often equal, if not superior, in intelligence to hearing children of their age, and that results from their being forced into the companionship of books, so that they rise higher and higher mentally, but the congenitally deaf as a class do not read books, and they lose ground mentally after leaving school; that is not because they are congenitally deaf, it is because they do not know language, and cannot therefore read with profit and enjoyment.

21,835. Do you consider it possible that the higher education of the deaf could be carried on wholly by lip reading, could a lecture ever be delivered to the deaf by the lip?—If the classes were small it could, in large numbers it could not.

21,836. Without having recourse to the manual alphabet?—Undoubtedly. I do not mean to say that you could deliver a lecture to a large number in the hope of its being understood by all the class, but if you had a dozen intelligent young men who were earnest in their studies, and who had acquired the power of reading from the mouth, they would follow the lecture, and if any one of the dozen did not understand a point here and there he could ask for an explanation. I do not see any impossibility in it where you have a small number in the class.

21,837. (*Mr. Johnson.*) It would require acute eyesight, would it not?—No; my impression is that the congenitally deaf as a class have better eyesight than the non-congenitally deaf, but they do not come up to those who are termed semi-mutes in the power of reading from the mouth. The difficulty is the language difficulty. It is a mental problem that the pupil has to solve, not merely a visual problem. He sees merely a portion of speech and has to make out the rest by his knowledge of language: he sees enough to fill up what he loses by the context, just as if I gave you a piece of printed matter and left out a word here and there, or mutilated a word: if you had a good knowledge of language you would read it all perfectly clearly. It is not a question of eyesight, it is not even a question of intelligence, it is a question of knowledge and familiarity with the English language. All those who have familiarity with the English language have the key to speech-reading, those who have not have not.

21,838. Do you not think that amongst the deaf and dumb there are a great number of persons who have feeble sight?—It is not a general characteristic, but the proportion is greater than in the normal population.

21,839. (*Rev. Mr. Sleight.*) Are you aware that Dr. Ed. Gallaudet, the President of the College, says, "We know it would be useless to attempt to give "lectures *vivâ voce* even to those who read well by "the lips"?—My answer to that is it is difficult to believe that he could ever have attempted it.

21,840. To what age do you keep your pupils in the American Institutions?—Very many are kept up to the commencement of adult life, but some do not enter till the commencement of adult life.

21,841. Do the orally taught inter-marry as much as those who are taught by the combined method or by the manual method?—There are too few cases of marriage among the orally taught as yet for us to base reliable conclusions on, but judging from the few cases that have occurred, I should say that a larger proportion of the orally taught marry hearing persons than of those taught on what is called the combined method. I would here refer to a practice which promotes inter-marriage in our institutions; it is a common habit in many of our institutions to call together periodically the former pupils of the institutions; the boys and girls of former years meet together as men and women to have a nice time in honour of their *alma mater*. The Clarke Institution in Northampton was the first to adopt the plan of having no periodical reunions of this kind, and there have been no inter-marriages of pupils of that institution. All the pupils have either married hearing persons or have married deaf mutes belonging to other institutions.

21,842. Have you known any cases of pupils who have received auricular instruction being drafted off into the elementary schools?—Yes, the auricular teachers lament that process very greatly, they say they lose their best pupils. The principal of the institution in Arkansas says that this auricular work is very discouraging work because when visitors come to see his school and he shows what he has been doing to develop the hearing of the pupils, and they find the pupils hearing what the teacher says to them they say, That is not a deaf mute at all, and they turn away and take no further interest in the work. In Nebraska pupils have left and gone into ordinary schools for the hearing and carried on their education there.

21,843. (*Chairman.*) I will just ask you a question or two bearing upon what you have said to-day. You spoke of the advisability of giving technical instruction, not of a distinctive, but of a general character in schools for the deaf; that plan has not been adopted in England for the reason that the teachers think it undesirable to diminish the short time that many pupils have for the study of language; at what age do you think that pupils might fairly begin to receive such general technical instruction?—I do not know that my opinion is entitled to any weight upon that subject, but I should think that a year before their graduation would be sufficient.

21,844. It has been suggested that if technical schools were started for the general population, pupils who have been educated in deaf and dumb institutions and who have received there a certain amount of technical education might after the age of 16 or so enter those technical schools to finish the technical education which they had begun in their special schools, do you think that would be a desirable thing?—I think it would be a very desirable thing. I see no reason why a deaf person could not attend one of those technical schools just as well as a hearing person.

21,845. Who appoints the principals of these deaf and dumb institutions in the United States?—I think they are appointed by the governors of the States.*

21,846. They are political appointments?—I think so. In one or two cases those political appointments have given very great dissatisfaction. I must say I condemn that system.

21,847. Then I will ask you a question on another point; would you be in favour of the appointment of a certain number of deaf mutes on the governing body of the institutions for the deaf and dumb?—I think it might, perhaps, be advantageous to have a minority representation of such persons, not a majority representation. I have not given that question much thought. The feeling in America is against it, I think.

* The governor appoints trustees, and the trustees appoint the principal. The principal appoints the teachers and employés.

Adjourned to Tuesday next at 11 o'clock.

SIXTY-EIGHTH DAY.

6, Old Palace Yard, S.W.

Tuesday, 26th June, 1888.

PRESENT:

THE RIGHT HON. THE LORD EGERTON OF TATTON IN THE CHAIR.

The RIGHT HON. SIR LYON PLAYFAIR, K.C.B., M.P.
SIR TINDAL ROBERTSON, M.P.
B. ST. JOHN ACKERS, ESQ.
F. J. CAMPBELL, ESQ., LL.D.
EDMUND C. JOHNSON, ESQ.
THE REV. W. BLOMEFIELD SLEIGHT, M.A.
THE REV. CHARLES MANSFIELD OWEN, M.A.
L. VAN OVEN, ESQ.
CHARLES E. D. BLACK, ESQ., *Secretary*.

MR. ALEXANDER GRAHAM BELL recalled and further examined.

21,848. (*Chairman.*) Before asking you any questions with regard to visible speech, have you anything further to add with regard to intermarriage of deaf mutes?—I have some tabulated statements relating to the intermarriage of deaf mutes (*see Q.* 21,522). I have here a table showing an analysis of 757 cases of intermarriage between deaf mutes (*handing in the following Table*).

Mr. A. G. Bell.

26 June 1888.

MARRIAGE OF DEAF MUTES.

Analysis of 757 Cases.

				Females. Deaf Mutes. Cause of Deafness. Congenital.	Non-congenital.	Not stated.	Hearing persons.	Total Males.
Males.	Deaf Mutes.	Cause of Deafness.	Congenital	86	93	48	13	240
			Non-congenital.	108	115	53	26	302
			Not stated	27	35	121	10	193
	Hearing persons -			8	6	8	—	22
Total females. -				229	249	230	49	757

Of 757 males, 22 were hearing persons, and 735 were deaf mutes.

Of 757 females, 49 were hearing persons, and 708 were deaf mutes.

Hence of 1,514 persons, 71 were hearing persons, and 1,443 were deaf mutes.

The general result that that table shows is, that of the 1,514 persons who intermarried in those 757 cases, 1,443 were deaf mutes, and 71 were hearing persons, and of the 1,443 deaf mutes, 71 or 5 per cent. married hearing persons, and 1,371 or 95 per cent. married among themselves.

Then there is another point which I did not touch on on Friday, which is very important on the question of heredity. We have hitherto had absolutely no statistics relating to the proportion of the congenitally deaf who marry partners who are themselves congenitally deaf. I have here a table (*handing it in*) showing an analysis of 402 cases of intermarriage of deaf mutes out of the 757 cases in the table I have just handed in.

INTERMARRIAGE OF DEAF MUTES.

Analysis of 402 Cases.

		Females. Congenital.	Non-congenital.	Total Males.
Males.	Congenital - - - -	86	93	179
	Non-congenital - - -	108	115	223
Total females - - -		194	208	402

Of 179 congenital deaf males, 86 married congenitally deaf, and 93 non-congenitally deaf females.

Of 194 congenitally deaf females, 86 married congenitally deaf, and 108 non-congenitally deaf males.

Hence of 373 congenitally deaf persons, 172, or 46.11 per cent., married congenitally deaf persons and 201, or 53·89 per cent., married non-congenitally deaf persons.

Of 223 non-congenitally deaf males, 108 married congenitally deaf, and 115 married non congenitally deaf females. Of 208 non-congenitally deaf females, 93 married congenitally deaf, and 115 married non-congenitally deaf males. Hence of 431 non-congenitally deaf persons 201, or 46·64 per cent., married congenitally deaf persons, and 230, or 53·36 per cent., married non-congenitally deaf persons. I would also present the Commission with an analysis of the 607 cases of deaf children of deaf mute parents referred to in Queries 21,530 and 21,531.

The witness handed in the following table.

DEAF-MUTE CHILDREN OF DEAF-MUTE PARENTS.

Analysis of 607 Cases.

Sex.		Cause of deafness.	
Males - - - -	271	Congenital - -	328
Females - - -	275	Non-congenital -	40
Not stated - - -	61	Not stated - -	239
	607		607

Of 368 deaf-mute children of deaf-mute parents, 328 or 89·1 per cent. were congenitally deaf, and 40 or 10·9 per cent. were non-congenitally deaf.

PERIOD OF BIRTH.	Father deaf, mother unknown.	Mother deaf, father unknown.	Both parents deaf.	Total.
1800-'9 - - - - -	8	—	—	3
1810-'9 - - - - -	1	2	—	3
1820-'9 - - - - -	6	6	1	13
1830-'9 - - - - -	14	11	11	36
1840-'9 - - - - -	23	14	20	57
1850-'9 - - - - -	31	30	41	102
1860-'9 - - - - -	32	35	61	128
1870-'9 - - - - -	21	37	120	178
Ascertained - - - -	131	135	254	520
Not ascertained - - -	35	8	44	87
Total - - - -	166	143	298	607

21,849. (*Dr. Campbell.*) Before admitting a deaf-mute child into an institution in America, are specialists employed to diagnose the causes of the deafness, or is the statement of any practitioner practising in the locality taken?—Neither the one nor the other, the institutions simply take what the parents say.

21,850. (*Chairman.*) Then how do you ascertain that out of those 607 cases, 328 were congenitally deaf?—From the census and from the records of the institutions.

21,851. Founded upon the statements of the deaf children?—Yes.

21,852. The parents would be able to say pretty accurately whether the children were congenitally deaf, unless they were cases which were from infantine diseases?—Yes, the statement of the parents is all you have to guide you.

21,853. Practically the congenitally deaf cases in your table would be cases where the child had never been known to speak?—Yes, cases reported in the census as congenitally deaf, or cases in which the parents had stated that the child had been born deaf, whatever that means.

21,854. (*Chairman.*) You say you are not able to ascertain whether those children were actually born deaf or whether their deafness was owing to some infantine disease?—No.

21,855. There is that element of uncertainty about the statistics?—Yes. That the majority of those who are reported to be congenitally deaf were congenitally deaf I think will appear from the fact that 54 per cent. of them have other members of the family deaf and dumb. That is strong evidence that we must not reject entirely the classification of congenital deafness and non-congenital deafness. When you come to analyze these cases according to the reported causes of deafness you find that of 368 deaf-mute children of deaf-mute parents, 328 or 89·1 per cent. were congenitally deaf, and 40 or 10·9 per cent. were non-congenitally deaf, which is enormously different from the proportion of those two classes in the deaf-mute population as a whole, and in the lower part of the table you will see the period of birth given. I have arranged these cases by their period of birth. You will observe that before the decade 1820–'9 there is no case in which both the parents were deaf. In those cases where I say "Father deaf" it may be that the mother was deaf also; and in those cases where I say "Mother deaf," it may be that the father was deaf also, but in nearly all the cases born in the first three decades, I have ascertained that only one parent was deaf.

21,856. The records I suppose are very imperfect before 1820?—These cases are all taken from the census of 1880 or from the cases mentioned in my memoir upon "The Formation of a Deaf Variety of the Human Race."

21,857. When was the first census taken in America?—In 1790, but there was no record of deaf mutes in that census. The first census in which deaf mutes were taken note of was 1830. I was enabled to investigate in detail the history of deaf mute cases by the discovery of an immense mass of genealogical information in Washington. The original sheets of paper containing the names of all the persons in the United States from which the census returns were made had not been destroyed. I found them piled away in a dark vault in the basement of the Patent Office, and the Secretary of the Interior had them bound and arranged so as form a special Library which contains many thousands of volumes, and there one can hunt back deaf mute families from one census to the other without any trouble. It is sometimes difficult in examining the ancestry of deaf mutes to get your starting point; you cannot get information concerning the families themselves directly at first. From these census returns you can work the family back as far as 1830, and the heads of the families back to the census of 1790. In the New England States we have such a mass of genealogical material printed in the shape of town histories and separate genealogies that in many cases the census returns give us information that can be continued in detail backwards through genealogical publications. It is chiefly in this way that I have collected my material relating to the ancestry of the deaf of the New England States.

21,858. Perhaps as we are on the question of heredity you will explain any of the most typical genealogies which you have hung upon the wall?—I have already directed attention to the fact that in the Island of Martha's Vineyard, a map of which I have here, there is a township called Chilmark, a very isolated place containing a total population of only about 500. In 1880 there were 20 deaf mutes in this township, which is a proportion of one to 25 of the population. In examining the history of the appearance of deafness in that township, I found there had been deaf mutes in that part of the island for 200 years. I found from records that two deaf mutes were born somewhere about the year 1680, and that deaf mutes had appeared at different times ever since then, and the appearance of deafness is confined to that particular part of the island. The geological character of that part of the island is different from the rest of the island. The surface is undulating and hilly, whereas the rest of the island is flat. It has a subsoil of very curious variegated clays that crop out in the form of a bold headland that is so beautifully coloured by these clays as to have acquired the name of Gay Head. Whether that has anything to do with the deafness I do not know, but it is a very curious fact that it is in that part of the island alone where the deafness occurs although the bulk of the population lies outside. I have a list of no less than 72 deaf mutes who have either been born in this place or whose ancestors have come from the place. I have traced the ancestry of those deaf mutes in every branch, and I found a great deal of intermarrying and a great many consanguineous marriages in the ancestry. So my theory of the origin of the deafness here is that a deaf-mute stock was very early introduced into the island, and that the defect has been perpetuated among the descendants by consanguineous marriages. I have here a manuscript volume which I will submit to the inspection of the Commission, showing all the lines of ancestry of those deaf mutes. In determining the important strains of blood in those deaf mutes, it seemed to me that one ought to look for focal points in the ancestry, to find out how many of those deaf mutes had common ancestors, and to find out in that way the important blood in the deaf mutes. I have examined every surname that appears in their ancestry, and they group themselves into three important strains of blood. (1.) One is the Tilton blood. All these black dots which you see here are deaf mutes, and they run up to the same ancestor, but on account of consanguineous marriages the same deaf mute may trace up by more than one line to an ancestor. There are 32 deaf mutes that trace up to Samuel Tilton out of the 72, so there are 40 which do not. That is the first strain of blood.

21,859. Are members of these families still living now?—Yes. (2.) Then comes the Mayhew blood. This chart shows the deaf mute descendants of Governor Mayhew, the Governor of the island. The island originally belonged to the Indians; then a charter was given to Thomas Mayhew who became the first Governor of the island; his son became a missionary to the Indians and people were brought over to cultivate the soil. So we had three very strongly differentiated classes of people on the island. First, the Indians; second, the common working people who came over to cultivate the land for Governor Mayhew; and third, the few families who constituted the aristocracy, that was Governor Mayhew's family, the Skiff family, and one or two others. The aristocratic families for a number of generations married among themselves.

21,860. Is there any evidence that any of Governor Mayhew's family married Indians?—No, I think it is pretty certain that there is no Indian blood in the descendants. Governor Mayhew's grandson had a manorial estate in the Island; he was Lord of the manor. Martha's Vineyard being one of the few places where a manorial estate was set up. Of the total number of deaf mutes I find that 41 trace up to Governor Mayhew and 31 do not, out of the 72. (3.) Now on this large chart we have the third important blood—the one that I think to be the really important blood—viz., the Skiff blood. This shows the descent of the Martha's Vineyard deaf mutes from James Skiff, and I find that 63 deaf mutes trace up to James Skiff, and only nine do not; those nine are cases in which I have very little information concerning the ancestry, and they might possibly turn out to trace up to James Skiff, but at all events 63 of the 72 do trace up to him.

21,861. When did James Skiff live?—In the 17th century. Now the important lesson to be learnt I think from such a diagram as that is that there may be handed down from generation to generation what you may term latent deafness. There can be no manner of doubt that these ancestors were not deaf mutes, that there has been something handed down that has come out as deaf mutism in the children. The proof to my mind that the Skiff blood is the important blood is that groups of deaf mutes who have never been near Martha's Vineyard trace up to that Skiff blood; that is the important point.

21,862. Those were not born on the island?—No; there is an important group here.

21,863. (*Dr. Campbell.*) Those 72 are in the island, are not they?—No, the 72 are not all in the island; but in all those cases ancestors came from the island. This group (the Newcomb group) is not in the island. This woman had children who could

Mr. A. G. Bell.

26 June 1888.

all hear and speak; she had grandchildren who could all hear and speak, and of her great grandchildren 19 were deaf mutes.

21,864. There was an introduction of fresh blood in the case of the parents of the grandchildren?—Yes, fresh blood was introduced. Yet there are 19 deaf mutes among her great grandchildren.

21,865. Is that the same blood as the 63?—Yes.

21,866. Do any of those 19 intermarry with any of the 31 or 41?—No.

21,867. (*Chairman.*) Are there present representatives of that branch?—Yes, some of them are dead. This is the Newcomb family of Sandwich, Massachusetts, in which there are seven children deaf and dumb, they are now old men. In these charts I have shown the ancestry of the deaf mutes; it would be impossible to include the hearing members on such a scale as this, so I have only shown the connections of the deaf mutes themselves. In this lower chart which shows the genealogy of the Lovejoy family I have given you all the hearing members as well as the deaf members. If there are any differences between the large diagram and the lower diagram, the lower one is the more reliable; and if the Commission would desire I should be very glad to present this diagram to them, and to write a brief account of the family to accompany the diagram without troubling you with any description of it at the present time. If you look at the large diagram* you will see that in the Sidney Branch deafness has been handed down in this Lovejoy family through five generations, we actually have five successive generations of deaf mutes, and these down here are quite young children. Then as I mentioned the other day we have the defect of hereditary blindness in the same family as a collateral defect. I could give you full details of that if desired. I have not included those cases here, because this simply refers to deaf mutes.

21,868. Will you kindly explain to the Commission the principles upon which visible speech is founded, and the reasons which led you to the adoption of it as a means of teaching the deaf and dumb?—Visible speech is the name of a phonetic alphabet devised by my father (Prof. A. Melville Bell) a number of years ago. It differs from all other phonetic alphabets in this respect, that the elementary characters do not represent sounds. When you examine the shapes of the letters of any other alphabet you will find that the little curves and straight lines of which the letters are composed have no significance, but in the visible speech alphabet, the curves and straight lines of which the characters are composed, denote the vocal organs that are used in uttering sounds, and they are built together into a compound form or character just as the parts of the mouth are put together in forming the sounds. The alphabet was devised as a universal alphabet for scientific purposes, with no thought of the deaf and dumb, but my father suggested its use in this connexion in the inaugural edition of his work, entitled "Visible Speech: The Science of Universal Alphabitics" (1864). The appearance of this work marked the commencement of a new era in the science of phonetics comparable to the era that was inaugurated in chemistry by the adoption of chemical symbols. Before the adoption of chemical symbols, chemists were in the habit of giving a distinct name to every different substance on the face of the earth, and chemistry was burdened by the very multitude of names that had to be learned. The moment it was determined to abandon this method, and give to the elements of which substances are composed distinct symbols, simplicity at once resulted. Supposing you did not know what water was; if you had its symbol, H_2O., you would know that it was composed of two parts of hydrogen, and one of oxygen, and all you had to do was to put the substances together, and you would produce the substance water. Now in a similar manner, before the appearance of my father's work, philologists and linguists, and men of science, sought to give to every sound a distinct character, and when it was sought to put in one alphabet the sounds of all languages, it was found that this was impracticable; it was found that the sounds that could be produced by the vocal organs were practically infinite in number. Now, my father, like those who devised the system of symbols in chemistry, set to work to symbolise elements. However many sounds it may be possible to produce with the vocal organs, they are all produced by the adjustment of a very small number of organs. We have only one tongue, and only two lips, and he thought if he could represent the organs themselves by symbols, he would represent sound in a much more accurate way than could be done by simply giving an arbitrary character for every sound. So if you were to take one of his symbols, and analyse it, it would mean, "Put your tongue in this position," or "put your lips in this position," or "make a certain attempt to expel breath," and such and such a sound will be the result; just as in the case of chemical symbols, we take the elements and produce the compound. Thus, my father has been able to form a universal alphabet that is capable of expressing, in a scientific manner, the sounds of any and all languages. There are only 10 characters in my father's alphabet, but those can be compounded to make compound characters to an indefinite extent. This is a diagram by means of which we teach the system to the deaf (*exhibiting it*). This alphabet was produced in 1864 as a method of writing all sounds, all languages in one alphabet, and in the experiments my father made, it was shown that the actual pronunciation of words in foreign languages could be deduced from the symbols. I was one of the young men who assisted my father in demonstrating his system, and one day, during my absence from the room, a distinguished Hindustani scholar pronounced to my father some words in Hindustani containing some very curious sounds. Instead of relying on his ear, my father studied the mouth of this gentleman, and he saw that in uttering the words, the tongue was in a particular position, and the lips were in a particular position, and the positions of the tongue and the mouth in forming the particular sounds were registered by my father by certain of these symbols. By-and-bye I was called into the room, and I examined these mysterious symbols, and I obtained from them a direction, "Put your tongue in this position, and your lips in this position." I did so, and to my surprise the gentleman clapped his hands and said, "That is splendid." I did not know what it was, it was a Hindustani word, and he said he had laboured with students for years to get them to pronounce that sound, and he could not do it, and here I had pronounced it without having heard it. Now, looking to the fact that deaf mutes do not speak, simply because they have never heard language, it at once dawned upon my father that this was a means by which they could deduce a language unknown to them, the English language, without having heard it. That was the origin of the application to the deaf.

21,869. (*Mr. Johnson.*) Are there any symbols for the action of any other organs besides the tongue and the lips?—Yes, the vocal chords and the soft palate.

21,870. (*Chairman.*) A knowledge of these symbols implies a thorough knowledge of the action of all the vocal organs?—Yes.

21,871. And for that reason the acquisition of such knowledge would be of very great use to teachers of the dumb?—Undoubtedly. If you examine the answers to the queries that have been handed in from the various institutions you will find that whatever difference of opinion there may be as to the use of the symbols with pupils, there is no difference of opinion as to the great value of a knowledge of this method of symbolising speech to teachers. Many say it is essential to a teacher to get a knowledge of the mechanism of speech, which he gets by the

*See diagram and explanatory note of the Lovejoy family in the Appendix.

study of speech expressed symbolically in this way. I wish to make it clear to you that my idea is that some such system as this (and I know of nothing to take its place) is essential in teaching the congenitally deaf. We can get intelligible speech from the congenitally deaf without any such system, but we can get perfect speech with such a tool as this in the hands of a trained teacher, it will not do anything itself, it wants a specially skilled teacher, but with a specially skilled teacher it is possible to give perfect speech to the congenitally deaf, without it you can get intelligible speech, but I do not think you will get much more.

21,872. (*Dr. Campbell.*) When you used the words "perfect speech," did you mean natural speech, or distinct speech?—As perfect as our own.

21,873. That which would sound natural to us?—Yes, perfect enunciation I would say. These characters are the elementary characters of visible speech, and you will see that they are the outlines of the organs that they represent, hence the name "Visible Speech." This is the character that means lip, and it is the outline of the lip; this is the character that means the point of the tongue; this is the character that means the top part of the tongue, and this is the outline that means the back part of the tongue. This is an outline of what scientifically is the soft palate, but in teaching deaf mutes we call it the nose, as the effect of depressing the soft palate is to direct the breath through the nose. This is a narrow chink between the vocal chords; that means that the vocal chords are placed parallel to one another with a very fine line between them; that is the vocalising condition of the glottis. Then when we present these symbols to a deaf child this would mean back part of the tongue; this would mean top part of the tongue; this would mean point of tongue: this would mean the lip; this would mean the nose; that would mean expulsion of air. Now there are two other characters here which do not mean organs; they mean passages. This indicates a narrow passage through which air may pass. In this case the passage is stopped up at one end and the air cannot get out. Now these may be built into compound characters or letters *ad infinitum*. You see a few of them here. (*Dr. Bell then described the compound characters, and showed how a person using his vocal organs in the way indicated by the symbols could enunciate not only words in the English language, but words in other languages difficult of pronunciation by an English speaking person.*) I have endeavoured to give you the underlying idea in this mode of teaching visible speech, and those who desire to read further upon the subject will find an article of mine in the American Annals of the Deaf and Dumb for January, 1872 (Vol. XVII, pp. 1-21), describing the mode of teaching the deaf and dumb by this system.

21,874. You think it very advisable that all teachers of the deaf should make themselves acquainted with this system as an aid in their work of teaching the deaf?—I think so undoubtedly.

21,875. I see in answer to your query whether visible speech has been employed in the institution, the Principal of the Illinois Institution says, "Used "to a very limited extent. It is of advantage to "teachers, as it enables them to comprehend physi-"ological facts involved in speech; but for pupils "while it is thus helpful it requires an amount of "time and labour to acquire that can better be im-"proved with the use of diacritical marks"?—Those are the dictionary marks.

21,876. Do you agree with that?—Not at all.

21,877. You think it is adapted for pupils as well for teachers?—I think when we come to teach speech to deaf children it is absolutely essential that we should present books and writing to them in a phonetic form; they must see the pronunciation of words as others hear. It is not enough to teach pronunciation of the words used by means of diacritical marks. The ordinary spelling does not show the pronunciation.

21,878. Except in a language like Italian?—Except in a language like Italian; but written English is unphonetical; the spelling does not represent the pronunciation, and the pupil cannot see the pronunciation distinctly from the mouth; he sees enough to enable him to understand what is said when he is familiar with the language, but he does not get at the details of pronunciation. To those who are taught pronunciation by diacritical marks and who do not see the word phonetically written, the idea of pronunciation becomes vague, and to that fact I attribute what we very commonly find in all oral schools, that the pronunciation of the older pupils is more defective than the pronunciation of the younger ones; they have forgotten the pronunciation.

21,879. (*Sir Lyon Playfair.*) Teaching them in the way you propose would, I presume, increase their general intelligence and so enable them to get on quicker?—I do not know that: I think that teaching them the ordinary written language of the people would develop their minds and make them intelligent and able to read books, but I think it is necessary to use a phonetic alphabet to develop their pronunciation. For this purpose I do not know that one form of alphabet has any special advantage over others—any form of alphabet will do—but what is necessary is that they should be accustomed to read books in which the words are spelt as they are pronounced; that is for their mouths, apart from their minds. If you are to get good speakers, especially among the congenitally deaf, they must see the pronunciation; it must not be taught simply as a school exercise; the words that are spoken by the mouth must come clearly differentiated to the eye again and again until the eye becomes familiar with them. Now I have found that the speech in our oral schools is somewhat defective, and I have tried to find out the cause of that defect. For example, Mrs. Bell's speech is very defective.

21,880. I do not think I should so characterise it; I have spoken for 20 minutes with her without knowing that she was deaf?—Mrs. Bell lost her hearing at 4½ years of age. I consider that her speech is very defective, not because she cannot pronounce the elementary sounds of language, she knows them all, but because her idea of pronunciation is vague; she relies more on the recollection of childhood. The moment she is asked to write phonetically what she thinks the pronunciation should be the trouble is revealed. She does not know how the words should be pronounced. When a word is written phonetically she says, "Is the word pronounced that way? I did not know it before," or, "I had forgotten that." Speech reading had not recalled the precise pronunciation.

21,881 (*Mr. Johnson.*) Does she usually write phonetically?—No; her speech is partially the result of recollection of early childhood, partially the result of the instruction of her mother, and partly the result of instruction in oral schools in Germany, for when she became deaf there was no school in the whole of America where a child who had become deaf at 4½ years of age could be taught speech, and she was sent to Germany, where she was taught to speak German; and I am told by German scholars that she pronounces that language better than English. Her deafness had one good effect—it led to the establishment of the Clarke Institution in Northampton, for her father, the Honourable Gardner G. Hubbard, stung by the fact that there was no school in the United States where his daughter's speech could be preserved and improved, determined that there should be such a school, and, shoulder to shoulder with Dr. Howe and Mr. F. B. Sanborn, Mr. Hubbard fought the American Asylum in the legislature of Massachusetts for years, and at last there was established the Clarke Institution. That was the first, or one of the first, oral schools established in our country, and Mr. Hubbard was for a number of years the president of it; and here I may

Mr. A. G. Bell.

26 June 1888.

say that I hope you may be able to examine some one on the oral side in America. I am generally looked on by teachers of the sign system as an oralist, but I think I have shown you that I am not a pure oralist, and I would suggest that the Commission should examine an advocate of the pure oral system as taught in some of the institutions in America. I would direct your attention to the fact that you have two gentlemen on this side of the Atlantic who could give you much information concerning the deaf of America. Mr. Hubbard (a pure oralist) is in France; and Rev. Thomas Gallaudet (an advocate of the sign method) is in England. Dr. Thomas Gallaudet is a brother of President Gallaudet, who testified before the Royal Commission last year. He is the head of the Church Mission to adult deaf mutes, and could undoubtedly give you much information concerning the adult deaf mutes of America.

21,882. (*Chairman.*) I see in the answer from the Maryland School this statement: "Visible speech has "not been employed directly in the instruction of "pupils. They have not been taught to read and "write its forms. Our principal teacher of articu"lation was taught visible speech and used it for a "year at Northampton. Her knowledge of the "organs of speech and their use obtained by this "study I consider of great value. Visible speech "has not been used because in my judgment the "learning of the symbols by pupils lengthens rather "than shortens the process of instruction"?—I have said that I consider that a phonetic representation of speech is absolutely necessary, but it does not follow that it should be visible speech (although I think it advisable)—any phonetic alphabet will serve the purpose, and I would call attention to the fact that you have in this country a library of works printed in phonetic type, in the Pitman and Ellis type (a supply of which I think of taking home as reading matter for the pupils in the oral schools). Now, in regard to visible speech, it fulfils a function that no other alphabet can do, in teaching the pronunciation of speech, and there I differ entirely with the principals who have dissented from that view. There is no alphabet that we have on the face of the earth that will do what this will.

21,883. When would you teach this symbolical alphabet? Would you teach it, in the case of the deaf, at the very commencement of their education?—At the very commencement; I would teach it with the ordinary symbols of writing. My idea of teaching the deaf and dumb is to carry on their general education by ordinary writing in the outset, and at the same time you should train their mouths by the use of visible speech.

21,884. I see the Principal of the New Jersey School says, "Not used in the instruction of pupils. "I have used the system as a guide for my teachers "in their study of the production of sound by the "human organs of speech. My reason for not ex"tending its use to my pupils is, that while I think "it an aid to the forming of a correct habit of "vocalisation, I have observed in pupils trained on "this system a difficulty in passing from the use of "symbols to that of alphabetic characters." You say the two ought go on side by side?—Yes.

21,885. Do you think children of ordinary intelligence who were being instructed by competent teachers could learn two modes of speech side by side?—There would be no trouble about it.

21,886. Are there any cases that you actually know of where that has been tried?—Yes.

21,887. And where it has been successful?—Yes. A number of institutions have abandoned the use of symbols for the little pupils, retaining it only for the teachers. The invention of the telephone took my personal attention away from the work, and there has been therefore no one in America to push the system and supply teachers; the best teachers, who are chiefly ladies, leave the work.

21,888. Have they gone to telephone work?—No, they marry and leave the profession. I think the difficulty is the lack of trained teachers, for this system is only a tool, it will not do anything by itself; it is a powerful instrument in the hands of trained teachers. I will give you my idea how I would teach speech to a congenital deaf child. I go with the oral teachers in this:—I would teach every child to speak; I would teach every child to read from the mouth, but I differ from oral teachers in the means I would take, and I think the object would be best attained by the plan I propose. I would propose to keep to the natural method of learning to speak as closely as possible. What do we do in the case of hearing children? In the first place we present sounds to the ears of hearing children; they do not at first imitate them at all, not for two years, but they perceive them, and they also instinctively produce sounds themselves; for example, they cry and laugh. The ear becomes a means of comparison between the sounds the child makes himself and the sounds that other people make. By and by as his organs and faculties improve he is struck by the resemblance between some of the sounds he makes and some of the sounds other people make, and then commences the process of imitation; the child consciously attempts to imitate sounds. Does he imitate them correctly? No, very far from it. The speech of a hearing child is imperfect, he imitates crudely, but his ear tells him how far off from the correct sound his own is, and by constant practice he approximates more and more closely to the correct enunciation. The natural process may be compared to the process by which we learn to shoot. You aim at the bull's eye, but do not hit it; at least, at the first attempt. You observe the point struck by your bullet, and its distance from the centre, and the next shot probably goes on the other side. Now you strike too high, now too low, now too much to the right, and now again to the left. Your eye tells you at a glance how far off from the bull's eye your shot has struck, and you get a practical direction that guides you in your next attempt. By constant practice your approximations become more exact, and finally you become a good marksman. Now you will observe that it is not enough that you should see the bull's eye; it is not enough that you should know you have missed. That knowledge alone would never lead to perfect shooting. You must know *where you struck*. You must see the relation of the point struck to the bull's eye. That is the knowledge that determines your progress. So in learning to speak, it is not enough that the deaf pupil should observe the teacher's mouth; it is not enough that he should know he failed to imitate correctly. He must know what he did when *he failed*. It is just here that visible speech is of assistance. The teacher presents the symbol for the English sound, and then the symbol for the incorrect position. The pupil sees at a glance the relation of one to the other, and obtains a practical direction that guides him in his next attempt. "Why! My tongue was too far forward, or too high, or too low, or too far back," &c. At the next effort he fails again, but whatever he may do he produces a sound of some kind, and whatever it may be, whether a cough! or a sneeze! or a Hottentot click! it can be written in visible speech. That is: The position of the vocal organs can be symbolically expressed, so as to show the relation of the position to that which he intended to assume. That is the kind of knowledge that is essential to progress in speech. Without it we can get rude approximations, but not perfect speech. I do not know of any other means of imparting this knowledge excepting visible speech. But visible speech is only the tool; it will do nothing by itself. It is only of such value for this purpose in the hands of a trained teacher. I would refer the Commission to another paper of mine upon this subject, which was read before the Eighth Convention of American Instructors of the deaf in Belleville, Ontario, 1874. *See* Proceedings of that Convention published in 1876 by the Belleville Institution, pp. 103–109.

Mr. A. G. Bell.

26 June 1888.

21,889. As you say, this is a system for the teaching of which you require thoroughly qualified teachers. Speaking from your own knowledge, do you know how long it would take any teacher to become so thoroughly imbued with the system as to be able to teach it to others?—You have persons in this country who could teach it to others, but there is at present hardly any one in America who could do so except myself and my father; that is the reason why it has not progressed as it otherwise would no doubt have done.

21,890. How many persons are there in this country who could teach it to others?—A large number.

21,891. Have they learned it entirely from your books?—From my father's books.

21,892. (*Mr. Johnson.*) Are they connected with institutions?—No. Mr. Sweet is one, Dr. Murray another, and Mr. Ellis another.

21,893. (*Chairman.*) I am not speaking of scientists. Do you know a single person engaged in practical teaching either in this country or in America, who has sufficiently mastered this system of visible speech to be able to communicate it to others?—I think Miss Hull, of Bexley, in Kent, and Mr. Kinsey,* Principal of the Training College at Ealing, have a good knowledge of the basis of the system, but not a sufficient knowledge of it to use it in the way I have described. There are certain persons, and you find them here and there, who have a wonderful faculty for imitating sound and analysing the mechanism of speech; a person who has not that faculty cannot be taught to use the system in the way described. Anyone may learn in a few days to use the system so as to represent English sounds; but it requires very special abilities to analyse and present to the pupil in symbolical form *the incorrect* sounds that deaf children make. It is the latter process that I consider to be essential in the instruction of the deaf.

21,894. Would not that rather lead to the conclusion that it is a system which it would be difficult to introduce into general use in this country?—I admit that it does require very special abilities, and the question is how to get teachers with those special abilities.

21,895. You say this system has been used a certain number of years in America, and the teachers of schools have taken it up more or less; but you say owing to the absence of your personal supervision to press the thing on it has not progressed very much?—I find a large number carrying it on.

21,896. But it has gradually been discontinued?—In some Institutions. In quite a number of others it is still used, although it is 12 years since I left the work.

21,897. Would not it be very difficult to introduce in this country an entirely new system without some such preceding influence as your own would be in America, supposing you had time to take up the question again?—My opinion is this: if the British Government will make the acquisition of speech by deaf children a matter of attention, and if they will afford pecuniary aid to teachers in proportion to results obtained, then they will have teachers adopting the best methods, whatever they are. If speech were taught to all the deaf, a great many articulation teachers would be employed, and out of those articulation teachers some would appear who were specially competent, and who might be capable of teaching the deaf and dumb in the way described. The first thing is to create a demand for articulation teachers; that demand would lead to a supply, and then a demand would be created for improved methods of teaching.

21,898. Supposing it were possible to get a certain number of teachers to teach speech by means of visible speech, the class of teachers who would take it up and master it would have to be more highly paid; how would that greater expense be met; would you propose that the Government give a larger amount of grant to teachers who taught on that system, or who taught speech in the best way?—I would propose that the Government should give a larger amount to those teachers who produced the best results. I would not have the Government say, You shall teach by this or that system. I would have all systems free, but I would have the Government throw the different systems into competition with one another. I would create by artificial means a struggle for existence, and then the survival of the fittest would do the rest.

21,899. (*Dr. Campbell.*) Supposing you found a dozen persons who really had the necessary aptitude for acquiring a knowledge of this system, and for teaching the deaf and dumb by it, how long would it take you to teach them?—A very short time if they had natural abilities: never if they had not. If they had not natural abilities they might be able to use the system, but they would not be able to use it in the way I think right, that is to depict the strange sounds that deaf children make when you are teaching them. In respect to this matter of teachers, I would say it is not only of importance to the deaf, but of importance to the hearing that the mechanism of speech should be studied by teachers; it should be a subject of study in your normal schools: in all your public schools you have children with defective speech, and in the vast majority of such cases the defects are associated with perfect vocal organs—there are very few cases in which defects of speech arise from malformations of the organs. Now if you were to include in the curriculum of your normal schools all over the country the study of the mechanism of speech then articulation teachers could be selected from among the most competent to go into this special work of teaching the deaf by this method; and not only would the deaf benefit, but the hearing would benefit; many of these little defects that arise could very readily be corrected by the teacher.

21,900. (*Mr. Johnson.*) Is the mechanism of speech studied in all your normal schools in America?—No. I am urging upon the Government of America that attention should be devoted to the study of the mechanism of speech in the schools, because we have a large foreign population in Wisconsin, Illinois, and other States; and if we want to preserve the purity of the English tongue in America, we must teach speech to the pupils in the public schools, and that means that we must teach the mechanism of speech to teachers. If we do that there will be no difficulty in getting trained teachers of articulation for the deaf.

21,901. (*Dr. Campbell.*) Have you ever tried to teach singing by means of visible speech?—No, but there is no doubt that the quality of the voice can be very much benefited, for the quality of the voice depends in a very minor degree upon the vocal chords; it depends more upon the positions of organs further forward than the vocal chords. My attention was directed to the applicability of this system in this direction by endeavouring to correct the disagreeable tone of voice of some deaf children in the American Asylum at Hartford. Some pupils when they first try to speak make sounds more like the cry of a peacock than anything else, and in such cases the teacher would often suppose that the disease which caused deafness had also affected the vocal chords, and that such pupils should be dropped from articulation work. I ventured to express the opinion that the quality of the voice very little depends upon the throat, but more depends on the position of the organs further forward than the throat; and I took a number of these cases and endeavoured to deal with them, and I discovered that there were certain parts of the mouth that had not hitherto been included among the vocal organs, viz., the posterior pillars of the soft palate, that have a power of approximation towards one another in the pharynx, and the more closely they approximate the more disagreeable is the character of the voice. I took these same pupils and gave them a looking-glass apiece, and taught them to depress the tongue and control these muscles so that they could ap-

* Since deceased.

Mr. A. G. Bell.

26 June 1888.

proximate the posterior pillars of the soft palate or separate them at will. Their voices became more natural and pleasant in quality the moment the pharyngeal cavity was expanded.

21,902. (*Mr. Johnson.*) Altering the arch of the palate?—Yes. The more the pharynx is contracted the more disagreeable is the quality of the voice, and the more it is expanded the more agreeable is the voice, and we converted those voices into agreeable voices. That same principle applied to singers would improve the quality of the voice.

21,903. (*Chairman.*) As we know, the voices of the deaf and dumb are generally harsh, do not you think that that harshness could be avoided if instruction in speech were given them very early in life?—That is my opinion.

21,904. The voice when it once gets set cannot be improved I presume?—I think it can.

21,905. Even in mature years?—Yes.

21,906. By proper teaching?—Yes, but we want properly qualified teachers.

21,907. You think it of the utmost importance in teaching speech to the deaf that the teacher should be thoroughly acquainted with the physiology of the throat and other vocal organs?—Yes, it is the blind leading the blind without that knowledge, and it is the absence of that knowledge on the part of the teacher that is the cause of the bad speech we get from our pupils. If you ask these teachers of articulation what they do with their mouths in uttering sounds they do not know; the instruction to the pupil is, look at my mouth when I am uttering sounds and find out what I do, the teacher himself knowing very little of the physiology of the vocal organs which are brought into play in uttering those sounds, and yet with all that ignorance on the part of the teachers it is the case that they succeed in giving intelligible speech; speech may be very imperfect and yet intelligible. If we encourage the teaching of speech, if we create a demand for teaching articulation, then will come the supply and then will come the improvements in the methods.

21,908. (*Mr. Johnson.*) Do you find much tonsilar defect among deaf and dumb children?—Not so much as I should have anticipated; there are some cases of enlarged tonsils. From my observation I do not think the proportion of children in institutions who have enlarged tonsils is larger than in the community at large.

21,909. (*Chairman.*) Have you anything further to say with regard to visible speech?—I would like to supplement what I have said about visible speech by a few remarks on my father's system of "line writing." I would have the Commission realise the fact that speaking and reading speech by the eye are two different arts, in either one of which a pupil may excel while he may not excel in the other. My own individual opinion is that all deaf children can be taught to speak, but that there is a difficulty in teaching them to read speech, especially in the case of the congenital deaf. That has led to a new departure in the art of teaching articulation which I would like to explain to you.

21,910. You mean with the view of facilitating speech reading?—Yes, and with the view of facilitating articulation teaching also. I have found that there is a difficulty in the use of visible speech in a school-room on account of the slowness with which you make the characters. My father in bringing forward his system gave us several different forms, one was a printed form, another was a current handwriting form, and the other was a stenographic form for shorthand reporting in all languages. If you were to take ordinary print and to do all your writing with capital letters there would be a great loss of time, and that is what is done with visible speech in the institutions. They use the capital letters of the printed fount exclusively. The writing is so slow that I wonder so many institutions still use the system. To my mind that continued use is conclusive evidence of the great value of the system. An attempt has been made to employ the stenographic alphabet of visible speech; and my father has specially adapted it for the use of the deaf under the name of "Line writing." I present to the members of the Commission a pamphlet by my father describing his system of "Line writing" (*handing it in*). I may say that the little experimental school which I carried on at Washington for a couple of years was specially established to test the applicability of this line writing to the teaching of the deaf. The stenographic characters of visible speech have been taken and slightly modified so as to form distinct characters, and to make them still more distinct they are written separately instead of being united together as in shorthand. The result is that the word makes a very compact picture to the eye of a deaf child. If you take any English word composed of the ordinary letter and compare the number of lines of which the word picture is composed in the English print with the number of lines of which it is composed in the line writing you will see at once that the line writing picture is simpler and more definite to the eye than the word picture, and in my little school the pupils were taught one-half the day by the line writing, and the other half of the day by the ordinary letters in the same subjects. I wanted to have a phonetic writing that we could use rapidly and speedily. This is capable of being written much faster than ordinary writing, but not so fast as ordinary shorthand, and I found that these little congenital deaf children always learnt the line writing form before the Roman letter form, though they had an equal opportunity of learning each. This line writing is phonetic and identical with visible speech. It is the shorthand form of visible speech. In visible speech print the vowels are brought out more prominently to the eye than the consonants. In line writing it is the reverse, it is the consonants that stand out prominently to the eye and the vowels that are subordinate; the little ticks are the vowels and the more prominent characters all consonants. Now there is a great advantage in this. In speech reading it is the consonants which are ambiguous to the eye, the vowels are all more or less clearly differentiated to the eye, so that a child finds a difficulty in arriving at a perception of the distinction between the different consonants, the eye being directed too prominently to the vowels. Speech is perfectly intelligible without any definite vowels; you can easily supply the vowels by context. I will read a passage to you without any definite vowels, and I think I shall make myself perfectly intelligible. [*Dr. Bell read a passage leaving out the vowels.*] Speech depends for its intelligibility upon the consonants; the vowels are liable to great variations in the mouths of individual speakers. Thus it is that pupils understand very readily the pronunciation of their teachers and friends, whereas they experience difficulty in understanding strangers. This is largely due to too great reliance upon vowels. These are clear to the eye, but they vary in the mouths of different speakers. Now we get in "line writing" a comparatively clear picture of what the pupil sees in the mouth of a speaker. In reading this line writing the pupil goes through a useful mental exercise, for in the same way as the consonants are ambiguous to the eye when the pupil reads from the mouth, they are to a certain extent ambiguous in line writing. In printed line writing they are perfectly clear, but in pencil writing you cannot distinguish very well between a thick line and a thin line, the thick line means voice and the thin line means no voice. The general slope of the characters shows the part of the mouth that is used, but the absence or presence of voice is indicated simply by the different thickness of the line. The absence or presence of voice the pupil cannot see in reading from the lips, he cannot see the distinction between P and B. So when a pupil writes this line writing in pencil you get a writing that presents to the eye the very same ambiguity that the mouth presents, and there is a mental exercise of exactly the same character as the mental exercise when you read from the mouth. The pupils learn to group words that have the same general outline, that is to say, homophenous words, words having the same appearance to the eye when they are spoken. So this method of line writing has the advantage of giving the child what he sees in the mouth when he tries to understand a speaker; but it is on paper permanently he can study it out.

21,911. There is no difference between P and B, or T and D, or K and G, except the thickness of the line?—That is so. The difference between P and B or T and D is not distinguished to the eye of the speech reader when he comes to look at your mouth in uttering those sounds. P is the same to the eye of the speech reader as B; the only difference is the presence or absence of voice; in the "line writing" the only difference is in thickness of the line, and when a pupil writes in pencil it is difficult to distinguish between P and B or T and D.

21,912. You create a difficulty in "line writing" in order to make it more like the difficulty with which the pupil has to contend in reading speech from the lips?—Yes, and there is this advantage in the line writing over speech reading. When you speak by word of mouth the positions vary successively, and the pupil has to rely on his memory in order to accumulate a sufficient number of words to enable him to decide by the context what the meaning of the sentence is; but in line writing he gets the sentence as a whole at once. So I hold that in the teaching of articulation the printed characters of visible speech are of great value, for there the differences of pronunciation are clearly differentiated to the eye; in the printed line-writing the pronunciation is also clear; but in the written line-writing (especially where pencil is used) we have a great advantage resulting from the fact that the ambiguities in the line writing correspond with those which exercise the mind of the student in reading from the mouth. It is training in speech reading. Another great advantage is that it can be much more rapidly written than ordinary writing.

21,913. (*Mr. St. John Ackers.*) When you use the expression "voice," you mean the vibration of the vocal chords?—Yes.

21,914. (*Sir Lyon Playfair.*) One of your recommendations, as I understand, is that in our normal schools the teachers should acquire a scientific, as well as a mere technical, knowledge of what they are doing?—Undoubtedly.

21,915. You think that knowledge would be a great value to him in his future occupation as a teacher?—That is my idea.

21,916. And you think also a better result would be attained in the case of the pupil if he was taught the science as well as the practice of speech?—Certainly. I may amplify that somewhat. A pupil who is taught the science of speech can acquire the pronunciation of a foreign tongue as perfectly as his own.

21,917. In our normal schools for teaching teachers the certificates are of different classes, and the amount paid to the teacher is determined by the knowledge which he possesses. Do you think it would be advisable that the Government should make articulation a specific subject, and induce not only ordinary teachers, but teachers for the deaf, to acquire a higher certificate and a higher payment by showing proficiency in that subject?—I think that would be a very important thing. I think that such certificates would be of enormous use in this country. A great number of people are preying upon the public—quacks, trying to cure defects of speech as if they were diseases instead of bad habits—certificated teachers of articulation would do an enormous good among the hearing as well as among the deaf by taking hold of such cases and giving proper and suitable instruction how to use the vocal organs.

21,918. In large towns where special rooms could be provided in board schools in different parts of the town, do you think certificated teachers of articulation might be advantageously employed in the teaching of the deaf?—Undoubtedly. I think we should aim to get such little schools established, not simply in the large centres of population, but in small centres of population wherever a sufficient number of pupils could be brought together to warrant the appointment of a teacher. I would advocate pushing that system of classes in affiliation with public day schools as far as practicable into rural districts.

21,919. I gather from what you said in an earlier part of your evidence that you see considerable advantages in bringing the deaf and dumb in contact with hearing children in school life?—Yes, undoubtedly. I see advantages in that association, and that quite apart from other benefits which may arise from associations formed in school being continued.

21,920. (*Mr. Johnson.*) Are you acquainted with the three great institutions that profess to teach the oral system in London, Mr. Van Praagh's, Mr. Schöntheil, and the college at Ealing?—No, I am not conversant with them from personal knowledge; I have not visited them yet. I have devoted all my time in preparing my evidence for this Commission. I hope to visit those institutions before my return to America.

21,921. Do you think that it would be possible to graft your system on to the present system of oral teaching?—I think it could be grafted on to any system.

21,922. You could graft it on to what we call the combined, or on to the oral, or on to any of the existing methods which are used in England now?—Certainly. I think that teaching a child articulation need not be the same thing as teaching it *by* articulation. It is ridiculous that in our schools in America arithmetic, geography, and history should be preferred to articulation. Articulation should be a compulsory subject of study in all schools, whatever method of instruction was employed. As the pupils advanced, it could then be seen what number were best fitted to be taught on what you call the pure oral, but which, I think, would be better called the speech reading method.

21,923. Then you think signs might be used together with your system in a sign school?—Undoubtedly; I do not advise that, but in my opinion the two would go on together.

21,924. You do not think the teaching by the one system would interfere with the teaching by the other?—No, they might run together as much as ordinary writing and signs go together now. I have already expressed my own opinion against using sign language, but this system could be combined with sign language.

21,925. I gather that it would take a very long time to teach your system to teachers, and it would take an equally long time for pupils to learn your system. Supposing a child to be educated entirely by your method, how long would it take to educate that child so as to perfect him fairly in your system?—Speaking from my own experience, for I am an expert in the use of the system, I have found in the case of the pupils I have had under instruction, that in two or three months I have such a control over the mouth that I can make the deaf pupil pronounce foreign sounds.

21,926. How long would it take to produce something like a useful result?—I should say at the outside one year. I would advocate that no child should be dropped from the articulation class who has not had one year's instruction. In that time you can certainly find out those who can be usefully taught and those that cannot.

21,927. Amongst the institutions in America is there a very large number that follow your plan?—Fifteen institutions. My attention has been taken away from this subject for no less than 12 years, and it really is this Commission that is bringing my mind back to it, so I am not familiar with what is being done now with my father's system in the institutions, except from the statistics I have collected. My impression had been that it had been very largely abandoned, but to my delight I find it is not. Twenty-

Mr. A. G. Bell.

26 June 1888.

four schools have failed to reply to my query about visible speech. Of the remaining 55, 32 have used visible speech and 23 have not. Of the 32 schools 15 continue to use it with their pupils; 9 make a limited use of it; 1 uses the line-writing form, and 7 have abandoned it altogether.

21,928. Do they use the phonetic system in developing the mouths of the pupils in any of those institutions?—Not that I am aware of.

21,929. You advocate that?—Yes, they simply use the symbols to teach the elementary sounds of the language, but they have no practice in reading from phonetic type: that I advocate. I do not insist that it should be visible speech especially (although I think that advisable); it may be any phonetic type so long as the language is printed as it is spoken.

21,930. Do you know whether Dr. Murray, or Mr. Sweet, or Miss Hull have practised this system in this country to any extent?—Dr. Murray has made it the basis of the phonetic notation in the Oxford dictionary, and Mr. Sweet has made it the basis of his studies in Icelandic; Mr. Ellis has also employed it as the basis of his method of noting early English pronunciation. In fact in England you have a number of scientific men who are thoroughly acquainted with the system in its scientific aspect, and I should strongly recommend if anything was done in this country in the way of applying it to the education of the deaf and dumb that they should be got to take an interest in it; and I would say further that I think it would be very beneficial if some of your philologists could be interested in the work of teaching speech to the deaf. A great many philologists have new theories relating to the mechanism of sounds; those ideas they can test in a novel way by trying to teach those sounds to deaf children. A great deal of light would be obtained by them in that process. No doubt some of your philologists might be got to take an interest in the work of articulation teaching, and it would be a very great advantage if they could.

21,931. None of those people to whom you have referred have turned their attention to the education of deaf and dumb children on your father's system?—Except Miss Hull, and it was due to Miss Hull that the system was adopted for the deaf at all. She was the first practical teacher to see that it had any advantages for the deaf, and it was here in London that my interest was first aroused in the deaf by witnessing the effect of some instruction given by her to her pupils.

21,932. (*Rev. Mr. Sleight.*) In schools in which this system is now used, how have the teachers acquired their knowledge of it?—Some of them acquired a knowledge of it at the time when I had a Normal Training College in Boston. The telephone took my attention away from the subject, and I do not know where the later teachers acquired their knowledge. Professor Butterfield, of Boston, has trained some teachers.

21,933. What number of teachers would you have attending your school at that time?—If I remember rightly I had about 60 altogether. I do not know how many graduated. I gave certificates of competency, and comparatively a small number graduated, but nearly all those 60 entered into the work.

21,934. And all found employment?—Nearly all found employment, and a large number of them are still at work in the various institutions in the country.

21,935. Would those teachers require higher salaries than ordinary teachers?—I think that those who obtained diplomas of competency did. In some of our oral schools while all the teachers are articulation teachers some one teacher is employed who is a specialist in the work, and then the difficult cases are handed over to her; when there is any special difficulty it is taken to the special teacher. In the Clarke Institution Miss Worcester is the special teacher of articulation. That is a good plan, I think, in a school.

21,936. I observe that in the answer from the Clarke Institution it is stated that Miss Worcester's method was substituted for visible speech; can you explain what Miss Worcester's method is?—I am sorry I cannot very fully; I would refer the Commission to a paper by Miss Worcester, read at the last meeting of the Convention of Articulation Teachers. I wrote to Miss Worcester asking from her a full description of her method to present to the Commission, and Miss Yale, the Principal, informed me that Miss Worcester was very ill, and in fact that her life was despaired of, so that I am unable to give the latest details of her method. All I can do is to refer you to the report of the proceedings at the Convention of Articulation Teachers, and in that Miss Worcester gives her plan, and it seems that of late years Miss Worcester's method has been very largely introduced into other institutions.

21,937. (*Rev. Mr. Owen.*) You said that whilst you would not suggest that the Government should dictate the method, you would advise that they should so act as to create a struggle for existence among the systems in the country; will you explain that a little more fully?—I think the Governmental aid should be largely given in accordance with the results of instruction, and that the Government should leave the different schools free to adopt their own methods; and I think that the basis on which they should go should be the ability of the children to use the English language in its written form, for that is an end that all the methods have in view. I would recommend that payment should be made according to a certain scale, having regard to the results obtained in written English, due consideration being had to the natural condition of the pupil, that is to say the age at which the deafness occurred should be known, so that the teacher should not be paid for producing results that were due to natural causes, as in the case of knowledge of the English language possessed by those who became deaf at the age of five or six. The practical test is to find out how far they are able to communicate by writing with hearing persons unfamiliar with the deaf. And then in addition to that we should have as a higher branch articulation and speech reading. The common basis would be a knowledge of written language, and in the higher branch a knowledge of articulation and speech reading.

21,938. When you spoke of the struggle for existence, you would not suggest that a higher grant should be given for one method as compared with another?—No. I should suggest that the highest grant should be given for the best results, irrespective of methods, and then teachers would strive to produce the best results.

21,939. (*Dr. Campbell.*) Has any modification of your father's system been tried at all as a means of giving musical instruction to the blind?—My father has proposed a modification of it for the instruction of the blind, but no one has appeared yet to make experiments with it in the case of the blind. My own attention was chiefly devoted to the deaf. My father has proposed a special form of visible speech consisting of raised letters for the blind that are specially legible to the sense of touch, his idea being that the blind want an alphabet that will render them independent of the seeing, and that therefore that alphabet should be phonetical. I showed this system of raised letters at the South Boston Blind Institution a number of years ago, but, as I have said, I have not directed my attention to that department of instruction.

21,940. In teaching singing to the blind, we find a great difficulty in getting out the natural voice, and I wish to know from you whether your system, which appears to be calculated to bring out all the inflexions of the voice in speaking was capable of being used in the teaching of the blind so as to bring out the natural voice in singing?—It has not been used in the musical education of the blind, but I have no doubt it might be advantageously.

21,941. (*Mr. Johnson.*) Are you aware that a system of phonetic characters for the blind was adopted some years ago in England, and that it has been really virtually abandoned?—I am not aware of that fact.

21,942. Mr. Frere published a great number of books in phonetic characters, but those are not now in use?—My father holds that the blind very readily acquire the pronunciation of foreign languages, and that they would very readily read foreign books in raised letters if the spelling corresponded to the pronunciation. Thus English works in phonetical type might obtain a circulation in foreign countries which would be impossible if the ordinary unphonetical spelling were adopted, and the cost of production would be thereby diminished. So too French works in raised letters would be of use to our blind if spelled phonetically, whereas they would be practically illegible to the English-speaking blind if the ordinary French spelling were adopted. The raised letters of visible speech are eminently adapted for international use, as the sounds of all languages could be written by the same alphabet.

21,943. He would use a phonetic system to carry out that object?—Yes.

21,944. Have you any experience at all of the knowledge which blind people have of foreign languages, or the way in which they acquire that knowledge?—None whatever.

21,945. You are not aware of the fact that they learn a great deal by the ear?—No. I have not devoted my attention to that subject.

21,946. (*Mr. Van-Oven.*) From the limited extent to which this system of visible speech has been adopted in the schools in America, and from what I see of the system myself, I gather that it is rather difficult to acquire a knowledge of it, but do you consider that it is desirable that all teachers of the deaf should learn this system of visible speech, so as to be furnished with a means of correcting the speech of the children they are teaching?—I think that the knowledge of the mechanism of speech which is acquired in the study of visible speech is important for teachers, and I also think it is important for the children.

21,947. But supposing it was found that to teach the children by means of visible speech was troublesome, or it was considered by the managers of the school unadvisable, you think it exceedingly important that the teachers in the school should be acquainted with it?—That is my opinion.

21,948. Consequently you would recommend that under all circumstances a knowledge of this system of visible speech should be acquired by teachers of the deaf and dumb?—That is my opinion; but I do not wish to force my opinion on anybody.

21,949. As a means of correcting the speech of deaf children you consider that a knowledge of this system is exceedingly desirable?—Yes.

21,950. (*Mr. St. John Ackers.*) You have already stated that in your opinion it is absolutely necessary that the teachers of the deaf should understand the mechanism of speech; do you consider that it is possible to acquire that knowledge equally well by any other method than that which you have been putting before us, for instance the German method by which teachers are instructed in the anatomy and physiology of the vocal organs, and if, in your opinion, "visible speech" is superior to that, will you explain to the Commission why you think so?—I think it is perfectly possible for a person to obtain a thoroughly competent knowledge of the mechanism of speech without going through a course of instruction in "visible speech"; but I think it is of very great assistance in acquiring such a knowledge; it affords the same kind of assistance that chemical symbols afford in acquiring a competent knowledge of chemistry; in fact these symbols bear precisely the same relation to phonetics that chemical symbols bear to chemistry.

21,951. Then all you insist on is, that it is essential that teachers should have that knowlege, and in your opinion if it is not got in one way it should be got in another?—Yes.

21,952. Do you think that those children who are taught by visible speech dream in visible speech?—It has not been used sufficiently to bring about any such result; they dream I think in movements of the mouth. The symbols have not been used to such an extent in any school as to make them so familiar to the eyes of the children as the ordinary print of a book. The process of forming the capital letters is so slow that it has not yet been used so thoroughly as I should like to see it used. That has led to the idea of the line writing form which is a more rapid form.

21,953. (*Sir Lyon Playfair.*) Do deaf persons speak when they dream?—Yes, they speak audibly.

21,954. (*Mr. St. John Ackers.*) We know that orally taught pupils talk in their sleep?—Yes.

21,955. You probably know that it has been stated by those opposed to visible speech that those who are taught by it do think in visible speech and therefore practically it is a sort of a second language to them which they have to translate?—It is the first time I have ever heard that idea brought forward.

21,956. I have often heard it myself. Perhaps you will give us your reasons why you think that is a false view of your system?—We have no experience to guide us, but in my opinion it is false, and for this reason: that visible speech is never used directly to express ideas. The characters recall, not ideas, but positions of the mouth; they recall the speech, and the speech recalls the ideas. It is the speech that is connected directly with the ideas, and the visible speech-writing simply recalls the speech; it recalls the positions of the mouth. You see the distinction. So that between visible speech and the mind of the child is spoken language in its ordinary form. It is this spoken language that is most closely connected with the mind, but supposing it were the case that people thought in visible speech, then we should have the same condition of affairs that we have with ordinary writing. You can analyse that, and see how far you think in ordinary writing; we do it to a very limited extent. As a general rule, ordinary writing recalls the speech, and partially illiterate people have a difficulty in gathering ideas from a printed page unless they read the words aloud. Well-educated persons do to a certain extent recall the ordinary spelling of words. When we forget how a word is spelt, how often we have to write it to see how it looks! That shows that we have its form associated in the mind independently of the sound. But in the use of a character which more closely corresponds with speech than the ordinary written form, it would be more closely connected with speech in the mind than the ordinary form.

21,957. Do you find that it in any way affects ordinary writing; do the pupils first of all begin to write as it were in their minds in visible speech, and then write in their ordinary practice?—There is one of the chief advantages to my mind of the use of a phonetical alphabet that is not based on Roman letters. Where you use a phonetical system which is based upon Roman letters, there is a confusion of spelling, the same letters being used in two different ways. But, so far as I have observed, there is not that difficulty where the phonetical alphabet is entirely distinct from the other. The words are translated as wholes, and it does not interfere with spelling. That is my experience.

21,958. You have already stated to the Commission that in your opinion the methods of teaching the congenitally deaf should be different from the methods adopted in teaching those who have lost hearing after they have obtained speech; would you teach all by visible speech, both those who had already speech as well as those who were congenitally deaf; or would you simply teach the congenitally deaf by visible speech?—My personal opinion is that it would be an advantage to all.

21,959. (*Chairman.*) One of the reasons why you said that in your opinion visible speech was so useful to the deaf and dumb was that it prevented them

Mr. A. G. Bell.

26 June 1888.

from falling into the error of mistaking one word for another, which is so easily done in English, where there are so many similar words with different significations, what you called "homophenes," whereas in German and Italian, where every word is pronounced as nearly as possible as it is written, there is not the same liability to error in lip reading. I understood you to say that English in that respect was at a disadvantage as compared with German or Italian?—Yes, in German and Italian the written form of the words conform very closely to the spoken forms, so that every lesson in articulation given by a teacher is supplemented by the written language in a book and by the printed notices and shop signs in the streets. Every shop sign is a lesson in articulation. A boy goes into a street, and he sees the name of the street phonetically spelt, so that the pronunciation of the words is all the time kept clearly before his eyes. In English it is not so. In English the written form differs in a very remarkable and absurd degree from the spoken form, so that in teaching articulation to the deaf in our country, they are left to acquire their knowledge of the spoken form from what they can find out from the mouth of the teacher, or from what specific instruction they receive when words are first taught.

21,960. In Germany, by the pure oral system, the language can be taught more easily, can it not, than English can be taught in England?—Yes, on the oral method.

21,961. Therefore, in teaching the oral method in England, the language being different from German or Italian, you want something to supplement and facilitate that instruction in lip reading which you say is essential to the understanding of speech by the deaf?—Yes. The English language is easier than the German language as a language; the difficulty is entirely artificial. It is easier to teach a child to speak English than to speak German. I know that, because I know that in English the consonants are the parts of speech upon which intelligibility depends, and of the consonants more than 75 per cent. in English are formed by the point of the tongue. The elements that are difficult to teach, the guttural sounds, which are very prevalent in German, are formed by the back of the tongue and the top part of the tongue; but in English these guttural sounds occur so comparatively rarely that a child may pronounce them very imperfectly and yet be perfectly intelligible. What I think is necessary in teaching speech to English children is that they should have a phonetical representation of the speech, for the purpose of simply letting them see what our pronounciation is; but as to the nature of the alphabet that is used for this special purpose I think it is entirely immaterial. Any system will do, so long as they are accustomed to read from a phonetical representation of speech. That will impress upon the memory of a child what the correct pronunciation should be, which an ordinary book would not do.

21,962. (*Mr. Johnson.*) And which an ordinary symbol would not do?—The symbols of visible speech would do as well for this purpose as any other phonetical character; I think better. But books and reading matter would have to be printed in the symbols in order to afford reading exercises. For such a purpose any phonetical alphabet would do; but visible speech has a special field of usefulness that no other alphabet can touch. Its special advantage lies, not so much in representing English sounds, as *in representing the sounds that the child makes itself*, because the principle is to go from the known to the unknown, and the known sound to the deaf child is the sound that he makes himself spontaneously, whatever it may be. It may not be an English sound.

21,963. (*Chairman.*) Do you wish to say anything further with regard to visible speech and line writing?—I should like to supplement with one word what I have said about visible speech and line writing. You see what institutions are now using visible speech. One institution, the Florida Institution, is using line-writing. That institution was actually using visible speech without knowing it.

21,964. Although the Principal of that Institution says: "We do not use visible speech, and have never done so," he has been doing it without knowing it?—Yes. My father is still active in this work; and he has produced a still further development this year, which should be known, at all events by title, to the Commission. He has produced a phonetical system, the object of which is to make the English language the universal language. He has been interested in Volapük, and attempts of that sort, and he has just published a work entitled "World English," in which he proposes a modified scheme of Roman letters. I mention that for this reason; that the Principal of the Western New York Institution, Mr. Westervelt, is going to introduce "World English," as a means of teaching articulation in his school. Now that is a school where articulation has been neglected; it is a school where the manual alphabet method is used. Great advance has been made in a knowledge of written English, but speech has been neglected, and the Principal of that school is going to make an independent experiment this autumn with "World English," and has set his teachers at work to study it.

21,965. Is that "World English" to be carried out in line writing?—No, it is a new system based upon Roman letters, the idea being to enable foreigners to acquire English more readily. That book is just published.

21,966. Is it phonetic?—It is phonetic, the idea being that the difficulty of making English an universal language is entirely its unphonetical alphabet. The book is published in London by Trübner and Company, and it is entitled "World English, the Universal Language," by Alexander Melville Bell. I mention that because it is going to be used in an institution for the deaf and dumb.

21,967. Are the teachers in deaf and dumb schools in America more highly paid than the teachers in the ordinary schools?—I do not think I am competent to answer the question. I have the impression that they have salaries that compare favourable with the salaries of teachers in ordinary schools.

22,968. (*Dr. Campbell.*) Of course in addition to their salary they have their board and lodging; consequently although they get a small sum in actual money it means more than ordinary teachers get?—Yes, it means more in such cases.

21,969. (*Mr. St. John Ackers.*) When I was in America a considerable number of those teaching in the institstions were not boarded in the institutions. They are not all boarded in the institutions, are they?—I think not.

21,970. (*Dr. Campbell.*) But those are usually termed Professors. When you speak of teachers in America, we understand by that, resident teachers?—I did not intend to use the word in that restricted sense. I use the term generally without reference to residence or non-residence.

21,971. (*Chairman.*) I think you said that there were some other points upon which you wished to supplement your previous evidence?—I was asked a question relating to the separation of the sexes. I think that one evil very often leads to another. I should look upon the whole Institution plan as in itself an evil to be avoided as much as possible, and on the Institution plan as the pupils grow up it would be advisable to have the elder boys in a separate school, but I would not debar them from associating with hearing persons of the opposite sex. In regard to the others, I think it would be much better to adopt what is known as the cottage system. Instead of having the pupils in dormitories, where they have nothing approximating to home life, I would rather have the living part of the institution in the shape of small cottages where you could have the little boys and the little girls and the elder girls arrayed more in a family relation. The cottage system I think would be infinitely preferable to the institution plan. The institution plan with its dormitories is subversive of the very basis of society, the family relation. The family is the basis of society, and if we must take these children away from their homes, let us try to bring about a family relation as much as possible, and I think it would be advantageous to associate the elder girls, who would have a motherly disposition, in little cottages with the younger children of both sexes making a little family group in each cottage.

21,972. Do you desire to say anything as to the desirability of having conventions of teachers?—In regard to suggestions for improving our methods of instruction, I think that the British Government should assist the bringing together of teachers for the purpose of discussing the methods of instruction. I cannot over estimate the benefit to America which has resulted from the periodical conventions of teachers which are held, where the most free discussions take place, teachers of the most opposite methods urge their views, and nothing but good comes from these teachers' conventions. The travelling expenses of some of the teachers and principals are sometimes paid by the States to enable them to attend conventions. Then again, in America we have an organ of communication between teachers, and that I think is of very great importance. I need hardly direct your attention to the "American Annals of the Deaf," an admirable journal, admirably conducted, containing within its pages nearly the whole literature of the world in relation to the deaf. That is of enormous importance in stimulating and improving methods of instruction.

21,973. Is there any other point to which you wish to refer?—There is another point. A very great deal can be done for deaf children at a very much younger age than is ordinarily supposed, and in many cases parents, especially mothers, would devote time to the instruction of their little ones if they knew what to do. The diffusion among parents of information relating to methods of home instruction giving specific directions how they are to act is of the very greatest importance.

21,974. Do you think that there might be any improvement in the mode of taking the census with regard to the deaf and dumb?—In the census returns I think it is of the greatest importance that we should study all the causes of deafness and the inheritance of the defect, and that to that end we should obtain not merely a census of those whom we may term deaf mutes, but that we should have a census of the deaf; we should know the adults who are afflicted with deafness as well as children, and if we ask for these two elements to which I direct the attention of the Commission, the amount of deafness and the age at which the deafness occurred, we can separate those that belong to the class deaf and dumb from the others. We want to study the whole subject. I would recommend that there should be a census of the deaf, and not merely a census of the deaf and dumb.

21,975. Can you suggest any improvement upon the existing schedule in the census relating to the deaf and dumb which would be applicable to this country as well as to America?—I am not prepared just now to make very specific recommendations, but I brought that subject before the late convention of principals that met at Jackson, Mississippi, and I have been appointed one of a Committee to confer with the Committee of Congress on the census with the object of proposing modifications in the questions to be asked relating to the deaf and dumb; and if it would be of any value to the Commission I should be glad to forward to the Commission whatever recommendations that committee make to Congress, because we shall have a meeting very shortly after my return to America.

21,976. That, we think, would be very valuable?—The chief point that I have recommended so far is the insertion of the simple question "Are there "any people deaf or hard of hearing in this house, "and if so at what age did the deafness occur?"

21,977. (*Mr. St. John Ackers.*) Leaving entirely out the question "Are there any deaf and dumb?"—I would put that in afterwards. Specialists can deduce from the answers to those two questions the number of deaf and dumb, but it would be safer to ask in addition after that question: "Are there any deaf and dumb?"

21,978. (*Sir Tindal Robertson.*) When will your next census be taken?—In 1890. The Federal Government takes a census every 10 years, and the different State Governments (or some of them) take a census every ten years, and they are so arranged that the State censuses come midway between two Federal censuses.

21,979. Is the next census in America to be a Federal Census or a State census?—It will be a Federal census in 1890, and then in 1895 some of the States will take a census.

21,980. (*Dr. Campbell.*) With reference to the dormitory system, I fully recognise the objections to it and have acted against it for many years, but do you find any ill effects from the deaf pupils being only say two in a room under the cottage system?—I am afraid that the Commission could not rely upon my testimony upon that point; but certainly I think that the cottage system is preferable to the dormitory system, and that home is preferable to the cottage system.

21,981. We all recognise that amongst the blind there is a great tendency to secret vices, and it is a growing evil, an evil which we must meet in some way. I wanted to know whether you have that in America amongst the deaf?—I do not know much about this subject. But I should think that exclusive segregation of persons of one sex is an unnatural thing, and would tend to produce morbid conditions.

21,982. (*Sir Tindal Robertson.*) I think that medical men generally would traverse that opinion?—I may of course be entirely wrong.

21,983. (*Chairman.*) Do you desire to say anything further in regard to sign language?—There are some points which I should like to enlarge upon a little in relation to signs and the sign language. I think it is very important that we should thoroughly understand what we mean when we use the word "signs"; and if I might be allowed to do so I should like to put in my testimony here my reply to Dr. Gallaudet in the discussion that we had upon this subject in Washington, because the main argument upon which he relied is universally used throughout America. It is that the sign language is the *natural language* of the deaf and dumb, and that therefore it *must* be used. I attempted to combat that, and this is what I said in reply to that point. *See* Annals vol. XXIX., p. 67. "There are "signs *and* signs. There is the same distinction "between pantomime and the sign-language that "there is between a picture and the Egyptian hiero-"glyphics. Pictures are naturally understood by "all the world, but it would be illogical to argue "from this that a picture-language like that devel-"oped by the ancient Egyptians must also be uni-"versally intelligible. Pantomime is understood "by all the world, but who among us can under-"stand the sign language of the deaf and dumb "without much instruction and practice? Panto-"mime and dramatic action can be used, and with "perfect propriety to illustrate English expres-"sions, so as actually to facilitate the acquisition of "our language by the deaf; but the abbreviated "and conventionalised pantomime known as the "'sign language' is used *in place* of the English "language, and becomes itself the vernacular of the "deaf child. All the arguments that have been ad-"vanced respecting pantomime and pantomime "language are equally applicable to pictures and a "picture language. We may say, for instance, that "a picture language is more natural than any of "the spoken languages of the world, because pic-"tures are naturally understood by all mankind. "We may even arrive, by a further process of gen-"eralisation, at the idea that picture writing in the "wider sense constitutes the only form of language "that is 'natural' at all, for all the other languages

Mr. A. G. Bell.

26 June 1888.

"appear to be entirely arbitrary and conventional. "If we pursue the parallel we shall arrive at the "conclusion that a picture language of some kind "must necessarily be the vernacular of our pupils, "by means of which the other more conventional "languages may be explained and taught. It is "immaterial whether such statements are fallacies "or not, so long as we do not apply them to edu- "cational purposes. But let us see how they work "in practice. No one will deny that the exhibition "of a picture may add interest to the fairy tale or "story that we tell the child. It illustrates the "language we use, and it may be of invaluable as- "sistance to him in realising our meaning. But "is that any reason why we should teach him "Egyptian hieroglyphics? Granting the premises, "is the conclusion sound that we should teach him "English *by means of* hieroglyphics? If such "conclusions are illogical, then the fundamental "ideas upon which our whole system of education "by signs is based are also fallacious and unsound."

21,984. Have you anything further to add with regard to the value of the sign language in social intercourse?—The sign language is not of any value whatever in promoting social intercourse with the hearing; its value as a means of social intercourse is with deaf mutes alone. It promotes their intercourse with one another, but hearing people do not know it. Now there is one very curious difference in the moral result of education by signs and education by oral methods. It is in the *amour propre* or self-respect of the pupil. A person who is taught by any of the oral methods comes to consider himself as the same as other people, and he desires to have as little difference as possible between him and other people. But a person who has been taught by a special language comes to look upon himself as belonging to a different race, of which he is proud. He comes to look upon himself as different from other people and glories in the fact. Now that leads to very curious results and misunderstandings. A sign teacher will misunderstand and misconstrue the conduct and actions of an orally taught person, because he does not realise that this feeling of *amour propre* or self-respect leads that orally taught person to avoid making a public exhibition of himself. So that an orally taught person will very often avoid conversation with a stranger if he cannot talk easily in company, because he does not like to have attention directed to his defect. You will find that in Dr. Gallaudet's speech before the National Educational Association at Madison, Wisconsin (1884); he makes a comparison between the public actions of persons taught orally and persons taught by the sign system. He says on page 47 of the Proceedings:—"I "have seen these two classes of persons mingling "in society. I have seen persons that depended "upon speech and lip reading entirely, without any "power of resorting to the manual alphabet or signs, "converse with strangers; I have seen the conver- "sation flag in a few moments after a few common- "places had been passed. I have seen strangers "striving to make themselves understood, and failing, "and I have seen these persons far more isolated in "society than others with whom I have been equally "familiar, who, having no speech, resorted to that "definite and complete means of communication, "writing," and so forth. He does not realise that those orally taught persons could have communicated by writing also. Why is it that after a few commonplaces had been passed they did not resort to paper and pencil? It was the feeling of *amour propre*. They did not desire to advertise themselves in public as being deaf. They preferred in public not to speak to a person at all, rather than direct attention to their infirmity. Now I may give an illustration of that, because I happen to know the whole details of the case. A deaf lady of Washington, who is a good speech-reader, found herself one day on board of a steamer bound for Mount Vernon in company with a lady friend. She was very much distressed to find on board a party of deaf mutes headed by Dr. Edward M. Gallaudet, and became very desirous of avoiding their notice. But Dr. Gallaudet recognised her, and in the politeness of his heart he came forward to talk to her. In vain this lady tried to show him by her actions that she did not want him to talk to her in that public place, because it directed attention to her infirmity, and she did not want to be recognised as a deaf mute. But Dr. Gallaudet, like other sign teachers, had become habituated to the stare of the public, and he failed to appreciate her feelings or understand her motives for desiring to be left alone. In his Madison address to which I have already alluded (page 47), he describes the above incident, and this is what he says:—"I call "to mind a trip that I made a short time ago "upon a steamer going from Washington to Mount "Vernon. On the steamer there were several "members of my own family. There were several "students from the college with which I am con- "nected. There was a lady who has had every "opportunity that any one could have for the acquisi- "tion of speech and reading from the lips. Social "intercourse, the free interchange of thought, the "flow of wit and repartee, went on where signs and "the manual alphabet were used freely: and I asked "a friend of this lady who had declined, during "many years, to use the manual alphabet, and who "had never learned to use signs, whether he thought "that that lady ever enjoyed such free social inter- "course in the social circle as did the young men "that were enjoying that day on the Mount Vernon "excursion with the manual alphabet and with "signs; and this friend of the lady who depended "on speech and upon lip reading, and who was a "fine speaker, and a fine lip reader, told me that "he was certain that she had never been able to "enjoy through the means of speech and lip read- "ing such heart satisfying social intercourse as was "being enjoyed by those who used the manual "alphabet and signs." Now in all this matter Dr. Gallaudet was sadly mistaken, and the "friend" to whom he refers was a gentleman who had rarely been inside her house, and who, on this occasion, simply acted as escort. Now I think I know a great deal better than Dr. Gallaudet what is the value of speech and speech-reading to the deaf. I have daily, hourly experience of their value in my own home. I know something of the sign-language; I am expert in the use of all forms of manual alphabet, but I have no need for these artificial instrumentalities in my own home. "Social intercourse," "the free interchange of thought," "the flow of wit and repartee," "heart-satisfying social intercourse" are all possible without signs or manual alphabets. I know it from experience. I know it from observation. And the paper and pencil which would not be produced in public, I have seen freely used in the privacy of home to set the stranger at ease and welcome him to the family circle. And when the ice has been broken I have seen that paper thrown aside as unnecessary, and conversation carried on freely by word of mouth. I know what I am speaking about when I testify to the value of speech and speech-reading. There is no other means by which the deaf can be brought into such intimate contact with the hearing.

21,985. (*Rev. Mr. Sleight.*) It is curious that you did not refute it at the time?—I did not know at the time the details of the case or the name of the person to whom Dr. Gallaudet referred. By the way, in talking with a deaf lady recently upon this subject of *amour propre* she suddenly startled me by the queries:—"If you had false teeth, would "you care to exhibit them in public? How would "you like, when you go into society, to have people "stare at your mouth and take notice of your teeth? "What would you think of the delicacy of feeling "that would prompt a stranger to congratulate you "upon the way in which art had supplemented the "deficiencies of nature? Can you wonder then that "I should seek to conceal my infirmity in every "way I can?" I have brought forward the above story to show you how the feeling of self-respect, of *amour propre*, which prevented an orally taught person from making an exhibition of herself or directing public attention to the fact that she had an infirmity, can be mistranslated and misconstrued by one who is accustomed to a system under which the deaf glory in being deaf. Now, I think that is a very proper spirit, and I think the spirit of the oral system is to make the deaf persons feel that they are the same as other people, to make them object to exhibit their infirmity to the world; whereas on the special language method they glory in the defect, they glory in being deaf mutes, they glory in being distinct from the world. These two radical tendencies are very important to consider, and our object should be, I am sure, to create the former feeling rather than the latter.

21,986. Do you approve of the Greenberger system, which, like some of the French and German systems in teaching simple words, teaches the words all at once, instead of spelling them to the deaf and dumb?—I do. I will go further and take the complete sentence. It is my belief that sentences and phrases are of more use to deaf children than words. They will understand from the mouth a phrase better than they will understand a word, and they will understand a word better than they will understand an elementary sound.

21,987. (*Sir Tindal Robertson.*) Is that because they guess to a certain extent?—Yes, they have more to guess at. A sentence also is expressive of a concrete idea. What a child wants to express is an idea. A word does not do that as a general rule; it is a complete phrase or sentence that is wanted.

21,988. (*Chairman.*) Have you found or heard of any difficulty in giving religious instruction to the deaf and dumb by means of the oral system or by language, because it has been contended that the only way in which such instruction can be given to the deaf and dumb is on the sign and manual system?—I think that may be perfectly answered by directing you attention to the list of schools for the United States at the end of this volume—"Facts and Opinions relating to the Deaf," page 194. You will see that one of the denominational schools started especially for the purpose of giving religious instruction where religious instruction is the first and foremost and most prominent thing in the minds of the teachers, and where everything gives way to religion is a pure oral school. That is the German Evangelical Lutheran Institution for the Deaf and Dumb. The fact that they do not use the sign language, but use the pure oral method, shows that it is suitable for religious instruction. I may say that I have great pleasure in presenting the Royal Commission with 100 copies of this book.

21,989. The Commission thank you for you generous gift. Have you heard that in the United States those who are deaf and dumb, and who have been taught on the oral system, attend the ordinary places of religious worship rather than the places of worship where the deaf and dumb talk on the sign and manual system are congregated together?—I have no statistics upon that point. I may say that Mrs. Bell finds no difficulty in following the Episcopal service where there is a regular service, although she cannot follow the sermon.

21,990. (*Rev. Mr. Sleight.*) Why is she not able to follow the sermon?—Partly because she is very short sighted, and secondly, because it would involve a very great strain upon her attention.

21,991. I see, mentioned here, Whipple's Home School for Deaf Mutes, and Whipple's Natural Alphabet, what is there peculiar about that?—I have already directed your attention to the origin of Whipple's school. Mr. Whipple established a school, he died, and one of his sons carried on this school, and this son devised an alphabet for the purpose of teaching speech that is very akin to visible speech, and it is a remarkable alphabet as having been developed for this special purpose of teaching the deaf. It is crude, of course, compared to a scientific alphabet like visible speech, but it possesses very great interest, and as Mr. Whipple, junr., is himself dead, it should be preserved and studied. The school still exists among the private schools.

21,992. I see that you mentioned the schools for the deaf in Canada: have you ever visited them, and can you give us any opinion about them? I think they are mostly either combined or manual, and that there is no pure oral school there?—No, I think there are no pure oral schools there. I believe I have visited them all with the exception of the New Brunswick Deaf and Dumb Institution, and the Federicton Institution. They are mentioned on page 195, and the replies are given on page 167.

21,993. Are they generally superior or inferior to the schools in the United States?—I think they are about the same. The same methods are adopted, and indeed, although they come under another political government, we always include the Canadian schools with the American schools.

21,994. In your conferences?—In our conferences we make no distinction between American and Canadian. The principals of these institutions meet our principals, and they have a vote in our conventions of principals. The teachers from these institutions meet the teachers of the deaf, and vote exactly in the same way. There are no political lines of demarcation regarding the instruction of the deaf. They are to all intents and purposes American schools.

21,995. (*Mr. St. John Ackers.*) Are there no private schools in Canada?—I do not know exactly the status of these schools. The New Brunswick Institution and the Fredericton Institution I know nothing about. The Mackay Institution comes more under the designation of a private school; it is now supported by a fund, but it is denominational. In Montreal there are two Roman Catholic Institutions, one for males and the other for females, and the Mackay Institution grew out of that as a Protestant school. It was started as a private school, and is now largely supported from a fund left by Mr. Mackay. It does not follow that none of those are private schools because they are not so designated in this report, because we do not go into that classification of Canadian schools; we simply lump them together as Canadian schools.

21,996. (*Chairman.*) I think you advocate that every child's hearing should be tested when it first enters a school, and that its education should be more or less guided by the amount of hearing that it possesses?—Yes.

21,997. Would you explain to us these instruments which you have been good enough to bring with you?—Certainly. [*Mr. Bell then exhibited to the Commission in operation the two forms of audiometer he had brought from America.*]

21,998 Can you state shortly the general recommendations which you would desire to make?—The chief points I would lay stress upon are the following:—

1. Decentralisation as the policy to be adopted by the Government in dealing with the deaf.
2. Non-interference with methods of instruction.
3. Certificated teachers whose qualifications shall be tested by the Government.
4. Governmental inspection of schools, and payment by results.
5. Government aid to apprentice the deaf when their education is completed.

21,999. Have you anything further to say with regard to the answers you have received to the queries which you sent to the institutions?—I shall

Mr. A. G. Bell.

26 June 1888.

simply direct your attention to the very cordial way in which the superintendents and principals have responded to my queries. I have printed their replies in full for your information; but I regret that I have been unable to include in the volume the many kind expressions of interest in your work that have reached me from all parts of America. I am sure that the teachers of the deaf in our country, one and all, unite with me in expressing the hope that your conclusions will result in a unanimous report. A division would seriously weaken the value of you recommendations and be detrimental to the best interests of the deaf. A unanimous verdict, on the other hand, will carry weight throughout the whole world, and profoundly modify the destinies of the deaf in every civilised land.

EXHIBITS.

The following Exhibits were made by Dr. Alexander Graham Bell during the course of his evidence before the Royal Commission.

Exhibit to Query 21,357.

CENSUS RETURNS.

[This Exhibit contained the names of 2,581 deaf-mutes living on the 1st of June, 1880, in the States of Maine, New Hampshire, Vermont, Massachusetts, Connecticut, and Rhode Island, with all the details concerning them as reported in the tenth census of the United States. The Exhibit is too voluminous to be printed here.]

Exhibit to Query 21,360.

AN OPEN LETTER

CONCERNING THE BILL RELATING TO THE INSTRUCTION OF DEAF-MUTES IN INCORPORATED CITIES AND VILLAGES.

Madison, Wis., Feb. 18, 1885.

To the Committees on Education of the Senate and Assembly of the Legislature of Wisconsin.

Necessity of further provision for instruction of deaf-mutes.

Gentlemen: His Excellency Gov. Rusk, in his recent message to the legislature, has called attention to the large number of deaf children in the State who are growing up in ignorance, and to the fact that the provision made for their education is yet inadequate. In 1880, according to the recent census, there were in the State of Wisconsin 1,079 deaf-mutes, of whom 600 were from 6 to 20 years of age. The total number of deaf-mutes returned as then in school was only 199. The following facts show that the means adopted by the other States have also failed to bring under instruction a large number of the deaf-mutes of school age. (This age is assumed in the census returns to be from 6 to 20 years.) Out of a total of 33,878 deaf-mutes in the United States in 1880, 15,059 were of school age; and the total number of deaf-mutes returned as then in the institutions and schools of the United States was only 5,393. It is obvious that the best means of reaching and bringing under instruction the uneducated deaf children of the country is a subject demanding immediate and serious attention. The Bill you are now discussing relating to the instruction of deaf-mutes in incorporated cities and villages touches this question.

The Institution plan has failed to reach a large number.

How are we to bring them under instruction?

It has given me great pleasure to respond to your cordial invitation to participate in your deliberations, and I think I would be wanting in my duty to the deaf, to whose interests I have given so many years of earnest thought, were I to leave Wisconsin without placing in your hands, in some permanent form, the views I have attempted to express to you orally.

Importance of the proposed measure.

The moment my attention was directed to the bill now under consideration, I recognized the fact that a new phase of legislation for the benefit of the deaf and dumb had been reached, of vast importance to the deaf and to society. The bill represents the first attempt that has been made in the United States to embody, in the form of a law, a principle of dealing with the deaf and dumb that has long been seen to be advisable from a theoretical point of view; and the example of Wisconsin will undoubtedly be speedily followed by other States. The principle involved may be tersely described as the policy of decentralization,—the policy of keeping deaf-mutes separated from one another as much as possible during the period of education, and in contact as much as possible with hearing and speaking children of their own age. The difficulty hitherto has been how to accomplish this. The proposed bill promises a partial solution of the problem, and is an important step in advance.

A new principle involved.

Decentralization.

Plan hitherto adopted.

When the subject of the education of the deaf first engaged the attention of the legislature, the State was thinly populated, and deaf-mutes were few in number. They were so scattered throughout the State that the only practicable method of reaching them appeared to be to collect them together into one school.

Centralization.

This policy of centralization had also, up to that time, been uniformly adopted by the older States. In pursuance of this policy, it became necessary to remove the children from their homes in order to instruct them, and this forced the State to assume the cost of support as well as tuition. Dormitories and special school buildings were erected, and in 1852 the Wisconsin institution for the education of the deaf was open at Delavan. A few years ago the buildings were destroyed by fire, and in 1880 the institution was rebuilt, with increased accommodations. The institution is now comfortably well filled; but the returns of the census show, that, even if crowded to its utmost capacity, it could not accommodate one-half of the deaf-mutes of school age in the State. It is now necessary to consider what additional facilities should be provided. Shall the Delavan institution be enlarged? Shall a new institution be erected in another part of the State? Or, shall schools of a different kind be established? The promoters of the bill propose a new departure.

The proposed measure.

They believe that in many of the incorporated cities and villages of Wisconsin the deaf children could, with limited State aid, be educated in the localities where they reside. By the passage of the bill the State will offer facilities for the establishment of small day schools for deaf children wherever the parents desire to keep them at home during the period of instruction. This desire, I am sure, is very general; and it is to be feared that in many cases the struggle between parental affection and the good of the child results in the retention of the child at home instead of sending it to school. By sending the teachers to the children, instead of the children to the teachers, wherever possible, the State will accommodate its policy to the wishes of parents, and bring comfort and happiness to many an afflicted family. The State, also, will be benefited by having deaf children brought under educational influences who would not otherwise, without compulsion, be sent to an institution, or who would enter school so late in life as to receive but little benefit from the course of instruction.

Advantages to the families.

Advantages to the State.

The condition of uneducated deaf-mutes

It is now well known that those whom we term "deaf-mutes" have no other natural defect save that of deafness. They are simply persons who are deaf from childhood, and many of them are only hard of hearing. The lack of articulate speech which has led to their denomination as "mutes" results from lack of instruction, and not from any defect of the vocal organs. No one naturally acquires without instruction a language he has never heard. But, if children who are born deaf or hard of hearing do not naturally speak, how then do they think? It is difficult for us to realize the possibility of a train of thought carried on without words; but what words can a deaf child know who has never heard the sounds of speech? When *we* think, we think in words, though we may not actually utter sounds. Let us eliminate from our consciousness the train of words, and what remains? I do not venture to answer the question; but it is this, and this alone, that belongs to the thoughts of a deaf child. Even written words, as found in books and periodicals, though appealing to a sense possessed by the deaf child, mean no more to him without instruction than a Russian or Chinese book would mean to us. Who, then, can picture the profound depth of the ignorance of the uneducated deaf-mute?

pitiable in the extreme,

If you would try to realize the black darkness of his mind, consider what your mental condition would be were you to wipe out from your memory everything you have ever heard of and everything you have read. Naturally intelligent, the deaf child looks out upon the world and longs for knowledge. Common humanity demands that we use every means—even to compulsion—to bring under instruction the deaf children of Wisconsin. Upon other grounds also the education of deaf children is a matter of importance; for deaf-mutes, if allowed to grow up without instruction, have all the passions of men and women, without the restraining influences that spring from a cultivated understanding.

and a danger to society.

Condition of educated deaf-mutes.

Under the enlightening influences of education they become good citizens, amenable to the laws of society, and able to exercise the franchise intelligently. As deafness is not necessarily a bar to intellectual culture, some are found capable of the very highest education. This has been recognized by Congress by the establishment of the National College for Deaf-Mutes, at Washington, which is open to the deaf-mutes of Wisconsin. To show the intellectual condition they can assume, I may say that a number in this country support themselves by literature. Some are editors, and contributors to the magazines and daily journals. Two deaf-mute brothers in Belleville, Ontario, are successful lawyers. There are very few positions in life which can not be occupied by deaf persons. Nearly all the arts and industries are open to them, and many of the professions. Even when uneducated they are rarely a burden upon the community; for deafness is no bar to physical labor. Indeed, it is to be feared that deaf-mutes are sometimes deprived of education on account of the value of their labor at home. By education, deaf-mutes are raised from a condition of mental degradation that is absolutely inconceivable, and from a social position but little removed from slavery, to become intelligent and valuable members of society, and sources of wealth to the State.

Advisability of early education.

The possibility of the education of the deaf and dumb is based on the possibility of teaching them a language whereby ideas may be imparted and the mind cultivated. But it is in very early childhood that language is most easily acquired. By adopting a policy of centralization the State has rendered it impossible to bring deaf children under instruction until after the most impressionable period of life has been passed. Wisconsin in her constitution defines the school age of her children as from four to twenty years; but deaf children, to whom education is so vitally important, can not enter your institution until they reach the age of ten. Why should deaf children be debarred from the benefits guaranteed to all by the constitution itself?

Local and day schools render this possible.

The nearer the school can be brought to the home the earlier can instruction be profitably commenced. Little day schools scattered throughout the State will meet a want that is sorely felt. The necessary smallness of the schools will be an element in promoting their efficiency.

Smallness of school promotes efficiency of instruction.

Under equal circumstances of instruction the pupils of small schools make greater progress than those of large ones, because the teacher can give more individual attention to the children.

Day schools promote home instruction.

Another advantage of the small day school is the influence on the home surroundings exerted by the teacher. There is no one so capable of instructing a little child as its own mother; but parents, as a rule, are utterly ignorant of all matters connected with the education of the deaf. The proximity of the home and school must lead to frequent personal contact between the parents and teacher. Information will be sought and given, and in many cases the parents and family will be brought to co-operate intelligently in the work of instruction.

Parents and families brought to co-operate in work of instruction.

The day schools to be a part of the general public-school system of the State.

The bill contemplates making the day schools for the deaf a part of the general public-school system of the State, and school-rooms will be provided by the incorporated cities and villages in which such schools are opened. As a very small school-room will accommodate as many deaf children as one teacher can profitably instruct, economical and other considerations will usually lead to the selection of a room in some building already occupied as a public school, and thus the deaf children will be brought into close proximity to large numbers of hearing children in the same building. This proximity will favor the growth of friendships between the deaf and the hearing pupils, which will be invaluable in adult life, leading to business and social relations of the greatest importance. Constant association with hearing and speaking children will accustom the deaf child to the society in which he is to live in the future. His hearing school-fellows and playmates will be the men and women by whom he will be surrounded in adult life. How important, then, that deaf-mutes should have the opportunity of cultivating the acquaintance of hearing persons of their own age. The friendships formed in childhood often last through life. Living constantly in the midst of the industries and activities of the communities in which they have interested personal friends to encourage and aid them, the ways are open to them to acquire any trade, business, or profession for which they have aptness or inclination. The broad fields and avenues of life invite them as they do the hearing; whereas, in institutions they are limited to a few mechanical trades merely, not so easily turned to account for want of that personal acquaintance so helpful in obtaining desirable employment. Furthermore, industrial education is being brought into the educational systems of the large towns, affording advantages of a broader and more thorough kind than institutions offer.

Advantages.

Every means that will bring the deaf child into closer association and affiliation with hearing children of his own age will promote his happiness and success in adult life. Association in the games and plays of hearing children will be an important element in bringing this about. Partial co-education with the hearing children of the public schools will also be of use. Partial co-education is not only perfectly feasible, but will be of advantage to the deaf child, and a means of economizing the time of the special teacher. Deaf children require a great deal of individual instruction, especially in the early steps of education. Some of the brightest children can be withdrawn from the special school-room for short periods of time, with advantage to the duller pupils, who could then receive the individual attention of the specially skilled teacher. There are subjects taught in the public schools in which information is gained through the eye, and in such branches deaf children could profitably enter the same classes with the hearing; for instance, they could join the classes for practice in writing, drawing, and arithmetic from the blackboard and on the slate, map drawing, sewing, etc. For other subjects, special methods of instruction would be necessary, es-

Partial co-education with hearing children.

pecially in the earlier stages, and this necessitates the employment of a special teacher and school-room.

Complete co-education.

I have no doubt that some of the brighter pupils might ultimately be able to dispense with the special teacher altogether, as cases are known in the United States where deaf children have successfully taken the full course in the public school, and graduated with honor to themselves and their teachers. It must be remembered, however, that those are exceptional cases; and, while they show the possibility of complete co-education in some cases, the experience of the past has demonstrated the impossibility of this in the great majority of cases.

Conditions created by the bill favorable to the acquisition of articulate speech.

The power of speech and reading speech from the mouth would evidently be of the greatest assistance in establishing communication between deaf and hearing children. Constant association with hearing and speaking children will act as a stimulus to the acquisition of speech, which stimulus is wanting in an institution where all the playmates and associates are deaf, and where some of the teachers themselves can not hear. It is well known to all instructors of the deaf, that, in other countries than our own, deaf-mutes are taught to speak, and that International Conventions of teachers of the deaf have decided that speech and speech reading should be taught to all deaf-mutes, as a regular branch of their education. That this is not more done in America is due to many causes, among the most important being the extraordinary ignorance of the American people concerning the mechanism of speech and the consequent difficulty in obtaining competent articulation teachers. I doubt whether one person in ten thousand could give an intelligible account of the movements of his mouth in uttering the simplest sentence. Indeed, so gross is the popular ignorance of the whole subject that, when a deaf-mute is taught to speak, people look upon it as a sort of miracle, and few persons seem to be aware that what is here regarded as a miracle is in other countries an every-day fact. All the deaf-mutes of Germany are taught to speak. In fact, so general is instruction of this kind that in 1882 more than 65 per cent. of the deaf-mutes under instruction in the world, outside the shores of America, were taught to speak and understand the speech of others in purely oral schools. Inside our shores less than 9 per cent. were to be found in oral schools. In most of our institutions, however, though they may not be classed as oral schools, speech is taught to a selected few of the pupils. The latest statistics on this subject show that in May, 1883, 14 per cent. of the deaf-mutes of America were using speech in the school-room as the means of communication with their teachers, 18 per cent. were taught to speak as an accomplishment, and 68 per cent. received no instruction whatever in articulation. In view of the lamentable neglect of articulation teaching in this country, it is encouraging to know, that, of the deaf-mutes in the institutions and day schools of the New England States, more than 54 per cent. are taught to speak.

German method of educating teachers for the deaf.

In the light of the great success of articulation teaching in Germany, the following fact is significant: I am informed that in that country instruction in the mechanism of speech and the anatomy of the vocal organs forms a part of the regular curriculum of the normal schools. Courses of lectures are also given on the methods of teaching defective children. It then becomes easy to select from the normal schools suitable persons for teachers of the deaf and dumb. Such persons require a thorough knowledge of the theory and art of teaching and of the mechanism of speech. Then, with a limited amount of practical experience in a school for the deaf under the superintendence of an experienced principal, they are qualified for their work.

Applicable to Wisconsin.

Such a plan is perfectly feasible in Wisconsin, and is viewed with favor, I understand, by the State Superintendent. A general knowledge of the mechanism of speech will be of value to the teachers of your public schools on account of the large number of children of foreign-born parents in your schools. If you would preserve the purity of the English tongue in Wisconsin, you must teach speech to the pupils of the public schools, and this involves a knowledge of the mechanism of speech on the part of the teachers. Should the subject of the mechanism of speech receive attention in your normal schools, there will be no difficulty in selecting from the students persons who show special natural abilities for articulation work to become the teachers in the small day schools for deaf children to be established under the provisions of the bill. Let the bill be passed, and a demand will arise for the schools. This will create a demand for teachers, and the demand will lead to a supply.

Advantages to the public schools.

No restriction relating to methods of instruction.

The promoters of this bill have wisely abstained from restricting in any way the methods of instruction to be used in the schools. The measure expresses a willingness on the part of the State to accommodate its policy to the wishes of the parents of deaf children to retain them at home; and, in pursuance of this spirit of accommodation, the bill leaves the parents and local authorities some liberty of choice regarding methods of instruction. When the most experienced teachers are divided as to the value of the different methods of instruction, who is competent to decide? The State may rest assured, that, when the interests of their afflicted children are at stake, the parents will be apt to make a careful choice. The State is secured against rash experiments of a doubtful nature by the general control to be exercised over all the schools by the State Superintendent and the State Board of Supervision, who also control the operations of the Delavan institution. By this provision also the harmonious relations of the small day schools to the central institution are guaranteed.

The State guaranteed against rash experiments, incompetent teachers, and inefficient management.

Harmonious relation of the local schools to the central institution assured.

The liability of the State limited to a per capita of $100 per annum.

It is to me a matter of regret that the amount of the State aid should have been limited to $100 per annum for each child instructed; for it is obvious that the higher the limit fixed by the State the more will it be possible to extend the benefits of the measure into the smaller centres of population. To my mind, the limit should ultimately be fixed at that amount, whatever it may be, which represents the average per capita cost at the State institution. I believe, however, that the amount of $100 per annum is sufficient to test the operations of the plan. Experience will show how far the measure fulfils the expectations of its promoters, and if successful the State can then consider what further increase of State aid may be advisable or necessary.

Advantages derived by country districts.

Each centre of instruction, established under the provisions of the bill, will radiate an influence into the surrounding country districts, and tend to attract into the schools deaf-mutes from those districts. In this way many deaf-mutes in rural districts may be reached whose parents would object to send their children far away from home to the State institution. It may also be possible, under the provisions of the bill, to establish a school in an incorporated village where there may not be a sufficient number of deaf children to support a teacher, by collecting into that centre a sufficient number of children from the surrounding country. The nearer the school approaches to the home of a child the less likelihood is there that he will escape instruction. Little by little, as the measure is put into operation, new centres of instruction will arise, each radiating its influence into the neighboring places, so that ultimately the benefits of the bill will reach into every nook and corner of the State.

Conditions created by the bill favorable to the growth of improvements in the methods of instruction.

The multiplication of small schools upon diverse plans, renders it possible for the first time in the history of the country to settle by a natural process the disputed points concerning the education of the deaf. A single State school with an established method of instruction, like an established religion, tends to intolerance. A number of small schools depending for life upon the results produced is favorable to progress. It should be the duty of the State Superintendent and State Board of Supervision to keep careful note of the processes employed in the various schools; and it should also be their duty to collect statistics that would demonstrate the influence of the methods of instruction upon the after lives of the pupils. Then we may expect progress, and the State of Wisconsin will point the way for the other States to follow.

Recapitulation.

In the above argument I have attempted to show:

1. That the operation of the bill is calculated to bring under instruction a larger number of the uneducated deaf children of the State than would be possible on the institution plan.

2. That their instruction may be commenced at an earlier age than has heretofore been practicable.

3. That by her constitution Wisconsin is pledged to offer the benefits of education to all her children between the ages of four and twenty years, and that in the case of the deaf she can not fulfil this obligation, excepting upon some such plan as that provided for in the bill.

4. That the conditions created by the bill are eminently favorable to the cultivation of speech and speech reading, and

5. That the conditions are also favorable to the growth of improvements in the methods of instruction.

In conclusion allow me to express my earnest and heartfelt desire that you may see fit to recommend to the legislature the passage of this bill, which in my opinion, is destined to confer untold blessings on the deaf and upon society.

I am gentlemen, yours, very respectfully,

ALEXANDER GRAHAM BELL.

EXTRACTS FROM THE LAWS OF WISCONSIN.

CHAPTER 315.

AN ACT in relation to the instruction of Deaf-mutes in incorporated cities and villages.

The people of the State of Wisconsin, represented in Senate and Assembly, do enact as follows:

SECTION 1. Upon application by the mayor and common council of any incorporated city, or by the president and board of trustees of any incorporated village in the State, to the State superintendent of public instruction, he shall, by and with the consent of the State board of supervision, grant permission to such city or village to establish and maintain, within its corporate limits, one or more schools for the instruction of deaf-mutes, residents of the State of Wisconsin.

SECTION 2. The mayor of any incorporated city, and the president of any incorporated village, which shall maintain one or more schools for the instruction of deaf-mutes, shall report to the State superintendent of public instruction and to the State board of supervision, annually, and as often as said State superintendent or board may direct, such facts concerning such school or schools as said State superintendent or board may require.

SECTION 3. There shall be paid out of the State treasury, in the month of July in each year, to the treasurer of every incorporated city or village maintaining a school or schools for the instruction of deaf-mutes, under the charge of one or more teachers of approved qualifications, to be ascertained by the State superintendent of public instruction, the sum of 100 dollars for each deaf-mute pupil instructed in any such school at least nine months during the year next preceding the first day of July, and a share of such sum proportionate to the term of instruction of any such pupil as shall be so instructed less than nine months during such year.

SECTION 4. The sums to be paid, as provided in next preceding section, shall be audited by the Secretary of State upon the certificate of the president and secretary of the school board and the superintendent of schools of such city maintaining such school, setting forth the number of pupils instructed in such school or schools, and the period of time each such pupil shall have been so instructed in such school or schools next preceding the first day of July; and in case any such school shall be maintained in an incorporated village, then upon the certificate of the county superintendent of schools of the proper county, accompanied by the affidavit of the teacher or principal of such school, setting forth the same facts last aforesaid, all of which such certificates and affidavits shall be first approved in writing by the State superintendent of public instruction and the president of the State board of supervision, which certificates and affidavits so approved shall be filed with the Secretary of State, who shall thereupon issue his warrant upon the State treasurer in favor of the treasurer of such city or village, as the case may be, for the sum which shall appear to be due pursuant to the provisions of this act; provided, that not more than two-fifths of the amount appropriated by this act shall be expended in any one county.

SECTION 5. A biennial appropriation is hereby made to pay the sums which shall each year become due and payable under this act; said appropriation shall not exceed five thousand dollars per annum for the years 1885 and 1886.

SECTION 6. This act shall take effect and be in force from and after its passage and publication.

Approved April 4, 1885.

CHAPTER 40.

AN ACT in relation to the instruction of Deaf-mutes, and amendatory of Section 4, of Chapter 315, of the Laws of 1885.

The people of the State of Wisconsin, represented in Senate and Assembly, do enact as follows:

SECTION 1. Section 4 of chapter 315 of the laws of 1885, is hereby amended by striking from said section the following words at the end thereof, to wit: "Provided that no more than two-fifths of the amount appropriated by this act shall be expended in any one county;" so that said section when so amended will read as follows: SECTION 4. The sums to be paid, as provided in next preceding section, shall be audited by the Secretary of State upon the certificate of the president and secretary of the school board and the superintendent of schools of such city maintaining such school, setting forth the number of pupils instructed in such school or schools and the period of time each such pupil shall have been so instructed in such school or schools next preceding the first day of July; and in case any such school shall be maintained in an incorporated village, then, upon the certificate of the county superintendent of schools of the proper county, accompanied by the affidavit of the teacher or principal of such schools, setting forth the same facts last aforesaid, all of which such certificates and affidavits shall be first approved in writing by the State superintendent of public instruction and the president of the State board of supervision, which certificates and affidavits so approved shall be filed with the Secretary of State, who shall thereupon issue his warrant upon the State treasurer in favor of the treasurer of such city or village, as the case may be, for the sum which shall appear to be due, pursuant to the provisions of this act.

SECTION 2. This act shall take effect and be in force upon its passage and publication.

Approved March 12, 1887.

FACTS AND OPINIONS RELATING TO THE DEAF,

FROM AMERICA.

[This Exhibit consisted of a circular letter of enquiry which had been sent to the Superintendents and Principals of American and Canadian Schools for the Deaf, with the replies thereto. These papers were presented to the members of the Royal Commission in a printed volume entitled Facts and Opinions Relating to the Deaf. From America.]

Circular Letter of Inquiry sent to the Superintendents and Principals of American and Canadian Schools for the Deaf.

1336 Nineteenth Street,
Washington, D. C., April 30, 1888.

DEAR SIR: I have been invited to appear before the Royal Commission appointed by the British Government to inquire into the condition of the deaf, and propose sailing for Europe very shortly for this purpose.

Allow me to request your co-operation in obtaining the latest information concerning American Institutions for the Deaf.

The subjects upon which information is specially desired by the Royal Commission are stated to be:

'1. Visible Speech. (We know very little about this.)

'2. Aural Method. (We know very little about this.)

'3. Intermarriage of deaf-mutes and possibility of a deaf variety of the human race. Any trustworthy statistics on this would be most valuable.

'4. Any general views which you might have on our inquiry, which is briefly to inquire into the education and training of deaf-mutes in the United Kingdom so as to make them more generally self-supporting than now.'

5. Information is also desired concerning the general work of articulation teaching.

May I trouble you to answer the following queries?

I shall be thankful for whatever information you may be kind enough to send, but to be of use it must be sent at once.

I am, dear sir, yours truly,
ALEXANDER GRAHAM BELL.

QUERIES.

I. Has 'Visible Speech' been employed in your institution?

Is it still employed, and to what extent?

If not, what cause do you assign for its discontinuance?

II. Auricular Instruction.—Do you make any special efforts to develop and utilize the hearing-power of your semi-deaf pupils?

If so, how many pupils do you have under auricular instruction?

How many of them are deaf from birth?

I shall be glad of any details regarding the methods of instruction employed in such cases, and the results. Do you use instrumental aids, such as hearing-tubes or trumpets, audiphones, dentaphones, &c.?

What is your opinion concerning the relative merits of such apparatus?

Do you know of any facts indicating improvement of hearing power at or about the age of puberty?

How many pupils in your institution do you consider to be 'semi-deaf'?

How many of these were deaf from birth?

How many pupils in your institution were deaf from birth?

So few statistics have been collected concerning the numbers of the semi-deaf, that I trust you will give all the assistance in your power in determining some reliable percentage.

Statistics concerning the number of pupils who can hear the ringing of a dinner-bell would be of use.

III. I should be pleased to receive your opinion relating to the intermarriages of the deaf, and the inheritance of deafness by the offspring; and any statistics relating to the subject.

IV. I shall also be glad to have you communicate any facts relating to the instruction of the deaf which you think would be of value to the Commission, and it will give me pleasure to lay your views before the members.

Space for brief replies to these questions (III and IV) will be found on the other side of this sheet, but I trust you will not deem it necessary to confine yourself to this limit if you desire to submit any views.

V. General Articulation work.—How many Articulation teachers do you employ?

Kindly fill out the following table relating to articulation:

	Total number of pupils.	Period of life when deafness occurred.			
		Birth or infancy (less than 2 years of age).	Early childhood (2 and less than 5 years of age).	Late childhood (5 or more years of age).	Unknown.
TAUGHT ARTICULATION:					
Articulation used as means of instruction	....	....	....	....	....
Articulation not used as means of instruction	....	....	....	....	....
NOT TAUGHT ARTICULATION:					
Dropped from articulation classes	....	....	....	....	....
Received no instruction in articulation	....	....	....	....	....
Grand total	....	....	....	....	....

I enclose a table relating to the teaching of articulation in the institutions of the United States, compiled May, 1883, by the Principal of the Clarke Institution. Please inform me if you observe any errors or omissions.

A. G. B.

I. VISIBLE SPEECH.

Replies of Superintendents and Principals of American and Canadian Schools for the Deaf to the first Query in the Circular Letter of Inquiry.

Name of Institution.	(a) Has visible speech been employed in your Institution?	(b) Is it still employed?	(c) If not, what cause do you assign for its discontinuance? / GENERAL REMARKS.
1. American Asylum	Yes...	No...	Because we found that we could accomplish the same results in less time by using diacritical marks of the dictionary. I consider it very essential that the teacher should have a thorough training in visible speech.—JOB WILLIAMS, *Principal.*
2. New York Institution....	....	....	J. L. Peet, Principal. No reply to circular letter to date, June 2, 1888.
3. Pennsylvania Institution.	Yes...	No...	Too difficult. Valuable aid for teachers.—A. L. E. CROUTER, *Principal.*
4. Kentucky Institution	No...	No...	W. K. Argo, Principal.
5. Ohio Institution...........	....	....	Just now I am *very full* of work, arranging for examinations and the close of school. I will endeavour to have the work done for you soon.—AMASA PRATT, *Superintendent.* No further reply received to date, June 2, 1888.
6. Virginia Institution.......	Yes...	Yes...	Used at intervals for the last twenty years, steadily since 1874. We have one teacher who has twenty-four pupils under instruction.—THOS. A. DOYLE, *Principal.*
7. Indiana Institution	Yes...	Yes...	Used as a basis for articulating system.—WILLIAM GLENN, *Superintendent.*
8. Tennessee Institution....	Yes...	No...	The time required for a child to become familiar with the symbols and to translate them in reading or writing we think can be otherwise more profitably employed, in most cases.—THOS. L. MOSES, *Principal.*
9. North Carolina Institution.	No...	No...	W. J. Young, Principal.
10. Illinois Institution.........	Yes...	Yes...	Used to a very limited extent. It is of advantage to teachers, as it enables them to comprehend physiological facts involved in speech; but for pupils, while it is thus helpful, it requires an amount of time and labour to acquire that can be better improved with the use of diacritical marks.—PHILIP G. GILLETT, *Superintendent.*
11. Georgia Institution.......	No...	No...	Have never been able to introduce it on account of want of funds to pay a specialist.—W. O. CONNOR, *Principal.*
12. South Carolina............	Yes...	Yes...	Used with all of our articulation pupils.—NEWTON F. WALKER, *Superintendent.*
13. Missouri Institution.......	Yes...	No...	Have discontinued symbols in class-room, but the principles are constantly used, and we consider a knowledge of visible speech invaluable to a teacher. Too complicated and easily forgotten by pupils after leaving School.—JAMES N. TATE, *Principal.*
14. Louisiana Institution	....	....	John Jastremski, Superintendent. No reply to circular letter to date, June 2, 1888.
15. Wisconsin School..........	Yes...	No...	Used for four years by Misses E. Eddy and R. Ritsher. We hold it of value to the teacher as an aid in securing the pronunciation of difficult and obscure sounds and combinations. But seemed to require too much time from the pupils to require them to learn to read and write it.—J. W. SWILER, *Principal.*
16. Michigan School	Yes...	Yes...	It is used only with those who show a faculty to readily improve by it.—M. T. GASS, *Superintendent.*
17. Mississippi Institution ...	Yes...	Yes...	One class of eight is instructed by lip-reading and articulation altogether. About twenty-five are being taught to speak and read lips by the use of Bell's system. Several of our pupils are becoming fine lip-readers.—J. R. DOBYNS, *Superintendent.*
18. Iowa Institution...........	....	....	G. L. Wyckoff, Principal. No reply to circular letter to date, June 2, 1888.
19. Texas Asylum...............	No...	No...	W. H. Kendall, Superintendent.
20. Columbia Institution:			
A. Kendall School	Yes...	Yes...	Used in the initiatory steps, and as a foundation for explanation and correction.—JAMES DENISON, *Principal.*
B. National College	....	....	Mr. Denison has sent you statements regarding the Kendall School. As to the College, there is nothing to say, as we do not teach speech therein.—E. M. GALLAUDET, *President.*
21. Alabama Institution	No...	No...	Jos. H. Johnson, Principal.
22. California Institution....	No...	No...	Warring Wilkinson, Principal.
23. Kansas Institution........	Yes...	No...	It is thought that the time required to become adept in the use of symbols can be better spent in actual drill of vocal organs directed by teacher. It is deemed desirable, however, for teachers to be familiar with symbols.—S. T. WALKER, *Principal.*
24. Le Couteulx St. Mary's Institution.	Yes...	Yes...	Used with older pupils who have come from other schools without speech until they have learned the elements. With younger pupils we prefer the phonetic or word method.—SISTER MARY ANN BURKE, *Principal.*
25. Minnesota School	Yes...	No...	Used for two years; not at all used now. It takes too much of the pupils' time, and small returns. It is well for the teachers to understand it. It does not give the help to pupils that I fully expected when I introduced it.—JONATHAN L. NOYES, *Principal.*
26. N. Y. Inst. for Improved Instruction.	No...	No...	D. Greenberger, Principal.
27. Clarke Institution.........	Yes...	No...	Not used, except in training teachers. We found that by substituting Miss Worcester's method for visible speech we gained much time, obtained quite as good results in speech, far better results in lip-reading, and speech became a much more spontaneous method of expression for the pupils.—CAROLINE A. YALE, *Principal.*
28. Arkansas Institution......	....	....	F. D. Clarke, Principal, did not reply to this question.
29. Maryland School..........	No...	No...	Visible speech has not been employed directly in the instruction of pupils. They have not been taught to read and write its forms. Our principal teacher of articulation was taught visible speech, and used it for a year at Northampton. Her knowledge of the organs of speech and their use obtained by this study I consider of great value. Visible speech has not been used because, in my judgment, the learning of the symbols by pupils lengthens rather than shortens the process of instruction.—C. W. ELY, *Principal.*

Name of Institution.	(a) Has visible speech been employed in your Institution?	(b) Is it still employed?	(c) If not, what cause do you assign for its discontinuance? GENERAL REMARKS.
30. Nebraska Institution	....	....	John A. Gillespie, Principal, did not reply to this question.
31. Horace Mann School	Yes...	Yes...	It is occasionally used in the instruction to the older pupils. All of the teachers are required to have a knowledge of visible speech. Its use was discontinued with younger pupils because we thought it better to give no written representation of the elements until after the pupils are able to pronounce words containing them.—SARAH FULLER, *Principal.*
32. St. Joseph's Institution	Yes..	No ...	We did use it to some extent, but not within the past eight or ten years.—ERNESTINE NARDIN, *President.*
33. West Virginia School	....	....	H. B. Gilkeson, Principal. No reply to circular letter received to date, June 2, 1888.
34. Oregon School	No...	No ...	We have never been able to introduce it for lack of funds.—P. S. KNIGHT, *Superintendent.*
35. Maryland Institute for Colored Persons.	....	....	F. D. Morrison, Superintendent. No reply to circular letter received to date, June 2, 1888.
36. Colorado Institution	Yes...	Yes...	Fourteen out of forty-two receive instruction in articulation.—JOHN E. RAY, *Superintendent.*
37. Chicago Day Schools	Yes...	No ...	Philip A. Emery, Principal. No remarks.
38. Central N. Y. Institution.	Yes...	Yes...	Used as far as it is practicable in each case.—E. B. NELSON, *Principal.*
39. Cincinnati Public School.	....	....	A. F. Wood, Principal. No reply to circular letter received to date, June 2, 1888.
40. West Pennsylvania Institution.	Yes...	No ...	Used several years ago. Not at all now, because the pupils learn sounds just as quickly and accurately with diacritical marks, which we regard to be more simple.—JOHN G. BROWN, *Principal.*
41. Western N. Y. Institution.	....	....	Z. F. Westervelt, Principal. No reply to circular letter received to date, June 2, 1888.
42. Portland School	Yes...	Yes...	Used with all pupils.—ELLEN L. BARTON, *Principal.*
43. Rhode Island School	No ...	No ...	Not used at all to my knowledge. I have been Principal of the R. I. School for the Deaf for nearly three years now, and have always used the German method, with later improvements. I have made some study of the "Bell System," but must say I fail to see that it holds any advantage over the German or is quite equal to it. The only symbols we use are the Dictionary (Webster's) diacritical marks. Our charts are made as simple as possible, and we drill unceasingly on the combination of elements in word-building. Just as soon as the pupil strikes a combination which has a significant meaning, the teacher explains by illustrations. In this way he slowly gains a vocabulary of words. Our method is a sort of cross between the strictly elementary and the word method.—ANNA M. BLACK, *Principal.*
44. St. Louis Day School	....	....	D. A. Simpson, Principal. No reply to circular letter received to date, June 2, 1888.
45. New England Industrial School.	Yes...	No ...	The Principal taught it for a short period, but, owing to pressure of business and lack of time, was compelled to discontinue it. The school, since its opening in 1879, has labored under financial difficulties, consequently has been unable to employ a fully qualified teacher of articulation.—NELLIE H. SWETT, *Principal.*
46. Dakota School	....	....	James Simpson, Superintendent. No reply to circular letter received to date, June 2, 1888.
47. Milwaukee Day School	No ...	No ...	Paul Binner, Principal.
48. Pennsylvania Oral School.	No ...	No ...	Emma Garrett, Principal. No remarks.
49. New Jersey School	No ...	No ...	Not used in the instruction of pupils. I have used the system as a guide for my teachers in their study of the production of sound by the human organs of speech. My reason for not extending its use to my pupils is that, while I think it an aid to the forming of a correct habit of vocalisation, I have observed in pupils trained on this system a difficulty in passing from the use of symbols to that of alphabetic characters.—WESTON JENKINS, *Superintendent.*
50. Utah School	....	....	Henry C. White, Principal. No reply to circular letter received to date, June 2, 1888.
51. Northern N. Y. Institution.	....	....	Henry C. Rider, Superintendent. No reply to circular letter received to date, June 2, 1888.
52. Florida Institution	Yes...	Yes...	We do not use "visible speech," and have never done so. When we started, it was with your "line writing," which, in the hands of an able teacher, met every need, and our pupils made much more rapid progress than any I had ever observed where other means were used. Whether it is the method or the teacher to whom the success is due, is an open question; but I think each is entitled to some share of the credit. It has been our experience (limited to three years in this school) that every deaf child of fair mental powers can be taught to speak with sufficient clearness to be understood by those unaccustomed to hearing "semi-mutes" talk, if the articulation training begin while the child is very young—say 4 to 8 years of age. But little can be done with children over 15 years of age.—PARK TERRELL, *Principal.* [Line writing is the stenographic form of "visible speech." I have therefore changed Mr. Terrell's reply from the negative to the affirmative.—A. G. B.]
53. Washington Territory School.	No ...	No ...	James Watson, Director. No remarks.
54. New Orleans Public School.	No ...	No ...	This school, being established in 1886, is a sign-language one, but I intend introducing an articulation class into this school shortly.—R. B. LAWRENCE, *Principal.*
55. Evansville School	No ...	No ...	We will introduce it in the near future, when our school is large enough.—CHARLES KERNEY, *Principal.*
56. La Crosse School	....	....	Albert Hardy, Superintendent. No reply to this question.
57. New Mexico School	No ...	No ...	Lars M. Larson, Principal. No remarks.

I. VISIBLE SPEECH—Continued.

Name of Institution.	(a) Has visible speech been employed in your Institution?	(b) Is it still employed?	(c) If not, what cause do you assign for its discontinuance? / General Remarks.
PRIVATE AND DENOMINATIONAL SCHOOLS.			
1. Whipple's Home School.	Yes...	Yes...	It is used whenever we find it difficult to teach the pupil to articulate distinctly.—MARGARET HAMMOND, *Principal.* The following question was also asked: Is "Whipple's Natural Alphabet" still used in the school? Would you kindly send me a copy of this ingenious alphabet to present to the Royal Commission? It would give me pleasure to receive any communication relating to the late Mr. Whipple's methods, and to lay it before the members. No reply to this question received to date, June 2, 1888.
2. German Evangelical Lutheran Institution.	Yes...	Yes...	Used exclusively.—D. H. UHLIG, *Director.*
3. St. John's Catholic Institution.	Yes...	Yes...	Used only in special class.—CHARLES FESSLER, *President.*
4. Frederick Knapp Institution.	....	....	Frederick Knapp, Principal. No reply to circular letter received to date, June 2, 1888.
5. Voice and Hearing School.	....	....	Mary McCowen, Principal. No reply to this question.
6. Mary Garrett's School ...	No ...	No ...	I studied visible speech with great pleasure to myself, and consider the symbols much superior to our English alphabet in that they represent the sounds as they are in words, while the names of the letters of the alphabet (with the exception of the long sounds of the vowels) are so different from their power in words. I do not use it with deaf pupils, because I want to teach them to understand the text in common use (faulty though it is) as early in their training as possible. I obviate the difficulty of there being several sounds for each vowel by teaching them their appropriate diacritical marks as soon as they begin to learn to write, so that they soon learn their different sounds. I also call their attention to the silent letters found in words.—MARY S. GARRETT, *Principal.*
7. Maria Consilia Institute.	Yes...	Yes...	Eight pupils receive instruction in it for one hour daily.—SISTER ADELE, *Principal.*
8. Cincinnati Oral School...	....	....	Cath. Westendorf, Principal. No reply to circular letter received to date, June 2, 1888.
9. Chicago Catholic School.	....	....	No reply to circular letter received to date, June 2, 1888.
10. Miss Keeler's Class	....	....	Sarah Warren Keeler, Principal. No reply to this question.
11. Cathedral Catholic School.	....	No ...	We do not employ visible speech, nor have we tried the auricular method. Our course of instruction is the same as that pursued at the Philadelphia Institute, except that we, for want of means, do not teach articulation or give industrial training.—E. P. CLEARY, *Principal.*
12. Sarah Fuller Home	(?)	(?)	Sarah Fuller, Supervising Principal. *See* remarks of Principal of Horace Mann School.
SCHOOLS IN THE DOMINION OF CANADA.			
1. Catholic Institute (Male)	....	....	J. B. Manseau, Principal. No reply to circular letter received to date, June 2, 1888.
2. Catholic Institute (Female).	....	....	Sister Mary of Mercy, Superioress. No reply to circular letter received to date, June 2, 1888.
3. Halifax Institute..........	No ...	No ...	J. Scott Hutton, Principal.
4. Ontario Institute..........	Yes...	No ...	Beginning in 1879, but dropped after about three years' trial. The system seems to be too difficult to be understood by young pupils. A thorough knowledge of visible speech, however, has been found of great assistance to the teacher of articulation.—R. MATHISON, *Superintendent.*
5. Mackay Institute..........	Yes...	Yes...	Used for seven years with every pupil to whom articulation is taught.—HARRIET E. McGANN, *Superintendent.*
6. New Brunswick Inst......	....	....	A. H. Abell, Principal. No reply to circular letter received to date, June 2, 1888.
7. Fredericton Institute ...	....	....	Albert F. Woodbridge, Principal. No reply to circular letter received to date, June 2, 1888.

Professor J. C. Gordon, of the National Deaf-mute College, writes: 'In reference to visible speech I feel that you will be fully justified in urging that all teachers of articulation should be thoroughly grounded in the mechanism of speech, and to this end "Visible Speech" gives a completeness and definiteness and sense of mastery not readily acquired by any purely experimental system.'

Statistics relating to Auricular Instruction and Description of Methods employed in American Schools to develop latent hearing power. Replies of Superintendents and Principals to the Second List of Queries in the Circular Letter.

(a) Do you make any special efforts to develop and utilise the hearing power of your semi-deaf pupils?
(b) I shall be glad of any details regarding the methods of instruction employed in such cases and the results.
(c) Do you use instrumental aids, such as hearing tubes or trumpets, audiphones, dentaphones, &c.?
(d) What is your opinion concerning the relative merits of such apparatus?
(e) Do you know of any facts indicating improvement of hearing power at or about the age of puberty?

(f) How many pupils in your institution do you consider to be semi-deaf?	(g) How many of these were deaf from birth?	(h) How many pupils in your institution were deaf from birth?	(i) How many pupils do you have under Auricular instruction?	(j) How many of these were deaf from birth?	(k) Number of pupils who can hear the ringing of a dinner-bell.	GENERAL REMARKS.
						1. AMERICAN ASYLUM.
8	4	......	......	......	......	(a) No systematic efforts. (k) I cannot tell.—JOB WILLIAMS, *Principal.*
						2. NEW YORK INSTITUTION.
......	......	......	......	......	......	J. L. Peet, Principal. No reply received to circular letter to date, June 2, 1888.
						3. PENNSYLVANIA INSTITUTION.
10	4	145	10	0	......	(a) To a limited extent. (c) We use hearing-tubes. (d) All have their value. (e) I have no information upon this point. (i) About 10. (j) None of them. (k) The majority *say* they can hear a bell ring.—A. L. E. CROUTER, *Principal.*
						4. KENTUCKY INSTITUTION.
8	2	112	8	2	26	(a) In cases where hearing promises to prove of use as a means of instruction—yes. (c) Yes. (d) In the majority of cases of little practical value. Trumpet gives most satisfactory results. (e) On the contrary, since 1880 we have had 8 pupils whose deafness came upon them about this period, in most cases gradually. (k) 57 older pupils tested—26 heard.—W. K. ARGO, *Superintendent.*
						5. OHIO INSTITUTION.
......	......	......	......	......	......	Just now I am *very full* of work arranging for examinations and the close of school. I will endeavour to have the work done for you soon.—AMASA PRATT, *Superintendent.* No further reply received to date, June 2, 1888.
						6. VIRGINIA INSTITUTION.
9	7	80	......	......	......	(a) Very little. (c) We have one of the Currier double tubes, which we use sometimes—but not continually with any pupil. (d) All the dentaphones, so called, that I have seen I regard as humbugs. Currier's tube is the best piece of apparatus that I know. (e) I do not. Edward Green, who entered here as a pupil in 1865 and was discharged in 1872, is said to have recovered his hearing since leaving. He is ranked in the record as a "semi-mute," who lost his hearing at two years of age by scarlet fever. (h) 80 I should say, although some of this 80 have been reported as going deaf at any age less than two years.—THOMAS A. DOYLE, *Principal.*
						7. INDIANA INSTITUTION.
......	......	......	20	9	......	(a) To a limited extent—limited by lack of time. (c) Use hearing-tubes. (d) Not of much use. (e) None.—WM. GLENN, *Superintendent.*
						8. TENNESSEE SCHOOL.
20	3	......	8	3	......	(a) We do. (b) By putting them in the "articulation" or "oral" class, believing that training of this kind teaches children to discriminate between the sounds of different words, or that such training improves the hearing—which we regard as one and the same thing—*in results.* (c) We have used tubes, trumpets, and dentaphones. (d) They are helps in some cases. (e) No; unless the fact that a larger per cent. of our pupils who have reached that age are semi-deaf than is found among the pupils under that age. (g) 3 so reported; but information as to others is not reliable. (h) About one-third born deaf, but above remark applies in this case. (k) 25 per cent.—THOS. L. MOSES, *Principal.*
						9. NORTH CAROLINA INSTITUTION.
10	......	50	......	......	......	(a) No. (c) We use no instrumental aids. (e) None. (h) "About 50" born deaf.—W. J. YOUNG, *Principal.*
						10. ILLINOIS INSTITUTION.
40	23	......	40	23	......	(a) We do, to utilise the modicum of hearing they have, and I have always done this; but I do not think we improve the hearing, though in some cases we teach them to better use the little hearing they have. (c) Every aid I can obtain we use. (d) The hearing-tube aids more than any other instrument. (e) I have watched closely for this, but have found no cases improved by that physical change. The tendency is rather to become worse. (h) "About one-half" deaf from birth. (i) 40 under auricular training at this date, May 8, 1888. (j) 23 deaf from birth; 2 became deaf under one year; 4 at 1 year; 5 at 2; 3 at 3; 1 at 4; 1 at 7; 1 at 9. (k) They all seem to hear the *dinner-bell* (!), but only about 5 per cent. hear the school bell.—PHILIP G. GILLETT, *Superintendent.*
						11. GEORGIA INSTITUTION.
4	2	32	......	......	......	(a) No. (c) No, speaking after 26 years' work in the Georgia Institution. (f) Of 300 pupils (admitted 1867 to 1888) 31 were semi-deaf. (h) 32 born deaf out of a total of 57.—W. O. CONNOR, *Principal.*

II. AURICULAR INSTRUCTION—Continued.

(f) How many pupils in your Institution do you consider to be semi-deaf?	(g) How many of these were deaf from birth?	(h) How many pupils in your Institution were deaf from birth?	(i) How many pupils do you have under Auricular Instruction?	(j) How many of these were deaf from birth?	(k) Number of pupils who can hear the ringing of a dinner-bell.	(a) Do you make any special efforts to develop and utilise the hearing power of your semi-deaf pupils? (b) I shall be glad of any details regarding the methods of instruction employed in such cases and the results. (c) Do you use instrumental aids, such as hearing tubes or trumpets, audiphones, dentaphones, &c.? (d) What is your opinion concerning the relative merits of such apparatus? (e) Do you know of any facts indicating improvement of hearing power at or about the age of puberty? GENERAL REMARKS.
						12. SOUTH CAROLINA INSTITUTION.
6	2	42	......	......	......	(a) No. (e) No.—NEWTON F. WALKER, *Superintendent*.
						13. MISSOURI INSTITUTION.
17	......	......	......	......	30	(a) Have tried to utilise with all in class, and in some cases have succeeded in developing. (b) No aural class, but pupils in oral class have some aural instruction. (c) We use a hearing-tube, and find it helpful in some cases. (d) Have used but one, and cannot speak relatively. (e) No. (f) We know there are 17 semi-deaf, but the hearing of the whole school has never been tested. (k) About 30 out of 199 hear the bell.—JAMES N. TATE, *Principal*.
						14. LOUISIANA INSTITUTION.
......	......	......	......	......	......	John Jastremski, Superintendent. No reply to circular letter received to date, June 2, 1888.
						15. WISCONSIN SCHOOL.
10	2	101	......	......	20	(a) We endeavor to use hearing where it is serviceable without instruments—used flexible *tubes* (single) for two years without decided benefit. (c) No instrumental aids now in use. (d) After persistent use of flexible tubes two years could not see any decided utility in them.—JOHN W. SWILER, *Superintendent*.
						16. MICHIGAN SCHOOL.
14	2	......	......	......	......	(a) We do not make any special efforts, although we as much as possible communicate with such pupils through the sense of hearing. (c) We have used a hearing-tube to a limited extent on account of sensitive ears; no systematic efforts have been made with the instrument. (e) I do not know.—M. T. GASS, *Superintendent*.
						17. MISSISSIPPI INSTITUTION.
6	1	......	8	4	6	(a) Yes. (b) One pupil about four years ago could not understand a word. She has been practised with the flexible tube until she can hear and understand from 1 to 8 feet behind her (the person speaking standing behind her). (c) We use only the flexible tube. (d) As far as my experience goes, I think this tube is the best. (e) I do not. (g) Not more than one of these born deaf. (h) Have not all statistics.—J. R. DOBYNS, *Superintendent*. [The figures given by Mr. Dobyns seem inconsistent with one another. I am unable to correct the error.—A. G. B.]
						18. IOWA INSTITUTION.
......	......	......	......	......	......	G. L. Wyckoff, Principal. No reply to circular letter received to date, June 2, 1888.
						19. TEXAS ASYLUM.
14	5	67	......	......	23	(a) No, but expect to. (e) One case of slight improvement. (f) About 9 per cent. semi-deaf. (h) 67 supposed to be born deaf.
						20. COLUMBIA INSTITUTION. A. KENDALL SCHOOL.
6	1	24	6	1	19	(a) No systematic work in classes in this direction, but occasional work and testing of hearing in individual cases, which show possibility of improvement and give hope for the future. (c) Yes. English conversational tube, Mr. Currier's duplex, and Mr. Maloney's. (d) The English conversational tube is very helpful if used with care; Mr. Currier's duplex tube very useful in helping to develop the voice as well as the hearing; Mr. Maloney's less liable to cause injury than others, as it does not enter the ear, and in some cases more powerful. (e) No. (k) 19 out of the 61 pupils claim they can hear it when in the same room with the bell.—JAMES DENISON, *Principal*.
						B. NATIONAL COLLEGE.
......	......	......	......	......	......	Mr. Denison has sent you statements regarding the Kendall School. As to the College, there is nothing to say, as we do not teach speech therein.—E. M. GALLAUDET, *President*.
						21. ALABAMA INSTITUTION.
6	0	53	......	......	......	(a) No. (c) Yes. (d) We don't think they are of any practical value, except to improve the quality of the voice in those pupils where we teach articulation. (e) No. (g) None of them.—JAMES H. JOHNSON, *Principal*.
						22. CALIFORNIA INSTITUTION.
14	12	......	......	......	......	(a) No. (e) No. (h) 102 deaf from birth or under 2 years.—WARRING WILKINSON, *Principal*.

(f) How many pupils in your Institution do you consider to be semi-deaf?	(g) How many of these were deaf from birth?	(h) How many pupils in your Institution were deaf from birth?	(i) How many pupils do you have under Auricular Instruction?	(j) How many of these were deaf from birth?	(k) Number of pupils who can hear the ringing of a dinner-bell.	(a) Do you make any special efforts to develop and utilise the hearing power of your semi-deaf pupils? (b) I shall be glad of any details regarding the methods of instruction employed in such cases and the results. (c) Do you use instrumental aids, such as hearing tubes or trumpets, audiphones, dentaphones, &c.? (d) What is your opinion concerning the relative merits of such apparatus? (e) Do you know of any facts indicating improvement of hearing power at or about the age of puberty? — GENERAL REMARKS.
						23. KANSAS INSTITUTION.
11	4	......	10	2	40	(a) Yes, with pupils who have some considerable perceptible degree of hearing. (b) Our regular articulation teachers take the class for 40 minutes each day. (c) Instrumental aid used very little. Have tried tubes, trumpets, audiphone, and dentaphone. (d) Currier's tube is best. (h) 157 deaf from birth or under 2 years. (k) 161 tested, 88 said they could hear, but 48 of these also said they heard when the bell was not rung. In a letter the superintendent says: "In regard to the experiment of hearing the dinner bell I will say that a large per cent. of those tried said they heard the bell, when I afterwards proved conclusively that they did not. I had them turn their backs to me each trial, and at a signal face me and tell who heard. These trials were repeated several times, and one or two of them were false trials, when the bell was not touched. Notwithstanding, 48 of the 161 tried answered that they heard the bell *every time*, even when it was not touched. Knowing that to make statistics of real effect (or rather the conclusions drawn from them) they should be as nearly correct as possible, I was careful to have these tests correct. I am convinced that fully one-half of any set of pupils give incorrect answers to questions relative to their powers of hearing. Why? I can't tell. They may not understand just what *hearing* is and *guess* that they hear, or they may like to appear to hear, and so say they do hear more than they can. It is so common for deaf children to deceive (intentionally or unintentionally I can't say), especially those who do not give their condition much thought. People in general believe more than is told them by or about deaf-mutes, especially their accomplishments.—S. T. WALKER, *Superintendent*.
						24. LE COUTEULX ST. MARY'S INSTITUTION.
14	9	40	14	9	6	(a) Yes. (b) With beginners or those whose hearing has not been trained the word is first taken from the lips, then spoken into the ear until they become familiar with the sound. (c) Seldom. Have tried all the above-mentioned aids. (d) We find that they shook the nerves of many of the pupils. (e) No. (k) 6 can hear the ringing of a dinner bell from a distance.—SISTER MARY ANNE BURKE, *Principal*.
						25. MINNESOTA SCHOOL.
20	......	66	7	3	......	(a) In a very few cases I do. (c) Yes. Currier's ear-trumpet. The audiphone gave no help compared with the ear-trumpet. (d) In some cases it is of service; some of our pupils complain of soreness in the ear after using it, and do not like to use it. It is only a temporary aid, except in a very few cases. (e) I do not. (f) 20 more or less deaf. (h) 111 under 1 year, 66 of these congenital. (i) 7 more or less. (k) 15 hear the steam-whistle sound in the morning.
						26. INSTITUTION FOR IMPROVED INSTRUCTION, N. Y.
18	6	53	......	......	......	(a) Yes. (c) We use ear-trumpets. (d) We prefer the conical shaped to the others. (e) No.—D. GREENBERGER, *Principal*.
						27. THE CLARKE INSTITUTION.
18	10	26	18	10	22	(a) Yes. (c) Hearing-tubes and trumpets. (d) None but those named have proved of any use. (e) No. (f) We class as semi-deaf any who can be given any word through hearing, or can distinguish most of the vowel sounds. (h) 28 born deaf and three others possibly.—CAROLINE A. YALE, *Principal*.
						28. THE ARKANSAS INSTITUTE.
15	9	53	9	7	......	(a) Yes. (b) [Mr. F. D. Clarke, Principal, has prepared a paper upon Auricular Training for the information of the Royal Commission, which is printed at the conclusion of this synopsis, among other papers upon the same subject.—A. G. B.]
						29. MARYLAND SCHOOL.
4	2	49	......	......	12	(a) To utilise it, yes; to develop it also if by that is meant the removal of any obstacles to hearing. I am sceptical of any development in the sense of growth of hearing *power*, as meant when we speak of growth of muscle. From some cases under my observation I am inclined to believe that apparent increase of hearing power is due to increased attention and mental development. (c) Not at present. I do not like to go on record as opposed to the use of aids to hearing, but believe fully in their use where practicable. We have now only two pupils who could use such appliances, and these can be reached by the voice. (c) Not at present. (d) In a series of experiments conducted with my pupils a year or two ago, I was led to the conclusion that so far as these cases were concerned the hearing-tube was to be preferred. (e) No. (k) 12 can hear the bell when near.—C. W. ELY, *Principal*.
						30. NEBRASKA INSTITUTE.
18	12	48	16	10	......	(a) Yes. (b) [Mr. J. A. Gillespie, Superintendent, has prepared a paper upon Auricular Training for the information of the Royal Commission, which is printed at the conclusion of this synopsis, among other papers upon the same subject. The Nebraska Institute was the first in America to establish a separate auricular department. Mrs. Taylor and Miss McCowen, who have also contributed papers upon this subject, were teachers of the auricular class in this institution. Miss McCowen has since established a "Voice and Hearing School" of her own in Englewood, Illinois, where she makes a specialty of Auricular Training.—A. G. B.]

(f) How many pupils in your Institution do you consider to be semi-deaf?	(g) How many of these were deaf from birth?	(h) How many pupils in your Institution were deaf from birth?	(i) How many pupils do you have under Auricular Instruction?	(j) How many of these were deaf from birth?	(k) Number of pupils who can hear the ringing of a dinner-bell.	(a) Do you make any special efforts to develop and utilise the hearing power of your semi-deaf pupils? (b) I shall be glad of any details regarding the methods of instruction employed in such cases and the results. (c) Do you use instrumental aids, such as hearing tubes or trumpets, audiphones, dentaphones, &c.? (d) What is your opinion concerning the relative merits of such apparatus? (e) Do you know of any facts indicating improvement of hearing power at or about the age of puberty? General Remarks.
						31. THE HORACE MANN SCHOOL.
15	8	22	......	......	23	(a) Yes. (b) We try to train the pupils to hear the sound of the teacher's voice without artificial aids. We think there is danger of harm to the child if it is quite young in the frequent use of tubes. We have no separate classes for such instruction. (d) We prefer instruments which are not inserted in the ear passage. (e) Yes. Several pupils have shown great improvement in their power to hear at that period. (g) Possibly 8 deaf from birth. (h) 14 deaf from birth, reported by parents. These do not include the 8 mentioned above. (k) 8 who are not semi-deaf can hear the ringing of a dinner-bell.—Sarah Fuller, *Principal.*
						32. ST. JOSEPH'S INSTITUTE.
35	19	85	35	19	......	(a) Yes, but do not separate them from those who are entirely deaf. (c) We use convex tubes, single and duplex, and ear trumpets. We used the audiphones for some time, but did not find them of much value to our pupils. (d) We obtain the best results from the use of the convex tube. (e) No.
						33. WEST VIRGINIA SCHOOL.
......	......	......	......	......	......	H. B. Gilkeson, Principal. No reply to circular letter received to date, June 2, 1888.
						34. OREGON SCHOOL.
......	......	9	......	......	4	(a) We are careful to exercise both hearing and speaking on part of those semi-deaf. (d) It depends *entirely* on the nature of the defect. Have found the audiphone and dentaphone absolutely useless in most cases. (e) Do not. But have one or two in whom defective hearing has been greatly improved by *simple exercise.* (f) "Semi-deaf" is a very indefinite term. Several in my classes can hear sharp sounds who are beyond the possibility of being reached by articulate speech. Have only one such in 30. (k) 4 out of 30.—P. S. Knight, *Superintendent.*
						35. MARYLAND SCHOOL FOR COLORED DEAF-MUTES.
......	......	......	......	......	......	F. D. Morrison, Superintendent. No reply to circular letter received to date, June 2, 1888.
						36. COLORADO INSTITUTE.
3	2	8	......	......	......	(a) Not just yet, but hope to begin soon. (e) None.—John E. Ray, *Superintendent.*
						37. CHICAGO DAY SCHOOLS.
3	......	......	......	......	......	(a) No. (d) The tests we have made have been useless.—Philip A. Emery, *Principal.*
						38. CENTRAL NEW YORK INSTITUTION.
......	......	......	......	......	......	(a) No, except by the use of Currier's conical tube. (c) We use Currier's conical tube. (d) It is the best I have ever seen. (e) No.—E. R. Nelson, *Principal.*
						39. THE CINCINNATI PUBLIC SCHOOL.
......	......	......	......	......	......	A. F. Wood, Principal. No reply to circular letter received to date, June 2, 1888.
						40. WEST PENNSYLVANIA INSTITUTION.
14	4	......	4	0	39	(a) Yes. (b) We have pupils listen to vowel sounds with their eyes closed until they can distinguish them. (c) We do not use any at present. (d) Have not found any that were very satisfactory. (e) One girl under auricular instruction 2 years; shows marked improvement during the present term. (i) 4 at present. (k) 39 out of 148.—John G. Brown, *Principal.*
						41. WESTERN NEW YORK INSTITUTION.
......	......	......	......	......	......	Z. F. Westervelt, Superintendent and Principal. No reply to circular letter received to date, June 2, 1888.
						42. PORTLAND SCHOOL.
10	10	34	10	10	......	(a) I do. (c) Make use of hearing-tubes. (e) I do not.—E. L. Barton, *Principal.*
						43. RHODE ISLAND STATE SCHOOL.
6	3	9	6	3	8	(a) Yes. (b) There are 5 or 6 of our pupils to whom we give a daily drill or practice with a flexible ear-tube, as a means of securing correctness of articulation or enunciation and improving the timbre of voice. As to this practice increasing their ability to understand spoken language to any extent, I am rather sceptical. I do not consider myself an enthusiast for auricular instruction. I have seen more children kept back by it than improved. There are people and people outside of our schools for the deaf, at the homes of the pupils and elsewhere, who, in spite of all that is reasonable and sensible, will scream at deaf persons, be they totally or only partially deaf. It seems so much more important in our crowd of necessary and practical instruction to give them the best facility for speech-reading possible. I thoroughly believe in its persistent and exclusive practice; that is, as compared with the manual alphabet or signs. Vide my report for 1887, which I send with this. (d) I never knew but one person who could hear any better by the use of an audiphone or dentaphone. (e) I do not. (f) 6 at present. (g) 3 at present. (h) Probably 9 at present. Possibly there have been nearly 25 in all, since the school was organised in 1877. (k) The 6 mentioned above and probably 2 others.—Anna M. Black, *Principal.*

(*f*) How many pupils in your Institution do you consider to be semi-deaf?	(*g*) How many of these were deaf from birth?	(*h*) How many pupils in your Institution were deaf from birth?	(*i*) How many pupils do you have under Auricular Instruction?	(*j*) How many of these were deaf from birth?	(*k*) Number of pupils who can hear the ringing of a dinner-bell.	(*a*) Do you make any special efforts to develop and utilize the hearing power of your semi-deaf pupils? (*b*) I shall be glad of any details regarding the methods of instruction employed in such cases and the results. (*c*) Do you use instrumental aids, such as hearing tubes or trumpets, audiphones, dentaphones, &c.? (*d*) What is your opinion concerning the relative merits of such apparatus? (*e*) Do you know of any facts indicating improvement of hearing power at or about the age of puberty? — General Remarks.
						44. ST. LOUIS DAY SCHOOL.
......	......	......	......	......	......	D. A. Simpson, Principal. No reply to circular letter received to date, June 2, 1888.
						45. NEW ENGLAND INDUSTRIAL SCHOOL.
6	5	11	3	1	6	(*a*) Yes, when we have such cases. (*e*) No. (*h*) Of 23 now present 11 were born deaf. (*i*) We have had 3.—Nellie H. Swett, *Principal.*
						46. DAKOTA SCHOOL.
	......	......	......	......	......	James Simpson, Superintendent. No reply to circular letter received to date, June 2, 1888.
						47. MILWAUKEE DAY SCHOOL.
1	1	17	......	......	9	(*a*) No. (*e*) Among the 45 pupils which I have had in my school within the last 4 years I have in vain sought for development of hearing power at that age. (*f*) One semi-deaf. She was congenitally deaf. She was completely deaf when she entered in 1885. From 1886 to 1887 her hearing developed considerably, though she was only 9 years of age. Within the last year no improvement in hearing has taken place, although she is improving physically and mentally. Her ear is so sensitive now that she cannot bear the loud voice close to her ear, nor even the careful use of an ear-trumpet, latest pattern, made by a gentleman in Washington (I cannot recall his name just now). [Probably Maloney.—A. G. B.] (*h*) 17 out of 45 congenitally deaf. (*k*) Used a very large dinner-bell; diameter at mouth, 7½ inches; height, 5 inches. Nine out of 35 pupils heard this bell within a range of from 4 to 6 feet.—Paul Binner, *Principal.*
						48. PENNSYLVANIA ORAL SCHOOL.
2	1	15	......	......	......	(*d*) I think above instrumental aids are useful to some. Some seemed to be helped as well without instrumental aid. (*f*) I have at present but 2 pupils who would be called "semi-deaf." One entered a few days ago. Latter speaks some words imperfectly. The other one did not speak on entering—hearing seemed to develop while she was acquiring speech through the eye. I have had but one assistant with 26 pupils this winter, therefore I could not form an aural class with *one* semi-deaf pupil. Still, as the teacher speaks distinctly to her, I have felt she would certainly gain somewhat *if* her deafness is of a nature to admit of aural development. I had a child who showed good results in aural development who left me to go to Philadelphia because it was a *boarding-school.* (*h*) Fifteen supposed to be deaf from birth.—Emma Garrett, *Principal.*
						49. NEW JERSEY SCHOOL.
13	6	......	10	5	......	(*a*) I use the ordinary flexible conical tubes. (*c*) As stated above. Have found metallic trumpets of little aid, on account of lack of clearness proportional to intensity of sound. Have met but 1 case in which the audiphone was helpful. (*d*) In my own practice I have found the flexible tubes useful in a greater or less degree in all cases of not too profound deafness; the metal trumpets helpful only where there was some recollection of the sounds of speech. Have never tried the dentaphone. (*e*) No case in which I could say positively that such facts were shown, but 2 or 3 in which my observation, not confirmed by careful tests, gave me the impression that such improvement took place. (*g*) 6 born deaf; only one after 2 years. (*j*) 6 born deaf, the others from 2 years and under.—Weston Jenkins, *Superintendent.*
						50. UTAH SCHOOL.
......	......	......	......	......	......	Henry C. White, Principal. No reply to circular letter to date, June 2, 1888.
						51. NORTHERN NEW YORK INSTITUTION.
......	......	......		......	......	Henry C. Rider, Superintendent. No reply to circular letter to date, June 2, 1888.
						52. FLORIDA INSTITUTE.
2	0	......	......			Two of the pupils can hear a little (semi-deaf). One became deaf at 2 years of age, and the other gradually lost her hearing, cause not known. We have never made any effort to develop the hearing of these pupils, though I doubt not that at least one of them could be much benefited by a systematic course of training.—Park Terrell, *Principal.*
						53. WASHINGTON SCHOOL (VANCOUVER, W. T.).
5	0	5	......	......	......	(*a*) No. (*c*) No.—James Watson, *Director.*
						54. NEW ORLEANS PUBLIC SCHOOL.
3	......	7	......	......	2	(*a*) Have not tried any yet. (*d*) I cannot form any opinion, as I have no experience as to the matter. (*e*) I don't know any. (*f*) 3 semi-deaf. (*g*) 7 of them deaf from birth [? A. G. B.]. (*h*) 7 born deaf.—R. B. Lawrence, *Principal.*
						55. EVANSVILLE SCHOOL.
4	0	5	......	......	12	(*a*) No. (*d*) I once witnessed such apparatus at the Illinois Institution. I should think they are of great value to those who can hear.—Charles Kerney, *Principal.*

(f) How many pupils in your institution do you consider to be semi-deaf?	(g) How many of these were deaf from birth?	(h) How many pupils in your institution were deaf from birth?	(i) How many pupils do you have under Auricular instruction?	(j) How many of these were deaf from birth?	(k) Number of pupils who can hear the ringing of a dinner-bell.	(a) Do you make any special efforts to develop and utilise the hearing power of your semi-deaf pupils? (b) I shall be glad of any details regarding the methods of instruction employed in such cases and the results. (c) Do you use instrumental aids, such as hearing tubes or trumpets, audiphones, dentaphones, &c.? (d) What is your opinion concerning the relative merits of such apparatus? (e) Do you know of any facts indicating improvement of hearing power at or about the age of puberty? GENERAL REMARKS.
						56. LA CROSSE SCHOOL.
0	......	3	......	......	......	(a) None —ALBERT HARDY, *Superintendent of Schools.*
						57. NEW MEXICO SCHOOL.
2	0	2	......	......	1	(a) I do think some of having articulation here if a good number of semi-deaf scholars can be had, but the people here in this Territory, being mostly Mexican, speak Spanish, and if their deaf youths be taught to speak in English in this school it would be of *no* use to them, as they cannot talk orally to their Spanish-speaking folks. They generally want them to get education here—especially in the Roman Catholic creeds. English is now taught here according to the Committee's decision. (k) One can hear the door-knock if about 7 yards near the door.—LARS M. LARSON, *Superintendent.*
						DENOMINATIONAL AND PRIVATE SCHOOLS.
						1. WHIPPLE'S HOME SCHOOL.
2	1	......	......	......	2	(a) No. (d) We have had no experience with the instruments mentioned. (e) No. (k) Two can hear the dinner-bell when rung in the room.—MARGARET HAMMOND, *Principal.*
						2. GERMAN EVANGELICAL LUTHERAN INSTITUTION.
1	0	19	1	0	......	(a) No, but we utilise it for the best advantage of teacher and pupil. (c) No. (d) We don't care anything about it. We have tried it, but found it almost useless. (e) No; we have not yet investigated this matter, nor have we heard or read anything about it.—D. H. UHLIG, *Director.*
						3. ST. JOHN'S CATHOLIC INSTITUTE.
4	0	3	......	......	......	(a) No. (e) Nothing reliable.—Rev. CHAS. FESSLER, *President.*
						4. KNAPP'S INSTITUTE.
......	......	......	......	......	......	F. Knapp, Principal. No reply to circular letter to date, June 2, 1888.
						5. VOICE AND HEARING SCHOOL.
......	......	......	......	......	......	(a) Yes. (b) [Miss McCowen, Principal, was one of the teachers of the first auricular class in the Nebraska Institution, and has since established a "Voice and Hearing School" at Englewood, near Chicago, Ill. She forwards a statement respecting her school, which is printed at the end of this synopsis, among other papers referring to auricular work.—A. G. B.]
						6. MARY GARRETT'S SCHOOL.
3	1	7	2	0	......	(a) Yes. (b) Whenever I can find a pupil who can hear vowel sounds I endeavor to develop the hearing by use, and by teaching him words in his ear. If he cannot at first copy the sound or word I repeat it in his ear. I show him what it is with my lips, and then repeat it in his ear to teach him the meaning of the sound. The pupils I have so trained improve in hearing, and the two I have under instruction now have learned to recognise many words if spoken within a quarter of a yard of their ears. (c) I have tried the audiphone and the Currier tube. (d) In the cases I have tried I prefer the tube, but while the pupils admit that they can hear better through a tube, they object to its use and prefer that I should speak near their ears. (f) 3, but they are more than "semi-deaf." (h) 1 from birth, 1 at 6 months, 1 at 18 months.—MARY S. GARRETT, *Principal.*
						7. MARIA CONSILIA INSTITUTE.
6	3	28	2	0	6	(a) We do in a few cases only. (c) We do not use any instrumental aids. (k) Five of our pupils can hear the large bell, 1 can hear the door-bell.—SISTER ADELE, *Principal.*
						8. CINCINNATI ORAL SCHOOL.
......	......	......	......	......	......	Mrs. Katharine Westendorf, Principal. No reply to circular letter received to date, June 2, 1888.
						9. CHICAGO CATHOLIC SCHOOL.
......	......	......	......	......	......	No reply to circular letter received to date, June 2, 1888.
						10. MISS KEELER'S ARTICULATION CLASS.
2	......	6	2	......	......	The 2 semi-deaf children have only a *very* slight degree of hearing. I have used speaking tubes with success in the cases of the 2 semi deaf-mutes.—SARAH WARREN KEELER, *Principal.*
						11. CATHEDRAL SCHOOL.
......	......	......	......	......	......	(a) We have not tried the auricular method.—E. P. CLEARY, *Principal.*
						12. THE SARAH FULLER HOME.
......	......	......	......	......	......	[Just organised. No report.—A. G. B.]

II. AURICULAR INSTRUCTION—Continued.

(f) How many pupils in your institution do you consider to be semi-deaf?	(g) How many of these were deaf from birth?	(h) How many pupils in your institution were deaf from birth?	(i) How many pupils do you have under Auricular Instruction?	(j) How many of these were deaf from birth?	(k) Number of pupils who can hear the ringing of a dinner-bell.	(a) Do you make any special efforts to develop and utilise the hearing power of your semi-deaf pupils? (b) I shall be glad of any details regarding the methods of instruction employed in such cases and the results. (c) Do you use instrumental aids, such as hearing tubes or trumpets, audiphones, dentaphones, &c.? (d) What is your opinion concerning the relative merits of such apparatus? (e) Do you know of any facts indicating improvement of hearing power at or about the age of puberty? GENERAL REMARKS.
						SCHOOLS FOR THE DEAF IN CANADA.
						1. MONTREAL CATHOLIC INSTITUTION FOR MALES.
......	......	......	......	......	......	Rev. J. B. Manseau, Principal. No reply to circular letter received to date, June 2, 1888.
						2. MONTREAL CATHOLIC INSTITUTION FOR FEMALES.
......	......	......	......	......	......	Sister Mary of Mercy, Superioress. No reply to circular letter received to date, June 2, 1888.
						3. HALIFAX INSTITUTION.
2	1	56	......	......	21	(a) No special efforts have been made in this direction. (c) Have used the audiphone and dentaphone to some extent. (d) I have not found either the audiphone or dentaphone of much value in teaching articulation. (e) Have not had my attention called to any instance of this kind. (f) By "semi-deaf," I understand such as can distinguish sounds or words by ear. (h) Probably 56 out of 75 pupils. (k) 21 out of 75 can hear a dinner-bell more or less distinctly when rung close to the head or ear. Six of these in one ear only—chiefly the right ear. One can distinguish the sounds *o* and *e*, and 2 of them most of the vowel sounds, and many words, as well as the bell at a considerable distance.—J. SCOTT HUTTON, *Principal.*
						4. ONTARIO INSTITUTION.
5	......	......	......	......	......	(a) No. (c) We have tried all the aids mentioned with little results. (d) I know of 1 case where the audiphone is of great benefit to a lady in Belleville. With it she can hear ordinary conversations—without it she is very hard of hearing. (e) No. (f) Four or five. (g) Have no information on this point. (h) See Reports. (k) Cannot give reliable statistics—so many of the smaller ones mistake hearing for vibration.—R. MATHISON, *Superintendent.*
						5. MACKAY INSTITUTION.
3	3	29	3	3	9	(a) We have done so, but were obliged to discontinue for want of time. (b) We used no instruments, merely spoke in a loud key into the child's ear, and I have no doubt much could have been accomplished, as the improvement in the hearing of each one so instructed was much improved. (e) No.—HARRIET E. MCGANN, *Superintendent.*
						6. NEW BRUNSWICK INSTITUTION.
......	......	......	......	......	......	A. H. Abell, Principal. No reply to circular letter received to date, June 2. 1888.
						7. FREDERICKTON INSTITUTION.
......	......	......	......	......	......	Albert F. Woodbridge, Principal. No reply to circular letter received to date, June 2, 1888

'Nebraska Institute for the Deaf and Dumb, Omaha, Neb.,
'May 4, 1888.

'MY DEAR PROF. BELL: Herewith please find a brief history of the aural work, with the tables you desire. This is as condensed as I could very well make it and give what you desire. Hoping it may prove to be what you wish, and to be of use to you,

'I am, very truly yours,

'J. A. GILLESPIE.

'Prof. A. G. Bell, Washington, D. C.'

'CONDENSED HISTORY OF AURAL INSTRUCTION.

'The history of the development of the aural method of instruction for the semi-deaf is as follows:

'Eight years ago a class of the older semi-deaf was organized as an experimental class, and supplied with the Rhodes audiphone.

'By a patient and laborious course those children were taught to recognize sounds, by repeating again and again various vowel sounds, and finally words and sentences. This result was obtained after about a three months' drill, half an hour each day, beginning at a point with them where they did not recognize sounds as such, but simply as noises.

'The next class in order was one of the smaller children of the school. In this case, after a similar drill, the results were equally or more satisfactory.

'In the fall of 1882 a class of the younger semi-deaf children was organized, whose instruction in all school work was to be carried on by this method.

'On the close of the school year, June following, this class had accomplished all, in an intellectual point of view, that could be expected of a beginning class taught by the ordinary methods. They had a vocabulary of two hundred to five hundred words which they could recognize by sound, speak fairly well, and use with facility in language exercises. A portion of these pupils left the State, some to attend the public schools and others to continue the work elsewhere. This method has been pursued uninterruptedly until the present time. In all, thirty-six pupils have been instructed by it. Of these, nineteen are congenital, fifteen from disease (two not stated), twenty-four males, twelve females. Of those deaf from disease, three lost hearing under one year of age, five between one and two years, remainder not stated.

'At present there are one hundred pupils in attendance. We have sixteen under aural instruction;

of these, nine will leave school as hard-of-hearing speaking people, with perhaps no greater degree of disadvantage from deafness than those who have become partially deaf in adult life.

'After eight years of experience in this work and of observation elsewhere, it is my firm belief that at least fifteen per cent. of our deaf-mute population are fit subjects for aural instruction, and that a majority of these can be graduated as hard-of-hearing speaking people, and the condition of the remainder greatly elevated above that of the ordinary deaf-mute.

'As to what takes place in a scientific point of view in aural work, my opinion is that in some cases there is a development in the hearing power, as well as improvement due to an increased knowledge of spoken language. In the majority of cases I think it proper to say that there is an improvement in both directions.

'As to the best means of testing the hearing power, I know of nothing better than the small class-room bell. We have used the audiometer, but the results with the bell have been equally as satisfactory.

'As to artificial aids to hearing, the ordinary flexible tube is as good as anything. The audiphone is useful in some cases, its value dependent upon the cause of deafness and condition of the auditory nerve and of the teeth.

'In three cases which have come under my notice there has been a decided change for the better in the condition of the hearing as the individuals entered the age of puberty. My confidence in the possibilities of this method is but strengthened by experience and observation.

'J. A. GILLESPIE, *Superintendent*,
'*Nebraska Institute for the Deaf and Dumb.*'

Cause of Deafness.	Number of Pupils in School.	Number of Pupils capable of Auricular Instruction.	Number actually under Auricular Instruction.
Congenital.......	48	12	10
Adventitious....	44	4	4*
Not stated.......	8	1 (adult 1)	1 (adult 1)
Total.........	100	18	16

*One at the age of 3 years, 1 at the age of 2 years, and 2 at the age of 1 year.

'National Deaf-Mute College,
'Kendall Green, near Washington, D. C.,
'May 7, 1888.

'MY DEAR PROFESSOR BELL: Let me thank you for your kind note of the 1st inst., and while I fear that I cannot at present write anything that would be of any value for your purpose, perhaps the enclosures may be of some use to you. At one time I thought of making at least a little memorandum for our "Philosophical Society" upon auricular work, and the enclosures were sent to me in reply to my requests for information.

'I also had letters from Dr. Gillett and Mr. Crouter, but these added no information of consequence.

'I have made no use of Mrs. Taylor's interesting paper, and turn it over to you.

'One point of considerable importance in regard to auricular work is this: very imperfect audition may be utilized with profit in improving the modulation of voice and the general quality of the articulation if persistently appealed to by the teacher of articulation. Another point is that many cases of feeble hearing power are to be found among the so-called "congenitally deaf," where the deaf habit has been formed largely through neglect.

'In reference to visible speech, I feel that you will be fully justified in urging that all teachers of articulation should be thoroughly grounded in the mechanism of speech; and to this end "visible speech" gives a completeness and definiteness and sense of mastery not readily acquired by any purely experimental system. And, finally, let me say I am very glad you have accepted the invitation to appear before the Commission, and if I can serve you, or the work rather, in any way, please let me know it. Excuse delay in answering your note and present haste.

'Yours truly,
'J. C. GORDON.'

'Nebraska Institute for the Deaf and Dumb,
'Omaha, Neb., February 15, 1888.

'MY DEAR PROFESSOR: I owe you an apology for not replying sooner, but I seemed to be so busy, I did not get round to it. As to aural work, there is nothing new to say. It is a fact, and, as an established fact, has become a part of our regular school work. I enclose a paper by Mrs. W. E. Taylor (Miss Plum), which will give you an idea of what she thinks. She has been our aural teacher for four years, and knows what she is talking about. I have had no reason to modify my views with reference to this matter as yet. Everything I see in connection with it but confirms me in the opinion that all semi-deaf children should be taught by this method, and also that the percentage of pupils that can be instructed this way will not fall below that we have already suggested.

'Very truly, 'J. A. GILLESPIE.
'Professor J. C. Gordon, Washington, D. C.'

By Mrs. W. E. TAYLOR (*formerly Miss* PLUM).

'Aural work has been so long an established fact that the history of the past three years presents few new features, and gives the results of few new experiments, but is merely a continuation and elaboration of the work begun five years ago.

'During these three years we have had twenty-one pupils under this instruction. Of these, one was removed to enter the public schools, and others to different States, leaving us sixteen in our school of one hundred. Our work with these leads us to believe that, generally, development is in educating the sense already possessed. In three instances the hearing power itself has increased.

'We do not now use the audiphone, because the ear-trumpet is preferred when any artificial aid is used for our present needs. By this means the pupil is to correct his speech by hearing his own voice as well as that of the speaker. This will not always answer, however, as there are on record cases where the audiphone has been beneficial when the trumpet would not meet the demand. In this connection we mention one boy who was started by the audiphone when his prospects of using his ears were decidedly slight. He continued its use for a few months, when it was thought no longer necessary to use any instrument for his further assistance. His hearing grew stronger, and with it his speech rapidly improved. In three years he became able to converse with his family by the use of his hearing, and to respond to their calls when not in the same room. His voice became natural and pleasant. This last is a fact that scarcely needs mention, as the speech of all aural subjects is more perfect and more easily made so than those of articulation, while the voices are infinitely better modulated.

'There have been several interesting cases in the Institution during the time you mention.

'Ernest Clark, of Columbus, Neb., had considerable hearing, being able to recognize sounds made by a voice from a distance of sixteen feet. He had been taught the elements of sound at home by what his mother described as a "natural method," but which we would designate "aural." Pursuing our usual line, the boy soon took school-room conversation. Being greatly interested in machinery, he was taught the names and movements of machines in the buildings. These names he pronounced easily, and with an articulation as perfect as could be desired; nor did he have any help in that direction. His hearing did not increase, but training helped him to use what he had. He is now in the public schools.

'Another boy, John McCartney, of Willow Springs, Neb., entered with us after some years' teaching in a sign class. After four years—one spent on the farm—he is able to do without signs, and, hearing him talk, a stranger would imagine him to be anything but a congenital mute. This is one of the cases in which there has been a growth of the hearing as well as education.

'A few weeks ago, a young man, eighteen years of age, never before in school, came to us. His hearing is very slight, and as yet he has not a large amount of voice. His first training was the shouting of sounds in various degrees of pitch or volume for him to imitate. This was to help him use his voice, and, by aid of the trumpet, the point was gained. The next step was to teach him the long, easily-heard sounds, as $\bar{o}$, *o*, $\bar{a}$, *a*, and simple words containing them. To get a correct utterance of the consonant's articulation, help was given, because he has not yet a sufficient quantity of hearing to enable him to imitate them. His hearing is rapidly improving, and he recognizes known sounds and notices new ones farther and more quickly than at first. His present work is the learning of "action words," having previously taken about fifteen nouns, names of things with which he was familiar.

'In our beginning class now, we follow the same outline that we should were these sign children, being careful to select those words whose vowel element is most easily recognized, and whose consonants are easiest to reproduce.'

'Voice and Hearing School for the Deaf,
'Wabash Avenue, near Sixty-third Street, Englewood, Ill.,
'May 1, 1888.

'DEAR SIR: Your letter of inquiry received. Am glad to furnish the desired information with regard to my own school, hoping it will aid the cause of this afflicted class, in whom I am so deeply interested.

'In answer to your questions, will state briefly:

'Have had two cases in which I considered there was real increase of hearing power, both quite marked—one due to the removal of a large mass of hardened wax from the ear, and the other to increased bodily vigor (the result, no doubt, of more active exercise and regular habits).

'*Apparent* improvement in hearing is usually increase in knowledge, due to *cultivation* of (1) *attention* and (2) accurate *perception* of *sounds*, that *without training* were but *disturbing noises*, if heard at all.

'I have only one pupil who appears to be in the least benefited by the audiphone.

'The London Dome is a favorite with all who hear *when listening to music*. The flexible ear-tubes are relied on for conversation when any instrument is used.

'1. Will further add: the only means of communication used in our home or school is idiomatic English.

'2. All class instruction is given through lip-reading, as there are some in every class who are totally deaf, and those who hear most hear not enough to dispense with lip-reading.

'3. Aural instruction is special, and given individually or introduced in their games, and the pupils helped to use each other's hearing, &c., &c.

'4. All hand work—Kindergarten, drawing, painting, modelling, type-setting, and wood-carving (in all of which boys and girls engage together with equal success), are used as a means of recreation and as a pleasurable *incentive* to *speech* as well as for the hand and eye training.

'Have tabulated answers to your remaining questions, which I hope will be available.

'Very respectfully,

'MARY MCCOWEN.

'Mr. Alexander Graham Bell, Washington, D. C.'

	Whole number of pupils in my school since its opening.	Number capable of being taught through hearing.	Number with very slight hearing.	At what age became deaf.						
				Under 1 year.	Between 2 and 3 years.	Between 3 and 4 years.	Between 4 and 5 years.	Between 5 and 6 years.	At 7 years.	At 12 years.
Congenital	26	7	5	....	....	....	....	....	....	....
Adventitious	23	11	2	1	7	2	3	7	2	1
Total.........	49	18	7	....	....	....	....	....	....	....

'One of the above pupils was also born *blind*, but has slight sight now, as the result of an operation. Her improvement in every way is very satisfactory. Another pupil not enumerated in either table heard perfectly, but was dumb from feeble-mindedness. I taught her to speak in short sentences, and she is now progressing satisfactorily under a private teacher.

'Kindergarten Class (in 2 divisions), 8 pupils.

'Daily exercises in Kindergarten games, Kindergarten occupations, aural drill, voice building, writing and blackboard drawing, incidental language, lessons whenever possible.

'Second Class, 2 pupils.

'All above lessons continued with the addition of special—1. Language lessons on all common objects and every-day actions, with easy idiomatic descriptions of same; 2. Writing with ink; 3. Drawing in charcoal (from the object); 4. Clay modelling (easy objects).

'Third Class, 6 pupils.

'All previous work continued and expanded. More difficult idiomatic descriptions of all that is done, seen, heard, and spoken in actual life, here, or in lesson books. Regular lessons in reading and arithmetic with book, and oral geography with map.

'Fourth Class, 3 pupils.

'Read *fluently* in any Third Reader. This year will *complete* Barton's "Language Lessons in Arithmetic," Barnes' "Primary History of United States," Swinton's "Introductory Geography." Daily lessons in general information in advanced idiomatic language, using objects, animals, plants, children's magazines, and the daily papers. Clay modelling continued and wood-carving begun.

'MARY MCCOWEN.'

	No. of pupils.	Age.	Age when entered school.	Time in this School.	Totally Deaf	Hear shrill metallic noise, but not voice.	Undecided as to hearing.	Hear easy words spoken very loud.	Hear and understand perfectly everything spoken distinctly very close to the ear.	Receiving daily auricular instruction.	Had some use of hearing when entered School.	Had no use of hearing when entered School.	Congenital.	Adventitious.	Age when became Deaf.	Cause of Deafness.	Knowledge of Language when entered this School.
	1	3 yrs.	3 yrs.	7 ms.	...	......	+	......	....	+	......	+		...	....	....	None.
	2	5 yrs.	5 yrs.	2 wks.	...	......	...	......	+*	+	+	......	...	+	2 yrs.	Scarlet fever.	Makes himself understood in baby vocabulary.
	3	6 yrs.	6 yrs.	2 wks.	...	......	+	......	....	+	......	+	...	+	2 yrs.	....	Lost speech entirely. Has been taught to speak twenty words by private teacher this year.
	4	6 yrs.	4½ yrs.	21 ms.	+	......	...	......	......	......	......	......	+	...	....	....	None.
5	5	6 yrs.	5 yrs.	7 ms.	+	......	...	......	....	......	......	......	...	+	2½ yrs.	Spinal meningitis.	Used an occasional word under excitement which his mother only could understand.
	6	6 yrs.	5 yrs.	4 ms.	...	......	+	......	....	+	......	+	+	...	....	....	None.
	7	6 yrs.	5 yrs.	7 ms.	...	......	+	......	....	+	......	+	+	...	....	....	None.
2	8	7 yrs.	5¾ yrs.	15 ms.	...	......	...	+	....	+	......	+	+	...	....	....	Had been taught by sign eight months, with a long vacation following. Remembered 15 written words. Spoke none.
	9	7 yrs.	5 yrs.	27 ms.	...	......	...	+	....	+	......	+	+	...	....	....	None.
	10	8 yrs.	6 yrs.	17 ms.	+	......	...	......	....	......	......	......	+	...	....	....	None.
2	11	8 yrs.	5 yrs.	3 yrs.	...	+	...	......	....	......	......	+	+	...	....	....	None.
2	12	9 yrs.	7 yrs.	27 ms.	...	......	...	+	....	+	......	+	+	...	....	....	Had been in private school taught by sign 1 year. Seemed to remember no words.
	13	9 yrs.	8 yrs.	7 ms.	...	......	...	+	....	+	......	+	+	...	....	....	None.
	14	11 yrs.	9 yrs.	15 ms.	...	......	...	......	+	+	+	......	...	+	3 yrs.	Scarlet fever.	Used slightly imperfect speech; did not read lips; wrote nothing.
	15	13 yrs.	7 yrs.	5 yrs. &7ms.	...	......	...	......	+	+	......	+	+	...	....	....	None.
	16	13 yrs.	7 yrs.	4 yrs. &7ms.	...	......	...	......	+	+	......	+	+	...	....	....	None.
4	17	13 yrs.	11 yrs.	13 ms.	...	......	...	......	+*	+	+	......	...	+	1½ yrs.	Spinal meningitis.	Talked but only an occasional word that a stranger could understand; wrote nothing.
	18	13 yrs.	8 yrs.	4 yrs.	...	+	...	......	....	......	......	+	+	...	....	....	Had been in sign school 3 years; knew 100 written words.
	19	15 yrs.	11 yrs.	4 yrs.	+	......	...	......	....	......	......	......	...	+	2 ms.	A fall.	Had been in a morning session oral school 2 years. Knew 30 words, spoken and written.
	20	19 yrs.	15 yrs.	4 yrs.	...	......	...	+	....	+	+†	......	...	+	5 yrs.	Scarlet fever.	Had attended sign institution 3 years. Spoke 25 words; wrote 400 words; construction of sentences very poor.
	20	....	....	....	4	2	4	5	3	14	4	12	13	7			

'New York Institution for the Deaf and Dumb, Station M.,
'New York City, February 17, 1887.

'MY DEAR MR. BELL: In reply to your communications of February 10 and 12, I would state that the work of developing the latent hearing of such pupils as we find, upon careful examination, possess any appreciation of sound, has been carried on in this institution for nearly two years with the most gratifying as well as the most convincing results.

'That the hearing power is increased I will not claim, but it is certain that voice sounds are more readily recognized and interpreted after a systematic course of aural training, and therefore, for practical purposes, it may not seem incorrect to assert that the hearing power is made available, if not increased, to such an extent, that many sounds which, before instruction was given, passed unnoticed, become readily appreciated and interpreted by the hitherto dormant ear.

'About seventeen per cent. of our pupils have the ability to comprehend sounds to a degree sufficient to warrant the training of the auditory apparatus to perform, with instrumental aid, the functions which belong to the organ of hearing in its normal condition.

'Experiments with the various "phones," trumpets, and tubes led to the perfecting of my conico-cylindrical tube, for which, from the testimony of teachers using it, as well as from my own observation, I feel justified in claiming that it is the most powerful conductor of voice sounds yet devised, and it has this superiority over any of the wholly metallic trumpets—in its use none of the unpleasant "roarings" are perceived. Besides, being flexible, it is easily carried. My duplex ear-piece with two conico-cylindrical tubes attached thereto gives, in many instances, a most perfect bridge across the chasm between hearing and actual deafness, because the deaf person is enabled to hear his own voice as well as that of the person speaking to him, and thus he is placed in as nearly a normal condition as is possible.

'You can readily understand, from your past experience, of what great value this becomes in the culture of the voice.

'For conducting musical sounds the London dome ear trumpet is very useful, but for voice sounds it does not equal my conico-cylindrical tube.

'The audiphone was thoroughly tested here, but it was not of sufficient conducting power to render its use available in our work. It has a value, however, and for many cases, slightly deaf as we should term them, in which a greater degree of hearing has existed and education has been acquired prior to the diminution of that sense, is an all-sufficient aid to an understanding and appreciation of sound.

'In a paper on "Aural Development," which I wrote, at the request of Mr. Gillespie, for presentation to the Convention of last summer, I gave an outline of my method of procedure in the class-room as follows:

'"Begin by accustoming the ear to interpret the sounds of the short vowels and their modifications combined with the consonants, for the reason that a very large proportion of the syllables in the English language have the short vowel sounds, and also, because the first efforts required to master the pronunciation of our language are facilitated by a limited number of easy rules. The class being furnished with the double instrument before mentioned, write a sentence on the large slates, one in which short *a* only is used: That cat has a rat. Placing the ear-pieces firmly in the external meatus, speak the sentence slowly into the bells of the tubes gathered in a cluster and require each pupil to repeat the words as nearly as it may be possible for him. Next, repeat the sentence naturally and urge the pupil to attempt it in the same way without assistance. The pupil should be allowed to observe the lips of his teacher at the same time in order that he may the more readily imitate the required sounds. If, however, this watching proves insufficient, his attention should be directed to the proper placing of the vocal organs for the production of such

* Have a very limited vocabulary, but are learning fast. † Attention easily attracted by a noise, but did not understand a word—is gradually losing her hearing this year. Gives her whole time to language and art work—Drawing, painting, designing, modelling in clay, wood-carving.

sounds. Do not expect or demand perfection; approximation should be regarded as progress at the first. You will discourage if you criticize too closely.

'" Bear in mind that the child possessing normal hearing requires years of practice, and under the most favorable circumstances, before he can secure correctness of enunciation. Recall the recitations of 'Mother Goose' and kindred rhymes by your own little friends, in which scarcely a word would be spoken with correctness. Should we demand more from our pupils?

'" Take up, seriatim, the sounds composing the words in the sentence: th-a-t—that, c-a-t—cat, h-a-s—has, a—a, r-a-t—rat, combining both eye and ear in assisting the pupil to reproduce the sounds uttered, thus securing lip-reading, hearing, and articulation.

'" As soon as short *a* is mastered, take short *e*, as in pen; short *i*, as in pin; short *o*, as in not; short *u*, as in but; and develop them in the same way.

'" In like manner take up the long vowels, and when you have completed them you will not only have laid a good foundation, but you will also have stimulated the acuity and increased the ability to perceive and comprehend sound."

'I am certain that in time to come, as men become broader in sentiment and feeling, we shall find a better classification of the deaf, so that each class will have the instruction best adapted to its peculiar needs, regardless of sign, oral, or aural methods, and that in the same institution and under the same direction each of these systems will be honestly and faithfully carried out, to the end that each deaf person shall be so taught as shall best enable him to overcome his defectiveness and enjoy the society of the world about him.

'In the hope that your efforts to enlighten the members of the Royal Commission will be rewarded by an increased endeavor to still further ameliorate the condition of the deaf, not only abroad but at home, I am faithfully yours,

'E. H. CURRIER.

'To Dr. Alexander Graham Bell,
'1500 Rhode Island Avenue, Washington, D. C.'

'The Arkansas Deaf-Mute Institute,
'Little Rock, Ark., April 30, 1888.

'DEAR SIR: In reply to yours of the 26th I would say:

'1st. Professor J. A. Gillespie stated at the Convention of Teachers of Articulation held at New York in 1884 that "a majority of 15 per cent. of all the pupils of our schools for the deaf could be graduated as hard-of-hearing speaking persons." He meant by this that 15 per cent. could be taught auricularly, and of these a majority would graduate as stated. I think this statement true; but after a long and careful trial I would prefer to place all those whose hearing was dullest in the regular articulation and lip-reading class, keeping only the most promising cases under special auricular instruction.

'2d. In my experience the large majority of those pupils who hear best are found among the congenitally deaf. Their deafness is so slight that had it occurred after becoming familiar with the sounds of spoken language, it would have caused no great inconvenience; but occurring before, prevented their learning to speak as normal children learn. I do not mean that this degree of deafness is more frequently congenital than adventitious, but that only those who are thus afflicted from birth or very early infancy are sent to our special schools for the deaf.

'3d. In my opinion, in most cases there is no increase in the hearing power, only an increase in the power of the mind to distinguish what it hears—a mental, not a physical, improvement. Still, I am convinced that, especially in congenital cases, there is occasionally a real physical improvement in hearing.

'4th. To ascertain the hearing power of a large number of deaf pupils, I would prefer to make a preliminary test with the audiometer, submitting all who heard as high as 10° to further tests with the voice, tube, and audiphone or tuning-fork. In my own practice, after my new pupils feel at home with me and their surroundings, I go into their class-room and test them by shouting, when they are not expecting it. Afterwards I use the tube, &c.

'5th. My attention has been directed to this subject for only four years. I share the general impression, that hearing sometimes improves about the age of puberty. It certainly has been noticed for the first time then. I have no evidence to offer, however. There *can* be no positive evidence till tests of hearing have been made and recorded for some years.

'6th. The audiphone, or its equivalent, a thin piece of hard wood veneer, slightly bent, is valuable as a test in some cases. However, even in those cases that at first seem to hear best by its use, it is usually laid aside after a while, and the pupil seems to hear without it. Out of 797 cases that I have examined carefully, I only know two who continued to think it an assistance. A good tuning-fork in the hands of a careful experimenter is an equally good test, but there is more danger of mistaking feeling for hearing than with the audiphone.

'In conclusion, allow me to say that I have found no facts contrary to the report of the Committee of which you were chairman, published in the "Annals" some three years ago.

'Any further information or assistance that I can render you will be a pleasure.

'Yours very sincerely,

'FRANCIS D. CLARKE, *Principal.*

'Alexander Graham Bell, Ph. D., Washington, D. C.'

AURICULAR INSTRUCTION IN ARKANSAS INSTITUTE.

Age at which Deafness occurred.	No. Pupils actually present.	No. considered capable of Auricular Instruction.	No. actually under Auricular Instruction.	
Unknown	3			
Congenital	53	9	7	4 taught entirely through the ear; the other 3 for one hour a day.
1 year or under	9			
1 year to 2 years	23	2		Both this year's pupils, and inconvenient to put them in class till after they learn to write.
2 years to 3 years	7	2	1	One of these is a new pupil; can't write yet.
3 years to 4 years	4	1	1	This boy says that he never could hear well. Father says he lost hearing at 4 from meningitis. Taught entirely through the ear.
4 years to 5 years	2	0	0	
5 years to 6 years				
6 years to 7 years	2			
10 years	1	1		Can be taught auricularly as well as any way, but is very dull.
12 years	1			
16 years	1			
Total	108	15	9*	

* 5 (4 congenital, 1 the doubtful case between 3 and 4) can hear ordinary conversational tones if slow and distinct, and say or understand anything.
2 (congenital) hear well, but have a very limited vocabulary.
2 (1 congenital, 1 between 2 and 3) can hear very loud talking, or with the tube.

III. INTERMARRIAGES OF THE DEAF.

Opinions and Statistics Submitted by Superintendents and Principals of American and Canadian Schools for the Deaf in answer to the Circular Letter of Inquiry.

1. AMERICAN ASYLUM.

Mr. Job Williams, Principal, directs attention to the following extract from the 1887 Report of the American Asylum:—

'Much has been said of late concerning hereditary deafness and of the tendency from the intermarriage of deaf-mutes "to form a deaf-mute variety of the human race." This impending catastrophe has been strongly set forth by Professor A. G. Bell, of Washington, D. C., who has industriously gathered statistics to sustain his theories, but whose data are too limited and too unreliable to draw therefrom any reliable conclusions. It is very difficult to get reliable statistics even in regard to those now living and at school, and time and distance increase the difficulty more than in proportion to the square of the time and distance. Let me illustrate. A deaf child entered our school a short time ago, and in answer to the question, "What deaf-mute relatives has she?" the reply came back, "None." Happening to know that the father was a deaf-mute, I divided the above general question into six or eight specific questions, and found that the child had *ten* deaf-mute relatives. Again, correct statistics as given are often very misleading; *e. g.*, we have in school 13 children, both of whose parents are deaf-mutes; or to state the case differently:—

'Three pupils have both parents, 2 brothers, 2 sisters, 2 uncles, 1 aunt, and 1 cousin.

'Two pupils have both parents, 3 brothers, 1 sister, 2 uncles, 2 aunts, and 1 cousin.

'Two pupils have 2 grandparents, both parents, 1 brother, 2 sisters, 2 uncles, 1 aunt, and 4 cousins.

'Two pupils have 2 grandparents, both parents, 2 brothers, 1 sister, 2 uncles, 1 aunt, and 4 cousins.

'Two pupils have both parents, 2 brothers, 1 sister, 1 uncle, and two cousins.

'Two pupils have both parents, 1 brother, 2 sisters, 1 uncle, and 2 cousins.

'Here are 13 children, and though an intelligent guess might be made as to the number of families from which they come, it would be impossible to be sure of that point from the above data. There might be 3 families, or there might be 13, or any number between those, so far as could be determined from the facts given. The truth of the matter is, there are *three* families, having respectively 4, 4, and 5 deaf-mute children.

'Glance again at the above table. Would it not puzzle one to be sure how many people were really involved in the figures there given? There might be *sixty-one* so far as one could tell from the table itself, but there really are only *twenty-seven*. Not a few of the published facts relating to deaf-mutes are as useless as the above tables as bases from which to draw conclusions.

'Moreover, almost anything may be proved by facts, provided the line of investigation be carefully chosen, and as carefully restricted within narrow limits. To take a very few families, in which both parents are deaf-mutes and prolific in deaf-mute offspring, gather the facts most carefully in regard to them, and draw therefrom general conclusions, while ignoring the hundreds of other families in which also both parents are deaf-mutes, gives results of little scientific value. For instance, we have had in school, in the decade under review, pupils from eleven families, in which the number of children is 73, of whom 30 are deaf-mutes. Now, so far as can be ascertained, there is no blood relationship between the parents in these families, nor was there any deafness in any previous generation which could be inherited; yet *forty-one per cent.* of the children are deaf-mutes. Should we confine our investigation to this narrow limit, we might conclude that there was a strong tendency in the whole human race to produce deaf-mute offspring, and therefore all marriage should be discouraged. That would be a no more hasty conclusion than some that have been drawn concerning the tendency of deaf-mute parents to produce deaf offspring.

'A more thorough investigation than has yet been made is needed before any reliable conclusions can be drawn. If Professor Bell, with the ample means at his command, would take the whole pupilage of the American Asylum, or of the institution at Washington Heights in New York City, or of the Institution in Philadelphia, and trace the descendants of every pupil in attendance since the opening of the school about seventy years ago, he might give us facts from which reliable and broad general conclusions could be drawn.

'In the absence of any such general investigation, we can give only the few facts that we have been able to gather. Perhaps, in time, enough fragmentary reports may be collected to be of value.

'Since the last decennial report of this school 289 pupils have been admitted. In regard to these, great pains have been taken to get reliable facts. Of these, 118, or nearly 41 per cent., were born deaf.

'Sixty-seven pupils, coming from 47 different families, have deaf-mute relatives, and in the same families there are 154 hearing children, and 19 other deaf-mute children, not at school here in the last ten years. So that *thirty per cent.* of the children in these 47 families are deaf.

'In 8 families, both parents being deaf-mutes, there are 21 children, of whom 15, or *seventy-one per cent.*, are deaf, all congenitally so.

'In 2 families, 2 grandparents and both parents being deaf, there are 5 children, all congenitally deaf.

'In 1 family, both grandfathers, 1 grandmother, and mother being deaf, there are 2 hearing children, and 2 children, or *fifty per cent.*, congenitally deaf.

'In 1 family, the mother being hard of hearing, there are 7 children, 4 of whom, or *fifty-seven per cent.*, are deaf.

'Were this a fair representation of the average condition of the offspring of deaf-mute parents, the facts would be appalling, but it is not. Revert again to the 2 families in which 5 children have both parents and two grandparents who are deaf. All these children are congenitally deaf. But this statement, in order to give it value as a scientific fact, should be modified by the further statement that 4 out of the 5 children come from 1 family, and that a daughter of the same grandparents, herself a deaf-mute, married a deaf-mute and has 4 children, all of whom can hear. So that the offspring of the 2 pairs of grandparents, instead of being 100 per cent. deaf-mutes, as appeared by the first statement, is in reality *only fifty-five per cent.*

'Again, it was stated that in 8 families, from which we have received pupils in the last ten years, both parents being deaf-mutes, there were in all 21 children, of whom 15, or *seventy-one per cent.*, were deaf-mutes. With this statement compare the following: From 1850 to 1874, inclusive, there were five general gatherings at the American Asylum of its former pupils. Among those assembled were the heads of 127 families having children. In 97 of these families both parents were deaf-mutes, and the aggregate number of their children was 266, of whom 32, or *twelve per cent.*, were deaf-mutes.

'In 30 other families but 1 parent was a deaf-mute, and there were 76 children, of whom 5, or *six and one-half per cent.*, were deaf-mutes.

'Let us look at another set of facts. In 25 families who have sent children to this school since the report of 1877, hearing parents, related by blood, have had 124 children, of whom 37, or *thirty per cent.*, were born deaf, and 20, or *sixteen per cent.*, were accidentally deaf—*i. e.*, *fifty-three per cent.* of their children were deaf.

'In 7 of these families the parents are first cousins, and have 45 children, of whom 6, or *thirteen per cent.*, are congenitally deaf, and 7, or *fifteen per cent.*, are accidentally deaf.

'In 3 of these families the parents are second cousins, and have 18 children, of whom 5, or *twenty seven per cent.*, are congenitally deaf, and 1, or *six per cent.*, are accidentally so.

'In 4 of these families the parents are third cousins, and have 10 children, of whom 2, or *twenty per cent.*, are congenitally deaf, and 2, or *twenty per cent.*, are accidentally deaf.

'In 9 of these families the parents are cousins (degree not specified), and have 43 children, of whom 6, or *thirteen and one-half per cent.*, are congenitally deaf, and 6, or *thirteen and one-half per cent.*, are accidentally deaf.

'In 2 families the parents are uncle and niece, and have 8 children, of whom 1 is congenitally deaf, and 1 accidentally so.

'Seventeen of the above 25 families have no deaf-mute relatives.

'One more point. It is claimed by some that the large schools of this county, by allowing the use of the sign language, foster a clannish spirit, and promote the marriage of deaf-mutes to deaf-mutes, and so have a strong tendency to produce deaf-mute offspring, which would be avoided were the oral method adopted. Statistics do not sustain this theory, for in Germany, the home and chief advocate of oral schools for more than a century and a quarter, there are 96 deaf-mutes to 100,000 of population, while in the United States there are only 66 deaf-mutes to 100,000 of the population. It might not be amiss in both cases to take into account human nature as an important factor in the solution of the problem.

'The following table shows all the children admitted to this school since May, 1877, who have deaf-mute relatives, and also all children admitted during the same time whose parents are related by blood. Cases connected by a brace belong to the same family:

PUPILS HAVING DEAF RELATIVES.

Case.	Register No.	Age at which Deafness occurred.	Consanguinity of Parents.	No. of Hearing Children in Family.	Deaf-Mute Relatives. Grandfather.	Grandmother.	Father.	Mother.	Brother.	Sister.	Uncle.	Aunt.	First Cousin.	Second Cousin.	
1	2145	Congenital...		0	1	1	1	1	1	2	2	1	4		
2	2362	Congenital...		0	1	1	1	1	1	1	2	1	4		
3	2327	Congenital...		0	1	1	1	1	1	2	2	1	4		
4	2146	Congenital...		0	1	1	1	1	2	1	2	1	4		
5	2150	Congenital...	2d cousins...	5					3						
6	2285	Congenital...	2d cousins...	5					2	1					
7	2152	Congenital...		0			1	1	3	1	2	1	1		One cousin of mother is deaf and dumb.
8	2386	Congenital...		0			1	1	3	1	2	1	1		One cousin of mother is deaf and dumb.
9	2257	Congenital...		0			1	1	2	2	2	1	1		One cousin of mother is deaf and dumb.
10	2308	Congenital...		0			1	1	2	2	2	1	1		One cousin of mother is deaf and dumb.
11	2153	Congenital...		0			1	1	2	2	2	1	1		One cousin of mother is deaf and dumb.
12	2378	Congenital...		1			1	1	2	1	1		2		
13	2198	Congenital...		1			1	1	2	1	1		2		
14	2199	Congenital...		1			1	1	1	2	1		2		
15	2247	Congenital...		2	2	1	1			1		2	2	2	
16	2264	Congenital...		0	1	1	1	1				1	1		
17	1140	Congenital...		1			1	1		1	1		4		
18	2336	Congenital...		3			1	1			8*				Her paternal grandparents were second cousins, and had 9 deaf children.
19	2214	Congenital...		0			1	1				2	1		
20	2388	Congenital...		0			1	1			1	2	5		One cousin of father.
21	2125	(?)		5					1						
22	2126	(?)		5					1						
23	2391	Congenital...	1st cousins...	8					1	1					
24	2128	4 years	1st cousins...	8						2					
25	2134	4 years	Cousins......	2											
26	2136	Congenital...		1					1						
27	2103	Congenital...		1					1						
28	2140	Congenital...	3d cousins...												
29	2141	1 year		5											Mother has 1 deaf-mute cousin.
30	2273	3 years	1st cousins...	0					1				2		Father's sister married her 1st cousin, and had two deaf-mute children.
31	2172	Congenital...	1st cousins...	0					1				2		
32	2173	Congenital...		2						1					
33	2176	1½ years		3					2	1					
34	2178	Congenital...	Cousins......	3						1					
35	2232	Congenital...	Cousins......	5						1					
36	2204	Congenital...	Cousins......	5					1						
37	2322	Congenital...		5						2					
38	2209	Congenital...		5						2					
39	2308	Congenital...		5						2					
40	2139			1					1	1					
41	2326	Congenital...									2		5	8	
42	2329	Congenital...		4					1	2					Two cousins of father.
43	2330	Congenital...		4					1	2					Two cousins of father.
44	2331	Congenital...		4					2	1					Two cousins of father.
45	2335	Congenital...		1						3					
46	2338	Congenital...	1st cousins...	7					1						
47	2315	1½ years		9									1		
48	2349	Congenital...		3				(†)		3					
49	2350	Congenital...		3				(†)	1	2					

* Eight aunts and uncles together. † Partially deaf.

Case.	Register No.	Age at which Deafness occurred.	Consanguinity of Parents.	No. of Hearing Children in Family.	Deaf-Mute Relatives. Grandfather.	Grandmother.	Father.	Mother.	Brother.	Sister.	Uncle.	Aunt.	First Cousin.	Second Cousin.	
50	2352	9 months	3d cousins	4											Grandfather, uncles, and aunt grew deaf at about twenty-five years of age.
51	2354	Congenital	Father uncle to mother.	2											
52	2360	Congenital	1st cousins	2							1		1		
53	2361	Congenital					1	1			1				
54	2310			3						1					
55	2375			3					1						
56	2377	Congenital		0											Grandparents were 1st cousins.
57	2381	4 yrs. 5 mos.		4											Father has 2 cousins and 2 nieces partially deaf.
58	2387	6 years	Cousins	4											
59	2389			3											One third cousin.
60	2394	Congenital		6						1					
61	2217	2 years	1st cousins	1					1	1					
62	2283	Congenital	1st cousins							2					
63	2222	1½ years	Father half brother to wife's mother.	4											
64	2227	1 year	Cousins	3											
65	2228	Congenital		1			1	1			2				
66	2230	Congenital		8					1						
67	2239	Congenital	1st cousins	2									1		
68	2251	1 year	2d cousins	6											
69	2252	Congenital		3					3	1					
70	2284	Congenital		3					4						
71	2259	1 year	Cousins	2											
72	2260	2 years	Distant cousins.	5											
73	2268	Congenital	3d cousins	0											
74	2278	3½ years	3d cousins	2											
75	2280	2 years		4									2		
76	2288	Congenital		4						1					
77	2289	Congenital	Cousins	1						1					
78	2293	12 years	Cousins	6											
79	2302	Congenital	1st cousins	3											
80	2309	3 years		11							1				
81	2313	Congenital	2d cousins	1									1		
82	2319	Congenital		3					3						
83	2320	3 years		1						1					

ALLEGED CAUSES OF DEAFNESS OF 289 PUPILS ADMITTED FROM MAY, 1877, TO MAY, 1887.

Bilious and catarrhal fever	1
Boils on head	1
Brain fever	5
Brain and bilious fever	1
Brain and catarrhal fever	1
Cholera infantum	3
Colds	2
Congenital	118
Congestion of brain	1
Diphtheria	2
Disease in head	7
Falls	10
Fever	5
Fits	4
Fright	1
Idiotic	3
Inflammation of the ears	1
Inflammation of the spine	1
Lung fever	1
Measles	8
Meningitis	21
Poisoned by toy	1
Salt rheum	1
Scarlet fever	53
Scrofula	2
Sickness	8
Small-pox	2
Spotted fever	1
Teething	1
Typhoid fever	4
Unknown	16
Whooping cough	4
	289

AGE AT WHICH DEAFNESS OCCURRED.

Congenital	118
Doubtful	18
Under 1 year	28
Between 1 and 2 years	39
" 2 and 3 years	26
Between 3 and 4 years	21
" 4 and 5 years	15
" 5 and 6 years	8
" 6 and 7 years	7
" 7 and 8 years	2
" 8 and 9 years	1
" 10 and 11 years	2
" 12 and 13 years	1
Idiotic	3
	289

'JOB WILLIAMS, *Principal.*'

2. NEW YORK INSTITUTION.

I. L. Peet, Principal. No reply to circular letter received to date, June 2, 1888.

3. PENNSYLVANIA INSTITUTION.

'I am of the opinion that the intermarriage of the deaf, particularly the congenitally deaf, should be discouraged.

'A. L. E. CROUTER, *Principal.*'

4. KENTUCKY INSTITUTION.

'As to the intermarriage of the deaf, my observation and experience is that those who were rendered deaf by accident or sickness are no more liable to have deaf offspring than people in possession of all their faculties. In the case of those born deaf there have been a number of cases where intermarriage has led to deaf-mute offspring. Such cases are infrequent, however, and confined mostly to one or two families that seem to have an inherited taint in the blood. In my judgment there is no danger of the formation of a deaf variety of the human race. . . .

'W. K. ARGO, *Superintendent.*'

5. OHIO INSTITUTION.

'Just now I am *very full* of work, arranging for examinations and the close of school. I will endeavor to have the work done for you soon.

'AMASA PRATT, *Superintendent.*'

No reply to circular letter received to date, June 2, 1888.

6. VIRGINIA INSTITUTION.

'On our general register of pupils we have the names of some 600 persons. This register includes all who have been here since the opening of the school in 1839. In looking over this list I find that there have been a number of marriages in which both parties were mutes, and know of but three of these marriages which have produced deaf-mute offspring. In the case of the Rev. Job Turner, who married a deaf-mute, there were two children—sons—one of whom married a Miss Bean, of Rockingham county. Miss Bean can hear and speak perfectly, but has three first cousins on her father's side who are congenital mutes. There are two children—grandchildren of Rev. Job Turner—both of whom can hear and talk. A first cousin of Mrs. Turner (last-mentioned) married a semi-mute, and they have three children who can hear and speak. Another first cousin married a semi-mute. This couple has one child which can hear and speak. I know of several families in Virginia (as many as ten, I think) in which deafness is common, but I have been able to hear of no children born to any of our old pupils that are deaf, beyond the cases cited above. . . .

'THOMAS A. DOYLE, *Principal.*'

N. B.—The Rev. Job Turner is a deaf-mute; his children can hear and speak.—A. G. B.

7. INDIANA INSTITUTION.

William Glenn, superintendent, expresses no opinion upon this question.

8. TENNESSEE SCHOOL.

Thomas L. Moses, principal, expresses no opinion upon this question.

9. NORTH CAROLINA INSTITUTION.

'I know of one family in our State where both of the parents are deaf and dumb, and all their children, nine in number, deaf and dumb; also two other families where both parents are deaf and dumb, and two or three children in each deaf and dumb. I have known of four families in this city (Raleigh) where the parents are deaf and dumb, and several children in each, none of whom are deaf.

'W. J. YOUNG, *Principal.*'

10. ILLINOIS INSTITUTION.

'I do not discourage the intermarriage of the deaf, as they are usually more happily mated thus than where one of the parties only is deaf. The deaf need the companionship of married life more than those who hear, and it is a gross wrong to discourage it.

'Deafness is not so frequently inherited by the offspring of deaf parents as by the offspring of parents who have deaf relatives other than children. There is a susceptibility to deafness in some kindreds which asserts itself whenever favoring conditions present themselves. These may occur in a family where both parents are deaf, or in some other family of the kindred. But the fact of the presence of deafness in the parents does not render the susceptibility more intense than in other families of the same kindred.

'I enclose some extracts from my last report, which may be of some aid to you:

'I have been endeavoring to collect vital statistics concerning the deaf and dumb for thirty-two years, but, notwithstanding my favorable situation, I have often found it very difficult to obtain the truthful information which is of so great importance. The strange reluctance of some persons to give information of their personal and family history is of such strength, that neither a corkscrew could draw, nor an hydraulic press could squeeze it out of them. Others have no intelligent knowledge of the circumstances which induced the deafness we seek information about, and sometimes assign causes purely imaginary. These statistics, I fear, are not entirely exact, for I frequently get new information about cases I had long known; but they are approximately so, and are probably as near exact, as far as they go, as can be obtained.

'From the information thus far obtained I find that deafness occurred—

				Cases.
At birth in				490
Under 1 year of age				167
At 1 and under 2 years of age				138
At 2	"	3	"	150
At 3	"	4	"	102
At 4	"	5	"	64
At 5	"	6	"	51
At 6	"	7	"	29
At 7	"	8	"	25
At 8	"	9	"	16
At 9	"	10	"	7
At 10	"	11	"	11
At 11	"	12	"	2
At 12	"	13	"	4
At 13	"	14	"	7
At 14	"	15	"	7
At 15	"	16	"	1
At 17	"	18	"	1
At 20	"	21	"	1

'The causes of deafness among the pupils of this institution, so far as known, have been—

	Cases.
Congenital, in	490
Cerebro-spinal meningitis	299
Inflammation of the brain	36
Brain fever	92
Scarlet fever	135
Erysipelas	4
Diphtheria	12
Measles	42
Small-pox	2
Chicken-pox	1
Fever	63
Nervous fever	6
Typhoid fever	45
Intermittent fever	11
Congestive fever	7
Catarrh	12
Colds	27
Sickness (nature, not given)	72
Falls	35
Gathering in head	44
Whooping-cough	24
Pneumonia	22
Spasms	21
Scrofula	10
Hydrocephalus	12
Congestion of the brain	11
Cutting teeth	5
Excessive use of quinine	15
Disease of the ear	8
Mumps	7
Gradual decadence of hearing	4
Paralysis	3
Fright	2
Shock of lightning	2
Sea-sickness	2
Cholera infantum	2
Burned with lye	2
Cholera	2
Concussion of brain	1
Influenza	1
Croup	1
Vaccination	1
Rickets	1
Disease of the spine	1
Worm fever	1
Burn	1
Scald-head	1
Drinking lye	1
Apoplexy	1
Scald	1
Cold plague	1
Cancer	1
Jaundice	1
Disease of kidneys	1

Bronchial affection	1
Sunstroke	1
Sprain in neck	1
Exposure to heat	1
A blow on the head	1
Washing in cold spring	1
Hemorrhage from the mouth	1
Throat diseases	1

'The 1,886 pupils represent 1,705 families.

'Of these 1 family contained 5 deaf-mutes.
" 11 families " 4 "
" 50 " " 3 "
" 103 " " 2 "
" 1,541 " " 1 deaf-mute.

'Among the 1,705 families, in 8 families the father and mother were deaf; in 1 family the father was deaf.

'Four hundred and fifty-two had deaf-mute relationships numbering 770, a detailed statement of which, as far as ascertained, is as follows:

	Cases.
Father and mother in	5
Father and sister in	2
Father, mother, 1 uncle and 1 aunt, in	1
Father, mother, and 1 brother, in	3
Father, mother, and sister, in	1
Father, mother, and 1 second cousin, in	1
Father, mother, 1 sister, 1 brother, 2 uncles, and 1 aunt, in	1
Father, mother, 2 brothers, 2 uncles, and 1 aunt, in	1
Grandmother, in	1
One brother, in	82
Two brothers, in	27
Three brothers, in	2
One brother and 1 sister, in	49
One brother and 2 sisters, in	13
Two brothers and 1 sister, in	13
One brother, 1 sister, and 3 cousins, in	2
One brother and 1 fourth cousin, in	2
Two brothers and 3 cousins, in	1
One brother and 2 great-uncles, in	1
One brother and 1 third cousin, in	1
One brother, 1 uncle, and 1 aunt, in	1
One brother and 3 cousins, in	1
One brother, 1 sister, and 1 uncle, in	1
One brother and 3 third cousins, in	2
One brother and 1 second cousin, in	3
One brother, 2 sisters, 1 uncle, and 2 aunts, in	1
Two brothers and 3 second cousins, in	3
One brother, 1 sister, and 1 cousin, in	3
Two brothers and 1 cousin, in	1
Two brothers, 1 sister, 1 uncle, and 2 aunts, in	1
One brother and 2 cousins, in	1
One brother, 1 sister, and 1 uncle, in	1
Two brothers and 1 uncle, in	1
One brother, 2 sisters, and 1 second cousin, in	1
One brother, 1 sister, and 2 cousins, in	2
Two brothers and 2 cousins, in	1
One brother, 1 great uncle, and 1 great aunt, in	1
One brother and 1 fourth cousin, in	1
One brother and 1 cousin, in	2
One brother and 1 great uncle, in	2
One sister, in	83
Two sisters, in	16
Three sisters, in	2
One sister and 2 great uncles, in	1
One sister and 1 second cousin, in	4
One sister and 1 third cousin, in	1
Two sisters and 1 second cousin, in	2
One sister, 1 great uncle, and 1 great aunt, in	1
One sister and 1 fourth cousin, in	2
One cousin, in	46
Two cousins, in	1
Three cousins, in	2
Five cousins, in	1
One second cousin, in	19
One third cousin, in	7
Two third cousins, in	2
Three second cousins, in	1
Four second cousins, in	1
One fourth cousin, in	2
Two fourth cousins, in	1
Two second cousins and 2 fourth cousins, in	1
One cousin and 1 third cousin, in	1
One second cousin and 1 third cousin, in	1
Two cousins and 1 nephew, in	1
One uncle, in	7
One uncle and 2 aunts, in	1
Two uncles and 1 aunt, in	1
One uncle and 1 great uncle, in	1
Two great grand-uncles, in	1
One uncle and 1 niece, in	1
One great uncle, in	1
One aunt, in	2
One great aunt, in	1
Two great aunts, in	1
One aunt and 2 cousins, in	1
One nephew, in	1
Two nephews and 1 niece, in	1

'It is a very interesting and striking fact that while the 450 deaf-mutes enumerated in the foregoing statement had 770 relationships to other deaf-mutes, making a total of 1,222, that only 12 of them had deaf-mute parents and only two of them one deaf-mute parent, the mother of these having been able to hear, and that in no case was the mother alone a deaf-mute.

'Of the deaf-mutes who have been connected with the institution as pupils and have left it, 272 have married deaf-mutes, and 21 have married hearing persons. These marriages have been as fruitful in offspring as the average of marriages in society at large, some of them resulting in large families of children. It is interesting to know that among all these only 16 have deaf-mute children. In some of the families having a deaf child there are other children who hear. These facts clearly indicate that the probability of deaf offspring from deaf parentage is remote, while other facts, set forth herein, very clearly indicate a deaf person probably has or will have a deaf relative other than a child.

'The family descent of the 1,886 pupils have been—

	Cases.
American	1,284
German	271
Irish	161
Swede	44
English	29
French	25
Hebrew	13
Scotch	13
Colored	11
Polish	10
Portuguese	4
Canadian	4
Russian	4
Italian	3
Norwegian	3
Hungarian	2
Bohemian	2
French and Indian	2
Mexican	1

'Very nearly 6 per cent. (110) of the pupils who have been admitted to this institution are reported as children of parents having consanguineous origin, as follows:

	Cases.
Children of first cousins	76
Children of second cousins	17
Children of third cousins	9
Children of fourth cousins	9
Grandchild of first cousins	1
Child of uncle and niece	1

'These came from 88 different families, of which

Two families had four deaf children.
Five families had three deaf children.
Ten families had two deaf children.
Seventy-two families had one deaf child.

'I have experienced considerable difficulty in ascertaining facts on this point, and I believe there are some cases of this kind upon which we are not correctly informed. If all the cases of the offspring of parents related by blood were reported, I have no doubt the percentage of such would be larger, certainly not less than 8, and probably quite 10 per cent. 'PHILIP G. GILLETT, *Superintendent.*'

11. GEORGIA INSTITUTION.

'I enclose answers to questions and also some tables containing statistics.

TABLE I.

Causes of Deafness as given by Parents.

	Cases.
17 unknown	·077
112 congenital	·511
19 meningitis	·086
12 sickness	·054
8 brain fever	·036
5 scarlet fever	·022
2 typhoid fever	·009
1 worm fever	·004
1 malignant fever	·004
6 fever	·027
7 pneumonia	·033
7 rising in the head	·032

4	whooping cough	·018
2	measles	·009
1	mumps	·004
1	erysipelas	·004
1	convulsions	·004
1	catarrh	·004
1	milk scab	·004
1	scrofula	·004
2	strong medicine	·004
4	quinine	·018
1	paralysis of the drum	·004
1	concussion—kicked by a mule	·004
1	concussion—thrown from a horse	·004
1	concussion—firing gun while head was in a kettle	·004
219		·995+
	Whole number of cases	219

TABLE II.

Giving Age at which Deafness occurred.

17	unknown	·077
112	congenital	·511
15	under one year	·068
19	over one and under two	·086
17	over two and under three	·077
12	over three and under four	·054
10	over four and under five	·045
7	over five and under six	·032
3	over six and under seven	·013
2	over seven and under eight	·009
3	over eleven and under twelve	·013
1	over fourteen and under fifteen	·004
1	over eighteen and under nineteen	·004
219		·993
	Whole number of cases	219

TABLE III.

Giving Number of Deaf-mutes to each Family.

		Cases.
142	families have one deaf-mute each	142
23	families have two deaf-mutes each	46
13	families have three deaf-mutes each	39
4	families have four deaf-mutes each	16
3	families have five deaf-mutes each	15
185		258

The 219 deaf-mutes are representatives of 185 families, which contain altogether 258 children (deaf.)

Of the 219 deaf-mutes, 93 have deaf-mute brothers, sisters, or other relatives.

In 5 families the parents are deaf-mutes, producing 14 deaf-mute children, and in *each* case the mothers, and in 3 cases the fathers, congenitally so.

One of the 219 has 11 deaf-mute relatives—1 brother, 2 sisters, 3 cousins in 1 family, 1 each in 3 other families.

In 1 family the father, mother, and 5 children are all deaf-mutes.

TABLE IV.

Showing the Consanguinity of the Parents as given by the Parents themselves.

In 20 families the parents were first cousins, producing 33 deaf-mutes, or nearly 12½ per cent. of the 258.

In 11 families the parents were second cousins, producing 18 deaf-mutes, or nearly 7 per cent. of the 258.

In 4 families the parents were third cousins, producing 7 deaf-mutes, or about 3 per cent. of the 258.

In 1 family the parents were fourth cousins, producing 5 deaf-mutes, or nearly 2 per cent. of the 258.

In 1 family the parents were half-cousins, producing 1 deaf-mute, or about ⅓ of 1 per cent. of the 258.

In 3 families the parents were distantly related, producing 5 deaf-mutes, or nearly 2 per cent. of the 258.

From the above it is seen that in 40 of the 185 families the parents were more or less related—a number equal to nearly 21½ per cent. of the whole.

From these 40 families emanated 69 deaf-mutes, or .267 per cent. of the 258.

TABLE V.

Giving Progeny of Former Pupils of the Georgia Institution who have Married each other, as well as those who have Married Hearing Persons, in all the Cases of which the Principal has knowledge.

1. William Jones, congenital, to Margaret McLeod, congenital, and 1 of 2; 5 children, all deaf-mutes.
2. James Jones, congenital, and son of above, to hearing lady; 3 children, all hear perfectly.
3. Henry Taylor, congenital, 1 of 3, to Mary Jones, congenital, daughter of No. 1; 1 child deaf-mute and 1 hears perfectly.
4. Lucius Prior, congenital, 1 of 5, to Mary Hoge, congenital, 1 of 3; 6 children, all hear perfectly.
5. Samuel Potts, congenital, 1 of 4, to Angeline Prior, congenital, 1 of 5; 4 children by this marriage, all hear perfectly.
6. Jackson Payne, congenital, 1 of 4, to Angeline Potts, widow; 2 children, all hear perfectly.
6. James Jernigan, 1, to 6½, Rebecca Whiteside, 1 deaf at 15 months; 6 children, all hear perfectly.
7. John Wright, 1, to 7½, Amanda Ray, congenital, and 1 of 4; 1 deaf-mute, 1 hears perfectly; first marriage.
8. David Payne, congenital, 1 of 4, to 7½, Amanda Wright, widow; 2 children, all hear perfectly.
9. David Payne, married second time to 9½, Dollie Highfill, congenital, and 1 of 2; 1 deaf-mute. Dollie has 1 cousin and 1 sister deaf.
10. Samuel Bruce, hard of hearing and brother to two deaf-mutes, to Margaret Jones 1; 5 children, all hear perfectly.
11. John Ray, congenital, brother to 7½, to hearing lady; 5 children, all hear perfectly.
12. George Ray, congenital, brother to 7½, to hearing lady; 4 children, all hear perfectly.
13. Joshua Davis, congenital, 1 of 3, to 13½, Nancy Morris, congenital, 1 of 3; 5 children deaf-mutes, 1 very hard of hearing, 1 hears perfectly. Davis's grandmother deaf-mute.
14. Henry Morris, congenital, brother to 13½, to 14½, Emma Edwards, congenital, and child of deaf-mute parents, both of whom were congenitally so; 2 children deaf-mutes and 1 very hard of hearing.
15. — Sweetman, one, to 15½, Kate Morris, sister to 13½; 5 children, all hear perfectly.
16. John Payne, congenital, brother to 8; Mattie Harris, 1; 3 children, all deaf-mutes.
17. John Burks, congenital, 1, to Susan Gaines, congenital, 1; 3 children, all hear perfectly.
18. Abner Davis, congenital, 1 of 3, brother to No. 13, to Mary Davis (not related), congenital, 1 of 3; 5 children, all hear perfectly.
19. W. B. Lathrop, 5 years, 1, to Miss Wright, hearing lady, but daughter of No. 7; 1 child, hears perfectly.
20. Styles Philips, congenital, 1 of 2, to Ida Wright, congenital, 1, daughter of No. 7; 1 deaf-mute, 1 hears perfectly.
21. Charles Davis, congenital, 1 of 3, brother to No. 13, to Barthella Darden, 3 years, 1; 1 child, hears perfectly.
22. Zachary T. Wood, congenital, 1, to hearing lady; 2 children, hear perfectly.
22. Joe White, congenital, 1, to Catherine Worrel, congenital, 1; 2 children, all hear perfectly.
23. William Bailey, congenital, 1 of 2, to Mallie Pendergrass, 3 years, 1; 1 child, hears perfectly.
24. James Shannon, 1, 12 years, to Martha Tootle, congenital, 1 of 2; 3 children, all hear.

Sixteen marriages of congenital deaf-mutes produced 59 children, 19 or 32½ per cent. of which were deaf-mutes.

'W. O. CONNOR, *Principal.*'

12. SOUTH CAROLINA INSTITUTION.

'I think the intermarriage of the congenital deaf tends strongly towards an increase of the deaf as a class. See no special reason why a congenital deaf-mute should not marry another deaf person, so from disease or other cause. I send accompanying statement of a family living near here:

'Robert P. Rogers, a deaf-mute, having one brother and two sisters deaf, of Freeport, Maine, married Sarah Holmes, a deaf lady of S. C., having one deaf brother. This marriage resulted in a family of five children, three girls and two boys, all deaf.

'1. The eldest of these, Jane, married a deaf man; they have five children, four deaf and one *probably* semi-deaf.

'2. The second, William H., married a deaf lady; they have two children, both deaf.

'3. The third, David S., married a deaf lady; no children.

'4. The fourth, Laura A., married a deaf man (not congenital); they have two children, both can hear.

'5. The fifth, Clara A., married a deaf man (am not certain if congenital or not); one child, can hear.

'N. B.—All of above-mentioned are congenital deaf-mutes, except those designated otherwise.

'NEWTON F. WALKER, *Superintendent.*'

13. MISSOURI INSTITUTION.

James N. Tate, Principal, expresses no opinion upon this question.

14. LOUISIANA INSTITUTION.

John Jastromski, Superintendent. No reply received to date, June 2, 1888.

15. WISCONSIN SCHOOL.

'In considering the welfare and social life of the deaf, I would advise, first, celibacy; but if nothing short of the married state will satisfy, then I would advise the deaf to marry the deaf, believing peace, happiness, and prosperity will thereby be promoted, and the probabilities of deaf offspring but slightly increased.

'J. W. SWILER, *Superintendent.*'

16. MICHIGAN SCHOOL.

'All that can be said is very speculative. Very few deaf-mutes in my own school have deaf parents. The proportion is so small that it does not go far, in my opinion, to establish the theory that deaf-mute marriages tended to produce a deaf-mute offspring. 'M. T. GASS, *Superintendent.*'

17. MISSISSIPPI INSTITUTION.

'I know a great many married deaf-mutes. I do not know of a deaf-mute couple who have deaf-mute children. I know a deaf man who married a hearing and speaking lady; they have a deaf-mute daughter. I have not been convinced that deafness is hereditary. 'J. R. DOBYNS, *Superintendent.*'

18. IOWA INSTITUTION.

'H. W. Rothert, Superintendent. No reply to circular letter received to date, June 2, 1888.

19. TEXAS ASYLUM.

'The parents of but one of our children are both deaf. There is another, however, whose father is a mute, the mother being hearing and speaking. Out of a total of 158, 40 have deaf relatives. There are 36 instances where such relations are of the same generation, being sisters and brothers and cousins; one case of third cousin; six instances where relatives are in the next generation above; three where they are in the second generation above, and six instances where generation is not stated. The number 40 given above represents 28 families, as in ten cases there are two to a family and in one case three to a family, and four of these children, representing two families, are not congenitally deaf; four others, representing four families, are not congenitally deaf; making six families in all out of the 28 represented whose children are not congenitally deaf. 'W. H. KENDALL, *Superintendent.*'

20. COLUMBIA INSTITUTION.

(*a.*) Kendall School. James Denison, Principal, expresses no opinion upon this question.

(*b.*) National College, E. M. Gallaudet, President, expresses no opinion upon this question.

21. ALABAMA INSTITUTION.

'We have had eighteen couples married, former pupils of this institution. So far as we can learn, not a single case of deafness amongst their children. One child suspected of being deaf died before the matter was definitely settled.

'JOS. H. JOHNSON, *Principal.*'

22. CALIFORNIA INSTITUTION.

'Any defect in parents is more likely to appear in offspring than if such defect did not exist in the parents. This abnormal tendency is especially seen following the marriage of cousins or second cousins. Among the pupils graduates of this institution there have been many marriages and many children, but there has never been a child inheriting the affliction of its parents.

'WARRING WILKINSON, *Principal.*'

23. KANSAS INSTITUTION.

'Not a sufficient number of cases of offspring of deaf-mutes is under my knowledge for me to speak with much force on the question. And yet I am acquainted with several such families, but do not now recall but two cases where offspring are also deaf. 'S. T. WALKER, *Principal.*'

24. LE COUTEULX ST. MARY'S INSTITUTION, BUFFALO, NEW YORK.

'Of the 442 pupils who have been under instruction in our school there is only one instance of a deaf-mute born of deaf-mute parents.

'Sister MARY ANN BURKE, *Principal.*'

25. MINNESOTA SCHOOL.

'In regard to the intermarriage of the deaf, I have seen very few instances of children of deaf parents inheriting their infirmity during the 36 years I have labored among these children. For 22 years I have been superintendent of the Minnesota School, have had about 500 deaf children under my care; during that time over 30 of them were married and have children, but none of these are deaf. Not a child received here has had deaf and dumb parents. In one case a mother is hard of hearing but the father is all right. I regard the intermarriage of own cousins as much more dangerous to the well-being of offspring than the intermarriage of deaf-mutes. Still, I would be very guarded not to allow two who were congenitally deaf to marry each other. Moreover, after considerable observation and careful consideration, I feel confident that happiness follows the intermarriage of the deaf far more frequently than it does when one of the couple is deaf and the other hears and speaks. I am confident this is the rule. 'J. L. NOYES, *Superintendent.*'

26. INSTITUTION FOR THE IMPROVED INSTRUCTION OF DEAF-MUTES, LEXINGTON AVENUE, NEW YORK.

D. Greenberger, Principal, expresses no opinion upon this question.

27. CLARKE INSTITUTION.

Miss Caroline A. Yale, Principal, expresses no opinion upon this question.

In answer to a special request for information regarding the marriages of former pupils, Miss Yale submits the following report:

'Seventeen pupils have married, twelve have married deaf-mutes educated in other schools, 5 have married hearing persons. We know of no deaf child born to any former pupil of this school.

'Below are given, as requested, all the information we have in regard to those marrying deaf-mutes:

Allen, James D. (dead), Montague, Mass., one child—not deaf.
Annan, Josephine A., East Boston, Mass., Mrs. Beltis.
Bosworth, Mary, Eastford, Conn.
Brown, Mary Lizzie, Kensington, N. H.
Forbes, Alice V., Sherborn, Mass., Mrs. Henry A. Porter.
Kelly, Mary E., Lynn, Mass., Mrs. C. E. Burrill, one child—not deaf.
Nevers, Harry W., Bridgeport, Conn.
Nicholls, Marietta, Arlington, Mass.
Porter, Isabel E., Santa Fé, New Mexico, Mrs. Lars M. Larson, one child—not deaf.
Robinson, Hattie F., Boston, Mass.
Towle, Lewella, East Boston, Mass., Mrs. Ivary W. Allen.
Whittier, Mary Emma, Brooklyn, N. Y., Mrs. Leo Greis.'

28. ARKANSAS INSTITUTION.

F. D. Clarke, Principal, expresses no opinion upon this question.

29. MARYLAND SCHOOL.

'While the vast majority of deaf-mutes are not the result of deaf-mute marriages, and do not show hereditary influence, there is in my mind no question that the marriage of congenital deaf-mutes is *liable* to be followed by a deaf-mute issue—that the chances of deaf-mute offspring in such cases is many times greater than in ordinary marriages.

'C. W. ELY, *Principal.*

'May 10, 1888.'

30. NEBRASKA INSTITUTE.

J. A. Gillespie, Superintendent, expresses no opinion upon this question.

31. HORACE MANN SCHOOL.

Miss Sarah Fuller, Principal, expresses no opinion upon this question. In answer to a special request for information regarding the marriages of former pupils, Miss Fuller submits the following list of pupils married; and a personal letter from which the following is quoted:

'. . . Three marriages are the probable result of association in classes in the Horace Mann School. The others, I think, may be traced directly to "Deaf-Mute Associations" and "Deaf-Mute Conventions," which seem to exert every possible influence to bring together young deaf people. I have learned to-day that there are four societies in Boston under the direction of deaf persons. . . . The so-called religious societies continually attract to their meetings young persons whose parents do not take the trouble to interest and help them at home. As all of the exercises are in signs, and a free use of signs is not only allowed but encouraged, one cannot wonder that there is some confusion in the minds of children, or rather young persons, when they reflect upon the different methods of instruction. The criticisms which sometimes come to me are so exactly those that I have heard from teachers of signs that I think our children must have most

MARRIAGES OF THE PUPILS OF THE HORACE MANN SCHOOL.

Name.	Time of deafness.	Where educated.	Business.	When married.	Number of children.	Hearing or deaf.
Emma Collins	Infancy	Horace Mann School.				
Michael Lynch	Infancy; hears slightly.	Horace Mann School.	Marble worker	1883	Three	Hearing.
Hannah Ryan	Infancy	Horace Mann School.				
Joseph E. Finnegan	Congenital	Horace Mann School.	Shoemaker	1886	One; died at birth.	
Jane A. Bragg	7 years of age	Horace Mann School.				
Frank L. Cole	2½ years of age	Horace Mann and Providence Schools.	Do not know	Oct., 1886	None	
Mary E. Moriarty	5 years of age	Horace Mann School and N. Y. Improved Institute.				
George Neville	A hearing man		Actor	Aug., 1886	None	
Mary J. Carton	10 years of age	Horace Mann School.				
James H. Farley	13 years of age	American Asylum		Jan., 1881	Three	Hearing.
Ida L. Marshall	Infancy	Horace Mann School.				
John N. Davis	Was not born deaf (speaks).	Public Schools in Winchendon.	Operative in pail factory.	Dec., 1887	None	
Gelia H. Towksbury	At 10 years of age	Public School and Horace Mann Sch'l.				
Charles C. Fisher	At 8 or 10 years of age.	American Asylum	Engraver and designer.	June, 1887	None	
Susan Simons (wid.)	Congenital	American Asylum				
Frederick Roberts	At 6 years of age	Horace Mann School, and later Hartford.	Works in market	Think in 1885	None	
Mary Carroll	Infancy	American Asylum and Horace Mann School.				
Amos A. Ladd	Congenital	American Asylum	Clockmaker	Sept., 1884	None	
Lizzie M. Sargent	Unknown	American Asylum	Works in a rubber factory.	Nov., 1881	None	
Isaac A. Blanchard.	Infancy	New York Institution. and few mos. at Horace Mann School.				
Alice V. Forbes	Infancy	Nearly a year at the Horace Mann, later at Clarke Institution and American Asylum.				
Henry A. Porter	Unknown	Montreal and New York.	Mill operative	Aug., 1884	One	Hearing.
Luella Towle	Infancy	Northampton, and a few months at the Horace Mann Sch'l.				
Ivory W. Allen	6 years of age	Educated in public schools.	Steward	Mar., 1885	One	Hearing.
Harriet F. Robinson	Congenital	Northampton, American Asylum, and a short time at the Horace Mann Sch'l.				
Elbridge A. Wellington.	Infancy	American Asylum	Works in car shop.	May, 1883	None	
Mary O'Neil	Congenital	American Asylum				
William F. Young	Infancy	American Asylum, and a few months at the Horace Mann School.	Do not know	Think in 1880	Four; all died in infancy.	
Amelia McCallum	Unknown	Think American Asylum.				
Alvah W. Orrutt	At 4 years of age	Horace Mann School, later American Asylum.	Do not know	Dec., 1886	None	
Nora C. Noyes	Congenital	American Asylum				
Samuel S. Cross	Congenital	American Asylum, and one year at the Horace Mann Sch'l.	Shoemaker	May, 1887	None	
Mollie Mann	Unknown	Think Columbus Inst., Ohio.				
Henry White	At 5 years of age	Hartford Asylum, Horace Mann Sch'l, National College.	Teacher	June, 1885	One	Hearing.

emphatic teaching from the sign-makers in regard to the *value of signs*. With so much adverse influence about our young people, I do not wonder that they marry among deaf persons and spend their social hours in criticisms of each other. I remember that you once thought I was mistaken in wishing that the young deaf people were not encouraged to meet together. My longer experience and knowledge of young deaf persons confirms my belief that even if some of the joys of social life are lost through separation from other deaf persons, they gain greatly in moral strength by meeting only persons who hear. It seems to me to be a great wrong to deaf persons to encourage them to meet together. Possibly you remember the remark that was made about our restricting our pupils in the use of signs: "It is cruel" - I think it *cruel* to encourage their use. Did I not know that there are many of our pupils who use and enjoy using speech, and who mingle freely with friends and with strangers, and who *do not* meet with societies of deaf persons, I should at times be disheartened.

The names reported in the preceding list have probably been given by the Principal of the American Asylum, or by the New York reports. Nevertheless I give them, thinking they might aid in making fuller statements than would be possible without them. Ten of the persons were never pupils of the Horace Mann School, and none were there for a long period.'

32. ST. JOSEPH'S INSTITUTE.

Madame Ernestine Nardin, President, expresses no opinion upon this question.

33. WEST VIRGINIA SCHOOL.

H. G. Gilkeson, Principal. No reply to circular letter received to date, June 2, 1888.

34. OREGON SCHOOL.

'I know personally 9 deaf-mute families. In 6 of these families there are children, in all 14, none deaf. In eighteen years I have had 90 pupils in all. One of these, only partially deaf, was of deaf-mute parentage.

'P. S. KNIGHT, *Superintendent*.

'Salem, Oregon, May, 1888.'

35. MARYLAND INSTITUTION FOR COLORED DEAF-MUTES.

F. D. Morrison, Superintendent. No reply to circular letter received up to date, June 2, 1888.

36. COLORADO INSTITUTE.

John E. Ray, Superintendent, expresses no opinion upon this question.

37. CHICAGO DAY SCHOOL.

In reply to this question, Mr. Emery forwarded a number of pamphlets which he has published bearing upon the subject, and directs special attention to an article entitled 'Intermarrying of Mutes,' from which the following is quoted: 'Permit us a few words about mutes marrying mutes. Is it *selfishness* or unselfishness in parents and friends who *fear* the ways of Providence in deafness, and do not want their deaf son or deaf daughter to marry and enjoy the highest state of *use* and happiness on earth to man? . . . . . Even suppose this intermarrying of mutes does *actually* tend to, and *will* in time, produce a new "variety of the human race," is it not the will of Providence to that end for a *purpose?* Where is our authority to thwart this purpose? Would it not savor more of wisdom to aid Providence by a more normal development of the physical and mental natures of the deaf than by prohibition or discouraging of intermarrying among them? Our duty is to *develop*, and not to suppress, whatever Providence gives or sends us.

'Let us admit, for argument's sake, or even if the figures *do prove*, that the intermarrying of the deaf with the deaf *tends* to produce a new variety of the human family, just how long will it take to cause the whole world—all people—to become deaf? A billion, if not a trillion of years! unless you can show an *increasing* ratio of deafness greater than the increase of hearing people, for the increase of deaf and dumb by intermarrying is a very small mote in fact, and far from being a beam. Will it be wise and philanthropic to interfere with Providence even in *theory?* Or are you riding a hobby under the mantle of *human* wisdom? Better mount the hobby of *preventiveness* of deafness, as "an ounce of prevention is worth a pound of cure." . . . .

'Allow us to repeat, by asking that in case a new variety of the human family from the intermarrying of deaf-mutes is to be regretted as a social disaster, would not Providence have *foreseen* it and have prescribed a prevention of it in deafness by causing deafness or some other effect to neutralize or paralyze the love of sex—amativeness? Or may He not do this yet? Or may He not yet stop the cause of deafness ere we reach the dreaded new variety? It seems to us that it will be well to keep "hands off" of what is so remote and problematic.

'PHILIP A. EMERY, *Principal*.'

For the full text of Mr. Emery's communication see volume marked 'Emery Pamphlets.'

38. CENTRAL NEW YORK INSTITUTION.

E. B. Nelson, Principal, expresses no opinion upon this subject.

39. CINCINNATI PUBLIC SCHOOL.

A. F. Wood, Principal. No reply to circular letter received up to date, June 2, 1888.

40. WEST PENNSYLVANIA INSTITUTION.

'I regret to say that I have no statistics at present bearing upon this question. So far as the range of my observation goes, however, in the majority of cases of intermarriage between the deaf, the children are similarly affected. I find among our pupils a very considerable number have one or both parents deaf, or have deaf grandparents or deaf uncles, aunts, or other relatives.

'JOHN G. BROWN, *Principal*.'

41. WESTERN NEW YORK INSTITUTION.

Z. F. Westervelt, Principal. No reply to circular letter received up to date, June 2, 1888.

42. PORTLAND SCHOOL, MAINE.

Ellen L. Barton, Principal, expresses no opinion upon this question.

43. RHODE ISLAND STATE SCHOOL.

'In regard to the intermarriage of the deaf, I think the least that can be said is, that they run a great risk in regard to the offspring being deaf, or at least predisposed to deafness. I have observed that in some families there is an inherited predisposition to deafness. Many of those, I think, who are not actually deaf, have this inherited tendency, and it takes but a slight cause to render them partially if not wholly deaf. Frank Lamont Cole, now of Pawtucket, R. I., attended this school from February, 1877 (at its founding) to June, 1880. Was 13 when admitted. Became deaf from scarlet fever at 2½ years. After leaving school married a deaf-mute, Jennie Bragg, who was *not a congenital*. They had twins, who died soon after their birth. Mary Emily Bauer, now living at Green, R. I., married Frank Brown, congenital deaf-mute. They have 1 child, now nearly a year old, *not deaf*. Emily Bauer attended the R. I. School from April, 1877, to May, 1880. 'ANNA M. BLACK, *Principal*.'

44. ST. LOUIS DAY SCHOOL.

D. A. Simpson, Principal. No reply to circular letter received up to date, June 2, 1888.

45. NEW ENGLAND INDUSTRIAL SCHOOL.

'One of our graduates married a deaf-mute—no children. 'NELLIE H. SWETT, *Principal.*'

46. DAKOTA SCHOOL.

James Simpson, Superintendent. No reply to circular letter received up to date, June 2, 1888.

47. MILWAUKEE DAY SCHOOL.

'So far as my observation has gone, deaf-mutism is not *direct* hereditary, but in very few cases. I find that a deaf-mute couple will very seldom have deaf-mute children; but the offspring of these hearing and speaking children is sure to be tainted. Deaf-mutism is undoubtedly hereditary.

'PAUL BINNER, *Principal.*'

48. PENNSYLVANIA ORAL SCHOOL, SCRANTON.

'When educated by *pure* oral method, I think large numbers will marry hearing people.

'EMMA GARRETT, *Principal.*'

49. NEW JERSEY SCHOOL.

The Superintendent submits the following extract from his 1885 Report, and adds: 'I feel obliged to recant the opinion cautiously hazarded in my Report of 1885 as to the probable comparative results of intermarriages among the deaf, and of marriage between deaf and hearing persons in respect to the proportion of the deaf to the hearing children of the two classes of unions respectively.'

(*Extract from* 1885 *Report.*)

'During the past year considerable interest has been awakened not only among those who are immediately interested in deaf-mute instruction, but in scientific circles and among the community at large by the discussion, in which Professor A. Graham Bell has taken a leading part, of the question how far the intermarriage of deaf-mutes tends to form an increasing class of deaf persons, differentiated more and more from those who hear.

'Very little can be positively said as to the antenatal causes of deafness in the present state of knowledge on the subject, and while deafness in the parents undoubtedly tends, with a certain degree of force, to reproduce itself in the children, it cannot yet be pronounced, with any degree of certainty, that there are not other and more obscure causes which have a larger share in producing congenital deafness.

'As a slight contribution towards the solution of this question I give below the information on this subject furnished by the records of this school.

'Of the 134 pupils who have received instruction in this school since its opening, there have been twenty-nine who have each one or more deaf relatives.

'These twenty-nine pupils represent twenty-four families, in one of which there have been five deaf-mute children, while two families have had four each, three families have had three each, and seven families have had two each of children thus afflicted. In three families, with a total of five deaf-mute children, both parents were deaf-mutes; and in four families, with a total of five deaf-mute children, one parent was deaf in a greater or less degree.

'In the eight remaining cases representing the same number of families, the deaf relatives were outside of the immediate family circle, being uncles, cousins, or those still more distantly related.

'As regards the relationship of parents before marriage, in the case of two out of our 134 pupils the parents were cousins, in two cases they were second cousins, and in one case they were third cousins.

'In none of these five families were there two or more deaf-mute children, and the proportion of related parents (less than four per cent. of the whole) is perhaps not greater in the 129 families from which these statistics are gathered than in the community as a whole.

'In the six families reported above as containing each three or more deaf-mute children, I am satisfied (although the point does not admit of exact statement) that the parents were in no case below the average in physique, in morals, or in their sanitary surroundings, and in no case was either of the parents deaf, while the 22 deaf-mute children of those families are, on the whole, rather above than below the average in health and vigor.

'While the number of cases covered by this Report is not large enough to furnish a safe basis for drawing any general conclusions, yet the indications which they afford will have a certain value, especially when they harmonize with the results of other investigations independently conducted.

'It would appear, then, that while the great majority of cases occur singly in unrelated families, there is yet a considerable number of marriages which give rise each to several deaf-mute children. Nor, if we may generalize from our figures, are the parents of a numerous deaf-mute progeny generally deaf themselves or from an ancestry characterized by deafness. It would seem, too, that, contrary to a rather wide-spread notion, neither consanguinity nor low vitality of the parents is a frequent cause of deafness in the children. I believe that these conclusions are in general harmony with the results of other investigations, except that deafness is probably rather more common among the classes surrounded by unfavorable conditions as to health than among those more fortunate in this respect.

'It is a curious fact that more marriages between deaf and hearing persons have furnished deaf children to this school than marriages in which both parties were deaf-mutes.

'While I would not attach too much importance to this circumstance, it is not without significance as suggesting that, so far as deafness is hereditary, we might expect the birth of fewer deaf-mute children to result from the intermarriage of the deaf among themselves than from the union of every marriageable deaf person with a hearing partner.

'In the latter case the number of marriages involving the danger of transmitting deafness to the children would be twice as many as in the former case, while our figures suggest the probability of inheriting the infirmity may not be doubled when both parents, instead of one, are deaf.

'Again, the fact that in so many cases *partial* deafness in a parent is followed by deaf-mutism in a child may be of more importance than at first appears.

'Partial deafness, as is well known, is in many cases, and especially where its intensity varies very much from time to time, caused by catarrh; and it is established by medical examination that a considerable share of congenital deafness is also of a catarrhal nature.

'There is, I believe, high medical authority for holding that the tendency to catarrhal disease is apt to be inherited, and the inference would be that this disease, affecting as it does the mucous membrane, may, when inherited, attack any mucous surface, whether or not it be the same which was affected in the parent.

'In this view, not only would the children of a parent whose hearing is dulled by catarrh be more likely than others to be deaf, but there would be an intelligible reason why a couple who have perfect hearing and excellent general health may have several deaf-mute children, as we have found to be often the case.

'The explanation would be that catarrh, which in the parents may have shown itself in some other mucous surface, has in the children passed to the auditory apparatus.

'This would be similar to what observers have reported in regard to scrofula, a disease which is undoubtedly inheritable, and of which the indications may be noticed in a considerable proportion of deaf-mutes.

'On the other hand, where deafness is caused by an acute disease, as brain fever, scarlet fever, or cerebro-spinal meningitis, it does not seem probable that there would be a tendency to transmit deafness to the children.

'The whole subject is one in which the general public, as well as specialists, have an interest; and it deserves, and is likely to receive, careful investigation.

'While Dr. Bell deserves great credit for his patient gathering of statistics of deafness, as well as for his ingenious analysis and interpretation of his own figures, and while later observers have contributed additional information, the subject awaits treatment at the hands of some member of the medical faculty who unites high professional skill to familiarity with the mass of recorded facts.

'WESTON JENKINS, *Superintendent.*'

50. UTAH SCHOOL, SALT LAKE CITY.

H. C. White, Principal. No reply to circular letter received up to date, June 2, 1888. For Mr. White's views upon this subject see article quoted by the Principal of the Cathedral School, Cincinnati, p. 83.

51. NORTHERN NEW YORK INSTITUTION.

Henry C. Rider, Superintendent. No reply to circular letter received up to date, June 2, 1888.

52. FLORIDA INSTITUTE.

Park Terrell, Principal. A reply to circular letter was sent, but through some unexplained delay in the mails it had not been received up to date, June 2, 1888. In a private note Mr. Terrell says: 'I have known of several cases of inherited deafness. Two little boys at this school, the children of W. F. Pape, of Branson, Levy County, Florida. The father was born deaf, and the mother a semi-mute. Perhaps Dr. E. M. Gallaudet can give you further account of Mr. Pape, as he was at the college one or two years.'

53. WASHINGTON TERRITORY SCHOOL.

James Watson, Director, expresses no opinion upon this question.

54. NEW ORLEANS PUBLIC SCHOOL.

'My opinion is that to make any effort to secure the passage of a law to prohibit the intermarriage of the deaf would amount to a most tyrannical thing; but as the best way to put a stop to the increase of the deaf I would earnestly recommend the passage of a law to prohibit the intermarriages of blood cousins.

'R. B. LAWRENCE, *Principal.*'

55. EVANSVILLE DEAF-MUTE SCHOOL, INDIANA.

'A deaf-mute in Iowa married a woman whose hearing was perfect, and had two children by her—one a deaf-mute son who died childless, the other a hearing daughter who married a hearing man, and gave birth to two deaf-mute daughters and a hearing son. This son married a hearing woman, and had by her a deaf-mute son. One of the daughters married a deaf-mute, and bore a hearing son. I have no confidence in the inheritance of deafness by offspring, as I doubt if there has been a deaf child born among about 1,000 schoolmates of mine who went to school with me at the Danville, Ky., Indianapolis, Ind., and Washington, D. C., Institutions.

'CHARLES KERNEY, *Principal.*'

56. LA CROSSE DAY SCHOOL, WISCONSIN.

'I have no data whatever. So far as I can judge, this matter is simply a "bugbear." I do not think there is even a possibility of a "race of deaf-mutes" resulting from intermarriage of deaf-mutes.

'ALBERT HARDY, *Superintendent of Schools.*'

57. NEW MEXICO SCHOOL.

'All the pupils here except one, who has a deaf cousin (probably a young man in Kansas), have no deaf relatives. I was made deaf by some unknown sickness at the age of nearly two years, and graduated from the Wisconsin School. Mrs. Larsan, a graduate from the Clarke Institute, became deaf at the age of thirteen years. We now have one child nearly two years old neither deaf nor dumb. He can hear and talk. There are three deaf families, having deaf children in Wisconsin, and two in Chicago Ill. This is all I know of.

'LARS M. LARSAN, *Principal.*'

PRIVATE AND DENOMINATIONAL SCHOOLS.

1. WHIPPLE'S HOME SCHOOL, CONN.

'I think it would be much better for the deaf never to marry, as I have known of no instance where there were not more deaf people brought into the world as the result, and I consider them an unfortunate class.

'MARGARET HAMMOND, *Principal.*'

2. GERMAN EVANGELICAL LUTHERAN INSTITUTE, NORRIS, MICHIGAN.

'We know very little about it.

'D. H. UHLIG, *Principal.*'

3. ST. JOHN'S CATHOLIC INSTITUTE, ST. FRANCIS, WISCONSIN.

Rev. Chas. Fessler, Principal, expressed no opinion upon this question.

4. FREDERICK KNAPP INSTITUTE, BALTIMORE.

Frederick Knapp, Principal. No reply to circular letter received up to date, June 2, 1888.

5. VOICE AND HEARING SCHOOL, ENGLEWOOD, ILLINOIS.

Mary McCowen expresses no opinion upon this question.

6. MARY GARRETT'S PRIVATE SCHOOL, PHILADELPHIA.

'Cases of intermarriages of the deaf have not come under my notice, and I have not had time to investigate the subject, although it is one of great interest. I have known of cases where deaf and idiotic offspring were the result of the marriage of cousins. In trying to obtain reliable statistics about my pupils I find that when parents are related or have deaf relatives they are loth to admit it, and frequently do not state the facts as they are. The parents of a bright little fellow of four who is rapidly learning articulation and language told me he had no deaf relatives, and I afterwards discovered he has a deaf uncle in a feeble-minded school. I think, therefore, that it requires a great deal of careful investigation to get at the real facts.

'MARY S. GARRETT, *Principal.*'

7. MARIA CONSILIA INSTITUTE.

Sister Adèle, Principal, expresses no opinion upon this question.

8. CINCINNATI ORAL SCHOOL.

Katharine Westendorf, Principal. No reply to circular letter received to date, June 2, 1888.

9. CHICAGO CATHOLIC SCHOOL.

No reply to circular letter received to date, June 2, 1888.

10. MISS KEELER'S ARTICULATION CLASS, NEW YORK.

Sarah Warren Keeler, Principal, expresses no opinion upon this question.

11. CATHEDRAL SCHOOL (CATHOLIC), CINCINNATI.

'The accompanying clipping will show how we stand as to the question of intermarriage of the deaf.

'E. P. CLEARY, *Principal*.'

(*From the Salt Lake City Daily Tribune.*)

'EDITOR *Tribune*: In your last Sunday issue there was a remark quoted from the Chicago *Herald* to the effect that a deaf race of men seems to be the inevitable result of schools for deaf-mutes. "The close association with one another leads to intermarriage, with offspring inheriting the common infirmity." This is what the *Herald* says is the result.

'This is a curious study in human heredity, one well worth the best efforts of the scientists, one of whom, Prof. Bell, of telephone fame, has made exhaustive researches upon the subject. As to whether it is true that deafness is inevitably transmitted from generation to generation by the intermarriage of deaf-mutes, the following facts will show:

'1. The world is 6,000 years old, and during all these years deaf-mutes have been born; they have intermarried and died, leaving children after children, yet nowhere on the face of the earth is a hereditary race of deaf-mutes found.

'2. The proportion of adventitious or accidental deafness caused by sickness is greater than that of congenital "born-so" deafness, as the records of all institutions for the deaf show. The annual report of the Ohio Institution for 1887 gives a list of 2.216 deaf-mutes as having been taught within its walls during the 61 years of its existence, and the number is divided as follows:

Adventitious deafness	1,314
Congenital "	663
Unknown "	239
Total	2,216

'3. Deaf-mutes, in the majority of cases, have borne children that have lived to maturity, married others, and died in perfect possession of all their senses without transmitting the infirmity of the first generation. This is a well-authenticated fact among the deaf-mutes of Boston and New York City, "where they most do congregate."

'4. While there happens in several cases to be a deaf-mute offspring in deaf-mute families, the same thing is true in cases where a deaf-mute had married a hearing person. How do you account for this reversion of nature—viz., deaf-mutes bearing hearing children, and mixed couples bearing deaf-mute children? This shows that there is evidently no law of heredity in deafness. It may be acquired independently of nature.

'5. While there is the least danger of transmission between deaf-mutes who have become accidentally deaf, it is greater in cases of congenital deafness—that is, when both parents were born deaf—but by a curious law of affinity, marriages between congenitals is rare among the deaf-mutes; therefore, the infirmity is likely to be wiped out in the second generation.

'6. The sage remark of the Chicago *Herald*, "the close association with one another leads to offspring inheriting the common infirmity," has been refuted by an experiment that was made thirty years ago by a colony of deaf-mutes in Kansas. Like birds of a feather, deaf-mutes gathered there from the hills of New England, from the plains of the Middle States, and from the Sunny South, to form a community, or, as the Chicago *Herald* put it, "a race of deaf men." A town government was set up with a deaf mayor and deaf selectmen, and the experiment seemed to progress favorably. But the projectors had forgotten their hearing children, who multiplied in number and usurped the government. Doubtless the leading men longed for a race of deaf offspring, but it was not given to them to be so blessed. Where is that deaf community now? Go ask the four winds of heaven. The new order of things brought on dissensions among the silent community, and it broke up, scattering them all over the Union, and the much-dreaded deaf race was blotted from the face of the earth like the extinct race of mastodons of "ye ancient times." There is no more danger of a hereditary race of deaf-mutes spreading than there is of the revival of the gigantic animal just mentioned. The Chicago *Herald* man may rest his soul in peace. He will never live to see a deaf race of men.

'7. Here in Utah there are over two hundred deaf-mutes, and as yet no case of deaf-mute parents having deaf-mute children has been reported; while, on the other hand, there are several married deaf-mutes who have children in perfect possession of all their senses. Neither my wife nor myself were born deaf, neither of us has any deaf-mute relatives living or dead, and our child is blessed with perfect auditory and vocal organs, and the danger of deafness is no greater in her case than in that of any other children. If she ever becomes deaf, it will not be through heredity, but from scarlet fever or cerebro-spinal meningitis, those dreaded diseases from whose fatal effects children escape only by giving up one of their most important senses as a sort of propitiatory sacrifice to death.

'8. Other statistics serve to show that intermarriage of blood relations is the most frequent cause of deafness. Degrees of consanguinity as between cousins are productive of more "ills that the flesh is heir to" than any other known cause of heredity. The deaf-mutes of Oregon are said to owe their infirmity more to blood relationship than to accidental sickness, on account of the intermarriage of the first families there. As every breeder of horses knows, the highest and best qualities of race-horses are frequently obtained by what is called inbreeding, so the worst defects may also be transmitted from the same cause. 'H. C. WHITE,

'*Principal of the Utah School for the Deaf*.'

12. SARAH FULLER HOME.

Sarah Fuller, Supervising Principal. See report of Horace Mann School.

SCHOOLS IN THE DOMINION OF CANADA.

1. CATHOLIC INSTITUTION (MALE), MONTREAL.

J. B. Manseau, Principal. No reply to circular letter received to date, June 2, 1888.

2. CATHOLIC INSTITUTION (FEMALE), MONTREAL.

Sister Mary of Mercy, Superioress. No reply to circular letter received to date, June 2, 1888.

3. HALIFAX INSTITUTION.

'Such marriages should not be encouraged, but cannot be prevented or prohibited. Out of 30 marriages among my own former pupils, 20 have been to deaf-mutes and 10 to hearing persons. So far there are probably between 30 and 40 children in these families, and only in one case do the offspring of these unions share the infirmity of the parents; but that case is sadly noteworthy, all the children, five in number, being deaf-mutes (one of the five is dead and the mother also). In this instance, however, the children were, so to speak, *doubly stamped*, there being several deaf and dumb in the families on both sides, as well as deafness in one of them three generations back.

'Out of 72 families connected with the Halifax Institution, where the pupils were all *congenital* mutes, 39 families had an average of about 3 congenital deaf-mutes to each; 73 families had an average of about 2 congenital deaf-mutes to each.

'Out of 147 families, there were 68 cases where the pupils had brothers and sisters or other relatives deaf and dumb or otherwise defective.

'Out of 120 families containing 189 deaf-mutes, of whom 131 were congenital, 45 were consanguineous marriages, *five-ninths* of the parents being *first cousins*. Further figures may be found in my Report for 1877.

'J. SCOTT HUTTON, *Principal*.'

4. ONTARIO INSTITUTION.

In a note, dated May 10, 1885, the Superintendent says: 'In reply to yours of April 30, I have filled up some of the blanks, and for the information asked for in some of the others referred you to some printed reports, copies of which I send you. In addition thereto I may say that, in Sept., 1885, we admitted a small boy named Gregg, whose mother is deaf and dumb—the only one that has ever been received. Up to this time I have not learned of any of the children of deaf-mute couples in Ontario being mutes.'

(*Extract from* 1883-4 *Report*.)

'Much has been said and written during the last three months about a deaf-mute variety of the human race, and fears were expressed by the writers that the intermarriage of deaf-mutes perpetuated a race of deaf-mutes, and was strongly disapproved of. A great many statistics were collected from various sources to prove the theory. Of course, I cannot tell what the facts are in connection with other institutions, but, from the information we have here, I am led to believe that the conclusions drawn are erroneous. Six hundred and sixty-one children have attended, or are in attendance, at this institution, and from the records I learn that not a single parent of these children is deaf and dumb. A few of their grandparents were mutes, and some of their great-great-grandparents. Of those who have been here and have intermarried, I have been unable to find that one of their offspring is deaf and dumb. The facts would seem to indicate that the intermarriage amongst the deaf and dumb is not the means of bringing into the world children similarly afflicted, and that deaf and dumb children are usually the offspring of hearing and speaking persons.

'R. MATHISON, *Superintendent*.'

Under date May 16, 1888, Mr. Mathison forwards the following particulars concerning an apparently deaf child in Ontario, both of whose parents are deaf:

'I forward you extended history of the Terrell family.

'William Terrell, Maria Terrell, parents of 8 children noted below:

'Both hearing persons, not related in the slightest degree; no deaf-mutes have been known in either of their families, but they are the parents of 5 mutes in a family of 8.

'1. William James, aged 39, mute, married. His wife and her sister both lost their hearing at an early age by sickness. Has had 3 children: one died in infancy, one at 13 months old, *and the other, now* 2½ *years of age, is apparently deaf and dumb*.

'2. Benjamin, mute, married, wife also deaf; 6 children, who can all hear.

'3. Rose, deaf-mute, married; has had five children—4 living; husband also deaf: children's faculties unimpaired.

'4. Mary, deaf-mute, husband also deaf; 1 child, who can hear and speak.

'5. Samuel, hearing, married, wife can hear; 2 children, both can hear.

'6. Bessie, hearing, married, husband semi-mute; 1 child, who can hear.

'7. John, deaf-mute, single.

'8. Maria, hearing, single.

'The 2½-year old child of William Terrell is the only congenital deaf-mute child of a deaf-mute father I have heard of here. In the Gregg case the mother lost hearing at 4 years of age, and this child at 2 years of age.'

5. MACKAY INSTITUTE, MONTREAL.

Harriet E. McGann, Superintendent, expresses no opinion upon this question.

6. NEW BRUNSWICK INSTITUTION.

A. H. Abell, Principal. No reply to circular letter received to date, June 2, 1888.

7. FREDERICKTON INSTITUTION.

Albert F. Woodbridge, Principal. No reply to circular letter received to date, June 2, 1888.

SCIENTIFIC TESTIMONY.

Relating to the possibility of the formation of a deaf variety of the human race in America and the conditions necessary to establish it.

From Professor EDWARD D. COPE, *Editor of the 'American Naturalist' and member of the National Academy of Sciences.*

'No. 2102 Pine street, Phila., May 8, 1888.

'DEAR MR. BELL: Your letter of May 5th is at hand. You desire my opinion relative to the possibility of the formation of a deaf variety of the human race. Also, given certain conditions, a deaf variety should arise. But what are these conditions? This is the point on which you wish my assistance.

'According to my views of evolution it is quite possible for a deaf or deaf-mute variety of man to arise and be perpetuated. It is not more improbable than that blind species of animals should arise and be perpetuated, a circumstance which has often occurred in the evolution of animals. The subject can be considered under two heads—first, the origin of such deaf-mutes; second, the perpetuation.

'First, as to the origin. Of this matter I know but little. In the case of sight, disuse is supposed to be the sufficient cause. Disuse of hearing is, however, difficult to experience in this world. Excessive use, that is, the constant presence of excessive noise, might, and does, cause deafness. The greater number of cases are, however, to be accounted for probably by disease. Dumbness would ultimately follow deafness.

'Second, as to perpetuation. The interbreeding of deaf-mutes should produce a deaf-mute race after a considerable lapse of time. Hearing is a sense of great antiquity, and the tendency to reproduce normal organs of hearing is so strong that they are to be looked for in the children of deaf-mutes for a long period. Reversions to hearing children would be frequent. But the number, *i. e.*, proportion, of deaf-mute children would constantly increase with succeeding intermarriages. It would, however, take a long period to produce a race of deaf-mutes which would not from time to time revert by producing normal children. But by preventing all marriages with normal persons such a result could in time be brought about.

'The fact that you mention—viz., that the proportion of deaf-mutes born of deaf-mutes is larger than in the case of normal people—is consistent with the view you take, which I believe to be a correct one. It is sustained by what we know of the evolution of vertebrated animals.

I am, very truly, yours,

'EDWD. D. COPE.

'P. S.—I may be more specific with regard to some of the vertebrata. In the Batrachian class the organs of hearing have undergone with time a great degeneracy in the series of the *Urodelæ* (the tailed division). The semicircular canals only exist with their auditory nerve branches; but there are no ossicles, except the lid-shaped stapes, and no external ear. They are descended from types (*Ganocephala* and *Rhachitomi*) which had both. The *Urodelæ* (salamanders) are probably not entirely deaf, but their hearing must be very obscure. They are mute, except the species of *Desmognathus*, which chirrup sometimes, and *Amphiuma*, which does the same. They are all more or less subterranean or aquatic, and the condition of their auditory organs may be therefore due to disuse. The history of these regions will be found in the June number of the "American Naturalist."'

From Professor ALPHEUS HYATT, *Professor in Harvard University, Member of the National Academy of Sciences.*

'Boston Society of Natural History,
'Berkeley street, Boston, Mass., May 8, 1888.

'DEAR PROFESSOR BELL: If congenitally deaf-mutes have been led by association, or otherwise, to seek each other in marriage, there can be no doubt that the most favorable conditions for the formation of a race of deaf-mutes has been brought about.

'This goes without saying on the principle of the transmission of hereditary tendencies, and certainly it cannot be a wise system which fosters such marriages.

'If such marriages should continue through several generations, I should regard it as almost certain that a deaf-mute race would be produced. It would be, to my mind, no serious objection that a proportion of the first generation of the offspring of deaf-mutes should be normally formed (*i.e.*, have good hearing); I should expect that the following generations would have a steadily-increasing proportion of deaf-mutes, and, in a certain number of generations, that the major number, or all, would be deaf. I am not a practical breeder, but have been accustomed to study series of animals, with the view of testing what characteristics were hereditary. I have found that my experience coincided with that of breeders and the opinions of writers like Ribot and others, who hold that all characteristics tend to become inherited.

'It would be a very strange contradiction of experience and theory if a deaf and dumb race were not produced by continual intermarriage of persons afflicted in this way. In fact, the onus of proof lies with those who assume the negative rather than with those who take the affirmative on this question.

'Wishing you success in your humanitarian efforts, I am very sincerely yours,

'ALPHEUS HYATT.'

From Dr. BOWDITCH, *Professor in Harvard University, Member of the National Academy of Sciences.*

'Physiological Laboratory, Harvard Medical School,
'Boylston and Exeter Streets, Boston, May 13, 1888.

'DEAR PROFESSOR BELL: I have received your letter of May 5, relating to the formation of a deaf variety of the human race.

'I do not consider myself an authority on questions of heredity and breeding, but, as I understand the doctrine of evolution, there can be no doubt that you are perfectly right in maintaining that for the production of a true breed of deaf-mutes it is not necessary that the *majority* of the children of congenital deaf-mute parents should be born deaf, but only that the *proportion* of deaf offspring of such marriages should be greater than in the case of marriages between persons who are not deaf-mutes. That this is really the case I think you have shown very conclusively, and I have always considered your paper as a very valuable demonstration that the human race is capable of modification by selective breeding, as well as a useful warning of the danger which attends the purely philanthropic method of dealing with social problems.

Yours very truly,

'H. P. BOWDITCH.'

From Professor WILLIAM H. BREWER, *Norton Professor of Agriculture in Yale University, Member of the National Academy of Sciences.*

'New Haven, Conn., May 25, 1888.

'MY DEAR SIR: You ask me for a statement of my "views upon the possibility of the formation of a deaf variety of the human race by the continued intermarriage of congenitally deaf-mutes." Of such a possibility I have no doubt whatever.

'As the subject is one of great interest and importance, I will give you at some length the general grounds of my opinion.

'The term *Breed*, as used by farmers, stock-breeders and fanciers, means a variety of domestic animals. Two attributes are necessary in the constitution of a breed—namely, the members must have some distinctive and recognizable character, and this character must be hereditary. The distinctive character may be but one single "point," to be bred for, and the special development of any one "point" may become the foundation of a breed.

'In practice, however, breeders usually recognize a combination of points more or less correlated to each other, and all bearing on the special uses or beauties of the breed.

'The heredity of the distinctive character is essential, because, if not transmitted to the offspring as a rule, then the special points are but individual peculiarities. Individual peculiarities may or may not be transmitted by heredity, but they are liable to be, however acquired. Such peculiarities may be transmitted to some of the descendants and not to others; they may be transmitted entire or only in part; they may be transmitted to the immediate offspring, or they may be dormant in the offspring and reappear in succeeding descendants.

'A breed is uniform only in those points which are considered essential to that breed. It may vary greatly in other characters. For example, the English thoroughbred (horse) is of many colors; the Trakene is of but one color; Shorthorns are variously colored; Devons are of but one color, and so of other examples. But if from changes in the fashion, changes in the market, or any other cause, it becomes desirable to fix any character before varied, that is easily brought about.

'As to the origin of existing breeds, some are ancient, and their actual origin is unknown. Others are modern, and of some of these historical breeds we have a reasonably complete history. Some of these breeds are already completed and finished, as is the English thoroughbred; others are in process of evolution, as is the American trotter. Both these breeds are especially bred for speed, but are varied in their other characters. Other modern breeds are uniform in many characters, as for example the Poland-China hog and the Plymouth Rock fowl. Many of the ancient breeds which were well defined long before herd-books or flock-registers were known, have been changed in modern times; characters have become strictly hereditary ("fixed") which were before uncertain; and other characters have become uniform which formerly varied. For example, the Galloway cattle were formerly mostly horned, but are now polled; Jersey cattle and Newfoundland dogs were formerly mostly spotted, but have now solid colors: the ancient Merino sheep have diverged into distinct sub-breeds, of which the Saxon, the French, and the American Merino are well-known examples.

'We have so complete a history of the processes employed by which new breeds have been created and old ones changed, that the principles involved are as well understood as are those pertaining to any other branch of biological science.

'However different the details may have been in practice, the essential and controlling factor has been *artificial selection*.

'A breed may be founded on any character which is transmissible. Almost any character is sometimes transmissible, and, if so at all, its heredity may be increased and fixed by continued selection. The uniformity of transmission by heredity is related to pedigree, and the individuals vary much more during the early history of a breed than later, and after herd-books or pedigree registers are established. These differences between individuals are sometimes very profound, extending even to important anatomical characters. For example, the middle of the last century the cattle of the Galloway breed were mostly horned, and that character continued so long as the presence or absence of horns was a mere fancy of the breeder. The time came when the hornless ones brought a slightly higher price; such were then selected more commonly for breeding, and during the first years of the present century most of the individuals were hornless, or with only scurs—that is, small horns attached to the skin only, and not to the skull by a bony core. After the herd-books were established for recording their pedigree, and associations for deciding what points of character the breed must have, and what they may not, and which denied record to an animal with even a scur, these disappeared, and now the breed is entirely hornless. Other equally instructive examples might be cited.

'In the creation of a new breed, or the changing of an old one, we may say that we determine the character by selection; we establish and fix it by heredity, and we ensure it by pedigree.

'It is conceded that the same biological laws apply to man and brute alike. I am not aware that any eminent biologist, naturalist, or breeder denies this. Let us now consider the especial case under discussion.

'1st. Let considerable numbers of deaf-mutes marry. This is the selection, and deafness is the character.

'2d. If they have any congenitally deaf offspring (and we know they do), let these again intermarry. This increases the heredity of the character.

'3d. Continue this process for a few generations. This establishes the pedigree and enhances the results. How many generations are required to establish a new breed out of old materials has never been determined, but numerous authorities and associations have agreed as to the number of generations of ancestors of an established breed which should be required as equivalent to pure blood for record in herd-books and pedigree registers, and therefore suitable for perpetuating the breed. Five generations of sires and four of dams is a common rule, and I imagine that the chances of a child being born with hearing would be small if all its ancestors for a like number of generations had been congenitally deaf. It is, however, only in modern times, and since the days of printed pedigree records, that breeds have been kept so pure, and the special characters so uniformly transmitted. Such is still the case with all races of civilized man, where we have a greater variety of character than in the better defined breeds of animals, because of less purity of pedigree. So in the case of the intermarriage of the deaf, the liability of being born deaf would be diminished by intermarriage with hearing persons.

'The only argument against the formation of a breed of men in whom complete or partial deafness will be a prevalent character is, that many of the deaf-mutes have become so by disease or accident, and not by heredity. But no fact is better established or more universally recognized among breeders, than that many forms of unsoundness that may be of accidental origin may become hereditary. Ring-bone, spavin, and similar diseases are often as truly the result of accident as deafness, and these are considered fit cause of rejection in the prize stallion shows, as note the recent practice and the abundant literature on the subject. Defects of the organs of sense are especially noted in this connection, more especially those of the eye.

'In the light of present biological science, and of the breeder's art, it is inconceivable that the process of selection of deaf parents should not establish a deaf variety of the human race.

'Yours truly,

'WM. H. BREWER.

'Professor Alexander Graham Bell, Washington, D. C.'

From Professor SIMON NEWCOMB, *Superintendent of the United States 'Nautical Almanac,' Member of the National Academy of Sciences.*

'Washington, D. C., May 2, 1888.

'DEAR PROFESSOR BELL,—I have your circular of April 30, to which you append a request for my opinion regarding the possibility of the formation of a deaf variety of the human race by the continual intermarriage of congenital deaf-mutes.

'That the continual intermarriage of persons possessing any peculiarity tends to make that peculiarity permanent is, I believe, a recognized law, constantly applied by breeders of new species in the animal and vegetable world. The result will, however, depend upon the general policy adopted.

'If we take all the congenital deaf-mutes now living, and form them into a community into which no new blood enters in subsequent generations, there would be no tendency towards the formation of a deaf variety. The second generation would, as you have shown, contain an undue proportion of congenitally deaf, but these deaf would still constitute a minority of the total population, and continuous intermarriage of the whole mass would only result in the formation of a community in which an undue proportion of the members would be congenitally deaf. To form a permanent type it is necessary that the hearing offspring should be continually eliminated from the community, and their places taken by deaf persons born outside. All the conditions necessary to the ultimate formation of a permanent deaf-mute variety would then be fulfilled. Moreover, to bring about this result, it is not at all necessary that a separate community of the deaf should be formed. The system of deaf marrying deaf will lead to the same result, although the parties may be scattered through the whole population, instead of being aggregated into a community.

'But this general statement does not give us any conception of the time which might be required to form the variety in question. Could breeders of human beings do as breeders of plants and certain animals can do, produce hundreds of offspring from a single pair, select those having the required peculiarity and eliminate the rest, the process would be very rapid. But, as human beings breed, it would be very slow. I have essayed a calculation as to the result of the policy in question on certain hypotheses; but I am unable to say how near these hypotheses approach the truth.

'What we really want is a complete census of children born of marriages between the deaf. The proportion of deaf children to hearing children would then give us the probability that a child so born would be deaf.

'In your memoir upon the formation of a deaf variety of the human race, you found that among the cases received into American institutions for the deaf and dumb 124 had both parents deaf. I also conclude from the table in Appendix Z that you found about 327 cases of marriages between deaf-mutes. In the absence of more complete statistics I shall assume that the ratio of deaf-mute children, both of whose parents were deaf-mutes, as collected by you, to the number of deaf who married deaf-mutes (654) gives a rude approximation to the required probability that deaf-mute parents will have deaf-mute offspring in the first generation. I assume this proportion to be one fifth.

'According to the law of heredity, the probability will increase in the case of each successive generation. In the absence of any exact knowledge of this law, I shall assume that the probability of deaf-mute parents having deaf-mute children increases through consecutive generations according to the series

$$\tfrac{1}{5},\ \tfrac{1}{3},\ \tfrac{1}{2},\ \tfrac{2}{3},\ \tfrac{3}{4},\ \tfrac{4}{5},\ \&c.$$

'Then assuming that we form an ideal community of n intermarried deaf-mutes, that in each generation we eliminate from this community the hearing children, and add n deaf-mutes from outside, and that each couple has, on the average, two children who grow up and marry, the number of the community at the end of $m + 2$ generation will be given by the series

$$\tfrac{2}{3}n + \tfrac{n}{5}\left(1 + \tfrac{1}{2} + \tfrac{1}{3} + \tfrac{1}{4} + \tfrac{1}{m}\right).$$

'The series within parentheses would correspond to the numbers of the community who were more likely than not to have deaf-mute children. In this case the formation of the deaf variety would be very slow, though ultimately it would be quite sure. At the end of the twelfth generation we should have only $\frac{n}{5}$ deaf-mutes more likely than not to have offspring of the same kind; at the end of the twentieth generation about $\frac{n}{4}$; but in each succeeding generation the probability of deaf-mute offspring would go on increasing.

'Until we have more exact statistics of heredity I do not see how it is possible to do more than suppose a hypothetical case of this kind. The most precise statement I can make would be in the following form:—

'1. The continual intermarriage of deaf-mutes through successive generations would ultimately result in the gradual formation of a deaf-mute variety.

'2. But this tendency would be very slow, and many generations would have to pass away before the variety would be permanently established.

'Yours very faithfully,

'SIMON NEWCOMB.'

From Professor W. K. BROOKS, *Professor of Morphology in Johns Hopkins University, Baltimore, Md., and Member of the National Academy of Sciences.*

'I MUST preface the discussion of this subject by a definition. An *inherited characteristic* is one which the organism has derived from the fertilized germ. It may or may not have been manifested by the parents or other ancestors. If it is more common among either the ancestors, or the brothers and sisters and cousins of the organism, than it is in the race at large, this fact is scientific proof that it is an inherited characteristic according to the definition, for the germ out of which it developed is its only bond of connection with its collateral relations or its ancestors.

'The experience of all breeders of domesticated animals and cultivated plants proves that only two conditions are necessary for the establishment of a new race or breed with any designated characteristic: 1st, the existence, in sufficient numbers to permit of propagation for a number of generations, without interbreeding, of individuals in which the desired peculiarity is inherited; and 2d, the rigorous selection for breeding, generation after generation, of those children who inherit the designated characteristic.

'All experience shows that if the peculiarity is *inherited*, as the word is defined above—that is, if the organism has received it from the fertilized germ, and if it has offspring by another organism with *the same* inherited peculiarity, the progeny of this union will contain a marked percentage of children with the same peculiarity; and that this percentage will increase rapidly in successive generations, and will soon approximate to 100.

'Proof of this statement will be given soon. It is necessary, first, to point out that a congenital peculiarity is not necessarily an inherited peculiarity.

'For example, so-called congenital deafness in human children may be divided into four classes: 1st. Cases where there is no disposition to deafness, and where the hearing is lost by accidents after birth, but before the time when normal children manifest consciousness of sounds. 2d. Cases where there is no predisposition to deafness, but where hearing is lost by accident before birth. 3d. Cases where there is an inherited predisposition to deafness. 4th. Cases where actual deafness is inherited.

'These four classes cannot be distinguished by any intrinsic evidence. If, however, a deaf child has more deaf brothers, or sisters, or cousins, or ancestors, than the average, for the community, this fact may be regarded as scientific evidence that it belongs to either class 3 or class 4.

'The question whether classes 1 and 2 transmit their peculiarities by inheritance is still under discussion, and much difference of opinion exists, but we have abundant proof that this is true of classes 3 and 4.

'It has been asserted, however, that inasmuch as each child is descended not only from its parents, but also from a long line of more remote ancestors, the influence, in inheritance, of an abnormal or exceptional parental peculiarity may be so overbalanced by the influence of the innumerable series of normal ancestors that the child will not resemble its parents, but will tend to revert to the normal type.

'This is undoubtedly true when the characteristic is not inherited by the parent, but is induced by other influences. It is not true, however, in cases where both parents have *the same inherited* peculiarity.

'It is only in a figurative sense that a child is descended from remote ancestors as distinguished from its parents, for all the matter in the germ comes to it from the bodies of its parents. If, then, each parent has the same inherited peculiarity—for example, a predisposition to deafness—this signifies that the sum or resultant of the combined influence of their ancestry tended to this result, to which it must necessarily tend in the child as well. All authorities upon inheritance are fully agreed that in such cases the child is enormously more likely than a child with normal parents to exhibit and to transmit the same peculiarity.

'So far as I am aware, the only authority which can be quoted as apparently opposed to this opinion is that of Galton; and an examination of this paper will, I think, show that in this case the opposition is apparent rather than real, and that his results are quite reconcilable with the view which has been advocated above.

'He says ("Nature," September 4, 1885), "It is some years since I made an extensive series of experiments in the produce of seeds of different sizes, but of the same species. * * * It appears from these experiments that the offspring did *not* tend to resemble their parent seeds in size, but to be always more mediocre than they; to be smaller than they if the parents were large; to be larger than the parents if the parents were very small;" and that the analysis of the family records of heights of 205 human parents and 930 children fully confirms and goes far beyond the conclusions obtained from seeds, as it gives with great precision and unexpected coherence the numerical value of the regression towards mediocrity. He says that this regression is a necessary result of the fact that "the child inherits partly from his parents, partly from his ancestors. Speaking generally, the farther his genealogy goes back, the more numerous and varied will his ancestors become, until they cease to differ from any equally numerous sample taken at haphazard from the race at large. Their mean stature will then be the same as that of the race; in other words, it will be mediocre." He illustrates this by comparing the result of the combination in the child of the mean stature of the race with the peculiarities of its parents to the result of pouring a uniform proportion of pure water into a vessel of wine. It dilutes the wine to a certain fraction of its original strength, whatever that strength may have been.

'He then goes on to the deduction that the law of regression to the type of the race "tells heavily against the full hereditary transmission of any rare and valuable gift, as only a few of the many children would resemble the parents. The more exceptional the gift the more exceptional will be the good fortune of a parent who has a son who equals, and still more if he has a son who surpasses him. The law is even-handed; it levies the same heavy succession tax on the transmission of badness as well as goodness. If it discourages the extravagant expectations of gifted parents that their children will inherit all their powers, it no less discountenances extravagant fears that they will inherit all their weaknesses and diseases. * * * Let it not for a moment be supposed that the figures invalidate the general doctrine that the children of a gifted pair are much more likely to be gifted than the children of a mediocre pair; what it asserts is that the ablest of the children of one gifted pair is not likely to be as gifted as the ablest of all the children of many mediocre pairs."

'Interesting and valuable as these results from the study of stature are, a little examination will show that they have no application to the case stated above; and there is ample evidence that if Galton had studied by themselves the cases where the parents were alike in stature, both short or both tall, and had picked out from among these the ones where the exceptional stature was due to the same peculiarity—*for example*, a very long femur—and if from these he had again selected those in which each parent had relatives with the same peculiarity, he would have obtained a very different result.

'It is well known that an hereditary peculiarity—that is, one which is shared by other members of the family—often shows an astonishing tendency to persist in later generations, quite independently of the time it has already persisted, and that, too, when one of the parents in each generation is normal.

'Of this a most remarkable illustration may be found on page 30 of Professor Bell's memoir on "The Formation of a Deaf Variety of the Human Race."

'In the H. family of Kentucky two brothers and a sister inherited from their parents a common predisposition towards deafness, as is shown by the fact that they all became ancestors of congenital deaf-mutes, although only one of them was deaf.

'We have no information regarding the first generation—the parents—although they were probably not deaf. In the second generation one of the three children was deaf. In the third generation all the grandchildren were deaf. In the fourth generation the records are incomplete, but all the children which are known, six in number, are deaf.

'In the fifth generation selection was introduced, as three of the children married deaf-mutes. The records are very incomplete, but of the six descendants known one is deaf.

'This remarkable case is given in the following table, and it seems to show that in the case of an inherited peculiarity the tendency of the children to resemble their parents may be vastly greater than their tendency to revert to the normal type of the race, even when there is no selection and one of the parents in each generation is normal:

First generation.	No information concerning their hearing.				
Second generation.	Son deaf.	Daughter hearing.	Daughter hearing.		
Third generation.	Seven deaf children.	Two deaf children.	Two deaf sons.		
Fourth generation.	No information concerning the descendants.	One child had two deaf children; no information concerning the other.	One son did not marry; the other had two deaf daughters, D¹, D², and one deaf son, S.		
Fifth generation.	No information.	No information.	D¹. Married a deaf man. One deaf son.	D². Married a deaf man. No children.	S. Married a deaf woman. Five hearing children. In this case the mother is not known to have inherited deafness.

'I find among the notes which Professor Bell has kindly placed in my hands another instructive case. O. H. was the only deaf child in a family of 11 children. He had 4 children, 2 of them deaf, and 3 grandchildren, 2 of them deaf, so that the relative predisposition of his parents, himself, and his children to transmit deafness may be represented by the series of fractions $\frac{1}{11}$, $\frac{1}{3}$, $\frac{2}{3}$, $= \frac{3}{33}$, $\frac{11}{33}$, $\frac{22}{33}$.

'These facts, and many more which might be quoted from our stock of information regarding domesticated animals, show that hereditary peculiarities are often very persistent, independently of selection, and the experience of all breeders shows that this tendency is greatly intensified when both parents have *the same* inherited peculiarity.

'Not only is this the case, but it is also well known, and proved by many observations, that the normal or type to which the average children of exceptional parents tend to revert may itself be rapidly modified in any desired direction.

'In proof of this I refer to the following experiments in selection by Fritz Müller (Ein Zuchtungsversuch an Mais. Kosmos, 1886, 2, 1, p. 22).

'Yellow corn is very variable in many respects. The number of rows of kernels on the cob is usually from 8 to 16, cobs with 10 or 12 rows being the most common, while one with 18 or 20 rows is very seldom found. After searching through several hundred cobs, Fr. Müller found one ear with 18 rows, but none with more.

'In 1867 he sowed at different times, and in such a way as to prevent crossing, (1) seed from the cob with 18 rows; (2) the seed from the finest 16-rowed ear; and (3) the seed from the finest 14-rowed ear. In 1868 he sowed (1) seed from a 16-rowed ear which had grown from seed from a 16-rowed ear; (2) seed from an 18-rowed ear from 16-rowed seed; and (3) seed from an 18-rowed ear from 18-rowed seed. In 1869 he sowed (1) seed from an 18-rowed ear with 18-rowed parents and grandparents; (2) seed from a 20-rowed ear with 18-rowed parents and grandparents; and (3) seed from a 22-rowed ear from seed from an 18-rowed ear produced from seed from a 16-rowed ear. The results are given in the accompanying table:

	1867.			1868.			1869.		
Number of rows on cob from which seed were taken.	14	16	18	16 16	16 18	18 18	18 18 18	18 18 20	16 18 22
Total number of cobs produced.	658	385	206	1,789	262	400	2,486	740	373
	%	%	%	%	%	%	%	%	%
8-rowed cobs......	·3	......	·3	·1	......	......	......	......	......
10-rowed cobs......	14·4	3·	1·	1·4	·8	·2	·1	......	......
12-rowed cobs......	48·0	22·8	13·	22·6	14·5	7·8	6·1	6·1	2·7
14-rowed cobs......	35·6	48·6	37·8	48·5	40·7	35·4	37·3	28·5	25·3
16-rowed cobs......	3·2	18·7	34·5	22·2	23·7	33·8	33·5	41·6	41·8
18-rowed cobs......	·5	6·8	12·6	4·9	12·3	18·2	18·6	20·2	24·1
20-rowed cobs......	......	·1	·3	·3	1·2	4·4	3·9	2·8	4·8
22-rowed cobs......	......	......	·3	......	·8	·2	·5	·8	1·
26-rowed cobs......	......	......	......	......	......	......	......	......	·5
Average.........	12·61	14·08	14·9	14·15	14·30	15·52	15·57	15·70	16·15

'It will be seen from this table that the number of ears with few rows decreases very rapidly in plants grown from seed taken from ears with many rows, and that the greater the number of rows on the ear from which the seed is taken the smaller is the number of ears produced with a small number of rows. It is also plain that, as the number of rows on the ear from which the seed was taken increases, the number of ears produced with a large number of rows increases, and that we have in each case a very considerable number of ears which equal their parents and a few which excel them, even when the parent seeds are far beyond the maximum for all ordinary corn. Fritz Müller says he has never, under ordinary conditions, except in three instances, found an ear with more than 18 rows, and Darwin puts the maximum at 20 rows; yet we have among the children of seed from a 22-rowed ear no less than 4.8 per cent., or 18 ears out of 373, with 20 rows, and one ear out of 373 with 26 rows, and it will also be seen that the number of children which equal their parents increases in each case in each successive generation.

'Thus the seed planted in 1867 from an 18-rowed ear produced 12.6% of 18-rowed children. The 18-rowed ear planted in 1868 from an 18-rowed parent produced 18.2% of 18-rowed children, and the 18-rowed seed planted in 1869 from 18-rowed parents and grandparents produced 18.6% of 18-rowed children. The series is 12.6%, 18.2%, 18.6%.

'The rapid change which took place in the "type" after only three years of selection is well shown by the following table, which gives the dominant number of rows at each sowing, and also the percentage of ears which had this number:

1867.	12 rows,	48%.	1868.	14 rows,	35.4%.
1867.	14 "	48.6%.	1869.	14 "	37.3%.
1867.	14 "	37.8%.	1869.	16 "	41.6%.
1868.	14 "	48.5%.	1869.	16 "	41.8%.

'The minimum for the third generation is equal to the mean for the first; the mean for the third generation, 16 rows, is very near the maximum for ordinary corn, and the maximum for the third generation is far beyond the maximum for the grandparents.

'I believe that a deaf race might be produced under less rigorous conditions than those which I have stated on the first page, but I am sure all authorities will agree that if these conditions are given the result will be as certain as any result can be which involves the phenomena of life. These are always so extremely complex that categorical answers to definite problems are seldom possible.'

IV. INSTRUCTION OF THE DEAF.

Views expressed by Superintendents and Principals of American and Canadian Schools for the Deaf in answer to a Circular Letter of Inquiry.

1. AMERICAN ASYLUM, HARTFORD.

'I give you statistics so far as I have time to get them accurately. For the last three years a much larger proportion of our pupils have been taught articulation than formerly, and a large share of those not taught now are those who entered before that date. Of the 57 pupils who have entered our school in the last three years only thirteen were dropped as showing too little ability or aptness in the line of articulation and lip-reading to make it worth while to continue their instruction in those branches, though some of them are excellent scholars.

'From experience here and repeated examinations of the work in oral schools I feel fully convinced that the combined system accomplishes the greatest good to the greatest number.

'JOB WILLIAMS, *Principal.*'

2. NEW YORK INSTITUTION, WASHINGTON HEIGHTS.

Chauncey N. Brainard, Superintendent, Isaac L. Peet, Principal. No reply to circular letter received to date, June 2, 1888.

3. PENNSYLVANIA INSTITUTION, PHILADELPHIA.

'The combined system has no place in our school at present. Our pupils are taught either *orally* or *manually*. * * * I believe in *oral* instruction (separate oral) for all deaf children who can be successfully instructed by that method, and in *sign* instruction for those who cannot.

'A. L. E. CROUTER, *Principal.*'

4. KENTUCKY INSTITUTION, DANVILLE.

'I think, in all cases possible, articulation should be taught when it is even probable that the pupils will improve sufficiently to render it of practical benefit to them in after life, but at the same time I think that the semi-mutes and a few of the exceptionally bright congenitally deaf, in the proportion of about 15 to 25 per cent. of the whole, are all that can be successfully educated by this method.

'W. K. ARGO, *Superintendent.*'

5. OHIO INSTITUTION.

'Just now I am very full of work arranging for examinations and the close of school. I will endeavor to have the work done for you soon.

'AMASA PRATT, *Superintendent.*'

No reply to circular letter received to date, June 2, 1888.

6. VIRGINIA INSTITUTION.

'I do not think that more than 20 per cent of the pupils at this institution could be educated by the articulation method. I am satisfied that the "combined system" is not practicable. Children who are taught by the articulation method should be kept away from sign schools if possible. In the case of semi-mutes the articulation is useful, even in such schools as this, in enabling the pupil to retain what power of speech he possesses upon entrance, and to help him in learning to read from the lips; for congenital mutes it is, we may say, useless. I intend to make an effort to induce the three States, Maryland, Virginia, and West Virginia, to establish a branch school at Winchester, let us say, to which pupils from each of the States named can be sent, and in which instruction will be given in articulation, and by means of articulation alone, being satisfied, as I said above, that no deaf-mute who is permitted to run with other mutes out of school, using signs as their sole means of communication, will ever profit much by instruction in articulation which is given only for a brief period in each day (from ½ to 1 hour), while the rest of the 24 hours is spent either in a sign class or in company with deaf-mutes who use signs alone as a means of communication. Understand that I speak here only of what I have observed in *this* school in the course of the last 14 years. I do not pretend to make an issue with the advocates of the so-called "combined" system. They are welcome to their opinion, and I claim to be entitled to mine, and I believe I am warranted in saying that I can establish mine so far as *this* school is concerned.

'THOMAS S. DOYLE, *Principal.*'

7. INDIANA INSTITUTION.

Eli P. Baker, Superintendent, expresses no opinion upon this question.

8. TENNESSEE SCHOOL.

'We believe, that putting semi-deaf pupils in the "articulation" or "oral" class, teaches children to discriminate between the sounds of different words, or that such training improves the hearing, which we regard as one and the same thing *in results.*

'THOMAS L. MOSES, *Principal.*'

9. NORTH CAROLINA INSTITUTION.

W. J. Young, Principal, expresses no opinion upon this question.

10. ILLINOIS INSTITUTION.

'All pupils on entering the institution are examined and tried, to ascertain those who give promise of doing well in articulation. * * * Articulation is not used as the sole means of instruction in any case, but in most of these cases it is one of the means of instruction. The number varies as pupils improve.

'PHILIP G. GILLETT, *Superintendent.*'

11. GEORGIA INSTITUTION.

'We have always tried to improve the speech of those who come to us having the ability to use spoken language to even a very limited extent. * * * I have nothing to suggest relating to the instruction of the deaf that would be of value to the Commission.

'W. O. CONNOR, *Principal.*'

12. SOUTH CAROLINA INSTITUTION.

N. F. Walker, Superintendent, expresses no opinion upon this question.

13. MISSOURI INSTITUTION.

William D. Kerr, Superintendent, expresses no opinion upon this question.

14. LOUISIANA INSTITUTION.

John Jastremski, Superintendent. No reply to circular letter received to date, June 2, 1888.

15. WISCONSIN SCHOOL.

'In regard to methods of instruction, I believe that instruction by means of articulation should be closely adhered to in all cases where oral instruction is imparted, and in cases where pupils cannot avail themselves of the oral method in being taught, I would place them in classes taught by the manual method, by spelling and writing. I regard the combined method as the best for all cases, and consider manual instruction a necessity for the great majority of deaf-mutes.

'JOHN W. SWILER, *Superintendent.*'

16. MICHIGAN SCHOOL.

M. T. Gass, Superintendent, expresses no opinion upon this question.

17. MISSISSIPPI INSTITUTION.

'I am satisfied we do not have enough teachers in our institutions for the number of pupils. The smaller our classes, the better the results. While it might seem extravagant on the part of the Government to employ a teacher for every 5 or 10 pupils, yet if such a teacher is competent and faithful it would not be many years before the Government would be repaid in a large ratio by the intelligent productive power of the pupils.

'J. R. DOBYNS, *Superintendent.*'

18. IOWA INSTITUTION.

Henry W. Rothert, Superintendent, G. L. Wyckoff, Principal. No reply to circular letter received to date, June 2, 1888.

19. TEXAS ASYLUM.

W. H. Kendall, Superintendent, expresses no opinion upon this question.

20. COLUMBIA INSTITUTION.

E. M. GALLAUDET, *President.*

'(A.) Kendall School. I think that Dr. E. M. Gallaudet's statements to the Royal Commission render anything I might say in the same connection superfluous.

'JAMES DENISON, *Principal.*'

(B.) National College. E. M. Gallaudet, President. Statement made to Royal Commission, 1887.

21. ALABAMA INSTITUTION.

Jos. H. Johnson, Principal, expresses no opinion upon this question.

22. CALIFORNIA INSTITUTION.

Warring Wilkinson, Principal, expresses no opinion upon this question.

23. KANSAS INSTITUTION.

'My belief, after fifteen years experience in the work of educating the deaf, and after having made the methods used in our American institutions a careful study, with the purpose of ascertaining the best methods, or combination of methods, is that the ideal institution for the instruction of the deaf is the one where it is practicable to put into use both the sign, pure oral, and auricular methods. To do this with the greatest amount of success, however, necessarily involves a very small number of pupils to each teacher, and is therefore in most cases impracticable.

'S. T. WALKER, *Superintendent.*'

24. LE COUTEULX ST. MARY'S, BUFFALO, N. Y.

Sister Mary Ann Burke, Principal, expresses no opinion upon this question.

25. MINNESOTA SCHOOL.

'I have no hesitation in saying that for the education of the deaf at public expense, where from seven to ten years are allowed for this purpose, the combined or eclectic system succeeds in more cases than the oral. The oral system does fail in giving the necessary discipline and education for citizenship where the combined system succeeds. No conscientious man can consistently use the precious time of youth, and expend public funds for the purpose of giving a lad an accomplishment liable to fall into disuse in a few years, when he can in the same time, and with the same means, give a much better mental and moral training without the accomplishment of very imperfect and often unintelligible speech. Both systems are valuable, and neither is to be discarded entirely.

'J. L. NOYES, *Superintendent.*'

26. INSTITUTION FOR IMPROVED INSTRUCTION, NEW YORK CITY.

D. Greenberger, Principal, expresses no opinion upon this question.

27. CLARKE INSTITUTION.

Caroline A. Yale, Principal, expresses no opinion upon this subject.

28. ARKANSAS INSTITUTION.

F. D. Clarke, Principal, expresses no opinion upon this question.

29. MARYLAND SCHOOL.

'I could not, without taking more time than would be allowable, submit anything under the fourth heading, and doubt whether I could add anything to the common stock on this point.

'CHARLES W. ELY, *Principal.*'

30. NEBRASKA INSTITUTE.

John A. Gillespie, Principal, expresses no opinion upon this question.

31. HORACE MANN SCHOOL.

Sarah Fuller, Principal, expresses no opinion upon this question.

32. ST. JOSEPH'S INSTITUTE, FORDHAM, N. Y.

Madame Ernestine Nardin, President, expresses no opinion upon this question.

33. WEST VIRGINIA SCHOOL.

H. B. Gilkeson, Principal. No reply to circular letter received to date, June 2, 1888.

34. OREGON SCHOOL.

P. S. Knight, Superintendent, expresses no opinion upon this question.

35. MARYLAND SCHOOL FOR COLORED DEAF-MUTES.

F. D. Morrison, Superintendent. No reply to circular letter received to date, June 2, 1888.

36. COLORADO INSTITUTE.

John E. Ray, Superintendent, expresses no opinion upon this question.

37. CHICAGO DAY SCHOOLS.

[The Principal of these affiliated schools, Mr. Philip A. Emery, has forwarded a number of printed pamphlets containing his views relating to the instruction of the deaf. These have been bound into one volume marked 'Emery Pamphlets.'

The following extracts are passages from Mr. Emery's pamphlets which he marked as expressing his ideas. Mr. Emery is himself deaf, and was educated in one of our institutions. It should be noted that the expression 'oral children' refers to ordinary hearing and speaking children, and not to deaf children taught orally. And 'oral schools' are ordinary public schools for hearing children, and not schools for the deaf on the oral plan.—A. G. B.]

EXTRACTS.

From Pamphlet No. 1.—'A Plea for Early Mute Education, Deaf-mute Day Schools, and the Objections to them Answered.'

'Aside from the State Schools, every town and city that can muster five deaf-mute children of school age should have a deaf-mute department connected with its town or city school, under the control of the School Board, and supported out of the school fund; and arrangements should also be made to send such children to the nearest State school, after three to five years of instruction in the day school, if the State school is within easy reach (not over one hundred miles at most). But if not, and the city and adjoining counties have about 300,000 inhabitants, they should have an institution of their own. The day school system can be kept up till it has two or three classes of eight or ten pupils each, then the city should have a regularly organized institution. Hence, all those cities like Cincinnati, Louisville, Chicago, Quincy, Milwaukee, Green Bay, Toledo, Cleveland, Buffalo, Savannah, Ga., New Orleans, Fort Wayne, Lafayette, Logansport, and other cities, should by all means have day schools and a mute high school of their own.

'The high schools should be located in a healthy suburb, and should allow those pupils living in the city who desire to go home at the close of school on Fridays and return on Mondays to do so, in order to save that much of boarding expense to the State, and also that the children may be more or less under the direct home and parental influences and prevented from being entirely weaned from the same.

'A deaf-mute taken from all the good influences of a home, and thrust into a crowd of fellows of misfortune like himself, in an elegant and imposing building, and *subjected to a change of habits and exercises almost if not entirely foreign to that of a home*, is sure to acquire *habits, tastes, and ideas that render him shiftless, capricious, and visionary in after life.*

'The carrying out of false ideas narrows the educational chances of the mutes, and limits their acquirements to *one-fourth*, if that much, to what is given oral children. The very reverse should be the idea and the aim. To give mutes the most varied, the broadest, and the largest possible school training, with the least amount of State boarding, should be the prevailing idea of all the teachers and friends of the mutes. This should also be the aim and acts of the State. It savors more of *true benevolence* than sailing under the cloak of charity, which is a farce, a fraud!

'The common school law only limits the schooling of oral children from six to twenty-one—*i. e.*, as a free gift, it schools them FIFTEEN YEARS. In the mute State schools the pupils formerly got only FIVE YEARS from their A B C to graduation! By what authority and moral right the State or Trustees of mute schools can limit the mutes to only five years, or a day less than allowed oral children, we are at a loss to understand, unless it be the great cost of boarding. In some of the mute schools the time has been lengthened to eight and ten years, which is an advance in justice; but, as the mute needs a schooling far more than an oral child, he should not be limited to a less length of time. His boarding should never be subtracted from his school time at all. Every mute has a just moral claim to at least FIFTEEN full school years of instruction, and no State or Trustees have any legal or moral right to shorten the time a single day. It is not only grossly unjust, but also *unconstitutional*, to legislate away a single day from the mute's moral right to schooling. The Legislature or Trustees may, if they choose, *lengthen* the time, but they can never curtail it.

'But as it is a *moral and social disaster* to take a mute away from home, and from the entire control of parents and home influences, from ten years old till he is fifteen or twenty, some auxiliary plan must be adopted to prevent this in a large measure, if not altogether, and to give him an earlier start and a larger privilege, equal to that of oral children at least, from six to twenty-one years. In some of the boarding mute schools they have been admitting mutes as young as seven or eight, but the experiment seems to have proved a failure, not because the children were too young *to learn*, but because too young for the rules and military-like care of such schools, and the Trustees in some instances have revoked the terms of admission back to ten years. While this is just one way, it is unjust another. For a child that is a mute should receive attention in the educational line, in its broadest sense, the moment it becomes deaf; and not be left to ignorance, sensuality, till ten years old. Schooling a mute at home is a splendid preventive of indolency of both mind and body, and thus bars the mutes from the tendency to stupidness, blank ignorance, sensuality, &c., that they acquire by being neglected after six years of age till ten or twelve, and which gives so much trouble when they do enter school, and takes so much valuable time to start them in book learning, and break them of bad habits.

'General Eaton says, on page ccxii of his report for 1881:—

'"The education of the deaf-mute child should be commenced in the home at the earliest practicable moment. He should be encouraged in all active exercises, since they occupy his mind and strengthen his body. He should be shown novel and interesting objects, that his powers of observation may be quickened and his mind furnished with material for thought. The *finger alphabet*, simple writing and drawing, and the meaning of figures may be taught by parents or by older brothers or sisters. Above all, the *moral education* of the child should not be neglected, as his future acquirements depend largely upon it. * * * As the deaf child has more than ordinary difficulties to overcome in obtaining an education, there should be no obstacle placed in the way of his entrance upon school-life at as early an age as may be deemed advisable."

'The mute day school seems to meet this want quite well. In the first place, it DOES NOT take the child away from home except during school days—9 A. M. to 3 P. M.—and leave him to live and board with his parents, and be under their entire control, the same as oral children. In the second place, it admits him when he is six years old, and CANNOT stop him till he graduates, be it fifteen or more years. In the third place, it costs the State nothing for board.

'True, this may not be done for all of the mutes, as will be seen further on, as to how the isolated mutes should be provided for. As for those living in a city, we have already explained the way for them.

'Schools similar to those in Chicago have been established in London, and placed by the School Board under the supervision of Rev. William Stainer. In order to extend their benefits, *homes have been opened* near them for the accommodation of children *living at a distance*. An account of these homes says:—

'"Mr. Stainer, aided by benevolent friends, has opened at two or three points near the schools 'ladies' Christian homes', where the children are brought together and provided with board and lodgings from Monday until Friday, returning to their homes for Saturday and Sunday. Each home has accommodation for forty children, and they are received as young as four years of age. Their parents pay the cost of their food. Besides the weekly boarders, there are some children who, having no homes of their own, are placed in these establishments as permanent boarders by boards of guardians, the Royal Association in Aid of the Deaf and Dumb, and benevolent individuals. The advantage of the homes is not only that children living at a distance are brought near to the schools, but also that out of school hours they are surrounded with educational and moral influences, while still maintaining their family relations and home ties by weekly visits." '—[From *Report of the Commissioner of Education*, 1881.]

'*Objections to Mute Day Schools Answered.*

'The first, and perhaps the strongest objection to these schools is, that regular attendance is impossible, on account of the unreliableness of continued good weather.

'True, these day-schools, like the oral common schools, are more or less subjected to the weather. On this account they cannot be as regularly attended as the State boarding-schools—deaf and dumb institutions. Yet they (mute day-schools) are as regularly attended as the oral schools. Because storms or very bad weather interrupt the regular attendance of oral schools, is that a good reason *against* their existence, and a proof that they should exist, or that they should exist only as boarding schools? Our mute day pupils are just as anxious to attend these day-schools as the boarding-school pupils are to get back to school at the close of their vacation, and for the same reason too!—and this during bad weather also. We are often amazed at their regular attendance during inclement weather. If they do now and then miss a day on account of bad weather, it does not always detract from their school-room progress. On the contrary, it often whets their mental appetite. The home jars, street sights and episodes, and their contact with people, &c., not only increases their stock of general knowledge, but also their desire for learning. The principal of the St. Louis day-school, Mr. D. A. Simpson, presents many arguments to prove that it is best for deaf children to remain at home during their school days, and answers the objections to day-schools as follows, in his letter to the Commissioner of Education, page ccxi of Report of 1881:—

'"The only strong point which opponents of day-schools can advance is the difficulty of classification of pupils and the large percentage of daily absence from school. To this it may be replied that some of the very important advantages which a day-school has over a State institution more than compensate for this difficulty of classification, and, as to absence from school, it is not at all true, as far as the St. Louis day-school is concerned, that the percentage of daily absence is large. Here, with forty-one pupils enrolled, the average daily absences do not exceed four, less than one from each class."

'Is not this very objection also more than counterbalanced by *better* health, caused by the daily exercises of a "long, free run" in going to and returning from school in the open air, than that of the boarding-school pupils?—not only of stronger physical health, but also *clearer and stronger mental powers?* Is it not a fact that more children are broken down, and the germs of consumption planted, by too close and long confinement than by outdoor exposures? Compare the pupils of a day-school and those of a boarding school as to health and mental vigor, and see if this is not so. We are not here contending against boarding schools as such at all; at least *not against small ones*, if the children are under no military-like rules, and who have more open-air and home-like freedom than can be allowed in large boarding schools. Again, is not this objection to day-schools, on account of irregular attendance, more than *overbalanced* in the instructing and training of mute children some three or four years earlier than they are in boarding schools?—and that, too, though the instruction on this account may not be quite so good. Is not this early, though ever so irregular, teaching of mutes, worth something as a PREVENTIVE against many bad habits and *blank mental crusting*, or spiritual blindness and mental callousness, so common with mutes who have been allowed to grow up in ignorance, unschooled till nine, ten, or more years old? The school year of many of the State mute schools runs from the second Wednesday in September to the second Wednesday in June, or thirty-eight weeks. Five days in school each week makes 190 school days: this, on a ten years' course, which is the longest time in any State schools, makes 1,900 school days; and, in those of eight years' course, 1,520 school-room days.

'In the day-schools, the school year has forty weeks—or 200 school days—and from six years old to twenty-one gives the mutes FIFTEEN YEARS! or 3,000 school days!! If he averages one day each week for absence on account of bad weather, which is a large allowance, it will leave him 2,400 days in school, and 500 days, or two and a half years, longer than the ten-year course; and 880 days, or four years, more than the eight-year course! What now has become of the objection?

'Besides the fact that the mute's boarding at home FORCES his folks to learn to talk with him in his easy, natural, and quick way, which is far better and easier in most cases than to force him to *lose much valuable school time* in learning articulation, it also more or less *educates the public* in the mute's peculiar characteristics and his language. This is of vast importance to the mute. For it is not after all the mode or manner by which the mute carries on communication, as it is the familiar acquaintance with the mutes by the public. Where mutes are well known by the public, especially mutes of good morals, they have far less trouble to get along, and in communication by signs, than they do where they are strangers or people do not know much about them. While we are not opposed to mute institutions for the country mutes, yet it is a fact that institution-mutes *too often* get entirely too much weaned from the public as well as from home, and when their school course is run, and they return home, they are strangers—foreigners to the neighborhood; and this *acts against* them, no matter how well educated. Some people think them semi-gods in learning, and "stand off!" And as most people can't write well nor understand overwell the gruntal and peculiar enunciation of articulation, &c., it causes them to act cold and distant, and thus leave the mute too severely alone, even when they would like his help, if they were only FAMILIAR by ACQUAINTANCE with him.

'This *unfamiliarity*, and therefore coldness and distance of the mute's relatives and the public, soon breeds in him discouragement, if not disgust, and off he goes to see the world or seek the companionship of his old school acquaintances, here, there, and yonder. If he can't do this, he lingers around home like a drone. Education is a fine thing, but when it, or rather the necessity of boarding away from home so early and so long, lifts him *above* his home and relations, it does him harm, and raises that ugly question, "Is it not more of a curse than a blessing?"

'There is still another point, and that is, the day-school not only familiarizes the business public with mutes in seeing them so often, but it familiarizes the *oral school children* with the mutes, and enables them both to learn to communicate with each other while going to and returning home from school together, and playing together, and thus they *grow up together*, and live and die old friends of childhood and school-days. This interweaves them together, as it were, into social and business life, and thus prevents in a large measure that alienation of mutes from the oral people that is so ugly in a business and social way.* Raise a cat and dog *together* from birth to maturity and they will always be friendly, no matter about the vast difference in their natures, but raise them *apart*, and lo, "a cat and dog life!" Apply the illustration to the different classes of children, and it needs no prophet to foretell the results. We speak here not from a theoretical point, but from many a sad experience, and thirty years among mutes out of school.

'*A Summary.*—Now let us briefly recast the advantages of a mute day-school, and see how stand the advantages *versus* the disadvantages by comparison.

'1. It begins the education of mutes at or near their home, where they can board AT HOME, and thus be under the direct care and influence of their parents, for at least the first few years, and prevents them in a large measure *from getting weaned* from their home and losing their *love* for their parents and home, which is too often the case when mutes receive *all* their education away from home. Therefore they are more INDEPENDENT and less INSTITUTIONIZED.

'2. It gives mute children more years of schooling—the same number of years that oral children receive, which in many States is from six to twenty-one; while State boarding-schools, are limited on account of the vast expense of boarding, &c., generally making the best scholarship of mutes about equal to oral children of the ages of ten and twelve years! As mutes need schooling far more than oral children, they should by all means receive as much and not *less*. Hence day-schools give mutes the same length of time as oral children, and save to the State at least one-half of the special appropriation for making that much less needed for boarding, by reducing the time necessary in a boarding-school to one-half—*i.e.*, schooling a mute from six to sixteen in a day-school, and then five years (sixteen to twenty-one) in a boarding-school will give a mute three times better education than can be had without going to a day-school.* That, too, without any greater cost to the State.

'3. It prevents the mutes from growing up in ignorance, stupidity, crustiness, and bad habits in a large measure, if not altogether. A mute at six is often "bright," and if not taken in hand while young, will grow sour, morose, and vicious as he grows older; uncared for, the more he feels and broods over his misfortune; which is checked if his education is commenced early; while, if left till ten, he often becomes a "hard case," or a "dull boy." This is illustrated in the *start* and advantage that semi-mutes have over others on entering an institution for mutes, which is not so much on account of their ability to hear or talk a little, as these are no mental advantages, but mostly from their having had some *early* schooling, and on this account enter at once an advanced class and sometimes the high class. This is also so with all who have been more or less to day-schools or have had several years of private instruction.

'4. It tends to expand and ennoble the mute's better nature, and increase his knowledge and experience of the world, men, and things, by daily observation at home, and while going to and returning from school, and in the discharge of his varied home duties.

'5. It gives the mute more *self-reliance* † and more *business push* to earn his own living, which is so often lacking in mutes educated wholly housed up and away from home. And it teaches him what is justice and the rights of man, and that others have rights, &c., as well as he; thus teaching him to regard and respect the claims and rights of others; and to curb his pride, *conceit* and *educational arrogance*.

'6. It *forces* his parents, brothers, sisters, relatives, and friends to learn to talk with him in *his own language* far better than when he is educated altogether away from home. This is of vast importance to him. And it is far less troublesome for relations to learn to talk with the mute by signs than it is for him to learn articulation! *A fact!*

'7. It builds up better physical health and makes him stronger and more robust, with less tendency to consumption, which is often the result of long confinement to rooms and limited yard range, and which has broken down the health and shortened the life of many a promising mute boy and girl; for which an education ever so good never compen-

---

* Prof. A. G. Bell, of telephone fame, has publicly taken the same view of the question, and insists upon it that the mutes must be raised and *schooled* with the oral children.

* Though common sense, justice, and the common law give the mute the same amount of schooling, yet in some States the Legislature should enact a special law requiring School Boards to open a day-school wherever five or more mutes can be got together, as it saves to the State four to six years of boarding expenses; and this saving of boarding more than covers the cost of the day-schooling: thus giving mutes a far better education at no greater cost, if as much, than all schooling in the institution. Hence what is taken from the school fund for day-schools is saved in turn in special appropriation to the State institution. And the same is so, if the State makes special appropriation for the day-schools. For it is only a different way, which amounts to the same in the Ledger, but gives the mutes a better education.

† The Massachusetts State Board of Charities says that children brought up in *asylums* and *charitable* institutions DO NOT LEARN SELF-RELIANCE, and that however good situations are procured for them on their becoming of proper age—graduated—to go out into the world, sooner or later they are almost sure to be found in some charitable institution!—in fact '*institutionized*!!—Small *manual* schools teach self-reliance and tend less to institutionization.

sates. Parents having their child boarding at home with them while young, or between six and sixteen, can doctor and care for it while sick, and are not annoyed by anxiety and uneasiness about sickness and epidemics like those whose children are away from home when sick, or with others who are sick with some violent or contagious disease. Among these are the *sore eyes*, so *common* in all institutions, among little children, and which is the great enemy of the deaf-mutes, but which is rarely known in a mute day-school.

'8. The chances and prevalence of evil, or the "epidemic of wickedness," is far less, if not one hundred times less, among day-school pupils than among those of a boarding-school. In day-schools the company and familiarity of good children with the evil and vicious ones is only for a few hours during the day, and *never at night*, the evil hour to man. Children well guarded against evil and bad company, and taken good care of, especially at night, will come to manhood and womanhood with better morals than all the lectures on morality and sermons on religion put together can do for them without this moral care. Children, like animals, need no reasoning but *forcible restraint* from evil, and must be compelled to do right, until their moral character is well formed, developed, and matured. No one can do this so easily and so well as parents—at least, not with those under sixteen. Our stress upon morality may seem too strong, but we must remember that it is the GREATEST *need*. An educated man without good morals is an evil and a curse to society, while a good moral man without an education is a blessing. It is the latter and not the former who deserves, and can make the right use of, an education.

'9. It gives the mute a larger circle of acquaintance among oral people at home, and this prevents the excessive clannishness so prevalent among mutes educated wholly from home and the world. The larger *familiar* acquaintance the mute has at home among his parents and neighbors, the less apt is he to become dissatisfied with his home life and to wander off among strangers.

'10. It prevents the parents from being *over-indulgent* and *foolish* with and about their mute child, to a great extent. Absence tends to lax requirements in duties and morality by parents on the return of an absent child, and allowance and indulgence that are wrong and injurious are permitted. But when a child is educated near home and boards at home while young or under sixteen, the parents see the ignorance and gloom of their child's mind daily dispelled, which *disarms* them of their *excess* of sorrow and pity (which is worse than not quite enough of it) for their child's misfortune, and causes them to treat him on an equality, as to duty, morality, *work*, &c., with the other children. A mute does not need pity, but a good *domestic and moral training* as well as a good school education, instead of pity, indulgence, and lax requirements.

'If a mute's education is begun when he is six years old in a day-school, and he is kept there till sixteen years old, and then sent for five years to a *Mute High School*—a separate and distinct school from the primary, not a high class of it, nor in any way connected with it officially or otherwise, nor on the same plat-location—where the SCIENCE of manual labor, trades* best suited for boys, and gardening, fruit-culture, &c., and culinary affairs—*household science*, &c.—for the girls, are FULLY AND THOROUGHLY TAUGHT as well as advanced studies, would he not get in these *fifteen years* of schooling a pretty good command of written language, and that too by *signs*, as well as a good education otherwise? And if to this he could add a full *Mute College* course (six years) would we not then have mutes of still broader views and more extended culture than now? Surely we would; for is not the narrowness and conceit of many of our mutes owing much to the too brief schooling and too lax moral training in their primary course?

'Times indicate a radical change coming. We fancy we see rising o'er the mountain-tops of error and misapplied philanthropy the morning star of a better day for the misunderstood, abused, and illy-educated mute; and that in the near future "the *many*" instead of "the *few*" will attain to a high degree of intelligence in scholarship, science, and morality. We ask the prayers and aid of all good men to the end that God will *bless and prosper the deaf-mute schools*, and speed the day when *all* mutes shall be as well educated *every way* as any one.

'*Remarks.*—The MS. of this pamphlet was written some two or three years ago, long before we knew anything about Prof. A. G. Bell's day-school views. The MS. was given to the printer in March, 1884.

'The good points of Prof. Bell as to day-schools *vs.* institutions seem to be anticipated in this pamphlet. But it seems that the author's *personal experience with deafness, articulation, signs*, and over a quarter of a century's experience as a teacher of the deaf, against Mr. Bell's *inexperience* in *deafness or signs*, or what it *actually* is as to *learning articulation without hearing*, saved the author from Mr. Bell's extreme views of articulation.

'While the author has written strongly in favor of day-schools, he wishes it distinctly understood that he is not a puller-down, but an advocate of progress—advancement. He believes it absolutely necessary to have State mute boarding-schools for the mutes of villages and those scattered over the country. But his own sad experience in an institution life, and a long business and social relation with the graduates of large and small mute institutions, forces him to conclude that the small institutions fare generally the best; and that these State schools should be more on the industrial plan, where farm work, gardening, and fruit culture are the leading features outside of the school-room, and the science and art part of these are taught in earnest. These, the most healthful and independent pursuits of man, and in which deafness is less a bar, if any at all, than in the trades and other pursuits, are not taught as they should be; and too much stress laid upon trades. A good mute who is a *good* farm-hand has far less trouble to get work and to get along than a mute with a trade, because deafness is not so much in the way with the former as it is with the latter.

'But for large cities the author believes that the city schools should have a deaf-mute department with "a special teacher in charge" well versed in the mute's own language—*signs*, with a high class boarding-school in the suburbs where trades can also be taught for the city boys. But the day-schools cannot be in the same room with the oral children. A small, separate room for such is necessary, the same as they *already* have in Chicago, Cincinnati, and St. Louis.

'These have maintained a harmonious connection for some ten years! And that too with excellent results, with none of the imagined disagreeableness, &c., between the oral and deaf children that institution folks fancy there would be, being also favorable for the development of character, business tact, self-reliance, &c.

'One of Mr. Bell's critics does not meet the issue by telling all about the attempts and failures of day-schools in Europe! This is *America!* not Europe.* Besides, these foreign day-schools for mutes were schools by themselves, and not *departments* to a school system like our great common school system.

*Only boys of good mechanical talents should be allowed to learn a trade. And they should be at least fifteen or sixteen years old.

*A brother critic uses this same foreign argument to prove the contrary! thus stabbing one another with a two-edged sword, instead of standing united on the argument.

Many of them were started in early days when people did not *demand* schools for children—not even for oral children, much less for the deaf—as they do in this age, and especially in this great country.

'There is another point his critic overlooked, and that is, that all or most of those foreign day-schools used the articulation system only, instead of the "combined."

'In this country we believe that the *eclectic* or *combined system* in the mute school *department* of the public schools will meet the great need of mute schools near home, at least for the present age. This American *eclectic day-school* system is the one used in the Chicago Mute Schools. Thus Chicago takes the lead.

'Mr. Bell's critic puts stress upon the idea that institution pupils are at home three months in the year while going to school, as if that was sufficient *home life* for a mute! He knows, we suppose, as well as any one, that if it was three months instead of seven, *away from home* every year for ten years, between the ages of ten and twenty, it would spoil most any oral child as to *home life* and *home ties*, &c. We venture to say he himself would not care to try the experiment with his oral children, if he has any, much less with an *unfortunate* child, if he had one.

'Another objector admits all that Prof. Bell says about *home ties* and *home influence*, but says "that not all homes are what they should be," therefore the mute should be taken away from its mother and home! If so, why not take away all the other children too? If the institution cared for the mutes till death, it would be less objectionable. But it does not, and after the school course is run it returns the mute to his humble and "*ought not to be*" home, to stay there! But being raised, by an institution life, *above* his parental station, he soon becomes dissatisfied with it, and then commences a life of discontentment, which often ends in something worse, such as travelling from place to place, begging, visiting and hanging round saloons, pool-rooms, base-ball grounds! Because of no home and no work? No; because home life is "too lonely!" too "work much!" &c. Parents are too lax with them, or have lost their control and influence over their mute child by long absence from home. A city daily paper went so far as to state that all the educated mutes in the city gambled, because so many of them were seen so often in pool-rooms, and that they were beer-drinkers too, because they were often seen congregated in saloons! And he might have added, with much show of truth, that they always (?) have beer at their picnics, dancing at their sociables, and wine at their parties! Would not this have been too true? Are these parties as they should be? Should not such be the exception instead of the rule? Does not this reflect severely on institution life? We beg, in the name of all that is sacred in home ties, all that is good in morality, that the institution folks look more closely to the *social and moral habits* of their charge, and not trust altogether to chapel service, so that their graduates will be more like the day-school pupils, who stick more to home and home duties, &c., even if many of these homes are "not what they should be." Remember that Providence rules and not man, or else even these "should not be homes" would not exist. And we would kindly suggest to parents that it will be well for them to see *where*, *how* and *with whom* their mute spends his idle time.

'To expect these institution children *not to become inflated with pride and arrogance from the effects of fine buildings, nice surroundings, and a domestic life of comfort and ease* not always found in the homes of the wealthy, is expecting entirely too much from poor human nature. It is said, "put a horse in *clover*, and he will *kick*," thus being *less useful* and *more dangerous*. Is not this so of man, and especially of *children*, *particularly* when gathered into "*a great crowd*"?

'"*Seven children*" are considered to be a *full* family, and all that a man and wife can raise as they *should be*; and that "twelve children is *too many*" for any man to care for and raise right. If so, what is the law of ratio or the largest number of deaf-mutes (who *need so much* and *constant personal attention*) that can be in *one* school, and be *cared for*, *taught*, and *trained* as they *should be*?

From Pamphlet No. 2.—'Are Signs or Articulation the best Means or Channel of Instruction?' 'By an Old Teacher *who was himself taught both Articulation and Signs, and* KNOWS *from personal experience and long observation which system is the* BEST IN THE SCHOOL-ROOM.'

'By whose authority do the oral people presume to speak and *dictate* to the deaf and dumb? Who gave the oral people exclusive authority to sit in judgment on the deaf and dumb without their consent? Have the deaf and dumb no voice nor rights that the oral are bound to respect? Why are intelligent deaf-mute teachers not consulted as to the needs, &c., of their people, even at teacher's conventions? Are they *dummy-numps?* or human educational chattel?'

'Is "the pure oral" method a jargon and gruntal intonation of vocal sounds, or an easy, clear, and distinct utterance—a mastery of vowel and consonant sounds?'

'Teaching the deaf and dumb to talk is *not* educating them at all. If it was, why do those children who can hear and talk need any schooling, even when they are splendid talkers?'

'True, one must have a language whereby to be educated. But it must be his mother tongue; and, if this is impossible, then the next, or the one the most EASY to learn and to remember, and *easiest and most fluent to use*, with the least possible mental *strain*; and not the driest and hardest. If so, why select or elect articulation, which to the deaf and dumb is not only foreign, but UNNATURAL and exceedingly hard and dry, taxing his memory ten times more than the driest and hardest dead or foreign language does the oral student? The sign language is *easier* to a mute than the mother tongue is to the oral child!—it is, as it were, HIS MOTHER TONGUE! Though a mute child, uneducated, knows but little and uses but little of the sign language, yet he takes to it as easily and as naturally as a duck to water; and in a little while, at school, gathers it up with such rapidity and *avidity* that he often astonishes his teacher with his accuracy and fluency in its use. He often surpasses, as a master of this language, the very best teachers of it among teachers of mutes who hear and speak!—thus opening wide the door to his mind whereby the teacher can readily talk with him on every subject, even on abstract ideas, &c., as though he (the mute) had command of a spoken language! And this is accomplished in an incredibly short time; thus losing but little time from the school-room studies in acquiring a language that to him is as easy as the English is to an Englishman, or French to a Frenchman. Yea, more so; for the mute is often his own instructor in the language of signs, and sometimes the teacher of it to his teacher! So simple, easy, *natural*, and *philosophical* is the language of signs that you can tell a mute child a pretty good story of a "cat and mouse" in signs almost the moment he has learned the signs for *cat* and *mouse*; and that, too, before he knows another word. This cannot be done in any spoken language to those who can hear and talk, much less to those deaf and dumb by articulation. These are *facts*—facts that we do not only believe to be true, but *know* to be true from our own personal experience and observation among mutes for over a quarter of a century as a teacher.

'Here we could stop and rest upon these facts, and defy the world and a thousand *Milan Conventions* to disprove them, and prove, not by resolutions, but *by facts*, that articulation is *inferior* to signs as a means or channel whereby to *educate* the deaf and dumb—not two out of ten, but nine out of ten.

'The sign language is so new and strange to many that we feel constrained to further remark upon it, for the special benefit of the parents of mutes who should fully know its merits and claims, and fully impress upon them these claims and merits, and that teaching the deaf and dumb to talk is *not educating them* any more than the learning of a foreign language by a vocal child is educating that child—at least, not as he should be educated on the start.

'The *art* of speaking by arbitrary rules, without sense or sound,* is not and cannot be the natural and proper channel through which to EDUCATE the deaf and dumb. It is more of *an accomplishment* than a channel to his mind. In this respect, we are *not*, and *never* have been opposed to mutes learning articulation or any other accomplishment that will *embellish* their education or mind; as it is to them what music or a foreign language is to the oral student. This and nothing more. But what we do oppose is the unjust and "cruel"† proceeding of FORCING a mute to learn articulation *before he is educated*, and the still worse policy of attempting to educate him by it only. That which severely taxes the mental powers and takes the strength of mind and memory *too much* from ideas, &c., is surely not a good thing to study while being educated. Language is not the *chief* thing to life and action, but *intelligence, good ideas, good judgment*, &c., are; and these should *always* take the *precedence* of a foreign language. Knowledge, not language, is power. Ideas *first*, language *last*.

'To a mute, spoken words are soulless as well as soundless, and do not and cannot convey the nature or meaning of an object or idea in their chirographical construction or mimic sounds, while SIGNS DO! Signs to a great extent are their own interpreters! There is no spoken language that does this. If not, and signs do and are so easily acquired and readily understood by mutes, then why, in the name of common sense, reason, and justice, attempt to educate the mute by prohibiting the use of signs? Why deny to him an *easy* and *pleasant* road to education? Why repeat with an unfortunate mute the foolish idea of the long-ago college authorities, that "Greek and Latin is the best *education*" a child could have?

'AFTER a mute is educated, or after he has a good start in knowledge *via* signs, he then, and *not before*, may be taught articulation, as an *accomplishment*. He can then, and more willingly, more easily, be taught it. For then he often has a *desire* to learn it. "A *desire* is half-way."

'In none of the sign schools are the mutes *prohibited* from learning to talk all they like, but rather encouraged to, while in the articulate schools they are FORBIDDEN to learn or to use signs, and are reprimanded if they break over this injunction! The plea that signs hinder a child from learning is not true. This is a thing we never knew in a single case in all our long intercourse with them—a thing we cannot account for.

'Most mutes who have learned both signs and articulation prefer to use signs. This being so,—and it is, so far as we have observed,—is it right to keep signs from them? Signs, we believe, are the great Providential compensation to a mute for the loss of hearing and speech—and a splendid compensation too, as nine-tenths of the mutes, if not every mute, can testify. Deny him the use of his own language, and you render his life sombre, solemn, and desolate. If you want proofs of these statements, go visit mutes who are married, or gathered together at parties, and see for yourself who are the most lively, cheerful, and intelligent,—those who have been educated by the sign system, or those educated by articulation only and who know no signs. What! though Providence stopped up my ears, tied my tongue, for some wise purpose, you, a friend (!?), would tie up my hands and send me along down the long journey of life sad and solemn, with only the *artificial* light of the articulate-lantern to guide me, in order that I might always, for *your selfishness*, remember to say "papa" and "mamma"—to talk parrot-fashion—rather than that I should not be able or forget how to say these, though I became ever so wise, happy and useful in an unbroken silence, by the beautiful and effective sign language!

'If we write in rather too severe a strain, remember that we are the victim of the attempt to educate us by the oral process, and that we are not pleading for others in what we have not had actual personal experience, but *vs.* a system in which we have had sad experience. Nor is it so much what the Gallaudets, the Peets, the Jacobs, and Brown, Williams, Wilkinson, Fay, McIntire, Gillett, De Motte, Noyes, Swiler, and many other staunch friends and defenders of the sign system say, that we are thus urged to plead, but from the fact that the deaf-mutes *themselves* all say it is the best, who surely are better judges of what is the best mode of expression for them, than those who were never dumb, judging from their volubility in what they have no personal experience of; though they seem to be deaf, as they seem not to hear the facts; yet they have no experience in deafness physically. Why any one with common sense can contend against signs in the face of all these facts we are at a loss to understand on the grounds of benevolence, common sense, and *education*.

'If signs were as hard to teach as articulation, and as unpleasant and as difficult for mutes to use, and had no advantage in conveying the nature, meaning, &c., of objects, we surely would be the last one in the world to write thus. The articulate system would in that case stand on equal grounds with it. But as articulation is hard to learn and unnatural, it can NEVER be the best method of instruction. We should remember that the learning to talk is one thing and education quite another; and that it is not the ability to communicate with others orally that mutes so much need as a good stock of ideas as to the world, men and things, which can be given mutes by signs in far less time (some say in one-fourth of the time) than by articulation. If so, why force a mute to take the *longest, hardest* and *driest* road to knowledge, *via* articulation, instead of the shortest and easiest, by signs? Why tax his memory on the start with that which he should learn last? Do we teach oral children Greek or Latin, or a foreign language, before they are educated in their own? NEVER! Would not such a foolish course tend to overtax and weaken their memories, and *hinder* their acquisition of knowledge?

'But when a mute is wholly or half educated, and is fourteen or sixteen years old, and is able to stand the *severe extra strain* on his memory, he can begin to learn to articulate. In this normal order of things we are as strong a friend to articulation as any one can be who is not blinded by false ideas or prejudice. Had the friends of articulation

* The Committee of the Chicago Deaf-Mute Day Schools, in its report for the year ending July 31, 1881, in speaking of the progress of the mutes, says 'The wonder, however, is not that as a class they accomplish so little, but really that they accomplish as much as they do in getting command of a language based upon *sound* which has *no sound*, nor sense in its articulate sound, to them.'

The progress referred to has been through *signs* as the means of instruction.

† See article on lip reading in *Am. Annals for Deaf and Dumb* for 1883.

gone to work on this idea, and opened their schools to mutes who had graduated from the sign schools, *desirous* of learning to talk as an accomplishment, the same as oral children do about music, they would have started right, and would have met with no opposition from the sign schools, and a great deal less from the mutes themselves. They would have secured the patronage that is now given to the articulate department of the sign schools, which would never have been opened, perhaps, had it not been for the wrong or extreme course pursued by articulate schools.

'If the oralists would confine themselves to teaching the pupils to articulate *common* words of every-day life in the common way of people, the same as the oral teacher in the oral department of mute schools, and leave school studies to the sign schools, they would be far more successful and do more good.

'To master common words, pronounce, and to be able to read the same on the lips of most people, is a task severe enough at all times on the mind of the pupil at the time. As learning to talk is not education, it therefore is a special or particular *art*, which requires a constant and close attention, for the time being, to master.

'The moment we undertake to divide the pupil's attention while learning to talk by teaching the sciences along with it, we retard the progress in articulation and waste the pupil's time in learning words used in books that are not common, and which the deaf often soon forget because so seldom used by the people. For it depends upon daily practice at home that enables a mute not to forget how to pronounce words learned.

'There are, no doubt, some semi-deaf, especially those who have become more or less deaf *after* ten years of age, who could be quite well educated by the "pure oral" system alone. But a system that embraces both articulation and signs would be the best, even for these. For when they fail to "catch" the teacher's utterance or words, or pronounce incorrect, &c., signs would instantly give them the right word or words, and aid them to pronounce more correct. This was so with ourselves, and other semi-deaf said it was so with them.

'We now come to what we consider the best social point in signs and the poorest in articulation, and which is "cruel"* in our friends as well as a great bugbear. We mean the objection to signs as leading to clannishness among mutes; and that, on this ground, short-sighted people say signs should not be learned. And that articulation without signs was the way to "*restore the deaf to society*," which is "a nice thing on paper," but not true in the full sense in reality, because the deaf are *still deaf*. Though they learned to talk ever so well, it is not so much what the deaf say as it is what the public want to say to them!—as people want to do the *talking*, and want *you* to *listen*. If you cannot listen or hear because deaf, then the people have little social interest in you. "A good listener" is a good friend, but a poor listener is not a desirable friend. Now, as these are stubborn facts, even with the best of people, what becomes of the restoration of the deaf to society?

'*We*, with all our fine *articulate powers*, are not on social equalities with those who hear. And why not? Simply because we are still deaf, and therefore barred out; because we cannot hear, and that, too, notwithstanding our good speaking powers!

'But in the companionship of our deaf and dumb wife, and all our mute acquaintance, we stand upon an equal footing, because deafness is *no bar* to the language of signs. As it is a sort of an every-day theatre, it makes life bearable because it transcribes nature so full and well that much of gloom and lonesomeness is driven away. For he who walks with nature, walks near God. And as signs bring one *closer* to nature than spoken language, he must in the very nature of things live a life less lonely and less cheerless than he who is deaf to all the world, but knows not nature's beautiful language of signs. For, is it not in signs that all nature speaks, and so spoke to Adam long before speech was developed?

'Give an *ignorant* deaf man hearing, and that moment he is the equal of any one, and is *talked to* and treated as a man. For his hearing has you by the nose, so to speak. If you slight him in the least because he is not well educated, you do so at your social peril.

'Give speech, even perfect speech, to the deaf man who is well educated—yea, a classical scholar —yet he is "the deaf man," "the dummy"! You may be able to hear him well, but because *he is deaf* you are *brief* in your talk *to* him, and often say nothing *yourself*. And you speak *less* to him when in company than when behind the barn. And why? Simply because *he is deaf*! Do you fancy he does not *see* and *feel* this *brevity*?

'Is not this a universal and stubborn fact? And has articulation restored him to society in the face of this fact?

'Can a deaf man with perfect speech be a society man fully and freely? We know of a number of very intelligent and highly respected semi-mute ladies and gentlemen who are treated with much silence in society simply because *they are deaf*. In a social gathering the company of even a person hard of hearing is avoided as far as practicable without causing him or her to feel slighted. Why so? Because of an inferior social relation? *No!* but because he or she is *deaf*. Ah! it is this everlasting deafness or want of hearing that plays the mischief.

'And as the wise seek the society of the educated, the rich the society of the wealthy, the poor those of like condition, the spiritualists those of like belief, the Methodists seek out and associate *mostly* with Methodists, and so of the Presbyterians and all other classes of people. If so, why not allow the deaf to associate with the deaf? You *never* condemn this clannishness in the former; why do you in the latter? Simply because you are liberal-minded and charitable with the former, but *narrow* and *uncharitable* with the latter! If this touches you to the quick, let it do so and burn you till you are just, for we have been the ones insulted, lo! these many years, and hope and pray that these words may wake you to the *wants* and *wishes* of THE MUTES, and less to those of your own, in regard to a people whom you want to unclan.

'Are deaf people devoid of modesty and sensibility?—No! This causes them to get out and keep out of the way—to sit in corners or on a back seat.

'Why do deaf people *prefer* deaf people for companions? Is it not because of like conditions—*equality?* If true, why deny them this *full companionship?*

'As a deaf man spends his idle time mostly by himself or in company with those like himself, why not allow him the fullest of this narrow social enjoyment, by enlarging it, and by permitting him the use of his own language—signs—as it is by *this*, and not by articulation, that he *loves* to talk to and be talked to by those who are deaf? We are not pleading against articulation, for it is *useful*, but we protest against the iron-jacketing of the deaf with restriction to articulation alone, or prohibiting their making use of signs. For they will use signs in spite of your rule, behind the house or when out of your sight, and thus practise deception—the first step in immorality.

'Is there not something radically wrong in that system which must needs put a muzzle on the deaf to

*A writer in the *Annals for the Deaf and Dumb*, for 1883, on Lip Reading so branded the exclusive articulation system.

prevent them from using signs?—the language of nature, which they love so well that they instinctively learn it with little and often with no instruction!

'Superintendent Ely, of the Maryland Mute School, in his Report for 1881-83, says:

'"It has been urged by extreme advocates of articulation that pupils cannot be successfully taught in schools where the sign language is used. Our experience disproves this conclusively, and also shows the great value of the sign language in stimulating the minds of the children, and *preparing them to receive more readily instruction in speech.*" [This is the belief of ALL teachers in mute institutions.]

'Were the articulate schools places for the deaf to learn to *talk only* (and that is all they should be), and not a school of learning, there would, no doubt, be a reason for forbidding the use of signs by the pupils. But if in teaching in English, grammar, or any science, you have a class who are Germans, or who understand that language better than English, and your explanation happens not to be clear in English, but would be in German, you would not be wise not to speak so, if you could, for the time being; and a tyrant or tyrannical not to allow your pupils to reply in their native tongue when they found they could not do it in English. Hence those teachers of "French and German" who undertake to teach English to these foreign people are the best teachers when they can speak these languages as well as the English. For they make the foreign language the "*stepping-stone" to the English.* Just so with the deaf—we are *obliged to use signs* and to allow them to use signs in order to get them to rightly understand us and we them, so as to make the best progress possible in school studies.

'Is not lip-reading, or the watching of the mouth of the speaker by the deaf, a vast machinery of "guess-work," guessing at the *tens of thousands* of words, more or less differently pronounced by a great many people, even by parents, brothers, sisters, and friends? And with men who have moustaches the fact of lip-reading is not only more difficult, but too often *impossible.*

'Is it not a fact that articulation teachers only can talk to their pupils best, while others, even parents, have more or less difficulty in making their child understand them? Were this not so, the articulate system would be better than it is. But so long as people speak *differently* and *indifferently*, it can only be an ACCOMPLISHMENT, but cannot compare with signs at all as a school-room medium between teacher and pupil.

'He who admits nothing, claims too much to be just. Therefore, the pure oralists are not just, for they admit nothing as true or useful in signs, the universal language of nature, particularly that of those who cannot hear or talk. He who admits what is true on his opponent's side, is *just.* Therefore the manualists are more just and wiser than the oralists, for they admit that some mutes can be taught to articulate to a certain extent, and a *few* others quite well.

'Why do not the articulate schools add a sign-department to their schools, like the sign-schools have done (in adding an articulation department), and thus give their pupils a more *intelligent* education, and thereby get more scholars and do more good? Is it not because the sign-department would soon become the largest department, and many of the articulate teachers be obliged to learn signs or else give way to those versed in signs? Would it not look wiser and more philanthropic for them to give the sign system a *full* and fair trial in their schools, and then, if found not to be of any use, nor to be what is claimed for it, to discontinue it? Would they dare to try it just a *little* while, and on a small scale? If not, why not? Ah! look behind, and you may see why.

'He who knows *both sides*—the practice, as well as the theory—is the best judge. Who, therefore, is the best judge, he who has *fully* and *fairly* TRIED *both* signs and articulation, or he who has tried articulation only?

'How many oralists are there who understand signs well, and yet prefer the oral system as the best *schoolroom* language-medium by which to teach the deaf to read, write, and cipher, and to learn geography, drawing, &c.? None! We have known cases of oralists coming over to the manual system, but not a case of a manualist going over to the oralist. People don't go back on Providence—nature, but sometimes they do on *art.*

'There are a great many manualists (sign-makers) who have taught or can teach articulation, but prefer the signs as the best channel to teach mutes to read, write, cipher, the study of geography, and all other school studies, including morality and religion.

'"Visible speech," with all its merits, is not of so much use to the deaf, who read so well what their teacher says that way, because, as it would seem, the common people do not speak altogether that way. It is *an unusual* way of speaking, and the deaf who talk this way attract attention at once, and everybody within hearing stops and stares at them! This cuts them to the quick, as they are more sensitive than other people because deafness makes them so.

'You can satisfy yourself by sitting a little out of the reach of the voice, and watching the motion of the lips of people. You will find that many people do not open and shut their mouths and move their lips exactly alike in pronouncing the same words, and you, like the deaf, soon get lost and bewildered. If the vowels had but *one* clear and distinct *lip-motion-sound*, and each and *all* people pronounced or *lip-uttered* words *alike*, the deaf would have far less trouble.

'Articulation must be confined to the common way, such as the people use, or else be of little use to the deaf in business life. Otherwise the deaf will miss and misunderstand much that people say to them, no matter how well they learn to read the lips of their teacher, who speaks not as common people do.

'When our State schools are reduced to a *normal* size (like the model one in Europe, where not over twenty-five pupils are permitted to be collected together), say not over 100 pupils in *one* locality, giving America about 600 schools instead of only about sixty, we will then be able to show a standard of excellency in *language, science, art, morality, industry, and trades*, that is not now attained, and impossible in over-large schools. Enlarge the little oral schools to 300 and 500 children of all grades of mental capacity, and where then would be their *few* excellent successes? The oral schools have been very fortunate in keeping their schools *small*, while the sign schools have been unfortunate in being permitted to grow entirely too large, and thereby lessening the individual attention that deafness makes absolutely necessary with the deaf.

'We have not said all we would like to, but we hope we have satisfied inquirers. We close by repeating that articulation is a nice accomplishment to those who can master it, but signs are the best medium of educating the deaf.'

From Pamphlet No. 3.—'Facts for Parents of Mutes, Ideas for the People, and Suggestions for the Law-makers.'

'The trustees of the various institutes should be composed in part of mutes, selected on account of their pre-eminent qualities of good sense, good judgment, and sterling honesty, for such people are much better acquainted with the needs of their own class than those who are able to hear, and who are, under the present system, appointed as trustees, but who are too often entire strangers to deaf-mutes and their peculiarities of language, &c., and, in their ignorance of such, are forced to rely upon the explanation and dictation of interested and sometimes selfish parties.

'As the superintendent is generally, if not always, present at the meetings of the board of trustees, he can, and should, interpret the proceedings of the board to the mute members. In fact, the importance of having deaf-mutes and semi-mutes as members of such bodies is so great as to justify the employment of an impartial and faithful interpreter, in case the superintendent cannot perform that duty.

'We do not see why deaf-mutes, with the intelligence, liberal-mindedness, and mature judgment of John Carlin, M. A., H. C. Rider, Editor of the *Deaf-Mutes' Journal* (N. Y.), with many others of equal honesty and intelligence scattered all over the Union, should not be on the board of trustees of their respective State schools for mutes.*

'We firmly believe that with such men, from among the deaf-mutes, on the board of trustees, deaf-mute education would be generally better promoted, many abuses prevented, and many wrongs redressed; and the general management of these institutions run less in the interest of speculators, selfish and individual interest, and more in the moral, intellectual, and industrial interest of those for whom the institutions were built.

'PHILIP A. EMERY, *Principal.*'

38. CENTRAL NEW YORK INSTITUTION, ROME, N. Y.

E. B. Nelson, Principal, expresses no opinion upon this question.

39. CINCINNATI PUBLIC SCHOOL.

A. F. Wood, Principal, expresses no opinion upon this question.

40. WEST PENNSYLVANIA INSTITUTION.

'My conviction is that the best method of instruction for the large majority of the deaf is what is usually termed in this country the combined method. The use of signs, in my judgment, cannot be discarded entirely; in fact, to a limited extent they are absolutely necessary, with rare exceptions, to the successful instruction of the deaf; and yet they should be employed as little as possible. Deaf children should be taught the English language from the very beginning. They should learn to use the manual alphabet at once, and be compelled to spell or write, and not be permitted to use the signs in the schoolroom.

'JOHN G. BROWN, *Principal.*'

41. WESTERN NEW YORK INSTITUTION.

Z. F. Westervelt, Superintendent and Principal. No reply to circular received to date, June 2, 1888.

42. PORTLAND SCHOOL, MAINE.

Ellen L. Barton, Principal, expresses no opinion upon this question.

43. RHODE ISLAND STATE SCHOOL.

'I thoroughly believe in speech reading, * * * in the constant drill of the elements and combinations, but not to the exclusion of words; for instance, if in an articulation exercise we should strike upon the combination *shoo* or *to*, I should stop and explain to the pupil that they are the same; that is, have the same sound (requiring the same muscular action in their formation) as *shoe* and *toe*; and I should show the pupil the objects which the words represent; in short, give him as thorough an understanding of the phonetic word as possible. Then he has one, yes, two words for his vocabulary. We go on building in this way until in the ten months (one school year's time) the new beginner, if he has ordinary intelligence, will have a list from 30 to 60, possibly 100 words. While all the while he adds a little and holds on to the building materials, all the time becoming more and more proficient in their adaptation and use. This method differs somewhat from the Northampton method, and altogether from Mr. Greenberger's *latest*.

'ANNA M. BLACK, *Principal.*'

Vide Reports for further information.

44. ST. LOUIS DAY SCHOOL.

D. A. Simpson, Principal. No reply to circular letter received to date, June 2, 1888.

45. NEW ENGLAND INDUSTRIAL SCHOOL.

Nellie H. Swett, Principal, expresses no opinion upon this question.

46. DAKOTA SCHOOL.

James Simpson, Superintendent. No reply to circular letter received to date, June 2, 1888.

47. MILWAUKEE DAY SCHOOL.

'In regard to question 4 I have written a brief paper and sent it to the Royal Commission through the Rev. Dr. Stainer, of London, who delivered it into their hands. I did this because I heard that Dr. Gallaudet had been asked to appear before them, and I feared the fact that articulation was taught in America, and that we had pure oral schools, might not come to their knowledge. This paper was written more than a year ago, and undoubtedly is still in the hands of the Commission. * * * Enclosed find the law relating to the establishment of day schools for the deaf in our State, also the amendment. The latter really makes the law of value. The amendment was a part of the law of 1885—that is, of the original Bill—but in order to gain our point we yielded a little to circumstances. We were then enabled to start our Milwaukee school, and in 1887 we obtained what we originally asked for—the 100 dollars per child.

'PAUL BINNER, *Principal.*'

EXTRACTS FROM THE LAWS OF WISCONSIN.

CHAPTER 315.

AN ACT in relation to the instruction of deaf-mutes in incorporated cities and villages.

The people of the State of Wisconsin, represented in Senate and Assembly, do enact as follows:

SECTION 1. Upon application by the mayor and common council of any incorporated city, or by the president and board of trustees of any incorporated village in the State, to the State superintendent of public instruction, he shall, by and with the consent of the State board of supervision, grant permission to such city or village to establish and maintain, within its corporate limits, one or more schools for the instruction of deaf-mutes, residents of the State of Wisconsin.

SECTION 2. The mayor of any incorporated city, and the president of any incorporated village, which shall maintain one or more schools for the instruction of deaf-mutes, shall report to the State superintendent of public instruction and to the State board of supervision, annually, and as often as said State superintendent or board may direct, such facts concerning such school or schools as said State superintendent or board may require.

SECTION 3. There shall be paid out of the State treasury, in the month of July in each year, to the treasurer of every incorporated city or village maintaining a school or schools for the instruction of deaf-mutes, under the charge of one or more teachers of approved qualifications, to be ascertained by the State superintendent of public instruction, the sum of 100 dollars for each deaf-mute pupil instructed in any such school at least nine months during the year next preceding the first day of July, and a share of such sum proportionate to the term of instruction of any such pupil as shall be so instructed less than nine months during such year.

SECTION 4. The sums to be paid, as provided in next preceding section, shall be audited by the Secretary of State upon the certificate of the president and secretary of the school board and the superintendent of schools of such city maintaining such school, setting forth the number of pupils in-

* Good sense, good general judgment on all business matters, good understanding of what a deaf-mute school should be, should entitle any mute to a trusteeship, and that, too, even if he is not a good English scholar. For, pray, how many of the oral people who hold such positions are good scholars?

structed in such school or schools and the period of time each such pupil shall have been so instructed in such school or schools next preceding the first day of July; and in case any such school shall be maintained in an incorporated village, then upon the certificate of the county superintendent of schools of the proper county, accompanied by the affidavit of the teacher or principal of such school, setting forth the same facts last aforesaid, all of which such certificates and affidavits shall be first approved in writing by the State superintendent of public instruction and the president of the State board of supervision, which certificates and affidavits so approved shall be filed with the Secretary of State, who shall thereupon issue his warrant upon the State treasurer in favor of the treasurer of such city or village, as the case may be, for the sum which shall appear to be due pursuant to the provisions of this Act; provided, that not more than two-fifths of the amount appropriated by this Act shall be expended in any one county.

SECTION 5. A biennial appropriation is hereby made to pay the sums which shall each year become due and payable under this Act; said appropriation shall not exceed five thousand dollars per annum for the years 1885 and 1886.

SECTION 6. This act shall take effect and be in force from and after its passage and publication.

Approved April 4, 1885.

CHAPTER 40.

AN ACT in Relation to the Instruction of Deaf-Mutes, and Amendatory of Section 4, of Chapter 315, of the Laws of 1885.

The people of the State of Wisconsin, represented in Senate and Assembly, do enact as follows:

SECTION 1. Section 4 of chapter 315 of the laws of 1885 is hereby amended by striking from said section the following words at the end thereof, to wit: 'Provided that no more than two-fifths of the amount appropriated by this Act shall be expended in any one county;' so that said section when so amended will read as follows: SECTION 4. The sums to be paid, as provided in next preceding section, shall be audited by the Secretary of State upon the certificate of the president and secretary of the school board and the superintendent of schools of such city maintaining such school, setting forth the number of pupils instructed in such school or schools, and the period of time each such pupil shall have been so instructed in such school or schools next preceding the first day of July; and in case any such school shall be maintained in an incorporated village, then upon the certificate of the county superintendent of schools of the proper county, accompanied by the affidavit of the teacher or principal of such schools, setting forth the same facts last aforesaid, all of which such certificates and affidavits shall be first approved in writing by the State superintendent of public instruction and the president of the State board of supervision, which certificates and affidavits so approved shall be filed with the Secretary of State, who shall thereupon issue his warrant upon the State treasurer in favor of the treasurer of such city or village, as the case may be, for the sum which shall appear to be due, pursuant to the provisions of this Act.

SECTION 2. This Act shall take effect and be in force upon its passage and publication.

Approved March 12, 1887.

48. PENNSYLVANIA ORAL SCHOOL, SCRANTON.

Miss Emma Garrett, Principal, says:—'I gather from a hasty reading of an article by Mr. R. Laichley that he suggests (in last number of "Quarterly Review of Deaf-mute Education," London), establishing day schools. Possibly where he wants to have them they will be practicable. I think the time will come when it will be practicable to have many of them in the United States. I think *present* need is for small oral boarding-schools here. While we have so many sign boarding-schools poor parents, ignorant of *methods*, will let their children slip into them. It was practicable to have a *day* school in large Philadelphia. I demonstrated that. Had eighty pupils.'

The following paper 'contains much that I would gladly say to any one studying the interests of the deaf':—

Conditions necessary to giving every Deaf Child a Chance to Learn to Speak, &c.

When the glorious Milan International Convention of Teachers of the Deaf, held in 1880, decided by a vote of 160 to 4 that the oral method ought to be preferred to that of signs for the education and instruction of the deaf, and that all new pupils be taught by oral method, it recommended that they should be separated from the old pupils who were finishing their course by signs and manual alphabets.

I read in the report of 11th National Convention of American Instructors of the Deaf in California in 1886 that the following resolution, with two amendments, was adopted: 'That earnest and persistent endeavors should be made in every school for the deaf to teach every pupil to speak and read from the lips, and that such efforts should be abandoned only when it is plainly evident that the measure of success attained does not justify the necessary amount of labor.'

The amendments to this resolution were as follows: 'First, that the trial was to be made by articulation teachers trained for the work; and secondly, that such pupils who had sufficient hearing should be taught aurally.' These amendments were good; but I looked anxiously, but without finding it, for an amendment to the effect that the pupils given this trial should be absolutely separated from pupils instructed by signs and manual alphabets, this being recommended as a necessary condition to success by the Milan Convention.

Believing that it is a 'necessary condition to success,' I should have proposed this amendment had I been present at the California Convention. As teachers at the Milan Convention decided, deaf children are not given a 'chance' to learn to speak unless they are kept away from signs and manual alphabets while the trial is being made.

I sometimes read in reports of large sign institutions that the small number of pupils they have taught orally compare favorably with those taught in purely oral schools. I do not grant this; but if I did, it would not prove that the same pupils would not do better in oral schools.

Most of our oral schools are in their infancy, and are very small. None of them are large, comparing them with our large sign institutions. Therefore, we must naturally suppose that the sign institutions, being so much more numerous, and, as a rule, so much larger, have a larger number of bright pupils, and a fair comparison cannot be drawn between the few selected pupils orally instructed in large sign schools and the pupils in small pure oral schools.

The charge sometimes made, that oral schools refuse dull subjects, cannot be sustained. I have never refused them, nor have I ever known any pure oral principal to do so.

A child deaf from early infancy was admitted to my school. He was afflicted with chorea, or St. Vitus's dance, had sores on his mouth and hands, and was exceedingly careless and impatient. He had had some instruction from a sign teacher and some from an articulation teacher. His mother told me they had failed in their efforts. His nervous twitching was so bad that he would sometimes turn around a dozen times before he could look at a word on my lips. His upper teeth seemed almost to cover the under teeth. His hand shook so, that it was with difficulty that he could hold a pencil. Sickness kept him at home a great deal. Omitting time lost in this way, he has been under my instruction about three years. In that time he has learned to speak about two thousand words, writes quite legibly, and has gained much general information under the head of language and geography lessons. Though he is still very nervous at times, he has slowly but steadily improved physically; and, if he can remain with me as long as sign institutions ask for the education of their pupils, he will have a good education and speak with sufficient distinctness. I tell of his case only in the interest of difficult subjects. Of course it was necessary to give careful thought to the proper treatment of his physical condition while giving him speech, lip-reading, mental development, and writing; and, I may add, I needed to help him to be morally strong to overcome his extreme impatience and carelessness.

I have had nine years' experience with the deaf, and I consider him one of the most difficult subjects I have ever known.

Dr. Buxton quoted a sentiment of Sir Arthur Helps at the Milan Convention that we would all do well to remember. 'Human nature,' he says, 'is a thing to which we can put no limits, and which requires to be treated with unbounded hopefulness.'

I have been an advocate of day schools for the deaf. I still believe such conditions are more natural, and that they are better, provided the child has a home within reasonable distance of school, and where parents and friends communicate with it only through speech. When these conditions do not exist the principal of an oral day school is at an immense disadvantage. This also would prevent any just comparison between articulation pupils in a boarding-school like our sign institutions and the pupils in an oral day school, where many of their homes are so far from school as to cause irregular attendance.

If orally taught deaf children cannot be with judicious parents and friends out of school hours, I think they are better off in an oral boarding-school, *provided* they have intelligent attendants out of school hours who are pledged to talk to the pupils, and who hold their positions on condition of their fulfilling this pledge. Thus always being surrounded with talking influences, they will naturally acquire the habit of speech.

It has been said that articulation teaching is injurious to the health of teachers. Facts do not support this statement when the teaching is done in purely oral schools. Special articulation work in sign schools may be unusually wearing. Worry is always more harmful than work, and our pure oral teachers may be sick at heart to feel how few American schools for the deaf employ the methods they believe in. 'Hope deferred maketh the heart sick.'

Deaf children should be early taught to speak. In the future, when their parents are blessed with a knowledge of the truths contained in Miss Mary S. Garrett's 'Directions to Parents of Deaf Children,'* they will in many cases begin this work. Until this good time comes I heartily recommend their being placed in moderate-sized oral boarding-schools at four or five years. I say moderate sized, for it seems to me it is impossible to give deaf or hearing children the 'mothering' they crave and need in very large schools. Very large schools for young people are sad sights, whether for the deaf or hearing.

That noble and now powerful organization in many of our largest cities—the Children's Aid Society—is rapidly doing away with large institutions for hearing children, preferring to risk placing poor hearing children in families who are willing to receive a child rather than to surround them with the many evils of life in a large institution. A little child begets love, and in some cases elevates the home it enters in this way.

In conversation with one of the most active workers in the Children's Aid Society—I think one of its projectors—I spoke of the necessity for boarding-schools for many deaf children *at present*. I unfolded the case as clearly as I could to her, and she agreed with me in thinking that a boarding-school on the cottage plan for about one hundred pupils was about the best we could hope to do for the deaf 'at present.' I emphasized 'at present' because the world moves, and what may be the best now may not be years hence.

* See Mary Garrett's Private School, No. 6.

Many touching stories are told by this Society of the unnatural little children it has found in these large institutions—one of a little girl who did not understand when asked to kiss some one, so completely had this very ordinary expression of affection been left out of her young life. If large institutions are sad for hearing children, how inexpressibly so are they for afflicted deaf children!

We may not look for a deaf child of four or five years to remember or make use of as much as a child of eight or nine would; but those who are taught early to speak will not form so strong a habit of expressing their wants in signs; their voices will ultimately be more natural, lip-reading more true, &c.

In reviewing the work done in Miss Mary S. Garrett's school the past year in her last report, she says, in reference to the *present conditions* by which the deaf are surrounded: 'The improvement in the speech and lip-reading of the pupils which it is the main object of the school to teach is all that could be expected under the circumstances. Before every deaf child can have the advantage of the best circumstances, almost as great a revolution must take place in the knowledge of those by whom they are surrounded from their birth as took place when the general belief of the world that the deaf are necessarily idiotic gave way a couple or more centuries ago to the knowledge that they are not.

It is known now by some that when every person who has any communication with a deaf child talks to it from infancy on, just as to a hearing child, and never uses a motion, sign, or manual alphabet with it, that the child learns the habit of depending on the lips alone and to understand spoken language readily, and the terrible barrier which makes it alone in the world is removed.

When this knowledge becomes general, and hearing people take advantage of it and act accordingly, then, and not until then, will the oral method be taught under the best circumstances. In the meantime hundreds of deaf children are being sacrificed to the ignorance of those who control them, just as thousands were sacrificed in the old times to the ignorance of the age.

Our pupils improve just in proportion to their several advantages in this respect; the more constantly they are talked with the faster they improve. I have never used any medium of communication with them except the speech and lip-reading they have learned, and they naturally always talked to me and always understand me; and if every one else did the same, and had always done so, speech and lip-reading would be easy and natural to them. They need the constant practice which makes speech and lip-reading a habit. EMMA GARRETT.

49. NEW JERSEY SCHOOL.

Weston Jenkins, Superintendent, expresses no opinion upon this question.

50. UTAH SCHOOL.

H. C. White, Principal. No reply to circular letter received to date, June 2, 1888.

51. NORTHERN NEW YORK INSTITUTION.

Henry C. Rider, Superintendent. No reply to circular letter received to date, June 2, 1888.

52. FLORIDA INSTITUTE.

St. Augustine, Fla., May 26, 1888.

'DR. A. G. BELL.—Dear Sir,—Am sorry the reply to your circular letter has not reached you. I hope it has ere this. I wrote it and left it on my desk for mailing, and can trace it no further. I will try to answer some of the questions as I remember them. We have 18 deaf pupils. Several of them were over 12 years of age when they entered, but even in this case we are teaching articulation to 12.

With 11 articulation is used as a means of instruction; 2 have never been taught articulation; and 4 have been tried without success. Two of the pupils can hear a little (semi-deaf); one became deaf at two years of age; and the other gradually lost her hearing. Cause unknown. We have never made any effort to develop the hearing of these pupils, though I doubt not at least one of them could be much benefited by a systematic course of training. * * *

'It has been our experience that every deaf child of fair mental powers can be taught to speak with sufficient clearness to be understood by those accustomed to hearing "semi-mutes" talk, if the articulation training begin while the child is very young—say 4 to 8 years of age. But little can be done with children over 15 years of age. * * *

'PARK TERRELL, *Principal*.'

53. WASHINGTON (TERRITORY) SCHOOL.

James Watson, Director. No reply to circular letter received to date, June 2, 1888.

54. NEW ORLEANS PUBLIC SCHOOL.

'As to the instruction of the deaf, in order to enable them to be well-educated, self-sustaining, and useful citizens, they should be sent early to school, but not to large State institutions, as home influences and the daily observations of life exert a powerful effect in improving the minds and manners of this class of children. The fact is that all growing children require close watching on the part of their own parents and relatives. Therefore day schools are far preferable to the large State institutions.

'R. B. LAWRENCE, *Principal*.'

55. EVANSVILLE SCHOOL, INDIANA.

Charles Kerney, Principal, expresses no opinion upon this question.

56. LA CROSSE DAY SCHOOL.

'I think that much valuable time and teaching force are thrown away trying to teach many deaf-mutes to talk. It is like Gratiano's "grain of wheat in a bushel of chaff"—an infinite deal of trouble and of little value when acquired. I speak this of the majority, who *never learn* to talk with ease, facility, and pleasure to themselves and others; still I would not cease to try to give all a chance.

'ALBERT HARDY, *Superintendent of Schools*.'

57. NEW MEXICO SCHOOL, SANTA FÉ

'I think some of having articulation here, if a good number of scholars can be had; but the people here in the Territory, being mostly Mexican, speak Spanish, and if their deaf youths be taught to speak in English in this school it would be of no use to them, as they cannot talk then to their Spanish-speaking folks. They generally want them to get education here, especially in the Roman Catholic creed. English is now taught here according to the Committee's decision. * * * This school is a new one, which has recently become the public property of this Territory. * * * There are now six scholars in attendance here. Two out of the six scholars here are semi-deaf and can speak Spanish, but they are learning English here. Their deafness occurred at the age of ten years. Before it occurred they were taught to speak at home. Two were born deaf, and the rest became deaf during early childhood. * * *

'LARS M. LARSON, *Superintendent*.'

PRIVATE AND DENOMINATIONAL SCHOOLS.

1. WHIPPLE'S HOME SCHOOL.

'We make articulation a specialty, teaching it to every child who enters school. We find all can be taught to articulate who have any degree of intelligence. 'MARGARET HAMMOND, *Principal*.'

2. GERMAN EVANGELICAL LUTHERAN INSTITUTION.

D. H. Uhlig, Director, expresses no opinion upon this question.

3. ST. JOHN'S CATHOLIC INSTITUTE.

Charles Fessler, President, expresses no opinion upon this question.

KNAPP'S INSTITUTE.

Fred. Knapp, Principal.—No reply to circular letter received up to date, June 2, 1888.

5. VOICE AND HEARING SCHOOL.

Mary McCowen, Principal, expresses no opinion upon this question.

The following passage marked by Miss McCowen is quoted from *The New Method* (April, 1888), a paper issued monthly by 'The Voice and Hearing School':

'Our little three-year-old pupil (supposed to have been totally deaf from birth, and so far developing no hearing), who had never learned at home to speak even the word "mamma," is getting to be a regular chatter-box—not that she has perfect speech, but her voice can be heard every hour of the day in spontaneous baby chatterings, using words intelligently which she has been taught, and day after day gaining new ones. At the same time her voice is losing the screech (no other word expresses the noise) which terrified the neighbors when she first came, and she is also fast forgetting the signs (because she does not need them to make herself understood) which had been specially taught her at home by a deaf-mute teacher. Her parents visited her last month, and expressed themselves delighted with her progress in every way.'

6. MARY GARRETT'S SCHOOL.

'Every year that I work among the deaf I feel more and more convinced that if *every* deaf child was guided to speech and lip-reading from infancy, and carefully kept from motions, signs, and manual alphabets, and allowed *only speech* for all communications with others, that the results would be satisfactory to us and most comforting to the afflicted deaf.

'We cannot expect the best results unless we use all the means. 'MARY S. GARRETT, *Principal*.'

Some of the views Miss Mary Garrett would desire to express will be found in the following article, written by her and published in the *Medical and Surgical Reporter* of June 12, 1886. This is the article referred to by her sister, Miss Emma Garrett, Principal of the Pennsylvania Oral School (No. 47):—

'DIRECTIONS TO PARENTS OF DEAF CHILDREN.

'All deaf children whose eyesight is good and who are not idiotic, can with extremely rare exceptions, be taught to talk and can learn lip-reading, provided their parents, care-takers, and teachers know how to guide and teach them. When parents discover an infant to be deaf, they should continue to talk to it, just as every mother does to a hearing baby when it is learning to talk; she does not use motions to it, because it has not yet commenced to understand her language, but she repeats over and over again to it the pet names she calls it, tells it again and again to "say papa," "say mamma," &c., &c., until it learns to understand and then to copy her words. She is keen to discover, encourage, and correct its first attempts at articulation.

'The attention of the deaf infant should be directed to the mouth with the same persistence, and it should be talked to just the same by every one who is with it. No more motions should be used with it than with a hearing child; its attention should be always guided to the mouth of the speaker and concentrated there. Little by little it will begin to attach meaning to the words and sentences it sees, just as the hearing child little by little learns to attach meaning to the words and sentences that it hears. People almost universally, when they wish to take an infant from its mother, hold out their arms and say, "Come," watching the little one for an indication in its face of its desire to be taken, or to see if it will hold out its arms to come. Thus the child learns the meaning of the word "come," but as it grows older the parent or others simply call it to come, without holding out the arms, dropping the motion as soon as the child understands the word. No more motions should be used with a deaf child than this, which amounts simply to showing the action represented by a word; the words should be indefinitely repeated, that the child may become familiar with their looks on the mouth, while the representation of an action should be dropped as soon as possible, and should never be made without at the same time showing the child the word representing it. The names of objects may be taught with the objects, which is really the way in which hearing children learn them in their homes. We must always remember that when a hearing child is learning to talk its hearing gives it the advantage of every word spoken in its presence, while the deaf child only has the advantage of seeing the mouth of the person it happens to be looking at, or who is talking with it, and this difference must be made up to the deaf child by a great amount of repetition of the words and language we are teaching it.

'Every one with whom a deaf child comes in contact should talk to it and encourage and aid it to articulate. Deaf babies begin to say "Ma-ma-ma" just as hearing babies do, but as a rule it is not encouraged in them; if it were, and the child properly guided to further articulation, it would talk.

'Miss Fuller, Principal of the Horace Mann School at Boston, quotes in her report for 1885 a part of a letter which she received "from the mother of a congenitally deaf pupil, now seven years of age, who is able to use speech and to understand it upon the lips of others to a remarkable degree." Miss Fuller says further that the letter "shows what a mother had done before her child entered school at the age of four years."

'The mother writes: "In trying to recall what Bertha learned in the first three years of her life, I realize the fact that it was through ignorance of her total deafness that we taught her anything. Thinking all the time that she was very backward in learning to talk, we took unusual pains with her, saying over the simple words that children catch so easily. If we had known at the beginning that she heard nothing when we spoke to her, I am afraid, instead of teaching her what little we did, we should have been discouraged and used signs. As it was, she had learned to speak many words before she entered school. "Papa" and "Mamma" were the first words that she learned. We would say, "Come and see papa," or "Come and see mamma," and at the same time hold out our hands to her. In a short time she learned to recognize us by these names and call us by them. To be sure, the words sounded very much alike when she spoke them, but hearing children often speak imperfectly at first. When she was sitting on the floor, I would say "Up" to her, and partly lift her, so that she soon learned what the word signified, and would say, "Mamma, up." She always lived among uncles and aunts, who have helped us in teaching her to talk. None of them ever used signs with her, but talked as with a hearing child. When quite young she learned to call them by their respective names. If she wanted to go to one of them she was induced to say, "Auntie Jennie," or "Uncle George," before she was gratified. In the same manner she learned to speak the name of any object that interested her. To teach her that she must not play with the stove, I showed her that it soiled her hands, and told her they were "all black." If she disobeyed, she would come to me, hold up her hands, and say, "All black." At one time we lived in a house with a family to whom Bertha became very much attached. She learned to call them by name, and when we took her to see them we always asked her if she wanted to go up-stairs. It was not long before she would say "Up-stairs" to us, many times in a day, meaning to ask us if she could go up.

'In this way we did what we could for her until we took her to school. The manner in which we had begun with her was very kindly commended, and we were advised to continue talking with her and teaching her words, which we have done. None of her questions, and they are very numerous, are ever allowed to go unanswered. We always encouraged her to talk to us about her play and everything that interests her, and try to explain what she does not understand. But our feeble efforts seem like nothing in comparison with what her teacher has done and is still doing for her. We appreciate it all, and only hope that Bertha may long remain under her skilful guidance and care.

'No one should be allowed to make motions or signs to the child, or to teach it the manual alphabet, as it grows older. It should be strictly trained to depend on lip-reading and that alone. When the child is old enough, it may be taught to write words and sentences as soon as it can articulate them and read them from the lips, but not before.

'There are no doubt mothers who would be skilful enough in training their children from the beginning so that they would never need to go to special schools for the deaf, but could be taught with the hearing; probably, however, the majority of parents would need to send their children to school taught by specially trained articulation teachers, for a while at least. Such teachers should be equally strict that all communications with their pupils, in classes and out of classes, at the table, on the play-ground, and on all occasions, should be through speech and speech alone. It is the universal experience that hearing children who study French and German in English schools, where all their lessons, outside of these special classes, are recited in English, do not learn to speak these languages. If deaf children are given special lessons in articulation in schools where they see signs and the manual alphabet used constantly around them, and where they use them in the play-ground, at the table, or in their classes, the cases where they become proficient in the actual use of speech and lip-reading will be as rare as those hearing children who become proficient in French and German under similar circumstances.

'Children or grown persons who lose their hearing through sickness should at once be trained to read the lips and encouraged to talk just as they did before, and they should as studiously be kept from all contact with signs or manual alphabet as the congenitally deaf.

'Miss Emma Garrett, Principal of the Pennsylvania Oral School for the Deaf at Scranton, Pa., describes in the January number of the *Annals of the Deaf* for 1886 the case of a pupil of hers. He was a young lad who lost his hearing in May, 1885. Under her direction he was induced to continue to talk as before and to depend on lip-reading alone for his communication with others; after spending a very few weeks under her instruction in the autumn, he was able to take his place in the hearing school which he had formerly attended, and all his communication there is through lip and speech-reading. There is a great difference in the aptitude of this class of the deaf for acquiring lip-reading; some seem to be what might be called natural lip-readers, and learn it from their associates simply by watching their lips, while others need training from special teachers. All such persons should, however, train themselves or be trained to depend on lip-reading and speech, and not on writing.

'It needs very little reflection on the part of intelligent minds to estimate the difference in the life of a person who is able to understand the speech of those around him, and to make himself understood by them, from the life of one who knows only signs and the manual alphabet, which are almost unknown outside of the institutions where they are taught.

'As there is only one deaf person to every 1,500 hearing persons in our population, it behooves us to help that one deaf person to fit himself for communication with those 1,500. We cannot expect the 1,500 to learn manual alphabets or arbitrary signs to suit the one deaf person.

'There is a popular delusion that the vocal organs of deaf children are defective; the fact is, that such cases are rare exceptions, and that as a rule their vocal organs are normal. The articulation of consonant sounds depends on certain positions of the lips, tongue, teeth, and palate. The quality of vowel sounds depends on certain positions of the tongue. Any deaf child who can cry and scream, and has lips, tongue, teeth, and palate, has the necessary vocal organs.

'The deaf children are capable of being taught by the *Pure Oral Method*, and the method is a success when parents, care-takers, and teachers know how to apply it. It is possible for deaf born children to learn speech and lip-reading after they begin to go to school, if they have competent teachers; but much time would be saved and far better results obtained if parents would do their part before the child is sent to school.

'*Great results have already been gained through the Oral Method, and I have no doubt that greater and better results than any already obtained await us in the future, as the method becomes more widely and more strictly and intelligently applied. The oral pupil who has the least amount of intelligible speech and of lip-reading compared with his fellow oral pupils, has just that much advantage over the most expert maker of arbitrary signs and the manual alphabet, which are sure to be as unintelligible to the general public as our speech is to the sign maker.*

'*The more perfect we can make the speech of the deaf, and the more skilful we can train them to be in lip-reading, and the greater the amount of language we can teach them, the happier and more independent they will be.* 'MARY S. GARRETT.'

7. MARIA CONSILIA INSTITUTE.

Sister Adèle, Principal, expresses no opinion upon this question.

8. CINCINNATI ORAL SCHOOL.

Katharine Westendorf, Principal. No reply to circular letter received to date, June 2, 1888.

9. CHICAGO CATHOLIC SCHOOL.

No reply to circular letter received to date, June 2, 1888.

10. MISS KEELER'S ARTICULATION CLASS.

'I have a private class for deaf-mutes taught by the same system as that used in the New York Institution for the Improved Instruction for Deaf-Mutes, in which I was an instructor from 1873 till 1885. 'SARAH WARREN KEELER, *Instructor*.'

11. CINCINNATI CATHOLIC SCHOOL.

'As I have been in the profession only since last September, I do not feel warranted in making any observations. Our course of instruction is the same as that pursued at the Philadelphia Institute, except that we, for want of means, do not teach articulation or give industrial training. * * *

'E. P. CLEARY, *Principal*.'

12. SARAH FULLER HOME FOR LITTLE CHILDREN WHO CANNOT HEAR.

[This is the first infant school for the deaf in America. The members of the Royal Commission may desire to know something of the origin and purposes of the school. I, therefore, take the liberty of quoting from a personal letter received from the Principal of the Horace Mann School.—A. G. B.]

'Newton Lower Falls, Mass., May 8, 1888.

'MY DEAR MR. BELL,—* * * I want to tell you a little about the beginning of our home school for little deaf children, as it will soon open. If you have had time to read the articles which I have sent to you, you know our object.

'During the years of my work for deaf children I have often been pained to know that bright eager little minds were found to wait for needed direction until, through neglect, they became listless and indifferent to natural helps. No institution would receive them, day schools were too distant to allow them to live in their homes and go back and forth without much trouble and expense, and private teaching cost too much for the returns to be gained, so no practical way seemed to lead out of the many difficulties until Mrs. Francis Brooks said emphatically: "We will have a little school." She has through friends secured enough money to warrant a good beginning, and we shall probably open the school next month with three pupils. One child is two and a half, deaf from cerebro-spinal meningitis, with some perception of sound, good antecedents, and a bright, attractive child. Another probable pupil was born deaf, good parentage, and is nearly three years of age. We have rented a small house near Mrs. Brooks's home in West Medford, and have two admirable persons to take charge—one as matron, and the other as teacher. Nothing has been so full of interest to me since the opening of the Horace Mann School as this ideal home for very young deaf children. I can scarcely resist the wish to go to it myself. I would like very much to have an opportunity to tell you more about it. To-night I cannot write longer, but you shall know of my plans for it from time to time.

'I am, sincerely yours, 'SARAH FULLER.'

[The letter of Mrs. Brooks which has led to the establishment of this school is full of interest, and should be preserved. I therefore take the liberty of appending it.—A. G. B.]

'THE SARAH FULLER HOME FOR LITTLE CHILDREN WHO CANNOT HEAR.

'It is proposed to establish in the country, near Boston, a home for children who, being deaf, cannot gain a knowledge of language unless taught.

'It is believed that in such a home, surrounded by the fostering care so needful to all young children, much may be done to mitigate the misfortune of deafness for these little ones.

'While teaching them to speak and to read the lips of those who speak to them, it will be possible to give them at an early age such knowledge of the rudiments of language, both spoken and written, as is usual with young hearing children.

'If this be accomplished, they will start in life less heavily weighted than if they are neglected until they are of the proper school age.

'It is not proposed to retain these children in the home after they are old enough to go to the Horace Mann School, only to prepare them for that and to utilize their earliest years before the organs of speech have lost their elasticity.

'If you are inclined to aid us in this undertaking, will you kindly sign this paper and name the amount of your gift?

'The money thus promised will be collected and acknowledged promptly.

'Please address and return to Mrs. Francis Brooks, 97 Beacon Street, Boston.

Name..............................

Address..............................

Amount..............................

SCHOOLS IN THE DOMINION OF CANADA.

1. CATHOLIC INSTITUTION (MALE), MONTREAL.

J. B. Manseau, Principal. No reply to circular letter up to date, June 2, 1888.

2. CATHOLIC INSTITUTION (FEMALE), MONTREAL.

Sister Mary of Mercy, Superioress. No reply to circular letter up to date, June 2, 1888.

3. HALIFAX INSTITUTION.

'As a native of the mother country, and for many years engaged in the instruction of the deaf and dumb there, I feel anxious to see the education of the deaf placed upon a proper basis. To accomplish this, in my view, the following things are necessary:

'1. Adequate financial support guaranteed by law to lift the institutions above the precarious and fluctuating support of *voluntary contribution*.

'2. A lengthened term of instruction—eight years at least, as in our own Nova Scotia law.

'3. Better remuneration of teachers.

'4. Elevation of teachers' qualifications and status.

'The last two would almost follow from the first, the want of funds being one chief source of the backwardness of deaf-mute education in Great Britain. Inadequate remuneration leads to inferior qualification and status of teachers, and that again to inferior work.

'The best basis for an institution for the deaf is to have its management organized as a voluntary corporation, subject to public election, drawing a *per capita* allowance for the support of its pupils, payable partly by the State and partly by the municipality or parish to which the pupils belong, an allowance sufficient to cover the cost of maintenance and education. Voluntary contributions need not be excluded, but the work should be regarded as *national*, not *private*—a matter of *right*, not an *eleemosynary dole*. The State to satisfy itself as to the quality of the work done by competent inspection or by tests applied according to a standard and method arranged by experts in the education of the deaf.

'Such a system would produce the maximum of results with the minimum of friction and waste.

'One evil to be dreaded is the subordination of the work to party politics, and another the employment of non-experts as inspectors or supervisors of the educational work. This has done serious mischief to the cause of late years in some parts of America. In the old country there is less danger from political interference, but more from the appointment of merely professional men, chiefly clergymen, as inspectors who have no special acquaintance with deaf-mute education. No general educational qualifications or attainments, however eminent, can supply the lack of special training here, where more than anywhere else the adage applies, "A little knowledge is a dangerous thing."

'J. SCOTT HUTTON, *Principal*.

'May 17, 1888.'

4. ONTARIO INSTITUTION.

R. Mathison, Superintendent, forwards reports of his Institution. The following passages, marked by Mr. Mathison, are quoted from the 1885 and 1887 Reports:—

From the 1885 *Report*.

'In each class there has been an average of twenty pupils, a number really in excess of what ought to be. Experience has demonstrated that sixteen deaf and dumb children are sufficient to tax the most painstaking and conscientious teacher. Although gratifying success has been shown by our teachers in the past with the larger number, still it is too much to expect that the same rate of progress can be maintained. The difficulties of teaching the deaf are greater than in teaching speaking children, as it is largely an individual work. With our present number of teachers, we are still obliged to place twenty or twenty-one pupils in each class. It is to be hoped that arrangements will be made whereby additional teachers may be obtained, so that the pupils now here, and to come, may receive an increased amount of benefit during their term of instruction.

'During the past year we have pursued the same methods of instruction as have been in vogue in former years, making every study subordinate to the teaching of language—the great want of the deaf. The Province owes every deaf-mute child an education, and a good one. It is even more necessary that a deaf child should be educated than a speaking one, and this leads me to remark that the time allowed in this institution, seven years, is too short for the proper instruction of the majority of deaf-mutes. Pupils are admitted at seven years of age and are supposed to complete their studies when fourteen, at which age most speaking children are still at school. A deaf child has to be taught more than a speaking one, and yet it is allowed fewer years in which to receive the necessary instruction. An extension to ten years, with a course of study for that period, would enable us to impart a good knowledge of language to a majority of the children who attend here.

'We have 235 pupils at the present time. About thirty of these are young children, all of whom are stated to be over seven years of age. They require constant, watchful care and attention, and were it not that the law compels us to receive them, it would be far better if they remained at home with their mothers until a more mature age had been reached. Their minds do not seem capable of grasping ideas, and for two or three years they are only taught the alphabet, and the names of a few objects which could be taught them in their own homes. The children who come here when nine or ten years of age take up the work much more readily than those who come younger, and are as far advanced at the end of one year as the younger ones who have spent two or three years here. Primary instruction could be given these little ones just as well by their parents, if they would interest themselves in the matter. A child may be taught quite early to write the letters of the alphabet and combine them into words indicating objects which can be shown to them. Its own name and names of persons in the family may also be learned in the same way. When a number of words are memorized, short and easy sentences may be written and understood by the child. Counting with objects may also be undertaken, and afford a pleasant pastime for the little one, shut out as it is in many instances from enjoying the play of speaking children. A little attention given in this way would help the young deaf and dumb child materially.

'Considerable discussion has taken place during the past year in England and the United States in reference to the establishment of day-schools for the deaf, in connection with ordinary public schools, but no definite conclusion seems to have been reached as to their desirability, as opposed to gathering them together in institutions. It has been contended that deaf-mutes brought into communication with hearing and speaking children in ordinary schools would derive great benefit from the association. The experiment was tried under the auspices of the School Board of London, England, but it was found impracticable to have them in the same rooms, and the deaf-mutes were relegated to classes in class-rooms by themselves. It was also seen that the deaf children did not associate and assimilate with the others, and that their powers of speech were insufficient to enable them to communicate with them. As a solution of the difficulties attending the day-school methods, homes were established in different parts of the city where they were kept and cared for the same as in an ordinary institution. In the United States a number of experiments have been made in the same direction, but with varying success, and where they still exist they are looked upon as only preliminary training places to fit pupils for the more thoroughly organized institutions. Professor J. C. Gordon, an eminent scholar, at the National Deaf-Mute College at Washington, has given a great deal of attention to this matter, and after thoroughly investigating the subject in a dispassionate manner, and consulting authorities at hand in the extensive library at his command, says "that disappointment and failure have uniformly followed the attempted extension and adaptation of the common school system to the needs of deaf children; that in Europe the systematic and organized efforts in that direction have been abandoned, and the education of the deaf has been confined to trained specialists in organized institutions; that a complete and satisfactory education of children who have never heard, in the same class with hearing children, has never been accomplished; that the satisfactory instruction of the deaf requires teachers having special fitness for the work, special training, and that special institutions remain the necessity for the great mass of deaf children, as they continue to afford satisfactory results with the greatest economy of time and money."

'Most of the institutions in the United States and Canada recognize the importance of industrial training for deaf-mutes. In the British institutions, however, an opposite opinion seems to prevail, for at a convention of the head-masters of these latter, held in Doncaster, a resolution was unanimously passed to the effect that the intellectual and moral training of the deaf and dumb was of more paramount importance to them than the teaching of trades. The principal objections then raised were, that when they left school they did not follow those trades which they had been taught, but preferred something else; that if they did continue to work at their respective trades, they were obliged to serve the full apprenticeship outside, no account being taken of the three or four years which they had spent at it while at school; and that the expense was too great. Since then, however, one at least of the British instructors has changed his opinion, namely the Rev. Wm. Stainer, who has charge of the London Day School. In a letter to the London *Times*, some time since, he says: "There are known to be at the present time hundreds of deaf and dumb people in the metropolis either wanting employment, or, for want of knowing a trade, incapable of supporting themselves by their own labor. Most of these have had all the advantages that an expensive school education could bestow, and yet are not self-supporting. * * * Hitherto I have advocated the entire separation of industrial and school occupations, on the ground that they would interfere with each other; but more recent experience, gained on the Continent and in the United States, convinces me that we are behind in this matter, and ought, without delay, to adopt practical measures in this direction."'

From the 1887 *Report.*

'I have no new departure in the way of imparting instruction to deaf children to announce, as we have pursued the methods which we have found to be most effective in the past. Our system is known as the *Combined* one, and by its use we are advancing side by side with the best institutions in America. The convention of instructors which met at Berkeley, California, last year came to the conclusion that the experience of many years in the instruction of the deaf has plainly shown that among the members of this class of persons great differences exist in mental and physical conditions and in capacity for improvement, making results easily possible in certain cases which are actually unattainable in others, and that the system of instruction existing at present recommends itself for the reason that its tendency is to include all known methods and expedients which have been found to be of value in the education of the deaf, while it allows diversity and independence of action, working at the same time in harmony, and aiming at the attainment of a common object.

'R. MATHISON, *Superintendent.*'

5. MACKAY INSTITUTION.

'We discourage the use of signs in the class-rooms, and encourage written and spoken language. * * *

'The advanced ones can readily communicate with hearing people and with each other without resorting to pen and paper.

'HARRIET E. MCGANN, *Superintendent.*'

6. NEW BRUNSWICK INSTITUTION.

A. H. Abell, Principal. No reply to circular letter to date, June 2, 1888.

7. FREDERICTON INSTITUTION.

Albert F. Woodbridge, Principal. No reply to circular letter to date, June 2, 1888.

LETTERS.

From the Principal of the Clarke Institution.

'Boulder, Colorado, May 5, 1888.

'DEAR SIR: Your circular came this morning. I have been out of the work of deaf-mute teaching for nearly four years, and you need more recent statistics than anything I can give you. I cannot add anything to those which Miss Yale will give you. I am very glad that you are sending out these "Queries," and hope you will receive full and prompt replies. I had a great deal of trouble to gather the tabulated statement we made in 1883, in some instances having to make *several* requests before obtaining a reply. I have just been comparing our statement with that in the last January *Annals*; it shows a gain in the teaching of articulation, but not as great a gain as I would like to see.

'The change at Hartford is quite marked, now giving some instruction in articulation to 85 out of 180, and in 1883 teaching 35 out of 188. In writing to Mr. Williams recently I commented on this increase, and he replies: "We have three teachers in our articulation department now, and are doing more than we have before done in that line. Some of our congenital mutes are doing remarkably well. I would have more rather than less of speech and speech-reading, but at the same time I believe as firmly as ever that there is a large percentage of the children in all schools for the deaf to whom speech and speech-reading can give no adequate compensation for the loss they would suffer in being deprived of the aid of the sign language in getting their education." When I think how the American Asylum fought the establishing of our school, I feel that "the world *does* move."

'I hope the *Annals* will receive the benefit of information you gather, and that you will be able to convince the Royal Commission of the advantages of articulation.

'With thanks for your kind wishes for my health, and love to Mrs. Bell,

'Yours truly, 'H. B. ROGERS.

'Professor A. Graham Bell,
'1336 Nineteenth Street, Washington, D. C.'

From the Editor of the 'American Annals of the Deaf.'

'Kendall Green, Washington, D. C., May 5, 1888.

'MY DEAR PROFESSOR BELL: I thank you for your circular, which I was glad to see; also for your courteous invitation to express my views. To express them fully would require a good deal of explanation and qualification, and I do not think it best to undertake it at present. I will only express the hope that you will urge the British Government to afford liberal support to existing schools of all kinds, and to establish new ones, without hampering them by close restrictions of any kind as to the methods to be pursued, trusting rather to "the survival of the fittest," which will be the inevitable result of the free discussion which has been going on for some time, and is not yet ended.

'Hoping you will have a pleasant and prosperous trip, and that your mission will result in much good,

'I am very truly yours, 'E. A. FAY.'

V.—STATISTICS OF ARTICULATION TEACHING.

Statistics forwarded by Superintendents and Principals of American and Canadian Schools for the Deaf in response to the Fifth Query of the Circular Letter.

Name of School.	Number of Articulation Teachers employed.	Grand total of Pupils.	Summary of Results. Totals.		Taught Articulation.		Not taught Articulation.		Analysis of Returns. Taught Articulation. Articulation used as means of instruction. Period of life when Deafness occurred.				Articulation not used as means of instruction. Period of life when deafness occurred.				Not taught Articulation. Dropped from Articulation Classes. Period of life when deafness occurred.				Received no instruction in Articulation. Period of life when deafness occurred.				Totals. Period of life when deafness occurred.				Remarks.
			Taught Articulation.	Not taught Articulation.	Articulation used as means of instruction.	Articulation not used as means of instruction.	Dropped from Articulation Classes.	Received no instruction in Articulation.	Birth or infancy (less than 2 years of age).	Early childhood (2 and less than 5 years of age).	Late childhood (5 or more years of age).	Unknown.	Birth or infancy (less than 2 years of age).	Early childhood (2 and less than 5 years of age).	Late childhood (5 or more years of age).	Unknown.	Birth or infancy (less than 2 years of age).	Early childhood (2 and less than 5 years of age).	Late childhood (5 or more years of age).	Unknown.	Birth or infancy (less than 2 years of age).	Early childhood (2 and less than 5 years of age).	Late childhood (5 or more years of age).	Unknown.	Birth or infancy (less than 2 years of age).	Early childhood (2 and less than 5 years of age).	Late childhood (5 or more years of age).	Unknown.	
PUBLIC SCHOOLS.																													
1. American Asylum	3	139	66	73	0	66	19	64	0	0	0	0	44	12	5	5	15	4	0	0	...	...	...	...	...	...	...	...	
2. New York Institution	...	...	...	...	...	...	...	...	...	...	...	...	...	...	...	...	...	...	...	...	...	...	...	...	...	...	...	...	No reply to circular letter.
3. Pennsylvania Institution	12	436	116	320	116	0	18	302	36	46	34	0	0	0	0	0	12	6	0	0	97	194	11	0	146	246	45	0	
4. Kentucky Institution	1	130	12	118	7	5	9	109	2	0	5	0	4	1	0	0	6	3	0	0	...	...	...	...	...	...	...	...	
5. Ohio Institution	...	...	...	...	...	...	...	...	...	...	...	...	...	...	...	...	...	...	...	...	...	...	...	...	...	...	...	...	Examinations prevented sending statistics.
6. Virginia Institution	1	148	86	62	24	62	14	48	...	...	...	...	...	...	...	...	...	...	...	...	...	...	...	...	...	...	...	...	
7. Indiana Institution	1	...	60	...	60	...	2	...	18	14	17	11	...	...	...	...	...	...	...	...	...	...	...	...	...	...	...	...	
8. Tennessee School*	1	108	14	94	14	0	1	93	...	...	...	...	...	...	...	...	...	...	...	...	...	...	...	...	...	...	...	...	
9. North Carolina Institution	1	...	17	...	8	9	7	...	...	...	...	...	...	...	...	...	...	...	...	...	...	...	...	...	...	...	...	...	
10. Illinois Institution	5	506	150	356	*	150	†	356	...	...	...	...	...	...	...	...	...	...	...	...	...	...	...	...	...	...	...	...	
11. Georgia Institution	*	57	5	52	0	5	0	52	0	0	0	0	2	2	1	0	0	0	0	0	...	...	...	...	...	...	...	...	
12. South Carolina Institution	2	54	23	31	15	8	4	27	...	...	...	...	...	...	...	...	...	...	...	...	...	...	...	...	...	...	...	...	
13. Missouri Institution	2	199	50	149	17	33	0	149	...	...	...	...	...	...	...	...	...	...	...	...	...	...	...	...	...	...	...	...	
14. Louisiana Institution	...	...	...	...	...	...	...	...	...	...	...	...	...	...	...	...	...	...	...	...	...	...	...	...	...	...	...	...	No reply to circular letter.
15. Wisconsin School	3	220	47	173	32	15	29	144	18	2	4	8	8	4	3	0	25	4	0	0	50	...	...	...	101	...	...	...	
16. Michigan School*	1	301	56	245	0	56	11	234	0	0	0	0	17	20	18	1	5	4	2	0	...	...	...	...	...	...	...	...	
17. Mississippi Institution	1	78	28	50	8	20	15	35	8	0	0	0	...	...	...	...	...	...	...	...	...	...	...	...	...	...	...	...	
18. Iowa Institution	...	...	...	...	...	...	...	...	...	...	...	...	...	...	...	...	...	...	...	...	...	...	...	...	...	...	...	...	No reply to circular letter.
19. Texas Asylum	1	158	45	113	0	45	12	101	0	0	0	0	28	8	9	*	10	1	1	†	...	...	...	...	...	...	...	...	
20. Columbia Institution:																													
A. Kendall School	2	61	37	24	*	37	3	21†	0	0	0	0	15	10	3	9	2	0	0	1	...	...	...	...	...	...	...	...	
B. National College	...	...	...	...	...	...	...	...	...	...	...	...	...	...	...	...	...	...	...	...	...	...	...	...	...	...	...	...	
21. Alabama Institution	2	59	15	44	12	3	2	42	...	...	...	...	...	...	...	...	...	...	...	...	...	...	...	...	...	...	...	...	
22. California Institution	1	137	32	105	0	32	21	84	0	0	0	0	...	...	...	...	...	...	...	...	...	...	...	...	102	26	6	1	
23. Kansas Institution	2	209	69	140	*	69	4	136	0	0	0	0	44	19	6	0	3	1	0	0	110	21	3	2	157	41	9	2	
24. Le Couteulx St. Mary's Institution	10	140	132	8	15	117	4	4	0	0	15	0	97	20	0	0	4	0	0	0	4	0	0	0	105	20	15	140	
25. Minnesota School	2	170	55	115	16	39	7	108	6	1	8	1	...	...	...	...	...	...	...	...	...	...	...	...	...	...	...	...	
26. Institution for Improved Instruction, N. Y.	14	183	183	0	183	0	0	0	104	43	27	9	...	...	...	...	...	...	...	...	...	...	...	...	104	43	27	9	
27. Clarke Institution	12	98	98	0	98	0	0	0	65	19	11	3	0	0	0	0	0	0	0	0	0	0	0	0	66	19	11	3	
28. Arkansas Institute	...	108	...	...	...	...	...	...	...	...	...	...	...	...	...	...	...	...	...	...	...	...	...	...	87	13	5	3	
29. Maryland School	2	95	62	33	14	48	33	0	13	0	0	1	33	10	3	2	22	10	1	0	0	0	0	0	68	20	4	3	
30. Nebraska Institute	...	100	...	...	...	...	...	...	...	...	...	...	...	...	...	...	...	...	...	...	...	...	...	...	...	...	...	...	
31. Horace Mann School	8	75	75	0	75	0	0	0	34	19	10	12	0	0	0	0	0	0	0	0	0	0	0	0	34	19	10	2	
32. St. Joseph's Institute	14	272	249	23	224	25	28	0	...	...	...	...	...	...	...	...	...	...	...	...	...	...	...	...	188	41	27	16	

33. West Virginia School																													No reply to circular letter.
34. Oregon School	1	30	6		6				2	1	3	0																	
35. Maryland School for Colored																													No reply to circular letter.
36. Colorado Institute	1	42	14	28	14	0	28	0					0	0	0	0					0	0	0	0	17	6	0	19*	
37. Chicago Day Schools (Central)	1	27	8	19	0	8	6	13	0	0	0	0	0	7	1	0													
38. Central New York Institution	1	158	30	128	15	15	3	125																					
39. Cincinnati Public School																													No reply to circular letter.
40. West Pennsylvania Institution	1	152	27	125	0	27	17	108	0	0	0	0	11	3	5	8	9	3	2	3	57	33	14	4	77	39	21	16	
41. Western New York Institution																													No reply to circular letter.
42. Portland School	5	50	50	0	50	0	0	0	33	14	2	1	0	0	0	0	0	0	0	0	0	0	0	0	33	14	2	1	
43. Rhode Island State School	4	30	30	0	30	0	0	0	16	8	4	2	0	0	0	0	0	0	0	0	0	0	0	0	16	8	4	2	
44. St. Louis Day School																													No reply to circular letter.
45. New England Industrial School	1	22	16	6	0	16	2	4	0	0	0	0	12	4	0	0	2	0	0	0	4	0	0	0	18	4	0	0	
46. Dakota School																													No reply to circular letter.
47. Milwaukee Day School	4	35	35	0	35	0	0	0	22	8	5	0	0	0	0	0	0	0	0	0	0	0	0	0	22	8	5	0	
48. Pennsylvania Oral School	2	24	24	0	24	0	0	0	18	4	2	0	0	0	0	0	0	0	0	0	0	0	0	0	18	4	2	0	
49. New Jersey School	2	96	39	57	13	26	8	49	5	8	0	0	17	4	5	0	8	0	0	0	49	0	0	0	79	12	5	0	
50. Utah School																													No reply to circular letter.
51. Northern New York Institution																													No reply to circular letter.
52. Florida Institute		18	12	6	11	1	4	2																					
53. Washington Territory School	1*	19	7	12	0	7	0	12	0	0	0	0	2	4	1	0	0	0	0	0	7	3	2	0	9	7	3	0	
54. New Orleans Public School*																													
55. Evansville School																													
56. La Crosse Day School	1	6	6	0	6	0	0	0	3	3	0	0	0	0	0	0	0	0	0	0	0	0	0	0	3	3	0	0	
57. New Mexico School																													
PRIVATE SCHOOLS.																													
1. Whipple's Home School	4	25	25	0	25	0	0	0																					
2. German Evangelical Lutheran Institute	3	132	132	0	132	0	0	0	76	46	10	0	0	0	0	0	0	0	0	0	0	0	0	0	76	46	10	0	
3. St. John's Catholic Institute	2	17	12	5	1	11	1	4	0	0	1	0	1	9	1	1	0	0	0	0	2	1	0	1	3	10	2	2	
4. Mr. Knapp's Institute																													No reply to circular letter.
5. Chicago Voice and Hearing School		20	20	0	20	0	0	0	15	3	2	0	0	0	0	0	0	0	0	0	0	0	0	0	15	3	2	0	
6. Mary Garrett's School	1	12	12	0	12	0	0	0	12	0	0	0	0	0	0	0	0	0	0	0	0	0	0	0	12	0	0	0	
7. Maria Consilia Institute	1	31	8	23	8	0	0	23	5	1	2	0	0	0	0	0	0	0	0	0									
8. Cincinnati Oral School																													No reply to circular letter.
9. Chicago Catholic School																													No reply to circular letter.
10. Miss Keeler's Articulation Class		10	10	0	10	0	0	0	6	1	1	2	0	0	0	0	0	0	0	0	0	0	0	0	6	1	1	2	
11. Cincinnati Catholic School																													No reply to circular letter.
12. Sarah Fuller Home	1	3	3	0	3	0	0	0	3	0	0	0	0	0	0	0	0	0	0	0	0	0	0	0	3	0	0	0	
CANADIAN SCHOOLS.																													
1. Catholic Institution (Male)																													No reply to circular letter.
2. Catholic Institution (Female)																													No reply to circular letter.
3. Halifax Institution	2	75	15	60	2	13	0	60									0	0	0	0					56	14	4	1	
4. Ontario Institution																													
5. Mackay Institution (Protestant)	2	43	15	28	0	15	6	22	0	0	0	0													29	12	2	0	
6. New Brunswick Institution																													No reply to circular letter.
7. Fredericton Institution																													No reply to circular letter.

No. 8. * Figures so far as given reliable, but for details Principal says: 'Statistics not accurate enough for use.'

No. 10. * 'Articulation is not used as the sole means of instruction in any case, but in most of these cases it is one of the means of instruction. The number varies as pupils improve.' † 'All pupils on entering the Institution are examined and tried to ascertain those who give promise of doing well in articulation.'

No. 11. * 'No specialist. We have always tried to improve the speech of those who came to us having the *ability* to use spoken language to even a very limited extent.'

No. 16. * 'We have 1 Articulation teacher and contemplate another.'

No. 19. * 'Four' noted, but addition of figures reveals error. † 'Two' noted, but addition reveals error.

No. 20A. * 'Thirty-seven taught articulation. Articulation used as means of instruction, but not as the sole means.' 'Two teachers of Articulation, one of whom teaches nothing else; the other devotes herself to Articulation teaching only a part of her time.' † 'Mostly deaf from birth.'

No. 23. * 'Several are talked to and talk in their regular classes, but no classes are formed where articulation is used as the sole means of instruction.'

No. 36. * 'Ten,' but addition of figures reveals 9 more unaccounted for.

No. 53. * 'No special teacher. Director and one teacher have had some experience in Articulation teaching.'

No. 54. * 'I intend introducing an Articulation class into this school shortly.'

VI. MISCELLANEOUS MATERIAL.

A DEAF-MUTE'S MEMORIAL TO CONGRESS TO ESTABLISH A DEAF-MUTE STATE.

Letter to the Editor from the 'Gallaudet Guide and Deaf-Mutes' Companion,' Vol. I, No. 12.—Boston, Mass., December, 1860.

'Near Athens, September 30, 1860.

'WM. M. CHAMBERLAIN. Dear Sir: The following is a copy of a memorial I have written and placed in the hands of our representative, Hon. James Jackson, for presentation to Congress early in December. It is sent you that, if any of our class within your reach would like a similar petition, they may do so, and send it before the Congress meet by the representative from Massachusetts, residing in Boston, who will meet and confer with Mr. Jackson at Washington.'

MEMORIAL.

'*To the Honorable the Congress of the United States—House and Senate:*

'The memorial of John James Flournoy, deaf-mute, now residing in the State of Georgia, respectfully showeth:

'That there are several deaf and dumb persons in the United States, having education, but in poor circumstances, who are incapable of competing with hearing persons in the means of making a living other than manual, and secondary to leading ones, employed by capitalists, which is that of common mechanic, or laborer; incapable from prejudice or want of situation of capacity (for none are tested) of election by the people, preferment by Government, or the usages of a profession—of having offices or emoluments, and thus contracted to the means of a day or job laborer:—that your Petitioner believes his unfortunate class of people are capable of performing many things denied their ability. But that there is no possibility of putting to effect our powers derived from education, except we could settle some territory out West, have a community of our own, and build up a small State, the government of which being ourselves (the deaf and dumb), by our management may exhibit our capacities and sources. That, unless the right to the pre-emption and government of such a territory be accorded us by the Congress and Executive, we would have no sufficient chance of evincing capacity.

'Your Petitioner therefore earnestly invokes the deliberation of the Congress. In the West, yet unchanged unto States, may be tracts of land in a territorial condition, adapted to this purpose. We pray that about forty or fifty square miles may be permitted us to select and lay off for a State and Government, devoted to the control and settlement, subject to the payment of the Government price per acre, of the deaf population of the United States and Europe, and subject, like other States, when admitted to a Republican form of Government and to the Constitution of the United States; and to be a reservation for our use and government.

'And so your Petitioner will ever humbly pray.

'JOHN JAMES FLOURNEY.'

MARRIAGE LAWS IN THEIR RELATION TO THE DEAF.

Extract from the 'Deaf-Mutes' Journal,' August 7, 1884.

'William Hebing, a young German, living on Hamilton Place, is the happy father of a ten-pound boy. The only peculiar feature in the case is that the parents are deaf-mutes, while the child, like most all children, has a strong pair of lungs, as neighbors can testify, and its organs of sound are apparently perfectly developed. Mr. Hebing is about twenty-eight years of age, and is a nephew of ex-Alderman Henry Hebing. He is an optician, and works for Bausch & Lomb. He was born dumb, as was his wife. Both are graduates of the Mute Institute in New York, where they resided for seven years. Removing to Rochester, they were married last fall in St. Boniface Church. Mr. Hebing states that he and his wife are not disturbed in their rest by baby crying.

'The matter seemed strange, and the facts were communicated to Dr. Fenno. He said that the child crying was no sign that it would talk. If the parents were born dumb and the child could talk, the doctor said he would think it strange.'—*Rochester Union and Advertiser*, July 30.

'William Hebing states that neither he nor his wife were born mutes. He merely wishes it stated, as the laws of the State forbid persons born mutes to be joined in marriage.'—*Rochester Union and Advertiser*, August 2, 1884.

Letter from the Librarian of the Law Library of Congress in reference to the above.

'Law Library, Capitol, Washington, D. C., May 23, 1888.

'MY DEAR SIR: In reply to your recent communication I have to report that, if there be a law in the State of New York "forbidding persons born mute to be joined in matrimony," I am unable to find it, and I can further say that, after considerable search, I cannot see that such was ever the law in any of the United States. It is true that persons *non compos mentis* have always been considered incapable of marriage, and in early days there was a disposition to rank mutes among this class. But that notion has long been dissipated, and it is now understood to be the law, as was decided in the year 1820 in the case of Brower *v.* Fisher, 4 Johnson's Chancery (New York), 441, that "a person though deaf and dumb from his nativity is not, therefore, an idiot or *non compos mentis*."

'Bishop, the leading American authority on the law of Marriage and Divorce (6th ed., 1881), says: "A person deaf and dumb may be competent to contract matrimony." Stewart, "On Marriage and Divorce in England and the United States," still more recent (1884), says: "Deaf and dumb persons are not idiots at law, and are mentally competent to marry." Fraser, in his well-known book on the Domestic Relations (Edinburgh, 1846), states the general conclusion to be: "Though a party be deaf and dumb, he is capable of marriage, because this corporeal infirmity is not mental incapacity, nor does it prevent the consummation of marriage by copula." And he refers at length to the great work of Sanchez (our copy is 3 vols., fol., Antwerp, 1614), where the matter is fully discussed, and the author expresses his decided opinion in favor of the validity of the marriage of parties deaf and dumb, his arguments in favor of this conclusion being strengthened by "the acknowledged fact that persons labor under this disease who are frequently of high intellectual capacity; and he adds, *durissimum esset eos compellere continenter vivere*."

'Thus, it may be concluded, such a regulation as the prohibition of the marriage of born mutes not only does not obtain in New York, but is the law nowhere in Christendom.

'Glad to be of service to you.

'I am yours very sincerely,

'CHAS. W. HOFFMAN.

'Prof. ALEXANDER GRAHAM BELL,
1336 Nineteenth Street.'

FREE INSTRUCTION OF DEAF CHILDREN.

RECENT LEGISLATION IN MASSACHUSETTS.

CHAPTER 179.

AN ACT to provide for the free instruction of deaf-mutes or deaf children.

Be it enacted, &c., as follows:—

SECTION 1. With the approval of the board of education the governor may send such deaf-mutes or deaf children as he may deem fit subjects for education, for a term not exceeding ten years in the case of any pupil, to the American Asylum at Hartford, the Clarke Institution for Deaf-Mutes at Northampton, or to the Horace Mann School at Boston, or to any other school for deaf-mutes in the Commonwealth, as the parents or guardians may prefer; and with the approval of the board he may make at the expense of the Commonwealth such provision for the care and education of children who are both deaf-mutes and blind as he may deem expedient. In the exercise of the discretionary power conferred by this act no distinction shall be made on account of the wealth or poverty of the parents or guardians of such children; no such pupil shall be withdrawn from such institution or school except with the consent of the proper authorities thereof or of the governor, and the sums necessary for the instruction and support of such pupils in such institution or school shall be paid by the Commonwealth: *Provided, nevertheless,* That nothing herein contained shall be held to prevent the voluntary payment of the whole or any part of such sums by the parents or guardians of said pupils.

SECTION 2. Section sixteen of chapter forty-one of the Public Statutes and chapter two hundred and forty-one of the acts of the year eighteen hundred and eighty-six are hereby repealed.

SECTION 3. This act shall take effect upon its passage.

Approved April 14, 1887.

GROWTH OF AMERICAN SCHOOLS FOR THE DEAF FROM 1857 TO 1887.

Statistics compiled from the American Annals of the Deaf.

Date.	Total number of Schools.	Total number of Pupils.	Number of pupils taught Articulation.	Total number of Teachers.	Number of deaf teachers.	Number of Articulation teachers.
1857	20	1,721	....	95	....	....
1863	22	2,012	....	....	....	....
1866	24	2,469	....	119	....	....
1867	24	2,576	....	120	....	....
1868	27	2,898	....	170	71	....
1869	30	3,246	....	187	77	....
1870	34	3,784	....	222	94	....
1871	38	4,068	....	260	(?)	....
1872	36	4,253	....	271	107	....
1873	38	4,252	....	274	104	....
1874	44	4,892	....	290	98	....
1875	48	5,309	....	321	111	....
1876	49	5,010	....	304	104	....
1877	49	5,711	....	356	111	....
1878	49	6,166	....	375	126	....
1879	51	6,431	....	388	113	....
1880	55	6,798	....	425	132	....
1881	55	7,019	....	444	147	....
1882	55	7,155	....	481	154	....
1883	58	7,169	....	497	151	....
1884	61	7,485	2,041	508	155	....
1885	64	7,801	2,618	540	156	....
1886	66	8,050	2,484	566	158	134
1887	69	7,978	2,556	577	155	171

ANALYSIS OF TENTH CENSUS OF THE UNITED STATES RELATING TO THE DEAF AND DUMB.

Results compiled from the published statements of the Rev. Fred. H. Wines, Expert and Special Agent of the Tenth Census for the Defective, Dependent, and Delinquent Classes.

DEAF AND DUMB OF THE UNITED STATES, 1880.

Where Found.

At home or in private families	27,867
In schools (including day schools)	5,393
In almshouses	511
In benevolent institutions	79
In hospitals or asylums for the insane	24
In prisons	4
Total	33,878

Sexes.

Males	18,567
Females	15,311
Total	33,878

Ages.

Under 6 years of age	1,437
6 to 16 years of age	10,046
Over 16 and under 21	5,013
21 years of age and over	17,382
Total	33,878

Age When Deafness Occurred.

Born deaf	12,155
Under 5 years of age	7,289
5 to 9 years of age	2,235
10 to 14 years of age	694
15 years of age	100
Unknown	11,405
Total	33,878

Causes of Deafness.

Congenital	12,155
Adventitious	10,318
Not stated	11,405
Total	33,878

Causes of Adventitious Deafness.

Causes assigned, accepted, and tabulated	9,209
Causes assigned, rejected as too vague or improbable to be counted or classified	978
No cause assigned	131
Total	10,318

Causes of Adventitious Deafness Assigned with More or Less Definiteness and Probability in the Following Cases.

Accident	593
Diseases of ear	366
Other diseases	8,250
Total	9,209

ANALYSIS OF THE CAUSES OF ADVENTITIOUS DEAFNESS IN THE UNITED STATES.

The list of causes accepted and tallied by the officers of the 1880 Census.

Meningitis	2,856
Scarlet Fever	2,695
Malarial and Typhoid Fevers	571
Measles	448
Fevers (non malarial)	381
Catarrh and Catarrhal Fevers	324
Other Inflammations of Air-passages	142
Falls	323
Abscesses	281
Whooping-cough	195
Nervous Affections	170
Scrofula	131
Quinine	78
Blows and Contusions	74
Inflammations of the Ear	72
Diphtheria	70
Hydrocephalus	63
Teething	54
Mumps	51
Small pox and Variola	47
Erysipelas	36
Fright	32
Water in the Ear	25
Sun-stroke	21
Noises and Concussions	21
Tumors	11
Chicken-pox	10
Struck by Lightning	10
Foreign Bodies in the Ear	9
Salt Rheum	3
Malformation of the Ear	2
Syphilis	2
Consumption	1
Total	9,209

SCHOOLS FOR THE DEAF IN THE UNITED STATES, 1888.

Name.	Location.	Method of instruction.	Date of opening.	Chief executive officer.
A.—PUBLIC SCHOOLS.				
1. American Asylum for the Education of the Deaf and Dumb.	Hartford, Conn	Combined	1817	Job Williams, M.A., Principal.
2. New York Institution for the Instruction of the Deaf and Dumb.	Washington Heights, New York, N. Y.	Combined	1819	Isaac Lewis Peet, LL.D., Principal. Chauncey N. Brainerd, Superintendent.
3. Pennsylvania Institution for the Deaf and Dumb.	Philadelphia (3), Pa	Manual and oral	1821	A. L. E. Crouter, M.A., Principal.
4. Kentucky Institution for the Education of Deaf-Mutes.	Danville, Ky	Combined	1823	W. K. Argo, B.A., Superintendent.
5. Ohio Institution for the Education of the Deaf and Dumb.	Columbus, Ohio	Combined	1829	Amasa Pratt, M.A., Superintendent.
6. Virginia Institution for the Education of the Deaf and Dumb and the Blind.	Staunton, Va	Combined	1839	Thomas S. Doyle, Principal.
7. Indiana Institution for the Education of the Deaf and Dumb.	Indianapolis, Ind	Combined	1844	Eli P. Baker, Superintendent.
8. Tennessee School for the Deaf and Dumb.	Knoxville, Tenn	Combined	1845	Thomas L. Moses, Principal.
9. North Carolina Institution for the Deaf and Dumb and the Blind.	Raleigh, N. C	Oral and manual	1845	W. J. Young, M.A., Principal.
10. Illinois Institution for the Education of the Deaf and Dumb.	Jacksonville, Ill	Combined	1846	Philip G. Gillett, M.A., LL.D., Superintendent.
11. Georgia Institution for the Education of the Deaf and Dumb.	Cave Spring, Ga	Manual	1846	W. O. Connor, Principal.
12. South Carolina Institution for the Education of the Deaf and Dumb and the Blind.	Cedar Spring, S. C	Combined	1849	Newton F. Walker, Superintendent.
13. Missouri Institution for the Education of the Deaf and Dumb.	Fulton, Mo	Combined	1851	William D. Kerr, M.A., Superintendent.
14. Louisiana Institution for the Deaf and Dumb.	Baton Rouge, La		1852	John Jastremski, M.D., Superintendent.
15. Wisconsin School for the Deaf	Delavan, Wis	Combined	1852	John W. Swiler, M.A., Superintendent.
16. Michigan School for the Deaf	Flint, Mich	Combined	1854	M. T. Gass, M.A., Superintendent.
17. Mississippi Institution for the Education of the Deaf and Dumb.	Jackson, Miss	Combined	1854	J. R. Dobyns, M.A., Superintendent.
18. Iowa Institution for the Education of the Deaf and Dumb.	Council Bluffs, Iowa	Combined	1855	Henry W. Rothert, Superintendent. G. L. Wyckoff, Principal.
19. Texas Deaf and Dumb Asylum	Austin, Tex	Combined	1857	W. H. Kendall, Superintendent.
20. Columbia Institution for the Deaf and Dumb.	Kendall Green, near Washington, D. C.		1857	E. M. Gallaudet, Ph.D., LL.D., President.
A. Kendall School for the Deaf	Kendall Green, near Washington, D. C.	Combined	1857	James Denison, M.A., Principal.
B. National Deaf-Mute College	Kendall Green, near Washington, D. C.	Manual	1864	E. M. Gallaudet, Ph.D., LL.D., President.
21. Alabama Institution for the Deaf	Talladega, Ala	Combined	1858	Joseph H. Johnson, M.D., Principal.
22. California Institution for the Deaf and Dumb and the Blind.	Berkeley, Cal	Combined	1860	Warring Wilkinson, M.A., Principal.
23. Kansas Institution for the Education of the Deaf and Dumb.	Olathe, Kans	Combined	1861	S. T. Walker, M.A., Superintendent.
24. Le Couteulx St. Mary's Institution for Improved Instruction of Deaf-Mutes.	Buffalo, N. Y	Manual, oral, and combined.	1862	Sister Mary Anne Burke, Principal.
25. Minnesota School for the Deaf	Faribault, Minn	Combined	1863	Jonathan L. Noyes, M.A., Superintendent.
26. Institution for the Improved Instruction of Deaf-Mutes.	New York, N. Y	Oral	1867	D. Greenberger, Principal.
27. Clarke Institution for Deaf-Mutes	Northampton, Mass	Oral	1867	Miss Caroline A. Yale, Principal.
28. Arkansas Deaf-Mute Institute	Little Rock, Ark	Combined	1867	Francis D. Clarke, M.A., Principal.
29. Maryland School for the Deaf and Dumb.	Frederick City, Md	Combined	1868	Chas. W. Ely, M.A., Principal.
30. Nebraska Institute for the Deaf and Dumb.	Omaha, Neb	Combined and aural	1869	John A. Gillespie, M.A., Principal.
31. Horace Mann School for the Deaf	Boston, Mass	Oral	1869	Miss Sarah Fuller, Principal.
32. St. Joseph's Institute for the Improved Instruction of Deaf-Mutes.	Fordham, N. Y	Combined and oral	1869	Madame Ernestine Nardin, President.
33. West Virginia School for the Deaf and the Blind.	Romney, W. Va	Combined	1870	H. B. Gilkeson, Principal.
34. Oregon School for Deaf-Mutes	Salem, Oregon	Combined	1870	Rev. P. S. Knight, Superintendent.
35. Maryland School for Colored Blind and Deaf-Mutes.	Baltimore, Md	Combined	1872	F. D. Morrison, M.A., Superintendent.
36. Colorado Institute for the Mute and Blind.	Colorado Springs, Colo.	Combined	1874	John E. Ray, M.A., Superintendent.
37. Chicago Deaf-Mute Day-Schools	Chicago, Ill	Manual and oral	1875	Philip A. Emery, M.A., Principal.
38. Central New York Institution for Deaf-Mutes.	Rome, N. Y	Combined	1875	Edward B. Nelson, B.A., Principal.

SCHOOLS FOR THE DEAF IN THE UNITED STATES, 1888—Continued.

Name.	Location.	Method of instruction.	Date of opening.	Chief executive officer.
		A.—PUBLIC SCHOOLS—Continued.		
39. Cincinnati Public School for Deaf-Mutes.	Cincinnati, Ohio	Manual	1875	A. F. Wood, Principal.
40. West Pennsylvania Institution for the Instruction of the Deaf and Dumb.	Edgewood, near Wilkinsburg, Pa.	Combined	1876	Rev. J. G. Brown, D.D., Principal.
41. Western New York Institution for Deaf-Mutes.	Rochester, N. Y	Combined	1876	Z. F. Westervelt, Principal and Superintendent.
42. Portland School for the Deaf	Portland, Me	Oral	1876	Miss Ellen L. Barton, Principal.
43. Rhode Island State School for the Deaf.	Providence, R. I	Oral	1877	Miss Anna M. Black, Principal.
44. St. Louis Day-School for the Deaf	St. Louis, Mo	Manual	1878	D. A. Simpson, B.A., Principal.
45. New England Industrial School for Deaf-Mutes.	Beverly, Mass	Combined	1879	Miss Nellie H. Swett, Principal.
46. Dakota School for Deaf-Mutes	Sioux Falls, Dakota	Combined	1880	James Simpson, Superintendent.
47. Milwaukee Day-School for the Deaf.	Milwaukee, Wis	Oral	1883	Paul Binner, Principal.
48. Pennsylvania Oral School for the Deaf.	Scranton, Pa	Oral	1883	Miss Emma Garrett, Principal.
49. New Jersey School for Deaf-Mutes	Chambersburg, near Trenton, N. J.	Combined	1883	Weston Jenkins, M.A., Superintendent.
50. Utah School for the Deaf	Salt Lake City, Utah	Manual	1884	Henry C. White, B.A., Principal.
51. Northern New York Institution for Deaf-Mutes.	Malone, N. Y	Combined	1884	Henry C. Rider, Superintendent.
52. Florida Blind and Deaf-Mute Institute.	St. Augustine, Fla	Combined	1885	Park Terrell, Principal.
53. Washington School for Defective Youth.	Vancouver, Wash	Combined	1886	James Watson, Director.
54. New Orleans Public School for Deaf-Mutes.	New Orleans, La	Manual	1886	R. B. Lawrence, Principal.
55. Evansville Deaf-Mute School	Evansville, Ind	Manual	1886	Chas. Kerney, B.A., Principal.
56. La Crosse Day-School	La Crosse, Wis	Oral	1886	Albert Hardy, Superintendent of Schools.
57. New Mexico School for the Deaf and Dumb.	Santa Fé, N. Mex.	Manual	1887	Lars M. Larson, B.A., Superintendent.
		B.—DENOMINATIONAL AND PRIVATE SCHOOLS, 1888.		
1. Whipple's Home School for Deaf-Mutes.	Mystic River, Conn	Oral	1869	Margaret Hammond, Principal.
2. German Evangelical Lutheran Institution for Deaf and Dumb.	Norris, Mich	Oral	1873	D. H. Uhlig, Director.
3. St. John's Catholic Deaf-Mute Institute.	St. Francis, Wis	Combined	1876	Rev. Chas. Fessler, President.
4. Mr. Knapp's Institute	Baltimore, Md	Oral	1877	Frederick Knapp, Principal.
5. Chicago Voice and Hearing School for the Deaf.	Englewood, Ill	Oral and aural	1882	Miss Mary McCowen, Principal.
6. Private School for Teaching Deaf Children to Speak.	Philadelphia, Pa	Oral	1885	Miss Mary S. Garrett, Principal.
7. Maria Consilia Deaf-Mute Institute	St. Louis, Mo	Combined	1885	Sister Adèle, Principal.
8. Cincinnati Oral School for the Deaf.	Cincinnati, Ohio	Oral	1886	Mrs. Katharine Westendorf, Principal.
9. Chicago Catholic School for Deaf-Mutes.	Chicago, Ill			
10. Miss Keeler's Articulation Class	New York, N. Y	Oral	1886	Miss Sarah Warren Keeler, Principal.
11. Cincinnati Catholic School for Deaf-Mutes.	Cincinnati, Ohio	Manual	1887	E. P. Cleary, B.A., Principal.
12. Sarah Fuller Home for Little Children who cannot Hear.	West Medford, Mass	Oral	1888	Sarah Fuller, Supervising Principal.
		C.—SCHOOLS FOR THE DEAF IN CANADA, 1888.		
1. Catholic Male Deaf and Dumb Institution for the Province of Quebec.	Mile-End, near Montreal, Canada.	Manual and oral	1848	Rev. J. B. Manseau, C.S.V., Principal.
2. Institution for the Female Deaf and Dumb of the Province of Quebec.	Montreal, Canada	Manual and oral	1851	Rev. Sister Mary of Mercy, Superioress.
3. Halifax Institution for the Deaf and Dumb.	Halifax, N. S	Combined	1857	J. Scott Hutton, M.A., Principal.
4. Ontario Institution for the Deaf and Dumb.	Belleville, Ontario	Combined	1870	R. Mathison, Superintendent.
5. Mackay Institution for Protestant Deaf-Mutes and the Blind.	Montreal, Canada	Combined	1870	Miss Harriett E. McGann, Superintendent.
6. New Brunswick Deaf and Dumb Institution.	Portland, N. B	Manual	1873	A. H. Abell, Principal.
7. Fredericton Institution for the Education of the Deaf and Dumb.	Fredericton, N. B	Combined	1882	Albert F. Woodbridge, Principal.

A. (3) Broad and Pine and (Oral Branch) Eleventh and Clinton Streets.
(24) No. 125 Edward Street.
(26) Lexington Avenue, between 67th and 68th Streets.
(31) No. 63 Warrenton Street.
(32) This institution has three branches: One at Fordham, another at 510 Henry Street, Brooklyn, and another at Throgg's Neck, Westchester county, N. Y.
(35) No. 649 W. Saratoga Street.
(37) There are five schools in different parts of the city. Mr. Emery's address is 43 So. May Street.
(39) Ninth Street, between Walnut and Main Streets.
(43) Corner Fountain and Beverly Streets.
(44) Corner Ninth and Washington Streets.
(47) Corner Seventh and Prairie Streets.
(54) Corner of Girod and Rampart Streets.

B. (4) Nos. 29, 31, and 33 Halliday Street.
(5) Wabash Avenue, near 63d Street.
(6) No. 16 South Broad Street.
(7) No. 1849 Cass Avenue.
(8) Seventh and Race Streets.
(9) St. Joseph's Home, May Street.
(10) No. 597 Lexington Avenue.

C. (2) No. 401 St. Denis Street.
(5) Notre Dame de Grâce.

EXHIBIT TO QUERY 21,379.

ARTICULATION TEACHING IN 1883.

[A table relating to Articulation Teaching in the United States May, 1883, compiled by Harriet B. Rogers, Principal of the Clarke Institution, Northampton, Mass., from replies received to a circular letter of enquiry. Reprinted from the Sixteenth Annual Report of the Clarke Institution, 1883. Appendix B.]

Tabular Statement concerning the Teaching of Articulation in the Institutions of the United States—May, 1883.

Name.	Location.	Date of opening.	Chief Executive Officer.	Articulation Teacher first employed.	Employed constantly since.	Number of teachers of Articulation now employed.	Number of pupils in Institution.	Number receiving instruction in Articulation.	Number using it as a means of instruction.	Number taught Articulation, but not using it as a means of instruction.
1 American Asylum	Hartford, Conn.	1817	Job Williams, M. A., Principal	1855	No (a).	2	188	35	None.	35
2 New York Institution	Washington Heights New York, N. Y.	1818	Isaac Lewis Peet, LL. D., Prin.; Carlton Carson, M. D., Sup't & Res't Physician.	1818	No (b).	8	448	200	33	167
3 Pennsylvania do	Philadelphia, Pa	1820	Joshua Foster, Principal	1870	Yes.	2	315	70	None.	70
4 Kentucky do	Danville, Ky.	1823	D. C. Dudley, M. A., Superintendent	......	......	None.	146	6	(c)6	None.
5 Ohio do	Columbus, Ohio	1829	Benj. Talbot, M. A., Acting Sup't	1868	Yes.	2	430	80	None.	80
6 Virginia do	Staunton, Va.	1839	Charles S. Roller, Principal	1876	Yes.	1	57	16	10	6
7 Indiana do	Indianapolis, Ind.	1844	William Glenn, Superintendent	1876	Yes.	1	327	41	None.	41
8 Tennessee School	Knoxville, Tenn	1845	Thomas L. Moses, Principal	1880	Yes.	1	102	13	13	None.
9 North Carolina Institution	Raleigh, N. C.	1844	W. J. Young do	1880	Yes.	1	80	10	10	None.
10 Illinois do	Jacksonville, Ill	1846	Philip G. Gillett, LL. D., Sup't	1868	Yes.	3	523	133	None.	133
11 Georgia do	Cave Spring, Ga	1846	W. O. Connor, Principal	......	......	None.	76	8	None.	8
12 South Carolina do	Cedar Spring, S. C.	1849	Newton F. Walker, Superintendent	1880	Yes.	1	48	6	6	None.
13 Missouri do	Fulton, Mo	1851	Wm. D. Kerr, M. A. do	1874	Yes.	2	192	55	None.	55
14 Louisiana do	Baton Rouge, La.	1852	R. G. Ferguson, M. A. do	......	......	None.	32	(d) 4	None.	4
15 Wisconsin do	Delavan, Wis.	1852	John W. Swiler, M. A. do	1868	Yes.	1	190	30	33	None.
16 Michigan do	Flint, Mich	1854	F. A. Platt, M. A., Principal; Dan. H. Church, Superintendent.	1876	Yes.	1	243	28	(e) 28	None.
17 Iowa do	Council Bluffs, Iowa	1855	Rev. A. Rogers, Superintendent	1878	No (f).	1	270	28	10	18
18 Mississippi do	Jackson, Miss	1856	J. R. Dobyns do	1882	Yes.	1	72	24	None.	24
19 Texas Asylum	Austin, Texas	1857	John S. Ford do	g1879	No (h).	None.	87	None.	None.	None.
20 Columbia Institution	Washington, D. C.	1857	E. M. Gallaudet, Ph. D., LL. D., Pres't	1870	Yes.	1	51	34	None.	34
21 Alabama do	Talladega, Ala.	1860	Joseph H. Johnson, M. D., Principal	......	......	None.	45	None.	None.	None.
22 California do	Berkeley, Cal.	1860	Warren Wilkinson, M. A. do	1881	Yes.	1	116	45	None.	45
23 Kansas do	Olathe, Kansas	1862	G. L. Wyckoff, Acting Superintendent	1882	Yes.	1	157	32	12	20
24 Le Conteulx St. Mary's Inst.	Buffalo, N. Y.	1862	Sister Mary Anne Burke, Principal	1873	Yes.	1	153	91	17	74
25 Minnesota Institution	Faribault, Minn.	1863	Jonathan L. Noyes, M. A., Sup't	1880	Yes.	1	127	32	6	26
26 Inst'n for Improved Instr'n	New York, N. Y	1867	D. Greenberger, Principal	1867	Yes.	14	166	166	166	None.
27 Clarke Institution	Northampton, Mass.	1867	Miss Harriet B. Rogers, Principal	1867	Yes.	12	85	86	85	None.
28 Arkansas Institute	Little Rock, Ark.	1868	H. C. Hammond, M. A., Principal	......	......	None.	52	None.	None.	None.
29 Maryland School	Frederick City, Md.	1868	Chas. W. Ely, M. A., Principal	1871	Yes.	2	89	66	None.	(r) 66
30 Nebraska Institute	Omaha, Neb	1869	J. A. Gillespie, B. D., Principal	1881	Yes.	2	94	56	13	43
31 Horace Mann School	Boston, Mass.	1869	Miss Sarah Fuller, Principal	1869	Yes.	8	83	83	83	None.
32 Whipple's Home School	Mystic River, Conn.	1869	J. Whipple, Proprietor	1868	Yes.	2	12	12	12	None.
33 St. Joseph's Institute	Fordham, N. Y.	1869	Miss Mary B. Morgan, Sup't	1870	Yes.	6	241	(i) 89	75	14
34 West Virginia Institution	Romney, W. Va	1870	J. C. Covell, M. A., Principal	1877	No (k).	None.	66	None.	None.	None.
35 Oregon School	Salem, Oregon.	1870	Rev. P. S. Knight do	......	......	None.	29	None.	None.	None.
36 Institution for Colored	Baltimore, Md	1872	F. D. Morrison, M. A., Superintendent	......	......	None.	13	None.	None.	None.
37 Ev. Lutheran Institution	Norris, Mich.	1873	H. D. Uhlig, Principal	1873	Yes.	3	40	40	40	None.
38 Colorado Institute	Colorado Spg's, Col.	1874	P. W. Downing, Principal; J. R. Kennedy, Superintendent.	......	......	None.	37	(l) 7	2	5
39 Erie Day School	Erie, Pa	1874	Miss Mary Welsh, Teacher	1874	Yes.	1	10	10	10	None.
40 Chicago Day Schools	Chicago, Ill	1875	P. A. Emery, M. A., Principal	1882	Yes.	1	(m)			
41 Central N. Y. Institution	Rome, N. Y	1875	Edward B. Nelson, B. A., Principal	1877	Yes.	1	164	25	20	5
42 Cincinnati Day School	Cincinnati, Ohio	1875	A. F. Wood do	......	......	None.	26	None.	None.	None.
43 Western Penna. Institution	Turtle Creek, Pa.	1876	Thos. MacIntire, Ph. D. do	1882	Yes.	1	102	13	6	7
44 Western New York Inst'n	Rochester, N. Y	1876	Z. F. Westervelt do	1876	Yes.	4	136	125	5	(s)120
45 Portland Day School	Portland, Me.	1876	Miss Ellen L. Barton do	1877	Yes.	4	33	33	33	None.
46 St. John's Cath. Institute	St. Francis, Wis	1876	Rev. Chas. Fessler do	1876	Yes.	2	42	34	None.	34
47 Rhode Island School	Providence, R. I	1877	Miss Katharine H. Austin do	1877	Yes.	3	30	30	30	None.
48 Mr. Knapp's School	Baltimore, Md.	1877	Frederick Knapp do	1877	Yes.	4	40	40	40	None.
49 Phonological Institute	Milwaukee, Wis.	1878	Adam Stettner do	1878	Yes.	2	21	21	21	None.
50 St. Louis Day School	St. Louis, Mo	1878	D. A. Simpson, B. A do	......	......	None.	41	None.	None.	None.
51 N. E. Industrial School	Beverly, Mass	1878	William B. Swett, Superintendent	1880	Yes.	1	19	6	1	5
52 School of Articulation	Marquette, Mich	1877	Mrs. A. M. Kelsey, Principal	1870	Yes.	(n)				
53 Dakota School	Sioux Falls, D. T.	1880	James Simpson, Superintendent	......	......	None.	10	None.	None.	2(o)
54 Scranton Day School	Scranton, Pa.	1880	Jacob M. Koehler, Principal	......	......	None.	12	None.	None.	None.
55 Oral Branch Pa. Inst'n	Philadelphia, Pa	1881	Miss Emma Garrett, Teacher in charge	1881	Yes.	7	60	60	60	None.
55 Institutions in the U. S						112	6232	1988	886	1105
National College	Washington, D. C	1864	E. M. Gallaudet, Ph. D., LL. D., Pres't	1877	No (p).	None.	31	None.	None.	None.

(a.) "Interval of 5 years, 1863-1868." (b.) "Employed, 1818-1821; 1846 one year, and from 1867 to present time." (c.) "Semi-mutes, taught almost wholly by lip-reading." (d.) "Taught by Principal." (e.) "To some extent." (f.) "Fire interrupted." (g.) "Also in 1880 and 1882." (h.) "Could not procure teacher." (i.) These figures seem not to do justice to the articulation work done. (k.) "Only two years." (l.) "Taught by Principal and a hearing teacher." (m.) "No further definite information." (n.) "School closed June, 1882." (o.) "Semi-mutes, who converse orally with all who can hear." (p.) Employed for 3 or 4 years; "discontinued because of interference with legitimate work of the college. With a few lip-readers, considerable use is made of speech in recitation." (r.) "We now give all our young pupils at least a year's careful instruction in speech before deciding whether the effort shall be discontinued or not." (s.) "All will have practical use made of articulation as a means of instruction."

THE SEMI-DEAF.

[The following returns from Facts and Opinions relating to the number of pupils who could hear the ringing of a dinner-bell were used in calculating the percentage given at the end of Query 21,395.]

NAME OF SCHOOL.	Number of pupils tested.	Number who heard bell.	Percentage.
Kentucky Institution	57	26	45.6
Wisconsin School	220	23	10.4
Mississippi Institution	78	6	7.7
Texas Asylum	158	23	14.5
Kendall School	61	19	31.1
Kansas Institution	161	40	24.8
Clarke Institution	98	22	22.4
Maryland Institution	95	12	12.6
Horace Mann School	75	23	30.6
Oregon School	30	4	13.3
Chicago Day School	27	5	18.5
West Pennsylvania Institution	148	39	26.3
Rhode Island School	30	8	26.6
N. E. Industrial School	22	6	27.2
Milwaukee Day School	35	9	25.7
New Mexico School	6	1	16.6
Whipple's Home School	25	2	8.
Maria Consilia Institute	31	6	19.3
Halifax Institution	75	21	28.
Mackay Institution	43	9	20.9
	1,475	304	20.6

The following returns were not used in calculating percentages:

Mississippi Institution	"About 30 of 199 hear the bell."
Pennsylvania Institution	"The majority say they can hear a bell ring."
Illinois Institution	"They all seem to hear the *dinner-bell* (!) but only about 5 per cent hear the school bell."
Le Couteulx St. Mary	"Out of 140 pupils 6 can hear the ringing of a dinner-bell from a distance."
Minnesota School	"15 hear the steam-whistle in the morning."
New Orleans Public School	"2 pupils could hear the ringing of the dinner-bell."
Evansville School	"12 pupils could hear the bell, but total number of pupils not given."
New Mexico School	"1 can hear the doorknock if about 7 yards near the door."
Ontario Institution	"Cannot give reliable statistics—so many of the smaller ones mistake hearing for vibration."

EXHIBIT TO QUERY 21,400.

PHOTOGRAPH OF AN AURICULAR CLASS.

[This Exhibit consisted of a photograph of an auricular class in the New York Institution, showing the use of the Currier "Conico-cylindrical conversation tubes with duplex ear-piece," a copy of the photograph is appended.]

EXHIBIT TO QUERY 21,408.

SCHOOL REPORTS.

[The following Reports of American and Canadian Schools for the Deaf were laid before the Royal Commission and left for their inspection.]

American Asylum, 1836-'46, 1847-'57, 1858-'67.
American Asylum, 1877, 1884, 1885, 1887.
Minnesota Institution, 1866-1874.
Minnesota Institution, 1875-1886.
Clarke Institution, 1867-1887.
Columbia Institution, 1868, 1883, 1884, 1886.
Conference of Principals and Superintendents, 1868, at Washington (Columbia Rep.).
Conference of Principals and Superintendents, 1884, at Faribault (Minn. Rep.).
Convention of American Instructors, 1876, at Belleville, Ontario.
Convention of American Instructors, 1886, at Berkeley, California.
Report of the Third Convention of Articulation Teachers, New York, 1884.
Groning Institute, 1887.
Institution for the Improved Instruction of Deaf-Mutes, 1870, 1874, 1882, 1883, 1884, 1885.
Halifax Institution, 1877, 1880, 1883, 1884, 1886.
Mackay Institution, Montreal, 1880, 1881, 1884, 1886.
Ontario Institution, Belleville, 1881, 1884, 1885, 1886, 1887.
Quebec Catholic Institution, 1882.
Georgia Institution, Cave Spring, 1871, 1880.
Wisconsin Institution, Delavan, 1871, 1880, 1882.
Wisconsin Phonological Institution, Milwaukee, 1880.
Wisconsin State Board of Supervision, 1882.
Milwaukee School Board Proceedings, 1886, 1888.
Pennsylvania Institution, Philadelphia, 1871, 1873, 1876, 1879, 1880, 1882, 1884, 1885.
Pennsylvania Oral School (Scranton), 1867.
Philadelphia Oral School, Mary S. Garrett, Principal, 1886, 1887, 1888.
Western Pennsylvania Institution, Pittsburg, 1883.
New York Institution, Washington Heights, 1861-1868 (1 vol.)
New York Institution, Washington Heights, 1871, 1875.
Western New York Institution, Rochester, 1881, 1884.
Miss S. W. Keeler's Articulation Class, New York, 1888.
Church Mission, New York, 1873.
Le Couteulx St. Mary's Institution, Buffalo, N. Y., 1875, 1884.
Horace Mann School, Boston, Mass., 1874, 1884, 1887.
New England Industrial School, Beverly, Mass., 1884, 1885, 1887.
Colorado Institution, 1875.
Kansas Institution, 1876, 1884, 1886.
Louisiana Institution, 1876.
Missouri Institution, 1876, 1878, 1884.
Alabama Institution, 1878.
Tennessee Institution, 1878, 1886.
South Carolina Institution, Cedar Springs, 1887.
North Carolina Institution, Raleigh, 1883.
Mississippi Institution, Jackson, 1883, 1887.
Maryland Institution, Frederick City, 1883, 1885.
Kentucky Institution, Danville, 1881, 1883, 1885, 1887.
Texas Institution, Austin, 1881.
Rhode Island Institution, 1879, 1883, 1885, 1886, 1887.
New Jersey Institution, 1883, 1884, 1885, 1886.
Portland, Maine, School Committee, 1888.
Illinois Institution, Jacksonville, 1882, 1884, 1886.
Illinois Board of Public Charities, 1872, 1874, 1876, 1878, 1880, 1882, 1884, 1886.
Ohio Institution, Columbus, 1883.
Iowa Institution, 1883.
Michigan Institution, Flint, 1880.
California Institution, Berkeley, 1880, 1884.
National Deaf-Mute College, Washington, Historical Sketch, 1880.

Exhibit to Query 21,409.

MEMOIR.

[This Exhibit consisted of a memoir "Upon the Formation of a Deaf Variety of the Human Race," by Alexander Graham Bell, published among the Memoirs of the National Academy of Sciences, 1883, Vol. II, pp. 177 to 262.

The Memoir is too long to be reprinted here, but copies of a reprint may be found in the libraries of American and Canadian Schools for the Deaf; and the chief libraries of the world contain either the reprint or the original.]

Exhibit to Query 21,446.

ANCESTRY OF THE DEAF.

[This Exhibit consisted of genealogical charts showing the ancestry of about one hundred New England families, in each of which three or more children have been born deaf. The charts form an index to the full genealogical material collected relating to these families.]

EXHIBIT TO QUERY 21,449.

IS THERE A CORRELATION BETWEEN DEFECTS OF THE SENSES?

People sometimes assume that a defect of any important sense is balanced to the individual by the increased perception of the remaining senses. For instance: it is often thought that deaf persons have better eye-sight than those who hear, and that blind persons have better hearing than those who see. The returns of the tenth census of the United States (1880) concerning the defective classes show clearly the fallacy of such a belief. They indicate that the deaf are much more liable to blindness than the hearing, and the blind more liable to deafness than the seeing.

About one person in every thousand of the population is blind, and one in every fifteen hundred deaf and dumb. Now, if these proportions held good for the defective classes themselves, we should expect to find one in a thousand of the deaf-mute population blind, or one in fifteen hundred of the blind population deaf and dumb: in other words, we should expect to find no more than thirty-four blind deaf-mutes in the country; whereas, as a matter of fact, no less than 493 blind deaf-mutes are returned in the census.

In the following table, I., I present an analysis of the doubly and trebly defective classes. The information has been compiled from the published statements of Rev. Fred. H. Wines (who had charge of the department of the census relating to the defective classes*), supplemented by unpublished information kindly furnished by the census office.

TABLE I.

Analysis of the Defective Classes as returned in the Tenth Census of the United States (1880).

Singly defective.		
Deaf and dumb†	30,995	
Blind	46,721	
Idiotic	73,370	
Insane	91,133	
Total singly defective		242,219
Doubly defective.		
Blind deaf-mutes	246	
Idiotic deaf-mutes	2,122	
Insane deaf-mutes	268	
Blind idiots	1,186	
Insane blind	528	
Total doubly defective		4,350
Trebly defective.		
Blind idiotic deaf-mutes	217	
Blind insane deaf-mutes	30	
Total trebly defective		247
Total defective population		246,816

In the following tables, II–VII., I have reduced these figures to percentages.

TABLE II.

Percentage of the Population of the United States who are Defective.

—	Totals.	Percentage.
Deaf and dumb	33,878	0·0675
Blind	48,928	0·0975
Idiotic	76,895	0·1533
Insane	91,959	0·1833
Defective population	246,816	0·4921
Population not defective	49,908,967	99·5079
Total population	50,155,783	100·0000

* *See* American Annals of the Deaf and Dumb for January, 1885.

† The "deaf and dumb" have no other natural defect save that of deafness. They are simply persons who are deaf from childhood, and many of them are only "hard of hearing." They have no defect of the vocal organs to prevent them from speaking. A child who cannot hear our language with sufficient distinctness to imitate it remains dumb until specially instructed in the use of his vocal organs. In the above table, the "deaf and dumb" are therefore classified with those having a single defect.

TABLE III.

Percentage of the Deaf-Mute Population who are otherwise Defective.

—	Totals.	Percentage.
Deaf-mutes returned as also blind	493	1·45
Deaf-mutes returned as also idiotic	2,330	6·90
Deaf-mutes returned as also insane	298	0·88
Deaf-mutes returned as otherwise defective	2,883	8·51
Deaf-mutes returned as simply deaf	30,995	91·49
Total deaf and dumb	33,878	100·00

TABLE IV.

Percentage of the Blind Population who are otherwise Defective.

—	Totals.	Percentage.
Blind persons returned as also deaf and dumb	493	1·01
Blind persons returned as also idiotic	1,403	2·87
Blind persons returned as also insane	558	1·14
Blind persons returned as otherwise defective	2,207	4·50
Blind persons returned as simply blind	46,721	95·49
Total blind	48,928	100·00

TABLE V.

Percentage of the Idiotic Population who are otherwise Defective.

—	Totals.	Percentage.
Idiots returned as also deaf and dumb	2,339	3·04
Idiots returned as also blind	1,403	1·82
Idiots returned as otherwise defective	3,525	4·58
Idiots returned as simply idiotic	73,370	95·42
Total idiots	76,895	100·00

TABLE VI.

Percentage of the Insane Population who are otherwise Defective.

—	Totals.	Percentage.
Insane persons returned as also deaf and dumb	298	0·32
Insane persons returned as also blind	558	0·61
Insane persons returned as otherwise defective	826	0·90
Insane persons returned as simply insane	91,133	99·10
Total insane	91,959	100·00

TABLE VII.

Percentage of the Doubly Defective who are also Trebly Defective.

Of 493 blind deaf-mutes, 217, or 44·02 per cent., are returned as also idiotic.

Of 493 blind deaf-mutes, 30, or 6·09 per cent., are returned as also insane.

Of 2,339 idiotic deaf-mutes, 217, or 9·28 per cent., are returned as also blind.

Of 298 insane deaf-mutes, 30, or 10·07 per cent., are returned as also blind.

Of 1,403 blind idiots, 217, or 15·47 per cent., are returned as also deaf and dumb.

Of 558 insane blind persons, 30, or 5·38 per cent., are returned as also deaf and dumb.

The tables seem to indicate that in the case of deafness, blindness, idiocy, and insanity, some correlation exists: for persons having one of those defects appear more liable to the others than persons normally constituted, and doubly defective persons appear to be more liable to be otherwise defective than persons having a single defect. For instance:

(*a.*) Of 50,155,783 persons in the United States, 246,816, or 0·4921 per cent., are defective.

(*b.*) Of 246,816 defective persons, 4,597, or 1·86 per cent., are doubly defective.

(*c.*) Of 4,597 doubly defective persons, 247, or 5·37 per cent., are trebly defective.

The results obtained above, I think, merit the consideration of scientific men, and are calculated to throw light upon the subject of correlated defects.

Although the proportion of the insane who are deaf or blind is abnormally large, the evidences of a correlation between insanity and the other defects noted above are not well marked; but in regard to deafness, blindness, and idiocy, a marked correlation appears to exist.

1. *Deaf-mutes.*—There are fourteen and a half times as many blind persons among the deaf and dumb in proportion to the population as there are in the community at large, and forty-six times as many idiotic.

2. *Blind.*—There are fourteen times as many deaf-mutes among the blind in proportion to the population as there are in the community at large, and nineteen times as many idiots.

3. *Idiotic.*—There are forty-three times as many deaf-mutes among the idiotic in proportion to the population as there are in the community at large, and eighteen times as many blind.

The apparent correlation between deafness, blindness, and idiocy, may possibly indicate that in a certain proportion of cases these defects arise from a common cause, perhaps arrested development of the nervous system.

It is, of course, possible that some of the persons returned as "blind deaf-mutes" may have lost sight and hearing from the same disease. The returns have not yet been sufficiently analyzed to enable us even to separate the congenital from the adventitious cases. We cannot, therefore, tell at the present time how far the evidences of correlation may be weakened by a closer inspection of details.

The large number of deaf-mutes who have been classified as idiots, also suggests caution in accepting the returns. I recently met a young lady—one of the brightest and best pupils of the Illinois institution for the deaf and dumb—who commenced her school-life in an idiot asylum. She was there discovered to be simply deaf, and was transferred to the Institution for the deaf and dumb at Jacksonville, where she not only received a good education, but was successfully taught to speak. Not only are children who are simply deaf sometimes sent to idiot schools, but idiotic children who hear perfectly are often sent to institutions for the deaf and dumb, when it becomes the painful duty of the principal to undeceive the parents as to the real condition of their child. The difficulty in distinguishing these two classes of defective persons arises from the absence of articulate speech. Children who are deaf from infancy, and idiots, do not naturally speak, but from very different causes. In the one case, the cause is lack of hearing; in the other, lack of intelligence. The judgment of unskilled persons regarding the intelligence of deaf-mutes should evidently be received with caution. It is only to be hoped that the number of idiotic deaf-mutes returned in the census has been overestimated. Before accepting the results as thoroughly reliable, it would be well to know whether or not the persons who made the returns were competent to judge in the matter.

ALEXANDER GRAHAM BELL.

(Extracted from "Science" for Feb. 13, 1885.)

EXHIBIT TO QUERY 21,454.

THE BROWN FAMILY.

[This exhibit consisted of a genealogical chart showing the ancestry and the descendants of Nahum Brown, a congenital deaf-mute. This chart will be found reproduced among the Postscripts with a description of the family under the general head of Ancestry of the Deaf.]

EXHIBIT TO QUERY 21,455.

THE ALLEN FAMILY.

[This exhibit consisted of a genealogical chart of the Allen Family, illustrating the prevalence of twins in that family. This chart will be found reproduced among the Postscripts with a description of the family under the general head of the Ancestry of the Deaf.]

WHAT KIND OF TRADES SHALL BE TAUGHT?

[This exhibit consisted of the following article by the Rev. Edward Everett Hale, D. D., as reprinted in the *American Annals of the Deaf*, Vol. XXXII, pp. 16-20, Jan., 1887, from *Lend a Hand* for June, 1886.]

All establishments for orphans or other poor children are obliged to consider the complicated and difficult question of the occupations to which these children shall be trained. The question has all the difficulties which the question of prison labor has, and, besides these, has some of its own.

For, to a considerable extent, the choice of the handiwork to which the child is bred regulates the grade of life in which he is afterwards to move. If we train a boy to be a shoemaker, so far as we are concerned we make him a shoemaker for his lifetime. If, on the other hand, we train him for a watchmaker, or for a locomotive engineer, we have given quite another turn to his life.

We have, unfortunately, inherited from Europe and the old charities, whether consciously or not, the idea that orphan children or other children in public institutions are necessarily to occupy a certain humble position in life. The statement of the greater part of the old world would be, that "they do not deserve" as good an education as the sons or daughters of the higher classes. To this tradition, superstition, or inheritance, we owe it that the children in our institutions are generally trained to the very lowest grades of handiwork or to domestic service.

It may be feared, indeed, that in the management of all "institutions" there slips in a good deal of the laziness which, according to Mr. Emerson, is latent in all human nature. It must be confessed that it is much easier to take every child of Adam as he comes, and make him, as a matter of course, a little shoemaker or a little tailor, than it would be to examine carefully the tastes and faculties of each child, so that he may do his duty in that state of life for which a good God has endowed him.

But a very little thought will show that the simpler callings of human life are exactly those which will take care of themselves in social order, so that we need not use the machinery of large and liberally endowed institutions to provide for them. Thus, as shoes are now made, largely with the assistance of machinery, a very few months of training will make a boy or a girl into a good shoemaker. An accomplished teacher of cooking assures us that in eighty lessons of one hour each a girl of fourteen can be initiated into all the essential mysteries of the kitchen. It is evident that occupations which require so little preparation will always be crowded, on the whole, though, in special localities, there may be a lack of workmen for a time. On the other hand, any calling which requires years of preparation will, on the whole, command higher wages, and offer "more room" for new-comers.

Now, suppose we satisfy ourselves with training our orphan children to these simplest walks of labor. What happens when they leave our institution but that they find themselves in competition with the largest class of working people, and with the class which receives the lowest wages?

We have had these children under our care for ten years. We certainly leave them better than we found them. But could we not have left them a great deal better?

Carefully study the charge of orphan asylums and other similar institutions, and it will appear that nine-tenths of that charge is the charge for the food of the children and their clothing. Now this element must be the same, whether we give to them the most careful education which the most fond parent can give to his children, or whether we leave them just a grade higher than hewers of wood and drawers of water. Ought we not, then, to look further, both to the interests of the children and the interests of the community, and inquire what future calling will be most remunerative to them and in what they will do best service to the world? What is it which, on the whole, the community stands most in need of? If we will fairly ask such questions, we shall be compelled to answer that we are to consult the tastes and talents of the children, and give to each of them the best education in our power. It has been proved, indeed, by figures, that an orphan asylum which would train its boys to be scholars, machinists, surveyors, engravers, or printers, if it could keep them in its service until they were twenty-one years of age, would make money by its liberality.

That is to say, it has been calculated that the money wages of such young people, from the time they are sixteen to twenty-one years of age, would reimburse those who had the care of them for the costly charge of education.

We have no wish to found an argument on considerations so carnal. The benefit of training as careful as we propose is much more than a gain of dollars and cents. Let the pupils of the institutions have it and let the public have it. But the fact that such a calculation can be made shows that, so far as the community is concerned, all parties would be benefited most by the highest possible standard given to the training in our institutions for children.

It will sometimes be in the power of the directors of such an institution to introduce an industry wholly new in that neighborhood. For this they have some special advantages. They are not under the direction of the public-school system, which of necessity compels us to work on a child on an average plan, as if we were turning out shoe-lasts in a factory. The success of the Rauhe-Haus, near Hamburg, was due to the introduction of first-class printing and first-class book-binding. The result, of course, is not simply the advantage to the treasury of the institution. The more important result is that to the country. The printers and book-binders trained in such an institution may be better trained than in the ordinary apprenticeship, where the object of a selfish master is simply to get the most possible out of his boys. Every one knows this who has seen the work of the best technical schools. It may happen that a machine-shop will keep a boy at work for a year in punching rivet-holes, a process which he learns completely in three or four days. He will be subject to no such useless drudgery in a properly adjusted school.

If a boy have a real taste for mechanism and machinery, a well-equipped school will make a good machinist of him by the time he is nineteen years old. The wages he will then begin to earn will be twice what they would be had you made him a shoemaker or a tailor.

There is a constant complaint that one or another branch of industry is crowded. This complaint seldom means anything. But when it does mean anything, it means that, in the particular spot where it is uttered, there are more people in that line than can be employed to advantage.

But this is only the same thing which is observed when we find that there is a cord of wood cut in the Adirondacks which nobody wants to burn, while in every crowded city people would be glad to give ten dollars for it.

Now, all branches of duty which are least apt to be crowded are those for which a most careful preparation is needed. As Mr. Webster said, "There is always room enough higher up."

Jenny Lind had not many competitors. George Stephenson always had occupation enough, and all his services were in demand. Mr. Brassey was never troubled by hard times. And, in general, just in proportion as we give to those who are entrusted to us an education of the higher grades, in that proportion do we relieve them from the anxieties which belong to crowded industries. We relieve them, at the same time, from the discontent of following for years, and perhaps for life, an avocation which is distasteful to them.

As we write these lines, it is with the recollection of a lad in an asylum, handicapped for the rest of his life by the complete loss of the sense of hearing.* When he left the institution where he was trained, at about the age of sixteen, he had been taught the use of tools, and initiated into the art and mystery of cabinet-making. But he said frankly to his friends that he should never succeed in that calling because he did not like it. He had the gifts of an artist; he was, indeed, an artist by nature, and his advisers had the courage and the faith to place him as an apprentice with one of our best engravers. What follows is, that at the end of ten years he is happy in his calling and not unhappy, for he is one of that remarkable group of men who have done so much to place the wood-engraving of America in the very forefront of the best work in the world.

* Joseph C. Davis, Roxbury, Mass.

The country has gained an artist of the first rank; it has lost a cabinet-maker of the lowest rank. This last loss is one which is easily supplied.

It is from such experience, and from the principles which lie beneath such considerations, that we are led to beg the managers of all schools and institutions which have the constant charge of children to study with care into the dispositions of those children, and to be not afraid to carry to the highest point the education which is given to them.

In brief, a boy who is willing to work should be encouraged where we best can encourage him to work in the line of his genius, if we have the wit to find out what that is.

The mere mechanical convenience of institutions is not to be considered in comparison with the advantage gained by the community whenever we have succeeded in putting the right peg in the right hole.

The progress of civilization consists in our steadily substituting well-trained workmen, using their knowledge in the subduing of the world, in the place of the mere drudges or laborers of the world. There is toil necessary, but toil or labor is more and more to be done in the future by the steam-engines and other slaves which we harness to our will.

Our business is, so far as we can, to change the untrained laborer into the skilled workman.

He shall cease from his labors, and his works shall follow him.

REV. EDWARD EVERETT HALE, D. D.,
Boston, Mass.

AURICULAR INSTRUCTION.

[This exhibit consisted of the Report of the Committee appointed by the Third Convention of Articulation Teachers to make a thorough investigation of the whole subject of Auricular Instruction. The report was written by Prof. J. C. Gordon, and includes extracts from a report written by Mr. F. D. Clarke upon tests of hearing in New York. See *Annals*, Vol. XXX, p. 59.]

The Committee "to make thorough investigation of the subject of tests of hearing, together with the best methods of the treatment and cultivation of latent aural power," constituted by the Third Convention of American Articulation Teachers of the Deaf, beg leave to submit, through the *Annals*, the following preliminary report:

Deeply impressed by Mr. Gillespie's paper on "The Aural Instruction of the Semi-Deaf," and the discussion which followed the reading of this paper, the members of the Committee promptly took up the work assigned them. Prominent otologists of the country have been consulted upon certain points; and the American Otological Society, at its annual meeting, courteously received Mr. Clarke, discussed questions submitted by him, and appointed a committee to confer with this Committee and to report to the Society. The various instruments and means in use to test the hearing have been noted, and several instruments have been designed and constructed. The utility of an instrumental test has been demonstrated by Mr. Clarke's experiments with the audiometer referred to in his report submitted herewith.* The Committee, however, hope to be able to present an instrument which will serve the same practical purpose, and also furnish a standard of great scientific value in the comparison of all the different degrees of hearing power.

The tests already made confirm the impression that a very large proportion of "deaf-mutes," so called, possess hearing, the degree ranging from a slight impairment to sensations not distinguishable from feeling.

A long and thorough course of experiment is required to determine the number and proportion of those having a utilizable amount of hearing.

The prevailing opinion appears to be against the assumption that the physiological instrument of hearing, the auditory apparatus, can be cultivated and improved (as, for instance, a weak muscle may be strengthened) by judicious exercise; but we should not lose sight of the *possible* improvement connected with the general physical development and improved physiological conditions of maturing youth, and if the improvement sometimes noted be intellectual instead of physical, or partly both, it probably does not materially affect the course to be pursued by him who would render this faculty useful to his pupils.

The genius, skill, and experience of Dr. Itard† give great weight to the conclusions expressed in his memoir upon "*l'Education physiologique du sens auditif chez les sourds-muets.*"

A commission of the Royal Academy of Medicine, after a thorough examination of the processes employed by Itard, convinced of the exactness of Dr. Itard's statements, presented a report, which was adopted unanimously.‡ This report states that "Mr. Itard has, in the first place, demonstrated the rarity of total deafness. He allows that one-fifth of the deaf-mutes are totally deaf.§ Of the remaining four-fifths, two-fifths confound speech with other sounds. There remain two-fifths who hear speech more or less distinctly, and these may be divided into four classes:

"1. Deaf-mutes who distinguish all the vocal sounds when addressed directly to them, slowly, in a loud voice, and with considerable repetition.

"2. Those who distinguish both vowels and consonants, but who confound such analogous forms as *ba* and *pa*, *fa* and *va*, *ta* and *da*; and also *ou* and *o*, *é* and *eu*.

"3. Those who confound all syllabic sounds or very unlike consonants, such as *pain* and *faim*, *gant* and *dent*, but can readily distinguish vowels.

"4. Those who can distinguish the voice from other sounds, but confound all vocal sounds.

"These semi-deaf or '*sourds-entendants*,' to whatever class they belong, present this remarkable phenomenon: that, submitted to methodical exercises, they quickly acquire one higher degree of hearing, and sometimes, though rarely, two."*

In conclusion, "the Commission regards it as demonstrated that, *by means of the special education of the auditory sense, practised by Itard, from one-tenth to one-twelfth of the pupils admitted as deaf-mutes can communicate by speech with their families upon leaving the institution.*" "It recognizes the necessity for the special class for these semi-deaf demanded by Itard and the Council of Administration."†

Twenty-five years later the subject was discussed at length in the Imperial Academy of Medicine, and, in response to a question submitted by the Minister of the Interior, "Whether among the pupils entering the National Institution each year there was to be found a certain number susceptible of amelioration or cure, who might attain to the perception of speech directly by the ear or through the aid of acoustic instruments or by other means?" the Academy formulated this reply: Among the pupils entering each year there is found generally a certain number‡ who appear susceptible of amelioration, and who ought to be placed under special treatment; but experience has not yet taught us that they are susceptible of complete cure."§

In the same direction we may cite more recent authorities.

One thinks "hearing might be improved by a course of exercises that appealed to the hearing and not to the sight. He cannot say that there is any positive improvement of the organ, but the mind learns to recognize the impressions it receives. He has great hopes of improvement in every case where the voice can be heard at all. A superintendent of a telephone exchange tells him that in cases where employés at first had great difficulty in understanding the telephone, after some months' use the difficulty entirely disappeared."‖

Another authority says: "In some cases of considerable deafness I have found the continued use of the conversation tube to be of benefit to the hearing.

"In cases, for instance, of impaired mobility of the sound-transmitting portions of the ear, the re-

*The hearing of the pupils in the Columbia Institution for the Deaf and Dumb has been tested by the same instrument, with results not differing materially from those in New York.

†Born 1774; died 1838. Resident physician and aural surgeon to the Paris Institution, 1779-1838. For Biographical Sketch see the *Annals*, vol. v, pp. 110-124.

‡May 6, 1828. See Menière: Surdi-Mutité, 1853, p. 29.

§In a previous publication Itard had placed the proportion of the totally deaf at more than one-half of the whole number.

*Maladies de l'oreille, Itard, t. II, p. 401.

†Mém. de l'Acad. de Méd., t. II, p. 178.

‡The Commission of the Academy, which had had the matter under examination for nearly four years, placed this number at 20 to 25 *per cent.* See De la Surdi-Mutité, par A. Houdin, 1855, p. 129. For Report in full, see pp. 115-130.

§Menière: Surdi-Mutité, p. 350.

‖Dr. Samuel J. Jones, of Chicago.

peated impact of sound-waves increases the mobility of the parts, and in cases of deaf-mutism, where there is hearing for words through the conversation tube, daily exercise of the kind assists in the modulation of the voice materially.

"The number of cases, among children usually classed as deaf-mutes, in which utilizable hearing exists, and also in which the hearing may be improved, is, I am convinced, much larger than is generally supposed, and suggests the advisability of some arrangement for qualified examination in this respect of children in deaf-mute institutions."*

Still another holds that the portion of the brain receiving impressions through the auditory nerve has lain dormant for so long a time that it responds slowly and with great difficulty to those impressions when first received, but if the impressions are continued it will finally respond more easily, and may even perceive impressions that were formerly unable to rouse it at all.†

In some cases the hearing appears to improve without any treatment or course of exercises. Two of these cases of improvement have been so marked as to attract the attention of all their friends. In one of those there is an ability to repeat words correctly from hearing, without the least idea of the meaning, though when the word was spelled on the hand it was at once recognized.

While the Committee is not prepared to recommend any set system of experiments or of training where hearing power is suspected or has been discovered that would not suggest itself readily to any instructor, it seems specially due to the older pupils, whose school life is almost over, that immediate efforts be made to test their hearing by such means as may be at hand, passing from the faintest to the loudest sounds; drums and bells, large and small, tuning-forks, musical instruments, the audiphone, and the voice, for instance, may be used. In all cases care should be taken to avoid possible injury to the ear by shouting into it, or into the flexible ear-tube which is recommended for aural experiments.

Wherever any vowels or words can be distinguished by a pupil when blindfolded, either directly or through a tube or an audiphone, efforts to utilize the hearing should not be lightly abandoned.

Talk to the pupil, and talk loud. Teach the elementary sounds of the English language as you would to a child that has no hearing, but remember that your pupil does hear. In an articulation class, let the teacher speak with at least a natural, if not a raised voice, and abandon the habit that some teachers have of simply moving the organs of speech and making no sound; and let the children use an audiphone or ear-trumpet, if either is of any use or the pupil thinks so.

Perhaps at some time in the future we may find a test of hearing such that we can say, all who come up to a certain point by this standard can be taught by the ear, and it is useless to waste time on those who do not. At present there is no such test.

The instrument, which in Mr. Clarke's hands has been so efficient, stimulates the desire of the Committee to furnish the profession as perfect a testing instrument as possible at an early date. The Washington members of the Committee commend to the attention of educators of the deaf the extracts from Mr. Clarke's report to the Committee herewith printed.

The Committee reserves important matters for future consideration, and, thankful for assistance already received, invites the further co-operation of all who can in any way contribute to the success of its labors.

ALEXANDER GRAHAM BELL,
JOSEPH C. GORDON,
F. D. CLARKE, *Committee.*

WASHINGTON, D. C., *Dec.* 13, 1884.

* Dr. Clarence J. Blake, of Boston. † Dr. Samuel Sexton, of New York.

Extracts from Mr. Clarke's Report on the Tests of Hearing at New York.

I received the first audiometer on September 25th, 1884, and at once began testing the hearing of the pupils and officers of the New York Institution.

On October 6th I spent the day at the Institution for the Improved Instruction of Deaf-Mutes, at 67th st. and Lexington ave., testing the hearing of all the pupils there.

At the New York Institution the total number of tests made was 368. Of this number 27 were rejected as doubtful tests. By this it is meant that for some reason the pupils fancied that the sound was heard when the audiometer was silent, or that it was impossible to find out whether they heard or not, owing to want of development of mind. This latter class were mostly very young pupils.

The remaining 341 cases and their hearing by the audiometer are given below, grouped into classes of 5 centimeters on the audiometer scale:

Audiometer.	*Number.*	*Percentage.*
0	70	20.52 +
0 and under 5	9	2.63 +
5 " 10	30	8.79 +
10 " 15	112	32.96 +
15 " 20	63	18.47 +
20 " 25	25	7.33 +
25 " 30	10	2.93 +
30 " 35	5	1.46 +
35 " 40	4	1.17 +
40 " 45	2	0.58 +
45 " 50	4	1.17 +
50 " 55	2	0.58 +
55 and upwards	8*	2.34 +
	341	

In this table those whose hearing is marked 0 may not be absolutely deaf, but they could not hear the loudest sound of the instrument used. For all practical purposes they may be put down as totally deaf.

The group of 55 and upwards includes all those who heard to the limit of the audiometer used, which was some distance above absolute silence.

At the Institution for the Improved Instruction of Deaf-Mutes there were 148 tests made, 31 of which were rejected as doubtful, leaving 117, who heard as follows:

Audiometer.	*Number.*	*Percentage.*
0	7	5.98.
0 to 5	1	0.86.
5 " 10	12	10.26.
10 " 15	43	36.75.
15 " 20	24	20.51.
20 " 25	19	16.24.
25 " 30	1	0.86.
30 " 35	3	2.56.
35 " 40	2	1.71.
40 " 45	1	0.86.
45 " 50	1	0.86.
55 and over	3	2.56.

The experimenters at New York soon fixed on the point 20 as about that which separates those who hear enough to be instructed through the ear from those who do not; at least, they thought that all above that number should be carefully tried for several weeks before being excluded from an aural class; subsequent experiments have induced them to lower this number to 15, or perhaps 14.

The facts that more than half of those tested heard between 10 and 20 on the audiometer scale, and that when the air was enclosed the vibration of the telephone could be *felt* to about the same point, raised the doubt that perhaps the experimenters had mistaken feeling for hearing.

The writer has twice before been connected with pretty extensive tests of the hearing of deaf-mutes, and was well aware of this danger. It was one of the points he had brought before the Otological Society for discussion. Both he and Professor E. H. Currier, in charge of the articulation department

* Includes 2 who are reported as dumb and not deaf.

of the New York Institution, who has given, and continues to give, most intelligent assistance, criticism, and advice in these experiments, had noticed this vibration before a single test was made, and had, as they thought, taken precautions to guard against its being mistaken for hearing. As all of the tests made at New York were made by Professor Currier or the writer, in person, they felt reasonably sure that they were right, but wished to make it equally clear to others.

It was argued, if this is feeling the reading for each ear should be the same. The record was carefully gone over, and all who heard equally in both ears were selected for re-examination. Professor Currier, who has experimented with most of the "aids of hearing," recommended for this test the "conical conversation tube" as more likely to give satisfactory results than any other. After many of these tests had been made it was found necessary to have some scale of marking, and the following was adopted:

Those able to recognize any one vowel only (generally ō) . 1.
Any two sounds .... 2.
All the following: ā, ē, ī, ō, ōō, a̤, ow, ä, but unable clearly to distinguish one or two, usually ā, ī .... 3.
No mistakes in the above .... 4.
Other sounds recognized .... 5.
If thought capable of being taught through the ear ...... 6.
To which was added another class:
If there is no doubt about capability of teaching through the ear .... 6.6.

After rejecting those whose hearing was 0.—0,* who certainly neither heard nor felt, and those whose hearing was 55, who certainly heard, there remained nine with equal readings for each ear, who heard as follows:

1. Audiometer 16½ Tube 5
2. " 16 " 0. Hears with audiphone, 6.
3. " 11 " 0.
4. " 13½ " 5.
5. " 11 " Not tested; absent.
6. " 22 " 6.6. Can carry on a conversation.
7. " 22 " 6.6.
8. " 9½ " 1. Doubtful.
9. " 10½ " 0.

In these cases, with the exception of No. 2, the tube tests confirm the audiometer tests. The case where the audiphone made the pupil hear, when the tube did not, will be spoken of later.

At the 67th-st. Institution there were only two whose hearing was equal in both ears. No farther test has been made of them.

It was farther ascertained that there was quite a large number who heard 0 in one ear, and various degrees of the instrument in the other. These are tabulated according to their hearing in the other ear, as follows:

Totally deaf one ear; hearing in other.

New York Institution.			67th-St. Institution.	
Audiometer.	Number.	Per cent.	Number.	Per cent.
Under 5......	10	10.63 +	1	6.66 +
5 " 10.......	13	13.82	4	26.66 +
10 " 15.......	46	48.93	5	33.33
15 " 20.......	16	17.12 +	3	20.00
20 " 25.......	4	4.28 +	1	6.66
25 " 30.......	1	1.06 +	0	0.00
30 " 35.......	1	1.06 +	1	6.66
35 " 40.......	1	1.06 +	—	—
40 " 45.......	0	0.00	—	—
45 " 50.......	1	1.06 +	—	—
50 " 55.......	1	1.06 +	—	—
Total.......	94		Total, 15	

The percentage of those whose hearing is between 10 and 20 is as large here as before; in the New York Institution much larger. If these are not tests of hearing, we must conclude that deaf-mutes have more feeling on one side than on the other.

*In giving audiometer readings the right ear is always given first if there is a difference in the two ears.

Dr. Peet has selected two classes of ten each from two other classes that numbered twenty-five and twenty-six. These classes are now known as the Aural Classes of the Institution; and Professor Currier has formed from the classes under his instruction in articulation two classes of 7 and 5 members, respectively, to be instructed orally. Both of these classes confirm the opinion of the value of the audiometer tests, though there are in them two cases whose audiometer readings are 14 and 14½. These two cases determined us to test all those whose audiometer test was above 15, and also several of those doubtful cases that seemed most promising.

Audiometer test, 15 or above.

No. selected, 126; not tested, 7; No. of tests, 119.

Tube-hearing.	Number.	Percentage of tube tests, 119.	Percentage of Aud. tests, 341.
0	8	6.67	2.33
1	4	3.36	1.16
2	3	2.57	0.86
3	12	10.03	3.51
4	4	3.36	1.16
5	16	13.44	4.66
6	25	21.00	7.33
6.6	46	38.65	13.48
Doubtful.	1	—	—

If it is desired to give aural instruction a favorable trial, all except those whose tube test is 0 ought to have at least a few weeks of aural training. They number in this table 110, or over 92 per cent. of those hearing 15 or over by the audiometer—more than 32 per cent. of all the tests made.

But if, convinced that the more unpromising cases will not improve, we only take those who hear all the open vowels without training (above 3 in this table); there are still 91 left, or over 26 per, cent. of the whole number tested.

Of course these are tests of the present condition, and it may be that the hearing power of these children is already as fully trained and educated as it ever will be; but, until the attempt to develop it has been made and failed, we have no right to say so.

Making 20 of the audiometer scale the standard above which all should hear the tube, we drop out all those whose hearing by the tube is 0, but we also drop 10 whose hearing is 6, and 13 whose hearing is 6.6. This proves that 15 is more nearly right than 20. Some tube tests have been made below 15, but, with the exception of those mentioned above, no promising results have been found. These tube tests have entirely re-established the confidence that the New York experimenters had in the audiometer tests at first. The audiometer will not tell whether a pupil can or cannot be taught to speak as certainly as the thermometer tells the temperature, but it gives us very reliable indications of what to expect in a tenth part of the time that we could otherwise ascertain it.

Why the tube tests and the audiometer tests do not exactly coincide I cannot at present say with certainty, but the following reasons seem to me to have weight.

First. In the tube test the memory and judgment of sound form very important factors, and the test is as much a test of these as of the hearing power. Given two pupils of equal audiometer reading, but of great difference in mental capacity and knowledge, I think I am safe in saying that the tube test of the more intelligent would be the higher.

Second. For accurate comparison the tests should have been made at the same time. I think that the hearing of our pupils varies considerably within quite short periods. Tests on this point are too few to generalize from.

Third. The audiometer seems to test all the hearing the pupil has. Its reading is the sum of what has been called the "aerial" and "bone conduction." I think the tube only tests the aerial and not the bone conduction. This view was first suggested to me by an experiment made by Mr. Currier with the audiphone.

A few tests have been made with this instrument. They go to show that in nearly every case where there was an audiometer reading of over 15 and a tube test of 0 or 1, the pupil hears with the audiphone.

Fourth. The strength of the tube should bear some relation to the amount of deafness. Several of these cases seem more annoyed than helped by the tube used, and we think that very possibly a weaker one may help them.

The New York member of the Committee feels fully that he has not done all that should be done in investigating this matter. The time at his disposal has been very limited. In his opinion, thoroughly to test the aural ability of all the pupils at this Institution, and to decide absolutely upon what means are best for this purpose, would take the undivided time and thought of a well-read and intelligent man for several months.

If to this is added the other work suggested by the resolution appointing the Committee, it is difficuly to set any limit to the time necessary.

The importance of a little more powerful aid to hearing than any of those we now have cannot be too strongly urged. If we had one that would reach the great percentage of those between 10 and 15 as well as the tube does those above 15, one-half of our pupils could be taught through the ear.

We have before us a vast field for experiment, and, if we only arouse the attention of the teachers of the deaf to its importance, we feel sure that the experiments will be faithfully made.

F. D. CLARKE.

EXHIBIT TO QUERY 21,518.

DEAF-MUTE NEWSPAPERS.

[This Exhibit consisted of a bound volume, containing the *Deaf-Mutes' Journal* for the years 1884, 1885, 1886.]

EXHIBIT TO QUERY 21,531.

DEAF CHILDREN OF DEAF PARENTS.

[This Exhibit consisted of a card catalogue, containing the names of 607 deaf-mutes who were believed to be the children of deaf parents.

Some uncertainty attached to 276 of these cases, as they were deduced from the Census returns of the deaf and dumb [in the manner described in the answer to Query 21,530] without verification by comparison with the population schedules.

The corrected figures after verification will be found in a Postscript headed "Deaf Children of Deaf Parents." In this same Postscript an analysis will be given correcting the tables presented in answer to Query 21,848. (See this volume, Part III).]

EXHIBIT TO QUERY 21,630.

VISIBLE SPEECH CHARTS.

[This Exhibit consisted of the visible-speech charts in use in American Schools for the deaf. These charts will be reproduced in the Postscript headed Visible Speech, and a description will be appended thereto.]

VISIBLE SPEECH AS A MEANS OF COMMUNICATING ARTICULATION TO DEAF-MUTES.

[This Exhibit consisted of an article by Alexander Graham Bell published in the *American Annals of the Deaf* for January, 1872, Vol. XVII, pp. 1-24.]

The system of "Visible Speech" was invented by my father, Mr. A. Melville Bell, professor of vocal physiology; and it constitutes a new species of phonetic writing, based, not upon sounds, but upon the actions of the vocal organs in producing them.

The plan originated fully a quarter of a century ago; and the germ of the invention was published in the first edition of "The Principles of Speech," (1849).

The idea conceived was that of representing the sounds of all languages by means of one alphabet, the characters of which should reveal to the eye the organic formation of the sounds. Although my father's professional duties as a corrector of the defects of utterance directly favored the study of the organic formation of sounds, still, the difficulties in the way of carrying out the idea were so great that it was not until 1864 that the plan took definite shape. Then, indeed, a scheme of letters was produced which claimed to be so perfect as to represent *any sound the human mouth could utter.*

Linguists and men of science were invited to test the truth of this assertion. The invitation was accepted; and for three years the most searching tests were applied in public and in private. The following facts were abundantly proved:

1st. That the sounds of any language could be written by means of Visible Speech; and,

2d. That a person unacquainted with a language could pronounce it at sight, with vernacular correctness, while deducing his pronunciation solely from the physiological symbols.

An account of a few of the earlier experiments was published in a pamphlet entitled "Visible Speech; a New Fact Demonstrated," (1864).

To convey an idea of the nature of these experiments, I quote a description of one from a letter to the *Reader*, by Mr. A. J. Ellis, the distinguished author of the "Essential of Phonetics." Mr. Ellis says:

> The mode of procedure was as follows: Mr. Bell sent his two sons, who were to read the writing, out of the room—it is interesting to know that the elder, who read all the words in this case, had only had five weeks' instruction in the use of the alphabet—and I dictated slowly and distinctly the sounds which I wished to be written.
>
> These consisted of a few words in Latin, pronounced first as at Eton, then as in Italy, and then according to some theoretical notions of how the Latins might have uttered them. Then came some English provincialisms and affected pronunciations; the words "how odd" being given in several distinct ways.
>
> Suddenly German provincialisms were introduced. Then discriminations of sounds often confused: *ess, is'*, (Polish;) *eesh, ich*, (German;) *ich*, (Dutch;) *ich*, (Swiss;) *oui, oui*, (French;) *wee*, (English;) *wie*, (German;) *vie*, (French.) Then some Arabic, some Cockney-English, with an introduced Arabic guttural, some mispronounced Spanish, and a variety of shades of vowels and diphthongs.
>
> * * * * The result was perfectly satisfactory; that is, Mr. Bell wrote down my queer and purposely-exaggerated pronunciations and mispronunciations, and delicate distinctions, in such a manner that his sons, not having heard them, so uttered them as to surprise me by the extremely correct echo of my own voice. * * Accent, tone, drawl, brevity, indistinctness, were all reproduced with surprising accuracy. Being on the watch, I could, as it were, trace the alphabet in the lips of the readers. I think, then, that Mr. Bell is justified in the somewhat bold title which he has assumed for his mode of writing—"Visible Speech."

This examination of the capabilities of the system, which may fairly be called an *experimentum crucis*, was made before the symbols of Visible Speech had been exhibited to Mr. Ellis. As he is, perhaps, the best living authority on the subject of phonetics, it may be interesting to know the opinion he formed of the *theoretical details* of the system when these were presented to him. I quote from another letter of his.

After referring to his own works, those of Amman, De Kempelen, Johannas Müller, K. M. Rapp, C. R. Lepsius, E. Brücke, S. S. Haldeman, Max Müller, and "a host of other works of more or less pretensions and value," (the treatises enumerated containing perhaps "a complete account of the present state of phonetical knowledge,") he says:

> Now, it is with this full and distinct recollection of works which I have not only read, but studied, many of them with great care and attention, that I feel called upon to declare that until Mr. Melville Bell unfolded to me his careful, elaborate, yet simple and complete system, I had no knowledge of alphabetics as a science. Much had been done. * * * But alphabetics as a science—and I have looked for it far and wide—did not exist. We did not know what elementary sounds or modifications of sound should be expressed, and the art of expressing such as had been pretty generally received was in a state of the greatest confusion.

USES OF THE INVENTION.

Among the uses of the system most interesting to the general reader, I may note:

1st. *The correction of stammering and other defects of speech; and the communication of articulation to deaf-mutes, by showing the proper position of the mouth in forming sounds.*

2d. *The teaching of illiterate adults in all countries to read their own language from books printed in the system.*

The imperfectly phonetic character of all previous alphabets has been the cause of the great length of time required to master the art of reading. Had each sound an invariable representative, and each letter an invariable sound, a pupil would commence to read whenever the powers of the letters had been acquired. Hence, the hope is indulged, that, when works have been printed in the Visible Speech typography, illiterate adults may be enabled to read such books *in a few days.*

3d. *The formation of a system of raised letters, of universal applicability, for the use of the blind.*

This is a development of the stenographic alphabet of Visible Speech. The words are capable of contraction according to the rules of stenography, so that works printed in this system need not be nearly so bulky as those at present used by the blind.

4th. *The writing of hitherto unwritten tongues for missionary and other purposes.*

No instance of failure has yet occured in the representation of the most difficult sounds, taken from over fifty languages.

5th. To the comparative philologist Visible Speech is invaluable, as a means whereby fast-disappearing dialects may be preserved for study and comparison, and the affinities of words be exhibited to the eye.

It must not be supposed that this list exhausts the applications of the system. It has been adapted to the wants of stenographic reporters in all countries, to the telegraphing of all languages without translation, and other new uses are constantly suggested.

The applications of the system were early seen to be so many and important that the British press was loud in its support of the inventor in his appeal to the English government for aid in publishing and applying his system. This appeal was unsuccessful; and so, in 1867, Professor Bell produced the inaugural edition of the system, entitled "Visible Speech; the Science of Universal Alphabetics."

APPLICATION TO DEAF-MUTES.

In 1869, the first attempt was made to communicate a knowledge of the symbols to deaf-mutes. This experiment was tried at a private establishment in South Kensington, England, conducted by Miss Hull.

No difficulty was found in giving the idea of the symbols to four children, the eldest about twelve and the youngest about seven years of age, and nearly all the elementary sounds of English were obtained from them *in a few days*.

It was at once evident that Visible Speech would be an instrument of great power in the hands of teachers of the deaf and dumb; and it became an absorbing problem how best to use it. Becoming, myself, intensely interested in the subject, I wrote to Mr. Peet, of New York, wishing to experiment with the symbols in the institution for deaf-mutes there. This was impossible at that time; but Mr. Peet brought the subject before the notice of American teachers at the recent Indianapolis Convention.

Since the experiment in South Kensington, a theoretical plan of instruction has been devised, but no opportunity was found of applying it till the spring of the present year.

In the meantime, Miss Hull, though laboring under the disadvantage of having no definite plan to work by, has been experimenting further with the symbols in her school. In a letter just received from her, referring to a visit from Miss Rogers, the principal of the Clarke Institution, she says: "My school will be the representative in England of your father's system applied to the deaf, which I, too, believe to be the true philosophical foundation for instruction in articulation."

Comparing the results obtained by her with those produced by Mr. Van Praagh, in London, working upon the German method, she says: "I certainly think our pupils spoke much plainer and more readily after six months' instruction than his did after twelve; but of course I am a prejudiced judge in that matter. I look to Visible Speech to obtain much greater and more certain results than any yet produced."

The lectures given by the inventor in the various towns of the United States during the last three years drew the attention of educationists to the subject; and mainly through the exertions of the late Hon. Dexter S. King, it was resolved that the system should be experimented with in the Boston school for deaf-mutes. The committee of that school invited me to visit Boston for the purpose of instructing the teachers in the use of the symbols. During the month of April, 1871, all the teachers were close students of the system. By the 1st of May, they had acquired sufficient knowledge of the symbols to conduct experiments under my superintendence; and by the 1st of June I was enabled to relinquish the conduct of the experiment into the hands of Miss Fuller, the principal of the school.

On the 13th of June, a public exhibition was given of the condition of the school, and it was shown that the very youngest children had comprehended the meaning of the symbols. Taking the school as a whole, it was found that, during the month of May, over three hundred English sounds, which the pupils had formerly failed to utter by imitation, had been obtained by means of Visible Speech. Class illustration was given of the pronunciation of syllables with differences of accent and quantity, and individual illustration of the *perfect utterance* of words and sentences. Adult deaf-mutes were present who had aquired all the sounds of the English language in ten lessons, and who could articulate a large number of words with absolute correctness. One pupil of the school, to whom special instructions had been given in the principles of elocution, read Longfellow's "Psalm of Life," from elocutionary marks, with natural and expressive inflections of the voice.

The following letters have recently been received concerning the experiment in the Boston school:

From the Committee of the Boston School for Deaf-Mutes.

BOSTON, *Nov.* 1, 1871.

A. GRAHAM BELL, Esq.

DEAR SIR: The system of Visible Speech, invented by your father, and so successfully introduced by you into the Boston school for deaf-mutes, has given the teachers an instrument of incalculable value in teaching deaf-mutes (congenital as well as others) to articulate clearly and correctly.

It has been heartily adopted as the system of the school, and the surprising results exhibited by the pupils at the close of your brief course of instruction are increasingly apparent every day.

Trusting you may be as successful in your future labors as in those we have witnessed, we remain, very cordially, your friends,

IRA ALLEN, *Chairman.*
GEO. F. BIGELOW.

From the Principal of the Boston School for Deaf-Mutes.

SCHOOL FOR DEAF-MUTES,
BOSTON, *Nov.* 4, 1871.

A. GRAHAM BELL, Esq.

DEAR SIR: In compliance with your request, I am happy to give you my opinion regarding the value of Visible Speech in teaching articulation to deaf-mutes.

I can say, with confidence, that I have found it of the greatest assistance. The consonants *b*, *d*, and *g*, which are the most difficult to obtain by imitation, are, by means of the symbols, produced with great ease and accuracy; and the consonant combinations, such as *ct*, *ks*, *nd*, etc., which were often very faulty, are, by this system, acquired perfectly.

In teaching vowels it is of especial value. The Visible Speech symbols make the child conscious of the correct positions of the mouth for producing these sounds. Hitherto such elements have been our greatest difficulties. I have been able to correct in several cases very imperfect vowel sounds which had baffled all attempts under the old system of imitation.

Although I have had but little experience in the use of Visible Speech, I am quite convinced that if we begun our work with a full knowledge of this system, we should have been spared a great amount of difficult and often discouraging labor, and produced much better results.

Yours, respectfully,

SARAH FULLER.

From the Superintendent of Public Schools in Boston.

CITY OF BOSTON, DEPARTMENT OF PUBLIC INSTRUCTION,
SUPERINTENDENT'S OFFICE, CITY HALL, *Oct.* 7, 1871.

A. GRAHAM BELL, Esq.

MY DEAR SIR: I congratulate you most cordially on the success of your experiment in the application of the science of Visible Speech, which was invented and developed by your father, to the instruction of the pupils in our Boston deaf-mute school. Heretofore, instruction of deaf-mutes in artificial articulation has been wholly imitative and empirical, and although the system is extensively employed, it has produced useful results only at the expense of incredible labor and patience on the part of both teachers and pupils.

You have, by your experiment in our school, proved the practicability of producing in congenital deaf-mutes *perfect* articulation, with vastly less labor than has been required to produce only imperfect articulation.

What is still more wonderful, if possible, you have succeeded in enabling deaf-mute pupils to modulate the voice, by giving a higher and lower pitch, and the upward and downward and circumflex inflections.

What you have done in the short time you have been engaged in our school has convinced me that the science of Visible Speech is to become a powerful and an indispensable instrumentality in the instruction of deaf-mutes.

I know of no greater step of progress, in this speciality of education, than this you have introduced, since the days of the Abbé de l'Epée and Samuel Heinicke.

Very truly, yours,

JOHN D. PHILBRICK.

I am at present engaged in conducting experiments with Visible Speech privately in Boston. An account of the results obtained will be presented to the readers of the *Annals* in due time.

The system is now undergoing experiment in the Northampton Institution for Deaf-Mutes, and it will be introduced into the American Asylum, Hartford, in May, 1872.

POPULAR ERRORS CONCERNING THE FUNCTIONS OF THE NEW ALPHABET.

I have attempted, in the preceding pages, to convey an idea of the nature and uses of Visible Speech; to give an outline of the history of the invention, and to state the results of its introduction into the Boston school.

I shall now supplement this by a brief description of the symbols themselves, the mode of communicating them to deaf-mutes, and the plan of instruction so far as developed. But before doing this, I think it right to correct any misapprehensions that may arise concerning the functions of the new alphabet.

1st. In regard to general applications.

There is no intention of superseding existing alphabets by the new letters. The system must, therefore, not be confounded with any phonetic movement, such as that at present existing in England. It is intended solely for international and scientific purposes, and as a key to other alphabets. In the words of Prof. de Morgan, it forms "a sound-bridge" from language to language, from no speech to speech.

2d. In its application to deaf-mutes.

(*a.*) The system does not interfere with any existing plan of education. Visible Speech takes *no part* in the contest between articulation, on the one hand, and signs and manual alphabets on the other. In presenting his system for adoption, all that the inventor means to say is this: "Here is a means by which you can obtain perfect articulation from deaf-mutes; *make what of it you choose.*" He places the *tool* in the hands of teachers, with general directions how to use it.

(*b.*) Visible Speech is not *necessarily* associated with lip-reading. There is no doubt that, in schools where lip-reading is employed, the symbols will materially assist the pupils by showing them *what to look for* in the mouths of hearing persons, but this is apart from its greater sphere of usefulness as a means of communicating articulation.

(*c.*) Visible speech does not profess to teach the deaf to *modulate their voices;* it deals with articulation pure and simple.

There is no doubt that, by means of the symbols, the quality or "timbre" of voice may be influenced; and future experiments will show how far a harsh and disagreeable voice may be made soft and pleasing by means of them.

Deaf-mutes may be taught to modulate their voices, and to read with expression, by means of an (at present) unpublished development of Visible Speech, which aims at representing pictorially the changes of the voice in regard to force, duration, and pitch. This system constitutes an elocutionary, and, in its fullest development, a musical notation, accomplishing for the throat what Visible Speech does for the mouth.

We all know that our deaf-mute pupils give on the play-ground and elsewhere *perfectly natural inflections.* They laugh and cry like other children. The problem is to make them *conscious* of the movements of their voices. Experiments in the Boston school have proved that this can be done.

MODE OF COMMUNICATING VISIBLE SPEECH TO DEAF-MUTES.

The elementary symbols are pictorial of parts of the mouth and of their modes of action. As the various organs of speech are disposed in forming any particular sound, the corresponding symbols are put together to build up a compound character indicative of the position of the mouth. This compound character most truly represents the sound intended, because no person can put his mouth into the position indicated without producing it.

The symbols have been successfully explained to deaf-mutes in the following manner: The outline of a face turned toward the right is drawn upon the blackboard (see illustration) and a representation of the inside of the mouth is added. The pupil's attention is directed to the various parts of the diagram, and he shows his appreciation by touching the corresponding portions of his own face or mouth. When the teacher points to the arrow head, a motion of the hand is made to suggest that it means "air coming out of the mouth."

Those portions of the face represented in the illustration by dotted lines are then erased from the board, and attention is directed to the broken remains of the diagram. When the teacher points to the fragmentary nose, lip, or tongue, etc., the pupil touches his own nose, lip, or tongue.

It will be observed that these disjointed portions of the diagram are *the Visible Speech symbols for the corresponding parts of the mouth.* The symbol for "lip" is the outline of a lip; that for the point of the tongue its picture, and so with other parts.

The sign for the lip is used for every sound formed by the lips; so with the point of the tongue, the top or "front" of the tongue, and the back of the tongue.

The sign for the throat represents a mere chink or slit in the throat, and is pictorial of the vocalizing condition of the glottis. It therefore means "voice."

The sign for the nose is, in reality, pictorial of the uvula, the pendulous extremity of the soft palate. When the soft palate is depressed, the breath passes up behind it and escapes through the nostrils. When it is raised the communication between nose and mouth is cut off. Hence the application of a symbol originally pictorial of the soft palate to the nose. It means "air passing through the nostrils."

But to return to our pupil. He knows nothing of the deep meaning underlying these symbols. To him the strange lines upon the board are only the remains of a picture. Filling up the gaps, in imagination he recognizes the crooked line as a portion of the nose, the curves as so many parts of the mouth, and the straight line as the throat.

The next step is to isolate the symbols, so that our deaf-mute shall recognize them independently of their position in the diagram. They are accordingly written in one line below the fragmentary picture.

The crooked character is shown, by reference to the face above, to be the same as the nose; the straight line, the throat; and the curves, the various parts of the mouth.

The elementary forms are then built up into more complex shapes.

The second line illustrates the junction of the curves with the straight line.

In the first symbol the curve is seen to be the under lip, and the straight line the throat. The name of the symbol is "lip-voice." The child describes it by pointing to his lip and then to his throat.

The third line shows the union of the nose sign with the various curves; and the fourth exhibits a triple combination, viz: a part of the mouth, with nose and voice signs added.

A character indicating a peculiar position of the vocal organs is next introduced. Observe the first symbol in the fifth line. The space enclosed by the curve is symbolically *shut in* by a line drawn across the ends.

Thus a straight line (made thin to distinguish it from "voice") is called "shut." The idea is conveyed by forcibly closing a book before the eyes of the pupil. Whenever he names the sign he imitates this motion.

The fifth line exhibits the union of this symbol with the various curves. The first character in the line, named "lip-shut," is described by touching the under lip, and then imitating with the hands the closing of a book. Here, for the first time, the idea of the directive nature of the symbols begins to dawn upon the deaf-mute. In conducting classes I have invariably found that when this point has been reached, at least one of the pupils would illustrate the symbol by *shutting his lips.*

The characters in the sixth line are composed of a curve and the signs "shut, voice."

Those in the seventh contain a curve and "shut, nose;" and the symbols in the eighth line are analyzed into a curve and "shut, voice, nose."

The broken outline of the face, which has been retained as an assistance to the memory, is now dispensed with, and the pupil is required to describe all the symbols again.

For the convenience of the reader, I give below the names of the symbols, in a tabular form, using

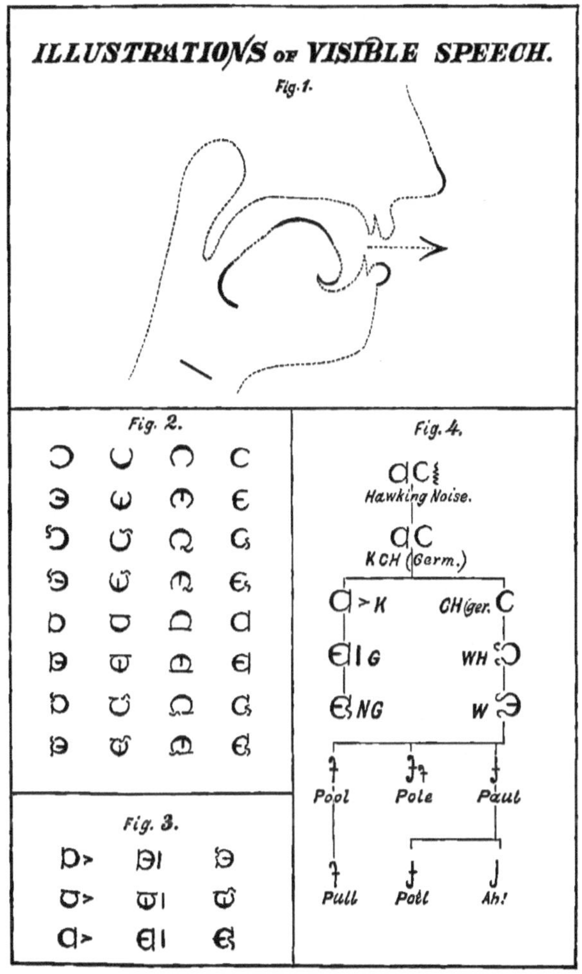

the initial letters of the words Shut, Voice, Nose, Lip, Point, Front, Back:

(*Key to Fig.* 2.)

L	P	F	B
LV	PV	FV	BV
LN	PN	FN	BN
LVN	PVN	FVN	BVN
LS	PS	FS	BS
LSV	PSV	FSV	BSV
LSN	PSN	FSN	BSN
LSVN	PSVN	FSVN	BSVN

It will be observed that, though at the first lesson thirty-four characters have been introduced, the memory is burdened with only four forms, viz: a curve (turned in different directions), a crooked line, a thick, straight line, and a thin one.

Though the sounds of speech may be *infinite* in variety, they are all formed by a limited number of organs; and they can all be represented by the combinations of ten elementary symbols.

The name of a sound-symbol is in reality a command *to do something with the mouth.*

Take, for example, the first character in the eighth line (see illustration), "lip, shut, voice, nose." This is, in effect, a direction to shut the lips and pass the voice through the nose. In explaining this symbol to a deaf-mute, one of his hands is placed upon the teacher's throat, and the other against the nose. If, then, the teacher makes the sound of the letter M, the pupil *sees* that the lips are shut, and *feels* a vibration in the throat and nose.

The symbols in fig. 3 represent the sounds of the following letters as taught to the children in the Boston school:

P B M
T D N
K G NG.

All one can say concerning the Roman letters is, that P is P, B B, etc. But the symbols tell us that P is formed by shutting the lips, and then making a puff of air, while for B, the lips are to be shut while the voice is sounded, and then a puff of voice is to be given, etc.

The characters exhibit to the eye all the relations that the sounds themselves do to the ear; and the organic relations are just as clearly shown:

As P is to B, so is T to D, and K to G.
As B is to M, so is D to N, and G to NG.
As P is to T, so is B to D, and M to N.
As P is to K, so is B to G, and M to NG.

P, B, and M have the "lip" and "shut" signs in common; and in sounding all, the lips are shut.

T, D, N, agree in shutting off the breath by means of the point of the tongue, and K, G, NG, in the closing action being performed by the back of the tongue.

Furthermore, the sounds P, T, K (represented by the same symbol turned in different directions), are made by the same organic action performed at different parts of the mouth; so with B, D, G, and M, N, NG.

When a deaf-mute has thoroughly mastered the meaning of the symbols, he is required to sound one of the characters; that is, the attempt is to be made to do with the mouth what the symbol directs.

The pupil, having little or no control over the movements of the vocal organs, will probably make a very different sound from that intended; but the first point gained is, that he makes a noise of some kind. Whatever it happens to be—whether a cough, or a growl, or a sneeze (!)—it can be written symbolically.

From this sound as a starting point, others can be developed in every direction, until all the English elements have been obtained.

I shall illustrate by a case that has actually occured.

A middle-aged deaf-mute, a resident of Boston, was studying the symbols with me.

I directed his attention to the vibration of my throat in sounding voice. He attempted to imitate this by a peculiar hawking noise—somewhat as if he were coughing up phlegm.

After repeating the sound several times, he analyzed my representation of it (see fig. 4), and thus became conscious of what his mouth was doing. In forming this sound the tongue is first put back so as to shut off the air from the mouth. The breath is then forced out between the tongue and soft palate in such a way as to set the uvula vibrating.

Upon presenting the symbols to him, minus the "trill" or shake, he made the sound gently, and without vibrating the uvula. What he gave was in reality an English element (K), followed by the German sound of *ch*.

The next point to be attained was to separate these elements, so as to have the English sound on one side, and the foreign one on the other. The first element of his sound was accordingly written with the sign for a puff of breath after it. He gave at once the letter K. The German *ch* was also obtained at sight of its symbol.

The attempt to pronounce K with voice produced G; and NG resulted from passing the voice through the nose.

By sounding the German *ch* with the lips nearly closed the English WH was obtained. W was given by adding voice. This sound may be considered, for all practical purposes, identical with the vowel *oo* in "pool." From this vowel five others were obtained by merely opening the mouth very gradually.

Thus from the original hawking noise eleven English sounds were developed by the directive power of the symbols.

This method of leading from one sound to another renders the acquisition of the English elements a matter of absolute certainty; but it is inapplicable to very young children. In all cases, however, mechanical assistance will accomplish what the intellect of the child is unable to do. The symbols inform the teacher of the correct position of the organs in producing any sound. By the exercise of a little ingenuity the child's tongue can be pushed into the required position by means of a pencil or pen-holder.

Mechanical assistance has been found to be so absolutely necessary that a manipulator of a convenient shape has been constructed of ivory.

Suppose we fail to obtain K from a child; a sound of *similar formation, but further forward in the mouth*, may be experimented upon. We shall presume our pupil can pronounce T. In T, the shutting action is performed by the point of the tongue; in K, by the back. (See fig. 3.)

If the teacher holds the manipulator so as to prevent any portion of the tongue from rising *except the back*, the attempt on the part of the pupil to say T will produce K. The manipulator is at once placed in the hands of the pupil himself, and the experiment is repeated. A mirror held before his face shows him the position of his tongue. It invariably follows that after a few attempts the child is enabled to pronounce the sound without any assistance whatever.

A plan for the development of sounds by means of the manipulator has been devised. It may be interesting to know that twenty-six English elements can be *forced* from the sound TH.

PLAN OF INSTRUCTION.

In teaching articulation a radical difference must be made at the outset between the semi-mute and the deaf-mute proper. The former has already *learned to talk*—the latter has everything to learn.

Our object should be to *keep up the knowledge* of spoken language possessed by the semi-mute, and to teach him the pronounciation of new words. This can be accomplished by the symbols of Visible Speech; and his voice may be prevented from becoming monotonous by the use of the allied elocutionary notation.

But the congenital deaf-mute (who may be taken as the type of the other class) has had no practice in the use of his vocal organs; and his mouth is at first incapable of using the language of hearing persons. The instrument of speech must be mastered like any other instrument—*by slow degrees*.

Hearing children (being guided only by imitation) require five or six years' practice in order to talk correctly, and even then it is astonishing how many grow up with defective articulation.

To expect the congenital deaf-mute to talk the moment he has mastered the elements of speech would be as unreasonable as to expect a child to play one of Beethoven's sonatas when he only knew the notes of his piano. He must have long and patient practice of scales and exercises, in order to obtain command over his instrument; he must have oral gymnastics, as a preparation for speech.

Should any one try the experiment of teaching a novice in music to play a sonata correctly, we may predict the result. Rapid passages would be slurred over, and many false notes be given.

The difficulties of execution would cause the performance to appear, at best, labored and mechanical, and the pupil would probably be disheartened. Should there be any approach toward correct playing, it could only be made through indomitable perseverance on the part of both teacher and pupil.

Analogy reveals the cause of the only partial success that has hitherto attended the efforts to teach articulation to the congenital deaf-mute. The attempt to make him utter words and sentences *from the very outset of his education* can only be productive of imperfect articulation. It will be difficult, and in many cases impossible, to correct afterwards the defects engendered by too great anxiety for progress on the part of his teacher.

The mouth must be educated to produce sounds before the difficulties of spoken language can be successfully grappled with. By means of the symbols the elementary sounds may be combined in all sorts of ways to form *senseless* compounds analogous to syllables, words, and sentences. These should be uttered at first very slowly; then, by degrees, faster and faster, until the power of correct and rapid utterance has been attained. Then, and not till then will it be safe to introduce articulation with sense attached.

I have suggested the following plan of instruction, which is suited to the capability of the very youngest beginner.

The imitative faculty of the child should be educated to the utmost, by causing him to copy the motions of the teacher's mouth. Direct him to make his tongue hard or soft, round or spread out flat; let him move it backward and forward, up and down, or in any way the fancy of the teacher may dictate.

English sounds may be obtained by imitation, and associated arbitrarily with their symbols.

The teacher should be careful not to spend too much time in laborious and disheartening efforts to obtain by imitation what will be more easily and certainly acquired afterwards. What is wanted is a mere foundation to work upon in the future. A skilful teacher will not confine himself to English elements, but will take whatever sound the child happens to make, and associate *that* with its correct symbol.

The sounds obtained are to be practiced in easy monosyllabic combinations, until they can be certainly discriminated.

When the child's attention is capable of being fixed, the meaning of the Visible Speech symbols may be explained to him. After this, he must *describe* as well as *sound* the elements mastered. No difficulty will be found with children of five or six years of age.

New sounds should next be developed by appealing to the mind through the analogies of the symbols, and by forcing the tongue into new positions by means of the manipulator. Thus the mind, the eye, and the sense of touch in the pupil co-operate with the mechanical skill of the teacher to produce sure and certain results.

No articulation, however perfect, will be *agreeable* unless strict attention is paid to the accent and quantity of syllables, and to the modulation of the voice. I have therefore recommended that the study of rhythm, and the cultivation of the voice, should be added as *separate branches of education*, as soon as possible.

It is apart from my present subject to enter into a description of the notation for rhythm and modulation. Suffice it to say that a rhythmical exercise may be written upon the board. The children are required, at first, to clap their hands, or tap their slates, or make some other visible motion, *in concert*, while marching round the room. The rhythmical repetition of a syllable can then be substituted for the clapping of the hands, the pupils marching as before. Finally, the marching is relinquished, and the teacher beats time with his hand instead. In this way an appreciation of rhythm is developed before applying it to words. Classes can be exercised with regular rhythm, as it occurs in poetry; and individuals, with the irregular rhythm of prose.

In regard to the modulations of the voice, all deaf-mutes can be trained to recognize at least five indefinite pitches. These may be called, "very high, high, medium, low, very low." By gliding from one to another, inflection can be produced. When these have once been obtained, we may seek to associate them with *feelings*.

Suppose the word "farm" to be uttered with a rising inflection suggestive of interrogation. Let the teacher *look* interrogatively. The pupil will unconsciously imbibe the idea that the word "farm," with such a rise of the voice, is equivalent to the sentence, "Is it a farm?" So with other inflections. Modulations of the voice, expressive of surprise, sorrow, anger, etc., should have their meanings visibly apparent in the face of the teacher.

I look forward with confidence to the time when deaf articulators will be taught the principles of elocution, so as to be enabled to read and speak with expression.

The following is a brief recapitulation of the plan of instruction:

I. 1. Educate the imitative faculty.
2. Obtain sounds by imitation, and associate them arbitrarily with their symbols.

II. 1. Understand the symbols of Visible Speech, and describe the sounds obtained by imitation.
2. Utter easy monosyllables, formed from the sounds obtained by imitation.
3. Commence the study of rhythmical motions.
4. Obtain differences of pitch.

III. 1. Develop the remainder of the English alphabet from the sounds obtained by imitation.
2. Give oral gymnastics, with monosyllabic combinations of all the sounds perfectly uttered.
3. Repeat a syllable rhythmically.
4. Glide from pitch to pitch, so as to obtain as great a variety of inflections as possible.

IV. 1. Practice oral gymnastics with polysyllabic combinations, giving differences of accent and quantity.
2. Repeat a monosyllable, with differences of accent and quantity, and with inflections of the voice.

V. 1. Utter polysyllables containing difficult combinations of consonants.
2. Give polysyllabic combinations analogous to sentences, attending to accent, quantity, and to the movements of the voice.
3. Teach the spoken names of familiar objects. Seek merely to form a vocabulary.
4. Repeat words with different inflections, so as to convey an idea of the expressiveness of the various tones.

VI. Articulate sentences with fluency and distinctness, attending to accent, quantity, and to the inflections of the voice.

Space has not permitted me to give more than a mere idea of the nature of the symbols of Visible Speech. For further particulars the reader is referred to the Inaugural Edition of the system.*

In conclusion, I should like to draw attention to the fact that Visible Speech can be explained by means of diagrams, so that foreign teachers of the deaf and dumb can reap the advantages of the system without the necessity of studying our language.

* This may be obtained from Messrs. Lee & Shepard, publishers, Boston.

UPON A METHOD OF TEACHING LANGUAGE TO A VERY YOUNG CONGENITALLY DEAF CHILD.

[This Exhibit consists of the following article by Alexander Graham Bell, reprinted from the *American Annals of the Deaf* for April, 1883, Vol. XXVIII, pp. 124–130.]

[A few months ago, Mr. Denison, Principal of the Primary Department of the Columbia Institution for the Deaf and Dumb, called the attention of the editor of the *Annals* to a new member of his class who possessed a remarkable command of language. His attainments in other respects were not extraordinary; but he used the English language with a freedom and accuracy quite exceptional in a congenital deaf-mute. His education was begun and carried on for three years by Professor Alexander Graham Bell. For several years past he had had no teacher. Inquiry of Professor Bell as to the method by which results so unusual had been attained led to the preparation of this paper. We are sure the narrative will prove no less interesting to our readers than it was to Mr. Denison and the editor, and we trust it will not only afford encouragement and aid to parents in beginning the education of deaf children at home, but will also have a stimulating and inspiring effect upon every teacher who reads it. Much of the method described is no less applicable to a class of pupils than to a single pupil; and we have no doubt that in the hands of capable and devoted teachers it would go far toward solving the great problem of the mastery of the English language by the congenitally deaf.—ED. *Annals*.]

To the Editor of the American Annals of the Deaf and Dumb:

SIR: You have been kind enough to express the opinion that the readers of the *Annals* would be interested in knowing the method I adopted in educating a very young congenitally deaf child, who became my pupil in 1872, and who has since acquired a vernacular knowledge of the English language in its spoken and written forms.

This boy was only about five years old when his education was commenced, and the results obtained in his case during the first two years indicate that the education of congenitally deaf children might profitably be commenced at home, and that they might even acquire a vernacular knowledge of English at least in its written form—before being sent to school.

The value of early home training in language cannot be overestimated. Our pupils, as a rule, do not enter school until after the age when children most readily acquire language. If they could commence their school course with even an imperfect and rudimentary knowledge of English, the labor of the teacher would be enormously reduced and the progress of the pupil immensely accelerated.

In the autumn of 1872 I became interested in the boy whose education forms the subject of this paper, and the following extract from one of my note-books will give an idea of the general plan which guided my first steps:

"*October 1st*, 1872.

"Master George S———, aged 5 years, became my pupil this morning.

"He was born totally deaf, and has never spoken a word in his life. He has never been to school, but has received private instruction for three weeks from Miss Fuller, Principal of the Boston School for the Deaf and Dumb.

"He seems a fine, bright, intelligent boy, and there is no apparent defect in his vocal organs.

"For my own guidance, and for the information of friends, I shall briefly sketch out the course I intend to pursue with him.

"It is well for a teacher not to burden himself with too many rules, but rather to grasp *general principles*, and to leave the details of instruction to be worked out by experience.

"I propose to divide his education into two great branches—one relating to articulation, the other to mental development.

"The method of teaching articulation has been explained at length in the *American Annals of the Deaf and Dumb for January*, 1872.

"The general principle is this: *The pronunciation of words and sentences is not to be attempted until the vocal organs have been well drilled on elementary sounds and exercises.**

"While then, the mouth is being brought under control by the use of the Visible-Speech symbols, the mind is to be educated by ordinary letters. The pupil must learn to read and write.

"I believe that George Dalgarno (in his work entitled 'Didascalocophus, or the Deaf and Dumb Man's Tutor,' published in 1680†), has given us the true principle to work upon when he asserts that *a deaf person should be taught to read and write in as nearly as possible the same way that young ones are taught to speak and understand their mother tongue.*

"We should talk to the deaf child just as we do to the hearing one, with the exception that our words are to be addressed to his eye instead of his ear.

"Indeed, George Dalgarno carries his theory so far as to assert that the deaf infant would as soon come to understand written language as a hearing child does speech, 'had the mother or nurse but as nimble a hand as commonly they have a tongue!'

"The principles inculcated by Prendergast (in his 'Mastery of Languages,' 1864‡), and by Marcel (in his 'Study of Languages, or the Art of Thinking in a Foreign Language,' 1869‡), would, if applied to deaf-mutes, point to the same result and to the same method of teaching.

"The principles of Froebel's Kindergarten Method of teaching are applicable to deaf-mutes.

"Froebel believes that *the natural instinct of the child to play should be utilized in his education.*

"His ideas would seem to indicate that the successful teacher must appeal to the faculties of *imagination and imitation*, and encourage *self-activity* in his pupil.

"*I propose, then, to blend the principles of Dalgarno and Froebel—to familiarize the child with written language by means of play.*"

In pursuance of this plan the school-room was converted into a play-room, and language lessons were given through the instrumentality of toys and games.

I was fortunate in securing the co-operation of a very excellent teacher—Miss Abbie Locke, now Mrs. Stone, of St. Louis—with whose assistance George's education was carried on.

Every toy was labelled with its proper name. The different parts of the room, the articles of furniture, and the various objects in the room were also all labelled, as far as possible. Each window had pasted upon it a piece of paper on which was written the word "window;" so with the doors, mantel-piece, table, blackboard, etc., etc.

The words were written in ordinary script characters, with the letters slightly separated. Against one wall was a card rack arranged to display from one to two hundred little cards, each about one inch square.

Upon these cards were written from time to time the names of his toys, and of all the different objects for which he had invented sign-names. Most of his playthings were kept locked up, and were only produced one or two at a time, so as to afford constant variety.

Word Exercises.

1. Our exercises would commence somewhat as follows: George would make his appearance in the morning anxious for play—making vigorous signs

* Experience and reflection have led me to modify this principle.

† Reprinted in the *Annals*, vol. ix, pp. 15–64.

‡ Reviewed in the *Annals*, vol. xiv, pp. 193–204.

for some of his most valued toys. For instance, he would fold his arms and beat his shoulders rapidly with his hands. This was his sign for "doll." The doll was accordingly produced, and his attention was directed to the word "doll" pasted upon the forehead. We compared this word with the words written upon the cards, to see who would first find that card with the word "doll" upon it. Of course in the beginning much to his chagrin—I would generally be the successful searcher. Having found the proper card, we would play with it a sort of game of hide-and-seek, which interested him exceedingly. He would turn away or shut his eyes while I replaced the card in the rack in some place to him unknown. The game consisted in finding it again.

Doll in hand, he would search for the card, comparing each written word with the word on the doll's forehead. He would shake his head gravely at each wrong word, and nod vigorously when he thought he had found the correct one.

When he made a mistake I pointed out the proper card and made fun of him. He was very sensitive to ridicule, and was generally ambitious to try again and again until he succeeded without my assistance. He was also much interested in my (pretended) unsuccessful efforts to find a card placed by him in the rack while my back was turned.

George seemed to enjoy this game exceedingly, but we rarely continued it for more than a few minutes at a time, and even then we constantly varied the names sought for, so as to avoid monotony.

In the beginning the cards were all blank, and the first day I filled in about half a dozen names, but required him to find only one card. Next day we sought not only for that card, but for one or two of the others. After a lapse of a few days he became pretty familiar with all the names, and then each day two or three new names were added, until he had quite an extensive collection of words at command.

2. When he became familiar with a few names I would get him to seek for the proper card without first consulting the label upon the toy. He would pick out some card and then compare it with the word pasted upon the toy. Great was his mortification when the two did not correspond, and great also was his triumph when they did.

I made a mental note of the names he learned by heart in this way, and then pretended not to understand his signs for the corresponding objects.

For instance, I remember that one morning he came down stairs in high spirits, very anxious to play with his doll. He frantically beat his shoulders with his hands, but I could not understand what he meant. I produced a toy-horse; but that was not what he wanted. A table; still he was disappointed. He seemed quite perplexed to know what to do, and evidently considered me very stupid. At last, in desperation, he went to the card-rack, and, after a moment's consideration, pulled out the word "doll" and presented it to me. It is needless to say that the coveted toy was at once placed in his possession. I always pretended to have great difficulty in understanding his signs when we were anywhere near the card-rack, so he soon became accustomed to pick out the words for any objects he desired.

3. The same plan was pursued at meals. A little card-rack was prepared for the dinner-table, so that he might have written words at hand for everything he required to eat or drink.

4. Another word exercise, pursued for a few minutes each day, consisted in the recognition of such words as "stand," "sit," "walk," "run," "jump," etc., which were written upon the blackboard and illustrated by standing, sitting, walking, running, and jumping.

Sentence Exercises.

The greater portion of our time was taken up—even from the first day—with the recognition of complete sentences instead of single words.

The exercises appeared under two forms: (1) impromptu written conversation, and (2) regular sentence exercises.

1. The impromptu conversation was going on all the time. I constantly asked myself the question, "If George could hear, what would I say to him now?" and whatever came into my head I wrote. I kept on writing to him all the time until the blackboard was covered with writing and my arm ached.

I emphasized words to his eye, and grouped them together on the board as I would have grouped them in utterance, leaving gaps here and there where one would naturally pause in speaking. In a word, *I tried to exhibit to his eye all the relations that would have met his ear could he have heard my speech.*

I believed thoroughly in the principle announced by Dalgarno that *it is the frequency with which words are presented to the mind that impresses them upon the memory*, and hence aimed at *much writing* as the accompaniment of everything we did.

I followed up my blackboard conversation by a liberal use of pantomime, bearing always in mind the general principle that I had formulated for myself, viz., that *the use of pantomime is to illustrate language, not to take its place.* In carrying out this principle, therefore, I always wrote first, and acted afterwards—avoiding the converse.

As an example of these impromptu exercises, I will give an imaginary conversation just as I might have written it upon the board:

Specimen of Impromptu Conversation.

Now George I wouldn't **whip** that poor horse if I were you.
You should be **kind** and **gentle** to it.
Please don't whip it any **more**.
You will be **naughty** if you **go on** whipping it like that.
You **mustn't** whip it any more.
Now be a **good boy** and give the **poor horse** something to **eat**.
That's right. **Kiss it**.
You're a **good boy** to **pat** the **horse** so **gently**.
Give the doll a **ride** on the **horse's back**.
Take care!— or the **doll** will **fall off!**

&c., ad libitum.

2. Regular sentence exercises. These exercises formed a regular daily game, which could be varied *ad libitum*. A number of directions were written upon the blackboard which were to be acted out. The game consisted in distinguishing one direction from another.

For example the following sentences might have been written:

Walk very slowly to the window.
Give the doll a drink of water.
Run round the table.
Go and look out of the window.
Make the doll dance.
Put the doll to bed.

We would then act out the sentences, one by one, and afterwards I would take a pointer and indicate one of the sentences at random for him to act out without assistance. Of course he would make frequent mistakes. For instance, when I pointed to the sentence, "Run round the table," he might proceed to give the doll an imaginary drink of water! Under such circumstances I would laugh at him, and write somewhat as follows: "No, that's not right; you are giving the doll a drink of water!!" I would then point to the sentence, "Give the doll a drink of water," and write "That's what you did," and make fun of him.

This exercise would be varied by George playing the master while I became his pupil.

I would test his knowledge by occasionally acting out the wrong sentence, and it gave him great delight to correct me.

In this way he learned very readily to distinguish about half a dozen different sentences, partly from their position on the board, partly by their differences in length, and partly by the recognition of individual words.

At first, however, the sentences were not recognized independently of their position on the board, and, as a general rule, by next day he had forgotten their meaning, excepting when they had been left on the board over night, so that they occupied the same relative positions as before.

WRITING.

He was extremely fond of these sentence exercises: but when he played the master, he was not contented with merely pointing at sentences that I had written—he wished to write them himself! This desire was forced upon my attention one day in the following manner: He took the chalk and scribbled all over the board and *then made signs for me to act that out!* After consideration of the subject, I came to the conclusion that this was a clear indication that the time had come to teach him to write. The great difficulty in the way of doing this lay in the fact that at this time he did not know a single letter of the alphabet—he recognized words and sentences only as wholes.

I determined to make the experiment of teaching him to write sentences as wholes, and the result was as surprising as it was gratifying.

I commenced by writing on the board some direction he wished me to carry out. After partially erasing this so as to leave the writing faintly visible, I placed the chalk in his hand and allowed him to trace over what I had written.

It is true that his first attempts resulted in rather ludicrous caricatures of the originals; but *he never forgot the meaning of a sentence he had traced over in this way a few times.*

The attempt to imitate my writing forced him to observe minutiæ that had hitherto escaped his attention, so that sentences began to be recognized quite independently of their position on the board, and were remembered from day to day.

His imitation of my writing improved with practice, and soon became quite legible. I observed also that his comprehension of my impromptu writing seemed to improve at the same time, and he evidently experienced a desire to use words in his communication with others. He had not progressed sufficiently to be able to write without tracing, but he would often come into the school-room out of school hours for the purpose of taking cards from the card-rack to give to servants or friends to make them understand what he wished.

SPELLING.

The moment he evinced the independent desire to communicate with others by written words, I felt that the time had come to give him a means of forming written words for himself by teaching him his letters and a manual alphabet.

For this purpose I adopted the plan, recommended by George Dalgarno, of writing the alphabet upon a glove. The arrangement of the alphabet I adopted is shown in the diagram on the following page.

This glove I presented to him one morning as a new plaything. He put it on his left hand, and then went to the card-rack, as usual, and presented me with the word for some object he desired; we shall suppose the word "doll." I then covered up the word with the exception of the first letter, "d," and directed his attention to the glove. After a little searching he discovered the corresponding letter upon the glove. I then showed him the letter "o" on the card, and he soon found it on the glove; and so with the other letters.

After a little practice of this kind he became so familiar with the places of the letters that he no longer required to search, but pointed at once to the proper letter upon the glove. Every time he required a card from the card-rack I made him spell the word upon his fingers.

Occasionally I would test his memory by requiring him to spell the word while I held the card behind my back. When I became convinced that he knew the word by heart I tore up the card.

In this way, one by one, all the cards disappeared from the rack. For a long time he was very proud of his glove, and was delighted to find that he could communicate with his parents and friends, and they with him, by simply pointing at the letters on his hand.

In communicating with me it was unnecessary for him to wear the glove, as we both remembered the places of the letters. I kept up the practice of writing to him, as before, but required him to spell the words upon his hand while I wrote them on the board. He soon became so expert that he could spell faster than I could write, and often finished his sentence by guessing what I was going to add before I had written more than two-thirds. When this stage had been reached I often used the manual alphabet with him instead of writing. I took his hand in mine and touched the places of the letters upon his hand. He did not require to look; he could *feel* where he was touched. He recognized the words in this way, however rapidly I spelled them upon his hand. As I had five fingers I could touch five letters simultaneously, if I so desired, and a little practice enabled me to play upon his hand as one would play upon the keys of a piano, and quite as rapidly.

have spoken to a hearing child by speech, and I believed (with George Dalgarno) that he would in time come to understand written language by the same process that children learn to understand their mother tongue.

It seemed to me that hearing children, in acquiring their vernacular, derived great assistance from the free use of the eye as an interpreter of words addressed to the ear, and that therefore my pupil would derive similar assistance from his eye, as the interpreter of words addressed to the sense of touch.

In addition, therefore, to the "regular sentence exercises" and "impromptu written conversation," I would talk to him a great deal upon his hand.

We would go to the window and chat by the half

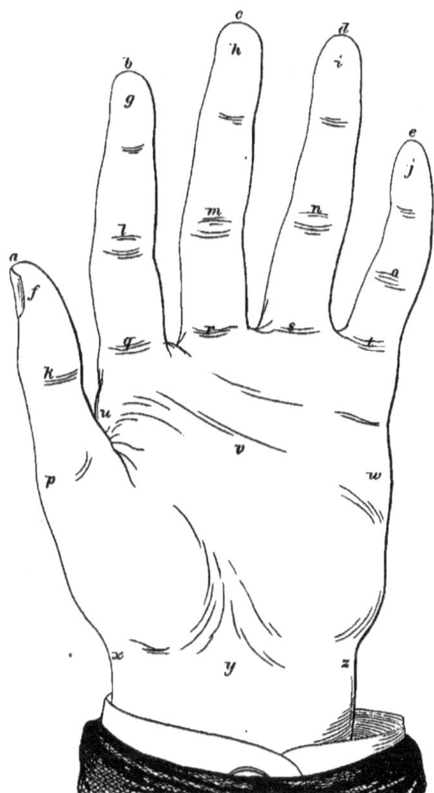

I could also give emphasis by pressure upon the fingers, and group the words together as they would be grouped in utterance, leaving pauses here and there corresponding to the pauses made in actual speech.

The more I used with him this means of communication the more I rejoiced in the fact that I had decided to employ an alphabet addressed to the sense of touch, instead of sight. It left his eye free to observe the expression of my face and the actions and objects which formed the subject of our conversation.

The general principle upon which I was working was to speak to him by written words, as I would

hour at a time about what was going on in the street. At night also I would frequently visit him in his bedroom for the purpose of satisfying myself that I could communicate with him as readily in the dark as by day.

His progress now became very rapid, and he commenced to talk to me by words, instead of signs. I placed no other pressure upon him than my pretended difficulty in understanding his gestures, and allowed him to express himself in any way he chose.

From the moment we commenced to employ the manual alphabet I myself abstained from the use of any other gestures than those I would have employed in talking to a hearing child under the same circumstances. My pretended difficulty in understanding his signs increased from day to day, so as to force him more and more to attempt to express his thoughts by English words. I would assist him in this by translating his signs for him from time to time and making him repeat the sentence independently upon his fingers.

In all conversations I was careful to employ natural and complete sentences, but his first attempts at independent expression (like the first independent utterances of a hearing child) consisted of isolated words.

The use of the glove alphabet was so little noticeable that I could talk to him very freely in a crowd without attracting the attention of others. I took him to Barnum's museum and talked to him all the time the lions were being fed, and I am sure that no one among the spectators had the slightest suspicion that the boy was deaf.

From the moment he learned the alphabet I gave him regular writing lessons, so that he should form his letters properly and write with ease. I then made him keep writing materials about him, and encouraged him to use them constantly in communicating with friends.

Before six months had elapsed I frequently found the floor littered with scraps of paper that he had used in this way, and I am sorry that it did not occur to me at the time to preserve them for future reference. It was not until late in 1873 that I made the attempt to collect a few scraps of this description, and those that are preserved in my note-book possess great interest.

I shall conclude this paper by the following specimens of his composition, which will show that at little more than six years of age this congenitally deaf boy had acquired a vernacular knowledge of the English language sufficient to enable him to communicate by writing with hearing persons.

SPECIMENS OF COMPOSITION.

July 1st, 1873. Scrap found upon the floor in his father's house in Haverhill.

Gurdon is sick to Haverhill in the other Room in the sofa.

2. *August 14th*, 1873. Letter to his mother, written from Brantford, Canada:

Dear Mama

The small cat loves the large cat. Mary will go to Haverhill. Grandma S— will go to Haverhill. I will go home in the train and let I will sleep in the cars. Mama and Nat and I will drive in Haverhill. The many flags is in Haverhill. I will go upstairs in Haverhill to flags. Richards and John and nurse and I and Mr. Bell will go home. After breakfast I will go to see Freddy. Is sleep. I will Eat fast. I love Gurdon and auntie.

3. *November 3d*, 1873. Scrap found upon the floor:

Are those mine? there to see the letters? if you please? Yes Dear Mr. Bell.

4. *November 4th*, 1873. Two scraps containing a conversation between George and myself:

First scrap.

Mr. Bell. I think you are tired and *hot* now, so we will be *quiet* and *rest* now. What does "rest" mean?

George. "Rest" means stop.

Mr. Bell. Yes, dear. It means "stop" or "still."

George. Or "wait."

Mr. Bell. Yes.

George. Please may I put a your handkerchief and be like an old woman?

Note in my record book: "After playing for a while he remembered that his grandmamma had made fun of him for pretending to be a woman, so he wrote:"

Second scrap.

I am not put on my towel on my head and be like an old woman and Grandma said not now Grandma will be so very *sorry* now.

5. *November 23d*, 1873. Letter written by George to his mamma in Haverhill. No person saw this letter until it was finished. Everything in it, even to the emphasizing of certain words, is his own. The omission of capital letters can be traced to the too frequent use of the manual alphabet in place of writing:

"this is *sunday* to-day & to-morrow will be Monday. the people are going to *church*. Mary and Nat are *grown* by and bye.* *john* is not sick now. I *love* daniel now. I am going to *bed* bye and bye. the kitten is alive.† *Mr. Bell* is *reading the book* but papa and mamma are *not* coming to be glad and I matched the lamp on fire. I looked at my little watch from my ka.‡ we will not drive with Mr. Bell. I will say please may I be excused.§ grandpa is tired to drive very fast home. we are walk very fast and go to franks horse and drive the colt on wednesday to see the eggs and hens and kitten and hay and cracker are on dog is not eat the kitten fall to die to the grave. and I am well and I think that Mr. Bell is sick to be tired and go to Boston to the house to go to bed to die to lie down on on my pocket to put the pretty to keys.‖ I looked at the kitten fast asleep on my straw. dan is going to the cow milk on Monday.

your loving
from George.

6. *December 14th*, 1873. Another original letter from George to his mamma.

Salem
Sunday, Dec. 14th.

"My Dear Mama

"I think that Mr. Bell is sorry that I wrote that to say My Dear Mama.¶

"I am sorry that papa and mama are not coming back now. I think that Dan is going to church on sunday with Ellen and Maggie now. By and bye Ellen and Maggie and Dan will come after church. Maggie will stay here with the house. Dan and I went out to the cow milked at the fair. It was dark and it is light. grandma is afraid but I will not go but tomorrow. Ellen is not afraid to see the cow too. I may not kick the cow with be sorry not glad to be still on sunday but bye and bye mary and nat is going to bed. Bye and bye Dan will cut.** but grandma is reading on sunday. I think that grandma has gone to church with Mr. Bell. Mr. Bell's beard is coming now.†† is like are the calendar. I am the deers in Boston.‡‡ The snow is stopping. The rain is not well but rain is sick but the snow is well. Mr. Bell is reading too. Grandma is not reading but after dinner it is the sun too. Haverhill is very far away over here. are papa stay in Haverhill.

7. *March 26*, 1874. Letter to Mrs. H——, written without any assistance.

Salem, Mass
March 26th 1874.

My Dear Grandma H——

I have been to the stable. I am very Glad that Mary will come back tomorrow. I loves Grandma H——. I love Grandpa H—— too and I have finished school before dinner. I have new wheel barrow and there is Grandma's pig in the stable. Maggie is not going to church but maggie is going to church on Sunday. Mr. Bell is writing to you, but I am busy to write to you too. I have a new doll. The dolls are sitting in Mary's chair here. Nat has a old bird and the new piano.§§ Mr. Bell has a new piano in Boston and play with me and Lilly.‖‖ I am laughing at you. I am not laughing at Grandpa H——. I have been the ladies last night and many days.¶¶ I love Maggie. I love Maggie dear pet I must not go near the horse because the horse is large and I may go near the cow. slept in the train from Canada. but now I am in Salem. I will go to Haverhill in a few days. Isa is upstairs sewing. She is not finished sewing.

Your loving
George T. S——.

---

* Mary and Nat (his brother and sister) will grow up by and by.

† The kitten had been crushed behind a book-case and nearly killed.

‡ "Ka" was the children's name for George's nurse.

§ He had just been taught to use this expression when he wished to leave the dinner-table before the others had finished.

‖ This referred to some incident with which I was not acquainted. He went through a pantomime about it, showing that there was some definite idea he wished to express, but no one could understand what he meant.

¶ When George had written "Salem, Sunday, Dec. 14," he attracted my attention that I might see he was going to write a letter. As he seemed in doubt to whom to address it, I suggested that he should begin "Dear Mr. Bell," but he wrote "My Dear Mamma." Upon which I looked very sorry, pretended to cry, and went out of the room, much to his amusement. When he was about half through his letter I returned and read a book till he had finished.

** Will saw firewood.

†† George had seen me before I had shaved.

‡‡ He had been pretending to be a deer.

§§ A toy bird and a toy piano.

‖‖ Mr. Bell had a new piano in Boston *a long time ago* and played for me & Lilly.

¶¶ "There were a number of ladies here a few days ago."

FALLACIES CONCERNING THE DEAF.*

[This Exhibit consisted of a paper by Alexander Graham Bell, read before the Philosophical Society of Washington, D. C., on the 27th day of October, 1883, with discussion by President Gallaudet and the Hon. G. G. Hubbard. (See Bulletin of the Phil. Soc. of Washington, D. C., Vol. VI, p. 48.) Reprinted in the *American Annals of the Deaf* for Jan., 1884, Vol. XXIX, pp. 32-69.]

I am glad to have the opportunity of saying a few words to the members of the Philosophical Society upon a subject that has occupied much of my thoughts of late, namely: Fallacies concerning the deaf, and the influence of those fallacies in preventing the amelioration of their condition.

It is difficult to form an adequate conception of the prevalence of deafness in the community. There is hardly a man in the country who has not in his circle of friends and acquaintances at least one deaf person with whom he finds it difficult to converse, excepting by means of a hearing-tube or trumpet. Now, is it not an extraordinary fact that these deaf friends are nearly all adults? Where are the little children who are similarly afflicted? Have any of us seen a child with a hearing-tube or trumpet? If not, why not? The fact is that very young children who are "hard of hearing," or who cannot hear at all, do not naturally speak, and this fact has given origin to the term "deaf-mute," by which it is customary to designate a person who is deaf from childhood.

"But are there no deaf children," you may ask, "excepting those whom we term deaf-mutes?" No, none. In the Tenth Census of the United States, (1880,) persons who became deaf under the age of sixteen years were returned as "deaf and dumb." Such facts as these give support to the fallacy that deafness, unaccompanied by any other natural defect, is confined to adult life, and is specially characteristic of advancing old age.

So constant is the association of defective speech with defective hearing in childhood, that if one of your children whom you have left at home, hearing perfectly and talking perfectly, should from some accident lose his hearing, he would also naturally lose his speech. Why is this, and why are those who are born deaf always also dumb?

FALLACIES CONCERNING THE DUMBNESS OF DEAF CHILDREN.

The most ingenious and fallacious arguments have been advanced in explanation. Anthony Deusing,† in 1656, claimed that the nerves of the tongue and larynx were connected with the nerves of the ear, "and from this communion of the vessels proceeds the sympathy between the ear, the tongue and larynx, and the very affection of those parts are easily communicated one with the other. Hence it is that the pulling of the membrane of the ear causeth a dry cough in the party, and that is the reason why most deaf men are dumb, or else speak with great difficulty, that is, are not capable of framing true words or of articulate pronunciation, by reason of the want of that convenient influx of the animal spirits; and for this cause also it is that those who are thick of hearing have a kind of hoarse speech.

The value of Deusing's reasoning may be judged of by the further information he gives us concerning the uses of the Eustachian tube. "By this it is," he says, "that smokers, puffing up their cheeks, having taken in the fume of tobacco, send it out at their ears. Therefore, the opinion of *Alcmaeon* is not ridiculous, who held that she-goats did breathe through their ears," etc., etc.

It is easy for us to laugh at the fallacies of the past, but are we ourselves any less liable to error on that account? The majority of people at the present day believe that those who are born deaf are also dumb *because of defective vocal organs.* Now let us examine this proposition. It is a more ridiculous and absurd fallacy than that of Deusing and more easily disposed of.

The hypothesis that congenitally deaf children do not naturally speak because their vocal organs are defective involves the assumption that were their vocal organs perfect such children *would* naturally speak. But why should they speak a language they have never heard? Do we speak any language that we have not heard? Are our vocal organs defective because we do not talk Chinese? It is a fallacy. The deaf have as perfect vocal organs as our own, and do not naturally speak because they do not hear. I have myself examined the vocal organs of more than four hundred deaf-mutes without discovering any other peculiarities than those to be found among hearing and speaking children. The deaf children of Italy and Germany are almost universally taught to speak, and why should we not teach ours? Wherever determined efforts have been made in this country success has followed and articulation schools have been established.

FALLACY CONCERNING THE INTELLIGENCE OF DEAF CHILDREN.

The use of the word "mute" engenders another fallacy concerning the mental condition of deaf children. There are two classes of persons who do not naturally speak: those who are dumb on account of defective hearing, and those who are dumb on account of defective minds. All idiots are dumb.

Deaf children are gathered into institutions and schools that have been established for their benefit away from the general observation of the public, and even in adult life they hold themselves aloof from hearing people; while idiots and feeble-minded persons are not so generally withdrawn from their families. Hence the greater number of "mutes" who are accessible to public observation are dumb on account of defective minds and not of defective hearing. No wonder, therefore, that the two classes are often confounded together. It is the hard task of every principal of an institution for the deaf and dumb to turn idiots and feeble-minded children away from his school—children who hear perfectly but cannot speak. Although it is evidently fallacious to argue that "because all deaf infants are dumb and all idiots are dumb, therefore all deaf infants are idiots," still this kind of reasoning is unconsciously indulged in by a large proportion of our population, and the majority of those who for the first time visit an institution for the deaf and dumb express unfeigned astonishment at the brightness and intelligence displayed by the pupils.

WHY HEARING CHILDREN WHO BECOME DEAF ALSO BECOME DUMB.

I have stated above that children who are born deaf do not naturally speak because they cannot hear. For the same reason children who lose their hearing after having learned to speak naturally tend to lose their speech. They acquired speech through the ear by imitating the utterances of their friends and relatives, and when they become deaf they gradually forget the true pronunciation of the words they

*An address delivered at the two hundred and thirty-ninth meeting of the Philosophical Society of Washington, D. C., held on Saturday, October 27th, 1883, and reprinted by permission from the Bulletin of the Philosophical Society by the American Annals of the Deaf and Dumb.

†"Dissertatio de surdis ab ortu." Groningæ: 1656. Translated into English by Geo. Sibscota under the title, "The Deaf and Dumb Man's Discourse." London: 1670.

know, and have naturally no means of learning the pronunciation of new words; hence, their speech tends to become more and more defective until they finally cease to use spoken words at all.

Adults who become deaf do not usually have defective speech, for in their case the habit of speaking has been so fully formed that the mere practice of the vocal organs in talking to friends prevents loss of distinctness. We can learn, however, from the case of Alexander Selkirk how important is constant practice of the vocal organs. This man, after about one year's solitary residence upon an island, was found to have nearly forgotten his mother tongue; and we find that deaf adults who shrink from society and use their vocal organs only on rare occasions acquire peculiarities of utterance that are characteristic of persons in their condition, although the general intelligibility of their speech is not affected.

FALLACIES REGARDING THE NATURE OF SPEECH.

The fallacies I have already alluded to respecting the difference between those who become deaf in childhood and those who become deaf in adult life have their origin in a fallacy concerning the nature of speech itself. To most people who do not reflect upon the subject it appears that speech is acquired by a natural process similar to that by which we acquire our teeth. We are all born dumb and without teeth. At a certain age the teeth make their appearance, and at another age we begin to talk. To unreflecting minds it appears that we *grow into speech*—that speech is a natural product of the vocal organs produced without instruction and education; and this leads directly to the fallacy that where speech is wanting or imperfect the vocal organs are defective.

I have already stated that this cause has been assigned in explanation of the dumbness of children who are deaf. The idea gives rise also to the popular notion that stammering and other defects of speech are diseases to be "cured," and the attempt has been made to do so even by heroic treatment. It is not so very long ago that slices have been cut from the tongue of a stammerer in the vain hope of "curing" what was after all but a bad habit of speech. I have myself known of cases where the uvula has been excised to correct the same defect. The dumbness of the deaf and the defective speech of the hearing are some of the penalties we pay for acquiring speech ignorantly by mere imitation. If parents realized that stammering and other defects of speech were caused by ignorance of the actions of the vocal organs, and not necessarily through any defect of the mouth, they would have their children taught the use of the vocal organs by articulation teachers instead of patronizing the widely-advertised specialty physicians who pretend by secret means to "cure" what is not a disease. Speech is naturally acquired by imitation and through the same agency defects of speech are propagated. A child copies the defective utterance of his father. A school-fellow mocks a stammering companion and becomes himself similarly affected. In the one case the fallacy that the supposed disease is hereditary prevents attempts at instruction and correction and in the other the idea that the affliction is the judgment of God in the way of punishment discourages the afflicted person, and renders him utterly hopeless of any escape excepting by a miracle.

A practical illustration of the fact that defective speech is propagated by imitation is shown in my own case. When I was a boy my father was a teacher of elocution, and had living with him at one time one or two pupils who stammered. While under the care of my father these boys spoke clearly and well without any apparent defect, but owing to his being called away for a protracted period of time his pupils relapsed, and the boys commenced to stammer as badly as at first. Upon my father's return he found a house full of stammerers. *His own sons were stammering too!* I can well remember the process of instruction through which I went before the defect was corrected in my own case.

IGNORANCE THE REAL DIFFICULTY IN THE WAY OF TEACHING DEAF CHILDREN TO SPEAK.

Speech is the mechanical result of certain adjustments of the vocal organs, and if we can teach deaf children the correct adjustments of the perfect organs they possess, they will speak. The difficulty lies with us. We learn to speak by imitating the sounds we hear, in utter ignorance of the action of the organs that accompanies the sounds. I find myself addressing an audience composed of scientific men, including many of the most eminent persons in the country; and I wonder how many there are in this room who could give an intelligible account of the movements of their vocal organs in uttering the simplest sentence? We must study the mechanism of speech, and when we know what are the correct adjustments of the organs concerned, ingenuity and skill will find the means of teaching *perfect* articulation to the deaf.

THE OLD FALLACY—"WITHOUT SPEECH, NO REASON."

I have already stated that children who are born deaf are also always dumb. How then can they think? It is difficult for us to realize the possibility of a train of thought being carried on without words; but what words can a deaf child know who has never heard the sounds of speech?

When we think we think in words, though we may not actually utter sounds. Let us eliminate from our consciousness the train of words and what remains? I do not venture to answer the question, but it is this, and this alone, that belongs to the thoughts of a deaf child.

It is hardly to be wondered at, therefore, that the fallacy should have arisen in the past that there could be no thought without speech, and this fallacy prevented for hundreds of years any attempt at the education of the deaf. Before the end of the last century deaf-mutes were classed among the idiots and insane; they had no civil rights, could hold no property; they were irresponsible beings. Even those interested in the religious welfare of the world consigned their souls to the wrong place; for "faith comes by hearing," and how could a deaf child be saved! I say that for hundreds of years the old fallacy that "without speech there could be no reason" hindered and prevented any attempt at the amelioration of the condition of the deaf. But strange to say, it was this very fallacy that first led to their education. It was attempted—by a miracle—to teach them to speak.

In Bede's History of the Anglo-Saxon Church, we read "how bishopp John cured a dumme man with blessing him:"

"And when one weeke of Lent was past, the next soundey he willed the poore man to come unto him; when he was come, he bydd him put out his tounge and show it unto him, and taking him by the chinne, made the signe of the holy crosse upon his tounge, and when he had so signed and blessed it, he commaunded him to plucke it in again, and speake saying, speake, me one word, say *gea, gea*, which in the english tounge is a worde of affirmation and consent in such signification as yea, yea.* In continent the stringes of his tounge were loosed, and he said that which was commaunded him to say. The bishopp added certain letters by name, and bid him say A: he said A: say B, he said B, and when he had said and recited after the bishopp the whole cross rewe he put upon him sillables and hole wordes to be pronounced. Unto which when he answered in all pointes orderly, he commaunded him to speake long sentences, and so he did; and ceased not all that day and night following, so longe as he could hold up his head from sleepe (as they make report that were present) to speake and declare his secret thoughtes and purposes, which before that day he could never utter to any man."†

* It will be remembered that the original of this was in Latin and that "the english tounge" here means what we now call the Anglo-Saxon.

†*American Annals of the Deaf and Dumb*, vol. 1, p. 33.

Now, stripped of the miraculous, this is simply a case of articulation teaching. In the other countries of Europe the first attempts at the education of the deaf were also made by teaching them to speak, and, as the early teachers were monks of the Roman Catholic church, it is probable that these schools resulted from the attempts to perform the miracle of healing the dumb. A large proportion of the deaf and dumb who were thus brought together were successfully taught to articulate.

But now comes a marvel. It was found by the old monks that their pupils came to understand the utterances of others by watching the mouth. Such a statement appears more marvellous to those who understand the mechanism of speech than to those who are ignorant of it, and there is a general tendency to consider this accomplishment as among the fictitious embellishments of the old narratives. But the experience of modern teachers confirms the fact. John Bulwer, who is said to have been the earliest English writer upon the subject of the instruction of the deaf and dumb, published in the year 1648 a treatise entitled "Philocophus, or the Deaf and Dumb Man's friend. Exhibiting the Philosophicall verity of that subtile Art, which may inable one with an *observant Eie*, to *Heare* what any man speaks by the moving of his lips. Upon the same Ground, with the advantage of an Historicall Exemplification, apparently proving, That a Man Borne Deafe and Dumbe may be taught to *Heare* the sound of *words* with his *Eie*, and thence learn to speak with his tongue."

ARTICULATION TEACHING IN AMERICA.

In Europe at the present time deaf children are much more commonly taught to speak and understand speech than in this country.

In the majority of our schools and institutions articulation and speech-reading are taught to only a favored few, and in these schools no use is made of articulation as a means of communication. A considerable number of the deaf children in our institutions could once hear and speak, and those pupils who retain some knowledge of spoken language have their vocal organs exercised for an hour or so a day in an articulation class under a special articulation teacher, but this is not enough exercise to retain the speech. I have seen a boy who became deaf at twelve years of age, and who had previously attended one of our public schools, go into an institution for the deaf and dumb talking as readily as you or I, *and come out a deaf-mute.*.

Few, if any, attempts are made to teach articulation to those who have not naturally spoken, except at the special request of parents who desire that the experiment shall be tried with their children.

I have seen a congenital deaf-mute—who also had a sister deaf and dumb—who was taught to speak in adult life, and I found upon experiment that he could understand by ear the words and sentences that he had been taught to articulate when they were spoken in an ordinary tone of voice about a foot behind his head; yet this young man had been educated at one of our best institutions without acquiring articulation, and as a consequence he grew up a deaf-mute and married a deaf mute. He informed me himself that he could hear the people talking in the workshop where he was employed but did not understand what they said.

As a matter of personal observation I am convinced that a large proportion of the congenitally deaf are only hard of hearing, and this belief is supported by the fact that it used to be the custom in some of our institutions to summon the pupils from the playground *by the ringing of a bell!* Does this not indicate that a large number of the pupils could hear the ringing of the bell and that they told the others who could not hear at all? Such pupils could have been taught to speak at home by their friends if artificial assistance had been given to their hearing. There was no necessity for their ever becoming deaf and dumb.

It is only within the last fifteen years or thereabouts that schools have been established in the United States where all the deaf children admitted are taught articulation and speech-reading; but such schools are rapidly increasing in number. Still, it is not generally known that the experimental stage has passed and that all deaf-mutes can be taught intelligible speech. This is now done in Italy and Germany, and the International conventions of teachers of the deaf and dumb held recently at Milan and Brussels have decided in favor of articulation for the deaf.

I have stated before that the difficulties in the way of teaching articulation are external to the deaf. They lie with us and in our general ignorance of the mechanism of speech. A teacher who does not himself understand the mechanism of speech is hardly competent to produce the best results. So dense is the general ignorance upon this subject that it is probable that of the 50,000,000 of people in this country the number of persons who are familiar with all that is known concerning the mechanism of speech might be numbered on the two hands. Considering this, the success obtained in our articulation schools is gratifying and wonderful.

UPON THE ART OF UNDERSTANDING SPEECH BY THE EYE.

It has been found in the articulation schools of this country that deaf children can acquire the art of understanding by eye the utterances of their friends and relatives; this fact has led some teachers to suppose that speech is as clearly visible to the eye as it is to the ear, and this fallacy tends to hinder the acquisition of the art by their pupils.

When we examine the visibility of the elementary sounds of our language, we find that the majority can not be clearly distinguished by the eye. How then, you may ask, can a deaf child who cannot distinguish the elements understand words which are combinations of these elements?

When the lips are closed we cannot see what is going on inside the mouth. The elementary sounds of our language, represented by the letters *p*, *b*, and *m*, involve a closure of the lips. Hence the differences of adjustment that originate the differences of sound are interior and cannot be seen.

But while the deaf child may not be able to say definitely whether the sound you utter is *p*, *b*, or *m*, he knows certainly that it must be one of these three; for no other sounds involve a closure of the lips. And so with the other elements of our language. While he may not be able to tell definitely the particular element to which you give utterance, he can generally refer it to a group of sounds that present the same appearance to the eye. In the same manner he may not be able to tell the precise word that you utter, but he can refer it to a group of words having the same appearance. For instance, the words "*pat*," "*bat*," and "*mat*" have the same appearance to the eye. While he cannot tell which of these words you mean when it is uttered singly, he readily distinguishes it in a sentence by the context. For instance, were you to say that you had wiped your feet upon a "*mat*," the word could not be "*pat*" and it could not be "*bat*."

Here we come to the key to the art of understanding speech by the eye: Context. But this involves as a prerequisite, a competent knowledge of the English language, and we may particularly distinguish those children who have acquired the art from those who have not by their superior attainments in this respect. We can, therefore, see why children who have become deaf after having learned to speak, naturally acquire this power to a greater extent than those who are born deaf.

There are many cases of congenitally deaf children who have acquired this art as perfectly as those who have become deaf from disease, but in every case such children have been thoroughly familiar with the English language at least in its written form.

FALLACIES REGARDING SPEECH-READING.

The fallacy that speech is as clearly visible to the eye as it is audible to the ear hinders the acquisition of the art by causing the teacher to articulate slowly, and word by word, even opening the mouth to its widest extent to make the actions of the organs more visible. When we realize that context is the key to speech-reading, theory asserts that ordinary conversational speech should be more intelligible than slow and labored articulation. This is amply proved by the experience of the most accomplished speech-readers. I have been told by one who has acquired this art that, when introduced to strangers, their speech is more readily understood if they are not aware they are speaking to one who cannot hear. The moment they are told, they commence to speak slowly, and open their mouths to an unnatural extent, thus rendering their articulation partially unintelligible. The change brought about by the knowledge that the listener could not hear was sometimes sudden and great.

I have lately made an examination of the visibility of all the words in our language contained in a small pocket dictionary, and the result has assured me that there are glorious possibilities in the way of teaching speech-reading to the deaf if teachers will give special attention to the subject.

One of the results of my investigation has been that the ambiguities of speech are confined to the little words, chiefly to monosyllables. The longer words are nearly all clearly intelligible. The reason is obvious, for the greater number of elements there are in a word the less likelihood is there that another word can be found that presents exactly the same outline to the eye.

We need never be afraid, therefore, of using long words to a deaf child if they are within his comprehension. We are apt to have the idea that short words will be simpler, and we sometimes try to compose sentences consisting as much as possible of monosyllabic words, under the impression that such words are easy for the pupil to pronounce and read from the mouth. It is more common, therefore, to present such sentences to beginners than to more advanced pupils. Now, I do not mean to say that these sentences may not be easier for a child to pronounce, but the words used are the most ambiguous to the eye. Such a simple word as "man," for instance, is homophenous with no less than thirteen other words.

A few years ago I dictated a string of words to some pupils with the object of testing whether they judged by context or were able to distinguish words clearly by the eye. The results are instructive. Among the words dictated occurred the following: "Hit—rate—ferry—aren't—hat—four—that—reason—high—knit—donned—co." I told the pupils not to mind whether they understood what I said or not, but simply to write down what they thought the words looked like, and what do you think they wrote? Upon examining their slates I found that nearly every child had written the following sentence: "It rained very hard, and for that reason I did not go." I told the pupils to be very careful to observe whether they could distinguish any difference between the words I uttered and the words they wrote. I therefore went over the whole string of words again, articulating them one by one very distinctly. No difference whatever was detected. The mother of one of my pupils was present, and was greatly astonished to see her daughter writing down words so different from those I had pronounced. She said that she could not have believed that her daughter could have been so stupid, but her surprise was increased when she found that the other children had written the same sentence.

I told her there was no difference in appearance between the words I had uttered and the words they had written. She desired to test the matter herself with her own child. She asked her daughter to repeat after *her* the words I had written, but the result was the same. The last part of the sentence she repeated at least a dozen times without shaking her daughter's confidence in the belief that the words she had uttered were precisely the same as those spoken by her mother. To one who could hear, it was a startling revelation to observe the confidence of the child in the accuracy of her replies.

"Repeat after me," said the mother, as she pronounced the words singly and with deliberate distinctness: "high;" answer, "I:" "knit:" answer, "did:" "donned;" answer, "not:" "co;" answer, "go." "Are you sure you have pronounced the words exactly as I have said them?" Answer, "Yes, perfectly certain." "Try again: knit;" answer, "did:" "donned;" answer, "not." "Are you *sure* I said that?" Answer: "Yes, absolutely sure." "Try again," and here the mother mouthed the word "donned;" answer, "not." The mother was convinced; and she left the room with the remark that she felt that she had been very cruel to her child, through ignorance of the fact that words that were very different to her ear looked alike to her child, and could not possibly be distinguished excepting by context.

I have seen a teacher attempting to impart instruction to a deaf child by word of mouth. She would speak word by word and the pupil would repeat after her. Upon one occasion the pupil gave utterance to a very different word from that which had been spoken by the teacher. The latter repeated the word a number of times, opening her mouth to the widest extent, and the boy each time repeated the incorrect expression. The teacher grew annoyed at the supposed stupidity of the pupil, and the pupil grew sulky, and was discouraged in his attempt to read from the mouth, whereas in reality it was not the stupidity of the boy that was in his way of progress, but the ignorance of the teacher, who did not know that the words that were so different to her ear were absolutely alike to his eye. Some teachers in their anxiety to teach speech-reading to their pupils have the idea that they should refrain from every other mode of communication so that their pupils may be forced to observe the movements of the mouth and the mouth alone.

For instance, it is easy to write an ambiguous word, or to spell it by a manual alphabet, but some teachers refrain from doing so under the impression that this practice leads the pupil to depend upon the hand, instead of the mouth.

Again, deaf persons gather an idea of the emotion that actuates a speaker by the expression of his countenance. In fact, facial expression is to the eye what the modulation of the voice is to the ear. It gives life to the inaudible utterances of the mouth; but there are some teachers who are so afraid that their pupils may come to depend upon the face instead of the mouth that they think they should assume an impassive countenance from which nothing could be inferred.

REQUISITES TO THE ART OF SPEECH-READING.

If we examine the visibility of speech and the causes of its intelligibility we shall find that there are three qualifications that must be possessed by a deaf child in order that he may understand readily the utterances of his friends. Omit any one of these qualifications and good speech-reading is an impossibility.

I. The eye must be trained to recognize readily those movements of the vocal organs that are visible. Has this ever been done? Have not pupils been required to grapple with all the difficulties of speech-reading at once, and to observe not only the movements of the vocal organs but to find out the meaning of what is said?

II. I have already explained that certain words

have the same appearance to the eye, and it is necessary, if the pupil is to understand general conversation, that he shall know the words that look alike, so that a given series of movements of the vocal organs shall suggest to his mind not a single word but a group of words from which selection is to be made by context.

An illustration will explain what I mean. There are many words which have the same sound to the ear, but different significations. For instance, were I to ask you to spell the word "rane," you could not tell whether I meant "rain," "rein," or "reign." These words sound alike, but they lead to no confusion, for they are readily distinguished by context. In the same way "homophenous words," or words that have the same appearance to the eye, are readily distinguished by context.

As a general rule, when a teacher finds that her pupil does not understand a given word she supposes the non-comprehension to be due to an untrained eye, and this leads to the patient repetition of the word with widely opened mouth, to make the action of the organs more visible.

This, unintentionally, enables the pupil to acquire a knowledge of homophenous words; for, when he fails to understand in the first instance, he is requested to try again. He then guesses at the meaning. He thinks of all the words that past experience has taught him looked something like the word proposed, and after a series of guesses generally succeeds in his attempt to unravel the meaning.

In this way success comes at last, and not in consequence of the pupil seeing more than he saw at first, but in consequence of knowledge gained by experience of failure. He learns what words present the same appearance to the eye. Let teachers find out the words that look alike, and teach them in groups to their pupils. In this way instruction will take the place of knowledge gained at present by painful experience.

III. The third requisite to good speech-reading is familiarity with the English language. Familiarity with our language either in its written or spoken form is absolutely essential in order that a deaf person may make use of context in his attempt to decipher our speech. It is a mental problem that the deaf child has to solve, and not solely a problem of vision. The eyes of the congenitally deaf, if there is any difference at all, are rather stronger and better than the eyes of those who become deaf from disease; and yet, as a class, the congenitally deaf acquire the art of speech-reading with much more difficulty than those who could speak before they became deaf. The reason is that, as a class, the former have not a vernacular knowledge of our language even in its written form, while the latter have. Children who become deaf in infancy from disease are at as great a disadvantage in this respect as the congenitally deaf, and for the same reason.

I shall enquire more particularly into the cause of this lack of familiarity with the English language, and I shall show that it results from a wide-spread fallacy regarding the nature of language and the means by which our language should be taught. In the meantime I shall simply direct attention to the fact that those who are deaf from infancy do not, as a general rule become familiar with the English language even in its written form.

It is obvious that if we talk to deaf children by word of mouth and refrain from explaining the words that are ambiguous, by writing or some other clearly visible means, those pupils who are already familiar with the language have very great advantages over the others. They have a fund of words from which to draw; they can guess at the ambiguous word and substitute other words within their knowledge, so as finally to arrive at the correct meaning. But young children who have been deaf from infancy, and who never therefore have known our language, are not qualified at once for this species of guess-work. They know no words excepting those we teach them, and have therefore no fund to draw upon in case of perplexity. If we commence the education of such children by speech-reading alone they are plunged into difficulties to which they have not the key.

To such children it becomes a matter of absolute necessity that our language should be presented to them in an unambiguous form.

With such pupils writing should be the main reliance; and speech-reading can only be satisfactorily acquired by the constant accompaniment of writing, or its equivalent—a manual alphabet. I have no hesitation in saying that the attempt to carry on the general education of young children who are deaf from infancy by means of articulation and speech-reading alone, without the habitual use of English in a more clearly visible form, would tend to retard their mental development. I do not mean to say that this is ever actually done, but I know there is a tendency among teachers of articulation to rely too much upon the general intelligibility of their speech. Let them realize that the intelligibility is almost entirely due to context, and they will rely more upon writing and less upon the mouth in their instructions to young congenitally deaf children.

After a probationary period pupils who could speak before they became deaf become so expert in speech-reading that the regular instruction of the school-room can be carried on through its means without detriment to the pupil's progress. The exceptional cases of congenitally deaf persons who have become expert in this art assure us that, with all who are deaf from infancy, we can certainly achieve the same results if only we can give them a sufficient knowledge of our language at least in its written form. In the early stages of the education of the congenitally deaf it appears to me that written English should be made the vernacular of the school-room, and that all words or sentences written should also be spoken by the teacher and read by the pupils from the mouth.

When the English language has become vernacular there is no reason why instruction should not also be given by word of mouth alone, (as in the case of those who could speak before they became deaf,) without interfering with mental development. Before leaving this subject I would say that it is of importance to remember that speaking and understanding speech by the eye are two very different things. We can all of us speak very readily, but I fancy it would puzzle most of us to be called upon to tell what a speaker says by watching his mouth. The congenitally deaf can certainly be taught to speak intelligibly even by persons unfamiliar with the mechanism of articulation. Such pupils should therefore be taught to articulate, and their vocal organs should be continually exercised in the school room by causing them to speak as well as to write. The congenitally deaf can be taught to articulate even *before* they are familiar with English, but I do not think they can acquire the power of understanding ordinary conversational speech by watching the mouth, at least to any great extent, until *after* they have become familiar with our language.

GESTURE-LANGUAGE.

I have already stated that the old fallacy "without speech there can be no reason" prevented for hundreds of years any attempt at the education of the deaf and dumb, and now I come to the memorable experiment that forever exploded the fallacy. Towards the latter end of the last century the Abbe de l'Epée, during the course of his ministrations in Paris, entered a room in which two girls were sewing. He addressed some remarks to them but received no reply. These girls were deaf and dumb. At once the kind heart of the good Abbe was touched and he determined to devote his life to the amelioration of the condition of the deaf and dumb. He gathered together quite a number of deaf children who made their home with him. He spent his time in their society and devoted to their comfort all that he possessed, reducing himself even to poverty for their sake. He soon observed that these children were communicating with one another, but not by speech. They were inventing a language of their own unlike any of the spoken languages of the earth—a language of gestures. These children were reasoning by means of this language, they were thinking in gestures instead of in words, and the idea occurred to the Abbe de l'Epée that the old dogma that had for so many hundred years prevented the education of the deaf was a fallacy. Here was nature developing an instrument of reason with which speech had nothing to do. Why should he not study this gesture-language and assist these children in their attempts to perfect a means of communication of this kind, and why should he not use this means of communication so as to lead their minds to higher and ever higher thoughts? He did so, and succeeded in developing the "sign-language" that is now so extensively employed in this country in the education of the deaf. The experiment at once attracted attention; kings and emperors visited the humble abode of the Abbe de l'Epée and were astonished by what they saw. He conversed with his pupils in the gesture-language, and he taught them through its means the meaning of written French, so that they were enabled to communicate with hearing persons by writing.

THE FALLACY THAT A GESTURE-LANGUAGE IS THE ONLY FORM OF LANGUAGE THAT IS NATURAL TO THE CONGENITALLY DEAF.

The old fallacy was done away with, but a new one immediately took its place, which has been introduced into our country with the language of signs and is now the main obstacle to the acquisition of English by the congenitally deaf. The fallacy to which I allude is that this gesture-language is the only language that is natural to the congenitally deaf; and that, therefore, such children must acquire this language as their vernacular before learning the English language and must be taught the meaning of the latter through its means. The proposition that the sign-language is the only language that is natural to congenitally deaf children is like the proposition that the English language is the only language that is natural to hearing children. It is natural only in the same sense that English is natural to an American child. It is the language of the people by whom he is surrounded.

A congenitally deaf child who for the first time enters an institution for the deaf and dumb finds the pupils and teachers employing a gesture-language which he does not understand, but in time he comes to understand it, and learns by imitation to use it just as an American child in Germany comes in time to understand and speak German. Although congenitally deaf children when they enter an institution do not understand or use the sign-language as there employed, they each know and use a gesture-language of some kind, which they employ at home in communicating with their friends and relatives.

Hence it is argued that if the "sign-language" employed in our institutions is not the only one, a gesture-language of some kind is necessarily the vernacular of the congenitally deaf child. The scope of the statement is thus widened, and the proposition we have now to consider may be thus expressed: Gesture-language, in the wider sense, is the only form of language that is natural to those who are congenitally deaf.

It is a matter of great importance to the 34,000 deaf-mutes of this country and to their friends and relatives, as well as to all persons who are interested in the amelioration of the condition of the deaf and dumb, that we examine this proposition with care and decide whether it is a fallacy or not. To my mind it is a fallacy based upon another concerning the nature of language itself, namely, that there is such a thing as a natural language. Such an idea has led to errors in the past and will ever continue to do so. We have all read of the monarch of ancient times who is recorded to have shut up a number of little children by themselves and to have given orders to their attendants to hold no communication with them, so that he might observe what language they would naturally speak as they grew up. It is recorded that the first word uttered was a Greek word; from which it was argued that the Greek language was the natural language of mankind.

In the 17th century the ingenious Van Helmont was imbued with the idea that the Hebrew language was of Divine origin, from which he argued that Hebrew was the natural language of mankind, and that the shapes of the Hebrew letters had some natural relation to the sounds they represented; that they pictured, in fact, the positions of the vocal organs in forming the sounds. The latter idea led him to employ the characters as a means of teaching articulation to a deaf-mute, but the former idea led him to teach his deaf-mute Hebrew instead of his native tongue. When we examine the languages of the world that are naturally acquired by hearing children, we fail to discover any natural connection between the words and the things they represent; everything is arbitrary and conventional.

ORIGIN AND MODE OF GROWTH OF A GESTURE-LANGUAGE.

Now let us examine for a moment the nature of a gesture-language and the manner in which it comes into existence. You may be, we shall suppose, a farmer, and your little deaf boy comes running into the house in great excitement, anxious to tell you something he has observed. How does he do so?

We shall imagine a case. He commences by placing his hands above his head, bowing low, and marching about the room, after which he points out of the window.

You shake your head, you have not the remotest idea what he means.

His face assumes an anxious look and down he goes upon his hands and knees and scrambles over the floor, touching the carpet with his mouth from time to time, and then again he points out of the window. Still you do not comprehend. A look of perplexity crosses his face. What can he do to make you understand? At last his face lights up as a new thought comes into his mind, and he touches the bridge of his nose and again points out of the window.

But alas! alas! you cannot understand.

The little fellow is perplexed and troubled. At last, in despair, he takes hold of your coat and pulls you out of the door around the corner and—*you find your cow in the turnip patch.*

Now you begin to understand what it was he meant to say: he had tried to picture the cow, and to imitate its actions. The hands held above the head had indicated the horns; the scrambling on the floor on his hands and knees had imitated the action of a four-footed animal, and his mouth to the carpet meant the cow eating the turnips.

But how about the bridge of his nose?

You will probably observe that the cow to which he referred had some white spot or other mark upon the nose, and the gesture of the child had not indicated a cow in general, but your black cow "Bessie," with the white spot on her nose, in particular.

Having advanced thus far in the comprehension of his meaning, do you think that the child will take the trouble to go through this same pantomime the next time he wishes to tell you about your cow? No: he may commence such a pantomime, but before he gets half through you understand what he means, and he never completes it. A process of abbreviation commences, until finally a touch on the bridge of his nose alone becomes the name of your cow "Bessie," and the simple holding of his hands above his head conveys to your mind the idea of a cow in general.

By a natural process of abbreviation the child arrives at a simple gesture or sign for every object or thing in which he is interested.

But there are many thoughts he desires to express which are abstract in their nature. How, for instance, can he indicate by any sign the color of an object? Suppose, by way of illustration, that he desired to communicate to you the idea that he had seen in the road a cow that was perfectly white.

I shall try to depict the conversation between yourself and your deaf boy as it might actually have occurred:

The Boy. The boy points to the road, touches his teeth, and holds his hands above his head.

You gather from this a vague idea of some connection between that road, the boy's teeth, and a cow.

Here is a problem: What did he mean? It is pretty clear that he had seen a cow in the road, but what connection had his teeth with that? Perhaps the cow's teeth were peculiar. You think you had better get him to explain, so—

The Father. You touch your teeth with an interrogative and puzzled look.

The Boy. The boy responds by showing you his shirt sleeve and pointing to the road.

Can he mean that there was any connection between his shirt sleeve and the cow? To clear this point—

The Father. You touch his shirt sleeve and raise your hands above your head with a look of interrogation.

The Boy. The boy nods vigorously, raises his hands above his head, and makes his sign for "snow," followed by other signs for other objects that are white.

After he has presented a sufficient number of such signs you perceive that the one thing common to them all was their color—they were white. And thus you gain the idea that the cow was white.

Do you suppose he goes through this process every time he desires to communicate the idea of white? No; he remembers the object which had conveyed to your mind the idea that that cow was white, and the sign for this object is ever after used as an adjective qualifying the object the whiteness of which he desires to indicate. Of course you cannot predicate what this particular sign may be. I have seen children who have conveyed the idea by touching their teeth; others who expressed it by an undulatory downward movement of the hand, expressive of the way in which a snowflake falls to the ground.

It will thus be understood that a deaf child first commences to express his ideas by pantomime, and that by a process of abbreviation pantomimic gestures come to be used in a conventional manner. Pantomime is no more entitled to the name of language than a picture is, although many ideas can be conveyed through its means. In proportion as it becomes more conventional and arbitrary it becomes more and more worthy of the name of language.

THE SIGN-LANGUAGE OF OUR INSTITUTIONS.

Now, when the deaf children who lived with the Abbe de l'Epée were first brought together, each of them used a gesture-language he had invented for himself as a means of communicating with his friends at home. Thus there were as many gesture-languages as there were children. The only element common to these languages was probably the pantomime from which they had all sprung. But now what happened? Association, and the necessity of intercommunication, led to their adoption of common signs. Each child presented his gestures to his fellows, and by a process of selection those signs that appeared to the majority to be most fitting survived, and were adopted by the whole, and the synonymous signs which were not so well fitted were either forgotten by disuse or used in a new meaning to express other ideas.

I do not wonder at the interest displayed in this growth by the Abbe de l'Epée and his contemporaries. To my mind, it was the most interesting and instructive spectacle that has ever been presented to the mind of man—the gradual evolution of an organized language from simple pantomime.

When, in 1817, the first school for the deaf and dumb was opened in America the sign-language as used in the school of the Abbe de l'Epée, then under the charge of his successor, the Abbe Sicard, was imported from France, and it became the medium of instruction. The teachers trained in this school naturally became the principals of other institutions established upon its model, and thus the sign-language has been diffused over the length and breadth of our land.

I heartily agree with all that experienced teachers of the deaf have urged concerning the beauty and great interest of this gesture-language. It is indeed most interesting to observe how pantomimic gestures have been abbreviated to simple signs expressive of concrete ideas; how these have been compounded or have changed their meaning to indicate abstract thoughts; and how the sequence of the sign-words has to a certain extent become obligatory, thus forming a sort of gesture syntax or grammar.

The original stock or stocks from which our languages are derived must have disappeared from earth ages before historic times; but in the gesture-speech of the deaf we have a language whose history can be traced *ab origine*, and it has appeared to me that this fact should give it a unique and independent value. In the year 1878, in a paper read before the Anthropological Society of London, I advocated the study of the gesture-language by men of science; for it seemed to me that the study of the mode in which the sign-language has arisen from pantomime might throw a flood of light upon the origin and mode of growth of all languages.

You may ask why it is that with my high appreciation of this language, *as a language*, I should advocate its entire abolition in our institutions for the deaf.

I admit all that has been urged by experienced teachers concerning the ease with which a deaf child acquires this language, and its perfect adaptability for the purpose of developing his mind; but after all it is not the language of the millions of people among whom his lot in life is cast. It is to them a foreign tongue, and the more he becomes habituated to its use, the more he becomes a stranger in his own country.

This is not denied by teachers of the deaf and dumb, but the argument is made, as I have stated above, that it is the only language that is natural to congenitally deaf children, or that, at all events, some form of gesture-language must necessarily be their vernacular, and be employed to teach our English tongue.

THE FALLACY THAT A GESTURE-LANGUAGE IS THE ONLY FORM OF LANGUAGE IN WHICH A CONGENITALLY DEAF CHILD CAN THINK.

Now, what do we mean by a language being "natural" or not? I cannot believe that in this nineteenth century any one really entertains the fallacy that there is a natural language *per se*. So I presume that that language is considered natural to a person in which he thinks. Under this meaning the proposition assumes this shape: The sign-language taught in our institutions, or a gesture-language of some kind, is the only form of language in which a congenitally deaf child can think. That is, it is the only language of which the elements can be associated directly with the ideas they express.

In this form the fallacy is easily exploded, for in the course of the last 100 years so many experiments have been made in the education of the deaf that we now know with absolute certainty that deaf children can be taught to associate written words directly with the ideas they represent; and when they are taught to spell these words by a manual alphabet, the movements of the fingers become so natural a method of giving vent to their thoughts that even in sleep their fingers move when they dream.

Not only has written English been made the vernacular of congenitally deaf children, but the same result has been achieved with written French, German, Spanish, Dutch, and other languages.

Congenitally deaf children who have been taught articulation move their mouths in their sleep and give utterance to words when they dream.

Laura Bridgman, the blind deaf-mute, was taught by the late Dr. Howe to gather ideas through the sense of touch. English words printed in raised letters were presented to her sense of touch in connection with the objects which they represented, and she associated the impressions produced upon the ends of her fingers with the objects themselves. The English language in a tangible form became her vernacular.

All these facts assure us that any form of language may become natural to a deaf child by usage so long as it is presented to the senses he possesses. There is only one way that language is naturally acquired, and that is by usage and imitation. Any form of language that can be clearly appreciated by the senses the deaf child possesses will become his vernacular if it is used by those about him.

WHY THE DEAF EMPLOY A GESTURE-LANGUAGE.

A gesture-language is employed by a deaf child at home, not because it is the only language that is natural to one in his condition, but because his friends neglect to use in his presence any other form of language that can be appreciated by his senses. Speech is addressed to his ear; but his ear is dead, and the motions of the mouth cannot be fully interpreted without previous familiarity with the language. On account, therefore, of the neglect of parents and friends to present to his eye any clearly visible form of language, the deaf child is forced to invent such a means of communication, which his friends then adopt by imitation. I venture to express the opinion that no gesture-language would be developed at home by a deaf child if his parents and friends habitually employed, in his presence, the English language in a clearly visible form. He would come to understand it by usage and use it by imitation.

An old writer, George Dalgarno, in 1680, has expressed the opinion, in which I fully concur, that "there might be successful addresses made to a dumb child, even in its cradle—*risu cognoscere matrem*—if the mother or nurse had but as nimble a hand as usually they have a tongue."

When deaf children enter an institution they find the other pupils and teachers using a form of gesture-language which they do not understand. For the first time in their lives they find a language used by those about them that is addressed to the senses they possess. After a longer or shorter time they discard the language which they had themselves devised, and acquire *by imitation* the sign-language of the institution.

HARMFUL RESULTS OF THE SIGN-LANGUAGE.

After a few months' residence in the institution the children return to their friends in the holidays using easily and fluently a language that is foreign to them, while of the English language they know no more than the average school-boy does of French or German after the same period of instruction. The only language they can employ in talking to their friends is the crude gesture-language of their own invention, which they had long before discarded at school; and they perpetually contrast the difficulty and slowness of comprehension of their friends with the ease with which their school-fellows and teachers could understand what they mean. They have learned by experience how sweet a thing it is to communicate freely with other minds, and they are continually hampered and annoyed by the difficulty they meet with in conversing with their own parents and friends.

Can it be wondered at, therefore, that such a child soon tires of home? He longs for the school play-ground and the deaf companions with whom he can converse so easily. Little by little the ties of blood and relationship are weakened, and *the institution becomes his home.*

Nor are these all the harmful effects that are directly traceable to the habitual use in school of a language that is different from that of the people. Disastrous results are traceable inwards in the operations of his mind, and outwards in his relation to the external world in adult life. He has learned to *think* in the gesture-language, and his most perfected English expressions are only translations of his sign-speech.

As a general rule, when his education is completed, his knowledge of the English language is like the knowledge of French or German possessed by the average hearing child on leaving school. He cannot read an ordinary book intelligently, without frequent recourse to a dictionary. He can understand of what he sees in the newspapers, especially if it concerns what interests him personally, and he can generally manage to make people understand what he wishes by writing, but he writes in broken English as a foreigner would speak.

Let us consider for a moment the condition of a person whose vernacular is different from that of the people by whom he is surrounded. Place one of our American school-boys just graduated from school in the heart of Germany. He finds that his knowledge of German is not sufficient to enable him to communicate freely with the people. He thinks in English, and has to go through a mental process of translation before he can understand what is said or can himself say what he means. Constant communication with the people involves constant effort and a mental strain. Under such circumstances what a pleasure it is for him to meet with a person who can speak the English tongue! What a relief to be able to converse freely once more in his own vernacular! Words arise so spontaneously in the mind that the thought seems to evoke the proper expression.

But mark the result: The more he associates with English-speaking people the less desire does he have to converse in German. The practice of the English language prevents progress in the acquisition of German. I have known of English people who have lived for twenty years in Germany without acquiring the language.

If our American school-boy desires to become familiar with the German language he must resolutely avoid the society of English-speaking people. He then finds that the mental effort involved in conversation becomes less and less until, finally, he learns to think in German and his difficulties cease.

Now, consider the case of a deaf boy just graduated from an institution where the sign-language has been employed as a means of communication. His vernacular is different from that of the people by whom he is surrounded. He thinks in the gesture-language, and has to go through a mental process of translation before he can understand what is said or written to him in English, and before he can himself speak or write in English what he desires to say. He finds himself, in America, in the same condition as that of the American boy in Germany. If he avoids association with those who use the sign-language, and courts the society of hearing persons, the mental effort involved in conversation becomes less and less, and finally he learns to think in English, and his difficulties cease.

But such a course involves great determination and perseverance on the part of the deaf boy, and few, indeed, are those who succeed.

Not only do the other deaf-mutes in his locality have the same vernacular as his own, but they were his school-fellows and they have a common recollection of pleasant years of childhood spent in each other's society. Can it be wondered at, therefore, that the vast majority of the deaf graduates of our institutions keep up acquaintance with one another in adult life? The more they communicate with one another the less desire do they have to associate with hearing persons, and the practice of the gesture-language forms an obstacle to further progress in the acquisition of the English language.

These two causes (*a*) previous exclusive acquaintance with one another in the same school and (*b*) a common knowledge of a form of language specially adapted for the communication of the deaf with the deaf, operate to attract together into the large cities large numbers of deaf persons who form a sort of deaf community or society having very little intercourse with the outside world. They work at trades or business in these towns, and their leisure hours are spent almost exclusively in each other's society. Under such circumstances can we be surprised that the majority of these deaf persons marry deaf persons, and that we should have as a result a small but necessarily increasing number of cases of hereditary deafness due to this cause? Such unions do not generally result in the production of deaf offspring, because the deafness of the parents in a large proportion of cases is of accidental origin, and accidental deafness is no more likely to be inherited than the accidental loss of a limb. Still I would submit that the constant selection of the deaf by the deaf in marriage is fraught with danger to the community.

WHY THE ENGLISH LANGUAGE SHOULD BE SUBSTITUTED FOR THE SIGN-LANGUAGE AS A VERNACULAR.

If we examine the position in adult life of deaf children who have been taught to speak, or who have acquired the English language as a vernacular, whether in its written or spoken forms, we find an entirely different set of tendencies coming into play, especially if these persons have not been forced in childhood to make the acquaintance of large numbers of other deaf children, by social imprisonment for years together in the same school or institution apart from the hearing world.

Their vernacular use of the English language renders it easy for them to communicate with hearing persons by writing, or by word of mouth if they have been taught to articulate; and hearing persons can easily communicate with them by writing, or by word of mouth if they have been taught the use of the eye as a substitute for the ear. The restraints placed upon their intercourse with the world by their lack of hearing leads them to seek the society of books, and thus they tend to rise mentally to an ever higher and higher plane. A cultivated mind delights in the society of educated people, and their knowledge of passing events derived from newspapers forms an additional bond of union between them and the hearing world.

If they have formed in childhood few deaf acquaintances, they meet in real life hundreds of hearing persons for every deaf acquaintance; and, if they marry, the chances are immensely in favor of their marrying hearing persons.

There is nothing in the deaf-mute societies in the large cities to attract them, and much to repel them; for the more highly-educated deaf-mutes in those societies speak what is to them a foreign language, while the greater number of the deaf-mutes to be found there are so ignorant that self-respect forbids them from mingling with them.

Thus, the extent of their knowledge of the English language is the main determining cause of the congregation or separation of the deaf in adult life. A good vernacular knowledge of the English language operates to effect their absorption into society at large, and to weaken the bonds that tend to bring them together; whereas a poor knowledge of the language of the country they live in causes them to be repelled by society and attracted by one another; and these attractive and repulsive tendencies are increased and intensified if they have been taught at school a language foreign to society and specially adapted for intercommunication among themselves. I say, then, let us banish the sign-language from our schools. Let the teachers be careful in their intercourse with their pupils to use English, and English alone. They can write, they can speak by word of mouth, they can spell the English words by a manual alphabet, and by any or all of these methods they can teach English to their pupils as a native tongue.

CONCLUSION.

In conclusion allow me to say—

1. That those whom we term "deaf-mutes" have no other natural defect than that of hearing. They are simply persons who are deaf from childhood, and many of them are only "hard of hearing."

2. Deaf children are dumb, not on account of lack of hearing, but of lack of instruction. No one teaches them to speak.

3. A gesture-language is developed by a deaf child at home, not because it is the only form of language that is natural to one in his condition, but because his parents and friends neglect to use the English language in his presence in a clearly visible form.

4. (*a*) The sign-language of our institutions is an artificial and conventional language derived from pantomime.

(*b*) So far from being natural either to deaf or hearing persons, it is not understood by deaf children on their entrance to an institution. Nor do hearing persons become sufficiently familiar with the language to be thoroughly qualified as teachers until after one or more years' residence in an institution for the deaf and dumb.

(*c*) The practice of the sign-language hinders the acquisition of the English language.

(*d*) It makes deaf-mutes associate together in adult life, and avoid the society of hearing people.

(*e*) It thus causes the intermarriage of deaf-mutes and the propagation of their physical defect.

5. Written words can be associated directly with the ideas they express, without the intervention of signs, and written English can be taught to deaf children by usage so as to become their vernacular.

6. A language can only be made vernacular by constant use as a means of communication, without translation.

7. Deaf children who are familiar with the English language in either its written or spoken forms can be taught to understand the utterances of their friends by watching the mouth.

8. The requisites to the art of speech-reading are:

(*a*) An eye trained to distinguish quickly those movements of the vocal organs that are visible (independently of the meaning of what is uttered);

(*b*) A knowledge of *homophenes**—that is, a knowledge of those words that present the same appearance to the eye; and,

(*c*) Sufficient familiarity with the English language to enable the speech-reader to judge by context which word of a homophenous group is the word intended by the speaker.

If we look back upon the history of the education of the deaf, we see progress hindered at every stage

*This word was suggested to me some years ago by Mr. Homer, late principal of the Providence (R. I.) School for Deaf-Mutes, and has now been permanently adopted.

by fallacies. Let us strive, by discussion and thought, to remove these fallacies from our minds so that we may see the deaf child in the condition that nature has given him to us. If we do this, I think we shall recognize the fact that the afflictions of his life are *mainly due to ourselves*, and we can remove them.

Nature has been kind to the deaf child; man, cruel. Nature has inflicted upon the deaf child but one defect, imperfect hearing; man's neglect has made him dumb and forced him to invent a language, which has separated him from the hearing world.

Let us, then, remove the afflictions that we ourselves have caused.

1. Let us teach deaf children to think in English by using English in their presence in a clearly visible form.

2. Let us teach them to speak by giving them instruction in the use of their vocal organs.

3. Let us teach them the use of the eye as a substitute for the ear in understanding the utterances of their friends.

4. Let us give them instruction in the ordinary branches of education by means of the English language.

5. And last, but not least, let us banish the sign-language from our schools.

If it were our object to fit deaf children to live together in adult life, and hold communication with the outside world as we hold communication with other nationalities than our own, then no better plan could be devised than to assist the development of a special language suitable for intercommunication among the deaf.

But if, on the other hand, it is our object to destroy the barriers that separate them from the outside world and take away the isolation of their lives, then I hold that our energies should be devoted to the acquisition of the language of the people *as a vernacular* in its spoken and written forms. With such an object in view we should bring the deaf together as little as possible, and only for the purpose of instruction. After school-hours we should separate the deaf children from one another to prevent the development of a special language, and scatter them among hearing children and their friends in the outside world.

Dr. E. M. GALLAUDET replied to Professor Bell with some remarks, of which the following is an abstract:

Mr. President: I have listened with great interest to the remarks of Professor Bell this evening, and am ready to agree in many particulars with the views he has so well presented.

I am, however, compelled to differ with him at several points, and as these involve matters of vital importance in the treatment of the deaf I will beg the indulgence of the Society for a short time while I attempt to show to what extent some of Professor Bell's views are erroneous.

In proving the generally received opinion that the vocal organs of persons deaf from infancy are defective to be a fallacy, Professor Bell declares that difficulties encountered by such persons in acquiring speech are wholly external to themselves, and that all persons so situated can, with proper instruction, be taught to speak and to understand the motions of the lips of others.

That this is a grave error has been proved by the experience of more than a century of oral teaching in Germany. The late Moritz Hill, of Weissenfels, Prussia, a man of the widest experience and highest standing among the oral teachers of Europe, expressed to me the opinion a few years since that out of one hundred deaf-mutes, including the semi-mute and semi-deaf, only "eleven could converse readily with strangers on ordinary subjects on leaving school." Of course a much larger number would be able to converse with their teachers, family, and intimate friends on common-place subjects; but it would be found that very many could never attain to any real command of speech.

The explanation of this lies in the fact that a child deaf from infancy, in order to succeed with speech and lip-reading, must possess a certain quickness of vision, a power of perception, and a control over the muscles of the vocal organs by no means common to all such children.

Professor Bell's view has been held by many instructors with more or less tenacity, and *this* fact is explained by a readiness on their part to argue from the particular to the general. Having attained marked success with certain individuals, they draw, in their enthusiasm, the mistaken conclusion that success is possible in the case of every other deaf child, overlooking the fact that many things besides the mere deafness of the child may affect the result.

Experience has demonstrated the fact that in attempting to teach the deaf to speak, failure in many cases must be anticipated.

Professor Bell is mistaken in supposing ignorance as to the mechanism of the vocal organs to be a prominent cause of failure to impart speech to the deaf. It is no doubt true that among persons unfamiliar with the training of the deaf few have made the mechanism of speech a study; but in Germany, Italy, and France, not to speak of our own country, many are to be found who may be said to have mastered this subject. The results of their labors have been made available to instructors of the deaf, and all the best oral schools are profiting thereby.

Professor Bell is mistaken when he says that "in a majority of our schools and institutions articulation and speech-reading are taught to only a favored few, and in these schools no use of articulation is made as a means of communication;" and that "few, if any, attempts are made to teach articulation to those who have not naturally spoken."

In most of the larger institutions for the deaf in this country every pupil is afforded an opportunity to acquire speech, and instruction in this is discontinued only when success seems plainly unattainable.

It is a great error to suppose it to be true of a deaf person, educated on what Professor Bell calls the sign method, that "as a general rule, when his education is completed, his knowledge of the English language is like the knowledge of French or German possessed by the average hearing child on leaving school," or to say that "he cannot read an ordinary book intelligently without frequent recourse to a dictionary."

On the contrary, a majority of persons thus educated have a good knowledge of their vernacular, are able to use it readily as a means of communication with hearing persons, and *are* able to read intelligently without frequent recourse to the dictionary.

When Professor Bell has become familiar with the peculiarities of the deaf, by personal contact with a large number of this class of persons, I am confident he will not repeat his assertion that "nature has inflicted upon the deaf child but one defect—imperfect hearing." For he will then have discovered, what has long been known to teachers of experience, that deaf children, in addition to their principal disability, are often found to be lacking in mental capacity, in the imitative faculty, in the power of visual or tactile perception, and in other respects, all of which deficiencies, though they do not amount even to feeble mindedness, much less to idiocy, do operate against the attainment of success in speech, as well as in other things which go to complete the education of such children.

Passing over several points of relatively small importance, in regard to which I believe Professor Bell's views to be subject to criticism, I come to his characterization as a fallacy of the opinion held by many "that the language of gestures is the only language natural to the child born deaf or who has become deaf in infancy."

I think, that in order to sustain his view that this is a fallacy, Professor Bell gives a strained and very unusual meaning to the words "natural language." If, as he explains, a natural language is any one that a child may happen to be first taught by those with whom he is associated, then I should have no controversy with him. But I understand a natural language to be one that is mainly spontaneous, and not at all one that is borne in upon a child from without.

Moritz Hill, to whom I have already alluded, speaks of the language of signs as "one of the two universally intelligible innate forms of expression granted by God to mankind," the other being speech. Now it is hardly necessary to urge that speech is the form of expression natural to hearing persons, and I think a little reflection will satisfy most persons that with the deaf the language of signs is the only truly natural mode of expressing their thoughts.

Professor Bell urges that the use of signs in the education of the deaf is a hindrance rather than a help, and that it would be better to banish them altogether.

To this view I must give my very earnest dissent.

I might, of course, cite the opinions of very many successful instructors of the deaf who have followed only the sign method to sustain my position, but I prefer to call in again the testimony of Moritz Hill, a man whose whole life was devoted to the instruction of the deaf by the oral method.

In an exhaustive work on the education of the deaf* Hill says, speaking of those who pretend that in the "German method" every species of pantomimic language is proscribed:

Such an idea must be attributed to malevolence or to unpardonable levity. This pretence is contrary to nature and repugnant to the rules of sound educational science.

If this system were put into execution the moral life, the intellectual development of the deaf and dumb, would be inhumanly hampered. It would be acting contrary to nature to forbid the deaf-mute a means of expression employed by even hearing and speaking persons. It is nonsense to dream of depriving him of this means until he is in a position to express himself orally. Even in teaching itself we cannot lay aside the language of gestures (with the exception of that which consists in artificial signs and in the manual alphabet, two elements proscribed by the German school), the language which the deaf-mute brings with him to school, and which ought to serve as a basis for his education. To banish the language of natural signs from the school-room, and limit ourselves to articulation, is like employing a gold key which does not fit the lock of the door we would open, and refusing to use the iron one made for it At the best it would be *drilling* the deaf-mute, but not *moulding* him intellectually or morally.

Hill then follows with thirteen carefully-formulated reasons why the use of signs is important and even indispensable in the education of the deaf

Professor Bell is in error when he supposes that in the so-called sign-schools verbal language is only imparted through the intervention of the sign-language. In many well-ordered schools of this class language is taught without the use of signs, and in such schools the language of signs is kept in its proper position of subordination.

It goes without saying that in schools for the deaf there may be an injudicious and excessive use of signs. This is always to be guarded against, and where it is I am convinced that no harm but great good results from the use of signs in teaching the deaf.

Furthermore, it is well known that the attempt to banish signs from a school for the deaf rarely succeeds. Miss Sarah Porter, for three years an instructor in the Clarke Institution at Northampton, Mass., an oral school in which most excellent results have been attained, shows candor as well as judgment when she says in a recent article in the *American Annals of the Deaf and Dumb,** "Every oral teacher knows that fighting signs is like fighting original sin. Put deaf children together and they will make signs secretly, if not openly, in their intercourse with each other."

It is not true as a matter of fact that the use of signs necessarily prevents the deaf from acquiring an idiomatic use of verbal language and from thinking in such language. Large numbers of them who have never been taught orally have come into such a use of verbal language, and while it is granted that many educated under the sign system do not use verbal language freely and correctly, the same is found to be true of very many who have been educated entirely in oral schools.

In one important particular the language of signs performs a most valuable service for the deaf, and one of which nothing has yet been found to take the place. Through signs large numbers of deaf persons can be addressed, their minds and hearts being moved as those of hearing persons are by public speaking in its various forms.

Having seen the good effects on the deaf of the discreet use of the sign-language, through a period of many years, I am confident that its banishment from all schools for the deaf would work great injury to this class of persons, intellectually, socially, and morally.

The Hon. GARDINER G. HUBBARD, in reply to Dr. Gallaudet's remarks, said he had been connected with the Clarke Institution for many years. The deaf pupils in that school are taught entirely by articulation. From recent inquiries which have been made to ascertain how far the graduates had profited by instruction in articulation, it appeared that in almost every instance they could carry on conversation with others sufficiently to engage in many kinds of business from which they would have been excluded if they had only used signs.

It was true, as Dr. Gallaudet said, the congenitally deaf were frequently able to articulate more distinctly than those who lost their hearing at an early age, and this arises from the fact that the disease that caused the deafness affected the organs of articulation to a greater or less degree; but the congenitally deaf do not make as rapid progress in their studies as those who had once spoken, for these have a knowledge of language which the former could only obtain by long protracted study.

Mr. Hubbard believed that the pupils at the Clarke Institution made at least as rapid progress in all their studies as those taught by signs, while at the same time they acquired the power of reading from the lips and speaking, in which those taught by signs were deficient.

When the first application was made to the legislature of Massachusetts for the incorporation of the Clarke Institution, Mr. Dudley, of Northampton, chairman of the committee to whom the petition was referred, had a congenitally deaf child under instruction at Hartford; the petitioners were opposed by the professors from the asylum, as they believed an articulating school would retard the education of the deaf, as it was impracticable to teach the deaf by articulation (that system having been tried and proved a failure), and the new method was stigmatized as one of the visionary theories of Dr. Howe, (the principal of the Perkins Institute for the Blind and the teacher of Laura Bridgman, the blind deaf-mute) who was associated with the petitioners in the hearing.

The application was rejected, through the influence

* Der gegenwärtige Zustand des Taubstummen-Bildungswesens in Deutschland; von Hill, Inspector der Taubstummen-Anstalt zu Weissenfels, Ritter des St. Olafs, &c. Weimar: H. Böhlau. 1866.

* Vol. xxviii, p. 191.

of these professors and of Mr. Dudley, "who knew from experience with his own child that it was impossible to teach the congenitally deaf to talk."

Two years after the application was renewed and with better success

Mr. Hubbard in the meantime, with the aid of Miss Rogers, had opened a small school where the deaf were taught to speak; this school was visited and examined by the committee, and the progress made was so great that Mr. Dudley became a warm convert, convinced that the impossible was possible, and the application was granted, although again opposed by the gentlemen from Hartford.

The school was opened at Northampton, and has been in operation for nearly fifteen years, and teaching by articulation has ceased to be a visionary theory

Many of the warmest friends of the Institution now are, like Dr. Gallaudet, connected with institutions where signs are used. In almost every institution for the deaf classes are now taught to articulate, though articulation is not used as the instrument for instruction.

Dr. Gallaudet had taken exception to the remark of Mr Bell that idiots were born dumb, and said that in every school for idiots there were many feeble-minded children who could talk readily; but Mr. Bell used the word idiot, not as simply a feeble-minded person, but according to its ordinary meaning, "A human being destitute of reason or the ordinary intellectual powers of man."

Mr. Hubbard was very much surprised and pained to hear Dr. Gallaudet advocating, even to a limited extent, the marriage of deaf-mutes with one another.*

It has always been the policy at Northampton to prevent as far as possible such marriages, for the records show that the children born of such intermarriages are often deaf, and even where a congenitally deaf person marries a hearing person the children sometimes are deaf

The tendency of the intermarriage of the deaf would be to raise a deaf race in our midst.

About one in 1,500 of the population are deaf; but if these intermarriages should take place, and a deaf race be created, the proportion would rapidly increase, and the object of all friends of the deaf should be to prevent the deaf from congregating, and to induce them to associate with hearing people.

In bringing the deaf together in institutions where they are taught by signs, the tendency is to make the deaf deafer and the dumb more dumb.

It was originally intended to have only a family or small school at Northampton, but it was soon found that signs could not be excluded from the playground, as the young children could not communicate in any other way. This plan was changed, the number of pupils was largely increased, and a preparatory department established in which signs were tolerated in the playground. On the removal of the pupils to the higher departments the use of signs is forbidden, and they are rarely used on the playground or between the pupils, either in or out of school hours.

In the latter years of instruction they acquire great facility in articulation and reading from the lips, though there is almost always some difficulty for a stranger to understand them.

Dr. Gallaudet had referred to the International Convention of deaf-mute teachers and their friends at Milan three years ago. Mr. Hubbard was present at the Convention held this year at Brussels, and was there informed that a delegate had been sent from France to attend the Convention at Milan and investigate the method of instruction in Italy, where articulation was used, for the purpose of deciding whether the instruction in the French schools should continue to be by signs or instruction by articulation be substituted for signs. The preference of the delegate had been for signs; but on witnessing the results obtained in the Italian schools, and hearing the discussion, he was led to advise that the instruction in the French schools hereafter be by articulation instead of signs, and such a change has, Mr. Hubbard understands, been made in the most of the schools in France.

Mr. Hubbard learned from the reports at Brussels that almost all the European schools were taught by articulation, and that this means of instruction was being rapidly substituted for the sign-language in England as well as in France.

Professor BELL said:

Mr. President: Allow me to say a few words in reply to Dr. Gallaudet. There are signs *and* signs. There is the same distinction between pantomime and the sign-language that there is between a picture and the Egyptian hieroglyphics.

Pictures are naturally understood by all the world, but it would be illogical to argue from this that a picture-language like that developed by the ancient Egyptians must also be universally intelligible.

Pantomime is understood by all the world, but who among us can understand the sign-language of the deaf and dumb without much instruction and practice?

Pantomime and dramatic action can be used—and with perfect propriety—to illustrate English expressions, so as actually to facilitate the acquisition of our language by the deaf; but the abbreviated and conventionalized pantomime known as the "sign-language" is used *in place* of the English language and becomes itself the vernacular of the deaf child. Judging by the quotations made by Dr. Gallaudet, Moritz Hill himself makes a clear distinction between "pantomime" and the sign-language, retaining the former and proscribing the latter. "Every species of pantomime language," he says, is not proscribed. "Natural signs," or signs such as those "employed by hearing and speaking persons," are retained, while "artificial signs are proscribed."

All the arguments that have been advanced respecting pantomime and pantomime-language are equally applicable to pictures and a picture-language. We may say, for instance, that a picture-language is more natural than any of the spoken languages of the world, because pictures are naturally understood by all mankind. We may even arrive, by a further process of generalization, at the idea that picture-writing in the wider sense constitutes the only form of language that is "natural" at all, for all the other languages appear to be entirely arbitrary and conventional. If we pursue the parallel, we shall arrive at the conclusion that a picture-language of some kind must necessarily be the vernacular of our pupils, by means of which the other more conventional languages may be explained and taught.

It is immaterial whether such statements are fallacies or not, so long as we do not apply them to educational purposes. But let us see how they work in practice. No one will deny that the exhibition of a picture may add interest to the fairy tale or story that we tell a child. It illustrates the language we use, and it may be of invaluable assistance to him in realizing our meaning. But is that any reason why we should teach him Egyptian hieroglyphics? Granting the premises, is the conclusion sound that we should teach him English *by means* of hieroglyphics? If such conclusions are illogical, then the fundamental ideas upon which

* Mr. Hubbard misunderstood Dr. Gallaudet if he thought he *advocated* the marriage of the deaf with the deaf. Dr. Gallaudet in his reply to Professor Bell, while he expressed his disapproval of such marriages, said they were not without some compensating benefits, or words to that effect; but he wrote in the *Annals* (vol. xviii. p. 202) that "intermarriage among deaf-mutes" he was "constrained to deprecate *in toto*," and we understand that he has not changed his views on this subject.—ED. *Annals*.

our whole system of education by signs is based are also fallacious and unsound.

One word in conclusion regarding speech. The main cause of the fallacies that fog our conception of the condition of the deaf child is *his lack of speech*. A deaf person who speaks, however imperfectly, is regarded by the public more as a foreigner than as a deaf-mute. Speech breaks through the barriers of prejudice that separate him from the world, and he is recognized *as one of ourselves*.

Dr. Gallaudet under-estimates the value of speech to a deaf child. He seems to think that speech is of little or no use unless it is as perfect as our own. The fact is that the value of speech to a deaf child must be measured by its *intelligibility* rather than by its perfection.

It is astonishing how imperfect speech may be and yet be intelligible.

We may substitute a mere indefinite murmur of the voice for all our vowel sounds without loss of intelligibility. [Professor Bell spoke a few sentences in this manner and was understood by all present.] Here at once we get rid of the most difficult elements we are called upon to teach. If now we examine the relative frequency of the other elements of speech—the consonantal sounds—we find that 75 per cent. of the consonants we use are formed by the point of the tongue, and that the majority of the remainder are formed by the lips. The consonants that are difficult to teach are chiefly formed by the top or back of the tongue, but on account of their comparative rarity of occurrence they may be very imperfectly articulated without loss of intelligibility. Hence I see no reason why —in spite of our general ignorance of the mechanism of speech—we may not hope to teach all deaf children an intelligible pronunciation. Let teachers appreciate the value of speech to a deaf child, and they will make the attempt to give it to him. At the present time lack of appreciation operates to prevent experiment upon the large scale. Skilled teachers of articulation will become more numerous as the demand for their services increases; and their ingenuity, intelligently applied, will increase the perfection of the artificial speech obtained.

In the meantime do not let us discard speech from the difficulty of obtaining it in perfection. Do not let us be misled by the idea that intelligible but defective speech is of no use, and must necessarily be painful and disagreeable to all who hear it. Those who have seen the tears of joy shed by a mother over the first utterances of her deaf child will tell you a different tale. None but a parent can fully appreciate how sweet and pleasant may be the imperfect articulation of a deaf child.

DEAF CLASSES IN THE PUBLIC SCHOOLS.

[This Exhibit consists of the following report of a discussion between Dr. Alexander Graham Bell and Dr. Philip G. Gillett in Chicago. Published in the *American Annals of the Deaf* for Jan., 1884, Vol. XXIX, pp. 312-325.]

By invitation of the Chicago Board of Education, Dr. ALEXANDER GRAHAM BELL and Dr. PHILIP G. GILLETT addressed that Board and an interested audience of ladies and gentlemen in Chicago on the evening of July 20, 1884, on the subject of the relative advantages of teaching deaf children in classes connected with public schools as compared with special institutions.

The Rev. FRED. H. WINES, Secretary of the Illinois State Board of Charities, in introducing Dr. Bell, said that the census showed 1,083 deaf persons of school age in Illinois, and that according to Dr. Gillett's last Report there were more deaf persons under twenty-one years of age in the State who have never reached the Institution at Jacksonville than there were on the rolls of that Institution as pupils. Under these circumstances, the duty of the State government to its deaf and dumb was a very serious question. If the deaf were not to be left to grow up in ignorance, one of three things must be done: either the Institution at Jacksonville must be enlarged, a new institution must be created, or provision must be made for their education outside of any institution. The Institution at Jacksonville was already the largest in the world, and, in the opinion of the State Commissioners of Public Charities, too large. They would oppose any further enlargement of it. There existed in the State a very wide and deep-seated feeling of opposition to the creation of any new institution. The situation was therefore full of difficulty.

Professor Bell was an advocate of the instruction of deaf children, in connection with those who can speak and hear, in the public schools; not in the same rooms, except for certain portions of their school-training, but in the same buildings. Professor Bell also advocated the imparting of instruction by the oral method, which, it is conceded, is applicable to a certain number of cases; whether, as he thinks, it is applicable to all deaf children was another question. The State Commissioners of Public Charities, without design to take any position upon these disputed points, and without committing themselves to the advocacy of any position or opinion held by Professor Bell, were anxious that he should have a hearing, since they desired to learn the truth, and to awaken public interest in the subject by means of public discussion. The eminence, ability, and attainments of Professor Bell entitled his views to candid and serious consideration. The city of Chicago and the county of Cook, with one-fifth of the entire population of the State, have a special interest in the question of adequate provision for the education of the deaf, and he thanked the city Board of Education, in the name and on behalf of the State Board, for its courteous response to their request to extend to Professor Bell the invitation by virtue of which he was present with them that evening.

Dr. Bell said * that the State of Illinois had shown great earnestness and sincerity in the education of her people. Colleges, seminaries, and schools of various kinds are to be found everywhere in the State, and she evidently appreciates the fact that the safety of her government and of the government of all the States depends upon their educational institutions. With regard to the education of the deaf and dumb, the State of Illinois can boast of the largest institution of the kind in the world; it is also one of the most efficient and most economically administered; but there are more than 500 deaf and dumb children in the State of Illinois under twenty years of age not attending school: in fact, as Dr. Gillett shows in his last official report, not more than half the deaf children have entered the Institution.

Should they enlarge the largest Institution in the world to accommodate these children, or should they provide new facilities for the education of these neglected deaf-mutes? The problem which they had to solve was one in which the whole country would be interested, for the recent census shows that there are in the United States about as many deaf children of school-age growing up without education as there are in all our institutions and schools put together.

Of the deaf children in our institutions few were admitted before they were ten or twelve years old, a considerable number did not commence their education until they were seventeen or eighteen years of age, and a few made their appearance at twenty-five years of age, or even older. In such cases it often turns out that the natural affection of the parents has made them reluctant to part with their child. They have retained him at home in unconsciousness of the lapse of years, until the signs of approaching manhood become so evident as to outweigh every other consideration, and they send him to school.

It is a hard thing for a mother to part with her child. The very affliction of her little one binds him closer to her. The right of the parent to the possession of the child is one of those natural, inalienable rights that all men are bound to respect. It is true that the rights of the community must take place over those of individuals. An uneducated deaf-mute may become a dangerous member of society, and society has therefore the right to demand, as a matter of self-protection, that deaf children shall be educated; but society has no right to demand the compulsory separation of a deaf child from its parents unless it can be clearly shown that the education of the child necessitates removal from home. It is, therefore, the duty of the State to establish day-schools for the deaf wherever possible. If this were done, the present institutions would be sufficient to accommodate all who could not attend day-schools.

Mr. BELL therefore recommended that we should supplement our present schools and institutions by an extensive development of day-schools, and he suggested as the most practical, most useful, and most economical kind of school to be established the formation of classes for deaf children in the public schools. He suggested that they set apart a small room in a public school building for the use of the deaf children of the neighborhood, and that a teacher should be employed who has been carefully trained in the methods of instructing the deaf. It would be economical to utilize a room of this kind for this purpose, as the appliances of a large school might thus be obtained without special cost. He did not advocate the complete co-education of deaf with hearing children. This had been tried before, and had usually been a failure. Nor did he advocate the present plan of exclusive segregation of the deaf, for it makes them a class apart from the hearing world. He suggested the adoption of an intermediate plan. He would educate the deaf by themselves, in as small numbers as possible, in the same building with hearing children in large numbers. He would promote inter-

* For this abstract of Dr. Bell's address we are indebted to his private secretary, Mr. FRANCIS Z. MAGUIRE, of Washington.—E. A. F.

course between the deaf and hearing children by throwing them together during play hours, and by placing the deaf children in the same classes with the hearing children for practice in subjects where information is gained through the eye. He would never bring together more children than one teacher could conveniently handle. He thought that about ten deaf children should constitute the extreme limit. In cities like Chicago, where more than a hundred deaf children could attend day-schools, and a number of teachers would be required, he advocated giving each teacher a small school-room in a different public-school building, rather than bring all the deaf children into one school. In this case a superintendent of deaf-mute instruction should be appointed to superintend the work.

The expense for instruction could easily be kept within $10,000 per annum, which, for a hundred pupils, would give a *per capita* cost of $100 per annum instead of $223.28, which is the average *per capita* cost of the education of a deaf child in an American institution.* The above figures are based upon the supposition that for a hundred pupils we employ ten teachers at $800 per annum and a superintendent at a salary of $2,000. Not only would the cost be less, but the advantage greater, for it is well known that under similar circumstances the pupils of small classes make greater progress than those of large classes, because the teacher can give more individual attention to the pupils. The cost at an institution includes board and industrial training. Upon the day-school plan the parents would generally assume the expenses of maintenance, and some special provision would have to be made for industrial training. This need give no concern, for so many deaf-mutes who were *not* taught in institutions are to-day earning their livelihood by trades as to demonstrate the practicability of apprenticing deaf-mutes in ordinary shops. In country places, where four deaf children could be collected together, it would cost no more to form them into a class than to send them to an institution where the State must assume the cost of board as well as education. The expenses of such a class under a properly qualified teacher could easily be kept within $800 per annum, which would give a *per capita* cost of $200 instead of $223.28. The great difficulty in carrying out such a plan is the difficulty of obtaining teachers. There is no school in America where teachers of the deaf are trained. Mr. BELL suggested that provision should be made for the education of teachers of the deaf in our normal schools, and that a certain amount of practical experience in teaching in approved institutions or day-schools be required before granting diplomas of competency to teach the deaf. The boards of education should demand such proof of competency in all teachers employed by them.

At the present time parents who are not in wealthy circumstances are usually forced to send their children away from home to be educated because the State only recognizes certain institutions. If teachers who obtain proper certificates of competency were entitled, under suitable restrictions, to receive the usual *per capita* amount appropriated by the State for the education of her deaf children, parents in very moderate circumstances, and in country localities where a school or class for the deaf could not be established, would in many cases be able to afford the expense of a private teacher if they were assisted by the State appropriation. Mr. BELL would urge upon the States the propriety of encouraging education at home, whereas the present policy practically compels the separation of the deaf child from its parents and hearing friends.

In regard to the methods of instruction that should be adopted, Mr. BELL thought it would be advantageous to allow considerable latitude. There were certain points, however, which he considered important. In most of our institutions the language through which instruction is given is a special language, which has been devised for communication between deaf-mutes, and does not facilitate communication with hearing persons. The deaf mutes think in this language, and have to translate their thoughts into English as into a foreign tongue. They remain foreigners in their own country, and associate almost exclusively with persons who can use the gesture-language. This common language is an important element in bringing them together in adult life and promoting intermarriage. While there was considerable difference of opinion among the most prominent teachers of the deaf as to the proportion of the deaf and dumb who could be taught to speak, it had been amply demonstrated that deaf children could be taught to read and to express their thoughts in writing without a knowledge of the gesture-language that separates the American deaf-mute from the community in which he lives. He would therefore urge that whatever method of education might be adopted, the English language should be substituted for the sign-language as the instrument of thought.

Then, again, there was no difference of opinion as to the desirability of teaching speech and speech-reading to as many of the deaf and dumb as possible. He would urge that articulation and speech-reading be taught to all the pupils, as this was the only way possible to ascertain how many could be taught. Home life and association with hearing children would act as a stimulus to the acquisition of speech, which stimulus was entirely wanting in an institution where all the playmates and associates were deaf, and where nearly one-third of the teachers themselves could not hear. Personally, he believed that all deaf-mutes could acquire an intelligible articulation, and this conclusion was borne out by the fact that all the deaf-mutes of Germany were taught to speak.

In giving speech to the deaf this country was really in arrears of other countries. Taking into consideration all the institutions of the world, 239 were oral schools, 32 were manual, and in 91 the combined system was used. Of 7,155 deaf-mutes in American institutions in 1882, only 584, or less than 9 per cent., were using speech in the school-room as a means of communication; whereas out of 19,318 deaf-mutes in foreign schools, 12,662, or more than 65 per cent., were taught to speak and understand the speech of others in purely oral schools.*

According to more recent statistics, collected by the Clarke Institution,† there were 1,991 deaf children in American institutions in May, 1883, who were receiving instruction in articulation. Of these, 1,105 were taught speech merely as an accomplishment, and 886 were using speech in the school-room as a means of communication. It should be added that in these same institutions there were at that time no less than 4,241 deaf-mutes who received no instruction in articulation. It will thus be seen that the vast majority of the deaf-mutes in foreign countries are taught to speak and understand the speech of others, whereas in our country no attempts are made to teach speech to the majority of our deaf-mutes.

DR. GILLETT said‡ that he and Professor Bell were both laboring for one end, the best possible results in deaf-mute education, though by somewhat different methods. For more than thirty years he had

* See the Report of the Illinois Institution for 1882.

* See the *Annals*, January, 1883, vol. xxviii, pp. 47 61.

† See Appendix to Sixteenth Report Clarke Institution, "Tabular Statement Concerning the Teaching of Articulation in the United States."

‡ Dr. Gillett's Address, of which an abstract is here given, is published in full in the *Deaf-Mute Advance* of August 2, 1884.—E. A. F.

never turned aside to engage in other enterprises, and he did not defer to Professor Bell or any other person in an earnest desire and purpose to accomplish the greatest possible good to the greatest possible number of the deaf. He had never in any way discouraged any project or proposal that claimed to tend to their betterment, though it to his mind was clearly impracticable. He had never advised a parent not to exhaust all medical and scientific means to cure the deafness of a child, though he had been acquainted with more than two thousand such endeavors without knowing of one successful case of treatment. In efforts to teach articulation and lip-reading he had, under the direction of the trustees of the Illinois Institution, within the last sixteen years expended over twenty-five thousand dollars and the energies and life of one of the best teachers that ever stood before a class of deaf children. The Institution endeavors to afford the best possible advantages to its pupils, embracing within its organization departments for literary instruction, oral and aural teaching, art and manual training.

Professor Bell had been careful to put his position hypothetically, and to state what he would have rather then what is known as attainable in the light of experience. He (Dr. Gillett) was willing to surrender any method, or preferences, or opinions that he now had whenever a better method was found, by the test of practical experience, to secure better results. As a practical man, entrusted with the expenditure of large sums of public money, however much he might desire, as a matter of sentiment, to try new things, he could not discard that which for a hundred years had been found useful and efficient without a positive knowledge that we have something better as a substitute. His hearers would not do so in their private business, and they would not have him do so in a public enterprise.

Dr. GILLETT said that Dr. Bell's project was not a new one. It might be new to some persons present, but, if so, it was because it was so old, and had been so long discarded that it had been forgotten, and our grandparents had not thought it worthy of handing down to us. It was assiduously tried during the last century in various parts of Germany with characteristic German zeal and patience, in the light of economy, of home attachments, of social associations, and of all the phases which Professor Bell had set forth. In every case it was found a failure, and abandoned. But he (the speaker) did not wish to be understood as opposed to trying it in America. Possibly it might succeed here. Republican government was tried in Europe and declared a failure, but succeeded in this great land. But let us be careful in trying experiments not to lose anything we already have, for, while it may be interesting and amusing to us, whatever loss, if any, may attend it will fall on unfortunate deaf children. Let it be remembered, also, that the hearing children of the common schools must be an important factor in this question. It might be that, as Chicago was a phenomenal city in so many respects, the children of Chicago schools have a little less depravity and a good deal more of a self-sacrificing spirit than common mortals, and would gladly forego the pleasure of sports with one another to give a few deaf-mutes practice in articulation and lip-reading on the play-ground, but he doubted it. The youth of our common schools, full of animal spirits and vivacity, would not, in fact, so far sacrifice their own enjoyments as to modify their games to suit them to a few deaf-mutes, and it would be unjust to require it of them.

As to the desirability of teaching deaf and dumb children to use speech he agreed with Dr. Bell. But, as to its practicability for *all* deaf children, he asserted that, while there are some who can be taught to use speech with satisfaction to themselves and pleasure to their friends, there are many who cannot. Science has not yet furnished us with a method of instruction that brings this boon within the attainment of *all* deaf children. He was looking with much hopefulness to Mr. Bell to furnish us this method, but we have not yet received it. Mr. Greenberger, Principal of the Institution for the Improved Instruction of Deaf-Mutes in New York, the acknowledged leader of oral teachers of the deaf in America, said recently, in substance, that we must have an American system of teaching articulation; that the German system will not do for America, however well it may answer in Germany, and that no system of teaching articulation we now have meets the conditions in America.* Dr. GILLETT said that his own observation agreed with what Mr. Greenberger had stated. Though the deaf—many of them—have learned to use speech so as to be intelligible to their teachers and frequent associates, yet, after leaving the institution, they disuse their acquired speech, and, in nearly all cases, when they desire precision, distrust their speech and lip-reading, and resort to writing. What particular conditions Mr. Greenberger referred to he was unable to say, but he conjectured that one of them was the superior results attained in those American institutions where the combined method obtains; where the instruction imparted is suited to the respective conditions of the various pupils.

Dr. GILLETT referred to several oral schools in America where the results had been more or less unsatisfactory in certain respects, which he specified. Some of these failures had been explained by saying that the teachers were incompetent, but, in the speaker's opinion, not the teachers but the system was at fault. An important number of deaf children may acquire a practical use of speech, helpful to themselves and satisfactory to their friends, but the best cases of such had not come from the articulation schools any more frequently than from the schools where an eclectic system prevails, teaching articulation to such as are capable of profiting by it, and calling other helps to the aid of the teacher in school-room work where required. The discussion concerning articulation and signs was not a new one. It had continued for more than a hundred years, and had not always been carried on in as friendly a spirit as that evening. It had been said that this was a question of the survival of the fittest. If so, both would survive, as one is the fittest for some cases, and the other is the fittest for others. That they have each existed for more than a hundred years proves that both have merit. Let us accord a proper meed of justice to each, and practise each where it can do the most good; then shall we achieve the best results for the deaf and dumb.

Professor Bell had given some interesting statistics relative to the effect of the intermarriage of deaf persons, and the principles he had deduced deserved serious consideration, not so much as indicating a real danger to society as showing the law of heredity. If there is a serious danger in this, we have no remedy. So long as love laughs at locksmiths, he will smile at all the admonitions anxious friends of the unborn may give him. This, however, was not a question for such a meeting as this so much as for an anthropological society, and he would not discuss it here.

Professor Bell's remarks upon trades for the deaf did not harmonize well with his views upon large institutions. He objected to the trades now taught because so limited in range, and yet insisted that the schools should be so small that no trades at all can be taught in them. And, again, that those taught are a failure, because some deaf-mutes, after learning one trade, have subsequently followed another. Some such cases there were, but their percentage was no larger than in society at large. Did not others often do this same thing? How many of the

*See the October (1881) number of the *Annals*, page 241.

members of the Board of Education of Chicago had at some time been engaged in a pursuit different from the one they were now following? Did not their previous experience the better equip them for their present pursuits? If any deaf-mutes after learning one trade at an institution were now pursuing others, the fact showed that their industrial education, their industrious habits, and their use of tools was well looked after while at the institution. Could Professor Bell refer to any cases of deaf-mutes who had done as well after receiving their education outside of an institution? The industrial education of deaf-mutes was by no means to be despised. It was one of the important elements of the institutions where the combined system obtains. The articulation schools in America had neglected this very important matter. The foremost of American workers in that method lately stated, in advocating the superiority of the articulation method, that comparing the pupils of an articulation school with those of a sign school was like comparing a Fifth Avenue congregation to the convicts of a penitentiary! What must be the spirit and extremity of a system that resorts to such an argument as that? Why select the inmates of a penitentiary rather than the students of a technical institute? In each case trades are pursued, and not only so, but the same trades. Those large institutions using the combined method are true technical schools, and for half a century have been practising the principles of teaching that are just now being adopted in the schools for hearing youth, both in elementary branches and technics. The audience present was about equally divided between hearing people and deaf-mutes, and Dr. GILLETT asked the Chairman to look into the faces of the ladies and gentlemen on the right, who were deaf, and then into the faces of the Board of Education and the ladies and gentlemen on the left, and say whether either company looked any more like the inmates of a penitentiary than the other. He himself would not state any opinion on the subject, for he probably could not give an impartial opinion, as most of the former had been his pupils, to whom he was attached as to his own children. Some of the sweetest experiences of his life has been the successes of some of his pupils in the use of speech. Their voices, that to strangers seemed unpleasant, to him were full of music, like the prattle of his own children in their early endeavors to talk.

Professor Bell had truly said that congenitally deaf children are dumb, not from the want of vocal organs, but from ignorance, having never been taught. He did not state, however, what is true, that the auditory apparatus is as necessary for perfect speech as the vocal apparatus. He says we learn speech by imitation. True; but we imitate sound, and there is no consciousness of sound where there is no hearing. The auditory apparatus is the organ that governs speech in nine hundred and ninety-nine cases in every thousand, though the vocal apparatus is the organ which executes the speech. The one reports to the mind the speech of another, or of one's self; the other performs the direction of the mind in producing speech. Both are alike involved in perfect normal speech, and the visual apparatus has nothing at all to do with it, as is shown in the case of persons born blind, who not only speak well, but become superior orators and musicians. The sight is the sense through which we are brought into relation with physical nature, and its functions lie wholly within the domain of the material. Hearing is the sense through which mind comes in contact with mind, and its functions are in the domain of the intellectual and æsthetic, and are consequently of a higher order than those of sight. We can readily conceive of a higher power performing the functions of a lower, but how can we expect the lower well to perform the functions of a higher power? Yet this is the very task we require of a deaf-mute when we ask him to perform with his eye the duty which is performed by the ear in ourselves. True, the eye has to do with the intellectual and æsthetic through letters and art, but never until the mind has been so cultivated through instruction by way of the ear as to have an appreciation of literature and art.

Professor Bell had said he would have all the deaf think in the English language, though he was careful not to say it could be done, but he would have it so. So would the speaker if it could be done. He would abandon everything he had, except his wife and children, for a system of instruction that would make the English language the vernacular of all deaf-mutes. He did not care especially about their thinking in English if they could only be made to speak in English. We do not any of us think in English. We formulate our thoughts in English. There is no natural language of thought. If there were, all mankind would use that language. One formulates his thoughts in the language he understands best. Persons have been known whose thought at one time was formulated in one language, but subsequently, by reason of the use of another language, it was formulated in the latter. It is just so with the deaf-mute. When he has acquired an adequate knowledge of English he will formulate his thought in the idiom of English, and no sooner, no matter by what system he has been taught. If any one doubted this, let him examine the compositions of pupils instructed without the aid of signs, quoted by Mr. Williams in a paper read before the recent Conference of Principals.* Even hearing persons, who had a good knowledge of English were often conscious of thought which they found language to express with great difficulty. They had the thought none the less because the language to express it in did not come to them.

Dr. GILLETT confirmed the statement, already made by Mr. Wines and Dr. Bell, that there were over five hundred deaf-mutes of a school age in Illinois who had never reached the Institution. What should be done for these was an important question. For four years past the speaker, in his reports to the State Government, had recommended the establishment of another institution, and he expected to make the same recommendation in the report shortly to be prepared. If, however, Professor Bell's suggestion to try the efficacy of classes in the common schools should meet with favor, he would most gladly co-operate to that end, though he was bound to confess that it did not commend itself to his judgment as feasible. He valued so highly the influences of home that he would gladly see all deaf-mutes educated at their homes. It was not to be forgotten, however, that not all homes are what they should be, and that often the education of the street paralyzes the good influences of the home. He had often urged parents to take up a residence near the Institution that they might retain the care and oversight of their children. In most cases when they had done so, after a little while, they insisted on their children remaining most of the time at the Institution. He had had some amusing experiences in this direction.

In conclusion, Dr. GILLETT said that he had appeared to-night not at his own desire. It had been arranged by those who called the meeting that he should sustain this side of the question in the debate, though it was the first time he had done so in sixteen years. He had been used to defend the other side. He had the honor of being the first superintendent of any of the old and long-established institutions in America to organize a zealous effort to confer speech upon the deaf. He had constantly maintained that all that is possible in this direction should be done. He intended to do so, as far as the

*See the October (1881) number of the *Annals*, pp. 294–296.

means entrusted to him would allow, and to try every proposal that gave any hope of better results; not to trifle with it, but to nurse it, and give it every opportunity possible, without sacrificing what was already possessed. He was ready to build up, but not to tear down at one fell swoop, as Professor Bell proposed, a fair structure which, though not perfect, is the best we have, and which for a hundred years has numbered among its adherents some of the noblest philanthropists that have graced the annals of mankind—De l'Épée and Sicard in France; Elliot and others in England; Gallaudet and Clerc and Weld and Stone and Turner and Peet and Hutton and Foster in America—and had lifted out of the densest ignorance thousands of deaf-mutes to the dignity of honest, honorable, and respectable citizens, many of them heads of families, where all the reciprocal duties of husband and wife, parent and child, were as well recognized and as faithfully performed as among those of their brothers and sisters more highly favored, on whom the loss of the most important sense God has bestowed upon man had not fallen.

Mr. LESTER GOODMAN, a graduate of the Illinois Institution and of the National College, then addressed the audience, speaking orally. He said that Dr. Bell seemed to have lost sight of the general in the particular. He had stated, as a conclusive and powerful argument against institutions, that a semimute lost his speech while attending one, totally ignoring the fact that hundreds, like the speaker, had had their speech perfected in the institution. The fundamental principle must be the greatest good for the greatest number.

A prime objection to having deaf-mutes taught in public schools was that no provision is there made for teaching trades. The idea was impracticable and injurious. Impracticable, because it would shut out the children of parents of limited means; because the majority of deaf children were widely separated, and hundreds of them live in isolated places. Injurious, because the home influence in a great many cases is bad. The institution, by taking deaf-mutes from some parents who have the worst kind of poverty—mental destitution—and from others who are vicious and shiftless, placed them at once on a higher level of thought, feeling and action.

Mr. GOODMAN said that in the Chicago post-office there were three former pupils of the Illinois Institution who fill responsible positions, their salaries aggregating $2,440 a year. They were married. They fulfilled their social and political duties. They were warmly in favor of institutions, and regarded with coldness any scheme calculated to cripple them. They thought that, in general, institutions should be managed on the cottage system; that the number of pupils to a teacher should be decreased; that greater endeavors should be made to secure the best talent for the work of instruction, recognizing in the meantime and warmly appreciating the great efforts made by superintendents who are eager and anxious to advance, but are hampered by lack of means.

Dr. BELL spoke again, and several other persons, both deaf and hearing, continued the discussion with much animation, until finally the chairman was obliged, by the lateness of the hour, to bring the meeting to a close.

E. A. F.

NOTIONS OF THE DEAF AND DUMB BEFORE INSTRUCTION.

[This Exhibit consisted of the following article by the late Dr. Harvey P. Peet, entitled "Notions of the Deaf and Dumb before Instruction, especially in regard to Religious Subjects," published in the *Bibliotheca Sacra* for July, 1855, reprinted in the *American Annals for the Deaf* for October, 1855, Vol. VIII, pp. 1–41.]

There are, we suppose, few reading men who have not met with that curious anecdote, transmitted to us by Herodotus,* of the plan devised by an ancient king of Egypt (Psammetichus) to ascertain what was the original language of mankind, by causing two infants to be nurtured in such strict seclusion that, no words being uttered in their hearing, they could not learn a language in the usual mode, by imitation, and, it was taken for granted, must return to the original speech of man. The sagacious monarch seems to have contented himself with obtaining a single word of the primitive language. The word *bec* (or *becco*), which, after some time, the children uttered when their attendant came in (some moderns have plausibly argued that they expressed hunger by calling for their foster-mother, a she-goat, by imitating the bleating of which, a sound like *bec* may have been produced), this word *bec* being on inquiry found to be good Phrygian for *bread*, the Egyptians thenceforward, waiving their own previous claim to be the most ancient race of men, admitted the Phrygians to be the oldest of nations; and their language the primitive speech of man.

We can never read this story without believing that it was part of the royal philosopher's design to ascertain also what was the original *religion* of mankind, though on account of the failure of any satisfactory result on that point, this part of the experiment was hushed up.

It seems to be some such feeling as that of the old Egyptian king, that children, cut off from intellectual commerce with mankind, must have an instinctive language, and innate ideas of religion, that is at the bottom of the curiosity so generally felt, and the more strongly among the most intellectual and reflecting, to know what ideas the deaf and dumb have before instruction, and in what mode they express their ideas; for in the case of each child who comes into the world without the sense of hearing, and is brought up among persons unaccustomed to communicate by gestures, the experiment of Psammetichus, as every intelligent reader will perceive, both in regard to language and religion, is tried over again. It is to be hoped the greater light we now possess will enable us to draw more careful and rational conclusions than he arrived at.

Many, perhaps most, of the popular notions respecting the intellectual and moral condition of the uneducated deaf and dumb, are as wide of the truth as would be our conjectures respecting the religion, language and institutions of the inhabitants of another planet. On the former subject, however, the erroneous notions that prevail have their foundation, not in the impossibility of acquiring correct information, but in the want of observation and reflection. It is natural to suppose that men and women of our own race, brought up among us, and externally not different from ourselves, must have not merely the *elements* of thoughts, feelings, and faculties like our own, but these thoughts, feelings, and faculties *developed* in the same manner that ours are. And the imitative character of the deaf and dumb tends to confirm this impression. When we see them act precisely like those around them, it is difficult to realize that they do not act from the same motives; or that their thoughts are not of a tissue similar to our own.

For instance, there are many who, if they should be introduced to a deaf-mute said to be suddenly and recently restored to hearing, would consider it a matter of course that he should be able at once to speak, and to understand what is spoken to him. Yet a very little reflection would teach them that, as the power of speech is an acquisition of slow growth, requiring the diligent use both of the faculty of hearing and of the organs of speech for years; the child or man who, having been deaf from birth or early infancy, should have his hearing restored, would, in respect to speech, be, at best, in the condition of the infant who has not yet begun to speak; and might as reasonably be expected to understand Greek or Hebrew as his own mother's tongue. Such unreflecting people have not yet attained even the degree of intelligence that prompted the experiment of old Psammetichus, much less the sagacity with which good Duke Humphrey detected the impostor who, professing to have been born blind, and to have been, just before, miraculously restored to sight, yet named correctly colors he was supposed never to have previously seen.* To parody the duke's dictum:

> Hearing restored may distinguish words; but suddenly
> To understand them is impossible.

Others, moved by the destitution of the ordinary means of religious instruction to which untaught deaf-mutes are condemned, less irrationally, but, so far as all the facts now known prove, quite as erroneously, suppose that, in the case of some of these unfortunate beings, who, from the mere faculty of imitation, attend public and private worship with apparent enjoyment and devotion, God has made a special revelation of himself which only the want of language prevented the deaf-mute from making known. Yet why should we look for special revelations to deaf-mutes, when they are withheld from so many millions of heathens?

As there are thousands of deaf-mute children yet uneducated in our own country (to say nothing of other Christian countries), besides, alas! hundreds who have been suffered to outlive the hope of education, there are doubtless thousands to whom, as parents, or relatives, or neighbors of uneducated deaf-mutes, or as pastors having such deaf-mutes in one or more families of their charge, the moral and religious state of these unfortunate beings is a subject of deep and painful interest. Neither is their mere intellectual condition without great interest to every inquirer into the structure of the human mind. The phenomena presented by the mind in such circumstances of difficulty, and in great measure of isolation from the influence of other minds, furnish an *experimentum crucis* to test the merits of any given theory on certain important points in mental and moral philosophy. Philanthropy, religion, and science are thus all interested on the subject we propose to discuss.

To begin with language; it is hardly necessary to say that the phenomena presented by the deaf from birth, or early infancy, without a recorded exception, seem at the first view fatal to the theory that there is any spoken language instinctive in man's mouth.

*Of this anecdote we have met several different versions. The one here followed, being apparently a literal translation of the original, the reader will find in Blackwood's Magazine for April, 1845, p. 474. The Article to which it forms the text, is a very curious one, on the absurd attempts of certain Dutch and Irish antiquaries to deduce the ancient universality of their respective languages from the accidental coincidence of one or two words, and forced and far-fetched analogies of others. This word *beck*, happens to signify *bread* in Dutch, and *becker*, as with us, a *baker*. From this slight foundation one Goropius, in the sixteenth century, brought out huge folios to prove that the language of Phrygia was Dutch, and hence that the latter was the primitive speech of man.

*Shakspeare's King Henry VI., Part II., Act II.

Those unfortunate children spontaneously utter rude cries indicative of their emotions; but never articulate words; or, at least, never sounds that can be recognized as belonging to any known language of men; and this not from any defect or peculiarity in their organs of speech, for, with great and long continued labor, they may be taught to articulate after a fashion; but because the acquisition of vocal speech, easily and rapidly made in flexible childhood, through the ear, becomes very difficult when that organ ceases to guide the voice. The deaf-mute carries out the experiment of Psammetichus to a result of which the sage monarch probably never dreamed. Finding himself unable to learn the language of those around him, he sets himself to work, at first from instinct, and then from design, to make a language of his own, in his circumstances necessarily a language addressed to the eye, a language of motion and expression, that is, of gestures. This language he endeavors to teach to those around him; and greatly is the shadow resting on his earlier years lightened, if he can find companions ready in perception, gifted in mimicry, and kind in heart, who will learn his language, aid him to develop and improve it, and put it to such use as shall afford him some share of social enjoyment: implying, of course, a certain degree of moral and intellectual development.

It may not be aside from our purpose to venture a few remarks on the much-vexed question of the origin of language; for there can be no religion where there is no language; and the condition of the uneducated deaf and dumb presents phenomena that may aid in elucidating the origin of the one as well as of the other.

That, as man had a beginning on the earth, so language also had a beginning, is the starting point of the inquiry. In the present stage of psychological science, we may assume as a fact proved by all experience, that there can be no considerable intellectual development without a language, whether of words or of gestures. And the converse holds equally good that there can be no language, worthy to be called such, where there is not a certain degree of intellectual development.

There are two rival hypotheses that have long exercised the dialectical skill of philosophers and theologians. The one party hold that the Creator made Adam a perfectly developed man, implying of course the possession of a language in copiousness, definiteness, expressiveness and harmony, adequate to his wants and capable of ministering to his enjoyments. The other party hold that the first man came into the world in a state of literal *infancy;* of course without a language; and that speech, like the arts and sciences, has been gradually invented and improved from feeble, if not accidental, beginnings. Between these two extremes there are, of course, various shades of opinion, but, in our view, logical consistency requires the choice of one or the other of the two theories we have stated.

To the unreflecting, speech seems as natural to man as his erect form. The first steps of philosophical research, however, show that men do not speak instinctively, but acquire language through the ear. A child born without hearing remains dumb: and a child even, losing hearing at an early age, becomes nearly or quite dumb. Nor is this owing merely, as was once supposed, to the sympathy between the nerves of the organs of hearing and of speech,* for there have been several instances of children born with all their faculties, who, having been lost or abandoned in deserts, are afterward found to have grown up possessed, perhaps, of acute hearing, but without anything like human speech.* Add that the total diversity that not only now exists, but has existed from time immemorial, between the languages spoken by neighboring races, as the Hindûs and Chinese, is hardly explicable on the theory of a common origin of languages; and a very fair case seems made out for the hypothesis of the gradual invention of speech. The arguments on the other side rest on deeper research and nicer observation.

There are writers who, admitting that all men learned language from their elders, meet the arguments just stated by denying that ignorant savages, as men must have been without language, could possibly invent speech. Says Rousseau: "Speech could only have been instituted by a series of conventions: but how shall those conventions be established, unless the parties are already in possession of a language through which to communicate and mutually understand each other?" The solution of the difficulty, in the view of this class of writers, is found in referring the origin of each primitive language to a direct interposition of Divine power. Adam, they hold, learned a language ready formed, as his descendants do; except that in his case, the teachers were superhuman beings. And, if any languages exist wholly and radically distinct from the first language, a similar solution can no doubt be found for the difficulty. A literal interpretation of the Mosaic narrative concerning the confusion at Babel, is one of the most obvious.

It is singular, say other writers, that these reasoners, who hold that speech must have been divinely communicated to man, because the previous possession of a language is necessary to the invention of a language, should not perceive that their argument is confuted by the very fact of their own possession of speech. Every child who learns language from his mother's lips, establishes with her the supposed series of conventions, just as much as if two children should invent a language between them. The natural language of gestures is usually brought forward to solve this difficulty, for the gestures, actions and looks of those who speak, present an obvious and important aid both to a foreigner learning our language orally, and to a child learning his mother's tongue.†

But those who make the language of gestures the principal original interpreter of speech, overlook the case of children born blind, who learn speech as readily as those who see, though their ideas of the meaning of many words must at first necessarily be less clear and definite. To this we shall again recur. We have here only to remark that the theory of the original Divine communication of speech is neither philosophically necessary, nor even consonant with Scripture. The Scripture narrative represents Adam as giving names to all animals, not as learning them from any teacher whatever.

Setting aside the last-named theory, we have to choose between the two first mentioned, each of which has the authority of eminent names; of men of intense reflection and laborious research. Says William von Humboldt: "Speech must be regarded as naturally inherent in man: for it is altogether inexplicable as a work of his understanding in its simple consciousness. There could be no invention of language unless its type already existed in the human understanding." So far we can readily agree with him. But when the great philosopher adds: "Man is man only by means of speech, but in order to in-

* It was a dogma of the ancient physicians, said to have come down from Galen, that the conjunction of deafness and dumbness in the same individuals, was to be accounted for by "a common organic lesion of the lingual and auditory nerves, arising as they do from a neighboring origin in the brain."—See the able Article in the Edinburgh Review, Vol. LXI., p. 409.

* One of these cases was that of Peter, the Wild Boy, who was found in the woods of Hanover in 1726, and taken to England, where vain attempts were made to teach him language. He lived to the age of seventy. Another remarkable case was that of a boy of twelve found in the forest of Aveyron in France, about the beginning of this century. He also was destitute of speech, and all efforts to teach him failed.

† See the North American Review for April, 1834; Article on the Education of the Deaf and Dumb.

vent speech he must be already man," he must either mean by *speech* (as we often mean by language), any possible means of communicating ideas, by signs whether audible or visible, or he must have strangely overlooked the phenomena presented by the deaf and dumb. The latter supposition is the most probable, especially as Humboldt is a German; for the Germans are slow to admit that the language of gestures can supply, to any considerable extent, the place of speech.

And yet, to those who are conversant with the deaf and dumb, and have studied their modes of thought and expression, nothing is clearer than that the language of gestures, in the improved and expanded stage which it soon reaches wherever a number of intelligent deaf-mutes are collected together, is sufficient, not merely for the communication of all ideas whatever, that can be expressed by words; but also as an instrument of thought, and of moral and intellectual development. Man cannot be man without some mode of communication with his fellows, sufficient not merely for calling, warning, entreating, threatening, for which the instinctive cries of many species of animals suffice, but also for narrating, describing, questioning, answering, comparing, reasoning. But there are multitudes of deaf-mutes, capable of all this, and well developed mentally and morally, who yet never heard and never uttered a word; and whose knowledge of the conventional signs for words, furnished by alphabetic language, was not a means of mental development, but an accomplishment, necessary to intercourse with those who hear and speak, which had to be slowly and laboriously acquired by explanation and translation in their own language of gestures. Some cases we know in which the mental and moral development has reached a point decidedly beyond the average of unlettered speaking men, where yet there is either a very slight knowledge of words, or even none at all.

While, then, we are ready to admit that speech is "the spontaneous result of man's organization, just as reason is,"* we must add that the language of gestures is also a "spontaneous result of man's organization." A language of articulation and intonation wakes sympathetic chords in the ear and brain; a language of gesture and expression equally speaks to the sympathies and *synideas* (if we may be allowed to make a word). Widely different as are the two languages in material, in structure, in the sense which they address, and in the mode of internal consciousness by which their signs are received, and by which they are used as the machinery of thought and reasoning; still, either alone, once well developed, is sufficient for all the wants of the human intellect. If speech is better adapted to generalization and abstraction, and hence to reasoning; pantomime is superior in graphic power, and sway over the passions. The man whose language is a language of gestures, because by the want of hearing he has been cut off from speech, is still, not less than his brother who possesses speech, undeniably a man.

This assertion may surprise those who recall the fearful state of ignorance and degradation of which so many deaf-mutes are painful examples. But the cause of this ignorance and degradation is not only the want of speech, but the want also of an improved and developed language of gestures. They were ignorant because those around them, either through dullness, stiffness, or indolence, were disqualified to aid them in developing their instinctive language of gestures to the degree necessary to enable them to profit by the experience of others, and to share in social communion. They were thus left without due exercise of the faculties in those years when that exercise is most important; and, above all, were cut off from all that mass of traditional knowledge of which language is the great store-house.

* W. C. Fowler's English Grammar, etc., p. 18.

The language of gestures is, indeed, obviously less convenient than speech in many circumstances: as, for instance, in darkness, or with any other obstacle to vision; or, which is yet more important, in case of intent occupation of the eye and hand, with work in hand, or game, or enemies in front. Still, when we recollect that it is far more self-explanatory than speech, as is proved by the fact that every wanderer, cast among people of an unknown tongue, has instinctive recourse to such skill in pantomime as he can command, we are tempted to believe that the language of gestures, mixed, of course, with instinctive cries, was the language of the first men; and that the instinctive cries, from being merely auxiliary, became the nucleus from which spoken languages were slowly developed.

But, though the *elements* of the language of gestures, by being far less variable, and by admitting of much more obvious analogies with the visible forms and actions of objects, are far more generally intelligible among men of diverse speech, and hence seem more *natural* than the elements of any known, or even conceivable language of words; yet, on closer research, we shall find that speech is the more natural and instinctive, as well as the more convenient of two rival channels of thought and feeling. Children readily and spontaneously learn speech, because spoken words cling with a natural cohesion to the memory; because they are prompted by a natural instinct to utter sounds; in short, because the acquisition of speech is a natural exercise of organs and faculties given them to that end. The case of blind children shows that gestures, however useful, are not *necessary* as interpreters of speech. And we have no evidence that there ever existed any community of men, not deprived of hearing, with whom speech was not in use at least as early as gesticulation.

Even deaf children, not less than children who hear, give natural and unconscious expression to their first feelings by utterances. In them, as well as in others, the cry of pain or of hunger precedes by months the gesture of anger or of supplication. Their inability to hear the speech of others is not the only cause of their becoming or remaining dumb. Their inability to hear *themselves*—leaving them unconscious of the sounds they utter—checks the natural overflow of thought and feeling by the muscles of the larynx, and turns it, except in moments of strong emotion, exclusively to the other natural channel, that of gestures and expressions of the eye and features.

The most remarkable instance on record of the instinctive expression of *ideas* (not *emotions*) by utterances, is found in the history of the blind deaf-mute, Laura Bridgman. She has been observed to utter a distinct sound; in some cases approaching a monosyllabic word, in others a clucking or other inarticulate noise, for each of her acquaintances, and even to change this uttered name (of which she can be conscious only by the muscular effort of producing it), when she becomes aware of any considerable change in the individual to whom it is applied.*

We are not aware that such a fact is recorded of any deaf-mute who can see, and hence it is, as we have before remarked, that the phenomena observed in *their* case *seem* to demolish the theory that any language of utterances, beyond mere emotional cries, is instinctive in man's mouth. But where deaf children are not objects of attention, these sounds will not be remarked, and, where they are objects of attention, the development of the visible language of gestures, as we have already observed, cuts off the other natural channel for the overflow of thought.

Here we have doubtless the germ of that faculty by which, fully developed in the first man, he be-

* See Dr. Lieber's paper, On the Vocal Sounds of Laura Bridgman, published in the Smithsonian Contributions to Knowledge.

came possessed of spontaneous speech. In his infant descendants it is not developed, because there is no room for its development. Children who cannot hear, are not conscious of its existence: and children who hear, have enough to do in learning words by imitation. The wild men who have been found in forests, where they had grown up with no more language than the wild beasts with whom they lived, and by some of whom they were probably at first nursed, may seem at first view an exception; but these, so far as we recollect, were all solitary; and it is unnecessary to remind the reader that a solitary child or man, having no use for language, far from being likely to form one, is apt to lose one already possessed.*

There are writers who attempt to describe the gradual formation of a language, beginning with mere instinctive cries of emotion, thence passing to single words or names, which, by the aid of the verb, are finally strung together in sentences, and made more definite by terminations or by particles. All this is ingenious; but wholly unsupported by any pertinent historical evidence. These writers affect to find "vestiges" of the successive stages of development through which they assume languages to have passed, in the different structures of the language spoken by different races of men.† But neither now, nor at any past time of which we have any authentic record, do we find a nation or tribe whose language has not passed through all the earlier and more difficult processes of its supposed formation. Tribes are yet found that, in respect to all other arts, and to all knowledge, are in as primitive a state as any progressive theorist can well dream of; but none whose language has not already, and, so far as we have any means of judging, ages since, passed far beyond the stage when all words were names, and the connection supplied by gestures.

We do not deny the possibility that men may thus form a language. On the contrary, we are inclined to believe that, if the subjects of the old Egyptian king's experiment had been kept in seclusion a few years longer, provided by being left together, they could have a taste of the pleasures and convenience of having a mode of communication, and could mutually aid and encourage each other in the formation of language; they would have added other sounds, more or less articulate, to the word *bec*; and thus would have gradually developed a dialect, imperfect no doubt, and requiring the aid of natural gestures, but yet with a considerable number of sounds resembling words. It is not improbable, as we may presently have occasion to show, that there may be savage tribes whose languages were thus formed. But if there be any languages thus formed, they must have been rapidly and spontaneously developed *pari passu* with the development of ideas in the first generation; for as the first ancestors of the tribe grew into rigid maturity of age, their modes of thought and forms of language would both crystallize into a determinate form, which, in accordance to a universal law of nature, would be impressed on the yet plastic minds of their children. The forms of the language being thus determined by some idiosyncrasy of the first progenitors, would henceforward remain nearly stationary for ages. Particular words change, assume new meanings, or are forgotten; but the grammatical forms of a language, unless broken by a mixture of races, and fused again into a new dialect, either remain substantially the same for ages, or, when they change, it is in a reverse manner to that which is implied by the theory of the slow formation of language during many generations. The changes of grammatical structure that history discloses are all changes from a more complex to a more simple structure. Some of the most ancient languages known possessed numerous inflections both of nouns and verbs. The modern languages derived from them have lost many of these inflections. Other ancient languages, as the Chinese, possessed no such inflections, and so have remained during thousands of years. Facts like these indicate that the first language was an inflected one, not a mere jargon of names without inflections or syntax.*

This monosyllabic and non-inflected structure of the Chinese language tempts us to conjecture, that this singular nation and singular language may have had their origin from a pair or more of children providentially cast out from human society while they possessed as yet, if any speech, but such a broken speech as is heard in the first efforts of children. This may, indeed, seem a more probable conjecture for the origin of a tribe of ignorant savages, than of a people so renowned for early civilization. There is, however, another mode in which a new tribe or even nation, might take its origin; a mode in which, while totally cut off from all tradition either of the language or the historical lore of the race whence it sprang, it might still preserve a certain civilization and skill in the arts necessary to subsistence or comfort.

In all ages of the world there have probably been deaf-mutes, for the words expressing this calamity are found in the most ancient languages known. Sometimes too, as we know, several deaf-mutes are found in the same family or neighborhood. They are generally quick in learning all the arts that depend on the eye and hand; hunting, fishing, agriculture, and the mechanic arts. Their sexual instincts are often strong, and their passions violent. May we not suppose that, in some very remote period, while the greater part of the earth was yet an unpeopled waste, a pair of deaf-mutes, rebelling against the restraint of some patriarchal family dwelling on the very verge of human habitation, and feeling their own ability to provide for themselves, may have wandered off into the boundless uninhabited wilds before them, there to found a new race? A race so founded would doubtless present many remarkable peculiarities. While it might well possess a certain traditional skill in the arts necessary to its mode of life, perhaps far beyond the range of its inventive faculties; it would have lost all tradition of the true origin and early history of mankind; and would possess a language resembling no other language of men; a language, most probably, of few elements, and without inflections, for the idioms of the dialect of gestures used by the first pair would be apt to give such a character to it in its first stage of formation. And, we may add, in anticipation of that part of our subject, that a people of such an origin might very probably retain some rites of the external worship of the race from which they sprang, while utterly ignorant of its meaning and spirit.

We have presented these two hypotheses (of which we suppose the latter to be quite new), to show that it is quite unnecessary to resort either to the older theory of the existence of the human race during generations in a savage or rather pre-savage state, with only the faint rudiments of speech, which developed differently in different tribes; or to the newer and more attractive, but equally unscriptural theory of a plurality of Adams and Eves placed in different regions; in order to account for the widest

* "Sir Kenelm Digby, in his Treaties of Bodies, mentions a remarkable instance of one John of Liege, who, from the apprehensions of danger from an approaching enemy, took refuge in a forest and was lost, where he remained so long that he lost the use of speech, and had to learn it again."—*Vox Oculis Subjecta*, p. 50.

† As a specimen of this sort of philosophizing, see a recent flippant and pretentious work, entitled "Vestiges of Civilization."

* The English has fewer inflections than the Anglo-Saxon; the Italian, French, and other languages of Southern Europe, than the Latin; the present dialects of India, than the Sanskrit. We are aware of no case in which a modern language has more varied inflections than the ancient language or languages from which it is derived. The Sanskrit, one of the most ancient languages preserved by writing, abounds in inflections beyond all others.

diversities of language (even if we suppose the confusion at Babel to have only produced differences of dialect), or, if any weight be due to tradition on such a point, for the most contradictory traditions, as to the origin of mankind.

From the theory which we have advanced, it will naturally result that the language spoken by the first man, and inherited by his immediate descendants, having its origin in a fuller development of faculties, joined to more perfect flexibility of the organs of speech, was probably a more perfect and harmonious language than any that may since, by such accidents as we have supposed, have had an entirely independent origin. And this primitive language we may easily suppose the stem from which all the languages of the Caucasian race have branched: thus accounting for the numerous points of resemblance among the languages of that race.

For we find in our philosophy no reason to reject the Scriptural doctrine, that the first man was the type of the highest perfection, mental and physical, of his descendants. Races of men sometimes improve, but, in other circumstances, they as notoriously degenerate. It is at least full as philosophical to suppose the inferior races of men to have been degenerate descendants from the superior races, as to suppose the converse. And those who hold that the Hottentot has gradually improved by migration to more favorable climates, till, passing through the intermediate grades, his remote descendants came upon the stage of life as a tribe of Caucasians, to be consistent, ought also to hold that the Hottentot himself was an improved offshoot from the Chimpanzee, and the latter from some remarkable baboon or monkey.

And such, as every reader will recollect, is the precise ground taken by that school of philosophers, represented by Lord Monboddo in the last century, and by the author of the noted work "Vestiges of the Natural History of Creation" in this, who seem possessed with a monomania of accounting for all phenomena without reference to a First Cause, wherever, by any effort of speculative ingenuity, the necessity for such a reference may seem to be removed a step further back. *Their* theory of the origin of man and of language, however insufficient it may be, has at least the merit of consistency. They do not suppose the first man to have been created and left by his Creator in a state of bodily maturity and intellectual infancy, or rather imbecility. According to their views the first man, the last of a long series of successive developments from the first germ of life (which itself, in the view of some, was merely a product of a new chemical combination), this first man, the lineal descendant of the *infusoria*, through the fishes, the frogs, and the monkeys, had of course an infancy, as the orang-outang or chimpanzee, from whom he was born, had before him. An infant with orang-outang parents can not well be supposed to have any other language than the howling, chattering and mowing of his own father and mother; and marvellous as is the formation, in whatever number of generations, of a human language from such an origin, it is no greater marvel than the birth of a rational man from an irrational ape. The difficulty with this theory is, that in seeking to escape the necessity of admitting a direct interposition of Divine power, it supposes a series of metamorphoses, each a greater miracle, as measured by human experience since the record of history began, than is implied in the most literal interpretation of the Mosaic account of the creation.

According to all human experience, every oak sprung from an acorn; nor has an acorn been ever known to produce a tree of a different species from its parent oak. But geology teaches that there was a time when the earth was unfit for the growth of oaks. There must have been a first oak. Is it easier to conceive this first oak, in direct contradiction to all experience, to have sprung from the seed of some less perfect plant, than to conceive it, not in contradiction to, but simply in addition to, because beyond the reach of experience, as springing from the ground at the will of the Creator?

If it be granted that the first pair were created with *adult bodies;* possessed at once of that stature, muscular development, and power over their motions, which, in the case of each of their descendants, are only acquired by the slow growth and slowly treasured experience of long years of infancy and childhood; it can hardly be denied to be equally probable that they were created also with *adult minds*, that is, mental faculties, not, as in the case of infants, merely in the germ, but well developed, and possessed of an instinctive power of speech, which, in fact, is hardly a greater marvel than an instinctive power of walking to the nearest tree, and plucking fruit to satisfy the first call of hunger. Milton makes Adam say, describing his first awakening into conscious life:

"Straight towards Heaven my wondering eyes I turned,
And gazed awhile the ample sky, till raised
By quick *instinctive motion up I sprung*,
As thitherward endeavoring, and *upright*
Stood on my feet; about me round I saw
Hill, dale, and shady woods, and sunny plains,
And liquid lapse of murmuring streams; by these,
Creatures that lived, and moved, and walked, or flew:
Birds on the branches warbling; all things smiled;
With fragrance and with joy my heart o'erflowed.
Myself I then perused, and limb by limb
Surveyed, and *sometimes went, and sometimes ran*
With supple joints, as lively vigor led:
But who I was, or where, or from what cause,
Knew not: *to speak I tried, and forthwith spake;*
My tongue obeyed, and readily could name
Whate'er I saw."

And this fine description contains philosophy as well as poetry. The Creator can dispense, if it so please him, with the long infancy of the mind, as well as with that of the body. There is nothing in itself more incredible in the representation of the first man, as instinctively naming whatever he saw, than in his instinctively standing upright, and moving over the earth at will. None of his descendants, for long months after birth, can do either the first or the last. If a human being should be nurtured from infancy up to adult age without ever having been suffered to use his limbs, he would be as utterly unable to stand and walk, as he would be unable to speak, if from the loss of hearing or other cause, he he should grow up without having ever exercised his organs of speech. And equally unable would he be to remember, think, and reason, if he had been always deprived of all opportunity of development and exercise of his intellectual faculties.

It is no serious objection to this view of the case that the possession of a language implies the possession of a considerable store of ideas, which can only be acquired by the use of the external senses. The Scriptures inform us that Adam named "every beast of the field, and every fowl of the air," when brought to him. Evidently the names came spontaneously to his tongue, as a natural result of the perfect organization and overflowing energy of his organs of speech. We do not suppose that he ever used, or was conscious of possessing a word for *elephant*, or *lion*, or *tree*, or *bird*, before he saw, and seeing tried to name those objects; or that he would have a word to express *love*, for instance, before he had experienced that feeling, which, of course, implies the perception of a beloved object.

The formation of a language of gestures by a deaf-mute child presents phenomena which may serve to illustrate the plastic power of a language in its vigorous and flexible youth. A sprightly deaf-mute child, once accustomed to have his pantomimic efforts received with kind interest, at the first sight of an elephant or a lion, will give this new animal a fitting sign-name; and, at the first perception of some new feeling, or mental relation, will devise some suitable mode of expressing it in pantomime. And his signs will be intelligible to his companions, if of quick perceptions, and accustomed to his mode of communication, provided they have seen the same objects, and experienced the same feelings, though the particular combination of signs made use of in the new case should be quite new to them. Can not we imagine that the Creator should endow the first pair with a power of speech as spontaneous, and to each other as self-interpreting, as the pantomime of the deaf and dumb still is? Is there any improbability in supposing that they were gifted with, as they needed greater propensity to, and facility in speech than is possessed by any of their descendants?

Whatever differences of opinion may obtain on the origin of language, there can be none that the possession or the capacity of acquiring a language is one of the surest tests of humanity. The want of a language in any adult being of admitted human origin, where the senses concerned in the use of language are not deficient, at once marks a low grade of idiocy. Language furnishes the machinery of the intellect; it is the multiplier of mental power, the treasury of the accumulating experience and reflections of the whole race, and hence is the great means of intellectual progress for the human race, as well as for each individual man. Another prerogative that distinguishes man from the most sagacious of the mere animal creation, a prerogative yet higher than language, and hardly less universal, is religion. As there is no known tribe of men without an articulate language, so there is hardly one without a religion, that is, without traditions more or less distinct, and having more or less sway through the conscience, on opinion and conduct; of a God and of a life beyond the grave.

This general consent of mankind on certain fundamental points of religious belief, is accounted for as we have seen in the case with the general prevalence of articulate speech, in two different ways. One class of philosophers and theologians hold, that whatever knowledge on such points is possessed by nations on whom the light of revelation has not dawned, is derived through dim traditions, transmitted from the remote patriarchal times. Another class regard the crude notions of the heathen on religious subjects as the spontaneous development of man's religious nature; which they hold leads every man, or at least every community, at a certain stage of mental and moral development, to recognize a God in his works, and infer the soul's immortality from the instinctive horror with which we recoil from the idea of entire extinction of being.

The two theories have this in common, that they take for granted that certain elements of religious belief are natural to the human mind. If man were not so constituted that a belief in a God and in a future life is accepted and clung to, as consonant with his nature, religious traditions could never keep such firm hold of the popular belief through countless generations. But when we say that the vine reaches to and twines round the stake, when presented to it, we do not mean that the vine can make its own support, or without painful and random trailings along the ground, reach a distant support; it but accepts the nearest support offered to it. The human mind (with rare exceptions) instinctively accepts and clings to the great truths embodied in the words, God and Immortality: does it follow that these truths are so near and open to human apprehension that the mind, in its vague and unaided reachings forth, can discover and grasp them?

It is in this point of view that the inquiries into the notions of the uninstructed deaf and dumb possess the greatest interest. The results of these inquiries we now proceed to give.

A series of questions as to their ideas before instruction on religious and other analogous subjects was recently proposed to the members of the three most advanced classes in the New York Institution for the Deaf and Dumb. The answers obtained were entirely their own, both in thoughts and in language. We here present a sufficient number to give a just idea of the whole.

Question 1. "Had you, before instruction, any idea of a God, or of any being in the sky more wise and powerful than man? Did you consider this being as benevolent and just, or as powerful, cruel, and awful?"

Answer. "Before instruction I had no conceptions with reference to the character of God; my grandmother and her daughter endeavored to instruct me, and make me understand that God was good and powerful, but I did not obtain any clear idea. They taught me in signs that the eye of God was so great that he could perceive with ease and quickness. When I learned the letters of the alphabet with one hand, a good lady pointed to some letters in a thin pamphlet, saying 'God is good,' but I did not clearly understand what this meant until the dawn of education beamed upon me."

"No, Sir; I had no idea of God."

"I thought that some one was in the sky. I feared that he was powerful and wise, because he turned a grindstone, and made it thunder and lighten." *

"Before I was instructed I had no idea of God, but I thought that some one caused thunder and lightning over the earth, which quaked."

"I had no idea of any being more wise and powerful than man."

"I knew nothing of God. I had no idea of considering his character."

"Yes, Sir, I had an idea of God before I came to school. During my stay at home my mother often told me that God was good, but I had not much knowledge about him."

"Nothing of a being in the sky more powerful than man was known to me till my brother told me through gestures that he was of greater strength and height than we, and put the corpse of a wicked man to the bottom of a hollow place, and then burnt it; and would take a dead person possessing goodness into the sky. My feelings were divided between fear of the being and determination to be good, so that I might be taken by him to his abode in the sky. On my mother's return home from a visit, she, being informed by him that he had taught me of the being, confirmed the statement."

"I had but a very imperfect idea of God originally imprinted on my mind by my mother, who gave me, through signs, the impression that he was entirely made of iron, by pointing to the stove round which we were sitting one Sabbath morning in winter; and that he was enthroned on high, by placing herself in an armchair, and touching it, and pointing upward, as if something resembling it were elevated above the blue azure vault. As far as I can remember, I thought that he was more powerful than man, and that he would be highly offended and extremely angry should I ever do anything disagreeable or offensive. After the most intense reflection, I can hardly say whether I ever thought he was benevolent and just or not."

"Before instruction I never had any conception of God, or of any being in the sky more wise and powerful than man."

"I had, before being instructed, no idea of God, nor of any being more wise and powerful in the sky than a man in the world, but I was taught in French by my nurse in Paris that there was such a being called 'Dieu.' I considered the being very cruel. While I was on the wharf at Beaufort, with my father, when quite a boy, we were waiting for the coming of a steamboat. It was an exceedingly hot day, and we were out of patience. I told him that 'Dieu' was very cruel."

"I have no recollection of having formed any idea

* This idea, though less poetical, is not more unphilosophical than the Homeric notion of thunderbolts forged on Vulcan's anvil.

that there was a God, or any other being superior to man."

Extracts like the foregoing might be multiplied indefinitely. Thousands of deaf-mutes in Europe and America, after becoming able to give an account of their early thoughts, have been questioned as to their ideas of God; and their answers have been perfectly uniform in the point that no one of them ever originated the idea of a Creator and Governor of the world from his own unaided reflections. What ideas some of them had attached to the word God, pointed out to them in books, were derived from the imperfectly understood signs of their anxious friends, or from pictures. In this way, many of the deaf and dumb acquired the notion that there was a great and strong man in the sky, a being to be feared rather than loved. Others received from pictures the notion that the being, so often pointed to in the sky, was a venerable old man, with a long beard and flowing robes. For instance, Massieu, the celebrated pupil of Sicard, gave the following account of the impressions he received from the attempts of his parents to make known to him the existence and the duty of worshipping God: *

"My father made me make prayers by signs, morning and evening. I put myself on my knees; I joined my hands and moved my lips, in imitation of those who speak when they pray to God."

"In my infancy I adored the heavens and not God; I did not see God, I saw the heaven (the sky). When I prayed on my knees I thought of the heaven. I prayed in order to make it descend by night upon the earth, to the end that the vegetables which I had planted should grow, and that the sick should be restored to health."

When asked if he gave a figure or form to this *heaven*, Massieu replied: "My father had shown me a large statue in a church in my country; it represented an old man with a long beard; he held a globe in his hand; I believed that he dwelt beyond the sun." Massieu further relates that he felt joy when his prayers were answered to his wishes; and, on the contrary, was accustomed to threaten heaven with angry gestures when he saw that hail destroyed the crops, or his parents continued sick.

It should be understood that the failure of so many anxious parents and relatives of uneducated mutes to impart to these unfortunates any correct or consoling ideas on religious subjects, is owing, not to any want of adaptation in the language of gestures for the communication of such ideas, but to their own want of skill in its use. As it exists in our institutions, this language is fully adequate to the clear and vivid expression of religious truths.†

Questions, 2. "Had you any idea that the world was created; that some wise and powerful being made plants, animals, men, and all things?"

"Did you ever try to reflect about the origin of the world and its inhabitants?"

Answers. "I had no idea that it was created by the word of God, and never thought of the origin of the world."

"No, I had no idea about it. I did not think of the first inhabitants of the world."

"I had no idea of the creation of the world, and that plants, animals, and all things, and men were made—No, sir."

"I did not know that it was created, but I felt as if it existed. I thought that plants, animals, men, and all things made themselves. No, I never endeavored to reflect about the origin of the world and its inhabitants."

"It was my opinion that the sun created the world, and all things, and animals, and the farmers caused the plants and vegetables to grow up. I never tried to reflect about the origin of the inhabitants."

"I can not recollect anything of what I thought with regard to the manner in which the world, and plants, animals, men, and all things were made. To the best of my recollection, I never tried to reflect about the origin of the world and its inhabitants."

"My ideas of the creation of the world, plants and other things were enveloped in the darkness of ignorance, till my dormant faculties were enlightened by the dawn of education when I came into the New York Institution for the Deaf and Dumb."

"I had no idea at all that the world was created, or that some wise and powerful being made plants, animals, men, and all things, as I thought they had ever been and would ever be in existence, and that the world was an endless level plain. It is impossible for me to assert whether I had ever tried to reflect about the origin of the world and its inhabitants."

"No, sir; I thought that some animals came from the south to this country, where they staid till the winter, when they flew away to the south, but some animals were born here. I believed that some great things raised themselves. I did not know that God made plants, but persons gathered some in the fall and kept them till spring, when they planted seeds in the earth. The seeds grew up by the influence of the water which some women poured upon them. I tried to think (about the origin of the world and its inhabitants) but could not do it. I thought that the inhabitants came from the south."

The writer of the last cited answer, it will be seen, was the only one that "tried to think" about the origin of the world and its inhabitants. It is worthy of remark that her education did not begin till she had attained the age of fifteen, and she had thus more time before instruction to "try to think," or to attempt to make original theories, than most of the others whose answers are given above, who generally came to school at eleven or twelve, or even earlier. With deaf-mute children, unless their friends are skilled in the language of signs, the reflective powers usually develop much more slowly than with children who hear; because the possession of signs for those ideas that are beyond the sphere of direct intuition, and the exercise of the faculties by intercourse with other minds, are necessary to any considerable development of those powers. The dialect which a deaf-mute, with the assistance of his relations and playmates, invents to serve for necessary and simple communications, is usually too meagre, imperfect, and often ambiguous, to favor the development of the higher intellectual faculties. And if these faculties are slowly and imperfectly developed, we should rationally expect, what appears to be the fact, that few, if any, of these unfortunate children seem ever to have reflected on the origin of the universe, or on the necessity of a First Cause for the phenomena of nature. As one of them expresses it, they "thought it was natural" that the world should be as it is. Some even fancied that those whom they saw to be old, had ever been so, and that they themselves would ever remain children. Those who had learned, by observation and testimony, the general law of progress from infancy to old age, supposed, if they attempted to think on the subject at all, that there had been an endless series of generations. But probably there are very few uninstructed deaf-mute children of ten or twelve who have reached such a point of intellectual development as even this idea implies. At least, we do not recall more than one case in which a deaf-mute has professed to have had such an idea, and his recollections do not seem to be clear.* It is much

*Those who may wish to read in full this interesting account of his own infancy by Massieu, may refer to Sicard's "Théorie des Signes," to Bébian's "Journal des Sourds-Muets et des Aveugles," (I. 333), or to the Appendix to Akerly's "Elementary Exercises for the Deaf and Dumb" [New York, 1826].

†The rude and uncultivated dialects of gestures generally serve only to recall ideas with which both parties are already familiar. It requires an improved dialect, and a master in its uses, to impart new ideas, especially if elevated and intricate.

*"*I believe* I used to think that this world stood itself always, and that the people, too, were descended from generation to generation without origin."—Twenty-second Report, American Asylum (1838), p. 17.

easier to give to a deaf-mute, by means of rude and imperfect signs, the idea that there is some powerful being in the sky, than to explain or even hint that this being made the world.* Hence it is that very few deaf-mutes have ever acquired, either from their own reflections or from the imperfect signs of their friends, any idea of the creation of the world, or even of the plants and animals on its surface. Nor need this surprise us when we reflect that the most enlightened nations of antiquity had not mastered this great idea. Ovid, writing in the learned and polished time of Augustus, expressed the popular belief of his time in the theory, that all things were produced by the due union of heat and moisture.†

Many deaf-mutes, however, whether from their own meditations or from misunderstanding the signs of their friends, have acquired child-like ideas, respecting the causes of certain natural phenomena; such as rain, thunder, and the motions of the heavenly bodies. Quite a number supposed that there were men in the sky, who, at certain times, made themselves busy in pouring down water and firing guns. The notions of deaf-mutes on such matters are often amusing enough, but when not derived from a misconception of the signs of their friends, ‡ are evidently formed in a spirit of analogy, which, indeed, has a great effect on the formation of their language of gestures. Where there is a resemblance in effects, they naturally suppose a resemblance in causes. An English deaf-mute boy, § observing that he could raise quite a strong wind with his mother's bellows, naturally concluded that the wind that sometimes blew off his cap in the street came from the mouth of a gigantic bellows. Neither does it seem that this belief was troubled by his inability to find the operator or the location of this bellows, for to one whose sphere of observation was so limited, and who could learn so little of the world beyond it from the testimony of others, the region beyond a circle of a few miles was as wholly unknown, and as open to the occupancy of imaginary giants and engines, and other figments of the imagination, as was ever the land of the Cimmerians to the Greeks, or the Fairy Land to the popular belief of the Middle Ages. Similar to this was the notion already given, of a girl who seems to have imagined that the plants which spring up annually in the fields and woods were, like those in her mother's garden, planted and watered by "some women:" an infantile conception in which, however, may be traced the first germ of the old Greek notions respecting nymphs and dryads.

A few more of these infantile attempts to account for the phenomena of nature, may be acceptable to the reader. One lad, struck with the similarity between flour falling in a mill, and snow falling from the clouds, concluded that snow was ground out of a mill in the sky. Others supposed that the men with whom their imaginations, or their misconceptions of the signs of their friends, had peopled the sky, brought up water from the rivers, or from some large neighboring sound or lake, and dashed it about from pails or tubs, through holes in the heavenly vault. The more general belief, however, seems to have been, that there was a great store of rain and snow in the sky, a matter no more to be wondered at than the abundance of earth and water below. Some supposed thunder and lightning to be the discharges of guns or cannon in the sky: a notion the converse of that well-known one of the savages who, when they first met in battle a European armed with a musket, believed they had encountered a God, armed with thunder and lightning. Others say that they believed lightning to be struck from the sky with iron bars, a fancy rather more difficult to account for than the other, though they had doubtless remarked the sparks struck by iron from stone.

In answer to the question whether they had any idea how the sun, moon, and stars were upheld in the sky, the uniform reply was that they had never thought about it. It seems as natural to children that these bodies should keep their places above us as that the clouds or the sky itself should. One lad had imagined a hole through the earth by which the sun could find a passage back to the east. Others supposed that after setting he continued his journey round under the northern horizon to the east again. There were even some who supposed that a new sun rose every morning, and was extinguished at night!

They all believed, of course, that the earth was flat. No one will wonder at this, for there are still many people, possessed of the advantages of speech and hearing, who on this point have not yielded the testimony of their eyes to the demonstrations of science.

The stars, in the view of many, were candles or lamps, lighted every evening for their own convenience by the inhabitants of the sky; a notion very natural to those who had had opportunities of watching the regular lighting, at night, of the street-lamps of a city. The moon was, to most of those whose answers are before us, an object of greater interest than any others of the heavenly bodies. One imaginative girl fancied that she recognized in the moon the pale but kind face of a deceased friend. Others thought that she continually followed them and watched their actions, moving some to "make saucy faces at her," and others to run and hide themselves in the fear that she would seize and cruelly treat them.* These were, probably, only momentary fancies. The greater number looked on the moon with pleasure, or at least without dread. Some say they believed she loved them.

The answers of some of them, from their imperfect command of language, probably express more than they intended; and, in several cases, their recollections of the ideas they had before instruction may have become mixed up with, or colored by, the ideas they have acquired since. It is difficult to judge how much the girl meant who professes to have had an opinion that "the sun created the world," and the difficulty is not diminished by the incoherency of the different parts of her statement. She may have observed that the sun caused the annual disappearance of snow and return of animal and vegetable life.

The answers to the question "Had you any idea of the existence of the soul as something distinct from the body, and which might be separated from it?" were so uniformly in the negative that it is unnecessary to quote more than two or three: *e. g.*, "No, Sir, I had no idea of the soul." "I had not the least notion of the existence of the soul." "I had no understanding of the existence of the soul; but now I understand that the soul exists in every person, and when death seizes them the soul is immediately separated from it" [the body]. The replies of pupils of the American Asylum to a similar question were to the same effect. One of them will serve as a specimen of the whole: "I had not any idea of my own soul nor of any spirit whatever."

It is remarkable that only one out of more than forty whose statements are before us seems to have

* "When I saw a large stone, I asked a friend of mine how it came. She pointed to heaven, but I did not know what it meant." Ib. p. 11.

† Quippe ubi temperiem sumsēre humorque calorque
Concipiunt: et ab his oriuntur cuncta duobus.
Metamorphoses, 1. 8.

‡ One girl, probably from misunderstanding the signs of her friends, had imbibed the idea that the priest made rain.

§ "A Voice from the Dumb," by W. Sleight of Brighton. Other deaf-mutes say they fancied the wind was blown from the mouth of some unseen being. This notion may have been derived from pictures.

* A pupil of the Hartford School wrote: "I had some faint idea that there was one in the moon who looked on every one of us, and would take any one that was angry or bad in some ways to his prison for life."—Twenty-second Report, American Asylum, p. 14. Other deaf-mutes have related similar fancies of their early years.

imbibed any of the popular superstitions respecting ghosts. If the misfortune of the deaf and dumb prevents them from learning much truth, it also protects them in most cases from receiving those early impressions of superstitious terror and folly which it is often so difficult to get rid of in later life.

Question 8. "What were your thoughts and feelings on the subject of death? Did you know that you must yourself die?"

Answers. "I had terrible dreams about death, which stimulated me to take some possible means to save my life from being destroyed, by hiding myself under the ground."

"I cannot recollect that I thought I must die myself."

"I had always regarded death with painful terror and superstition: it seemed to me an unnatural and ghastly thing, and a sort of punishment inflicted on bad human beings. I did not know that I must die like others, nor that all must die."

"I considered death as an unpleasant subject of reflection, and hated it from the bottom of my heart, but could not help dreadful reflection on it whenever I saw man or animal die. I knew it was the extinction of human, as well as animal life, but had no idea that all men, animals and vegetables must come to an end. When I saw men and animals die, I had no feelings of sympathy toward them, as I usually thought they were killed by taking things that were destructive to life, and was so much afraid of it [death] that I formed a resolution to defend myself against its baleful effects, expecting never to be its victim in all my life."

"My thoughts were that a person would never appear in life after his death. I was afraid of death. I did not think we must all die. I had an idea that I should possibly die."

"I thought death awful and terrible, and my feelings on it were great and painful. I guess that I had thought that I myself must die."

"I often saw the old people failing till they died and were buried in the grave, but I did not fear it, because I would not die like them."

"I really knew that I should myself die, as my dear friend, Mrs. S. R. D., often told me by the signs that I should die, and would be taken from the grave to be in a happy place up where she pointed with her hand; but I knew nothing about God and heaven."

"I did not know, but I cherished the hope that I was not appointed to be caught by sickness or death. I did not know that I myself must die."

"Yes, sir, I thought that death was God and I knew that I would die, but I was in a deeply, fearful, sorrowful manner in which I thought I should never see my parents hereafter."

"Before I came to be educated, the subject of death affected my thoughts and feelings. I considered it to be the most dangerous of all calamities, and sometimes dreaded it. I generally thought that I should never die, but live for eternity."

From these extracts, and similar ones might be indefinitely multiplied, it will be seen that to most of the uneducated deaf and dumb, death is truly the king of terrors. Those who had not been taught the contrary by the signs of their friends, cherished the belief that they could evade the power of death and live on forever. We have heard of a lad who, having observed that people who died had taken medicine, resolved to abstain from medicine, as well as other hurtful things; and it might in some cases be well if those who are not deaf and dumb were equally prudent.* Other deaf-mutes are recorded to have been unwilling to betake themselves to their beds, when unwell, from having observed that those sick persons who kept their beds generally died.

Other deaf-mute children, of less experience, or of a happier temperament, profess to have had, or at least to be able to recollect, no thoughts or feelings on the subject of death. Some state that all that troubled them at the sight of a corpse, was the weeping of those around them.

To the question whether they were ever led by dreaming of a deceased person to suppose that that person, though dead and buried, yet lived, thought, and felt somewhere; the general reply was that they recollected no such dreams. A few recollected having dreamed of the death of friends whom on awaking they found alive.

So far as we can learn from their statements, none of the deaf and dumb have originated the idea of the existence of the soul, after death, in a state separate from the body; and it is only in rare cases that their friends have had skill in the language of gestures to impart to them any correct notions on that point. The attempts made for this end by many anxious parents, have at most given the child-like idea that the dead are taken from their graves bodily into the sky, or are bodily thrown into a fire. We have seen that one lad derived from his brother's signs the idea that the corpse of a wicked person was burned in "a hollow place." Of a like character were the early impressions of certain German deaf-mutes, recorded by one of their number, O. F. Kruse of Schleswig, that the bodies of the good remain uncorrupted in the grave, where they only slumber to be hereafter awakened; while those of the wicked rot and become the prey of worms. It is easy to understand that children, who have never seen a corpse except in the brief interval between death and burial, may suppose that the dead only sleep in the grave. One of the pupils of the New York Institution had been haunted by the terrible idea that, should she die and be buried, she might awake in the grave, and would be unable to call for help. Kruse describes the shock to his feelings when he first, by seeing a skeleton, came to know that the body returns to dust in the grave.

Question 10. "What did you think when you saw people assemble at church every seventh day? or when you attended family prayer?"

Answer. "I could not understand what it meant."

"I often thought why people assembled at church every Sabbath-day but I did not know what they did so" [*i. e.* for what reason] "I never attended family prayer, only prayer meeting."

"I don't recollect." (Several answered to this effect.)

"I don't know what I thought." (This also was the answer of several.)

"I often saw people assemble at church, but I did not know what it meant."

"I did not think about the church before any one taught me."

"I thought people were fond of attending on church, but I did not know why they used to have family prayer."

"I thought that they loved to read the Bible, and to hear their preacher speaking, but I did not understand why family prayer was attended."

"I assure you that I had no thought of the people's assemblage at the church as if a stone were in my head."

"I thought that the people were in the church to worship the clergyman of the highest dignity and splendor."

"I thought that the people assembled at the church with great pleasure in studying various branches of knowledge, and thought that the family played."

"I thought that there was a Sabbath in the heaven every seventh day while the people were assembled

* A pupil of the Hartford School had formed the notion that "A doctor wished to give poison to sick persons that they might die." The reader will recollect that savage tribes have at times risen in fury and murdered missionaries, because the sick to whom they had given medicine had died. A dreadful tragedy of this kind was enacted in Oregon, in November, 1847.

at church, because my mother pointed her fingers to the sky and held up her hands on each side of her head when I refused to go to church."

"It seemed strange to see the people assembled at church on Sunday, and to see them read their prayer-books, but I did not know to whom they prayed. I did not attend the family prayer, but when I was quite a boy I used to go to a Catholic church with my nurse, and saw the people; but I remember I was full of mischief." (This is the boy that told his father that "Dieu" was very cruel.)

From the above extracts it will be seen, that most of the deaf and dumb before instruction never had any ideas whatever of the object of public or private worship, some probably taking the weekly assemblage at church as being as much a matter of course as any other periodical event; while others, if they tried to think about it, only added it to the long list of human actions which, in their darkened state, were incomprehensible to them. One or two of them seem to have made rather a shrewd guess at the secret motives of some outward professors when they considered public worship as a recreation, and family prayer as a play; and the idea of another, that people met to worship or to do honor to the clergyman, might in some cases be warranted by the fact. Only one bright lad seems to have connected anything like religious ideas with public worship. His mother's signs gave him the impression that men met on the seventh day on earth because the people in heaven or in the sky did the same.

To the same purport as the foregoing, on all the points we have considered, is the testimony of many other deaf-mutes as well in Europe as in America. Nor have we ever heard of any well authenticated case of a deaf-mute who gained any correct ideas on religious subjects by his own unaided powers of observation and reflection. There are some who, having been able to hear and speak in childhood, have retained, after becoming deaf, the knowledge of God, the soul, and the life to come, previously acquired: and in very rare cases, tolerably correct ideas on such subjects have been imparted to an uneducated deaf child by a friend remarkably expert in the language of gestures. But we feel authorized by the evidence before us to deny that any deaf-mute has given evidence of having any innate or self-originating ideas of a Supreme Being to whom love and obedience were due: of a Creator, or a Superintending Providence, of spiritual existences, or of a future state of rewards and punishments. On this point we will quote the testimony of two or three eminent teachers, out of many that might be cited. The late excellent Thomas H. Gallaudet, the father of deaf-mute instruction in America, thus expresses himself! "I do not think it possible to produce the instance of a deaf-mute, from birth, who, *without instruction on the subject from some friend, or at some institution for his benefit*, has originated, from his own reflections, the idea of a Creator and moral Governor of the world, or who has formed any notions of the immateriality and immortality of his own soul." *

Equally decided is the testimony of the Rev. W. W. Turner, the present Principal of the American Asylum: "It avails little to theorize on questions of this nature, or to show by a process of reasoning, what the human mind can or cannot apprehend. The fact is simply this: The most intelligent deaf-mutes, after a careful inquiry made at different stages of their education, uniformly testify that they never had any idea of a God, or of their own soul, previous to instruction; that they either had never thought on the subject, or if they had, concluded that all things had ever been; and that death was the termination of existence."

And Mr. A. B. Hutton, the estimable Principal of the Philadelphia Institution, bears this testimony: "In the whole course of my sixteen years' experience in the instruction of deaf-mutes, I have never found any evidence for believing that the deaf and dumb from birth, possessed before instruction any idea of a spiritual, Supreme Being, who created and governs everything around us, the idea of God. I have observed that many have crude notions of a being like a man whom they conceived as dwelling in the sky, of great size, age, and muscular power who possessed cannon to thunder with, and soldiers to flash powder for lightning, and lamps for stars; but even these conceptions they have referred to pictures and the signs of their friends as their source."

The testimony of European teachers is not less decisive than that of the Americans. As one of the most favorable to the intellectual and moral capacity of the uninstructed deaf and dumb, we will cite M. Berthier, himself, a deaf-mute, and for many years a distinguished professor in the Institution of Paris. In one of his letters (as quoted by the Abbé Montaigne), he says: "It is possible that some deaf-mutes may attribute certain effects, as storms, wind, and hail, to a certain cause, and may figure to themselves one or more extraordinary beings commanding the rain, the lightning, and other natural phenomena; but a deaf and dumb person, without instruction, will never have a notion, even vague and confused, of a superior existence, whom it is his duty to love, revere, and obey, and to whom he must give an account of his thoughts and of his actions."*

In opposition to all this mass of testimony, may be cited the merely speculative opinion of Deger-

* This testimony of Messrs. Gallaudet, Turner and Hutton is cited from the Twenty-second Report of the American Asylum.

* The Abbé Montaigne, in his "Recherches sur les Connoissances intellectuelles des Sourds-Muets, considérés par rapport à l'administration des Sacremens," cites the testimony of many eminent European teachers, who, so far from supposing that the uninstructed deaf and dumb could have any idea of a Creator, or of their moral responsibility to a superior being, considered them as hardly superior, intellectually and morally, to animals or to idiots. This judgment is much too severe. Either those teachers must have expressed such opinions before they had made due inquiry into the condition of the uneducated deaf and dumb; or they must have taken, as a general rule, some exceptional cases of deaf-mutes who had been neglected and thrust out of society.

Bebian, who was intimately and thoroughly acquainted with the language and character of the deaf and dumb, says: "The greater number of the deaf and dumb had, already before instruction, the idea, I will not say of a first cause, a notion too complicated for the feebleness of their intellect, but that of a sovereign being. They all have, if not the idea, at least the sentiment, of good and evil." And we agree with him on both points, except that, as we have shown, their ideas of a powerful being in the sky are in all cases, so far as we have any evidence, derived from the signs of their friends.

The Abbé Montaigne, holding with Bonald, that "Language is the necessary instrument of every intellectual operation, and the means of every moral existence," and that "Words are indispensable to moral ideas," naturally concludes that uninstructed deaf-mutes should not be admitted to any of the sacraments, except those (as baptism) which are ordinarily administered to infants; and he supports his views by the authority, among other names eminent in the Catholic church, of St. Augustine, who says (lib. III. contra Julianum, cap. IV.) of the deaf from birth: "Quod vitium etiam ipsam impedit fidem; nam surdus natus litteras, quibus lectis fidem concipiat, discere non potest."

Though one of the most venerated of the fathers has thus pronounced faith impossible to those who could neither hear nor read the word, yet many Catholic priests have endeavored to instruct deaf-mutes in the dogmas of their religion by means of signs and pictures; and have thought the results authorized their admission to the sacraments. In many cases, probably, they have deceived themselves as to the clearness with which their instructions were comprehended; still their benevolence is praiseworthy, and the possibility of communicating the most elevated moral and religious ideas by means of the language of gestures will be questioned only by those who are ignorant of the power of that language. Indeed, if religious instruction must be deferred till it could be fully comprehended in words alone, it would become hopeless for a large proportion of the deaf and dumb. Many there are who leave our institutions with a very im-

ando,* that, since the deaf-mute possesses the like powers of observation and reflection with other men, he is capable, time and opportunity being granted to the development of his faculties, of arriving at the conception of "a supreme power, an intelligence that has right to our gratitude," and of divining that the worship he witnesses is offered to such a being; and the assertion of Dr. Howe, that his favorite blind and deaf-mute pupil, Laura Bridgman, "alone and unguided sought God, and found him in the Creator."

If we admit, for the argument's sake, the abstract possibility that a deaf-mute may, by the independent exercise of his own faculties, attain the conception of a Creator, to whom gratitude and obedience are due; still we must observe that the intellectual development implied in such an achievement of the reflective powers is quite incredible, unless we suppose the possession of a language, whether of words or gestures;† and the possession of a language necessarily implies both a power and a long habit of communicating with other minds. The deaf-mute who possesses the intellectual ability to trace the Creator in his works, must, therefore, possess a corresponding ability to converse with his fellows, and, in a Christian land, unless we suppose a general conspiracy to keep him in ignorance, he can hardly possess this ability without becoming acquainted with the prevalent belief long before he is able to work out a theology for himself.

And, in spite of Dr. Howe's assertion, which indeed he qualifies as "to the best of his knowledge and belief,"‡ we doubt if this was not, in a good measure, the case with Laura Bridgman. Her eminent teacher wished in her case to carry out a favorite theory, that the spontaneous development of man's religious nature would lead the creature to a correct knowledge of the Creator. She had been several years under instruction, and had acquired a fair intellectual development, and, for a deaf-mute, a very considerable command of language, before her teacher made any effort to lead her thoughts to religious subjects. He then found that, having attained an "acquaintance with the extent of human creative power," she seemed conscious of "the necessity of superhuman power for the explanation of a thousand daily recurring phenomena." But is it not at least full as probable that she had unconsciously imbibed the idea of a Creator from her free communications, every day and almost every hour of the day for years, with a whole school of intelligent and well-taught blind girls? The statement that Laura "by herself conceived the existence of God," first appears, if we mistake not, in Dr. Howe's report for 1845.* In his Report for 1843, two years earlier, he says of Laura, then in her fifth year of instruction: "The various attempts which I have made during the year to lead her thoughts to God and spiritual affairs, have been, for the most part, forced upon me by her questions, which I am sure were prompted by expressions dropped carelessly by others; such as God, Heaven, Soul, etc., and about which she would afterwards ask me."† In the interval between the writing of these two statements, the Doctor had been absent more than a year in Europe. Is not there here room to suppose that, between zeal for a favorite theory, and just pride in the remarkable powers of his pupil, he may have overlooked the possibility, nay, the probability, of her having acquired, in familiar conversation, hints, at least, of truths which he supposed to be discoveries of her unaided intellect?

However this may be, we hold that to expect that children in general, deaf-mute or not, will by their own unaided reflections, acquire correct ideas of God and immortality, because some child of very uncommon mental power and activity is supposed to have done so, is about as rational as to expect that every boy who plays with a pair of compasses may out of his own head construct thirty-two of the first problems in Euclid, because Pascal is said to have done so. Tell a bright youth that *the three angles of a triangle are equal to two right angles*, or that *in a right-angled triangle the square of the hypothenuse equals the sum of the squares of the legs*, and, with some previous training and preparation, he may be able to construct an original demonstration; but how many out of a thousand, or even a million, if launched without a chart upon the sea of geometry, will make the independent discovery of these propositions?

Even to the mighty ones of our race, the Confuciuses, the Zoroasters, the Platos, can hardly be conceded the ability, unaided by direct revelation, to form just and ennobling conceptions of the Most High, and of man's destiny. With the great mass of mankind, their religious nature suffices to enable them to receive, and understand, and cling to a religion, but not unaided to make one; at least, one that can be, by the most liberal Christian, supposed acceptable to the Creator; else how shall we account for the gross and unworthy conceptions of God prevalent not only among nearly all rude tribes, but even among the most polished people of antiquity? It may, indeed, be said that the reverence imbibed in childhood for the faith of their fathers, prevented them from developing a more rational belief, but this argument only removes the difficulty a step further back. And, moreover, there are examples, rare it is true, of tribes not wholly destitute of intellectual power, and having at least a language far more precise and copious than is possessed by most uneducated deaf-mutes who yet seem as utterly destitute of religious ideas as we have shown the latter to be. The devoted missionary Moffat testifies that, when he preached the existence of God and the immortality of the soul to the barbarous tribes of the Griquas and Bechuanas in South Africa, he was heard with an amazement that found vent in bursts of deafening laughter. Such things had never, even in a shadow of tradition, been heard of among them. According to their views death is nothing less than annihilation, and they never for a moment allow their thoughts to dwell on it.

Whatever difference of opinion may prevail as to the ability of man to form for himself a religion not altogether repugnant to reason or, in some essential points, to revelation, there is unfortunately no question as to his ability, and his strong propensity

---

perfect knowledge of written language, but, notwithstanding, well instructed in the leading truths of religion.

The legitimate and indeed avowed conclusion from the Abbé's doctrine is, that deaf-mutes who can not read and write, can have no moral sense, and must be classed with infants and idiots, who being incapable of sin themselves, and hence only bearing the taint of the original sin, which, according to the Romish faith, baptism washes away, are saved without religious instruction, if they have been baptized. In Italy, these conclusions have been carried out to a point which probably our Abbé would not sanction; some Italians having opposed the instruction of deaf-mutes on the ground that, if uninstructed, not being morally accountable, their salvation was certain, whereas, if instructed, they would become morally accountable, and might incur, by their own sins, damnation. Alas for the happiness of mankind when superstition opposes by such arguments the efforts of benevolence to sweeten their bitter lot of ignorance and affliction!

* De l'Education des Sourds-Muets de Naissance (Paris. 1827), Tome I. pp. 92, 93.

† Dr. Howe says (Report for 1843, p. 25): "The intellect cannot be developed unless *all* the modifications of thought have some sign, by which they can be recalled. Hence men are compelled by a kind of inward force to form languages, and they do form them under all and every circumstance." We think, however, that, with the uneducated deaf and dumb, the development of the intellect is usually somewhat in advance of the ability to communicate with others; but by no means sufficiently so to affect the present argument.

‡ Report for 1850, p. 65.

* P. 29.

† Report for 1843, p. 37.

too, to materialize rather than spiritualize the object of his worship; to make his God a being of terror and wrath rather than of love; of partiality to himself rather than of equal justice to all men: and rather to transplant to his hoped-for heaven the sensual joys of this world than to look forward to spiritual or even intellectual enjoyment in another life. Reasoning from these well-known traits of humanity, we find it much easier to believe that what dim glimpses of religious truth are found among heathen tribes are vestiges of a purer belief held by their remote ancestors than that any just and ennobling religious conceptions have spontaneously been developed among such tribes.

This subject has an important practical application The American instructors of the deaf and dumb have held it to be their duty to begin the religious instruction of their pupils at the earliest practicable stage of their education; that is, say, within the first few months or even weeks. Dr. Howe considered it his duty to defer any instruction to Laura Bridgman on such subjects as God and the Soul to the fifth year of her instruction, and then it was forced upon him by her having picked up notions on such subjects in casual conversations. His reasons we suppose were that such ideas should not be presented till the pupil has attained a stage of intellectual development that will enable him fully to comprehend them, and that he should even rather be led to make such ideas his own by right of discovery than to have them presented as dogmas which he must accept. Much of this difference of practice is to be ascribed to the difference of circumstances and of plans of instruction. On Dr. Howe's plan, perhaps the best which the peculiar case he had to deal with admitted, he had no means of intellectual intercourse with his pupil, and the pupil no means of intellectual development except by a language of words, the acquisition of which, for deaf-mutes, is always slow and laborious. On the system prevailing in our institutions for the deaf and dumb the teacher can, at a very early stage of instruction, reach the understanding, the heart, and the conscience of his pupil through the latter's own language of pantomime. And, when the deaf-mute pupil first finds himself in a community where everyone talks his own language in an improved dialect, the development of his hitherto dormant faculties makes as much progress in a few months as it probably would in as many years were he rigorously confined to words, written or spelled on his fingers, as the signs of ideas and the means of social intercourse. This preference for signs, indeed, sometimes causes our pupils to neglect and forget words; still the use of signs has great and positive advantages as a *means* (not, as some have strangely supposed, an *end*) of instruction.

It is this ability which, if our pupils do not bring to school with them, they very soon acquire, to converse on intellectual and moral subjects in the language of gestures that enables us to begin their religious instruction so early. The teacher, in a numerous class of newly-arrived deaf-mutes, is almost precisely in the condition of a missionary to some tribe of heathens. He must first learn their language, and after seek to make it better adapted to the communication of spiritual ideas, but he need not and does not defer the preaching of the Gospel till they can learn his own language.

Moreover, in a numerous class, early religious instruction is necessary to moral control over the pupils. The uneducated deaf and dumb, if they have no religious ideas, still have a moral sense, a sense of right and wrong, as regards the relations of property, and certain other important checks on the animal propensities. But this moral sense, unsustained by any feeling of accountability to an almighty, just, and omniscient God, is at best weak and dim. And there are not wanting those among them in whom the moral sentiments have been designedly perverted by vicious associates. When the teacher has to deal with but one or two pupils, and can guard against evil communications, watchfulness and correct example may be sufficient to preserve or restore moral purity, till the time comes when the teacher may think his pupil intellectually ripe for the reception of doctrines that may supply higher motives to virtue. But in the case of a whole community, some of the members of which there is reason to fear, may be already corrupt, there is an evident necessity to invoke, at the earliest possible period, that consciousness of God's all-seeing eye, and wholesome fear of his sure, if slow, justice, by which men in general are restrained from gross transgressions. And the facts and reasonings presented in this Article tend to show that this plan, not the less a sound one we conceive because sanctioned by the practice of the wise and pious for so many centuries, is, also, in most cases, the sure one. Deaf-mutes readily accept religious truths offered to their yet unprejudiced belief. We have no satisfactory evidence that any of them, even after considerable mental culture, have, in their own vague seekings for the causes of things and the future destiny of man, attain unaided the truth. If we leave them uninstructed on such points till the latter part of an ordinary course of instruction, not a few may be taken from our care before that important part of education is reached; and those who remain to the end will be in danger of picking up, by reading and conversation, false and absurd notions, which it may be difficult afterward to eradicate.

Another cogent consideration, in favor of the early inculcation of religious truth, is found in its influence on the development of character. We do not consider religion as merely some higher science, to be reserved to the closing years of education—the capital which is to crown the column. On the contrary, we hold to the good old belief, that children should be brought up in the nurture and admonition of the Lord: that the precept of Moses is still applicable: "Command your children to observe to do all the words of this law; for it is not a vain thing for you, because it is your life."* We can not leave our children ignorant of the observances of public and private worship, and would not if we could. And we must either leave them to suppose that they are a mere recreation or a "play," or we must teach them that these observances have a deep and solemn significance.

History teaches us that the religion of a nation influences the formation and development of the national character. The nations of Europe and America are not Christian because they are the most enlightened races of mankind, but they are the most enlightened because they are Christian. As with a race so with an individual. A pure and elevated religious faith, either originally accepted through the evidence of miracles, and from its own excellency, or impressed by parental teaching in infancy, tends to purify and elevate the individual as well as the national character. When the Divine law is made the rule of conscience, the tone of private and public morals is higher, and there are stronger safeguards against secret transgressions than when the formation of the moral character is left to the natural development of a happy constitution of the moral sentiments. May the time come when no child in the world, whether deaf-mute or not, shall grow up without knowledge of his Creator.

* Deut. 32: 46, 47.

SINGULAR OBSERVATION OF DR. ITARD.

[This Exhibit consisted of an editorial under the above heading, published in the *American Annals of the Deaf* for January, 1856, pp. 104-110.]

Our friend, Mr. Burnet, sends us a passage, which he says he takes from a note by Dr. Itard, to the chapter of Hoffbauer's *Médecine Légale* (Medical Jurisprudence), relating to the deaf and dumb, (Chambeyron's translation, Paris: 1827, p. 210). The extract, translated, is as follows, with Mr. Burnet's note annexed:

"It is certain that whenever we observe a deaf-mute—one who is educated I mean—by himself, and absorbed in meditation, or transported by a violent passion of any kind, we do not see him bring into use his natural language; whether it be that his meditations are never coherent or profound, or whether that this language, formed of unwieldy and complicate movements, cannot adapt itself to the rapid and wandering course of our solitary thoughts. But there is, related to this, another not less remarkable phenomenon, which has never before been brought to notice. In acute disorders, in inflammation of the brain, for example, to which the deaf and dumb are particularly liable, the convulsions, the drowsiness, the complete suspension of the intellectual functions supervene as in ordinary cases, but the most common symptom, that of delirium, does not appear. Only sometimes it is indicated by some attempts which the patient makes to get up, and by picking at the bed-clothing a little (*un peu de carphologie*), but never by any of those pantomimic signs, which might naturally be looked for, in place of the talkativeness which attends delirium in disorders of this nature. There is in this case, a delirium of movements, with no evidence of delirium of thought. I would adduce on this point, an important parallel instance, namely, that the same may be observed in infancy, the age when reflection is exercised in only a very superficial manner," *etc.*

"MR. EDITOR: I send you the foregoing *citation textuelle*, because if the fact is correctly stated (and Itard had uncommon opportunities for an observation of that kind), it is certainly a curious and pregnant one. I have not time to translate the passage for you. You can easily do it, or get it done. Please ascertain whether the experience of your physicians and nurses confirms the observations of Itard. *I* should be disposed to account for the fact (if it be one) on Bébian's theory, that the deaf and dumb do not think either in signs or words, but only in images and ideas; hence, when their minds wander, the wandering is internal only, there is no propensity to manifest it by outward loquacity, as in the case of those who think in words or other signs, rather than in naked ideas. But I have not time to enlarge, or even to follow out the train of thought here suggested.

"Yours truly,

"J. R. BURNET."

In pursuance of Mr. Burnet's suggestion, we have made inquiry of the Principal of the American Asylum, and also of the Matron, whose long experience and good judgment entitle her testimony in such a matter to the highest confidence; and we have thus far found nothing whatever, from them or from any other quarter, to confirm the observation of Dr. Itard. The Matron, who has always had the oversight of the sick in the institution, gives it, in unqualified terms, as the result of her experience, that the deaf and dumb are as liable to delirium in acute disease as other people are, and that their mental wanderings when so affected, are expressed by signs much in the same way as in ordinary cases by speech. She mentions instances in which the patients talked incessantly by signs, addressing either the unreal beings present to their imagination, or soliloquizing or talking to those around them, in relation to the chimeras conjured up by their disordered fancy.

Mr. Turner's observations coincide in general with those of the Matron. He mentions, moreover, the case of a pupil of the Asylum, who while apparently in ordinary health, became mentally deranged; and the first notice had of it was that he was observed making signs to himself, or rather addressing the imaginary beings by which he was beset.

We believe it is no more uncommon for the deaf and dumb to talk in their dreams during sleep than for speaking persons to do the same. We know also, that they do sometimes in their solitary musings, let out their thoughts in signs. We doubt not they may be observed to do so, not less often than speaking persons may be overheard giving utterance to their private meditations; for many speaking persons never do this, and those who do are not usually overheard by others. That we do not see the deaf and dumb using the sign language in their meditations is certainly a slender reason on which to hang an important inference.

There is in the case of Julia Brace, the girl in the American Asylum who is deaf, dumb, and blind, a fact of importance in its bearing on this subject. Her means of communication with others are signs, substantially such as are used by the deaf and dumb around her; and though communication with her is limited, compared with that of the deaf and dumb with each other, yet it can be carried on to an extent truly surprising. When made *to* her, the signs are of course addressed to her sense of feeling. The fact we now refer to, is that she is often observed making signs to herself, when any subject of exciting interest to her occupies her mind. It may be said indeed, that as she cannot see, it is the same to her whether persons are present or absent; the signs she makes being addressed to the sight of others. It is not, however, exactly so; for when wishing to converse with others, she comes near and in contact with them, so as to be in a condition to receive a response. She may not unfrequently be observed wrapped in reverie, manifestly unconscious of the presence of any one with her, the workings of her face showing that something is passing in her mind; and it will not be long perhaps, before her signs will reveal to the observer what it is which interests her;—it may be some event, trivial or important, recently transpired or soon anticipated, of which she has been informed, concerning some one within the circle of her acquaintance, which of course does not extend much beyond those connected with the institution—or it may be, though not often so, that some trespass, real or imaginary, upon her rights of property or person, or something she has noticed which she deems an outrage upon established propriety, has roused her indignation—or, not unfrequently, it is some desired or newly possessed article of dress or ornament which absorbs her thought, as such things do the thoughts of wiser people. The fact may be taken as beyond question, that it is her habit to talk much in this way to herself, with no idea of communicating her thoughts to others.

In the Thirty-eighth Report of the American Asylum, among the specimens of compositions appended to the Report is one by a young man who is yet a pupil of the Asylum, entitled "About my Delirium," of so much interest in this connection that we can hardly do better than to copy it entire. It shows, at least, that the imaginations of the deaf and dumb may be as active as any person's in the delirium of a fever. It seems to us somewhat remarkable that the young man should after his recovery be able to give so full and connected an account of his fancies, but that the relation is genuine there can be no room for doubt. Much more than this he actually wrote, and much more still he recollected and could relate, as he said. What is still more to the point, he talked much by signs in his delirium, and his talk as remembered by those who were with him agreed well with his after recollections as thus detailed by himself. His account of it is as follows:

ABOUT MY DELIRIUM.

"When I was sick with lung-fever, last November, I was involved in darkness, and became delirious. I had many dreams. I am going to tell you some of them. One day, in the afternoon, I was told that there was a serious mob in the city of Hartford. I feared that the men would kill all the pupils in the American Asylum. I thought that I had been placed in the hospital, southwest of the State House, on the Little River, but I did not like it, because I was not happy to hear of the mob. While I slept in the bed I was told that the mob came very near me and they broke the wall.

"Many men from Wethersfield came to me and told me that they would save me from danger of being killed by the mob. They wished me to be placed in Wethersfield, but they could not do so because many men surrounded the house. While they were saying this to me I wished to be saved from danger. I could not save myself. But I believed that God would preserve me from danger. I thought about my sins, and knew that I had done wickedly, and confessed it to God, for I had done wrong. I asked God to forgive me, and I soon was peaceful, and gave myself to Him, and believed that he alone could save me. I was happy, and expected that he would save me. At last the mob was victorious over Hartford, and treated the people cruelly. Soon I besought God to help me to escape from danger to Wethersfield, and I began to be moved over the mob towards Wethersfield. When they saw me moving they intended to fire at me. Soon, when I saw that a man was about to fire at me, I shut my eyes and knew that I was going to die, but I heard a noise of firing, and I was saved, and I felt very thankful to God, for he had preserved me. Immediately I was brought to the house, and awoke. Soon I slept again, and dreamed that I was again moved towards Wethersfield, but the men were going to fire at me. I was not afraid that I would be killed, because I believed that God would preserve me. And the men were much amazed that I was not killed. They fired at me, but the same kind Providence protected me. Then they drove several mad dogs to me, and, if they should bite me, I would die of hydrophobia. At the time one of my hands was touched by the dogs. I knew that I should not live long. Then I was conveyed to the house again. I could not escape to Wethersfield, and it was quite tedious to stay in the house. I was not quiet to sleep till the night came. Before the midnight the men brought a locomotive to the house, and carried it away to another place. While the locomotive was carrying it on the ground I saw the floor began to be torn, and I thought I would be destroyed, and looked at the floor very carefully, but I found that I would not be destroyed. Then I slept again, but I heard a noise of running of the house. I looked round, and thought about the mob. Soon the house was placed by a hill. Then they brought many ants and threw them down upon the roof and the ants fell down upon me. So I did not like them.

"At that time I saw many small animals in the house. While I looked round, I saw several rabbits and their young ones. The young ones were as small as young mice. I was much pleased at seeing them. Soon I saw several other animals coming out of the fire place, they looked like quails. The quails stepped in a row. Some of them fell into a bottle. Their friends were sorry and mourned for them. One of them was large and came up to the top of the bottle and it stretched forth its head into the bottle and brought several quails out of the bottle. When it had taken them out of the bottle, it shouted for joy. It again brought several others out, but the neck of one of them in the bottle was cut off. It cried with a loud voice for pain, and I heard it. So I pitied it for its distress. All the quails went away. Soon I heard a roaring of an animal, and I looked under the bed in which A. T. from Billerica, Mass., slept. Soon I saw a cat's head which was hanged in a blanket. I saw its head was much injured. And I saw that several other animals were in the similar fate of the cat. Soon I saw a blue animal under the bed of A. T. and I looked under the bed, and saw the blue animal moving. It was as large as a cat, but it was stronger than the cat. Soon it came under my bed and proceeded into a small bed to catch some other animals. Some time after it crawled up T's bed very silently to suck his blood. I told him that the blue animal had come into his bed to suck his blood, but he did not believe me. I looked at it very interestingly. Soon it came out upon the blanket. Then I fixed my eyes at it and it was vexed and began to open its mouth in pretty large width. I bade it to shut its mouth, but it was more angry and opened its mouth wider and wider, and soon its mouth was torn. This animal looked like a lizard, but it had more legs than a lizard. Its skin looked like a bat's.

"After this I saw several black and red animals in the ventilator of the hospital, looking at me. When I moved myself in my bed, they were afraid and hid themselves. Some of them were red and looked like foxes, and some others were black. Soon I saw something in the clock swinging. I found it was a very little person, but it was made of wood, and held a pail in each hand.

"Soon I dreamed another dream and I opened my eyes and looked up and saw that the ceiling began to be broken, and the water was turned into ice and I saw there a horse on the ice moving over me. So I thought that the horse was a mad quadruped. I saw it beginning to fall down upon me. At the same time I asked the boys who watched with me that I might spring from the bed, but they refused to let me rise from the bed. Soon it disappeared and I slept again. At length I was better, but I talked with none, except Miss F. and Mrs. W. the matron of the Asylum a little. Soon I began to be hungry and at last I became as well as I had been before. And now I am very grateful to God for healing me.

"G. C."

Possibly the experience of others connected with other institutions might produce some peculiar cases as concerns this matter. How it may have happened that Dr. Itard should be quite mistaken in the facts, if he was so, we shall not attempt to explain. We believe, however, that his attainments in a knowledge of the sign language were exceedingly limited.

EXHIBIT TO QUERIES 21,858-'59-'60.

DEAF-MUTES OF CHILMARK.

[This Exhibit consisted of three genealogical charts, showing the descent of the Chilmark Deaf-Mutes, (1) from Samuel Tilton, (2) from Governor Mayhew, (3) from James Skiff.

These charts are reproduced in a Postscript under the head of Ancestry of the Deaf. The information concerning the ancestry of the deaf of Chilmark (Martha's Vineyard, Mass.), was obtained chiefly through the researches of the late Hon. Richard L. Pease, the genealogist of the island. Shortly before his death Mr. Pease expressed the opinion that Mr. Bell's statement in Query 21,859, that "there was an aristocratical class in Martha's Vineyard," was incorrect.]

THE LOVEJOY FAMILY.

(Explanation of the Graphical Chart.)*

The chart shows the descent from John Lovejoy of twenty-seven congenital deaf-mutes, all bearing the surname Lovejoy, except those marked "Lord," "Berry," and "Jellison."

These deaf-mutes group themselves into three families only remotely connected through the Lovejoy blood.

I. CONCORD BRANCH.—In the Lovejoy family of Concord, New Hampshire, there were four deaf-mutes, two brothers and two sisters. The ancestry on the mother's side is unknown.† The only member of this family who seems to have married was a hearing brother of the deaf-mutes (who was at one time insane). He married his father's sister's daughter, by whom he had four children. The oldest was a deaf-mute. She was one of the early pupils of the Illinois Institution. She married a deaf-mute but had no offspring. She died of consumption.

The deaf-mutes in this branch of the family have left no descendants.

II. SEBEC BRANCH.—In the Lovejoy family of Sebec, Maine, two out of eleven children were born deaf. Six of the children died young: two of them (one a deaf-mute) from accidental causes, another from scrofula.

There was no deafness in the ancestry so far as has been ascertained, but the mother traces up by two lines of ancestors to persons who are also ancestors of deaf-mutes in Chilmark, Martha's Vineyard, a township in Massachusetts, remarkable for the number of deaf-mutes that have been born in it. In 1880 one person in every twenty-five of the population was a deaf-mute.

The deaf tendency in the mother's family is well marked. She had a sister who had five deaf and dumb children, and another who had deaf grandchildren. She also had a cousin who had seven deaf and dumb children, another who had two, and a third who had three. (See Newcomb diagram on Lovejoy chart.)

Her surviving deaf-mute child (see Lovejoy chart) married a hearing woman (not a relative) who was slightly insane, and is said to have had insane relatives. They had four children, three of them deaf-mutes. The hearing daughter married and had one child (a son). This son married and has one son, now a baby in arms.

One of the deaf-mutes (a daughter) married a deaf-mute, but had no offspring. She died of consumption.

The other deaf-mutes are unmarried.

III. SIDNEY BRANCH.—In the Lovejoy family of Sidney, Maine, deaf-mutes have appeared for five successive generations in increasing numbers and the younger deaf-mutes are marrying deaf-mutes. All these deaf-mutes are believed to have been born deaf.

First Generation.—The first deaf-mute was the sixth child in a family of sixteen children; his father was the sixth child in a family of eleven; and his mother was one of the eldest of a family of twenty-five children (by two marriages of their father).

The deaf-mute married a hearing woman of the surname "Smith" (not a relative), by whom he had seven children. One, the fifth, was a deaf-mute.

Second Generation.—This deaf-mute son married twice.

His first wife (a hearing woman) was a Smith (probably a distant relative of the mother, but this does not certainly appear). By her he had three children, the eldest a deaf-mute.

By his second wife (a hearing woman, not a relative) he had seven children, three of them deaf-mutes. One of the hearing children was born deaf in one ear, but this did not make him a deaf-mute, nor would he be even called deaf, for he hears well with the other ear.

The eldest daughter of the first deaf-mute in the Sidney Branch had two deaf-mute children (both illegitimate); one, a male living 1888, unmarried; the other a female of the surname Lord. She is deceased.

Returning to the descendants of the second deaf-mute:

Third Generation.—Two of the four deaf-mutes in his family married. The oldest, a son, married a hearing woman (not a relative), by whom he had eight children, three of them deaf-mutes. [So far there had been no intermarriages with deaf-mutes or with near relatives. The deafness had persisted in the family through four successive generations in spite of the introduction of fresh blood at each marriage. This fact shows how strong sometimes may be the hereditary character of the defect.]

Another child of the second deaf-mute (a deaf-mute daughter) married a congenital deaf-mute of the surname Berry, who has a brother and other relatives deaf and dumb.

They have had eight children, three of them deaf-mutes. At the present time, 1888, these children are very young. I enclose a graphical chart showing some of the consanguineous marriages in the father's family. [See Berry Group on Lovejoy chart.]

Another child of the second deaf-mute (the hearing son who was born deaf in one ear) married a congenital deaf-mute of the surname "Marr," who had two brothers and one sister deaf and dumb. They have had three children (one a deaf-mute). The youngest child is now (1888) a baby in arms.

Fourth Generation.—Two of the deaf-mutes of the fourth generation have married.

The first married a congenital deaf-mute of the surname "Jellison," who has a deaf-mute brother and sister; and the sister has a son who is deaf and dumb. Of the five children of this marriage two are deaf-mutes. The children are very young—the youngest a baby in arms (1888).

The other deaf-mute of the fourth generation who married, married a hearing man (not a relative).

They have three children (all hearing) who are now (1888) very young.

Fifth Generation.—The "Jellison" children constitute the fifth generation of deaf-mutes in the Sidney Branch of the Lovejoy family.

GENERAL REMARKS.

The Lovejoys of the New England States all appear to be descendants of John Lovejoy, one of the early settlers of Andover, Massachusetts. He came from England and settled in Andover before the year 1640. He was a farmer. He had twelve children, seven sons and five daughters. The descendants are very numerous. I have collected records of several hundreds of them. I am indebted for much of my material to the researches of Mrs. A. C. Pratt, of Chelsea, Mass., who is preparing a Lovejoy genealogy for the use of the family.

Longevity seems to have been a characteristic of the earlier members of the family, several living to be over 90 years of age. There was great mortality among the young children of the third generation from "throat distemper," some families being almost wholly swept away.

The descendants spread from Andover as a centre and settled in the neighboring towns and States, and many of them in the later generations emigrated to the West. They occupy all sorts of positions in society. Some are found among the wealthy and

* The Graphical Chart and Explanation have been revised since they were presented to the Royal Commission.

† It has been ascertained that the parents of this family were first cousins; and also, that the mother had a brother who was insane.

cultivated classes, others occupy very humble stations in life. Very many of them are found among the best and most respected citizens of the Republic.

Allow me to draw attention to some of the peculiarities found in the Lovejoy family which may perhaps have some bearing upon the deafness in the family.

Blindness.—The eldest brother of the first deaf-mute in the Sidney Branch (see chart) became blind in middle life, and several of the other brothers and sisters had failing eye-sight as they advanced in years. The father of the deaf-mute also became blind in middle life, and his mother (grandmother of the deaf-mute) was blind at the time of her death, which took place in her 102d year.

The deaf-mute himself and most of his descendants enjoyed good eye-sight, but blindness has appeared among the descendants of his blind brother. One of the children was blind, two grandsons lost their sight in middle life from cataract. One had his vision restored by an operation; a daughter of this man has failing eye-sight (from what cause I do not yet know). Thus blindness, or a tendency to blindness, has appeared in this branch of the family for six successive generations* (see chart). A niece of the first deaf-mute (the daughter of one of his younger sisters) has been totally blind for more than thirteen years; and there are other instances reported of persons belonging to this family who have defective sight.

In this connection it may be interesting to note that the deaf-mute granddaughter of the first deaf-mute, surnamed "Lord" (see chart), had eyes of different color. One eye was dark and the other blue. One of her illegitimate children was born blind, or had undeveloped eyes. My informants state that "the child was born without eyes at all"—that there were no eye-balls in the sockets; but these same authorities assert that the child was deaf and dumb, a fact that could not have been definitely ascertained as the child died in early infancy.

Insanity and Genius.—The father of the first deaf-mute in the Sidney Branch was a man of energy and marked mental abilities. He worked himself up to a position of eminence and acquired considerable property. Indeed, he was quite a wealthy man. He was in every way a prominent man in his section of the country, "Justice of the Peace" and "Representative to The General Court." He was known far and wide as "Squire Lovejoy." In advanced years, after blindness came upon him, he became insane; Probate records show that the selectmen of the town where he resided declared him to be *non compos* and incapable of taking care of his property, and that at the request of his children the Judge appointed a guardian for him. They also show that he afterwards recovered and that the guardianship was removed.

His brother, the ancestor of the Sebec Branch, does not seem to have developed any special defect, but cases of insanity have appeared among his descendants, taking a suicidal form (see chart). Among the descendants of another brother (probably the only other who lived to adult life) men of great mental calibre have appeared—men even of genius. Two talented brothers who have made their mark in the history of their country were grandchildren. Their father was insane in his latter years.

Intemperance.—The father of the first deaf-mute in the Sidney Branch was born in December, 1731. Shortly afterwards the following entries relating to his father (grandfather of the deaf-mute) were made in the records of the church of which he had been a member:

"1732, Jan. 4. At a church meeting * * * Lovejoy being convicted before the church by sufficient testimony of the sins of speaking falsely and of being disguised with drink, thereupon it was voted: 1st. That in consideration of his having been so irregular in conversation since he had made an open and public confession of the very same sins (for name & kind) of which he is now convicted, therefore the accepting a second confession from him, should be deferred until there was some good ground to think that he has reformed his manner of life. And, 2d. That it was their desire that he should be admonished in public for his above-named scandals and be debarred from church privileges until there should be a reformation of his manners; and also, that they expected and desired that he would be present at the time of his public admonition. All which the Pastor (before or in the presence of the church) informed him of, as also, showed him the reasonableness of what they had done, and moreover, told him that if he refused to give his attendance at the time of his public admonition, viz: the next Sabbath after sermon in the afternoon, it would be construed as a further breach of covenant, inasmuch as he had expressly obliged himself when he owned the covt. to submit to the laws of Christ's Kingdom as they are administered among his people. Note.—It was plain and obvious to the whole church that the person above named made no discovery at all of repentance but the contrary."

"1732, Jan. 9. * * * Lovejoy's admonition declared and published, and he was pronounced debarred from church privileges till he should reform his life according to the aforesaid votes.—The sd. person not present."

The church records afford no evidence of any subsequent reformation. On the contrary, they show that all his children born after this date were baptized "on their mother's account."

Of his ten children, five died young. Of the youngest child I know nothing save the fact of his birth. He probably also died young. The other children, three sons and one daughter, lived to adult life and were married. Of the daughter (Phebe) I know little; she may have been the Phebe who married an Abbott and had a blind son, but of this I cannot be sure. The three sons turned out well and lived to advanced years. They were all men of marked ability and acquired property by their own energy. The only one who seems to have developed a defect in his own person was the one born December, 1731 (the father of the deaf-mute). As has already been stated he became blind in middle life, and afterwards temporarily insane; and blindness and deafness have appeared in a hereditary form among his descendants. It may, perhaps, be worthy of notice that his birth occurred at a period between the date of "the open and public confession" of his father and the date of the entry in the church record quoted above. The father of the deaf-mute in his best days was a convivial man, but not a drunkard. Like most men of his time he enjoyed his glass, and he bought his liquor by the barrel. The following anecdote of him is preserved among his descendants: When his eyes began to fail him his physician warned him that he must abstain from stimulants or lose his sight. His resolution was soon taken. Pouring out a glass of his favorite beverage, he held it up to the light and surveyed it fondly for a few moments. He then tossed it off, to the toast of "Farewell Eyes." Whatever may be the truth of this story he became blind, and the habit of drinking grew upon him until finally he became a drunkard. He died very suddenly at an advanced age.

How far the habit of intemperance has been handed down in the family I do not know.

ALEXANDER GRAHAM BELL.

* In my original communication to the Royal Commission it was stated that there was a gap in the succession at the fourth generation, but on consulting my notes I find there was no gap.

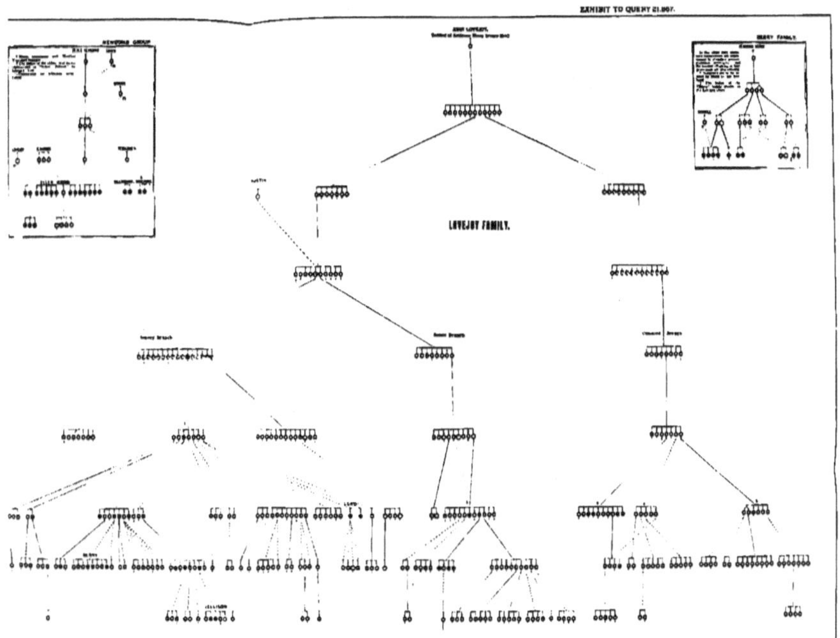
EXHIBIT TO QUERY 21,907.
LOVEJOY FAMILY.

VISIBLE SPEECH AT THE BELLEVILLE CONVENTION.

[This Exhibit consisted of the following address concerning Visible Speech, by Alexander Graham Bell, delivered before the Eighth Convention of American Instructors of the Deaf at Belleville, Ontario, Canada, July 17, 1874. (See proceedings of that Convention, published in 1876, by the Ontario Institution, pp. 103-109.)]

Prof. A. G. Bell said:

MR. PRESIDENT, LADIES AND GENTLEMEN: At this late hour I shall not seek to tire you with any more papers. If you will grant me your patience for a little while—and I promise you that it *will* be for a little while—I should prefer to explain to you at once what these mysterious looking characters mean (pointing to some diagrams). I should like to show you how simple they are, and to illustrate to you the mode of using them in the instruction of the deaf.

With the President's leave I shall therefore lay aside my paper. I feel sure you do not want to hear me talk *about* visible speech, but would prefer to see and understand the thing itself.

I see before me teachers gathered together from all parts of America, and I am glad that I am called upon to introduce this subject to your notice *here*. For Canada is the adopted country of the inventor of visible speech, and he has made his home in this very Province of Ontario.

It is gratifying to Prof. Melville Bell to know that his system of visible speech, the fruit of over twenty years of toil, is at last forcing its way into public notice. As an instrument of philological research it has long been acknowledged to have no equal. In China, in the mission-field, it has commenced a career of usefulness that is already attracting attention. And now its success in the instruction of the deaf recommends it to *your* notice.

Its applicability to general Linguistic Studies—to Universal Stenography—and to Universal Printing for the Blind—will doubtless soon come to be acknowledged too.

I shall commence by asking some of the teachers of visible speech who are present to-day to form themselves into a class, so that I may illustrate the mode of explaining the symbols to deaf children. (See diagram this Volume, Part II, page 147, also diagrams in Postscript relating to Visible Speech, this Volume, Part III.)

A class of five teachers was formed, and Mr. Bell proceeded to explain the symbols by means of gestures and diagrams—occasionally addressing a few words to the audience. He then continued:

I trust that the explanation you have just witnessed will have shown you that the system is neither difficult nor complicated. Indeed it has been proved in the Boston Day School for the Deaf that children of five years of age are not too young to understand the symbols.

The point that I want you specially to observe is, that the symbols are plastic enough to represent any imagined position of the vocal organs. Hence, if we can only discover the exact position of the organs assumed in uttering any sound, we can express it symbolically. By means of the symbols, it is as easy to spell the sound of a cough or a sneeze as of an English word. Or (what is more to our purpose) we can spell the strange noises that our deaf pupils gave utterance to.

Not only can we assign symbols to such sounds, but we can lead the pupil, through their means, first to observe the motions of his own organs, and then to control such motions, even when the organs themselves are concealed from direct observation.

I had a little pupil five and a half years of age (congenitally deaf), upon whom I experimented. The little boy soon caught the idea that I could represent symbolically any movement of the vocal organs he chose to make. This, of course, led him to observe himself closely. One day it suddenly struck him that his mouth was moving while he was eating. He stopped—thought for a moment—and then attracted my attention. In an excited way he made believe to taste something, and then made signs to know whether I could write that. I symbolized the motions of the mouth during the act of tasting. A minute or two afterwards, he stopped in the middle of a drink of water—made me place my hand upon his throat to observe the motion when he swallowed the water—and made signs for me to write. This also was written to his satisfaction. But the next day he was delighted to find a motion that could *not* be symbolized by visible speech. He came running to me and placed my hand upon his left side. He then made pulsatory gestures and wanted me to write.

He wished me to write *the beating of his heart.*

This child, though otherwise unusually bright, was very backward in imitating sounds. I well remember the difficulty I had in teaching him, by imitation, such a simple element as the sound of p. Innumerable feathers had to be blown away from the back of his hand before he uttered the sound correctly. T, d, n, k and g were nevertheless developed at once *from the act of tasting* by the analogies of the symbols.

Mr. Bell here illustrated upon the blackboard the process of development, and the symbols employed. He then requested two of the teachers of visible speech to leave the hall, so that tests might be put to show that sounds of any kind could be obtained from a person, without assistance from the sense of hearing. Members of the audience dictated to Mr. Bell words and sentences in English, French, German, and other languages, to be written on the blackboard in the symbols of visible speech. Ventriloquial noises were made, such as an imitation of the crowing of a cock—the hum of a bee—the sawing and planing of wood—and a peculiar kind of whistle. A few English words incorrectly pronounced were also added. The two teachers, who had been out of earshot while the test sounds were being made, were then recalled, and after studying the symbols upon the board for a moment, reproduced the words and noises as originally uttered.

Mr. Bell then continued:

The experiment we have just made, proves that *a person may be directed by these symbols, how to pronounce sounds that he has never heard.* Deafness need therefore be no bar to the acquirement of articulation, if your teachers will accept assistance from visible speech. I know that there is an idea prevalent, even among teachers of the deaf, that there is some real defect in the vocal organs of deaf-mutes that incapacitates them from acquiring a good pronunciation. We do not sufficiently realize the fact that deaf-mutes are dumb merely because they are deaf. No one would dream of supposing that our mouths were defective because we do not talk Chinese. The simple fact of the matter is, that we have never heard that language. It is the same with the deaf-mute. He lives in a world of hearing people, and has been surrounded from his birth by those who talk; but alas! not one sound has ever entered the closed portals of his ears. With all the organs of speech perfect, he is dumb merely because he does not know what to do. If we would teach the deaf-mute to speak, we must of course appeal to other senses than that of hearing. If it were possible for the unassisted eye to discover the mechanism of speech, deaf-mutes would have learned to articulate of themselves long ago; but it is not the case. Many sounds depend upon the adjustment of organs that are quite concealed from observation. By means of these physiological symbols alone can we reveal to the deaf-mute's eye the concealed mechanism of speech. Since there is in the deaf-mute no other natural defect than that of hearing, it is certainly possible to make him like hearing people in every other respect. The time is coming when the terms "dumb" or "mute" will be considered as a reproach when applied to the deaf. The old dogma, "without hearing, no speech; without speech, no reason," placed deaf-mutes hopelessly among the idiots and insane. We know how recently they have been elevated to the rank of civilized human beings. We see the injustice of former times, but alas! we are too often blind to that of our own. We recognize at once that deaf-mutes can be taught to think without speech, but alas! how few are they who believe that they can be taught to speak without hearing. People outside of the profession look with incredulity at deaf-mutes, and wonder that they can be taught to think in written words as we think in speech. When deaf-mutes are taught to speak, as well as to think, people look upon it as a kind of miracle. The results that are now looked upon with so much wonder, will ere long become every-day facts, and future generations will look back with surprise to the time when civilized nations could allow children that were merely deaf, to grow up with undeveloped minds, and dumb.

Mr. Greenberger wished to know how many characters were employed in visible speech.

Prof A. G. Bell said that was a question much more easily asked than answered. Compound symbols, like those upon the board, could be numbered by hundreds, and they might be increased *ad infinitum*. Yet they were all composed of ten elementary symbols, just as the words in Webster's Unabridged Dictionary were all compounded of twenty-six letters. A deaf child had only to learn the meaning of a few elementary forms, and at once the compound symbols became directions how to place the organs. There were just as many symbols as there were sounds in speech.

Mr. Greenberger meant to ask how many characters were considered as English? How many sounds were taught to a deaf-mute as English elements?

Prof. A. G. Bell said that he considered it sufficient to teach thirty-six sounds as English elements to deaf-mutes, although he was aware that orthoepists distinguished more. He did not consider it necessary, however, to go into nice distinctions with deaf pupils. He thought it was sufficient to teach twenty-three consonants and thirteen vowels.

Mr. D. Greenberger would request Mr. Bell to make another experiment. He wanted to see how he could aid his pupils in producing articulate sounds. He wished to see what could be done with deaf-mutes.

Prof. A. G. Bell did not think rapidity of acquirement was what should be aimed at, but thoroughness. We could not expect to perform miracles. He thought that congenital deaf-mutes might, with the aid of visible speech, learn to articulate in a shorter time than hearing children. Few children talk well under three or four years of practice. Indeed, he had seen many children who talked imperfectly at five years of age. He thought it would be a good plan to give congenital deaf-mutes a couple of years' practice with oral gymnastics before requiring them to use speech as a means of communication with hearing persons. Their articulation would doubtless be benefited by a long previous training of the vocal organs. He did not wish it to be understood that he considered two years' practice as necessary. Experience would show how long training was advisable. With semi-mutes, speech and lip-reading might be used from the outset without danger to the perfection of the articulation, as they had acquired the necessary flexibility of the organs before becoming deaf. He would not commence with congenital deaf-mutes in the way shown by Mr. Greenberger. He would not seek to teach them English sounds merely by imitation. He would try to direct their attention, not to any specific sound, but to the movements occurring in their mouths, in making the noises that all deaf-mutes do spontaneously. He would represent such actions upon the board by means of the physiological symbols, and make them describe the symbols by signs. Deaf children are delighted to see their own noises represented upon the blackboard. It encourages them to make new attempts to vary upon the original sounds. The children emulate each other to see who will produce the greatest variety of noises. They describe the symbols for all these sounds by the means of signs. In process of time they discover that these signs are really descriptive of the physiological actions that accompany the sounds. They are thus led to observe the movements that occur in the larynx, pharynx, or back parts of the mouth, while they are uttering their noises. In this way they are taught to recognize and to control the movements of organs concealed from direct observation. When this stage has been reached, the teacher, instead of following the lead of the pupil, turns round and requires the pupil to follow *his* guidance. He leads him, by the analogies of the symbols, from his own animal noises to the articulation of English sounds. Every stage of the process is pleasant to the child. He is not discouraged by disheartening repetitions. The process may seem slow and round-about, but it is *sure*.

If pupils could learn to articulate by merely watching the mouths of hearing persons, deaf-mutes would have learned to speak long ago by themselves. A good description of the position of the organs required—even if understood by the pupil—is not all that is necessary. You may describe to a deaf child the mechanism of English sounds, by visible speech or otherwise; your pupil may understand you, and yet be utterly unable to perform what you want him to do.

Try it yourselves. Ask any ordinary speaking person to pronounce the sound of k. Don't tell him that it is k. Describe what he is to do with his tongue. Although he performs the action hundreds of times every day of his life *unconsciously*, the chances are that he will make strange facial contortions, roll his tongue about in his mouth, utter certain gurgling noises, and *give the matter up in despair*.

Tell him it is the sound of k, or let him hear you pronounce it, and he will make the correct sound at the first attempt.

Are deaf children less liable to these difficulties than hearing persons? Some may say that they are. At all events, such an experiment as that just mentioned may assure us that a deaf child may be perfectly able to pronounce a sound, may understand perfectly what to do, and yet may not do it, and this not through obstinacy or any fault of his own. Under such circumstances, constant repetition will be useless—nay, it will be worse than useless—it will be disheartening. In such a case it is the teacher that is wrong and not the child. The failure or difficulty shows that the method of teaching is either wrong for that particular child or it is hard for it. Of course the teacher must be guided in the outset by the peculiarities of each pupil. Some will do more by imitation than others. Mr. Bell would use imitation with all, so far as it will go; but he would not force it beyond that point. When a child fails to pronounce a sound by imitating his teacher, after the mechanism of the sound has been explained to him and after a few repetitions, he would have the teacher approach the sound by a new route. He would try to lead him to it by showing him how it differed from some one or more of the noises the child had previously made and analyzed. No failure could be possible upon such a plan. He would try to explain to the

Convention by means of a simile that had been suggested to him by a friend.

Place a man in the middle of a large town with a map of the city in his hand, and require him to find his way to your house. He may see the place upon the map—understand the arrangement of the streets—but he will be utterly unable to go to the place until he first finds the precise spot upon which he stands.

Show him, "Here is the hotel where you are staying, and here is the street where I live," and he at once sees, "First turning to the right—second to the left—and there you are."

Now, it is somewhat similar with visible speech. Take some sound that your pupil can do—whether an English sound or an outlandish noise does not matter—and show him the place of that sound upon the map of the mouth. That is, assign to it some symbol that will show its place. Then show him the symbol for some English sound you want to teach him. He sees—he understands—some practical direction like this, "Keep your tongue in the same position in which it was when you uttered that noise, but contract your lips, and then you will be uttering this English sound."

He has something definite to go by. He has a known starting-point from which he may try to reach the new sound. But may he not fail? Yes, certainly he may; but whatever he does, he will give utterance to *some* sound in place of the right one. It is then the teacher's duty to locate this new sound—to assign to it its proper symbol—and in this way convert his failure into a success. The pupil is surprised and delighted that he has obtained a new sound he did not intend to get. He is encouraged—tries again. Each fresh attempt brings him nearer and nearer to the position desired by the teacher, and at last he gets it.

Consider again the simile of the map. The man alluded to before may leave his hotel and take a wrong turning. Tell him merely that he is wrong, and the chances are he will become confused--lose his way—and get lost in the intricacies of the city. Should he stumble upon his friend's house, it will probably be by accident.

On the other hand, let him take his map in his pocket. See him standing at the street corner. He ascertains the name of the street he is on—consults his map—and obtains at a glance a practical direction that will set him right: "Why, I turned to the left instead of to the right!"

He finds no difficulty in retracing his steps to the hotel, or in finding his friend's house, so long as he carries his map with him.

He may make many errors—he may turn down wrong streets—but, sooner or later, he finds the right place—and a hearty welcome he receives when he gets there.

Visible speech in the hands of an experienced teacher is to the deaf articulator what a good clear map is to the traveller in a strange city, and the more he wanders through the city the better will he come to know it in the end. The difficulties of articulation teaching will be diminished a hundredfold if teachers will accept assistance from visible speech. It comes into conflict with no existing method of instruction. Those who wished to see the practical working of the system would find it in many institutions represented there. He would not take up the time of the Convention in making useless experiments upon deaf-mutes.

MISS WORCESTER'S METHOD.

[This Exhibit consisted of a paper by the late Miss Alice E. Worcester, entitled "How shall our Children be Taught to Read," published in the proceedings of the Third Convention of Articulation Teachers of the Deaf, New York, 1884, pp. 81–91.]

In the simple sense of ability to pronounce at sight the words of our written language (in which, alone, it will be discussed in the present paper), this question is one whose difficulty and importance are both sufficiently attested by its continual agitation in the public schools. To any learner, young or old, English spelling must make not a little hard the first steps in the crooked road to knowledge which lies that way; and no one feels more keenly the embarrassment arising from its irregularities and inconsistencies than does the teacher of speaking, deaf children who realizes afresh daily, what a relief it would be to little, puzzled minds and over-burdened memories, if words were spelled as they are pronounced and pronounced as they are spelled. Every such teacher must grow more and more to feel that a pass-key to reading would be placed in the hands of thousands of ignorant people in America and England, to-day, if the words they speak and understand were represented upon the printed page by characters which stood as the unvarying equivalents of the sounds which produce them. Only about forty-two such sounds are needful for English speech. This short alphabet of phonetics once learned, then a little practice for power of combination given—and, *presto*, the work is done! And with what an "Open Sesame" to all that great treasure of wisdom and beauty which lies behind the gates of print, would the youngest, the poorest, the most meagrely-taught enter upon life! "Visible Speech," with its dream of a wider application as a "Universal Alphabet," was only one of the outgrowths of discussion among scholars of the need of some such boon to the masses as this.

Meanwhile, however, our troublesome spelling remains unchanged; and, while it is what it is, our question can hardly cease to be asked. Nor do such millennial visions of delightful improbabilities give us much help in answering it, unless we may gain from them a light by which to see present possibilities. If, indeed, we agree that the thing which would make an answer simple would be a perfect system of phonetics, we may well look to see what there is in present conditions which might be made, to any extent, to yield a similar result. But what, let us ask first, would be the advantage, to the deaf, of such a system?

It is safe to assume, in general, that the best principles of work with other children are best also for the deaf, however the methods of their application may need to differ. And, in this case, the solution of the hearing child's difficulty would be also that of the deaf child's greatest troubles. For—

1. The aid of lip-reading would be almost incalculable. The words which the deaf child saw pronounced would, in the very action of speech, *write themselves* simultaneously in his mind, if each sound had, as was said, its unvarying representative in a letter or letters. Spoken and written language would thus become, in a fundamental sense, the same; and, while such obstacles would still remain as arise from sounds which look alike in position, and from inability to see all the positions of rapid speech, the great "Hill of Difficulty" would have been removed from the way of lip-reading.

2. The aid of speech would, perhaps, be even greater. Not simply because the deaf articulator would be able to pronounce any and every word at sight, but because words would be written in pronunciation to him, *pronounced to his eye* whenever he saw them; so articulation would be reiterated to his mind at every turn, supplying, in large measure, his present, greatest lack—that mental impression produced by the incessant recurrence of the same sounds, by which, under ordinary circumstances, a child learns to talk. If, then, written words carried with them their own pronunciation, the deaf child would think in speech as far as he thought in words, would read speech, write speech, and every word he met would be an articulation teacher to him.

To whatever extent, therefore, spoken language can be made to write itself and written language to pronounce itself, to the eyes and understanding of the deaf, just so far the same thing has been accomplished which the ideal spelling would do. But can this be done to any extent? and how?

The involuntary answer of my own mind comes always in some words said to me by my father, when, years ago, I stood at his knee, myself a little child just learning to read. I suppose it must have been in spring or early summer that those lessons were given which opened Wonderland to me; for it is always morning in my thought of them, with a glimpse of blue mountains through the open window and a sweet, windy breath from the garden outside to freshen the memory of the kind face into which I looked as I said my alphabet—an alphabet of sounds, by which, in the midst of a busy life, my father found time to teach all his children to read. "What are the four sounds of A?" "What is the sound of B?" "How many sounds has C, and what are they?" So the lesson ran, and following this came the first steps of simple combination. "Give the sound of B; now the first sound of A: now speak them slowly together—now quickly, as you would talk!" A few such lessons, too, I can recall. But the time of which I wish to speak is that which came next; the day when my father opened for me a little, blue-covered story-book. Slowly, one at a time, he telling me at first which vowel sounds to give, I pronounced, and wonderingly recognized, the words which seemed to speak themselves as I put sound with sound. "Say them as you would talk," my father said, "and the book will talk to you." And the book did, indeed! Many little rules, hints as to "silent letters," etc., were given as I went on; but, beyond this point, the only direct help I received was help to use my wits. "Does that sound like any word you ever heard? You have the wrong sound of some letter. Try another, and see if that makes sense. Look at the other words and see what ought to make sense. Think of other words spelled like this, and how they were pronounced. Use your reason and your judgment. *Use your reason and your judgment.*" These were my father's often-repeated words; and, in them and in the sturdy common-sense of his method, lies, I think, a germ of help for this much-vexed question. To do as he did, in gaining for our children all possible help from simple rules, while teaching, still, that all rules are not final; to lead them, from the first, to think and compare and decide; to introduce them at once to that with which they must evidently deal; to use reason always rather than memory; herein lies the secret of the best success. My father's success with his children was rapid and complete.

A few months of such instruction found us, every one, devouring with intense enjoyment, every child's book within reach; and let me say, in passing, that deaf children in a new class taught in a somewhat similar fashion this year, were able at the end of five months to read any ordinarily simple text at sight, with sufficient correctness to be perfectly intelligible; though the rules for pronunciation which enabled them to do so had been learned only in course of the development of their articulation, and at that time they had had no "reading lessons" whatever. Take, for example, this, which I heard a little girl of seven pronouncing to herself as she sat in class, one day, from a Bible-roll upon the wall, whose large, bright picture had, I suppose, attracted her attention. I noted, and here italicize certain words which she mispronounced. The rest were perfectly clear, and neither I nor another teacher, who was asked to listen without seeing the text, failed to understand what was meant by any word.

"Jesus *asked** them where they had *buried*† Lazarus.‡ Then they *brought*§ him to the grave. It was a cave, and a stone was rolled to the door of it. Jesus *said*.‖ 'Take away the stone.' And after the stone was taken away Jesus cried with a loud voice, '*Lazarus* come forth.' As soon as he had spoken these *words*.** *Lazarus* came out alive, with his hands and his feet bound with grave clothes, and his face tied around with a napkin."

Said the teacher of this class, afterward: "I have a bright little sister, seven years old, at home, who has been a year in school. She can read those pages from her primer which she has learned to read in school, but she could not begin to take unfamiliar text and read it at sight like that." Could not this be said of many and many another bright little child after its first year of instruction in a primary school?

For the teaching of articulation and of reading, a strong voice has been heard of late in favor of the "syllable" method for the one, and the "word" method for the other. It seems to me, however, that in behalf of our question it may be urged:

1. That this fact remains: Speech, however taught, is made up of a limited number of sounds, produced by definite positions of the vocal organs. Also words, though each be a unit, are made up of combinations of a limited number of letters, which, in their exact order and number in each instance, the mind must grasp and retain, to enable children later to distinguish between words or reproduce them in writing. If, then, there is any correspondence between the spoken and written representatives of the same idea which will make it possible to learn them, not as two things—separate, arbitrary, and distinct, to be connected only by an especial act of memory in each case—but as one, through some essential likeness, time is saved when time is short and very precious, and reason assists memory where the load upon memory at the least is very great.

2. Whether, consciously or not, these positions of the vocal organs must be taken, and with reasonable accuracy, to produce even intelligible speech. The debt our own speech owes to our continual hearing of the same sounds, is demonstrated not only by the speed with which speech becomes indistinct or imperfect when hearing is destroyed, but also, most significantly, by the effect of hearing another language for any length of time to the total exclusion of our own. If, therefore, the printed words he sees can be made to *speak* to the deaf child by emphasizing continually, to his mind, essential things in his pronunciation of them, we have a help for the preservation and distinctness of his speech, which we cannot lightly pass over in considering how reading is to be made of most avail.

3. The aid to lip-reading from an established habit of connecting positions with spellings, instinctively, is also to be considered and is not less important. But I only pause to urge that—

* Pronounced ask-ed.
† " bur-ied.
‡ " Lazar-us.
§ " sounding the *g*.
‖ " as if rhyming with *laid*.
** " " " " " *cords*.

4. In point of fact, elementary sounds, even when taught only in combination, are made distinct to the pupil's apprehension to a considerable extent, by the necessity, in correcting articulation, of emphasizing the point in fault; and, in teaching it, of bringing out the point to be attained. Such knowledge of them, therefore, as is needful for the intelligent study of their representatives in words, may be given, at the same time, with very slight addition to the work, and without dwelling more upon them in direct articulation-drill than would otherwise be thought desirable.

Among those who teach by sound, two methods of representation are in common use; the symbols of "Visible Speech" and the diacritical marks of the dictionary.

The cause of articulation for the deaf, in this country, owes much to Visible Speech, both from the study of vocal physiology to which it has led, and from the fact that it has offered, through its students, almost the only source of supply for the recent and urgent demand for articulation teachers. I am glad to express here my great personal obligation to it; and it has been with reluctance that I have gradually come to the belief (after using Visible Speech six years, with a large number of classes, and with an earnest purpose to gain from it every advantage for the children), that the use of symbols, with the classes of our institutions, is a hindrance rather than a help at every point. A hindrance, first, to lip-reading; not, as has so often been urged against it, because of the time it takes from the lip-reading of words as ordinarily spelled, by being taught first, but for the reason, not enough considered and far more vital, that it leads the pupil to look only for unvarying representatives of the positions he sees, and to expect, also, to find words spelled by a number of letters corresponding to their number of sounds, bringing a long period of confusion, later, among that multitude of spellings amidst which all his previous ideas must be readjusted. To attain freedom in speech-reading he must be trained, from the first, to consider different spellings of the same sound; he needs to see "silent" letters, and to know that it may be a combination of a number of letters, as well as a single letter, which represents a given sound.

As to speech, no little, undeveloped deaf child ever learned to talk by taking of himself, from his understanding of them, the positions indicated by such symbols. He must be shown how to take them, must be taught, in short, to imitate, as much when they are used as under any other circumstances. They never create speech, what actually happens is the exact reverse of this; their correspondence is explained to positions taken through power thus *already acquired* in another way, or to actions which are involuntary. Moreover, only the simplest, most evident things about such symbols can be explained to a little child at all. At first, and for a long time, they remain, practically, arbitrary signs to him. Better, then, that letters, with which sounds thus learned can be just as easily associated, and which will be in daily use throughout all the years of his growing intelligence, should be taught first. If there is value to him in physiological symbols, let it be secured by teaching them when he has such mental development that they can be understood.

Diacritical marks are open to the same objection as Visible Speech, while they have not the merit of real, symbolic value. They are purely arbitrary; they are not consistent: and the effort to construct from them any satisfactory representation of such a table of sounds as is necessary for English speech, is indeed a discouraging one. Webster counts eighteen vowel sounds. Ten of these are to be represented by the two marks (—) and (◡) over five letters. The same marks stands for a different sound in every instance, though they are consistent in indicating, in each case, the length of the vowel marked. Let us, then, go on a little. *A* and *e*, marked (*â*, *ê*), are to be pronounced respectively as in *air* and *there*. But the same mark over *u* (*û*) gives the sound heard in *urge* and over *o* (*ô*) the sound of "broad *a*," says Webster; while "broad *a*" is marked (*a*), and to give the *û* sound to *er* and *ir* they must be written (*ẽr* and *ĩr*), while the two dots which turn (*a*) to *ar*, turn (*u* and *o*) to *oo*. Take a much simpler matter of consonants. Voice added to the sound of *s* gives that of *z*, and to *th* the sound of "hard" *th*. But the addition of voice to *s* is to be indicated by a line below that letter (*s*), while the same addition to *th* is written with a line through it. Not exactly logical or clear, it seems to me, to the mind of a little child whose "reason and judgment" are to be used!

The reason urged in behalf of using these marks in articulation teaching is, of course, that the pupil will thus be prepared to use a dictionary. But, some time must surely elapse before a deaf child, or any other child, just in school, will obtain much practical help from a dictionary. Meanwhile, apart from the teacher and the school-room, he sees symbols and marks nowhere. The proportion of the words, too, which he will ever look up in a dictionary and deliberately fix in his memory, to those which will thrust themselves upon his notice at every turn—upon the printed page, in his home letters, on the very signs that line the streets—is as one to a million! To give a child, who comes to the dictionary as the rest of us do, with sounds already made to be marked, a key to the "key," which will enable him to use it easily is, in my own experience, not a difficult matter. But, for daily use, the mischievous thing about them both is this: that marks and symbols tend directly to lead the mind away from the habit of reasoning and discrimination. Not finding them except as they are written for him, the average pupil waits to *have* them written and expects to do little or nothing by himself except to commit to memory. With the habit of using them, too, any but the most self-denying of teachers will continually dash them down to mark the pronunciation of new words, rather than to take the precious time from other work to make the pupil reason out the application of rules. The difference in value between that which is memorized simply and that which the mind makes its own by understanding, need hardly be discussed.

And the worst of it is, we do a long work, only to undo it! We spend months in teaching children that certain sounds have certain symbols, or we mark one letter "long" and another "short" only to find in the end that we *must*, if children are ever to be able to pronounce a new word for themselves, give them reasons; teach them rules and different spellings; lead them to think, to judge by comparison and to decide. If, then, this must be done at last, why not at first? We waste time always too short; we confuse our pupils by obliging them to go through one process only to change to another; we retard progress by necessitating a constant, mental translation, if we do anything else.

In venturing to ask, for a few moments, your kindly consideration of a simple plan used the past two years with my own classes, it is not at all because I can claim it to be a sufficient answer to all these hard questions, or even to be a perfected system. The charts referred to below, and given in full in an appendix to this paper, present the result of two years' practical experiments. But they have been brought to this form through many changes suggested by the daily experience of the school-room; which, while confirming the principles they seek to embody, has constantly opened new possibilities of application. Other changes in details of representation are doubtless still to be made I only offer them here as a suggestion of work in the direction in which, more and more, I seem to see the light.

Considering that written language, as it meets our children in daily life, comes only in the shape of letters and combinations of letters, my effort has been to see how far it might be possible to lay aside all marks and symbols, and to deal directly with the problem in the form under which it presents itself. It does, indeed, seem essential to have some standard representative for each English sound. It is from this need, of course, that marks and symbols have arisen.

1. As far, then, as I have been able to discover any unfailing letter or spelling which gives one of these sounds, I have used it for the foundation of work upon each These stand first in each group upon the chart. (See Appendix.) Where not even one invariable representative has been found for a given sound, one of those most common is meant to stand in this place. But next, and more needful perhaps, has been the attempt—

2. To make letters *mark themselves* for pronunciation to the greatest possible extent by their position in words and their connection with other letters. Take, for example, the sound of long *a*. The simplest and most nearly invariable rule for its pronunciation is that for monosyllables ending in "silent *e*." When this vowel sound is taught as an element, therefore, it is first represented to the pupil in his way: *—a —e*. (See Appendix, Vowel Chart.) Work upon combination at once fills those blanks with consonant letters in endless variety,—

—a —e

c k
—a —e

pl t
—a —e

f t
—a —e

n m
—a —e

etc.

And the quick teaching of the child's sight, which shows him that the relative position and connection of the *—a —e* remain unaltered, whatever the letters may be which fill the other places or, however they may be changed, makes its pronunciation a matter of established fact to him very speedily.

Again, *a*, in a similar position without the *e*, has always its short sound. Representing this element, then, by the position of the letter which produces it, *—a—*, the child fills the blanks as before,—

—a—

c t
—a—

m n
—a—

th t
—a—

etc.

seeing, more and more clearly that the unchanging *a* is left always in a position which will, in future, carry its own pronunciation with it to him. So (see Appendix) with *i* and *y*. So (though with more exceptions in the case of the long sound) with *o*. The child will see these letters, in these relative positions, all his life where he will see neither marks nor symbols. He has no small advantage, then, in being independent of such helps. For, to just such an extent as these rules apply, the pronunciation of written language becomes not a matter of memory but of sight. It is true, indeed, that there is scarcely a rule for English spelling that is not "proved by its exceptions," many or few! But, under this method of teaching, the work of memory is reduced to its minimum. A child, who *knows* that, in general, the position of certain letters in words tells him their pronunciation, has only to remember the exceptions to his rules—as very different, and much lighter matter.

I cannot speak too strongly upon this point. Would that we had a spelling which made infallible rules possible! But as it is, how often does the teacher, baffled by exceptions to the simplest rules he can frame, give up the effort altogether; and fail even to gain for his pupils the benefit of that "half loaf" of the proverb! Because we cannot say, of all words similarly spelled, that they are pronounced alike, shall we teach the pronunciation of each separately, with no reference to the rest,—leaving thus a mere confusion of likenesses and differences? Or shall we clearly separate from the mass, that portion, often very large and never despicable, of which we can say to our pupils: "Words spelled in this way follow a general rule; knowing that, you need only to learn these, among them, which must be remembered as exceptions." In short, shall we anywhere teach fifty separate words where we need teach only a dozen, or a dozen where we need teach but one? "It is forgotten," says Prof. Bonamy Price in a recent article on Education, "that memory is far severer for the brain than the exercise of intelligence, and thus the thinking power is struck with paralysis."

Of another point I wish to speak here: The fact that this direction of thought at once leads the child to consider "silent letters," so-called, and their real value in words. To return to the example already used; in—*a*—*e* the *e* ceases to be a superfluity and becomes a component part of the vowel, avoiding a puzzle of lip-reading which always arises under other methods of teaching. A child sees, we will say, the word *same* spoken for the first time. We will suppose that sounds are represented to him by unvarying, physiological symbols. This word, then, writes itself to his mind thus:

Ʊ [ɪʙ

He also knows the written word "same" and its meaning, but what is there, in the picture that this pronunciation makes, to suggest it? Or he has been taught letters, and has learned to represent the long *a*-sound by the letter which bears that name. Then this mental transcription of the word is this, "s-a-m;" which not only fails to suggest the correct written word, but gives a spelling which actually stands for quite a different pronunciation. If, however, he has been taught that vowel in the way which has been suggested, his—*a*—*e* at once makes the framework of the written word he knows; the pronunciation and the spelling coincide and become reasonable to his thought. The real importance of this seemingly simple matter would, I think, be quite apparent, if time would permit a full discussion, here, of the part which a secondary letter plays in the actual spelling of words which contain our long vowel sounds. We find the *a*-sound represented in monosyllables by—*a*—*e*, *ai*, *ay*, etc.; but rarely, if ever, by the letter *a* alone. It often is represented by this letter in polysyllables, but in a great majority of cases is dependent for its value on these same "silent letters" of the root, which must be present to the mind in deciding the pronunciation of the derivative word. A glance at any table of vowel spellings, like that in the key to a dictionary, is enough to open an interesting subject for thought in this direction.

3. Of important letters and spellings having more than one sound, for whose pronunciation no fixed rules can be given, it is taught, at once, what and how many sounds each has to be remembered and decided between. So if the pupil cannot be surely told, for instance, when *ow* will have one sound and when another, he may, at least, know that it will have one of two, and that if his first pronunciation is wrong the second must be right. Such spellings are repeated on the chart, each one standing in the group under every sound it may represent; they are numbered also, after the first of each instance, the better to be connected in memory. (See chart for *ea*, *ow*, *oo*, *u*.)

4. The most common spellings of each sound are grouped so that they may stand clearly together before the eye and be inseparably connected with the thought of that position, when seen in speech, to assist the mind in its discriminating process.

5. The attempt has been to represent on such a chart just those rules for pronunciation which the elementary language of classes always obliges them to learn as early as possible; the most nearly invariable and the most frequent in application. And then—

6. To connect these so intimately with the very sight of letters and act of speech, that they shall not need to be remembered, but can be made the base of a continual addition in the shape of short lists of exceptions, or of rules that apply only to small classes of words and the words to which they apply, which must be largely matters of memory.

This basis may well seem a slight affair for so complicated a structure as English spelling to build upon. But, though some of the commonest words, and those first taught are found as exceptions to the rules here represented, of their general applicability let me give an instance. With the new class of deaf children at the Clarke Institution, last year, the first part of the well-known "Jacobs' Reader" was used a short time daily, during the last few months of the year, for the sake of its picture-teaching and simple language. Counting the different words in it, one day, I noted as follows:

Whole number	677
Number coming directly under rules on chart	510
Number coming directly under first additional rules taught	35
Number which conform to chart by 1. Crossing out a superfluous letter. (Example: *calf*). 2. Showing double force of a letter. (Example: *deer*).	68
Number which contradict chart. (Example: *shoe*)	64

Out of 677 different words, then, 545 should be pronounced at sight by the child well trained in his first year's work, the utmost help needed being a number pencilled over a letter here and there. Of the remaining 132 many were, in point of fact, pronounced rightly to the children who used this book, through that instinct of selection, curious to watch in them as in hearing children, which seems to come with growing familiarity with print. If, on the other hand, such charts seem too cumbersome to present to young pupils, the result of work with this same little class may help to prove that, practically, they are not so. The time, from September 23 to Christmas, was given up to such drill on elementary sounds, combinations, and control of breath and voice as seems to us essential to secure good speech. All this work was done from the lips; but while the teacher did not write the children did! With each sound was taught, as its equivalent, the key-spelling on the charts. Then, if a child spent a minute working over a sound, *s*, for example, he wrote that letter on his slate afterward, no matter how many times a day. If it was a combination which he repeated from his teacher's lips, he wrote that. As the first spellings grew familiar, more were added, building his charts up slowly and by degrees. A daily time for penmanship, needful, with other exercises for rest and change of work, helped in the correct formation of the letters thus learned. All was done gradually, with no separate time for this teaching, and no appreciable effort on the child's part—done chiefly in moments when otherwise he would have been unoccupied, or waiting for his turn to recite. But when language-work began in earnest, there was no need in teaching the meaning of such words as *foot*, *feet*, *toe*, *leg*, *arm*, *hand*, *cheek*, *nose*, *mouth*, *tooth*, *teeth*, *cat*, *book*, *boy*, *man*, etc., to teach the written form. We gave the spoken word; that—If I may be allowed the expression—*wrote itself* to the child's mind, and he knew what the spelling would be without being told. Of course, the first words taught in this class were chosen with some care, that they might fall under rules. But the ease and rapidity with which the children learned, later, the many words that did not, in all respects, conform to their charts, showed how lightly memory was taxed in other directions, and confirmed our belief in the right principle of the work while it greatly exceeded our expectations. More language, more independent use of language, more talking, better speech and lip-reading than I ever knew in a class of the same grade before, was the result of the year's work; with ability to read at sight, of which I have spoken, and to write from the lips with a degree of correctness that was most encouraging. The rules those children learned in a year, almost without effort, were the same that I have sometimes failed, in all the five years of their primary course, to instil into classes so thoroughly that the children need not stop to *remember* to apply them. The class of the year before made the same quick response of intelligence to that which strove to simplify their early work and to adapt itself to their reason. The reason even of a very little child is a great power.

APPENDIX.

NOTE.—Dashes show the position of a given letter or letters in words, as,

y— y initial
—y=y final, etc.

Prepared for young classes, these charts are based upon monosyllables to a considerable extent. Rules for accent, which in polysyllables change, in some instances, the pronunciations here indicated are to be taught later; while for little ones who cannot understand, at once, much about syllables, the length of a dash may be used to show a "long" or "very short" word to the eye; as the final *y* (——*y*) in a two syllabled word like *money*, and the final *y* (—*y*) of different pronunciation in a tiny monosyllable like *my*. (See Chart.)

It is also to be noted that *final r* not being a full consonant but a glide, the rules for vowels with consonants in general do not apply to that letter when final. Always influencing the sound of the vowel preceding it, it is considered separately in each case in that relation, as will be seen below. (See *er*, *ir*, *ur*, *ar*, etc.)

Final *b*, *d*, *g*, are taught ending with a little breath-sound to relieve the tension; this is indicated by the ———b (bp), etc., of the Consonant Chart.

CONSONANT CHART.

p		sh
t	f	
	v	r——
k ck c		l
b—— ——b (bp)	th th^{2}	wh
		ch tch
d—— ——d (dt)	s c (ce, ci, cy)	
g—— ——g (gk)		j g ——ge (dch)
	z s^{2}	
m		h
n		x
ng		qu

VOWEL CHART.

ee ea	er	oo u^{3} —w	
—i— —y— y——	ir yr ur ———ar	oo^{2} w—— u^{4}	
—a—e ai ay	——or ——re	—o—e oa ——o ow^{3}	
—e—— ———y ea^{2}	ar —u^{2}— ——a	or au aw	
——a—		——o—	
you u	—i—e —y—e igh —y	ou ow	oi oy

Key to Vowel Chart.

see *seat*	*her*	*boot* *rude* *screw*	
sit *hymn* *yard*	*sir* *martyr* *fur*	*book* *put* *want*	
came *pail* *day*	*collar* *doctor* *fire*	*home* *coat* *potato* *throw*	
bell *sorry* *head*	*cart* *cup* *sofa*	*short* *because* *claw*	
cat		*not*	
youth *use*	*mine* *scythe* *right* *my*	*out* *owl*	*oil* *boy*

Exhibit to Query 21,976.

THE DEAF IN THE ELEVENTH CENSUS.

In response to the desire of the Commission, the following papers were forwarded to London:

1. Letter from A. Graham Bell to Senator Hale, printed in a Senate document entitled "Communications received by Committee on the Census, United States Senate, relating to Census bill (H. R. 1659), pp. 31–37."

2. Report of Census Committee appointed by the Conference of Superintendents and Principals of American Schools for the Deaf, published in the *Annals*, Vol. XXXIV, p. 232.

3. Final form of amended Census schedule submitted by A. Graham Bell, to the Hon. Robert P. Porter, Superintendent of the Eleventh Census of the United States.

(1.) COMMUNICATION TO SENATOR HALE.

1336 19th Street, Washington, D. C.,
December 28, 1888.

Dear Senator: In accordance with your recommendation, I beg to submit a few suggestions relating to the Eleventh Census of the United States, and relating especially to the enumeration of the defective classes.

Yours, very respectfully,
Alexander Graham Bell.

Senator Eugene Hale,
Chairman of Census Committee of the United States Senate.

SUGGESTIONS RELATING TO THE ELEVENTH CENSUS OF THE UNITED STATES, 1890.

Introductory Remarks.

(1) According to the census returns, the defective classes have increased 400 per cent. in thirty years, while the general population of the country has simply doubled. The following table shows the relative figures at each census since 1850:

Years.	Total Population of the United States.	Total Blind Population.	Total Deaf-and-Dumb Population.	Total Idiotic Population.	Total Insane Population.
1850........	23, 191, 876	9, 794	9, 803	15, 787	15, 610
1860........	31, 443, 321	12, 658	12, 821	18, 930	24, 042
1870........	38, 558, 371	20, 320	16, 205	24, 527	37, 432
1880..	50, 155, 783	48, 928	33, 878	76, 895	91, 997

(2) I have examined with care the statistics of the Tenth Census relating to the deaf and dumb, and find internal evidence to show that in their case there has been a real increase greater than the increase of the general population, and not simply an apparent increase due to greater accuracy of enumeration; for, when the whole population of the United States are classified according to their age in 1880, the proportion of deaf-mutes among the younger persons is seen to be greater than among the older; indeed it is proportionally greater as the age is younger, until quite young children are reached.

(3) The following are the numbers of the deaf and dumb returned in the Tenth Census:

Period when Deafness occurred.	Number of Deaf-Mutes.
At or before birth................................	12, 155
After birth..	10, 318
Not stated...........	11, 405
Total	33, 878

(4) Classification of these cases according to their age in 1880 shows that there has been an enormous increase of recent years in the numbers of the non-congenitally deaf; but this need hardly be considered as a permanent condition, for it appears to be due to an epidemic of cerebro-spinal meningitis, which will probably die away, as former epidemics have done.

(5.) The following table shows the percentage of the whole population of the United States born at each decade, and also the percentage of the congenitally deaf population:

Period of Birth.	Total Population Living in 1880.	Congenital Deaf-Mutes Living in 1880.	Percentage of the whole Population Living in 1880.	Percentage of Congenitally Deaf Population Living in 1880.
Before 1780.....	4, 016	—	0.0080	—
1781-90..........	20, 863	9	0.0416	0.074
1791 1800........	196, 197	63	0.3912	0.518
1801-10...........	776, 507	241	1.5482	1.983
1811-20...........	1, 830, 095	472	3.6488	3.883
1821-30.....	3, 111, 317	751	6.2033	6.179
1831-40...........	4, 558, 256	1, 078	9.0882	8.870
1841 50...........	6, 369, 362	1, 614	12.6992	13.280
1851-60..........	9, 168, 303	2, 460	18.2798	20.240
1861- 70..........	10, 726, 601	3, 398	21.3866	27.958
1871-80...........	13, 394, 176	2, 068	26.7051	17.015
Total....	50, 155, 783	12, 154	100.0000	100.000

(6) These results are shown in graphical form in the following diagram. The continuous line indicates the percentage of the general population, and the broken line that of the congenitally deaf population, born at each decade:

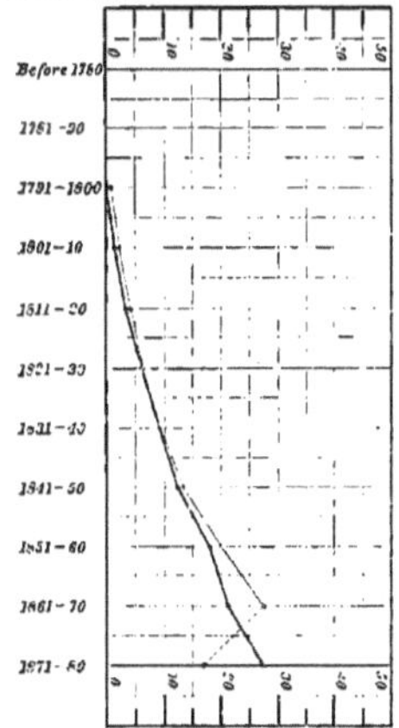

(7) The indications are that the congenital deaf-mutes of the country are increasing at a greater rate than the general population.

(8) The great and sudden decrease in the numbers of deaf children born in the last decade (1871–80) is probably due to imperfect returns of deaf-mutes under ten years of age; for, though 54 per cent. of all the deaf and dumb were deaf from birth, only 30 deaf infants were reported in the census of 1880, and only 49 between the ages of one and two, out of a total deaf-mute population of 33,878.

(9) Statistics in my possession show that in the year 1819 deaf-mutes began to marry partners who were themselves deaf and dumb.

(10) The percentage of intermarriages has continuously increased, until now not less than 90 per cent. of all deaf-mutes who marry, marry partners who are themselves deaf and dumb.

(11) The latest statistics collected by me include 1,443 cases of marriage. Of these 1,443 deaf-mutes, I find that 71 (or five per cent.) had married hearing persons, and 1,372 (or 95 per cent.) had intermarried among themselves.

(12) In 1828 a deaf-mute child was born of a deaf-mute father and mother, and now such cases can be numbered by the hundred. My statistics are based upon a list of 528 deaf-mutes, mostly young, who have one or both parents deaf.

(13) Some of these children have already married deaf husbands or wives, and deaf offspring have appeared in the third generation.

(14) I can cite families in which the deafness has been handed down through four generations, and can give in minute detail particulars relating to a family in Maine in which congenital deaf-mutes have appeared for five successive generations in increasing numbers, and in which the younger deaf-mutes are marrying deaf-mutes.

(15) My list of deaf children of deaf parents (all, excepting one, born before 1880) comprises 528 cases (mostly young), 91.6 per cent. of whom were deaf from birth.

(16) Upon the assumption that 528 such cases were living when the Tenth Census was taken, we obtain the following results:

(*a*) One person in every 1,480 of the general population was deaf and dumb, and one person in every 64 of the deaf-mute population was a child of deaf-mute parents.

(*b*) One person in every 2,736 of the general population was deaf from birth, and one person in every 38 of the congenitally deaf population was a child of deaf-mute parents.

(17) The laws of heredity indicate, that, if these deaf children should marry congenitally deaf husbands or wives, an increased proportion of deaf-offspring will appear in the next generation; and that the continuous intermarriage of congenital deaf-mutes from generation to generation may ultimately result in the formation of a deaf variety of the human race in America, in which all or most of the children will be born deaf.

(18) In these conclusions I am supported by the following American men of science, all members of the National Academy of Sciences, and most of them experts on the subject of heredity. These gentlemen are Professor Edward D. Cope, editor of the *American Naturalist*; Professor Alpheus Hyatt, of Harvard University; Professor William H. Brewer, of Yale University; Dr. Bowditch, of Harvard University; Professor Simon Newcomb, of Washington, D. C.; and Professor W. K. Brooks, of Johns Hopkins University.

(19) I would therefore urge upon the United States the importance of examining in the next census the marital relations of defective persons, and the extent to which their defects have been inherited by their offspring.

THE ENUMERATION OF THE DEFECTIVE CLASSES.

(20) The enumeration of the defective classes is always found to be itself defective.

(21) However perfect the classification may be, the returns of these classes will always be incomplete, on account of a natural objection to expose the defects of relatives, especially when these are very young.

(22) Accuracy of enumeration will be promoted by eliminating from the census schedules (as far as may be possible) every question that could wound the feelings of parents or friends of afflicted persons. For example: if the enumerator approached the subject of defects by asking whether the persons enumerated were perfect in sight, hearing, mind, and body, he would be more likely to secure the information desired than if he asked a fond mother whether her child was "blind, deaf and dumb, idiotic, insane, maimed, crippled, bed-ridden, or otherwise disabled."

(23) There are degrees in every defect, and the lesser forms are more capable of amelioration than the graver. Classification under the graver forms tends to the exclusion of the lesser from the returns; but classification under the lesser forms would include the graver, and be less objectionable to friends, so that evasions would be fewer, and the returns more accurate and complete. For example: the blind, deaf and dumb, idiotic, insane, maimed, crippled, bed-ridden, and otherwise disabled, would all be returned under the head of defects of sight, hearing, mind, or body; but the converse would not necessarily be true.

(24) The returns should include all persons laboring under disabilities of sight, hearing, mind, or body, of sufficient magnitude to prevent education in ordinary schools, lessen wealth-producing power, and incapacitate for military service.

(25) The deaf and the blind should be grouped into a sub-class by themselves, and separated as much as possible from the other defective classes, because they are enumerated chiefly for educational purposes, whereas the others need eleemosynary care or restraint.

(26) Public establishments for purely educational purposes should be classified as "schools," and not as "asylums." They should be included in statistics relating to the general education of the people, and excluded from those relating to charitable institutions.

(27) Many children who cannot profitably attend ordinary public schools on account of disabilities are allowed to grow up without instruction, because parents object to send them to asylums, or institutions governed by State boards of charity.

(28) The statistics of the Tenth Census show the following figures relating to defective children of school age:

	Total in the United States.	Total in Special Schools.
Blind	7,768	1,534
Deaf-and-dumb	15,059	4,893
Idiotic	29,373	1,942
Insane	3,184	—

(29) The term "deaf and dumb" is not only objectionable in itself, but is incorrect, because it classifies those who belong to this class as laboring under a double disability instead of a single one.

(30) Deaf-mutes are simply persons who are deaf from childhood; and dumbness or muteness is the result of the natural defect, and not a defect in itself. The vocal organs are not defective.

(31) Many of the so-called deaf and dumb can speak. Some had acquired the art before hearing was lost, and others acquired it by instruction in school.

(32) In the census of 1880 all persons who lost hearing before they reached the age of sixteen years are classified as "deaf and dumb," whether they could speak or not.

(33) This incorrect and very objectionable classification leads to evasion and inaccurate returns.

(34) Dumbness by itself is not a defect calling for enumeration in the census (unless, indeed, for statistical purposes and the determination of causes), for defective speech alone is not a disability that prevents instruction in ordinary schools. It does not materially lessen wealth-producing power, nor does it incapacitate the person for military service.

(35) Persons who have not studied the subject generally fail to realize that deaf-mutes should be classified among the deaf, and not among the dumb; and enumerators, therefore, can hardly be expected to follow the classification.

(36) For the sake of accuracy in the returns, therefore, it would be well to make defective speech a subject of inquiry in the primary schedule relating to population. The dumb who are deaf, and the dumb who are idiotic, will appear on supplementary schedules relating to the deaf or the feeble-minded; and the dumb who are neither deficient in mind nor hearing need have no special schedule of inquiry.

(37) Special schedules relating to all the defective classes (except the dumb) should be prepared with the assistance of experts of two kinds, viz., specialists who have studied the causes of the defects, and teachers who are familiar with the special methods of instruction necessary.

(38) The gravity of the disabilities resulting from deafness can be ascertained from two elements: (1) the age or period of life at which the defect occurred; and (2) the amount of deafness (whether total or partial). The former element is the more important of the two, for a slight defect of hearing in an infant results in graver disabilities than total deafness occurring in adult life. For example: in the case of the deaf infant, the defect interferes with the acquisition of language through the ear, and the child remains dumb. His thoughts are carried on without words, so that a mental condition exists which is abnormal. His ignorance is so great as to be appalling; for his mind is deprived of everything that other people have ever heard of or read about that is not derived directly from their own observation. Without special instruction, such children grow to adult life with all the passions of men and women, but without the restraining influences that spring from a cultivated understanding.

(39) Persons who become deaf in adult life have no greater disability than the defect itself; but, where deafness occurs in childhood, incidental disabilities arise which are greater than the natural defect; but because they are incidental, and not natural, they are capable of amelioration, and even complete removal, by suitable instruction in special schools. Hence the very great importance of a correct enumeration of the younger deaf children.

(40) FORM OF INQUIRY.

PHYSICAL AND MENTAL CONDITION.							
	CONDITION OF—						
	The Senses.			The Mind.		The Body.	
Is the person (on the day of the enumerator's visit) sick or temporarily disabled, so as to be unable to attend to ordinary business or duties? If so, what is the sickness or disability?	Sight.	Hearing.	Speech {of persons 5 or more years of age.	Mental Development.	Mental Health.	Bodily Condition.	Bodily Health.

In the primary schedule relating to population the defective classes should be grouped together under the head of "physical and mental condition," instead of under "health," as was done in 1880. The preceding form is suggested for incorporation in the primary schedule relating to population.

(41) The enumerator should be instructed to ask (*a*) whether the person has perfectly normal sight, hearing, and speech; whether the mind is normally developed and in a healthy condition; and whether the bodily condition is normal and the general health good. If the answer is "yes," the enumerator should indicate the reply by a horizontal mark (—) placed in the proper column; if "no," by a mark sloping from right to left (/); and, if the question is not answered in a satisfactory and reliable manner, the column should be left blank. (*b*) If the physical or mental condition is reported as "not perfectly normal" (/), the enumerator should then inquire whether the disability is sufficiently great to prevent instruction in an ordinary school, to interfere with the acquisition of a suitable means of livelihood, and to incapacitate for military service. If this is found to be the case he should convert the sloping mark (/) into a cross (×), and proceed to put the interrogatories contained in the supplementary schedule relating to the special class of defect noted.

(42) As the supplementary schedules should be prepared with the assistance of specialists, it may perhaps not be advisable for me at the present time to refer to the details, excepting so far as to say that inquiries should be instituted relating to the causes of defects and their inheritance by offspring. The marital relations of defective persons should be noted and the results tabulated. The total number of children born to them should be recorded, and the number who died young. The record should also note the number of defective and normal offspring.

NATIVITY AND PARENTAGE.

In examining the ancestry of deaf-mutes, I have had occasion to consult the original population schedules of former censuses, which are preserved in the Department of the Interior; and I have found little difficulty in tracing the families backward from census to census in the male line of ascent. If the name of the father had been given in former censuses, it might now be possible for genealogical experts to trace from these records the American ancestry of every person now living in the United States in every branch, for the name of the father would give the maiden name of females. I therefore suggest that in the census of 1890 the father's name should be noted in that part of the schedule that relates to the nativity of the parents, so that the people of the United States may leave to their descendants genealogical records from which their full ancestry may at any future time be ascertained. The following letter and enclosed resolutions show that this recommendation has been endorsed by the New England Historic Genealogical Society.

Yours respectfully,

ALEXANDER GRAHAM BELL.

Senator EUGENE HALE,
Chairman of the Senate Committee on the Eleventh Census.

Letter from the President of the New England Historic Genealogical Society.

SALEM, MASS., 15*th February*, 1889.

MY DEAR MR. BELL:

The accompanying paper was received by me to-day from the Recording Secretary of the New England Historic Genealogical Society, of which I am president. It carries its own explanation so far as the action of our Society is concerned, but it may interest you to know that this action was brought about through the instrumentality of Dr. S. A. Green, librarian of the Massachusetts Historical Society, who referred to me your letter to him and the accompanying papers.

I lost no time in bringing the subject to the attention of the N. E. H. G. Society; though, as such bodies move slowly, I have not been able to give you the proof of our deep interest in your project until now.

Yours, &c.,

A. C. GOODELL.

DR. ALEXANDER GRAHAM BELL,
1336 *19th Street, Washington, D. C.*

Enclosed Resolutions.

SOCIETY'S HOUSE, 18 SOMERSET STREET,
BOSTON, MASS., *13th February*, 1889.

At a meeting of the council of this Society, held Tuesday the 5th inst., a communication was presented from Professor Alexander Graham Bell, of Washington, D. C., suggesting an improvement in the next United States Census, which communication was referred to a committee consisting of the following gentlemen: Hamilton Andrews Hill; the Hon. Wm. Claflin; William Endicott, Jr.; Robert C. Winthrop, Jr.; the Rev. Andrew P. Peabody, D. D.; John Ward Dean; Henry Austin Whitney; the Rev. David D. Haskins, S. T. D.; John J. Hassam; Col. Thomas Wentworth Higginson; Grenville H. Norcross; and the Hon. Geo. S. Hale.

This committee presented at the meeting of the Society held on the 6th inst., the following report, which was adopted:

The committee to which was referred a communication from Dr. Alexander Graham Bell, of Washington, inviting attention to a recommendation made by him to the Census Committee of the Senate for an extension of one of the schedules of population, in the next census, begs to report:

Dr. Bell's statement of the case (see Senate document relating to the Census, p. 37) is as follows:

"In examining the ancestry of deaf-mutes, I have had occasion to consult the original population schedules of former censuses, which are preserved in the Department of the Interior, and I have found little difficulty in tracing the families backward from census to census in the male line of ascent. If the name of the father had been given in former censuses it might now be possible for geneological experts to trace from these records the American ancestry of every person now living in the United States in every branch, for the name of the father would give the maiden name of females. I therefore suggest, that in the census of 1890 the father's name should be noted in that part of the schedule that relates to the nativity of the parents, so that the people of the United States may leave to their descendants genealogical records from which their full ancestry may at any time be ascertained."

This suggestion is full of interest to the genealogists of the country, and if carried into effect would undoubtedly prove of great value to them. The Committee therefore recommends that the Society address a letter to the Hon. Eugene Hale, chairman of the Census Committee of the Senate, expressing its sense of the importance of the suggestion of Dr. Bell, and asking for it the careful consideration of Congress, and, if practicable, its incorporation in the scheme for taking the census of 1890.

Respectfully submitted.

At a subsequent meeting of the Council, held Monday the 11th inst., it was voted that the report of the committee to whom was referred the communication of Dr. Alexander Graham Bell relating to the extension of one of the schedules of population in the next census is hereby accepted, and the chairman of the committee is authorized and requested to address a letter to the Hon. Eugene Hale, Chairman of the Census Committee of the Senate of the United States, expressing the sense of the Society of the importance of Dr. Bell's suggestion.

Voted, that any letter addressed to Senator Hale shall be signed by all members of the committee, and that the secretary be ordered to send forthwith a copy of the resolution, with the names of the members of the committee, to Dr. Bell.

Attest:

DAVID G. HASKINS, Jr.,
Recording Secretary.

(2.) REPORT OF CENSUS COMMITTEE.

[From the *American Annals for the Deaf* for July, 1889, Vol. XXXIV, p. 202.]

A meeting of the Standing Executive Committee of the Convention of American Instructors of the Deaf was held at the National Deaf-Mute College, May 9, 1889, to consider the best method of enumerating the deaf in the next Census, and confer with the Hon. Robert P. Porter, Superintendent of the Census, on the subject. Dr. Alexander Graham Bell and Mr. Frederick Howard Wines, in accordance with the action of the Sixth Conference of Principals and Superintendents, were invited to act with the Committee. All the members of the Executive Committee and Dr. Bell were present: Mr. Wines was unable to attend. The Committee discussed the subject for several hours, and had a pleasant interview with Mr. Porter and Dr. J. S. Billings, who has charge of the mortality and vital statistics of the Eleventh Census. Mr. Porter acceded at once to the request of the Committee that, in the publication of the results of the Census, the deaf should be separated from the pauper and criminal classes, and promised to give his respectful and careful consideration to all suggestions that might be made by the Committee. The Committee subsequently addressed the following letter to Mr. Porter:

WASHINGTON, *June* 21, 1889.

Hon. ROBERT P. PORTER,
Superintendent of the Census.

DEAR SIR: At the Sixth Conference of Principals and Superintendents of American Schools for the Deaf, held at Jackson, Mississippi, April 14-17, 1888—a body representing all the Schools for the Deaf in the United States, numbering last year 8,372 pupils—we were appointed a committee to endeavor to effect a reform in the method of enumerating the deaf in the United States Census, in the hope of securing fuller and more accurate statistics in 1890 than have heretofore been obtained. In accordance with your request at our interview on the 9th of May last, that we should make such suggestions as might seem desirable in this direction, we respectfully submit the following recommendations:

1. Section 17 of the act of Congress entitled "An Act to provide for taking the tenth and subsequent censuses" [Approved March 3, 1879] provides that "Schedule number one shall contain inquiries * * * as to the physical and mental health of each person enumerated, whether active or disabled, maimed, crippled, bedridden, deaf, dumb, blind, insane or idiotic, and whether employed, or unemployed, and if unemployed during what portion of the year."

In accordance with this provision inquiries were made in the Tenth Census concerning the disabled; and full returns were sought of all the classes named in the act, excepting the deaf and the dumb. Only those dumb were enumerated who were also deaf; and only those deaf who had lost hearing before the age of sixteen years.

We urge that in the Eleventh Census all the classes named in the act be fully enumerated; and we specially urge that the returns of the deaf be not limited to the sub-class of the deaf formerly denominated the "deaf and dumb."

If the requirements of the law are fully complied with, the returns will be much more useful to us, as teachers of the deaf, than if the plan pursued in former censuses of inquiring only for the "deaf and dumb" is continued. Pupils are admitted to the schools we represent not on account of their dumbness, but on account of their deafness. Persons who are merely dumb are not received; persons who are merely deaf are received. Our schools are open to all children of school age who are debarred by deafness from attending ordinary schools for hearing persons. We wish the aid of the Census in obtaining the names and post-office addresses of such children, in order to bring them into the special schools suited to their condition.

2. The age or period of life at which deafness occurred is a more reliable element in determining the sub-class of the deaf to which a person belongs than the presence or absence of the power of speech, or the exact amount of muteness involved.

We therefore recommend that in taking a census of the deaf, the enumerators be specially required to ascertain the age or period of life at which the deafness occurred. They should be instructed that this point is of such vital importance to the correct classification of the deaf that an answer must be obtained in every case, or a reason assigned for non-reply. This reason may, in some cases, itself reveal the point desired.

3. We recommend that in schedule number one the physical and mental condition of each person be noted. The following form is suggested for incorporation in that schedule:

PHYSICAL AND MENTAL CONDITION.	
Sight.	Good — Not good / Cannot see well enough to read X.
Hearing.	Good — Not good / Cannot hear loud conversation X.
Speech.	Good — Not good / Cannot speak so as to be understood X.
Mind.	Mental condition good — Not good / Mentally disabled X.
Body.	Physical condition good — Not good / Physically disabled X.

To ascertain the condition of the hearing, the enumerator should be instructed to ask, first, whether the person can hear well. If the answer is "Yes," the enumerator should indicate the reply by a horizontal mark (—) placed in the "Hearing" column; if the hearing is not good, by a mark sloping from right to left (/); and if the question is not answered the column should be left blank.

If the hearing is reported as "not good" (/), the enumerator should then ascertain the extent of the disability. If the person is too deaf to be taught in ordinary schools for hearing persons, or cannot hear conversation in a loud tone of voice, the enumerator should convert the sloping mark (/) into a (X), and proceed to put the interrogatories contained in the supplementary schedule or card relating to the deaf. (See paragraph 4, below.) If, on the other hand, the person is merely "hard of hearing," or if there is doubt whether the deafness is sufficient to constitute the disability above specified, the cross should not be made, and the person should not be entered on the supplementary schedule or card relating to the deaf.

The condition of the speech should be ascertained and recorded in a similar manner. If the person speaks well, the enumerator should make a horizontal mark (—) in the "Speech" column; if not, a sloping mark (/); and if the person cannot speak so as to be understood, or cannot speak at all, the sloping mark should be converted into a cross (X).

The deaf and the dumb would then be indicated as follows, in schedule number one:

	CONDITION OF THE—				
	Sight.	Hearing.	Speech.	Mind.	Body.
The deaf..........................	......	X	......	......	......
The dumb (because of deafness).	......	X	X	......	......
The dumb (because of idiocy)....	......	......	X	X	......
The dumb (because of defective vocal organs)........................	......	......	X	......	......

The fact that there are three classes of dumb persons shows the liability to error when the enumerator is instructed, as heretofore, to inquire for the "deaf and dumb." Out of 29,776 idiots, whose powers of speech were ascertained from physicians in the last Census, 7,396, or about one-fourth of the whole number, could not articulate at all, or had no use of spoken language; 14,707, or about one-half, could articulate but imperfectly, or their use of language was very defective; the number who spoke intelligibly was only 7,673. It thus appears that a large proportion of the idiotic are no less "dumb" than deaf-mutes, and it is almost inevitable that when *dumbness* is made prominent (as in the term "deaf and dumb") the one class should be confused with the other, resulting in the return of intelligent deaf-mutes as "idiotic" and of idiotic hearing persons as "deaf and dumb." In the last Census, moreover, 2,339 persons were returned as both "deaf-mutes and idiotic." It is extremely probable that among these were some deaf-mutes of good mind, and some idiots who could hear. If a census of *the deaf* is taken this source of error will be removed. Other advantages of the form of questions above proposed over the former plan of asking for the "blind, deaf and dumb, idiotic, insane, maimed, crippled, bedridden, or otherwise disabled," are explained in Dr. Alexander Graham Bell's communication to Senator Hale (paragraphs 20-30), a copy of which is herewith inclosed.

4. Mr. F. H. Wines, of Springfield, Illinois, Special Agent of the Tenth Census in charge of the statistics relating to the deaf and other special classes of the population, who was invited to act with this Committee but was unable to be present at our meeting, suggested to us by letter that, instead of supplementary schedules, the enumerators should be provided with special cards, on which the questions to be asked in the case of each deaf person should be printed, with spaces for the answers, and that the enumerators be required to fill out these cards in duplicate, one copy for use and the other for preservation. We approve of the suggestion of special cards, and recommend the following form, in addition to such references as may be necessary for identification with schedule number one:

[Face of Card.]

[This space may be used for the necessary references for identification with schedule number one.]

THE DEAF.

Instructions to the Enumerator.

Note A. The questions on this card should be asked in the case of every person who is too deaf to be taught in ordinary schools for hearing persons, or who cannot hear conversation in a loud tone of voice.

Note B. Question No. 5 is very important, and every possible effort must be made to obtain a correct answer.

If the person was born deaf, write B; if not, state the age at which the hearing was lost.

If it is difficult to find out the exact age at which the person became deaf, ask *at what period of life* deafness occurred, as, for instance, whether it was in infancy (under 4 years of age), in childhood (under 10), in youth (under 20), in adult life (from 20 to 50), or in old age.

If you cannot get an answer to Question No. 5, state here the reason why you cannot.

Note C. In answering Question No. 8, use the same check-marks as in schedule number one.

---

1. Name of the deaf person?
2. Residence when at home: Town?
County? State?
Post-office address?
3. Name of this person's father?

[Reverse of Card.]

4. Race or color of this person? Sex? Age?
5. **At what age or period of life did this person become deaf?** (See *Note B.*)
6. Cause of deafness?
7. Did the deafness result from military service?
8. Physical and mental condition [See *Note C*]. Sight? Hearing? Speech? Mind? Body?
9. Can this person hear sufficiently to perceive a warning shout in case of danger?
10. Is this person educated? Where taught?
11. What is this person's occupation?
Monthly earnings? $ Value of property? $
12. Is this person a pauper?
13. Were the parents of this person first cousins?
14. Has this person had any deaf brothers or sisters?
15. Is this person single (s); married (m); widowed (wid); or divorced (d)? If married, name of the wife (or husband)?
16. Name of the wife's (or husband's) father?
17. Has the wife (or husband) had any deaf brothers or sisters?
18. How many children have been born of this marriage? How many of the children were deaf? How many died young?
19. Is the wife (or husband) deaf? If so, became deaf at what age or period of life? (See *Note B.*)

5. In addition to the statistics gathered by the enumerators, much valuable information relating to the deaf can be obtained by means of inquiries addressed to principals of schools for the deaf, teachers of common schools, physicians, and intelligent deaf persons. We recommend that special cards with suitable questions be addressed to each of these classes of persons.

6. We recommend that some one thoroughly qualified by familiarity with the deaf be placed in charge of the entire work of the Census relating to this class.

7. We recommend that in the publication of the results of the Census the deaf be separated from the pauper and criminal classes.

8. In the last census 4,599 persons were returned as doubly or trebly afflicted with deaf-mutism, idiocy, insanity, and blindness. Those who were returned as "deaf and dumb and idiotic," were reported among "the deaf and dumb" and again among "the idiotic," etc., etc.; each of the doubly afflicted persons being thus counted twice, and each of the trebly afflicted persons thrice. In this way the 4,597 doubly and trebly afflicted persons counted in the summing up of the insane, idiots, blind, and deaf-mutes (Tenth Census, vol. xxi, page vii), as 9,441 persons, more than double their actual number, making the total of these classes appear greater by 4,844 individuals than it really was. In order to insure accuracy with respect to these classes, we recommend that the returns of persons doubly and trebly afflicted be not classed with the deaf, the idiotic, etc., respectively, but be grouped in classes by themselves, and placed in charge of some specially qualified person for the careful examination and verification of the returns, and for an investigation into the causes of these terrible afflictions.

9. An impression is prevalent that deafness, blindness, idiocy, and insanity are often due to consanguinity in the parents, and statistics have been collected which show that a considerable percentage of the deaf, blind, idiotic, and insane are the children of first cousins. These statistics, however, can be of little value in determining the questions involved until we know what percentage of the general population are offspring of such unions. We therefore recommend that in schedule number one the question be asked, "Were the parents of this person first cousins?"

We trust that these suggestions will commend themselves to your judgment, and believe that, if adopted, they will result in a more accurate and satisfactory census of the class in whose welfare we are especially interested than has yet been obtained.

Respectfully and truly yours,

EDWARD M. GALLAUDET,
ISAAC LEWIS PEET,
PHILIP G. GILLETT,
J. L. NOYES,
CAROLINE A. YALE,
ALEXANDER GRAHAM BELL,
EDWARD ALLEN FAY,
Committee.

(3.) FINAL FORM OF SCHEDULE

Submitted to the Hon. Robert P. Porter, Superintendent of the Eleventh Census of the United States, by Alexander Graham Bell.

FORM OF QUESTIONS USED IN SCHEDULE No. 1 OF THE TENTH CENSUS [1880.]

HEALTH.						EDUCATION.			NATIVITY.		
Is the person [on the day of the Enumerator's visit] sick or temporarily disabled so as to be unable to attend to ordinary business or duties? If so, what is the sickness or disability?	Blind, /.	Deaf and Dumb, /.	Idiotic, /.	Insane, /.	Maimed, Crippled, Bedridden, or otherwise disabled, /.	Attended school within the census year, /.	Cannot read, /.	Cannot write, /.	Place of birth of this person, naming State or Territory of United States, or the country if of foreign birth.	Place of birth of the FATHER of this person, naming the State or Territory of United States, or the country if of foreign birth.	Place of birth of the MOTHER of this person, naming the State or Territory of the United States, or the country if of foreign birth.
15	16	17	18	19	20	21	22	23	24	25	26

FIG. 1.

SUGGESTED FORM OF QUESTIONS FOR SCHEDULE No. 1 OF THE ELEVENTH CENSUS [1890].

PHYSICAL AND MENTAL CONDITION.						EDUCATION.			NATIVITY AND PARENTAGE.				
Is the person [on the day of the Enumerator's visit] sick or temporarily disabled so as to be unable to attend to ordinary business or duties? If so, what is the sickness or disability?	Sight. Good — Not good / Cannot see well enough to read X.	Hearing. Good — Not good / Cannot hear loud conversation X.	Speech. Good — Not good / Cannot speak so as to be understood X.	Mind. Mental condition good — Not good / Mentally disabled X.	Body. Physical condition good — Not good / Physically disabled X.	Attended school within the census year? Yes — No X.	Can this person read? Yes — No X.	Can this person write? Yes — No X.	Place of birth of this person, naming State or Territory of United States, or the country if of foreign birth.	Place of birth of the FATHER of this person, naming State or Territory of the United States, or the country if of foreign birth.	Place of birth of the MOTHER of this person, naming State or Territory of the United States, or the country if of foreign birth.	Were the parents of this person first cousins? Yes, —. No, X.	Name of the FATHER of this person.
15	16	17	18	19	20	21	22	23	24	25	26	27	28

FIG. 2.

PART III.

POSTSCRIPTS.

COMMENTS

ON POINTS IN PROFESSOR BELL'S EVIDENCE BEFORE THE ROYAL COMMISSION, PRESENTED IN CRITICISM OF CERTAIN POINTS IN PRESIDENT GALLAUDET'S EVIDENCE.

PREFATORY NOTE.

For the opportunity of presenting the following comments to the public in this volume I am indebted to the courtesy of Professor Bell, to whom I beg to tender my thanks for this mark of his esteem and confidence. In accepting the privilege thus accorded me, I have written, as I am sure Professor Bell would prefer, with entire freedom in the interest of those benevolent ends we have equally at heart, but at the same time without the slightest abatement of that great respect and warm regard I have entertained these many years towards him who, though sometimes my opponent in debate, I am glad to believe has long been my friend.

E. M. GALLAUDET.

CENSUS RESULTS.

Professor Bell criticizes the opinion expressed in my evidence, Q. 13,105, that the ratio of deaf-mutes to the whole population of the United States was not greater in 1880 than 1 to 1,800, and endeavors to show that the number of deaf-mutes reported in the country by the Census of 1880, viz., 33,878, is under rather than over the actual aggregate at that time. [See Prof. Bell's evidence, Q. 21,357.]

The record of my evidence makes me base my criticism of the results of the Census entirely on errors in duplicating names. I do not think the report correctly states what I said; at all events, it was far from my purpose to take such narrow ground in questioning the accuracy of the Census Report. I am, therefore, especially obliged to Prof. Bell for giving me this opportunity of stating fully my reasons for the opinion I expressed to the Commission.

The Rev. F. H. Wines, Special Agent of the Census Office, who had entire charge of the enumeration of the so-called "Defective, Dependent, and Delinquent Classes," says, in his introduction to the volume in which the results of his labors are given to the public:

> "There is no sufficient reason to believe that the number of insane, idiots, blind, and deaf has increased at anything like the rate shown in the tables. Either the ratios to the total population, as here shown, are excessive, or those deduced from the figures of former years fall below the truth."

The figures of 1870 showed 1 deaf-mute to 2,379 inhabitants, and the proportions indicated by the census returns of 1860 and 1850 were substantially the same. Applying the ratio of 1870 to the total of population in 1880, 50,155,783, we have as the number of deaf-mutes 21,082, instead of 33,878 as reported, a difference of over 12,000.

I quite agree with Mr. Wines that the ratio "deduced from the figures" of 1870 is too low, and, in my estimate, have given him an advance of over 6,000. Why I ought not to give him the other 6,000 can be made easily evident.

In the original returns of the Census more than 3,000 idiots were included with the deaf-mutes. In the final report the number of deaf-mute idiots was given as 2,122.

I know of no teacher of the deaf, of long experience, who entertains any other opinion than that nearly all persons reported as deaf-mute idiots, even in this final statement, are *merely* idiots—mute perhaps, but not so because of deafness, but only because of feebleness of mind; and I am sure that had Prof. Bell been at the head of a large school for the deaf during a generation, where he might have personally examined the numbers of children seeking admission as so-called deaf-mutes, but who were idiots, pure and simple, he would have closed his comments on the unreliability of the Census returns, published in *Science*, Feb. 13, 1885, in language much more emphatic than the following:

> "The judgment of unskilled persons regarding the intelligence of deaf-mutes should evidently be received with caution. It is only to be hoped that the number of idiotic deaf-mutes returned in the Census has been overestimated. Before accepting the results as thoroughly reliable, it would be well to know whether or not the persons who made the returns were competent to judge the matter."

Mr. Wines, in addressing the Convention of American Instructors of the Deaf, held at Jacksonville, Illinois, in the summer of 1882, said, in regard to the work then in progress in classifying and verifying the Census returns:

> "One of our greatest difficulties has been the fact that so many are reported as belonging to more than one of the defective classes. * * * The possible complications of misfortune are numerous and distressing, as well as perplexing. We are now engaged in an effort to reduce their number, and we do not feel justified in publishing any of the results until we have *completed* the task of correcting, not one class only, such as the deaf or blind, but all the classes, all our lists, of which there are seven. We cannot depend upon our results as final *for any one class* until we are through; and how long it will take to get through no one can tell. It depends upon the number of clerks and the amount of money the Superintendent of the Census places at my disposal. In statistical work it may be taken as an axiom, *that we cannot have any degree of accuracy the cost of which we are not willing to meet.*"

That the means of completing Mr. Wines' work were not furnished is well known, and he himself says, in his letter transmitting his volume to the Acting Superintendent of Census, March 3, 1885:

> "I think it right to say that these tables do not represent the entire result of the investigation projected by me with the approval of General Francis A. Walker, former Superintendent of Census. A portion of the work, begun and partially finished, was in the end abandoned, owing to the closing of the office."

That this cutting short of the work throws a cloud over the accuracy of every portion of it, we have Mr. Wines' own opinion quoted above. And evidences of inaccuracy in the final report are not wanting.

A single discovered instance cannot fail to suggest the possibility of many not brought to light.

Professor Bell, in his evidence, No. 21,530, speaks of a family of deaf-mutes as follows:

> "I will show you the sort of information I get from the Census return. Here is a case. Here is a family all of the surname of Rank, all living in the same house; here is Daniel, aged 40; Annie, aged 38: Elias, aged 17; Eddy, aged 12; and Mary, aged 3, all deaf-mutes living in the same house with the same surname."

This is the sort of information Professor Bell gets from the Census and relies on, but from a much more trustworthy source, namely, the assurance of the father of the family himself, in answer to inquiries made by Professor Fay in connection with his work, now in progress, of securing marriage statistics of the deaf, I have the information that *neither of the three* children, Elias, Eddy, and Mary, is deaf.

Mr. Wines in his zeal to secure a complete enumeration of the classes committed to his charge, made use of one method which certainly was *liable* to lead to error. This was the inducement of extra pay to enumerators for every name added to the list of defectives. Mr. Wines says, in his introduction:

"For this extra service the enumerator was offered additional compensation; and it was impressed upon him that he should exert himself to find these defective persons, and make a full report of each case."

That the enumerators placed many names on their lists of which they did *not* make full reports is shown from the fact that of 11,405 cases reported as deaf and dumb, nothing is given as to the *age when deafness occurred, nor as to the cause of deafness:* information of such prime importance as to warrant at least a *presumption*, if not a conclusion, that the whole 11,405 were persons who became deaf in adult life, and hence were not properly classed as deaf-mutes at all. [See Professor Bell's evidence, Q. 21,487.]

No enumeration of "the deaf" was made in the Census of 1880, but this class of persons was considered, in the Massachusetts Census of 1885, quite apart from the "deaf and dumb." The report of this Census gives 2,973 deaf persons in the State, not including 828 reported as deaf-mutes. If this proportion between "the deaf" and the "deaf and dumb" held throughout the country in 1880, there were upwards of 80.000 persons whose disability was of a nature to make it easy for ignorant, careless, not to say mercenary, enumerators to improperly enroll large numbers of them among the deaf and dumb. This source of possible error, in connection with the probable blunders as to deaf-mute idiots, and the fact above alluded to, that of 11,405 alleged deaf-mutes nothing is given on the two points of greatest importance in settling the question whether they are deaf-mutes or only "deaf," leads to the conclusion that the number of deaf-mutes, correctly so termed, in the country in 1880, was less by several thousand than the Census returns claim.

But the confirmation of my expressed opinion, that the *true ratio* of the "deaf and dumb" of the country to the whole population was not greater than 1 to 1800, does not stop here.

It is probable that the Census of 1880 was as correctly taken in Massachusetts as in any State; undoubtedly more correctly than in many of the States and Territories. In 1880 there were, according to the U. S. Census, 978 deaf-mutes in a total population of 1,783,085, or 1 in 1,823, a proportion slightly under the figure named by me to the Royal Commission.

But in 1885, the State Census of Massachusetts, undoubtedly more accurate than the Federal enumeration of 1880, gives only 828 deaf-mutes, less by 150 than the number reported in 1880, while the total population had increased to 1,942,141, making the proportion of deaf-mutes 1 in 2,345, essentially the same as that deduced from the United States Censuses of the whole country in 1850, '60, and '70, at which Mr. Wines and Professor Bell have been wont to point the finger of scorn.

PRIVATE SCHOOLS.

In my evidence before the Commission, Q. 13,131, I say that "For all practical purposes the private schools are hardly worth considering," having said concerning them:

"Of these schools, eleven in number, five are oral schools, three are combined, one is experimental and in two the method is not given. The number of pupils is, altogether, only 165."

Professor Bell says, in his evidence, Q. 21,366:

"There is a great lesson to be learnt from private schools. The existence of private schools in a country like ours, where the States are munificent in their benefactions to the deaf-and dumb, is an anomaly. Why do these private schools exist? They express the existence of grave dissatisfaction with the institutions—that is, their significance—and when you come to examine the statistics of those private schools you will find that they are of two classes, one purely religious, the other purely oral."

That Professor Bell does not speak with his usual accuracy in his classification of these eleven schools is evident, when the fact is noted that two of these schools are neither "purely religious" nor "purely oral," namely, the New-Mexico school—manual in its method, and Professor Bell's own school, carefully returned by him as following the "experimental method."

But it is from his broad statement that the existence of these private schools is at once an anomaly and a protest I desire especially to dissent. They no more present an anomaly in education than does the existence, in a country where public provision for general education is "munificent," of large numbers of private schools established for purposes of gain, and to provide means of instruction for children whose parents prefer, for personal reasons, not to send them to public schools.

Five of these eleven schools can justly be said to exist mainly from considerations of personal advantage to those who maintain them, with the hope, perhaps, that the support of their schools may ultimately be assumed by the State.

Four schools are purely denominational, and their existence means nothing more than that their promoters are not satisfied with undenominational religious instruction, which is necessary in establishments supported by taxes levied on the whole community.

Without wishing to extend discussion on this point, I will only record my opinion that Prof. Bell entirely overestimates the importance of the private schools as expressive of dissatisfaction with the methods followed in the public institutions.

WHAT IS THE COMBINED SYSTEM?

Prof. Bell, Q. 21,374, objects to my claim that the Combined Sytem exists in the Pennsylvania Institution, and quotes Mr. Crouter, the Principal, as saying, "The combined system has no place in our school, at present."

With all respect to Prof. Bell and Mr. Crouter, I believe I may claim to have invented the terms "combined system" and "combined method" in 1867, when I made an extensive examination of schools for the deaf in Europe.

In reporting on the establishments then visited, I named twenty which I considered as being conducted under what might properly be termed "the combined system," the last of which I found at Copenhagen. There, as now, in Philadelphia, a separate oral school existed, not far removed from one in which signs were freely used. Both schools were under the external control of certain State officers, and pupils were passed from one to the other according to the ability they showed to succeed under the respective methods used. In one of the schools the "oral method" was exclusively employed—as is the case in Philadelphia, and yet the two schools moved on under a "combined system," the details and arrangements of which may be justly commended.

Much confusion has often arisen because of the use by many writers of the terms "method" and "system" interchangeably. I have endeavored for some time never to speak of the "oral system" or the "sign or manual system," but always of the oral method, the manual method, the auricular method, but not of the "combined method," reserving the term "system" to be coupled with the word "combined," as possessing a broader meaning.

I should, therefore, hold, as I did twenty years ago, that an establishment conducted on the "combined system" may employ many methods and may include more than one school. But my statement before the Commission in 1886, that the Pennsylvania Institution "was conducted under what is called the combined system," Q. 13.141, has a much more positive confirmation than any mere opinion as to the meaning of words.

Among the books and pamphlets laid before the Commission in connection with my evidence was a paper prepared by Mr. Crouter, the principal of the Pennsylvania Institution, and read to the California Convention in July, 1886. Two months later the author furnished me a printed copy of this paper in advance of its publication, that I might lay it before the Commission with my evidence. The title of this paper is, "The True Combined System of Instruction."

In the second paragraph of his article, Mr. Crouter quotes a definition of the "combined method" given by Professor Fay in the *Annals* as long ago as January, 1882, as follows:

"The combined method is not so easy to define [as the oral and manual] as the term is applied to several distinct methods, such as: (1) the free use of signs and articulation with the same pupils and by the same instructors throughout the course of instruction; (2) the general instruction of all the pupils by the manual method with the special training of part of them in articulation and lip-reading as an accomplishment; (3) the instruction of some pupils by the manual method and others by the oral method in the same institution; (4) although this is rather a combined system, the employment of the manual method and the oral method in separate schools and under the same general management, pupils being placed in one establishment or the other, as seems best in each individual case.'

Mr. Crouter criticises at some length the methods described under the first and second heads, and expresses the opinion that the third form is not wholly free from objection.

The fourth form he commends as the "true combined system of instruction," and says it

"Includes under one management manual instruction, pure and unadulterated, for all who may most profitably be so taught, and oral instruction, pure and unadulterated, for all who can most effectually be educated by that method. It discards all attempts to provide accomplishments of any kind, and confines itself to what appears wisest, best, and most practicable for each individual case."

This "true combined system of instruction," Mr. Crouter says, has been adopted in the Pennsylvania Institution "after a trial for several years of the second method of instruction as defined by Professor Fay," with results "unsatisfactory as regards articulation and speech-reading;" and in closing his article he declares—

"We consider our departure no longer within the domain of experiment; it has become an accomplished fact."

Whether an appeal from Mr. Crouter in "Facts and Opinions" to Mr. Crouter before the California convention will be counted as conclusive as the old time appeal from "Philip drunk to Philip sober," is for the reader to determine, but I think all will allow that with the above testimony of the Principal of the Pennsylvania Institution, furnished me by himself on the eve of my departure for England in the autumn of 1886, I was justified, in the absence of any cablegram withdrawing or modifying his paper, in citing the Pennsylvania Institution as a school conducted under the "Combined System."

Alluding as he does in several places in his evidence to the "Combined System," Professor Bell, seemingly carried away by excess of zeal for his favorite "method," makes use of language which, I am confident, he will wish, on reflection, to modify. In answer to a question, No. 21,654, "Now in America the system of instruction generally followed is what is called the combined system, I believe?" Professor Bell says:

"Yes; in my opinion that is the sign-language in disguise."

And again, No. 21,718:

"I do not believe there is any 'Combined System' in America. What is known as the 'Combined System' is simply the sign language in disguise."

And again, No. 21,825:

"In schools where they claim to have the combined method, as a general rule they have sign-language as the language of communication with the mind, and the pupils study written language and spoken language as our hearing children study French and German in the public schools, and with similar results; the sign-language is their language when they come out of school, and the other is a foreign tongue."

To say that there is no "Combined System in America," when for many years the official tables published annually in the *Annals* have reported the method of instruction in a majority of the schools for the deaf in the United States and Canada as "combined," is inconsistent with Professor Bell's usual accuracy; and if, as his language implies, he means to charge many honored and venerable teachers of the deaf in America with resorting to "disguises," and making unwarranted "claims," this would be a departure from his ordinary courtesy and fairness. But more serious than these two slips is the criticism cast in Q. 21,825 on the results of the education carried on under the Combined System.

It is not true that to the graduates of our Combined System schools written and spoken language are "foreign tongues." All that can be said with truth is that a certain proportion of their children, *under whatever method they are educated*, leave school with an imperfect command of verbal language. But the proportion is not larger in Combined, or even in Manual schools, than in those employing the oral method.

Hundreds of graduates from any respectable "combined" institution in the country can be named who are able to write their vernacular more correctly and intelligently than the average graduate of the common-schools.

The pupils of the elder Gallaudet and the elder Peet, as well as those of their associates and immediate successors, all trained under the manual method, with a free use of the sign-language, and without a lisp of speech, attained a facility in the use of their vernacular not surpassed by the graduates of the best oral schools, and if the criticism of Professor Bell be true of the graduates of any single school for the deaf at the present time, it is because its teachers are of less ability and fitness than those brought into the profession in the early days.

It is high time that the absurd idea were banished from every sensible mind, that accuracy in the use of verbal language cannot be attained by deaf-mutes educated on the manual method, including as free a use of the sign-language as any manual teacher in his senses would wish to make. Far from being a hindrance in the education of the deaf, the language of pantomime, discreetly used, is a help in every method and at every stage of the pupil's progress. And in making this statement it gives me pleasure to direct attention to the fact that Professor Bell, notwithstanding his evident misapprehension as to results, assures the Commission of his high appreciation of the value of signs in teaching the deaf. In Q. 21,819, he says:

"There is no objection in any method of instruction to the use of natural signs so long as they do not supersede language. * * * It is impossible to reach the mind of a child without the use of natural signs. Hearing children use natural signs in the same way; the only objection is to this conventional *language* of signs. The advocates of sign-language muddle the minds of people who have not studied the question by confusing the subject of sign-language with the more general subject of signs. I have read a little of what the German teachers have said on the subject of signs. They do not object to natural signs, and there is no such thing as a school in existence where natural signs are not employed, natural signs being understood to mean the signs that ordinary people employ."

The only comment I need to make on the foregoing quotation is to assure Prof. Bell that the "muddle in the minds of people" in regard to the distinction between "signs" and "sign-language" is of their own making, and exists mainly because some of them, "not having studied the question," and having little or no knowledge of the much maligned and misrepresented language, persist in declaiming against the evil effects of its use, quite ignorant, all the time, of the fact that the "sign-language," which they condemn, is made up in the proportion of at least nine to one, of "natural signs" which they approve, and that even the "conventional" or "arbitrary" signs, which some oral teachers would have us believe come direct from the evil one, are, with rare exceptions, ideographic.* And Professor Bell seems not to have gotten wholly out of the "muddle" himself when he says, in answer to question 21,817, "Did that child express her first ideas in natural signs?"—"In natural pantomime, helped out by crude conventional signs it had devised for itself;" for what signs could be more truly "natural" than *any* that an uninstructed deaf-mute child would be likely to make in attempting to express its simple ideas? The calling of any such signs "conventional" reminds one who has "studied the question" of a remark made years ago by the eminent teacher of the deaf, John A. Jacobs, in an article on the "Philosophy of Signs in the Instruction of Deaf-Mutes," appearing in the *Annals* for July, 1855.

Mr. Jacobs was complaining of the different ideas attaching in the minds of different persons to certain terms in quite common use, such as "methodical," in connection with signs, a word long taken as the synonym of "arbitrary" and "conventional." Mr. Jacobs says:

"It will be impossible to come to any agreement about the matter in controversy, while the term 'methodical signs' is continued to be used. In spite of any definition that may be given to it, the previous notions of the reader will cling to the use of the term. It is by no means appropriate or clear. As long as it is employed, an interminable logomachy will be kept up."

And so, to avoid falling into the use of words against which Mr. Jacobs warns those who undertake to write on conventional signs, I will pass on to another topic in Professor Bell's evidence.

I have been seriously puzzled over the answer given in No. 21,839, to the following question:

"Are you aware that Dr. Ed. Gallaudet, the President of the College, says, 'we know it would be useless to attempt to give lectures *viva voce* even to those who read well by the lips?'"

Professor Bell says:

"My answer to that is, it is difficult to believe that he could ever have attempted it."

After several endeavors to reconcile this with Prof. Bell's well-known great faith in the practically unlimited scope of oral communication with well-taught deaf-mutes, I have been compelled to perceive in the answer an ingenious covering of his own retreat, by a delicate compliment to me in his quick admission that I would be unlikely to attempt the impossible.

AMOUR PROPRE vs. MAUVAISE HONTE.

Towards the close of his evidence, Professor Bell, undertaking to point out "a very curious difference in the moral result of education by signs and education by oral methods" falls into a series of errors which ought not to be allowed to pass uncorrected. He begins by saying, (Q. 21,984):

"It [this difference] is in the *amour propre* or self-respect of the pupil. A person who is taught by any of the oral methods comes to consider himself as the same as other people, and he desires to have as little difference as possible between him and other people. But a person who has been taught by a special language comes to look upon himself as belonging to a different race, of which he is proud. He comes to look upon himself as different from other people, and glories in the fact. Now that leads to very curious results and misunderstandings. A sign-teacher will misunderstand and misconstrue the conduct and actions of an orally-taught person, because he does not realize that this feeling of *amour propre* or self-respect leads that orally-taught person to avoid making a public exhibition of himself. So that an orally-taught person will very often avoid conversation with a stranger if he cannot talk easily in company, because he does not like to have attention directed to his defect."

In commenting on this passage I must first criticise Prof. Bell's use of words, for the term *amour propre* has a very different meaning from "self-respect," which is given as its synonym or equivalent.

If Prof. Bell uses the words *amour propre* in their true sense, viz., self-love, vanity, a sentiment which Rochefoucauld declares to be the "greatest of all flatterers," the "moral result of education by oral methods" would hardly seem to deserve the commendation he bestows. If, on the other hand, Prof. Bell conveys his exact meaning in the English word "self-respect," it is not easy to understand how *that* sentiment would be built up by a course of conduct involving attempted deceit, accompanied always by a fear of detection.

If Professor Bell will allow me I will suggest a term which, in my opinion, expresses much more accurately than either *amour propre*, or "self-respect," the actual mental condition of many orally-taught persons, and I will then endeavor to show that this state of mind, however characterized, and however brought about, is morbid and greatly to be deprecated.

It is the *mauvaise honte* or false modesty, which Littré defines as "a false shame for that which is not blamable, and which may sometimes even be worthy of praise."

Surely the deaf are not to blame for their inability to hear, nor is it anything to be ashamed of; and yet the admitted tendency of oral teaching, which *aims* to make a deaf person "the same as other people," with "as little difference as possible between them and other people," is to lead him to shrink from having "attention directed to his defect," for as Professor Bell says (further on in 21,984), he prefers "in public not to speak to a person at all, rather than direct attention to [his] infirmity." Now, I ask the curious reader to refer to the answer to question 21,984, and, having read it through, to observe that while, according to Prof. Bell, "the spirit of the oral system is to make the deaf person feel that he is the same as other people;" this same orally-taught person still has an "infirmity," the keen consciousness of which, and the false shame for which, continually reminds him, like a grim spectre, that after all his much-vaunted oral teaching he is *not* "the same as other people," and that under many circumstances, when engaged in social converse, he must, "after a few common-places have been passed," lapse into silence (not even resorting to the use of pencil and paper, in which he is not above the level of the manually-taught deaf-mute), lest, forsooth, he should "exhibit his infirmity to the world."

I believe the candid reader will agree with me that the mental attitude, however termed, which would lead a well-educated person to pursue the course indicated by Prof. Bell, and for the reason he gives, may be justly criticised and must be deprecated.

And now to consider for a moment, the mental attitude of manually-taught deaf persons, greatly misrepresented by Prof. Bell, when he says, as he does repeatedly, that "they glory in the defect, they glory in being deaf-mutes, they glory in being distinct from the world."

My personal acquaintance with manually-taught deaf-mutes extends to several thousands, and I am sure I am justified in saying that as a rule they accept their "infirmity," their "defect," as a dispensation of Providence, for which they have no reason to be ashamed, and which no proper feeling of self-respect calls on them to try to conceal.

That they do not try to hide their defect from

* No word in our language is found to express precisely the idea attempted to be conveyed. One might be coined, such as "ideogestic," or "ideomimic."

the world is because they have been wisely told by their teachers that they will more frequently find the world kind and considerate of this defect than otherwise.

The result is, that compared with the orally-taught, for which so much is claimed in the matter of their being "restored to society," the manually-taught, even though they have no speech, are, as a rule, the less isolated in general society, and this for reasons that Prof. Bell has made perfectly clear, though he intended all the time to prove the contrary.

POLITICAL APPOINTMENTS.

In closing these comments, I will take the liberty of referring to a statement made by Prof. Bell, Q. 21,846, which does not come strictly within the scope suggested by my title.

Prof. Bell says, in answer to a question relating to the mode of appointing the principals of institutions in the United States, "They are political appointments?"

"I think so. In one or two cases those political appointments have given very great dissatisfaction."

This answer conveys the idea that as a rule the principals of the American schools for the deaf are appointed from political considerations.

This is so far from being true that it cannot be stated of more than five or six principals now in office in this country. That such appointments are to be condemned, all well-thinking persons will agree with Professor Bell. And it is to be hoped that the practice, limited, though it has, happily, been, will soon be entirely abandoned.

E. M. GALLAUDET.

THE CENSUS OF 1880: A REPLY TO PRESIDENT GALLAUDET'S COMMENTS BY REV. FRED. H. WINES.

COPY OF A LETTER FROM DR. BELL TO REV. F. H. WINES.

1336 NINETEENTH STREET,
WASHINGTON, D. C., *March* 27, 1890.

DEAR MR. WINES: Allow me to direct your attention to President Gallaudet's comments upon my evidence before the Royal Commission, a copy of which I enclose.

You will observe that in support of his charges against the accuracy of the Census of the deaf (taken by you in 1880), President Gallaudet has introduced new matter not presented to the Royal Commission.

I would, therefore, invite your attention to the same, and shall be pleased to publish any remarks you desire to make relating to the matter.

Yours truly,
(Signed) ALEXANDER GRAHAM BELL.

DR. F. H. WINES,
Riggs House, Washington, D. C.

REPLY OF REV. F. H. WINES.

CENSUS OFFICE,
WASHINGTON, D. C., *March* 30, 1890.

MY DEAR SIR: I thank you for calling my attention to the argument advanced by Professor Gallaudet in opposition to the accuracy of the census of the deaf made under my direction in 1880, and for giving me an opportunity to reply to it.

He expresses the opinion that "the ratio of deaf-mutes to the whole population of the United States was not greater in 1880 than 1 to 1,600." This is a negative opinion. But in his testimony before the Royal Commission he expressed the positive side of the same opinion, in the words: "It may be presumed that 1 in 1,800 would represent accurately the proportion."

The returns by the census enumerators, on the other hand, made the ratio 1 in 1,480, which, he thinks, should have been "corrected for error."

I certainly do not know, and it is difficult to see how any one can know, which of these ratios is nearer to the truth. The natural presumption would be in favor of figures based upon the results of personal inquiry by the census enumerators. Still, the uncertainty which attends all statistical work admits of the possibility that President Gallaudet's personal impressions may be entitled to greater weight than that which attaches to the enumerators' statements. I cannot decide this question; my attitude toward it is that of a judge, not of an advocate.

But it is clear to me that, whether his opinion is correct or incorrect, the reasons assigned by him in its favor will not bear examination.

He observes: "The record of my evidence makes me base my criticism of the results of the census entirely on errors in duplicating names. I do not think the report correctly states what I said; at all events it was far from my purpose to take such narrow ground."

What did he say, as reported by the stenographer of the Royal Commission? (See vol. 3, p. 456.) The italics are mine. "*An examination of the actual reports* made in the taking of this 1880 Census shows that the officers in this special branch of the Census, in their zeal to have a very full and perfect census of deaf-mutes, erred on the other side, and in many cases *enumerated the same person twice, and even three times. A sufficient number of errors of the character I have mentioned have been found*, in examining the report, to make it practically certain that the ratio of the deaf to the whole population has not materially increased over the figures of the previous censuses."

My attention being called to this language, I wrote to President Gallaudet, courteously asking him to inform me by whom the examination of which he speaks was made. To this question, addressed to him more than a year ago, he has as yet made no reply.

It is quite true that the enumerators in many cases reported the same person twice. The same was true of all previous censuses, and will occur again in the Census of 1890. But this was not due to the zeal of the officers in charge. The same person is enumerated, in a certain percentage of cases, at his home and again away from it; if zeal has anything to do in causing this error, it can only be the zeal of the enumerators. And the implication contained in the words, "if it had been corrected for error," as though it had not been so corrected, is most unjust.

In round numbers, the number of deaf-mutes returned by the enumerators, instead of being 33,878, was 38,500. The number reported by physicians was 1,500, making a total of 40,000. From this total I caused to be erased more than 6,000 names, of which about 2,500 were duplicates; the rest were idiots, or deaf or dumb only. The net reduction in the number, as it would have stood, had it not been corrected for error, was between 4,500 and 5,000. I would give the exact figures, but a small portion of my memoranda on this subject has been lost; the portion which remains includes five-sixths of the population of the United States, and is therefore sufficiently large to establish the substantial accuracy of the foregoing statement. Your own evidence (vol. 3, p. 803), that you had prepared a card catalogue including more than two-thirds of all the deaf-mutes enumerated in 1880, and had arranged them alphabetically, without discovering any considerable number of duplicates, is a strong corroboration of my own belief that the work of correction was carried as far as was at all practicable. However, President Gallaudet has abandoned this ground of attack, and it is needless to say more about it.

In his comments upon your evidence he speaks of "the blunders as to deaf-mute idiots." Whether there were, in fact, so many as 2,122 persons in the United States who were thus doubly afflicted, may be fairly questioned. All that can be positively asserted is that the enumerators reported a much greater number. His quotation from my remarks at Jacksonville, in 1882, shows that I was keenly alive to the possibility of error in this direction. He probably does not know that a personal letter was written to the head of every family from which a deaf-idiot was reported, containing specific questions, carefully framed, so as to determine with certainty whether the case was, in fact, one of double misfortune, or of simple deafness, or idiocy. In every instance where the first letter was not answered, he was written to again, and in a very large number of cases three letters were sent him. After the third call no further effort was made in this direction, because it seemed to be useless. The replies were examined with equal care, and showed that, in a large number of instances, this double infirmity actually exists; those reported to be deaf only, or feeble-minded only, were eliminated, so far as the information furnished would permit, but, of course, many of the letters remained unanswered. President Gallaudet is mistaken in supposing that my language in the introduction to vol. xxi of the Tenth Census had any reference to this inquiry. What I had chiefly in mind was a different inquiry, relating wholly to the criminal classes and the administration of public justice.

He says: "Mr. Wines, in his zeal to secure a complete enumeration of the deaf, made use of one method which certainly was liable to lead to error. This was the inducement of extra pay to enumerators for every name added to the list of defectives." This statement is inaccurate, and conveys an erroneous impression. The pay offered was not for names added to this list, but for full particulars respecting each case, involving as many answers and as much labor as the work done upon the population schedule. Not to have paid for it would have been unfair, and precisely the same compensation is offered in the Census of 1890. The extent of the error arising from this source is estimated by Dr. Gallaudet at 6,000 (the difference between one in 1,480 and one in 1,800 of the total population), for which, at 3 cents per name, the "mercenary" enumerators received the enormous sum of $180, which was divided among some 40,000 of them.

As to the suggestion that the Census was unworthy of confidence, because in 11,405 cases the age at which deafness occurred was not stated, this is a question which, in the nature of things, cannot be answered for all deaf-mutes. The deaf-mute himself does not know, perhaps; or, if he does, he may not be present to answer the enumerator in person; or he may be an uneducated deaf-mute, incapable of communicating with him. The presumption which President Gallaudet supposes to be warranted, that "the whole 11,405 were persons who became deaf in adult life," is so violent as to amaze a statistician, and it is refuted by the fact that the ages of these very persons are known, and that a large percentage of them were still children when the Census was taken.

Equally surprising is the allusion to a single family in which three children were reported as deaf-mutes, who were not even deaf, as if an isolated fact of this description could establish, or even indicate, any conclusion. Doubtless there are hundreds of persons listed as deaf-mutes on the census rolls who were not deaf. But there are hundreds of others, who are unquestionably deaf and dumb, whose names are omitted. It is an axiom in statistics, that the errors on one side must be presumed to be balanced by an equal number of errors on the other; else there could be no statistical reasoning whatever.

Finally, as to the vaunted superiority of the Massachusetts Census, far be it from me to deny it. But it is not proved. I would respectfully suggest that, if the State of Massachusetts desires to put this question to a conclusive test, and if it will produce its list of deaf-mutes, either in 1880 or in 1885, or in both years, for comparison, the United States list has been preserved, and the two can be compared name by name. I wish that this might be done. But the apparent falling-off in the number of deaf-mutes in 1885, in that State, is easily to be accounted for, on the ground that in the latter year an attempt was made to enumerate all the deaf, and many who were really deaf-mutes did not appear as such in the returns, because they were reported as deaf only. I apprehend that the same cause is likely to lead to the same result in the Federal Census to be taken on the first day of next June.

President Gallaudet unintentionally misrepresents my actual position on this whole question, in saying: "I quite agree with Mr. Wines that the ratio deduced from the figures of 1870 is too low." I think that I have never said that. I am not aware that I have pointed at any previous census of the deaf the "finger of scorn," though I certainly have ridiculed previous censuses of pauperism and crime in this country. What I have said about the deaf is that the figures of 1870 and of 1880 cannot both be right. But which will stand is, in my mind, as yet undetermined. We must wait and see what the Census of 1890 will show. If those who have it in charge shall not exercise the same indomitable patience in detecting and eliminating errors which characterized the census of 1880, the ratio of the deaf to the total population is likely to be larger on the face of the returns than it was after the necessary corrections had been made ten years ago. A number of improvements have been made in the schedule, and, unless confusion should arise in the minds of the enumerators as to the real distinction between the deaf and dumb and the deaf or dumb only, (which is not impossible), the Census of 1890 ought to settle this vexed question. But it must be approached without prepossession for or against any preconceived ratio. It is difficult to understand, in the absence of explanation, how President Gallaudet arrived at his decision to "give Mr. Wines" half the apparent relative increase in the number of the deaf, but to refuse him the other half. So far as appears, he ventures a guess, which may be right or wrong. The Census Office cannot indulge itself in guessing. It is bound to use due diligence in eliminating all palpable or ascertainable errors, and, having done this, to state the facts as they appear in evidence. Any charge that a different course was pursued in taking the last census of the deaf can be founded only in misapprehension.

I am, my dear sir, most sincerely yours,

FRED. H. WINES.

DR. ALEXANDER GRAHAM BELL.

THE CENSUS OF 1880: CONCERNING THE COMMENTS OF REV. F. H. WINES.

NATIONAL DEAF-MUTE COLLEGE,
KENDALL GREEN,
NEAR WASHINGTON, D. C.,

July 17, 1890.

DR. A. GRAHAM BELL.

DEAR SIR: I thank you for allowing me to see Rev. F. H. Wines' letter to you of March 30th last, in which he makes several comments on my criticisms of the 1880 Census of the "Deaf and Dumb."

There are a number of points in the letter to which I might reply, but I have no desire to continue the discussion; I am quite willing that the intelligent reader should form his own estimate as to effect of Mr. Wines' letter in weakening the force of my Comments.

There is, however, one statement in the letter which I think is likely to convey an impression other than that intended by Mr. Wines. He says:

"My attention being called to the language, I wrote President Gallaudet, courteously asking him to inform me by whom the examination of which he speaks was made. To this question, addressed to him more than a year ago, he has as yet made no reply."

I have submitted this paragraph to several intelligent persons and without an exception they gathered from it that a courteous letter to me had been left unreplied to for more than a year.

The letter to which Mr. Wines refers was received by me in the summer of 1888. I am not able to give the date, for unfortunately during that season the letter was lost. At that time I had no copy of my evidence before the Royal Commission, none had even been sent me. I at once wrote Mr. Wines saying that as soon as I could secure a copy of my evidence from England I would reply to his letter. Some months elapsed before my evidence reached my hands. Under date of December 13, 1888, I find in my press-book a letter to Mr. Wines which begins as follows:

"DEAR SIR: I received a few days since a copy of my testimony before the English Royal Commission, and have looked carefully over my statements bearing on the Census."

I then give Mr. Wines the essential points which I elaborated in my Comments last winter. Of course I cannot say that Mr. Wines received either of my two letters. But what I wish to direct attention to is, that he does not say he did not, while leaving this to be inferred,—no doubt without intention on his part.

Very truly yours,

E. M. GALLAUDET.

DEAF CHILDREN OF DEAF PARENTS: RESULT OF RE-EXAMINATION OF THE CASES REPORTED TO THE ROYAL COMMISSION.

A card-catalogue was exhibited to the Royal Commission containing details obtained from census returns concerning 607 persons who were believed to be deaf offspring of deaf parents (see queries 21,530, 21,531), and a table compiled from this catalogue was given on page 52 (see query 21,848). Some uncertainty attached to these figures, for in a number of cases the relationship in households had been assumed upon *prima facie* evidence, as stated in query 21,530, without verification by comparison with the schedules of the general population which were at that time inaccessible. By the courtesy of the Census Bureau I have since had access to the original population schedules of the census of 1880, and I have been enabled to identify names, verify details, and correct errors in all but 28 cases. As a result of this investigation I find that 63 cases reported to the Royal Commission were erroneously assumed to be deaf children of deaf parents. In these cases deaf-mutes of the same surname had been reported as living in the same house at the time the census was taken; for example (see query 21,530), in one house were found four deaf-mutes of the name of Holman: Richard, aged 40; Ruth, aged 30; George, aged 4; and Levi, aged 2. In such cases it was assumed that these were deaf children of deaf parents. Upon examining the relationships noted in the original population-schedules, it was found that in 11 cases the deaf children were nephews or nieces of the deaf persons supposed to be their parents; in 17 cases they turned out to be brothers and sisters of the persons assumed to be their parents, and in 27 cases they proved to be the wives of the persons supposed to be their fathers. In these 27 cases the husband was twenty-five or more years older than the wife. In one case, that of the Runk family (query 21,530), it has been ascertained that the enumerator's return of the children as deaf was erroneous (see page 207).

516 cases are believed to have been correctly reported to the Commission as deaf children of deaf parents, but it has been thought advisable, in the following tables, to omit 10 cases in which the surnames are unknown, as in such cases there is a possibility of duplication. The annexed tables contain an analysis of the remaining 506 cases.

In 148 cases the age at which deafness occurred is not stated; of the 358 remaining, 327, or 91.3 *per cent.*, were reported as congenitally deaf, and 31, or 8.7 *per cent.*, as adventitiously deaf. Applying this percentage to the 506 cases tabulated, gives 462 as congenitally deaf. The estimated congenitally deaf-mute population of the United States in 1880 was 18,328 (see Memoir, Table 17). From these numbers it would appear that one deaf-mute in 40, of the congenitally deaf-mute population, is of deaf-mute parentage, instead of one in 34, as stated at the end of query 21,531.*

* NOTE BY THE EDITOR.—If the computation be limited to those cases actually returned as congenitally deaf in the population-schedules of 1880, the proportion is larger than Dr. Bell's estimate; for the returns give 12,154 persons deaf from birth, of whom 327, or more than one in 37, were of deaf-mute parentage. It is obvious that whatever reasonable disposition be made of the doubtful cases, the ratio of deaf-mute children of deaf-born parents to the congenitally deaf population is a very large one. J. C. G.

A correction should be noted in query 21,855. The text should read: * * * "before the decade 1830-'9, there is no case in which both the parents were deaf."

In the following tables, presenting an analysis of 506 cases of deaf children of deaf parentage, verified by an examination of the original and unpublished population-schedules of the Census of 1880, "Deaf from Infancy" designates those becoming deaf under 4 years of age; "Childhood," at 4 and under 10 years; "Youth," at 10 and under 20 years; "Not stated," under 20 years of age.

A. G. B.

TABLE I.

Deaf Children of Deaf Parents.

Result of the re-examination of the 607 cases reported to the Royal Commission. (See Queries 21,530 21,531, and 21,848.)

Verified		506
Verified, but may be duplicates		10
Awaiting verification		28
Nephews or nieces instead of children	11	
Brothers or sisters instead of children	17	
Wives instead of daughters	27	
Other cases	8	
Erroneous		63
Total		607

TABLE II.

Deaf Children of Deaf Parents.

Analysis by Sex and Period of Life when Deafness Occurred.

Period of life when deafness occurred.	Total.	Male.	Female.	Sex not stated.
Deaf from birth	327	169	150	8
Deaf from infancy	23	10	13	—
Deaf from childhood	6	3	3	—
Deaf from youth	2	1	1	—
Not stated*	148	57	56	35
Total	506	240	223	43

* These cases were returned as "deaf-mute" or "deaf and dumb," but the age at which deafness occurred was not given.

TABLE III.

Deaf Children of Deaf Parents:

Analysis by Character of Deafness and Period of Birth.

PERIOD OF BIRTH.	Total.	CHARACTER OF DEAFNESS.		
		Congenital.	Non-Congenital.	Not stated.
1800 to 1809.........	4	4	—	—
1810 to 1819.........	5	3	—	2
1820 to 1829.........	10	8	1	1
1830 to 1839.........	34	18	3	13
1840 to 1849.........	54	27	3	24
1850 to 1859.........	96	46	10	40
1860 to 1869.........	112	77	10	25
1870 to 1879.........	167	134	4	29
1880 to 1889.........	12	8	—	4
Unknown............	12	2	—	10
Total............	506	327	31	148

TABLE IV.

Deaf Children of Deaf Parents:

Analysis by Period of Birth and Parentage.

PERIOD OF BIRTH.	Total.	PARENTAGE.		
		Both parents deaf in youth.	One parent not deaf.	Balance of cases.
1800 to 1809....	4	—	4	—
1810 to 1819....	5	—	5	—
1820 to 1829....	10	—	9	1
1830 to 1839....	34	13	11	10
1840 to 1849....	54	25	13	16
1850 to 1859....	96	46	22	28
1860 to 1869....	112	64	26	22
1870 to 1879....	167	128	21	18
1880 to 1889....	12	9	2	1
Unknown.......	12	5	1	6
Total.........	506	290	114	102

TABLE V.

Deaf Children of Deaf Parents:

Analysis by Character of Deafness in both Parents and Children.

EXPLANATION OF ABBREVIATIONS.

C.: *Congenitally deaf.*

N. C.: *Non-congenitally deaf*—lost hearing before reaching the age of 20 years.

N. S.: *Not stated.* Period of life when deafness occurred not stated, but person was reported to be "deaf and dumb," so that deafness occurred before reaching the age of 20 years.

A. L.: *Adult life.* The person became deaf in adult life after reaching the age of 20 years.

N. D.: *Not deaf.*

X.: *Unknown* whether this is a *deaf* or a *hearing* person.

CHARACTER OF DEAFNESS OF PARENTS.		Number of Deaf Children.	CHARACTER OF DEAFNESS OF CHILDREN.		
One Parent.	The other Parent.		Congenital.	Non-Congenital.	Not stated.
C	C.........	147	127	3	17
C	N. C......	53	44	4	5
C	N. S......	25	14	1	10
C	A. L......	—	—	—	—
C	N. D......	53	51	1	1
C	X..........	25	24	1	—
N. C........	N. C......	9	4	4	1
N. C........	N. S.....	2	1	1	—
N. C........	A. L......	—	—	—	—
N. C........	N. D......	2	—	1	1
N. C........	X..........	5	2	2	1
N. S........	N. S......	54	19	2	33
N. S........	A. L......	—	—	—	—
N. S........	N. D......	59	28	4	27
N. S........	X..........	28	4	—	24
A. L........	A. L......	2	—	—	2
A. L........	N. D......	39	9	4	26
A. L........	X..........	3	—	3	—
Totals..............		506	327	31	148

TABLE VI.—DEAF CHILDREN OF DEAF PARENTS:
Detailed Analysis of Parentage.

FATHER			Deaf Children. Totals: Both sexes.					
			MOTHER. Deaf in Youth. Character of Deafness. Congenital	Non-congenital	Not stated	Deaf in adult life	Not deaf	Unknown
Deaf in Youth.	Character of Deafness.	Congenital	147	24	11	...	27	9
		Non-congenital	20	9	1	...	1	2
		Not stated	14	1	54	...	32	19
Deaf in adult life			...	...	...	2	20	1
Not deaf			26	1	27	19		
Unknown			16	3	9	2		

TABLE VII.—DEAF CHILDREN OF DEAF PARENTS:
Analysis of Character of Deafness.

FATHER	DEAF CHILDREN: CHARACTER OF DEAFNESS. Congenital.						Non-congenital.						Not stated.					
	MOTHER. Deaf in Youth. Character of Deafness. Congenital	Non-congenital	Not stated	Deaf in adult life	Not deaf	Unknown	MOTHER. Deaf in Youth. Character of Deafness. Congenital	Non-congenital	Not stated	Deaf in adult life	Not deaf	Unknown	MOTHER. Deaf in Youth. Character of Deafness. Congenital	Non-congenital	Not stated	Deaf in adult life	Not deaf	Unknown
Deaf in Youth. Character of Deafness. Congenital	127	18	7	....	25	8	3	3	1	....	1	1	17	3	3	....	1	
Non-congenital	26	4	1	....	....	....	1	4	....	....	1	2	2	1				
Not stated	7	....	19	....	20	3	....	1	2	....	2	....	7	....	33	....	10	16
Deaf in adult life	......	....	....	....	6	....	....	....	....	....	2	1	....	....	....	2	12	
Not deaf	26	....	8	3	....	....	....	....	2	2	....	....	....	1	17	14		
Unknown	16	2	1	....	....	....	....	....	....	2	....	....	....	1	8			

TABLE VIII.—DEAF CHILDREN OF DEAF PARENTS:
Analysis by Sex.

FATHER	DEAF CHILDREN: SEX. Males.						Females.						Not stated.					
	MOTHER. Deaf in Youth. Character of Deafness. Congenital	Non-congenital	Not stated	Deaf in adult life	Not deaf	Unknown	MOTHER. Deaf in Youth. Character of Deafness. Congenital	Non-congenital	Not stated	Deaf in adult life	Not deaf	Unknown	MOTHER. Deaf in Youth. Character of Deafness. Congenital	Non-congenital	Not stated	Deaf in adult life	Not deaf	Unknown
Deaf in Youth. Character of Deafness. Congenital	80	13	3	....	14	4	56	11	5	....	12	5	11	....	3	....	1	
Non-congenital	14	6	1	....	....	1	14	3	....	....	1	1	1					
Not stated	4	....	26	....	11	2	7	1	27	....	10	1	3	....	1	....	2	16
Deaf in adult life	......	....	....	2	10	....	....	....	....	....	5	1	....	....	....	....	5	
Not deaf	14	1	10	9	....	....	12	....	17	10								
Unknown	6	1	6	2	....	....	10	2	3									

TABLE IX.—DEAF CHILDREN OF DEAF PARENTS:

Deaf from Birth.—327 cases.

Father		Males.										Females.										Sex not stated.									
		Mother deaf; period of life when mother's deafness occurred: In youth.					In adult life.			Mother not deaf	Mother unknown	Mother deaf; period of life when mother's deafness occurred: In youth.					In adult life.			Mother not deaf	Mother unknown	Mother deaf; period of life when mother's deafness occurred: In youth.					In adult life.			Mother not deaf	Mother unknown
		Birth	Infancy	Childhood	Youth	Not stated	Adult life	Old age	Not stated	Not deaf	Unknown	Birth	Infancy	Childhood	Youth	Not stated	Adult life	Old age	Not stated	Not deaf	Unknown	Birth	Infancy	Childhood	Youth	Not stated	Adult life	Old age	Not stated	Not deaf	Unknown
Deaf. Period of life when father's deafness occurred: In youth.	Birth	78	3	4	2	3				13	3	47	2	5	2	4				12	5	2									
	Infancy	11	2	1		1						14	1																		
	Childhood	1																													
	Youth																														
	Not stated	4				6				7	1	3				13				11	1									2	1
In adult life.	Adult life									1																				3	
	Old age									1																					
	Not stated									1																					
Not deaf		14				2			3			12				6															
Unknown		6				1						10			2																

Deaf from Infancy.—23 cases.

Father		Males.										Females.										Sex not stated.									
		Birth	Infancy	Childhood	Youth	Not stated	Adult life	Old age	Not stated	Not deaf	Unknown	Birth	Infancy	Childhood	Youth	Not stated	Adult life	Old age	Not stated	Not deaf	Unknown	Birth	Infancy	Childhood	Youth	Not stated	Adult life	Old age	Not stated	Not deaf	Unknown
Deaf. Period of life when father's deafness occurred: In youth.	Birth		1							1	1	2	2			1															
	Infancy	1	2										2							1	1										
	Childhood																														
	Youth																														
	Not stated					2							1							1											
In adult life.	Adult life																														
	Old age																														
	Not stated									1										1											
Not deaf						1										1															
Unknown																															

Deaf from Childhood.—6 cases.

Father		Males.										Females.										Sex not stated.									
		Birth	Infancy	Childhood	Youth	Not stated	Adult life	Old age	Not stated	Not deaf	Unknown	Birth	Infancy	Childhood	Youth	Not stated	Adult life	Old age	Not stated	Not deaf	Unknown	Birth	Infancy	Childhood	Youth	Not stated	Adult life	Old age	Not stated	Not deaf	Unknown
Deaf. Period of life when father's deafness occurred: In youth.	Birth																														
	Infancy																														
	Childhood										1																				
	Youth																														
	Not stated																			1											
In adult life.	Adult life																														
	Old age																				1										
	Not stated																														
Not deaf																	1														
Unknown							2																								

Deaf from Youth.—2 cases.

Father		Males.										Females.										Sex not stated.									
		Birth	Infancy	Childhood	Youth	Not stated	Adult life	Old age	Not stated	Not deaf	Unknown	Birth	Infancy	Childhood	Youth	Not stated	Adult life	Old age	Not stated	Not deaf	Unknown	Birth	Infancy	Childhood	Youth	Not stated	Adult life	Old age	Not stated	Not deaf	Unknown
Deaf. Period of life when father's deafness occurred: In youth.	Birth											1																			
	Infancy																														
	Childhood																														
	Youth																														
	Not stated																														
In adult life.	Adult life																														
	Old age																														
	Not stated																														
Not deaf							1																								
Unknown																															

Age at which deafness occurred not stated.—148 cases.

Father		Males.										Females.										Sex not stated.									
		Birth	Infancy	Childhood	Youth	Not stated	Adult life	Old age	Not stated	Not deaf	Unknown	Birth	Infancy	Childhood	Youth	Not stated	Adult life	Old age	Not stated	Not deaf	Unknown	Birth	Infancy	Childhood	Youth	Not stated	Adult life	Old age	Not stated	Not deaf	Unknown
Deaf. Period of life when father's deafness occurred: In youth.	Birth	2	3									6										9				3				1	
	Infancy	1	1																			1									
	Childhood																														
	Youth																														
	Not stated					18				4	1	4				14				6		3				1					15
In adult life.	Adult life																													2	
	Old age									1																					
	Not stated								2	5										4											
Not deaf				1		7			5							10	1		8												
Unknown					1	5										3															

Analysis by period of life in which deafness occurred.

TABLE X.—CHILDREN OF DEAF PARENTS—*Deaf from Birth.*

Father	Males										Females										Sex not stated									
Mother →	Deaf, in youth: Birth	Infancy	Childhood	Youth	Not stated	Deaf, in adult life: Adult life	Old age	Not stated	Not deaf	Unknown	Deaf, in youth: Birth	Infancy	Childhood	Youth	Not stated	Deaf, in adult life: Adult life	Old age	Not stated	Not deaf	Unknown	Deaf, in youth: Birth	Infancy	Childhood	Youth	Not stated	Deaf, in adult life: Adult life	Old age	Not stated	Not deaf	Unknown
Born 1800–1809.																														
Deaf, in youth: Birth									2										1											
Infancy																														
Childhood																														
Youth																														
Not stated																			1											
Deaf, in adult life: Adult life																														
Old age																														
Not stated																														
Not deaf																														
Unknown																														
Born 1810–1819.																														
Deaf, in youth: Birth																														
Infancy																														
Childhood																														
Youth																														
Not stated									1																					
Deaf, in adult life: Adult life																														
Old age																														
Not stated																														
Not deaf															2															
Unknown																														
Born 1820–1829.																														
Deaf, in youth: Birth									1																					
Infancy																														
Childhood																														
Youth																														
Not stated																			3											
Deaf, in adult life: Adult life																														
Old age																														
Not stated																														
Not deaf	2														2															
Unknown																														
Born 1830–1839.																														
Deaf, in youth: Birth	2								2	1	3								1											
Infancy	1																													
Childhood																														
Youth																														
Not stated									2						1				2											
Deaf, in adult life: Adult life																														
Old age																														
Not stated									1																					
Not deaf															1															
Unknown														1																
Born 1840–1849.																														
Deaf, in youth: Birth	5								1	1	2		1						2	2										
Infancy	1										2																			
Childhood																														
Youth																														
Not stated	1				1										1				2											
Deaf, in adult life: Adult life																														
Old age																														
Not stated																														
Not deaf	1							1			1				1															
Unknown														1																

Analysis by the decades in which deaf-born children of deaf parents were born.

(Row headings: FATHER. DEAF. Period of life when father's deafness occurred. Column headings: MOTHER. DEAF. Period of life when mother's deafness occurred.)

TABLE X.—CHILDREN OF DEAF PARENTS—*Deaf from Birth.*—Continued.

Born 1850-1859.

Father	Males: Mother deaf, in youth: Birth	Infancy	Childhood	Youth	Not stated	In adult life: Adult life	Old age	Not stated	Mother not deaf	Mother unknown	Females: Mother deaf, in youth: Birth	Infancy	Childhood	Youth	Not stated	In adult life: Adult life	Old age	Not stated	Mother not deaf	Mother unknown	Sex not stated: Mother deaf, in youth: Birth	Infancy	Childhood	Youth	Not stated	In adult life: Adult life	Old age	Not stated	Mother not deaf	Mother unknown
Deaf; period of life when father's deafness occurred: In youth: Birth	12		1								2								1											
Infancy					1																									
Childhood																														
Youth																														
Not stated	2				2				1	1	1				3				2											
In adult life: Adult life																													3	
Old age									1																					
Not stated																														
Not deaf	1				1						6																			
Unknown	2										3																			

Born 1860-1869.

Father	Males: Mother deaf, in youth: Birth	Infancy	Childhood	Youth	Not stated	In adult life: Adult life	Old age	Not stated	Mother not deaf	Mother unknown	Females: Mother deaf, in youth: Birth	Infancy	Childhood	Youth	Not stated	In adult life: Adult life	Old age	Not stated	Mother not deaf	Mother unknown	Sex not stated: Mother deaf, in youth: Birth	Infancy	Childhood	Youth	Not stated	In adult life: Adult life	Old age	Not stated	Mother not deaf	Mother unknown
Deaf; period of life when father's deafness occurred: In youth: Birth	16			1	1				3	1	10	1	1	2	2				4	1										
Infancy	2		1								4	1																		
Childhood	1																													
Youth																														
Not stated	1				3				3		1				2					1									1	
In adult life: Adult life									1																					
Old age																														
Not stated																														
Not deaf	4				1			1			2																			
Unknown	1										3																			

Born 1870-1879.

Father	Males: Mother deaf, in youth: Birth	Infancy	Childhood	Youth	Not stated	In adult life: Adult life	Old age	Not stated	Mother not deaf	Mother unknown	Females: Mother deaf, in youth: Birth	Infancy	Childhood	Youth	Not stated	In adult life: Adult life	Old age	Not stated	Mother not deaf	Mother unknown	Sex not stated: Mother deaf, in youth: Birth	Infancy	Childhood	Youth	Not stated	In adult life: Adult life	Old age	Not stated	Mother not deaf	Mother unknown
Deaf; period of life when father's deafness occurred: In youth: Birth	39	3	3	1	2				3		20	1	3		2				3	2										
Infancy	7	2									8																			
Childhood																														
Youth																														
Not stated											1				6				1										1	
In adult life: Adult life																														
Old age																														
Not stated																														
Not deaf	5							1			3																			
Unknown	3				1						4																			

Born 1880-1889.

Father	Males: Mother deaf, in youth: Birth	Infancy	Childhood	Youth	Not stated	In adult life: Adult life	Old age	Not stated	Mother not deaf	Mother unknown	Females: Mother deaf, in youth: Birth	Infancy	Childhood	Youth	Not stated	In adult life: Adult life	Old age	Not stated	Mother not deaf	Mother unknown	Sex not stated: Mother deaf, in youth: Birth	Infancy	Childhood	Youth	Not stated	In adult life: Adult life	Old age	Not stated	Mother not deaf	Mother unknown
Deaf; period of life when father's deafness occurred: In youth: Birth	4								1												2									
Infancy																														
Childhood																														
Youth																														
Not stated																														
In adult life: Adult life																														
Old age																														
Not stated																														
Not deaf	1																													
Unknown																														

Period of birth unknown.

Father	Males: Mother deaf, in youth: Birth	Infancy	Childhood	Youth	Not stated	In adult life: Adult life	Old age	Not stated	Mother not deaf	Mother unknown	Females: Mother deaf, in youth: Birth	Infancy	Childhood	Youth	Not stated	In adult life: Adult life	Old age	Not stated	Mother not deaf	Mother unknown	Sex not stated: Mother deaf, in youth: Birth	Infancy	Childhood	Youth	Not stated	In adult life: Adult life	Old age	Not stated	Mother not deaf	Mother unknown
Deaf; period of life when father's deafness occurred: In youth: Birth											1																			
Infancy																														
Childhood																														
Youth																														
Not stated																														1
In adult life: Adult life																														
Old age																														
Not stated																														
Not deaf																														
Unknown																														

Analysis by the decades in which deaf-born children of deaf parents were born.—Continued.

TABLE XI.—CHILDREN OF DEAF PARENTS—*Deaf from Infancy.*

Analysis by the decades in which children deaf from infancy were born.

Father (period of life when father's deafness occurred)	Males										Females										Sex not stated									
Mother:	Deaf in youth: Birth	Deaf in youth: Infancy	Deaf in youth: Childhood	Deaf in youth: Youth	Deaf in youth: Not stated	Deaf in adult life: Adult life	Deaf in adult life: Old age	Deaf in adult life: Not stated	Not deaf	Unknown	Deaf in youth: Birth	Deaf in youth: Infancy	Deaf in youth: Childhood	Deaf in youth: Youth	Deaf in youth: Not stated	Deaf in adult life: Adult life	Deaf in adult life: Old age	Deaf in adult life: Not stated	Not deaf	Unknown	Deaf in youth: Birth	Deaf in youth: Infancy	Deaf in youth: Childhood	Deaf in youth: Youth	Deaf in youth: Not stated	Deaf in adult life: Adult life	Deaf in adult life: Old age	Deaf in adult life: Not stated	Not deaf	Unknown
***Born* 1800-1809.**																														
Deaf, in youth: Birth																														
Deaf, in youth: Infancy																														
Deaf, in youth: Childhood																														
Deaf, in youth: Youth																														
Deaf, in youth: Not stated																														
Deaf, in adult life: Adult life																														
Deaf, in adult life: Old age																														
Deaf, in adult life: Not stated																														
Not deaf																														
Unknown																														
***Born* 1810-1819.**																														
Deaf, in youth: Birth																														
Deaf, in youth: Infancy																														
Deaf, in youth: Childhood																														
Deaf, in youth: Youth																														
Deaf, in youth: Not stated																														
Deaf, in adult life: Adult life																														
Deaf, in adult life: Old age																														
Deaf, in adult life: Not stated																														
Not deaf																														
Unknown																														
***Born* 1820-1829.**																														
Deaf, in youth: Birth																														
Deaf, in youth: Infancy																														
Deaf, in youth: Childhood																														
Deaf, in youth: Youth																														
Deaf, in youth: Not stated																														
Deaf, in adult life: Adult life																														
Deaf, in adult life: Old age																														
Deaf, in adult life: Not stated																				1										
Not deaf																														
Unknown																														
***Born* 1830-1839.**																														
Deaf, in youth: Birth																														
Deaf, in youth: Infancy																														
Deaf, in youth: Childhood																														
Deaf, in youth: Youth																														
Deaf, in youth: Not stated																														
Deaf, in adult life: Adult life																														
Deaf, in adult life: Old age																														
Deaf, in adult life: Not stated									1																					
Not deaf					1										1															
Unknown																														
***Born* 1840-1849.**																														
Deaf, in youth: Birth																														
Deaf, in youth: Infancy																														
Deaf, in youth: Childhood																														
Deaf, in youth: Youth																														
Deaf, in youth: Not stated					1																									
Deaf, in adult life: Adult life																														
Deaf, in adult life: Old age																														
Deaf, in adult life: Not stated																														
Not deaf																														
Unknown																														

TABLE XI.—CHILDREN OF DEAF PARENTS—*Deaf from Infancy*—Continued.

Analysis by the decades in which children deaf from infancy were born.

Born 1850–1859.

Father	Males: Mother deaf in youth: Birth	Males: Infancy	Males: Childhood	Males: Youth	Males: Not stated	Males: Mother deaf in adult life: Adult life	Males: Old age	Males: Not stated	Males: Mother not deaf	Males: Unknown	Females: Mother deaf in youth: Birth	Females: Infancy	Females: Childhood	Females: Youth	Females: Not stated	Females: Mother deaf in adult life: Adult life	Females: Old age	Females: Not stated	Females: Mother not deaf	Females: Unknown	Sex not stated: Mother deaf in youth: Birth	Sex not stated: Infancy	Sex not stated: Childhood	Sex not stated: Youth	Sex not stated: Not stated	Sex not stated: Mother deaf in adult life: Adult life	Sex not stated: Old age	Sex not stated: Not stated	Sex not stated: Mother not deaf	Sex not stated: Unknown
Deaf, in youth: Birth										1	2	1																		
Infancy		2																	1											
Childhood																														
Youth																														
Not stated																														
Deaf, in adult life: Adult life																														
Old age																														
Not stated																														
Not deaf																														
Unknown																														

Born 1860–1869.

Father	Males: Mother deaf in youth: Birth	Males: Infancy	Males: Childhood	Males: Youth	Males: Not stated	Males: Mother deaf in adult life: Adult life	Males: Old age	Males: Not stated	Males: Mother not deaf	Males: Unknown	Females: Mother deaf in youth: Birth	Females: Infancy	Females: Childhood	Females: Youth	Females: Not stated	Females: Mother deaf in adult life: Adult life	Females: Old age	Females: Not stated	Females: Mother not deaf	Females: Unknown	Sex not stated: Mother deaf in youth: Birth	Sex not stated: Infancy	Sex not stated: Childhood	Sex not stated: Youth	Sex not stated: Not stated	Sex not stated: Mother deaf in adult life: Adult life	Sex not stated: Old age	Sex not stated: Not stated	Sex not stated: Mother not deaf	Sex not stated: Unknown
Deaf, in youth: Birth		1													1															
Infancy	1											1																		
Childhood																														
Youth																														
Not stated					1							1							1											
Deaf, in adult life: Adult life																														
Old age																														
Not stated																														
Not deaf																														
Unknown																														

Born 1870–1879.

Father	Males: Mother deaf in youth: Birth	Males: Infancy	Males: Childhood	Males: Youth	Males: Not stated	Males: Mother deaf in adult life: Adult life	Males: Old age	Males: Not stated	Males: Mother not deaf	Males: Unknown	Females: Mother deaf in youth: Birth	Females: Infancy	Females: Childhood	Females: Youth	Females: Not stated	Females: Mother deaf in adult life: Adult life	Females: Old age	Females: Not stated	Females: Mother not deaf	Females: Unknown	Sex not stated: Mother deaf in youth: Birth	Sex not stated: Infancy	Sex not stated: Childhood	Sex not stated: Youth	Sex not stated: Not stated	Sex not stated: Mother deaf in adult life: Adult life	Sex not stated: Old age	Sex not stated: Not stated	Sex not stated: Mother not deaf	Sex not stated: Unknown
Deaf, in youth: Birth									1			1																		
Infancy												1								1										
Childhood																														
Youth																														
Not stated																														
Deaf, in adult life: Adult life																														
Old age																														
Not stated																														
Not deaf																														
Unknown																														

Born 1880–1889.

Father	Males: Mother deaf in youth: Birth	Males: Infancy	Males: Childhood	Males: Youth	Males: Not stated	Males: Mother deaf in adult life: Adult life	Males: Old age	Males: Not stated	Males: Mother not deaf	Males: Unknown	Females: Mother deaf in youth: Birth	Females: Infancy	Females: Childhood	Females: Youth	Females: Not stated	Females: Mother deaf in adult life: Adult life	Females: Old age	Females: Not stated	Females: Mother not deaf	Females: Unknown	Sex not stated: Mother deaf in youth: Birth	Sex not stated: Infancy	Sex not stated: Childhood	Sex not stated: Youth	Sex not stated: Not stated	Sex not stated: Mother deaf in adult life: Adult life	Sex not stated: Old age	Sex not stated: Not stated	Sex not stated: Mother not deaf	Sex not stated: Unknown
Deaf, in youth: Birth																														
Infancy																														
Childhood																														
Youth																														
Not stated																														
Deaf, in adult life: Adult life																														
Old age																														
Not stated																														
Not deaf																														
Unknown																														

Period of Birth Unknown.

Father	Males: Mother deaf in youth: Birth	Males: Infancy	Males: Childhood	Males: Youth	Males: Not stated	Males: Mother deaf in adult life: Adult life	Males: Old age	Males: Not stated	Males: Mother not deaf	Males: Unknown	Females: Mother deaf in youth: Birth	Females: Infancy	Females: Childhood	Females: Youth	Females: Not stated	Females: Mother deaf in adult life: Adult life	Females: Old age	Females: Not stated	Females: Mother not deaf	Females: Unknown	Sex not stated: Mother deaf in youth: Birth	Sex not stated: Infancy	Sex not stated: Childhood	Sex not stated: Youth	Sex not stated: Not stated	Sex not stated: Mother deaf in adult life: Adult life	Sex not stated: Old age	Sex not stated: Not stated	Sex not stated: Mother not deaf	Sex not stated: Unknown
Deaf, in youth: Birth																														
Infancy																														
Childhood																														
Youth																														
Not stated																														
Deaf, in adult life: Adult life																														
Old age																														
Not stated																														
Not deaf																														
Unknown																														

TABLE XII.—DEAF CHILDREN OF DEAF PARENTS—*Deaf from Childhood.*

Analysis by the decades in which children deaf from childhood and having deaf parents were born.

Columns: MOTHER. Deaf: Period of life when mother's deafness occurred — In youth (Birth, Infancy, Childhood, Youth, Not stated); In adult life (Adult life, Old age, Not stated); Not deaf; Unknown. Rows: FATHER. Deaf: Period of life when father's deafness occurred — In youth (Birth, Infancy, Childhood, Youth, Not stated); In adult life (Adult life, Old age, Not stated); Not deaf; Unknown.

Born 1800-1809.

Father	Males: Birth	Males: Infancy	Males: Childhood	Males: Youth	Males: Not stated	Males: Adult life	Males: Old age	Males: Not stated	Males: Not deaf	Males: Unknown	Females: Birth	Females: Infancy	Females: Childhood	Females: Youth	Females: Not stated	Females: Adult life	Females: Old age	Females: Not stated	Females: Not deaf	Females: Unknown	Sex not stated: Birth	Sex not stated: Infancy	Sex not stated: Childhood	Sex not stated: Youth	Sex not stated: Not stated	Sex not stated: Adult life	Sex not stated: Old age	Sex not stated: Not stated	Sex not stated: Not deaf	Sex not stated: Unknown
Deaf, in youth: Birth																														
Infancy																														
Childhood																														
Youth																														
Not stated																														
Deaf, in adult life: Adult life																														
Old age																														
Not stated																														
Not deaf																														
Unknown																														

Born 1810-1819.

Father	Males: Birth	Males: Infancy	Males: Childhood	Males: Youth	Males: Not stated	Males: Adult life	Males: Old age	Males: Not stated	Males: Not deaf	Males: Unknown	Females: Birth	Females: Infancy	Females: Childhood	Females: Youth	Females: Not stated	Females: Adult life	Females: Old age	Females: Not stated	Females: Not deaf	Females: Unknown	Sex not stated: Birth	Sex not stated: Infancy	Sex not stated: Childhood	Sex not stated: Youth	Sex not stated: Not stated	Sex not stated: Adult life	Sex not stated: Old age	Sex not stated: Not stated	Sex not stated: Not deaf	Sex not stated: Unknown
Deaf, in youth: Birth																														
Infancy																														
Childhood																														
Youth																														
Not stated																														
Deaf, in adult life: Adult life																														
Old age																														
Not stated																														
Not deaf																														
Unknown																														

Born 1820-1829.

Father	Males: Birth	Males: Infancy	Males: Childhood	Males: Youth	Males: Not stated	Males: Adult life	Males: Old age	Males: Not stated	Males: Not deaf	Males: Unknown	Females: Birth	Females: Infancy	Females: Childhood	Females: Youth	Females: Not stated	Females: Adult life	Females: Old age	Females: Not stated	Females: Not deaf	Females: Unknown	Sex not stated: Birth	Sex not stated: Infancy	Sex not stated: Childhood	Sex not stated: Youth	Sex not stated: Not stated	Sex not stated: Adult life	Sex not stated: Old age	Sex not stated: Not stated	Sex not stated: Not deaf	Sex not stated: Unknown
Deaf, in youth: Birth																														
Infancy																														
Childhood																														
Youth																														
Not stated																														
Deaf, in adult life: Adult life																														
Old age																														
Not stated																														
Not deaf																														
Unknown																														

Born 1830-1839.

Father	Males: Birth	Males: Infancy	Males: Childhood	Males: Youth	Males: Not stated	Males: Adult life	Males: Old age	Males: Not stated	Males: Not deaf	Males: Unknown	Females: Birth	Females: Infancy	Females: Childhood	Females: Youth	Females: Not stated	Females: Adult life	Females: Old age	Females: Not stated	Females: Not deaf	Females: Unknown	Sex not stated: Birth	Sex not stated: Infancy	Sex not stated: Childhood	Sex not stated: Youth	Sex not stated: Not stated	Sex not stated: Adult life	Sex not stated: Old age	Sex not stated: Not stated	Sex not stated: Not deaf	Sex not stated: Unknown
Deaf, in youth: Birth																														
Infancy																														
Childhood																														
Youth																														
Not stated																														
Deaf, in adult life: Adult life																														
Old age																														
Not stated																														
Not deaf																														
Unknown																														

Born 1840-1849.

Father	Males: Birth	Males: Infancy	Males: Childhood	Males: Youth	Males: Not stated	Males: Adult life	Males: Old age	Males: Not stated	Males: Not deaf	Males: Unknown	Females: Birth	Females: Infancy	Females: Childhood	Females: Youth	Females: Not stated	Females: Adult life	Females: Old age	Females: Not stated	Females: Not deaf	Females: Unknown	Sex not stated: Birth	Sex not stated: Infancy	Sex not stated: Childhood	Sex not stated: Youth	Sex not stated: Not stated	Sex not stated: Adult life	Sex not stated: Old age	Sex not stated: Not stated	Sex not stated: Not deaf	Sex not stated: Unknown
Deaf, in youth: Birth																														
Infancy																														
Childhood										1																				
Youth																														
Not stated																														
Deaf, in adult life: Adult life																														
Old age																				1										
Not stated																														
Not deaf																														
Unknown																														

TABLE XII.—DEAF CHILDREN OF DEAF PARENTS—*Deaf from Childhood.*—Continued.

Born 1850–1859.

FATHER.				Males.	Females.	Sex not stated.
Deaf. Period of life when father's deafness occurred.	In youth.	Birth				
		Infancy				
		Childhood				
		Youth				
		Not stated				
	In adult life.	Adult life				
		Old age				
		Not stated				
Not deaf						
Unknown				2		

Born 1860–1869.

FATHER.				Males.	Females.	Sex not stated.
Deaf. Period of life when father's deafness occurred.	In youth.	Birth				
		Infancy				
		Childhood				
		Youth				
		Not stated			1	
	In adult life.	Adult life				
		Old age				
		Not stated				
Not deaf					1	
Unknown						

Born 1870–1879.

FATHER.				Males.	Females.	Sex not stated.
Deaf. Period of life when father's deafness occurred.	In youth.	Birth				
		Infancy				
		Childhood				
		Youth				
		Not stated				
	In adult life.	Adult life				
		Old age				
		Not stated				
Not deaf						
Unknown						

Born 1880–1889.

FATHER.				Males.	Females.	Sex not stated.
Deaf. Period of life when father's deafness occurred.	In youth.	Birth				
		Infancy				
		Childhood				
		Youth				
		Not stated				
	In adult life.	Adult life				
		Old age				
		Not stated				
Not deaf						
Unknown						

Period of birth unknown.

FATHER.				Males.	Females.	Sex not stated.
Deaf. Period of life when father's deafness occurred.	In youth.	Birth				
		Infancy				
		Childhood				
		Youth				
		Not stated				
	In adult life.	Adult life				
		Old age				
		Not stated				
Not deaf						
Unknown						

Analysis by the decades in which children deaf from childhood and having deaf parents were born.—Continued.

MOTHER.			(repeated under Males, Females, Sex not stated)
Deaf. Period of life when mother's deafness occurred.	In youth.	Birth	
		Infancy	
		Childhood	
		Youth	
		Not stated	
	In adult life.	Adult life	
		Old age	
		Not stated	
Not deaf			
Unknown			

TABLE XIII.—DEAF CHILDREN OF DEAF PARENTS—*Deaf in youth, but exact period of life when deafness occurred not stated.*

Analysis by decades in which children of deaf parents became deaf during youth.

Males.

Father	Mother deaf, in youth: Birth	Infancy	Childhood	Youth	Not stated	Mother deaf, in adult life: Adult life	Old age	Not stated	Mother not deaf	Mother unknown
***Born* 1800–1809.**										
Deaf, in youth: Birth										
Infancy										
Childhood										
Youth										
Not stated										
Deaf, in adult life: Adult life										
Old age										
Not stated										
Not deaf										
Unknown										
***Born* 1810–1819.**										
Deaf, in youth: Birth										
Infancy										
Childhood										
Youth										
Not stated										
Deaf, in adult life: Adult life										
Old age										
Not stated										
Not deaf										
Unknown										
***Born* 1820–1829.**										
Deaf, in youth: Birth										
Infancy										
Childhood										
Youth										
Not stated										
Deaf, in adult life: Adult life										
Old age										
Not stated										
Not deaf										
Unknown										
***Born* 1830–1839.**										
Deaf, in youth: Birth	1									
Infancy										
Childhood										
Youth										
Not stated					1					
Deaf, in adult life: Adult life										
Old age										
Not stated										
Not deaf										
Unknown					2					
***Born* 1840–1849.**										
Deaf, in youth: Birth										
Infancy										
Childhood										
Youth										
Not stated					5					
Deaf, in adult life: Adult life										
Old age										
Not stated										
Not deaf					2					
Unknown										

Females.

Father	Mother deaf, in youth: Birth	Infancy	Childhood	Youth	Not stated	Mother deaf, in adult life: Adult life	Old age	Not stated	Mother not deaf	Mother unknown
***Born* 1800–1809.**										
Deaf, in youth: Birth										
Infancy										
Childhood										
Youth										
Not stated										
Deaf, in adult life: Adult life										
Old age										
Not stated										
Not deaf										
Unknown										
***Born* 1810–1819.**										
Deaf, in youth: Birth										
Infancy										
Childhood										
Youth										
Not stated										
Deaf, in adult life: Adult life										
Old age										
Not stated										
Not deaf					2					
Unknown										
***Born* 1820–1829.**										
Deaf, in youth: Birth										
Infancy										
Childhood										
Youth										
Not stated									1	
Deaf, in adult life: Adult life										
Old age										
Not stated										
Not deaf										
Unknown										
***Born* 1830–1839.**										
Deaf, in youth: Birth	1									
Infancy										
Childhood										
Youth										
Not stated	1				2					
Deaf, in adult life: Adult life										
Old age										
Not stated										
Not deaf					1					
Unknown										
***Born* 1840–1849.**										
Deaf, in youth: Birth										
Infancy										
Childhood										
Youth										
Not stated	1				1				2	
Deaf, in adult life: Adult life										
Old age										
Not stated									2	
Not deaf					1	1				
Unknown										

Sex not stated.

Father	Mother deaf, in youth: Birth	Infancy	Childhood	Youth	Not stated	Mother deaf, in adult life: Adult life	Old age	Not stated	Mother not deaf	Mother unknown
***Born* 1800–1809.**										
Deaf, in youth: Birth										
Infancy										
Childhood										
Youth										
Not stated										
Deaf, in adult life: Adult life										
Old age										
Not stated										
Not deaf										
Unknown										
***Born* 1810–1819.**										
Deaf, in youth: Birth										
Infancy										
Childhood										
Youth										
Not stated										
Deaf, in adult life: Adult life										
Old age										
Not stated										
Not deaf										
Unknown										
***Born* 1820–1829.**										
Deaf, in youth: Birth										
Infancy										
Childhood										
Youth										
Not stated										
Deaf, in adult life: Adult life										
Old age										
Not stated										
Not deaf										
Unknown										
***Born* 1830–1839.**										
Deaf, in youth: Birth										
Infancy										
Childhood										
Youth										
Not stated										4
Deaf, in adult life: Adult life										
Old age										
Not stated										
Not deaf										
Unknown										
***Born* 1840–1849.**										
Deaf, in youth: Birth	1									
Infancy										
Childhood										
Youth										
Not stated	2									6
Deaf, in adult life: Adult life										
Old age										
Not stated										
Not deaf										
Unknown										

TABLE XIII.—DEAF CHILDREN OF DEAF PARENTS—*Deaf in Youth, but exact period of life when deafness occurred not stated*—Continued.

Analysis by decades in which children of deaf parents became deaf during youth.

Born 1850—1859.

FATHER.	Males.										Females.										Sex not stated.									
MOTHER.	Deaf. Period of life when mother's deafness occurred. In youth. Birth	Infancy	Childhood	Youth	Not stated	In adult life. Adult life	Old age	Not stated	Not deaf	Unknown	Deaf. Period of life when mother's deafness occurred. In youth. Birth	Infancy	Childhood	Youth	Not stated	In adult life. Adult life	Old age	Not stated	Not deaf	Unknown	Deaf. Period of life when mother's deafness occurred. In youth. Birth	Infancy	Childhood	Youth	Not stated	In adult life. Adult life	Old age	Not stated	Not deaf	Unknown
Deaf. Period of life when father's deafness occurred. In youth. Birth																					3									
Infancy																														
Childhood																														
Youth																														
Not stated					6				4						7				2						1					1
In adult life. Adult life																													2	
Old age																														
Not stated								1	4										2											
Not deaf					1			2							2			2												
Unknown																														

Born 1860—1869.

FATHER.	Males.										Females.										Sex not stated.									
MOTHER.	Deaf. In youth. Birth	Infancy	Childhood	Youth	Not stated	In adult life. Adult life	Old age	Not stated	Not deaf	Unknown	Deaf. In youth. Birth	Infancy	Childhood	Youth	Not stated	In adult life. Adult life	Old age	Not stated	Not deaf	Unknown	Deaf. In youth. Birth	Infancy	Childhood	Youth	Not stated	In adult life. Adult life	Old age	Not stated	Not deaf	Unknown
Deaf. Period of life when father's deafness occurred. In youth. Birth																					1									
Infancy																														
Childhood																														
Youth																														
Not stated					3						1				1				1		1									
In adult life. Adult life																														
Old age									1																					
Not stated								1	1																					
Not deaf			1		3			1							1			3												
Unknown					3										2															

Born 1870—1879.

FATHER.	Males.										Females.										Sex not stated.									
MOTHER.	Deaf. In youth. Birth	Infancy	Childhood	Youth	Not stated	In adult life. Adult life	Old age	Not stated	Not deaf	Unknown	Deaf. In youth. Birth	Infancy	Childhood	Youth	Not stated	In adult life. Adult life	Old age	Not stated	Not deaf	Unknown	Deaf. In youth. Birth	Infancy	Childhood	Youth	Not stated	In adult life. Adult life	Old age	Not stated	Not deaf	Unknown
Deaf. Period of life when father's deafness occurred. In youth. Birth	1	3									4										2									
Infancy	1	1																												
Childhood																														
Youth																														
Not stated					3						1				3															
In adult life. Adult life																														
Old age																														
Not stated																														
Not deaf					1			2							3			3												
Unknown				1																										

Born 1880—1889.

FATHER.	Males.										Females.										Sex not stated.									
MOTHER.	Deaf. In youth. Birth	Infancy	Childhood	Youth	Not stated	In adult life. Adult life	Old age	Not stated	Not deaf	Unknown	Deaf. In youth. Birth	Infancy	Childhood	Youth	Not stated	In adult life. Adult life	Old age	Not stated	Not deaf	Unknown	Deaf. In youth. Birth	Infancy	Childhood	Youth	Not stated	In adult life. Adult life	Old age	Not stated	Not deaf	Unknown
Deaf. Period of life when father's deafness occurred. In youth. Birth											1										2									
Infancy																														
Childhood																														
Youth																														
Not stated																														
In adult life. Adult life																														
Old age																														
Not stated																														
Not deaf																														
Unknown															1															

Period of birth unknown.

FATHER.	Males.										Females.										Sex not stated.									
MOTHER.	Deaf. In youth. Birth	Infancy	Childhood	Youth	Not stated	In adult life. Adult life	Old age	Not stated	Not deaf	Unknown	Deaf. In youth. Birth	Infancy	Childhood	Youth	Not stated	In adult life. Adult life	Old age	Not stated	Not deaf	Unknown	Deaf. In youth. Birth	Infancy	Childhood	Youth	Not stated	In adult life. Adult life	Old age	Not stated	Not deaf	Unknown
Deaf. Period of life when father's deafness occurred. In youth. Birth																									3				1	
Infancy																					1									
Childhood																														
Youth																														
Not stated										1																				4
In adult life. Adult life																														
Old age																														
Not stated																														
Not deaf																														
Unknown																														

TABLE XIV.—DEAF CHILDREN OF DEAF PARENTS—*Deaf from Youth.*

Born 1800–1809.

FATHER.				Males.	Females.	Sex not stated.
Deaf.	Period of life when father's deafness occurred.	In youth.	Birth			
			Infancy			
			Childhood			
			Youth			
			Not stated			
		In adult life.	Adult life			
			Old age			
			Not stated			
Not deaf						
Unknown						

Born 1810–1819.

FATHER.				Males.	Females.	Sex not stated.
Deaf.	Period of life when father's deafness occurred.	In youth.	Birth			
			Infancy			
			Childhood			
			Youth			
			Not stated			
		In adult life.	Adult life			
			Old age			
			Not stated			
Not deaf						
Unknown						

Born 1820–1829.

FATHER.				Males.	Females.	Sex not stated.
Deaf.	Period of life when father's deafness occurred.	In youth.	Birth			
			Infancy			
			Childhood			
			Youth			
			Not stated			
		In adult life.	Adult life			
			Old age			
			Not stated			
Not deaf						
Unknown						

Born 1830–1839.

FATHER.				Males.	Females.	Sex not stated.
Deaf.	Period of life when father's deafness occurred.	In youth.	Birth			
			Infancy			
			Childhood			
			Youth			
			Not stated			
		In adult life.	Adult life			
			Old age			
			Not stated			
Not deaf						
Unknown						

Born 1840–1849.

FATHER.				Males.	Females.	Sex not stated.
Deaf.	Period of life when father's deafness occurred.	In youth.	Birth			
			Infancy			
			Childhood			
			Youth			
			Not stated			
		In adult life.	Adult life			
			Old age			
			Not stated			
Not deaf						
Unknown						

Analysis by the decades in which children deaf from Youth and having deaf parents were born.

Column headings below each of Males, Females and Sex not stated:

MOTHER.									
Deaf.								Not deaf	Unknown
Period of life when mother's deafness occurred.									
In youth.					In adult life.				
Birth	Infancy	Childhood	Youth	Not stated	Adult life	Old age	Not stated		

TABLE XIV.—DEAF CHILDREN OF DEAF PARENTS—*Deaf from Youth*—Continued.

Born 1850-1859.

FATHER.				Males.	Females.	Sex not stated.
Deaf.	Period of life when father's deafness occurred.	In youth.	Birth			
			Infancy			
			Childhood			
			Youth			
			Not stated			
		In adult life.	Adult life			
			Old age			
			Not stated			
Not deaf				1		
Unknown						

Born 1860-1869.

FATHER.				Males.	Females.	Sex not stated.
Deaf.	Period of life when father's deafness occurred.	In youth.	Birth		1	
			Infancy			
			Childhood			
			Youth			
			Not stated			
		In adult life.	Adult life			
			Old age			
			Not stated			
Not deaf						
Unknown						

Born 1870-1879.

FATHER.				Males.	Females.	Sex not stated.
Deaf.	Period of life when father's deafness occurred.	In youth.	Birth			
			Infancy			
			Childhood			
			Youth			
			Not stated			
		In adult life.	Adult life			
			Old age			
			Not stated			
Not deaf						
Unknown						

Born 1880-1889.

FATHER.				Males.	Females.	Sex not stated.
Deaf.	Period of life when father's deafness occurred.	In youth.	Birth			
			Infancy			
			Childhood			
			Youth			
			Not stated			
		In adult life.	Adult life			
			Old age			
			Not stated			
Not deaf						
Unknown						

Period of birth unknown.

FATHER.				Males: MOTHER. Deaf. In youth. Birth	Infancy	Childhood	Youth	Not stated	In adult life. Adult life	Old age	Not stated	Not deaf	Unknown	Females: MOTHER. Deaf. In youth. Birth	Infancy	Childhood	Youth	Not stated	In adult life. Adult life	Old age	Not stated	Not deaf	Unknown	Sex not stated: MOTHER. Deaf. In youth. Birth	Infancy	Childhood	Youth	Not stated	In adult life. Adult life	Old age	Not stated	Not deaf	Unknown
Deaf.	Period of life when father's deafness occurred.	In youth.	Birth																														
			Infancy																														
			Childhood																														
			Youth																														
			Not stated																														
		In adult life.	Adult life																														
			Old age																														
			Not stated																														
Not deaf																																	
Unknown																																	

(Mother column headings: MOTHER. — Deaf. Period of life when mother's deafness occurred. In youth: Birth, Infancy, Childhood, Youth, Not stated. In adult life: Adult life, Old age, Not stated. — Not deaf. — Unknown.)

Analysis by the decades in which children deaf from Youth and having deaf parents were born.—Continued.

The Massachusetts State Census of 1885, to which reference is made by President Gallaudet, p. 208, presents, beyond his contention, features of interest which arise from the exhaustive inquiries made in a special schedule relating to all persons of defective physical condition. These inquiries relate to the blind, the deaf, the dumb, the deaf and dumb, the insane, the idiotic, the maimed, the lame, the bed-ridden, the paralytic, and those suffering from acute and chronic diseases. In filling this schedule the enumerators were charged with a delicate and difficult task. The nature and the accuracy of the discrimination attempted in the classification of the *deaf*, the *dumb*, and the *deaf and dumb*, cannot be determined in the absence of the specific instructions to the enumerators, and the writer does not propose to interpret the results. How accurate a discrimination was actually exercised cannot be ascertained. In 1875 the number of persons returned as deaf was 7,255, while in 1885 the number was only 2,973. This decrease of 41 per cent. in the number returned and the much greater shrinkage as compared with the general population is accounted for by Mr. Carroll D. Wright, Chief of the Bureau of Statistics and Labor, by the supposition that the number in 1875 probably included many who were slightly "hard-of-hearing" only.

It is perhaps due to Mr. Carroll D. Wright and his assistants to say that they deserve unstinted commendation for the conscientious thoroughness and intelligence manifested in the preparation of the volume containing the statistics which suggested the more detailed treatment of topics relating to the deaf in this paper.

A portion of the tabular matter which follows is extracted from the statistics published in the Census of Massachusetts for 1885, but the principal tabulations have been prepared expressly for this volume from a re-examination of the original returns, and have not been printed heretofore.

The illustrative diagrams have been prepared from studies of the statistics by Dr. Alexander Graham Bell. The tables and diagrams are herewith submitted.

J. C. G.

KENDALL GREEN,
June 27, 1891.

TABLE I.

Extracted from Mr. Carroll D. Wright's Analysis of Massachusetts State Census of 1885.

DEFECTIVE PHYSICAL CONDITIONS.	Males.	Females.	Both sexes.
Deaf.			
Deaf only	1,043	1,523	2,566
Deaf and otherwise defective	212	195	407
Deaf and Dumb.			
Deaf and Dumb only	423	369	792
Deaf and Dumb and otherwise defective	15	21	36
Dumb.			
Dumb only	43	33	76
Dumb and otherwise defective	31	27	58

TABLE II.

Analysis of Massachusetts State Census of 1885, *compiled from tabulations, pp.* 1314-15, *Part II, Population and Social Statistics.*

Classification of persons and sex.	Total persons	Number in institutions.	Illiterate.	CONJUGAL CONDITION.		MEANS OF SUPPORT.								
				Single.	Married, etc.	Public aid.	Partially public aid.	Private aid.	Partially private aid.	Public and private aid.	Supported by parents.	Supported by relations.	Self-supporting.	Support not given.
DEAF.														
Males	1218	31	69	249	1006	27	5	28	25	4	36	37	1071	22
Females	1718	35	134	421	1291	35	13	38	39	5	44	109	1395	40
Aggregates	2973	66	203	670	2303	62	18	66	64	9	80	146	2466	62
DEAF AND DUMB.														
Males	438	63	60	315	123	19	4	24	8	30	74	13	261	5
Females	390	65	52	271	119	12	4	26	9	35	61	29	212	2
Aggregates	828	128	112	586	242	31	8	50	17	65	135	42	473	7
DUMB.														
Males	74	11	37	70	4	7	2	7	3	....	26	11	17	1
Females	60	10	33	50	10	7	2	4	1	....	20	9	17	
Aggregates	134	21	70	120	14	14	4	11	4	....	46	20	34	1

TABLE III.

Massachusetts Census of 1885: Cases of "Deaf," "Deaf and Dumb," and "Dumb" otherwise affected, compiled from tabulations of Defective Physical Conditions.

1. THE "DEAF."

	Number of persons.
Deaf and blind	98
" " and dumb	3
" " " insane	2
" " " idiotic	1
" " " paralytic	2
" " " deformed	2
" " dumb and insane	1
" " " " idiotic	1
" and insane	16
" " idiotic	13
" " paralytic	25
" " deformed	5
Total	169

2. THE "DEAF AND DUMB."

Deaf and dumb and insane	7
" " " " idiotic	9
" " " " paralytic	4
" " " " deformed	1
" " " " idiotic and paralytic	1
Total	22

3. THE "DUMB."

Dumb and insane	2
" " idiotic	33
" " paralytic	6
" " deformed	1
" idiotic and paralytic	3
Total	45

TABLE IV.

Massachusetts Census of 1885: Analysis of 3,788 cases of defective hearing, including 1,585 persons who became deaf under 17 years of age, tabulated from Mr. C. F. Pidgin's transcripts of the original returns.

	"Deaf."	"Deaf and Dumb."	Summation of both classes.
"Congenital"	112	403	515
"Non-Congenital"	2722	383	3105
Not stated	154	14	168
Total	2988	800	3788
Deaf from birth	112	403	515
Deaf from under 5 years of age	187	307	494
Deaf from 5 to 9 years of age	230	63	293
Deaf from 10 to 14 years of age	187	6	193
Deaf from 15 years of age	40	3	43
Deaf from 16 years of age	46	1	47
Total	802	783	1585

TABLE V.

Massachusetts Census of 1885: Analysis of 1585 cases of persons becoming deaf under 17 years of age, by sex and period when deafness occurred, compiled from Mr. C. F. Pidgin's transcripts of the original returns.

1. RETURNED AS "DEAF."

Age when affected.	Males.	Females.	Both sexes.
From birth	55	57	112
Became deaf under 12 months	3	8	11
" " between 1- 2 years of age	9	9	18
" " " 2- 3 " "	18	27	45
" " " 3- 4 " "	27	41	68
" " " 4- 5 " "	18	27	45
" " " 5- 6 " "	30	34	64
" " " 6- 7 " "	19	36	55
" " " 7- 8 " "	12	29	41
" " " 8- 9 " "	17	18	35
" " " 9-10 " "	17	18	35
" " " 10-11 " "	23	37	60
" " " 11-12 " "	5	11	16
" " " 12-13 " "	19	22	41
" " " 13-14 " "	15	19	34
" " " 14-15 " "	17	19	36
" " " 15-16 " "	15	25	40
" " " 16-17 " "	14	32	46
Total	333	469	802

2. RETURNED AS "DEAF AND DUMB."

From birth	208	195	403
Became deaf under 12 months	5	17	22
" " between 1- 2 years of age	42	31	73
" " " 2- 3 " "	56	50	106
" " " 3- 4 " "	33	27	60
" " " 4- 5 " "	27	19	46
" " " 5- 6 " "	18	13	31
" " " 6- 7 " "	7	6	13
" " " 7- 8 " "	3	3	6
" " " 8- 9 " "	6	4	10
" " " 9-10 " "	3	......	3
" " " 10-11 " "	2	1	3
" " " 11-12 " "	—	—	—
" " " 12-13 " "	2	......	2
" " " 13-14 " "	1	......	1
" " " 14-15 " "	—	—	-
" " " 15-16 " "	3	......	3
" " " 16-17 " "	......	1	1
Total	416	367	783

3. SUMMATION OF BOTH CLASSES.

From birth	263	252	515
Became deaf under 12 months	8	25	33
" " between 1- 2 years of age	51	40	91
" " " 2- 3 " "	74	77	151
" " " 3- 4 " "	60	68	128
" " " 4- 5 " "	45	46	91
" " " 5- 6 " "	48	47	95
" " " 6- 7 " "	26	42	68
" " " 7- 8 " "	15	32	47
" " " 8- 9 " "	23	22	45
" " " 9-10 " "	20	18	38
" " " 10-11 " "	25	38	63
" " " 11-12 " "	5	11	16
" " " 12-13 " "	21	22	43
" " " 13-14 " "	16	19	35
" " " 14-15 " "	17	19	36
" " " 15-16 " "	18	25	43
" " " 16-17 " "	14	33	47
Total	749	836	1585

TABLE VI.

Tabulation by sex, age, and age at occurrence of deafness, of the "Deaf" and the "Deaf and Dumb," with a summation of both classes. Columns B and C were compiled from the original returns.

1885. Present age.	Age at occurrence of deafness.	A. The "Deaf." Number affected at ages specified. M.	F.	Both sexes.	B. The "Deaf and Dumb." Number affected at ages specified. M.	F.	Both sexes.	C. Summation of "The Deaf" and "The Deaf and Dumb." Number affected at ages specified. M.	F.	Total.
2 years		1		1		1	1	1	1	2
	Birth	1		1		1	1	1	1	2
3 years		1	3	4		6	6	1	9	10
	Birth					2	2		2	2
	3 months					1	1		1	1
	6 months		1	1					1	1
	1 year		1	1		3	3		4	4
	3 years	1	1	2				1	1	2
4 years					6	2	8	6	2	8
	Birth				3		3	3		3
	3 months					1	1		1	1
	1 year					1	1		1	1
	2 years				2		2	2		2
	3 years				1		1	1		1
5 years		1		1	6	4	10	7	4	11
	Birth				2	1	3	2	1	3
	6 months				1		1	1		1
	1 year				1	1	2	1	1	2
	2 years				1	1	2	1	1	2
	3 years	1		1	1	1	2	2	1	3
6 years		3	5	8	6	4	10	9	9	18
	Birth	1	1	2	3	2	5	4	3	7
	6 months		1	1					1	1
	9 months					1	1		1	1
	1 year					1	1		1	1
	2 years	1		1	2		2	3		3
	3 years	1		1				1		1
	4 years		2	2	1		1	1	2	3
	6 years		1	1					1	1
7 years			2	2	8	6	14	8	8	16
	Birth				1	5	6	1	5	6
	6 months		1	1					1	1
	1 year				1		1	1		1
	2 years				3	1	4	3	1	4
	3 years				2		2	2		2
	4 years		1	1					1	1
	6 years				1		1	1		1
8 years		6	4	10	5	9	14	11	13	24
	Birth	1	1	2	5	2	7	6	3	9
	6 months					1	1		1	1
	1 year		1	1		3	3		4	4
	2 years					2	2		2	2
	3 years	1	1	2		1	1	1	2	3
	4 years	1		1				1		1
	6 years	3		3				3		3
	7 years		1	1					1	1
9 years		1	5	6	3	12	15	4	17	21
	Birth	1	2	3	3	5	8	4	7	11
	2 years					4	4		4	4
	3 years		2	2		2	2		4	4
	5 years		1	1					1	1
	6 years					1	1		1	1
10 years		5	4	9	10	7	17	15	11	26
	Birth	1		1	4	3	7	5	3	8
	3 months	1		1				1		1
	1 year				2		2	2		2
	2 years	1		1	1	1	2	2	1	3
	4 years	1	1	2	1	2	3	2	3	5
	5 years	1		1				1		1
	6 years					1	1		1	1
	7 years		2	2					2	2
	8 years				1		1	1		1
	9 years		1	1					1	1
	Unknown				1		1	1		1
11 years		5	5	10	6	14	20	11	19	30
	Birth		1	1	1	10	11	1	11	12
	11 months				1		1	1		1
	1 year				2	2	4	2	2	4
	2 years					2	2		2	2
	3 years	1		1	1		1	2		2
	4 years		1	1	1		1	1	1	2
	6 years	1		1				1		1
	7 years	2		2				2		2
	9 years		1	1					1	1
	10 years		1	1					1	1
	Unknown	1	1	2				1	1	2
12 years		5	5	10	11	11	22	16	16	32
	Birth		1	1	5	5	10	5	6	11
	4 months					1	1		1	1
	8 months				1		1	1		1
	9 months					1	1		1	1
	1 year				1	1	2	1	1	2
	2 years		1	1	4	2	6	4	3	7
	3 years		1	1					1	1
	7 years	1		1				1		1
	8 years	1		1		1	1	1	1	2
	9 years	2		2				2		2
	11 years		2	2					2	2
	Unknown	1		1				1		1

TABLE VI.—Continued.

1885. Present age.	Age at occurrence of deafness.	A. The "Deaf." Number affected at ages specified. M.	F.	Both sexes.	B. The "Deaf and Dumb." Number affected at ages specified. M.	F.	Both sexes.	C. Summation of "The Deaf" and "The Deaf and Dumb." Number affected at ages specified. M.	F.	Total.
13 years		6	12	18	12	12	24	18	23	41
	Birth		2	2	2	2	4	2	4	6
	3 months		1	1					1	1
	8 months					1	1		1	1
	1 year		1	1	3	3	6	3	4	7
	2 years	2	1	3	3	3	6	5	4	9
	3 years		3	3	4	2	6	4	5	9
	4 years		1	1					1	1
	7 years	1	1	2				1	1	2
	8 years		1	1					1	1
	10 years	1		1				1		1
	12 years		1	1					1	1
	Unknown	*2		*2		*1	*1	*2		2
14 years		5	9	14	24	15	39	29	24	53
	Birth				5	3	8	5	3	8
	4 months		1	1					1	1
	1 year				1	1	2	1	1	2
	2 years		3	3	6	6	12	6	9	15
	3 years	1		1	3	2	5	4	2	6
	4 years	1	2	3	4	2	6	5	4	9
	5 years	1		1	2		2	3		3
	6 years				1	1	2	1	1	2
	7 years		1	1	1		1	1	1	2
	8 years		1	1					1	1
	9 years	1		1				1		1
	12 years		1	1					1	1
	Unknown	1		1	1		1	2		2
15 years		7	10	17	9	7	16	16	17	33
	Birth		1	1	4	2	6	4	3	7
	1 year				1	1	2	1	1	2
	2 years				2	2	4	2	2	4
	3 years		2	2		1	1		3	3
	4 years	1	1	2	2	1	3	3	2	5
	5 years	1		1				1		1
	7 years		2	2					2	2
	8 years	1		1				1		1
	9 years		2	2					2	2
	10 years	2	2	4				2	2	4
	13 years	1		1				1		1
	Unknown	1		1				1		1
16 years		8	13	21	13	11	24	21	24	45
	Birth	3	2	5	6	3	9	9	5	14
	8 months					1	1		1	1
	1 year		1	1	2		2	2	1	3
	2 years		1	1	1	1	2	1	2	3
	3 years		2	2					2	2
	4 years		2	2	3	3	6	3	5	8
	5 years	2	1	3	1		1	3	1	4
	6 years					2	2		2	2
	7 years	1		1				1		1
	8 years		1	1		1	1		2	2
	11 years		1	1					1	1
	13 years	1		1				1		1
	14 years		1	1					1	1
	Unknown	1	1	2				1	1	2
17 years		6	10	16	12	6	18	18	16	34
	Birth		1	1	3	4	7	3	5	8
	1 year				3		3	3		3
	2 years		1	1					1	1
	3 years	1	1	2		1	1	1	2	3
	4 years				1		1	1		1
	5 years	2		2	3	1	4	5	1	6
	6 years	1		1				1		1
	7 years		2	2					2	2
	9 years	1		1				1		1
	10 years		1	1					1	1
	13 years		2	2	1		1	1	2	3
	15 years				1		1	1		1
	16 years	1	2	3				1	2	3
18 years		10	11	21	11	5	16	21	16	37
	Birth	2	2	4	5	2	7	7	4	11
	1 year				3		3	3		3
	2 years		1	1	1	3	4	1	4	5
	3 years				1		1	1		1
	4 years	1	1	2	1		1	2	1	3
	5 years	1	2	3				1	2	3
	6 years	1		1				1		1
	7 years		1	1					1	1
	9 years		2	2					2	2
	11 years	1		1				1		1
	12 years	2	1	3				2	1	3
	13 years		1	1					1	1
	14 years	1		1				1		1
	17 years	1		1				1		1
19 years		5	7	12	10	11	21	15	18	33
	Birth	1	1	2	6	4	10	7	5	12
	1 year				2	2	4	2	2	4
	2 years					1	1		1	1
	3 years	3		3				3		3
	4 years				1		1	1		1
	5 years					3	3		3	3
	6 years		1	1		1	1		2	2
	7 years		1	1					1	1
	8 years	1	1	2	1		1	2	1	8
	9 years		2	2					2	2
	16 years		1	1					1	1
20 years		5	8	13	4	11	15	9	19	28
	Birth		2	2	3	6	9	3	8	11
	1 year				1	2	3	1	2	3
	3 years					2	2		2	2
	4 years					1	1		1	1

* The slight discrepancy here noted was referred to Mr. C. F. Pidgin, who was not able to supply the correction without a re-examination of the original returns, and these had been re-classified for other purposes.—EDITOR.

TABLE VI.—Continued.

Present age.	Age at occurrence of deafness.	A. The "Deaf." Number affected at ages specified. M.	A. F.	A. Both sexes.	B. The "Deaf and Dumb." Number affected at ages specified. M.	B. F.	B. Both sexes.	C. Summation of "The Deaf" and "The Deaf and Dumb." Number affected at ages specified. M.	C. F.	C. Total.
1885.										
20 years—Continued.	5 years	1		1				1		1
	6 years		1	1					1	1
	8 years	1	1	2				1	1	2
	9 years		1	1					1	1
	10 years	1	1	2				1	1	2
	13 years	1	1	2				1	1	2
	14 years		1	1					1	1
	Unknown	1		1				1		1
21 years		5	4	9	5	5	10	10	9	19
	Birth	1		1	1	3	4	2	3	5
	1 year	1		1	1		1	2		2
	2 years				1		1	1		1
	3 years		1	1	1	1	2	1	2	3
	5 years				1	1	2	1	1	2
	9 years	1		1				1		1
	10 years		1	1					1	1
	12 years		1	1					1	1
	16 years		1	1					1	1
	18 years	1		1				1		1
	Unknown	1		1				1		1
22 years		9	13	22	9	2	11	18	15	33
	Birth				6	2	8	6	2	8
	6 months		1	1					1	1
	1 year	1		1				1		1
	2 years				2		2	2		2
	3 years	1	2	3				1	2	3
	5 years	1		1	1		1	2		2
	6 years	2	1	3				2	1	3
	7 years		2	2					2	2
	8 years	3		3				3		3
	10 years		2	2					2	2
	11 years	1		1				1		1
	13 years		1	1					1	1
	17 years		1	1					1	1
	20 years		2	2					2	2
	22 years		1	1					1	1
23 years		10	10	20	6	8	14	16	18	34
	Birth	1		1	4	6	10	5	6	11
	6 months					1	1		1	1
	1 year	1		1				1		1
	2 years	2		2	1		1	3		3
	3 years	1	1	2		1	1	1	2	3
	4 years		1	1					1	1
	5 years		2	2					2	2
	8 years		1	1					1	1
	10 years	1		1				1		1
	11 years	1	1	2				1	1	2
	12 years	1	1	2				1	1	2
	13 years	1		1				1		1
	14 years		1	1					1	1
	15 years				1		1	1		1
	19 years	1		1				1		1
	Unknown		2	2					2	2
24 years		3	10	13	8	10	18	11	20	31
	Birth		1	1	3	7	10	3	8	11
	1 year				2		2	2		2
	2 years		1	1	1	1	2	1	2	3
	3 years		1	1		1	1		2	2
	4 years		1	1	1		1	1	1	2
	5 years		2	2					2	2
	6 years	1		1	1		1	2		2
	7 years					1	1		1	1
	9 years		1	1					1	1
	10 years		1	1					1	1
	12 years	1		1				1		1
	18 years		2	2					2	2
	Unknown	1		1				1		1
25 years		7	13	20	8	10	18	15	23	38
	Birth		1	1	7	7	14	7	8	15
	6 months					1	1		1	1
	2 years	1		1				1		1
	3 years				1		1	1		1
	4 years		1	1		1	1		2	2
	5 years	1		1				1		1
	6 years		1	1					1	1
	8 years					1	1		1	1
	10 years		3	3					3	3
	12 years	1		1				1		1
	13 years	1	1	2				1	1	2
	14 years		1	1					1	1
	15 years	1	1	2				1	1	2
	17 years	1		1				1		1
	20 years		3	3					3	3
	22 years	1		1				1		1
	25 years		1	1					1	1
26 years		14	14	28	8	4	12	22	18	40
	Birth		1	1	6	4	10	6	5	11
	1 year				1		1	1		1
	2 years				1		1	1		1
	3 years	1		1				1		1
	4 years	1		1				1		1
	5 years	1	2	3				1	2	3
	6 years	1	2	3				1	2	3
	7 years	1	1	2				1	1	2
	8 years	1		1				1		1
	9 years	2		2				2		2
	10 years	1	1	2				1	1	2
	11 years	1		1				1		1
	12 years	1	1	2				1	1	2
	14 years		1	1					1	1
	15 years		1	1					1	1
	16 years	1	1	2				1	1	2
26 years—Continued.	18 years		1	1					1	1
	20 years	1		1				1		1
	21 years		1	1					1	1
	24 years	1	1	2				1	1	2
27 years		10	21	31	5	3	8	15	24	39
	Birth	1		1	3	2	5	4	2	6
	2 years	1		1	1	1	2	2	1	3
	3 years		1	1					1	1
	5 years	1	3	4				1	3	4
	7 years	1	2	3				1	2	3
	8 years		1	1	1		1	1	1	2
	10 years		1	1					1	1
	12 years		1	1					1	1
	13 years	1		1				1		1
	15 years	1	2	3				1	2	3
	16 years	2	1	3				2	1	3
	17 years		2	2					2	2
	19 years		1	1					1	1
	20 years	1		1				1		1
	21 years	1	1	2				1	1	2
	23 years		2	2					2	2
	24 years		3	3					3	3
28 years		8	18	26	10	8	18	18	26	44
	Birth		1	1	5	5	10	5	6	11
	1 year		1	1	2		2	2	1	3
	2 years		1	1	1	1	2	1	2	3
	3 years					2	2		2	2
	4 years	1		1	1		1	2		2
	5 years		2	2					2	2
	6 years	1		1				1		1
	7 years		1	1					1	1
	9 years	1	1	2				1	1	2
	13 years		1	1					1	1
	14 years	2		2				2		2
	15 years		1	1					1	1
	16 years	1	2	3				1	2	3
	18 years	1	2	3				1	2	3
	20 years		1	1					1	1
	23 years		1	1					1	1
	24 years		2	2					2	2
	25 years	1		1				1		1
	28 years		1	1					1	1
	Unknown				1		1	1		1
29 years		8	12	20	5	6	11	13	18	31
	Birth	2		2	2	3	5	4	3	7
	11 months					1	1		1	1
	2 years				3	1	4	3	1	4
	3 years		1	1					1	1
	4 years		2	2					2	2
	7 years		1	1					1	1
	10 years					1	1		1	1
	13 years	1		1				1		1
	14 years		1	1					1	1
	17 years		2	2					2	2
	18 years	1		1				1		1
	20 years	1		1				1		1
	21 years		1	1					1	1
	24 years		1	1					1	1
	25 years	1	1	2				1	1	2
	27 years		1	1					1	1
	Unknown	2	1	3				2	1	3
30 years		12	29	41	8	11	19	20	40	60
	Birth		1	1	5	4	9	5	5	10
	11 months					1	1		1	1
	2 years	1	1	2	1	3	4	2	4	6
	3 years	1		1		1	1	1	1	2
	4 years		2	2	1	1	2	1	3	4
	5 years	1	4	5				1	4	5
	6 years	1		1	1		1	2		2
	9 years	2		2				2		2
	10 years	1	1	2				1	1	2
	12 years		1	1					1	1
	14 years	1		1				1		1
	15 years		1	1					1	1
	16 years	1	1	2				1	1	2
	17 years		1	1					1	1
	20 years	1	6	7				1	6	7
	24 years	1		1				1		1
	25 years		2	2					2	2
	26 years	1	1	2				1	1	2
	27 years		1	1					1	1
	28 years		3	3					3	3
	29 years		2	2					2	2
	Unknown		1	1		1	1		2	2
31 years		6	20	26	15	2	17	21	22	43
	Birth	1	1	2	5		5	6	1	7
	1 year	1		1				1		1
	2 years		2	2	2	1	3	2	3	5
	3 years		2	2	3		3	3	2	5
	4 years				1		1	1		1
	5 years		1	1	1	1	2	1	2	3
	6 years		1	1	1		1	1	1	2
	8 years				1		1	1		1
	10 years		2	2	1		1	1	2	3
	11 years		1	1					1	1
	12 years		1	1					1	1
	14 years		1	1					1	1
	15 years		1	1					1	1
	19 years	1		1				1		1
	20 years		1	1					1	1
	21 years		2	2					2	2
	23 years		1	1					1	1
	24 years	1		1				1		1

TABLE VI.—Continued.

1885. Present age.	Age at occurrence of deafness.	A. The "Deaf." Number affected at ages specified. M.	F.	Both sexes.	B. The "Deaf and Dumb." Number affected at ages specified. M.	F.	Both sexes.	C. Summation of "The Deaf" and "The Deaf and Dumb." Number affected at ages specified. M.	F.	Total.
31 years—Continued.	26 years.......	....	1	1	....	....	....	....	1	1
	27 years.......	....	1	1	....	....	....	....	1	1
	30 years.......	....	1	1	....	....	....	....	1	1
	Unknown	2	....	2	....	....	....	2	....	2
32 years......	....	10	9	19	13	5	18	23	14	37
	Birth	1	....	1	8	2	10	9	2	11
	6 months......	....	....	....	....	1	1	....	1	1
	1 year..........	1	1	2	....	....	....	1	1	2
	2 years........	....	....	....	....	2	2	....	2	2
	3 years........	....	....	....	1	....	1	1	....	1
	4 years........	....	....	....	1	....	1	1	....	1
	6 years........	1	2	3	....	....	....	1	2	3
	9 years........	1	....	1	1	....	1	2	....	2
	10 years......	....	1	1	1	....	1	1	1	2
	12 years......	....	1	1	1	....	1	1	1	2
	17 years......	....	1	1	....	....	....	....	1	1
	24 years......	1	....	1	....	....	....	1	....	1
	27 years......	1	1	2	....	....	....	1	1	2
	28 years......	1	1	2	....	....	....	1	1	2
	29 years......	1	1	2	....	....	....	1	1	2
	30 years......	1	....	1	....	....	....	1	....	1
	Unknown	1	....	1	....	....	....	1	....	1
33 years......	....	12	20	32	8	4	12	20	24	44
	Birth	1	1	2	....	3	3	1	4	5
	1 year..........	....	....	....	1	1	2	1	1	2
	2 years........	....	2	2	1	....	1	1	2	3
	3 years........	....	1	1	2	....	2	2	1	3
	4 years........	1	....	1	1	....	1	2	....	2
	6 years........	....	2	2	1	....	1	1	2	3
	8 years........	....	1	1	1	....	1	1	1	2
	9 years........	....	1	1	1	....	1	1	1	2
	10 years......	1	....	1	....	....	....	1	....	1
	11 years......	....	1	1	....	....	....	....	1	1
	13 years......	1	....	1	....	....	....	1	....	1
	14 years......	1	1	2	....	....	....	1	1	2
	15 years......	1	....	1	....	....	....	1	....	1
	18 years......	....	1	1	....	....	....	....	1	1
	19 years......	....	2	2	....	....	....	....	2	2
	21 years......	....	2	2	....	....	....	....	2	2
	22 years......	1	....	1	....	....	....	1	....	1
	23 years......	2	2	4	....	....	....	2	2	4
	24 years......	1	....	1	....	....	....	1	....	1
	25 years......	1	1	2	....	....	....	1	1	2
	26 years......	1	....	1	....	....	....	1	....	1
	28 years......	....	1	1	....	....	....	....	1	1
	Unknown	....	1	1	....	....	....	....	1	1
34 years......	....	10	18	28	3	8	11	13	26	39
	Birth	1	2	3	3	5	8	4	7	11
	3 years........	....	....	....	....	2	2	....	2	2
	4 years........	1	....	1	....	1	1	1	1	2
	5 years........	1	1	2	....	....	....	1	1	2
	10 years......	1	....	1	....	....	....	1	....	1
	18 years......	1	2	3	....	....	....	1	2	3
	20 years......	1	1	2	....	....	....	1	1	2
	21 years......	1	1	2	....	....	....	1	1	2
	22 years......	....	3	3	....	....	....	....	3	3
	24 years......	1	2	3	....	....	....	1	2	3
	25 years......	....	1	1	....	....	....	....	1	1
	28 years......	1	1	2	....	....	....	1	1	2
	29 years......	....	1	1	....	....	....	....	1	1
	30 years......	1	1	2	....	....	....	1	1	2
	32 years......	....	2	2	....	....	....	....	2	2
35 years	....	14	18	32	8	7	15	22	25	47
	Birth	....	....	....	4	5	9	4	5	9
	3 months......	....	....	....	1	....	1	1	....	1
	4 months......	1	....	1	....	....	....	1	....	1
	1 year..........	1	....	1	1	....	1	2	....	2
	3 years........	....	1	1	1	1	2	1	2	3
	4 years........	1	....	1	....	....	....	1	....	1
	7 years........	....	....	....	....	1	1	....	1	1
	9 years........	....	1	1	....	....	....	....	1	1
	10 years......	1	1	2	....	....	....	1	1	2
	13 years......	1	1	2	....	....	....	1	1	2
	15 years......	2	....	2	....	....	....	2	....	2
	19 years......	1	....	1	....	....	....	1	....	1
	20 years......	2	1	3	....	....	....	2	1	3
	23 years......	1	....	1	....	....	....	1	....	1
	24 years......	1	1	2	....	....	....	1	1	2
	25 years......	1	1	2	....	....	....	1	1	2
	27 years......	....	2	2	....	....	....	....	2	2
	28 years......	....	2	2	....	....	....	....	2	2
	30 years......	....	3	3	....	....	....	....	3	3
	31 years......	....	1	1	....	....	....	....	1	1
	33 years......	1	2	3	....	....	....	1	2	3
	Unknown	....	1	1	1	....	1	1	1	2
36 years......	....	7	22	29	5	7	12	12	29	41
	Birth	2	2	4	3	3	6	5	5	10
	1 year..........	....	....	....	1	1	2	1	1	2
	3 years........	....	....	....	....	1	1	....	1	1
	4 years........	....	2	2	1	....	1	1	2	3
	5 years........	....	....	....	....	1	1	....	1	1
	10 years......	....	2	2	....	....	....	....	2	2
	13 years......	2	1	3	....	....	....	2	1	3
	14 years......	....	2	2	....	....	....	....	2	2
	16 years......	....	1	1	....	1	1	....	2	2
	17 years......	1	....	1	....	....	....	1	....	1
	19 years......	....	1	1	....	....	....	....	1	1
	21 years......	....	1	1	....	....	....	....	1	1
	23 years......	....	1	1	....	....	....	....	1	1
	24 years......	....	2	2	....	....	....	....	2	2
	26 years......	....	3	3	....	....	....	....	3	3
	27 years......	....	1	1	....	....	....	....	1	1
	30 years......	1	....	1	....	....	....	1	....	1

TABLE VI.—Continued.

1885. Present age.	Age at occurrence of deafness.	A. The "Deaf." Number affected at ages specified. M.	F.	Both sexes.	B. The "Deaf and Dumb." Number affected at ages specified. M.	F.	Both sexes.	C. Summation of "The Deaf" and "The Deaf and Dumb." Number affected at ages specified. M.	F.	Total.
36 years—Continued.	31 years......	....	1	1	....	....	....	....	1	1
	32 years......	....	1	1	....	....	....	....	1	1
	36 years......	....	1	1	....	....	....	....	1	1
	Unknown	1	....	1	....	....	....	1	....	1
37 years......	....	11	17	28	7	5	12	18	22	40
	Birth	....	....	....	4	2	6	4	2	6
	6 months......	....	....	....	....	1	1	....	1	1
	2 years........	1	....	1	2	1	3	3	1	4
	3 years........	1	....	1	....	1	1	1	1	2
	4 years........	1	....	1	1	....	1	2	....	2
	5 years........	....	1	1	....	....	....	....	1	1
	8 years........	1	....	1	....	....	....	1	....	1
	10 years......	....	1	1	....	....	....	....	1	1
	14 years......	1	....	1	....	....	....	1	....	1
	19 years......	2	....	2	....	....	....	2	....	2
	22 years......	....	1	1	....	....	....	....	1	1
	23 years......	....	1	1	....	....	....	....	1	1
	24 years......	1	....	1	....	....	....	1	....	1
	26 years......	....	1	1	....	....	....	....	1	1
	27 years......	1	6	7	....	....	....	1	6	7
	29 years......	....	1	1	....	....	....	....	1	1
	30 years......	....	1	1	....	....	....	....	1	1
	32 years......	....	1	1	....	....	....	....	1	1
	34 years......	....	1	1	....	....	....	....	1	1
	35 years......	1	....	1	....	....	....	1	....	1
	36 years......	....	1	1	....	....	....	....	1	1
	Unknown	1	1	2	....	....	....	1	1	2
38 years......	....	13	24	37	6	3	9	19	27	46
	Birth	3	....	3	3	1	4	6	1	7
	1 year..........	....	....	....	....	1	1	....	1	1
	2 years........	....	....	....	....	1	1	....	1	1
	3 years........	....	1	1	1	....	1	1	1	2
	5 years........	....	....	....	1	....	1	1	....	1
	6 years........	1	....	1	....	....	....	1	....	1
	8 years........	1	2	3	....	....	....	1	2	3
	9 years........	....	2	2	....	....	....	....	2	2
	10 years......	....	2	2	....	....	....	....	2	2
	14 years......	1	1	2	....	....	....	1	1	2
	15 years......	1	1	2	....	....	....	1	1	2
	16 years......	1	....	1	....	....	....	1	....	1
	20 years......	2	2	4	....	....	....	2	2	4
	23 years......	1	1	2	....	....	....	1	1	2
	24 years......	....	1	1	....	....	....	....	1	1
	25 years......	....	2	2	....	....	....	....	2	2
	27 years......	....	1	1	....	....	....	....	1	1
	28 years......	....	3	3	....	....	....	....	3	3
	30 years......	....	2	2	....	....	....	....	2	2
	33 years......	....	1	1	....	....	....	....	1	1
	34 years......	1	....	1	....	....	....	1	....	1
	38 years......	1	....	1	....	....	....	1	....	1
	Unknown	....	2	2	1	....	1	1	2	3
39 years......	....	20	14	34	10	2	12	30	16	46
	Birth	2	....	2	9	2	11	11	2	13
	1 year..........	1	....	1	....	....	....	1	....	1
	2 years........	....	....	....	1	....	1	1	....	1
	3 years........	....	1	1	....	....	....	....	1	1
	5 years........	3	....	3	....	....	....	3	....	3
	9 years........	1	....	1	....	....	....	1	....	1
	10 years......	1	....	1	....	....	....	1	....	1
	12 years......	1	....	1	....	....	....	1	....	1
	13 years......	....	1	1	....	....	....	....	1	1
	14 years......	1	....	1	....	....	....	1	....	1
	16 years......	2	....	2	....	....	....	2	....	2
	18 years......	1	....	1	....	....	....	1	....	1
	19 years......	4	2	6	....	....	....	4	2	6
	22 years......	....	1	1	....	....	....	....	1	1
	24 years......	....	2	2	....	....	....	....	2	2
	25 years......	....	2	2	....	....	....	....	2	2
	28 years......	1	....	1	....	....	....	1	....	1
	29 years......	1	2	3	....	....	....	1	2	3
	30 years......	....	1	1	....	....	....	....	1	1
	35 years......	1	....	1	....	....	....	1	....	1
	37 years......	....	1	1	....	....	....	....	1	1
	Unknown	....	1	1	....	....	....	....	1	1
40 years	....	19	35	54	9	3	12	28	38	66
	Birth	....	3	3	7	....	7	7	3	10
	1 year..........	....	....	....	....	1	1	....	1	1
	2 years........	....	1	1	....	1	1	....	2	2
	3 years........	1	2	3	1	....	1	2	2	4
	4 years........	....	1	1	....	1	1	....	2	2
	5 years........	....	2	2	....	....	....	....	2	2
	6 years........	1	....	1	....	....	....	1	....	1
	7 years........	....	1	1	....	....	....	....	1	1
	8 years........	1	3	4	....	....	....	1	3	4
	10 years......	1	1	2	....	....	....	1	1	2
	12 years......	....	2	2	....	....	....	....	2	2
	14 years......	2	1	3	....	....	....	2	1	3
	15 years......	....	1	1	....	....	....	....	1	1
	16 years......	....	2	2	....	....	....	....	2	2
	17 years......	1	....	1	....	....	....	1	....	1
	18 years......	1	2	3	....	....	....	1	2	3
	22 years......	1	....	1	....	....	....	1	....	1
	24 years......	....	1	1	....	....	....	....	1	1
	25 years......	2	4	6	1	....	1	3	4	7
	26 years......	1	1	2	....	....	....	1	1	2
	30 years......	3	1	4	....	....	....	3	1	4
	32 years......	1	1	2	....	....	....	1	1	2
	33 years......	1	....	1	....	....	....	1	....	1
	34 years......	....	1	1	....	....	....	....	1	1
	38 years......	....	2	2	....	....	....	....	2	2
	40 years......	1	....	1	....	....	....	1	....	1
	Unknown	1	2	3	....	....	....	1	2	3

TABLE VI.—Continued.

1885.		A			B			C		
		The "Deaf."			The "Deaf and Dumb."			Summation of "The Deaf" and "The Deaf and Dumb."		
Present age.	Age at occurrence of deafness.	Number affected at ages specified.			Number affected at ages specified.			Number affected at ages specified.		
		M.	F.	Both sexes.	M.	F.	Both sexes.	M.	F.	Total.
41 years	....	6	14	20	5	9	14	11	23	34
	Birth	....	....	....	2	6	8	2	6	8
	1 year	....	....	....	1	1	2	1	1	2
	2 years	....	....	....	2	1	3	2	1	3
	3 years	....	1	1	....	....	....	....	1	1
	5 years	....	1	1	....	....	....	....	1	1
	7 years	....	1	1	....	1	1	....	2	2
	9 years	1	....	1	....	....	....	1	....	1
	19 years	1	....	1	....	....	....	1	....	1
	20 years	1	....	1	....	....	....	1	....	1
	21 years	....	2	2	....	....	....	....	2	2
	26 years	....	1	1	....	....	....	....	1	1
	30 years	....	1	1	....	....	....	....	1	1
	31 years	....	4	4	....	....	....	....	4	4
	34 years	1	....	1	....	....	....	1	....	1
	35 years	1	....	1	....	....	....	1	....	1
	37 years	1	....	1	....	....	....	1	....	1
	38 years	....	2	2	....	....	....	....	2	2
	Unknown	....	1	1	....	....	....	....	1	1
42 years	....	14	21	35	4	2	6	18	23	41
	Birth	2	....	2	1	1	2	3	1	4
	1 year	1	1	2	....	1	1	1	2	3
	2 years	2	1	3	....	....	....	2	1	3
	4 years	....	1	1	....	....	....	....	1	1
	7 years	....	....	....	1	....	1	1	....	1
	9 years	....	1	1	....	....	....	....	1	1
	10 years	....	1	1	....	....	....	....	1	1
	13 years	....	1	1	....	....	....	....	1	1
	14 years	1	....	1	....	....	....	1	....	1
	15 years	....	....	....	1	....	1	1	....	1
	16 years	....	1	1	....	....	....	....	1	1
	18 years	....	1	1	....	....	....	....	1	1
	19 years	2	....	2	....	....	....	2	....	2
	20 years	1	1	2	....	....	....	1	1	2
	21 years	1	....	1	....	....	....	1	....	1
	22 years	....	1	1	....	....	....	....	1	1
	27 years	....	1	1	....	....	....	....	1	1
	28 years	1	1	2	....	....	....	1	1	2
	30 years	....	3	3	....	....	....	....	3	3
	32 years	....	1	1	....	....	....	....	1	1
	34 years	....	1	1	....	....	....	....	1	1
	35 years	1	....	1	....	....	....	1	....	1
	36 years	1	....	1	....	....	....	1	....	1
	37 years	1	....	1	....	....	....	1	....	1
	38 years	....	1	1	....	....	....	....	1	1
	Unknown	....	3	3	1	....	1	1	3	4
43 years	....	13	25	38	5	4	9	18	29	47
	Birth	....	....	....	2	2	4	2	2	4
	9 months	....	....	....	....	1	1	....	1	1
	2 years	....	....	....	1	1	2	1	1	2
	3 years	....	....	....	1	....	1	1	....	1
	4 years	....	....	....	1	....	1	1	....	1
	5 years	1	....	1	....	....	....	1	....	1
	6 years	....	1	1	....	....	....	....	1	1
	10 years	....	1	1	....	....	....	....	1	1
	12 years	....	1	1	....	....	....	....	1	1
	13 years	....	3	3	....	....	....	....	3	3
	15 years	1	1	2	....	....	....	1	1	2
	20 years	2	3	5	....	....	....	2	3	5
	21 years	1	1	2	....	....	....	1	1	2
	22 years	1	....	1	....	....	....	1	....	1
	24 years	1	2	3	....	....	....	1	2	3
	27 years	1	....	1	....	....	....	1	....	1
	28 years	1	....	1	....	....	....	1	....	1
	30 years	1	1	2	....	....	....	1	1	2
	33 years	....	4	4	....	....	....	....	4	4
	35 years	....	2	2	....	....	....	....	2	2
	37 years	....	2	2	....	....	....	....	2	2
	39 years	1	1	2	....	....	....	1	1	2
	40 years	....	1	1	....	....	....	....	1	1
	42 years	....	1	1	....	....	....	....	1	1
	Unknown	2	....	2	....	....	....	2	....	2
44 years	....	12	23	35	3	1	4	15	24	39
	Birth	2	1	3	1	1	2	3	2	5
	2 years	....	1	1	1	....	1	1	1	2
	3 years	....	1	1	....	....	....	....	1	1
	4 years	....	....	....	1	....	1	1	....	1
	6 years	....	1	1	....	....	....	....	1	1
	11 years	....	1	1	....	....	....	....	1	1
	12 years	1	....	1	....	....	....	1	....	1
	14 years	....	1	1	....	....	....	....	1	1
	15 years	....	1	1	....	....	....	....	1	1
	20 years	2	1	3	....	....	....	2	1	3
	21 years	3	1	4	....	....	....	3	1	4
	22 years	2	....	2	....	....	....	2	....	2
	23 years	....	1	1	....	....	....	....	1	1
	24 years	....	1	1	....	....	....	....	1	1
	26 years	....	1	1	....	....	....	....	1	1
	27 years	1	....	1	....	....	....	1	....	1
	28 years	....	1	1	....	....	....	....	1	1
	30 years	....	1	1	....	....	....	....	1	1
	34 years	....	1	1	....	....	....	....	1	1
	35 years	....	1	1	....	....	....	....	1	1
	36 years	....	2	2	....	....	....	....	2	2
	38 years	....	3	3	....	....	....	....	3	3
	43 years	1	1	2	....	....	....	1	1	2
	Unknown	....	1	1	....	....	....	....	1	1
45 years	....	16	33	49	4	6	10	20	39	59
	Birth	....	1	1	2	6	8	2	7	9
	2 years	1	....	1	....	....	....	1	....	1
	3 years	1	1	2	....	....	....	1	1	2
	5 years	1	1	2	....	....	....	1	1	2
	6 years	....	....	....	1	....	1	1	....	1
	7 years	1	....	1	....	....	....	1	....	1

TABLE VI.—Continued.

1885.		A			B			C		
		The "Deaf."			The "Deaf and Dumb."			Summation of "The Deaf" and "The Deaf and Dumb."		
Present age.	Age at occurrence of deafness.	Number affected at ages specified.			Number affected at ages specified.			Number affected at ages specified.		
		M.	F.	Both sexes.	M.	F.	Both sexes.	M.	F.	Total.
45 years—Continued.	9 years	....	....	....	1	....	1	1	....	1
	12 years	....	1	1	....	....	....	....	1	1
	13 years	....	1	1	....	....	....	....	1	1
	14 years	1	....	1	....	....	....	1	....	1
	15 years	....	1	1	....	....	....	....	1	1
	17 years	....	1	1	....	....	....	....	1	1
	19 years	....	1	1	....	....	....	....	1	1
	20 years	....	3	3	....	....	....	....	3	3
	22 years	1	....	1	....	....	....	1	....	1
	23 years	....	2	2	....	....	....	....	2	2
	25 years	3	3	6	....	....	....	3	3	6
	26 years	....	1	1	....	....	....	....	1	1
	27 years	....	1	1	....	....	....	....	1	1
	28 years	1	1	2	....	....	....	1	1	2
	29 years	1	....	1	....	....	....	1	....	1
	30 years	1	2	3	....	....	....	1	2	3
	33 years	1	1	2	....	....	....	1	1	2
	35 years	1	5	6	....	....	....	1	5	6
	38 years	1	....	1	....	....	....	1	....	1
	40 years	....	2	2	....	....	....	....	2	2
	41 years	1	....	1	....	....	....	1	....	1
	42 years	....	1	1	....	....	....	....	1	1
	43 years	....	1	1	....	....	....	....	1	1
	Unknown	....	2	2	....	....	....	....	2	2
46 years	....	13	31	44	6	1	7	19	32	51
	Birth	....	....	....	4	1	5	4	1	5
	1 year	....	....	....	1	....	1	1	....	1
	2 years	....	....	....	1	....	1	1	....	1
	3 years	1	....	1	....	....	....	1	....	1
	6 years	1	....	1	....	....	....	1	....	1
	7 years	1	2	3	....	....	....	1	2	3
	8 years	1	....	1	....	....	....	1	....	1
	10 years	1	....	1	....	....	....	1	....	1
	12 years	....	1	1	....	....	....	....	1	1
	13 years	....	2	2	....	....	....	....	2	2
	15 years	....	1	1	....	....	....	....	1	1
	16 years	....	1	1	....	....	....	....	1	1
	21 years	....	1	1	....	....	....	....	1	1
	22 years	1	....	1	....	....	....	1	....	1
	24 years	....	1	1	....	....	....	....	1	1
	25 years	1	2	3	....	....	....	1	2	3
	26 years	1	....	1	....	....	....	1	....	1
	30 years	....	5	5	....	....	....	....	5	5
	31 years	....	2	2	....	....	....	....	2	2
	34 years	1	2	3	....	....	....	1	2	3
	36 years	....	2	2	....	....	....	....	2	2
	37 years	....	1	1	....	....	....	....	1	1
	38 years	1	2	3	....	....	....	1	2	3
	40 years	....	1	1	....	....	....	....	1	1
	41 years	....	1	1	....	....	....	....	1	1
	42 years	1	2	3	....	....	....	1	2	3
	Unknown	2	2	4	....	....	....	2	2	4
47 years	....	16	31	47	2	3	5	18	34	52
	Birth	2	2	4	1	1	2	3	3	6
	6 months	....	....	....	....	1	1	....	1	1
	9 months	....	1	1	....	....	....	....	1	1
	1 year	....	....	....	....	1	1	....	1	1
	2 years	....	2	2	....	....	....	....	2	2
	3 years	1	....	1	1	....	1	2	....	2
	6 years	....	1	1	....	....	....	....	1	1
	7 years	1	1	2	....	....	....	1	1	2
	12 years	....	1	1	....	....	....	....	1	1
	16 years	....	1	1	....	....	....	....	1	1
	17 years	1	....	1	....	....	....	1	....	1
	20 years	2	1	3	....	....	....	2	1	3
	25 years	2	....	2	....	....	....	2	....	2
	26 years	1	....	1	....	....	....	1	....	1
	27 years	1	2	3	....	....	....	1	2	3
	28 years	....	1	1	....	....	....	....	1	1
	29 years	....	1	1	....	....	....	....	1	1
	30 years	2	3	5	....	....	....	2	3	5
	31 years	....	1	1	....	....	....	....	1	1
	32 years	....	2	2	....	....	....	....	2	2
	33 years	....	1	1	....	....	....	....	1	1
	35 years	....	3	3	....	....	....	....	3	3
	37 years	1	1	2	....	....	....	1	1	2
	40 years	....	1	1	....	....	....	....	1	1
	42 years	....	2	2	....	....	....	....	2	2
	43 years	....	1	1	....	....	....	....	1	1
	45 years	....	1	1	....	....	....	....	1	1
	46 years	1	....	1	....	....	....	1	....	1
	Unknown	1	1	2	....	....	....	1	1	2
48 years	....	12	36	48	3	4	7	15	40	55
	Birth	....	2	2	2	2	4	2	4	6
	1 year	....	....	....	....	2	2	....	2	2
	2 years	....	2	2	....	....	....	....	2	2
	4 years	2	....	2	....	....	....	2	....	2
	5 years	....	....	....	1	....	1	1	....	1
	8 years	....	1	1	....	....	....	....	1	1
	16 years	....	3	3	....	....	....	....	3	3
	18 years	2	1	3	....	....	....	2	1	3
	20 years	1	....	1	....	....	....	1	....	1
	21 years	....	2	2	....	....	....	....	2	2
	23 years	....	1	1	....	....	....	....	1	1
	24 years	1	1	2	....	....	....	1	1	2
	25 years	1	....	1	....	....	....	1	....	1
	26 years	....	1	1	....	....	....	....	1	1
	27 years	....	1	1	....	....	....	....	1	1
	28 years	3	2	5	....	....	....	3	2	5
	29 years	1	1	2	....	....	....	1	1	2
	30 years	....	2	2	....	....	....	....	2	2
	33 years	....	2	2	....	....	....	....	2	2
	34 years	....	2	2	....	....	....	....	2	2
	36 years	....	1	1	....	....	....	....	1	1
	38 years	....	3	3	....	....	....	....	3	3

TABLE VI.—Continued.

1885. Present age.	Age at occurrence of deafness.	A. The "Deaf." Number affected at ages specified. M.	F.	Both sexes.	B. The "Deaf and Dumb." Number affected at ages specified. M.	F.	Both sexes.	C. Summation of "The Deaf" and "The Deaf and Dumb." Number affected at ages specified. M.	F.	Total.
48 years—Continued.	40 years	....	2	2	....	....	....	....	2	2
	42 years	....	2	2	....	....	....	....	2	2
	43 years	1	2	3	....	....	....	1	2	3
	45 years	....	1	1	....	....	....	....	1	1
	Unknown	....	1	1	....	....	....	....	1	1
49 years	....	21	25	46	6	2	8	27	27	54
	Birth	1	....	1	4	1	5	5	1	6
	1 year	....	....	....	1	....	1	1	....	1
	2 years	1	....	1	1	....	1	2	....	2
	3 years	....	1	1	....	1	1	....	2	2
	5 years	2	....	2	....	....	....	2	....	2
	6 years	1	2	3	....	....	....	1	2	3
	7 years	....	1	1	....	....	....	....	1	1
	9 years	1	....	1	....	....	....	1	....	1
	10 years	....	1	1	....	....	....	....	1	1
	13 years	....	1	1	....	....	....	....	1	1
	14 years	1	1	2	....	....	....	1	1	2
	15 years	....	1	1	....	....	....	....	1	1
	18 years	1	1	2	....	....	....	1	1	2
	19 years	....	2	2	....	....	....	....	2	2
	20 years	....	2	2	....	....	....	....	2	2
	22 years	1	....	1	....	....	....	1	....	1
	24 years	....	1	1	....	....	....	....	1	1
	25 years	....	1	1	....	....	....	....	1	1
	26 years	1	....	1	....	....	....	1	....	1
	27 years	1	....	1	....	....	....	1	....	1
	28 years	2	1	3	....	....	....	2	1	3
	29 years	1	1	2	....	....	....	1	1	2
	33 years	....	1	1	....	....	....	....	1	1
	34 years	....	1	1	....	....	....	....	1	1
	35 years	1	3	4	....	....	....	1	3	4
	40 years	2	1	3	....	....	....	2	1	3
	41 years	1	1	2	....	....	....	1	1	2
	43 years	1	....	1	....	....	....	1	....	1
	44 years	....	1	1	....	....	....	....	1	1
	Unknown	2	....	2	....	....	....	2	....	2
50 years	....	26	44	70	5	11	16	31	55	86
	Birth	....	1	1	3	7	10	3	8	11
	1 year	....	....	....	....	1	1	....	1	1
	2 years	....	2	2	1	1	2	1	3	4
	3 years	1	....	1	....	1	1	1	1	2
	5 years	....	....	....	1	....	1	1	....	1
	7 years	....	1	1	....	....	....	....	1	1
	10 years	4	....	4	....	....	....	4	....	4
	12 years	2	1	3	....	....	....	2	1	3
	15 years	1	1	2	....	....	....	1	1	2
	16 years	....	1	1	....	....	....	....	1	1
	17 years	....	1	1	....	....	....	....	1	1
	18 years	....	2	2	....	....	....	....	2	2
	20 years	3	6	9	....	....	....	3	6	9
	21 years	2	....	2	....	....	....	2	....	2
	23 years	....	1	1	....	....	....	....	1	1
	25 years	1	1	2	....	....	....	1	1	2
	28 years	2	....	2	....	....	....	2	....	2
	29 years	1	1	2	....	....	....	1	1	2
	30 years	2	7	9	....	....	....	2	7	9
	31 years	1	1	2	....	....	....	1	1	2
	32 years	....	3	3	....	....	....	....	3	3
	33 years	....	2	2	....	....	....	....	2	2
	35 years	2	3	5	....	....	....	2	3	5
	38 years	1	....	1	....	....	....	1	....	1
	40 years	1	3	4	....	....	....	1	3	4
	42 years	....	1	1	....	....	....	....	1	1
	45 years	....	2	2	....	....	....	....	2	2
	49 years	....	1	1	....	....	....	....	1	1
	Unknown	2	2	4	....	1	1	2	3	5
51 years	....	16	25	41	2	3	5	18	28	46
	Birth	2	1	3	2	2	4	4	3	7
	1 year	....	1	1	....	....	....	....	1	1
	2 years	1	....	1	....	....	....	1	....	1
	4 years	....	....	....	....	1	1	....	1	1
	5 years	1	....	1	....	....	....	1	....	1
	6 years	....	1	1	....	....	....	....	1	1
	12 years	....	1	1	....	....	....	....	1	1
	13 years	1	....	1	....	....	....	1	....	1
	15 years	....	1	1	....	....	....	....	1	1
	21 years	....	2	2	....	....	....	....	2	2
	24 years	1	....	1	....	....	....	1	....	1
	25 years	2	1	3	....	....	....	2	1	3
	26 years	....	1	1	....	....	....	....	1	1
	28 years	1	....	1	....	....	....	1	....	1
	30 years	2	1	3	....	....	....	2	1	3
	31 years	1	5	6	....	....	....	1	5	6
	33 years	....	1	1	....	....	....	....	1	1
	34 years	....	1	1	....	....	....	....	1	1
	35 years	....	1	1	....	....	....	....	1	1
	36 years	....	2	2	....	....	....	....	2	2
	40 years	....	2	2	....	....	....	....	2	2
	41 years	....	1	1	....	....	....	....	1	1
	44 years	2	....	2	....	....	....	2	....	2
	45 years	1	....	1	....	....	....	1	....	1
	46 years	....	1	1	....	....	....	....	1	1
	49 years	1	....	1	....	....	....	1	....	1
	Unknown	....	1	1	....	....	....	....	1	1
52 years	....	20	31	51	3	6	9	23	37	60
	Birth	....	....	....	....	2	2	....	2	2
	6 months	....	....	....	....	1	1	....	1	1
	1 year	....	....	....	1	....	1	1	....	1
	2 years	....	....	....	....	1	1	....	1	1
	3 years	1	1	2	....	1	1	1	2	3
	4 years	....	....	....	....	1	1	....	1	1
	5 years	1	1	2	....	....	....	1	1	2
	6 years	....	1	1	....	....	....	....	1	1
	8 years	1	....	1	1	....	1	2	....	2

TABLE VI.—Continued.

1885. Present age.	Age at occurrence of deafness.	A. The "Deaf." Number affected at ages specified. M.	F.	Both sexes.	B. The "Deaf and Dumb." Number affected at ages specified. M.	F.	Both sexes.	C. Summation of "The Deaf" and "The Deaf and Dumb." Number affected at ages specified. M.	F.	Total.
52 years—Continued.	12 years	2	....	2	....	....	....	2	....	2
	16 years	....	1	1	....	....	....	....	1	1
	17 years	....	2	2	....	....	....	....	2	2
	18 years	1	....	1	....	....	....	1	....	1
	22 years	....	1	1	....	....	....	....	1	1
	23 years	....	1	1	....	....	....	....	1	1
	25 years	....	1	1	....	....	....	....	1	1
	27 years	2	3	5	....	....	....	2	3	5
	30 years	3	2	5	....	....	....	3	2	5
	31 years	1	....	1	....	....	....	1	....	1
	32 years	1	2	3	....	....	....	1	2	3
	33 years	....	....	....	1	....	1	1	....	1
	35 years	1	2	3	....	....	....	1	2	3
	36 years	1	1	2	....	....	....	1	1	2
	37 years	1	....	1	....	....	....	1	....	1
	40 years	2	3	5	....	....	....	2	3	5
	42 years	1	4	5	....	....	....	1	4	5
	43 years	....	1	1	....	....	....	....	1	1
	44 years	....	2	2	....	....	....	....	2	2
	46 years	....	1	1	....	....	....	....	1	1
	49 years	1	....	1	....	....	....	1	....	1
	Unknown	....	1	1	....	....	....	....	1	1
53 years	....	24	37	61	1	4	5	25	41	66
	Birth	....	1	1	1	3	4	1	4	5
	2 years	....	....	....	....	1	1	....	1	1
	5 years	....	1	1	....	....	....	....	1	1
	6 years	1	3	4	....	....	....	1	3	4
	7 years	1	....	1	....	....	....	1	....	1
	8 years	....	2	2	....	....	....	....	2	2
	10 years	....	2	2	....	....	....	....	2	2
	11 years	....	3	3	....	....	....	....	3	3
	12 years	1	....	1	....	....	....	1	....	1
	13 years	1	1	2	....	....	....	1	1	2
	15 years	....	2	2	....	....	....	....	2	2
	16 years	1	1	2	....	....	....	1	1	2
	18 years	....	1	1	....	....	....	....	1	1
	24 years	....	1	1	....	....	....	....	1	1
	25 years	....	1	1	....	....	....	....	1	1
	27 years	1	1	2	....	....	....	1	1	2
	28 years	3	....	3	....	....	....	3	....	3
	30 years	1	2	3	....	....	....	1	2	3
	31 years	1	1	2	....	....	....	1	1	2
	32 years	2	....	2	....	....	....	2	....	2
	33 years	4	2	6	....	....	....	4	2	6
	34 years	....	2	2	....	....	....	....	2	2
	35 years	2	....	2	....	....	....	2	....	2
	38 years	2	1	3	....	....	....	2	1	3
	40 years	....	1	1	....	....	....	....	1	1
	43 years	....	1	1	....	....	....	....	1	1
	45 years	1	1	2	....	....	....	1	1	2
	46 years	....	2	2	....	....	....	....	2	2
	47 years	....	1	1	....	....	....	....	1	1
	Unknown	2	3	5	....	....	....	2	3	5
54 years	....	25	30	55	6	1	7	31	31	62
	Birth	4	1	5	4	1	5	8	2	10
	3 years	....	1	1	2	....	2	2	1	3
	6 years	....	1	1	....	....	....	....	1	1
	10 years	1	2	3	....	....	....	1	2	3
	14 years	....	1	1	....	....	....	....	1	1
	15 years	....	1	1	....	....	....	....	1	1
	17 years	2	....	2	....	....	....	2	....	2
	18 years	1	....	1	....	....	....	1	....	1
	23 years	....	2	2	....	....	....	....	2	2
	24 years	1	....	1	....	....	....	1	....	1
	25 years	1	....	1	....	....	....	1	....	1
	30 years	1	2	3	....	....	....	1	2	3
	32 years	2	....	2	....	....	....	2	....	2
	33 years	2	1	3	....	....	....	2	1	3
	34 years	6	3	9	....	....	....	6	3	9
	36 years	1	1	2	....	....	....	1	1	2
	37 years	....	1	1	....	....	....	....	1	1
	38 years	1	....	1	....	....	....	1	....	1
	39 years	1	1	2	....	....	....	1	1	2
	40 years	....	1	1	....	....	....	....	1	1
	41 years	1	2	3	....	....	....	1	2	3
	46 years	....	2	2	....	....	....	....	2	2
	48 years	....	1	1	....	....	....	....	1	1
	50 years	....	3	3	....	....	....	....	3	3
	52 years	....	1	1	....	....	....	....	1	1
	Unknown	....	2	2	....	....	....	....	2	2
55 years	....	26	40	66	5	4	9	31	44	75
	Birth	2	1	3	2	3	5	4	4	8
	3 years	....	1	1	....	....	....	....	1	1
	4 years	....	....	....	1	....	1	1	....	1
	5 years	....	1	1	1	1	2	1	2	3
	6 years	....	2	2	....	....	....	....	2	2
	10 years	1	....	1	....	....	....	1	....	1
	14 years	1	....	1	....	....	....	1	....	1
	15 years	2	....	2	....	....	....	2	....	2
	16 years	1	1	2	....	....	....	1	1	2
	19 years	2	....	2	....	....	....	2	....	2
	20 years	1	2	3	....	....	....	1	2	3
	23 years	....	1	1	....	....	....	....	1	1
	25 years	1	3	4	....	....	....	1	3	4
	29 years	....	2	2	....	....	....	....	2	2
	30 years	2	7	9	....	....	....	2	7	9
	32 years	2	....	2	....	....	....	2	....	2
	35 years	2	3	5	....	....	....	2	3	5
	38 years	....	1	1	....	....	....	....	1	1
	40 years	2	....	2	....	....	....	2	....	2
	42 years	....	1	1	....	....	....	....	1	1
	45 years	4	4	8	....	....	....	4	4	8
	49 years	....	1	1	....	....	....	....	1	1
	50 years	2	1	3	....	....	....	2	1	3

TABLE VI.—Continued.

1885. Present age.	Age at occurrence of deafness.	A The "Deaf." Number affected at ages specified. M.	F.	Both sexes.	B The "Deaf and Dumb." Number affected at ages specified. M.	F.	Both sexes.	C Summation of "The Deaf" and "The Deaf and Dumb." Number affected at ages specified. M.	F.	Total.
55 years—Continued.	51 years	....	1	1	....	....	....	....	1	1
	52 years	....	2	2	....	....	....	....	2	2
	54 years	....	1	1	....	....	....	....	1	1
	Unknown	1	4	5	1	....	1	2	4	6
56 years		19	31	50	2	3	5	21	34	55
	Birth	1	1	2	1	1	2	2	2	4
	1 year	1	....	1	....	....	....	1	....	1
	3 years	1	....	1	....	....	....	1	....	1
	4 years	1	....	1	....	....	....	1	....	1
	5 years	1	....	1	....	1	1	1	1	2
	6 years	....	2	2	....	....	....	....	2	2
	8 years	....	....	....	....	1	1	....	1	1
	10 years	1	....	1	....	....	....	1	....	1
	19 years	1	....	1	....	....	....	1	....	1
	20 years	....	1	1	....	....	....	....	1	1
	22 years	....	1	1	....	....	....	....	1	1
	23 years	....	2	2	....	....	....	....	2	2
	25 years	....	1	1	....	....	....	....	1	1
	26 years	1	3	4	....	....	....	1	3	4
	28 years	1	....	1	....	....	....	1	....	1
	29 years	1	1	2	....	....	....	1	1	2
	30 years	....	1	1	....	....	....	....	1	1
	31 years	....	3	3	....	....	....	....	3	3
	32 years	1	....	1	....	....	....	1	....	1
	34 years	1	....	1	....	....	....	1	....	1
	36 years	....	2	2	....	....	....	....	2	2
	39 years	....	1	1	....	....	....	....	1	1
	40 years	....	1	1	....	....	....	....	1	1
	41 years	1	1	2	....	....	....	1	1	2
	42 years	....	1	1	....	....	....	....	1	1
	44 years	1	1	2	....	....	....	1	1	2
	45 years	....	1	1	....	....	....	....	1	1
	46 years	2	2	4	....	....	....	2	2	4
	48 years	....	1	1	....	....	....	....	1	1
	50 years	1	2	3	....	....	....	1	2	3
	51 years	1	....	1	....	....	....	1	....	1
	53 years	1	1	2	....	....	....	1	1	2
	55 years	....	1	1	....	....	....	....	1	1
	Unknown	....	....	....	1	....	1	1	....	1
57 years		16	39	55	1	5	6	17	44	61
	Birth	....	....	....	....	3	3	....	3	3
	1 year	....	....	....	1	....	1	1	....	1
	3 years	....	2	2	....	....	....	....	2	2
	4 years	1	....	1	....	....	....	1	....	1
	5 years	....	1	1	....	2	2	....	3	3
	6 years	....	1	1	....	....	....	....	1	1
	7 years	....	2	2	....	....	....	....	2	2
	10 years	....	1	1	....	....	....	....	1	1
	12 years	1	....	1	....	....	....	1	....	1
	14 years	....	1	1	....	....	....	....	1	1
	15 years	1	....	1	....	....	....	1	....	1
	16 years	....	2	2	....	....	....	....	2	2
	17 years	2	....	2	....	....	....	2	....	2
	18 years	....	2	2	....	....	....	....	2	2
	20 years	....	1	1	....	....	....	....	1	1
	25 years	1	2	3	....	....	....	1	2	3
	27 years	2	3	5	....	....	....	2	3	5
	29 years	....	1	1	....	....	....	....	1	1
	30 years	1	1	2	....	....	....	1	1	2
	32 years	1	2	3	....	....	....	1	2	3
	33 years	1	....	1	....	....	....	1	....	1
	34 years	....	1	1	....	....	....	....	1	1
	37 years	....	2	2	....	....	....	....	2	2
	39 years	1	3	4	....	....	....	1	3	4
	39 years	....	1	1	....	....	....	....	1	1
	40 years	....	1	1	....	....	....	....	1	1
	41 years	....	1	1	....	....	....	....	1	1
	42 years	1	1	2	....	....	....	1	1	2
	45 years	1	2	3	....	....	....	1	2	3
	46 years	....	1	1	....	....	....	....	1	1
	47 years	....	2	2	....	....	....	....	2	2
	52 years	....	1	1	....	....	....	....	1	1
	54 years	....	1	1	....	....	....	....	1	1
	55 years	1	....	1	....	....	....	1	....	1
	Unknown	1	....	1	....	....	....	1	....	1
58 years		15	27	42	3	2	5	18	29	47
	Birth	1	....	1	2	1	3	3	1	4
	4 years	....	....	....	....	1	1	....	1	1
	5 years	....	1	1	....	....	....	....	1	1
	6 years	....	2	2	....	....	....	....	2	2
	10 years	1	1	2	....	....	....	1	1	2
	12 years	1	1	2	....	....	....	1	1	2
	20 years	2	....	2	....	....	....	2	....	2
	25 years	....	2	2	....	....	....	....	2	2
	28 years	....	3	3	....	....	....	....	3	3
	30 years	....	2	2	....	....	....	....	2	2
	33 years	3	1	4	....	....	....	3	1	4
	35 years	1	....	1	....	....	....	1	....	1
	36 years	....	1	1	....	....	....	....	1	1
	37 years	1	....	1	....	....	....	1	....	1
	38 years	....	3	3	....	....	....	....	3	3
	39 years	....	1	1	....	....	....	....	1	1
	40 years	2	1	3	....	....	....	2	1	3
	44 years	....	1	1	....	....	....	....	1	1
	45 years	....	2	2	....	....	....	....	2	2
	46 years	....	1	1	....	....	....	....	1	1
	48 years	....	1	1	....	....	....	....	1	1
	49 years	....	1	1	....	....	....	....	1	1
	50 years	2	....	2	....	....	....	2	....	2
	54 years	1	....	1	....	....	....	1	....	1
	55 years	....	1	1	....	....	....	....	1	1
	Unknown	....	1	1	1	....	1	1	1	2

TABLE VI.—Continued.

1885. Present age.	Age at occurrence of deafness.	A The "Deaf." Number affected at ages specified. M.	F.	Both sexes.	B The "Deaf and Dumb." Number affected at ages specified. M.	F.	Both sexes.	C Summation of "The Deaf" and "The Deaf and Dumb." Number affected at ages specified. M.	F.	Total.
59 years		24	22	46	1	2	3	25	24	49
	Birth	....	1	1	1	2	3	1	3	4
	5 years	....	1	1	....	....	....	....	1	1
	19 years	2	1	3	....	....	....	2	1	3
	21 years	1	....	1	....	....	....	1	....	1
	24 years	2	....	2	....	....	....	2	....	2
	25 years	....	1	1	....	....	....	....	1	1
	28 years	1	....	1	....	....	....	1	....	1
	29 years	....	1	1	....	....	....	....	1	1
	32 years	1	....	1	....	....	....	1	....	1
	34 years	1	2	3	....	....	....	1	2	3
	35 years	2	1	3	....	....	....	2	1	3
	36 years	1	....	1	....	....	....	1	....	1
	37 years	2	3	5	....	....	....	2	3	5
	40 years	1	1	2	....	....	....	1	1	2
	41 years	1	....	1	....	....	....	1	....	1
	43 years	....	2	2	....	....	....	....	2	2
	44 years	....	2	2	....	....	....	....	2	2
	45 years	....	1	1	....	....	....	....	1	1
	49 years	1	1	2	....	....	....	1	1	2
	51 years	1	....	1	....	....	....	1	....	1
	53 years	1	....	1	....	....	....	1	....	1
	54 years	1	1	2	....	....	....	1	1	2
	56 years	1	....	1	....	....	....	1	....	1
	Unknown	4	3	7	....	....	....	4	3	7
60 years		27	38	65	4	6	10	31	44	75
	Birth	1	1	2	4	5	9	5	6	11
	1 year	....	1	1	....	....	....	....	1	1
	2 years	1	....	1	....	....	....	1	....	1
	4 years	....	....	....	....	1	1	....	1	1
	7 years	1	....	1	....	....	....	1	....	1
	8 years	3	....	3	....	....	....	3	....	3
	10 years	....	2	2	....	....	....	....	2	2
	12 years	1	1	2	....	....	....	1	1	2
	15 years	....	2	2	....	....	....	....	2	2
	16 years	....	1	1	....	....	....	....	1	1
	17 years	1	....	1	....	....	....	1	....	1
	18 years	1	1	2	....	....	....	1	1	2
	20 years	....	2	2	....	....	....	....	2	2
	25 years	....	1	1	....	....	....	....	1	1
	26 years	....	1	1	....	....	....	....	1	1
	30 years	4	2	6	....	....	....	4	2	6
	33 years	....	1	1	....	....	....	....	1	1
	35 years	1	2	3	....	....	....	1	2	3
	36 years	1	....	1	....	....	....	1	....	1
	38 years	2	....	2	....	....	....	2	....	2
	40 years	4	3	7	....	....	....	4	3	7
	45 years	1	4	5	....	....	....	1	4	5
	48 years	....	1	1	....	....	....	....	1	1
	49 years	1	....	1	....	....	....	1	....	1
	50 years	1	2	3	....	....	....	1	2	3
	52 years	....	1	1	....	....	....	....	1	1
	53 years	....	1	1	....	....	....	....	1	1
	54 years	....	2	2	....	....	....	....	2	2
	55 years	1	....	1	....	....	....	1	....	1
	57 years	1	2	3	....	....	....	1	2	3
	58 years	....	1	1	....	....	....	....	1	1
	60 years	1	....	1	....	....	....	1	....	1
	Unknown	....	3	3	....	....	....	....	3	3
61 years		23	25	48	2	....	2	25	25	50
	Birth	....	1	1	2	....	2	2	1	3
	2 years	1	....	1	....	....	....	1	....	1
	7 years	....	1	1	....	....	....	....	1	1
	11 years	....	1	1	....	....	....	....	1	1
	14 years	1	....	1	....	....	....	1	....	1
	15 years	1	1	2	....	....	....	1	1	2
	16 years	....	1	1	....	....	....	....	1	1
	17 years	1	....	1	....	....	....	1	....	1
	23 years	....	1	1	....	....	....	....	1	1
	26 years	2	....	2	....	....	....	2	....	2
	28 years	1	....	1	....	....	....	1	....	1
	30 years	....	4	4	....	....	....	....	4	4
	31 years	2	....	2	....	....	....	2	....	2
	32 years	....	1	1	....	....	....	....	1	1
	35 years	....	2	2	....	....	....	....	2	2
	36 years	1	....	1	....	....	....	1	....	1
	40 years	2	1	3	....	....	....	2	1	3
	41 years	3	1	4	....	....	....	3	1	4
	45 years	1	3	4	....	....	....	1	3	4
	46 years	1	....	1	....	....	....	1	....	1
	50 years	....	1	1	....	....	....	....	1	1
	51 years	2	....	2	....	....	....	2	....	2
	53 years	....	1	1	....	....	....	....	1	1
	55 years	1	....	1	....	....	....	1	....	1
	56 years	....	3	3	....	....	....	....	3	3
	57 years	....	1	1	....	....	....	....	1	1
	58 years	....	1	1	....	....	....	....	1	1
	59 years	1	....	1	....	....	....	1	....	1
	Unknown	2	....	2	....	....	....	2	....	2
62 years		20	28	48	5	....	5	25	28	53
	Birth	2	1	3	1	....	1	3	1	4
	1 year	....	....	....	2	....	2	2	....	2
	3 years	....	....	....	1	....	1	1	....	1
	7 years	....	1	1	....	....	....	....	1	1
	8 years	....	1	1	....	....	....	....	1	1
	9 years	1	....	1	....	....	....	1	....	1
	12 years	1	....	1	....	....	....	1	....	1
	18 years	....	2	2	....	....	....	....	2	2
	19 years	1	....	1	....	....	....	1	....	1
	20 years	....	2	2	1	....	1	1	2	3
	22 years	1	....	1	....	....	....	1	....	1
	23 years	....	2	2	....	....	....	....	2	2
	27 years	....	1	1	....	....	....	....	1	1
	30 years	....	2	2	....	....	....	....	2	2
	32 years	1	1	2	....	....	....	1	1	2

TABLE VI.—Continued.

1885.		A			B			C		
		The "Deaf."			The "Deaf and Dumb."			Summation of "The Deaf" and "The Deaf and Dumb."		
Present age.	Age at occurrence of deafness.	Number affected at ages specified.			Number affected at ages specified.			Number affected at ages specified.		
		M.	F.	Both sexes.	M.	F.	Both sexes.	M.	F.	Total.
62 years—Continued.	37 years	...	1	1	...	...	...	...	1	1
	40 years	2	2	4	...	...	...	2	2	4
	42 years	3	3	6	...	...	...	3	3	6
	45 years	2	1	3	...	...	...	2	1	3
	47 years	...	2	2	...	...	...	...	2	2
	48 years	1	...	1	...	...	...	1	...	1
	52 years	2	2	4	...	...	...	2	2	4
	55 years	1	...	1	...	...	...	1	...	1
	56 years	1	1	2	...	...	...	1	1	2
	57 years	...	1	1	...	...	...	...	1	1
	60 years	1	...	1	...	...	...	1	...	1
	61 years	...	1	1	...	...	...	...	1	1
	Unknown	...	1	1	...	...	...	...	1	1
63 years		28	33	61	2	...	2	30	33	63
	Birth	...	1	1	1	...	1	1	1	2
	3 months	...	1	1	...	...	...	...	1	1
	5 years	1	...	1	1	...	1	2	...	2
	6 years	...	1	1	...	...	...	...	1	1
	10 years	...	1	1	...	...	...	...	1	1
	13 years	1	...	1	...	...	...	1	...	1
	15 years	1	...	1	...	...	...	1	...	1
	16 years	...	1	1	...	...	...	...	1	1
	20 years	2	...	2	...	...	...	2	...	2
	21 years	...	1	1	...	...	...	...	1	1
	22 years	1	...	1	...	...	...	1	...	1
	23 years	1	1	2	...	...	...	1	1	2
	25 years	...	2	2	...	...	...	...	2	2
	26 years	...	2	2	...	...	...	...	2	2
	28 years	1	...	1	...	...	...	1	...	1
	30 years	...	4	4	...	...	...	...	4	4
	33 years	1	1	2	...	...	...	1	1	2
	35 years	...	2	2	...	...	...	...	2	2
	38 years	2	1	3	...	...	...	2	1	3
	40 years	...	1	1	...	...	...	...	1	1
	42 years	1	...	1	...	...	...	1	...	1
	43 years	...	5	5	...	...	...	...	5	5
	44 years	1	...	1	...	...	...	1	...	1
	45 years	2	...	2	...	...	...	2	...	2
	48 years	2	1	3	...	...	...	2	1	3
	49 years	2	...	2	...	...	...	2	...	2
	50 years	2	1	3	...	...	...	2	1	3
	51 years	1	...	1	...	...	...	1	...	1
	53 years	2	...	2	...	...	...	2	...	2
	54 years	...	1	1	...	...	...	...	1	1
	55 years	1	...	1	...	...	...	1	...	1
	56 years	...	1	1	...	...	...	...	1	1
	57 years	1	...	1	...	...	...	1	...	1
	Unknown	2	4	6	...	...	...	2	4	6
64 years		20	26	46	3	1	4	23	27	50
	Birth	1	...	1	1	1	2	2	1	3
	1 year	...	...	...	1	...	1	1	...	1
	2 years	...	...	...	1	...	1	1	...	1
	4 years	...	1	1	...	...	...	...	1	1
	5 years	...	1	1	...	...	...	...	1	1
	13 years	1	...	1	...	...	...	1	...	1
	14 years	2	...	2	...	...	...	2	...	2
	16 years	...	1	1	...	...	...	...	1	1
	20 years	...	2	2	...	...	...	...	2	2
	21 years	2	...	2	...	...	...	2	...	2
	22 years	...	1	1	...	...	...	...	1	1
	24 years	1	3	4	...	...	...	1	3	4
	25 years	1	...	1	...	...	...	1	...	1
	27 years	...	1	1	...	...	...	...	1	1
	30 years	1	1	2	...	...	...	1	1	2
	32 years	...	1	1	...	...	...	...	1	1
	34 years	2	2	4	...	...	...	2	2	4
	39 years	...	1	1	...	...	...	...	1	1
	40 years	...	2	2	...	...	...	...	2	2
	41 years	1	...	1	...	...	...	1	...	1
	44 years	1	1	2	...	...	...	1	1	2
	49 years	2	...	2	...	...	...	2	...	2
	50 years	...	3	3	...	...	...	...	3	3
	52 years	1	1	2	...	...	...	1	1	2
	54 years	1	2	3	...	...	...	1	2	3
	55 years	1	...	1	...	...	...	1	...	1
	59 years	...	1	1	...	...	...	...	1	1
	60 years	1	...	1	...	...	...	1	...	1
	Unknown	1	1	2	...	...	...	1	1	2
65 years		25	35	60	2	1	3	27	36	63
	Birth	1	2	3	1	...	1	2	2	4
	4 years	...	...	...	...	1	1	...	1	1
	5 years	1	...	1	...	...	...	1	...	1
	6 years	...	1	1	...	...	...	...	1	1
	8 years	...	1	1	...	...	...	...	1	1
	9 years	1	1	2	...	...	...	1	1	2
	10 years	1	...	1	...	...	...	1	...	1
	15 years	1	...	1	...	...	...	1	...	1
	18 years	1	...	1	...	...	...	1	...	1
	20 years	1	2	3	...	...	...	1	2	3
	22 years	...	1	1	...	...	...	...	1	1
	25 years	1	2	3	...	...	...	1	2	3
	30 years	3	4	7	...	...	...	3	4	7
	34 years	...	1	1	...	...	...	...	1	1
	35 years	1	2	3	...	...	...	1	2	3
	40 years	2	1	3	...	...	...	2	1	3
	43 years	1	1	2	...	...	...	1	1	2
	45 years	3	6	9	...	...	...	3	6	9
	47 years	1	...	1	...	...	...	1	...	1
	52 years	1	...	1	...	...	...	1	...	1
	53 years	...	2	2	...	...	...	...	2	2
	56 years	3	...	3	...	...	...	3	...	3
	57 years	1	...	1	...	...	...	1	...	1
	62 years	...	2	2	...	...	...	...	2	2
	63 years	...	2	2	...	...	...	...	2	2
	64 years	...	1	1	...	...	...	...	1	1

TABLE VI.—Continued.

1885.		A			B			C		
		The "Deaf."			The "Deaf and Dumb."			Summation of "The Deaf" and "The Deaf and Dumb."		
Present age.	Age at occurrence of deafness.	Number affected at ages specified.			Number affected at ages specified.			Number affected at ages specified.		
		M.	F.	Both sexes.	M.	F.	Both sexes.	M.	F.	Total.
65 years—Continued.	65 years	...	1	1	...	...	...	...	1	1
	Unknown	1	2	3	1	...	1	2	2	4
66 years		19	23	42	...	2	2	19	25	44
	Birth	...	1	1	...	1	1	...	2	2
	6 months	1	...	1	...	...	...	1	...	1
	2 years	...	...	...	...	1	1	...	1	1
	16 years	1	1	2	...	...	...	1	1	2
	25 years	...	2	2	...	...	...	...	2	2
	26 years	3	1	4	...	...	...	3	1	4
	30 years	...	3	3	...	...	...	...	3	3
	31 years	...	1	1	...	...	...	...	1	1
	36 years	1	2	3	...	...	...	1	2	3
	38 years	1	...	1	...	...	...	1	...	1
	39 years	...	1	1	...	...	...	...	1	1
	40 years	2	...	2	...	...	...	2	...	2
	41 years	2	2	4	...	...	...	2	2	4
	44 years	1	1	2	...	...	...	1	1	2
	47 years	1	...	1	...	...	...	1	...	1
	50 years	1	2	3	...	...	...	1	2	3
	51 years	...	1	1	...	...	...	...	1	1
	56 years	2	2	4	...	...	...	2	2	4
	57 years	...	1	1	...	...	...	...	1	1
	58 years	1	...	1	...	...	...	1	...	1
	59 years	1	...	1	...	...	...	1	...	1
	63 years	1	...	1	...	...	...	1	...	1
	64 years	...	1	1	...	...	...	...	1	1
	65 years	...	1	1	...	...	...	...	1	1
67 years		29	30	59	2	2	4	31	32	63
	Birth	...	1	1	1	2	3	1	3	4
	3 years	...	...	...	1	...	1	1	...	1
	4 years	1	...	1	...	...	...	1	...	1
	6 years	1	1	2	...	...	...	1	1	2
	12 years	1	...	1	...	...	...	1	...	1
	14 years	...	1	1	...	...	...	...	1	1
	15 years	...	1	1	...	...	...	...	1	1
	16 years	1	...	1	...	...	...	1	...	1
	18 years	...	1	1	...	...	...	...	1	1
	20 years	...	1	1	...	...	...	...	1	1
	22 years	1	...	1	...	...	...	1	...	1
	23 years	...	1	1	...	...	...	...	1	1
	25 years	2	2	4	...	...	...	2	2	4
	27 years	1	1	2	...	...	...	1	1	2
	30 years	1	2	3	...	...	...	1	2	3
	35 years	...	1	1	...	...	...	...	1	1
	37 years	1	1	2	...	...	...	1	1	2
	38 years	...	1	1	...	...	...	...	1	1
	40 years	2	2	4	...	...	...	2	2	4
	42 years	1	...	1	...	...	...	1	...	1
	47 years	5	...	5	...	...	...	5	...	5
	50 years	1	1	2	...	...	...	1	1	2
	52 years	...	1	1	...	...	...	...	1	1
	55 years	2	1	3	...	...	...	2	1	3
	56 years	...	1	1	...	...	...	...	1	1
	57 years	1	3	4	...	...	...	1	3	4
	60 years	...	1	1	...	...	...	...	1	1
	62 years	2	3	5	...	...	...	2	3	5
	64 years	3	1	4	...	...	...	3	1	4
	66 years	1	...	1	...	...	...	1	...	1
	Unknown	1	1	2	...	...	...	1	1	2
68 years		24	25	49	2	3	5	26	28	54
	Birth	...	...	...	...	2	2	...	2	2
	8 months	...	...	...	1	...	1	1	...	1
	3 years	...	...	...	1	...	1	1	...	1
	5 years	...	...	...	...	1	1	...	1	1
	16 years	1	1	2	...	...	...	1	1	2
	28 years	...	3	3	...	...	...	...	3	3
	30 years	2	1	3	...	...	...	2	1	3
	33 years	1	...	1	...	...	...	1	...	1
	35 years	1	...	1	...	...	...	1	...	1
	40 years	...	1	1	...	...	...	...	1	1
	43 years	2	1	3	...	...	...	2	1	3
	48 years	7	3	10	...	...	...	7	3	10
	50 years	...	1	1	...	...	...	...	1	1
	52 years	...	1	1	...	...	...	...	1	1
	53 years	1	...	1	...	...	...	1	...	1
	54 years	...	1	1	...	...	...	...	1	1
	55 years	1	1	2	...	...	...	1	1	2
	56 years	1	1	2	...	...	...	1	1	2
	58 years	1	2	3	...	...	...	1	2	3
	60 years	2	...	2	...	...	...	2	...	2
	61 years	...	1	1	...	...	...	...	1	1
	62 years	...	1	1	...	...	...	...	1	1
	64 years	1	...	1	...	...	...	1	...	1
	65 years	1	3	4	...	...	...	1	3	4
	Unknown	2	3	5	...	...	...	2	3	5
69 years		15	25	40	2	1	3	17	26	43
	Birth	1	...	1	1	...	1	2	...	2
	2 years	...	1	1	1	...	1	1	1	2
	3 years	1	1	2	...	1	1	1	2	3
	9 years	1	...	1	...	...	...	1	...	1
	16 years	...	1	1	...	...	...	...	1	1
	19 years	...	1	1	...	...	...	...	1	1
	24 years	1	1	2	...	...	...	1	1	2
	25 years	1	...	1	...	...	...	1	...	1
	30 years	...	2	2	...	...	...	...	2	2
	39 years	...	2	2	...	...	...	...	2	2
	40 years	...	1	1	...	...	...	...	1	1
	43 years	...	1	1	...	...	...	...	1	1
	44 years	...	1	1	...	...	...	...	1	1
	49 years	1	...	1	...	...	...	1	...	1
	50 years	1	3	4	...	...	...	1	3	4
	54 years	...	1	1	...	...	...	...	1	1
	55 years	...	1	1	...	...	...	...	1	1
	59 years	2	1	3	...	...	...	2	1	3

TABLE VI.—Continued.

1885.		A			B			C		
Present age.	Age at occurrence of deafness.	The "Deaf." Number affected at ages specified.			The "Deaf and Dumb." Number affected at ages specified.			Summation of "The Deaf" and "The Deaf and Dumb." Number affected at ages specified.		
		M.	F.	Both sexes.	M.	F.	Both sexes.	M.	F.	Total.
69 years—Continued.	62 years	......	1	1	......	......	......	......	1	1
	64 years	......	1	1	......	......	......	......	1	1
	65 years	2	......	2	......	......	......	2	......	2
	66 years	1	1	2	......	......	......	1	1	2
	68 years	1	1	2	......	......	......	1	1	2
	69 years	......	1	1	......	......	......	......	1	1
	Unknown	2	2	4	......	......	......	2	2	4
70 years	......	31	33	64	4	......	4	35	33	68
	Birth	......	1	1	2	......	2	2	1	3
	2 years	......	......	......	1	......	1	1	......	1
	5 years	......	......	......	1	......	1	1	......	1
	15 years	1	......	1	......	......	......	1	......	1
	18 years	1	......	1	......	......	......	1	......	1
	20 years	......	2	2	......	......	......	......	2	2
	25 years	1	......	1	......	......	......	1	......	1
	30 years	3	......	3	......	......	......	3	......	3
	31 years	1	......	1	......	......	......	1	......	1
	35 years	2	1	3	......	......	......	2	1	3
	38 years	1	1	2	......	......	......	1	1	2
	40 years	2	1	3	......	......	......	2	1	3
	45 years	1	1	2	......	......	......	1	1	2
	50 years	3	5	8	......	......	......	3	5	8
	51 years	1	......	1	......	......	......	1	......	1
	55 years	1	1	2	......	......	......	1	1	2
	56 years	1	......	1	......	......	......	1	......	1
	57 years	1	1	2	......	......	......	1	1	2
	58 years	1	......	1	......	......	......	1	......	1
	60 years	3	5	8	......	......	......	3	5	8
	61 years	......	1	1	......	......	......	......	1	1
	64 years	......	1	1	......	......	......	......	1	1
	65 years	......	4	4	......	......	......	......	4	4
	66 years	......	1	1	......	......	......	......	1	1
	67 years	......	1	1	......	......	......	......	1	1
	68 years	2	2	4	......	......	......	2	2	4
	69 years	......	2	2	......	......	......	......	2	2
	Unknown	5	2	7	......	......	......	5	2	7
71 years	......	20	17	37	2	3	5	22	20	42
	Birth	......	......	......	1	1	2	1	1	2
	1 year	......	......	......	1	......	1	1	......	1
	2 years	......	......	......	......	1	1	......	1	1
	3 years	......	1	1	......	......	......	......	1	1
	5 years	......	......	......	......	1	1	......	1	1
	16 years	......	1	1	......	......	......	......	1	1
	18 years	1	......	1	......	......	......	1	......	1
	20 years	......	1	1	......	......	......	......	1	1
	21 years	......	1	1	......	......	......	......	1	1
	22 years	1	......	1	......	......	......	1	......	1
	31 years	1	......	1	......	......	......	1	......	1
	35 years	......	1	1	......	......	......	......	1	1
	40 years	1	1	2	......	......	......	1	1	2
	41 years	2	1	3	......	......	......	2	1	3
	42 years	......	1	1	......	......	......	......	1	1
	46 years	1	2	3	......	......	......	1	2	3
	50 years	3	1	4	......	......	......	3	1	4
	51 years	1	1	2	......	......	......	1	1	2
	55 years	1	......	1	......	......	......	1	......	1
	56 years	1	1	2	......	......	......	1	1	2
	59 years	......	1	1	......	......	......	......	1	1
	60 years	......	1	1	......	......	......	......	1	1
	61 years	2	......	2	......	......	......	2	......	2
	65 years	......	1	1	......	......	......	......	1	1
	66 years	2	......	2	......	......	......	2	......	2
	68 years	1	......	1	......	......	......	1	......	1
	69 years	......	1	1	......	......	......	......	1	1
	71 years	1	......	1	......	......	......	1	......	1
	Unknown	1	......	1	......	......	......	1	......	1
72 years	......	24	21	45	2	1	3	26	22	48
	Birth	......	......	..	1	......	1	1	......	1
	2 years	......	1	1	......	......	......	......	1	1
	4 years	......	......	......	......	1	1	......	1	1
	5 years	......	......	......	1	......	1	1	......	1
	12 years	......	1	1	......	......	......	......	1	1
	19 years	......	1	1	......	......	......	......	1	1
	20 years	1	1	2	......	......	......	1	1	2
	21 years	......	1	1	......	......	......	......	1	1
	22 years	......	1	1	......	......	......	......	1	1
	28 years	......	1	1	......	......	......	......	1	1
	30 years	1	1	2	......	......	......	1	1	2
	32 years	......	1	1	......	......	......	......	1	1
	39 years	1	......	1	......	......	......	1	......	1
	42 years	3	2	5	......	......	......	3	2	5
	43 years	1	......	1	......	......	......	1	......	1
	44 years	1	......	1	......	......	......	1	......	1
	47 years	1	......	1	......	......	......	1	......	1
	50 years	1	......	1	......	......	......	1	......	1
	52 years	1	3	4	......	......	......	1	3	4
	54 years	......	1	1	......	......	......	......	1	1
	56 years	1	1	2	......	......	......	1	1	2
	60 years	1	......	1	......	......	......	1	......	1
	62 years	2	1	3	......	......	......	2	1	3
	65 years	2	......	2	......	......	......	2	......	2
	67 years	3	......	3	......	......	......	3	......	3
	68 years	1	......	1	......	......	......	1	......	1
	70 years	1	2	3	......	......	......	1	2	3
	71 years	1	1	2	......	......	......	1	1	2
	Unknown	1	1	2	......	......	......	1	1	2
73 years	......	31	19	50	4	1	5	35	20	55
	Birth	......	......	......	3	1	4	3	1	4
	3 years	1	......	1	......	......	......	1	......	1
	4 years	......	1	1	1	......	1	1	1	2
	5 years	1	......	1	......	......	......	1	......	1
	16 years	1	......	1	......	......	......	1	......	1
	18 years	......	1	1	......	......	......	......	1	1
	20 years	......	1	1	......	......	......	......	1	1

TABLE VI.—Continued.

1885.		A			B			C		
Present age.	Age at occurrence of deafness.	The "Deaf." Number affected at ages specified.			The "Deaf and Dumb." Number affected at ages specified.			Summation of "The Deaf" and "The Deaf and Dumb." Number affected at ages specified.		
		M.	F.	Both sexes.	M.	F.	Both sexes.	M.	F.	Total.
73 years—Continued.	23 years	1	......	1	......	......	......	1	......	1
	25 years	......	1	1	......	......	......	......	1	1
	30 years	1	1	2	......	......	......	1	1	2
	33 years	1	......	1	......	......	......	1	......	1
	34 years	1	1	2	......	......	......	1	1	2
	35 years	1	......	1	......	......	......	1	......	1
	40 years	1	1	2	......	......	......	1	1	2
	43 years	2	......	2	......	......	......	2	......	2
	48 years	......	1	1	......	......	......	......	1	1
	50 years	3	2	5	......	......	......	3	2	5
	51 years	1	......	1	......	......	......	1	......	1
	52 years	1	......	1	......	......	......	1	......	1
	53 years	3	1	4	......	......	......	3	1	4
	57 years	......	1	1	......	......	......	......	1	1
	63 years	2	1	3	......	......	......	2	1	3
	64 years	......	1	1	......	......	......	......	1	1
	65 years	2	......	2	......	......	......	2	......	2
	68 years	3	......	3	......	......	......	3	......	3
	69 years	2	2	4	......	......	......	2	2	4
	70 years	1	1	2	......	......	......	1	1	2
	71 years	......	2	2	......	......	......	......	2	2
	72 years	1	......	1	......	......	......	1	......	1
	Unknown	1	......	1	......	......	......	1	......	1
74 years	......	29	31	60	3	1	4	32	32	64
	Birth	......	......	......	1	1	2	1	1	2
	4 years	......	......	......	1	......	1	1	......	1
	6 years	......	1	1	......	......	......	......	1	1
	7 years	......	......	......	1	......	1	1	......	1
	14 years	......	1	1	......	......	......	......	1	1
	18 years	1	1	2	......	......	......	1	1	2
	24 years	......	1	1	......	......	......	......	1	1
	25 years	......	1	1	......	......	......	......	1	1
	30 years	1	......	1	......	......	......	1	......	1
	34 years	3	1	4	......	......	......	3	1	4
	35 years	......	1	1	......	......	......	......	1	1
	40 years	2	2	4	......	......	......	2	2	4
	44 years	4	1	5	......	......	......	4	1	5
	45 years	......	1	1	......	......	......	......	1	1
	47 years	......	1	1	......	......	......	......	1	1
	49 years	2	1	3	......	......	......	2	1	3
	50 years	1	......	1	......	......	......	1	......	1
	51 years	......	1	1	......	......	......	......	1	1
	54 years	......	3	3	......	......	......	......	3	3
	55 years	......	2	2	......	......	......	......	2	2
	59 years	......	2	2	......	......	......	......	2	2
	60 years	1	2	3	......	......	......	1	2	3
	64 years	3	1	4	......	......	......	3	1	4
	65 years	1	2	3	......	......	......	1	2	3
	66 years	1	......	1	......	......	......	1	......	1
	68 years	......	1	1	......	......	......	......	1	1
	69 years	......	1	1	......	......	......	......	1	1
	70 years	3	1	4	......	......	......	3	1	4
	71 years	1	1	2	......	......	......	1	1	2
	72 years	2	1	3	......	......	......	2	1	3
	74 years	1	......	1	......	......	......	1	......	1
	Unknown	2	......	2	......	......	......	2	......	2
75 years	......	32	32	64	3	3	6	35	35	70
	Birth	1	2	3	1	2	3	2	4	6
	2 years	......	......	......	......	1	1	......	1	1
	3 years	......	1	1	1	......	1	1	1	2
	4 years	......	1	1	......	......	......	......	1	1
	5 years	......	......	......	1	......	1	1	......	1
	8 years	1	......	1	......	......	......	1	......	1
	12 years	1	......	1	......	......	......	1	......	1
	15 years	......	2	2	......	......	......	......	2	2
	16 years	......	1	1	......	......	......	......	1	1
	18 years	1	......	1	......	......	......	1	......	1
	20 years	1	......	1	......	......	......	1	......	1
	25 years	3	1	4	......	......	......	3	1	4
	26 years	......	1	1	......	......	......	......	1	1
	30 years	......	3	3	......	......	......	......	3	3
	35 years	2	......	2	......	......	......	2	......	2
	37 years	......	1	1	......	......	......	......	1	1
	45 years	1	......	1	......	......	......	1	......	1
	50 years	1	2	3	......	......	......	1	2	3
	55 years	......	1	1	......	......	......	......	1	1
	57 years	......	1	1	......	......	......	......	1	1
	60 years	5	3	8	......	......	......	5	3	8
	65 years	4	5	9	......	......	......	4	5	9
	66 years	2	......	2	......	......	......	2	......	2
	67 years	2	1	3	......	......	......	2	1	3
	68 years	1	......	1	......	......	......	1	......	1
	69 years	1	......	1	......	......	......	1	......	1
	70 years	1	2	3	......	......	......	1	2	3
	72 years	1	1	2	......	......	......	1	1	2
	72 y'rs (73?)	2	3	5	......	......	......	2	3	5
	Unknown	1	......	1	......	......	......	1	......	1
76 years	......	27	20	47	3	1	4	30	21	51
	Birth	2	1	3	......	1	1	2	2	4
	2 years	......	......	......	1	......	1	1	......	1
	3 years	......	......	......	1	......	1	1	......	1
	4 years	1	......	1	......	......	......	1	......	1
	9 years	......	1	1	......	......	......	......	1	1
	12 years	......	......	......	1	......	1	1	......	1
	21 years	1	......	1	......	......	......	1	......	1
	25 years	......	1	1	......	......	......	......	1	1
	26 years	3	......	3	......	......	......	3	......	3
	28 years	1	......	1	......	......	......	1	......	1
	30 years	1	......	1	......	......	......	1	......	1
	36 years	......	3	3	......	......	......	......	3	3
	38 years	1	......	1	......	......	......	1	......	1
	46 years	2	......	2	......	......	......	2	......	2
	51 years	1	1	2	......	......	......	1	1	2
	53 years	1	......	1	......	......	......	1	......	1
	56 years	5	2	7	......	......	......	5	2	7

TABLE VI.—Continued.

1885. Present age.	Age at occurrence of deafness.	A. The "Deaf." Number affected at ages specified. M.	F.	Both sexes.	B. The "Deaf and Dumb." Number affected at ages specified. M.	F.	Both sexes.	C. Summation of "The Deaf" and "The Deaf and Dumb." Number affected at ages specified. M.	F.	Total.
76 years—Continued.	61 years	......	3	3	......	......	......	......	3	3
	62 years	1	......	1	......	......	......	1	......	1
	65 years	1	......	1	......	......	......	1	......	1
	66 years	......	3	3	......	......	......	......	3	3
	68 years	1	......	1	......	......	......	1	......	1
	70 years	......	1	1	......	......	......	......	1	1
	71 years	1	1	2	......	......	......	1	1	2
	74 years	2	1	3	......	......	......	2	1	3
	Unknown	2	2	4	......	......	......	2	2	4
77 years		**18**	**27**	**45**	**2**	......	**2**	**20**	**27**	**47**
	Birth	2	......	2	1	......	1	3	......	3
	3 years	......	1	1	......	......	......	......	1	1
	6 years	......	1	1	......	......	......	......	1	1
	20 years	......	1	1	......	......	......	......	1	1
	23 years	......	1	1	......	......	......	......	1	1
	26 years	1	......	1	......	......	......	1	......	1
	27 years	2	1	3	......	......	......	2	1	3
	30 years	......	1	1	......	......	......	......	1	1
	37 years	......	2	2	......	......	......	......	2	2
	40 years	......	3	3	......	......	......	......	3	3
	47 years	......	1	1	......	......	......	......	1	1
	50 years	1	......	1	......	......	......	1	......	1
	52 years	......	1	1	......	......	......	......	1	1
	55 years	2	......	2	......	......	......	2	......	2
	57 years	1	3	4	......	......	......	1	3	4
	62 years	1	1	2	......	......	......	1	1	2
	65 years	1	1	2	......	......	......	1	1	2
	67 years	1	1	2	......	......	......	1	1	2
	70 years	3	......	3	......	......	......	3	......	3
	71 years	......	1	1	......	......	......	......	1	1
	72 years	......	1	1	......	......	......	......	1	1
	73 years	1	......	1	......	......	......	1	......	1
	74 years	......	1	1	......	......	......	......	1	1
	75 years	1	3	4	......	......	......	1	3	4
	76 years	......	2	2	......	......	......	......	2	2
	Unknown	1	......	1	1	......	1	2	......	2
78 years		**26**	**12**	**38**	**2**	**1**	**3**	**28**	**13**	**41**
	Birth	......	......	......	1	1	2	1	1	2
	1 year	......	......	......	1	......	1	1	......	1
	3 years	1	......	1	......	......	......	1	......	1
	6 years	......	1	1	......	......	......	......	1	1
	25 years	1	......	1	......	......	......	1	......	1
	26 years	1	......	1	......	......	......	1	......	1
	48 years	2	1	3	......	......	......	2	1	3
	54 years	1	......	1	......	......	......	1	......	1
	55 years	2	......	2	......	......	......	2	......	2
	57 years	2	......	2	......	......	......	2	......	2
	58 years	1	......	1	......	......	......	1	......	1
	60 years	1	1	2	......	......	......	1	1	2
	63 years	2	......	2	......	......	......	2	......	2
	68 years	2	2	4	......	......	......	2	2	4
	70 years	4	1	5	......	......	......	4	1	5
	72 years	1	......	1	......	......	......	1	......	1
	73 years	1	2	3	......	......	......	1	2	3
	74 years	1	1	2	......	......	......	1	1	2
	75 years	......	1	1	......	......	......	......	1	1
	77 years	1	1	2	......	......	......	1	1	2
	Unknown	2	1	3	......	......	......	2	1	3
79 years		**30**	**26**	**56**	**1**	**1**	**2**	**31**	**27**	**58**
	Birth	......	......	......	......	1	1	......	1	1
	2 years	......	......	......	1	......	1	1	......	1
	5 years	1	......	1	......	......	......	1	......	1
	14 years	......	1	1	......	......	......	......	1	1
	17 years	......	1	1	......	......	......	......	1	1
	20 years	1	1	2	......	......	......	1	1	2
	21 years	1	......	1	......	......	......	1	......	1
	44 years	1	......	1	......	......	......	1	......	1
	47 years	1	......	1	......	......	......	1	......	1
	49 years	1	......	1	......	......	......	1	......	1
	50 years	1	1	2	......	......	......	1	1	2
	53 years	......	2	2	......	......	......	......	2	2
	54 years	1	......	1	......	......	......	1	......	1
	59 years	2	3	5	......	......	......	2	3	5
	60 years	2	......	2	......	......	......	2	......	2
	61 years	......	1	1	......	......	......	......	1	1
	62 years	1	......	1	......	......	......	1	......	1
	64 years	2	1	3	......	......	......	2	1	3
	65 years	1	......	1	......	......	......	1	......	1
	67 years	......	1	1	......	......	......	......	1	1
	69 years	5	......	5	......	......	......	5	......	5
	70 years	2	1	3	......	......	......	2	1	3
	71 years	1	......	1	......	......	......	1	......	1
	72 years	......	2	2	......	......	......	......	2	2
	73 years	1	1	2	......	......	......	1	1	2
	74 years	......	1	1	......	......	......	......	1	1
	75 years	1	3	4	......	......	......	1	3	4
	76 years	1	1	2	......	......	......	1	1	2
	77 years	1	1	2	......	......	......	1	1	2
	78 years	......	1	1	......	......	......	......	1	1
	79 years	......	1	1	......	......	......	......	1	1
	Unknown	2	2	4	......	......	......	2	2	4
80 years		**31**	**31**	**62**	**1**	**1**	**2**	**32**	**32**	**64**
	Birth	......	......	......	1	1	2	1	1	2
	18 years	......	1	1	......	......	......	......	1	1
	20 years	......	1	1	......	......	......	......	1	1
	27 years	......	1	1	......	......	......	......	1	1
	30 years	1	1	2	......	......	......	1	1	2
	32 years	......	1	1	......	......	......	......	1	1
	35 years	2	......	2	......	......	......	2	......	2
	40 years	2	1	3	......	......	......	2	1	3
	50 years	2	3	5	......	......	......	2	3	5
	52 years	......	1	1	......	......	......	......	1	1
	55 years	1	1	2	......	......	......	1	1	2
	60 years	4	......	4	......	......	......	4	......	4

TABLE VI.—Continued.

1885. Present age.	Age at occurrence of deafness.	A. The "Deaf." Number affected at ages specified. M.	F.	Both sexes.	B. The "Deaf and Dumb." Number affected at ages specified. M.	F.	Both sexes.	C. Summation of "The Deaf" and "The Deaf and Dumb." Number affected at ages specified. M.	F.	Total.
80 years—Continued.	64 years	......	1	1	......	......	......	......	1	1
	65 years	3	3	6	......	......	......	3	3	6
	66 years	......	1	1	......	......	......	......	1	1
	68 years	1	......	1	......	......	......	1	......	1
	70 years	4	3	7	......	......	......	4	3	7
	72 years	3	1	4	......	......	......	3	1	4
	74 years	3	......	3	......	......	......	3	......	3
	75 years	3	3	6	......	......	......	3	3	6
	76 years	1	......	1	......	......	......	1	......	1
	77 years	......	1	1	......	......	......	......	1	1
	78 years	1	2	3	......	......	......	1	2	3
	79 years	......	1	1	......	......	......	......	1	1
	80 years	......	1	1	......	......	......	......	1	1
	Unknown	......	3	3	......	......	......	......	3	3
81 years		**12**	**19**	**31**	......	......	......	**12**	**19**	**31**
	9 years	1	......	1	......	......	......	1	......	1
	12 years	......	1	1	......	......	......	......	1	1
	31 years	......	2	2	......	......	......	......	2	2
	34 years	......	1	1	......	......	......	......	1	1
	40 years	......	1	1	......	......	......	......	1	1
	46 years	......	1	1	......	......	......	......	1	1
	51 years	1	......	1	......	......	......	1	......	1
	61 years	1	2	3	......	......	......	1	2	3
	63 years	......	1	1	......	......	......	......	1	1
	69 years	2	......	2	......	......	......	2	......	2
	70 years	1	......	1	......	......	......	1	......	1
	71 years	2	2	4	......	......	......	2	2	4
	73 years	1	1	2	......	......	......	1	1	2
	75 years	1	1	2	......	......	......	1	1	2
	76 years	......	1	1	......	......	......	......	1	1
	79 years	......	1	1	......	......	......	......	1	1
	80 years	1	......	1	......	......	......	1	......	1
	Unknown	1	4	5	......	......	......	1	4	5
82 years		**17**	**18**	**35**	......	......	......	**17**	**18**	**35**
	Birth	......	1	1	......	......	......	......	1	1
	9 years	......	1	1	......	......	......	......	1	1
	10 years	1	......	1	......	......	......	1	......	1
	11 years	1	......	1	......	......	......	1	......	1
	24 years	......	1	1	......	......	......	......	1	1
	37 years	1	......	1	......	......	......	1	......	1
	39 years	......	1	1	......	......	......	......	1	1
	40 years	......	1	1	......	......	......	......	1	1
	42 years	1	2	3	......	......	......	1	2	3
	52 years	......	2	2	......	......	......	......	2	2
	55 years	......	1	1	......	......	......	......	1	1
	57 years	1	......	1	......	......	......	1	......	1
	60 years	2	2	4	......	......	......	2	2	4
	61 years	......	1	1	......	......	......	......	1	1
	62 years	1	......	1	......	......	......	1	......	1
	70 years	2	......	2	......	......	......	2	......	2
	72 years	5	......	5	......	......	......	5	......	5
	73 years	2	1	3	......	......	......	2	1	3
	76 years	......	1	1	......	......	......	......	1	1
	77 years	......	1	1	......	......	......	......	1	1
	78 years	......	1	1	......	......	......	......	1	1
	81 years	......	1	1	......	......	......	......	1	1
83 years		**16**	**20**	**36**	......	**1**	**1**	**16**	**21**	**37**
	Birth	......	......	......	......	1	1	......	1	1
	23 years	2	......	2	......	......	......	2	......	2
	39 years	1	1	2	......	......	......	1	1	2
	43 years	2	1	3	......	......	......	2	1	3
	53 years	......	1	1	......	......	......	......	1	1
	58 years	3	......	3	......	......	......	3	......	3
	60 years	2	......	2	......	......	......	2	......	2
	63 years	......	4	4	......	......	......	......	4	4
	65 years	......	1	1	......	......	......	......	1	1
	70 years	1	1	2	......	......	......	1	1	2
	71 years	......	1	1	......	......	......	......	1	1
	73 years	1	1	2	......	......	......	1	1	2
	75 years	2	1	3	......	......	......	2	1	3
	76 years	......	2	2	......	......	......	......	2	2
	78 years	......	2	2	......	......	......	......	2	2
	79 years	1	......	1	......	......	......	1	......	1
	80 years	1	......	1	......	......	......	1	......	1
	82 years	......	1	1	......	......	......	......	1	1
	83 years	......	1	1	......	......	......	......	1	1
	Unknown	......	2	2	......	......	......	......	2	2
84 years		**16**	**13**	**29**	......	......	......	**16**	**13**	**29**
	3 years	2	......	2	......	......	......	2	......	2
	44 years	1	1	2	......	......	......	1	1	2
	51 years	1	......	1	......	......	......	1	......	1
	54 years	2	2	4	......	......	......	2	2	4
	64 years	2	1	3	......	......	......	2	1	3
	65 years	1	1	2	......	......	......	1	1	2
	70 years	2	1	3	......	......	......	2	1	3
	72 years	......	1	1	......	......	......	......	1	1
	74 years	1	1	2	......	......	......	1	1	2
	75 years	1	......	1	......	......	......	1	......	1
	79 years	......	1	1	......	......	......	......	1	1
	80 years	1	1	2	......	......	......	1	1	2
	83 years	1	1	2	......	......	......	1	1	2
	Unknown	1	2	3	......	......	......	1	2	3
85 years		**18**	**15**	**33**	......	......	......	**18**	**15**	**33**
	5 years	1	......	1	......	......	......	1	......	1
	27 years	......	1	1	......	......	......	......	1	1
	30 years	1	......	1	......	......	......	1	......	1
	32 years	1	......	1	......	......	......	1	......	1
	40 years	......	2	2	......	......	......	......	2	2
	45 years	1	1	2	......	......	......	1	1	2
	50 years	1	......	1	......	......	......	1	......	1
	65 years	......	1	1	......	......	......	......	1	1
	68 years	......	1	1	......	......	......	......	1	1
	70 years	2	2	4	......	......	......	2	2	4

TABLE VI.—Continued.

1885.		A			B			C		
		The "Deaf."			The "Deaf and Dumb."			Summation of "The Deaf" and "The Deaf and Dumb."		
Present age.	Age at occurrence of deafness.	Number affected at ages specified.			Number affected at ages specified.			Number affected at ages specified.		
		M.	F.	Both sexes.	M.	F.	Both sexes.	M.	F.	Total.
85 years—Continued.	71 years		1	1					1	1
	73 years		1	1					1	1
	75 years	4	4	8				4	4	8
	76 years	1		1				1		1
	79 years	1		1				1		1
	80 years	1		1				1		1
	82 years	2		2				2		2
	83 years	1		1				1		1
	85 years		1	1					1	1
	Unknown	1		1				1		1
86 years		3	13	16				3	13	16
	4 years		1	1					1	1
	26 years		1	1					1	1
	46 years		1	1					1	1
	50 years		1	1					1	1
	60 years		1	1					1	1
	63 years		1	1					1	1
	66 years		1	1					1	1
	73 years		1	1					1	1
	76 years	1		1				1		1
	78 years		1	1					1	1
	81 years	1	1	2				1	1	2
	84 years		1	1					1	1
	85 years		1	1					1	1
	86 years	1		1				1		1
	Unknown		1	1					1	1
87 years		6	9	15				6	9	15
	37 years	1		1				1		1
	62 years		1	1					1	1
	65 years		1	1					1	1
	72 years	1		1				1		1
	74 years		1	1					1	1
	77 years	1	2	3				1	2	3
	78 years		1	1					1	1
	80 years	2	1	3				2	1	3
	82 years		1	1					1	1
	Unknown	1	1	2				1	1	2
88 years		5	9	14				5	9	14
	38 years		1	1					1	1
	40 years	1		1				1		1
	65 years		1	1					1	1
	68 years	1	2	3				1	2	3
	73 years	1	1	2				1	1	2
	75 years	1		1				1		1
	78 years	1	1	2				1	1	2
	80 years		2	2					2	2
	83 years		1	1					1	1
89 years		6	8	14				6	8	14
	60 years	1		1				1		1
	74 years		2	2					2	2
	75 years	1		1				1		1
	78 years		1	1					1	1
	79 years	1	1	2				1	1	2

TABLE VI.—Continued.

1885.		A			B			C		
		The "Deaf."			The "Deaf and Dumb."			Summation of "The Deaf" and "The Deaf and Dumb."		
Present age.	Age at occurrence of deafness.	Number affected at ages specified.			Number affected at ages specified.			Number affected at ages specified.		
		M.	F.	Both sexes.	M.	F.	Both sexes.	M.	F.	Total.
89 years—Continued.	80 years	1	2	3				1	2	3
	83 years		1	1					1	1
	84 years	1		1				1		1
	86 years	1		1				1		1
	Unknown		1	1					1	1
90 years		1	6	7				1	6	7
	20 years		1	1					1	1
	35 years		1	1					1	1
	50 years		1	1					1	1
	70 years	1	2	3				1	2	3
	75 years		1	1					1	1
91 years		2	4	6				2	4	6
	2 years	1	1	2				1	1	2
	41 years		1	1					1	1
	80 years		1	1					1	1
	85 years		1	1					1	1
	Unknown	1		1				1		1
92 years		1	6	7				1	6	7
	42 years		1	1					1	1
	52 years	1		1				1		1
	72 years		2	2					2	2
	80 years		1	1					1	1
	88 years		2	2					2	2
93 years		1	3	4				1	3	4
	43 years		1	1					1	1
	86 years		1	1					1	1
	88 years	1		1				1		1
	Unknown		1	1					1	1
94 years		2	4	6				2	4	6
	79 years		1	1					1	1
	80 years	1		1				1		1
	82 years		1	1					1	1
	86 years		1	1					1	1
	89 years	1		1				1		1
	92 years		1	1					1	1
95 years		2	3	5				2	3	5
	53 years	1		1				1		1
	70 years		1	1					1	1
	89 years	1		1				1		1
	Unknown		2	2					2	2
96 years			1	1					1	1
	85 years		1	1					1	1
97 years			2	2					2	2
	85 years		1	1					1	1
	Unknown		1	1					1	1
108 years			1	1					1	1
	Unknown		1	1					1	1

SUMMARY.

Present age, 1885.	A The "Deaf." M.	F.	Both sexes.	B The "Deaf and Dumb." M.	F.	Both sexes.	C Summation of "The Deaf" and "The Deaf and Dumb." M.	F.	Both sexes.
2 years	1	......	1	......	1	1	1	1	2
3 years	1	3	4	......	6	6	1	9	10
4 years	......	......	......	6	2	8	6	2	8
5 years	1	......	1	6	4	10	7	4	11
6 years	3	5	8	6	4	10	9	9	18
7 years	......	2	2	8	6	14	8	8	16
8 years	6	4	10	5	9	14	11	13	24
9 years	1	5	6	3	12	15	4	17	21
10 years	5	4	9	10	7	17	15	11	26
11 years	5	5	10	6	14	20	11	19	30
12 years	5	5	10	11	11	22	16	16	32
13 years	6	11	17	12	12	24	18	23	41
14 years	5	9	14	24	15	39	29	24	53
15 years	7	10	17	9	7	16	16	17	33
16 years	8	13	21	13	11	24	21	24	45
17 years	6	10	16	12	6	18	18	16	34
18 years	10	11	21	11	5	16	21	16	37
19 years	5	7	12	10	11	21	15	18	33
20 years	5	8	13	4	11	15	9	19	28
21 years	5	4	9	5	5	10	10	9	19
22 years	9	13	22	9	2	11	18	15	33
23 years	10	10	20	6	8	14	16	18	34
24 years	3	10	13	8	10	18	11	20	31
25 years	7	13	20	8	10	18	15	23	38
26 years	14	14	28	8	4	12	22	18	40
27 years	10	21	31	5	3	8	15	24	39
28 years	8	18	26	10	8	18	18	26	44
29 years	8	12	20	5	6	11	13	18	31
30 years	12	29	41	8	11	19	20	40	60
31 years	6	20	26	15	2	17	21	22	43
32 years	10	9	19	13	5	18	23	14	37
33 years	12	20	32	8	4	12	20	24	44
34 years	10	18	28	3	8	11	13	26	39
35 years	14	18	32	8	7	15	22	25	47
36 years	7	22	29	5	7	12	12	29	41
37 years	11	17	28	7	5	12	18	22	40
38 years	13	24	37	6	3	9	19	27	46
39 years	20	14	34	10	2	12	30	16	46
40 years	19	35	54	9	3	12	28	38	66
41 years	6	14	20	5	9	14	11	23	34
42 years	14	21	35	4	2	6	18	23	41
43 years	13	25	38	5	4	9	18	29	47
44 years	12	23	35	3	1	4	15	24	39
45 years	16	33	49	4	6	10	20	39	59
46 years	13	31	44	6	1	7	19	32	51
47 years	16	31	47	2	3	5	18	34	52
48 years	12	36	48	3	4	7	15	40	55
49 years	21	25	46	6	2	8	27	27	54
50 years	26	44	70	5	11	16	31	55	86
51 years	16	25	41	2	3	5	18	28	46

SUMMARY.—Continued.

Present age, 1885.	A The "Deaf." M.	F.	Both sexes.	B The "Deaf and Dumb." M.	F.	Both sexes.	C Summation of "The Deaf" and "The Deaf and Dumb." M.	F.	Both sexes.
52 years	20	31	51	3	6	9	23	37	60
53 years	24	37	61	1	4	5	25	41	66
54 years	25	30	55	6	1	7	31	31	62
55 years	26	40	66	5	4	9	31	44	75
56 years	19	31	50	2	3	5	21	34	55
57 years	16	39	55	1	5	6	17	44	61
58 years	15	27	42	3	2	5	18	29	47
59 years	24	22	46	1	2	3	25	24	49
60 years	27	38	65	4	6	10	31	44	75
61 years	23	25	48	2	......	2	25	25	50
62 years	20	28	48	5	......	5	25	28	53
63 years	28	33	61	2	......	2	30	33	63
64 years	20	26	46	3	1	4	23	27	50
65 years	25	35	60	2	1	3	27	36	63
66 years	19	23	42	......	2	2	19	25	44
67 years	29	30	59	2	2	4	31	32	63
68 years	24	25	49	2	3	5	26	28	54
69 years	15	25	40	2	1	3	17	26	43
70 years	31	33	64	4	......	4	35	33	68
71 years	20	17	37	2	3	5	22	20	42
72 years	24	21	45	2	1	3	26	22	48
73 years	31	19	50	4	1	5	35	20	55
74 years	29	31	60	3	1	4	32	32	64
75 years	32	32	64	3	3	6	35	35	70
76 years	27	20	47	3	1	4	30	21	51
77 years	18	27	45	2	......	2	20	27	47
78 years	26	12	38	2	1	3	28	13	41
79 years	30	26	56	1	1	2	31	27	58
80 years	31	31	62	1	1	2	32	32	64
81 years	12	19	31	......	......	......	12	19	31
82 years	17	18	35	......	......	......	17	18	35
83 years	16	20	36	......	1	1	16	21	37
84 years	16	13	29	......	......	......	16	13	29
85 years	18	15	33	......	......	......	18	15	33
86 years	3	13	16	......	......	......	3	13	16
87 years	6	9	15	......	......	......	6	9	15
88 years	5	9	14	......	......	......	5	9	14
89 years	6	8	14	......	......	......	6	8	14
90 years	1	6	7	......	......	......	1	6	7
91 years	2	4	6	......	......	......	2	4	6
92 years	1	6	7	......	......	......	1	6	7
93 years	1	3	4	......	......	......	1	3	4
94 years	2	4	6	......	......	......	2	4	6
95 years	2	3	5	......	......	......	2	3	5
96 years	......	1	1	......	......	......	......	1	1
97 years	......	2	2	......	......	......	......	2	2
108 years	......	1	1	......	......	......	......	1	1
Total	1259	1729	2988	430	370	800	1689	2099	3788

A.—AGES OF THE DEAF BY DECENNIAL PERIODS.

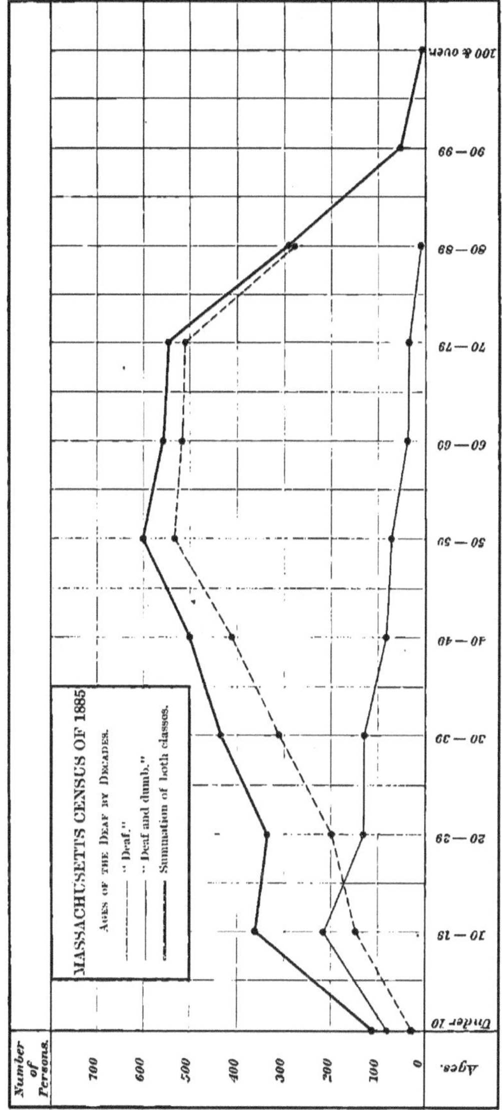

B.—AGES OF THE DEAF BY QUINQUENNIAL PERIODS.

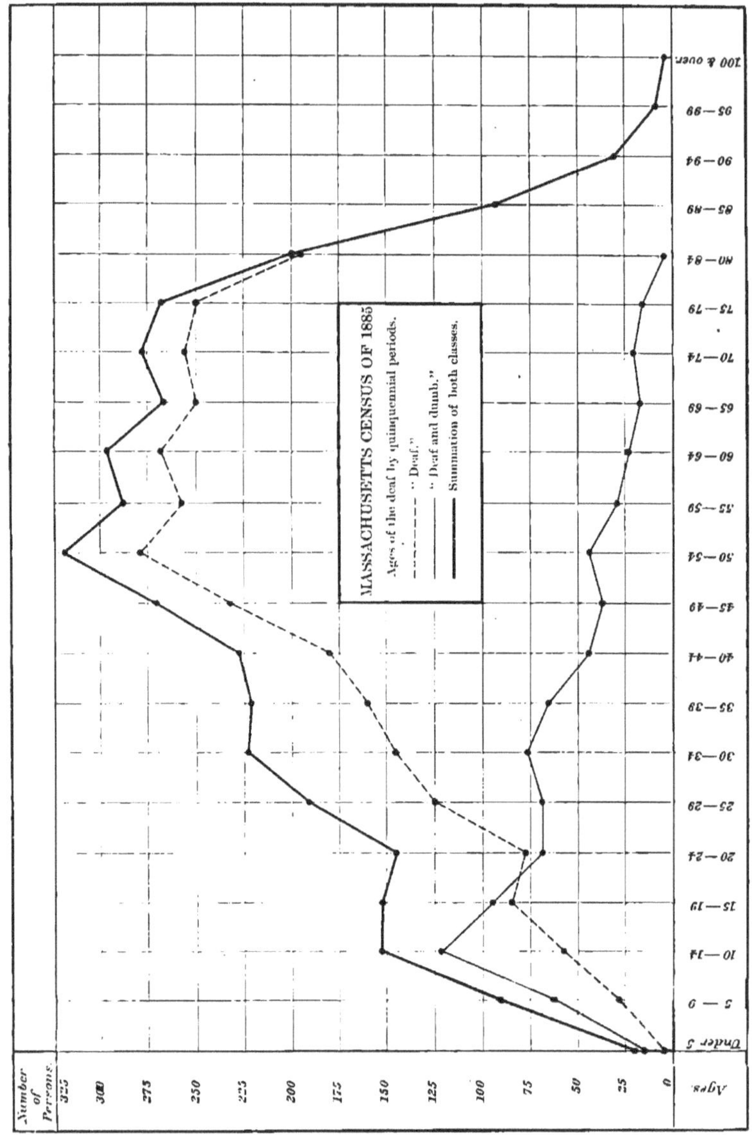

C.—AGES OF THE CONGENITALLY DEAF BY DECENNIAL PERIODS.

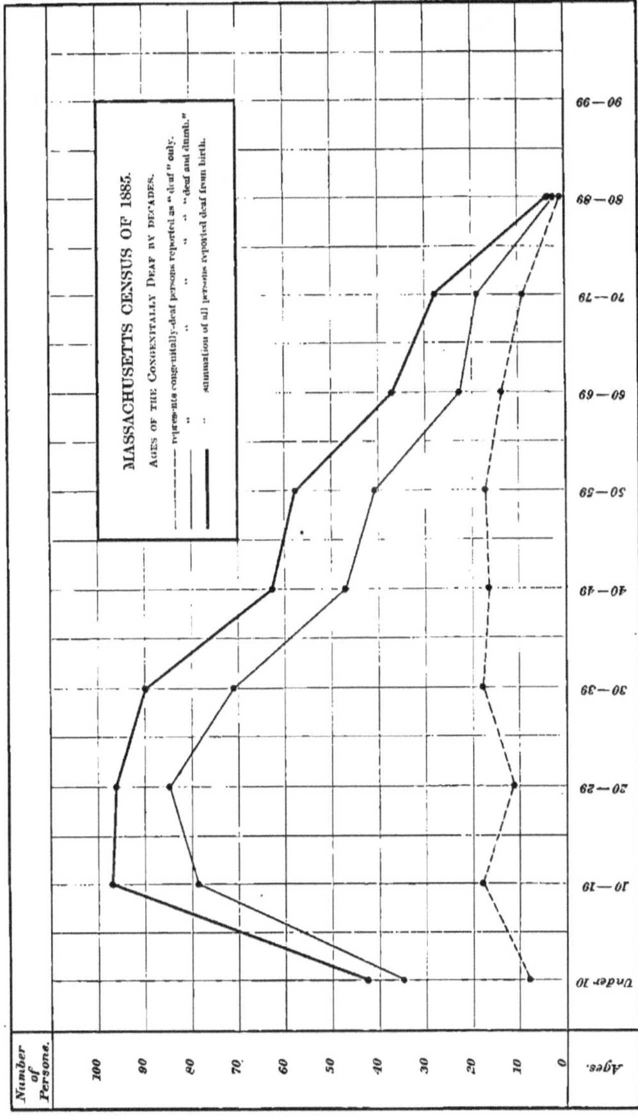

D.—AGES OF THE CONGENITALLY DEAF BY QUINQUENNIAL PERIODS.

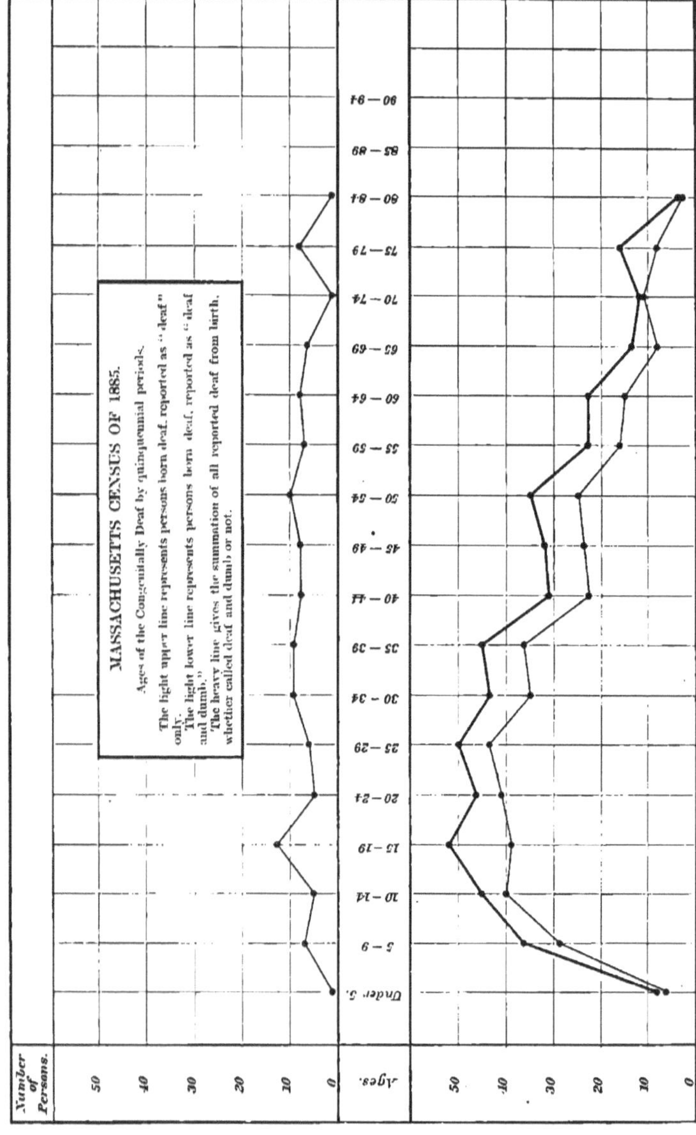

E.—Ages at which Deafness Occurred by Decennial Periods.

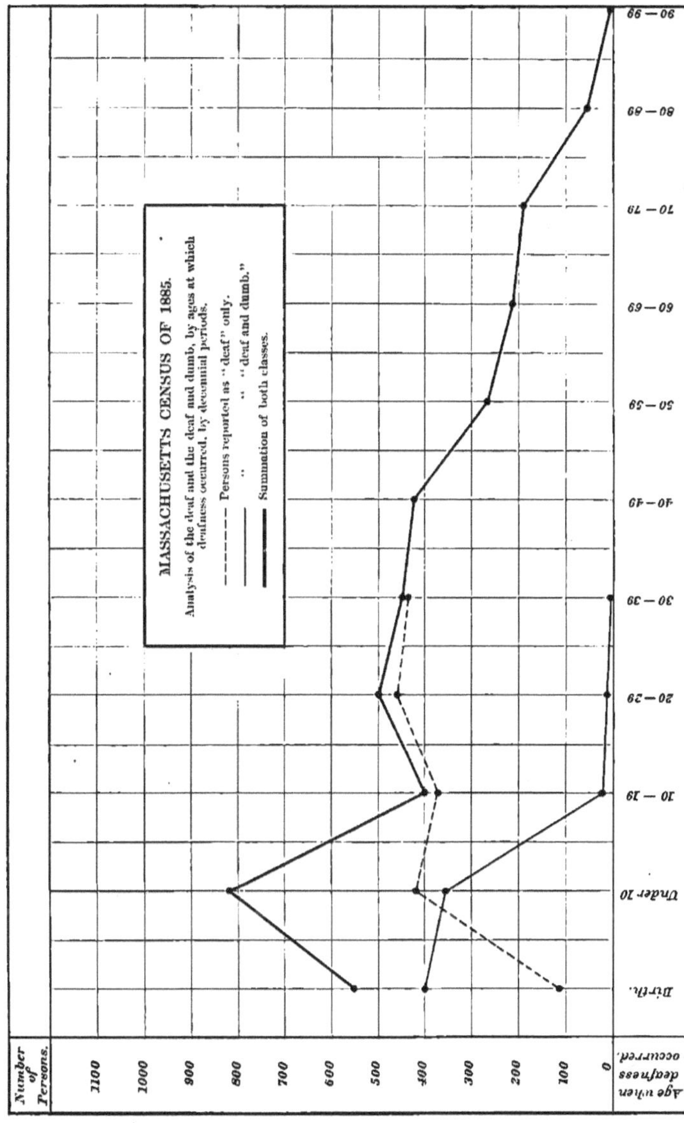

F.—AGES AT WHICH DEAFNESS OCCURRED BY DECENNIAL PERIODS, INCLUDING THE CONGENITALLY DEAF IN THE FIRST PERIOD.

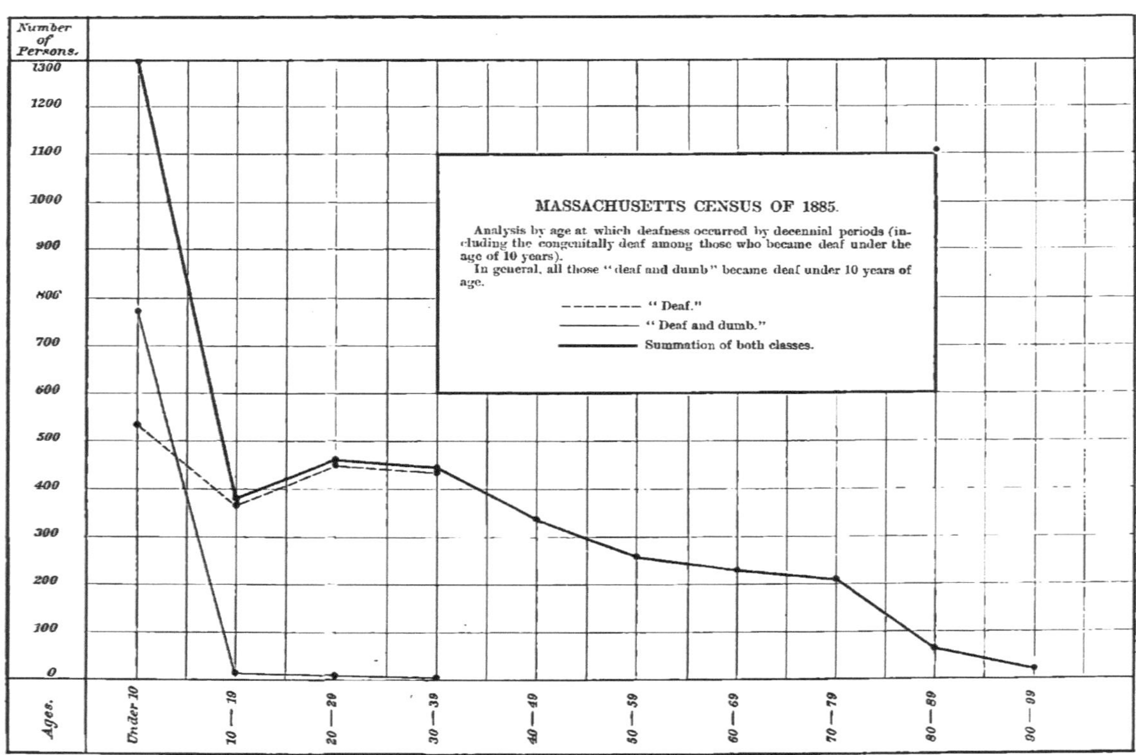

G.—Ages at which Deafness Occurred by Quinquennial Periods.

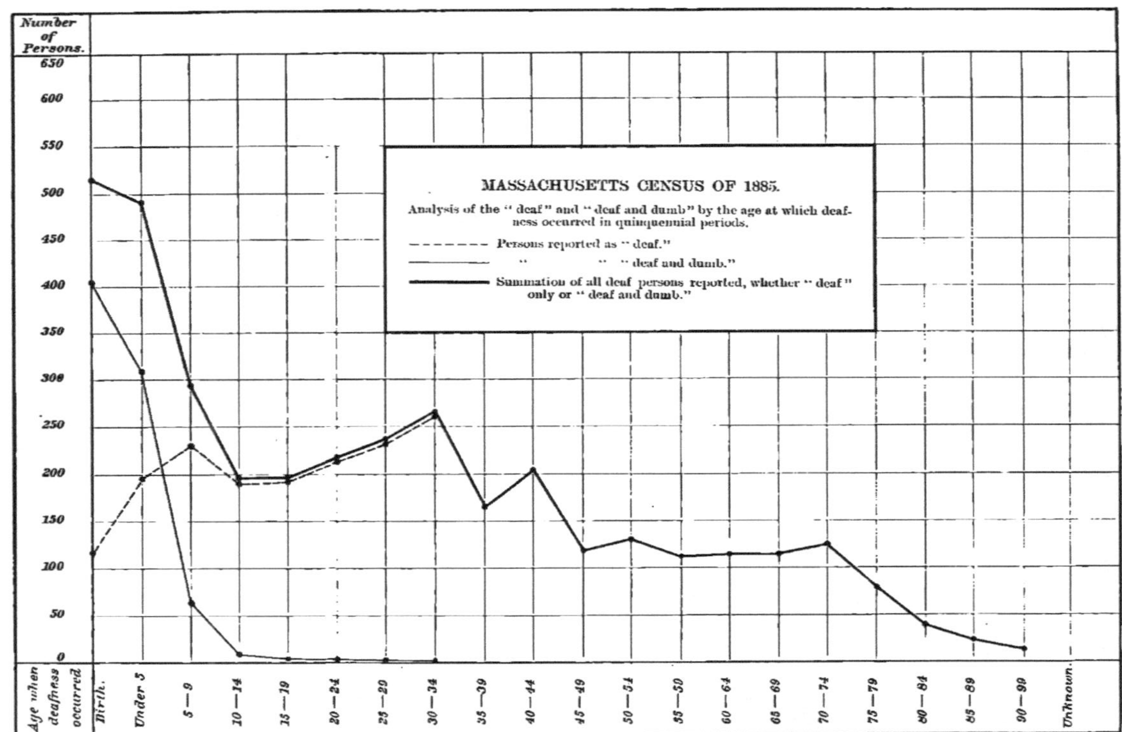

VISIBLE-SPEECH CHARTS.

This exhibit consisted of the following charts, which are employed in American schools for the purpose of explaining to deaf children the meaning of my father's "Visible Speech" symbols.

In Chart I. certain elementary symbols are shown which are compounded in charts II. and III. to express positions of the vocal organs which yield consonant sounds. In Chart IV. we have other elementary symbols which are combined in chart V. to express vowel positions. Chart VI. illustrates symbolically the positions of the vocal organs in uttering English consonants, and chart VII. symbolizes positions that yield English vowels.

CHART I.

The teacher selects some member of her class, and pretends to draw upon the blackboard the profile of the pupil's face. She then looks into the pupil's mouth and proceeds to draw a picture of the interior of the mouth. The whole picture, when completed, constitutes a diagram like that shown in Chart I. The teacher then proceeds to test the children's comprehension of the drawing. She points to different parts of the diagram, for example the forehead, nose, upper lip, lower lip, chin, lower part of jaw, throat, etc. The children indicate their comprehension of the diagram by touching the corresponding parts of their own faces. Attention is then directed to the interior of the mouth, and the teacher points to the picture of the upper teeth, upper gum, top of the hard palate, soft palate, etc. The children touch, or attempt to touch, the corresponding parts of their own mouths. So with the lower organs—the under teeth, the point of the tongue, the top or "front" part of the tongue, the back of the tongue, etc.

When the comprehension of the class has been well tested the teacher erases from the blackboard all those parts of the diagram which are shown in dotted lines in Chart I., leaving the visible-speech symbols in position as shown by the heavy lines.

It will be observed that the symbols are themselves the outlines of the organs they represent, hence the origin of the term "Visible Speech." The teacher points to the fragmentary remains of the picture upon the blackboard, and the pupils recognize the symbols as "the nose," "the under lip," "the point of the tongue," "the top, or front, of the tongue," "the back of the tongue," and "the throat." The arrow-head, which represents a sudden emission, or puff, of air from the mouth, is indicated by a sudden motion of the hand away from the mouth.

The next step is to have the pupils recognize the symbols independently of their position on the blackboard. The symbols are therefore written in one line below the fragments of the head (see Chart I). The heavy lines alone are written, the dotted lines not appearing at all.

The pupils then compare these symbols with the fragments of the drawing above and identify them as (1) the throat, (2) the back of the tongue, (3) the top, or "front" part, of the tongue, (4) the point of the tongue, (5) the under lip, (6) the nose, and (7) puff of air from the mouth.

Finally the upper drawing is entirely removed from the blackboard, and the lower line of symbols alone is left. Each pupil describes these as follows: (1) he touches his throat; (2) he points backwards into his mouth with a little jerk of the hand, indicating a part of the tongue further back in the mouth than he can well touch with his finger; (3) he touches the top, or front part, of his tongue; (4) he touches the tip, or point, of his tongue; (5) he touches his under lip; (6) he touches his nose; (7) he places his hand near his mouth and then moves it suddenly away from the mouth to indicate a sudden emission, or puff, of air.

After the meanings of these have been mastered, two new symbols, shown at the bottom of Chart I., are introduced. Here again it should be noticed that the symbols drawn on the blackboard consist only of the parts in heavy lines, the parts in dotted lines being omitted. The first of these new marks symbolizes a pipe or passage through which air may pass. In the second case the pipe is shut or stopped up at one end. The first indicates a narrow central aperture or passage somewhere in the mouth; the second indicates the complete closure or shutting of the mouth-passage at some part. The idea is of too abstract a character to be explained at once to a deaf child who knows no language; hence these symbols are taught arbitrarily as positions of the fingers without any attempt being made to explain their significance. As a matter of fact, deaf children come to understand their meaning when applied to the explanation of positions of the mouth.

The pupils are taught to indicate the first symbol at the bottom of Chart I. by holding the thumb and forefinger of the right hand near to one another without touching. This sign we may translate as "centre aperture." The second or "shut" symbol is shown by bringing the thumb and forefinger together with a shutting action.

We may here notice that the straight line or throat symbol is used in the sense of "voice." When a deaf child places his hand upon the throat of his teacher he can feel a vibration or tremor in the throat, whenever the voice is sounded. Hence he soon comes to associate the throat sign with a vibration of the vocal cords, and he indicates "voice" by touching his throat.

It should also be noticed that the "nose" sign is really pictorial of the pendulous extremity of the soft palate, and it indicates "soft palate depressed," so as to allow air to pass into the nasal passages. In English, only three elements, M, N, and NG, involve the depression of the soft palate. When a deaf child places his finger against the nose of his teacher while she pronounces M, N, or NG, he can feel a vibration or tremor of the nostrils, and to him the soft-palate symbol means voice or breath passing through the nose.

The symbols shown upon Chart I. are capable of being combined into compound forms, some of which are shown in Charts II. and III. Before proceeding, however, to the analysis of the compound characters on these charts it may be well to assign brief names to the elementary symbols of Chart I., which we can use to designate the gestures or signs employed by the deaf child which have been explained above.

In the following charts I shall refer to the symbols at the bottom of Chart I., as—

1, voice; 2, back; 3, front; 4, point; 5, lip; 6, nose; 7, puff of air; 8, centre-aperture; and 9, shut.

CHART II.

The symbols on this chart are named by the deaf child by analyzing them into the elementary symbols of which they are composed. We may translate his signs as follows:

1st Line.—1. Lip centre-aperture; 2. Point centre-aperture; 3. Front centre-aperture; 4. Back centre-aperture.

2d Line.—1. Lip centre-aperture, voice; 2. Point centre-aperture, voice; 3. Front centre-aperture, voice; 4. Back center-aperture, voice.

3d Line.—1. Lip centre-aperture, nose; 2. Point centre-aperture, nose; 3. Front centre-aperture, nose; 4. Back centre-aperture, nose.

4th Line.—1. Lip centre-aperture, voice, nose; 2. Point centre-aperture, voice, nose; 3. Front centre-aperture, voice, nose; 4. Back centre-aperture, voice, nose.

5th Line.—1. Lip shut; 2. Point shut; 3. Front shut; 4. Back shut.

EXHIBIT TO QUERY 21,868.

·CHART I·

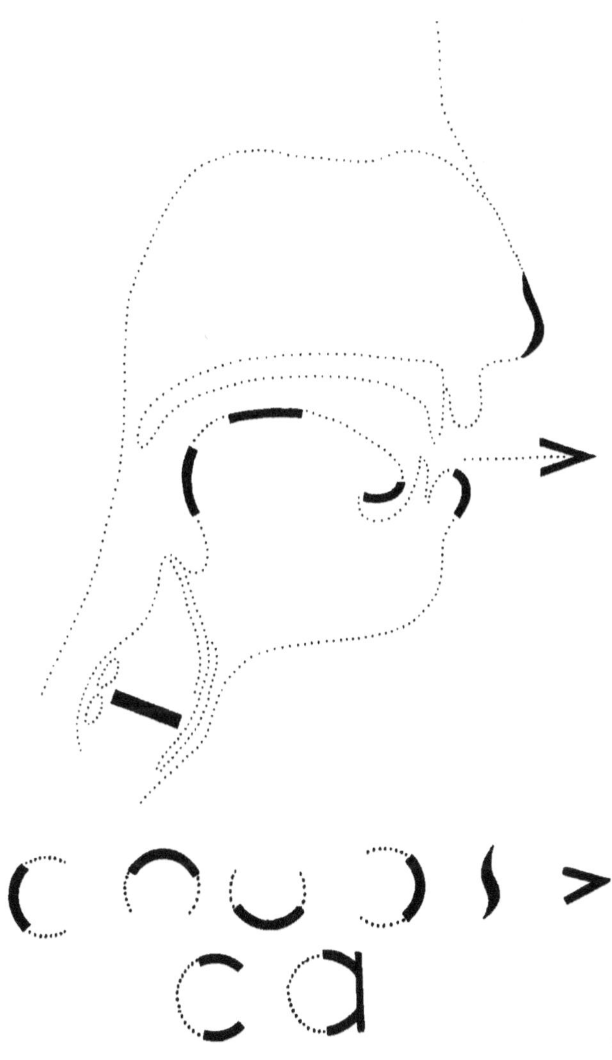

VISIBLE SPEECH.

INVENTED BY PROF. MELVILLE BELL.

EXHIBIT TO QUERY 21,868.

·CHART II·

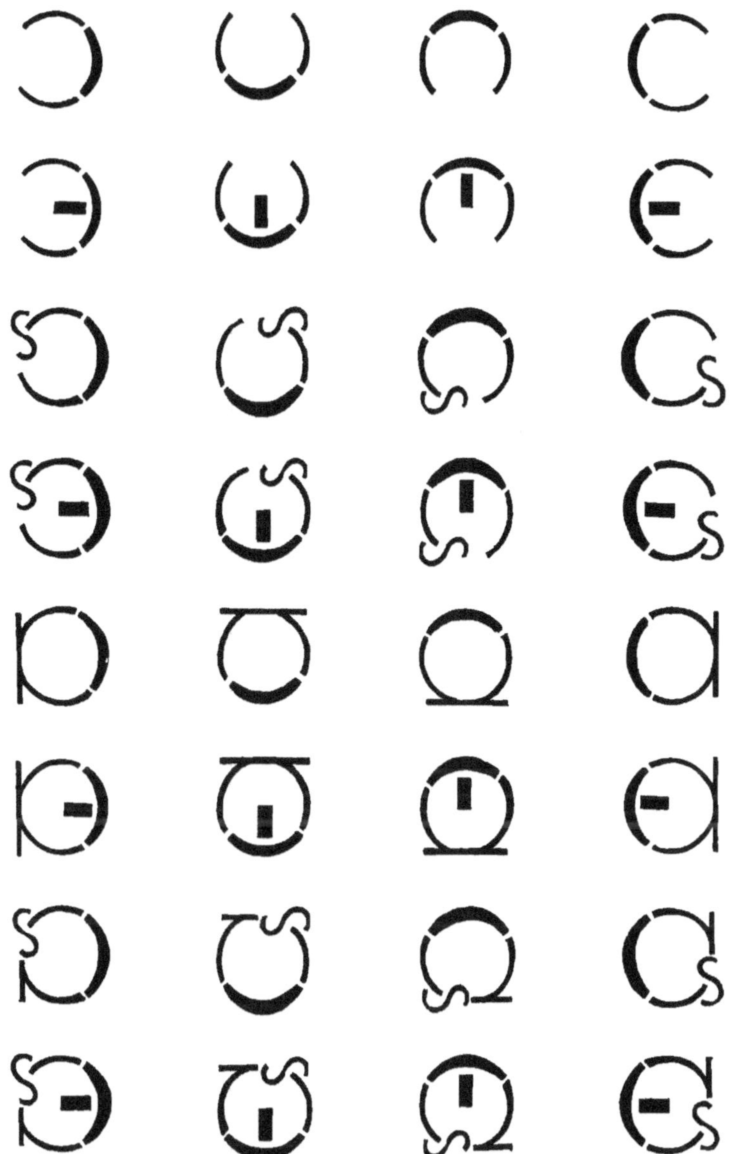

VISIBLE SPEECH.

INVENTED BY PROF. MELVILLE BELL.

EXHIBIT TO QUERY 21,868.

· CHART III ·

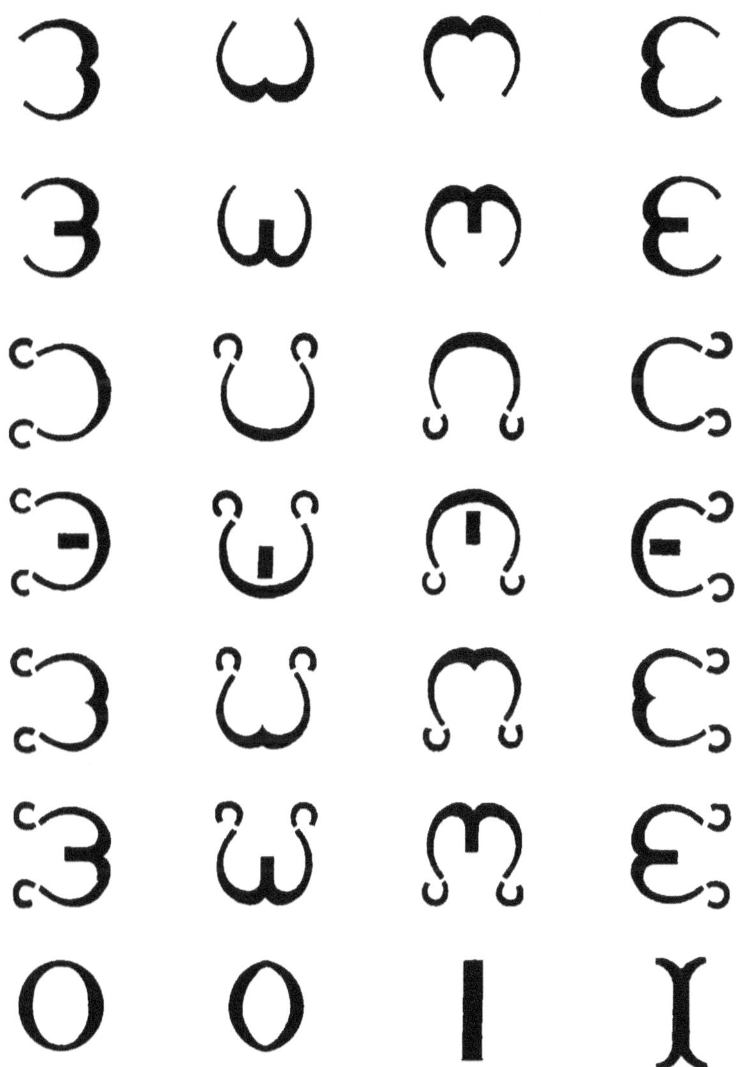

VISIBLE SPEECH.

INVENTED BY PROF. MELVILLE BELL.

EXHIBIT TO QUERY 21,868.

· CHART IV ·

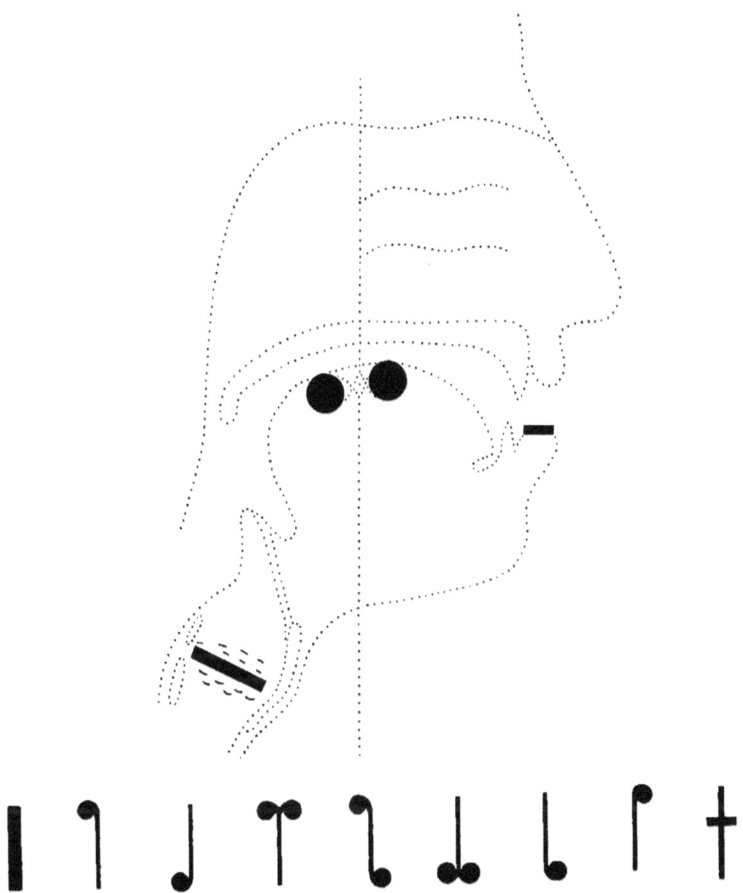

VISIBLE SPEECH.

INVENTED BY PROF. MELVILLE BELL.

EXHIBIT TO QUERY 21,868.

· CHART V ·

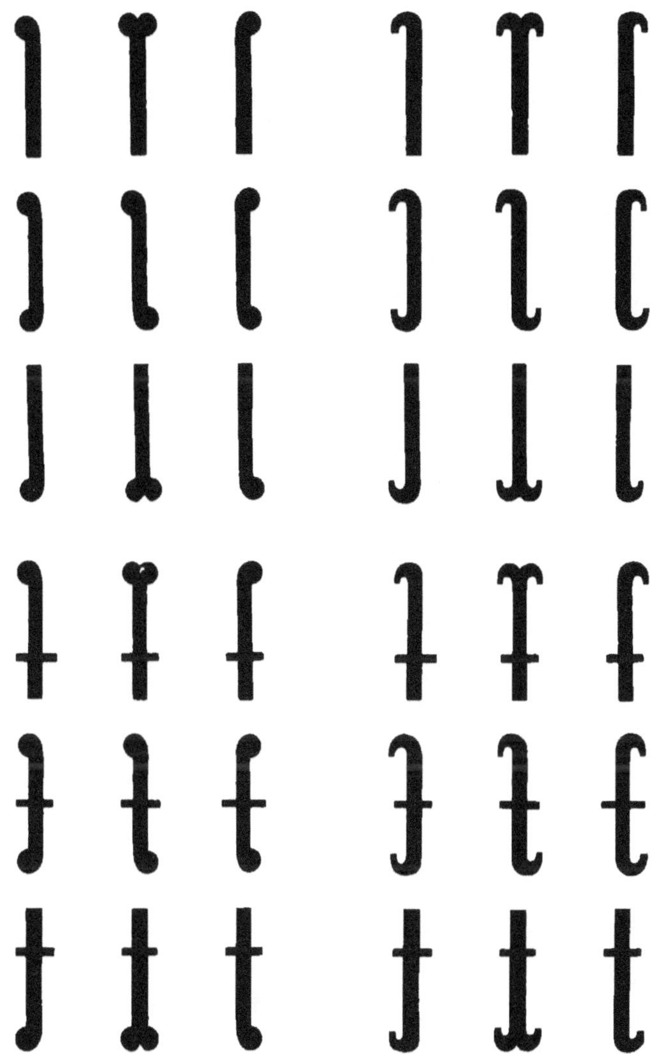

VISIBLE SPEECH.

INVENTED BY PROF. MELVILLE BELL

·CHART VI·

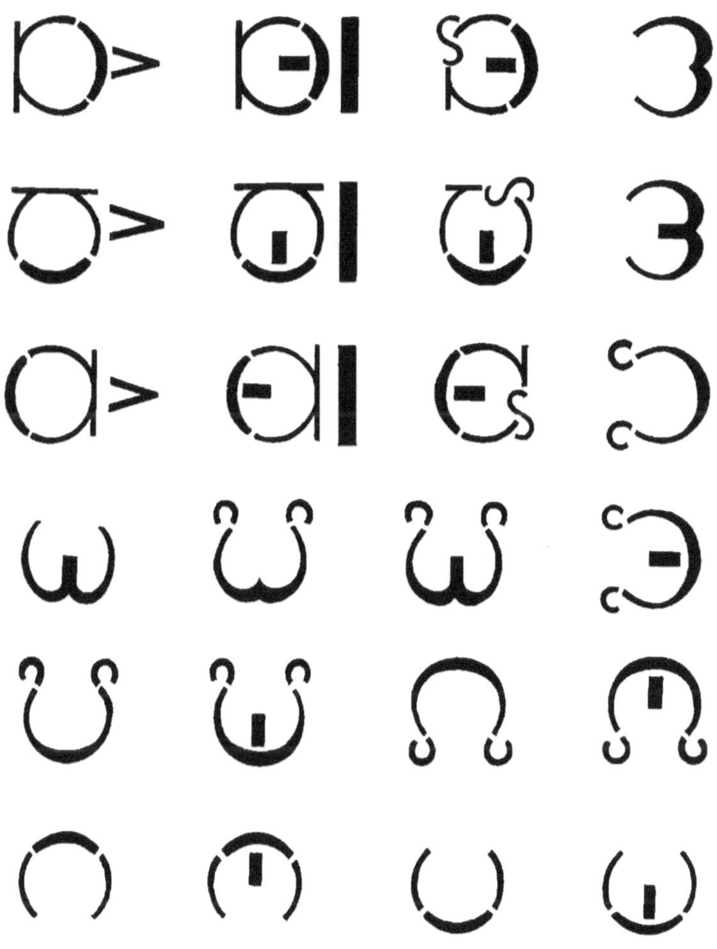

VISIBLE SPEECH.

INVENTED BY PROF. MELVILLE BELL.

EXHIBIT TO QUERY 21,868.

·CHART VII·

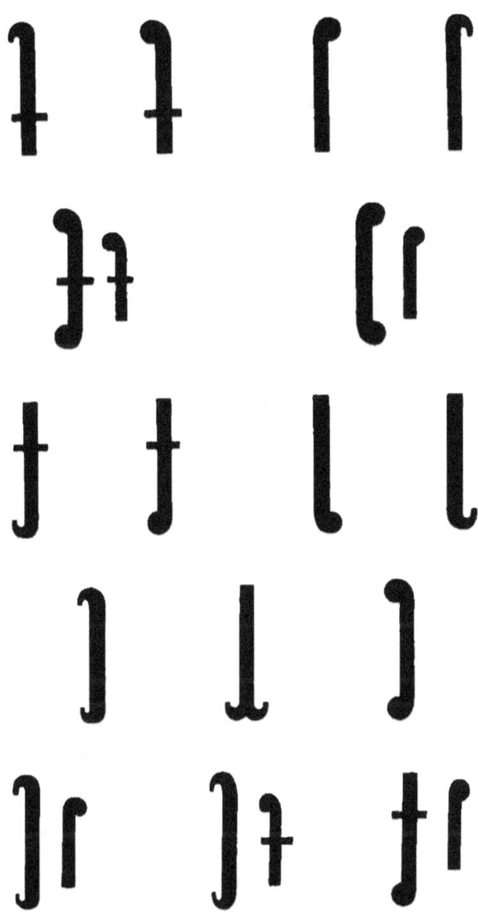

VISIBLE SPEECH.

INVENTED BY PROF. MELVILLE BELL.

6th Line.—1. Lip shut, voice; 2. Point shut, voice; 3. Front shut, voice; 4. Back shut, voice.

7th Line.—1. Lip shut, nose; 2. Point shut, nose; 3. Front shut, nose; 4. Back shut, nose.

8th Line.—1. Lip shut, voice, nose; 2. Point shut, voice, nose; 3. Front shut, voice, nose; 4. Back shut, voice, nose.

Long before a class has finished describing these symbols, the pupils begin to obtain the idea that the symbols are directions to do something with the mouth. For example, when they describe the first symbol in the fifth line, "Lip shut," some of them usually shut their lips. After the whole Chart has been described it then becomes the teacher's duty to make the children understand that the compound symbols they have been describing indicate positions of the mouth. The teacher directs attention to her mouth while she assumes some of the positions symbolized. For example, she describes *seriatim* the symbols in the first line.

1. "Lip centre-aperture." She places her lips close together, leaving a small aperture between them. She then takes a pupil's hand and blows through this small centre-aperture against his hand. The resulting sound is not an English element of speech, but is the sound produced by blowing to cool something.

2. She describes the next symbol "point centre-aperture." With her hand she lifts up the point of her tongue and brings it into position against the upper gum, and makes the pupil look into her mouth and observe that there is a small aperture or hole between the point of her tongue and the upper gum. She then, without moving her tongue, blows air through the point centre-aperture against the pupil's hand. The resultant sound is that of the French "R" in the word "*théatre*," or the English "R" (non-vocal) in the word "tree."

3. In a similar manner she shows that in pronouncing the third symbol "front centre-aperture," the tongue is humped up in the middle, assuming somewhat the shape of the symbol itself. The top or front part of the tongue is pressed up into the arch of the palate, leaving a small centre passage or channel over the middle of the tongue through which she can blow air against the pupil's hand. The resultant sound is that of the letter "H" in the word "hue."

4. In pronouncing the fourth symbol she pushes her tongue towards the back part of the mouth with her hand, and shows that her tongue remains back when her hand is removed. She then lets the pupil feel that air can be blown upon his hand without moving the tongue. The resulting sound is that of the German "Ch" in the word "nach."

Proceeding next to the second line:

1. She shows that the first symbol, "lip centre-aperture, voice," is the same as the first symbol in the first line, "lip centre-aperture," excepting that a straight line is placed within the curve. She shows then that the lips are in the same position, but that a tremor or vibration can be felt in her throat which could not be felt when the other symbol was sounded. She takes the two hands of her pupil and places one against her throat, and holds the other in front of her mouth while she produces "lip centre-aperture, voice." The pupil sees the small centre-aperture between the lips, and feels the emission of air against his hand, and also perceives the trembling of the throat when the voice is sounded. The resulting sound being the German "W" in the word "wie."

2. In a similar manner, keeping one of the pupil's hands on her throat and the other in front of the mouth, she produces the second symbol in the second line, "point centre-aperture, voice," contrasting it with the second symbol in the first line which has no voice. He sees the centre aperture over the point of the tongue, and feels the vibration of the voice and the emission of the air from the mouth. The resulting sound is that of the letter "R" in the word "run."

3. In a similar manner she exemplifies the third symbol in the second line, "Front centre-aperture, voice." The resultant sound is that of the consonant "Y" in "you." In teaching the deaf, this may be considered identical with the vowel "ee."

4. The fourth symbol in the second line, "Back centre-aperture, voice," is shown to be the same as the German "Ch" (Back centre-aperture), excepting that a vibration is felt in the throat.

Proceeding next to the eighth line:

1. The teacher describes the first symbol, "Lip shut, voice, nose." In forming this sound the lips are shut and the voice is passed through the nose. She places one of the pupil's hands against her throat, and the other against her nose, and pronounces the sound of the letter "M." The pupil sees the closure of the lips and feels a vibration in the throat and nose.

2. The second symbol in the eighth line, "Point shut, voice, nose," represents the position of the organs in forming the letter "N." The pupil sees the point of the tongue shut against the upper gum and feels a vibration in the throat and nose.

4. The last symbol in the eighth line, "Back shut, voice, nose," expresses the position of the organs when producing "ng" in such a word as "sing." Here the pupil sees that the back of the tongue is raised, and feels a vibration in the throat and nose. The object of this exemplification is simply to make the pupils understand what the symbols mean, and not to get them to make the sounds themselves. Still, the children generally try to imitate what the teacher does, and of course, in most cases, they fail because they have not yet acquired control over their vocal organs. As it is not the object of their teacher at this stage to cause the pupil to make sounds, she should not take any notice of their failures for fear of discouragement. She should be satisfied with evidences of comprehension of the meaning of the symbols. Most children are able to take Charts I. and II. in one lesson. After reviewing these at a subsequent time, the third Chart is explained.

CHART III.

The pupil's attention is directed to the symbol "lip centre-aperture" (see the first symbol in Chart II.), which he describes by touching the under lip and then holding the thumb and forefinger close together without touching. The teacher then directs attention to the mouth, and shows that there is only one small hole through which the air passes. She then holds her lips together in the middle and allows air to escape through two side apertures, one at each corner of the mouth, showing the pupil that now there are two holes through which the air escapes instead of one. This fact she symbolizes by writing two "lip centre-aperture" symbols one above the other, thus forming a character somewhat like the Arabic numeral 3. This the pupil describes by touching his lip, and then holding near the thumb, not one finger alone, but two, indicating that the aperture is divided into two parts. Thus the thumb and forefinger held near together indicates one central aperture, and the thumb held near the fore and middle fingers indicates "divided aperture."

Turning now to Chart III. the symbols are described as follows:

1st Line.—1. Lip divided-aperture: 2. Point divided-aperture; 3. Front divided-aperture; 4. Back divided-aperture.

2d Line.—1. Lip divided-aperture, voice; 2. Point divided-aperture, voice; 3. Front divided-aperture, voice; 4. Back divided-aperture, voice.

The 2d symbol in the second line, "point divided-aperture, voice," expresses the position of the tongue in forming the sound of "L" in such a word as "love." The point of the tongue is placed against the upper gum, and voice is passed through two side apertures, one on each side of the tongue. The symbols in the 3d, 4th, 5th, and 6th lines are what my father terms "mixed" symbols, involving two positions of the organs assumed simultaneously. The 1st symbol in the 3d line is composed of a large "lip centre-aperture" symbol with a small "back centre-aperture" hooked on to one end of the curve. For the sake of symmetry another small "back centre-aperture" is attached to the other end of the curve, but this has no organic significance. This compound symbol expresses the position of the organs in sounding the English element represented by the letters "wh" in such a word as "whistle." The back of the tongue is in the position for the German "ch" (back centre-aperture), while at the same time a small centre-aperture is formed by the lips. The labial aperture being more obstructive than the back aperture characterizes the sound as a labial letter. For this reason the "Lip centre-aperture" sign is made the most prominent part of the compound symbol. Deaf pupils dedescribe this symbol as "Lip centre-aperture, back centre-aperture."

Proceeding now with the description of the remaining symbols upon chart III. we have:

3d Line.—1. Lip centre-aperture, back centre-aperture. 2. Point centre-aperture, front centre-aperture. 3. Front centre-aperture, point centre-aperture. 4. Back centre-aperture, lip centre-aperture.

4th Line.—1. Lip centre-aperture, back centre-aperture, voice. 2. Point centre-aperture, front centre-aperture, voice. 3. Front centre-aperture, point centre-aperture, voice. 4. Back centre-aperture, lip centre-aperture, voice.

5th Line.—1. Lip divided-aperture, back centre-aperture. 2. Point divided-aperture, front centre-aperture. 3. Front divided aperture, point centre-aperture. 4. Back divided-aperture, lip centre-aperture.

6th Line.—1. Lip divided-aperture, back centre-aperture, voice. 2. Point divided aperture, front centre-aperture, voice. 3. Front divided-aperture, point centre-aperture, voice. 4. Back divided aperture, lip centre-aperture, voice.

Numerous other compound symbols might be built up out of the elementary signs shown in Chart I., expressing both possible and impossible positions of the organs. The forms shown in Charts II. and III. are not intended to be pronounced by the pupil, but are given simply as exercises in analysis. If the pupils can be made to understand the meaning of the compound symbols by analyzing them into their elementary forms, Visible Speech becomes a symbolic language, whereby any imaginable position of the vocal organs may be expressed so as to be understood by the children.

The remaining symbols on Chart III., seventh line, are throat symbols. They picture various conditions of the glottis.

1. The first character, shaped like the letter "O," pictures a wide aperture in the throat. The vocal cords are wide apart, leaving a large opening between them through which air may freely pass without obstruction. This is the condition of the glottis in uttering the letter "H" and all non-vocal or breath consonants. The letter "H" may, indeed, be considered as the non-vocal or breath form of a vowel. It has just as many different sounds as there are vowels. Pronounce such words as "he," "hay," "ha," "hoe;" and "who;" it will be observed that the mouth-position for the sound of "H" is different in each word. "H" only occurs as an element of speech before a vowel. Under such circumstances the mouth-position for "H" is the same as for the succeeding vowel, but the opening in the glottis is so wide as to allow the breath to pass into the mouth without sensible obstruction in the throat.

2. The second symbol in the seventh line pictures a smaller aperture in the throat than the first. The vocal cords are brought near enough together to obstruct in some degree the passage of air between them, giving rise to a rustling sort of sound which is universally denominated "whisper." This is the condition of the glottis when we whisper vowel sounds. This position of the throat may also be assumed in uttering consonants, thus giving rise to the "whispered" consonants, which, in some languages, are significant elements of speech, quite distinct in meaning from the "breath" and "voiced" consonants of similar formation occurring in the same languages.

3. We have already become familiar with the third symbol in the seventh line, as the representative of "voice." It pictures a still smaller aperture in the throat than either of the preceding. The vocal cords are placed parallel to one another, and the aperture between them is reduced to a mere slit (pictured by a straight line). In this condition of the glottis the passage of air through the slit-like aperture occasions a vibration of the vocal cords, producing voice.* This is the condition of the glottis in uttering vocal consonants and vowels.

4. The fourth symbol in the seventh line pictures complete closure of the glottis. The vocal cords are pressed together so as to completely shut the aperture between them, and prevent the escape of air. This is the condition of the glottis aimed at by singers in practising what is called the "*coup de glotte*." It also occurs as an element of speech in certain dialects. For example: In the Scotch dialect as spoken in Glasgow "throat shut" is substituted for T (point shut) in such words as butter, water, etc. In English also it occurs as an unrecognized element of speech in words commencing with vowels. In ordinary utterance every syllable really commences with a consonant. When words are supposed to begin with vowels, the "throat shut" consonant really precedes the vowel sound, although it is not usually recognized as an element of speech by orthoepists. Pronounce with considerable force the names of the five vowel letters A, E, I, O, U. A closure of the glottis takes place before each vowel, excepting the last. The "throat shut" consonant precedes the vowels A, E, I, and O; but U is preceded by the consonant Y. Indeed the name of the vowel might have been spelled YOU without affecting the pronunciation. The "throat shut" consonant, followed by a forcible emission of air from the lungs, is familiar to every one in the form of a cough.

The meaning of the throat symbols shown in the seventh line is explained to deaf children in the following way:

1. Touch the throat, and then hold the two hands together palm to palm, curving the fingers so as to cause the space between the hands to assume the shape of the first symbol. The idea to be conveyed is that the aperture in the throat is somewhat of that shape, and very large.

2. Touch the throat, and then hold the hands together palm to palm as before, but reduce the space between the hands so as to cause the aperture to assume the shape of the second symbol. The idea to be conveyed is that the aperture in the throat is more contracted than in the former case.

3. Touch the throat, and hold the hands together palm to palm as before, so that the aperture between the hands is reduced to a mere slit. At the same time give a quivering or trembling motion to the hands. The idea to be conveyed is that the aperture in the throat is a mere slit, and that a trembling or quivering motion occurs in the throat which the pupil may perceive for himself by placing his hand upon the teacher's throat while the teacher produces voice.

4. Touch the throat, and then press the two hands together palm to palm with a shutting action, causing the hands to assume the appearance of the fourth symbol in the seventh line.

* See "*Voice*" in Webster's International Dictionary, 1891. —EDITOR.

We may translate these gestures into words, and give names to these symbols in the following manner:

7th line.—1. Throat open. 2. Throat contracted. 3. Throat a-slit (voice). 4. Throat shut.

CHART IV.

When we compare the symbols shown on Charts II. and III. with those on Chart V., we notice a radical difference between them. The most prominent feature of the symbols on Charts II. and III. is a curve of some sort, whereas the characteristic of those on Chart V. is a straight line. By reference to Chart I. it will be seen that a curve is indicative of some part of the mouth, and that a straight line represents voice. The symbols on Charts II. and III. represent positions of the organs that yield consonant, and those on Chart V., positions that yield vowel sounds. The generic difference between consonants and vowels is thus portrayed in the symbols. In consonant symbols the mouth position is made the characteristic feature of the symbol, the voice where it occurs being written subordinately by a straight line within the curve. In vowel symbols, on the other hand, the voice sign is made the characteristic feature, and the mouth position is represented subordinately by curves or dots or other marks appended to the voice line. Chart IV. is used for the purpose of explaining to deaf children the meaning of these appendages. The chief parts of the tongue employed in forming vowel sounds are the back and the front parts of the tongue. When we draw a vertical line centrally through the diagram on Chart IV., we find that a dot or other mark on the right-hand side of the line rests on the front part of the tongue, whereas a mark on the left-hand side of the line rests on the back of the tongue. In vowel symbols a mark on the right hand side of the voice line indicates the front part of the tongue, a mark on the left indicates the back of the tongue, and a short horizontal line drawn across the vowel stem indicates that the lips are employed. Thus the symbols at the bottom of Chart IV. indicate (1) the voice; (2) the back of the tongue; (3) the back of the tongue: (4) both back and front of the tongue used simultaneously. [This is what my father terms a "mixed" position]. (5) back and front ["mixed"]; (6) back and front ["mixed"]; (7) the front of the tongue; (8) the front of the tongue; (9) the lips.

It will be observed that the appendages are placed sometimes at the top of the vowel stem, sometimes at the bottom, and sometimes at both ends. This pictures the elevation of the tongue in the mouth. When the mark is at the top of the vowel stem the part of the tongue indicated is placed high up in the mouth, leaving a small aperture between the tongue and the palate; when the mark is at the bottom the tongue is low with a large aperture; and when it is at both ends the tongue occupies an intermediate position with an intermediate aperture. Reading again the symbols at the bottom of Chart IV., we have (1) the voice; (2) back of the tongue high; (3) back of the tongue low; (4) back and front both high ["high mixed"]; (5) back and front both mid position ["mid mixed"]; (6) back and front both low ["low mixed"]; (7) front low; (8) front high; (9) this symbol means not only that the lips are used, but that the aperture between them is of a rounded form.

The deaf child is taught to indicate the small aperture formed by the high position of the tongue by holding his thumb and forefinger close together without touching. [This is the same sign formerly described as meaning "centre-aperture."] The low tongue position with large aperture is indicated by holding the finger and thumb far apart; and the intermediate position is represented by a half-way position of the thumb and forefinger. Thus degrees of aperture are indicated by degrees of separation of thumb and forefinger.

We are now prepared to analyze the symbols on Chart V.

CHART V.—*Vowels.*

The vowels on Chart V. may be divided into four groups, of nine symbols each:

FIRST GROUP.—*Primary Vowels.*

Reading downwards we have:

First line.—1. High Back. 2. Mid Back. 3. Low Back.

Second line.—1. High mixed. 2. Mid Mixed. 3. Low Mixed.

Third line.—1. High Front. 2. Mid Front. 3. Low Front.

SECOND GROUP.—*Wide Vowels.*

Reading downwards we have:

First line.—1. High Back Wide. 2. Mid Back Wide. 3. Low Back Wide.

Second line.—1. High Mixed Wide. 2. Mid Mixed Wide. 3. Low Mixed Wide.

Third line.—1. High Front Wide. 2. Mid Front Wide. 3. Low Front Wide.

THIRD GROUP.—*Primary Round Vowels.*

Reading downwards we have:

First line.—1. High Back Round. 2. Mid Back Round. 3. Low Back Round.

Second line.—1. High Mixed Round. 2. Mid Mixed Round. 3. Low Mixed Round.

Third line.—1. High front round. 2. Mid front round. 3. Low front round.

FOURTH GROUP.—*Wide Round Vowels.*

Reading downwards we have:

First line.—1. High Back Wide Round. 2. Mid Back Wide Round. 3. Low Back Wide Round.

Second line.—1. High Mixed Wide Round. 2. Mid Mixed Wide Round. 3. Low Mixed Wide Round.

Third line.—1. High Front Wide Round. 2. Mid Front Wide Round. 3. Low Front Wide Round.

Wide vowels differ from primary vowels by a slight widening of the oral passage; for example: Contrast the high front vowel (*ea* in the word "eat") with the high front wide vowel (*i* in the word "it"). The oral passage for the latter is slightly larger than for *ee*, and Prof. Melville Bell believes also that the back part of the mouth, or the cavity of the pharynx, is more expanded in wide vowels than in primary. Widening the oral passage is indicated by a hook instead of a dot. Groups 3 and 4 are rounded vowels, that is, the passage between the lips is of a rounded form.

Deaf children describe these symbols by using the signs already mentioned in describing chart IV, and we may translate their signs for the symbols on chart V as follows:

FIRST GROUP.

Reading downwards we have:

First line.—1. Voice, back small-aperture. 2. Voice, back mid-aperture. 3. Voice, back large-aperture.

Second line.—1. Voice, back small-aperture, front small-aperture. 2. Voice, back mid-aperture, front mid-aperture. 3. Voice, back large-aperture, front large-aperture.

Third line.—1. Voice, front small-aperture. 2. Voice, front mid-aperture. 3. Voice, front large-aperture.

SECOND GROUP.—*Wide Vowels.*

In teaching deaf children, the symbols of this group are considered as identical with those of group I, and are described in the same manner. When the pupils have become familiar with the analysis of visible-speech symbols, they are shown, by means of the thumb and forefinger, that the positions symbolized in the second group have a slightly wider aperture than the corresponding positions in the first group.

Prof. Melville Bell's conception of the expansion of the pharynx during the utterance of wide vowels is a difficult one to convey to deaf children who know no language; I have therefore not attempted to do more than convey the idea that the mouth passage for wide vowels is slightly wider than for primary vowels, so that the primary and wide symbols, taken together, represent six degrees of aperture; for example: Take the front vowels, commencing with the smallest aperture and ending with the largest, we have the following series of apertures:

1. High front.
2. High front wide.
3. Mid front.
4. Mid front wide.
5. Low front.
6. Low front wide.

THIRD GROUP.—*Primary Round Vowels.*

Reading downwards we have:

First line.—1. Voice, back small-aperture, lip small-aperture. 2. Voice, back mid-aperture, lip mid-aperture. 3. Voice, back large-aperture, lip large-aperture.

Second line.—1. Voice, back small-aperture, front small-aperture, lip small-aperture. 2. Voice, back mid-aperture, front mid-aperture, lip mid-aperture. 3. Voice, back large-aperture, front large-aperture, lip large-aperture.

Third line.—1. Voice, front small-aperture, lip small-aperture. 2. Voice, front mid-aperture, lip mid-aperture. 3. Voice, front large-aperture, lip large-aperture.

The labial apertures described are of a rounded form, but as the pupils can see for themselves the shape of labial apertures, it has not been considered necessary to give them a distinct sign for a rounded aperture; they simply describe the size of aperture by the separation of finger and thumb.

FOURTH GROUP.—*Wide Round Vowels.*

In teaching deaf children, the symbols of this group are considered as identical with those of group III, and are described in a similar manner. The differences are explained later on. The symbols of group IV bear the same relation to those of group III that the symbols of group II bear to those of group I. (See note above relating to group II.)

CHART VI.

Chart VI. shows the mechanism of the English consonants as explained to the deaf.

First line:

(1) "Lip shut," followed by "a puff of air." We have here two symbols, the first of which (Lip shut) represents *p*, as in *put*, *cup*, &c. It is not advisable to teach "shut" consonants as separate elements. They are best taught in connection with vowels. The most elementary form of *p* taught is the final *p*, as in *cup*, where the "Lip-shut" position is followed by a puff of air, as shown in the Chart.

(2) "Lip-shut, voice," followed by "voice." The first of these symbols (Lip-shut voice) represents *b* in *but*, *cub*, &c. This is not taught elementarily, but in connection with a vowel. The simplest form is that shown in the Chart where the "Lip-shut, voice" position is followed by an indefinite murmur of voice, forming a syllable somewhat like *bir* in *bird*.

(3) "Lip-shut, voice, nose," represents *m* in *man*, *come*, &c.

(4) "Lip divided-aperture," represents *f* in *fie*, *luff*, &c. The upper organ in this case is the edge of the teeth, instead of the upper lip.

Second line:

(1) "Point-shut," followed by "a puff of air." The first symbol (point-shut) represents *t*, as in *to*, *not*, &c. When *t* occurs as a final letter, as in *not*, the "point-shut" position is followed by a puff of air, as shown in the Chart.

(2) "Point-shut, voice," followed by "voice." The first symbol (point-shut voice) represents *d*, as in *do*, *nod*, &c. In the symbols shown in the Chart the "point-shut, voice" position is followed by an indefinite murmur of voice, thus representing a syllable somewhat like *dir* in *dirk*.

(3) "Point-shut, voice, nose" represents *n*, as in *no*, *nun*, &c.

(4) "Lip-divided-aperture, voice" represents *v*, as in *vie*, *love*, &c.

Third line:

(1) "Back-shut" followed by "a puff of air." The first symbol (back-shut) represents *k* in *key*, *sick*, &c. When *k* occurs as a final letter, as in *sick*, the "back-shut" position is followed by a puff of air, as shown in the Chart.

(2) "Back-shut, voice," followed by "voice." The first of these symbols (back-shut, voice) represents *g*, as in *go*, *log*, &c. The "back-shut, voice" position is followed by an indefinite murmur of voice, forming a syllable somewhat like *gir* in *girl*.

(3) "Back-shut, voice, nose" represents *ng*, as in *lung*, *tongue*, &c.

(4) "Lip-centre-aperture, back-centre-aperture" represents *wh*, as in *whet*. It is taught to the deaf as "back-centre-aperture" (German *ch*), with the lips rounded as in the act of whistling. In obtaining this sound from a deaf child it is found essential to direct attention to the "*back-centre-aperture*" position.

Fourth line:

(1) "Point-divided aperture, voice" represents *l*, as in *lull*.

(2) "Point-divided aperture, front-centre aperture" represents *th*, as in *thin*, *kith*, &c.

(3) "Point-divided aperture, front-centre aperture, voice" represents *th*, as in *then*, *with*, &c.

(4) "Lip-centre aperture," "back-centre aperture, voice" represents *w* in the word *wet*. In teaching the deaf it is essential to direct attention to the "back-centre aperture" position, and the sound is taught as identical with the vowel *oo* in *pool*.

Fifth line:

(1) "Point-centre aperture, front-centre aperture" represents *s*, as in *sown*, *hiss*, &c.

(2) "Point-centre aperture, front-centre aperture, voice" represents *z* in *zone* and *s* in *his*.

(3) "Front-centre aperture, point-centre aperture" represents *sh*, as in *she*, and *s*, as in *assure*. It also occurs after point-shut in such a word as church (tshurtsh).

(4) "Front-centre aperture, point-centre aperture, voice" represents *s* in *measure* and *z* in *azure*. It is heard in *j* or in *g soft* after "point-shut, voice" in such a word as *judge* (dzhŭdzh).

Sixth line:

(1) "Front-centre aperture" represents the sound given to *h* in *hue*, for which we have no letter. As it is the non-vocal form of the consonant *y*, it may be represented by *yh*. It also occurs after non-vocal consonants, as in few (f*yh*oo), tune (t*yh*oon), cue (k*yh*oo).

(2) "Front-centre aperture, voice" represents *y* in the word *you*. In teaching the deaf it is considered as identical with the vowel *e*.

(3) "Point-centre aperture." This sound has no letter, and may be represented by *rh*, as it is the non-vocal form of *r*. The deaf are taught that the letter *r* has this sound when it comes after a non-vocal consonant, as in pry (p*rh*y), try (t*rh*y), cry (c*rh*y).

(4) "Point-centre aperture, voice" represents *r* in such a word as *run* also *r* after a vocal consonant, as *bride*, *dry*, &c.

Seventh line.—"Throat-large-aperture" represents *h* in such words as *heat*, *hit*, *hate*, *head*, *hat*, *hoot, hook, hope, hall, hot, half, hurl, hut, high, how, hoist.*

CHART VII.

The symbols in Chart VII. represent the positions for English vowel sounds.

First line:

(1) "High-back-wide, round" represents the vowel heard in the following words: *foot, put,* &c.

(2) "High-back, round" represents the vowel heard in *pool, move, through, true, flew.*

(3) "High-front" represents the vowel heard in *eel, eat, field, key, seize,* &c.

(4) "High-front, wide" represents the vowel heard in *ill, build,* &c.

Second line:

(1) "Mid-back, round," followed by a glide towards "high-back, round," represents the vowel heard in *pole, coal, soul, dough, bowl,* &c.

(2) "Mid-front," followed by a glide towards "high-front," represents the vowel heard in *ale, ail, eight, great, say, they,* &c.

Third line:

(1) "Low-back-wide, round" represents the vowel heard in *doll, what,* &c.

(2) "Low-back, round" represents the vowel heard in *all, paul, paw, thought,* &c.

(3) "Low-front" represents the vowel heard in *shell, head, said,* &c.

(4) "Low-front-wide" represents the vowel heard in *shall,* &c.

Fourth line:

(1) "Mid-back-wide" represents the vowel heard in *ah, father,* &c.

(2) "Low-mixed-wide" represents the vowel heard in *her, pearl, girl, fur,* &c.

(3) "Mid-back" represents the vowel heard in *gull, come, rough,* &c.

Fifth line:

(1) "Mid-back-wide," followed by a glide towards "high-front," represents the vowel heard in *pile, sleight, buy, eye,* &c.

(2) "Mid-back-wide," followed by a glide towards "high-back-round," represents the vowel heard in *cow, bough, round,* &c.

(3) "Low-back-round," followed by a glide towards "high-front," represents the vowel heard in *oil, boy,* &c.

The sound of *h* only occurs before a vowel, and it is advisable to give the deaf pupil the idea that there are as many sounds of *h* as there are vowel sounds. Defective pronunciation results from the attempt to give a uniform value to the sound. The deaf pupil is taught that the mouth position for *h* is always the same as that of the succeeding vowel; in fact, that *h* is the *breath form* of the succeeding vowel. For example, contrast the *h* in *he* with that in *who* (hoo). In the former case the mouth position for *h* is the same as that for the vowel *ē*; in the latter it is the same as that for the vowel *ōō*.

SUMMARY OF RECOMMENDATIONS, EXTRACTED FROM THE OFFICIAL REPORT OF THE ROYAL COMMISSION.

We recommend :—

1. That the provisions of the Education Acts be extended to the deaf and dumb, and power be obtained to enforce the compulsory attendance of children at a day-school or institution up to the age of 16.

2. That where the number under any school authority is too small to form a class, or where the child is unable to attend an elementary school, the school authority should have the power, and be required, either to send a child to an institution or to board out such child under proper inspection, and to contribute to his education and maintenance such annual grant as would be equivalent to the contribution now allowed to be paid by Boards of Guardians; and if there should be neither institution nor school available or willing to receive such child, the school authority should have the power, either by itself or in combination with other school authorities, to establish a school or institution for the purpose, and to educate such children under proper inspection.

3. That, independently of the position of the parent, a capitation grant not less than half the cost of the education of such child, with a maximum grant of £10, should be given for all in the same way as in ordinary elementary schools, and that the fees payable by necessitous parents should not exceed those payable in the case of ordinary children, but that in all cases parents should contribute according to their ability.

4. That the age of entry should, as far as possible, be seven; that pupils should, as a rule, be admitted once a year; that the school attendance should be compulsorily enforced for at least eight years, without any existing limit of distance from school; and that power should be given to the local authority to pay the rail or tram fare of children when necessary.

5. That, on admission, the cause of deafness should be stated in the school register on the certificate of a medical practitioner.

6. That in all schools and institutions the general health, hearing, and sight of deaf children should be periodically inspected by a medical practitioner; and that those possessing some hearing capacity should be carefully and frequently examined, so as to test and improve their hearing, pronunciation, and intonation by mechanical means, such as ear-trumpets, etc.

7. That technical instruction in industrial handicrafts should be under the Education Department as part of the curriculum in schools for the deaf and dumb after the age of 12 or 13, and that this training be continued to 16. After 16 it may be left to institutions to apprentice their pupils, or to send them to the technical or industrial schools provided for ordinary children.

8. That a special code for the deaf and dumb be issued, and that drawing, wood-carving, or modelling be made part of the regular curriculum of instruction for both sexes.

9. That every child who is deaf should have full opportunity of being educated on the pure oral system. In all schools which receive Government grants, whether conducted on the oral, sign and manual, or combined system, all children should be, for the first year at least, instructed on the oral system, and after the first year they should be taught to speak and lip-read on the pure oral system, unless they are physically or mentally disqualified, in which case, with the consent of the parents, they should be either removed from the oral department of the school or taught elsewhere on the sign and manual system in schools recognized by the Education Department. The parent shall, as far as practicable, have the liberty of selecting the school to which his child should be sent.

10. That children who have partial hearing or remains of speech should in all cases be educated on the pure oral system. The children should in all schools be classified according to their ability.

11. [It must be understood that our suggestions are not intended to be applicable to all children now under instruction, and that the recommendations indicated will, by their very nature, have to be carried out according as circumstances permit.]

12. That there should be teachers in the proportion of one to 8 or 10 pupils in pure oral schools, and of one to 14 or 15 in sign and manual schools.

13. That in institutions the principal or head-master should reside in the school.

14. That the inspectors should be selected by the Education Department as far as possible from those who have had previous acquaintance with the work of inspection in ordinary elementary schools, and who in addition shall have become fully qualified by the knowledge of the systems of instruction practised both at home and abroad. They should also certify that the teachers are properly qualified.

15. That they should see that the schools are properly furnished with all the appliances necessary, and the internal arrangements requisite, for the proper teaching of the pure oral system where it is adopted.

16. That they should report on the knowledge of written language, speech, and the general efficiency of the schools, under whatever system.

17. That the individual examination by the inspector should be a means for merely testing the general progress of the scholars, and not for the purpose of paying individual grants, and that the grants should be proportionate to the higher cost of educating the deaf on any system.

18. That the different methods or systems of teaching should be left free from the control of the inspector, so long as the result in written or spoken language is satisfactory.

19. We think that the present training colleges for the teachers of the deaf do not now fulfil all the conditions which ought to be required by the Educational Department, nor can they be expected to arrive at that standard without Government assistance, examination, and inspection, all of which are enjoyed by ordinary training colleges, and with compulsory enforcement of two years' training for the students.

We recommend—

20. That if the Educational Department should approve of them, or of any other well qualified institution, they should be recognized as training colleges for teachers of the deaf, and should receive a grant at least equal to that given to ordinary training colleges.

21. That, except in schools where the sign and manual system is exclusively used, all teachers should be in possession of all their faculties and have had previous experience in teaching hearing children.

22. That trained teachers of the deaf should, as in Germany, receive salaries such as would induce teachers of special attainments to enter the profession, and on a higher scale than those enjoyed by trained teachers of ordinary children.

23. That after sufficient time shall have elapsed to give full effect to the recommendations above given, the Educational Department should enforce such regulations with regard to certified teachers for the deaf as may be in force in ordinary public elementary schools, and that the certificates of any self-constituted bodies shall not then be recognized.

24. That there should be one uniform schedule of inquiry of the deaf for the census returns of the whole of the United Kingdom.

25. That the class should be spoken of as the deaf; the terms "deaf-mute" and "deaf and dumb" should be strictly applied to such only as are totally deaf and completely dumb.

26. That the deaf and dumb should be kept as far as possible from being a class apart. We think that the mixture of the sexes in school, and especially in after life, is in all cases unadvisable. We also think that the intermarriage of the congenital deaf should be strongly discouraged, as well as the intermarriage of blood relations, especially where any hereditary tendency to deaf-mutism prevails in the family.

27. That the children who are deaf, dumb, and blind could be taught in a school for the blind rather than in one for the deaf.

GOVERNMENTAL BILL DRAWN BY VISCOUNT CRANBROOK, LORD PRESIDENT OF DEPARTMENT OF EDUCATION FOR ENGLAND AND WALES.

[Ordered to be printed, 1 July, 1890.]

ARRANGEMENT OF CLAUSES.

Clause.

1. Obligation of parents as to blind and deaf children.
2. Duty of school authority with respect to blind and deaf children.
3. Powers of school authorities for providing school accommodation for blind and deaf children.
4. Contributions to blind or deaf institution.
5. Arrangement for boarding out blind and deaf children.
6. Regard to be had to religious persuasion of child.
7. Provision as to attendance order in cases of blind or deaf children.
8. Provision in case of failure of duty by school authority.
9. Parliamentary grant for education of blind and deaf children.
10. Liability of parent for education of blind or deaf child.
11. Saving for rights of parent.
12. Contribution of county councils.
13. Application of Act to young persons between 14 and 16.
14. Repeal of powers of guardians to send blind or deaf children to school.
15. Provisions as to school authorities.
16. Interpretation of terms.
17. Extent of Act.
18. Commencement of Act.
19. Short titles.

A BILL

INTITULED

An Act to make better Provision for the Elementary Education of Blind and Deaf Children in England and Wales.

Be it enacted by the Queen's most Excellent Majesty, by and with the advice and consent of the Lords Spiritual and Temporal, and Commons, in this present Parliament assembled, and by the authority of the same, as follows:

1.—(1.) The fact of a child being blind or deaf shall not of itself be a reasonable excuse for not causing the child to attend school, except in the case of a deaf child under seven years of age.

(2.) In the case of a blind or deaf child, the fact that there is not within any particular distance from the residence of the child any public elementary school which the child can attend shall not of itself be a reasonable excuse for not causing the child to attend school, or for neglecting to provide efficient elementary instruction for the child.

2.—(1.) It shall be the duty of every school authority to enable blind and deaf children resident in its district who are not idiots or imbeciles, and for whose elementary education efficient and suitable provision is not otherwise made, to obtain such education in some school or institution for the time being certified by the Education Department as suitable for that purpose.

(2.) Every school or institution so certified (in this Act referred to as a certified school or institution) shall be open at all times to the inspection of Her Majesty's Inspectors of Schools, and shall be deemed to be a certified efficient school within the meaning of the Elementary Education Act, 1876, but a school or institution conducted for private profit shall not be so certified.

3.—(1.) For the purpose of providing sufficient school accommodation for its own district, a school board may contribute such sums of money and on such conditions as it thinks fit towards the provision of public school accommodation for blind or deaf children by the school board of another district.

(2.) The school boards of two or more districts may combine for any purpose relating to the provision or maintenance of public school accommodation for blind or deaf children of their districts.

(3.) In pursuance of any arrangement or combination under this section, or of any arrangement made with a school attendance committee, the school board of a school district may provide public school accommodation for blind or deaf children resident in another district, and for that purpose shall have the same powers as it has of providing sufficient school accommodation for its own district.

4. A school authority may in the case of any blind or deaf child resident in its district contribute towards the expenses of and incidental to the attendance of the child at any certified school or institution and of and incidental to the maintenance of the child while so attending, such reasonable sum as may, subject to regulations of the Education Department, be agreed on.

5. A school authority may, subject to regulations by the Education Department, make arrangements for boarding out any blind or deaf child in a home conveniently near to the school or institution where the child is receiving elementary education, and the expenses of any child so boarded out shall be expenses of the maintenance of the child within the meaning of this Act.

6. In the performance of its duties under this Act with respect to a child, a school authority shall have regard to the religious persuasion of the parents of the child, and the child shall in no case be compelled to receive religious instruction contrary to the wishes of the parent.

7. Where an attendance order is made under section eleven of the Elementary Education Act, 1876, with respect to a blind or deaf child, the court may, if the parent does not select any school which is reasonably available, order that the child attend such certified school or institution willing to receive the child as the court thinks expedient, having regard to the provisions of the last foregoing section.

8. If the Education Department are satisfied, after such inquiry and such notice to a school authority as they think expedient, that the school authority has failed to perform its duty under this Act, the Education Department may either—

(1) proceed in manner directed by section twenty-seven of the Elementary Education Act, 1876; or

(2) order that the school authority pay to any certified school or institution specified in the order, towards the expenses of and incidental to the attendance of any particular child in the school or institution, or of his maintenance while so attending, such annual or other sum as may be fixed by general or special order of the Department, and any sum so fixed shall be a simple contract debt to the school or institution from the school authority, or where it is a committee appointed by a council or guardians, from that council or guardians.

9. Nothing in the Elementary Education Act, 1876, shall prevent the Education Department from giving aid from the parliamentary grant to a certified school or institution in respect of the education of blind or deaf children, to such amount and on such conditions as may be directed by or in pursuance of the minutes of the Education Department in force for the time being.

10.—(1.) Where a school authority incur any expense under this Act by the provision of school accommodation or contribution or otherwise in respect of any blind or deaf child, whether as regards its education or its maintenance, the parent of the child shall be liable to contribute towards the expenses of the child such weekly sum as may be agreed on between the school authority and the parent, or in the absence of any such agreement, such weekly sum not exceeding the expenses of the child as may be ordered by a court of summary jurisdiction, and that sum may, without prejudice to any other remedy, be recovered by the school authority summarily as a civil debt.

(2.) It shall be the duty of the school authority to enforce this order, and any sum paid under the order may be applied by the school authority in aid of its general expenses.

(3.) A court competent to make an order under this section may at any time revoke or vary any order so made.

11.—(1.) The parent of a blind or deaf child shall not, by reason of any payment made under this Act in respect of the child, be deprived of any franchise, right, or privilege, or be subject to any disability or disqualification.

(2.) Payments under this Act shall not be made on condition of a child attending any certified school or institution other than such as may be reasonably selected by the parent, nor refused because the child attends or does not attend any particular certified school or institution.

12.—(1.) The council of each administrative county shall, out of the county fund, pay to each school authority acting within their county one-half of the net expenses reasonably incurred under this Act by the school authority in respect of a blind or deaf child, after deducting any sum recovered from the parent.

(2.) If any question arises as to whether any such expenses are reasonably incurred, the question may on the application either of a school authority or of a county council be referred to the Education Department, whose decision shall be final.

(3.) Where the district of a school authority is situate in more administrative counties than one, the payment under this section to the school authority shall be borne by the administrative counties in which each portion of the district is situate in proportion to the rateable value of that portion ascertained on such day as the Education Department may fix.

(4.) This section shall not apply to the council of a county borough, or in the case of the London School Board, and where a school district is situate partly within and partly without a county borough, this section shall apply to the part outside that borough as if it were alone the school district of the school authority.

13. The provisions of this Act shall apply as if a blind or deaf young person between the ages of fourteen and *sixteen* years were a child, but nothing in this Act shall extend the age of compulsory education.

14. The powers of boards of guardians to send blind or deaf children to school shall cease as from the commencement of this Act, except as to children who are idiots or imbeciles, or who are resident in a workhouse, or whose parents are in receipt of parochial or union relief, or who have been deserted by their parents.

Provided that where any blind or deaf child with respect to whom the powers of guardians cease in pursuance of this section is at the commencement of this Act relieved in any institution by a board of guardians, the child shall continue chargeable as if this Act had not passed, until the expiration of *six months* notice to be given by the guardians to the school authority of the district from which the child was sent.

15. The powers and expenses of a school authority under this Act shall be deemed to be powers and expenses of the authority under the Elementary Education Acts, and the provisions of those Acts shall apply thereto accordingly, and in the case of a school attendance committee section thirty-one of the Elementary Education Act, 1876, shall apply to those expenses, save that such consent of the council or guardians as is mentioned in that section shall not be required.

16.—(1.) In this Act—

The expression "blind" means too blind to be able to read the ordinary school books used by seeing children.

The expression "deaf" means too deaf to be taught in a class of ordinary children in an elementary school:

The expression "school authority" means a school board or school attendance committee;

Other expressions have, unless the contrary intention appears, the same meaning as in the Elementary Education Acts.

(2.) For the purposes of this act a child shall not be deemed to alter its residence by reason only of its being sent to another district by a board of guardians or under the powers conferred by this Act.

17. This Act shall not extend to Scotland or Ireland.

18. This Act shall come into operation on the *first day of January, one thousand eight hundred and ninety-one.*

19.—(1.) This Act may be cited as the Elementary Education (Blind and Deaf) Act, 1890.

(2.) The Elementary Education Act, 1870, and the Acts amending the same are in this Act referred to as the Elementary Education Acts.

(3.) The Elementary Education Acts and this Act may be cited collectively as the Elementary Education Acts, 1870 to 1890.

METHODS OF INSTRUCTION IN AMERICAN SCHOOLS IN 1891, WITH A SUMMARY OF STATISTICS.

[The *American Annals of the Deaf* for January, 1892, contains the detailed statistics of American schools for 1891, tabulated by Dr. E. A. Fay, editor of the *Annals*. The following account of methods of instruction with a summary of the latest statistics is extracted from the text accompanying Dr. Fay's tables.—Ed.]

The "Methods of Instruction" named in the Tabular Statement of American Schools may be defined as follows:

I. *The Manual Method.*—The sign-language, the manual alphabet, and writing are the chief means used in the instruction of the pupils, and the principal objects aimed at are mental development and facility in the comprehension and use of written language. The degree of relative importance given to these three means varies in different schools; but it is a difference only in degree, and the end aimed at is the same in all. If the pupils have some power of speech before coming to school, or if they possess a considerable degree of hearing, their teachers, if they themselves hear and speak, usually try to improve their utterance by practice; but no special teachers are employed for this purpose, and comparatively little attention is given to articulation and speech-reading.

The schools in America following this method are seven in number, viz., the Maryland Colored, Cincinnati Public, New Mexico, Evansville, Toledo, Eastern Iowa, and Chinchuba schools. The whole number of pupils during the year was 94.

II. *The Oral Method.*—Articulation and speech-reading, together with writing, are made the chief means of instruction, and facility in articulation and speech-reading, as well as mental development and written language, is aimed at. Signs are used as little as possible, and the manual alphabet is generally discarded altogether. There is a difference in different schools in the extent to which the use of natural signs is allowed in the early part of the course, and also in the prominence given to writing as an auxiliary to articulation and speech-reading in the course of instruction; but they are differences only of degree, and the end aimed at is the same in all. The schools in America following this method are eighteen in number, viz., the New York Improved Instruction, Clarke, Horace Mann, Portland, Rhode Island, Milwaukee, Pennsylvania Oral, Cincinnati Oral, La Crosse, Wausau, Whipple's, German Lutheran, Mr. Knapp's, McCowen, Miss Keeler's, Sarah Fuller, Albany, and Miss Kugler's schools. Total number of pupils during the year (not including those of Mr. Knapp's Institute from which returns were not received), 833.

III. *The Combined System.*—Articulation and speech-reading are regarded as very important, but mental development and the acquisition of language are regarded as still more important. It is believed that in many cases mental development and the acquisition of language can be better attained by some other method than the Oral, and, so far as circumstances permit, such method is chosen for each pupil as seems best adapted to his individual case. Articulation and speech-reading are taught where the measure of success seems likely to justify the labor expended. The schools in America using some form of the Combined System are fify-nine in number, viz., the American, New York, Pennsylvania,* Kentucky, Ohio, Virginia,* Indiana, Tennessee, North Carolina, Illinois, Georgia, South Carolina, Missouri, Louisiana, Wisconsin, Michigan, Mississippi, Iowa, Texas, Kendall, Alabama, California, Kansas, Le Couteulx St. Mary's, Minnesota, Arkansas, Maryland, Nebraska, St. Joseph's,* West Virginia, Oregon, Colorado, Chicago, Central New York, Western Pennsylvania, St. Louis, Western New York, New England Industrial, Dakota, New Jersey, Utah, Northern New York, Florida, Washington State, Texas Colored, North Dakota, St. John's Catholic, Ephpheta, Maria Consilia, St. Mary's, Notre Dame, Montreal Catholic (both Male and Female), Halifax, Ontario, Mackay, Fredericton, and Manitoba schools, and the National College. The schools during the year contained 9,098 pupils, of whom 3,652 were taught articulation and speech-reading.

The various methods in which the Combined System is applied in American schools may be classified as follows:

A. The general instruction of the pupils is carried on chiefly by the Manual Method. Part or all of them receive special training in articulation and speech-reading. The schools following this method are twenty-three in number, viz., the American, Ohio, Virginia, Indiana, Georgia, Louisiana, Mississippi, Texas, Kansas, Oregon, Chicago, Western Pennsylvania, St. Louis, New England Industrial, Dakota, Northern New York, Texas Colored, North Dakota, Maria Consilia, Halifax, Ontario, and Fredericton schools, and the National College. Total number of pupils during the year, 2,981; number taught articulation and speech-reading, 852.

A. B. Part of the pupils are taught by the Manual method, others by the Oral method. Of the former, part receive special training in articulation and speech-reading. All are permitted to mingle freely with one another out of school-hours. This is the method of twelve schools, viz., the Kentucky, Illinois, Missouri, Wisconsin, Michigan, California, Minnesota,* Arkansas, Maryland, St. Joseph's, Colorado, and Florida schools. Total number of pupils, 2,859; number taught articulation and speech-reading, 1,190.

A. E. The general instruction of the pupils is carried on chiefly by the Manual method. Part of them receive special training in articulation and speech-reading. Some of the teachers also use articulation and speech-reading, in addition to the manual alphabet and writing, as a means of instruction with part of their pupils. This is the method of the Kendall, Central New York, and New Jersey schools, containing during the year 367 pupils, of whom 229 were taught articulation and speech-reading.

B. Some of the pupils are taught by means of the Manual method, and others by the Oral method. These two classes are permitted to mingle freely with one another out of school-hours. This is the method of ten schools, viz., the Tennessee, North Carolina, South Carolina, Alabama, Nebraska, West Virginia, Utah, Ephpheta, St. Mary's, and Montreal

* The Principal of the Pennsylvania Institution prefers to designate the methods there pursued as "Manual and Oral" rather than "Combined," the Principal of the Virginia Institution the methods there pursued as "Manual," and the President of the St. Joseph's Institute the methods there pursued as "Oral and Combined."

* *Minnesota School.*—"It should also be remembered that all of our pupils make trial of articulation, and are dismissed from the oral classes upon the recommendation of the teacher of articulation, and only then when the teacher of articulation decides they are incapable of obtaining an education by the Oral method. Moreover, in class-rooms we lay great stress upon object teaching, writing from actions, and all real combinations of actions such as we are able to produce in the school-room. We resort to this method that the natural sign-language may not be made too prominent. The manual alphabet, writing, lip-reading, and articulation are freely used by the teachers and pupils in the class-room and in social intercourse. We have not yet organized a class in auricular training, although we use quite freely Currier's ear trumpet with those who are capable of receiving instruction through the sense of hearing. I claim to use every method of instruction that seems to me of service in educating deaf children."—J. L. Noyes, Superintendent.

Catholic Male schools, containing during the year 1,056 pupils, of whom 445 were taught by the Oral method.

B. C. Some of the pupils are taught by means of the Manual method, and others by the Oral method. Of the latter, part are permitted to mingle freely out of school-hours with the manually-taught pupils; others are kept entirely separate from them, and from those who mingle with them, out of school-hours as well as in the school-rooms. This is the method of the Pennsylvania Institution, containing during the year 490 pupils, of whom 130 were taught by the Oral method, 103 of them in a separate school. "Manual and Oral," rather than "Combined," are the terms Mr. Crouter prefers to use in describing the methods of the Institution.

B. D. Some of the pupils are taught by the Oral method; others by the manual alphabet and writing, without the use of the sign-language. The latter also receive special training in articulation and speech-reading. The two classes are permitted to mingle freely with one another out of school-hours. This is the method of the Cincinnati Notre Dame school, containing during the year 8 pupils, four of whom were taught by the Oral method.

C. Some of the pupils are taught by means of the Manual method, and others by the Oral method. These two classes are kept entirely separate out of school-hours as well as in the school-rooms. This is the method of the Montreal Catholic Female Institution, containing during the year 196 pupils, of whom 72 were taught by the Oral method.

D. The general instruction of the pupils is carried on chiefly by means of the manual alphabet and writing, without the use of the sign-language. All the pupils receive special training in articulation and speech-reading. This is the method of the Western New York Institution, which contained during the year 167 pupils. Mr. Westervelt calls this "The American Vernacular Method."

E. The sign-language, the manual alphabet, writing, articulation, and speech-reading are all used as means of instruction, by the same teachers and with the same pupils. This method is pursued in six schools, viz., the New York,* Le Couteulx St. Mary's, Washington State, St. John's Catholic, Mackay, and Manitoba schools. Total number of pupils during the year, 665; number taught articulation and speech-reading, 534.

F. In addition to one or more of the methods above described, auricular training is given to a part of the pupils in twelve "Combined System" schools, viz., the New York, Indiana, Illinois, Mississippi, Kendall, Kansas, Le Couteulx St. Mary's, Minnesota, Arkansas, Nebraska, and Colorado schools, and the National College. Auricular instruction is also made a prominent feature of the McCowen School.

G. The Iowa Institution was reported in 1890 as following the Combined System, but we are not informed as to which of the above sub-classes the method pursued belongs. Total number of pupils during the year, 309; number taught articulation and speech-reading, 25.

The following is a summary of the statistics of the methods of instruction in American schools, including Canada, for the year 1891:

Total number of pupils	10,025
Number in Manual method schools	94
" " Oral method schools	833
" " Combined System schools	9,098
Number taught exclusively by the Manual method	5,540
" " articulation and speech-reading	4,485
Number taught articulation and speech-reading in Combined System schools	3,652
Number taught exclusively by the Oral Method	1,481
" " articulation and speech-reading by the "Combined A" method	852
Number taught by the "Combined A. B" method	1,190
" " " " A. E" "	229
" " " " B" "	445
" " " " B. C" "	130
" " " " B. D" "	8
" " " " C" "	72
" " " " D" "	167
" " " " E" "	534
" " by Combined method not specified	25
Number of articulation teachers	288
Number of articulation teachers in Oral method schools (including principals)	98
" " in Combined System schools (not including principals)	190

* *New York Institution.*—"All the pupils are taught articulation for one hour daily."—I. L. PEET, Principal.

SUMMARY OF STATISTICS OF SCHOOLS FOR THE DEAF IN THE UNITED STATES FOR TWENTY-EIGHT YEARS.

[Compiled from the *American Annals of the Deaf* by Dr. Alexander Graham Bell.]

TABLE I.—*Table concerning the teachers employed in American schools for the deaf, showing what proportion of these teachers are themselves deaf.*

DATES.	Total teachers.	Total deaf teachers.	Total hearing teachers.	PERCENTAGES.	
				Deaf.	Hearing.
1857	95				
1863					
1866	119				
1867	120				
1868	170	71	99	41.7	58.3
1869	187	77	110	41.1	58.9
1870	222	94	128	42.3	57.7
1871	260	110	150	42.3	57.7
1872	271	107	164	39.5	60.5
1873	274	104	170	37.9	62.1
1874	290	98	192	33.7	66.3
1875	321	111	210	34.5	65.5
1876	304	104	200	34.2	65.8
1877	356	111	245	31.1	68.9
1878	375	126	249	33.6	66.4
1879	388	113	275	29.1	70.9
1880	425	132	293	31	69
1881	444	147	297	33.1	66.9
1882	481	154	327	32	68
1883	497	151	346	30.3	69.7
1884	508	155	353	30.5	69.5
1885	540	156	384	28.8	71.2
1886	566	158	408	27.9	72.1
1887	577	155	422	26.8	73.2
1888	606	154	452	25.4	74.6
1889	615	160	455	26	74
1890	641	170	471	26.5	73.5
1891	686	167	519	24.3	75.7

TABLE II.—*Table concerning the hearing teachers employed in American schools for the deaf, showing how many of them are teachers of articulation.*

DATES.	Total hearing teachers.	HEARING TEACHERS.		PERCENTAGES.	
		Articulation teachers.	Not articulation teachers.	Articulation teachers.	Not articulation teachers.
1866					
1867					
1868	99				
1869	110				
1870	128				
1871	150				
1872	164				
1873	170				
1874	192				
1875	210				
1876	200				
1877	245				
1878	249				
1879	275				
1880	293				
1881	297				
1882	327				
1883	346				
1884	353				
1885	384				
1886	408	134	274	32.8	67.2
1887	422	171	251	40.5	59.5
1888	452	199	253	44	56
1889	455	208	247	45.7	54.3
1890	471	213	258	45.2	54.8
1891	519	260	259	50.1	49.9

TABLE III.—*Statistics concerning the number of deaf-mutes who are taught to speak in American schools for the deaf.*

DATES.	Total schools.	Total pupils.	Pupils taught articulation.	Pupils not taught articulation.	Percentage of pupils taught articulation.	Percentage of pupils not taught articulation.
1857	20	1,721				
1863	22	2,012				
1866	24	2,469				
1867	24	2,576				
1868	27	2,898				
1869	30	3,246				
1870	34	3,784				
1871	38	4,068				
1872	36	4,253				
1873	38	4,252				
1874	44	4,892				
1875	48	5,309				
1876	49	5,010				
1877	49	5,711				
1878	49	6,166				
1879	51	6,431				
1880	55	6,798				
1881	55	7,019				
1882	55	7,155				
1883	58	7,169				
1884	61	7,482	2,041	5,441	27.2	72.8
1885	64	7,801	2,618	5,183	33.5	66.5
1886	66	8,050	2,484	5,576	31	69
1887	69	7,978	2,556	5,422	32	68
1888	73	8,372	3,251	5,121	38.8	61.2
1889	73	8,575	3,412	5,163	39.7	60.3
1890	77	8,901	3,682	5,219	41.3	58.7
1891	77	9,232	4,245	4,987	46	54

TABULAR STATEMENT OF SCHOOLS FOR THE DEAF IN THE UNITED KINGDOM.

Table A.

Statistics relating to pupils under instruction in the year 1892 in the Institutions for the Deaf in the United Kingdom. Tables A and B were compiled by Professor J. C. Gordon from tabulated returns collected for the Committee of the Cross Deaf and Dumb School for North and East Lancashire.

Institutions.	Pupils.												
	Total number.	Males.	Females.	Born deaf or partly deaf.	Cause of deafness unknown.	Lost hearing in early infancy.	Had speech before loss of hearing.	Semi-deaf.	Have defective sight.	Have other defects.	Offspring of blood relatives.	Offspring of deaf parent or parents.	Have deaf relatives.
1. London (Old Kent Road)	44	25	19	28	......	......	......	......	......	......	3	2	....
2. Margate	299	166	133	212	......	......	6	......	20	2	19	6	....
3. Edinburgh (Henderson Road)	60	37	23	45	2	11	2	2	11	3	3	1	7
4. Birmingham	141	79	62	88	5	37	10	......	23	......	7	3	....
5. Dublin (National)	32	14	18	23	0	9	1	5	2	0	4	0	6
6. Glasgow	134	67	67	57	15	......	......	30	......	1	3	3	26
7. Aberdeen	20	12	8	15	......	4	......	......	4	2	3	0	....
8. Manchester	200	120	80	120	......	80	45	? 15	20	10	4	2	....
9. Liverpool	120	73	47	......	......	54	......	2	24	2	10	0	4
10. Exeter	46	28	18	25	......	......	4	......	12	3	......	0	....
11. Doncaster	126	71	55	73	......	26	14	......	6	3	5	......	....
12. Belfast	91	59	32	82	......	......	10	......	7	......	17	3	9
13. Newcastle	120	75	45	60	6	46	7	3	2	2	0	5	12
14. Bristol	50	29	21	37	3	10	5	......	10	1	7	5	24
15. Brighton	89	50	39	......	......	......	......	......	4	0	......	1	12
16. Bath	14	4	10	10	......	......	1	......	2	......	......	......	....
17. Dundee	19	14	5	12	....	.....	1	......	......	......	......	2	....
18. Dublin (St. Mary's)	427	......	216	......	......	......	......	......	26	1	......	......	....
19. Dublin (St. Joseph's)		211	......	......	......	......	......	......	3	......	......	......	....
20. Swansea	56	37	19	21	......	28	7	5	7	2	6	0	6
21. Edinburgh (Donaldson's Hospital)	111	58	53	60	14	35	13	5	13	2	......	8	23
22. London (Clapton)	40	0	40	32	......	......	......	0	10	......	15	0	4
23. Llandaff	23	14	9	11	......	......	5	......	2	2	......	0	....
24. London (Notting Hill)	27	15	12	17	......	......	10	......	5	0	4	3	....
25. Boston Spa	124	62	62	62	......	......	9	.....	8	1	1	0	3
26. Hull	30	16	14	16	0	11	0	3	2	1	0	0	....
27. London (Fitzroy Square)	49	34	15	41	......	8	4	0	7	1	5	0	9
28. Lanark	24	15	9	12	......	......	7	......	4	......	......	1	....
29. Derby	58	36	22	34	7	17	1	2	13	5	0	1	1
30. London (Ealing)	18	11	7	10	......	......	1	......	0	3	1	0	....
Total	2592	1432	1160	1203	52	376	163	72	247	47	117	46	146

Table B.

Statistics of Institutions for the Deaf in the United Kingdom for the year 1892.

Name of Institution.	Teachers.		Pupils.			
	Male.	Female.	Under Oral Method.	Under Silent Method.	Under Combined Method.	Total number.
1. London (Old Kent Road)	12	8	44	0	0	44
2. Margate			207	45	47	299
3. Edinburgh (Henderson Rd)	3	2	24	13	23	60
4. Birmingham	4	6	0	97	44	141
5. Dublin (National)	3	1	32	0	0	32
6. Glasgow	5	7	12	0	122	134
7. Aberdeen	1	......	0	4	16	20
8. Manchester	12	8	160	40	0	200
9. Liverpool	8	4	90	30	0	120
10. Exeter	4	1	0	0	46	46
11. Doncaster	7	5	126	0	0	126
12. Belfast	5	1	0	78	13	91
13. Newcastle	6	2	0	0	120	120
14. Bristol	2	2	0	50	0	50
15. Brighton	3	2	0	77	12	89
16. Bath	......	3	0	14	0	14
17. Dundee	1	......	4	15	0	19
18. Dublin (St. Mary's)	......	16	0	216	0	427
19. Dublin (St. Joseph's)	13	......	0	211	0	
20. Swansea	2	3	0	20	36	56
21. Edinb'h (Donalds'n's Hos).	7	3	13	12	86	111
22. London (Clapton)	1	3	0	0	40	40
23. Llandaff	2	3	0	0	23	23
24. London (Notting Hill)	2	1	27	0	0	27
25. Boston Spa	......	16	101	0	23	124
26. Hull	2	1	0	0	30	30
27. London (Fitzroy Square)	2	4	49	0	0	49
28. Lanark	......	4	0	0	24	24
29. Derby	3	4	Derby Sys.			58
30. London (Ealing)	1	1	18	0	0	18
Total	111	111	907	922	705	2592

Table C.

Statistics of School Board Classes for the Deaf in England and Scotland, compiled from the Appendix to the Report of the Royal Commission by Professor J. C. Gordon.

Name of Class.	Teachers.		Pupils.			
	M.	F.	Under Oral Method.	Under Silent Method.	Under Combined Method.	Total number.
1. Bradford School Board Class for the Deaf.	......	2	20	....	....	20
2. Bristol Deaf Class	......	2	19	....	....	19
3. Leeds Deaf and Dumb Department, Leeds School Board.	......	2	....	22	16	38
4. Leicester: Elbow Lane B'd School.	......	2	12	....	....	12
4. Leicester: Milton Street B'd School.	......	2	12	....	..	12
5. London (14 classes in various parts of London).	8	29	373	..	....	373
6. Nottingham Deaf-Mute Class.	1	2	26	....	....	26
7. Sheffield School Board's Deaf and Dumb School.	1	......	....	....	32	32
8. Dundee Oral School for the Deaf and Dumb.	......	1	14	....	....	14
9. Govan Parish, Glasgow Deaf-Mute Class.	......	2	15	....	....	15
10. Greenock Oral School for Deaf-Mutes.	......	2	16	....	....	16
Total	10	46	507	22	48	577

TABULAR STATEMENT OF SCHOOLS FOR THE DEAF IN GERMANY AND IN ADJACENT COUNTRIES IN WHICH GERMAN IS SPOKEN.

Extracted from the *Organ* for September, 1891.

TABLE A.

STATE.	SCHOOLS.				NO. OF PUPILS.				TEACHERS.		
	Boarding.	Day.	Mixed.	Total.	Male.	Female.	Total.	Classes.	Male.	Female.	Total.
Prussia	6	33	8	47	2340	1766	4106	378	389	24	413
Bavaria	12	3	......	15	315	277	592	62	37	14	51
Würtemberg	5	2	1	8	182	162	344	40	28	10	38
Saxony	2	......	1	3	226	170	396	37	39	1	40
Baden	3	......	......	3	115	88	203	20	23	1	24
Hesse	......	2	......	2	69	46	115	12	14	......	14
Alsace-Lorraine	4	......	......	4	89	85	174	20	12	12	24
Other States	2	9	2	13	269	182	451	48	46	3	49
Total	34	49	12	95	3605	2776	6381	617	588	65	653

TABLE B.

STATE.	SCHOOLS.				NO. OF PUPILS.				TEACHERS.		
	Boarding.	Day.	Mixed.	Total.	Male.	Female.	Total.	Classes.	Male.	Female.	Total.
Germany	34	49	12	95	3605	2776	6381	617	588	65	653
Austria-Hung'y	16	5	4	25	858	698	1556	121	104	28	132
Switzerland	14	......	1	15	245	204	449	53	30	19	49
Luxembourg	1	......	......	1	16	7	23	3	3	......	3
Russian Baltic Provinces	2	1	1	4	83	77	160	15	10	6	16
Total	67	55	18	140	4807	3762	8569	809	735	118	853

ANCESTRY OF THE DEAF.

EXPLANATION OF SYMBOLS EMPLOYED IN GRAPHICAL CHARTS.

A family in which the order of birth is not followed.

A family in which the order of birth is followed. Read from right to left; the first born on the right, the youngest, on the left.

A family containing a case of twins.

A family containing a case of triplets.

Males.

Females.

A family in which the children died young.

A continuous line indicates descent from a male — a dotted line descent from a female. Where more than one line proceeds from a male, the children are by different mothers; where more than one line proceeds from a female, the children are by different fathers.

SYMBOLS FOR DEFECTS.

The character of the defect is indicated by the character of the shading (vertical, horizontal or oblique), and the amount of the defect, by the amount of the shading.

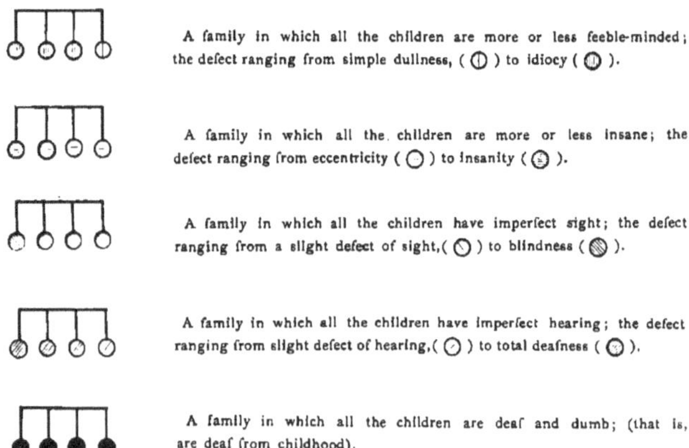

A family in which all the children are more or less feeble-minded; the defect ranging from simple dullness, ( ) to idiocy ( ).
A family in which all the children are more or less insane; the defect ranging from eccentricity ( ) to insanity ( ).
A family in which all the children have imperfect sight; the defect ranging from a slight defect of sight, ( ) to blindness ( ).
A family in which all the children have imperfect hearing; the defect ranging from slight defect of hearing, ( ) to total deafness ( ).
A family in which all the children are deaf and dumb; (that is, are deaf from childhood).

INDEX.

EXPLANATORY NOTE.

Titles of papers are in large bold-faced type, as "**Fallacies Concerning the Deaf**," "**Poetry of the Deaf.**"

Numerical references to the part and to the page are in bold-faced type, while the number of the question is indicated in ordinary type. The first two figures of the latter, (13) in President Gallaudet's, (21) in Dr. Bell's, have been omitted as unnecessary.

Examples: "Action of California Convention, **I**, 141, **7**," refers to Part I, question 13,141, page 7.

"Abolition of institutions not advocated, **II**, 463, **14**," refers to Part II, question 21,463, page 14.

Readers will bear in mind that there are *two series* of page-numbers: the first covers Part I, President Gallaudet's Evidence and Exhibits; the second covers the remainder of the work, Part II, Dr. Bell's Evidence and Exhibits, and Part III, Postscripts.

INDEX.

Ability of American instructors of the deaf, *Gallaudet*, **I**, 259, **19**; *Bell*, **II**, 791, **45**.
—— to read from the mouth, a third comparative test of efficiency, **II**, 748, **42**.
—— of deaf-mutes to earn their living, **I**, 285, **22**.
Abnormal increase of the non-congenitally deaf, **II**, 416, **9**.
Abolition of institutions, not advocated, **II**, 463, **14**.
Absolute necessity of using written form of language in the earlier stages of instruction **II**, 669, **35**.
Absolutely deaf, Pupils not, should be taught orally, *Gallaudet*, **I**, 424, **31**.
Abundant knowledge in America of the work in Europe, **I**, 339, **26**.
Accidental or Acquired deafness not transmitted, **I**, 252, **19**.
Accuracy of the statistical tables in the *American Annals*, **II**, 493, **18**.
Ackers, Mr. B. St. J., Questions by, **I**, 13,522; **II**, 21,361; 21,499; 21,558; 21,590; 21,913; 21,950; 21,954; 21,969; 21,977; 21,995.
—— Extract from paper at Milan Convention by, **I**, **100**.
—— Mrs. B. St. J., **I**, **106**.
Action of California Convention, **I**, 141, **7**.
—— of Milan Convention, **I**, **106**.
—— of Washington Conference of Principals, **I**, **59**.
Action-writing reverses the process of nature, **II**, 813, **48**.
Actual improvement in condition of backward, or dull pupils, **I**, **82**.
Acquaintance among the deaf promoted by philanthropists, **II**, 548, **24**.
Acquisition of Visible Speech, **II**, 880, 899, **57**: *See* Visible Speech.
Additional facilities for instruction, How to provide, **II**, **69**.
Adèle, Sister, on Visible Speech in Maria Consilia Inst., **II**, **77**; on Auricular Instruction, **83**.
Admiration for the sign-language, *Bell*, **II**, 560, **25**.
Adults, Cases of, taught to speak, **II**, **157**.
—— Effect of special language upon, **II**, 540, **23**.
—— generally should be rendered independent of special societies, **II**, 644, **32**.
—— Partially educated, must be reached, **II**, 741, **40**.
—— Societies for, **II**, 613, **31**.
—— —— Benefits of, **II**, 919, **59**.
—— —— Both sexes in, 621, **31**.
—— —— harmful but necessary for certain purposes, **II**, 643, **32**.
—— —— promote intermarriage, **II**, 618, **31**.
Advanced classes of Horace-Mann School in public-school building, **II**, 781, **44**.
Advantage of day-schools, *Bell*, **II**, **70**, **71**; **168**; *Emery*, **108-112**. *See* Day-schools.
—— controverted, *Gallaudet*, **I**, 192, **12**; *Gillett* and others, **II**, **169**.
Advantage of deaf child over one who hears, *Gallaudet*, **I**, 218, **15**; *Bell*, **II**, 834, **50**.
Advantage of acquaintance of the deaf with hearing children, **II**, **70**.
—— of deaf-mutes over the speaking deaf, **I**, **102**.
——, Practical, of German and Italian written languages over English, **II**, 961, **62**.
Advantages of decentralization, **II**, **69**.
—— of small schools, **II**, **70**. *See* Day-Schools.
—— of speech and speech-reading, **I**, 460, **33**.
Adventitious deafness, Causes of, tabulated, **II**, 487, **18**; **II**, **91**, **92**, **93**, **127**.
Adverse Statistics relating to children of deaf parents, Effect of analysis of, **II**, 612, **30**.
Advice as to unsuitable marriages, **I**, 353, **19**; 392, **29**.
—— —— —— *See* Classification of the Deaf into four groups as a Guide to Marriage, **II**, 473, **16**.
Advisability of early education, **II**, **70**.
African race, Deaf-mutism in, **I**, **44**; Mind in, **I**, 501, **36**.
After-life of pupils, **I**, 320, **25**.
Advocates of pure oral system opposed to use of manual alphabet, **II**, 719, **40**.
Age, Effect of, upon development of voice, **I**, 146, **8**.
——, Proper school, **I**, 144, **8**; 416, **30**.
—— of pupils at leaving school, **II**, 840, **51**.
—— —— ——, Proper, for taking up technical instruction, **II**, 843, **51**.
—— of occurrence of deafness, **II**, 422, **10**; 487, **17**.
—— an element in examining results of instruction, **II**, 585, **29**.
——, Statistics of, **II**, 487, **17**; **91**, **92**, **93**, **127**.
Ages of deaf-mutes, Classified, **II**, 487, **17**; **II**, **127**.
Aggregation of deaf-mutes in certain communities, **I**, **50**.
Aid, Governmental: How it may be given, *Bell*, **II**, 937, **60**; should be no discrimination between day-schools and institutions, *Bell*, **II**, 768, **43**; necessary, *Gallaudet*, **I**, 367, **28**; 309, **24**.
—— —— and private benevolence, **I**, 366, **28**; **II**, 740, **41**.
—— —— should depend upon certain results obtained, **II**, 748, **42**. Objections, 769, **42**; **I**, 265, **20**.
—— State, to day-schools in Wisconsin, **II**, **71**.
—— —— to various schools, *see* Table, **I**, **74**.
Aids to hearing, *See* Auricular instruction.
Alarms of war, a cause of deafness, **I**, **45**.
Alcmaeon, Opinion of, **II**, **155**.
All grades of mental ability reached by the combined system, *Williams*, **I**, **82**.
Allen family, The, **II**, 454, **13**; Chart, **III**, —, See "*Ancestry of the Deaf.*"
Alleviation, The greatest possible, **I**, 425, **31**.
All pupils are not taught to speak, Why, **I**, 359, **27**.
—— —— should have the opportunity to learn to speak, **I**, 500, **36**.
Alphabet, Universal, devised by Prof. A. Melville Bell, **II**, 868, **54**; Dalgarno, Glove, *and* Manual alphabets, *see these titles*, and Finger-Spelling.

Alternatives, Choice between, **I**, 441, **32**.
Ambiguity in speech-reading, **II**, 568, **26**; **II**, **158**.
— of the term "combined," **II**, 573, **27**.
— of the designation "oral method," **II**, 705, **39**.
Amendment to action of California Convention, Desirable, *Miss E. Garrett*, **II**, **117**.
American Annals of the Deaf, see *Annals*.
— **Asylum**, Sketch of, **I**, **54**.
— **delegates** at Milan represented 6,000 pupils, **I**, 522, **38**.
— **lady**, Case of, **I**, 473, **34**.
— **Manual alphabet**, **I**, 273, **21**.
— — — with plates, *Gordon*, **I**, **94-97**.
— **opinion** upon Milan Convention, **I**, 306, **24**.
— **pupils** are not all taught to speak, Why, **I**, 359, **27**.
system, An, *G. O. Fay*, **I**, **80**; Greenberger, **II**, **170**.
— **teachers**, Ability of, *Gallaudet*, **I**, 259, 263, **19**. *Bell*, **II**, 791, **45**.
Amorous relationships formed leading to marriage where the sexes are taught together, **II**, 524, **21**.
Amour propre as affecting the orally taught, **II**, 984, **64**; **II**, 985, **65**.
— — *vs. Mauvais honte*, *Gallaudet*, **III**, **210**.
Analysis of 22,172 cases of deaf-mutes living on 1st June, 1880; Diagram *to face*, **II**, **0**.
— **and comparison** of statistics for '30, '40, '50, *H. P. Peet*, **I**, **45**.
— **of the defective classes**, **II**, **134**.
— **of statistics** of deaf-mutes in Tenth Census, **II**, **127**.
Ancestral cause of deafness and other defects, **II**, 450, **13**.
Ancestry of the Deaf, Graphical Charts, etc., **III**, —.
— **of deaf mute population** of Chilmark, Martha's Vineyard, **II**, 858, **53**.
— **of New-England deaf-mutes** traced, **II**, 441, **12**.
Annals, American, of the Deaf, Accuracy of statistics in, **II**, 493, **18**.
citations: **I**, 105, **3**; 106, 109, 111, **4**; 125, **5**; 256, **19**; 274, **21**; 427, **31**; 470, **34**; 519, **37**; **II**, 472, **15**; 487, **17**; 492, **18**; 563, **26**; 599, **30**; 691, **37**; 738, *foot-note*, **41**; 812, **47**; 827, **50**; 873, **55**; 983, **63**.
— **commended**, **II**, 972, **63**.
— **described**, **I**, 270, **20**.
— **presented** to the Royal Commission, 271, **21**.
Annual cost of educating pupils, **I**, 125, **5**; in Paris, 143, **8**; in National College, West Point, and Annapolis, 236, **16**; in day-schools, **II**, 767, **43**; average *per capita* cost, 737, 738, *foot-note*, **41**.
Anomalous position of institutions in the school-system, **II**, 774, **42**.
Answer to argument that "the sign-language is the natural language of the deaf," **II**, 983, **63**.
Aphorisms from Dalgarno, **II**, 702, **39**.
Apparent Correlation between deafness, blindness, and idiocy, **II**, **134**.
decrease of deaf-mutes explained, **II**, 437, **11**.
— **increase** of deaf-mutes discussed, **I**, 105, **3**.
Appointments, Political, **III**, **211**; **II**, 816, **51**; **I**, 263, **20**.
Apprenticeship, System of, **I**, 286, **22**.
Argo, Mr. W. H., on auricular instruction, **II**, **78**; on intermarriage, **II**, **91**; on system of instruction, **II**, **106**.
Argument quoted from Salt-Lake City *Tribune*, p. 83, **II**, incorrect, **II**, 623, **31**.
Armitage, T. R., Esq., M. D., Questions by, **I**, 13,381, 13,419; 13,421.
Arrested development, a common cause of cases of deafness, blindness, and idiocy, **II**, 450, **13**; assigned as cause of deafness in blue-eyed, white cats, **II**, 448, **12**.
Arroll, W. A., Esq., Question by, 13,356.
Articulation, Action of California Convention, **I**, 141, **7**; **II**, 677, **36**.
— **Action of Milan Convention**, **I**, **106**.
— **Action of Washington Conference**, **I**, **59**.
— **in American Asylum**, *Williams*, **I**, **85**.
— **All pupils could be taught**, **II**, 377, **4**; controverted: *Gallaudet*, **I**, 360, **27**; *Kinsey*, **108**; *Williams*, **86**.
— **classes**, Proper size of, **II**, 496, **19**.
— **Distinction between, and speech-reading**, **II**, 575, **27**.
— **does not restore the deaf to society**, *Emery*, **II**, **114**.
— **Early example of**, **II**, **156**.
— **not used as a means of instruction in the National College**, **II**, 587, **29**; how used, **I**, 510, **37**.
— **of words before learning elements—case of Bertha**, **II**, **120**.
— **ought to have a more prominent place**, *Gallaudet*, **I**, **106**.
— **Percentage of pupils taught**, **II**, **71**; 676, **35**.
— **Proficiency in, a test of results**, **II**, 748, **42**.
— **should be compulsory**, **II**, 922, **59**.
— **Sketch of, in U. S.**, *Gallaudet*, **I**, 133, **6**, **57**; *Bell*, **II**, **157**.
— **Statistics of**, **II**, 377, **4**; 379, **5**; 380, **5** (*v. correction*, 469, **19**); 492, **18**; 497, **19**; 806, **46**; Table for '83, **II**, **130**; Table for '88, **II**, **124**.
— **taught as an accomplishment**, Result of, **II**, 582, **28**; *Ely*, **II**, **115**.
— **teachers**, Meaning of increased number of, **II**, 496, **19**.
— **the longest, hardest road**, *Emery*, **II**, **113**.
— *See* Oral Method, etc.
Artificial selection, the essential factor in creating new breeds, *Brewer*, **II**, **103**.
Art, Instruction in, **I**, 173, **11**; **II**, 472, **15**.
— **of understanding speech by the eye**, **II**, **157**.
Artists, Deaf: *J. C. Davis*, **II**, **138**; *Humphrey Moore*, **I**, 175, **11**.
Association of adult deaf-mutes, a subject for careful consideration, **II**, 613, **32**; beneficial, **II**, 919, **59**; Tendency to, irrespective of method, **I**, 442, **32**; *See* Adults, Societies for.
— **of deaf-mutes with deaf-mutes**, not essential to happiness, **II**, 722, **40**.
— **of deaf children with the hearing**, **II**, 465, **14**; 469, **15**; 651, **33**; 781, **44**; 919, **59**, **71**.
— **of deaf instructed youth with hearing**, for technical instruction, **II**, 468, **15**.
Asylums, Idea of, **I**, 477, **35**.
Attitude of Dr. Bell toward rival systems, **II**, 881, **56**.
Audiometer, and tests of hearing, **II**, 402, **8**; **II**, **140**.
— **Two forms of**, **II**, 997, **65**.
— **and hearing-tube tests compared**, **II**, **142**.
Audiphone, The, **II**, 402, **8**; **II**, **87**.
— **Description of**, **II**, 689, **37**.
— **Peculiar utility of, in certain cases**, **II**, 689, **37**.
— **Substitute for**, *Clarke*, **II**, **88**.
Audiphone used in 2 out of 707 cases, *Clarke*, **II**, **88**.

Audition, Very imperfect, utilizable in Articulation teaching, *Gordon*, **II, 85.** *See* Auricular instruction
—— essential to perfect speech, *Gillett*, **II, 171.**
Aural method, *see* Auricular instruction.
Auricular instruction : *American principals*, **II, 78 88.**
—— —— *Dr. Bell*, **II**, 392–406, **7** ; 483 487, **17** ; 681 689, **36** ; 810, **47.**
—— —— *F. D. Clarke*, **II, 88, 140.**
—— —— *Committee of New-York Convention*, **II, 139.**
—— —— *E. H. Currier*, **II, 87.**
—— —— *Dr. E. A. Fay*, **I, 70.**
—— —— *Pres. Gallaudet*, **I**, 147-157, **8-9.**
—— —— *J. A. Gillespie*, **II, 84, 85.**
—— —— *Prof. Gordon*, **II, 85, 139.**
—— —— *Miss McCowan*, **II, 86.**
—— —— *Mrs. Taylor*, **II, 85.**
—— —— Age of proper subjects, **II**, 810, **47.**
—— —— Case of Mr. W. G. Jones, **II**, 399, **8.**
—— —— Definition of the method, **II**, 387, **6.**
—— —— Hereditary aptitude for, **II**, 811, **47.**
—— —— Instrumental aids, **II**, c, **78-84, 85, 86, 87, 88** ; 400, **8.**
—— —— *Modus operandi of*, *Currier*, **II, 187 188.**
—— —— Nature of, **II**, 397, **7**, and *supra*.
—— —— Number and ratio of pupils capable of receiving, **II**, 403, **8** ; 684, **36** ; TABLE, columns *f, i, k*, **78 84** ; TABLES : *Nebraska*, **85** ; *Voice and Hearing School*, **87** ; *Arkansas*, **88.**
—— Photogravure of a class in, *to face*, **II, 132.**
—— —— possibly improves the organ of hearing in certain cases, **II**, 399, **7** ; *Gillespie*, **II, 85** ; *Mrs. Taylor*, **II, 85** ; *Miss McCowan*, **II, 86** ; *Clarke*, **II, 88.**
—— —— prepares certain pupils for education in ordinary schools, **II**, 812, **51.**
—— —— Selection of subjects for, **II**, 686, **36.**
—— —— Separate method for, in four schools, **II**, 400, **8** ; *Arkansas, New York, Nebraska*, Miss McCowan's *Voice and Hearing School*, **II**, 484-7, **17.**
—— —— Subjects, among the adventitiously deaf, **I**, 407, **33** ; among pupils hard-of-hearing from birth, **I**, 300, **24.**
—— —— Tests of Hearing, **II**, 395, **7** ; 402, **8, 85.**
—— —— *See titles*, Audiphone, Audiometer, Hearing.
Aurist, Examination of pupils by, not a general feature of day-schools, **II**, 799, **46.**
Available means of preventing certain marriages, **I**, 398, **29.**
Availability, Limited, of speech and speech-reading, **I**, 324, **25.**
Average cost of education, **I**, 125, **5** ; 143, **8** ; 236, **16** ; **II**, 458, **14** ; 737, **41** ; 767, **43.**
—— rate of speed for writing, finger-spelling, speech to children, and of reading to one's self, **II**, 813, **47.**

Backus, Mr. Levi S., the first deaf-mute editor of a newspaper, **I, 55.**
Backward children, [*dégénérés, arriérés*] System of instruction for, *Kinsey*, **I, 107** ; *Williams*, **I, 82.**
Barton, Miss Ellen L., On Auricular instruction. **II, 81** ; on Visible Speech, **II, 76.**
Basis of classification of methods of instruction. **II**, 385-387, **6.**
—— for education of the deaf in Great Britain, *Hutton*. **II, 122.**
—— —— —— of the congenitally deaf, **II**, 567, **26.**
—— of objections to Dr. Bell's theories, **II**, 605, **30.**
—— for testing results of education proposed, **II**, 937, **60.**
Bayard, Hon. T. F., On effects of the physical training of deaf college-students, **I**, 525, **38.**
Bebian's theory, **II**, 827, **50.**
Bede describes finger spelling, **II, 94** ; "How bishopp John cured a dumme man," **II, 156.**
Begin language-teaching, How to, **II**, 566, **26.**
Bell, Dr. Alex. Graham : [For subjects omitted below consult Index for topic desired, especially references to Part II.]
Ability and intelligence of the congenitally deaf, **II**, 589, **29.**
Articulation, *See titles*, Articulation, Oral, and Pure Oral.
Articulation and finger-spelling, **II**, 675, **35.**
Auricular instruction, **II**, 686, **36** ; 812, **51.**
Basis of classification of methods of instruction, **II**, 385, **6.**
Centralization, **II**, 762, **43.** *See this title.*
Census of 1880, etc., **II**, 356, **1** ; 598, **30.**
Census of 1890 : **Communication** to Senator Hale, **II, 197** ; **Final Form of Schedule** submitted to Hon. Robert P. Porter, **II, 203.**
Classification of the deaf, **II**, 383–388, **5 6.**
Classification as a guide to marriage, 473, **16.**
Combined system, **II**, 651, **33** ; 714, **39** ; 822, **49.** *See title.*
Is there a correlation between defects of the senses? II, 134 ; abnormal phenomena noted, 450, **13.**
Conditions of institution-life are unfavorable to practice in speech, **II**, 582, **28** ; 585, **29** ; 666, **34.**
On day-schools, **II**, 360, **2** ; 457, **13** ; 464, **14** ; 469, **15** ; 518, **24** ; 585, **29** ; 650, **43** ; 724, **40** ; 760, **43** ; 767, **43** ; 774, **44** ; 797, **45** ; **On deaf classes in the Public Schools, II, 168.**
Dalgarno's principle, **II**, 563, **25.**
Defects in three methods of instruction, 570, **27.**
Discovery as to vocal organs, **II**, 901, **57.**
Experience of, as an instructor and educator, **II**, 694, **37** ; **II, 150.**
Fallacies concerning the Deaf, II, 155.
Finger-spelling, **II**, 570, **26** ; 668, **34** ; 669, **35** ; 673, **35** ; 694, **38** ; 710, **39** ; 719, **40** ; 826, **50.**
How to teach speech to a child congenitally deaf, **II**, 888, **56.**
Heredity, **II**, 444, **11** ; 450, **13** ; 502, **19** ; 611, **30** ; 625, **31** ; 640, **32** ; 802, **46** ; 858, **53.**
Industrial instruction, **II**, 777, **44.**
Line-writing, **II**, 909, **58.**
"Lip" or Speech-reading, **II**, 568, **26** ; 585, **29** ; 705, **39** ; 836, **50.**
The Lovejoy Family, II, 197.
Marriage and intermarriage, **II**, 510-522, **20 21** ; TABLE, 818, **52.** *See these titles.*
Method of teaching language to a very young congenitally deaf child, II, 150.
Method of presenting English words to the eye of the deaf with rapidity, **II**, 813, **47.**

Bell, Dr. A. G.—*Continued:* Methods of measuring results, II, 579, **28.**

Missions for adult deaf, 721, **40.**

Open Letter to Committee of the Wisconsin Legislature, II, 69.

per capita cost of education, II, 737, **41.**

Remedial measures to check tendency to formation of a deaf variety, 457, **13**; 547, **24**; 624, **31**; 641, **32**; 784, **45.**

Semi-deaf, TABLE of, II, **131.**

Separation of instruction in written, and spoken language, II, 576, **27.**

Sign-language and signs, II, 819, **49**; 983, **16**; *see* these titles.

Statistics of Articulation-teaching, II, 380, **5**; 497, **19**; 806, **46.**

System of inspection, II, 678, **36**; 742, **41**; 998, **65.**

System of instruction, II, 570, **21**; 577, **28**; 584, **29**; 694, **38**; **150.**

Teachers and Teaching, II, 677, **36**; 754, **42**; 795, **45**; 907, **58**; 914, **59**; 933, **60.**

Teaching articulation and teaching *by* articulation, II, 922, **59.**

Summary of general recommendations, II, 998, **65.**

Views upon three broad varieties of methods of instruction, II, 570, **27.**

Visible Speech, II, 628, **31**; 868, **54**; 927, **59**; 946, **64**; *Charts*, III, —.

Visible Speech as a means of communicating articulation to deaf-mutes, 144; Visible Speech at the Belleville Convention, II, 189.

For subjects omitted above, see titles generally throughout the Index, especially references to Part II.

Bell, Mrs. A. G., II, 706, **39**; 881, **55**; 984, **65.**

—— Prof. A. Melville, Author of Line-writing, II, 910, **58**; Author of Visible Speech, II, 868-871, **54**; Author of World-English, II, 964, **62.**

Bell, Ringing of a, to test hearing, II, 375-7, **7.**

Beneficent effect of efforts in favor of oral teaching, I, 487, **35.**

Benevolence, Private, as affected by State-aid, I, 366, **28**; II, 740, **41.**

Bequests and legacies to American institutions, I, 366, **28.**

Bertha, Case of, Miss Fuller's pupil, II, **120.**

Berthier on ideas of uninstructed deaf-mutes, I, **182.**

Best form of external organization, I, 115, **4.**

—— pay for best results, II, 898, **57**; not practicable, I, 265, **20.**

—— results, To secure, requires reorganization of both sign-, and oral schools, *G. O. Fay*, I, **80.**

—— system, The, *Crouter*, I, **78.**

—— —— for a five years' course, II, 813, **47.**

Bicycler, deaf, Views of an orally instructed, I, 171, **11.**

Billiard-ball illustration, II, 570, **27.**

Binner, Mr. Paul, on auricular instruction, II, **82**; on hereditary deaf-mutism, II, **98**; on the pure oral method in America, II, **116**; on Visible Speech, II, **76.**

Biological laws apply to man and brute alike, *Brewer*, II, 625, **31**; II, **103.**

Bird, Mr. W. L. (*portrait*), Poem: The ocean, I, **90.**

Birth, Statistics of period of, for married deaf-mutes, by decades, II, 510, **20.**

Black, Miss A. M., on auricular instruction, II, **81**; on intermarriages, II, **97**; on method to be pursued with a beginner in speech, II, **116**; on Visible Speech, II, **76.**

Black race in America in relation to education I, 501, **36.**

Blackboard conversation described, II, **151.**

Blake, Dr. C. J., Otologist, on auricular training, II, **140.**

Blank form for Articulation-statistics, II, **74.**

Blind, Acquisition of foreign languages by the, II, 914, **61.**

—— Census returns of, in U. S., II, **134.**

—— deaf-mutes, II, 449, **12**, **134.**

—— —— Idiotic, II, **134.**

—— —— Insane, II, **134.**

—— Telephone-work, an avenue of employment of the, II, 783, **45.**

Boarding of deaf children by parents, II, 537, **23.**

—— -out system, preferable to the association-system, II, 798, **46.**

—— schools, Small oral, *Miss E. Garrett*, II, 48, **117.**

—— —— Superiority of, *Gallaudet*, I, 249, **18**; *controverted*, *see* Day-Schools.

Boards of Charity and Boards of Education, *Gallaudet*, I, 110, **4.**

—— of trustees should be composed in part of deaf-mutes, *Emery*, II, **115.**

Bolling, Col. W., I, **54.**

Boot and Shoe fund, Workings of, II, 774, **44.**

Borie, Urbain, deaf poet, I, **92.**

Boston Day-schools, All children well dressed in, II, 774, **44.**

—— —— arrange for technical training in the Institute of Technology, II, 468, **15.**

—— —— Visible Speech in, II, **145.**

Bowditch, Dr. H. P., On the possibility of a deaf variety, II, **102.**

Boy, A, who heard only through the audiphone, II, 689, **37.**

—— Case of a bright, sent to school for feeble-minded, *Williams*, I, **83.**

—— **How a little, six years old, learned English, II, 694-702, 37-39.**

Braidwood, Lines by ["C. S."], a pupil of, on seeing Garrick act, I, **91.**

Braidwoods, The, founders of [first] institution for instruction of deaf-mutes, I, **54.**

Breaking the line of intermarriages, Effect of, II, 505, **19.**

Breeding, Laws of, II, 625, **31**; *Bowditch*, II, **102**; *Brewer*, II, **102**; *Brooks*, II, **104.**

Brewer, Prof. W. H., Communication on the possibility of a deaf variety, II, **102**; Quotation from, II, 625, **31.**

Bright pupils transferred from oral schools to American Asylum, *Williams*, I, **83.**

Bridgman, Laura, Peculiar phenomena in case of, *H. P. Peet*, II, **175**; **183**; Poem (*portrait*), I, **90.**

Brotherhood of St. Gabriel, *Gallaudet*, I, **109.**

Brown, Dr. J. G., On auricular instruction, II, **81**; on best method of instruction, II, **116**; on intermarriages in Western Pennsylvania, II, **97**; on Visible Speech, II, **5.**

Brown, The, family of Henniker, II, 454, **13**; *Chart*, III, in "Ancestry of the Deaf."

Brooks, Mrs. Frances, Letter from, which led to establishment of the first infant school for the deaf, **II, 121.**

—— **Prof. W. K.,** Communication **on possibility of a deaf variety, II, 104.**

British Government should require teachers to be trained, II, 679, **36.**

"Bull's eye" illustration, **II,** 888, **56.**

Bulwer, John, author of Philocophus, etc., **II, 157.**

Burden on the people increased, How far, **II,** 528, **22.**

Burke, Sister Mary Ann, on auricular instruction, **II, 80;** "1 pupil out of 445 has deaf parents," **II, 95;** on Visible Speech, **II, 75.**

Burnet, Mr. J. R., deaf author and poet: "The Battle of Trenton," **I, 89;** On a singular observation by Dr. Itard, **II, 185.**

"Burying of the hatchet" in America, *Gallaudet*, **I,** 140, **7;** *Bell*, **II,** 592, **30.**

California Convention: Articulation, **I,** 139, **7;** 141, **7; II,** 673, **36;** Consensus of opinion, **I,** 140, **7; II,** 591, **29.**

Campbell, Dr. F. J., on the dormitory system, **II,** 980, **63;** on separate institutions for girls and boys, **II,** 539, **23;** Questions by, **I,** 13,233; 13,237; 13,278; 13,471; 13,493. **II,** 21,375; 21,381; 21,397; 21,451; 21,496; 21,498; 21,512; 21,538; 21,551; 21,639; 21,849; 21,863; 21,872; 21,899; 21,901; 21,939; 21,968; 21,970.

Canada, Auricular instruction in, **II, 84;** Methods of instruction in, 578, **28; 122;** Visible Speech in, **77.**

Can all the deaf succeed in acquiring speech and speech-reading? *Gallaudet*, **I,** 360, **27;** *Williams*, **86;** *Kinsey*, **108;** *Bell*, **II,** 377, **4.**

Can older deaf pupils acquire satisfactory speech? **II,** 578, **28.**

Capacity, Mental, of the Congenitally deaf, **II,** 588, **29.**

Carelessness of census-enumerators, *H. P. Peet*, **I, 44.**

Card-racks and cards, Employment of, **II, 150.**

Carlbom, F., a deaf poet, **I, 92.**

Carlin, John, deaf-mute poet and artist (*portrait*), **II, 87; "To the Fire-Flies," II, 87.**

Case of Dr. Bell's pupil taught by the Dalgarno method, **II,** 694-702, **37-39.**

—— —— Miss Gordon's pupil exhibited before the National Academy of Sciences, **I,** 149, **8.**

Cases of pupils transferred from oral schools to the Hartford Institution, **I, 83.**

—— of success under both methods, **I,** 461, **33.**

Catarrhal disease, a cause of congenital deafness, *Jenkins*, **II, 98.**

Cats, Deafness in blue-eyed, white, **II,** 448, **12.**

Causes of deafness, *see titles* Consanguinity, Intermarriage of deaf with the deaf, and Heredity.

—— —— —— as compiled in census from returns of 9,209 cases, **I, 65; II,** 487, **17, 18; II, 127.**

—— —— —— Improbable and vague, in many cases, **II,** 492, **18.**

—— —— —— Survey of, *H. P. Peet*, **I, 44;** *E. A. Fay*, **62-65.**

Cautions to the deaf in regard to marriages, *Gallaudet*, **I,** 392, **29;** *Fay*, **64;** *Bell*, **II, 16.**

Celibacy advised, *Seiler*, **II, 95;** *M. Hammond*, **II, 99.**

Census Returns for 1830, 1840, 1850, *H. P. Peet*, **I, 43.**

—— —— —— **1850, 1860, 1870,** *E. A. Fay*, **I, 49;** Comparative table, **I, 51.**

—— —— —— **1870,** Mass. State Board of Charities, 9th Report: Causes of error, etc., **I, 49.**

—— —— —— **1880,** Accuracy of, *Gallaudet*, **I,** 105, **3; III, 207;** *Bell*, **II,** 355, **1;** 808, **47;** *Wines*, **II,** 357, **1; III, 212.**

—— —— —— Analysis of Returns for deaf-mutes, **II,** 487, **17; 127;** By States, etc., **I, 51.**

—— —— —— Causes of deafness, tabulated, **II,** 487-8, **17-18; 127.**

—— —— —— Exhibit of returns for New-England, **II, 69.**

—— —— —— Deaf children of school-age, **II,** 359, **2.**

—— —— —— Deaf-mutes returned incorrectly as idiotic, *Bell*, **II,** 479, **16;** *See* **I, 49.**

—— —— —— Duplications, *E. A. Fay*, **I, 49;** *Gallaudet*, **I,** 105, **3; III, 207;** *Bell*, **II,** 357, **1;** *Wines*, **II,** 357, **1; III, 212;** *See Mass. Report*, **II, 49.**

—— —— —— Massachusetts, for 1880 and 1885, **III, 208, 213;** *Tables*, **214.**

—— —— —— Number of deaf-mutes, **II,** 357, **1;** 487, **17;** by States, *Table*, **I, 51;** *Analytical Table*, **II, 17; 127.**

—— —— Younger deaf-mutes are not fully enumerated, **II,** 411, **9; I, 47; 49.**

—— Federal and State, when and how often taken, **II,** 978, **3.**

—— of **1830,** the first to enumerate the deaf and dumb, **II,** 807, **46.**

—— questions, Form of, **II,** 383, **6;** 976, **63.**

—— —— **Schedule proposed, II, 201; 203.**

—— Returns afford a clue to deaf children of deaf parents, **II,** 530, **22.**

—— —— Important improvement in, **II,** 974-7, **63.**

—— —— should be verified by competent observers, **II,** 809, **47.**

—— of **1890,** *Bell*, **II, 197; 203;** *Gallaudet* and others, **II, 201.**

Certain families exhibit tendency to deafness, *Gallaudet*, **I,** 253, **19;** *H. P. Peet*, **44;** *Fay*, **63.**

Certificated teachers, Government grants only to, **II,** 753, **42.**

—— —— Field for, of Articulation, **II,** 917, **59.**

Certificates, not degrees, given by State-schools, **I,** 386, **29.**

—— of poverty not usually required for free admission to schools, **I,** 249, **18.**

"Centralisation" promoted by National and State governments, **II,** 359, **2;** Effect of, **II, 70;** described, **II, 69;** fails to reach many children, **II,** 359, **2;** 702, **43;** becomes intolerant, **II,** 366, **3.**

Cerebro-spinal meningitis, Epidemics of, and their effect upon statistics, **II,** 419, **9;** 420, **10.**

Chance, Small, of a hearing child in fifth generation of deaf parentage, **II,** 625-7, **31.**

Change of views regarding instruction, *Pres. Gallaudet*, **I,** 308, **24;** *Dr. Bell*, **II,** 691, **38.**

Characteristics of a race of deaf-mutes, *H. P. Peet*, **I, 176;** of uneducated deaf-mutes, *Fay*, **I, 66.**

Characteristics, Inherited, defined, *Brooks*, II, 104.
—— tend to become inherited, *Hyatt*, II, 102.
Charges against Manual-method schools, I, 82.
Charity, Boards of, Functions of, I, 110, 4.
—— in the education of the deaf, II, 740, 41.
—— promoted by day-schools, II, 774, 44.
—— -schools, an improper designation, I, 476, 34.
Châtelain, S. B., a deaf poet, I, 92.
Chemist, Deaf, [Geo. T. Dougherty], I, 240, 17.
Chicago Board of Education, Discussion before, II, 168.
Chief elements producing deaf-mute children, II, 518, 24.
Child four years old, Experiment with, II, 813, 48; Miss Fuller's pupil, Bertha, II, 120.
—— Deaf, should learn a language in two years, II, 833, 50.
Children are wilfully deprived of the power of articulation, II, 825, 50.
—— Deaf, of deaf parents, II, 520-535, 22, 23; *Tables*, II, 848, 52; Revised Table, III, —.
Children's books are not adapted to deaf children, *G. O. Fay*, I, 79.
Chilmark, Martha's Vineyard, Deaf-mute population of, II, 858, 53. *See* III, Ancestry of the Deaf.
Circular of inquiries to heads of American schools, *Bell*, II, 74.
Cities and Villages, Wisconsin law relating to schools in, II, 73.
Civilization, Progress of, defined, *E. E. Hale*, II, 138.
Clannish association of the deaf, I, 251, 18.
Clanship, Papers promoting, II, 522, 20.
Claims, Three, for the combined method, *Williams*, I, 85.
Clarke, Mr. F. D., II, 487, 17; co-inventor of the audiometer, II, 403, 8; Communication on Auricular Instruction, II, 88; Extracts from report of, on Tests of Hearing, II, 140.
—— and others, Report of Committee on Auricular Instruction, II, 139.
Clarke Institution, Account of, I, 58.
—— —— discountenances intermarriage, *Hubbard*, II, 166.
—— —— Founding of, II, 881, 55.
—— —— has received private aid, II, 740, 41.
—— —— No intermarriages of pupils with pupils of the institution, II, 841, 51.
—— —— Statistics of marriages from, II, 526, 21.
—— —— Statistics and names, II, 95.
Classification of the deaf, *Dr. Bell*, II, 383-388, 5-6; *Crouter*, I, 79; *E. A. Fay*, I, 60; *Gallaudet*, I, 417, 30; 100.
—— of the congenitally deaf, *Brooks*, II, 104.
—— as a guide to marriage, II, 173, 16.
—— of methods of instruction proposed by *Dr. Bell*, II, 385-8, 6.
—— of signs, II, 560, 25; only the fourth class is objectionable, II, 570, 27.
Class-rooms, Separate, I, 127, 6.
Cleary, Mr. E. P., on auricular instruction, II, 83; on intermarriage of the deaf, II, 100; on Visible Speech, II, 77.
Clerc, Laurent, II, 510, 23.
Cleveland, Grover, President of the United States, Letter from, I, 353, 27.
Climate, Influence of, *H. P. Peet*, II, 44.
Clothing, Expenses of, how provided for, II, 139, 41.
Clue, A, to those able to use speech, II, 489, 18.
Cogswell, Alice, Dr. T. H. Gallaudet's pupil, I, 54.
Collateral defects, II, 867, 54; 134.
College, National Deaf-Mute:
Account of, I, 211, 14; 57.
Bowling Alley, I, 524, 38.
Course of Study, I, 236, 16.
Diplomas, I, 384, 29.
Entrance-Examinations, I, 448, 32.
Faculty, I, 513, 37; 531, 39.
Gymnasium for physical culture, I, 389, 29; Effect of gymnasium, bowling, and swimming, I, 525, 38.
Lectures, I, 452, 32.
Occupations of graduates, I, 240, 17.
Organization, I, 101, 3; 119-123, 5.
Relation of President of U. S. to, I, 119-122, 5.
Routine of daily duties, I, 503, 37.
Sign-language little used in class-rooms, I, 237, 16.
Students from United Kingdom in, I, 239, 17.
See Columbia Institution.
Columbia Institution, History of, I, 57.
—— —— Colored pupils, Status of, I, 119, 12.
—— —— Land belonging to, I, 275, 21.
—— —— Oral instruction in, I, 333, 26; 492, 31.
—— —— *See* College, National Deaf-Mute.
Co-education with hearing children, II, 467, 14.
—— Complete, impracticable, II, 458, 14; 653, 33.
—— Objections to, *Goodman*, II, 172.
—— possible in exceptional cases, II, 71.
—— resulted in failure in Europe, *Gillett*, II, 170.
Colony of deaf-mutes, *White*, II, 100; *Flournoy*, 126.
Combined Method, Definition of, *E. A. Fay*, I, 59; 76.
Combined System, Ambiguity of, *Bell*, II, 573, 27.
—— —— Always includes sign-language, II, 714, 39.
—— —— As applied to Philadelphia Institution, *Bell*, II, 374, 4; *Crouter*, 106; *Gallaudet*, I, 139, 7; 141, 8; 349, 26; III, 208.
—— —— as defined by *Dr. E. A. Fay*, I, 59; 76.
—— —— as understood by *Dr. Bell*, II, 654, 33; 718, 40.
—— —— as understood by the Commissioners, II, 715, 40.
—— —— Comparative value of, *Gallaudet*, I, 427, 31.
—— —— Forms of, *Gallaudet*, I, 299, 24; 474, 34; 502, 36; 104.
—— —— Exposition of, *Gallaudet*, I, 291, 23; III, 208.
—— —— in New England, includes oral schools, *Gallaudet*, I, 108.
—— —— including pure oral schools, favored by generality of well-educated deaf-mutes in America, *Gallaudet*, I, 474, 34.
—— —— No place for, in a natural classification, *Bell*, II, 385, 6.
—— —— schools, Pupils think in sign language in, *Bell*, II, 825, 45.
—— —— The True, Exposition of, *Crouter*, II, 76.
—— —— Used in different senses in America, *Bell*, II, 573, 27.
—— —— Vague and unsatisfactory designation, *Bell*, II, 374, 4.
—— —— schools, Written conversation with young pupils in, impracticable, *Bell*, II, 833, 50.
—— —— and Aural, Meaning of, *Bell*, II, 824, 49.
Commencing with oral language impedes the progress of the congenitally deaf, II, 567, 23.

Comments on Dr. Bell's Evidence, *Gallaudet*, **III, 207.**
—— on Pres. Gallaudet's Evidence, *Wines*, **III, 212.**
—— on Rev. F. W. Wines' Reply, *Gallaudet*, **III, 213.**
Common cause, A, for certain defects, **II**, 450, **12.**
—— **error, A,** in regard to children of the congenitally deaf, **II**, 603, **30.**
Commissioners of Public Charities in Illinois, Views of, *Wines*, **II, 168.**
Committee on Auricular instruction, **II**, 487, **17** ; **Report, II, 130.**
—— on Improvement of Census Schedules, **II**, 975, **63** ; **Report, II, 201.**
—— on Registration of School-Statistics, **Report, I, 52.**
Communication, Means of, taught to deaf children by three systems, **II**, 579, **28.**
—— No restriction should be placed upon, between deaf, and hearing children, **II**, 668, **34.**
—— of the generality of the deaf with outer world, by speech or by writing? **I**, 441, **32.**
—— Possible means of, **I, 102.**
Companions, Advantage of hearing, for deaf children, **II**, 585, **29.**
Comparative industry, thrift, etc., of deaf-mutes and others, **I**, 462, **33.**
Comparison between deaf, and hearing children, **II**, 834, **50.**
—— between those born deaf and those born not deaf, **I**, 435, **32.**
—— between the Visible Speech and "German" methods of teaching articulation, **II, 145.**
—— of census-returns and school-attendance, *H. P. Peet*, **I, 48.**
—— of congenitally and non-congenitally deaf population (Diagram No. 1), *to face*, **II, 9.**
—— of congenitally deaf population with population at large (Diagram No. 3), *to face*, **II, 10.**
—— of methods of instruction, *G. O. Fay*, **I**, 201, **13** ; **79.**
—— of oral, and sign systems, **II**, 559, **24.**
—— of results, **I**, 172, **11** ; 341, **26** ; **104** ; with same pupil under different methods, **I, 83.**
—— of results in written language, the primary test for all schools, **II**, 748, **42.**
Competency of non-specialists to pass upon the mental state of deaf children denied, **II**, 482, **17.**
—— of teachers decided by principals, **II**, 702, **45.**
Competent teachers, Scarcity of, **II**, 677, **36.**
—— —— of Visible Speech, **II**, 890, **57.**
Competition needed by the State-institutions, **II**, 747, **42.**
Complete statistics of marriages and offspring from records of Georgia institution, **II**, 529, **22.**
Composition of California Convention, I, 140, **7.**
Compositions by same pupils under the oral, and manual methods, *Williams*, **I, 84.**
—— by backward or dull children, **I, 85.**
—— by young child, **II, 154.**
Comprehension precedes expression, **II**, 813, **47.**
Comprehensive education in its Philosophy and Practice, *G. O. Fay*, **I, 79.**
Compulsory attendance, I, 346, **26** ; **II**, 362, **3** ; **II**, 763, **43** ; and regulations as to distance, **II**, 771, **44.**
—— reading recommended, **II**, 813, **48.**
Concurrent speech-reading and "touch-spelling" practicable, **II**, 694, **38.**
Condensed history of aural instruction, *Gillespie*, **II, 84.**
Condition, Mental, of the deaf before instruction, **II**, 827, **50** ; *H. P. Peet*, **I, 69** ; *Fay*, **I, 66.**
—— of the deaf after leaving school, **I**, 246, **18.**
—— Physical, of deaf-mutes, **I**, 376, **28.**
Conditions producing deaf-mutes are artificial, **II**, 518, **24.**
—— that will result in formation of a deaf variety, **II**, 502, **19.**
—— of institution-life unfavorable to use of spoken language, **II**, 464, **14.**
Conferences of Principals of institutions, **I**, 266, **20.**
—— —— When and where held, **I, 110.**
—— —— Action of Washington Conference, 1868, on Articulation, **I**, 133, **6** ; **59.**
—— —— Action of Jackson, Miss., [*Faribault, Minn.?*] Conference on Statistical Forms, **II**, 599, **30** ; Report of Committee on School-Statistics, **I, 52** ; Report of Committee [appointed by the Jackson, Miss., Conference] on Recommendations for the Census of 1890, **II, 201.**
Congenital deafness, Causes of, **II**, 411, **11.**
—— —— Classification of, *Brooks*, **II, 104.**
—— —— Difference in diagrams of, explained, **II**, 428, **10.**
—— —— Element of uncertainty as to, **II**, 854, **52.**
—— —— not always distinguishable from non-congenital, **II**, 475, **16** ; a misleading distinction, *Fay*, **I, 62.**
—— deaf-mutes, increasing at a greater rate than general population, **II**, 431, **10** ; 435, **11.**
Congenitally deaf, The : as a class lose ground because they do not know language, **II**, 831, **50.**
—— —— Natural capacity of, **II**, 588, **29.**
—— —— use pantomime, **II**, 617, **49.**
—— —— Eye sight of, **II**, 837, **50.**
—— —— Proportion of, *Gallaudet*, **I**, 327, **27** ; *Fay*, **I, 61.**
Connor, Mr. W. O., on auricular instruction, **II, 78** ; on intermarriage, with full returns from Georgia, **93–94** ; on speech, **107** ; on Visible Speech, **75.**
Consanguineous marriages as a cause of deafness, *Fay*, **I, 64** ; *Bell*, **II**, 447, **12.**
—— —— in Martha's Vineyard, **II**, 858, **53.**
—— —— Statistics of 10 *c. m.* out of 185 families of deaf-mutes in Georgia, **II**, *Table IV*, **94.**
—— —— Statistics of deaf children from 25 families of hearing parents in American Asylum, **II, 89.**
—— —— Table of statistics from Illinois, **II, 93.**
—— —— Statistics from 35 British institutions, **II**, 147, **12.**
Conscientousness requires that speech be taught to every deaf child, **II**, 583, **28.**
Consonants, Intelligibility of speech depends upon, **II**, 910, **58.**
Constitutional provision for universal education in certain States, **II**, 732, **41.**
Context, the key to speech-reading in English, **II**, 585, **29** ; **157.**
Contrel of day-schools in Wisconsin, **II, 71.**
Convention, Milan ; *Ackers*, **I**, 522, **38** ; not truly representative, *Gallaudet*, **I**, 520, **38.**
—— *President Gallaudet's* **paper** on, **I, 105.**
Conventions of educators of the deaf, advisable, **II**, 972, **63.**
—— Free discussion in American, **II**, 592, **30.**
—— Nature of, **I**, 266, **20** ; When and where held, **I, 110.**
Minute adopted by California Convention, **I, 3.**
—— **Resolutions of California Convention concerning oral instruction, I**, 141, **7** ; *Int. Record of Charities and Correction*, **I**, 139, **7.**

Convention, Third of Articulation-teachers [1884], II, 936, 60; Miss Worcester's Paper, 192.
Conventions of deaf-mutes, I, 273, 21.
— of orally-taught deaf, use gestures, I, 464, 33.
Conversation in dreams of the deaf, II, 828, 50.
— Mode of, among orally-taught pupils, I, 317, 25.
— with a deaf boy six years old, II, 702, 39, 151.
— in writing, impracticable with young pupils in "combined" schools, II, 833, 50.
— Uncertainty and embarrassment in, depending upon speech-reading, *Gallaudet*, I, 102.
Conversion of French delegates at Milan to the oral method, 403, 30.
Co-operation of parents and teacher, II, 724, 40.
Cope, Prof. E. D., Communication on the possibility of the formation of a deaf variety and the conditions necessary to establish it, II, 101.
Corn, Fritz Müller's experiment with, *Brooks*, II, 105.
Corporate form of Organization, *Gallaudet*, I, 112, 4; 123, 5.
— shows best results, 115, 4.
Correlation between defects of the senses, II, 449, 12; Dr. Bell's paper, from *Science*, II, 134.
Cost of education, *per capita*, I, 141, 8; 344, 26; in Government-schools at Annapolis and West Point, 236, 16; in Paris, 141, 8; 344, 26; II, 458, 14; 737, 41; of deaf children of deaf parents, II, 531, 22.
— — how returned to the State, I, 248, 18.
— — in a system of day-schools, II, 169.
— of buildings and grounds, I, 125, 5.
Cottage-system, II, 798, 46; II, 971, 62.
Country districts, Day-schools, Advantages in, *Bell*, II, 71.
Courses of study in Am. Schools, *Gallaudet*, I, 173, 11.
Cousins, Marriage of, I, 254, 19.
— Deaf-mute children of, II, 417, 12: *See also* Marriages, Consanguineous.
Cramer, Mrs. M. A. M., a deaf writer and poet, I, 93.
Creator, Idea of, in uninstructed deaf, I, 182.
Cretinism allied to deaf-dumbness, I, 43.
Crime, A, not to try to teach deaf children to speak, II, 582, 29.
Criticism upon conclusions based upon incomplete data answered, II, 530, 22.
Crouter, Mr. A. L. E., on auricular instruction, II, 78; method of instruction, II, 705, 39; oral instruction, II, 661, 664, 34; intermarriages, II, 106, 91; Visible Speech, II, 75.
— Views of, expressed at California Convention, *Gallaudet*, I, 149, 7; III, 208.
— The True Combined System, I, 76.
Crude signs or *any* means of communication allowable between deaf, and hearing children, II, 673, 35.
Cruel restrictions, *Gallaudet*, I, 165, 9; 205, 14; *Miss Fuller*, II, 97.
Cultivation of habit of reading novels, plays, and children's story-books, a rational means of gaining a knowledge of language, II, 813, 48.
Currier, Mr. E. H., II, 487, 17; Communication on Auricular Instruction, II, 87; inventor of conico-cylindrical conversation-tubes, II, 400, 8.
Curve, Symmetrical, formed by the congenitally deaf, in diagram No. 1, II, 413, 9.

Dactylology, Advantages of, in presenting the English language to the deaf, *Bell*, II, 570, 26; 675, 35; 668, 34; 669, 35; 673, 35; 694, 38; 710, 39; 719, 40; 826, 50.
— Advantages to hearing-people, *Denison*, I, 98; Origin and utility of, *Gordon* I, 94. *See titles*, Finger-spelling, Manual Alphabet.
Dalby, Sir William, Arrested development a leading cause, II, 442, 11.
Dalgarno, George, II, 563, 25; II, 694, 37.
— — Aphorisms from, II, 702, 39.
— — Child taught on system of, by *Dr. Bell*, II, 694-702, 38, 39.
— — "Touch" alphabet of, II, 694, 38; II, 815, 48; 152.
Darwin, Dr. George, Researches in Consanguinity, II, 447, 12.
Davis, J. C., a deaf artist: engraver on wood, II, 138.
Day-schools, Advantages of, II, 464, 14; 463, 15; 527, 21; 649, 33; 724, 40; 770, 43; 780, 44; 784, 45; 830, 50; 70.
— and boarding schools, *Fay*, I, 69.
— American sentiment is against extension of, *Gallaudet*, I, 192, 12.
— Discrimination should not be made against, II, 770, 43.
— Distinct classes of, II, 650, 33.
— Exterior organization of, *Gallaudet*, I, 112, 4.
— Gymnasium for physical exercise in, II, 727, 40.
— Medical supervision, II, 790, 46.
— Technical training, II, 468, 15.
— tend to become institutions, II, 797, 46.
— occupy a field not open to institutions, II, 469, 15.
— preferable to residential schools, II, 649, 33; 760, 43.
— Plea for, *Emery*, II, 108.
— Public, Deaf classes in, Discussion, II, 168-172.
— Size of, II, 457, 13; 464, 14; 467, 15; 528, 21.
— Statistics of, *see* tables, I, 72; II, 128.
— Stimulate the acquisition of speech, II, 585, 29.
— Summary of advantages, *Emery*, II, 110.
— Support, II, 767, 43.
— in Wisconsin, II, 360, 2; 767, 43; 69; Extracts from laws, 116.
"Day-dreams of the Deaf," W. H. Simpson's, Extracts from, I, 92.
Deaf, Deaf-mute, Deaf and Dumb: *See* special title of topic desired relating to this class.
Deafness, Causes of:
Arrested development, II, 422, 11.
Catarrh, *Jenkins*, II, 98.
Cerebro-spinal meningitis, II, 416, 9.
Consanguinity of parents, II, 446, 12.
Direct and indirect, *Fay*, I, 62-65.
Hereditary abnormality in nervous system, II, 450, 13; hereditary predisposition, 441, 11.
Maternal impressions, II, 443, 11.
Scarlet fever, II, 419, 10.
Syphilis, II, 803, 46.
The most frequent, II, 802, 46.
Table of, from Census of 1880, II, 17, 18.
Uselessness of the classification into "congenital" and "non-congenital" in determining adventitious deafness, *Fay*, I, 62.

Deafness certainly runs in families, *H. P. Peet*, I, **44.**

— Degrees in, from slight to total, II, 392, **7.** *See* Audiometer.

— in blue-eyed, white cats, II, 148, **12.**

— is no bar to physical labor, II, **70.**

— is the only defect in deaf mutes, II, 392, **7.**

Deaf Children in institutions, Number of, II, 359, **2**; 761, **43**; **127.**

Deaf Children of deaf parents, II, 529, 530, 531, **22**; 611, **30**; *Tables*, 848, **52**; *Revised Tables*, III, —; Exhibit to Q. 21,531, II, **143.**

— — — — — Earliest instance of, II, 438, **11.**

— — — — — marry deaf-mutes, II, 507, **20.**

— — — of school-age, with, and without instruction, II, 359, **2**; 761, **43.**

— — Thirty, out of 73, from 11 families in which parents are not related, *Williams*, II, **89.**

— dumb and blind, in schools for the deaf, I, 281, **22**; *See* Dr. Bell's paper on correlated defects, II, **134.**

— **Classes in the public schools**, II, 812, **47**; **168.**

— families may be traced through Census-returns back to 1830, II, 857, **53.**

— habit due largely to neglect, II, **85.**

—, otherwise defective, I, **46**; II, **134.**

— pupils can attend technical schools, II, 844, **51.**

— race, How to make a, II, 547, **24**; **Scientific Testimony**, II, **101**; Characteristics of, *H. P. Peet*, II, **176.** *See* Deaf-mute Variety.

— relatives, as a basis of classification, II, 473, **16.**

Deaf-mutes, by Prof. E. A. Fay, Ph. D., I, **60-71.**

— — Class of, not transmitting deafness, II, 473, **16.**

— — : Classification into congenital and non-congenital misleading in studying heredity, I, **62.**

— — : Congenital and Non-congenital, Diagrams of, *facing*, II, 409, **8**; 416, **9.**

— — combined with general population, diagram *to face*, II, **10.**

— — in various countries, I, 356, **27.**

— — nearly all marry deaf-mutes, II, 507, **20.**

— — on governing bodies of institutions, II, 847, **51**; *Emery*, II, **115.**

— — Proportion of, greater in Germany than in U. S., *Williams*, II, **90.**

— — returned incorrectly as idiotic, II, 479, **16.**

— — self-supporting as a class, II, 471, **15.**

Deaf-mute Variety, Conditions requisite to produce, II, 502, **19**; 547, **24**; Preventive measures, II, 457, **13**; Quotations from Dr. Bell's Memoir presented to the National Academy of Sciences, II, 409, **9**; 411, **9**; 416, **9**; 431, **10**; 435, **10**; 450, **13**; 458, **14**; 510, **20**; 520, **22**; 856, **53.** **Scientific testimony upon possibility of**, II, **101-106.** Tendency to formation of, II, 457, **13.** Tables of deaf descendants from deaf ancestors, II, 848, **52**; *Revised*, III, —.

Deaf-mutisms, Examples of, I, **66.**

Death, Ideas of, *H. P. Peet*, II, **181.**

Decades, Birth of 607 deaf children of deaf parents grouped by, II, 531, **22.** *Revised Table*, III, —.

Decentralisation, begun, II, 360, **2**; 363, **3.**

— Desirability of, II, 548, **24.**

— Limitations of, II, 784, **45.**

Defect in deaf children is one-sided, II, 669, **35.**

Defects of the combined method, *Crouter*, I, **76.**

Defects of senses, Correlation between, II, 449, **12**; Dr. *Bell's* **Paper**, II, **134.**

Definition of methods, *Fay*, I, **59.**

Degeneracy in organs of hearing in Salamanders, *Cope*, II, **102.**

Delirium, Experience of deaf person in, I, **186.**

Denison, Mr. James, on auricular instruction and on Maloney's "otaphone," II, **72**; on Visible Speech, II, **75**; II, **79**; **The manual alphabet as a part of the public-school course**, II, **9.**

Dental transmission, *see* Audiphone.

Denominational, and Private Schools, Significance of, *Gallaudet*, I, 131, **6**; III, **208**; *Bell*, II, 366, **3**; 371, **4**; Statistics of, I, 130, **6**, **73**; B, **74**; II, **124, 129.**

Deusing, Anthony, II, **185.**

Diacritical Marks: **Paper** by Miss Worcester, II, **192**; *Dr. Brown*, II, 76; *Miss Black*, II, 76; *Miss Mary S. Garrett*, II, **77**; *Dr. Williams*, II, **75.**

Diagrams: Analysis of 22,472 cases of deaf-mutes, *faces* II, **9.** Comparison of congenitally and non-congenitally deaf, *faces* II, **8**; Comparison of deaf, and general population, *faces* II, **10**; Visible Speech, III, —.

Difference between institution, and census returns, II, 431, **10.**

— The point of, between Dr. Bell and the pure oralists, II, 669, 675, **35**; 694, **37.**

Didascolocophus, II, 563, **26.**

Difficulties in the way of early cases of intermarriage, II, 523, **21.**

Difficulty of introducing Visible Speech considered, II, **897**; **57.**

— of procuring competent teachers, II, 677, **36.**

Digby, Sir Kenelm, Case of loss of speech through disuse, II, **176.**

Dinner-bell *vs.* school-bell, II, 395, **7.**

Directions to parents of deaf children, *Miss Mary S. Garrett*, II, **119.**

Disagreeable tone of voice, Correction of, II, 901, **57.**

Discovery, Dr. Bell's, as to vocal organs, II, 901, **57.**

Discrimination against day-schools should not be made by the State, II, 770, **43.**

Diseases causing deafness, Statistics of, Wines, II, 488, **18**; **127.**

— and accidents causing deafness, *Fay*, I, **65.**

Disposition to deafness in certain families, *Gallaudet*, I, 253, **19.**

Disputed questions discussed amicably in American conventions, II, 592, **30.**

Dissatisfaction with institutions, II, 365-7, **3**; 371, **4.**

— with oral schools, I, 311, **24**; **84.**

Distinction between using signs in teaching and in lecturing, I, 205, **14.**

Diversity of methods, Effect of, II, 365, **3.**

Division of methods according to language of communication, II, 718, **40.**

Dobyns, Mr. J. R., on auricular instruction, II, **79**; intermarriage, II, **95**; size of classes, II, **107.** Visible Speech, II, **75.**

Doctor, Notion concerning, II, **181.**

Dogs, Newfoundland, formerly mostly spotted, *Brewer*, II, **102.**

Do orally-taught pupils use speech in adult life? II, 706, **39.**

Do principals generally discourage intermarriage? II, 519, **24.**

Dormitory plan is subversive of family relation, II, 971, **65.**

Doyle, Mr. T. S., on auricular instruction, **II, 78**; intermarriage, **II, 92**; system of instruction, **II, 106**; Visible Speech, **II, 75.**

Double-headed system of internal organization, I, 126, **5.**

Douglass, Hon. Fred., Lines to, **I, 92.**

Dramatic signs, II, 560, **25.**

Draper, Prof., A. G., Poem by, I, 211, **18**; **88.**

Dreaming in spoken language, II, 952, **61**; in Visible Speech, II, 953, **61**; on fingers in "combined" schools, II, 825, **49.**

Dull pupils under different systems, *Williams*, **I, 85.**

Dumb, an objectionable term, *Fay*, **I, 60.**

Dumbness, Fallacies concerning, II, 155.

—— due to neglect, **II, 164.**

Duplications in census returns of 1880, inconsiderable, II, 357, I; **III, 211.**

Duty of instructors to advise against unsuitable marriages, *Gallaudet*, I, 398, **29.**

—— of the State to the deaf, I, 249, **18**; **II, 168.**

—— requires that all deaf-mutes be taught speech, II, 583, **28.**

Dwarfs, II, 450, **13.**

Earlier stages of instruction, Reliance upon written language in, II, 572, **27.**

—— teachers, Views of, upon intermarriage of the deaf, II, 541, **23.**

Earliest effort to teach deaf-mutes in the United States, **I, 54.**

—— specimen of poetry by the deaf [printed in London newspapers and magazines about the end of the year 1768 over the initials "C. S."], **I, 91.**

Eaton, Hon. John, Views of, on early education of deaf children, *Emery*, **II, 108.**

Economy and Parsimony, *Gallaudet*, **I, 104.**

Edison, Mr. T. A., Efforts of, to invent an aid to hearing, II, 155, **9.**

Education of deaf-mutes, Early, advisable, **II, 70.**

—— —— —— —— Average *per capita* cost, I, 141, **8**; 344, **26**; compared with Annapolis and West Point, 236, **16**; in Paris, 141, **8**; 344, **26**; in U. S., II, 458, **14**; 737, **41**; of deaf children of deaf parents, II, 531, **22**; estimated for a system of day-schools, **II, 169.**

—— —— —— —— Privileges of, more restricted than for hearing children, II, 536, **23**; *Emery*, **II, 108.**

—— —— —— —— a question of language-teaching, II, 559, **25**; 566, **26**; 694 702, **37**-**39**; 813, **47**; 837, **50.**

—— —— —— ——: A system adapted to all deaf-mutes, not excluding the feebler-minded, *Dr. Williams*, **I, 82.**

—— —— —— —— in the United States, **History of,** *Gallaudet*, **I, 54-59.**

—— —— —— —— *See* special title for topic desired.

Educating teachers, German method of, **II, 71.**

Effect of adoption of oral system exclusively, *Pres. Gallaudet*, I, 340, **26**; **I, 101**; *Dr. G. O. Fay*, **I, 80**; *Kinsey*, **I, 108**; *Dr. Williams*, **I, 82.**

—— of making deaf-mutes think in a special language, II, 458, **24**; 552, **24.**

—— of old-world traditions upon manual training, *E. E. Hale*, **II, 137.**

—— of slight deafness, II, 392, **7.**

—— of State aid upon private benevolence, I, 366, **28.**

—— of tendency to deafness in certain families, I, 253, **19.** *See* Heredity, Marriage and Intermarriage, Ancestry of the Deaf, and other titles bearing upon this subject.

Egerton, Lord, of Tatton (Chairman), Queries by, 13,101; 13,178; 13,181; 13,208; 13,220; 13,227; 13,229; 13,234; 13,239; 13,244; 13,279; 13,294; 13,318; 13,374; 13,380; 13,420; 13,424; 13,431; 13,454; 13,472; 13,481; 13,495; 13,505; 13,523; 21,355; 21,362; 21,369; 21,382; 21,385; 21,392; 21,398; 21,405; 21,407; 21,416; 21,417; 21,419; 21,438; 21,446; 21,449; 21,453; 21,457; 21,461; 21,473; 21,497; 21,502; 21,511; 21,515; 21,520; 21,522; 21,524; 21,526; 21,533; 21,541; 21,547; 21,549; 21,552; 21,559; 21,627; 21,661; 21,674; 21,678; 21,843; 21,848; 21,850; 21,854; 21,867; 21,870; 21,882; 21,893; 21,903; 21,909; 21,959; 21,963; 21,971; 21,983; 21,988; 21,996.

Elements of trades to be taught, in preference to specific trades, II, 471, **15.**

Elimination of artificial causes of intermarriage, II, 547, **24.**

Ellis, Mr. A. J., uses Visible Speech in noting early English pronunciation, II, 930, **60.**

Elwin, Pa., School for the Idiotic, II, 449, **12.**

Ely, Mr. C. W., on auricular instruction, **II, 80**; on intermarriage, **II, 95**; on Visible Speech, **II, 75.**

Emery, Mr. P. A., on auricular instruction, **II, 81**; on intermarriage, **II, 97**; **Plea for Day-Schools, II, 108**; Superiority of sign over articulation system, **II, 112**; Suggestions to law-makers, **II, 115.**

Emigration and Climate, Influence of, *Table*, **I, 46.**

Emotion, Signs of, II, 560, **25.**

Emotions, The, as affected by the two methods, I, 445, **32.**

Employment of deaf teachers, I, 469, **34.**

—— No great difficulty in obtaining, I, 199, **13.**

—— obtained through school-acquaintance with hearing-pupils, II, 469, **15.**

Endowment of institutions, I, 116, **4**; 125, **5.**

—— Possible, for the Columbia Institution, I, 275, **22.**

Engelsmann, Mr. B., **I, 58.**

English language is unphonetical, thus differing from Italian, etc., II, 878, **55.**

—— ——, made a school-task, II, 813, **48.**

—— ——, more difficult than Italian, or German, II, 561, **25.**

—— —— Should we teach, by means of hieroglyphics? **II, 166.**

—— —— Sounds of, are easier than German, II, 961, **62.**

—— tongue, How to preserve the purity of, **II, 71.**

Enumerators' returns should be verified by competent observers, II, 809, **47.**

Enunciation, Perfect, possible, II, 873, **55.**

Environment, Retention of normal, II, 458, **14.**

Epidemic producing deafness, II, 416, **9.**

Errors in Census returns: **Previous to 1850**, *H. P. Peet*, **I, 44**; **1850**, One-half the whole number of aged deaf-mutes returned, credited to Mass. and Penn., *H. P. Peet*, **I, 47**; Returns between ages of 10 and 30, assumed to be tolerably correct, *H. P. Peet*, **I, 49**.
1850, 1860, 1870, Causes of liability to error, Mass. State Board of Charities, **I, 49**.
1880, Opinion of *Pres. Gallaudet*, **I**, 105, **3**; **III, 207**; *Dr. Bell*, **II**, 355, **1**; 808, **47**; *Rev. Wines*, **II**, 357, **1**; **III, 212**. *See* Census Returns.
Errors of the deaf in language, *Gallaudet*, **I**, 158-171, **9-11**. *See* Language, *also*, Bell, Dr. A. G., System of instruction, etc.
Everybody, Can, learn to speak? **II**, 576, **27**; 675, **35**; *Kinsey*, **I, 101**; **107**.
Evolution of breeds, *Brewer*, **II, 102**.
—— —— deaf batrachians, *Cope*, **II, 101**.
—— —— sign-language from pantomime, **II**, 560, **25**.
Examination of schools, *See* Inspection.
—— of European schools by Pres. Gaulladet in 1867, **I**, 138, **6**.
Executive management of institutions, **I**, 125, **5**; 263, **20**; **III**,—; **II**, 126, **5**.
Expense of education, **I**, 141, **8**; 344, **26**; 236, **16**; 141, **8**; 344, **26**. TABLE for 1885, **74**.
II, 458, **14**; 531, **22**; 737, **41**; *Estimated* for a system of day-schools, **169**.
Experience of a lady, **II**, 585, **29**; 706, **39**; 984, **64**; of a young man under different methods of instruction, **I, 103**.
Experiment, A suggestive, **II**, 813, **47**.
Experimental years, Use of signs in, **I**, 503, **36**.
Explanation of Symbols of graphical charts, **III**, *to face*, —.
Extent of deaf-mutism, *Fay*, **I, 61**. *See* Statistics.
Exterior organization of schools for the deaf, **I**, 112, **4**.
Extracts from laws of Wisconsin, **II, 73**.
Eyes and hair not "matched," Significance of, **II**, 448, **12**.
—— Blue, and deafness, **II**, 448, **12**.
—— of the congenitally deaf, **II**, 837, **50**.

Facts and Opinions relating to the Deaf, from America, collected by Dr. Bell, and presented to the Royal Commission, **II, 74-129**.
Facts bearing upon the formation of a deaf variety, **II**, 502, **19**.
Failures to acquire idiomatic use of language under different methods. **I**, 158, **9**.
Faith without words, St. Augustine on, **II, 182**.
Fallacies concerning the Deaf, *Bell*, **II, 155**;
HEADINGS:
Fallacies concerning the dumbness of deaf children, 155.
Fallacies concerning the intelligence of deaf children, 155.
Why hearing children who become deaf also become dumb, 155.
Fallacies regarding the nature of speech, 156.
Ignorance the real difficulty in the way of teaching deaf children to speak, 156.
The old fallacy—"without speech, no reason," 156.
Articulation-teaching in America, 157.
Upon the art of understanding speech by the eye, 157.
Fallacies regarding speech-reading, 158.
Requisites to the art of speech-reading, 158.
Gesture-language, 159.
The fallacy that a gesture-language is the only form of language that is natural to the deaf, 160.
The sign-language of our institutions, 161.
The fallacy that a gesture-language is the only form of language in which a congenitally deaf child can think, 161.
Why the deaf employ a gesture-language, 162.
Harmful results of the sign-language, 162.
Why the English language should be substituted for the sign-language as a vernacular, 163.
Conclusion, 163.
—— Discussion: *Gallaudet*, **II, 164**; *Hubbard*, **165**; *Bell*, **166**.
Familiarity with language a prerequisite to speech-reading, **II**, 667, **34**.
Family, or non-sporadic deafness, **II**, 473, *note*, **16**.
—— **tendencies** should be considered by persons contemplating marriage, *Gallaudet*, **I**, 392, **29**.
Families containing many deaf-mutes, **II**, 454, **13**; 530, **22**; 858, **53**; **133**; **136**; **186**; **187**; **III**, *Ancestry of the Deaf*, —.
False teeth illustration, **II**, 985, **64**.
Faribault conference, Dr. Bell's advocacy of the manual alphabet, **II**, 713, **39**; Report of Committee on **Improved form of school statistics, I, 52**.
Fay, Dr. E. A., Deaf-Mutes, I, 60-71;
HEADINGS: Definition and Classification, 60; Extent of Deaf-Mutism, 61; Causes: *Heredity*, 62; *Consanguinity*, 64; *Maternal Impressions*, 64; *Scrofula*, 64; *Social Circumstances*, 65; *Mountainous Regions*, 65; *Diseases and Accidents*, 65.
Mental Condition and Characteristics, 65; Morbidity, 66; Mortality, 67; Marriage, 67; Occupations, 67; Legal Rights and Responsibilities, 68; Origin and Growth of Schools and Methods, 68; School-Age, 69; Boarding-schools and Day-schools, 69; Private Instruction at Home, 69; Auricular Instruction, 70; Manual Alphabets, 70; Visible Speech and Line Writing, 70; Higher Education, 70; Religious Work for Adults, 71.
—— **Definitions of Methods, etc.**, **I, 59**; **76**.
—— **Letter on Governmental aid, II, 123**; on *per capita* **cost of instruction, II**, 738, **41**.
—— **Statistics of schools for 1885**, TABLES, **I, 72-75**; for 1888, TABLES, **II, 128-9**.
Fay, Dr. G. O., Comprehensive Education in its Philosophy and Practice, I, 79; *Gallaudet*, **I**, 140, **7**; 201, **13**.
Feeble-minded, Education of, favored, *note*, **II, 12**.
—— —— deaf, Method adapted to, **I, 82**; Acceptance of, by schools, **II**, 636, **32**.
Feelings as affected by the two methods. **I**, 445, **32**.
Female teachers, **II**, 782, **45**; 888, **56**.
Fessler, Rev. Charles, On auricular instruction, **II, 83**; on Visible Speech, **II, 77**.
Feuds, Cessation of. **II**, 594, **30**.
Florida institution uses line-writing, **II**, 963, **62**.
Flournoy, J. J., deaf author. Memorial to Congress to establish a deaf-mute State. **II, 126**.
Finger-language. *See* Finger-Spelling.
—— -**spelling**, Origin and general utility of, *Gordon*, **I, 94**.
—— —— Place of, in instruction. **II**, 576, **28**.
—— —— Speed of, **II**, 667, **34**.
—— —— useful in presenting our language to the deaf, *Bell*, **II**, 570, **26**; 668, **34**; 669, **35**; 673, **35**; 694, **38**; 710, **39**; 719, **40**; 826, **50**.

Finger-spelling useful to hearing-persons, *Denison*, **I, 98**; *Gordon*, **I, 94.**

First recorded intermarriage, Children of, **II**, 542, **23.**

Fluctuations in numbers of the non-congenitally deaf, **II**, 414, **9.**

Freedom as to methods with Governmental inspection of results, **II**, 751, **42.**

Formation of a deaf variety of the Human Race, Memoir upon. *See* Deaf-mute Variety.

Free instruction, generally provided for deaf children, **I**, 216, **15**; Tuition, board, and lodging are furnished free in the National College to students unable to pay—about 95%—**I**, 217, **15.**

——— **Recent legislation** in Mass., upon, **II**, **126.**

—— **passes** on railroads for pupils, **II**, 774, **44.**

Frequency of intermarriages of the deaf, in America, **I**, 390, **27.**

Frere's books in phonetic type, **II**, 942, **61.**

Froebel's principle, **II**, **170.**

Friendship promoted between deaf and hearing-children, **II**, **70.**

Fuller, Miss Angie A., deaf writer and poet, "The Semi-Mute's Soliloquy," **I**, **88.**

—— **Miss Sarah**, on auricular instruction, **II**, **81**; Marriages of pupils from Horace Mann School, **II**, **96**; The first Infant School for Deaf-Children, **II**, **121**; Visible Speech, **II**, **76**, **145.**

—— **The Sarah, Home** for little children, **II**, 774, **44.**

Fund to assist graduates in "making a start," **I**, 368, **28.**

Gabriel, Saint, Brothers of, their conversion to the pure oral method, **I**, **107.**

Gallaudet, Pres., E. M., [For many topics see desired title in index.]

—— GENERAL REFERENCES TO PART I:

Auricular instruction, 147, **8**; 202, **14**; 407, **33.**

Classification of the deaf, 417, **30.**

Conferences and conventions, 266, **20.**

Day-schools and Institutions, 192, **12**; 249, **18.**

Duration of pupilage, Course of study, 173, **11.**

Employment of deaf teachers, 458, **33**; 469, **34.**

Evidence before the Royal Commission, I **39.**

Higher education, 211, **14.**

History of the education of the Deaf in the U. S., 54.

How shall the Deaf be educated? 100.

Industrial training, 181, **12**; 401, **30**; 459, **33.**

Intermarriage of the deaf with the deaf, 252, **18**; 392, **29.**

Isolation of orally educated, 165, **9**; 171, **10.**

Language-teaching, 158, **9.** *See Methods of Instruction.*

Manual alphabet, 273, **21.**

Methods of instruction, 136, **6**; 290, **23**; 310, **24**; 349, **26**; 371, **28**; 403, **30**; 444, **32**; 498, **36.**

Milan Convention, 105-110; 520, **37.**

Occupations of well-educated deaf persons, 240, **17.**

Oral and aural training; Report of address, **81.**

Organization, external and internal, 111, **4.**

Physical culture, 528, **38.**

Result of tour of inspection, 1867, **58.**

Poetry of the Deaf, 87.

Separation of sexes, 198, **13.**

Sign-language, 166, **10**; 201, **13**; 205, **14**; *See* Methods of Instruction; Combined Method; How shall the deaf be educated? Milan Convention, etc.

Statistics, 105, **3**; 288, **23**; *also*, **II**, 355, **1**; **III, 207.**

Teachers and their qualifications, 257-267, **19-20**; 469, **34.**

Value of Speech and Speech-reading, 165, **10**; 171, **11**; 319, **25**; 460, **33.**

—— CITATIONS, QUOTATIONS, ETC., IN PART II:

On combined system (general), **II**, 374, **4**; 718, **40**; as illustrated in the Pennsylvania Institution, **II**, 374, **4.**

The consensus of opinion in the California Convention, **II**, 592, **30.**

On gymnastics, **II**, 727, **10.**

Main argument of, in favor of the sign language, **II**, 983, **63.**

Lectures, *viva voce*, to audiences of deaf-mutes, **II**, 839, **51.**

The isolation of the orally educated, **II**, 984, **64.**

Organization, **II**, 734, **41.**

Quotation from, concerning experience on an excursion, **II**, 984, **64.**

Ratio of deaf-mutes to general population, **II**, 356, **1.**

Significance of private schools in the U. S., **II**, 366, **3**; 371, **4.**

—— IN PART III:

Census Results, 207; Private Schools, **208**; **What is the Combined System? 208**; Amour propre *vs.* Mauvais honte, **210**; Political appointments, **211.**

—— **Rev. Dr. Thomas**, **I**, 396, **29**; **II**, 881, **56.**

—— **Dr. Thomas Hopkins**, **I**, **54.**

—— **Mrs. T. H.**, **I**, 444, **32**; **109.**

Galloway cattle, *Brewer*, **II**, **101.**

Galton's law of regression, *Brooks*, **II**, **104.**

Game of "word-hunting," **II**, 694, **38**; **151.**

Games and manly sports, **I**, 413, **30.**

Gardening for deaf-mutes, **I**, 190, **12.**

Garrett, Miss Emma, On auricular instruction, **II**, **82**; Communication on **Conditions necessary to giving every deaf child a chance to learn to speak, II, 117**; on small oral boarding-schools, **II**, **117.**

Garrett, Miss Mary S., **Directions to Parents of Deaf Children, II, 119**; auricular instruction, **II**, **83**; consanguinity and intermarriage, **II**, **99**; pure oral system, **II**, **119**; Visible Speech, **II**, **77.**

Gass, Mr. M. T., on auricular instruction, **II**, **79**; intermarriage, **II**, **95**; Visible speech, **II**, **75.**

"**German**" and "**French**" systems both needed, *Kinsey*, **I**, **107.**

German Articulation-teachers do not object to use of natural signs, **II**, 819, **49.**

German experience, in method of instruction, *Bell*, **II, 169**; as to organization, *Gillett*, **II, 170.**
—— How to learn, **II, 162.**
Germany, Proportion of deaf-mutes in, greater than in U. S., *Williams*, **II, 90.**
—— System in vogue in, does not meet conditions in America, **II, 170.**
—— Thorough method of educating teachers in, *Bell*, **II, 71.**
Genealogical information in general schedules of census returns, **II**, 857, **53.**
—— —— Accessible sources of, in New England, **II**, 857, **53.**
—— inquiry among families containing three or more deaf children, **II**, 444, **11**; as to correlation of defects, **II**, 450, **12**; extending to twelve generations, **II**, 451, **13**; Manuscript volume of, **II**, 858, **53.**
—— Studies, **II**, 530, **22**; 858, **53**; **133**; **130**; **186**; **187**; *also, see Chart*, facing **II, 188**; and *Ancestry of the Deaf*, **III, ——.**
Geological formation of Chilmark, Martha's Vineyard, **II**, 858, **53.**
George, S., Account of, **II, 150**; 694–702, **37 39.**
Georgia Institution, Marriage records and statistics from, **II**, 529, **22**; **II, 93.**
Gesture-method, Oral system is a, **I**, 455, **33.**
Gestures, Abuse and use of, **I**, 162, **9**; *See* Signs, Sign-language, Combined System, Fallacies, How shall the Deaf be educated? etc.
Gillett, Dr. P. G., all pupils given a trial in articulation in Illinois institution, **II, 107**; on auricular instruction, **II, 78**; on intermarriages of deaf with the deaf, **II**, 549, **24, 92**; **Tabulated Statistics**: age of deafness, causes, kinship, marriages, nationality or family descent, **II, 92-93**; Visible Speech, **II, 75.**
—— Report of address on **Deaf-classes in the public schools, II, 170.**
Gillespie, Mr. J. A., **II**, 483, **17**: Auricular class in the Nebraska institution, **II**, 402, **8**; Condensed **History of aural instruction, II, 84**; Letter on **aural work, II, 85.**
Glenn, Mr. W., on auricular instruction, **II, 78.** Visible Speech, **II, 75.**
Glove-Alphabet, **II**, 694, **38, 152**; *plate*, **153.**
God and immortality, Idea of, **II, 183.**
Goodman, Mr. L., **II, 172.**
Gordon, Prof. J. C., **I**, 273, **21**; **II**, 487, **17**; **77.**
—— The **"American" Manual Alphabet**, with plates, **I, 94.**
—— and others, Report of Committee on **Auricular Instruction, II, 139.**
—— Miss Mary T. G., Oral and auricular pupil of, exhibited before the National Academy of Sciences, **I, 81.**
Governing bodies, Deaf-mutes, as members of, **II**, 847, **51**; *Emery*, **II, 115.**
Governmental aid in Great Britain should be made dependent upon results obtained, **II**, 748, **42**; *Objections*, **II**, 749, **42**; **I**, 265, **20.**
—— inspection, No system of, in U. S., **II**, 678, **36.**
Gradation in hearing, **II**, 403, **8.**
Grade of life determined by choice of handicraft, *E. E. Hale*, **II, 137.**
"Graduates" of State-schools, **I**, 368, **29.**
Grant of land to American Asylum, **II**, 359, **2.**
Grants to aid graduates, **I**, 368, **28.**
Graphical Charts: *Lovejoy* chart, **II**, *to face*, **188**; *Brown* and *Allen* charts, see *Ancestry of the Deaf*, **III, ——**; Visible Speech charts, 1–7, **III, ——.**
Greenberger, Mr. D., **I, 58**; **II, 170**; on auricular instruction, **II, 80**; on Visible Speech, **II, 75.**
—— on insufficiency of the German system of teaching articulation for American conditions, *Gillett*, **II, 170.**
—— The, system, **II**, 986, **65.**
Groups of the Deaf with reference to marriage, *Table*, **II, 16.**
Groups, rather than single letters differentiated in speech-reading, **II**, 568, **26.**
Growth of American schools from 1857 to 1887, **II, 127.**
—— of Articulation teaching, **II**, 497, **19.**
Gymnasium, Bowling alley, and Swimming-pool, Effects of, **I**, 525, **38.**
—— in Horace-Mann Day-school, **II**, 780, **44.**
Gymnastics, Physical, **II**, 727, **40.**

Hale, Rev. E. E., on **occupations and trades, II**, 471, **15.**
—— Senator Eugene, communication to, on **Census of the Deaf, II, 97.**
Halifax institution, Recommendation of principal of, as to teachers, **II**, 679, **36**; Report of, on consanguineous marriages. **II**, 447, **12**; Statistics of, marriages, **II**, 535, **23.**
Hammond, Margaret, Experience of Whipple Home-school, **II, 19**; recommends celibacy, **II, 99.**
Hanson, Mr. Olof, Translation of poem from the Swedish by, **I, 93.**
Happiness of Deaf-mutes under the two methods of instruction, **I**, 444, **33.**
—— of the intermarried, **II**, 557, **24**; *Emery*, **II, 14.**
Hardy, Mr. A., on auricular instruction, **II, 83**; on articulation, **II, 119**; on intermarriage, **II, 99.**
Heady, Mr. Morrison, deaf, dumb, and blind author and poet, **I, 93.**
Hearing-child hears words repeated daily for two years before uttering them, **II**, 813, **48.**
Hearing, essential to perfect speech, *Gillet*, **II, 171.**
—— Improvement and utilization of, **II**, 392, **7**; **II, 140.**
See Auricular instruction.
—— **Report of committee on, II, 139.**
—— of 700 children in public schools tested, **II**, 403, **8.**
—— Partial, Number and percentage of deaf pupils having, **II**, 395, **7.**
—— power, Apparent increase of, explained, **II, 86**; **87**; **88.**
—— —— Probable improvement of, in a few cases, **II, 85**; **86**; **88.**
—— Teachers, Marriage of, to the deaf, **II**, 558, **24.**
Hereditary aptitude for auricular instruction, **II**, 811, **47.**
—— blindness as a collateral defect, **II**, 867, **54.**
—— character of deafness in Chilmark and other cases, **I, 50.**
—— predisposition, a cause of deafness, **II**, 441, **11.**

Heredity: Analysis of 402 cases of intermarriage of deaf with the deaf, II, 848, **52.**
—— Scientific experts upon, II, 502, **19**; **101-106.**
—— Study of, through families having three or more deaf children, II, 444, **11.**
—— Views of Dr. E. A. Fay, I, **62.** *See* Consanguinity, Intermarriages, Deaf children of Deaf parents, Deaf-mute Variety, etc.
Herodotus, Anecdote from, II, **173.**
Hermaphrodites, II, 454, **13.**
Hieroglyphics, Illustration, II, 983, **63.**
Higher education of the deaf, *Gallaudet*, I, 211, **14**; *Fay*, I, **70.**
Hill, Moritz, on natural signs, I, **103.**
History of deaf-mute education in U. S., I, **54.**
Hirsch, Mr. D., Pupil of, I, 471, **34.**
Hindustani reproduced by Visible Speech, II, 868, **54.**
Hoagland family, The, II, 530, **22**; Statistics of, II, **105.**
Hoffman, Dr. C. W., marriage laws in reference to the deaf, II, **126.**
Holman family, The, II, 530, **22.**
"Homes" for children, II, 796, **45.**
Home-ties, II, 548, **24.**
Home-instruction, Information relating to should be disseminated, II, 973, **63.**
"Homophenes," II, 759, **62**; **158.**
Hopeful feature, II, 518, **24.**
Horace-Mann School, Intermarriages from, II, 526, **21.**
Hours of School, *Table*, I, **73.**
House-work of the institutions, I, 189, **12.**
"Howard Glyndon," [Laura C. Redden Searing, Mrs.,] *portrait*, author and poet; "Which is best?" I, **89.**
How to compare families of the congenitally deaf with ordinary families, II, 606, **30.**
Howe, Dr. S. G., II, 881, **55**; on Development of religious idea, II, **183.**
Hubbard, Hon. Gardiner G., II, 881, **55**; **165.**
Hull, Miss S. E., of Bexley, I, **106**; **109**; the first to apply Visible Speech to instruction of the deaf, II, 931, **60**; 893, **57.**
Human race capable of modification by selective breeding, *Bowditch*, II, **102.**
Humboldt, W. von, "Speech naturally inherent in man," II, **147.**
Hutchinson's teeth, II, 803, **46.**
Hutton, Mr. A. B., ideas of uninstructed deaf-mutes, II, **182.**
Hutton, Mr. J. Scott, on articulation, II, **84**; on consanguinity and on intermarriage, with statistics, II, **100**; on placing the education of the deaf upon a proper basis, II, **122**; *see* Halifax institution.
Hyatt, Prof. Alpheus, On possibility of the formation of a deaf variety, II, **102.**

Idiocy, Causes of, inter-related to causes of deafness in many cases, II, *foot-note*, **12.**
—— and correlation of color of eyes and hair, II, 419, **12.**
Idiotic deaf-mutes, II, 449, **12**; II, **134.**
Idiots and deaf-mutes, liable to be confounded by Census-enumerators, II, 809, **47**; II, **135.**
—— and imbeciles, 450, **12**; 479, **16**; 809, **47.**
—— and feeble-minded, Need of provision for, II, 357, **2.**
Ignorance of mechanism of speech, Effect of, II, **71.**
—— Popular, of the tendency of intermarriages, II, 624, **31.**
—— The, of uneducated deaf-mutes, II, **70**; *H. P. Peet*, II, **173.**
Ill effect of conflicting systems, *Crouter*, I, **78.**
Illinois institution, Sketch of, I, **56**; Size of, II, **168**; Marriages of deaf-mutes from, II, 510, **20.** *See* Gillett, Dr. P. G.
Illiterate parents, and day-school plan, II, 724, **40.**
Illustrations of Visible Speech, *plates*, II, **147**; III, ——.
Imagination as affected by the two methods, I, 445, **32.**
Imitative signs, II, 560, **25.**
Importance of Visible Speech, II, 633, **32**; *see* title.
—— of conventions of instructors, I, 266, **20.**
Impossibility of judging of efficiency of teachers by results, I, 265, **20.**
Impromptu conversation, Specimen of, II, **151.**
Improvement in hearing in auricular training, discussed, II, 688, **36**; not due to medical treatment, I, 301, **24**; *see* auricular instruction; Nature of, II, 399, **7.**
Inaccuracy of Census returns for certain classes, *H. P. Peet*, I, **46.**
Incompetent heads of institutions, I, 127, **6**; III, **211.**
Inconsistency of certain pure oralists, I, **108.**
Increase of deaf children of deaf parents, by decades, II, 531, **22.**
—— of expense from separate oral department not great, *Crouter*, II, **78.**
Indiana institution, Sketch of, II, **56.**
Indianapolis convention, Views expressed by Dr. Gallaudet at, I, 166, **10.**
Indications of only partial success in education of the congenitally deaf, II, 585, **20.**
Induction-balance, Principle of, employed in audiometer, II, 405, **8.**
Industrial training, *Gallaudet*, I, 181, **12**; 284, **22**; 367; **27**; 400, **30**; 459, **33**; *Gillett*, II, **170**; *Bell*, II, 468, **15**; 777, **44**; 843, **51.**
Industries requiring greatest preparation apt to be least crowded, *E. E. Hale*, II, **137.**
Infant school for deaf children, The first, II, 774, **44**; is on the pure oral plan, II, 818, **49**; History of, II, **121.**
Infant schools as interfering with home-life, II, 830, **50.**
Infants not debarred from signs, but from the sign-language, II, 819, **49.**
Inferiority of the oral system, *Emery*, II, **112-115.**
Influence of private schools, II, 371, **4**; controverted, III, **208.**
Influences tending to intermarriages, II, 523, **21.**
Insane Deaf-mutes, II, 450, **12**; **134**; Insane who are otherwise defective, II, **134**; Insanity among relatives of the deaf, II, 450, **13.**
Inspection of schools, *Gallaudet*, 124, **5**; 276, **22**; 280, **22**; 347, **26**; 369, **28**; 718, **42**; *Bell*, II, 472, **41**; 678, **36**; 998, **65.**

Institutions, Abolition of, not advocated, **II**, 463, **14**;
—— as a cause of intermarriages, **II**, 526, **21**.
—— Discipline of, of doubtful advantage, **II**, 726, **40**.
—— do not get pupils at sufficiently early age, **II**, 725, **40**.
—— fail to reach one-half the deaf children, **II**, 469, **15**; **69**.
—— foster pride, *Emery*, **II**, **112**.
—— in Germany not a cause of intermarriages, **II**, 461, **14**.
—— Majority of children in, have no opportunity to learn speech, **II**, 583, **29**.
—— Medical men in, **II**, 799, **46**.
—— Not practicable to do away with, **II**, 553, **24**.
—— Separate, for the sexes, **II**, 539, **23**; *see* Sexes.
—— : boarding-schools preferable to day-schools, *Fay*, **I**, **69**; *Gallaudet*, **I**, 197, **13**; *Gillett*, **II**, **170**.
Instruction, New classification of methods, **II**, 385, **6**.
—— : Old classification of methods, **II**, 386, **6**.
—— Views of heads of institutions upon. **II**, **106-124**.
—— retarded by neglect of writing and finger-spelling, **II**, 672, **35**.
Instructors, *see* Teachers, etc.
Intelligence of deaf children, Fallacy concerning, **II**, **155**.
Intelligibility of speech depends upon the consonants, **II**, 910, **58**; **167**.
—— the proper test of value for speech, **II**, 579, **28**.
Interest in work of the Commission, general throughout America, **II**, 909, **66**.
—— of President in education of the deaf, **I**, 355, **27**.
Intermarriage of the deaf with the deaf, Effect of, **II**, **88-106**.
—— as affecting happiness, **II**, 557, **24**; *Gillett*, **II**, **92**.
—— between pupils of same institution, **II**, 516, **20**.
—— Causes of, **II**, 457, **14**.
—— deprecated, *Gallaudet, foot-note*, **II**, **166**.
—— discountenanced by Clarke Institution, **II**, **166**.
—— discouraged by earlier teachers, **II**, 511, **23**.
—— Early cases of, **II**, 523, **21**.
—— Effect of, *Gallaudet*, **I**, 252, **18**; 475, **34**.
—— Effect of breaking the line of, **II**, 505, **19**.
—— favored by majority of principals, **II**, 551, **24**.
—— How to eliminate artificial causes of, **II**, 547, **24**.
—— in Germany, **II**, 461, **14**.
—— may possibly reduce the total of deaf offspring, W. Jenkins, **II**, **98**.
—— not preventable, *Gillett*, **I**, **170**.
—— of the orally taught, **II**, 841. **51**.
—— promoted by reunions of former pupils, **II**, 811, **51**.
—— Results of, **II**, 528, **21**; 530, **22**; 540-543, **23**; 848, **52**; First case, **II**, 540, **23**.
—— Special language, the chief cause of, **II**, 554, **24**.
—— Statistics of, *see* title Marriage.
—— Views of Dr. Gillett upon, **II**, 519, **24**; Dr. W. W. Turner, and early teachers, **II**, 541, **23**; Scientific authorities, **II**, **101-106**.
Invention of language by children, **II**, 387, **6**.
—— of the telephone, **II**, 635, **32**.
Invitations to the Milan Convention, **I**, 521, **38**.
Isolation, Social, of the deaf, **I**, 165, **9**.
Is there a correlation between defects of the senses? *Dr. Bell*, **II**, **134**.
Itard, Dr. J. M. G., on the hearing of the deaf, **II**, **139**.
Itemizer, The, column, **II**, 518, **20**.
Itinerant missionaries among the deaf, **II**, 613-619, **31**.

Jackson Conference, Action of, in reference to statistical forms, **II**, 599, **30**; **Report of Committee**, **I**, **52**; Epitome of a paper on **a system of language-teaching** presented by Dr. Bell, **II**, 813, **47**.
Jenkins, Mr. Weston, **Ante-natal causes of deafness**, **II**, **98**; on auricular instruction, **II**, **82**; Catarrhal diseases and scrofula, as causes of deafness, **II**, **98**; on Visible Speech, **II**, 884, **56**; **76**.
Jennings, Miss Alice C., a deaf author and poet, **I**, **93**.
Jersey cattle, formerly mostly spotted, *Brewer*, **II**, **103**.
Johnson, Mr. E. C., Questions by, **I**, 13,207; 13,225; 13,243; 13,268; 13,296; 13,491; 13,504; 13,528.
——**II**, 21,389; 21,702; 21.788; 21,815; 21,820; 21,827; 21,837: 21,869; 21,881; 21,892; 21,900; 21,902; 21,908: 21,920; 21,941; 21,962.
—— Mr. J. H., on auricular instruction, **II**, **79**; intermarriages in Alabama, **II**, **95**; on Visible Speech, **II**, **75**.
Jones, Dr. S. J., otologist, on improvement in hearing, **II**, **139**.
Journalists, Deaf, **I**, 240, **17**.
Joy of parents over first utterances of deaf children, **II**, **167**.
Judgment of young men who have had experience of both methods, **I**, 474, **34**.

Kansas Institution, Test of hearing in, **II**, 396, **7**. *See* Walker, S. T.
Keeler, Miss S. W., Private class in articulation, **II**, **121**; auricular instruction, **II**, **83**.
Kendall, Mr. W. H., On intermarriage and relationship in Texas, **II**, **95**.
Kendall School, The, uses speech as one means of instruction in, **II**, 587, **29**. *See* Columbia Institution.
Kentucky Institution, Sketch of, **I**, **55**.
Kerney, Mr. C., On auricular instruction, **II**, **82**; peculiar case of transmission of deafness, **II**, **99**; Visible Speech, **II**, **76**.
Key to speech-reading, **II**, 585, **29**.
Kindergarten-principle, **II**, 775, **44**; -work, **I**, 179, **11**.
Kinsey, Mr. A., **II**, 893, **57**; Extracts from paper presented to Milan Convention favoring different methods of instruction for two classes of pupils, **I**, **101**; **I**, **107**.
Kitto, Dr. John, Verses by, **I**, **91**.
Knight, Mr. P. S., Auricular instruction, **II**, **81**; intermarriages in Oregon, **II**, **97**; Visible Speech, **II**, **76**.
Knowledge of language, Test of, in institutions visited by Dr. Bell, **II**, 832, **50**.
—— of Manual alphabet need harm no deaf child, **II**, 673, **35**.
——, not language, is power, *Emery*, **II**, **113**.
—— of physiology of vocal organs, essential to satisfactory teaching of speech, **II**, 907, **58**.
Kruse, Mr. Otto F., on early impressions, **II**, **181**.

Lady, Experience of a, relying upon speech-reading and finger-spelling, **I**, 171, **11**.

—— who relies upon speech-reading and rejects finger-spelling, **II**, 585, **29**; 984, **64**.

Land-grant to the American Asylum **I**, 478, **35**; **54**; **II**, 359, **2**.

Language acquired by instruction and imitation, **II**, 386, **6**.

—— Attainments in idiomatic use of, may be the same under oral and manual methods, *Gallaudet*, **I**, 313, **26**.

—— illustrated by natural pantomime *following* blackboard-writing, *Bell*, **II**, **151**; 560, **25**.

—— invented, **II**, 387, **6**.

—— Knowledge of, lacking in many schools, *Gallaudet*, **I**, 158, **9**.

—— of the people,—where found, **II**, 813, **48**.

—— of thought, No natural, *Gillett*, **II**, **171**.

—— Special, defined, **II**, 391, **7**.

——, Special and Ordinary, the true basis of classification of methods of instruction, **II**, 385, **6**.

—— Special, tends to bring adult deaf-mutes together, **II**, 540, **23**.

Language-teaching, Education of the deaf hinges upon, **II**, 559, **25**.

Large day-schools objectionable, **II**, 528, **21**.

Larson, Mr. L. M., on English language in a Spanish community, **II**, **83**; on intermarriage, **II**, **99**; on school at Santa Fé, N. M., **II**, **119**.

Latent deafness, **II**, 861, **53**.

Laura Bridgman, deaf, dumb, and blind, (*portrait*), Poem by, **I**, **90**; *See* Bridgman.

Law of Wisconsin aiding day-schools for the deaf, **II**, 360–367, **2**, **3**.

—— Extracts from, **II**, **73**; **II**, **116**.

Lawrence, Mr. R. B., auricular instruction, **II**, **82**; consanguineous marriages, **II**, **99**; day-schools, **II**, **119**.

Lawyers, Deaf, **I**, 240, **17**; **II**, **90**.

Learning to shoot, **II**, 883, **56**.

—— to swim before going into the water, **II**, 781, **45**.

Le Couteulx, St. Mary's institution, **II**, 822, **49**.

Lectures, by "lip-reading," **II**, 805–9, **50**; Should be given in signs, **I**, 208, **14**.

Legacies to American institutions, **I**, 366, **28**.

Legal Rights and Responsibilities, *Fay*, **I**, **68**.

Length of school-life, **II**, 536, **23**; under different methods, **I**, 437, **32**.

Letter to heads of institutions and of schools, **II**, **74**.

—— from President of United States, **I**, 355, **27**.

—— from former pupil of Prof. Porter, **I**, **102**.

——: **An Open Letter**, *Bell*, **II**, **69**.

Lightning, Origin of, **II**, **180**.

Limited facility in speech-reading not a proof of inefficiency in instruction, **I**, 324, **25**.

Line-writing, **II**, 909, **58**; as related to speech-reading, **II**, 912, **59**; used in Florida Institution, **II**, **76**; in Mr. Bell's school, **II**, 910, **158**.

Lip-readers resorting to finger-spelling, Cases of, **I**, 171, **11**.

Lip-reading, a sign-method, **I**, 455, **33**.

—— English elements are not clearly differentiated in, **II**, 567, **26**.

—— not practicable for all, **II**, 377, **4**.

—— Place of, in a course of instruction, **II**, 577, **28**.

Lip-reading rendered difficult by lack of uniformity in pronunciation, *Emery*, **II**, **115**.

—— *See* Speech-reading.

Literature, Special, for ordinary deaf-mutes, **I**, **79**.

Lithographers, Deaf, **I**, 171, **11**; 190, **12**.

Local homes, better than institutions, **II**, 770, **43**.

Location of schools, **II**, **71**.

Locke, Miss Abbie [Mrs. Stone], **II**, **150**.

London Dome-tube, **II**, **86**, **87**.

—— **School-board schools**, **II**, 466, **14**; Desirability of plan, **II**, 652, **33**.

Looking-glass, Use of, **I**, 511, **37**; **II**, 901, **57**.

Lovejoy, The, family, **II**, 803, **46**; 867, **54**; *Chart, to face*, **II**, **188**; Explanation of Symbols, **III**, —.

McCowen, Miss Mary, Account of a pupil three years old, **II**, **119**.

Blind deaf pupil, **II**, **86**.

Auricular instruction, with statistical tables, **II**, **86-87**.

McDonnel, Esq., M. D., Robert, Question by, **II**, 21,418.

McGann, Miss H. E., on auricular instruction, **II**, **84**; on method of instruction in Mackay Institution, **II**, **123**; on Visible Speech, **II**, **77**.

Madison (Wis.) **Meeting** of National Educational Association, **I**, 165, **9**; **II**, 360, **2**; **Extracts from address** by Pres. Gallaudet, *Bell*, **II**, 984, **64**.

Maginn, Mr. F., **I**, 239, **17**; 456, **33**.

Magnat, M., **I**, **106**.

Maintenance not included in allowance for day-schools, **II**, 773, **44**.

Majority of children of deaf parents are not deaf, **II**, 535, **23**.

—— of pupils do not have the opportunity to acquire speech, **II**, 677, **36**.

Malformation of vocal organs, Case of, [?] **I**, 418, **31**.

Maloney's otophone, **II**, 20, **79**; 47, **83**.

"Man," Words resembling, to the eye of speech-reader, **II**, 568, **26**.

Manly sports, Participation in, **I**, 413, **30**.

Mann, Horace, Influence of, **I**, 133, **6**; **I**, **58**.

Manual Alphabet, Advantages and Convenience of, *Bell*, **II**, 570, **26**; 576, **28**; 669, **35**; 710, **39**; 716, **40**; *Denison*, **I**, **98**; *Gordon*, **I**, **94**.

—— —— Educational value of, **II**, 574, **27**; 711, **39**; 716, **40**.

—— —— Effect of, to exclusion of signs, **II**, 666, **34**.

—— —— Forms of, *Bell*, **II**, **153**; *Fay*, **I**, **70**; *Gallaudet*, **I**, 274, **21**.

—— —— **General utility of**, for speaking persons, *Denison*, **I**, **98**; *Gordon*, **I**, **94**.

—— —— **History of**, *Gordon*, **I**, **94**.

—— —— Restrictions to be observed in using, **II**, 584, **29**; 673, **35**.

—— —— used to exclusion of sign-language at Rochester, **II**, 574, **27**.

—— —— Wide-spread knowledge of, in U. S., **I**, 411, **30**.

Manual Method described, *Fay*, **I**, **57**; defined, **II**, 387, **6**.

—— —— schools [14] in U. S., **I**, 291, **23**; the method first introduced, **I**, 132, **6**.

Manual Method, Utility of, for dull pupils, *Kinsey*, **I, 107**; *Williams*, **I, 82.**
—— —— Valid objection to, **II**, 570, **26.**
—— Schools neglect speech, **II**, 579, **28.**
Margate institution, **II**, 556, **33**; 666, **34.**
Marriage, Classification as a guide to, **II**, 473, **16.**
—— laws, Hoffman, **II**, 524, **21.**
—— Consanguineous, *see* Consanguineous marriages.
—— of deaf-mutes; Analysis of 757 cases, **II**, 848, **52.**
1,089 cases from 10 States, 293 cases from Illinois, 1,448 cases collated from deaf-mute newspapers, **II**, 522, **21.**
Cases from Clarke Inst. and Horace-Mann School, **II**, 526, **21.**
Cases from Georgia, **II**, 529, **122.**
—— —— —— reported by heads of institutions, &c.:
Alabama, **II, 95.**
American Asylum, **II, 89.**
California, **II, 95.**
Clarke Inst., **II, 95.**
Florida, **II, 99.**
Georgia, **II, 94.**
Halifax, **II, 100.**
Horace-Mann School, **II, 96.**
Illinois, **II, 92.**
Le Couteulx St. Mary's, **II, 95.**
Michigan, **II, 95.**
Minnesota, **II, 95.**
Mississippi, **II, 95.**
New Jersey, **II, 98.**
North Carolina, **II, 92.**
Ontario, **II, 101.**
Oregon, **II, 97.**
Rhode Island, **II, 97.**
South Carolina, **II, 94.**
Texas, **II, 95.**
Virginia, **II, 92.**
—— —— —— encouraged by officers of institutions, *Gallaudet*, **I**, 302, **29.**
—— —— —— defended, *Emery*, **II, 97**; *Gillett*, **II, 92**; Swiler, **II, 95.**
—— —— —— Results of, tending to perpetuate the physical peculiarity of deafness, **II**, 528, **21**; 530, **22**; 607 cases of deaf children of deaf parents, **II**, 848, **52**; First recorded case, **II**, 438, **11**; Meaning of incomplete returns, **II**, 530, **22.**
—— —— —— Percentage of, marrying hearing persons, **II**, 507, **20.**
—— —— —— Prof. Fay on, **II, 67.**
Martha's Vineyard, Deaf population of, **II**, 450, **13**; 858, **53.** *See* Ancestry of the Deaf, **III**, —— .
Maryland school, Peculiar organization of, **I**, 123, **5**; Visible Speech in, **II**, 882, **56.**
Massachusetts, recent legislation in, **II, 126**; **II, 185.**
Census of 1865, **I, 49.**
Census of 1885, **III**, —— .
Massieu, Ideas of, **II, 179.**
Mathison, Mr. R., Auricular instruction, **II, 84**; controverts Dr. Bell's views and gives statistics of Ontario institution, **II, 101**; the Terrell family, **II, 101**; upon methods of instruction and on day-schools, **II, 122**; on Visible Speech, **II, 77.**
Maternal impressions, *Fay*, **I, 64.**
Mayhew family, The, **II**, 859, **53.**
Meaning of incomplete returns. **II**, 530, **22.**
—— of "manual, oral, and combined," **II**, 823, **49.**
Mechanism of Speech, Few teachers proficient in, **II**, 677, **36.**
—— —— How to acquire knowledge of, **II**, 871, **55**; *Gordon*, **II, 77.**
—— —— should be studied, by all teachers of the deaf, **II**, 681, **36**; in public schools in U. S., to preserve purity of the language, **II**, 900, **57.**
Medical men attached to institutions, **II**, 378, **29**; Examination of new pupils by, **II**, 152, **9**; 305, **24.**
—— —— Opinion of, upon segregation of the sexes, *Sir T. Robertson*, **II**, 982, **63.**
—— study of a family through five generations, **II**, 803, **46.**
—— supervision, **II**, 799, **46.**
—— treatment of diseases of the ear, **II**, 801, **46.**
Memoir upon the Formation of a Deaf Variety of the Human Race, **II**, 409, **9**; 411, **9**; 416, **9**; 431, **10**; 435, **10**; 457, **13**; 458, **14**; 510, **20**; 529, **22**; 850, **53.**
Mental condition and characteristics of the deaf, *Fay*, **I, 65.**
—— **development more rapid under combined method**, *Williams*, **I, 85.**
—— **impressions as a cause of deafness**, **II**, 443, **11.**
Method and system distinguished, **I**, 141, **7**; 290, **23.**
—— The, recommended in America, **I**, 308, **24.**
Methods of instruction classified according to the language of communication used, **II**, 178, **40.**
—— —— Diagram of, **II, 6.**
—— —— Dr. Bell's views upon, **II**, 570, **27.**
Milan International Convention, Action of, **I, 106**; Constitution of, **I**, 520, **37**; Effect of, in England and America, **I**, 529, **39**; President Gallaudet's **Report** upon, **I, 105**; [For other reports and articles upon, *See American Annals*, xxv, 293; xxvi, 75; 93; 138; 163; 192; xxvii, 146; xxviii, 42.]
—— **Schools** visited, **I**, 485, **35.**
Misfortunes, Three, resulting from deafness, **II**, 570, **26.**
Milton, John, on origin of speech, **II, 177.**
Minnesota Conference of principals, **I**, 172, **11.**
Mischievous effects of certain forms of combined method, *Crouter*, **I, 76.**
Missionaries and missions, **I**, 321, **25**; 365, **27**; **II**, 613, **31**; 721, **40.**
Mixing of deaf children with hearing children at play, etc., **II**, 651, **33.**
Moffatt on idea of God and immortality, **II, 183.**
Monboddo, Lord, Philosophy of, **II, 177.**
Montaigne, Philosophy of, **II, 182.**
Money point of view, **II**, 528, **22.**
Monopoly among teachers, **II**, 792, **45.**
Montreal, Separation of sexes in, **II**, 787, **45.**
Moore, Mr. Humphrey, a deaf artist, **I**, 175, **11.**
Moral result of education by signs as compared with the oral method, **II**, 984, **64.**
—— **sentiment should be aroused against the criminal neglect of speech**, **II**, 583, **28.**
—— **training in institutions**, **II**, 726, **40.**
Morality of the deaf, **I**, 410, **30.**
Morbidity of the deaf, *Fay*, **I, 66.**
Mortality of the deaf, *Fay*, **I, 67.**
Mothers might do much for deaf children, **II**, 973, **63.**
Mount Vernon excursion, Incident of, **II**, 984, **64.**
Mountainous regions, Effect of, *Fay*, **I, 65.**

Moses, Mr. T. L., auricular instruction, II, 78; instruction of the semi-deaf, II, 106; Visible Speech, II, 75.

Murray, Dr. [J. A. H.], uses Visible Speech in the Oxford Dictionary, II, 930, 60.

Muscular improvement of deaf college-students, I, 526, 38.

Noyes, Mr. J. L., auricular instruction, II, 80; consanguinity and intermarriage, II, 95; superiority of the combined system, II, 107; Visible Speech, 75.

Number of children taught by different methods in U. S., I, 428, 31.

Nurses and Mothers "gabble" to children, at a rate of 200 words per minute, II, 813, 47.

Nack, Mr. James (a precocious deaf poet); Verses and *portrait*, I, 88.

Nardin, Madame E., on Visible Speech, II, 76.

National Academy of Sciences, I, 81.

—— College, II, 585, 29; 70. *See* College, National.

Nationality of the deaf; *See* Census of 1850, 1860, 1870.

—— of pupils in Illinois institution, II, 93.

Natural classification of the deaf, Diagram of, II, 5.

Natural method fails in one particular, II, 813, 47.

—— pantomime and the sign-language distinguished, II, 560, 25.

—— ——, Place for, II, 560, 25.

—— process reversed in the sign-schools, II, 813, 48.

—— signs, II, 560, 25; 819, 49; never given up, II, 820, 49; not prohibited in oral schools, II, 821, 49.

Nebraska institution, Mode of instruction in, II, 687, 36.

Necessities, Three, in the case of the congenitally deaf, II, 570, 27.

Necessity for greater educational facilities, in U. S., II, 69; in Illinois, II, 171.

Nelson, Mr. E. B., auricular instruction, II, 81; Visible Speech, II, 76.

Nervous shock, a cause of congenital deafness, II, 45.

Nervous system, Hereditary abnormality in the, a cause of deafness, II, 450, 13.

Newcomb family, The, II, 863, 53; 867, 54.

—— Prof. S., Communication from, on **possibility of the formation of a deaf variety, II, 103.**

New-England enumeration more complete than in newer sections, I, 50.

"New Departure" in teaching Articulation, II, 909, 58

New-Jersey school: History of, I, 55; Visible Speech in II, 884, 56.

Newspapers, Deaf-mute, I, 272, 21; II, 517, 20; Proper aim of, II, 522, 21.

New principle, A, of dealing with deaf-mutes, II, 69.

New-York institution, II, 518, 20; Percentage of fit subjects for auricular instruction in, II, 403, 8.

—— Original institution in, has been split up into 7 or 8 distinct institutions, II, 359, 2.

—— —— —— Sketch of, I, 54.

—— —— —— for Improved Instruction, Sketch of, I, 58.

—— —— institutions not State institutions, I, 491, 36.

Non-congenitally deaf, Majority of, debarred from Articulation, II, 596, 30.

No restrictions should be placed upon communication between hearing and deaf children, II, 668, 34.

North-Carolina institution, Sketch of, I, 56.

Notions of the Deaf and Dumb before instruction, *Dr. H. P. Peet*, **II, 173.**

Not practicable to do away with institutions, II, 553, 24.

Novels and Plays, Use for, II, 813, 48; 813, 47.

Objections, to Visible Speech, II, 955, 61; to institutions (boarding-schools) counterbalanced by advantages, I, 197, 13; to training children for simplest callings, *Hale*, II, 137.

Objectionable feature of "local homes," II, 770, 43.

Object of education is to *fit pupils to enter a world of hearing people*, II, 781, 44.

Obligation to provide education, recognized by the States, II, 735, 41.

Occupations of the deaf, *Fay*, I, 67; of graduates of the College, 210, 17.

Ohio institution, Sketch of, I, 55.

Omissions of deaf-mutes from census-returns, I, 49.

"One royal road" to learning a language, II, 563, 25.

Open Letter to Committee of Wisconsin Legislature, II, 69.

Oral method, Characteristic of, II, 385, 6.

—— Definition of, *Fay*, I, 59; *Bell*, II, 387, 6.

—— a vague designation, *Bell*, II, 705, 39.

—— —— Schools, established in London, II, 920, 59; in U. S., I, 132, 6; Cost of education in, Paris, I, 141, 8.

—— —— established by law in France, I, 374, 28.

—— —— Reaction against, as an exclusive system, I, 371, 28; Results unsatisfactory, I, 170; Inferior in scholarship, I, 80; Unfavorable opinion of pupils, I, 474, 34; Practically selects pupils, I, 438, 32; insufficient for education of all deaf-mutes, I, 141, 8; 371, 28.

—— —— Improvement of, *Gallaudet*, I, 315, 25; *G. O. Fay*, I, 80.

—— system desirable as tending to increase the independence of deaf-mutes, II, 644, 32.

—— —— to be tested by proficiency of pupils in written language, II, 580, 28.

—— —— unjustly ridiculed, II, 820, 49.

—— pupils think in motions of the mouth, II, 825, *a* 49.

—— schools fortunate in having small classes, II, 115.

—— —— Graduates of, are induced to join adult deaf-mute societies, II, 96.

—— —— neglect written language, II, 575, 28.

—— and aural training, Case of, exhibited by Pres. Gallaudet, I, 81.

—— ——: Religious services, Character of, *Gallaudet*, I, 465, 33.

Ordinary language, the characteristic of one method of instruction, II, 385, 6.

Organization of institutions, *Gallaudet*, Exterior, I, 112, 4; Interior, I, 125, 5; Peculiar organization of Maryland institution, I, 123, 5.

O'Rourke, Mr. J., Case of, I, 81.

Origin and growth of schools and methods, *Fay*, I, 68.

—— and perpetuation of deafness, *Cope*, II, 101.

Origin of language, *Dr. H. P. Peet*, **II, 176.**
— of religious ideas, **II, 178.**
Owen, Rev. C. M., Questions by, **I,** 13,309; 13,319; 13,530; **II,** 21,403; 21,690; 21,703.

Pains are taken to advise against contracting certain marriages, **I,** 394, **29.**
Pantomimic acting to explain reading, **II,** 813, **48.**
Pantomime, Proper use of, *Bell*, **II, 151; 166.**
Parents may choose either system in New England and New York, **I,** 498, **36.**
— Relation of, and teachers, **II,** 724, **40.**
Partial co-education of deaf, and hearing children possible, **II,** 458, **14; 70.**
Patronage and politics, **I,** 262, **20.**
Payment by results, **I,** 265, **20; II,** 748, 749, **42.**
Pease, Hon. Richard L., **II, 186.**
Peculiar organization of Maryland institution, **I,** 123, **5.**
Peet, Dr. Harvey Prindle, Principal N. Y. Inst. (1831–1867), *Gallaudet*, **I, 55.**
— — Census Returns for 1830, '40, '50, **I, 43.**
— — Notions of the Deaf and Dumb before Instruction, **II, 173.**
— Dr. I. L., **I, 54.**
— Mrs. Mary Toles, Verses and *portrait*, **I, 90.**
Pélissier, deaf author and poet, **I, 92.**
Pennsylvania Institution, History of, **I, 55.**
— — System of instruction in, **I, 77**; 141, **8; II,** 374, **4**; 659, **33; III, —.**
Percentage of deaf able to rely upon speech exclusively, **I,** 325, **25.**
— — — to population at large, *table*, **II, 11.**
— — — marrying hearing persons, **II,** 507, **20**; individuals or *couples?* **II,** 512, **20.**
— of semi-deaf pupils, **II, 131.**
Perfecting of education, Effect of, **II,** 523, **21.**
Permanent teachers, how secured, **I,** 260, **19.**
Pernicious use of the sign-language, **I,** 167, **10.**
Peter, the wild boy, **I, 174.**
Philanthropic Societies, **II,** 613, **31.**
Philbrick, John D., on Visible Speech, **II, 145.**
— Miss Rachel, deaf author, etc., **I, 93.**
Philocophus [1648], **II, 157.**
Philological Society of England, **II,** 560, **25.**
Phonetic Alphabet, Prof. A. Melville Bell's Universal, **II,** 868, **54**; *see also* Visible Speech.
— books, **II,** 942, **61**; Supply of, **II,** 882, **56.**
— characters for the blind, **II,** 941, **60.**
— form, essential in teaching pronunciation, **II,** 875, **55.**
— writing commended, **II,** 576, **28.**
Phrases and sentence-forms, not words, needed by the deaf child, **II,** 814, **48.**
Phonological Institute, **I,** 275, **21.**
Photogravure of an auricular class, *to face*, **II, 132.**
Physical condition of deaf-mutes a little lower than the average, **I,** 376, **28.**
— training, **I,** 389, **29**; Effects of, as measured at the National College, **I,** 527, **39.**
— — practicable in day-schools, **II,** 727, **40.**
Physicians, Aid of, in verifying census-returns, **II,** 809, **47.**
Pictures, Illustrative, to be shown *after* the text has been read, **II,** 813, **48.**
Plagiarism from Pélissier, **I, 93.**
Plan, A, to reach all deaf children, **II, 168.**
Playfair, K. C. B., M. P., Sir Lyon, Questions by, **II,** 21,879; 21,914; 21,953.
Play-hours, Association of deaf, and hearing children in, **II,** 465, **4.**
Poetry of the Deaf, (illustrations), *Gallaudet*, **I, 87.**
Polano, Mr., Mastery of speech and speech-reading by, **I,** 471, **34.**
Point of difference with pure oralists, *Bell*, **II,** 720, **40.**
Political appointments, **II,** 846, **51; III, 211.**
— influence avoided in corporate form of organization, **I,** 118, **4.**
Popular ignorance of the mechanism of speech, Effect of, **II, 71.**
Population returns, Examination of, to find deaf children of deaf parents, **II,** 531, **22.**
Portland Day-School, **II,** 797, **45.**
Porter, Miss Sarah H., quoted, **II, 165.**
Post-mortem examinations, **I,** 381, **29.**
Poverty, Certificates of, not required generally, **I,** 269, **18.**
Practicability of separate departments under one organization, *Crouter*, **I, 78.**
Practical probability of the formation of a deaf variety, **II,** 502, **19.**
Pratt, Mrs. A. C., genealogist, **II,** 450, **13.**
Preference of deaf-mutes for deaf-mutes, **II,** 555, **24.**
— of pupils, knowing both systems is for signs, *Emery*, **II, 113**; for combined system, *Gallaudet*, **I,** 474, **34.**
Prejudice toward the deaf, **I,** 200, **13; II,** 556, **24; 167.**
Preliminary Home-instruction, **II,** 973, **63.**
Presentation of "*Facts and Opinions*" to the Royal Commission, **II,** 988, **65.**
— of *American Annals*, **I,** 271, **21.**
Preventive measures, Guiding principle in search for, **II,** 458, **14.**
Principals and teachers, Ability of, **II,** 791, **45**; Mode of appointment of, **I,** 261, **19; II,** 845, **51; III, 211.**
— List of, TABLE, **II, 72.**
— express the desire to give all deaf children an opportunity to acquire speech, **II,** 677, **36.**
— Majority of, favor intermarriage, **II,** 551, **24.**
Primitive speech, Efforts to determine, **II, 173.**
Private instruction at home, *Fay*, **I, 69.**
Private schools, Classification of, *Gallaudet*, 130, **6.**
— — Significance of, *Gallaudet*, **I,** 131, **6; III, 208**; *Bell*, 365, **3**; 371, **4.**
— — Statistics of, **I,** 130, **6; 73**; D, **74; II, 124; 129.**
Proficiency in a language depends upon use, **II,** 464, **14.**
Proportion of adventitious, and congenital cases, **I, 61.**
— of deaf-mutes to general population, *See* Statistics.
— greater in Germany than in the U. S., *Williams*, **II, 90.**
— of oral graduates able to rely upon speech and speech-reading, **I,** 316, **25.**
Propriety of separation of the sexes in early school-life, **II,** 785, **45.**
Proximity with hearing children desirable, **II,** 528, **21.**
Psammeticus, Experiment of, **II, 173.**
Puberty, Improvement of hearing at, **II,** (*e*), **78-84; 88.**

Public aid to schools, II, 730, 41; TABLE, I, 74.
—— opinion, Pressure of, affects growth of oral teaching, II, 501, 19.
Public and Private schools, List and statistics of, I, 72-75; II, 128.
Pupilage, Duration of, I, 172, 11.
Pupils acquire a limited vocabulary under any system, I, 163, 9.
Pupils in American Asylum having deaf relatives. TABLE, II, 90.
Pupil-teacher system, II, 759, 43.
Pure oralists are not just, *Emery*, II, 115.
Pure oral method:—*Gallaudet*;
interpreted variously at the Milan Convention, I, 298, 3; 107.
a misleading designation, I, 134, 7.
Schools, in America, I, 289, 23.
in combined system schools, I, 292, 23.
—— —— ——:—*Bell*;
defined, II, 669, 35.
not suitable for all children, II, 560, 25.
should be adopted for children having natural speech, II, 568, 26.
Trial of, in America, II, 805, 46.
Percentage of pupils taught by, II, 806, 46.
—— —— ——. *See titles* Oral Method, Articulation.
Purity of English tongue, How to preserve, II, 71.

Quackery in curing defects of speech, II, 917, 59.
Quadrennial conventions of American instructors, I, 266, 20.
Qualifications of teachers, general and special, I, 257, 19; 264, 20; II, 754, 42; 756, 43; 791, 45; 998, 65.
Quality of voice, II, 901, 57.
Quickest means of exhibiting words to the deaf, II, 570, 27.
Quick perception, Bearing of, on method of instruction, I, 82.

Race of deaf-mutes, Origin and characteristics of an imaginary, *H. P. Peet*, II, 176.
—— Influence of, I, 44.
Rain and Snow, Explanation of, II, 180.
Rates of presenting thought by speech, writing, finger-spelling, and silent-reading, II, 813, 47; Rapidity of manual spelling, II, 570, 27; 669, 35.
Ratio of articulation-teachers increasing, II, 494, 18.
—— of deaf mutes to the general population, II, 356, 1.
Ray, Mr. J. E., on auricular instruction, II, 81; on Visible Speech, II, 76.
Reaction against the exclusive practice of the oral method, I, 371, 28.
Reading, Silent, Educational importance of, as the speediest way of presenting language to the deaf, II, 47.
—— should be compulsory, II, 813, 48.
Recapitulation of advantages of the Wisconsin-bill, II, 72.
Recommendations, Summary of, II, 998, 65.
Relationships, in American Asylum, II, 90; in Illinois institution, II, 93; in Georgia institution, II, 94.
Relationship, Ties of, strengthened by day-schools, II, 724, 40.
Relative value of methods, How to determine, II, 579, 28.
Reliance upon speech-reading in earlier stages defeats the end, II, 585, 29.
Religious instruction, *Moritz Hill*, I, 103; *Gallaudet*, I, 127, 6; 314, 25; 350, 26; 409, 30; 465, 33; *H. P. Peet*, II, 184; *Bell*, 369, 3; 988, 65.
—— Societies for adults, *Fay*, I, 71; *Miss Fuller*, II, 96.
Repetition of words, Extent of, in acquiring a language, II, 813, 47.
Repressive legislation not advocated, II, 457, 13.
Researches of Dr. W. W. Turner, II, 528, 22.
Restrictions upon use of finger-spelling, II, 584, 29; 673, 35; 576, 28.
Resolutions of N. E. H. G. Society, II, 200.
Results, The best, II, 574, 27.
—— How to compare, II, 579, 28; Three tests proposed, II, 748, 42.
—— of intermarriage. *See* Marriage *and* Intermarriage.
Reversion to normal type discussed, *Brooks*, II, 104; *Cope*, II, 101.
Robertson, Esq., W. Tindall, Questions by, I, 13,376; 13,381; 13,422; II, 21,384; 21,422; 21,443; 21,445; 21,455; 21,783; 21,978; 21,982; 21,987.
Rochester institution, Written conversation with young children practicable at, II, 833, 50.
—— —— Method, and results in, II, 575, 27.
Rogers, Miss H. B., I, 58; On progress in America, II, 123; Articulation teaching, *Table*, II, 130.
Rousseau, J. J., I, 174.
Royal Commission, Recommendations of, III, ——.
Runck family, The, II, 530, 22; *Gallaudet*, III, 207.
Russian work-shop system, II, 468, 15.

Salamanders, Degeneracy of organ of hearing in, *Cope*, II, 101.
Salaries of teachers, I, 258, 19; II, 679, 36; 907, 62; should not depend on "results," I, 265, 20.
Sanborn, Mr. F. B., I, 58; *Foot-note*, I, 49; II, 881, 55.
Sanchez on Marriage of the Deaf and Dumb (1614), II, 126.
Sarah-Fuller Home for little children who cannot hear, II, 771, 44; II, 121.
Sargent, Dr. D. A., I, 527, 38.
Scarlet fever, Rank of, as a cause of deafness, II, 419, 10.
Scientific testimony relating to possibility of formation of a deaf variety, II, 101-106.
Schleswig institution, Selection of teachers for, II, 681, 36.
School-age in America, II, 840, 51; *Fay*, I, 68.
School-Board schools, to a great extent separate schools, II, 669, 35; in buildings with hearing children, II, 466, 14.
School-hours, *Table*, I, 73.
School-life, Length of, II, 530, 538, 23.
—— Magazines, I, 273, 21; II, 518.

Schools, Table of, **II, 128.**

—— Proper size of, II, 457, **13**; 464, **14**; 467, **15**; 469, **15**; 528, **21.**

—— receiving State-aid are not inspected by competent persons, **II**, 742, **41.**

Scrofula, *Fay*, **I, 64.**

Secret vice, I, 480, **35**; **II**, 981, **63.**

Segregation, Effect of, **II**, 457, **14.**

Selection, Effect of continuous, **II**, 535, **23.**

Self-reliance promoted by day-schools, *Emery*, **II, 110.**

"**Semi-deaf**," Percentage of, **II**, 403, **8**; *Table*, **131.**

"**Semi-mutes**," Prof. Storrs on teaching, **II, 77.**

—— —— in the National College, **II**, 588, **29.**

Senses, Domain of, defined, *Gillett*, **II, 171.**

Sentence-exercises, Examples of, **II, 152.**

Sentences and phrases are more useful than separate words in speech-reading, **II**, 986, **65.**

Sentences taught as wholes, **II, 152.**

Separate institutions for girls and boys, **II**, 539, **23.**

—— language, Effect of, **II**, 552, **24.**

Separation of adult deaf-mutes from the hearing-world, Reason of, **II**, 389, **6.**

—— of orally, and sign-taught pupils, not desirable, I, 296, **23.**

Seven deaf children in one family, **II**, 455, **13.**

Sexes, Both, in adult societies, **II**, 621, **31**; in the same schools, **II**, 620, **31**; Separation of, **II**, 971, **62**; Separation of sexes in day-schools, **II**, 788, **45**; in institutions, **II**, 789, **45**; during school life, **II**, 646-648, **33**; 539, **23**; Separation of s. unnatural, **II**, 785, **45.** *Gallaudet* on separation, I, 198, **13.**

—— Statistics of, **II**, 487, **17.**

Sex peculiarities, **II**, 450, 454, **13.**

Sexton, Dr. Samuel, otologist, on improvement in the brain tract receiving impressions through the auditory nerve, **II, 140.**

Sheep, Merino, *Brewer*, **II, 102.**

Shouting, Effect of continuous, in development of hearing, **II**, 399, **7.**

Siamese twins, Deaf descendants of, **II**, 450, **13.**

Sibscota, George, **II, 155.**

Sight, **Feeble**, more common among the deaf than in the normal population, **II**, 838, **51.**

Signs, Advantage of, **II**, 570, **27**; divided into four classes, **II**, 560, **25**; Language of, reaches the mind of the deaf child quickest, **II**, 570, **26**; Proper use of, **II**, 560, **25.** *See* Fallacies.

Sign-language, abolished in the Western New-York Institution, **II**, 574, **27.**

—— —— Abuse of, I, 166-171, **10.**

—— —— a special language, **II**, 389, **6**; 391, **7.**

—— —— enables teacher to gauge capacity, *Williams*, **I, 83.**

—— —— eventually a hindrance to acquisition of English, **II**, 570, **26.**

—— —— General advantages and utility of, I, 202, **14.** *See* under *title* Gallaudet.

—— —— harmful to a dull child, **II**, 826, **50.**

—— —— methods defined, **II**, 387, **6.**

—— —— in relation to intermarriages, **II**, 525, **21**; 554, **24.**

—— —— in social intercourse, **II**, 984, **64**; I, 202, **14.**

—— —— teachers quibble about "signs," **II**, 819, **49.**

—— —— the mother-tongue of the deaf? Is the, **II**, 812, **47.**

—— —— *See* Oral, Pure Oral, Combined.

"**Silent World**," The, **II**, 519, **20.**

Similarity of letters in speech-reading, **II**, 568, **26.**

Simpson, Mr. W. H., deaf poet, Verses by, **I, 91.**

Singular observation of Dr. Itard, **II, 185.**

Six-fingered persons, **II**, 450, **13.**

Six hundred and seven deaf children of deaf parents, **II**, 530, **22**:—**Corrected Table**, **III**, ——.

Size of schools, **II**, 458, **14**; 464, **14**; 467, **15**; 469, **15**; 528, **21.**

Skiff family, The, **II**, 860, **53.**

Sleight, Rev. W. B., Questions by, 13,242; 13,416; 13,423; 13,425; 13,432; 13,455; **II**, 21,404; 21,421; 21,431; 21,698; 21,807; 21,816; 21,821; 21,825 *a*; 21,829; 21,839; 21,932; 21,985; 21,990.

Snow and Rain, Origin of, **II, 180.**

Social circumstances as a cause of deafness, *Fay*, **I, 64.**

—— **intercourse** of the deaf and dumb impeded by the "lip-system," I, 411, **30**; I, 984, **64.**

Sotheby, K. C. B., Admiral Sir E., Questions by, I, 13,400, 13,531; **II**, 21,545, 21,548.

Soul, Existence of the, **II, 180.**

Sounds, Organic relation of, **II, 148.**

Spanish language, Experiment in learning the, **II**, 813, **48.**

Spavin, *Brewer*, **II, 103.**

Speaking children known to lose their speech in a sign-language institution, **II**, 582, **28.**

Special advantage in use of Visible Speech, **II**, 962, **62.**

—— **language**, defined, **II**, 391, **7**; not necessary, **II**, 560, **25**; the chief cause of intermarriage, **II**, 554, **24**; Influence of, **II, 169**; peculiar characteristic of one method of instruction, **II**, 385, **6.**

Specialists among oral teachers, **II**, 935, **60.**

Speech, Fallacies concerning nature of, **II, 156.**

—— in oral schools, somewhat defective, **II**, 879, **55.**

—— **Intelligibility**, not perfection, the proper gauge of value of, **II**, 579, **28.**

—— of children becoming deaf in late childhood, **II**, 490, **18.**

—— **Ordinary**, more intelligible to speech-reader than labored articulation, **II**, 585, **29.**

—— proficiency in, A degree of, should be a condition of graduation, *G. O. Fay*, **I, 79.**

—— should be taught simultaneously, but not as an accomplishment, **II**, 571, **27.**

—— used in many cases in the College, I, 237, **16.**

Speech-reading of lectures and public addresses, **II**, 835, **50**; 839, **51**; **III, 210.**

—— may be acquired by all who know a language, **II**, 567, **26.**

—— **Positions** of English elements are not clearly differentiated in, **II**, 567, **26.**

—— method, **II**, 387, **6.**

—— for higher stages of education, **II**, 826, **50.**

—— not the only point to be considered, **II**, 666, **34.**

—— will not teach language, **II**, 668, **34.**

—— **Speed** of, compared with finger-spelling and writing, **II**, 667, **34.**

—— **Sufficiency** of, for social intercourse, **II**, 984, **64.**

Spiritual needs of the adult deaf, an important matter, **II**, 723, **40.**

Spoken words, soulless and soundless, *Emery*, **II, 113.**

Sporadic and non-sporadic deafness, **II**, 475, 478, **16.**

"**Spotted-fever**," **II**, 418, **9.**

Stainer-Home connected with London schools, **II**, 728, **41**; *Emery*, **II, 109.**

Stanford, Rev. John, pioneer in attempting to teach a class of deaf children in America, I, **54**.

State-aid, does away largely with annual subscriptions, but not with bequests, in U. S., I, 366, **28**.
—— —— Forms of, in U. S., I, 112, **4**.
—— —— granted as a right, and not simply as a charity, I, 367, **28**; 477, **35**; II, 732, **41**.
—— —— should be granted without restriction as to method of instruction, I, 309, **24**.
—— —— Scheme of, *Hutton*, II, **122**.
—— —— should be coupled with governmental inspection and payment by results, II, 998, **65**; 751, **42**; 748, **42**.
—— —— should be without discrimination against day-schools, II, 768, **43**.
—— —— should be given to specially and fully trained teachers, II, 679, **36**; 917, **59**.
—— —— *See*, How supported, Value of buildings and grounds, and Expenditures, in *Table*, I, **74**.
—— institutions, Organization of, I, 112, **4**.

Statistics: Analysis of the Census of 1880, II, 487, **17**.
—— Accuracy of Census of 1880, I, 105, **1**; II, 355, **1**; III, **207**.
—— Census Returns, *see* Census.
—— Consanguineous marriages as a cause of deafness: II, 447, **12**; American Asylum, II, **89**; 35 British institutions, II, 447, **12**; Georgia, II, **94**; *Table* of Illinois statistics, II, **93**.
—— Deaf children in institutions, II, 359, **2**.
—— Deaf children of school-age, II, 359, **2**.
—— Importance of proper classification, II, 598, **30**.
—— Number and ratio of pupils capable of receiving auricular instruction, II, 403, **8**.
—— Number of deaf-mutes in U. S., II, 357, **1**.
—— of American Asylum, II, **90**.
—— of Articulation teaching, II, **124**.
—— —— —— for the world, II, **71**; **169**.
—— of congenital deafness, Uncertainty in, II, 855, **52**.
—— of Illinois institution, II, **92**.
—— of intermarriages, *see* under title, Marriage.
—— of marriages, *see* under title, Marriage.
—— of muscular improvement in deaf students, I, 527, **39**.
—— of offspring of 24 marriages in Georgia, II, **94**; of ——, in Illinois, II, **93**; of 157, in New England, II, **89**.
—— of period of birth of married deaf-mutes, 510, **20**.
—— of pupils taught articulation '83-'87, II, **377**; **4**, **5**.
—— Ratio of deaf-mutes to population, II, 356, **1**.
—— School, Report of Committee on, I, **52**.
—— TABLE showing growth of American schools, '57 to '87, II, 492, **18**. TABLES for 1885, I, **72-75**.
—— 207 deaf-mute children of deaf-mute parents, II, 529, **22**; 607 deaf children of deaf parents, II, 530, **22**; III, ——.
—— of Visible Speech, II, 927, **59**.

Statistics: uniformity in returns, Value of, I, 109, **4**; II, 598-602, **30**.

Stature, Galton's study of, *Brooks*, II, **104**.

Stars, Origin of, II, **180**.

Stewart, Dr. Dugald, Discovery by, II, 563, **26**.

Stimulus to acquisition of speech, II, 585, **29**.

"**Struggle for existence**," II, 937, **60**. *See* "Survival of the Fittest."

Studies which might be pursued in common by deaf, and hearing children, II, 458, **14**.

Success of pupils transferred from one system to another, I, 312, **24**.

Superintendents of public instruction, II, 743, **41**.
—— and principals of Institutions, List of, I, **72**.
—— —— —— Character and qualifications of, I, 127, **6**.

Superiority of pupils in French, and American schools in scholarship, I, **79**.

Supplementing the institution-system by small day-schools, II, 762, **43**.

"**Survival** of the fittest," *Gillett*, II, **170**; *Fay*, II, **123**; *Bell*, II, 717, **42**; II, 937, **60**.

Sweet, Mr. Henry, uses Visible Speech in Icelandic studies, II, 930, **60**.

Swett, Miss N. H., on Auricular instruction, II, **82**; on Visible Speech, II, **76**.

Swiler, Mr. J. W., advises (1) celibacy, (2) intermarriage, II, **95**; on auricular instruction, II, **79**; on methods of instruction, II, **107**; on Visible Speech, II, **75**.

Swimming-pool at the Columbia Institution, I, 414, **30**.

Switzerland, Remarkable statistics of, I, **43**.

Symbolic signs, II, 560, **25**.

Syphilis, II, 803, **46**.

System, The, of the future, I, 470, **34**.

Tabular Statements of Statistics:
Articulation-teaching in 1883, II, **130**; Analytical Table, II, **124**; Growth of, '83-'88, II, **19**.
Auricular instruction, II, **78-84**; Arkansas, II, **88**; Miss McCowen's School, II, **87**; Tests of hearing, II, **140-141**.
Causes of Deafness, U. S. Census, II, **18**; Am. Asylum, II, **91**; Georgia, II, **93**; Illinois, II, **92**.
Correlation of Defects, II, **134**.
Census Returns, 1830, '40, '50, I, **45-48**; 1850, '60, '70, I, **50**; 1880, By States, I, **51**; Analysis of Census of 1880, II, **127**; of twelve countries, I, **61**; Defective classes, 1850, '60, '70, '80, II, **197**; Period of birth and percentage of the congenitally deaf population, II, **197**; Statistical forms for XIth Census, II, **201**.
Deaf children of Deaf parents, II, **52**; III, ——.
Deaf Relatives, II, **90-91**; **93**; **94**; **105**.
Marriages, II, **21**; **52**; **96**.
School-Statistics, I, **72-75**; **128-129**; Forms for, I, **52**; Pupils transferred to Am. Asylum, I, **85**.
Visible Speech, II, **75-77**.

Tarra, Cav. Sac. Giulio, **36**, Strictures upon the sign-language, I, **109**.

Tate, Mr. J. N., on auricular instruction, II, **79**; on Visible Speech, II, **75**.

Taylor, Mrs. W. E. [Miss Plum], Paper on **aural work**, II, **85**.

Teachers, Best, chiefly ladies, II, 887, **56**.
—— Boarding of, II, 969, **62**.
—— Competency of, II, 752, **42**.
—— Difficulty in retaining, illustrated, II, 703, **39**.
—— Female, II, 782, **45**; 887, **56**.
—— Few, specially trained in normal schools, II, 755, **42**.

Teachers, General and special qualifications of, II, 754, 42.
— German, Method of educating, II, 71.
— How to provide, II, 169.
— Intelligence and capacity of, II, 752, 42.
— Inferior, I, 244, 20.
— in America, extremists, II, 574, 27.
— of Visible Speech, Salaries of, II, 935, 60.
— Mistake made by, II, 580, 28.
— Salaries of, gauged by results, II, 748, 42; 749, 42; I, 265, 20.
— should be familiar with Visible Speech, II, 874, 55.
— should be selected from the general teachers and specially trained, II, 691, 36.
— should write or spell to the congenitally deaf child, II, 571, 21.
— Qualifications of, I, 257-260, 19; 263-265, 20.
Teaching articulation and teaching *by* articulation, II, 694, 37.
— speech to the congenitally deaf, *Modus operandi* of, II, 888, 56.
— to talk is not education, *Emery*, II, 112.
Technical instruction, Age for commencing, II, 843, 51.
Telephone, Invention of the, II, 635, 32.
Tennessee School, Sketch of, I, 56.
Ten per cent. only of graduates of the National College born deaf, II, 585, 29.
Terrell family, The, II, 101.
Terrell, Mr. P., on auricular instruction, II, 82; experience in the Florida Inst., II, 188; on inherited deafness, II, 99; on Line-writing and Visible Speech, II, 76.
Tests of hearing, II, 395, 7; *see* Auricular Instruction, Hearing.
— of methods, II, 366, 3; 748, 42.
Thinking in English not always possible, *Gillett*, II, 171.
Thinking, in a language, II, 385, 6; without speech, II, 826, 50.
Three Bears, Story of, how related, II, 815, 48.
Three forms of exterior organization, I, 112, 4.
Tilton family, The, II, 858, 53.
Time required to produce useful results by Bell's system, II, 926, 59.
Tonna, Mrs. E. (Charlotte Elizabeth), I, 91.
Tonsils, Diseased, not common, II, 908, 58.
"Touch" Alphabet, II, 691, 37; 815, 48; *plates*, II, 153.
Trades, What kind of, shall be taught? II, 472, 15; *E. E. Hale's* paper, II, 137.
— Teaching of, I, 181, 12; 187, 12; 73. *See* Industrial training.
Training College, A State, not advisable, II, 795, 45; 756, 42; Training-school at Washington contemplated, I, 258, 19.
— Gymnastic, in Horace-Mann school, II, 780, 44; in National College, I, 38.
Translation from one language to another not a satisfactory method, II, 563, 25.
Transportation facilities for pupils, II, 774, 44.
True, The, combined system, *Crouter*, I, 76.
True method of comparing systems, II, 579, 28.
Trustworthiness of Dr. Bell's Memoir upon a Deaf Variety, II, 531, 22.
Truth in all the systems, II, 570, 27.
Tubes, Hearing, *See* Auricular Instruction.
Turner, Dr. W. W., Researches of, II, 528, 22; Theory of, 541, 23; Ideas of the uninstructed deaf, II, 182.
Twins and Triplets, II, 450, 13; in Allen family, II, 454, 13. *See* charts of Allen and Brown families, III, —.
Two languages required in English-speaking countries, II, 576, 27.

Uhlig, Mr. D. H., on auricular instruction, II, 88; on Visible Speech, II, 77.
Unanimity in recommendations by the Commission, Importance of, II, 999, 66.
Unconstitutionality of Federal inspection of State institutions, I, 369, 28.
Understanding a language will come through seeing it, II, 813, 48.
Uneducated deaf, a danger to society, II, 70; rarely a burden, II, 70.
— think in pictures, II, 827, 50.
Uniformity in statistical forms, II, 599, 30.
Unique feature in the Horace-Mann school, II, 781, 44.
— power of Visible Speech, II, 882, 56.
Universal alphabet, Prof. A. Melville Bell's, II, 868, 54.
Unreliability of Census returns upon points requiring special knowledge in the enumerator, II, 808, 47.
Unsatisfactory results in certain oral schools, II, 170.
Use of Speech by orally-taught graduates, I, 319, 25.
Utah, Deaf-mutes in, *White*, II, 100.
Upon a method of teaching language to a very young congenitally deaf child, *Bell*, II, 150.

Vacations, Summer, of American schools for the deaf, *Table*, I, 74.
Value of buildings and grounds, *Table*, I, 74.
— of conventions of instructors, I, 266, 20.
Van Helmont, II, 160.
Van Oven, L., Esq., Questions by, II, 21,399; 21,406; 21,437; 21,514; 21,516; 21,544; 21,516; 21,588; 21,610; 21,664; 21,676; 21,680; 21,824; 21,937; 21,946.
Variability associated with congenital deafness, II, 450, 13.
Variety, Deaf, Memoir upon, II, 409, 9; 411, 9; 416, 9; 431, 10; 435, 10; 457, 13; 458, 14; 510, 20; 529, 22; 856, 53.
Vermont, Deaf farmer in, I, 241.
Vernacular of Laura Bridgman, II, 162.
"Vestiges of Creation," II, 177.
Vice, Secret, I, 480, 35; II, 981, 63.
Virginia Institution, Sketch of, I, 56.
Verdict, Effect of a unanimous, II, 999, 66.

Visible Speech, Prof. A. Melville Bell's, **II**, 628-635, **31**, **32**.
—— —— Acquisition of, by all teachers of the deaf advisable, **II**, 946, **61**.
—— —— advantageous to both classes of the deaf, **II**, 958, **61**.
—— —— and sign-writing, *Fay*, **I**, **70**.
—— —— as a means of communicating Articulation to Deaf-mutes, **II**, **144**.
—— —— at the Belleville Convention, **II**, **189**.
—— —— at the commencement of a child's education, **II**, 883, **56**.
—— —— cannot affect ordinary writing, **II**, 957, **61**.
—— —— compared with the German method, **II**, 950. **61**; **145**.
—— —— explained, **II**, 868-871, **54**.
—— —— for the blind, **II**, 939, **60**.
—— —— capable of representing all the sounds the deaf child makes, **II**, 962, **62**.
—— —— Illustrations of, **II**, 147; Charts, **III**, ——.
—— —— is not a kind of second language as asserted, **II**, 956, **61**.
—— —— Proper method of using, **II**, 899, **57**.
—— —— Recapitulation of plan of instruction in speech by means of, **II**, **140**.
—— —— takes no part in contest between systems, **II**, 694, **37**.
—— —— is used in at least fifteen institutions, **II**, 927, **59**.
Vocabulary of an auricular class, **II**, **84**.
Vocal organs, A discovery in regard to, **II**, 901, **57**.
—— —— of deaf children, perfect, **II**, 669, **35**; *foot-note*, **II**, **134**.
—— sounds of Laura Bridgman, **II**, **175**.
Voice may be improved even in mature years, **II**, 905, **58**.
—— Relation of, to early practice in speech, **II**, 579, **28**.
"Vox Oculis Subjecta," **I**, **91**.

Walker, Mr. N. F., on intermarriage, **II**, **94**; on Visible Speech, **II**, **75**.
Walker, Mr. S. T., on auricular instruction, **II**, **80**; on the ideal institution, **II**, **107**; on intermarriage, **II**, **95**; Test of hearing in Kansas Inst., **II**, 395, **7**; on Visible Speech, **II**, **75**.
Watson, Mr. J., on auricular instruction, **II**, **82**; on Visible Speech, **II**, **76**.
Weak-minded pupils, **II**, 636, **32**; **I**, **82**.
Western New-York Institution, Results in, **II**, 574, **27**.
Westervelt, Mr. Z. F., will introduce *World-English* as a means of teaching articulation, **II**, 964, **62**.
What kind of Trades shall be taught? *E. E. Hale*, **II**, **137**.
What shall deaf children read? **II**, 813, **48**.
Whipple's, Mr., experiment, **II**, 392, **7**; school, *foot-note*, **II**, **7**.
—— Mr. Zerah C., "Natural alphabet" for teaching articulation, **II**, 991, **65**.
White cats with blue eyes are deaf, **II**, 448, **12**.
White, Mr. H. C., Communication on intermarriages, **II**, **100**.
Why hearing children who become deaf also become dumb, **II**, **155**.
Why "semi-mutes" excel in speech-reading, **II**, 837, **50**.
Wilkinson, Mr. W., on consanguinity and intermarriage in California, **II**, **95**.
Williams, Mr. Job, on Articulation-teaching and the combined system, **II**, **106**; on intermarriages, **II**, **88**; on Visible Speech, **II**, **75**; **A system of education adapted to all deaf-mutes** not excluding the feebler-minded, **I**, **82**.
Will of Providence, *Emery*, **II**, **97**.
Wines, Rev. Fred. H., Analysis of Census, **II**, 487, **17**; Accuracy of Census, **II**, 357, **1**; **III**, **212**; Estimate of number of deaf-mutes, **II**, 358, **2**; Need of provision for idiotic and feeble-minded, **II**, 357, **2**; on *per capita* expense, *foot-note*, **II**, **41**; Remarks at Chicago, **II**, **168**.
Wisconsin, Law of, **II**, 360, **2**, **3**; Dr. Bell's **open letter**, **II**, **69**.
—— —— Extracts from, **II**, **73**; **116**.
Woodall, M. P., William, Esq., Questions by, **I**, 13,177; 13,179; 13,219; 13,224; 13,228; **II**, 21,368; 21,415; 21,420; 21,426; 21,432; 21,448; 21,452; 21,454; 21,458; 21,501; 21,518; 21,521; 21,523; 21,525; 21,531; 21,555; 21,575; 21,659; 21,696; 21,701; 21,730.
Wood-carving for deaf-mutes, **I**, 190, **12**.
—— Engraving in America; Case of J. C. Davis, **II**, **138**.
Women as teachers, **II**, 782, **45**.
Worcester, Miss Alice, Method of teaching articulation, **II**, 936, **60**; **Miss Worcester's method**, **II**, **192**.
Words, how impressed upon the memory, **II**, 564, **26**.
—— Memorizing of detached, condemned, **II**, 814, **48**.
Works family, The, **II**, 530, **22**.
World-English, **II**, 964, **62**.
Written form, The, may be kept to itself as a distinct language, **II**, 576, **27**.
—— language should be the basis of instruction for the congenitally deaf, 567, 570, **27**.
—— —— how best taught, **I**, 426, **31**.
Writing should be used for mental reasons, **II**, 665, **34**.
—— Speed of, compared with finger-spelling and speech, **II**, 667, **34**.
—— (Penmanship) may be taught at home, **I**, 172, **11**.

Yale, Miss C. A., on auricular instruction, **II**, **80**; on marriages of the deaf, **II**, **95**; on Visible Speech, **II**, **76**.
Young, Mr. W. J., on auricular instruction, **II**, **78**; on marriages of the deaf, **II**, **92**; on Visible Speech, **II**, **75**.

www.ingramcontent.com/pod-product-compliance
Lightning Source LLC
Chambersburg PA
CBHW020534300426
44111CB00008B/656

* 9 7 8 3 3 3 7 1 3 6 2 2 2 *